Monty Python's Flying Circus

An Utterly Complete, Thoroughly Unillustrated, Absolutely Unauthorized Guide to Possibly All the References

From Arthur "Two-Sheds" Jackson to Zambesi

Darl Larsen

The Scarecrow Press, Inc.
Lanham, Maryland • Toronto • Plymouth, UK
2008

SCARECROW PRESS, INC.

Published in the United States of America
by Scarecrow Press, Inc.
A wholly owned subsidiary of
The Rowman & Littlefield Publishing Group, Inc.
4501 Forbes Boulevard, Suite 200, Lanham, Maryland 20706
www.scarecrowpress.com

Estover Road
Plymouth PL6 7PY
United Kingdom

British Cataloging in Publication Information Available

Library of Congress Cataloging-in-Publication Data

Larsen, Darl, 1963–
  Monty Python's flying circus : an utterly complete, thoroughly unillustrated,
 absolutely unauthorized guide to possibly all the references from Arthur "Two-Sheds"
Jackson to Zambesi / Darl Larsen.
    p. cm.
  Includes bibliographical references and index.
  ISBN-13: 978-0-8108-6131-2 (hardback : alk. paper)
  ISBN-10: 0-8108-6131-3 (hardback : alk. paper)
  1. Monty Python's flying circus (Television program)—Dictionaries. I. Title.

PN1992.77.M583L37 2008
791.45'72—dc22
                                                                    007052082

∞™ The paper used in this publication meets the minimum requirements
of American National Standard for Information Sciences—Permanence of
Paper for Printed Library Materials, ANSI/NISO Z39.48-1992.
Manufactured in the United States of America.

For Nycole, Keir, Emrys, Brynmor,
Eamonn, Dathyl, Ransom, and Cuchulainn,

and

WPW

Contents

Acknowledgments

Dr. William P. Williams, University of Akron, has followed my progress and been a tireless supporter since our days together as teacher and student at Northern Illinois University, and I thank him again for his assistance and friendship.

Thanks is also extended to these Brigham Young University entities: the Center for the Study of Western Europe, the Kennedy Center for International Studies, the College of Fine Arts and Communications, and the Theatre & Media Arts Department—providing generous research and travel grants and wholehearted support for the completion of this project.

The good folks at the British Broadcasting Corporation's Written Archives Collection in Caversham Park were both gracious and helpful, allowing unfettered access to production files for the *Flying Circus* episodes. Thanks, Louise! Making life on the road much more amenable, the very gracious Richard Ogawa and Daniel Brown (and Livingston and Apollo) allowed me to invade their home during all of my research trips to the UK.

Special research thanks must go out to the original gang: Josh Abboud, Jason Allred, Brad Barber, Charlie Bird, Katie Bogner, Lisa Broberg, Jenn Bushman, Marcus Cano, Tawnya Cazier, Corey Chipman, Jeremy Coon, Travis Eberhard, Brian Endicott, Christy Gleave, Kynan Griffin, J.D. Hacken, Tressa Halcrow, Todd Hamilton, Molly Hart, Dan Heder, Sam Hoffman, Melanie Lamb, Cara Poulson, Tim Skousen, Kyle Snarr, Evelyn Steed, Nate Swain, Matt Whitney, Megan Wolfley, and Wyatt Woolley, all intrepid and long-suffering members of the TMA 498R Monty Python course brazenly offered for the first time in 2001. The second such course offering included student researchers David Aller, Dan Barnett, Trevor Campbell, Brandon Conway, Tawni Goldsberry, Brad Haymond, Kimball Maw, Dan Needham, Mike Ormond, Wil Haydt, Jed Robinson, Emily Yu, Stacey Snider, Paul Tuft, and Nat Wells. Of this latter bunch, Stacey Snider continued to work with me as a research assistant, providing compiling and indexical work in recent months. My students and research assistants Randy Astle and Megan Atkinson also provided significant legwork.

Fellow BYU professor Daryl Lee contributed French translations for the Pythons' jabberwock French, while Northern Illinois' Maria Krull performed the same service for the Italian translations. I'd also like to thank my colleagues here in the BYU Theatre & Media Arts program who acted as supporters from the earliest days, including Rodger Sorensen, Sharon Swenson, Dean Duncan, Tom Russell, Tom Lefler, Jeff Parkin, Amy Jensen, and Megan Jones. An interest in the interrogation of literature came to me from one of the great community college professors in the world, Ms. Betty Higdon of Reedley College, whose active influence haunts the edges of this work, and everything I read or write.

Also, warm thanks to my parents, Norbert and Patricia Larsen; Dean Stephen R. Jones; Robert Nelson; Andrew Black; Benji Harry; and Stephen Ryan and the brave folk at Scarecrow Press.

And lastly, a heartfelt thanks to my family including my wife, Nycole, and our seven wonderful children—Keir, Emrys, Brynmor, Eamonn, Dathyl, Ransom, and Cuchulainn. They put up with Dad's long hours and short fuse as this project came to be, and I'm very, very grateful.

Introduction

"So, what is this?"

A fair question, and one asked by not a few of my patient deans, bemused colleagues, confused family members, and the like. My interest in Monty Python began like most anyone's—I was young, it was the late-1970s, and they were that silly British group involved in some kind of circus that came on late at night when I was supposed to be abed. I watched a little, and understood as much. The interest was fanned as midnight showings of *Monty Python and the Holy Grail* and then the naughty *Life of Brian* visited local movie screens, and later the miracle of VHS tape provided a few treasured episodes of *Monty Python's Flying Circus* that could be watched again and again. But it wasn't until Professor William Proctor Williams and I half-jokingly (which also means half-seriously) happened to be discussing the creative language of insult and vilification in Jonson's *Volpone* and *The Alchemist*, as well as Shakespeare's dimly clever Dogberry in *Much Ado About Nothing*, that we agreed Monty Python owed a significant debt to these English Renaissance dramatists, and a thesis topic was conceived. The completed dissertation—*"It's" Shakespeare: English Renaissance Drama and Monty Python* (2000)—raised a few eyebrows, but before long became the more respectable *Monty Python, Shakespeare and English Renaissance Drama* (2003). The die was cast.

"So, what is this?"

The above explains my interest, but not the project before you. For that we must go, naturally, to *The Faerie Queene*. In A.C. Hamilton's General Introduction to his 1977 edition of Edmund Spenser's epic poem, the esteemed Queen's University (Canada) editor ultimately justified the new edition in a single, simple, portmanteau-like dictum: "What is chiefly needed to understand the allegory fully is to understand all the words" (18). So the Poet Laureate's massive, six-book, mythologized celebration of and paean to Elizabeth and the Tudor dynasty can be fathomed by merely reading and understanding the words? Done and done. It sounds simple, of course, until it's realized that there are twelve cantos in each book and tens of thousands of words to be understood. And while all the words may have been quite discernible (to the classical scholar, at least) in the sixteenth century, time has deformed English-speaking culture and society and especially its language to such an extent that many of these words have either fallen out of the cultural lexicon or, more often, been gradually transformed themselves, taking on new meanings and fresh, sometimes even contradictory inferences. Hamilton relies on the *Oxford English Dictionary* (*OED*) for as many etymologies as he can trace but even there, nearly four hundred years on from the poem's composition, many words have continued to "become," rendering their Spenserian usage sometimes either estimable or completely mysterious.

But it's also more than just individual words lost in time. Hamilton has to deal with Spenser's poetic language, his personal quiver of allusions and references and Tudor mythologies, the poet's attempt to reclaim (as Jonson noted) words and images that have been culturally "wrested from their true calling." In short, Spenser reclaims language as he writes, obligating the critic to discover the mechanisms of that reclamation—otherwise, the epic poem becomes opaque, oblique, and eventually unreadable except for its most basic, obvious, immemorial images. Understanding the "true meaning" of the words, then, illumines the poet's purpose as he allegorically celebrates the virtues of Elizabeth, the Tudors, and England.

And now the natural transition to *Monty Python's Flying Circus*, and this unusual *editio cum notis unius editoris*. The seeds of this project were sown as I prepared for doctoral comprehensive exams, especially as I studied Hamilton's carefully, exhaustively annotated edition of *FQ* mentioned above, but also Evans' *The Riverside Shakespeare* (1974), Fraser and Rabkin's *Drama of the English Renaissance* (1976), and Hughes' 1957 edition of Milton's *Complete Poems and Major Prose*. The notes provided by editors in these seminal texts have become invaluable—preserving as much as possible original etymologies, and glossing mythic and contemporary references in often densely populated texts. If, I reasoned, the modern reader—student and critic alike—could struggle with centuries-old texts, even those so well-glossed as the works of Shakespeare, Spenser, and Milton, then the same contemporary eyes would likely find unglossed, non-annotated offerings of the culturally and politically topical comedy of *Monty Python's Flying Circus* equally challenging, excepting the episodes' witty writing and silly situations. Admittedly, dead parrots, silly walks, and jabberwock French can be funny without any explanation, and a man with a stoat through his head probably doesn't need a footnote. But the Pythons did find much of their subject matter in contemporary British newspapers and television, as well, and those topical references are ephemeral at best—they tend to fade very quickly, constantly being supplanted by newer references, which are also destined to wane and be replaced, and on. Images of or references to current Cabinet ministers, government policy papers, and various party scandals for example, dissolved into the ether as the Tories replaced Labour in June 1970, and then Labour returned the favor just a few years later, all during the initial run of *Flying Circus*. The Pythons' other favorite comedy ore mine, English and European history, is already the playground of the educated, cultured elite, meaning many viewers will not be able to recognize or appreciate such esoteric referents as the political significance (to England) of Charles XII and the seizing of duchies, the Jarrow March, or even the more recent Profumo Affair, all either mentioned by name or alluded to in *Flying Circus* episodes. In short, with the currency of the show firmly anchored in the late 1960s and early 1970s, and with the Pythons' gleeful, sometimes smarty-pants wielding of their collective Oxbridge classical educations, *Monty Python's Flying Circus* has become funny to many subsequent audiences (including Brits) simply for its slapstick and surreal silliness—ironically, this cultural, social, and historical lingua franca is in danger of being misunderstood, or even silenced forever.

And so this project is of two minds, at least. One goal I set was to perform a simple identification of names, faces, places, musical cues, uncredited actors, slang terms, colloquial expressions, etc., the hope being that the interested reader (who is likely also a viewer) could better appreciate the fractured, polyglot, multilevel nature of the Pythonesque world. That was

the easy part. Second but far more important are the deeper dives into that created world to actually "understand all the words," providing explanations and explications that surface glossings can't fathom. It was this second thread that wove itself throughout not only the late 1960s-1970s London, but back through the warp and woof of English history and mythology, into Number 10 Downing Street and Westminster and the courts system, into the living rooms and ducks-on-the-wall kitchens of Hull and Bristol, across the green belts of Bucks and Berks and the beaches of Oban and Paignton, and onto the brightly lit stages of recent British television history—reference-wise, the Pythons are all over the map. Examples: In Episode 1, the American singer Vicki Carr is mentioned, and she is briefly glossed. Similarly, textual mentions of various Modernist painters ("Chagall" and "Picasso"), television practices ("BP," "caption"), and historical persons ("Jean d'Arc" and "A. Lincoln") are briefly referenced in the same episode and briefly glossed. Elsewhere, philosophical luminaries including Jean-Paul Sartre and Søren Kierkegaard are mentioned by name, but just in passing, and are glossed just as briefly. In later episodes, including Eps. 14, 27, and 28, these thinkers are not only mentioned, but certain Python characters and situations begin to clearly exhibit Sartrean and Kierkegaardian characteristics—there the glossings justifiably become much more meaningful and analytic. It then becomes possible to go deep *and* far, making connections between the world of the 1960s and classical or existentialist philosophy, for example, and consistently identifying allusions, intertextualities, references, parodies, and imitations, to name just a few areas of illumination. In this way I will hopefully satisfy the demands of myriad reader/viewers, as well as demonstrate the cultural significance of these constructions that become Monty Python's social history.

And perhaps without knowing it the Pythons were remembering their version of a common man's (or Englishman's) social history, one specifically informed by modern communication technology—the newspaper, radio, and most importantly, television—and the then-recently expanded availability of the classical Oxbridge education, but also an England still very much yoked to traditions stretching back to the end of the Roman occupation. This synchronic/diachronic tension is apparent whenever Attila the Hun or Mozart stars in his own TV show (Eps. 20 and 1), or one typical English viewer can request and be granted the death of another (Ep. 1), or as a twelfth-century Viking finds himself riding through a twentieth-century suburb of Greater London (Ep. 27). As will be seen, the world created by *Flying Circus* is most often defined as *English* as opposed to *British*, where class strictures are admitted and lampooned and foreigners are almost always suspect, and the settings also tend to be centered in the Midlands and South, the heart of provincial England where most of the troupe members grew up. The settings and textual mentions and characterizations tend to favor this working, middle-class Britain—Luton and Guildford and Swindon and Wolverhampton—as well as the whole of Greater London. Taken together, these seemingly oxymoronic influences allowed the Pythons to meld popular and high culture, middle class and aristocracy, juxtaposing "cabbages and kings," essentially, offering a world where pith-helmeted avatars of the former British colonial empire can dance and fish-slap each other silly.

And now the nuts and bolts. The glossings for the episodes are provided alphabetically in an encyclopedic format. A reader or viewer interested in finding a particular reference can access the index, of course, but can also turn directly to the particular episode and look up the term, spoken phrase, or name in its alphabetic order. No introduction or summary of the particular episodes are provided—it's assumed the reader has seen the episode in question, or at least heard about the "Dirty Hungarian Phrasebook" sketch, for instance, and may want to know more. Entries are also cross-referenced to other episodes wherever necessary. Quotations from characters are cited using quotation marks, while stage directions, scene descriptions, and titles are indicated by the use of italics. Factual information culled from the BBC's Written Archives Collection is cited (as requested by the BBC) by folder number (e.g., T12/1,084). Neither the printed *Flying Circus* scripts nor the taped episodes comprise an original text or *locus classicus* for our purposes—both are referenced as needed. Finally, the abbreviation "PSC" ("Printed Script Commentary") at the beginning of an annotation means the word or phrase being referenced comes directly from the printed script itself, and would not be available to the viewer, just the reader. These strange, "in-house joke" phenomena will be discussed in several annotations.

The bibliography is *not* comprehensive, but represents a broad collection of monographs and encyclopedia or reference-type books, journal and newspaper articles, Internet journals and particular websites either consulted as this work progressed, or mentioned by name, subject, or author in the episodes themselves. A work like this annotation is chimeric, admittedly, and the after material reflects that polymorphousness. The listed resources as a whole are not exhaustive or definitive but representative. The bricolage or even magpie nature of the Pythons' referencing demands the inclusion of discrete, focused, sometimes even bizarre personal and organizational websites, for instance, where informational odds and ends are curioed. Simply put, there is much information needed for these glossings that isn't gathered into books, and perhaps never will be, and is only found hiding in the far-flung corners of the World Wide Web. This is probably true for many pop culture subjects, and will only become more the case as information is saved to digital as opposed to paper pages in the future. The advantages of a Google-tapped world is gratefully acknowledged here.

Finally, it's hoped that this venture into an admittedly popular-culture-meets-academia world will be appreciated for what it purports to be— a close, rigorous but still friendly reading of a cultural phenomenon. Shakespeare was a talented, ambitious "upstart Crow" in 1592, and Hitchcock was for many years simply a competent director of pulpy genre films—both have transcended those early straits to become the respected, acculturating institutions they are today. Whither Monty Python? The *OED* accepted "Pythonesque" into its 1989 edition, after all. There were dozens of funny and influential shows on British television, but *Monty Python's Flying Circus* managed to live well beyond not only its natural lifespan and other shows' popularity—but its "Englishness" has ingrained itself into our cultural lexicon along the way. The following pages explore the longevity, the complexity, the reflexivity of *Monty Python*, and promise an illuminating read.

Episode 1: "Whither Canada?"

– A –

"A272 . . . Hindhead"—("Picasso/Cycling Race") The A272 is far south of Hindhead, which *is* on the A3—the A3 continues on north and east into London.

"AA"—("Picasso/Cycling Race") British Automobile Association, established in London in 1905. The organization doesn't regularly follow celebrity bicycle races, and will be mentioned prominently again in Ep. 44, when Mrs. S.C.U.M. (Jones) is wondering where to pay her AA bill after the impending nuclear holocaust.

"angel-drawers"—("*It's the Arts*") A variation of other terms like "angel face," and may also be an ironic term, since Ross doesn't appear terribly angelic or cherubic (see *OED*). This sketch is also an early indication of the "thesaurus sketch" structure as often created by the Cleese and Chapman writing team—in this instance multiple terms of endearment. The homoerotic subtext is apparent, though this subtext will be undercut by the interviewer's loss of interest as the interview concludes, then re-engaged in the exchange between interviewers off-camera.

In *At Last the 1948 Show* (1967), Cleese and Chapman had contributed a similarly homosocial linking element set in a courtroom, where the barrister (Cleese) asks: "Where were you on the evening of the 14th of July?" Chapman responds defensively, "Why?" Cleese then answers, petulant and pouty, "Well, I waited up all night for you and you never came home!"

Python's penchant for undercutting almost any proposition forwarded by the text/performance will become a hallmark of the show's structure.

animation—(PSC; link out of "*It's the Arts*") Prior to this Gilliam animation mentioned in the printed script, a five-section collage of artists and artwork appears, with the screen divided into fourths and a circular frame in the middle. In each of these spaces is projected a motion picture image. The upper left image appears to be a filmed image of Henry Moore at work (1898-1986), an English sculptor of the human form, including *Reclining Figure* (1939) (Wilkinson, *ODNB*). The bottom right image is a painter using a wide trowel or spatula, and could be Franz Kline (1910-1962), an American abstract expressionist. The lower left image could be violinist Yehudi Menuhin (1916-1999), who will be mentioned again in Ep. 31, as a judge in the "Summarize Proust" competition. The central image is a symphony orchestra, and could be the Royal Philharmonic Orchestra in the Royal Albert Hall. This collage is probably meant to serve as the closing "shot" for the *It's the Arts* program begun much earlier. The Gilliam animation interrupts before any credits can roll.

The music used underneath this arts image is from "Saturday Sports" by Wilfred Burns, played by the National Light Orchestra. "Saturday Sports" was the well-known theme of the BBC television show *Sportsview* (1954-1968), which featured Brian Johnston, the wildly popular cricket commentator mentioned later in Eps. 21 and 45. Music used in the ensuing animation (accompanying Gilliam's animated photos) includes "All the Fun of the Fairground" played on the 89-key "marenghi" fair organ (WAC T12/1,082). The titles/credits for *Sportsview* were structured much like the panelled titles used in *It's the Arts*.

"Ardennes"—("The Funniest Joke in the World") Why the six-month delay, if the joke was ready by January? The Battle of the Ardennes was fought between 16 December 1944 and 16 January 1945. In July 1944, the Battle of the Bulge (becoming the more popular name for the period) was under way, the last German ground offensive on the Western Front, and American and British forces were enjoying some success before a slowdown in autumn 1944. In Python's world, then, the Killer Joke turned the tide of war on the Western Front, effectively ending the Nazi threat in Europe.

"Awful"—(PSC; "The Funniest Joke in the World") This type of joke—a set-up followed by rim-shot pay-off—is the very kind of comedy that the Pythons had said they were reacting against as they fashioned *Flying Circus*. Whenever a character in *FC* makes or attempts to make such a joke, he/she is stopped mid-payoff (often fatally), or punished after the fact. In Ep. 18, when the Gents are trying to escape being "caught on film," one urges the others to "Run this way!" One (Idle) answers: "If I could run that way—." He is cut off by the raised fingers of the others, meaning that kind of joke won't be tolerated, and he stops, understanding completely.

In this the Pythons are also moving away from one of their hero groups, The Goons, who were not above delivering, without apology, these kinds of puns and "boom-boom" jokes in the mélange of their physical and cerebral comedy. Example: A character (played by Harry Secombe) is hiding inside the piano in the sketch "Napoleon's Piano." He is discovered, and another character (played by Peter Sellers) asks him what he's doing in the piano. "I'm hidin'," the man answers. "No, you're not," the questioner retorts. "Haydn's been dead for years." The audience responds well to this set-up–payoff joke structure, and the show moves briskly forward.

– B –

"Battersea"—("Picasso/Cycling Race") South side of the Thames in Wandsworth borough. The nearest major circular (roundabout) seems to be somewhat west of and south of Battersea at the confluence of the A27 and the A3205 in Wandsworth Town.

The mammoth, iconic, four-stacked Battersea Power Station is clearly visible over the housetops in Ep. 12, during the "Upperclass Twit" sketch.

Raymond Baxter type—(PSC; "Picasso/Cycling Race") Baxter (b. 1922) introduced the *Challenge* program on BBC in 1963, and was a presenter on *Tomorrow's World*, a BBC science and technology program, from 1965-1977. His "type" wears a winter coat, hat, horn-rimmed glasses, and small mustache. He cuts a similar figure to the "Eddie Waring" caricature depicted earlier.

beach—("It's Man" introduction) The beach where the "It's Man" comes ashore is located at Poole Harbour, Dorset, about ninety miles southeast of London. Palin takes viewers back to this setting some twenty years later in the *Pythonland* special show made for the BBC in 1989.

The Pythons and BBC scheduled multiple location shots for this type of excursion, shooting as many exterior locations for future episodes (links and entire sketches/films) as possible. In this same sand dune area, for instance, several exteriors for "The Funniest Joke in the World" and the "Genghis Khan" scenes were shot.

"Berkshire"—("The Funniest Joke in the World") Home to Windsor Castle, Eton College, and some of England's most prestigious families, Berkshire is an area bounded by Hampshire, Wiltshire, Oxfordshire, Buckinghamshire, and Surrey in the south-central part of England. The Pythons probably chose Berkshire as the Joke's burial place due to nearby Salisbury Plains' military installations and training grounds.

This shot was not recorded in the Berkshire countryside, but in the meadows outside of Saxmundham, Suffolk on 22 August 1969 (WAC T12/1,083).

"biblical laments"—("The Funniest Joke in the World") Laments are conventional, ritualized forms of mourning, and here referring to the *Book of Lamentations* in the Old Testament, which details the Chaldean destruction of Jerusalem.

The Chaldeans will be significant again, mentioned in Ep. 43, "Police Helmets."

bizarre things happen—(PSC; "Opening Titles") The final images in this Gilliam-created opening title sequence are the foot crushing the *Monty Python's Flying Circus* title, and the image of God "shushing" from above. The foot is from the Bronzino painting *An Allegory with Venus and Cupid* (c. 1540-1550), and the God figure is lifted from *The Immaculate Conception* by Carlo Gravelli (1492). Gilliam borrowed Cupid's right foot for the title sequence. Both the Bronzino and Gravelli have been displayed in the National Gallery in London for many years.

The "bizarre things happen" script comment means that the Pythons doing most of the writing (Chapman, Cleese, Idle, Jones, and Palin) would have been given only the scarcest of outlines for the proposed Gilliam animation sequence, and many times all they knew was that Gilliam was working on something thematically connected to the episode.

"black oval shapes"—(PSC; "Picasso/Cycling Race") This description could be referring to abstract Kandinsky paintings like *Black Spot I* (1912), *Ravine Improvisation* (1914), or *Cossacks* (1910-1911). *Cossacks* has been in the Tate's collection since 1938. Kandinsky gave himself over to abstract painting with the formation of the Munich group Der Blaue Reiter/The Blue Rider (1911-1914).

"blimey"—(PSC; "Famous Deaths") A common corruption of "blame me" or "blind me," and probably earlier from "God blame me" and/or "God blind me." Also, certainly incongruous and anachronistic that Mozart would utter such a word, since it is very much a British slang and wasn't coined (according to the *OED*) until the 1890s.

blow-up behind—(PSC; "Arthur 'Two-Sheds' Jackson") During this transition into the "Two-Sheds" Jackson interview on the typical two-chair set, a portion of the "Allegro Vivace" section of Beethoven's Symphony No. 4 plays beneath.

BP screen—(PSC; linking element) *Back Projection* screen. A projector throws a filmed image from behind onto a see-through screen, thus "back projection" or "back projected." This technology has become outdated with the advent of TV chroma-key technology, etc.

"Brancusi"—("Picasso/Cycling Race") Constantin Brancusi (1876-1957) was actually a sculptor, which really would have been a feat during a bicycle race. He was an abstractionist, and in the *FC* text he is cleverly described as "making a break on the outside." His *Bird in Space*, for example, wasn't even recognized as a work of art when it came to the United States for the first time in 1927, and was taxed (at a 40 percent rate) as a piece of industrial metal (*Time*, 7 March 1927). The Tate Gallery first collected a Brancusi sculpture in 1959.

"Braque"—("Picasso/Cycling Race") Georges Braque (1882-1963) was a colleague and competitor to Picasso, and practiced a more lyrical Cubism. He featured the bird motif in a number of his later works, including *Falconeers, Frontispiece* (1952), and especially *Untitled (3 birds)* (1955), *Untitled (flock birds)* (1955), and *Untitled (black bird)* (1955). Braque also produced the painting *Bicycle* (1952), depicting a bicycle in a forested area, with flowers and an open field in the background. This last painting may even have had some influence on the juxtaposition of bicycling and painting in the Python creation process for this episode. The Tate collected Braque works as early as 1926, and acquired at least two in the 1960s.

"Buffet, Bernard"—("Picasso/Cycling Race") Painter and printmaker Buffet (1928-1999) was influenced by the existentialist movement; his work was also Passion-oriented, and influenced by the hardships of the post-WWII era. In 1970 the Pope asked for and received—from the artist—a collection of Buffet works depicting the life of Christ. Buffet may be the most marginally known of all these artists, at least in the UK, which may just mean that he was a personal favorite of one of the Pythons.

The Tate Gallery collected Buffet's *Portrait of the Artist* (1954) in 1955, and then it would be thirty years before a second Buffet work would join the Tate's significant collection of Modern Art.

" . . . but which the Germans could"—("The Funniest Joke in the World") This scenario is reminiscent of wartime endeavors on both sides of the battle, including radar, the Manhattan Project for atomic weaponry, the German atomic research programs (heavy water [D_2O] research, etc.), as well as rocket and jet air warfare technology, etc.

– C –

caption—(PSC; "Famous Deaths") These captions are superimposed on the screen. Python's use of historical figures and settings will become essential to the structure and humor of *FC*. In this case, the incongruity of an eighteenth-century composer hosting a television show provides the jumping-off point for the sketch's humor. In most cases, there is no attempt to explain or account for the presence of long-dead figures, or characters separated by geography, time, or culture, as they interact or just appear in modern settings. This also becomes a Python trope, and reflects the significant influence that seminal Modernist works like Eliot's *The Waste Land*—where class and accent, the past and present, and even cultures and languages interact in a sort of ever-present, decaying London—exhibited in the works of Monty Python. Eliot's play *Murder in the Cathedral* (1935) will be referenced in Ep. 28.

Under this particular caption can be heard music from one of Mozart's quartets, "Pression No. 3," probably referring to Quartet No. 3 (WAC T12/1,082 5 October 1969).

"Carr, Vicki"—(closing credits) An American-born singer, Carr had performed in 1967 at a Royal Command Performance for Queen Elizabeth.

"Chagall"—("Picasso/Cycling Race") Russian-born Marc Chagall (1887-1985) combined influences of Expressionism, Cubism, the bright colors of Fauvism, etc., and his early experiences of simple folk life and persecution as a Jew.

The Tate Gallery acquired at least seven Chagall paintings between 1942 and 1953, all of which are still part of the museum's impressive collection of Modern Art.

"Chichester"—("Picasso/Cycling Race") Town on the A27 in West Sussex county, eighteen miles east of Portsmouth, and north of Chichester Harbour. In Ep. 10, Ron Obvious (Jones) will attempt to eat the Chichester Cathedral. The Chichester Festival is mentioned in Ep. 25, when a Shakespearean actor overplaying the Richard III role is admitted into hospital, to be operated on "just in time."

clearly labelled—(PSC; "The Funniest Joke in the World") This sign-carrying acts as both a means of instant identification and a source for incongruous humor. The silliness of the self-conscious signs may also help shake the stigma that depictions of the Nazis might still have engendered on British television and for British viewers, especially in comedic settings.

In the earliest days of cinematic animation, artists like Winsor McCay, William Nolan, and Raoul Barré regularly employed long-standing comic strip conventions, including labels and thought/dialogue balloons, etc. While at Warner Bros. in the 1930s Tex Avery used some of these same conventions, especially the sign-holding character ("Corny gag, isn't it?"). In this Gestapo scene the signs appear much like those used in the 1952 Bugs Bunny/Marvin Martian cartoon *Hasty Hare* (dir. Chuck Jones). After being captured by the Martians, Bugs is trussed up and labeled "One Overconfident Earth Creature." Later Bugs escapes and ties up Marvin and his dog, K-9, their labels reading "Two Disgruntled Martians."

"Cleveland, Carol"—(closing credits) Unofficial cast member Cleveland (b. 1942) appears here in the credits for Ep. 1, but not in the actual episode. She appears first in Ep. 2, which actually was recorded first but aired second. The credit sequence may have been created for the initial episode, then appended to this episode as it moved into the premier spot.

Cleveland had also posed with the Pythons for several of their publicity photos during the writing and recording of the initial episodes. This inclusion was clearly the BBC's attempt to broaden the show's demographic potentialities, and to be in line with the mixed cast structures of recent successful comedy shows such as *Do Not Adjust Your Set* (1967-1969), *At Last the 1948 Show* (1967), and the American hits *Your Show of Shows* (1950-1954) and *Laugh-In* (1968).

"comfort"—(PSC; "Arthur 'Two-Sheds' Jackson") Homosocial or homosexual? The significant number of allusions to male homosexuality in *FC* become all the more intriguing as the homosexuality of Graham Chapman is considered. Chapman himself plays some of the most "flaming" and outré characters and, conversely, shoots and kills the admittedly gay Algy (Palin) in Ep. 33, the "Biggles Dictates a Letter Sketch."

The significance of the Stonewall riots in June 1969 in Greenwich Village, New York, have to be considered when discussing the presence of obvious or even flamboyant gay characters in popular culture, and for our purposes, on public television. When New York police raided the known gay bar, the Stonewall Inn, beating cross-dressed and effeminate patrons and sparking a series of street riots, the once-hidden world of sexually active gay men (and, to a lesser degree, lesbians and the transgendered) was splashed across newspapers and evening news reports (see D'Emilio; Duberman). Just two months later the Pythons would record their first episodes, and the following month (October 1969) those episodes begin to air. Essentially, the very public and disturbing police and mob actions gave indirect license to the Pythons (and other creative entities, of course) to cross what may have been formerly an unfordable rubicon—the redemptive depiction and gentle comedic ribbing of gay characters.

Finally, the "Queer TV Database" lists gay characters appearing or who have appeared on British television, and the absences are quite telling. There are none listed for the 1950s, just seven for the 1960s (none of which seemed to be flaunting their sexuality), then twenty-seven in the decade of the 1970s. (The seven in the 1960s include roommates Bert and Ernie of *Sesame Street* fame, so the delimiting factors for inclusion in the database might be questionable.)

commentator—(PSC; "The Funniest Joke in the World") This man (Jones) is dressed in typical period attire for a newscaster—suit, tie, horn-rimmed glasses—so we are still in the present, assumedly. The timeline will quickly dissolve, however, and we will be back in the WWII era for the balance of the sketch.

"commissioned painting"—("Picasso/Cycling Race") Probably the most famous of Picasso's commissioned works was the mural requested by the Spanish Republican government in 1937—a work which ultimately became *Guernica*—for the Spanish Pavilion of the Paris Exposition. Picasso also painted the commissioned work *Stage Curtain for the Ballet "Parade"* (1917), and even the dove symbol commissioned by the Communist Party for the World Peace Congress in 1949.

Additionally, the BBC Radio and TV had been commissioning musical pieces, radio serials, and television shows since their beginnings, though admittedly few modern art paintings.

– D –

"d'Arc, Jean"—("Famous Deaths") Joan of Arc (1412-1431), also called Saint Joan, answered a divine call and led the French army to victory at Orléans during the Hundred Years' War. She was captured by the English (with the help of French collaborators), and was burned at the stake. Transcripts of the trial are extant (and fascinating), and were the basis of Carl Dreyer's celebrated 1932 film on Joan. She was canonized in 1920.

"Day, Robin"—("*It's the Arts*" and "Arthur 'Two-Sheds' Jackson") Later in this same episode, when an-

other Interviewer (Idle) is having trouble with an interviewee (Arthur "Two-Sheds" Jackson, played by Jones), the interviewers will gang up and throw Jackson from the studio set. This overtly aggressive and physical characterization is almost certainly based on the reputation earned by well-known Independent Television News (ITN) and BBC interviewer Robin Day (1923-2000), who created for himself an intense, pointed interview style, especially with previously almost untouchable government figures—including heads of state, members of Parliament, and even PM Macmillan in February 1959—asking direct questions and accepting only similarly direct and ingenuous answers. Day is credited with inventing the modern television interview. (For more on Day see his entry in the *ODNB*.) He stood for Parliament for the Liberal party from Hereford in 1959, and lost. (The Liberal party will be the focus of Ep. 45.)

See the fine columns/obituaries written about Day and published in *The Guardian* (8 August 2000). In the setting of the sketch, the interviewers become almost Western heroes cleaning up Dodge or Tombstone.

"Dead March"—(PSC; "The Funniest Joke in the World") Actually called "Funeral March," this version of the Beethoven work was arranged by Mayhew Lake (WAC T12/1,082).

"De Kooning"—("Picasso/Cycling Race") Willem De Kooning (1904-1997), a Dutch painter, was also a member of the New York School (see Pollock note below) and an "action" painter, alternating between "abstract and figural painting" (Tansey 860).

By 1969 the Tate Gallery could claim three De Kooning works as part of its collection, two of which were donated in 1969 by the painter himself, through the American Federation of Arts. The paintings which the Pythons could have viewed during this period in the Tate were completed in 1966-1967, some of the latest work cited in this sketch.

"Delaunay"—("Picasso/Cycling Race") Robert Delaunay, born in France (1885-1941), is credited with introducing vibrant colors into Cubism, leading to Orphism. Like Kandinsky, Delaunay was also a member of the Blue Rider movement.

The Tate had purchased two Delaunay works prior to the writing of this episode, one in 1958 (*Study for "The City,"* 1909-1910), and the other in 1967 (*Windows Open Simultaneously*, 1912).

"Derby-Doncaster rally"—("Picasso/Cycling Race") Derby and Doncaster are about fifty miles apart, and the presumed route might be north on the A38 to the A61 to the A630, and into Doncaster. No such race appears to have existed.

"Der ver . . . "—("The Funniest Joke in the World") A swipe at Germany's wartime propaganda beamed into Great Britain over the radio waves, where in this case the English syntax seems to have confused the Nazi translators:

> Radio Voice: There were two peanuts walking down the street, and one was a salted . . . peanut.

The confused looks on the faces of the Ma and Pa Britain listeners (Chapman and Idle) tell the whole story, and may have been the actual response of many Brits and especially Londoners who heard the Third Reich's attempts at persuasion by broadcast propaganda.

Words in the joke like "ver" ("were"), "valking" ("walking"), "peanuts" ("peanuts"), "von" ("one"), and "vas" ("was") are not, of course, actual German words, but Python's jabberwocky German.

There were significant attempts at such broadcast propaganda by the Third Reich during the war, including UK citizen William Joyce, known as "Lord Haw-Haw," who made light of the German threat to Great Britain in the late 1930s, and was listened to (and enjoyed) by millions in the UK. Joyce would be hanged for treason after the war. According to a surviving BBC internal memo dated 16 November 1939, the BBC's counteraction to these popular and subtly effective propaganda broadcasts was to create its own homespun version of the war effort, and broadcast at the same times as the enemy. (See the "BBC at War" sections of bbc.co.uk.)

Deutschland Über Alles—(PSC; "The Funniest Joke in the World") "German, Germany Above (Over) All." German national anthem (1922-present), with music by Haydn, and text by von Fallersleben. This version is drawn from the album *Hitler's Inferno: In Words and Music 1932-1945—Marching Songs of Nazi Germany* (WAC T12/1,082).

"Dibley Road"—("The Funniest Joke in the World") No such road exists. The setting, however, seems to be the same one used in the "Dull Life of a City Stockbroker" sketch in Ep. 6, as well. Production notes for the episode indicate that this is 48 Ullsworth Road, Barnes (WAC T12/1,083).

According to Palin, this name ("Dibley") comes from the "Gwen Dibley's Flying Circus" title that Palin had brought to the table as one possible name for the show (Morgan, 1999, 26).

"Different Gestapo Officer"—(PSC; "The Funniest Joke in the World") The transparent use of signs, names, and labels to make one thing or person into another is a Python staple, and was probably a holdover from the vaudeville and music hall stages, and even

Warner Brothers cartoons. Cf. the "Dead Parrot" sketch in Ep. 8, "The Chemist Sketch" in Ep. 17, and the "Conquistador Coffee Campaign" sketch in Ep. 24 for similar sign usage.

"Dobson's"—(linking element into "The Funniest Joke in the World") A name possibly borrowed from the Beerbohm 1911 novel, *Zuleika Dobson*. See entry for "know what I like" in Ep. 4 for more on this intriguing possible connection.

This entire sketch is something of a rare linking element to the eventual WWII-era setting of the latter part of the "The Funniest Joke in the World" sketch, foreshadowing the military applications of the lethal joke. It is rare because very few of the *FC* linking elements are anything more than a single person or image, completely decontextualized and distinct from the narrative action at hand. This one is much more of a smoothing device to propel us into the WWII setting of the following and abnormally lengthy sketch. The famous picture of Churchill flashing the "V for victory" hand sign adorns the wall behind, and the link between his ample face and the pigs on the map can't be missed. (Remember, Churchill would fall out of the public's favor very quickly after the war ended, being seen as an innovative wartime leader but a peacetime throwback to the Victorian era. Labour and Clement Attlee picked up 239 seats in the sweeping 1945 General Election, as well as almost 50 percent of the popular vote, and the Conservatives were out of power until 1951.)

Curiously, there is also a small "action figure" standing next to the map table, one clearly requested in the design requirements for the episode. The figure is a striped-shirt robber type, with mask and a gun, and made of balsa wood. It's well out of place, visually and thematically, and not referenced in the short scene at all (WAC T12/1,082). Cleese will dress just this way, however, in the "Bank Robber (Lingerie Shop)" sketch in Ep. 10. The model will finally appear in Ep. 13, in the *"Probe-Around* on Crime" sketch.

"Dufy, Raoul"—("Picasso/Cycling Race") Dufy (1877-1953) created bright, colorful paintings (Fauvist and Impressionist influences), many of scenes of pleasure. See Tansey.

By late 1969 the Tate Gallery held two Dufy watercolors, *Olive Trees by the Golfe Juan* (c. 1927) and *Deauville, Drying the Sails* (1933).

– E –

"Eddie"—(PSC; "Famous Deaths") The written script earlier identifies this character as an "Eddie Waring figure," though he is clearly supposed to be Eddie himself by the time Mozart (Cleese) thanks him. He is an "announcer type" or "presenter" characteristic of British TV then and now, thus a key figure in *FC's* television parody format. See the note for Waring below.

"Edward the Seventh, King"—("Famous Deaths") Edward VII (1841-1910) was Queen Victoria's eldest son, and is the only participant on the list to have died a somewhat natural death, which probably accounts for his low score (see "back marker" below). After his father Albert's death in 1861, Edward took on larger responsibilities as his mother grieved in seclusion, though political control was kept from him until he ascended the throne in 1901. His son, George V, succeeded him in 1910. See the *ODNB*.

Edward is slighted as the "back marker": "One who starts from scratch or has the least favorable handicap in a game, match or race" (*OED*). "Bertie's" death was much less dramatic, memorable, and/or tragic than any of the others, his life was characterized by his own epicurean profligacies, being blamed by his mother for his father's early demise, and he finally had the wretched bad luck of following his mother, the iconic and beloved Victoria, onto the throne.

Episode 1—This episode was actually recorded second, on 9 July 1969, then broadcast first on 5 October 1969. (The subtitle "Whither Canada?" is also the lone reference to Canada in the episode.) The stated budget for this episode was £4,000, then £3,800 for each subsequent show, according to Michael Mills of Light Entertainment. He would end the 31 July 1969 budget memo, written to John Howard Davies and Ian MacNaughton: "You have heard the word of the Lord . . . please heed it." (By way of comparison, the fourth and final series episodes had bloated to more than £100,000 per episode) (WAC T12/1,083).

Also, this episode was taped at the BBC Television Centre on Stage 6, with very few extras or walk-ons. The show was often bumped around from soundstage to soundstage as other more known or respected shows needed the space. On several occasions the show actually had to leave TV Centre and tape, for example, at Golders Green Hippodrome or Ealing Television-Film Studios. There are mentions of these somewhat capricious shuttlings in the day-to-day memos and notes found in the BBC's Written Archive Collection.

Lastly, this episode was sub-subtitled at the end of the typed graphics credits page, "A new comedy series for the Switched On." This subtitle did not appear in the finished episode (WAC T12/1,082).

"Ernst, Max"—("Picasso/Cycling Race") Ernst (1891-1976) was originally a Dadaist, then moved to Surrealism and the freedom of "chance associations" in his work (Tansey 830).

There were four Ernst works available for viewing in the Tate Gallery in 1969.

"evergreen bucket kickers"—("Famous Deaths") An indication that Lord Nelson continues to be a fascinating (and much-trumpeted) English historical figure, looming large in the elementary and secondary school history classrooms, undoubtedly. The phrase means simply a "favorite" or "popular" ("evergreen") public figure death, in this case one that has burrowed its way into English culture.

Nelson's name would have been in the news fairly recently, and spectacularly, when the Nelson Pillar in Dublin (erected in 1808) was blown up by Irish Republican forces in 1966, and had to be demolished completely. There are extant a number of political cartoons addressing the subject, including one from Keith Waite (*The Sun*, 9 March 1966), wherein Lord Nelson unexpectedly alights from his lofty column to read, concernedly, the Dublin newspaper headlines.

"Ewhurst"—("Picasso/Cycling Race") City in Surrey County on the B2127, and where Picasso is seemingly way off course when he crashes. His attempted shortcut "through Dorking via Gomslake and Peashall" is either cheating or simply impossible, since the towns in question are actually "Gomshall" and "Peaslake," with Dorking further along the A25.

– F –

"fairy"—("Arthur 'Two-Sheds' Jackson") Slang for a male homosexual. The term isn't used nearly as often in *FC* as some other homosexual put-downs, like "poof" and its derivatives. The term wouldn't be as significant except that the interviewers are about to share—off-camera but within earshot—a very homosocial/homosexual moment. In the context of this scene, then, a "fairy" is a man who allows himself to be given the bum's rush (pun slightly intended) by more "butch" gay men. The term will be used again, and prominently, in Ep. 33 when Captain Biggles (Chapman) asks Ginger (Gilliam) if he's gay, and in Ep. 13, where policemen become fairies with magic wands.

film of Hitler rally—(PSC; "The Funniest Joke in the World") This series of Hitler images is taken from a Pathé newsreel, Ref. No. 139, while the crowd scenes are lifted from "WWII Nuremberg Rally" footage from Associated British Pathé (BBC WAC T12/1,082).

"Fontwell"—("Picasso/Cycling Race") On the A27 in West Sussex, five miles west of Arundel. The A29 doesn't run to or from Chichester, however, being a north-south route between Bognor Regis and Fontwell. Picasso would then have to stay on the A29 northward to Billingshurst, where the A29 meets the A272, a major east-west road.

– G –

"gate in the country overlooking a field"—("Flying Sheep") This scene—gentlefolk leaning against a white fence in an idyllic northern setting, admiring the fields of green—is a tableau drawn almost directly from the more pastoral moments of novelist Thomas Hardy and perhaps especially D.H. Lawrence. Both authors will be specifically revisited in later episodes (Eps. 17 and 2, respectively), and their ethoi referenced throughout *FC*.

In Lawrence's *Sons and Lovers* (1913), mother Gertrude and beloved son Paul strike a similar pose as they watch cricketers, and as Gertrude falls in love with her youngest son.

"Geneva Convention"—("The Funniest Joke in the World") International agreements were made beginning about 1864 in Geneva, Switzerland, regarding conduct of combatants during times of war. Other kinds of Geneva Convention agreements include acceptable treatment of prisoners of war, civilians, and non-combatants, etc.

"Gerard's Cross"—(PSC; "Italian Lesson") Actually misspelled, it is correctly "Gerrards Cross," and is found in the county of Buckinghamshire, four miles northwest of Uxbridge, west of Greater London. This mention of a Greater London suburb elicits a laugh from the cobbled-together studio audience (who don't laugh much at all during this initial episode), perhaps just because the name is familiar. During this period, Gerrards Cross would have been located somewhat awkwardly, viz., its status as a recently incorporated town (1859), and its emerging attractiveness for London belt commuters.

"Gericault"—("Picasso/Cycling Race") Theodore Gericault (1791-1824) is seemingly well out of place in this bicycling group of modern artists, as he preceded most of the other artists mentioned by several generations. He was influenced by Michelangelo and Rubens and worked in the Romantic movement. Perhaps Gericault's (and Romanticism's in general) fascination with the physiognomy of death and the insane allows his inclusion by the Pythons. (See Tansey 733-37.) Gericault is the only artist in this race to not have a significant, continuing presence in London museums or galleries during the Pythons' lifetimes.

Gilliam's wonderfully visual mind—(PSC; "Whizzo Butter" link) Terry Gilliam's animated sequences ap-

pear throughout the *FC* series, and continue on into
the feature films. At the time of the script rehearsals,
Gilliam would have been off alone working on animated links, without consulting other cast members.
He would have had a copy of the script, but none of
the other Pythons knew, prior to taping, just what the
links might look like or contain, thematically. This is
why these scripts can only mention Gilliam and his
work, and almost never describe it (though the collected scripts' editor, Roger Wilmut, could well have
inserted descriptions, but chose not to). See Morgan's
Monty Python Speaks! or Gilliam's *Gilliam on Gilliam* for
more on Gilliam's animation process.

"gramophone records"—("The Funniest Joke in the
World") Both the gramophone (a vintage record player)
and records are now considered at least classics, and antiquated. At the time, available technology for sound
projection would have been limited to phonograph-
type players and reel-to-reel tape players. By Ep. 26, a
reel-to-reel player is used for similar sound projection.

This same kind of antiquated player will be
mounted on a bicycle and used to broadcast Nazi
propaganda and music in the "Minehead By-Election"
sketch. See Ep. 12.

"Grazie . . . gentilezza"—("Italian Lesson") Approximate translations for these sometimes mangled Italian
phrases are as follows (only the translated lines are included):

> Giuseppe: Il cucchiaio ("The spoon")
> Teacher: Molto bene, Giuseppe ("Very well, Giuseppe")
> Giuseppe: Grazie signor . . . grazie di tutta la sua gen-
> tilezza ("Thank you, Sir . . . thank you for your kind-
> ness")
> All: Sono Inglese di Gerrard's Cross ("I am an English-
> man from Gerrard's Cross")
> Teacher: Sono Italiano di Napoli ("I am an Italian from
> Naples")
> Mariolini: Ah, capisco, mille grazie signor ("Ah, I un-
> derstand, many [thousand] thanks, sir")
> Francesco: Per favore, Signor! ("Please, Sir!")
> Francesco: Non conosgreve parliamente, signor devo
> me parlo sono Italiano di Napoli quando il habitare
> de Milano ("I don't understand this language, Sir.
> Why do I have to say I am an Italian from Naples
> when I live in Milan?")
> Francesco: Milano è tanto meglio di Napoli. Milano è la
> citta la più bella di tutti . . . nel mondo ("Milan is
> much better than Naples. Milan is the most beautiful
> city in the world.")

As it turns out, the Pythons did fairly well with their
probably limited Italian language skills, with only the
"Non conosgreve" section exhibiting some "improper
Italian," according to Maria Krull, Northern Illinois
University, who provided these translations.

"Guernica . . . Vallauris"—("Picasso/Cycling Race")
These are titles of Picasso works as rattled off by the
cyclist Reg Moss (Chapman). *Guernica* is titled after
the Spanish city bombed in 1937 by German planes as
training for the nascent Nazi Blitzkrieg. *Guernica* is
actually a mural painting, because of its size (approx.
11'6" by 25'8"). *Les Demoiselles d'Avignon* (actual title)
is from 1907 and measures 8' by 7'8". At Vallauris,
France, the National Picasso Museum contains the
celebrated 1952 works *War* and *Peace*.

Secondly, how and why a sprint cyclist would have
such intimate knowledge of the history of modern
painting can only be answered by referring to
Python's penchant for allowing characters (like the
Pepperpots, for instance) access to knowledge well beyond their presented position or social station. Coal
miners in Ep. 15 will understand classical architecture
and European martial/treaty history, for instance;
Pepperpots will argue about the true meanings of
"freedom" in Sartre's existential masterworks in Ep.
27; and perhaps most famously, Middle Ages peasants
will be given intricate knowledge of anarchosyndical-
ist political structures in the feature film *Monty Python
and the Holy Grail* (1974).

"Guilford"—("Famous Deaths") A town in Surrey,
England, at a ford across the River Wey. Guilford is
about 28 miles from London, so at least 228 miles from
Hull, which means the Pythons probably just pulled
names out of a hat when writing this section. With
Palin hailing from the north, and several of the others
raised in the Midlands, it's easy to see how certain
place names might have been chosen based on childhood neighborhoods and regions.

Guilford will be mentioned again during the Picasso
sketch ("the Guilford Bypass") as it actually sits
astride the A3. No worthwhile bypass seems to have
existed in this area, however, since the A3 dissects
Guildford, and all other roads are much smaller.

"Guiseppe"—("Italian Lesson") It's already clear that
almost everyone in the classroom is Italian, and only
the teacher seems to have missed this point. The irony
of teaching introductory, conversational Italian to native Italians is the obvious joke, and it's compounded
by Python's characteristic "comic misunderstanding"
trope, thanks to the teacher's failure to recognize his
students' nationalities. This comic misunderstanding
occurs when peasants refuse to recognize kings, in the
Python world, or when Thomas Dekker's lower-class
characters consort with upper-class characters on the
same social level, and without self-consciousness, in
The Shoemaker's Holiday (1599). The tradition is also
carried on in myriad eighteenth-century plays (e.g.,

Sheridan's *The Rivals*) and novels (Fielding's *Tom Jones*). See Larsen's *MPSERD*.

– H –

Ham House—(PSC; "The Funniest Joke in the World") The home of the Duke and Duchess of Lauderdale in the late seventeenth century, located in Ham, on Ham Street, Richmond, Greater London. It's not absolutely certain from the shot itself whether they actually used the location, since it is a rather tight close-up, though Ham House figures prominently in Ep. 2, so the re-use of the location would be likely. (See notes for "Osborne" in Ep. 2.) BBC production notes confirm that Ham House was, indeed, secured as the setting for several scenes (WAC T12/1,083).

"Harriers"—("Picasso/Cycling Race") Interesting allusion, since the Manchester Harriers are and were a track-and-field club, not a cycling concern. (A harrier is a dog or a cross-country runner.) This YMCA club has been in existence since 1882.

"HEAVEN!"—("Whizzo Butter" animation) The final word displayed in Gilliam's Whizzo Butter ad, the music behind this hard-sell moment is a sped-up version of the "Hallelujah Chorus" taken from "Handel's *Messiah* Highlights No. 44" (WAC T12/1,082).

"hedgehog"—("It's the Arts") An important member of the Python bestiary, by Ep. 14 an enormous hedgehog named Spiny Norman is stalking the notorious criminal Dinsdale Piranha.

The fact that Robin Day has a hedgehog isn't so surprising when looking forward to Praline's (Cleese) encounter with a Post Office Worker (Palin) in Ep. 23. There, it's revealed that Praline himself has a pet halibut, and that prominent public figures such as Sir Gerald Nabarro, Dawn Palethorpe, Alan Bullock, Marcel Proust, and Kemal Ataturk also claim special and oddly named pets. See notes to Ep. 23 for entries on each of these people.

"hospital"—("The Funniest Joke in the World") This is also shot while on the dunes at Bournemouth, using the same tent seen in the "Genghis Khan" scene. This kind of doubling, especially on locations where film shooting is scheduled, reduced production costs (or kept costs near what the BBC would allow), and will be seen throughout the run of the show. Note, for example, the various shots throughout the first, second, and third series that feature the rugged highlands of Scotland near Glencoe (including, for instance, the "Lemon curry?" inserts in Ep. 33).

"Hull"—("Famous Deaths") Hull is 200 miles north of London, on the North Sea.

– I –

Indian-style background music—(PSC; "Famous Deaths") According to the music copyright requests for this episode, this piece is called "Tratalala Rhythm" (WAC T12/1,083).

"international cycling fame"—("Picasso/Cycling Race") At the end of the Picasso sketch, Picasso has fallen and failed to successfully combine his art and cycling. The incongruous elements of this scene create humor, of course, but there's more here. The Python choice of modern painting (and art) and abstractionism overall is significant. The goals of the various movements in modern art (and the Modernist movement in general) tended to be (a) the examination and even shattering of the boundaries of figurative representation, and (b) to push outward the limits of what had been accepted as appropriate media and subject matter in the arts. This is true of painting as well as literature, film, music, and all the plastic arts. Python played with the plasticity of their medium—they understood well the manipulative elements—making demands of both the medium and the audience as they took their Modernist-*cum*-Postmodernist television presentation and re-presentation to new limits. What was said of Brancusi in his use of whatever sculpting material he selected could be said of Monty Python: they "extracted from the material . . . its maximum effect" (Tansey 840).

interrogating him—(PSC; "The Funniest Joke in the World") This scene is perhaps inspired by similar scenes in films like Rossellini's *Rome: Open City*, or even popular BBC shows like *Spycatcher* (1959-1961), where Nazis were ferreted out by the intrepid Lt.-Col. Pinto.

"It's . . . "—(opening credits) Just after this utterance a bell sounds (probably a glockenspiel) and the show's theme music begins, the "Liberty Bell March" by John Philip Sousa, an American composer of martial music. The music was chosen, according to Palin and Gilliam, as these two sat and listened to many title song possibilities, with Gilliam saying that the initial bell sound was the clincher for him (see Johnson's *The First 20 Years of Monty Python* 21-22).

'It's' man . . . back to the sea—(closing credits) This is one of the few episodes with such an identifiable beginning and ending, a neat book-ending, perhaps attributable to the show's position (first episode) in the series.

It's the Arts—("It's the Arts") Would become a generic arts program title in a number of *FC* episodes, including Ep. 1 (*It's Wolfgang Amadeus Mozart*), Ep. 6, and Ep. 10, *It's A Tree* sketch. The titular use of "It's" is borrowed by Python from many British television shows, including *It's a Knockout* (BBC-1, 1966).

– K –

"Kandinsky"—("Picasso/Cycling Race") Russian-born Wassily Kandinsky (1866-1944) was one of the first pure abstractionists in modern painting. See the "black oval shapes" entry above for more on Kandinsky and his presence in London galleries.

The laundry list of twentieth-century artists competing in this race is significant, as these artists would have been shaking up the world of art, design, advertising, architecture, and even morality and culture as the Pythons were growing up and shaping their own sensibilities. Interesting also that Pythons would characterize the world of modern art as a heated contest, reflecting the competitive environment created and nurtured by the mass culture art world of the period. In fact, once the *l'art pour l'art* ("art for art's sake") period arrived in postwar era, and especially into the 1960s, competition for gallery space and, therefore, commercial and public exposure, intensified significantly. See Hughes' *The Shock of the New* for a discussion of this phenomenon.

Also, here is a fine example of significant knowledge given to seemingly insignificant characters, like a Pepperpot (Palin), who in this case is able to identify modern painters by sight, and will later correct commentator Trench (Cleese) as to the proper nationality of German expatriate Kurt Schwitters. (Cf. Shakespeare's use of Dogberry and his associates in *Much Ado*, as well as Python's use of the Pepperpots to discuss philosophy, politics, art, and literature throughout *FC*.)

"Khan, Genghis"—("Famous Deaths") Mongol conqueror (c. 1155-c. 1227) who is credited with the consolidation of nomadic tribes into a unified Mongolia. His empire eventually extended to the Adriatic Sea.

The larger-than-life Khan—along with Lord Nelson, Mozart, Attila, Stanley Baldwin, Churchill and Ramsay MacDonald and others—is just the type of historical figure the Pythons will consistently re-contextualize into contemporary settings, or surprise with modernity in their own time. This results in a constant "context smashing" (a Roberto Unger term) where the understood settings, preconceptions, structures, and even verisimilitudes are broken apart by the purposeful decontextualizing of, for example, historical figures (Unger 63). In such a postmodern world—where fragmentation is the only constant—the Pythons can posit and undercut, posit and undercut, rendering narrative instability the "stable" norm. This cult of context smashing becomes the new context, of course, and the new norm must then be overthrown, as well. The pressure for more and newer contexts to continually smash will contribute to the Pythons' eventual demise—the same fate, ironically, of most Modernist movements as their reactions to traditional art forms and subject matters were co-opted by mass culture (often in the form of commercial art).

This tent scene was shot on the location trip to the southern coastal town of Bournemouth in July 1969 (WAC T12/1,083).

"Kingston"—(Picasso/Cycling Race") Officially Kingston upon Thames, the city is several miles north of Tolworth, and west of Wimbledon Common. Explorer Brian Norris (Palin) will "discover" the Kingston Bypass as he searches for the most likely Surbiton to Hounslow migration trail (see Ep. 28).

"Kiss me, Hardy!"—("Famous Deaths") These famous last words were originally reported by Robert Southey in his *Life of Nelson* (1813). Thomas Hardy was Nelson's flag captain, and reportedly kissed Nelson on the forehead as the admiral lay dying. (Note the leap from a modern building [see "top window" note below]). Nelson also suffered a violent death, meaning he would rank high on the scoring board. See the note for Nelson below.

"Klee, Paul"—("Picasso/Cycling Race") Swiss-born Klee (1879-1940) employed "forced associations and distortions" as he commented on the modern world and human foibles, and may have questioned the efficacy of a technology-driven society (Tansey 832-33). Along with Kokoschka and Schwitters, Klee and the Swiss-Germans are at the back marker of the race.

The Tate Gallery had collected five Klee paintings by 1969, most purchased in 1946 as a part of a broad expansion into the neglected area of European Modernism by the Gallery. The Contemporary Art Society (founded in 1910) arranged for the purchase of many of these Modernist works, including race participants Dufy, Klee, Picasso, and Toulouse-Lautrec.

"Kokoschka, Oskar"—("Picasso/Cycling Race") Austrian artist Kokoschka (1886-1980) was an Expressionist whose works drew on high Romanticism (the late eighteenth and early nineteenth century) (Tansey 812). In the episode's cycling race Kokoschka is dropping off the pace, as is Klee, perhaps as the move toward abstraction in art (and away from the traditions of Romanticism) becomes more and more pronounced.

Kokoschka could boast two works owned by the Tate Gallery by 1969.

– L –

Lederhosen Teutonic figure—(PSC; "Italian Lesson") Here Chapman is wearing the traditional lederhosen costume of European Alpine regions, complete with cocked feather hat. This costume will reappear on both Palin and Idle as they play vigorous Bavarian waiters in "The Restaurant Sketch" for the second *Fliegender Zirkus* (Bavarian TV) episode. The German/Teuton is certainly an Other, and characterized by stereotypical dress, as are the Italians in the room. (In Ep. 29, the Welsh women's national costume will be used for the men singing the "Money" song, accompanied by a Welsh harpist.) This type of visual shorthand for character typing is common throughout *FC*, and is carried over from live stage (music hall and burlesque), radio, and television traditions.

The costume people working for the show at the BBC were given the following instructions for this character: "Leiderhousen [*sic*]. The full apple strudle [*sic*] bit" (WAC T12/1,082).

"Léger, Ferdinand"—("Picasso/Cycling Race") French artist Léger (1881-1955) developed "machine art," influenced by the original Cubists, which illustrated a fascination with the beauty of machinery, and would have reflected the interests of the Futurists of this period, as well. (Futurist prophet F.T. Marinetti will be discussed in the notes to Ep. 14, for his version of a "Silly Walk.") Léger's 1919 painting *The City* was on the "monumental scale" (7'7" by 9'9.5") cautioned against by Reg Moss (Chapman) early in the sketch.

The Pythons could have traveled to Edinburgh or Manchester to see Léger works during this period, but there were also four Léger works available for viewing at the Tate Gallery, all donated in 1949-1950. Léger had also painted *The Four Cyclists* in 1943-1948, *Big Julie* (1945), *Leisures on Red Background* (1949), and *The Acrobats* (1952)—*all* prominently featuring bicycles and riders.

"Lincoln, A."—("Famous Deaths") American Abraham Lincoln (1809-1865) was the sixteenth president of the United States, and was shot and killed at Ford's Theatre by John Wilkes Booth, an actor and ardent supporter of slavery. Eddie (Idle) characterizes Lincoln as "little," though he was actually abnormally tall for his era. Lincoln would sign his correspondence, normally, as "A. Lincoln," the same way the Pythons list him on the scoreboard.

– M –

Man—(PSC; opening titles) In this first episode, the introductory character played by Michael Palin is not called the "It's Man," merely "Man." In Ep. 2 he becomes the "It's Man" in the script, and remains so throughout his appearances in *Flying Circus*. This opening—featuring the "It's Man" in myriad situa-tions and settings—became Python's signature introduction, and was also used through *most* of the *FC* episodes. Interestingly, by the middle of the second season (Ep. 19 and beyond), the intro either moves further into the episode, even near the end at times, or is eliminated entirely. As the troupe became more comfortable in its writing ability and with the medium itself, manipulation and undercutting became more prevalent, especially in regard to the accepted television formats of the time.

The "It's Man" doesn't appear in Eps. 19, 21, 26, or 34, nor does he appear in the abbreviated fourth series at all (Eps. 40-45). In Ep. 43, the "Hamlet" episode, Palin will appear in an "It's Man"-type link—where he emerges from an explosion, blackened, but not ragged and tatty, with his own hair, and says "And then"—as if he's a more dignified or Shakespearean transitional element than the "It's Man." Frankly, the "And then" man's appearance makes no sense at all in the context of the show, because the transition is to black, the end of the show.

"Marat"—("Famous Deaths") Jean-Paul Marat (1743-1793) was a French politician, physician, and journalist, and was the leader of the Montagnard faction during the French Revolution. While resting in a medicinal bath (13 July 1793) he was stabbed to death by Charlotte Corday, a Girondin (royalist) conservative from Normandy (*EBO*).

The well-known death portrait (found in the Musées Royaux des Beaux-Arts, Brussels) painted by Jacques-Louis David is featured in Ep. 25, where characters in famous paintings call a strike and leave the paintings for picket lines. In life Marat also denounced Jacques Necker, who is prominently mentioned in Ep. 40, "The Golden Age of Ballooning."

"Miro"—("Picasso/Cycling Race") Jean Miro (1893-1983) was an "organic" Surrealist, and eventually became more interested in subject matter, as did many Surrealists (Tansey 830).

In 1969, the Tate held only one Miro painting, *Women and Bird in the Moonlight* (1949), which had been purchased in 1951.

"Mondrian, Piet"—("Picasso/Cycling Race") Painter Piet Mondrian (1872-1944) led the Dutch abstract "De Stijl" ("The Style") art movement, and his influence was felt and mimicked broadly in art, architecture, and graphic design. He is a "Neo-Plasticist" because he believed "that plastic art affirms that equilibrium can only be established through the balance of unequal but equivalent oppositions" (Gardner's 824). His work moved away from representation and into abstraction.

Two Mondrian paintings, including the well-known *Composition with Yellow, Blue and Red* (1937-1942), were part of the Tate's collection in 1969.

"Monty Python's Flying Circus"—(opening titles) In these first episodes, John Cleese speaks this line in a very straightforward, sober tone of voice. The delivery of the title (vocally) will change by Ep. 8, though will continue to be voiced by Cleese until the end of the second series, when Palin takes over from Ep. 27 on. (The tag line is not spoken in Eps. 19 or 26.) See notes to titles in Ep. 2.

The song underneath is a version of John Phillip Sousa's "Liberty Bell" theme, as recorded by the Band of Grenadier Guard (WAC T12/1,082 5 October 1969). This would become the show's (and Pythons') signature song, as well as the traditional version used throughout the series. The end theme will change in Ep. 45 fittingly, when "Liberty Bell" is played haltingly on a guitar.

Moss, Reg—(PSC; "Picasso/Cycling Race") These scenes were shot on and around the Walton on Thames roundabout and shopping precinct in Walton, Surrey (WAC T12/1,083).

Mozart—("It's Wolfgang Amadeus Mozart" and "Famous Deaths") Wolfgang Amadeus Mozart (1756-1791), the well-known Austrian composer. Colin Mozart (Palin), the son of Wolfgang, will appear in Ep. 21 as a ratcatcher.

In 1970, Peter Cook and Dudley Moore—who had, as part of the groundbreaking 1961-1964 satirical stage show *Beyond the Fringe* greatly influenced the Pythons—would create a recurring "Ludwig" (as in Beethoven) musical sketch for their *Not Only . . . But Also* comedy show.

– N –

"National Film Theatre"—("It's the Arts") Mentioned as the venue for Sir David Ross' film retrospective, the NFT is located on London's South Bank, and hosts internationally acclaimed film festivals, including the London Film Festival.

"Nelson, Admiral"—("Famous Deaths") Viscount Horatio Nelson (1758-1805) won the Battle of Trafalgar, making Britain safe from foreign invasion for perhaps the first time in her history. He lost his life to a sniper's bullet in the battle, allegedly uttering the famous "Kiss me, Hardy" as he died.

The cast of the original *Beyond the Fringe* (1960) satirical show (university wits Alan Bennett, Peter Cook, Jonathan Miller, and Dudley Moore) had included a lengthy sketch on Nelson and specifically the awkwardness of his purported last words (to wit: Hardy has to leave his command position, make his way to the wounded Nelson under fire, kiss him, etc.). Most

of the Pythons had seen the show (which premiered in 1960 in Edinburgh, then moved to the Fortune Theatre in London in 1961), and have admitted to being quite influenced by it.

A very short allusion to this obviously seminal and contested historical moment can also be found in the *Do Not Adjust Your Set* episodes, co-written by Idle, Jones, and Palin (and Denise Coffey and David Jason), from 1967. The children's show was produced by Humphrey Barclay for Associated Rediffusion TV, then Thames TV.

"Nicholson, Ben"—("Picasso/Cycling Race") The only Englishman facing Picasso in this race, Nicholson (1894-1982) is characterized as an austere geometric abstractionist, influenced by studying with Mondrian (see note on Mondrian above), and teaming with sculptor Barbara Hepworth. For more on Nicholson, see Sophie Bowness' article on the artist in the *ODNB*.

Not surprisingly, the Tate holds more works by British native Nicholson than any of the other (foreign) race participants. Approximately two dozen drawings, paintings, and collages, many presented by the artist himself, were part of the Tate collection by late 1969.

– O –

"Oh ja . . . Ach!"—("Italian Lesson") German to English translations for this scene: "Excuse me, sir. What is the word for stomachache?" and "Oh, yes. Thank you very much. Ah, the German classroom. I see!"

In medical terms, "mittelschmerz" is generally an abdominal pain in women associated with ovulation.

There is also a character named Mrs. Mittelschmerz in "Stake Your Claim," who claims to be able to "burrow through an elephant." This sketch can be heard on the Monty Python album *Another Monty Python Record* (side 2), and seen (and heard in German) on the first *Fliegender Zirkus* episode.

"organ and tympani"—("Arthur 'Two-Sheds' Jackson") Interesting combination of instruments, especially since the composition is being called a "symphony" (meaning at least wind, string, and percussion, and in some numbers), which at least hints at a full orchestral arrangement. No mention of what kind of organ; tympani are tunable kettledrums.

– P –

patriotic music . . . crescendo—(PSC; "The Funniest Joke in the World") According to surviving BBC payroll paperwork, bit-part players Cy Town and Lesley Weekes also appeared in this longer-than-usual sketch, filming their portions on 18 August 1969. Town would go on to appear on *Dr. Who* many times, often in costume as a monster, while Weekes had appeared on *Z Cars* earlier in 1969 (WAC T12/1,083).

See IMDb.com for more on these and other actors appearing in bit parts. Most of the extras and walk-ons who appeared in *Flying Circus* have not yet been credited (beyond the WAC records)—these appearances will be highlighted throughout these annotations.

"Peenemünde"—("The Funniest Joke in the World") This is the infamous Nazi "V" rocket base in northeast Germany, where German scientists (including many who would later work in the American space program, such as Werner Von Braun) had been building and testing V-1, V-2, and even V-10 rockets—initially for attacks on England, but to eventually combat the Russians and Americans. The V rocket program became a significant target for the Allies late in the war, since the Germans were well ahead of the rest of the world in rocket and atomic technology, and the war could have ended very differently had Peenemünde not been bombed so effectively by the Allies from 1943. Soviet troops overran the base in 1945, and took many scientists into the fledgling Russian space program.

Pepperpots—(PSC; linking element into "Whizzo Butter") A name probably based on the character Mrs. Pepperpot, created by Norwegian children's author Alf Prøysen. Mrs. Pepperpot never knew when she was going to shrink down to Pepperpot size and shape, a roundish pepper container. As rendered by the Pythons, these characters wear frumpy print dresses, wigs, carry purses, and speak in falsetto tones.

Additionally, playwright Terence Rattigan (1911-1977) wrote this character description in the preface to the second volume of his *Collected Plays* (1953):

> . . . there follows a simple truth, and for the purpose of its illustration let us invent a character, a nice, respectable, middle-class, middle-aged, maiden lady, with time on her hands and the money to help her pass it. She enjoys pictures, books, music, and the theatre and though to none of these arts (or rather, for consistency's sake, to none of these three arts and the one craft) does she bring much knowledge or discernment, at least, as she is apt to tell her cronies, she 'does know what she likes'. Let us call her Aunt Edna . . . Aunt Edna is a universal. . . . (xi-xiii)

Rattigan will be mentioned (and played by Cleese) in Ep. 30, where he is killed with a spear gun by HRH the Dummy Princess Margaret.

Lastly, there is another image of the pepperpot that may have informed, at least unconsciously, the totality of the Python housewife character who became known as a "Pepperpot." Lady Violet Bonham-Carter (1887-1969), daughter of Liberal PM H.H. Asquith (fl. 1908-1916), lists the fascinating contradictions of the Edwardian age, and includes the feminine but politically committed "suffragettes, hurling bricks at 10 Downing Street, attacking ministers, armed with dog whips, hatchets, and *pepperpots*" (audio transcription, *Eyewitness 1910-1919*, "Death of Edward VII and Political Battles of 1910"). In this instance, then, the traditional housewife as found in both the Edwardian era and the Pythons' world is capable of the odd "slit up a treat" when crossed.

"Picasso"—("Picasso/Cycling Race") Pablo Picasso (1881-1973) was a noted Spanish painter, sculptor, printmaker, etc., and considered by many to be the most significant figure in Modern Art, and Modernism in general. Python's description of Picasso and his influence on the world of art mentioned later in the episode is spot on, with the exception, perhaps, of his bike-and-painting expertise.

This cross-referencing of Picasso and cycling could certainly be an oblique reference to Picasso's celebrated bicycle-seat-and-handle-bars sculpture, *Head of a Bull*, from 1943.

There were approximately a dozen Picasso works available for viewing in the Tate collection by 1969, most bequeathed in 1933.

pig—(PSC; link into "It's Wolfgang Amadeus Mozart") Pigs becomes a recurring motif in this episode, and the references even cross over to Ep. 2 (or *from* Ep. 2, since these first two episodes were flip-flopped before broadcast). The pig appearances will include animation, props, audio (squeals), and a caption later in the episode.

"Pigs 3, Nelson 1"—(PSC; link into "Arthur 'Two-Sheds' Jackson") Not only prolonging the pig theme, but also the sport and scoring motif evident from the "Famous Deaths" sketch at the beginning of the episode. See Ep. 2 for the wrestling match to determine the existence of God.

"pig's head"—(PSC; "Picasso/Cycling Race") This is an actual pig's head, as asked for by designer Roger Limington (WAC T12/1,082).

pillbox—(PSC; "The Funniest Joke in the World") A concrete bunker created as a defensive and/or observation position, often with gun slits. These can still be seen throughout the coastal regions of Britain, Wales, Scotland, etc.

"Pollock, Jackson"—("Picasso/Cycling Race") American artist Pollock (1912-1956) was a member of the "New York School" of the late 1940s and 1950s, and much of his work falls into the "action painting" category; he often poured or dripped on a canvas on his studio floor.

In the Tate collection there were two Pollock works by 1969, both of the "poured" variety.

"pre-war joke"—("The Funniest Joke in the World") Perhaps one of Python's most scathing political moments, this allusion peels back the scab on a still-painful pre-WWII wound. Then-Prime Minister Neville Chamberlain had secured promises (the Munich Agreement) from "Herr Hitler" that German advances to that point (including the threats toward Czechoslovakia) would not continue, nor would Germany threaten the sovereignty of the rest of Europe and the world—a policy of appeasement. By 1 September 1939, of course, the "peace in our time" policy was in tatters, as Nazi tanks rolled through Poland. Chamberlain never politically escaped that onerous accomplishment, and the image (newsreel footage of worthless paper in hand) has become iconic. Not a wartime PM, he was replaced by the unpopular Churchill when the elder statesman lost Conservative support in 1940. Chamberlain died a short time later.

The satirical cast of *Beyond the Fringe* (Bennett, Cook, Miller and Moore) had also skewered Chamberlain in their stage show first performed in 1961 in Edinburgh, then later in London and New York. (Listen to "The Aftermyth of War" sketch on *The Complete* Beyond the Fringe CD [EMI, 1996].)

This Chamberlain newsreel image came from VIS-NEWS (Ref. No. 1450), according to the archival sources request/copyright forms (WAC T12/1,082). The BBC seemed to have been quite careful in checking for and paying for (when necessary) copyrighted material, including photos, film clips, music clips, and sounds of all kinds. See the Python files in the BBC's Written Archives Collection, Caversham Park.

There had also been an earlier attack along these same lines, when in a 1942 speech Michael Foot (b. 1913; editor of *The Evening Standard*) compared the oppressive, first-strike actions of Churchill's wartime government against the freedom of the newspaper industry to Hitler's actions during the "appeasement" days. In 1940, Foot had co-published *Guilty Men*, a direct attack on Chamberlain and appeasement.

– Q –

"Q Division"—("The Funniest Joke in the World") A division of Scotland Yard. Jack Slipper (1924-2005)—who became "Slipper of the Yard" after apprehending (then losing) the Great Train Robbers in 1963—was a member of Q Division. The Pythons' oft-heard "So-and-So of the Yard" declamations have been borrowed from at least two sources: Slipper, of course, who took many opportunities to appear in front of news cam-

eras, becoming something of a media celebrity in the 1960s and 1970s, but also the earlier Det. Insp. Robert Fabian of *Fabian of Scotland Yard* (1954) fame. Fabian (d. 1978) sported the trench coat, hat, and pipe ensemble, and usually appeared at the end of each fictionalized episode.

"Quando Caliente del Sol"—("Italian Lesson") The popular song "When the Sun is Hot . . . " is performed here by guitarist Miguel-Lopez Cortero, who was paid £10/50 for his services (WAC T12/1,082).

– R –

"Richard the Third"—("Famous Deaths") Richard (1452-1485) was the famed Plantagenet king later vilified by Tudor apologists, whose inflated villainy also made great dramatic fodder for Shakespeare. Richard died at Bosworth Field (22 August 1485), the ultimate War of the Roses. This battle and Richard's death allowed for the establishment of the Tudor dynasty under Henry VII. See Ross' *Wars of the Roses*.

"Ross"—("It's the Arts") The Sir Edward Ross character could be based on any number of distinguished and knighted British film directors, including Richard Attenborough (*Oh! What a Lovely War*), Alfred Hitchcock (*The Birds*), David Lean (*Doctor Zhivago*), even Michael Powell (*Peeping Tom*), etc. Attenborough will be sent-up (as "Dickie Attenborough") in Ep. 39, "The British Showbiz Awards" sketch.

Also, this "interviewer and guest" format (three camera set-up) is utilized and satirized throughout *FC*, and has been a staple on British television since its inception.

"Royal Festival Hall"—("It's the Arts") Situated on the banks of the Thames alongside the Hayward Gallery and opened in 1951, the one-hundredth anniversary of the Great Exhibition. The RFH has primarily been used for music, dance, and lecture series, as opposed to film retrospectives.

– S –

"Salisbury Plain"—("The Funniest Joke in the World") An open chalk plateau in Wiltshire and Berkshire, the Plain is home to significant prehistoric monuments, including Stonehenge. This area has been used for military exercises for many years, as well, which is why the Pythons would have interred the deadly joke here.

"Schwitters, Kurt"—("Picasso/Cycling Race") Schwitters (1887-1948) was a German collage artist (the Pepperpot is quite correct) and a Dadaist. Schwitters put his "Merz Pictures" together from garbage piles, bits of masonry and stone, found items, etc. Schwitters, then might not actually belong in the race (which might be why he's in last place), since he was not a painter, but a committed collagist.

There was only one Schwitters work, *Opened by Customs* (1937-1938), purchased by the Tate during this period.

scoreboard—(PSC; "Famous Deaths") The scoreboard created for this sketch does, indeed, look like the original scoreboard on the Eddie Waring–hosted *It's A Knockout* show. (*It's A Knockout* is featured on the 10 and 17 May 1969 *Radio Times* covers.) See the entry for "Eddie Waring" for more.

The *Sunday Times* published a scoreboard not unlike this in March 1969, revealing the popularity (as determined by readers) of the royal family. The complete scoreboard looked like this, as reprinted in *Private Eye*:

The results were scored as follows: a great deal, plus 1; quite a lot, plus ½; not very much, minus ½; not at all, minus 1; don't know, zero. This is how it turns out:

	Score
The Queen	63
Prince Philip	55
The Queen Mother	48
Lord Mountbatten	41
Prince Charles	39
Princess Alexandra	36
Princess Anne	26
Princess Margaret	2
Duke of Kent	−6 (Ingrams 227)

"Scotland Yard"—("The Funniest Joke in the World") Headquarters of the Metropolitan Police, originally at Whitehall, and founded by Sir Robert Peel in 1829. The building (completed in 1967) is found at Broadway and Victoria Street in Westminster.

"Scribbler"—(PSC; "The Funniest Joke in the World") "Ernest Scribbler," or, literally, one who is serious about his writings. This is an allusion to the Scriblerus Club, the ur-Monty Python learned literary troupe including Alexander Pope, Jonathan Swift, John Gay, Thomas Parnell, and John Arbuthnot. The five contributed to the *Memoirs of Martinus Scriblerus*, which was begun in 1713 and eventually published in 1741, and which ridiculed erudition and scholarly jargon. Pope occasionally used Martinus Scriblerus as a pseudonym, as did George Crabbe. (See Drabble's *Oxford Companion to English Literature*.)

"slit your face"—("Whizzo Butter" advert) Another possibility of violence from a seemingly harmless source, this phrase is adapted elsewhere in *FC* as the slangy "slit (you) up a treat" (cf. "Operating Theatre"

and Ep. 14's "The Piranha Brothers"). In Ep. 8, seemingly innocent grandmothers will rampage through London in "Hell's Grannies," and there is also a certain killer rabbit in *Holy Grail*, to name just two other such innocuous threats.

sound effect—(PSC; "The Funniest Joke in the World") With the Gestapo man (Chapman) providing his own sound effects, the result is like bringing the ever-present sound effects technicians out of the off-stage areas, or in the case of television, off-camera, and into full view. It also underscores the artificiality of the violent acts as presented in all movies and television—the soundtrack and visual elements are always separate and distinct, and must be artificially generated, then carefully synchronized for the illusion of reality to be achieved.

The Pythons, remember, were raised listening to the radio, including the sound effects–laden *The Goon Show*, as well as working and writing for the university revues at Cambridge and Oxford. The Goons made a regular point of identifying for the listening (and studio) audience the machinery behind the magic—whenever an LP-based sound effect was used, or when characters pretended to leave a room by walking away slightly from the microphone, etc. The radio dramas of the 1930s and 1940s on the BBC also employed a rich panoply of sound effects, and audience expectations of a certain level of verisimilitude could be fulfilled. By the same token, when the expectations of verisimilitude are fully in place for any art form, defying those same conventions becomes possible and—in silly comedy like the Goons delivered—even expected.

This becomes the Pythons' sort of *raison d'être*, creating, for example, as believable a medieval world as they can for the film *Monty Python and the Holy Grail*, then consistently undercutting that reality with anachronisms and general silliness.

"squawk"—(PSC; "Famous Deaths") Genghis Khan (1162-1227) dies here, almost the way the "Dead Parrot" sketch (Ep. 8) explains the demise of the bird in question, including the preference of the Norwegian Blue for "kipping on its back," and its supine condition being blamed on a "long squawk." Also, Cleese dies in the exact same manner later in this episode (lunging backwards into sudden death) as a Nazi hearing for the first time the "Funniest Joke in the World." In reality, Khan actually died rather peacefully, at the fairly old age of 65.

All that is missing from these deaths is the iconic flower clutched at the chest, and these would have been more like the deaths of animated characters. Screwy Squirrel dies just this way, for example, in Tex Avery's MGM cartoons. Cleese as a Nazi also very clearly calls out Woody Woodpecker's signature cry (voiced originally by Gracie Lantz, wife of Woody creator Walter Lantz) as he dies.

The Goon Show pioneered this cartoony-ness, an animated awareness that Peter Sellers characterized years later as being key in developing the show and writing the episodes with Harry Secombe, Michael Bentine, and Spike Milligan—writers and performers also emerging from collective service in WWII—setting the show apart from anything that had come before. Sellers remembers:

> We wanted to express ourselves in a sort of surrealistic form. We thought in cartoons, we thought in blackouts, we thought in sketches. We thought of mad characters. We thought of—take a situation and instead of letting it end normally, let it end the other way—twisted around. (Audio transcription, "The Last Goon Show")

This cartoony approach to structure and subject was adopted and adapted to include the visual elements the television medium would allow—the self-conscious signs (both held by characters and generated electronically), knowing glances, fourth-wall-shattering asides, pratfalls, the character squash and stretch, even, which had previously only been allowed in the cartoon world—as the Pythons created *Flying Circus*.

"stock film"—(PSC; "The Funniest Joke in the World") Stock film is generally film shot for one purpose, then used for another purpose, or used generically (for news footage, documentaries, commercials, even underfunded feature films). The BBC archives millions of feet of film (and now video) footage (and still photographs) from government information films, how-to films, documentary films, captured wartime footage, BBC TV and Radio performances, news footage, etc.

The Pythons plundered these archives whenever, for example, an establishing shot might be needed, such as the title shot for the "Spanish Inquisition" sketch (Ep. 15) showing the surface works of a coal mine, presumably in Wales; a photo of the plans for the Crystal Palace (Ep. 29); and the ubiquitous "Women's Institute" film clip, which appears in many episodes. (See the note for the Women's Institute in Ep. 2.)

"Strewth!"—("Famous Deaths") Historically, a necessary contraction of "God's truth," the type of oath that from at least Elizabethan times would not have been permissible on the English theatrical stage. In a more contemporary instance, a character in the 1969 film *Battle for Britain* (dir. Guy Hamilton; released just weeks before the first *FC* series went on the air) utters the invective as he plunges his Spitfire into combat. See also similar invectives like "zounds" ("by God's wounds") and "s'blood" ("God's blood"). This term is

used almost exclusively in *FC* by Chapman, and will be heard in Ep. 2 as the cycling Arthur Figgis (Chapman) realizes Arthur Frampton (Jones) actually has three buttocks.

Generally, BBC jitters over viewers' sensibilities led to synonyms or more metaphorical language rather than straight-out cursing or oaths ("coitus" and "intercourse the penguin" as invectives in Ep. 27; a raspberry instead of "sod" in Ep. 17). Television morality watchdog groups were also quite active during this period, including Mary Whitehouse (see entries in Eps. 8 and 32 notes), meaning there was always the niggling possibility of civil or even criminal action against blasphemers, contributors to public delinquency, etc. See Hewison's *Monty Python: The Case Against* for more on the Pythons' legal and censorial struggles.

Lastly, one of *The Goon Show* characters—William the Gardener—shouts "Strewth!" when he is startled awake in "The Pevensey Bay Disaster" (3 April 1956).

"St Stephen"—("Famous Deaths") Called the first Christian martyr, Stephen was charged with blasphemy by the Sanhedrin and stoned to death for his faith c. AD 36. The end of Stephen's ministry, life, and his concurrent vision are found in Acts 6–7.

"studio ain't"—("Arthur 'Two-Sheds' Jackson") Play on the oft-heard "This town ain't big enough for the two of us" from both Hollywood Western lore (apocryphal or otherwise) and especially cartoons spoofing those Westerns. (Bugs Bunny utters the phrase in *Bugs Bunny Rides Again* (1948), then rapidly builds a metropolis around the western town to provide more room for both of them.) The iconic cowboy figure appears occasionally in *FC*, including Cleese's all-in-black mustachioed cowboy "Southerner" who dispenses homilies to buck up Arthur Pewtey (Palin) in Ep. 2, the "Marriage Guidance Counsellor" sketch, as well as the "Cheese Westerns" sketch in Ep. 33, and in both of the *FZ* episodes.

– T –

"taken the A272"—("Picasso/Cycling Race") The humorous incongruity here, then, isn't just the fact that an internationally known artist is trying to paint a major work while riding a bicycle, but that a celebrity like Picasso (still alive in 1969) would use a road like the A272, and that he has to negotiate local traffic congestion. A similar bit of Python incongruity appears in the 1983 feature film *ML*, when an alleged "mosquito" bite on a British soldier—officer class—is recognized, even the raging Zulu Wars just outside the tent come to a complete halt.

"tea boy"—("*It's the Arts*") A "gofer" at the lowest level, this certainly refers to the guild-like tradition of working up through the film studio ranks in the early days of British (and even Hollywood) studio cinema, but could also reference more directly the following: Alfred Hitchcock, who began his film career as a title designer for silent films; David Lean, who started as a clapper boy and wardrobe assistant; and Michael Powell, who worked myriad odd jobs as a studio gofer before directing. See the note for "Ross" for additional comments.

"thirteen years"—(PSC; "The Funniest Joke in the World") This from the *printed* script's description of what Ernest Scribbler's mother "understands" as she reads the deadly joke note: " . . . *thinking it is a suicide note - for he has not been doing well for the last thirteen years.*" It is intriguing to read just how much non-visual, even non-essential information is included in these scripts meant for performance. Many of these ancillary elements can be characterized as editorializations, or asides for the discriminating reader only (the other Pythons?). These moments are a fascinating conceit on the writers' part, since the tidbits (1) do not end up on screen, and (2) would be completely lost without actually reading the performance texts. They often read as almost inside jokes—only available to and decipherable by other Pythons.

This is even more curious as we take into consideration the fact that Python was writing for itself, as Shakespeare did for the King's Men, and not for anyone else (technical BBC folk aside), as opposed, say, to Ben Jonson, who wrote knowing that his work would be published and actually read. Some of these moments—asides—would seem to be "givens" in this case—*understood*—but they're included, anyway.

"this week's request death"—("Famous Deaths") As early as 1967 there were radio shows on BBC Radio 1 playing listener requests. In the earlier *The Goon Show*, Neddie announces a series of requests from listeners who have allegedly written to the show:

> Neddie (Secombe): Now, first of all, for Mrs. Heironymous Clun of 4, The Villas, Cleethorpes Sinks, here is the very record she hasn't asked for. The Rites of Spring, by Ripsi-Korsettsoff played by the Gulf Stream Tearoom Quartet from the oblique position. . . . And now, Private Wretch of the 4th Mudguards has asked for a record of his sergeant falling down a manhole. And here it is, accompanied (without orchestra), by Geraldo. . . . Now on the serious side, Elsie Sprugg and Gladys Legg of Rowton House Champagne Bar have asked for a record of Sir Gwilym Cludge conducting the Four in Jeopardy with knee-bracket accompaniment and silent dogs with the Massed Bands of the Hybrid Spahi's Banjo Society and the 4th Coolies Harmonica

Chorus recorded in the natural surroundings of the living room of Jim Davidson's Saxophone Parlour and Part-Time Egg Hatchery with a solo by Rawicz and Landauer. Well, Elsie and Gladys, we haven't got it. But! Here is a record of Fred Clute and his Nubian Monsters playing cribbage! . . . Finally, Miss Frewina Kellogg would like to hear Sabrina sing. (transcribed excerpts from "The Great Tuscan Salami Scandal," 21 February 1956)

Other actual request shows from the period included *Memories For You* (BBC Home Service and Light Programme, Victor Sylvester's Ballroom Orchestra), *Housewive's Choice* (BBC Light Programme, 1946-1967), and *At Your Request* (Sandy MacPherson at the organ).

tinkling—(PSC; "It's Wolfgang Amadeus Mozart") The music being played is Mozart's "L'Oiseau-lyre: Gigue in G," according to the music requests for this week's show (WAC T12/1,082).

"Tolworth roundabout"—("Picasso/Cycling Race") There is a significant roundabout in Tolworth where the A3 and the A3210 meet, though according to archival sources, this scene was shot in Walton-on-Thames, Surrey, on 17 July 1969 (WAC T12/1,083).

"top window"—(PSC; "Famous Deaths") This dummy is thrown from flat 79, Slade House, Edgar Road, Hounslow (WAC T12/1,242). According to notes from director Ian MacNaughton, the residents were more than happy to allow the BBC the use of their flat. This tower is just east of Hounslow Heath.

"Toulouse-Lautrec"—("Picasso/Cycling Race") Toulouse-Lautrec (1864-1901) was a painter and poster maker, haunting and capturing the nightlife of Paris. He also was quite short of stature, which is why he is depicted riding a tricycle, and not a bicycle like everyone else. He is included by the Pythons, most likely, simply because of his size, and is effectively used in place of a verbal punchline. Toulouse-Lautrec will be revisited via a still photo—where he is wearing a "slenderizing garment" while painting—in Ep. 28, "Trim-Jeans Theatre."

The writers of *The Yellow Submarine* include a very brief cameo of a Toulouse-Lautrec character as John, George, Ringo, and Fred search for Paul.

In 1969 the Tate could claim two Toulouse-Lautrec works, one donated in 1940, the other in 1961.

"train-spotting"—("Arthur 'Two-Sheds' Jackson") The practice of watching for trains and recording their numbers is still a popular hobby in the UK. Referenced again in Ep. 7, the "You're No Fun Anymore" sketch.

"Two-Sheds"—("Arthur 'Two-Sheds' Jackson") This is a clear incongruity, where classical arts figures are given handles and nicknames as if they were sports figures or organized crime members. Also, the epithet has a certain "Two Gun" ring to it, as if from a Zane Grey novel, Hollywood Western, or crime drama.

Naming and the power of names/words do become very influential in the Python oeuvre. Here Jackson (Jones) won't be able to escape the implications of his nickname—it will define him and eventually cause a terminal disruption in the interview. Similarly, in Ep. 19 the character Raymond Luxury Yacht (Chapman) announces that though his name is spelled one way it should actually be pronounced "Throatwobbler Mangrove"; in Ep. 22 the new member (Jones) of the faculty at an Australian University isn't named Bruce, so his name is changed to Bruce to be in line with all the other faculty members. Also, see the power of words/names like "mattress" in Ep. 8, and "witch," "Ni," and especially "it" in the feature film *Holy Grail*.

For a discussion of Shakespeare's version of this same phenomenon, see Larsen's *MPSERD*, and specifically Richard III's abilities as a maker/director. For example, at the height of his powers, if Richard *says* someone is a traitor, that person *becomes* a traitor, and can be dealt with accordingly. A married woman can become an available woman; a cousin can become a foe; rightful heirs can become seditious, etc. Richard is perhaps the ultimate "maker" in English literary history.

– U –

"Unknown Joke"—("The Funniest Joke in the World") "Unknown soldier" tombs are in many countries; in England the tomb is located in Westminster Abbey.

The subjects treated in this initial episode—Britain's "darkest days" of WWII, television mores and formats, unattractive and even threatening middle-class women, homosexuality, a collage of modern art and sport, and Nazi aggression—anticipate Python's interest in pushing the bounds of subject matter and decency on television, as well as the value of vulgarity and shock in entertainment. These subjects and characters will reappear throughout the series, as well.

– V –

"Vicky"—("Picasso/Cycling Race") Not normally a man's name, but there was a well-known cartoonist active just prior to this period, pen-named "Vicky." His real name was Victor Weisz (1913-1966), and he was a significantly left-of-center artist who had committed suicide in 1966. Vicky drew for several papers, including *The Daily Mail*, *The Evening Standard*, and *The New Statesman*. His leftist stance and sometimes acid-

tipped pen probably endeared him to the young Pythons. There are two portraits of Weisz in the National Gallery collections. Weisz's collection of approximately 4,000 comic strips can be viewed at the British Cartoon Archive.

The Goons would occasionally employ this kind of effeminizing naming, as well. In "The Last Tram (From Clapham)" (23 November 1954) a chauffeur (played by the bandleader Ellington) appears, and Neddie calls him "Gladys," eliciting a hearty laugh from the audience. He answers to "Gladys" for the balance of the show.

viking . . . knight—(PSC; "Picasso/Cycling Race") This Viking, played by various members of the cast, appears throughout the *FC* series as a completely non sequitur linking element. Some of the links shot during this first series (and filmed in Scotland) will appear much later in the third series, as well. The knight also acted as a linking element and/or—using a rubber chicken as a mace—as the punishment for a delivered punchline, not unlike the archetypal vaudeville stage "hook" that appeared when a failed act was to be terminated (or the oversized hammer that will appear in *FC* later). The knight's "slapstick prop" appearances gradually wane as the Pythons mature in their utilization of links and transitions.

Terry Gilliam often plays the knight, and was paid a bit extra for the "walk-on" appearance, according to BBC records.

"V-Joke"—("The Funniest Joke in the World") A play on the German "V"-rocket program. See "Peenemünde" note above. It is quite fitting that later in the episode the German V-Joke falls flat (misses its target, simply bemusing British homefront radio listeners), since not only did many of the V-rockets miss significant targets, but during the war years German scientists—pursuing the same atomic weaponry ends as the Allies—relied in error on the capabilities of heavy water and carbon, rather than uranium, causing disastrous delays in German atomic research.

"Vott"—(PSC; "The Funniest Joke in the World") An example of the written form of the kind of fractured English Python demands of many of its Others, in this case foreigners, Germans (and evil Nazis, to boot). The troupe members adopt rather caricatured Germanic accents, which affects nearly all their dialogue and even its delivery, though this pervasiveness is only hinted at in the printed form of the scripts. (The Nazis and their Germanic accents are much more hyperbolized here than, say, the earlier Mozart dialogue.)

In this verbal shorthand, the Pythons are much like their Goon ancestors. The Goons did not have the visual element to rely on, however, so dressing a character like a City Gent or a Rustic would make little difference to a radio audience. They would employ often outrageously over-the-top accents to instantly identify nationalities and various Brits, including (East) Indians (Babu Banerjee), French (Moriarty), Germans (Naughty Prisoner), and every accent from English aristocrats to Yorkshire laborers to "Cockney idiots."

This is also not unlike Shakespeare and his approach to Katherine's foreigner status, as well as her maid, in *Henry V*. Shakespeare illustrates Katherine's "foreigner-ness" by skewing her English, reducing her lines, often, to nearly baby-talk. She asks: "Is it possible dat I sould love de ennemie of / France?" (5.2.169-70). After Henry gives her his much longer response, she counters with "I cannot tell wat is dat" (5.2.177). Her last words in butchered English (she does have one more speech in French) come soon after: "Den it sall also content me" (5.2.250). Her woman Alice is painted with the same brush, and though Alice is able to translate Henry's English into French, her accented English is nearly indecipherable; "*Oui*, dat de tongeus of de mans is be full of deceits: dat is de Princess" (5.2.119-20). (For more on this phenomenon, see *MPSERD* 67.)

The primacy of the English language is trumpeted here, as is English-ness. Marston performs the same lingual gymnastics in regard to a foreigner in *The Dutch Courtesan*, wherein Franischina can be heard to utter: "O mine aderliver love, vat sall me do to re- / quit dis your mush affection?" (1.2.87-88). Franischina's accent also seems to come and go as the play moves on, much like Python's characters can massacre some words and leave others alone. Cf. Python's take on the Japanese accent in Ep. 29, "Erizabeth L," or a Caribbean accent later in the same episode, both mangled by Jones.

– W –

Waring, Eddie—(PSC; "Famous Deaths") Game show co-host (with David Vine) on the BBC in the 1966-1987 show called *It's A Knockout* (another "*It's*"-titled show, see notes to Ep. 10). This was the Brit version of the pan-European show *Jeux San Frontieres* (*Games Without Borders*). See notes for Eddie Waring in Ep. 2.

wartime planning room—(PSC; link into "The Funniest Joke in the World") This would have been a very familiar setting for especially UK viewers, as many WWII films featured these planning room scenes. The most recent would have been the myriad scenes featured in the big budget, Hollywood-funded (by United Artists and Harry Saltzman, who will be parodied in Ep. 6) blockbuster *Battle of Britain*. Instead of

pigs being pushed around, of course, the primarily female operatives would manipulate models of planes to indicate Luftwaffe movement and RAF response.

"wartime radio"—(PSC; "The Funniest Joke in the World") Television broadcasts were halted abruptly by the BBC on 1 September 1939 (reportedly during a Mickey Mouse cartoon), and wouldn't return until June 1946, so radio became the critical source of information for the homefront audience during WWII. Broadcast propaganda was extremely significant during the war, naturally, and emanated from almost all of the major countries involved. Specifically, Germany broadcast English-language propaganda (negative battlefield reports, fascist doctrine and programming, etc.) from the earliest days of the war, and even back into Hitler's early days as National Socialist dignitary. The BBC also broadcast foreign-language programs into occupied countries throughout the war, and the evening news reports and addresses from Churchill became staples of the wartime listener's diet, especially during the Battle of Britain. (There is a poignant, haunting moment in the initial scenes of Rossellini's *Rome, Open City*, where, as Nazi troops bang on a door downstairs, an illegal and secreted radio can be heard droning out the familiar "This is London calling" broadcast.) This image of earnest citizens crouched around a radio would have been well known to the Pythons, all born between 1939 and 1943, most (excepting Gilliam, of course) having at least some memory of the war years in Britain.

"watching generals"—(PSC; "The Funniest Joke in the World") Many of these military scenes were shot 17-18 July 1969 at Pirbright Army Camp, Brookwood, Woking, Surrey (WAC T12/1,084 19 October 1969).

"Wenn . . . gersput!"—("The Funniest Joke in the World") Idle would later call the joke "written-down gibberish," as it was intended only for easy memorialization, not translation or meaning (Johnson *20 Years* 51).

"Whizzo Butter"—("Whizzo Butter" advert) Parodying television commercials will become a staple in Python's *FC* episodes. This particular instance is obviously modeled after the "Can you tell Stork from butter?" margarine advertising campaign in the UK circa 1956. Leslie Crowther was often the interviewer looking for comments from the man on the street, with "7 out of 10" generally choosing Stork over butter. (Crowther will be referenced again in Ep. 42, when his *The Black and White Minstrel Show* is featured.) Other margarine trade names in the UK of the period included Clover, Flora, and Echo.

The above scene was shot in the London suburb of Acton, just outside the F.J. Wallis store, Acton Branch.

There is a short memo included in the WAC asking for permission to shoot outside the store. (See WAC file number T12/1,242.) Acton and Ealing were often used for location shooting, as both were in close proximity to BBC TV Centre and Ealing TFS.

Later, in Ep. 6, the Whizzo Chocolate Company will be memorably featured for offering such tidbits as "Crunchy Frog" and "Anthrax Ripple."

"Wisborough Green"—("Picasso/Cycling Race") Wisborough Green is on the A272 between the A283 to the west and the A29 to the east. This mish-mash of directions isn't surprising, or even original to the Pythons. For example, look at Shakespeare's directions, as provided in *Richard III*, for another route:

> . . . from Northampton to London: "Last night, I [hear], they lay at Stony-Stratford / And at Northampton they do rest to-night. / Tomorrow, or next day, they will be here" (2.4.1-3).

Following these directions it certainly would not be to-morrow or the next day; one would find the Irish Sea quicker than the city of London. Phyllis Rackin offers that Shakespeare's dubious geography was certainly "careless," but "only because he had better things to do with his settings than plot their locations on a map . . . " (*MPSERD* 80) (All Shakespeare citations, unless otherwise indicated, are culled from G. Blakemore Evans' *The Riverside Shakespeare* [1974], and as nearly as possible employ the typesetting and spellings employed therein.) The Pythons, too, had more on their collective minds as they wrote this sketch than geographical correctness, with the humor revolving around the specter of Picasso biking and painting through English suburbia. Throughout *FC*, there are instances of nearly accurate historical/academic citations and namings, such

as *Horace* Walpole being given credit for *Rogue Herries* (Ep. 33) and the precise page (468) of Trevelyan's discussion of the Treaty of Utrecht in Ep. 26, among many others. (It was *Hugh* Walpole who wrote *Rogue Herries* [1930], and Trevelyan discusses the Treaty of Utrecht on page *486* in his 1952 edition. See notes for Eps. 26 and 33 for more.) It's clear that the Pythons more often than not relied on fairly accurate memorialized versions of history and people as they wrote.

One glaring exception will be seen in Ep. 37, where the Pythons quite obviously quote from a significant passage from G.M. Trevelyan (also the 1952 edition) and his discussion of Frederick William and the Seven Years' War.

"with him"—("Picasso/Cycling Race") In the Picasso painting/cycling sketch, it is only at this moment that this event or publicity stunt becomes an actual race. Prior to this, Picasso was seemingly alone, performing a Guinness-type bike stunt. Now the narrative has transmogrified the stunt into a full-out race, and Picasso becomes just another participant.

This stream-of-consciousness structure is borrowed from Modernist writers well known to the Pythons, including Gertrude Stein, James Joyce, and Virginia Woolf. The sheer number of Modernist painters, sculptors, essayists, novelists, philosophers, thinkers as well as Modernist public figures and the Modernist ethos in general informs everything the Pythons do in *FC* as they move away from and react to traditional broadcast TV material, formats, and subject matter. The shuffling between Modernism and Postmodernism in the Python oeuvre will be noted throughout.

"writes"—(The Funniest Joke in the World") The music beneath this intro is "Baywood Villa" (WAC T12/1,082).

Episode 2: "Sex & Violence"

– A –

"accounts"—("Marriage Guidance Counsellor") This last phrase seems to be leading to the possibility of a shared sexual experience on a twice-monthly basis for the Pewteys, but quickly caroms off into the keeping of financial accounts. Ep. 15 will look at the possibility of putting a tax on "thingy," meaning sexual activity, and the conclusion is that chartered accountancy could certainly become more interesting at that point. The Pewteys' sex life may vaguely be the point of discussion throughout Arthur Pewtey's long-winded explanation. There is almost a "nudge" moment from Mr. Pewtey, as if he's using a euphemism for his sexual prowess ("after-dinner speaker"), though it again becomes clear rather quickly that he's speaking more gibberish than anything else.

"Aldridge, Arthur"—("The Mouse Problem") "The late" Arthur Aldridge (by name only) appears in Ep. 3 as a dead witness in a coffin. Cleese and Chapman earlier used this same name in writing a character for *At Last the 1948 Show*.

"all run down"—("The Mouse Problem") Certainly some orgiastic implications here, especially in English Renaissance terms. Eric Partridge in *Shakespeare's Bawdy* glosses "climb," citing Marston and Chapman again: "To climb a woman's legs (as though they were the limbs of a tree) and then to 'enjoy' her" (*EH* 2.2.366). This "climb" is in this sketch performed all together, as in the mass orgies described by witnesses to the Profumo affair, and the "all run down" suggests a mass climax, as well.

The sordid events of the much later (and completely serious) film *Eyes Wide Shut* (1999; co-written and directed by Stanley Kubrick) bears striking resemblance to this sketch, and the film itself may have been based at least obliquely on the events surrounding the Pro-

fumo scandal. Kubrick was, interestingly, making his own dark, turgid comedy (*Dr. Strangelove*) in England at the time this scandal broke, and was fresh off of another sexually charged film, *Lolita* (1962).

"'ampstead"—("Working-Class Playwright") May be a reference to King's College, Hampstead, London. King's College is a city school, therefore more erudite and refined than Barnsley College, located in Barnsley, South Yorkshire. Barnsley was a major mining town in the nineteenth century. King's College is also affiliated with the National Theatre, specifically, and not the Royal Court Theatre. Barnsley, being a provincial college, would have been the preferred setting, ironically, for another "Angry Young Man" novelist, Kingsley Amis, author of *Lucky Jim* (1954) and *That Uncertain Feeling* (1955). See Drabble's *Oxford Companion to English Literature*. The Romantic poets set up camp in Hampstead in the nineteenth century, too, creating a more artistic sensibility for the region.

Lastly, the 1969 film *Kes*, directed by Ken Loach and set in the harsh, unforgiving Barnsley area, may have unusually forced this Yorkshire region into the public view during this period.

"And now for something completely different"—("A Man With Three Buttocks") Cleese and Chapman would actually bring this phrase with them from *At Last the 1948 Show*, where it was voiced by Aimee MacDonald, the linking girl and presenter for the show (listen to *At Last the 1948 Show* Album). This particular utterance (by Eric Idle as the Announcer) is one of the rare times that a troupe member other than Cleese speaks these words as either a linking or introductory element. The line doesn't become a catchphrase for the troupe until the second series (appearing in only two episodes of the first series, Eps. 2 and 9 [where Palin actually says it once, and Cleese, twice]), and is then uttered exclusively by Cleese in Eps. 14-17, 19-20, and

22-26. Idle says it again in Ep. 21, then it changes to just "And now," spoken by Cleese, in Eps. 27, 31, and 39. In many episodes, then, it doesn't appear at all, in any form.

"Arternoon"—(PSC; "Flying Sheep") Colloquial (and a printed approximation of an accent) version of "afternoon." The suggestion is that there is a coarse Northern accent being used, which is the case, but the accent can be heard on much more than just the odd word. Note the occasional textual mentions, like "Arternoon," "Ar," "'tis," and "Eh."

"Arthur"—(PCS; "Musical Mice") It should be apparent by now that the first name "Arthur" has some significance to Python, as they've named so many characters in just the first two episodes with that very name. "Arthur" will continue to be a favorite throughout *FC* and even into the feature films, such as *Holy Grail*. It could be that Alun Owen's influential screenplay for *Hard Day's Night* (1964; directed by Richard Lester)—wherein George tells a reporter that his hair is called "Arthur"—served as one inspiration.

Specifically an "Arthur" character appears in: Eps. 1, 2 (seven different characters), 3, 4 (the episode subtitle and a character), 5, 6, 9 (six different characters), 10, 14, 19 (five different mentions), 20 and 21 (two characters each), 22, 24 (two characters), 27 (three mentions), 31 (three mentions), 35 (two characters), 36 (four characters), 39, and 41.

"attracted to mice"—("The Mouse Problem") This looks very much like a nod to the then-current Dr. Thomas Harris book *I'm OK You're OK*, released in 1969. These mice-men, in Harris' co-opted "Transactional Analysis" scenario, would be the "not-OK" types who resort to secretive, ritualistic behaviors, including withdrawal and games to avoid the pains of intimacy with "OK" types. Mr. Jackson's comment that he felt more at ease with other mice seems to put us firmly in this new and dynamic world of interpersonal relationships. Interestingly, Harris quotes Kierkegaard and Sartre in his work, both of whom the Pythons also reference (and put great stock in, clearly). Harris' work was based on Eric Berne's earlier book (*Games People Play*, 1963), which may also have influenced this sketch (in its original iteration prior to *FC*).

– B –

"beating about the bush"—("Marriage Guidance Counsellor") These clichés anticipate the ones Mr. Pewtey will receive shortly from the American Southerner. The sexual connotation of the word "bush" (slang for female pubic hair) is important, especially if Pewtey's problem is his inability to sexually satisfy his young, nubile wife. The phrase itself refers to the act of one hunter scaring fowl out of brush or bracken, while another hunter waits with a snare or weapon to finish the job. The literary meaning of the term—to "expend labour of which the fruit is not gained by oneself" (*OED*)—applies aptly to Pewtey as he provides the prey, his wife, unwittingly, to the on-the-hunt marriage counselor.

"Belloc, Hillaire"—("The Mouse Problem") Belloc's first name was actually spelled "Hilaire." Born in France, Belloc (1870-1953) was a naturalized Englishman, and even stood for Parliament for the Liberal Party in 1906. A noted Edwardian poet and historian, Belloc was an ardent Catholic apologist and attacked high finance (even to the point, some said, of bigotry and anti-Semitism). See "Defender of the Faith" from *The New York Press* by William Bryk, 16 March 2000, and Belloc's entry (penned by Bergonzi) in the *ODNB*.

Why Belloc is included with Caesar and Napoleon as a closet mouse isn't clear, though it should be noted that all three qualify as "others" based on their non-Englishness, which may be all that's necessary. Belloc's clearly being used as a punchline of sorts—but there's no smoking gun as to why. It could be that any Frenchman who is of the papist faith and writes children's rhymes must be a closet sexual deviant, a "disgusting little pervert," the brush Python employs often in *FC* to paint "othered" authority figures. (The mention of Belloc's name also produces a significant laugh from the studio audience, even though he's been dead sixteen years by this time.)

"The Bells of St. Mary's"—("Musical Mice") A popular film and song title, the 1945 film starred Bing Crosby and Ingrid Bergman. Crosby sang the title song, as well. The film was directed by Leo McCarey.

"blast"—(link into "The Wrestling Epilogue") This somewhat tame imprecation is taken textually as an order, as off-screen we hear "Sir!" (Jones). The cannon fires in response, yet another example of the significance of language and the word, of the power of words in the Python world. It's also a great example of the fluid nature of Python's narrative structure, where bits of earlier material (here, flying sheep) can resurface, and even, in the case of the "Icelandic Saga" sketch in Ep. 27, can intrude, Viking-like, on another narrative.

"blue cheese films"—("The Mouse Problem") Blue (or bleu) cheese is whitish cheese with veins of blue mold. "Blue" films are off-color, vulgar, or obscene (or pornographic) films. The color blue is also often associated in England with the Conservative Party (see

OED and the "blue corner" note below), which adds a level of meaning to this already multivalent sketch.

"blue corner . . . red corner"—(PSC; "The Wrestling Epilogue") The corners in the wrestling ring are identified by the color of spit buckets in each. It should be no surprise that the red corner is located at announcer's left, based on the political spectrum, and that it is the academic who occupies that leftist/socialist position. The monsignor—as a representative of the church—would be characteristically more conservative, thus on the right, politically.

There are also many instances of political pundits fretting over Labour "going red," or forsaking Socialism for Communism, especially prevalent in the UK in the post-Bolshevik Revolution years. And as the Tories tended to be the landed gentry and moneyed merchant class, their "blue"-bloodedness was also a consistent appellation, especially in the post-Victorian era.

"books about belief"—("The Wrestling Epilogue") In the 1960s a number of religious books were penned by establishment figures such as Rudolf Bultmann, Paul Tillich, Dietrich Bonhoeffer, and perhaps especially Bishop John Robinson's *Honest to God* (1963).

Robinson (1919-1983) was the Bishop of Woolwich in South London. These books popularized "radical theologian discussion" in the UK, and Robinson was an important secular theologian (William P. Williams, communication to the author). Robinson, a "demythologizer," called for new assertions of faith that would transcend and replace old beliefs that had few adherents in modern England—he saw the need for a new "image of God" more real "to people of a secular scientific world" (James, *ODNB*). The firestorm that followed pitted luminaries such as the Archbishop of Canterbury against Robinson in what may have seemed to be epic wrestling matches for the soul of Man.

"Brian"—("French Lecture on Sheep-Aircraft") Brian is another name that appears repeatedly in the Python oeuvre. A Brian-named character appears in Eps. 2, 4, 9, 11, 13-14 (three characters), 19 (four characters), 20-23, 29, 36-37, 40-41, 43, and 45.

There are many possibilities for the high status this name seems to occupy in Python, including *FC* staff-member Brian Jones, and various BBC television commentators sharing the name. The titular character in the feature film *Life of Brian* (1979) is also a Brian (played by Chapman). The most likely, however, refers to Captain Brian Trubshaw, British test pilot and first pilot of the Concorde SST, whom the Queen referred to openly as "my Brian." Cf. the entry for "Trubshawe" below.

"Brie . . . Gouda"—("The Mouse Problem") Brie and Camembert are both soft cow's milk cheeses from northern France; Cheddar is a hard English cheese; and Gouda is a cheese from The Netherlands generally made in wheels. Cf. "Cheese Shop" sketch from Ep. 33, which features Mr. Mousebender (Cleese) trying to buy cheese from proprietor Wensleydale (Palin), who actually has no cheese to sell.

"Brighton"—("Marriage Guidance Counsellor") Resort town on the southern coast of England, less than an hour from London. Popularized in the 1750 book by Richard Russell, Brighton became an important resort destination after its publication.

Brighton became even more popular during the privations of the postwar years, as strict limits were imposed on how much British currency could be taken from the country. Many middle-class travelers found that their bank holiday and even summer excursions had to become in-country visits, so the lake country, holiday camps (e.g., Butlins), and southern seaside destinations like Paignton, Bournemouth, and Torbay boomed in popularity (see the entry for "holiday money" below, as well as Morgan's *Britain Since 1945*).

"botty"—("A Man With Three Buttocks") Another slang for "bottom." Not the first satirists to fixate on the human buttocks, see the rather protracted tale told by the Old Woman in *Candide*, chapters 9, 10, and 12, who lost one buttock (a "rumpsteak") to her captors, and bore "half a backside" ever after.

"bum"—("A Man With Three Buttocks") This is one of the naughty words which in Ep. 17 the BBC Man (Palin) announces will not be allowed to be mentioned on the show again.

– C –

caption—(PSC; "The Wrestling Epilogue") Title cards like these were requested from the graphics department at TV Centre on a weekly, as-needed basis, and at least initially described as being like cards "the BBC usual [*sic*] do," meaning these cards were a normal part of BBC production, broadcast, and viewing during this period, and part of the humor would be that the silly titles appeared official (WAC T12/1,083).

cards—(PSC; "Marriage Guidance Counsellor") Perhaps (1) a comment on the cost of these generated titles, which in Ep. 6 are jokingly calculated from the beginning of the show; and (2) another way to remind the audience that a link is under way, that a show is being produced and watched. The artifice of the text is not only forwarded, but it seems that the audience is actually being dared to lose interest, to be distracted by the constant reminders of the show's constructedness. Animator Tex Avery pioneered this sign-holding forwardness in his Warner Bros. and later MGM cartoons, borrowing the convention from fin de siècle comics and political cartoons.

carnivorous pram—(PSC; animated link into "The Mouse Problem") The baby carriage or pram (from "perambulator") eats old ladies who look in to coo at the baby. This motif—a lethal threat from a seemingly harmless entity—has been seen before and will be recurring, found in Ep. 20, where killer sheep are on the loose; Ep. 7, where a blanc mange eats humans; and most memorably in *HG*, as the white rabbit guarding the cave of Caerbannog kills several knights.

"Charlie Gardener"—("The Wacky Queen") "Charlie" is a slang name that in Britain was reportedly assigned to all night watchmen during the reign of Charles I, and was also used pejoratively to refer to any bumbling, inept person (*OED*). This is not necessarily a term that would be found in a Hollywood film.

"chartered accountant"—(PSC; "The Mouse Problem") In Ep. 10 chartered accountants are described as "appallingly dull fellow[s], unimaginative, timid, lacking in initiative, spineless, easily dominated, no sense of humour, tedious company and irrepressibly drab and awful." For dullness, in the Python oeuvre, no profession exceeds chartered accountancy. This is why in the featurette *The Crimson Permanent Assurance* (1983), chartered accountants can incongruously become pirates, pillaging financial concerns worldwide, and why in Ep. 15 a proposed tax on sexual relations could certainly "make chartered accountancy more interesting."

"Chateau La Tour"—("Working-Class Playwright") The working-class father's substance abuse of choice happens to be a highly respected (and quite expensive) fine red wine, not tobacco, opium or hashish, or whiskey, as might be typical.

"choice"—("The Mouse Problem") The Vicar (Cleese) is implicated here as advocating and perhaps even participating in aberrant behavior—akin to the Bishop (Jones) leering at the hint of physicality in Ep. 7, the vicar (Idle) rifling the donations box in Ep. 6, the vicar with his nude lady in Ep. 17 (also Idle), the sherry-swilling vicar (Palin, Ep. 36)—and especially as he gestures like a mouse after he finishes speaking.

city gent—(PSC; "Flying Sheep") A bowler hat and dark conservative suit (with vest), an umbrella, and a purposeful look and walk comprise the uniform of the "City Gent" in the Python oeuvre. (The costumers called for "bowler hat and brolly.") This is significant in that by the late 1960s this "uniform" had been out of style for some years, and would have been much more common in the postwar years. The Pythons, then, were

relying on a type that might have been out of sight, but certainly not out of mind, and would certainly have been the "look" of the conservative city businessman as the Pythons grew up. "City" refers to the City of London, that one-square-mile area where so much of the financial business of the UK is transacted, and City Gent types are thick.

This visual dichotomy in the sketch—between city and country folk—sets up a motif that Python will revisit over and over again, offering a visual, shorthand way for character (or caricature) depiction, and which also serves the narrative demand for brevity. This typological approach allows Python to present characters without resorting to the usually necessary (and often lengthy) character development, in favor of a pseudo-physiognomic assessment, followed by either narrative support for that assessment (with all the attendant cultural biases, expectations, etc.) or a narrative undercutting. In this case, the Rustic (Chapman) seems to have both more and more significant knowledge than the City Gent (Jones). The Python world allows for this typing, as later seen in Ep. 28, when all it takes to qualify as a woman or child in the "women and children first" abandonment of a sinking ship is for a grown man to dress like a woman or child (or "Flemish Merchant" or "Red Indian" or "Space Man").

This typology is not unlike the descriptive names Ben Jonson gave to some of his characters, including Drugger, Dapper, Dol Common, Mosca, Volpone, Zeal-of-the-Land-Busy, and Sir Politic Would-Be. Even the Elizabethan dramatists' penchant for making all bastards evil, simply because they are bastards (like *Much Ado*'s Don John), or all foreigners untrustworthy because they are foreigners (Aaron the Moor in *Titus Andronicus*) is a precursor of this typological dramatic practice.

Peter Ackroyd notes in *London: The Biography*, that London has always intermixed pantomime and life, which explains "why London has always been considered to be the home of stock theatrical characters—the 'shabby genteel,' the 'city slicker,' the 'wide boy.'" He continues: "In print-shop windows of the mid-eighteenth century there were caricatures of London 'types'" (142). The Pythons would have found their stock characters not in print shop windows, but in pantomimes, on the radio, in film and TV, and in the pages of *Private Eye*, where Bond-author Ian Fleming (called "Phlegm") is characterized as a "bored city gent" who's turned to fantasy writing (Ingrams 56).

Cleveland, Carol—(PSC; "Marriage Guidance Counsellor") This is the first appearance (by a character, not just a passerby) of a female in *FC*. Cleveland is included because she is a beautiful, buxom (real) woman, not a Pepperpot, and she is the object of lustful affection, not scorn or ridicule. This does set the trend for the balance of the series, because—with rare exceptions—the female characters in *FC* are not allowed to rise above the level of either dimwitted mark or bathing beauty, or dimwitted bathing beauty (as in the "Science Fiction" sketch, Ep. 7). Cleveland here is also nearly mute, excepting her ability to titter. She is certainly objectified here, and her second appearance—in Ep. 2, "Mouse Problem"—will be equally objectified (and equally silent).

It really won't be until Ep. 5 that Cleveland is allowed to be involved in the narrative in a contributive way—in other words, almost like one of the boys:

> Woman (Cleveland): I think it's silly to ask a lizard what it thinks, anyway.
> Chairman: (*off*) Why?
> Woman: I mean they should have asked Margaret Drabble.

See notes to Ep. 5, the "A Duck, a Cat and a Lizard (Discussion)" sketch.

"clever sheep"—("Flying Sheep") An oxymoron, and indicative of much of Python's incongruous humor. It will often be the seemingly least clever types (Pepperpots, plumbers, peasants) who display the most profound intelligence and canniness in the Python world.

"commercial possibilities"—("Flying Sheep") He may be a Rustic, but he is also a wily businessman, able to appreciate nuances missed by the City Gent. This will become the case for many lower-class types depicted by the Pythons, including the peasant Dennis (Palin) in *HG*, and many Pepperpots in *FC*. It is the Pepperpot in Ep. 1, after all, who is able to identify that collagist Kurt Schwitters is not English, but German.

Compère—(PSC; "Musical Mice") This unctuous character appears (played by either Palin or Idle) many times in *FC*, and is essentially a greasy emcee at an equally grungy nightclub. Dressed in garish red, he is meant to resemble entertainment hosts—known as "Redcoats"—at Butlins Holiday Camps (founded 1936-1966), where affordable family vacation and entertainment could be had. These would have been the kinds of destinations that British families were able to afford in the lean postwar years.

For the second series the Pythons shot some footage at the Butlins Holiday Camp in Bognor. See the notes for "Lake Pahoe" in Ep. 32.

"conjuror"—("The Mouse Problem") A magician, a user of sleight-of-hand tricks or prestidigitation.

"continental version"—("A Man With Three Buttocks") Referring to the practice of recording multiple versions of a particular radio/television show,

episode, etc., one for British audiences, and one for a French or German audience, for example. (The continental versions were often more racy than would have been allowed on "Auntie BBC," too.) Also, the BBC had for years provided broadcast material in scores of languages for the far-flung corners of the Empire. The Pythons would later themselves be asked to record two episodes of *FC* for German television, the first, at least, in German and subtitled in English. The new episodes featured a combination of new and already-broadcast sketches.

Credits—(end credits) A typed caption/title card was part of the end credits prior to filming/taping, but was not included in the episode. The note reads: "The second exploration into short, sharp, modern humour" (WAC T12/1,083). The Pythons, producer John Howard Davies, or director MacNaughton may have decided that post-commentary would be missed by most viewers, or they simply ran out of time and sacrificed the card. It also might be that, given JHD's rather droll assessment of the previous week's show (he called it "rubbish"), the producers felt the shows couldn't possibly live up to the boastful tagline (WAC T12/1,082).

– D –

deep Southern American voice—(PSC; "Marriage Guidance Counsellor") This look (black hat, mustache, black cowboy gear) as well as the affected drawl is very much a result of the significant presence on British TV of such American Western staples as *The Lone Ranger* (BBC, 1957), *Gunsmoke* (ITV, 1956), *Maverick* (ITV, 1959), *Rawhide* (ITV, 1959), *Bonanza* (ITV, 1960), and later *Big Valley* and *The High Chaparral*.

"Descartes, Rene"—("Pepperpots in Supermarket") Descartes (1596-1650) was a French mathematician, scientist, and philosopher, and is often called the father of modern philosophy. He is mentioned earlier in Gilliam's animation (when Rodin's "The Thinker" disappears in Ep. 1) and is also memorialized as a "drunken fart" in "The Philosopher's Drinking Song" (or "The Bruce's Song") on both the *Matching Tie and Handkerchief* and *Monty Python Live at Drury Lane* record albums. His influence is decidedly negative in Ep. 14, where Mrs. Simnel (Palin) will lament that children are being spoiled on Cartesian dualism. Descartes and "Cartesian Dualism" is also mentioned in the pre-Python song "Rhubarb Tart" in *At Last the 1948 Show* sung by Cleese. (See the "disappears too" entry below for more.)

desk—(PSC; "A Man With Three Buttocks") This is a standard BBC or ITV news/announcer set, complete with desk, chair, framing backdrop, and framed back-projection (BP) screen. A slide image of a walrus is projected on the BP screen behind the announcer, though it is never noticed or mentioned during the scene. Other slides that will appear without comment or context will include an illustration of an allosaurus, a naked sailor on a rug (photo by Robert Broeder, and which will be used again in Ep. 28), and the well-known 1934 photo taken by Dr. Robert Wilson, purportedly of the Loch Ness Monster. The photo was subsequently identified as a fake—it is in actuality a miniature floating model of the monster's head and neck.

"Dierdre"—("Marriage Guidance Counsellor") Actually, the name "Deirdre" is most often associated with a sorrowing and pitiful maiden, so the incongruity (for those who could appreciate the etymology) is understood. This also illustrates Python's interest in unusual naming, usually for incongruous humor. Cf. the impressive Scottish enchanter "Tim" and the mercurial peasant "Dennis," both in *HG*, or the poet reader "Harness Wombat" in Ep. 17, as well as "Mitzie" and "Vicky" (both men) in Ep. 1.

disappears too—(PSC; animated link into "A Man With Three Buttocks") A clever play on Descartes' "Cogito, ergo sum," his famous summation of his belief in the significance of human thought as clear evidence of existence. The "gag" here is simple and profound: remove a man's thoughts, and you remove the man.

This image is a retouched photo of Rodin's statue *The Thinker* (1880).

This also indicates the power of the animator, the creator, in relation to the characters and worlds he creates. Gilliam's hands will often enter the seemingly sacrosanct diegetic world of the animation frame to manipulate that world before our eyes. This "figuration of the artist" in animation goes back to its earliest days. Pioneers J. Stuart Blackton, Winsor McCay, and Max Fleischer, among others, created animated cartoons where the hand of the animator can be seen to initiate the action, to create the cartoon world, to give the breath of life to inanimate drawings. In Fleischer's "Out of the Inkwell" series (c. 1919-1923), Fleischer's hand and pen create and/or set free Ko-ko the Clown from his inkwell, and the cartoon can only end when Ko-ko is returned to his capped home. In Later *FC* episodes, Gilliam will even insert his face and body into the frame, and in the feature film *Monty Python and the Holy Grail*, the audience gets to see the animator die of a heart attack, ending the animated sequence.

The "thought bubble" that is pricked in the Descartes'/*Thinker* scene is an element used by cartoonists (and early animators like McCay, Wallace Carlson, Pat Nolan, Emile Cohl et al.) to indicate a character's thoughts. The thought bubble often looks more cloudlike (fluffy around the edges) than a speech bubble. These bubbles were also present in the pages of *Private Eye*, reportedly suggested by Peter Cook to enliven the boring but necessary ministerial photos (Ingrams 8).

– E –

"East Anglia"—("The Wrestling Epilogue") The University of East Anglia is in Norwich, and in Ep. 20 is also the school where undergraduate village idiots matriculate. The university was established in 1962, and was thus a very "new" university in Britain in 1969, and therefore suspect. Oxford and Cambridge—where most of the Pythons studied—have been in existence since the thirteenth and fourteenth centuries, respectively.

Eek Eek Club—(PSC; "The Mouse Problem") This is a reference to clubs like Berlin's famous KitKatKlub, but may also reach back further, to the political and literary Kit Cat (or Kit Kat) Club founded in the eighteenth century in London. Whig politics and associations were the board of fare, and members included writers Congreve, Vanbrugh, Addison, and Steele, and politicians like the Duke of Marlborough and Sir Robert Walpole. The salacious and political possibilities, however, indicate a mixture of both references—meaning these sex clubs might be gathering places for Conservative Party deviants. (See the entries for "blue cheese films" and "blue corner" above for more.)

Caerphilly is a cheese originally from Caerphilly (Glamorgan, Wales), and "a go-go" indicates this is essentially a cheese strip club. This dance club's sign notes that it is actually located in Soho.

"Epilogue"—("The Wrestling Epilogue") The signing-off show on early BBC-TV. A clergyman would read and then comment on scriptural passages. In *Hard Day's Night* (1964), the TV director (Victor Spinetti) driven toward a breakdown by The Beatles' antics is certain that his failure will result in a career-ending *Epilogue* assignment.

Episode 2—This is the second installment of the *Flying Circus* series, though it was recorded first on 30 August 1969, and broadcast 12 October 1969. (The calendar in the Marriage Councellor's office indicates 28 August, incidentally, meaning they must have pulled it off of someone's office wall as they prepped the shoot.) The filmed portions (outside of the studio) would have been shot earlier, in July 1969.

Throughout most of this show's pre-filmed life this episode was known in internal BBC memos and communiqués as "Bunn Wackett Buzzard Stubble & Boot," not "Sex & Violence" (WAC T12/1,083). This obviously created some confusion in the middle management levels of the BBC, leading the Head of Light Entertainment, Michael Mills, to ask that any such subtitles be either de-emphasized or gotten rid of altogether (WAC T12/1,242).

In an in-house memo (probably from the desk of John Howard Davies), the delayed reaction to Episode 1 is recorded: "This week's episode [Episode 2] stars as usual John Cleese, Michawl [*sic*] Palin, Terry Jones, Graham Chapman and Eric Idle, and deals with the same idiotic rubbish as the first show but, we hope, will be funnier" (WAC T12/1,082).

"escape"—("Flying Sheep") Perhaps even an obtuse reference to the recent hit film *The Great Escape* (1963), which is later satirized aptly in Ep. 28, as part of the "Trim-Jeans Theatre" sketch.

– F –

"farmer's wife"—("The Mouse Problem") Reenactments of mouse roles in various fairy tales and children's rhymes characterize these parties, clearly. This last reference (the farmer's wife) hints at a pleasure/pain sadomasochistic theme, complete with a knife-wielding dominatrix and her willing, squeaking victims. See the "perverts meet" note for more on sadomasochism. The "matron" chasing these micemen is Jones in drag, and with a full mustache.

"fellows"—("The Mouse Problem") This seems to confirm that participants at these deviant gatherings were all male, thus supporting and escalating the homoerotic reading, where young white males seek illicit sexual thrills.

"Figgis, Arthur"—(PSC; "A Man With Three Buttocks") Character played by Cleese (Ep. 20) and Chapman (Eps. 2 and 6). In Ep. 20, Figgis is a village idiot; otherwise he seems to be an interviewer/announcer for the BBC. Figgis is mentioned here as if the audience would know him, though there isn't an accompanying laugh, so this may just be a set-up for the cycling shot to come. It could be that Figgis is a borrowing from the group over at *Private Eye*, who castigate *Punch* and its ancient librarian, "Figgis" (see the first issue of *Private Eye*).

"fight for it"—("The Wrestling Epilogue") Classic confrontation between believers in God and believers in men, between religion and humanism, and probably a subtle comment on the "troubles" already under way among Northern Ireland's differing believers (Roman Catholic and Protestant), as well as recent religious conflicts in the Middle East where Britain found itself involved both militarily and diplomatically. There are also allusions here to the ongoing and often vitriolic debate between those who believe in a higher power and those who simply do not, and would have fit the contentions between men like Hilaire Belloc (see above) and Bishop John Robinson (see "books about belief" note above). The specter of two respected men wrestling for the existence of God isn't any less or more ridiculous, the Pythons seems to be saying, than two nations fighting and killing each other for essentially the same cause.

In the 5 April 1963 edition of *Private Eye*, cartoonist "Timothy" provides a two-page spread entitled "Britain Gets Wythe Itte, 1963," a spoof on Tory attempts to make over the party's image from fussy and Victorian to hip and au courant. One placard attached to St. Martin-in-the-Fields reads: "Debate—Is There a God?" and lists two bishops who will be arguing the point in a repeat BBC show (Ingrams 80-81).

"film"—("The Mouse Problem") In Ep. 18, the "*Blackmail*" sketch, the film presented is also of poor quality, as it is also a "hidden camera" film from the BBC.

Much of this footage was shot at or near 48 Ullsworth Road, Barnes, with the police station shots being filmed at Barnes Police Station, Lonsdale Road (WAC T12/1,083).

film leader—(PSC; "The Wacky Queen") Correctly a "universal leader," since a film leader is actually just blank film that allows for the threading of the film through a projector. A universal leader is a "leader designed according to the ANSI [American National Standards Institute] document PH22.55 for the current projection rate of 24 frames per second (1 1/2 feet per second), and recommended for use on all release prints. It was designed to replace the Academy [of Motion Picture Arts and Sciences] leader originally conceived when the motion picture projection rate was 16 frames per second" (Pincus 181).

"flying . . . slam"—("The Wrestling Epilogue") The flying mare and full body slam are professional wrestling moves.

– G –

"Gladstone"—("The Wacky Queen") William Gladstone (1809-1898) was a longtime and repeat British Prime Minister (1868-1874, 1880-1885, 1886, 1892-1894). His relationship with Victoria (see note below) soured late in his life, and in 1894 he tendered his resignation, rendering it highly unlikely that he would have later cavorted about with his Queen for a silent comedy film. See *ODNB*.

"Gosh"—("Marriage Guidance Counsellor") Probably a slight swipe at the American version of English, and American colloquialisms. Also, it sounds very much like what the awestruck young Joey Starrett might say in *Shane* (1953).

"Greaves, Jimmy"—(film leader link into "The Wacky Queen") The name "Jimmy Greaves" takes the place of the number "5" in the leader as broadcast. Greaves was an English national team and professional football star, appearing in the 1962 and 1966 World Cup tournaments. England won the World Cup in 1966.

– H –

"Harold"—("Flying Sheep") This very determined and clever "Harold" may be a reference to once Secretary of the Royal Aero Club, Commander Harold Perrin, known as "Harold the Hearty." Harold, who ran the Royal Aero Club from 1906 to 1945, was characterized as "brilliant," and a man obsessed with the possibilities and inevitability of flight.

"have a go"—("The Wacky Queen") This is much more a British phrase than American. All three citations in the *OED* are from Commonwealth sources. Again, just a slight malapropism as the Englishmen attempt an American monologue, obviously without consulting the lone American on the staff, Terry Gilliam. See entries for "hosepipe" and "wacky" for more.

"Hello Sailor"—("The Wrestling Epilogue") A phrase used many times in *FC* (and at least once in *The Goon Show*), and always associated with homosexuality (see Ep. 14, as well). The phrase alludes to (ostensibly) women picking up sailors, but is adapted to the homosocial world of *FC*. Both men's sexuality is called into question, one by name (Gay) and the other by the title of his work ("Hello Sailor").

This motif will run throughout the series, where Her Majesty's sailors are, when mentioned, gay and usually rather effeminate. See later "sailor" references in Eps. 10, 20, 28, and 30 for more. Peter Sellers had created a sailor character for *The Goon Show* (in the early 1950s) who was poncy, neat, and easily irritated, and who spoke with the now-familiar lisp, a portrayal that seems a direct influence on the Pythons.

"hole"—("The Mouse Problem") Can be read as either a homo- or heterosexual innuendo, especially in light of the secretive and perverse nature of the activity. Cf. Jonson's *Bartholomew Fair* where the puppet Leander tells Leatherhead to " . . . kiss my hole here, and smell" (5.4.135), suggesting the anal orifice, and the specter of love creeping "in at a mouse-hole" in Middleton and Rowley's *The Changeling* (3.3.100), to add the possibil-

ity of heterosexual encounters. See Henke's *Courtesans and Cuckolds* for more.

"holiday money"—("Marriage Guidance Counsellor") During the postwar period, austerity measures enacted by the government to combat a badly slumping economy included the strict control of currency. British travelers overseas were at one time only allowed to take £30 with them, meaning most never could actually afford to leave the island(s). Thus, as Kenneth Morgan mentions: "People traveled to seaside holidays (especially on the fixed 'August Bank Holidays') in tightly packed and unmodernized rolling stock, or perhaps in ancient coaches" (*Britain Since 1945* 77). By 1969, that £30 figure had risen, evidently, under a Labour government. In a "Mrs. Wilson's Diary" entry in *Private Eye*, Chancellor Jenkins has just returned from a continental holiday, suntanned and confident, while the Scilly-refreshed PM Wilson, a bit parky over Jenkins' cheek, asks: "As a matter of interest, how did you fiddle the fifty pound limit?"

In the sketch Palin seems to be offering a character who knows this controlled, penny-conscious life intimately well; perhaps because Palin himself grew up in that environment, as did the rest of the troupe. Mates of the Pythons The Beatles broached this territory, as well, in McCartney's "When I'm Sixty-Four": "Every summer we can rent a cottage on the Isle of Wight, if it's not too dear / We shall scrimp and save . . . " (audio transcription from the McCartney/Lennon song, *Sgt. Pepper's Lonely Hearts Club Band* album, 1967).

See the entry for "sharing the interests" below for more.

"holiday or . . . "—("Flying Sheep") Here the City Gent (Jones) looks the Rustic (Chapman) up and down from behind, doing a quick visual assessment of the rustic clothing, and by the look on his face, knows the answer to his own question—the man is a local. D.H. Lawrence approached this same kind of intercultural friction in the relationship between the gamekeeper Mellors and Lady Chatterley in *Lady Chatterley's Lover*:

> Mellors: "If yer want ter be 'ere, yo'll non want me messin' abaht a' th' time."
> Lady Chatterley: "Why don't you speak ordinary English?"

The Pythons will revisit this Lawrence-like world of haves and have-nots (of owners and workers) in the "Working-Class Playwright" scene later in this same episode, and throughout *FC*, whenever a toff meets a commoner.

"homosexual . . . drug-addict . . . footballer"—("Working-Class Playwright") A reference inspired by the *Private Eye* staff's take on Tony Richardson's 1961 film, *A Taste of Honey*:

We were lucky enough to find two exciting new cheap unknowns in Alfred Weights and Shirley-June Tush to play the lead parts of the *latently homosexual professional lacrosse player* Arthur Sidmouth, and Doreen, the girl who watches sympathetically from a bar stool in the film's opening shots as Arthur vomits up his half-pint of ginger shandy. (Ingrams 41; italics added)

The "homosexual nymphomaniac drug-addict" reference could also be an allusion to Chapman himself, who was known to struggle with alcoholism and his homosexuality (see Morgan, 1999, 57, 68, and 91). Cleveland said of Chapman: "[He] always did everything to excess, everything he did: obviously his drinking and the way he flaunted his homosexuality . . . caused a certain amount of embarrassment at the time" (Morgan, 1999, 68). Chapman's outré behavior may have been an embarrassment publicly, perhaps, but clearly not enough to steer clear of homosexual gibes throughout *FC*, many featuring Chapman chiming in with gusto.

This description of the father's play is also an amalgamation of "Angry Young Men" plots, including David Storey's *This Sporting Life* football theme (note the homosocial and even homoerotic post-match shower room scene), and homosexual themes and tension in many works of the period, including authors John Osborne (*A Patriot for Me*, 1965), Harold Pinter (*The Servant*, 1963), and Storey (*Radcliffe*, 1963). In *This Sporting Life*, the (anti)hero Frank Machin (played by Richard Harris) destroys himself and any relationship he may have been able to have with Margaret (Rachel Roberts) and her children with drink, angst, and self-doubt. (For more, see Aldgate's *Censorship and the Permissive Society* and Carpenter's *The Angry Young Men*.) *Private Eye* spoofs the critical fawning over the movement in its 4 May 1962 issue. Pinter, by the way, is also later lampooned in *FC* Ep. 10, "Arthur Tree" sketch, as "Harold Splinter."

"hosepipe"—("The Wacky Queen") A spigot or faucet, the term "hosepipe" isn't generally used in the United States, betraying the Pythons' British approach to American English.

"Hounslow"—("The Mouse Problem") In the West London borough, near Heathrow Airport. "MIDDLE-SEX." is actually shortened to "MIDDX." on the caption card.

This caption spot may very well have been the place in this episode where the then-current home address of former mate and employer David Frost was included. Immediately after the initial broadcast of the episode on 12 October, Frost (or his people) must have called the BBC higher-ups (including Tom Sloan, Head of Light Entertainment, and even the Postmaster General) to complain about the direct reference, prompting a memo dated 14 October 1969 from producer John Howard Davies to director Ian MacNaughton, asking (tiredly, it seems, as if he were talking to or about naughty children) that the caption be changed. JHD asks that Cleese come in and record a new voiceover, so that after the repeats Davies won't have to get "castrated again" by the BBC (WAC T12/1,084). Contemporary phone books list a "Frost, DP" (completely, his name is David Paradine Frost) living at 84 Alexandra Road, NW8 with the phone number 01-624 1568. This is in the fashionable St. Johns Wood suburb of London.

Davies was especially vexed since the Pythons had, in the previous episode, slipped Frost's phone number somewhere into the episode. Frost's *production* company, David Paradine Productions Ltd., had the phone number 01-584 5313 during this period, and his home number was MAIda Vale 1568, according to the British Telephone Historical Archives. Neither of these phone numbers appear or are mentioned in first two *FC* episodes as they survive today, nor in the printed scripts, meaning the requested changes must have been made. (By 1971, according to BT records, Paradine and Frost had moved to swankier digs in Mayfair, all the more reason for the Pythons to dislike him.)

The Pythons would take infrequent potshots at Frost in *FC*, who had parlayed his Cambridge Footlights secretary position into satirical shows for the BBC, and who eventually became a fixture on British and even American TV as an interviewer and presenter. Frost's rather naked ambition seems to have rubbed a number of people, Pythons and *Beyond the Fringe* types included, the wrong way (see Humphrey Carpenter's *That Was Satire, That Was* for more). *Private Eye* co-founder and contributor Richard Ingrams characterized Frost in this warmly unflattering way in 1971:

From the start Frost evinced a profound animosity from the founding fathers of the satire movement. There was something ungentlemanly about a man who was so obviously on the make. His astonishing industry ran counter to the spirit of public-school amateurism which characterized *Beyond the Fringe* and *Private Eye*. At the same time there was a strange charm about his barefaced ambition which was somehow endearing. (11)

It is no surprise then that the Pythons lump Frost in with the sexual deviants. By Ep. 19, Frost will be lampooned as Timmy Williams, an unctuous, insufferable TV hack.

– I –

"ici"—("French Lecture on Sheep-Aircraft") Translation: "The travelers, the luggage, they are here!" Just prior to this, Jean-Brian (Palin) asks (in Franglish) where the passengers and baggage might be, and his partner (Cleese) answers the question.

interviewer—(PSC; Pepperpot link out of "French Lecture on Sheep-Aircraft") These are the same Pepperpots who in Ep. 1 couldn't tell the difference between Whizzo Butter and a dead crab; here they are able to appreciate the abstract and often difficult contributions of noted French philosophers. (See the entry for "Pepperpots" in Ep. 1 and "Jean-Paul Sartre" in this episode for more.) This scene is also shot in the F.J. Wallis store in Acton (WAC T12/1,242). Two Pepperpots (Mrs. Premise and Mrs. Conclusion) will discuss Sartre's worldview—and especially his writings on freedom and materialism—in Ep. 27, even traveling to Paris to confront him directly.

– J –

"Jackson, Arthur"—("The Mouse Problem") Cf. Arthur "Two-Sheds" Jackson from Ep. 1. The address below this name on the caption may have been where the address of David Frost was broadcast, the inclusion of which caused a punch-up in BBC management, leading to JHD's memo to director Ian MacNaughton, and a change in the taped version for rebroadcast. See the entry for "Hounslow" above, and the entry for "*scoreboard*" in Ep. 1.

"Jehovah"—("The Wrestling Epilogue") God of the Old Testament, and well chosen since it translates to "God the Almighty" in later Christian usage.

– K –

"Kargol and Janet"—("The Mouse Problem") A hint of a narrative fracture here, especially as Janet (Cleveland) bursts into the frame, though acknowledgment of the rupture hasn't occurred, and the documentary atmosphere is still in force—at least at the diegetic level. In fact, the Linkman (Palin) will push the interview through/across this attempted narrative disruption by framing his questions to Kargol (Chapman) *the psychiatrist*, and not Kargol *the conjuror*. The smoothing over or resistance to the narrative disruption holds the presented diegetic world together, and the documentary can continue in earnest. This kind of fissure, in other episodes, will lead the narrative off into new directions, to "something completely different," as in Ep. 27, or stop it completely, as in Ep. 35, "Mortuary Hour," when an interruption by Badger (Idle) causes the sketch to be abandoned.

In the production notes for this episode, Janet's costume is supposed to look as if "she were assisting Mike and Bernie Winters" (WAC T12/1,083). The Winterses were comedians (and brothers) popular in the UK in the 1950s and 1960s, and who hosted their own TV shows in the early 1970s.

"Kierkegaard"—("The Wrestling Epilogue") Søren Kierkegaard (1813-1855) was a Danish religious philosopher, a critic of "systematic rational philosophy," and is seen as the father of the existentialist trends in philosophy (Drabble, 1985, 531). The continuing reference to Existentialist thought and thinkers should be noted, and displays the Pythons' debt to the Modernist period. For more on Kierkegaard and his influence on the Pythons (and the twentieth-century Existentialists), see notes to Eps. 14, 27, and 28, where his writings in *Either/Or* become significant, and specifically "Crop Rotation."

"kill 'em"—("The Mouse Problem") It's not entirely clear whether all voices are talking about men who want to be mice, or actual mice. In any case, many of the solutions read like rodenticide—meaning men who act like mice can/should be treated as such.

– L –

Lawrence, D.H.—(PSC; "Working-Class Playwright") Lawrence (1885-1930), a Northerner himself, born in Eastwood in Nottinghamshire, was first recognized as that newest and brashest of literary breeds, the working-class novelist. The Oedipal elements of his works have been identified as early examples of the psychoanalyzing of characters in modern literature (see Ep. 43 for *Hamlet* on the psychiatrist's couch). The Pythons writing into the script "right out of D.H. Lawrence" obviates the need for a physical description of the set, for the production designers and viewers, and eventually taps into the acculturated viewer's knowledge of Lawrence, his tropes and characters/settings, and television and cinematic adaptations of his work. The viewer (or reader?) who understood these allusions could sport his/her "badge of acculturation," and "get" the in-jokes and allusions, just like one who "knows" Shakespeare can similarly claim acculturation (*MPSERD* 24-25). This is an example of the Pythons' trotting out their academic credentials, where the similarly educated viewer can appreciate the allusions on multiple levels.

"Leamington"—("The Mouse Problem") A city in the Warwick district, Warwickshire, and home to the Royal Leamington Spa.

little man—(PSC; "Marriage Guidance Counsellor") The Man (Arthur Pewtey) is described in the production notes for this episode as wearing a "Herbert Arkwright suit, eventually to be torn by a Buffalo," which is probably an oblique reference to the character created by Ronnie Barker, Arkwright, in *Seven of One*, a series of comedy pilots (WAC T12/1,083), and was probably a new iteration of an earlier Barker character. The BBC described the character as a "stuttering, miserly, lustful shopkeeper." The mentioned buffalo—perhaps meant to appear in relation to Cleese's Southerner—never did materialize in the episode. (This may just be that portions of the potential shows each week were elided for time or taste, and any production-related requests would also have been canceled.) Another short sketch—called the "Quickie Duel" in the show's notes—was also written and reportedly even recorded, but never made part of the broadcast episode (see WAC files for 1969 and the First Series). Johnson in *The First 20 Years of Monty Python* carefully notes the variations from printed script to recorded show (as do a number of fan websites), so most of these changes won't be addressed in these notes.

"London"—("Working-Class Playwright") Again, a character defined by his speech, the way he talks and words he chooses. This satire is based entirely on the "Angry Young Men" and their "Kitchen Sink" dramas produced by young British novelists, filmmakers, and playwrights in the late 1950s and into the early 1960s, and often set in provincial mining and textile mill areas and featuring working-class antiheroes. Films like *Look Back in Anger* (1958), *Room at the Top* (1959), and *This Sporting Life* (1963) emerged from this social realist movement, a movement born of the British documentary "Free Cinema" of the postwar years. Significant playwrights of the period included John Braine, John Osborne, Harold Pinter, and David Storey. (See Aldgate's *Censorship and the Permissive Society* for more on the movement, as well as Carpenter's *The Angry Young Men: A Literary Comedy of the 1950s*.)

In *Room at the Top* (dir. Jack Clayton), for instance, the hero Joe Lampton (Laurence Harvey) wants nothing more than to stay out of his village and move up into the world of the upwardly mobile, and he's willing to do anything (and become anyone) to achieve his goals.

In the Pythons' world, though, instead of the working-class younger generation lashing out at the stultifying effects of life in the mines or mills, it's the older working-class artist blasting the effete notions of what real labor is, and where the really meaningful production is going on in Britain (on the stage, page, and screen). Python subverts expectations by almost reversing the Oedipal structure to favor the working-class playwright father over the "laborer" son. The Pythons are also subtly validating their own existence as artists—each from a working-class background.

The 4 May 1962 edition of *Private Eye* (1.10) spoofs this allegedly working-class literary and theatrical movement, as well, making fun of the "fee-paying school" grads like Osborne, and spoofing Richardson's *A Taste of Honey*.

– M –

"man's got to do"—("Marriage Guidance Counsellor") A Marlovian "mighty line," of sorts. Cf. Marcus Aurelius Antoninus's *Meditations*: "In the morning, when you are sluggish about getting up, let this thought be present: 'I am rising to a man's work'" (Book V, 1). American Negro League baseball pitcher Satchel Paige spoke similarly when he said, discussing his use of multiple pitches and "looks": "Man's got to do what he's got to do." There's also some very similar dialogue throughout the 1952 Western *High Noon*, where Sheriff Kane (Gary Cooper) must go back and face the evil Frank Miller, simply because it's what he must do. This is also essentially the reason, Shane (Alan Ladd) explains, why he must go to town and face the gunman in black (Jack Palance) in *Shane* (1953).

"men now known to have been mice"—("The Mouse Problem") "Veni Vidi, Vici" ("I came, I saw, I conquered") were Julius Caesar's words (by his own account) at the defeat of Pharnaces in Anatolia. Caesar lived from c. 100 BC to 44 BC. He is also featured (as he dies) in Ep. 15, the *"Julius Caesar* on an Aldis Lamp" scene. Napoleon Bonaparte (1769-1821), emperor of France, stands in his familiar hand-in-coat pose. These inserts were shot in the dunes near Bournemouth.

If this sketch is actually about closet homosexuality, as it seems, then what the presenter is doing is what—according to Wayne Dynes in *Homosexuality: A Research Guide*—began to appear among "homosexual scholars in German-speaking countries" in the nineteenth century—namely, lists of noteworthy homosexuals in history (182). Dynes continues, identifying the historians' justifications for such (somewhat fanciful) listwork:

> Parallel tendencies occur with scholars representing other minority groups, where such lists seem to function to provide historical witness of the collective worth of an ostracized group. This "hall of fame" approach has recently been criticized as skewing homosexual and lesbian history towards an unrepresentative elite, effacing historical variety and class differences. The search for famous homosexuals also provokes a largely fruitless series of debates over whether figures of the past, such as Socrates or Caesar, were truly homosexual. (182)

Not historians by trade, the Pythons aren't trying to recuperate their chosen historical figures by creating a newfound "collective worth," they are instead ridiculing these same figures by tagging them with the sexual diminishment label used so often in *FC*. Again, for the Pythons, power and closet perversion go hand in hand as they here also favor the "unrepresentative elite"— Napoleon, Caesar—with their satiric attentions.

A portion of this sex-power connection must be attributed to the many lurid stories in tabloid newspapers of important (often political) men doing questionable things of a sexual nature. For instance, in December 1958 the political career of Ian Harvey, a Harrow East Conservative, was brought to an ignominious end when he was arrested in the bushes of St. James Park in flagrante delicto with a young member of the Coldstream Guards. Harvey even tried to make a break for it, contemporary reports say, but was easily caught. Both parties were eventually charged with "breaching the park's regulations," fined £5, and released. (This was also discussed, soberly and in respect to the Profumo affair, in *Private Eye* in the 12 November 1965 issue [Ingrams 129].) No surprise, then, that the Pythons can see both the Coldstream Guards–type organizations and any member of the government as potential closet perverts. In Ep. 14, for example, the Household Cavalry will be alluded to as a bastion of homosexuality.

"Mice and Men"—("The Mouse Problem") Play on John Steinbeck novel title, *Of Mice and Men*, which is itself borrowed from noted Scotsman Robert Burns' 1785 poem, *To a Mouse*: "The best laid schemes o' mice and men / Gang aft a-gley" (stanza 7).

monsignor . . . skull cap—(PSC; "The Wrestling Epilogue") This prelate is wearing black robes with red lining, including a short cape and matching skull cap. The actor is Terry Medlicote, from the Tough Guys Agency (WAC T12/1,083), and is obviously a professional wrestler, as he has noticeable cauliflower ear. Given the originally religious nature of *Epilogue*, this prelate character fits rather well.

Not so his opponent, a so-called old Don figure. This wrestler appears to be the prototypical Cambridge don, with tweedy conservative attire. An "old Don" is actually a college fellow or tutor. This would have been the "type" of lecturer the Pythons encountered at Oxford and Cambridge, and even in their prep schools. The actor is Brian Lancaster from Tough Guys Agency (WAC T12/1,083).

"mouse organ"—("Musical Mice") Play on "mouthorgan," also known as a "Jew's Harp." This entire sketch was reportedly added to the episode's script after-the-fact (Johnson *20 Years* 49).

Mouse Problem—("The Mouse Problem") According to Cleese, this sketch was originally written prior to *FC*, when Cleese and Chapman were writing additional material for a Peter Sellers film, *The Magic Christian* (1969; screenplay by Terry Southern). Sellers rejected the idea, eventually, and Cleese and Chapman retooled it for *FC* (Johnson *20 Years* 50).

"The Mouse Problem" sketch is also significant in that it is sustained satire without the self-consciousness characteristic of much of *FC*. This continuity may be attributed to its earlier incarnation as a proposed section of a complete, narratively fluid film. Additionally, the undercutting and acknowledgment of the artifice is missing here, with the exception of Kargol's (Chapman) attempt to perform as a conjuror, not a psychiatrist. The interviewer (Palin) refuses to let him do so, and the narrative moves on without interruption.

"Must Go"—(PSC; "The Mouse Problem") These placards are based on then-current anti-Vietnam posters like "Ho Ho Ho Troops Must Go," "SHHHAME," and "Put the Nix-On War—Bring Peace Now," seen in the streets of London and across the United States Significant anti-war demonstrations had occurred in London in both March and October of 1968.

– N –

"National Theatre"—("Working-Class Playwright") The National Theatre (actually several theatre spaces) opened as a subsidized theatre in 1962, on the South Bank of the Thames. Its inaugural play was *Hamlet*, starring Peter O'Toole, in 1963. The National Theatre was actually home to more conventional plays, including Shakespeare and other English Renaissance drama revivals, whereas the Royal Court Theatre (English Stage Company, St. Martin's Lane, London) staged works from this "new" group of playwrights, including Osborne (and the 1956 premiere of *Look Back in Anger*), Wesker, Arden, Storey, and others, as well as important foreign plays from Brecht, Ionesco, Beckett, Sartre, and Duras. (See royalcourttheatre.com.)

"Old Vic" is the colloquial name for the venerable Royal Victorian Theatre (Waterloo Road, London), which had to be rebuilt after the bombings of WWII. It's worth noting that this radical middle-aged playwright (as played by Chapman) would be hanging out with the more "establishment" types (Olivier, Redgrave, Gielgud, etc.) at both the Old Vic and National Theatre, and not the Angry Young Men types. This is either a mistake in venues from the Pythons, or yet another subversion, the latter being more likely.

newspaper headlines—(PSC; "The Mouse Problem") This headline has been physically replaced (cut-and-pasted by Gilliam) on what appears to be an actual contemporary edition of *News of the World*. (The Pythons requested that these newspapers look like, specifically, *News of the World, Daily Express*, and *The Times* [WAC T12/1,083].) Another (actual) story running in the same issue is titled "The Rise and Fall of the Kennedy Clan" (this hard on the heels of Ted Kennedy's 18 July 1969 Chappaquiddick incident). The "Peer Faces Rodent Charges" headline appears on the Friday, 23 August 1969 edition of *The Daily Express*, also a touched-up version, and replaced the original headline. Images of these newspapers are still available on microfilm.

A following headline ("Mouse Clubs on Increase") is pasted onto the Monday, 28 July 1969 (late London) edition of *The Times*, which also features a story on new test results from Apollo mission moon rock samples. (The Apollo frenzy will be treated in Ep. 28, "*Life of Tschaikowsky*.") The headline and story "Rocks of Moon a Puzzle" occupy the far right column of the paper; a photo of the astronauts' wives visiting their husbands in isolation has been replaced by the mouse photo. Feature stories on Edward Kennedy's post-Chappaquiddick difficulties were replaced by the "Mouse Clubs on Increase" headline and story.

Northern couple—(PSC; "Working-Class Playwright") The son (Idle) is wearing a very nice business suit, while the Northern couple (Chapman and Jones) looks like comfortable working folk. In the costuming notes for this particular episode, the costume designer is given this prompt for these characters: "Both look like Mr. and Mrs. Trevor Howard in *Sons and Lovers*" (WAC T12/1,083). Actor Trevor Howard (1913-1988) starred (with Dean Stockwell and Wendy Hiller) in the 1960 film adaptation of the Lawrence novel directed by Jack Cardiff. *Sons and Lovers* is the 1913 D.H. Lawrence novel based on his own childhood in Eastwood, Nottinghamshire. This visual dichotomy (again, here and throughout *FC* used as shorthand for the audience) will become quite important as the scene plays out.

The term "Northern" also covers quite a bit of territory, including just about everything north of London or, more specifically, north of the Humber, or anything north of a line from Bristol to The Wash ("the fordable portion of the estuary between Lincolnshire and Norfolk"—*OED*).

not applauding—(PSC; link into "The Wrestling Epilogue") Another bit of stock footage, this time featuring Indian (and Asian) members of the Commonwealth. The fact that they aren't amused might be another example of Python's "othering" of everything and everyone not English. As Indians they are not part of the acculturated English club, thus they wouldn't "get" the joke, colloquial reference, etc. On the other hand, they could be unamused by the pranks of their colonizers, rendering this moment an indictment of the British Empire's presence in India, for example. Lastly, this clip could have been chosen only because it's kind of the "not applauding" version of the much-used Women's Institute clip.

"nowt"—("Working-Class Playwright") A Northern colloquialism meaning "nothing." A section from Lawrence's 1913 novel, *Sons and Lovers*, gives a clear indication of where the Pythons lifted their Northern characters' speech patterns, and where the cross-cultural, class-to-class tension originated. In this scene from the novel, bullying father Walter Morel is decrying the "hateful" authority figures in his pit:

> "Th' gaffer come down to our stal this morning, an' 'e says, 'You know, Walter, this 'ere'll not do. What about these props?' An' I says to him, 'Why, what art talkin' about? What d'st mean about th' props?' 'It'll never do, this 'ere,' 'e says. 'You'll be havin' th' roof in, one o' these days.' An' I says, 'Tha'd better stan' on a bit o' clunch, then, an' hold it up wi' thy 'ead.' So 'e wor that mad, 'e cossed an' 'e swore, an' t'other chaps they did laugh." (16)

– O –

"offences"—("The Mouse Problem") The same argument involving the legalization of drugs (thus making illicit drugs less attractive to young people) was made at the time and continues to be made today.

Perhaps the influence of former Harvard professor Timothy Leary (1920-1996) and his somewhat orgiastic advocacy of both clinical and recreational uses of marijuana, psilocybin, and LSD in the 1960s is significant here, as well. Leary was covered quite frequently in *The Times*, and often (as on 9 August 1969, for example) on the front page. Kargol may be fashioned at least obliquely after Leary, especially in Leary's role as a high-profile ivory tower intellectual (1959-1963) and media celebrity more than willing to admit his own involvement in illicit drug use. By giving these and other psychedelic drugs to grad students, and then anyone who cared to share his life, Leary certainly got "it out in the open," as Kargol admonishes.

"Osborne"—("The Wacky Queen") One of the royal family's residences during Queen Victoria's reign, Osborne is located on the Isle of Wight. After the Prince Consort's death, Victoria spent a great deal of time at Osborne and Balmoral—in other words, away from London and the demands of Westminster. This seclusion allowed her son, Bertie (later Edward VII, the "back marker" in "Famous Deaths" in Ep. 1), a more active role in the country's affairs. The Queen died at

Osborne in 1901. This *FC* location, however, was obviously shot at Ham House (Richmond-upon-Thames), which would have been a much easier location to utilize. For more on Ham House see Ep. 1 notes. Parts of the later "Superman" sketch were also shot at Ham House.

For Python's on-location shooting, the cast and crew would typically shoot most if not all of the entire series' exteriors during one, extended trip. Location doubling would have saved time and money.

"other mice"—("The Mouse Problem") Satirizing "probing" television documentaries, the writers have fetishized rodents, making dressing like a mouse akin to transvestitism, homosexuality, recreational drug use, or orgiastic sexual practices—or just about any other practice late-1960s British society might label as "deviant." The impetus for this sketch could have been documentaries about illicit drug use, spousal swapping, closeted homosexuals, etc., or, even more likely, a combination of many such documentaries dealing with obsessive-compulsive behaviors and alternative lifestyles of all kinds. Again, it's the unrelenting, unbroken (by irruptions of silliness or other narrative threads) nature of this narrative that sets this apart from most of Python's later work in *FC*.

It was in 1969 that groundbreaking documentary programs like *Civilisation* (written and hosted by Kenneth Clark [1903-1983]) first went out in color on BBC2, then BBC1. David Attenborough (b. 1926) was running the show at BBC2 during this period (1965-1968), and his enthusiasm for documentary film of all kinds fueled this flowering of nonfiction broadcast.

"ovine"—("Flying Sheep") Idle quite clearly says "avine" (of or pertaining to birds) and not "ovine" (of or referring to sheep), which may have been a slip of the tongue based on the following word ("aviation"), and simply missed during the editing and clean-up process. This voiceover would have been inserted after taping and playback, when the show was cleaned up for content, flow, and length. A later sketch ("Mouse Organ") was also inserted after principal recording had been completed.

– P –

paint on him—(PSC; "The Wacky Queen") There are hundreds of paint gags in silent comedy films and later cartoons, as well as Laurel and Hardy (*Towed in the Hole*, 1932) and the Three Stooges (*Tassels in the Air*, 1938) films.

The culminating "pie in the face" routine was a standard slapstick comedy bit from the music hall and vaudeville stage and myriad Keystone Cops (Mack Sennett) films, and especially later acts like Laurel and Hardy (*Their Purple Moment*, 1928; *The Battle of the Century*, 1927), the Three Stooges, and the Marx Brothers. The 1964 film *Dr. Strangelove*, co-written by Stanley Kubrick and Terry Southern, was originally supposed to end with an all-out pie fight in the War Room, but the scene was cut from the final release print of the film. The Pythons would later include a how-to "pie in the face" sketch in their live performance for *Live at the Hollywood Bowl* (1980).

Part 2—(PSC; titles) This episode did end up as *Episode* 2, coincidentally, even though it was recorded first. This kind of mislabeling or purposeful misspeaking occurs throughout *FC*, and is evident much earlier in many *Goon Show* episodes, *At Last the 1948 Show*, on the pages of *Private Eye*, and then later in the feature film *Holy Grail* (Arthur replacing "5" with "3" over and over again).

"Pascal"—(Pepperpot link out of "French Lecture on Sheep-Aircraft") Blaise Pascal (1623-1662) was a French mathematician, physicist, religious philosopher, and writer. His principle of "intuitionism" had an impact on Rousseau and Henri Bergson, the latter being prominently mentioned several times in *FC*. Author Hilaire Belloc (noted above), who will be mentioned later in the episode, was also greatly influenced by Pascal.

"pathos"—("Marriage Guidance Counsellor") From the Greek ("suffering," "feeling"). This mentioning supplements the use of "Deirdre" earlier, as well, adding a level to the allusion. Pathos may have actually been reached had the knight and chicken not appeared, prompting the caption and link, but then the Pythons wouldn't have been consistent in their undercutting of normal, expected dramatic structure and communication.

"Persian Radio"—("A Man With Three Buttocks") The BBC has long held broadcast interests throughout the Middle East and Arabia, meant to serve the Empire's colonial presence. The Persian Gulf area is serviced by a shortwave relay station on Masirah Island near Oman (*EBO*).

"perverts meet"—("The Mouse Problem") This entire satire—easily the most sustained satire in *FC*—is at least partially an allusion to the damaging Profumo scandal of just a few years earlier.

Elizabeth II's Secretary of State of War (1960-1963) John Profumo had an *affaire du coeur* with a young prostitute, Christine Keeler, who also happened to be bedding a Soviet naval attaché, Captain Eugene Ivanov. It was feared for years afterward that at the height of the Cold War the Soviets were given access to top secret "pillow talk" regarding the NATO alliance. There arose allegations (many reported also in publications ranging from *Private Eye* to *The New York Post*) that orgies were conducted in various palatial residences in and around London. These orgies included judges and ministers participating in acts of prostitution, sadomasochism, and the wearing of masks, according to *Lord Denning's Report*, compiled by Lord Alfred Thompson Denning (1963). The various young women involved also then sold their story to the London tabloids. Adding a sinister element to the whole fiasco, Profumo lied to the House of Commons about the affair. He resigned, but didn't have to do so ceremoniously, as was the norm. The U.S. FBI gathered 1,500-plus pages of documents as it quietly investigated the scandal that nearly toppled the Macmillan government.

"plummet"—(PSC; "Flying Sheep") An example of a word heavily accented but not depicted as such in the printed text. The Rustic lengthens the medial vowel, from an "uh" sound to the "oo" sound in "foot." He also delivers very hard [r] sounds in words like "birds" and "fair." Other such accentings occur on words like "much" (with the medial vowel pronounced like the vowels in "foot"), "my" ("mah-ee"), and "blind" (almost "blo-eend"). Other words, like "whole" and "Harold," are changed by aphaeresis, or the elision of the initial unstressed sound, resulting in "'oles" and "'arold," respectively. "Behavior" is altered in pronunciation via dissimilation, or the elision of the [h] due to its proximity to the medial [a].

The point here is not necessarily the eventual pronunciation, but to identify the speaker as a provincial, by his accent, and create a ready-made characterization (or caricaturization) at the same time. The Pythons do the same thing with the outrageous accents and delivery of "Upperclass Twits" in Ep. 12, so much so that the characters' speech must be subtitled for the viewer. A nod to G.B. Shaw and his well-known lament: "It is impossible for an Englishman to open his mouth, without making some other Englishman hate or despise him" (*Preface to Pygmalion*).

As will be seen, regional accents become very critical in *Flying Circus* as identifiers of class, education, and breeding, a trope borrowed, at least, from D.H. Lawrence. In *Sons and Lovers* (1913), for example, the significant class difference between young coal miner Walter Morel and the girl of his fancy, Gertrude Coppard, is evidenced simply by his listening to her:

> Walter Morel seemed to melt away before her. She was to the miner that thing of mystery and fascination, a lady. When she spoke to him, it was *with a southern pronunciation* and a *purity* of English which thrilled him to hear. (9; italics added)

Her speech gives her away, elevates her, endears him to her, engenders the distrust of her working-class neighbors, and eventually betokens the schism between them as they grow to loathe each other.

"PM"—("The Wacky Queen") Prime Minister. Leader of the government in power, though the PM can be selected from a coalition government. See entry for Gladstone above, or depictions of Heath (Ep. 10), Macmillan (Ep. 12), Chamberlain and Churchill (both Ep. 1).

"poncing"—("Working-Class Playwright") As "ponce" means to be or act effeminately, the father here implies that a more effete laborer like his son must also be a homosexual.

pseudo—(PSC; "French Lecture on Sheep-Aircraft") With some foreign language training in their elementary educations, the Pythons could easily create pseudo-French or German dialogue, and supplement this pseudo-speak with gestures and bastardized English words. In his journal entry for the day of the taping of Ep. 2, Palin would call the moment "two Frenchmen talking rubbish" (Johnson *20 Years* 47-48).

Reminiscent of the bias against the French that seems to have existed in Britain since the Norman invasion, at least, this aversion to the French language is probably one of the "honest prejudices which naturally cleave to the heart of a true Englishman" that Addison wrote of in *The Spectator* (number 383, 20 May 1712). P.G. Wodehouse would much later describe the "look of furtive shame, the shifty, hangdog look which announces that an Englishman is about to talk French" (*The Luck of the Bodkins* [1936]). Shuffling off furtiveness, Python moves toward Anglicizing and sending up the French they speak, while caricaturing the French themselves, perhaps following Voltaire, who in *Candide* was quite nasty toward his countrymen, noting that their "principal occupations" were, in order, "lovemaking," "slander," and finally "stupid talk" (ch. 21).

"put my mind at rest"—("Marriage Guidance Counsellor") Arthur Pewtey (Palin) is another in what will become a long line of Python characters who can't see what's going on in plain sight. Outrageous or absurd acts can be ignored entirely in the Python world. In Ep. 3 Cardinal Richelieu (Palin) is allowed to testify as a character witness in a modern courtroom; in Ep. 17 a family's living room is on a sidewalk; and in Ep. 6, "The Dull Life of a City Stockbroker" sketch, the stockbroker in question (also Palin) somehow can't see spear-throwing Africans, naked salesgirls, a guerilla war, and a hanged man over his desk.

The Pythons' Modernist impulse is apparent here, going right back to the work that announced the beginnings of Modernist Art, Manet's scandalous *Le*

Déjeuner sur l'Herbe (*Luncheon on the Grass*, 1863). Manet placed a provocatively posed nude (whose gaze directly implicates and challenges the viewer/voyeur) in a modern setting *and* in the company of two dressed males—even the Salon des Refusés was scandalized, but a sensation followed nonetheless. The men in the setting seem impassive; the woman seems defiant. The world of art would never be the same. See Hughes' discussion of this transition in *The Shock of the New*.

– R –

Rodin's . . . The Kiss—(PSC; animated link into "The Mouse Problem") Auguste Rodin's (1840-1917) *The Kiss* was finished in 1886. A number of Rodin's works are on display at the Tate Gallery in London, including *The Kiss*. This version (commissioned by American E.P. Warren) had also spent a few years in Lewes, and went on public display in 1914. It immediately aroused a furor over its depicted sensuality and nudity, and opponents wanted the statue draped, screened from public view. The Tate would buy this version outright in 1952. Cf. "Tory Housewives Clean-Up Campaign" in Ep. 32, where statues, sculptures, and paintings at various galleries are covered–Mary Whitehouse-type Pepperpots.

The erotic and troubling statue *The Kiss* is an apt transition into the following sketch, "The Mouse Problem," where men behave like mice.

rustic—(PSC; "Flying Sheep") The Rustic is a broadly drawn type, certainly meant to stand out in relation to the City Gent next to him. This "type" is universal, at least in Europe. The Rembrandt drawing *Portrait of Willem Bartholsz. Ruyter* (c. 1638) portrays the actor Ruyter in a burlesque costume of a yokel. The costume is clearly a smock and floppy hat, and represented, according to the Rijksmuseum, a popular leading role in the "boertigheden" playing in the theatres of Amsterdam (see Rijksmuseum.nl). The Pythons' knowledge of the Northern European (Holland, Germany, etc.) artists and their work is evident as early as Ep. 4 ("Art Gallery") and then Ep. 25 ("Art Gallery Strike"). There have been myriad paintings in the collections of the National Gallery from eminent Northern European artists (Rembrandt, Breughels, Vermeer et al.) since the 1830s, at least.

This rustic also looks very much like the village idiots characterized in Ep. 20, the "Idiot in Society" sketch, wearing the smock and floppy hat uniform. This uniform will also be worn by the "Bumpkin" character in Ep. 25, the "Art Gallery Strike" sketch, where he is supposed to be the figure from Constable's

The Hay Wain painting (also in the National Gallery). The costume requirements were simply "smock, floppy hat" (WAC T12/1,083).

"rump"—("A Man With Three Buttocks") Here begins a "thesaurus"-type sketch, where synonyms, metaphors, and variations-on-a-theme abound. Cf. the "Dead Parrot" sketch in Ep. 8, as well as the "What the Stars Foretell" sketch in Ep. 37, in which Cleese is himself being satirized (by others in the troupe) for his interest in thesaurus sketches. Voltaire provides an early example of this type of writing in *Candide*, when Martin has affirmed the constant foul nature of man, while Candide tries to see some hope:

> "Do you think," said Candide, "that mankind always massacred one another as they do now? Were they always guilty of lies, fraud, treachery, ingratitude, inconstancy, envy, ambition, and cruelty? Were they always thieves, fools, cowards, gluttons, drunkards, misers, calumniators, debauchees, fanatics, and hypocrites?" (chapter 21)

The Pythons (and especially writing partners Cleese and Chapman) will build on this foundation, adding a touch of the splenetic often, where the normally placid character—often the buttoned-down Cleese—will suddenly erupt into a vituperative verbal list. "Cheese Shop" in Ep. 33 is a textbook example of Cleese's escalation trope.

"runnin'"—(PSC; "Marriage Guidance Counsellor") Once again, the accent (here American, southern, which is as broad as saying England, northern) is partially implied by manipulating the written text. Also, this use of the "face up to the foe" verbal trope has a basis in Shakespeare, and involves both intestinal fortitude and a bridling of passions:

> *Nor.*   Be advis'd;
> Heat not a furnace for your foe so hot
> That it do singe yourself. We may outrun
> By violent swiftness that which we run at,
> And lose by overrunning. Know you not
> The fire that mounts the liquor till't run o'er
> In seeming to augment it wastes it? Be advis'd;
> I say again, there is no English soul
> More stronger to direct you than yourself,
> If with the sap of reason you would quench,
> Or but allay, the fire of passion. (*Henry VIII* 1.1.139-149)

The formerly puling Arthur Pewtey will turn and face his fears and foe, but the ending isn't nearly as neat as it is in countless Hollywood movies, or even in a Shakespeare play. Pewtey will collapse at the first sign of resistance, perhaps a Python comment on the more contemporary Englishman.

– S –

sand dune—(PSC; "It's Man") According to BBC files, these opening and closing "It's Man" scenes were shot near the foreshore and cliffs near Covehithe, north of Southwold (WAC T12/1,083). Most of the location excursions during the four-series run of FC were planned to be as geographically varied as possible, meaning proximity to mountainous terrain, plains, and the seashore. Initially the Oban and Glencoe regions of Scotland provided the needed vistas (and later for *Holy Grail*, as well), then the Devon region (Dartmoor, Paignton, Torbay), then Norwich, and finally the island of Jersey.

"Sartre, Jean-Paul"—(Pepperpot link out of "French Lecture on Sheep-Aircraft") Sartre (1905-1980) was a French novelist, playwright, and Existentialist—triumphing individual beings' freedom. He became something of a darling to idealistic students and various anti-establishment types (like the young Pythons) when in 1964 he was awarded but refused to accept the Nobel Prize for Literature. The Pepperpots mention him here, along with Pascal, Voltaire, and Descartes. In Ep. 27 the intelligent, peripatetic Pepperpots Mrs. Premise (Cleese) and Mrs. Conclusion (Chapman) travel to Paris to visit Sartre and discuss his work. See the entries "Marxist" and "Revisionist" in Ep. 27 for a lengthier discussion of Sartre and his work and influence.

These "Aunt Edna" types (Rattigan's term, see "Pepperpots" entry in Ep. 1) are certainly "universal and immortal," but the Pythons obviously take umbrage at Rattigan's discounting of their intelligence and significance in the world of letters, and as participators in narrative decision-making (see Ep. 27 for more). Rattigan describes Aunt Edna's "lowbrow" nature:

> Now Aunt Edna does not appreciate Kafka . . . she is upset by Picasso . . . and she is against [William] Walton. . . . She is, in short, a hopeless lowbrow, and the great novelist, the master painter, and the composer of genius are, and can afford to be, as disregarding of her tastes as she is unappreciative of their works. (*Collected Plays, Volume 2* xii)

The Pythons clearly have adopted the Aunt Edna type in their Pepperpots, but have more often than not gifted her with penetrating vision and encyclopedic knowledge, creating a very different "universal and immortal" type.

"Scotsman on a horse"—("A Scotsman on a Horse") This Scotsman will appear again in Ep. 6 and finish the sketch just begun here. The production design team for this location shoot also supplied three strategically placed thistle bushes near the Scotsman to create a believable ambience (the thistle being the heraldic emblem of Scotland). The stunt rider (except in close-ups) is Harry Woodley, not Cleese, and the church is The Old Place Chapel, Boveney, Windsor (WAC T12/1,083). The Old Place will be used again in Ep. 21, when the couple (Cleese and Cleveland) run into a church in the "Silly Vicar" sketch.

This obscure reference to a "Scotsman on" something is most likely borrowed from J.M. Barrie's play *What Every Woman Knows* (1918): "My lady, there are few more impressive sights in the world than a Scotsman on the make."

"sharing the interests . . . her feet"—("Marriage Guidance Counsellor") Spaniard-American George Santayana (1863-1952) would, in 1922, describe the "British Character" thusly: "England is the paradise of individuality, eccentricity, heresy, anomalies, hobbies, and humours" (Santayana 30). In the sketch there's really no indication that Deirdre and Arthur didn't actually share these stated interests—her encounter with the counselor notwithstanding—even though none of the interests may sound terribly interesting. Gardening, of course, is almost an English mania, and in most *FC* episodes even the tiniest yards behind row houses (see "The New Cooker Sketch," Ep. 14) feature carefully kept gardens. (During and after the war, for example, these gardens provided vegetables for a strictly rationed England, becoming ubiquitous by necessity.) Model aeroplane/airplane flying and clubs increased in popularity soon after the war, at places like Hibaldstow aerodrome (in North Lincolnshire, east of Doncaster), and remain a very popular family activity. The sheer number of hobbies and "spotting" societies in the UK is somewhat staggering, including trainspotters (Ep. 7), train switching box associations (Ep. 25), motorway interchange enthusiasts (Ep. 35), as well as bridge (foot, auto, and rail) and aerial antennae groups and websites.

The Pewteys might have been saving their money in a sixpenny bottle (see entry below) for a holiday to Brighton or Torquay, for instance. Postwar monetary controls limited the amount of money a British vacationer could take from the country, forcing many to find vacation spots in the UK (see Morgan's *Britain Since 1945*). See the notes for "Brighton" and "holiday" above for more on these fiscal restrictions and travel/life during the postwar period.

Sheep—("Flying Sheep") Ep. 1 offered the pig motif, and this episode will run with a sheep theme, the second major entry in the Python bestiary. Cf. Ep. 20, the "Killer Sheep" sketch. The presence of sheep in the economy and history of Great Britain could account for its significant presence in the *FC* episodes, though the frequent appearances and mentionings of penguins in the episodes aren't so easy (with the notable exception of the Penguin Books phenomenon, to be discussed later). Maybe it's just because penguins are (in Cleese's words) "comic, flightless web-footed little bastards" that they will additionally appear in episodes 5, 22, 23, and 38. See entries for those episodes for more.

showgirl's outfit—(PSC; "The Mouse Problem") This is Cleveland's second appearance in the series, and she is once again scantily clad and mute. Her role is an iconographic one—"pretty girl"—and thus far she has been objectified for her physical female attributes. There exists an early Monty Python publicity photo actually featuring the six Pythons and Cleveland—and she is not dressed scantily—though in the early part of the first season her contributions are purely gender-specific. See the "Kargol and Janet" entry above for a description of her outfit.

"sixpenny bottle"—("Marriage Guidance Counsellor") A bottle of ale (or ink or wine, etc.) costing six pence. See Jonson's *Bartholomew Fair* 2.2.

"skirting board"—("The Mouse Problem") Molding or base board installed along the lower part of an interior wall. In Ep. 20, the Killer Sheep also live behind the skirting boards and wainscotting.

"sparrows"—("The Mouse Problem") The "Man" depicted here is dressed as a milkman, including black-and-white striped apron, a white uniform, and a peaked cap.

The "sparrows" this milkman mentions have been glossed as alluding to lechery. "Sparrow," according to Henke, was used by the Greeks "as a euphemism for the erected penis" (249). Using this terminology, the milkman, then, is actually describing the act of fellatio. It is also interesting to note that the *OED* cites a December 1902 edition of the *Daily Chronicle*: "I should like to say a few words about the milkman's secret customers, otherwise 'sparrows'." These are the (primarily female?) customers who benefit from the milkman's visit in the form of illicit sexual congress. Cf. Ep. 3—where the siren traps milkmen in her attic—for the darker half of that equation.

Here again the accent issue comes to the fore, especially as a certain "type" is being forwarded. As this city "tough" (dressed as a milkman) speaks he substitutes the interdental fricative unvoiced "th" (q) sounds with the labiodental fricative unvoiced "f" sounds ("with" becomes "wif," and "throats" becomes "froats").

stock shot—(PSC; "A Man With Two Noses") The Pythons (and their researchers) culled the BBC archives and contemporary newspapers and maga-zines for still photos and film footage of politicians, royal events, and just everyday people, adding to the pastiche, collage effect of the series. See the "stock film" entry in Ep. 1.

stretching owls—(PSC; animated link into "Flying Sheep") The Gilliam animations here have nothing to do with owls, just as Ep. 1, entitled "Whither Canada?", never actually answered that question, or even mentioned Canada after the title. *Owl-Stretching Time* was just one of the many show title possibilities bandied about by Chapman, Cleese, Gilliam, Idle, Jones, and Palin. *Owl-Stretching Time* finally ended up as the title for Ep. 4. Other possible titles for the entire series included *Baron Von Took's Flying Circus*; *Gwen Dibley's Flying Circus*; *The Circus*; *Flying Circus*; *A Horse, a Spoon and a Basin*; *Bunn Wackett Buzzard Stubble and Boot*; and *The Toad Elevating Moment*. (See Morgan's *Monty Python Speaks!*, and Roger Wilmut's *From Fringe to Flying Circus*.)

The *Bunn, Wackett, Buzzard, Stubble, and Boot* possibility was reportedly penciled onto the cover page of the Ep. 2 script, and *Owl-Stretching Time* was penciled through (Johnson *20 Years* 49).

Once again, very little prior knowledge of Gilliam's final product for these animated links was available to other cast members. Now and again, Gilliam would pull in a fellow Python to do a voiceover during the week of production rehearsal, but otherwise there was little contact, hence little clear description of the animations in the shooting script. See *Monty Python Speaks!* and *Gilliam on Gilliam* for more.

"Strewth!"—("A Man With Three Buttocks") Cf. another character played by Chapman, Mr. Foster of Guildford, who dies suddenly in Ep. 1, uttering the same epithet. "Strewth" is a shortened version of "God's truth," and is used as an oath.

"succeed"—("Flying Sheep") Note that all of the action in this sketch is described; it takes place off-camera. The occasional sound effect helps create and preserve the ambience, but there are no cutaways from the talking heads to nesting sheep, real or animated. The characters' perspectives, perceptions, and descriptions of the events are, then, the source of comedy, and not the actual events themselves. In *Beyond the Fringe*, the "Royal Box" sketch is performed by the three participants (Peter Cook, Dudley Moore, and Alan Bennett) sitting on chairs next to each other—facing the audience—and looking out over the audience toward an imaginary royal box. In *At Last the 1948 Show*, Chapman and Tim Brooke-Taylor perform the same "offstage" comedy in the form of a sheepdog trial, where Chapman speaks with a recognizable and broad Yorkshire accent:

Brooke-Taylor: You have two dogs?

Chapman: Ssh!

Brooke-Taylor: (whispering) Where are they now?

Chapman: Oh, ah, well one of them's over, now where is he? Oh, ah, over there by that pile of dead sheep. Magnificent brute, treacherous to a fault. ("Sheepdog Trial," Series 1, Program 3, 1 March 1967)

All the action here is offscreen and therefore suggested, and when the dogs "Butcher" and "Crippen" attack and begin to eat the sheep, Brooke-Taylor recoils in revulsion, describing the rather graphic attack. (Cf. Ep. 33 notes for a Python reference to the infamous Crippen.) Another *At Last the 1948 Show* sketch, "Courier," features Cleese as a tour bus guide taking a busload of English tourists through myriad European capitals in record time. No other voices are heard at all, actually, just Cleese, pointing out distant capitals, barking instructions for photo opportunities, and threatening everyone with another hellish tour if they miss even one capital.

This "observational" structure (far more presentational than representational) keeps this type of setting and writing more akin to stand-up or club comedy, which was enjoying a rise in popularity in the 1950s and 1960s, thanks to American performers including Lenny Bruce and Woody Allen. The physical and financial constraints experienced by the troupe in pre-Python days at various revues in Oxford and Cambridge would have also cultivated this referential or associative structure (as would the significant influence of BBC Radio's *The Goon Show*). Once they reached the BBC's television stages, budgets didn't allow for complicated sets or process shots, so the offscreen references would continue through the third series. (In the fourth series, when budgets skyrocketed to approximately £100,000 an episode, everything—the costumes, props, sets, location work, and special effects—became more elaborate, intricate, and expensive.) This is also not unlike Shakespeare's descriptions of the Battle at Agincourt in *Henry V*, actions that take place offstage and are merely referred to by characters onstage.

– T –

"talkin'"—("Working-Class Playwright") The Northern, working-man accent here is quite pronounced, with the elision of words signaling at least part of this accent's particulars. Note, though, that a coarse accent (when compared, say, to the Queen's English spoken in London) doesn't mean the speaker is a rustic. Here it's quite the opposite. The coarse speaker turns out to be quite refined, in direct opposition to his *Sons and Lovers* "working-class" milieu, clothing, accent, etc., all reminiscent of Lawrence's brusque miner Walter Morel. Python undercuts its own undercutting on a regular basis. Significantly, the son has lost his Northern accent, in favor of English as spoken further south.

"Tennyson"—("The Wacky Queen") Alfred, Lord Tennyson (1809-1892) was an apt choice for this mock film, since Tennyson is considered to embody the Victorian age in his lyrical, often melancholic poetry. Tennyson spent most of his career in poetic pursuits, though he did attempt staged drama in 1874, somewhat unsuccessfully (*ODNB*). See notes to Ep. 17 for more on Tennyson, there installed in an East Midlands' bathtub. Tennyson was named Poet Laureate in 1850. See the "wax cylinders" entry below for more.

"they're birds"—("Flying Sheep") In Ep. 5, a cat is suffering from "the stockbroker syndrome, the suburban fin de siècle, ennui, angst, weltschmertz" and even "moping," and must be jarred from his "rut." This is Python's version of the classic beast fable, à la Dryden's *The Hind and the Panther*, as certain animals take on qualities not generally associated with a particular species, and/or are anthropomorphized.

"thirty minutes . . . up"—("The Mouse Problem") A moment where we can't be sure if the Linkman is referring to *The World Around Us* show he's hosting, or the episode of *FC* we've been watching that contains the *World* show. Phenomenologically, the boundaries between these shows have disappeared during this segment.

"tit"—("Working-Class Playwright") *OED*: "Fool."

"Trubshawe"—(PSC; "French Lecture on Sheep-Aircraft") Approximate translation: "Good evening, here we have the modern diagram of a French-English sheep. Now we have in the head, the cockpit. Here one finds the small English Captain Trubshawe." (Translations provided by Joshua Abboud.) This is clearly a reference to the then-famous Brian Trubshaw (1924-2001), Britain's first and very celebrated pilot for the new Anglo-French Concorde SST. In Ep. 37, the name "Concorde" will elicit quite a laugh from the audience, as there it will be given to Dennis Moore's horse. Lancelot's "horse" in *HG* (played by Idle) is also named Concorde.

This naming (or at least the spelling) could also refer obliquely to Michael Trubshawe (1905-1985), an actor who appeared in films such as *The Magic Christian* (1969; additional script material by Cleese and Chapman), *A Hard Day's Night* (1964), and *The Lavender Hill Mob* (1951). Trubshawe played an English aviator in *Scent of Mystery* (1960), and an armed forces officer in many other films. A prototypical role player—a type, even—Trubshawe seems a perfect choice for Python's sheep pilot. Cleese and Chapman would also later co-write *The Rise and Rise of Michael Rimmer* (1970), in which Trubshawe appeared.

"tungsten . . . operations"—("Working-Class Play-wright") Tungsten carbide-tipped drills are quite hard (on the Moh's Hardness Scale) and have been used extensively in coal mining operations since the 1920s. Preliminary operations might include drilling exploratory holes to mark the extent of the coal vein and preparing the face for the digging machinery. The coal face is the "working wall" of coal in a coal mine, or the line of coal deposits followed by coal miners as they drill and remove, drill and remove, etc. Palin, who grew up in mining country, would probably have been familiar with the coal mining industry, tools, etc., and there's little doubt that the Pythons' lower-school exposure to such a significant and controversial industry in the history of Great Britain would be significant, as well.

Coal's significance to the economy of the UK has been well documented, but in this sketch, coal mining is being sent up as an escape for "laborers" and a neat way to hide from the work of the real world.

"two . . . a day"—("The Mouse Problem") Sounds like a teenage masturbation statistic, possibly arising from David Reuben's 1969 book *Everything You Always Wanted to Know About Sex but Were Afraid to Ask*, or a similar quote from either Kinsey (*Sexual Behavior in the Human Male* [1948] and *Sexual Behavior in the Human Female* [1953]), or Masters and Johnson (*Human Sexual Response* [1966]). Reuben's book entered the mainstream culture, and was read by millions around the world. All of these landmark studies would have been prominently in the public view during this period, and could easily have influenced the Pythons' early lives and later writing.

– U –

"unique film"—("The Wacky Queen") Even the earliest (and unsubstantiated) claims that motion pictures were exhibited to a royal audience in England weren't any earlier than 1891, making 1880 a date the Pythons probably chose out of the air. The film does share a resemblance with early British film pioneer Cecil Hepworth's and American Edwin S. Porter's staged, sight-gag approach in their "flickers," but both were also working on such narrative-type films much later, around the turn of the century (1903-1905).

The "jolly American accent" called for in this film certainly isn't Tennyson (see note above), but is recognition of the Hollywood pedigree that this type of film and film narration represent.

– V –

"Victoria"—("The Wacky Queen") Queen Victoria (1819-1901) is considered by many to be Britain's most beloved monarch, and she reigned for sixty-three years. By the time films like the one in which the Pythons portray her could have existed (1895 and beyond), however, she would have been in her mid-70s, and rather frail. And since Gladstone (see note above) died in 1898, this fictional film would have to have been made between about December 1895 and May 1898.

"vole"—("The Mouse Problem") Type of field mouse. The vole is the Pythons' American film studio parody logo during *FC*, depicted as "Twentieth-Century Vole," which will reappear in Ep. 6. Prior to *FC*, Cleese mentions the vole as a potentially comedic beast in the "Ant" sketch in *At Last the 1948 Show*.

"Voltaire"—(Pepperpot link out of "French Lecture on Sheep-Aircraft") "Voltaire" (1694-1778) was a pseudonym of François-Marie Arouet, an often acerbic but consistently astute observer of French culture, and French society in general. Voltaire's influence on the Pythons—perhaps in forming the English-ness they trumpet and the "characteristic qualities" of the English mind—is obvious as the alliterations, grotesqueries, narrative manipulations, and just the black-tinged satire (against tyranny, bigotry, narrow-mindedness) of their work are appreciated. Voltaire enjoyed taking pokes at religion and government, targets the Pythons consistently take aim at, as well. See notes throughout for allusions to Voltaire and *Candide* in *FC*.

Vox pop films—(PSC; "The Mouse Problem") Many of these inserts were shot in the Saxmundham meadows area on 22 August 1969, as well as near the foreshore and cliffs of Covehithe, and on or near the Harbour Pier, on 21 August (WAC T12/1,083).

– W –

"wacky"—("The Wacky Queen") This is American slang (as are "a-plenty," "way-out," and "doggone it"), meaning Python was attempting to mimic not only the American accent, but also the use of American English idioms and colloquialisms. (See "hosepipe" and "have a go" notes for moments when the Pythons' English-ness betrays itself.)

The film as presented is reminiscent of the standard newsreel-type shorts popular in American movie theaters in the golden age of Hollywood, featuring slices of everyday life as well as news of the weird and celebrity from across the country and around the world. William Randolph Hearst, for example, had films made of his guests cavorting at Hearst Castle, his mansion in San Simeon, California, and audiences could see the likes of Mary Pickford, Douglas Fairbanks, Hal Roach, John Gilbert, and Charlie Chaplin engaged in the lives and leisures of the rich.

Waring, Arthur—("The Wrestling Epilogue") Yet another Arthur character, though probably meant to build on the Eddie Waring reference in Ep. 1. Eddie Waring is such a strong allusion here because of his close connection to sport, and for so many years. He was a well-known Rugby League broadcaster, using phrases that were parroted by many in the South. Waring was either loved or hated as Rugby League commentator, and the Pythons seemed to have loved/hated him enough to caricature him more than once.

"wax cylinders"—("The Wacky Queen") American inventor Thomas Edison had worked to perfect this type of audio recording and broadcasting technology, creating a working prototype by 1877.

In 1890, Poet Laureate Tennyson (1809-1892) himself recorded a version of both "Charge of the Light Brigade" (1864) and "Charge of the Heavy Brigade" (1882) on such wax cylinders, and the scratchy, sometimes inaudible (but still quite stirring) versions of both can be heard at poetryarchive.org. In Ep. 41, when John Hughman portrays Tennyson in the Victorian poetry sketch, his intonation and delivery ("Half an inch!") indicate he's most likely heard these recordings, as well.

"What's wrong wi' me? . . . yer tit!"—("Working-Class Playwright") The two men nearly come to blows here, and, as this scene is "right out of D.H. Lawrence," it's clear that Lawrence's penned kitchen confrontation between eldest son William and drunk father Walter in *Sons and Lovers* is the inspiration:

> Paul never forgot coming home from the Band of Hope one Monday evening and finding his mother with her eye swollen and discoloured, his father standing on the hearth-rug, feet astride, his head down, and William, just home from work, glaring at his father. . . . William was white to the lips, and his fists were clenched. He waited until the children were silent, watching with children's rage and hate, then he said:

> "You coward, you daren't do it when I was in."

> But Morel's blood was up. He swung around on his son. William was bigger, but Morel was hard-muscled, and mad with fury.

> "Dossn't I?" he shouted. "Dossn't I? Ha'e much more o' thy chelp, my young jockey, an' I'll rattle my fist about thee. Ay, an I sholl that, dost see."

> Morel crouched at the knees and showed his fist in an ugly, almost beast-like fashion. William was white with rage.

> "Will yer?" he said, quiet and intense. "It 'ud be the last time, though." (56)

William's mother (Morel's wife) will break up the fight before it gets out of hand, just as Mother (Jones) does in the *FC* episode. The roles are cleverly reversed from the original, where Morel is the hard-bitten, uneducated, and now bitter coal miner, and son William is destined for schooling and a job in the city.

"wheel"—("The Mouse Problem") Exercise wheel often found in rodent cages. Also, a "run in the wheel" suggests copulation, with "run" glossed as energetic copulation and "wheel" meaning the female pudendum. See John Marston and George Chapman's 1605 play *Eastward Ho* (2.2.363).

"where's the water?"—("The Wacky Queen") Reenactment of one of the seminal moments in film history, the Lumiere brothers' short film *Watering the Gardener*, or *The Sprinkler Sprinkled* (c. 1895). One of the earliest pseudo-narratives in surviving film, the action is based on a French comic strip of the period. Some of the Victoria-Gladstone film actually resembles these early slice-of-life "documentaries" (or "actualities") mixed with a healthy dose of silent comedy gaggery (which the French actually pioneered well before the Americans and then Hollywood came to the table).

"wherever you are"—("French Lecture on Sheep-Aircraft") Reminiscent of American vaudeville, radio, and television performer Jimmy Durante's signature closing line: "Good night, Mrs. Calabash, wherever you are."

"Wigan"—("The Wrestling Epilogue") West of Manchester, in Lancashire. Wigan is a coal and heavy industrial area, and probably more typically the home of a wrestler than a humanist. In 1936 George Orwell traveled north, eventually producing his *Road to Wigan Pier* (1937), a close look at unemployment in industrial Britain.

"Willie"—("The Wacky Queen") A shortening of "William" that most Brits would likely avoid, except derisively, since it can be mistaken for the childish reference for "penis," and in the hearing is homonymic.

Women's Institute—("A Man With Two Noses") Stock footage, probably from a Women's Institute gathering from the late 1940s or 1950s. This same footage is used many times in *FC*, and the women portrayed are at least partly the basis for the "look" of the Pepperpots as played by the Pythons. According to the weekly stock film and music requests cleared for usage (copyright clearance) by BBC staff for *FC*, this stock footage was paid for each time it appeared (see the Written Archives Collection files, *Monty Python's Flying Circus*).

The Women's Institute was originally established in Canada, and gained a foothold in England until just prior to WWI. Some of the Pythons' family members (mothers, aunts) may have been members, especially during the war years.

The World Around Us—("The Mouse Problem") A Python version of *Panorama*, the long-running current affairs show (BBC-TV, 1953-today), with elements of similar programs including Associated Rediffusion/Thames TV's *This Week* (AR, 1956-1968; Thames, 1968-1992), *World in Action* (Granada TV, 1963-1999), and even *The World About Us* (BBC-2, 1967-1986). *The World About Us* was a natural history series, which would account for the mice in "Mouse Problem," while *Panorama* employed in-depth, often abrasive (for the period) interviews and exposés. *World in Action* was Granada's popular and front-running public affairs program, and *This Week* served similar purposes for Associated Rediffusion, then Thames. (See Vahimagi's *British Television*.) Much of the material for *FC* came from the Pythons' growing up as the first television generation, and their satire often targets the confines and outlines of the television format and industry.

These public affairs–type programs together would produce, for example, at least eight filmed reports on the "troubles" in Northern Ireland during 1969 alone (see "Ten Years of TV Coverage" in *Belfast Bulletin* 6 [Spring 1979]: 20-25, published by the Belfast Workers Research Unit).

– Y –

Yorkshire—("Working-Class Playwright") Northern county between the Pennines and the North Sea. York-shire changed from a largely agrarian to a heavily industrial economy during the Industrial Revolution, and has become well known for its factories, row-houses, and wrenching work-to-live poverty. In the feature film *Meaning of Life*, one of the earliest sketches is set in a Yorkshire mill/mine town—specifically in one of the anonymous rowhouses—which the Pythons characterize as part of the Third World. Palin was born in Sheffield, South Yorkshire (D.H. Lawrence was also born in South Yorkshire), which may account for the significant attention paid to the region and its people, accents, and customs in *FC*. The neat suit Ken's wearing also subverts the expectations one might have of a caricatured Northerner, which is probably the intent, and fuels the humor of incongruity.

– Z –

"Zatapathique"—("French Lecture on Sheep-Aircraft") Approximate translation: "Agreed, agreed. Now, I present to you my colleague, the celebrated poof Jean-Brian Zatapathique." Jean-Brian Zatapathique (Palin) and Cleese's Frenchman also appear in Ep. 14, introducing the French version of a Silly Walk ("Le Marche Futile"). A "poof" is a homosexual or effeminate male, and is, along with "fairy," Pythons' term of choice for the homosexual male in *FC*. The term "poof" was, as recently as 1957, one of the banned words on the English stage, being removed from John Osborne's play *The Entertainer* before a production license was granted (see Aldgate).

"zinc"—("The Mouse Problem") This City Gent (Cleese) is as callous as his "type" can be, to the Pythons, with profit margins and capital being the essential elements of his final "solution." In regard to "widows and orphans" being commodified, in *ML* it is the laid-off Catholic laborer (Palin) who decides to sell all his children for medical experiments. Zinc also seems to be Python's mineral of choice (see Ep. 6).

Episode 3: "How to Recognize Different Types of Tree From Quite a Long Way Away"

"bar"—("Court Scene [Witness in Coffin/Cardinal Richelieu]") Simply, the barrier at which court business was transacted.

"barrister"—("Court Scene [Witness in Coffin/Cardinal Richilieu]") An attorney. Cleese was, indeed, a student of the law, and would have made a career of it if it hadn't been for writing jobs for television. See the Cleese musings in McCabe's *The Pythons*.

"Bartlett"—("Court Scene [Witness in Coffin/Cardinal Richilieu]") This same name will be used in Ep. 40 by a Glaswegian (played by Peter Brett) trying to see the Montgolfier brothers (Idle and Jones), along with another man posing as King Louis XIV, XV, and XVI (Palin).

"bloody"—("Court Scene [Witness in Coffin/Cardinal Richilieu]") Less a swear word than a "vague epithet" (*OED*) in Britain today. See the complete *OED* entry for more on the word's history, which is varied and evolving. In the feature film *Life of Brian*, however, the word is clearly used as a serious imprecation:

> Mr. Cheeky (Idle): Do you mind? I can't hear a word he's saying.
> Mrs. Big Nose (Gwen Taylor): Don't you "do you mind" me. I was talking to my husband.
> Mr. Cheeky: Well, go and talk to him somewhere else. I can't hear a bloody thing.
> Mr. Big Nose (Palin): Don't you swear at my wife. (Scene 2)

The Pythons tend to use the word as more of a "vague epithet" throughout *FC*. This is not one of the words which, in Ep. 17, will be banned from use on the program.

In the 1948 BBC internal memo "BBC Variety Programmes Policy Guide for Writers and Producers," the law on swearing is laid down in the section entitled "Expletives":

> Generally speaking the use of expletives and forceful language on the air can only be justified in a serious dramatic setting where the action of the play demands them. *They have no place at all in light entertainment* and all such words as God, Good God, My God, Blast, Hell, Damn, Bloody, Gorblimey, Ruddy, etc., etc., should be deleted from scripts and innocuous expressions substituted.

Though produced a full two decades before *FC* was even created, the document (also known as the "Green Book") remained in full force and effect in 1969, and may have been read to the offending Pythons, chapter and verse, as they trounced all the over its moralizing guidelines. A generation older than the Pythons, long-time BBC actor and then director/producer Ian Mac-Naughton would have been very familiar with the guidelines.

"bowler . . . innings"—("Stolen Newsreader") Cricket terms: A "bowler" is essentially the pitcher on the cricket field. "Innings" means to proceed successively as batsmen, the first two as a pair together, to the wicket and try to make as many runs as possible against the bowling and fielding of their opponents. See "wickets" below. As an incredibly popular sport in the UK, cricket (and football) personalities and terminology will appear throughout the four series. See cricinfo.com and Wisden for more.

"Bratbys"—("Court Scene [Witness in Coffin/Cardinal Richilieu]") John Randall Bratby (1928-1992), a British painter affiliated with the social-realist Kitchen Sink

School, is noted for producing hundreds of sketches and paintings even as his popularity declined. Bratby was quite active during this period, and could have been mentioned in the previous episode in relation to the "Working-Class Playwright" scene. He is at home, however, in the type of setting Mrs. Fiona Lewis (Chapman) describes—where goldfish could spit water on his work—as he was fascinated by the everyday, painting "cornflake packets," dustbins, kitchen table tops, and Monopoly boards (see Lambirth, *ODNB*).

bus—("Bicycle Repair Man") The bus conductor is played by Al Fleming, and the driver is Dennis McTighe; this bus sequence was shot on Lammas Park Road, in Ealing (WAC T12/1,083). Other Supermen on the bus include John Dickenson, Lionel Sansby (*Dr. Who*), David Segger, and Peter Kaukus (*Dr. Who*) (WAC T12/1,242).

– C –

Cardinal . . . beautiful robes—(PSC; "Court Scene [Witness in Coffin/Cardinal Richilieu]") Cardinal Richelieu (1585-1642) is fashioned here very much after the image available to the Pythons in the National Gallery, a full-body portrait by Champaigne (1602-1674), where the subject wears full-length, red-pink robes, white collar, an emblem of office on a blue collar, and a red skull cap. Richelieu also sports the recognizable upturned mustache and goatee. There is also a Champaigne triple portrait of the same subject in the National Gallery.

Continuing what will become a signature Python trope, no one seems to question the initial appearance of this long-dead historical figure, though Inspector Dim (Chapman) will eventually "out" him as an impersonator. See entry for "Dim" below.

Lastly, Richelieu is also carrying a microphone, which he holds like a lounge singer, and speaks here with a forced American/French accent. This characterization is somewhat out of character for the troupe, as French characters are usually forced to speak with thick French accents or in jabberwock French. This might be accounted for by the fact that this is an impersonator, and not the Cardinal himself.

"children's programme music"—(PSC; "Children's Stories") This is "Holiday Playtime" by King Palmer (WAC T12/1,084). The book Idle is allegedly reading from is actually the very popular children's book *What Do People Do All Day?*, published in 1968, by author/illustrator Richard Scarry (1919-1994).

chorus again with him—("Court Scene [Witness in Coffin/Cardinal Richilieu]") This moment of Dim's

unmotivated song is shared by all (including hand and body movements) and borrows from the genre of the American film musical, and of the 1950s, especially, but is quickly undercut as the Barrister (Cleese) takes over and is stared at, becoming nonplussed. In these musicals, the music tends to be non-diegetic (off-screen and *not* of the world of the film), and the passersby tend to "hear" the lead's music, as well, and join in the singing and dancing (see *Seven Brides For Seven Brothers* [1954], for example, as referenced in Ep. 18). See Rick Altman's *The American Film Musical*.

Church Warden—(PSC; "Bicycle Repair Man") Generally a layperson elected to assist the clerical staff in their duties.

"CID"—("Court Scene [Witness in Coffin/Cardinal Richilieu]") Criminal Investigation Department, a branch of Scotland Yard. Members of this branch had carried out the investigation of the Kray brothers several years earlier. See entries in Ep. 14.

Clerk of the Court—(PSC; "Court Scene [Witness in Coffin/Cardinal Richilieu]") Though not listed in the printed script or in the credits for the show, this actor is Paul Lindley (WAC T12/1,084). Lindley had appeared in *Till Death Do Us Part* (1966) and the very popular *Dixon of Dock Green* (1965, 1970).

As this and the following series unfold, it will become clear that most of those who appear on screen (extras, walk-ons) will not get credit on screen. In fact, for most of the extras and walk-ons, this volume will be the first time after their initial appearances that their participation in *Monty Python's Flying Circus* will be publicly acknowledged. Most of these citations are culled from the cast lists for payment in repeats, by the way, and are only extant in the WAC records for the entire series. A special thanks to the BBC's Written Archives Collection (Caversham Park, UK) for their cooperation in this area.

Cleveland, Carol—(PSC; "Seduced Milkmen") This actress is *not* Carol Cleveland, but Thelma Taylor (WAC T12/1,084). Carol's name is included in the script, and there's no record of why she did not appear in this role. It could be that Cleveland simply wasn't available for this on-location shoot—a skeleton crew and cast would have made the trek for this scene. Taylor had small parts in other TV series, including *The Benny Hill Show* (1965), *Carry on Cleo* (1964), and *The World of Beachcomber* (1969). This sequence was shot on 16 July 1969 (WAC T12/1,242).

"CLINK!"—("Bicycle Repair Man") These intertitles borrow from both the comic book and later TV traditions for campy American TV superhero shows like *Batman* (1966-1968) or *Mighty Thor* (1966).

Compère—(PSC; "Restaurant Sketch") The compère is both an organizer and a kind of director (for example, at Butlins Holiday Camps) of music and entertainment activities. By the late 1960s, the compère is appearing as an introducer/presenter on television, and as a linking element, which is where the Pythons place him. The Pythons' compères are generally greasy, unctuous, and even salivating. See the compère (Palin) introducing the "Science Fiction" sketch in Ep. 7, and the compère (Idle) introducing Harry Fink in Ep. 9.

"Cornwall"—("Stolen Newsreader") County in southwestern England, occupying a peninsula jutting into the Atlantic Ocean, and home to Penzance and Newquay. In Ep. 34, Jeremy Pither (Palin) will call Cornwall home, and the Chinese-British Ambassador (Chapman) will pretend to be familiar with the area.

"cruel to be kind"—("Court Scene [Witness in Coffin/ Cardinal Richilieu]") Cf. *Hamlet* 3.4.178. In the "Sheepdog Trials" sketch in *At Last the 1948 Show*, the sheepdog trainer (Chapman) admits how crucial cruelty is in training:

> Interviewer (Tim Brooke-Taylor): Well, how do you train the dogs?
> Trainer: Well that's very simple. We use a little kindness and a lot of cruelty.
> Interviewer: So you have to be cruel to the dogs?
> Trainer: Oh, yes, very cruel, very cruel indeed. I'm surprised it's allowed. Really nasty. Shocking! (*At Last the 1948 Show* album)

The Trainer is also obviously supposed to be a Yorkshireman, based on his accent (sounding very much like the rustic Chapman plays in Ep. 1), beginning most sentences with the regional "Ooh, ah. . . ."

– D –

"dead crab"—("Court Scene [Witness in Coffin/Cardinal Richilieu]") Cf. "Whizzo Butter" sketch from Ep. 1.

"Dim"—("Court Scene [Witness in Coffin/Cardinal Richilieu]") The incongruity between the inspector's name and his rather bare-faced cleverness (he's able to point out that Cardinal Richelieu died more than 300 years earlier) should be obvious. Dim's role as the unexpected resolution to the puzzle hearkens back to Dogberry's role in *Much Ado*, where the malapropistic (and, yes, probably dim) Constable actually ferrets out Don John's scheme (5.1).

Dim here is a CID man (Criminal Investigation Division), a branch of the Metropolitan police that had taken much of the blame for the drawn-out investigation, arrest, and prosecution of the noted Kray brothers just a few years earlier. Detective Chief Superintendent Frederick Gerrard, head of No. 3 District CID, had led the Kray investigation. The Kray arrests had been made in 1965, but convictions weren't achieved until March 1969, just weeks before the Pythons gathered to write the first series.

"Donkey Rides"—(PSC; link into "Restaurant Sketch") This is a silly sight or throwaway gag, of course, not unlike a Tex Avery or *Mad Magazine* gag, and shot on the beaches near Bournemouth. This gag will reappear in Ep. 35, where it's so dark it's nearly impossible to read the carried sign. In *LB*, a woman carrying a donkey on her shoulders walks past a stone-selling table saying she can't go to the stoning, her donkey's sick.

– E –

"East and West"—("Stolen Newsreader") This refers to the Cold War division between the NATO countries (including the United States, UK, Western Europe, etc.) as "west," and as "east" the Soviet Bloc countries. These terms have lost much of their cultural significance recently, especially with the collapse of the Soviet empire in the late 1980s.

"engine driver"—("Court Scene [Witness in Coffin/ Cardinal Richilieu]") A train engineer.

Episode 3—This episode was recorded third on 14 August 1969, and broadcast on 19 October 1969.

Some idea of the show's (a) middling popularity early and (b) its elevated level of corporate headache-inducement can be fathomed in another in-house memo—perhaps tongue-in-cheek (or just tired and cheeky)—from the office of John Howard Davies: "The third episode of 'Monty Python's Flying Circus' starring John Cleese, Michael Palin, Terry Jones, Graham Chapman and Eric Idle with animations by Terry Gilliam, please refer to episodes 1 and 2" (WAC T12/1,084). JHD will file another, similarly bleak memo for Ep. 4.

Walk-ons listed for this episode include Moira (or Moyra) Pearson, Elizabeth Broom, and Paul Lindley. Others being paid for appearing include Peter Blackburn, Philip Mutton, Joan Hayford-Hobbs, Peter Kaukus, Al Fleming, Thelma Taylor, Christine Young, and John Watters. See other entries in this episode for individual appearances by these actors (WAC T12/1,084).

– F –

"fair cop"—("Court Scene [Witness in Coffin/Cardinal Richilieu]") The phrase appears in *FC* (Eps. 3, 6, 27, and

29) and the later feature films, and is spoken by characters both historical and fictional. In *Holy Grail* it's the accused witch (Connie Booth) who mutters the phrase after she's been found a witch; in "Salvation Fuzz" sketch (Ep. 29) the murderer (Idle) of various bishops is fingered by the hand of God, and replies: "It's a fair cop, but society's to blame." The *OED* indicates that the phrase "It's a fair cop"—meaning "to capture"—first appeared in print in 1891 (from a quote attributed to an apprehended thief), and has since become a part of the British vernacular.

The phrase isn't just reserved for homey police shows like *Dixon of Dock Green*, either, or even just bad detective fiction, but can be found in a 16 July 1965 *Time* magazine article examining Tory vote-gerrymandering on a controversial capital gains tax cut amendment. It seems the Conservatives—who were in the minority 1964-1970, but by just three votes—lulled Labour to sleep in the wee hours of a legislative day, then surprised them by calling for a vote and showing up en masse to beat the sitting government, 180-166. Labour moaned and whined, but eventually termed the successful surprise attack "a fair cop," and the Wilson government took its second parliamentary defeat as the majority party (time.com/time/magazine/article/0,9171,833977-1,00 .html).

Fanfare of trumpets—(PSC; "Court Scene [Witness in Coffin/Cardinal Richilieu]") This fanfare music accompanying the entrance of the Cardinal is *not* accounted for in the usually comprehensive music rights requests (WAC T12/1,084). It may have been a public domain piece.

"freedom . . . much prized"—("Court Scene [Witness in Coffin/Cardinal Richilieu]") Cf. John Quincy Adams' *Poem*. Also, see Shakespeare's *The Tempest* 2.2.186-87, and *Julius Caesar* 3.1.

– G –

"Glamorgan"—("Stolen Newsreader") From the Welsh *Morgannwg*, Glamorgan is in southern Wales, and extends inland from the Bristol Channel coast between the Rivers Loughor and Rhymney. Swansea city and county are part of Glamorgan. This is the third Wales city mentioned in this sketch, including "Swansea" and "Porthcawl." Glamorgan's cricket club is a county team, and they play in Cardiff.

Noting that much of this newscast concerned Wales, this entire segment could be a jab at the BBC's regional news coverage, especially the silly details like a lost savings book somehow being of import to the entire region. In *Hard Day's Night*, the director of the TV special featuring The Beatles is certain that his failure will

lead to a posting doing "news in Welsh," a most unfortunate eventuality.

"go"—("Nudge, Nudge") Certainly a sexual reference as used here. See John Osborne's censor-exercising play *The Entertainer* (1957): "But I have a go, lady, don't I? I 'ave a go. I do." In the "Nudge, Nudge" sketch (written and performed by Idle), the sexual euphemisms include, "sport," "goer," "go," "games," "been around," "photographs," "Purley," "done it," and finally "slept with a lady," along with mildly suggestive hand gestures. Much of this sketch wouldn't have passed muster if the BBC's "Green Book" rules were still being strictly enforced. See the entry for "bloody" above for more on those restrictions.

"Gold Reserves"—("Stolen Newsreader") Gold bullion or coin held by a government or bank, not individuals.

Grocer, The—("Bicycle Repair Man") These titles represent Python's penchant for humor by incongruity, or the elevation of the mundane to the level of the heroic. See Fielding's *Tom Thumb* or Pope's *Rape of the Lock*, or even Simon Eyre and his "princely born" fellows in Dekker's *Shoemaker's Holiday*. Also, the Lord Mayor of London in Dekker's play, Sir Roger Otley, is a grocer by trade.

The satirical magazine *Private Eye* called Conservative PM Edward Heath (1916-1992) "The Grocer" or "Grocer Heath" from 1962 onwards. Heath would be PM 1970-1974, following the surprise-filled 1970 General Election, providing significant fodder for the *Private Eye* staff.

"guv"—("Bicycle Repair Man") Slang for "governor," often a term of deference to a more elevated, genteel person.

– H –

"hatchments"—("Court Scene [Witness in Coffin/ Cardinal Richilieu]") This word appears in *Hamlet* 4.5, and nowhere else in Shakespeare's plays:

> *Laer.*   Let this be so.
> His means of death, his obscure funeral—
> No trophy, sword, nor hatchment o'er his bones,
> No noble rite nor formal ostentation—
> Cry to be heard, as 'twere from heaven to earth,
> That I must call't in question. (4.5.213-218)

From the *OED* , there are two meanings, both rather obsolete: "1) An escutcheon or ensign armorial; esp. a square or lozenge-shaped tablet exhibiting the armorial bearings of a deceased person, which is affixed to the front of his dwelling-place," and "2) The 'hatching' with which the hilt of a sword is ornamented."

Both of these definitions can work for Python, but especially the latter, displaying the possible continuing cross-fertilization between art forms in Python's oeuvre. The Pythons were certainly aware of international cinemas, with the Japanese influence perhaps becoming apparent here. "The sword is the soul of the samurai" is part of the Bushido code, thus the "outward hatchments of his soul" operates on more than one level.

"hire purchase"—("Court Scene [Witness in Coffin/ Cardinal Richilieu]") Purchased on credit. The woman/ witness (Chapman) is running through a laundry list of everyday gossip, none of which seems to have any connection to the case at hand.

"his own hands"—("Bicycle Repair Man") Also borrowed from the *Superman* (1940-1951) radio show's preamble: "Superman! Who can change the course of mighty rivers, bend steel with his bare hands. . . ."

horse chestnut—(link into "Nudge, Nudge") A large, ornamental, nut-bearing tree introduced to England in about 1550. See *OED*.

"Huguenots"—("Court Scene [Witness in Coffin/ Cardinal Richilieu]") Protestants in France in the sixteenth and seventeenth centuries, many of whom suffered severe persecution for their faith. Richelieu tolerated these non-Catholics until they presented a military threat to Louis XIII and, even though the Huguenots were supported by the English, including the Duke of Buckingham, he led a war against them in 1628-1629, destroying their power base and ending the threat.

This period will be broached again in Ep. 37, when the aristocrats being robbed by Dennis Moore discuss in detail the Thirty Years War and England's embroilment in "continental affairs." The Pythons' source there, as here, seems to be eminent historian G.M. Trevelyan. See notes to Ep. 37 for more on this historical reference.

– I –

"immediatement"—("Restaurant Sketch") A mangled French-ified version of "immediately." Cf. the "Flying Sheep" sketch (Ep. 2), or encounters with French soldiers in *Holy Grail* for Python's assault on the French language. Also, see Shakespeare's similar treatment of the French language in *Henry V*.

"impersonator"—("Court Scene [Witness in Coffin/ Cardinal Richilieu]") Cf. the blancmange sketch, police station section, in Ep. 7, when the Detective In-

spector (Idle) is eaten by a blancmange whom he's confused for "Riley." In Ep. 14, Cleese plays an admitted "female impersonator" (the only time such a cross-dressing is admitted in the series.)

Inside—("Seduced Milkmen") The music that swells underneath as the man sees the other trapped milkmen here is Mantovani's version of "Charmaine" by Rupee (WAC T12/1,084).

Interesting Lives—(animated link into "Seduced Milkmen") Underneath this animated sequence, Gilliam utilizes "The Can-Can," as well as "Music Boxes 1-16" by Eddie Warner, and a portion of a Richard Rodger waltz (WAC T12/1,084).

"It's Bicycle Repair Man!"—("Bicycle Repair Man") Based on "It's a bird! It's a plane! No, it's Superman!" from the *Superman* TV series starring George Reeves. The preamble to the 1940s radio show *Superman* also featured this tagline.

A number of political cartoonists and pundits in the UK were producing cartoons of "Wilman" (attacking PM Wilson), a weak and ineffective Superman-type able to defeat, barely, tiny islands like Anguilla, which British forces invaded in early 1969. See William Papas' panel cartoon for 24 March 1969 in *The Guardian*, and the British Cartoon Archive for more.

– J –

jetty—("Stolen Newsreader") This is the end of Southwold Pier in Southwold, Suffolk. According to WAC records for the episode, Peter Lovell assists in pushing the Newsreader (Cleese) (WAC T12/1,083). Lovell would later work as production assistant on *Goodies Rule—OK?* (1973) and *Some Mothers Do 'Ave 'Em* (1975).

– K –

"KGB"—("Court Scene [Witness in Coffin/Cardinal Richilieu]") Former USSR secret police organization (Komitet Gosudarstvennoy Bezopasnosti ["Committee for State Security"]), 1917-1991. During this period, the KGB was very much a secretive and feared organization of political control. The KGB is mentioned again in Ep. 34, when Jeremy Pither and his bicycle tour somehow make it from Devon and Cornwall to the Soviet Union. This is one of the words, when mentioned by the witness (Chapman), that prompts a direct look toward the camera by counsel (Cleese), the other key words being "leg" and "womb."

"kosher car park"—("Court Scene [Witness in Coffin/ Cardinal Richilieu]") Presumably, a place where

Orthodox Jews (or Jewish cars?) can park without running afoul of Jewish law.

In *The Goon Show* episode "King's Solomon's Mines," Bluebottle (Sellers) is thrown into the river, and shouts out: "Help! I've fallen into non-kosher water!"

– L –

"larch"—(opening credits) This slide image, though overexposed, seems to actually be a rather scraggly larch tree. This is also the only tree recognized during the episode, despite the title.

laundrette—("Bicycle Repair Man") This is the Bendix Laundrette on Uxbridge Road in Acton, and the scene was shot on 14 July 1969 (WAC T12/1,083). Phone books for the period and area list the actual address as 261 High Street, which becomes Uxbridge Road.

"liver . . . head off"—("Court Scene [Witness in Coffin/Cardinal Richilieu]") Cf. the "Live Organ Transplants" sketch in *ML*, wherein a man has his liver removed with kitchen and carpentry tools while he's alive.

"London town"—("Restaurant Sketch") Probably the writing team of Cleese and Chapman, who had been writing together since their late Cambridge days. Neither were from London, however. Cleese was born in Weston-Super-Mare, Avonshire, and Chapman in Leicester, Leicestershire. All of the Pythons had been living in the Greater London area for most of the decade of the 1960s, writing for and performing in various TV shows.

lorry—("Stolen Newsreader") A large truck for transporting goods. The troupe's gear was transported in such vehicles, one of which (a green panel truck) is featured in Ep. 15, after the "Spanish Inquisition" sketch. The driver of the lorry stealing the Newsreader (Cleese) is Peter Blackburn, and these scenes were shot on 15 July 1969 (WAC T12/1,242).

– M –

magic lantern—(opening credits) A precursor of the motion picture projector, the nineteenth-century "magic lantern" was often used to display slides during scientific lectures and demonstrations. Since the magic lantern—as a term—had been passé for a number of years in broadcasting, it's not clear why they chose the term instead of "slide projector." As early as the 1890s, "slide projector" was the preferred term.

man in the suit of armour—(PSC; link into "Children's Stories") The man in the uncomfortable-looking suit

was almost always Terry Gilliam, and was a walk-on part, for which he would have been paid an additional £5/5, at least during the show's first season (WAC T12/1,083). These chestnut slapstick links become less and less frequent as the show progresses, seemingly as the Pythons feel more and more confident in their conception, writing, and performance skills.

"mangy"—("Restaurant Sketch") *OED*: "Mean, stingy, niggardly; disappointingly small."

"men dressed as ladies"—("Children's Stories") Certainly at least an intertextual reference to Python's own cross-dressing practices but, ironically, or perhaps maliciously, this might be a reference to author Richard Scarry's alleged arrest in 1965 for solicitation of a male undercover police officer (see the entry at http://en.wikipedia.org/wiki/Richard_scarry).

"Minister without Portfolio"—("Stolen Newsreader") A minister of the government who may be a member of the Cabinet but who is not at the head of any particular department. In 1963-1964 Lord Carrington (b. 1919) was the Minister without Portfolio in Macmillan's government, and then was opposition leader in the House of Lords after the Conservatives fell from power in October 1964. Lord Carrington will be later mentioned in Ep. 42, and has already been mentioned—yes, unfavorably—a number of times in the pages of *Private Eye*.

"m'lud"—("Court Scene [Witness in Coffin/Cardinal Richilieu]") A slang contraction of "My Lord," this is a term of respect for holders of office, specifically judges, as many were actually Lords. By the 1960s the usage is waning significantly, with overuse appearing obsequious and "patronising" (*OED*).

"Mungo"—("Restaurant Sketch") *OED*: "A typical name for a Black slave. Hence, a Negro." This name could be used here as a play on the character's servile status (he is a cook), as either slave or kitchen worker. Most likely, however, given the Pythons' penchant for Modernist literature, the name probably comes from "Mungo Jerry," a character found in T.S. Eliot's well-known book *Old Possum's Book of Practical Cats* (1939, and republished more contemporarily by Faber in 1962).

– N –

"National Savings"—("Stolen Newsreader") Currently England's second-largest savings institution, in business since 1861 when the Palmerston government set up the "Post Office Savings Bank" for ordinary workers across the UK. The loss of such a savings book and its mention on the national (even regional) news must be considered satirical, since it's highly unlikely the press would have much interest in such a trivial matter. Again, elevating the mundane to the level of the epic/heroic, or in this case, newsworthy, certainly applies here.

"NEDC"—("Stolen Newsreader") Acronym for National Economic Development Council, which was set up in 1962 as a national (UK) economic policy forum.

"ODCN"—Perhaps Oil-Dri du Canada (ODCN), which has been in business since 1963, and may well have had opportunity or need to talk with the National Economic Development Council (NEDC). More likely this is one of the many made-up, official-sounding acronyms offered throughout the series. The satirical magazine *Private Eye* (and its Oxbridge precedents) also employed similarly made-up names and acronyms mixed in with actual names and acronyms; the magazine was sued for libel ("issued a writ" by the allegedly defamed) on many occasions, and paid out damages for many of those offenses.

"NO. 3"—("The Larch") This is the same slide as image number one, clearly.

"nod's . . . bat"—("Nudge, Nudge") Taken from an old Irish proverb: "A nod's as good as a wink to a blind horse." A bat doesn't rely on its eyes anyway, of course, which may be the reason for its inclusion here.

"not at all well"—("Court Scene [Witness in Coffin/ Cardinal Richilieu]") This phrase has become something of a Python trope—quoted or misquoted from its appearance in *HG* (see below). The phrase, however, is earlier mentioned in *The Goon Show* by Peter Sellers ("The White Box of Bardfield"), which is where the Pythons may have heard it first. In *HG*, cf. the "plague cart" scene:

> Dead Person (John Young): I'm not dead!
> Mortician (Idle): Here—he says he's not dead!
> Customer (Cleese): Yes, he is.
> Dead Person: I'm not!
> Mortician: He isn't.
> Customer: Well, he will be soon, he's very ill.
> Dead Person: I'm getting better!
> Customer: No, you're not—you'll be stone dead in a moment. (Scene 2)

The same sentiments are voiced in "Salvation Fuzz," when the rabbit fish is described in Ep. 29:

> Man (Idle): What, rabbit fish?
> Woman (Jones): Yes. It's got fins.
> Man: Is it dead?
> Woman: Well, it was coughin' up blood last night.

"Not so fast!"—("Court Scene [Witness in Coffin/ Cardinal Richilieu]") This exchange is probably based on extant crime and courtroom television shows like *Perry Mason*, where witnesses typically (and easily) confess on the stand under the examination of persistent counsel or investigators.

– O –

Olivier impression—("Court Scene [Witness in Coffin/Cardinal Richilieu]") Olivier (1907-1989) was a renowned English actor and director, whose delivery and intonation became both well known and much imitated. The balance of the soliloquy is a typically Pythonesque farrago of "Shakespearean" language and syntax, sometimes glossable, and sometimes not. Idle will mimic Olivier's delivery and posture, and the rest will be an authentic-sounding soliloquy as if from Shakespeare or Marlowe.

This section also reads very much like the *Beyond the Fringe* sketch "So That's the Way You Like It," which is a rather bouncy and jangled conflation of jabberwock English Renaissance drama-speak:

> Sustain we now description of a time
> When petty lust and overweening tyranny
> Offend the ruck of state.
> Thus fly we now, as oft with Phoebus did
> Fair Asterope unto proud Flander's court.
> Where is the warlike Warwick
> Like to the mole that sat on Hector's brow,
> Fairset for England, and for war! (audio transcription, *Beyond the Fringe*)

"Omsk . . . Krakow"—("Stolen Newsreader") This is essentially fallacious geography, since Omsk is in Russia and Krakow is in Poland.

"Bulestan"—Not a country or a Soviet satellite, it is a term that appears in *Regesta Regis Æthelstani* (*The Anglo-Saxon Charters of King Æthelstan*, 924-39), and involving a land grant from the king to the brethren at Muchelney Abbey: " . . . on bulestan of bulanstane . . ." (Sawyer number 455). Obviously this name is supposed to sound like one of the Soviet Bloc regions (Kazakhstan, Kyrgyzstan, Tajikistan, Turkmenistan, Uzbekistan) but turns out to be very much of Old English derivation.

"Only . . . offence"—("Court Scene [Witness in Coffin/ Cardinal Richilieu]") Once again, Python elevates something minor to the epic level, not unlike Pope's *Rape of the Lock* (1712), Swift's description of the point of contention in Lilliput (ends of eggs) in *Gulliver's Travels* (1726), and Butler's *Erewhon* (1872). In the feature film *Life of Brian*, those who try and follow Brian as their messiah also argue over the spiritual significance of a gourd and a sandal, and one man wishes to be healed from thinning hair.

"out of the TV Centre"—("Stolen Newsreader") The thieves rush the Newsreader out of Studio 4 (*Flying Circus* was generally assigned to Studio 6).

– P –

"parking offence, schmarking offence"—("Court Scene [Witness in Coffin/Cardinal Richilieu]") This is a common American colloquialism borrowed from many Yiddish words that, according to the *OED*, "begin with this sequence of sounds, fused with or replacing the initial letter(s) of a word, so as to form a nonsense-word which is added to the original word in order to convey disparagement, dismissal, or derision." In essence, a nonsense (and even nonce) word is created for each iteration of this phrase.

Piano starts playing—(PSC; "Court Scene [Witness in Coffin/Cardinal Richilieu]") Offscreen, Bill McGuffie (1927-1987) is playing this live piano accompaniment (WAC T12/1,084). McGuffie would also write and play original songs later in the series.

"point on it"—("Court Scene [Witness in Coffin/Cardinal Richilieu]") Cf. Miguel de Cervantes' *La Gitanilla*: "Don't put too fine a point to your wit for fear it should get blunted."

"Porthcawl"—("Stolen Newsreader") Another Welsh location, Porthcawl is a coastal resort, a Bridgend county borough, and also a part of county of Glamorgan, Wales. Terry Jones was born in northern Wales.

"punch-line"—("Restaurant Sketch") When the Pythons do deliver a punchline, they usually either (a) point it up to the audience, thus undercutting the effectiveness of any surprise (by definition) punchline in general; or (b) assault the deliverer of the punchline, either physically or with derision. Again, the Pythons' comedic inspirations The Goons did employ punchlines on occasion, and often dreadful puns (but lustily, unflinchingly, unapologetically delivered). The Goons, however, didn't pause and wait for audience reaction to the tried and true jokes, but raced right on with their rather dizzying barrage. Listen to, for example, the sketch "Napoleon's Piano" (*Collected Goon Show* CD), or this exchange in the episode "The Man Who Never Was":

Prisoner (Secombe): Does your wife know this?
Maj. Bloodnok (Sellers): Shut up! Achtung! Gebluten geblutz! Admit it, you're a spy!
Prisoner: I'm not a spy, I'm a shepherd!

Maj. Bloodnok: Ah! Shepherd's pie! You can't fool us, you naughty German!

"Purley"—("Nudge, Nudge") An outer borough of southern London, in Surrey. When this sketch is performed in Los Angeles in 1980 for the film *Live at the Hollywood Bowl*, "Purley" is replaced by "Glendale," and to a healthy laugh from the LA audience.

– Q –

"Quantity Surveyor"—("Bicycle Repair Man") *OED*: "A surveyor who estimates the quantities of labour and materials required for building and engineering work." Mentioned because it simply sounds dull, and not heroic.

"Queen, Michael"—("Stolen Newsreader") A "queen" is slang for an effeminate homosexual man. See the description offered by Biggles' secretary (Nicki Howorth) in Ep. 33, "Biggles Dictates a Letter."

– R –

"red"—(link into "Children's Stories") Slang for Communist Party member or sympathizer, the usage also applies to "commies" uttered later in the diatribe. This originally referred to the color of the party badge (*OED*). Cleese is, if course, here depicting an over-the-top Enoch Powell, who had spoken of "reds in high places lighting their own funeral pyre" as he surveyed the left-leaning slump of England, his "green and pleasant land" (*Private Eye* 31 July 1970, page 10).

This period was significant in the history of the Cold War as both the United States and USSR struggled to keep control of their spheres of influence, especially in the face of the decolonization process throughout the Third World, and "Prague Spring"–type attempts at self-rule in Eastern Europe. The so-called Brezhnev Doctrine was implemented in November 1968, sending a distinctly chilly shiver into the world:

When forces that are hostile to socialism try to turn the development of some socialist country towards capitalism, it becomes not only a problem of the country concerned, but a common problem and concern of all socialist countries. (Leonid Brezhnev, Fifth Congress speech)

Armed suppression of any such "development" was thereafter justified, and the Cold War got a bit colder. Though treated comedically here, the anxiety level of the Western world must have been significantly elevated between the time when Soviet tanks rolled through Budapest, Hungary, in November 1956, and Czechoslovakia in August 1968.

referee blowing whistle—(end credits) This stock film was taken from the recent Scottish Cup Final film, shot in 1969. This title is part of the list of stock film requested by the show for Ep. 3 (WAC T12/1,084). This type of obvious "ending" to an episode disappears as the first season progresses, often in favor of mock endings.

"Rhodesia"—("Court Scene [Witness in Coffin/Cardinal Richilieu]") The subject of the African members of the Commonwealth comes up often in *Flying Circus*, and Rhodesia specifically in the fourth series' final episode (Ep. 45). See notes for Episode 45 on "Rhodesia" and "Ian Smith."

Rhodesia was significantly in the news in 1969 when students at the London School of Economics (LSE) rioted and tore down newly installed security gates. Problems had begun in 1966 when the school appointed its new director, Dr. Walter Adams, who had come to LSE from the University College of Rhodesia, sparking immediate (then smoldering) student unrest. Adams was criticized for his cozy relationship with Ian Smith's government, and his perceived complicity with the continuation of white rule in Rhodesia. The LSE was closed for three weeks after the January 1969 riots (see bbc.co.uk for 24 January 1969, and entries in the *ODNB*).

"Rotarian"—("Stolen Newsreader") A member of the Rotary Club, a philanthropic organization founded in the United States.

– S –

"saddle"—("Bicycle Repair Man") A bicycle seat.

"savage"—("Court Scene [Witness in Coffin/Cardinal Richilieu]") Cf. Shakespeare's *Merchant of Venice*: "Their savage eyes turn'd to a modest gaze / By the sweet power of music . . . " (5.1.78-79), and *King John*: "And tame the savage spirit of wild war" (5.2.74).

"scrubby"—("Restaurant Sketch") *OED*: "Stunted, under-developed."

"slept with a lady"—("Nudge, Nudge") This rather tame sexual reference (the first of many to come) was only possible during the reign of BBC Director-General Hugh Greene (fl. 1960-1969), whose more liberal approach to programming possibilities allowed the Pythons a time slot. As the Pythons subsequently explored the boundaries of the BBC's newfound permissiveness, they seemed to litaneutically employ the handbook "Variety Programmes Policy Guide for Writers and Producers," written in 1948 but still in use more than twenty years later. The handbook's banned references for television presentation included "lavatories," "effeminacy in men," and "immorality of any kind," all of which the Pythons visited and revisited as the series rolled on. Also forbidden (and regularly targeted by the Pythons) were "suggestive references" to newlyweds (Ep. 8), fig leaves (Ep. 6), prostitution (Eps. 14, 33), ladies' underwear (Eps. 5, 9), animal sexual habits (Ep. 20), religion or religious figures (Eps. 15, 17), and commercial travellers (Eps. 22, 28). The government and politicians were also off-limits, two targets that became Python favorites. Humphrey Carpenter discusses the handbook in relation to early 1960s satire shows in *That Was Satire, That Was* (205-6).

song—("Court Scene [Witness in Coffin/Cardinal Richilieu]") The tune borrowed here is "Someone Else I'd Like to Be" by Tom Sutton, sung by both Cleese and Chapman, with live piano by Bill McGuffie (WAC T12/1,084). McGuffie will figure in *FC* over the following several seasons, writing original songs for the performers and playing piano accompaniment, as he does here.

"soothe . . . quiet"—("Court Scene [Witness in Coffin/Cardinal Richilieu]") Cf. Congreve's *The Mourning Bride*: "Music has charms to soothe a savage breast" (1.1), and Shakespeare's *King Richard II*: " . . . truth hath a quiet breast" (1.3.96). Congreve was a member of the Kit Kat Club in eighteenth-century London (see entry for "Eek Eek Club" in Ep. 2).

spanner—(PSC; "Bicycle Repair Man") A wrench.

"storm toss'd"—("Court Scene [Witness in Coffin/Cardinal Richilieu]") Cf. *Romeo and Juliet*: "Thy tempest-tossed body . . . " (3.5.137).

"stuff and pith"—("Court Scene [Witness in Coffin/Cardinal Richilieu]") Cf. similar phraseology found in both *Henry V* and *Hamlet*, with the latter reading: "The pith and marrow of our attribute" (1.4.22).

suburban house—(PSC; "Seduced Milkmen") This was filmed on location in Barnes, Richmond upon Thames, according to Palin. See Palin's presentation in *Pythonland* (DVD, dir. Ralph Lee, 1999). BBC records indicate that the house was precisely located at 48 Ullsworth Road, Barnes, where portions of "The Mouse Problem" and "Deadliest Joke" were also filmed (WAC T12/1,083). Most of these sequences were shot on 16 July 1969.

Superboy—("Bicycle Repair Man") There actually was a Superboy character (meant to be simply a young Superman) created in 1944. The boy playing Superboy here is John Watters (WAC T12/1,083), who also appeared in *Oliver!* (1968), *Z Cars* (1969), and *Footprints in the Jungle* (1970). Watters shot his scene on 14 July 1969 (WAC T12/1,242).

"Superman"—("Bicycle Repair Man") American comic book character created in June 1938, written by Jerry Siegel and drawn by Joseph Shuster for Action Comics. Superman would appear on a radio show, TV cartoons, novels, a Broadway musical, several television series, and feature motion pictures. The American accents used by the commentator and those dressed as Superman remind the reader/viewer of the character's roots, and the credo by which he lives: "Truth, justice, and the American way."

The accompanying music is not a generic "chase martial" as listed in the WAC records, but is a portion of "March of the Insurgents" by Jack Shaindlin (WAC T12/1,084). This music will also be heard in Ep. 6 as the Frankenstein monster (Cleese) attacks a bus queue.

"Swansea"—("Stolen Newsreader") There are at least six nature reserves in the Swansea area. Swansea is a Welsh city in Glamorgan, southwestern Wales. It lies along the Bristol Channel at the mouth of the River Tawe (hence its Welsh name, Abertawe). Swansea is the second largest city in Wales.

– T –

"tangled web"—("Court Scene [Witness in Coffin/Cardinal Richilieu]") Cf. Sir Walter Scott's *The Last Day of the Minstrel*: "Oh, what a tangled web we weave, / When first we practice to deceive!" (canto VI, stanza 17). Scott is mentioned/alluded to at least two other times in *FC*. His book *Red Gauntlet* is woefully misread aloud in Ep. 38, and the other allusion is discussed below in the "Provost of Edinburgh" note in Ep. 7.

"trap"—("Court Scene [Witness in Coffin/Cardinal Richilieu]") Richelieu is now the woodcock to Dim's springe. See the entry for "woodcock" below.

TV Centre—("Stolen Newsreader") Main British Broadcasting Corporation complex, located in Shepherd's Bush. This was where most of the BBC's sound stages were located, and where *Flying Circus* was primarily recorded, when *en-studio*. The then-state-of-the-art studio space opened to much fanfare in 1960.

– U –

"unturned"—("Court Scene [Witness in Coffin/Cardinal Richilieu]") Cf. Euripides' *Heraclidae* (c. 428 BC). This is another insignificant moment elevated to high (mock-) seriousness. Cleese, having read law at Cam-

bridge, may have drawn upon his limited experience in the courts for this scene. In fact, in a publicity photo for *The Frost Report* (1966), Cleese appears dressed as a barrister.

"Uproar!"—("Court Scene [Witness in Coffin/Cardinal Richilieu]") The others in this scene include Fred Berman and William Curran as the Ushers, Maurice Quick as the Counsel, as well as Bill Gosling, Jim Delany, Alan Granville, Moira Pearson, and Elizabeth Broom (WAC T12.1,084). Several of these are bit-part actors who appeared regularly in many British TV shows during this period. Maurice Quick, for example, appeared in *Dixon of Dock Green*, *Doctor Who*, and *Z Cars*, and Bill Gosling (aka William Gossling) appeared in *Z Cars* (1971), *Upstairs, Downstairs* (1972), and *Hearts and Flowers* (1970). Elizabeth Broom and Jim Delany would take other bit/walk-on parts in shows like *Some Mothers Do 'Ave 'Em* (1973), a show produced by Michael Mills, with technical folk like James Balfour (camera) and Bernard Wilkie (visual effects designer), late of the *FC* crew. Alan Granville was an uncredited extra on *Dr. Who*, as are others who appear often on *FC*, including Maurice Quick, Peter Kaukus, Cy Town, and Bernadette Barry (see *The Encyclopedia of Fantastic Film & Television*).

Any actor hired to appear in any *FC* episode is noted in the accounting portions of the surviving records, for repeat fee purposes, though the actor's precise role ("walk-on," "speaking," "extra") isn't always noted.

– V –

"very big"—("Restaurant Sketch") This Cook looks very much like the hulking Cook figure appearing in Harold Lloyd's silent comedy film *Haunted Spooks* (1920), directed by Harold Roach. The Cook in this silent comedy film is called out from the kitchen to help throw out an unwanted suitor.

"Voleschtadt"—("Stolen Newsreader") Perhaps a homonym or just misspelling of Vollstadt, but may also be one of the earliest "vole" references in *FC*. It could translate essentially as "mouse city."

– W –

"wakes the drowsy apricot"—("Court Scene [Witness in Coffin/Cardinal Richilieu]") Rousing a sleepy drupe? Cf. Shakespeare's *A Midsummer Night's Dream*:

> Tit. Be kind and courteous to this gentleman,
> Hop in his walks and gambol in his eyes;
> Feed him with apricocks and dewberries,

With purple grapes, green figs, and mulberries;
The honey-bags steal from the humble-bees,
And for night-tapers crop their waxen thighs,
And light them at the fiery glow-worm's eyes,
To have my love to bed and to arise;
And pluck the wings from painted butterflies
To fan the moonbeams from his sleeping eyes:
Nod to him, elves, and do him courtesies. (3.1.164-174)

The drowsiness is here attributed to the object of the four Fairies' attention, Bottom. In *King Richard II*, "dangling apricocks" are compared by the Gardener to unruly children who demand much of their master (3.4.29-32).

"What frees . . . owl of Thebes?"—("Court Scene [Witness in Coffin/Cardinal Richilieu]") The phrase "owl of Thebes" does not appear in Shakespeare's corpus, and the owl, when mentioned by Shakespeare, is most often a harbinger of death or birth, or a sort of night watchman. Perhaps, though, the gist of the phrase can be attributable to Fortinbras in *Hamlet*: "This quarry cries on havoc. O proud death, / What feast is toward in thine eternal *cell*, / That thou so many princes at a shot / So bloodily hast strook?" (5.2.364-67).
Or even to the Greek likeness of Cymbeline:

Gui.   Out of your proof you speak; we poor unfledg'd,
Have never wing'd from view o' th' nest, nor [know] not
What air's from home. Happ'ly this life is best,
If quiet life be best; sweeter to you
That have a sharper known; well corresponding
With your stiff age; but unto us it is
A *cell* of ignorance, travelling a-bed,
A prison, or a debtor that not dares
To stride a limit. (3.3.27-34)

Perhaps an echo can be heard of Thomas Gray's *Elegy Written in a Country Church-Yard*, where are found the complaints of the "mopeing Owl," as well as the "narrow cell" containing "rude Forefathers" of the rural hamlet. Whatever the source, the Pythons consistently draw upon the rich panoply of English literature and literary figures for their comedy.

"What's-it like?"—("Nudge, Nudge") This highly euphemistic sketch plays on the fact that the audience understands the lewdness of Norman's (Idle) questions and allusions, and the gent (Jones) misses the true meaning of every wink and nudge almost completely. Notice, too, that the punchline receives an appropriately fake laugh track response, signaling the Python's continuing sneer at what they considered to be typically restraining comedic structures. The lameness of the ending didn't stop them from including the sketch, of course, and it reappears to much acclaim in most of the troupe's live stage performances, including *Live at the Hollywood Bowl* (1980).

"wickets"—("Stolen Newsreader") Cricket paraphernalia, a wicket consists of three stumps/stakes (about 28 inches tall) topped by two bails and arranged so that a ball cannot pass between the stumps. Two wickets are set up—the batsman defends and the bowler attacks. A cricket match will be depicted in Eps. 20 and 45, and two cricket teams will appear earlier in Ep. 20.
The match highlighted here (Yorkshire vs. Glamorgan) is an example of "county cricket," or matches between the various counties of the UK and a practice in place as early as 1827. These were also often amateur versus professional matches. Yorkshire dominated this inter-county play during the 1960s, probably much to the delight of South Yorkshire-native Palin.

"Wimbledon"—("Court Scene [Witness in Coffin/ Cardinal Richilieu]") Formerly a municipal borough of Surrey, though since 1965 Wimbledon has been part of Merton, a borough of Greater London. It is eight miles southwest of London. Most of Ep. 7 is centered on alien blancmanges playing for the tennis world crown at Wimbledon.

"woodcock in his springe"—("Court Scene [Witness in Coffin/Cardinal Richilieu]") Cf. Laertes' too-late realization in *Hamlet*: "Why, as a woodcock to mine own springe, Osric: / I am justly kill'd with mine own treachery" (5.2.306-7). A "springe" is a trap for small animals, especially birds, like the woodcock.

– Y –

"Yard"—("Court Scene [Witness in Coffin/Cardinal Richilieu]") Refers to Scotland Yard, headquarters of the London Metropolitan Police and located south of St. James's Park in Westminster. In *FC* episodes, appearances by characters from the Yard are generally greeted with some fanfare.

"Yorkshire"—("Stolen Newsreader") Largest historical county of England, in the north-central part of the country between the Pennines and the North Sea. Palin was born in Sheffield, South Yorkshire.
Yorkshire's cricket club was founded in Sheffield in 1863, and many of its best years were had before WWII.

"you-know-what"—("Court Scene [Witness in Coffin/ Cardinal Richilieu]") This kind of non-reference usually means something of a sexual nature, here probably gynecological. See the sketch about taxation on "thingy" (sexual acts) in Ep. 15.

Episode 4: "Owl-Stretching Time"

– A –

"Albania"—("Song [*And Did Those Feet*]") Zog ruled 1928-1939, when Italian fascists unseated him as they overran Albania. Zog lived in exile afterward.

"all the things you can read about in a book"—("Secret Service Dentists") Meaning, these things just listed won't be seen in this sketch, or even on this show. This "faux intro" motif is also used to build up other sketches in other episodes, viz., Ep. 8, the "Army Protection Racket" sketch, as well as the *"Black Eagle"* sketch in Ep. 25. There is also the very sober, historically reasonable intro to *HG*, which is quickly undercut.

"ancient time"—("Song [*And Did Those Feet*]") Here she stops his mouth with a kiss. Cf. Benedick to Beatrice in Shakespeare's *Much Ado*. The song is actually called "Jerusalem."

anti-tank gun—(PSC; "Secret Service Dentists") This is a weapon designed specifically to combat tanks in the field, featuring armor-piercing shells. The 1960s saw a significant increase in the interest in, production, and use of such weapons. The older model used in this episode looks very much like a version of the WWII-era M-20 bazooka. The rise in anti-colonial guerrilla actions in Africa and South America, for example, meant that these low-tech, shoulder-fired type weapons became quite prominent.

The increasing size and lethality of the weapons in this sketch seems a comment on the then-current arms race, as well, where the United States and USSR (and, by association, NATO and the Warsaw Pact countries) were building and deploying ever larger and more destructive weapons in the race for global supremacy. Bugs Bunny and Elmer Fudd had earlier spoofed this nihilistic build-up, as well, in the Warner Bros. cartoons *What's Opera, Doc?* and *Duck Dodgers*.

Great Britain's part in this arms race, for the most part, meant agreeing to host/deploy U.S. weapons systems, including nuclear submarines, B-52 bombers, and various missile systems. The decision to scuttle its own glitch-ridden Blue Streak missile project and cast in with the United States on the Skybolt system seemed a good idea in the very early 1960s, but soon thereafter the Americans announced the creation and deployment of long-range ICBMs, and the Skybolt system immediately became obsolete. Newspapers, Labour Party officials, and *Private Eye* had a field day skewering the seemingly shortsighted Macmillan administration for leaving the UK without a credible nuclear deterrent at the height of the Cold War.

"Art Gallery"—("Art Gallery") Cf. *"It's the Arts"* in Ep. 1. Pythons' forays into the world of high art (and literature, music, etc.) display their acculturation, and their university training. Their "working mothers" here are also given significant knowledge and appreciation of fine art, well beyond what might be expected of the working class.

Pete and Dud (Peter Cook and Dudley Moore) had performed a sketch called "Art Gallery" for their 1965 TV show, *Not Only . . . But Also*. In it Pete and Dud meet and discuss the efficacies of Rubens' "fat ladies," da Vinci's cartoons (which aren't "funny" at all), and the unmatched skill of wildlife painter Vernon Ward (the duck's eyes follow you as you pass the painting).

In the Python "Art Gallery," the women seem to be in a room of Constable-type (or at least nineteenth-century British) landscapes, and the Pythons had asked for the prop department to provide a copy of "Turner's *Bridge at Kew*." A painting that seems to be of a maritime setting (boats, a bridge in the background) can be glimpsed on the easel in the middle ground, but it is certainly not a Turner, nor Whistler, Constable, or similar. One of the paintings (third from left) may be a version of one of Constable's "Hampstead Heath" paintings (perhaps *Hampstead Heath with a Rainbow*, 1836); the painting on the far left resembles Turner's *Crossing the Brook* (1815). Most of the paintings can't be seen very well, but it's clear they're not eighteenth century or earlier. They may also be popularized prints of Constable followers, of which there were many.

See entry for "landscape artists" in this episode for more. Again, original versions of these English masters would have been available to the Pythons at the Tate, Victoria & Albert, and National Gallery museums, as they are today.

"Arthur"—("Opening Captions") Cf. the multiple uses of "Arthur" in Eps. 1 and 2, and then throughout *FC*, appearing in twenty-one different episodes. This episode features the exploits of Arthur Lemming. See below.

– B –

"back at two"—("Secret Service Dentists") Either a spoof on the dental profession for taking a regular lunch break no matter what they're involved with, or even the film/TV industry where actors can break character at the call for lunch and resume the situation later.

Not unlike the Warner Bros. cartoon characters (Ralph and Sam, a wolf and a sheepdog), who can be at each other's throats from 9 to 5 but come punch-out time they're friends again. The seven cartoons in which they appear and share this relationship date between 1953 and 1963. See Jerry Beck's *Looney Tunes and Merrie Melodies*.

"banana fiend"—("Self-Defence") The specter of incongruity is apparent here, since attack by fresh fruit is rarely a real threat. But, the incongruity is almost ameliorated by the fact that the RSM type has a noticeable tic, as well as a fixation on fresh fruit. Perhaps the intimation is that the RSM suffers some sort of post-traumatic stress disorder after his military service. And before the "fresh-fruit-as-dangerous" scenario can be wholly discounted, it must be remembered that in the Python world, sheep, rabbits, and even blancmanges can be deadly.

The Goons had treated this subject in the episode "The Affair of the Lone Banana" (26 October 1954), where a loaded banana is capable of killing a man.

"Baroque"—("Art Gallery") Period defined by dramatic themes and stylistic complexity, and roughly coinciding with the duration of the seventeeth century, and including painters such as Rubens, Rembrandt, and Velazquez.

beach—("Undressing in Public") Much of this sketch was shot at the beaches of Bournemouth, on Friday, 10 July 1969 (WAC T12/1,083).

"Big Cheese"—("Secret Service Dentists") American underworld or film noir slang for a boss, or a self-important person. Used just this way by Raymond Chandler in a *Black Mask* story (July 1934): "So the big cheese give me the job" (64).

blank English stare—(PSC; "Undressing in Public") Another example of the Englishness of the text and its cultural referents/references. The authors are careful to note that there is no judgment in the look, no "disapproval," just another thing that "we" (as Englishmen and -women) can share, and in sharing are therefore English. Voltaire also commented on Englishness, characterizing the entire population as "eaten up with melancholy," and this penchant for watching blankly appears in *Candide*, chapter 23:

> As they were chatting thus together they arrived at Portsmouth. The shore on each side the harbor was lined with a multitude of people, whose eyes were steadfastly fixed on a lusty man who was kneeling down on the deck of one of the men-of-war, with something tied before his eyes. Opposite to this personage stood four soldiers, each of whom shot three bullets into his skull, with all the composure imaginable; and when it was done, the whole company went away perfectly well satisfied.

These selfsame kinds of stares can be seen in the location shots when passersby are watching the recording. See the "Olympic Hide-and-Seek Final" in Ep. 35, and the somewhat disinterested bystanders in the "How to Give Up Being a Mason" sketch in Ep. 17, as well as holiday-goers in-shot during *Scott of the Antarctic* in Ep. 23.

This is also the same kind of look that often greeted Monsieur Hulot (Jacques Tati, 1909-1982) in films like *Mon. Hulot's Holiday* (1953) and *Mon Uncle* (1958). Both are gentle commentaries on the display of private actions in public settings, with Hulot blithely stumbling through modern French society—a kind of throwback to a gentler, kinder era that may or may not have ever existed.

bookseller—(PSC; "Secret Service Dentists") Voltaire notes that the job of bookselling had no equal, with Candide deciding "that there was no trade in the world with which one should be more disgusted" (chapter 19). No surprise, then, that the bookseller (Cleese) as depicted here moonlights as a spy of sorts.

Cleese earlier played a perturbed bookseller in a sketch with customer Marty Feldman on *At Last the 1948 Show*. In the later Python version, Jones takes the part of the customer.

bookshop—(PSC; "Secret Service Dentists") There are posters on the walls of this shop for various current and popular titles, including:

(1) A generic advertisement to read more Louis L'Amour books (noted American Western author)

(2) A title from a series of spy books featuring the cowardly Boysie Oakes, written by John E. Gardner, this one called *Madrigal* (1968). These books were quite popular during this period, and featured a super-spy who really wasn't terribly adept—not unlike the naughty dentists in the sketch

(3) *The Naked Ape* by Desmond Morris (published 1967, 1969) is prominently featured between Cleese and Idle (Cf. Ep. 12, where the caption "The Naked Ant" appears.)

(4) An advertisement for the latest book by Lobsang Rampa, *Beyond the Tenth* (1969), is also seen. Rampa had written *The Third Eye* in 1958, reportedly detailing his own life as a Tibetan lama, but he was later exposed as a Plympton-born Brit, Cyril Hoskin. He continued to write and live in this assumed monk character for many years. (See notes to the *"Erizabeth L"* sketch in Ep. 29 for more on Rampa.)

(5) There is a poster for the Roderick Thorp novel *The Detective* ("An Adult Look at a Detective") near the door, this a crossover poster for the film (1968) starring Frank Sinatra, as well

(6) There are also several Penguin books, including a green "crime" series book, and an orange-jacketed "classic." See notes to Ep. 38 for more on the Penguin book series, and the cultural significance of Penguin Publishing in the UK.

This particular sketch was actually shot on Stage 8, not Stage 6, where the episodes were normally staged, perhaps because the size of the set and moveable machinery demanded a differently equipped space. There is also the possibility that this taping just got bumped by another show on this date, 21 September 1969, which happens later in the series on several occasions (WAC T12/1,086).

breakwater—("Undressing in Public") *OED*: "A groyne or barrier on the beach to retain shingle." This breakwater seems to run from the top of the beach down to the low tide line.

"Bring me . . . chariot of fire"—(link into "It's a Man's Life in the Modern Army") The change of mood becomes very apparent here as the double-edged references appear. What was sacred in the hymnal setting must now be seen as sexual, especially as the girl enters. Henke notes that in English Renaissance literature "arrow" has been glossed as both "kiss" and a metaphor for "penis." He cites George Walton Williams (editor of the 1966 edition of *The Changeling*) who, following extant stage directions, glosses "arrow" as "kiss":

> *Ant.* No danger in me; I bring naught but love
> And his soft-wounding shafts to strike you with.
> Try but one arrow; if it hurt you,
> I'll stand you twenty back in recompense.
> [*Kisses her.*] (3.3.136-39)

(The format and spelling for quotes from Dekker, Middleton, Webster, et al., are included as found in Fraser and Rabkin's *Drama of the English Renaissance* [1976].)

Thus an arrow is merely a kiss, amorous but not overtly sexual. The ribaldry associated with the term is displayed by Robert Greene in *A Disputation Between a Hee Cony-Catcher and a Shee Cony-Catcher* (1592), with Greene remarking that the harlot's "quiuer is open to euery arrow" (6). The allusion is even more pronounced in the next line from "Jerusalem," where the arrow has enlarged/engorged into a "spear," and the quiver is the "unfolding clouds" of the female pudenda. "Fire" also has sexual connotations, suggesting inflamed passions. So this hymn purportedly about Christ's visit to the British Isles here becomes—thanks to the fawning and fondling female presence—something of a torch song full of probably unintended double entendres and sexual allusions. The mood has indeed changed, and will continue to do so for the singer (Idle) and the amorous girl (Katya Wyeth).

"British Dental Association"—("Secret Service Dentists") The BDA is the regulatory agency for the UK dental industry. This is one of the few times that an actual, active British organization is satirized, by name, in *FC*. Most of the time, the Pythons create a fictitious name for such things, perhaps to avoid litigation and/or libel entanglements. In Ep. 7, for example, a card that had been made to read "The President of British Footwear Ltd." was changed to "The President of Leisure Footwear Ltd."

bundle him out—(PSC; "Secret Service Dentists") Physically pushing him out the door (bundle meaning to go out in some disorder, according to the *OED*). Cf. the actions of the two interviewers in Ep. 1 who do the same to Arthur "Two-Sheds" Jackson.

– C –

"change the mood"—("Song [*And Did Those Feet*]") The mood will get sexually charged in the singer's next appearance when a woman (Katya Wyeth) appears and begins to fondle the singer (Idle).

"clever dick"—("Self-Defence") A smart, adept, adroit person (*OED*). In the "Top of the Form" sketch helmed by Cleese in *At Last the 1948 Show*, Cleese as moderator refuses to award points even as a contestant gives the correct answer, "Pyongyang," because the respondent is a "clever dick."

commissionaire—(PSC; "Undressing in Public") *OED*: "One entrusted with small commissions; a messenger or light porter; the designation of various subordinate employés in public offices, private businesses, hotels, etc., on the Continent." In an example of "the customer's always right," the commissionaire (Chapman) responds to the gentleman's mimed questioning by pulling his own pants down, a comic misunderstanding.

"Courtauld"—("Art Gallery") Small but influential gallery in Somerset House, the Strand, London. The Courtauld houses an impressive collection that includes Manet, Rubens, and Tiepolo. This comment also indicates that this particular scene is set somewhere other than the Courtauld, most likely the National Gallery, but perhaps the Tate Britain or Victoria & Albert Museum. The Pythons would use the facade of the Tate Britain (on Millbank) again in Ep. 32, when the "Tory Housewives Clean-Up Campaign" race in to cover up the obscene art.

cut-out animation—(PSC; "Sedan Chair" animated link out of "Self-Defence") Gilliam's technique of using bits and pieces of photos, drawings, etc., arranged on an animations stand or table, then photographed one frame or a few frames at a time. Animator Lotte Reiniger (1899-1981) had been working with cut-outs in silhouette in animation since as early as 1919, while Hans Richter (1888-1976) worked with cut-out shapes in the 1920s. Cut-out animation continued to be successful in Eastern Europe and the USSR into the 1960s (see Khitruk's *Man in the Frame* [1966]). Gilliam's professed inspiration for the cut-rate and experimental animation seen in *FC* is Stan Vanderbeek (1927-1984), an animator and collagist (*Gilliam on Gilliam* 38-40).

"cut to me"—("It's a Man's Life in the Modern Army) Playing the role of the tyrant (cf. T.W. Baldwin's typology in *Organisation and Personnel of the Shakespearean Company*), the Colonel (Chapman) can for a moment take control of the narrative, become the director, and move the narrative off in a different direction.

For an almost completely successful attempt at narrative tyranny, look at Richard's power in Shakespeare's *Richard III* as both maker and director, able to transform friends into enemies and foes into allies, and able to direct the plots around him (see *MPSERD*, chapter 6). This power endures until the demands of historicity and simply the completion of the play make sure that Richard falls. Falstaff also attempts to wield such power, boasting that his influence over Prince Harry-cum-King Henry is such that he is a "maker," and that he possesses almost godlike abilities. Falstaff to Shallow: "I will *make* the King . . . " (*HIV* 5.5.5-8). The Colonel's influence will be overcome by the nar-

rative, but the Colonel will have the last laugh, as he will eventually bring the program to a close, and even assist (off-screen) in tossing the "It's Man" back over the cliff.

– D –

"damsons . . . prunes"—("Self-Defence") A damson is a black or purple plum, and a prune is simply a dried plum. This is an early iteration of the Chapman/Cleese "thesaurus"-type sketch that will be seen in full flower by Ep. 33, "Cheese Shop."

dentist's gear—(PSC; "Secret Service Dentists") The Big Cheese is wearing all-black, form-fitting clothing, and looks more like Dick Shawn's character Lorenzo Saint DuBois (LSD) from Mel Brooks' film *The Producers* (1968) than a protoypical megalomaniac, à la a James Bond villain. Still, the chair, the furry animal, and the diabolical laughter and equally diabolical acting (cf. "Spanish Inquisition," Ep. 15) are present to conjure up images of Bond villains like the cat-lover Blofeld (Donald Pleasence) from *You Only Live Twice* (1967). The Big Cheese is also wearing lots of hippie-jewelry, including a large flower-power necklace, nudging him closer to the LSD character, as well.

"do your worst"—("Self-Defence") The supreme defensive challenge. Cf. the Old Woman being accosted by Arthur and Bedivere (over shrubbery) in *HG*. Also, see Jonson's *The Alchemist*: "Thy worst. I fart at thee" (1.1.2).

"Dresden Pottery"—("Art Gallery") Pottery from the Dresden, Germany, area where fine pottery products have been created since the seventeenth century. The city was nearly bombed out of existence in the last days of WWII as the Allies switched from strategic targets to all targets of opportunity, hoping to shorten the war.

– E –

Episode 4—Entitled "Owl-Stretching Time," which was one of the possible titles for the series, and was also considered as a possible title for Ep. 2, though it's still known by that title (in the WAC records). See the notes for "stretching owls" in Ep. 2, and Morgan, 1999, 49.

This episode was recorded 21 September 1969, and broadcast on 26 October 1969.

Additional folk not included in the cast list for this particular episode—but noted as being paid for appearing in the show in WAC documents—include Frank Littlewood, Albert Ward, Barry Took, and Peter Lovell. Littlewood appeared in the sci-fi TV program *The Escape of RD7* (1961). Albert Ward was a longtime

British TV figure, appearing in the radio and TV versions of *Welsh Rarebit* in 1952. Barry Took is given some credit for bringing all the Pythons to the BBC in 1969 for *FC*, and spent many years on BBC radio and TV as a writer and comedian. Peter Lovell was a production assistant on shows like *The Goodies*. Future episodes will include many more extras and walk-ons as the demands of the sketches increase and become more complicated and populated.

Still not convinced that they'd landed a winner in these earliest episodes, another John Howard Davies' admittedly droll memo referencing Ep. 4 reads somewhat unflatteringly: "The fourth episode of 'Monty Python's Flying Circus' stars as usual John Cleese, Graham Chapman, Michael Palin, Terry Jones and Eric Idle. More rubbish" (WAC T12/1,084).

One indicator of the uncertainty with which the audience and BBC were reacting to *FC* could be that Ep. 4 is *listed* as having gone to air "Mono," meaning monochrome, and not as a "colour" broadcast, as the first three episodes clearly enjoyed. This was the period when bemused befuddlement was the overarching reaction to *FC*, and many regions were opting out of broadcasting the show in favor of more attractive local programming. The WAC files contain memos of Pythons' concerns about unfriendly broadcast slots, as well as audience shares compared to other BBC shows (see WAC T12/1,082 through T12/1,094 for *FC* first series information).

An additional memo in the file for Ep. 4 is from Michael Mills (Head of Comedy, Light Entertainment Television, BBC) to Ian MacNaughton and JHD patting the show on the back ("very meritorious and very funny"). Mills does give some tips for better editing, and ends by assuring IM and JHD that the show is better than most anything else currently produced through Light Entertainment. The memo is dated 29 September 1969, about one week prior to the airing of the first episode (WAC T12/1,085).

"evil"—("Secret Service Dentists") Pronounced "ee-vil," with the schwa-sounding [i] replaced by the [i] as pronounced in "bid." Peter Sellers would use this same pronunciation in various character guises in *The Goon Show* (1951-1960).

"Excitement . . . Adventure"—(PSC; "Secret Service Dentists") The filmed black-and-white images that accompany each of these words are not accounted for in the WAC records of the episode or series.

explosion—(PSC; "Self-Defence") Undoubtedly part of Python's continuing satire on the nihilistic mentality of the military industrial complex of the world powers during this period. This same topic will be broached over and over again, including crime figures

shaking down Britain's weakened military in "Army Protection Racket" (Ep. 8), the proliferation of nuclear weapons ("Piranha Brothers," Ep. 14) in an era when Britain was relying on the United States for its nuclear deterrent, wars and rumors of wars ("Blood, Devastation, Death, War and Horror," Ep. 30), the increasing Chinese threat (Gilliam animation and "Bingo-Crazed Chinese," Ep. 34), the über-villain Richard Nixon (Eps. 5, 10, and 12; all written and recorded long before the Watergate revelations), and the soulless Soviet empire ("Mr. Pither," Ep. 34).

The *Beyond the Fringe* creative team had created a number of scathing Cold War skits in the early 1960s, as well, including "Civil War," "TV PM," and "Steppes in the Right Direction."

exposed again—(PSC; "Undressing in Public") This type of gag was Buster Keaton's stock-in-trade. In *Cops* (1922) he attempts an escape by climbing onto what appears to be a spare tire attached to a car. The car drives away, and we see that the tire is actually a display for a tire store. He also slips under a car to hide, and the car drives away, only to be replaced by another car before his pursuer can see him.

– **F** –

falling to the ground—(PSC; "Self-Defence") This lethality becomes the hallmark of the sketch, and is found throughout Python. Eventually, everyone in this sketch—including the RSM—is dead. The morbidity factor of Python's humor arose often from the troupe's attempts to "shock" or at least surprise the television audience, and must also be seen as a nod to the death and destruction seen on evening newscasts covering the recent civil and military disturbances around the world. In Ep. 8 the new recruit wants out of the military when he realizes that servicemen get "properly" dead; this could be a direct response to the Northern Ireland "troubles" featured on the front pages of all major English newspapers in 1969.

"Fighting Temeraire"—("Art Gallery") A lesser-known 1838 Turner work, it is fully titled *The Fighting Temeraire tugged to her Last Berth to be broken up, 1838*. This painting still hangs in the National Gallery, though it's considerably larger than depicted, and couldn't have been carried around by the Pepperpots. *The Slave Ship* (1840) is considered Turner's masterpiece by most art critics, though pedestrian art lovers rank "Temeraire" higher, according to the NG. In "Fighting Temeraire," J.M.W. Turner (1775-1851) is said to be depicting the decline of the British navy, which may account for Python choosing the painting for the sketch. It may also have been chosen simply because it was a well-known painting by a well-known British artist, and one that would have been (and still is today) the subject of lectures for visiting grade school students as they tour the National Gallery.

"fillings"—("Secret Service Dentists") In this parody, this mock epic, the Pythons have replaced the usual semantic elements of the spy thriller genre (international spies, nuclear weapons, microfilm, secret documents or tapes, etc.) with sillier items like fillings. They've even adapted the lingo ("appointment," "gas," "upper right two and four") from dentistry to tell their John le Carré, Alistair Maclean (or even Leon Uris) type spoof. In the usual Python genre-busting way, elements of American gangster films and pulp fiction novels also occupy this sketch, as will recognizable nods to Ian Fleming's "James Bond" novels and films.

"Flemish . . . Schools"—("Art Gallery") Flemish Renaissance masters include Jan Van Eyck (more interested in multi-surfaced, realistic detail), while Mannerists attempted to combine Gothic and Renaissance styles with very different Flemish and Italian traditions, and many of the masterpieces of the latter school are unattributable (see *Gardner's*). The Van Eyck painting *The Arnolfini Portrait* (1434) is later featured in Gilliam's animation in Ep. 6, at the close of the lengthy "Johann Gambolputty . . . " sketch. The Bronzino "An Allegory With Venus and Cupid"—from which Gilliam borrowed the famous Python foot—is an example of stylized, affected Mannerist painting. (This painting will reappear, touched-up and animated, in a Gilliam animation in Ep. 6.) The Tate, National Gallery, and V&A all offered significant Flemish and Mannerist pieces and artists (Bronzino, Tintoretto, El Greco) for the Pythons' reference.

"Flopsy"—("Secret Service Dentists") Character from Beatrix Potter's *Peter Rabbit* (1901). The rabbit depicted in the sketch is obviously stuffed, looking no more alive than will the attack rabbit in *HG*, and is reminiscent of the white cat fondled by several Bond villains. In another genre-busting moment, the gun the Big Cheese will use to shoot the rabbit is a shiny, long-barreled American six-shooter.

"Florentine"—("Art Gallery") Of or from Florence, Italy, including Raphael, who spent a short but important four years there (1504-1508). In the early fifteenth century, Florence was the locus of the learned and artistic world. According to historian John Symonds:

> Nowhere else except at Athens has the whole population of a city been so permeated with ideas, so highly intellectual by nature, so keen in perception, so witty so subtle, as at Florence. . . . The primacy of the Florentines in literature, the fine arts, law, scholarship, philosophy

and science was acknowledged throughout Italy. (*The Renaissance in Italy* 125)

The Pythons may have seen their London, and specifically their small digs at the BBC, as their own English version of that Florentine paradise. Florentine collections in the major museums and galleries in and around London had been significant and available for many years.

flunkey—(PSC; link into "Song [*And Did Those Feet*]") Originally, "flunkey" meant a male livery servant, with contempt implied (*OED*). Today, it refers to anyone who performs menial, drudge-like service.

– G –

"gelignite"—("Self-Defence") A blasting gelatin invented by Alfred Nobel, who also invented dynamite. Comprising a topical, news-generated item for the Pythons as they wrote the first series, gelignite explosive devices were the weapon of choice for Provisional IRA Campaign–type attacks beginning in 1969, and often directed at British targets. In August 1969 hundreds of homes and businesses were destroyed in sectarian fighting in Northern Ireland.

gilt frame—(PSC; "Art Gallery") A gilt-edged frame is one that is ornately adorned.

Girl in a bikini—("Undressing in Public") Probably walk-on Christine Young, as listed in the production records for the episode. This was shot on 10 July 1969 in Bournemouth (WAC T12/1,242). According to IMDb.com, Christine would also appear in 1970 in the television play *The Lie* (based on an Ingmar Bergman play), her only listed credit. (Where available, additional appearance credits for Python extras and walk-ons are primarily culled from the Internet Movie Database, as well as the British Film Institute archives.)

Graham knows the tune of—(PSC; link out of "Secret Service Dentists") Yet another unusual textual moment from the written scripts that would have no way of reaching any audience beyond the troupe and production personnel.

"greengages"—("Self-Defence") A type of plum.

– H –

hiss him—(PSC; "Secret Service Dentists") One of the few moments where the studio audience is brought in on the structured humor during the run of *FC*. Cf. "The Queen Will Be Watching" sketch, Episode 26. This hissing also flexes the genre boundaries even more broadly, this time to encompass staged melodramas, where black-attired villains were regularly hissed, and heroes and ladies saved were applauded. The English pantomime audience, for example, would have been well used to such participatory moments.

The hissing goes along with the "Gone, and never called me mother" sentiment from the *East Lynne* melodrama noted below (see "never called me mother" entry below).

Hotel—(PSC; "Undressing in Public") The name on the front of the building identifies this location as the doorway of the Palace Court Hotel, which is actually in the heart of London (64-65 Princes Square, London, W2 4PX). This shot would have been recorded after the Pythons returned from their countryside/seaside excursions for filmed segments.

– I –

"It's a Man's Life in the . . . "—("It's a Man's Life in the Modern Army") Slogan for the Royal Army (see Woodward).

Also, an LP entitled "This Is Free Belfast: Irish Rebel Songs From the Six Counties" would be recorded in 1971, featuring a new traditional song from the time of the "Troubles," "It's a Man's Life in the Army," an anti-Crown folksong.

– J –

"Jerusalem . . . time"—("Song [*And Did Those Feet*]") "Jerusalem" is a very English hymn adapted from a William Blake poem, with music by Charles H.H. Parry. The hymn is used several times in *FC*. Cf. Ep. 8, when bedding sales associates have to sing the hymn as an antidote to the utterance of the word "mattress." After the successful conclusion of the arrest in "Salvation Fuzz" (Ep. 29), the family is directed to sing this hymn, where it segues into the following sketch. The text of the hymn (from the Preface to *Milton: A Poem* [1804]) is as follows:

And did those feet in ancient time
Walk upon England's mountains green?
And was the Holy Lamb of God
On England's pleasant pastures seen?
And did the countenance divine
Shine forth upon our clouded hills?
And was Jerusalem builded here
Among these dark satanic mills?

Bring me my bow of burning gold!
Bring me my arrows of desire!
Bring me my spear! O clouds, unfold!
Bring me my chariots of fire!

I will not cease from mental fight,
Nor shall my sword sleep in my hand,
Till we have built Jerusalem
In England's green and pleasant land.

There is certainly a nineteenth-century and even Northern flavoring to the text ("satanic mills"). The text is dated 1804, and the music 1916. Its Englishness is apparent in the supposition that Christ visited England, thus Englishmen can lay claim to the Saviour (just like an Englishman can claim Shakespeare and Monty Python). Teeth aren't mentioned anywhere in the actual hymn.

– K –

"know what I like"—("Art Gallery") A paraphrase from several sources. First, Henry James' *Portrait of a Lady* (1881): "I don't care anything about reasons, but I know what I like" (ch. 24); and also (mentioned earlier) Max Beerbohm's 1911 novel *Zuleika Dobson*: "She was one of the people who say: 'I don't know anything about music really, but I know what I like'" (ch. 2).

Beerbohm (1872-1956) was a noted English author, parodist, and caricaturist (*ODNB*). His novel *Zuleika Dobson* was a burlesque of Oxford life, and should have been very familiar to all the Oxbridge Pythons. James' novel features Americans variously assimilating into English/European society, with the "hard, repellent" wife figure perhaps serving as inspiration for the women in this sketch, and Pepperpots throughout the Python oeuvre (Drabble, 1985, 780).

Samuel Courtauld (see entries for "Courtauld," "Rubens," "Utrillo," "Van Gogh") gathered his enormous and influential collection (1923-1929) based on his own emotional responses to the works, and admitted his intense subjectivity (see courtauld.ac.uk). Courtauld "knew what he liked," and, as it turned out, what he liked happened to be shared by both critics and patrons.

Victor Weisz (pen name "Vicky") produced a UK political cartoon in February 1966 depicting Soviet Premier Kruschev looking at a painting of PM Macmillan, with the caption: "'Well, I don't know anything about art, but I know what I like!' (The first major British art exhibition opened in Moscow yesterday)."

This phrase is also the trodden-upon punchline for the "Michelangelo" sketch in the Pythons' *Live at the Hollywood Bowl* concert film production.

– L –

"landscape artists"—("Art Gallery") British nineteenth-century landscape artists included names like Turner and the prolific John Constable (1776-1837). Constable's

The Hay Wain (1821) will figure prominently later in *FC*, in Ep. 25, when the central figure from the painting and many other painted figures go out on strike.

It's no surprise that the Pythons would choose these landscape artists for inclusion here. Both Turner and Constable separated themselves, to varying degrees, from the Italianate (or just continental) influence of the classical landscape, and, especially Constable, who focused on the English countryside for many years.

"Lemming of the BDA"—("Secret Service Dentists") There was a classic BBC serial produced on the cusp of the silent-to-sound era called *Lloyd of the CID* (1932).

"Libya"—("Song [*And Did Those Feet*]") The Cardiff Rooms would be the name of a lounge or restaurant setting at a hotel somewhere in Libya, perhaps Tripoli. Such venues would have been named after known, familiar locations in Great Britain, and would have attracted locals as well as significant numbers of nostalgic Brit expatriates working in the far-flung reaches of the Empire. Libya was promised by Great Britain in 1942 that the decades-long Italian rule would end and never reappear, and Libya became independent in 1952.

"loganberries"—("Self-Defence") A hybridized fruit created from the raspberry and blackberry. Created in 1881 in California, the loganberry is also grown in England.

looks slightly outraged—(PSC; "Undressing in Public") Here the man looks directly at the camera, acknowledging its presence. He isn't outraged that the camera (and, by association, an audience) is sharing his private space, but the supposed peeping tom does raise his hackles. This is again a nod to the silent comedy and even classic cartoon trope where the character looks at the camera and both acknowledges and implicates the audience.

– M –

machine—(PSC; "Undressing in Public") A nickelodeon "peep show" machine that holds either a loop of film or a series of cards, both of which would be turned by a hand crank. (The Edison versions featured early and cumbersome electric motors and light bulbs.) Both also work on the same principle of providing successive images to the eye to create the illusion of motion. The view we see (as recorded by the Pythons) is from a different angle and distance-to-object than could have been provided by the machine, and the image is even reversed. The "flickering" effect provided by this projected image is what gave the earliest films their nickname—"flickers."

This "What the Butler Saw" (Mutoscope-type) machine is a fixture at seaside resorts, and is also seen in

Osbert Lancaster's political cartoon of 16 July 1969 published in the *Daily Express*, where media campaigner Mary Whitehouse is lampooned ("You can save your money—I'd say at a guess that this butler must have been in service with Mrs. Whitehouse"). Whitehouse and her group would lock horns with the Pythons in 1979, as *Life of Brian* was being produced and then distributed.

"Malaya"—("Self-Defence") Actually, this was most likely learned from watching cartoons, where anvils and pianos and large rocks often fall from the sky and crush characters, including Blackie (Tex Avery) and Wile E. Coyote (Chuck Jones).

Malaya is now (and was at the episode's writing) called Malaysia (after 1963), is located in the South China Sea, and had a significant British presence until at least 1960. British troops and administrators were a significant part of that presence, since the beginning of the Communist (Chinese) guerrilla actions there in about 1948. Many National Service members just older than the Pythons would have served their tours of duty in Malaya during this postwar period, and many died in the hit-and-run attacks employed by the rebel forces (*Eyewitness: 1950-59*, "Malaya"). The many stirring accounts of British fortitude in the face of danger recounted in the newspapers and on the radio back home may account for the inclusion of Malaya and this RSM.

Spoofing the newest intercontinental ballistic missile (ICBM) technology sought by the British government in the 1950s, the Goons had launched a self-propelled guided NAAFI to British troops stationed in Malaya in "The Jet-Propelled Guided NAAFI" episode (24 January 1956). The Navy, Army, and Air Force Institutes were military canteens, where homefront goods could be purchased in far-flung locations.

"mangoes"—("Secret Service Dentists") A return of the fruit obsession from the earlier "Self-Defence" sketch. These are tropical fruits, and would have been imported during this period from former members of the Empire like India.

"Mazarin . . . Versailles"—("Song [*And Did Those Feet*]") Mazarin (1602-1661) was a cardinal (he followed Richelieu), as well as a tutor and minister to Louis XIV (1638-1715). Versailles is the massive palace built by Louis XIV, and was a palatial retreat for the French monarchy. References to Louis XIV (and XV and XVI) will reappear in Ep. 40.

"Mountains Green"—(link into "Secret Service Dentists") The glossing of "England's Mountains Green" as overtly sexual becomes much easier here, especially if "a man's life" is meant to include copulation. The color green has long been associated with sexual promiscuity and prostitution (Henke 114), hence

Spencer glossing "green women" as unchaste women (referencing *Bartholomew Fair* 4.5. 127-29). "Mountains" can be either (or both) the female's breasts or pubic area. See Sidney's *Astrophil and Stella* and his object of lustful affection's "Cupid's hill." Also, cf. the Gardens of Adonis in Spenser's *Faerie Queene*, where the "stately Mount" is just one erotic section of this highly sexualized landscape:

> Right in the middest of that Paradise,
> There stood a stately Mount, on whose round top
> A gloomy groue of mirtle trees did rise,
> Whose shadie boughes sharpe steele did neuer lop,
> Nor wicked beasts their tender buds did crop,
> But like a girlond compassed the hight,
> And from their fruitfull sides sweet gum did drop,
> That all the ground with precious deaw bedight,
> Threw forth most dainty odours, & most sweet delight.
>
> And in the thickest couert oif that shade,
> There was a pleasant arbour. . . . (3.6.43-44)

See A.C. Hamilton's edition of *The Faerie Queene*, as well as his *The Spenser Encyclopedia*.

For more on this more Ovidian Sidney and his connection to Monty Python, see notes to Ep. 36, "Pornographic Bookshop" sketch.

"Mr Apricot"—("Self-Defence") Further proof that the RSM has lost touch with non-fruit-related reality. The apricot is also mentioned in Ep. 3, during the defendant's soliloquy.

"my only line"—(link into "Undressing in Public") Cf. Ian Davidson's appearances in Ep. 19, where he asks if he can mention that he's currently appearing on television. Otherwise, in an example of Python's "equal opportunity" tenet (where they try and offend everyone), the male character here is ridiculed just as the female character was earlier, though the consequences for the male character aren't nearly as fatal as for the female. See Ep. 8 where the Art Critic (Palin) strangles his wife. The woman (Katya Wyeth), at least, was intelligent enough to deliver a pun. Also, this line is accurate, in that Gilliam was given very little to do in the performance of the episodes, especially in the earlier episodes, and especially with any speaking roles. If he appeared, it was generally in full costume (i.e., he played the knight in armor a few times).

– N –

"natter"—("Art Critic") To prattle, talk incessantly.

"naughty dentists"—("Secret Service Dentists") There are naughty chemists in Ep. 17, and they get their comeuppance as well. "Naughty" is a descriptor used constantly in *The Goon Show*, especially by Sellers (as Major Bloodnok and Henry Crun) and Spike Milligan (as Minnie Bannister).

"never called me mother"—("Secret Service Dentists") A phrase adapted from the nineteenth-century stage melodrama *East Lynne or The Earl's Daughter*, it is heard when the disguised heroine has returned home from her illicit romance only to have her formerly abandoned child die in her arms. The grief-stricken mother cries: "Gone! Gone, and never called me mother!"

Harry Secombe uses the phrase, as well, in *The Goon Show* episodes "Shifting Sands" (24 January 1957), and "Scradje" (13 March 1956). In these instances, sappy-violin-and-old-piano-style music ("Hearts and Flowers") accompanies the utterance, further supporting the "mellerdrammer" citation above. (In *FC* Ep. 11, the Goon word/name "F'tang" [from "The Call of the West," 20 January 1959] is borrowed several times, and including Eps. 17 and 18.)

The pervasiveness of the reference is reinforced by other mentionings in popular culture, including Dashiell Hammett's *Red Harvest* (1929), where the unnamed lead character compares the soap opera–type goings-on in "Poisonville" to something out of "East Lynne."

"never used to like Turner"—("Art Gallery") Equating art and food—both involve preferences and acquired tastes. The specter of the mass consumption of art is also addressed in Ep. 1, where Picasso races other artists, turning the relative singularity of a painter and his/her painting into a consumer-driven, mass-consumption form—a comment on the "acquisitive culture" that will reach its apotheosis in *FC* in Ep. 41. Walter Benjamin discussed this phenomenon—the loss of an artwork's "aura" and traditional "authority"—in his landmark essay, "The Work of Art in the Age of Mechanical Reproduction" (*Illuminations* 1968; also available in the third edition of the Mast and Cohen reader, *Film Theory & Criticism* [Oxford 1985]: 675-94.)

Python certainly violates the so-called natural distance that prior to the flowering of the Modernist period had existed between artwork and audience. They manipulate a reproduced image—segmenting, fragmenting, scrutinizing closer than the museum setting would ever allow. In this case, the characters get to actually *taste* the work of art, bringing to bear a sense that heretofore had no bearing on the artform or its appreciation.

This comment is also significant in that Turner himself and his work did, at least occasionally, suffer in comparison to others around and before him. In most of the texts written about him, he is described as taciturn and distant at best, and downright abusive when in a mood. His art would also cause an American investor to bemoan the artist's "indistinctness," so perhaps Turner was an acquired taste for many, including the Pepperpots in this scene (see Gage [1975] and Ackroyd [2006]). See the entry for Turner below for more on the influential English artist, and Herrmann's article on Turner in the *ODNB*.

"not good enough for you"—("Self-Defence") This "taking on airs" ridicule is seen in Ep. 33, the "Biggles Dictates a Letter" sketch, when Biggles' secretary quibbles with him over whether she's a "courtesan" or a "harlot." The same theme is also seen in *ML*, when the Sergeant-Major wants to march "up and down the square," and none of his men do.

"number was on that one"—("Self-Defence") A familiar colloquialism, primarily used in pulp fiction genres, meaning a lottery (or draft) number. The Third Man (Jones) is then rightly perplexed that one's number could be on something other than a bullet or the like—he's obviously familiar with the normal usage of the phrase. By Ep. 38, a character (played by Jones there, as well) won't be able to recognize a similarly colloquial and acceptable phrase, "No time to lose."

– O –

"out of them"—("Secret Service Dentists") Cf. the cheese shop without any cheese in Ep. 33, as well the Tudor job agency offering no Tudor jobs (Ep. 36). This is one of many attempted transactions in the *Flying Circus* world that will go awry.

– P –

Part 7—(Introductory link into "Song [*And Did Those Feet*]") *FC* often begins as if in medias res (Ep. 3 was numbered "12B" in the captions), probably a nod to the serialized histories (extended tellings of the Wars of the Roses, history of monarchs, etc.) available on British television and radio for many years. This structure will also apply to sketches throughout *FC*, where very few are allowed to play out to a logical conclusion, and especially to a punchline. And if the sketch involves a transaction ("Cheese Shop," "Dead Parrot," "Argument Clinic"), this same structural weakness almost always negates the successful transaction, sending the narrative, the customer, and the proprietor off into a completely new direction. In Ep. 22 the patient/customer (Chapman) manages to get the doctor/proprietor (Cleese) to agree to a homosexual encounter, but not plastic surgery ("Cosmetic Surgery").

The Monty Python feature films and live stage shows are a different matter. This same structure is more difficult, of course, in live settings, where the nature of the theatrical stage demands certain conventions—acknowledgment of the proscenium, opening and closing curtains, the inability to present inserts or cutaways at a moment's notice, etc. In these settings the sketches tend to dominate, naturally, and the stream-of-consciousness structure must necessarily recede. This is why the early feature film *And Now For Something Completely Different* (1971)—a collection of restaged and reshot (on film) sketches from the first two seasons of *FC*—seems to drag throughout, even though the funnier sketches are all included, and the performances are lively. What is missing are the quick cuts, the inserts, the interruptions from other sketches and characters, etc., that the television medium allows.

"passion fruit"—("Self-Defence") The edible fruit of the Passion-flower (*OED*). The Passion-flower is named after the final events in Christ's mortality, so the passion fruit could actually be a fruit associated with suffering and death. This fruit, along with many on the list of dangerous fruits, would have been imported from tropical and subtropical Commonwealth countries.

"peckish"—("Art Gallery") Hungry. Cf. the "Cheese Shop" sketch (Ep. 33), and the "Undertaker" sketch (Ep. 26).

"pig's life"—(link into "Self-Defence") Cf. Episode 1 (and just a bit of Ep. 2) for the well-traveled pig motif.

"Pip"—("Song [*And Did Those Feet*]") Python mentions a "Pip" (P.F. Jones) on several occasions, but almost always in relation to his more famous wife, tennis star Ann Haydon-Jones. Cf. Ep. 7, the "Blancmange" sketch, as well as notes to Eps. 19 and 22.

"pointed stick"—("Self-Defence") This becomes the Fourth Man's (Idle) hobbyhorse, as he'll keep coming back to it; he's not unlike Uncle Toby (Sterne's *Tristram Shandy*) in his fixations.

This reappearing motif isn't foreign to Idle, who also plays a Scotsman in Ep. 35 who barges into sketches and demands payment to not interrupt the sketch, while in Ep. 19 he'll drone on and on about tourists and Watney's Red Barrel in his tourist monologue.

"pomegranates"—("Self-Defence") Far from a threat, both the wandering children of Israel and the prophet Muhammad saw the pomegranate as the most desirable of fruits (*EBO*). The pomegranate is another fruit mentioned in the Self-Defence class that must be imported into the UK from former colonies, including Malaya, mentioned earlier.

"producer"—("Rustic Monologue" link into "Secret Service Dentists") Referring to the well-known gossip that many eager but undiscovered Hollywood in-genues had sexual relations with studio higher-ups to get a foot in the door. Less known would be the male actor being forced to sleep with a producer—but it wasn't unheard of. This may also be a questioning of this rustic's sexuality.

promenade—(PSC; "Undressing in Public") Paved area at the top of the beach.

pulls them up—(PSC; "Undressing in Public") Here a musical score reminiscent of silent comedy films begins. The music is played on a movie palace–type Wurlitzer organ, and the song is the "Colonel Bogey March" from *The Bridge on the River Kwai* (1957). (Performed by Reginald Dixon [WAC T12/1,085].) The film itself—though not black and white or grainy—resembles a Roscoe "Fatty" Arbuckle film from his Mack Sennett days (c. 1917). The action also appears to be slightly faster than normal, meaning either the playback has been accelerated, or the camera was purposely "undercranked" when the film was shot. Either way, it's meant to look like a silent comedy film, which would have been shot at about sixteen to eighteen frames per second.

– Q –

"**quinces**"—("Self-Defence") A yellowish pear-type fruit, also grown commercially only outside of Britain.

– R –

rabbit lying in his lap—(PSC; "Secret Service Dentists") This rather affected character with the associated affected performance (precise, exaggerated pronunciations, strange attire and mannerisms, etc.) is an interesting example of what Robert K. Jones described in his book *The Shudder Pulps*. The villains of the mid-'30s American detective stories began to overshadow the heroes, and the abominable nature of the villains (like Dr. Death) demanded a transformation of the hero. The so-called defective detective came about in response to these "weird menace" stories, and the morally, physically, ethically, or spiritually handicapped detective came to the fore (see Sam Spade's moral ambivalence in *The Maltese Falcon*, or Jeff Bailey's in *Out of the Past*).

Pythons' villain is of course an agglomeration of evilness from various genres, with a healthy dose of campiness, and the "hero" in this case is a dentist—not a detective at all. Garyn Roberts notes the penchant for pulp characters—both evil and good—to assume the characteristics of contemporary world leaders, with some adapting FDR's wheelchair-bound figure (see

Happenstand, Roberts, and Browne, *More Tales of the Defective Detective in the Pulps* 1-9). The most powerful man in the world, then, must be defective in some way. The Big Cheese appears in a chair, as do many of the early Bond villains—ruling from a permanently seated position. Python creates a whole host of "defective" characters—ugly Pepperpots, unassuming Pewteymen, Gumbys, pieced-together animations—who just happen to be able to function in narratively strong and significant ways.

"**Raphael's Baby Jesus**"—("Art Gallery") Perhaps referring to *The Madonna and Child* (c. 1508) or *The Madonna and Child with the Infant Baptist* (c. 1509-1510). Both Raphael works are displayed in the National Gallery; he and many other Renaissance artists painted similarly themed "virgin and child" pictures. Actually, considering the effects of time, pollution, misguided repainting and touch-up work, and even purposeful defacement, spilling ketchup on a painting might not be the worst a gallery could expect to endure.

"**rat**"—("Secret Service Dentists") Almost a quote from a 1928 issue of *Collier's*: "'You're a double-crossing rat,' I said" (18 August 1928). The terms "double-cross" and "rat" are aligned in a 1927 *Vanity Fair* issue where the term "rat" is glossed as "a double-crosser or a worthless person" (*OED*). No surprise, then, that the term would show up so prominently in the gangster, underworld, and pulp fiction–type films and novels of the late 1920s and through the 1940s. "Rat" is also glossed (in the *OED* and attributed to Lytton) as one who changes sides, so "double-crossing rat" is actually a doubled term.

"**roscoe**"—("Secret Service Dentists") Quite a specialized term actually, it is an American slang for "gun." Here the word is used by an obvious northern European (Van der Berg). In American gangster films of the 1930s and beyond, terms like "rod," "heater," "gat," even "bean shooter" are much more prevalent. (See the Hollywood gangster films *The Public Enemy* [1931], *Scarface* [1932] and *Little Caesar* [1931].)

One of the pulpiest of pulp fiction writers of the 1930s and 1940s, Robert Leslie Bellem (d. 1968), and his hard-nosed detective Dan Turner (in *Spicy Detective*), used the term "roscoe" constantly and seemingly without effort. Turner's milieu was the darker side of the Hollywood movie industry—fitting for the movie-like "Secret Service Dentist" sketch.

RSM—(PSC; "Self-Defence") Regimental Sergeant Major. Here he's (Cleese) even wearing his sergeant's stripes on both sleeves of his t-shirt. In Ep. 26, a hospital run by RSM-types features bandaged patients who have to work, perform calisthenics, and run races. Unlike their *Goon Show* predecessors, none of the Pythons served in WWII, nor would they perform National Service, meaning their "firsthand" exposure to such military types would have come through media depictions.

"Rubens . . . cherries"—("Art Critic") Peter Paul Rubens (1577-1640) was a Flemish Baroque master. As for fruit in his paintings, there are grapes in *Bacchus* (c. 1638), miscellaneous fruit in *Minerva Protects Pax From Mars* (c. 1629), and even an overflowing cornucopia in *The Union of Earth and Water* (c. 1618)—but not an abundance of cherries.

The Pythons may have been familiar with Rubens through both the commissioned ceiling painting, *The Allegory of War and Peace* (1629), found in the Banqueting House, Whitehall Palace, as well as the Rubens' works found throughout the National Gallery since the nineteenth century.

rustic accent—(PSC; link into "Secret Service Dentists") This does sound a bit like the rustic accent noted in Ep. 2, though the man is much less coarse in his dress.

The Rustic's aborted "rustic monologue" is perhaps an update of the pastoral-type piece that had become so popular in the seventeenth and eighteenth centuries in England, composed by John Gay and Alexander Pope, among others. That, or perhaps more akin to the rustic Scottish poetry uttered later in *FC* by the poet McTeagle in Ep. 16. See the note to Ep. 16 for more on this "coarse" poetry and its practitioners.

– S –

sedan chair—(link into "Song [*And Did Those Feet*]") Enclosed chair carried by two servants. This same chair and set-up will be used again in one of the *Fliegender Zirkus* episodes made for Bavarian television.

This short scene was shot near Covehithe, Suffolk on 21 August 1969 (WAC T12/1,083).

shale beach—("It's Man" link into "Song [*And Did Those Feet*]") Reminiscent of the "Famous Deaths" sketch from Ep. 1. The It's Man, however, survives the fall here at Covehithe (WAC T12/1,083). A shale beach is a beach consisting of shale, the most common sediment on Earth, as opposed to sand. Shale tends to fracture along horizontal planes, creating a very rocky, uncomfortable beach.

"sixteen-ton weight"—("Self-Defence") There appears to be no surviving record of this particular oversized, cartoon-like prop originally being requested from the BBC's property department. (Construction requests for other notable props—e.g., the giant penguin for "BBC Programme Planners," Ep. 38, or Mrs. Crump-Pinnet's green front door seen in

Ep. 14's "New Cooker" sketch—are extant in WAC records for the various series.) This is the first time the weight prop is used in the show. It may have been destroyed afterward to conserve storage space, as another sixteen-ton weight is requested (to be built) of the design department's "Construction Organiser" for use in the studio on 19 December 1969 (WAC T12/1,093). This new weight will be the prop seen in Ep. 12, when it will be dropped on a Presenter (Palin) and clearly broken. It was obviously broken beyond fixing because, on 2 July 1970, a request was submitted to have it repaired (WAC T12/1,242). The show was on hiatus at this time, after the final broadcast of the first series on 11 January 1970.

"sloppy . . . plagiarism"—("It's a Man's Life in the Modern Army") Could be Python's take on themselves. Idle wore shoulder-length hair throughout the run of the show, as did Gilliam, none of them performed National Service or served in the military, and they certainly felt free to pay homage to the parts of culture they liked, and to blast (by parody, satire) the parts of culture they didn't like.

"spits . . . again"—("Art Gallery") The Pepperpots' priorities here are clearly in place. Public defacement and vandalism are regrettable but acceptable, while spitting clearly is not. The amoral capabilities of the younger generation—including its propensity for violence and anti-social behavior—is an occasional trope in *FC*, since the Pythons obviously still considered themselves to be youthful anti-establishment types. See the letter in Ep. 5 where the writer bemoans the loss of appreciation for traditional values and blasts the "young hippies roaming the streets, raping, looting and killing." This is a fine line the Pythons have to walk, between becoming their parents and decrying the younger generation, and remaining true to the youthful arrogance they've obviously cultivated.

striped . . . flannels—(PSC; "Undressing in Public") The man stands out at the beach wearing the black-and-yellow striped jacket, the straw hat ("boater"), and light flannel pants. It looks more like a period costume than everyday beach attire. The boater is called such because it was originally used as a boater's hat. This same type of costume will be used again in the "*Salad Days*" sketch in Ep. 33.

striptease routine—(PSC; "Undressing in Public") The accompanying music is the well-known "The Stripper" (performed by David Rose and Orchestra), and Jones is performing in a sort of dinner theatre setting in front of a complete, purpose-built interior set (WAC T12/1,085). This is the "pier pavilion" (Bournemouth Pavilion) mentioned in the text, and can be glimpsed by name just before he enters.

swarthy—("Secret Service Dentists") Having a dark complexion, hair, etc.

"SW1"—(PSC; "Secret Service Dentists") London postal district, in this case the Westminster area, home to Parliament and, essentially, Her Majesty's government.

– T –

"Tarquin"—("Song [*And Did Those Feet*]") Perhaps a reference to Laurence Olivier's son, Tarquin Olivier, who would have been just a little older than the Pythons (b. 1937). Or, the noted painting *Tarquin and Lucretia* (c. 1695) by Giuseppe Maria Crespi may have influenced the Pythons, especially when the following scene ("Art Gallery") is taken into account. Shakespeare also mentions Tarquin often, especially in *The Rape of Lucrece*, where he is "[b]orne by the trustless wings of false desire, / Lust-breathed Tarquin" (stanza 1). The change of mood mentioned by the singer might account for this inflamed desire.

"tastes a bit"—(PSC; "Art Gallery") So destroying the paintings and sculpture isn't acceptable, but eating them somehow is? Perhaps the distinction lies in the utility of the acts—one is mere destruction, and the other is nourishment, consumption, even acquisition (in an endlessly acquisitive culture). The Visual Effects department at the BBC declined to build the edible painting, referring the Pythons to the Catering department, instead (WAC T12/1,085).

In Ep. 10, Ron Obvious (Jones) attempts to eat the Chichester Cathedral, cannibalism is discussed in Ep. 26, and there is also significant consumption in Gilliam's animations. In *HG*, cold weather forces Sir Robin to eat his minstrels, and in *ML*, Mr. Creosote is the über-glutton who takes one bite too many.

"terrible joke"—("Art Critic") This pun is actually no worse than any that the male Pythons have uttered, and actually fairly clever, but the female character here is singled out for derision, perhaps for violating the all-male club's rules by uttering a thoughtful witticism. The fact that she can pun may make her a threat, intellectually, to this boys' club.

terrible twitch on tic—("Self-Defence") This tic may be due to the ex-RSM's unpleasant experiences in Malaya, where British forces (and civilians) were constantly sniped and targeted for bombing, forcing families to live in concrete bungalows, drive armored cars, and generally fear for their lives every day, and especially at night in the dark jungle. The account given by Mrs. Dorothy Lucy of protecting her children and wielding a Bren gun against potential guerrilla ma-

rauders is representative of the tic-inducing life in colonial Malaya (*Eyewitness: 1950-59*, "Malaya 3").

"Thompson"—(PSC; "Self-Defence") Name of a fruit, as well, as in Thompson Seedless grapes.

tiger—("Self-Defence") The tiger appears again in the feature film *ML*, and there has taken a British officer's leg. The tiger here is obviously stuffed and mounted on wheels. This is also a somewhat rare example in *FC* of an actual, real-life predator (a wild, carnivorous animal) being used as a lethal—albeit stuffed—means of attack. Generally, it's the least likely animal (i.e., the rabbit) that poses the greatest threat in *FC*. The inclusion of the tiger indicates that the RSM may have actually served in Malaya, where tigers are endemic.

"tobacconist"—("Secret Service Dentists") Proprietor of a shop that sells tobacco (cigarettes, cigars), and sundry convenience store items. Tobacconists are featured in *FC* a number of times, including the "Dirty Hungarian Phrase-Book" sketch in Ep. 25, and the "Silly Walks" sketch begins in a tobacconist's shop (Ep. 14).

to camera—(PSC; "Secret Service Dentists") Moreso than Ep. 2's faux epilogue, this resembles an actual epilogue, where the show is wrapped up, the loose narrative threads brought together.

"ton of bricks"—(PSC; "Self-Defence") Actually, the usual punishment from above in Python is either a sixteen-ton weight or a giant hammer. See the following "Self-Defence" sketch. The phrase "ton of bricks" refers to the past dangers associated with walking near a brick-façade building under construction, when the bricks would have been loaded on a flat board and hoisted via a pulley system. Warner Bros. cartoons featured this type of punishment, as did Hanna & Barbera's "Tom & Jerry" series, and Tex Avery in cartoons like *Bad Luck Blackie* (1947).

trippers—(PSC; "Undressing in Public") Slang for resort visitors, vacationers.

trousers—(PSC; "Undressing in Public") This furtive "peeping" is exactly what social and moral activists feared the movies would lead to in the early days of cinema, when storefront nickelodeons were seen as inflammatory dens of lower-class iniquity. See Musser.

"Turner"—("Art Gallery") Joseph M. W. Turner (1775-1851) emotionalized nature (akin to a Romantic poet's literary work) in his English landscapes. Turner has consistently ranked at or near the top of "favorite artist" polls in the UK, being a favorite son for decades, probably for his attention to homegrown subjects and settings. Numerous Turner works have been on display in the National Gallery, including

Dido Building Carthage (1815) and *Sun Rising Through Vapour* (c. 1807), both part of the Turner Bequest of 1856. *The Fighting Temeraire* (1839), glossed above, was also part of this significant bequest. For more on Turner see the *ODNB*.

"two-timed me"—("Secret Service Dentists") The classic spy or film noir genre moment when a traitor is exposed, or a spy admits to counterintelligence, etc. In the film noir *Asphalt Jungle*, this type of exchange occurs when it's discovered that Emmerich (Louis Calhern) has double-crossed Doc Riedenschneider (Sam Jaffe) and Dix (Sterling Hayden). Gunfire, of course, erupts not long after, and both good guys and bad guys feel the "sting" of the coughing roscoe. (See the entry for "roscoe" above.)

– U –

"under the drill"—("Secret Service Dentists") This has become something of a euphemism for any kind of suffering, and here it replaces other similar genre devices in Bond films like the laser in *Goldfinger* (1964), or the rocket engine in *Dr. No* (1962).

"up against the wall"—("Secret Service Dentists") Probably a reference to the grisly St. Valentine's Day massacre in a Chicago garage in 1929, when men from Al Capone's gang killed men from Bugs Moran's gang over control of the illegal liquor trade (during Prohibition) in Chicago.

"Utrillo"—("Art Critic") Frenchman Maurice Utrillo (1883-1955) is known for paintings depicting the streets of his hometown Montmarte. Largely self-taught, Utrillo's brushwork was significant, as with "heavy, rich pigment he built up aging, cracked walls, often covered with large inscriptions" (*EBO*). The Art Critic is eating *Place du Tertre* (c. 1910), which is currently in the Tate Britain, and was originally purchased as part of the Courtauld Fund expenditures in 1926. See the entries for the "Art Gallery" sketch for more on these UK national collection purchases.

– V –

"Van Gogh"—("Art Gallery") Vincent Van Gogh (1853-1890) was a Dutch-born painter who worked as an "expressionist" of color. There are a number of Van Gogh works in London public collections, including *Sunflowers* (1888), *Self Portrait with Bandaged Ear* (1889), and *A Wheatfield, with Cypresses* (1889).

Courtauld funds (c. 1924) purchased most of the better-known continental "modern" art for the UK na-

tional collection, including Cezanne, Degas, Gauguin, Manet, Monet, Renoir, Van Gogh, and others. Thanks as well to the "National Gallery and Tate Gallery Act of 1955," paintings could be transferred back and forth between the museums, and may have been in either or both settings during this period.

"Vermeer's *Lady at the Window*"—("Art Gallery") Not actually the name of the painting in question (see below). Vermeer will be mentioned by the art critic later in this episode, and the name "Lady at a Window" is mentioned in Ep. 25 as one of the paintings gone on strike. Vermeer shouldn't have been included in a Renaissance or Mannerist schools exhibition, however, since he lived much later (1632-1675) and was known as one of the "Little Dutch Masters."

Jan Vermeer (1632-1675) lived and worked in Delft, and only about three dozen paintings have been ascribed to him. The National Gallery owns two Vermeer paintings, *A Young Woman Standing at a Virginal* and *A Young Woman Seated at a Virginal*, both c. 1670-1672. See the National Gallery's website for images of the paintings.

The painting in question is actually called *Young Woman with a Water Pitcher* (c. 1665), and has been part of the Metropolitan Museum of Art's (New York City) collection for more than 100 years.

"Vogler"—("Secret Service Dentists") Is this Arthur Lemming of the BDA betraying his real identity? To this point he's admitted only to being a tobacconist interested in books on false teeth, yet his is the first mentioning of "Vogler." None of the others notice the slip-up. There was a "Vogler" character (played by George Murcell) who appeared on the sleuthing show *The Saint* in 1963.

Vosburgh, Dick—(PSC; "Secret Service Dentists") An American actor and writer, Vosburgh (b. 1929) wrote for *The Frost Report* (1966) and appeared in *At Last the 1948 Show* (1967) and *How to Irritate People* (1968), working with several of the Pythons (especially Cleese) in both venues.

– W –

"Wait for it!"—("It's a Man's Life in the Modern Army") Standard military-type leader line in Python (and British cinema in general, as will be evidenced below. Cf. Episode 5, the "Confuse-a-Cat" sketch, as well as the crucifix party scene in *LB*.

This phrase is borrowed from many film sources, including the one movie produced by their comedy heroes, the Goons, called *Down With the Z Men* (1952). In a scene where Harry is mistaken for a new army recruit, he is hustled into rank, and a Sergeant readies the men for drilling. A dog barks offscreen, and the men mistake that for their Sergeant's command, and begin to move. He must call out "Wait for it!" several times before he is understood apart from the dog. The line also can be heard in the 1969 blockbuster *Battle of Britain*, when an old sergeant is maneuvering a squad of equally aged Home Guard types.

The Sergeant character in *Z Men* is very much copied by Palin for his drill sergeant portrayal in the feature film *Meaning of Life* (1983).

"Watteau"—("Art Critic") Antoine Watteau (1684-1721) was a Rococo artist influenced by the lyrical commedia dell'arte and French comedy. The studio audience seems to miss entirely the homonymic pun, though they respond to the throttling scene later.

Watteau's *The Scale of Love* (1715-1718) has been part of the National Gallery's collection since 1912, and the chalk sketches *Study of an Antique Statue—Jason or Cincinnatus* and *Two Monkeys in Costume, Smoking* were received in 1952. See the online collections information for both the Courtauld and National Gallery.

wellingtons—("Secret Service Dentists") A kind of waterproof boot designed by Hoby of St. James Street, London for the Duke of Wellington in the nineteenth century. Initially a mark of high fashion, even foppishness, the Wellington soon became the footwear of choice for the working middle class.

Also known as "gum boots," the "Gumbies" will sport Wellingtons as part of their uniform throughout *FC*, the characters appearing first (but not yet named) in Ep. 5.

"Whatever Happened to Baby Jane?"—("Secret Service Dentists") Play on the title of the 1962 Bette Davis film *Whatever Happened to Baby Jane?*, and based on the Henry Farrell novel.

"Wimpole St."—("Secret Service Dentists") The address 22a Wimpole is the home of the Barretts in *The Barretts of Wimpole Street* (1934, 1957). Also, cf. Ep. 32 where Lake Pahoe is actually located at 22A, Runcorn Avenue, and not 22 Runcorn Avenue.

Woman—(PSC; "Undressing in Public") This is a local woman, perhaps culled from the beachfront area as they shot, played by Joan Hayford-Hobbs of Bournemouth. The woman's "husband" in this scene is played by another local man, Philip Mutton (WAC T12/1,082).

working mothers—(PSC; "Art Gallery") Perhaps the "Pepperpot" term hadn't quite caught on by Ep. 4, since these two aren't dressed—nor do they act— much differently than Python's usual cross-dressed Pepperpots. The term "Pepperpot" makes its debut in an interview sketch in Ep. 2, the second episode broadcast but *written* as the first episode for the series. Whichever writing team (Chapman and Cleese, Jones and Palin, or Idle) contributed that scene seems to have coined the usage of the term for *Flying Circus*. They are officially called Pepperpots as early as Ep. 1.

– Y –

"You shot him!"—("Self-Defence") It's not often in the Python world that an outrageous act like this one actually gets noticed or commented upon, and is akin to the transvestite in Ep. 14 identifying him/herself as such.

Episode 5: "Man's Crisis of Identity in the Latter Half of the Twentieth Century"

"all evening"—("Erotic Film") The filmed sexually suggestive images are undercut by this admission, suggesting that the power of the image may occlude or even replace actual sexual experience. This sort of pop-Freudian allusiveness emerged between the wars, essentially, and worked its way into popular culture in movies, advertising, etc.

"All right!"—("Police Raid") Chapman's typical blustery entrance as a police figure. This characterization is perhaps in purposeful opposition to the most beloved TV constable available to the great British viewing public, PC Dixon on the long-running *Dixon of Dock Green* (1955-1973). Dixon (Jack Warner) was warm, considerate, helpful, and the epitome of quiet, folksy strength. Chapman often seems to go out of his way to be the opposite of all these traits. (An exception will be seen in Ep. 7, when Chapman's constable actually turns to the camera and utters Dixon's well-known catchphrase: "Evening all.")

animation—(animated link into "The Smuggler") During the animation sequence, Gilliam hums snatches of "Up, Up and Away," a song made popular by the Fifth Dimension (and written by Jim Webb) in June 1967.

applauding—(PSC; "Erotic Film") All these images are meant to suggest successful male orgasm, of course, and not female sexual pleasure. (And as it turns out, he [Jones] is the only one being "pleasured" in this sketch, and outside the sexual relationship, as well.) These types of images are borrowed from Hitchcock, whose well-known usage of similar images (train into a tunnel, fireworks) in *North By Northwest* (1959) indicated the sexual congress of the characters played by Cary Grant and Eva-Marie Saint.

The shot of planes refueling is a direct connection to the title sequence of Kubrick's *Dr. Strangelove* (1964), also suggesting copulation.

The inclusion of Richard Nixon was something of a running joke with the Pythons (and others, of course), especially since he was seen as unattractive and non-sexual, as compared to Jack Kennedy, for example. Nixon was mentioned earlier in Ep. 4, and will appear again in Eps. 10 and 12. Nixon had visited Britain in February 1969, and was lampooned in cartoons and caricatures in newspapers across the country (including, for example, *The Guardian*, 21 February 1969). See the British Cartoon Archive.

"Bagshot, Surrey"—("Letters and Vox Pops") Located southwest of London, adjoining the River Thames. It's not clear why the letter writer would address the letter to someone other than the BBC, unless it was a direct response to a/the previous letter, in this case from Mr. Grisewood.

"Bakewell, Joan"—("Erotic Film") Born in 1933, Bakewell was a presenter on BBC-2's *Late Night Lineup* (1964-1972). The Pythons will be admonished on 23 December 1970 by BBC higher-ups for "the further appearance of the programme team [the Pythons] on *Line-Up*, about which the producer" (JHD) hadn't informed superiors (WAC T47/216). Bakewell's TV work included shows at both the BBC and in independent television, with programs covering the arts, entertainment, and travel. Bakewell attended Newnham College, Cambridge, as did Margaret Drabble (see below for more on Drabble).

Bakewell is featured on the cover of the 29 November 1969 *Radio Times*.

battleship broadside—("Erotic Film") This is stock footage of a WWII-era battleship firing its large guns from the side, hence "broadside." There is no specific request for this footage in the WAC files.

"BBC Home Service"—("Letters and Vox Pops") The well-known 9 p.m. news (1939-1945) aired by the BBC attempted to provide accurate and honest information on the day's events during World War II, and was subsequently a bit of a thorn in the government's side. According to Wilson, Churchill consistently distrusted and attempted to corral the BBC during the war, calling the service "the enemy within the gates" (*After the Victorians* 429). According to Geoffrey Wheatcroft, this period ushered in the "golden age" of the BBC (*Atlantic Monthly* 287, no. 3 [Mar. 2001]: 53-58).

The cast of *Beyond the Fringe* had trod through this area in 1961 with their "Aftermyth of War" sketch, satirizing the alternating pluck and complacency of the British citizenry during WWII.

BBC Home Service would become Radio 4 in 1967.

"Berlin air lift"—("Letters and Vox Pops") Vital postwar (1948) military airlift conducted by the United States into Soviet-occupied Berlin. The Soviet Union had closed the only road across East Germany and into Berlin (administered by U.S., UK, French and Soviet forces in separate zones), hoping to squeeze the Allies out by starving the city of food, fuel, and supplies. Under the Marshall Plan, round-the-clock flights brought in everything a city would need to survive, until the Soviet and East German authorities relented.

"Bevis"—("Erotic Film") Cf. Ep. 9, where the lumberjack's girl (Connie Booth) cries about her formerly "rugged" boyfriend of the same name.

bowler—(PSC; "Confuse-a-Cat") A recognizable domed hat, it became the way to identify a "City Gent" in *FC* and earlier in the pages of *Private Eye*. In *Hard Day's Night* (1964), Paul similarly dons a bowler (and affects a posh accent) to make a "pull" on two young ladies in the dining coach.

boxer—(PSC; "Letters and Vox Pops") The boxer character has reappeared from the "Confuse-a-Cat" sketch earlier. He is perhaps attacking the somewhat stentorian woman as the Pythons' version of a dowdy, unattractive New Left female.

bra and pants—("Erotic Film") Cleveland is relegated to sexual object status again.

– C –

caber—("Erotic Film") A test of skill and strength and Scottish in origin, the caber is a large pole or spar, and is tossed. In Ep. 7, the surfeit of Scotsman forces the sharing of a single caber (which could be interpreted in a homosocial or homosexual way if we build on the image from the "Erotic Film").

"Camerer Cuss & Co."—(PSC; "Newsreader Arrested") This BP screen photo appears to be unretouched, and features the name of an actual business, Camerer Cuss & Co., founded 1788, and specializing in antique clocks and watches. The store was located in St. James's, London,

"Camp, Sandy"—("Police Raid") The pseudonymic Camp is referenced more than once in *FC*, including being noted as a "mighty fine director" by the Red Indian (Idle) in Ep. 6. (The Indian mentions that Camp is working at Leatherhead Rep.) This may also be an allusion to Sandy Wilson, a playwright who will be mentioned in Ep. 31, "Language Laboratory."

Also, the term "camp" may be important, as the man in question is both an artist (actor, director) and is in the company of another young man. The *OED* defines "camp": "Ostentatious, exaggerated, affected, theatrical; effeminate or homosexual; pertaining to or characteristic of homosexuals." So Sandy Camp may just be a catch-all name for the gay artist in Pythons work.

For the specific significance of this police raid in a celebrity's home, see the entry for "found on the premises" below.

cardinal hat—(PSC; Confuse-a-Cat) *OED*: The "cardinal" is one of the seventy in the College of Cardinals charged with electing the Pope. The cardinal's hat is a simple red skull cap.

"central London area"—("Newsreader Arrested") BBC's Broadcast Centre was built for BBC Radio broadcasting in 1932, and was completely torn down and rebuilt in 2005. Broadcast House (BH), as it became known, is located at Oxford Street and Regents Park, adjacent to Nash's All Souls Church. The building was heavily damaged by German bombs during the Blitz, and was significantly remodeled and expanded in 1961. Television Centre, where *FC* was recorded, is further from Central London, in Shepherd's Bush.

The BH building also purposely resembles a ship, and may have been an influence for the Python featurette *The Crimson Permenent Assurance* (1983), which features a Victorian office building that becomes a pirate ship. (See the feature film *Monty Python's Meaning of Life*.)

"check"—("Vox Pops" link into "Police Raid") This is another example of Python's use of these Vox Pops moments as smooth, almost effortless modes of transition between scenes. The character Sandy (Idle) moves fluidly from Vox Pop contributor to participant in the following sketch.

circle each other—(PSC; "Confuse-a-Cat") One of Thomas Edison's earliest films is known as *Glenroy Brothers* (c. 1895), a comic boxing match. Edison staged numerous such events for his electric-driven, static camera. Python (Gilliam) would refer back to early motion picture depictions of boxing, probably drawn from surviving Eadweard Muybridge photographs in Ep. 40, "The Golden Age of Ballooning."

Cleveland—("Letters and Vox Pops") This appearance for Cleveland (where she mentions Margaret Drabble) represents yet a second chance for a woman to "be one of the boys" and join in the humor. This will continue, to varying degrees, over the balance of the run of *FC*. Her usefulness as a sex object did not diminish, however, and she continues in that role as well.

crest—(PSC; "Confuse-a-Cat") This appears to be simply a BBC lorry, but the focus on a crest would indicate that it (the "Confuse-a-Cat" company) enjoys a Royal Charter, much like the BBC.

– D –

"dark days . . . wall"—("Letters and Vox Pops") Cf. Winston Churchill's address at Harrow School on 29 October 1941:

> Do not let us speak of darker days; let us speak rather of sterner days. These are not dark days: these are great days—the greatest days our country has ever lived; and we must all thank God that we have been allowed, each of us according to our stations, to play a part in making these days memorable in the history of our race. (Churchill Centre)

The stated age of this correspondent, 60, would have meant he was about 30 years old when war was declared in 1939, and thus eligible for military service.

"Dean, Michael"—("Erotic Film") Dean was also a presenter on *Late Night Line-Up*, along with Joan Bakewell, mentioned above. The other two members of the original *LNLU* staff were Denis Tuohy and Nicholas Tresilian (Vahimagi 129). Bill Cotton, BBC Light Entertainment, will later complain about the appearance of the Pythons on *Late Night Line-Up* (and, perhaps, the presence of a *LNLU* camera on the Python set), permission for which the Pythons had not asked or received (WAC T47/216).

"Distract-a-Bee"—("Confuse-a-Cat") Yet another "silly credits" motif, of which there will be many; see

the "Timmy Williams" sketch, Ep. 19, and *"The Black Eagle"* (Ep. 25), as well as *HG*. The bee would also figure into Python humor, with the "Eric the Half-a-Bee" song sung by Cleese and originally found on *Monty Python's Previous Record* LP (and now CD).

"Drabble, Margaret"—("Vox Pop" links) Noted British novelist and editor, Drabble was born in Sheffield, like Michael Palin, and attended Newnham College, Cambridge (graduating 1957, prior to Chapman or Cleese, both 1963). She joined the Royal Shakespeare Company upon completing university, where she understudied Vanessa Redgrave. Drabble's novels from this period include *A Summer Bird Cage* (1963), *The Garrick Year* (1964), *The Millstone* (1965), *Jerusalem the Golden* (1967), and *The Waterfall* (1969), and she also produced short stories and biographies (*ODNB*).

Interesting that rather than asking a lizard, the next best source would be author/historian Drabble, which seems a bit of a poke at the popular writer. Important as well is that this is really the first time in *Flying Circus* that a female character (played by a woman) is given a clever/funny line to deliver without some kind of textual, often violent retribution.

Dramatic music—(PSC; "Confuse-a-Cat" credits) The music clip here is "Action Station" by Dave Lindup, as played by the European Sound Stage Orchestra (WAC T12/1,086).

Drum roll and cymbals—("Confuse-a-Cat") The percussion accompaniment is played by Tony Taylor (WAC T12/1,086).

"duck, cat and lizard"—("A Duck, a Cat and a Lizard [Discussion]") The Montgolfier brothers—French balloonists later caricatured in Ep. 40—sent aloft a duck, a rooster, and a sheep in September 1783. Similarly, a section of the proposed Futurist film *Vita Futurista* (to be created by F.T. Marinetti) contained a section where "an argument between a foot, a hammer and an umbrella" was to take place (Weston 86). The Futurists were part of the Modernist movement, and were active in Italy prior to WWI. Marinetti also made a number of memorable personal appearances in the UK, touting the Futurist movement (Wilson, *After the Victorians*, 162).

"Dunkirk"—("Letters and Vox Pops") French beach from which thousands of Allied troops were rescued by civilian and military craft during WWII, May–June 1940. The name itself became a rallying cry, thanks to Churchill, to the unflagging sprit of the British people.

The Pythons, along with many their age, would have certainly grown up hearing this kind of litany from those that served during the "dark days" of the war, which is probably why it's being delivered here as more of a chanted liturgy than a rallying cry.

The grumpy man in *Hard Day's Night* (1964) who wants the train coach all to himself epitomized the sentiment:

Man (Richard Vernon): And don't take that tone with me. I fought the war for your type.
George: Yeah, and I'll bet you're sorry you won.

dustbin—(PSC; "Confuse-a-Cat") In this case, a large trash can. When two dustbins are presented moments later in the sketch, the scene looks very much like a performance of Beckett's Modernist and darkly absurd classic *Waiting for Godot*. (The play premiered in January 1953 in Paris.) The title of this third episode, "Man's Crisis of Identity in the Latter Half of the Twentieth Century" suggests yet another connection. Modern man's identity in an increasingly fragmented, technological world is a fundamental, vital concern for Beckett, certainly, and other Modernist figures of this period. In this world, successfully confusing a cat is the quintessential meaning given to the existence of these human characters—an absurd concept at which Beckett might have nodded approvingly.

– E –

"East Grinstead"—("Letters and Vox Pops") Located south of London in the Mid Sussex district. The BBC studios are/were not located in East Grinstead, an area which has for many years, by the BBC's own admission, been virtually ignored (as a news source or place of interest) because of its proximity to London. (See the BBC's history section on the southeast at tvradiobits .co.uk.)

"encyclopedia salesman"—("Burglar/Encyclopaedia Salesman") This gag is also found earlier in the satirical magazine *Private Eye* (1961).

Episode 5—This episode was recorded fifth on 10 March 1969, and broadcast 16 November 1969. Episodes 6-10 would be shuffled among themselves as the BBC tried to lift less-than-stellar ratings during this early period, though much of the problem could be blamed on the regional BBC entities opting for local programming instead of *Flying Circus*.

Early on, at least, the regions seemed to treat the show as a particularly and specifically *London* product, meaning a type of "city comedy" that might not appeal to (and may even offend) the historic counties. (This is ironic, in that none of the Pythons were actually from London, and the show did expend a great deal of time and energy mocking the life and people of London.) In the Elizabethan and then Jacobean city comedy, for instance, the wit and man-

ners of the metropolis—often in comic juxtaposition to the rustic, backward provinces—provide the mirth and satire. Playwrights Dekker, Lyly, Middleton, and especially Jonson worked in the genre, bringing to the stage "deeds and language such as men do use" (*Every Man in His Humour*) and especially men of the City. See Larsen's *MPSERD* for a discussion of Dekker and Jonson.

As late as August 1970, all regions outside of the Greater London area were still intermittently opting out of *FC* transmissions according to BBC records (WAC T47/216).

"Esher"—(PSC; "Confuse-a-Cat") A part of Greater London, located on the southwest corner of the city's outskirts. Most of this sketch (the filmed portions), however, was shot at or near 20 Edenfield Gardens, Worcester Park, Surrey on Monday, 18 August 1969 (WAC T12/1,083). In Ep. 36, Esher is the site where orgies seem to happen without much fuss, according to the "Man Who Says Words in the Wrong Order" (Palin). The city of Esher is mentioned in Eps. 5, 8, 28, 36, and 39.

"Excuse me a minute"—("Newsreader Arrested") This multivalent moment is a very nice example of Python playing with the conventions of not only TV, but the supposed sanctity of time and space. And since the new Newsreader (also Idle) on the screen has taken over the balance of the newscast, it must mean that we from thence onward are watching the goings-on in the world of the BP screen, and not the original news set. There is a bracketed time and space inferred here, not unlike the layered brackets of time exhibited in Bergman's influential film *Wild Strawberries* (1960). (Very aware of the various New Waves and important film directors of this period, the Pythons will imitate the famous final scene from Bergman's *The Seventh Seal* [1957] in Ep. 7, "Science Fiction" sketch, and skewer the perhaps more self-important French Nouvelle Vague directors like Godard in Ep. 23, the "French Subtitled Film.") The influence of Alain Resnais' enigmatic and difficult 1962 film *Last Year at Marienbad* is also felt here.

– F –

"fairy"—("Vox Pops" link into "Police Raid") Once again, using effeminating names as put downs, part of the "othering" process of Python. Cf. the Biggles sketch in Ep. 33.

fast motion—(PSC; "Confuse-a-Cat") Filmed action exposed at fewer than twenty-four frames per second (for sound film), meaning the camera is "undercranked," which makes motion appear faster than natural when projected. Silent film would have run about sixteen to eighteen fps. See "jerky motion" note below for more.

fez—(PSC; "Confuse-a-Cat") A wool or felt cap. Several Gilliam-drawn characters will be depicted wearing fez in the first *FZ* episode in 1971, as the "Albrecht Dürer" story is morphed into a more Middle Eastern version.

"found on the premises"—("Police Raid") This sketch is likely a composite reference to several much-celebrated celebrity arrests in 1968-1969:

1. In 1968, John Lennon—a Python acquaintance— was arrested by Police Sergeant Norman Pilcher for drug possession. Lennon would later say he was framed by Pilcher
2. On 12 March 1969, George Harrison (who would later help finance *Life of Brian*) was arrested at home by Sergeant Pilcher (using police dogs), and more than 100 marijuana cigarettes were found. Harrison claimed a frame-up by Pilcher, as well
3. And finally, the 1969 arrest of Mick Jagger (and then-girlfriend Marianne Faithfull) in Jagger's Chelsea flat for drug possession.

According to Jagger, local drug interdiction officer Detective Sgt. Robin Constable burst into Jagger's apartment, planted drugs, "found" them, and made an arrest. Jagger then said that Constable told him not to worry, that they could "sort it out," and a bribe of about $1,900 (£1,000) was allegedly solicited. Jagger was eventually fined about $200, and the police stood by their story of possession on Jagger's part, and found no malfeasance on Constable's part (see the National Archives, August 2005).

There was also, in fact, a police dog trained to sniff out drugs involved in the Jagger arrest. According to an affidavit in the National Archives, the dog handler was Sergeant Shearn. As for Pilcher, he would be indicted in late 1972 for planting evidence in other, unrelated cases and sentenced to more than four years in prison. (Pilcher's drug-sniffing dog was allegedly named "Willie.")

Tertiarily, there is also the case of Det. Sgt Harry Challenor, a West End Central officer who over a five-year period (c. 1958-1963) planted evidence of all sorts on myriad arrestees, and was eventually found to be schizophrenic and unfit for trial. (This characterization may have influenced the Pythons' rather loopy version of PC "Pan Am" in Ep. 17, also played by Chapman.) The fact that Challenor was a practicing and influential Freemason led many to believe that his psychiatric sentence as opposed to prison time was a fraternal favor. See freemasonrywatch.org

for more. For the Pythons' take on Freemasonry, see Ep. 17, as well.

"Fulham"—("Newsreader Arrested") An inner borough of London, home to Fulham Palace (early sixteenth century), the residence of the bishops of London until 1973, and now a museum. The BBC is headquartered in the Hammersmith and Fulham area.

(Incidentally, when the BBC studios were built in the Shepherd's Bush-White City area, corporation executives were adamant that "White City" not be used as the corporate address in internal communiqués—due to the BBC's acronym habit [i.e., Television Centre becomes "TC"]—as they didn't want to be constantly saying the BBC was in the "WC.")

– G –

"Gedderbong"—("Confuse-a-Cat") Also used in Ep. 18, as the Master of Ceremonies (Palin) introduces the combatants in the Ken Clean-Aire Systems (Cleese) fight. Gedderbong is slang for "gentlemen." Goon Harry Secombe uses the term in the episode "The Last Tram (From Clapham)" (23 November 1954) as he introduces the show.

"give the wife?"—("Police Raid") One of the few actual punchlines delivered, sans retribution or undercutting, in all of *FC*.

"glib"—("The Smuggler") Probably a reflexive moment, commenting on the writing, and not on the Man's (Palin) choice of words, per se. But if this can be construed as commenting on the comment itself, it could be that the Officer (Cleese) is reminding the traveler that he's in no position to be glib at all.

"Grisewood"—("Letters and Vox Pops") Peter Grisewood was an actor in the popular *Quatermass and the Pit* TV series (BBC, 1958). A tad closer to home, the BBC Third Programme planner and eventual Controller during the Pythons' early lives was Harman Grisewood (1906-1997), who is credited with creating *The Money Programme*, which will be satirized by the Pythons in Ep. 29. Grisewood left the BBC for *The Times* in 1966, and was much talked about in the press of the time (*ODNB*).

– H –

"helping police"—("Newsreader Arrested") Cf. Gilliam's later film *Brazil* (1986), where those under suspicion are "invited" by Ministry of Information officials to assist police in their investigations. In other words, it is a very polite euphemism for what might become a very unpleasant situation.

This isn't unusual language in the UK, especially in newspapers and on television. Duncan Campbell begins his report on a very recent "cash-for-peerages" scandal with the following: "One of the most enduring expressions in British policing is the phrase 'helping with inquiries.' A delicate euphemism, it can usually be taken to mean the exact opposite of what it says" (*Guardian Unlimited*, 1 February 2007). More to the Pythons' period, when the Kray brothers were arrested in 1968, the BBC reported the following:

> They [Ronnie, Reggie and Charlie Kray] are among 18 men currently being held at West End Central police station *helping with inquiries* relating to offences including conspiracy to murder, fraud, demanding money with menaces and assault. (news.bbc.co.uk/onthisday/hi/dates/stories/may/8/newsid_2518000/2518695.stm. Accessed 5 February 2007.)

For much more on the Krays, see notes to Ep. 14.

– I –

"I didn't want to be a barber anyway . . . "—("Lumberjack Song") This "bad faith" moment is a Sartrean concept, where the "waiter" is unhappy serving bourgeois customers, and therefore abusive—he wants to be an "artist," instead. See notes for Ep. 13, "abuse you" for more on the conceit.

"I'm sorry, I'm confused"—("Silly Job Interview") In this and other sketches like it—e.g., "Buying a Bed" (Ep. 8), and "Police Station (Silly Voices)" (Ep. 12)—the newcomer stumbles into a world he/she cannot comprehend, with lack of meaningful communication often the most obvious sign of this confusion. In all three, however, the novitiate can learn the rules that govern the world of the sketch and, with practice, even function in that world. Arthur and his knights learn how to deal with the Knights Who Say "Ni" in the same way.

"innit"—("Vox Pops" link) Vulgar form of "isn't it."

into shot—(PSC; "Erotic Film") As a nosy Scotsman, Idle will interrupt sketches in Ep. 35, and Chapman's "Major" character will interrupt "silly" sketches many times in the series.

During "The Flea" episode of BBC Radio's *The Goon Show*, announcer Wallace Greenslade steps in front of the action twice to remind the audience that actual fleas are not being used in the program.

– J –

jerky motion—(PSC; "Confuse-a-Cat") What's shown here is a mishmash combination of both fast motion and jump cut—several short shots of an object in different positions presented in quick succession (a man "sliding" across stage without walking). The camera is turned on and off, exposing a few frames when the figure is in the desired position, then moving the figure, exposing a few more frames, etc. Scottish-Canadian filmmaker Norman McLaren pioneered this technique in the groundbreaking "pixilated" film *Neighbours* (1952). See the note for "pixilated motion" below.

"jolly good laugh"—("Careers Advisory Board") This indicates that we might have been watching a promotional or training film, the kind of work that Cleese would move to (corporate training video) in the late 1970s. Cf. the currency discussion earlier between stuffed animals that followed on the heels of the customs sketch.

jump cut—(PSC; "Confuse-a-Cat") A filmmaking term used to describe when something is filmed with a break in time—but appears to happen in real time—so that the action appears to "jump" impossibly to a new position. This phenomenon was reportedly "discovered" by French magician-turned-filmmaker Georges Méliès (1861-1938). See entry for "various tricks" below.

– K –

"killing"—("Letters and Vox Pops") Perhaps a reference to the recent student riots seen in 1968 in Paris, the civil unrest in New York and Los Angeles of the same year, as well as many large cities globally, and the general increase in visibility of the "hippie" generation.

– L –

"Less race prejudice"—("Letters and Vox Pops") This "child on the street" interview format is also seen in Ep. 3, where the "children" request Idle's "Nudge, Nudge" sketch.

Also, this moment draws on the still-current racial unrest in the United States (specifically, riots in Watts [Los Angeles], in 1965 and Washington, D.C., in 1968, to name two), the race-related unrest in the "Asian" and "Caribbean" neighborhoods of Greater London (including Notting Hill in the late 1950s), and might also refer to the religious "troubles" rising in Northern Ireland.

"Liddell, Alvar"—("Letters and Vox Pops") A respected BBC newsreader (1908-1981), Liddell was certainly known to the Pythons for his radio presence during the dark days of WWII, his guest appearance in 1968 on the popular *Dad's Army*, as well as his mention in the "Aftermyth of War" sketch from the *Beyond the Fringe* cast, "when, every night at nine o'clock, Alvar Liddell brought us news of fresh disasters."

See the entries for "BBC Home Service" and "Dunkirk" for more.

locked camera—(PSC; "Confuse-a-Cat") When a camera head is fastened to its mounting so that it will not move (pan, tilt, etc.), it is then "locked down." The locked, immobile camera is necessary for animating, or exposing one or a few frames at a time. The images would be far less stable if the camera head were allowed to remain loose during the pixilation sequences.

Long John Silver—(PSC; "Confuse-a-Cat") Character from Robert Louis Stevenson's novel *Treasure Island* (1883). The characterization here looks very much like it is patterned after Disney's 1950 film version, starring Robert Newton as Long John Silver. And either the costume was easy to come by (in the BBC's costume shop) or, thanks to the very popular Christmastime *Treasure Island* pantomime, Long John Silver loomed large in the Pythons' collective juvenile impressions (along with the Pantomime Goose, the Pantomime Princess Margaret, and Dobbin the Pantomime Horse). (See the entries for panto characters in Ep. 30.) This iconic pirate appears in multiple *FC* episodes, including Eps. 10, 23, 25, and 32, and is further mentioned in audio sketches on Python LPs.

Pantomime performances had been staples of the BBC's Christmas Day broadcast line-up for many years, airing in the early afternoons (usually around 2:15 p.m.) since at least 1956, when both *Puss in Boots* and *Pantomania* (featuring *Dick Whittington*) aired in the afternoon and evening, respectively (*TV & Radio Bits*). In the years that followed, *Babes in the Wood* (1957), *Puss in Boots* (1962), *Dick Whittington* (1963), *Robinson Crusoe* (1963), *Mother Goose* (1965), *Aladdin* (1966), *Cinderella* (1967), and *Humpty Dumpty* (1968) aired.

– M –

"Match of the Day"—("Newsreader Arrested") A sports show featuring regularly scheduled portions of a selected football match and commentary that premiered on BBC2 in 1964, then moved to BBC1 in 1966. *Match of the Day* would become a fixture on British television for many years.

– N –

Napoleon—(PSC; "Confuse-a-Cat") The standard pose for depictions of Napoleon Bonaparte is hand in vest, and in full military uniform. Napoleon also appears in Ep. 2, the "Mouse Problem" sketch, where he pulls a wedge of cheese from his vest and takes a bite.

"No"—(PSC; "A Duck, a Cat and a Lizard [Discussion]") For a very similar "no response" response in this same interview format (in fact, identical), cf. Ep. 36, where dead men are interviewed.

– P –

penguin—(PSC; "Confuse-a-Cat") Significant to Python's bestiary, penguins in Ep. 38 are proven to be more intelligent than BBC program planners; and in Ep. 22, a penguin atop a TV set explodes. There is also a giant, tentacled, marauding penguin in Ep. 23. The prominence of Penguin Books in the UK as the Pythons grew up may help account for the presence of penguins. A Penguin title is clearly visible in the book rack during the "Secret Service Dentists" sketch in Ep. 4.

A satirical personal ad from the pages of *Private Eye*: "Old Penguins required by senile bird fancier and pervert" (Friday, 13 May 1966).

pixilated motion—(PSC; "Confuse-a-Cat") Photographing an image frame by frame, resulting in moving, seemingly "animated" objects, etc.

This type of animation (pixilation) is also called "stop-motion" animation, and is used again in Ep. 20 as furniture and appliances race at Epsom. The technique was utilized in animation by J.S. Blackton (*Haunted Hotel*, 1908), then Georges Méliès (fl. 1902-1912), and Ladislaw Starewicz (fl. 1912-1925). Scot-Canadian animator Norman McLaren would employ human figures in his pixilated animations as early as the 1940s, culminating in the celebrated *Neighbours* (1952). This particular work seems to be the predominant influence on the Pythons, as much of their animation work here very much resembles McLaren's "full body" pixilation.

pogostick—(PSC; "Confuse-a-Cat") Spring-loaded pole with foot rests, designed as a bouncing toy. In another early cinema connection, *Punch* magazine reported in 1921 that Charlie Chaplin intended to donate a pogo stick to each child attending the schools he'd attended in England.

"popularity"—("Letters and Vox Pops") This is spoken by a City Gent, obviously representing the monied, business-enriched Conservative sector of the country. This callous, money-class characterization appears throughout Python, and is reminiscent of Voltaire's character Pococurante (meaning "small care"), who—after laying waste to women and fidelity, the art of Raphael, eighteenth-century music and drama, Homer, Virgil, Horace, Cicero, the sciences, and Milton—justifies his malaise-tinged opining: "Anyhow, I say

what I think, and care very little whether other people agree with me" (ch. 25). (Voltaire has already been mentioned admiringly by the supermarket Pepperpots in Ep. 1.)

Enoch Powell and the more arch-conservative Tories of this period fit this mold, speaking strongly against immigration and foreigners on welfare rolls for the good of the country, as they would say, and not to court popularity. In June 1970, Tony Benn (b. 1925) spoke out against the Enoch Powells of the world, and against Powell and the Conservatives specifically:

> The flag of racialism, which has been hoisted in Wolverhampton [Powell's constituency and Idle's schoolboy home], is beginning to look like the one that fluttered twenty-five years ago over Dachau and Belsen. And if people don't speak up against filthy and obscene racialist propaganda still being issued under the imprint of the Conservative Central Office, by an official Conservative candidate, then the forces of hatred will mark up their first success, and mobilize for their next offensive. (audio transcription from *Eyewitness: 1970-79*, "Racial Discrimination and Immigration")

It was also this very refusal to court popularity that served Churchill so well in the "dark days" of the war, but served to alienate him from his cabinet, party, and the postwar populace—and he was soundly voted into the opposition (Wilson, *After the Victorians* 484-87).

"pre-sexual revolution"—("Letters and Vox Pops") Characteristic of the changing times, this intellectual female journalist spouts the key terms of the late '60s and early '70s, calling for the shrugging off of the last vestiges of so-called Victorian morality. Being a sort of "stuffed blouse" she gets punched in the face for voicing her opinion.

"Profumo case"—("Letters and Vox Pops") John Profumo, EII's Secretary of War (1960-1963), caused a scandal by having an affair with a prostitute who also happened to be seeing a Soviet naval attaché. The scandal and repercussions nearly toppled the sitting Macmillan government. See entry for Ep. 2, "Mouse Problem" sketch, for much more. There are also, not suprisingly, hundreds of extant political cartoons treating this sordid and entertaining subject (see the British Cartoon Archive).

proscenium—(PSC; "Confuse-a-Cat") The curtain, as well as the arch and framework holding the curtain up. This is an acknowledged, staged show, so the proscenium is not only visible, but expected.

– R –

"racialist"—("Vox Pops" link) Racialism is a belief in one's own superiority to another race to the end that living anywhere near "others" can be threatening, in essence. A racialist, then, would be one who practices or believes in racialism. In this case, it's curious that this Gumby somehow connects the eating of rodents to those who travel abroad.

Connecting this to the then-recent (April 1968) "Rivers of Blood" speech delivered by Enoch Powell (see entry for "taxpayers' expense" below) is possible through Conservative leader Edward Heath, who eventually called Powell a "racialist" when the storm over the inflammatory speech refused to subside, and finally sacked him. The Conservatives were still able to return to power in 1970, and under Heath.

This rift between Heath and Powell was also featured on the cover of the satirical magazine *Private Eye* on 19 June 1970. Heath and Powell sit next to each other at a dais:

> Heath: I give up. What is white and mad, sees blacks and reds all over the place and stabs me in the back at the last minute?
> Powell: (grinning) ME!

Private Eye was, of course, satirizing British culture and political figures, but also performing some first-rate investigative journalism. According to Bourke, the magazine welcomed hot potato stories the traditional press couldn't, including exposé work on the Ronan Point disaster (Ep. 17), early reporting on the Krays (Ep. 14), and Reginald Maudling's financial improprieties ("*Private Eye*" on BBC Audiobook *Eyewitness: 1960-69*).

recovers—("Careers Advisory Board") Chapman and Cleese both endured career changes. Chapman had qualified to practice medicine, and Cleese was on his way to a life in the courts as a barrister when both surrendered those careers for work on stage and in television. See Morgan *Speaks!* and McCabe's *The Pythons*.

– S –

"satire"—("Letters and Vox Pops") Which is, of course, what Python is doing, and how, for example, Doug Piranha will inspire fear in the London underworld in Ep. 14, causing grown men to "pull their own heads off" rather than face his sarcasm.

"Ned Sherrin"—Sherrin (b. 1931) was producer of *That Was the Week That Was* (1962, 1964-1965), the current events comedy show where Cleese had worked as a writer.

sedan chair—(PSC; "Confuse-a-Cat") In Ep. 4, a well-dressed eighteenth-century gentleman (Idle) arrives at the beach in a sedan chair, emerges, strips to his trunks, then gets back into the chair and is carried into the water. The sedan chair will reappear in the second episode of *Fliegender Zirkus* (1971), the two episodes written and recorded for Bavarian TV.

Several people get out—(PSC; "Confuse-a-Cat") The "crew" setting up the Confuse-a-Cat stage includes Palin, Idle and Jones, and also Len Howe (*The Professionals*), Marcelle Elliott (*Dr. Who*), and Ian Elliott (*Paul Temple*) (WAC T12/1,086).

"silly billy"—("Vox Pops" link into "Police Raid") *OED*: "A foolish or feeble-minded person; used specifically as a nickname of William Frederick, Duke of Gloucester (1776-1834), and of William IV (1765-1837)." Given the term's etymology, it's not clear why a French au pair (Cleveland) would use it.

stage whisper—(PSC; "Confuse-a-Cat") Loud enough to be heard by an audience; a purposely loud whisper.

Stetson—(PSC; "Confuse-a-Cat") John B. Stetson (1830-1906) was an American hat manufacturer whose broad-brimmed hats became popular in the American West, and became popularly associated with cowboys and the frontier life. The Southerner (Cleese) in Ep. 2 wears a black Stetson-type hat, as do the characters in the Dodge City version of "Albrecht Dürer" in the first FZ episode.

This obvious Americanism would also have run afoul of the BBC's "Variety Programmes" handbook, as well, as it makes it very clear that both making fun of Americans and adopting Americanisms is out of bounds. The goal was to keep the BBC from being culturally pillaged by the attractive and surging American culture already occupying the majority of England's movie screens, magazines, and music venues. See Barry Took's *Laughter in the Air* for more/most of the contents of the handbook.

"Stig"—("Silly Job Interview") The term (from Old Norse) actually means "to start in alarm," which comes pretty close to the character's reactions in this sketch. It is also perhaps an oblique reference to the work of Stig Kanger, a Swedish philosopher who was interested in logical necessity, possibility, and behaviors (*EOB*). The Stig in the sketch has a very difficult time following (perceiving, interpreting) the logic of his interviewer's actions.

Most likely, however, this is a casual reference to the character "Stig" from the very popular children's book *Stig of the Dump*, written by Clive King, and first published in the UK in 1962. King had graduated from Downing College, Cambridge, just as Cleese would later.

A "Stig O'Tracy" will appear as a character (played by Chapman) whose head is nailed to the floor by Dinsdale Piranha in Ep. 14.

"stoat"—("Confuse-a-Cat") The European ermine, just one of the many small animals tossed into Python's mix regularly. The stoat is also mentioned a number of times—all in silly ways—in the pages of *Private Eye*.

"stockbroker syndrome"—("Confuse-a-Cat") *Not* a reference to the Stockholm Syndrome, or the tendency for captives to bond with their captors during a period of detention, since that term wasn't coined until 1973. Instead, this is a clever turn-of-a-phrase that proffers a medical explanation for a career choice, and is akin to the gibing that chartered accountants receive in the Python oeuvre, as well as stockbrokers (see "Dull Life of a City Stockbroker" in Ep. 6). This phrase begins a short "thesaurus" moment endemic to Chapman and Cleese's team writing.

stove-pipe—(PSC; "Confuse-a-Cat") A tall, cylindrical hat, the description of such a hat is originally American. President Abraham Lincoln (see Ep. 1, "Famous Deaths") wore such a hat, as do a number of characters in the animated film *The Yellow Submarine* (1968).

"strip"—("The Smuggler") Vicars and churchmen in general are almost always suspect in the Python oeuvre, just as they were for Ben Jonson, Voltaire, and similar.

In *FC*, vicar-types dip into church funds, engage in perverse "mouse" activities, are entrées ignored by the careful diner, act as henchmen for bishops, keep nude ladies, drink gallons of sherry, etc. On *The Contractual Obligation Album* (LP, 1980) a Bishop performs voiceover work for energy drink commercials on the radio. In Jonson it is the Puritan sect attacked for its hypocritical double standards and money-grubbing activities (see Jonson's *Volpone* and *The Alchemist*). In Voltaire, Candide echoes Swift's Gulliver (from *Gulliver's Travels* 3.9) as Candide waxes incredulous over the absence of churchmen in El Dorado, Voltaire's perfect society: "What!" said Cacambo, "have you no monks among you to dispute, to govern, to intrigue, and to burn people who are not of the same opinion with themselves?" (ch. 18).

In other instances Voltaire's depictions of men of the cloth include forays into gluttony and sexual depravity of all kinds, and men generally immersed in the world's vices and pleasures. The Pythons will observe this as well in Ep. 24, when new-age religious men ask for only wealthy members, offer sexual license as part of membership, and deal in stolen merchandise ("Crackpot Religions Ltd.").

"suburban . . . what you will"—("Confuse-a-Cat") "Suburban fin-de-siecle ennui" is a "turn-of-the-century weariness and dissatisfaction" characteristic of changing epochs, but generally attached to the close of the nineteenth century and the increase in the presence and even threat of technology. Here it's relegated to the suburbs, as well, so less localized.

"Angst"—*OED*: "Anxiety, anguish, neurotic fear; guilt, remorse."

"Weltschmertz"—Essentially "world pain," a sorrow or sadness over the present or future evils or woes of the world in general; sentimental pessimism. The term first appeared in Johann Paul Friedreich Richter's *Selina; or, Above Immortality* (1827).

"Moping"—Dull and spiritless. This state has been attributed to animals before, including Drayton's *Eclogues* (1593) " . . . little moping Lambe of mine . . . ", and Gray's *Elegy* (1750) where the "moping owl" greets the evening.

All these terms certainly serve to anthropomorphize the cat, rendering it more like a moody teenager than a house pet.

– T –

"taxpayers' expense"—("Vox Pops" link) This entire diatribe sounds very much like ultra-Conservative Enoch Powell's "Rivers of Blood" speech delivered in 1968 in Birmingham, at the Annual General Meeting of the West Midlands Area Conservative Political Centre. Powell's fear that the foreign cultures coming with foreigners would inevitably erode his own culture is clearly evident:

> It almost passes belief that at this moment 20 or 30 additional immigrant children are arriving from overseas in Wolverhampton alone every week—and that means 15 or 20 additional families a decade or two hence. Those whom the gods wish to destroy, they first make mad. We must be mad, literally mad, as a nation to be permitting the annual inflow of some 50,000 dependants, who are for the most part the material of the future growth of the immigrant-descended population. It is like watching a nation busily engaged in heaping up its own funeral pyre . . . [a]s I look ahead, I am filled with foreboding. Like the Roman, I seem to see "the River Tiber foaming with much blood." (*Observer*, 21 April 1968)

Powell (1912-1998) supported an idea he and some Conservatives termed "re-emigration"—meaning repatriating former immigrants back to their home countries or to other countries of their choice, at some taxpayer expense. As a result of this speech—wherein ultimately Powell predicted an organized, incremental overthrow of England by "foreign nationals" (mentioned in Ep. 15)—Conservative leader Heath (calling Powell a "racialist") fired Powell from his Shadow Cabinet. Powell never returned to national political prominence. He will be mentioned again during the

Tourist's rant in Ep. 31. A timely book about Powell had appeared in this same year (1969), *The Rise of Enoch Powell: An Examination of Enoch Powell's Attitude to Immigration and Race* (Cornmarket: London), by Paul Foot.

Cf. Voltaire's *Candide*, wherein the people of El Dorado have adopted this same xenophobic attitude, barring citizens from traveling or studying abroad:

> Those princes of their family who remained in their native country acted more wisely. They ordained, with the consent of their whole nation, that none of the inhabitants of our little kingdom should ever quit it; and to this wise ordinance we owe the preservation of our innocence and happiness. The Spaniards had some confused notion of this country, to which they gave the name of El Dorado; and Sir Walter Raleigh, an Englishman, actually came very near it about three hundred years ago; but the inaccessible rocks and precipices with which our country is surrounded on all sides, has hitherto secured us from the rapacious fury of the people of Europe, who have an unaccountable fondness for the pebbles and dirt of our land, for the sake of which they would murder us all to the very last man. (chapter 18)

The Pythons' take on xenophobia is noteworthy in that their "othering" throughout FC identifies plenty of suspect persons and belief systems, including homosexuals, attractive and/or intelligent women, foreigners, religious leaders, Conservative politicians, upper-class types, and so on.

"Thatcher"—("Police Raid") Probably an allusion to Margaret Thatcher (b. 1925), by 1969 a well-known Conservative figure (the "Iron Lady") and subject of Python's barbs on more than one occasion.

Perceived now as the staunchest of conservatives, Thatcher was, according to biographers, during the late 1950s and through the 1960s quite liberal in contrast to her party, pushing for the decriminalization of homosexuality, the legalization of abortion, and the right for tenants to actually buy their Council Estate homes (*ODNB*). Her role in the elimination of a free milk program for low-income school children may be what the Pythons remember her for, however. In 1969, Thatcher was part of Heath's Shadow Cabinet. The fact that the policeman/authority figure "Thatcher" here is trampling on an artist's rights simply reinforces the more liberal bent of the troupe.

"things off"—(PSC; "Confuse-a-Cat") In between this bit of dialogue and the workmen is a wipe transition in the form of a "closing book, opening book." Wipes of this nature are characteristically used in television shows (as well as by contemporary filmmaker Akira Kurosawa) to denote the passage of time, so this is a form of ellipses. The wipe is not used often in *Flying Circus*.

"Thompson's Gazelle"—("Confuse-a-Cat") Misspelled—it's *Thomson's*—the East African gazelle is also called a "Tommy." Inspector Flying Thompson's Gazelle of the Yard (Idle) will appear in Ep. 29.

to the knees—(PSC; "Vox Pops" link) The Man standing in the stream is, in fact, a Gumby, though not identified as such in the written scripts. Obviously the name "Gumby" or "Gumbie" hadn't sufficiently worked itself into the Python lexicon by the writing of the fifth script/episode, unlike "Pepperpot," which quickly found common usage.

The first written description of this particular costume is found in the costuming requests for studio shooting (to be provided as copies of costumes used on location for continuity purposes), and is dated 12 October 1969: "5 Mr. Gumbies: 'Wellies, long trousers rolled up to the knee, braces. Collarless shirts. V. necked sleeveless pullovers (fairisle). All too small for the wearers. White knotted hankies on heads'" (WAC T12/1,083). The original idea for the costume allegedly came on location (shot in the summer of 1969), and so would have prefigured this in-studio iteration (see McCabe's *The Pythons*). This makes sense, since the location shots were all completed (on film) by July 1969, before entering the studio to record the videotape portions of the episode.

The Gumby costume itself might be inspired by the Alec Guinness character Henry Holland in *The Lavender Hill Mob* (1951), who sports the knotted handkerchief, wire glasses, etc. There is also the possibility that this look and performance came from a TV commercial character speaking for Toffo Deluxe toffees, and described as a "pathetic, cowering and servile, Yorkshire process worker, speaking from the shop floor, in his white surgical cap, and wellies" (see *1950s British TV Memories*).

"two hundred cigarettes"—("Vox Pops on Smuggling") Travelers entering Britain would have been considered smugglers (or "duty-not-paid" targets) if they carried 200 or more cigarettes and did not declare them for purposes of excise tax payment. Also, most law enforcement officials in Great Britain were *not* armed on a regular basis.

– V –

various tricks—(PSC; "Confuse-a-Cat") This entire scene is not unlike the early, presentational days of cinema, often called primitive cinema. In primitive cinema the spectacle is emphasized, the movement of the images, and the "to-be-looked-at-ness" of the images as entertainment. "Trickfilm" maker Georges Méliès utilized these editing elements to make objects and people appear and disappear, transmogrify, and "become" as an audience watches—cinematic sleight-of-hand, certainly. Borrowing on this tradition later would be Richard Lester, Peter Sellers, and Spike Milligan in their "home movie" *The Running, Jumping and Standing Still Film* (1959), where characters appear and disappear, and silly non sequiturs populate the disjointed narrative space.

viewer's letter . . . voice over—("Letters and Vox Pops") This format was actually a BBC staple from as early as 1962, when Robert Robinson (see below) hosted *Points of View*, a five-minute filler between programs on BBC-TV. The show was dedicated to viewer letters, and was primarily a place and time to air complaints from viewers about BBC programming. The graphics used on *Points of View* to give out the BBC mailing address were copied precisely by the Pythons, even down to the font selected:

POINTS OF VIEW
BBC Television Centre
London W12

Letters to the BBC also appear in Ep. 11, while similar letters to the *Daily Mirror* appear in Ep. 10, and offers to help re-start the "Icelandic Saga" are also given a similar address in Ep. 27. The satirical magazine *Private Eye* also employed alleged letters from alleged readers, though most were written by the magazine's staff.

The BBC's Robert Robinson (b. 1927) will be vilified in Ep. 32, when he comes to represent (for the moral Conservatives) all that is smutty on TV. See Ep. 32, the "Tory Housewives Clean-Up Campaign" section.

"vole"—("Confuse-a-Cat" end credits) A type of mouse, the vole has been mentioned already in Eps. 2 and 3; "Twentieth-Century Vole" is Python's generic Hollywood film studio.

– W –

"wait for it"—("Confuse-a-Cat") Phrase often used in a military parade kind of setting in the Python oeuvre, including the cross bearer contingent as they prepare to march to their crucifixion in *LB*, as well as the Colonel redirecting the show via camera two in *FC* Ep. 4. The phrase is uttered in a number of previous films (many British WWII pictures, of course), from the Goons' *Down Among the Z Men* (1952) to *Battle of Britain* (1969), and even Noel Coward's short play *Red Peppers* (from *Tonight at 8:30*) (1935).

"what we . . . call"—("Confuse-a-Cat") Kind of a Python verbal trope, see the doctor in *ML* who is examining a fellow officer who's lost a leg:

> Perkins (Idle): So, it'll, ehh—it'll just grow back again, then, will it?
>
> Doctor Livingstone (Chapman): Uhh . . . I think I'd better come clean with you about this. It's, um—it's not a virus, I'm afraid. You see, a virus is what we doctors call very, very small . . . ("Fighting Each Other")

Also used in Ep. 35 (" . . . what we scientists call, 'Sexy Underwear' or 'Erotic Lingerie' . . . ") and Ep. 45 (" . . . what we in the medical profession call a naughty complaint"). The word choice and tone is certainly condescending in these instances, as if the highly trained professional must "dumb down" the dialogue for the television viewing public—though this may actually be the case, and is probably based on actual BBC interviews familiar to the Pythons.

wimple—(PSC; "Confuse-a-Cat") Part of the nun's "costume," or habit.

window—("Burglar/Encyclopaedia Salesman") This "out-the-window" sequence was shot at Slade House, Hounslow, Middlesex (WAC T12/1,086). Similar deaths occur in Ep. 1, "Famous Deaths," as well as the suicides in Ep. 12.

"wonders"—("Burglar/Encyclopaedia Salesman") Other Python door-to-door salesmen items include naughty novelty gags (Ep. 15), "live" television documentaries (Ep. 32), Icelandic honey and Liberal Party candidates (Ep. 45), and the collection of liver donations (*Meaning of Life*),

"wood"—("Letters and Vox Pops") This same Scotsman will later be made entirely of tin. See Ep. 6. Scotsmen (and not the Welsh or Irish) will be consistent targets for the Pythons throughout the life of *FC* (cf. Ep. 7, the "Science Fiction" sketch).

– Y –

Y-fronts—("Erotic Film") "Briefs" underwear.

"You know I"—("Silly Job Interview") Like Shakespeare's Prelude in *Henry V*, this is a theatrical set-up, not unlike the cards used by the Marriage Guidance Counsellor in Ep. 2, or the characters pointing to the card reading "Life Insurance Ltd" later, in Ep. 26. The delivery is purposely clumsy in this case, and probably satirizing similar shows/sketches where the writing of the set-up is sincere, but achingly barefaced and obvious.

Episode 6

– A –

"acting and hunting"—("Red Indian in Theatre") As opposed to "hunting and gathering."

"All clear"—("Non-Illegal Robbery") The music beneath this lead-in to the garret set is borrowed from the film *From Russia With Love* (1963)—the title track—and is written by John Barry (WAC T12/1,088).

"anthrax"—("Crunchy Frog") A "splenic fever" (*Bacillus anthracis*) in sheep and cattle, anthrax can afflict humans, causing pustules and death. In a country at least historically linked to and even dependent on sheep, anthrax (and FMD and like diseases) would have been a topic of some public conversation.

More significantly, perhaps, is the World Health Organization's contemporary ongoing study into the devastating effects of weaponized anthrax. After WWII, several nations, including the Soviet Union, aggressively pursued weaponized (i.e., aerosol) versions of such bacteria for biological warfare ends. The WHO study's results—up to 250,000 killed in each large city without immediate vaccination—would have made sensational newspaper copy in the late 1960s and early 1970s. The U.S. supply of weaponized anthrax began to be destroyed in 1969 (*JAMA* 287 (2002): 2236-52).

assegai—(PSC; "The Dull Life of a City Stockbroker") *OED*: "A kind of slender spear or lance of hard wood, usually pointed with iron, used in battle . . . extended by the Portuguese to the light javelins of African tribespeople generally, *and most commonly applied by Englishmen to the missile weapons of the South African tribes*" (italics added). This inclusion, then, would have been an artifact of Britain's colonial presence in South and Eastern Africa.

"autograph"—(link into "It's the Arts") The hand (likely Gilliam's) signs "Best Wishes, Arthur Figgis" and underneath in parentheses he begins to write "account-ant," when the squiggle that was his first name gets away. (Figgis is the ancient librarian for *Punch* magazine, according to *Private Eye* contributors.) The squiggle runs wild for a bit, with the animator's hand trying to stop it, then it is squashed, displaying once again the ultimate power of the animator over his creation.

This trope—the visible, controlling hand of the animator—is as old as animation itself, going back to J.S. Blackton (*Humorous Phases of Funny Faces*, 1906), Winsor McCay (*Little Nemo*, 1911), Emile Cohl (*The Newlyweds*, 1912), Max Fleischer (*Out of the Inkwell*, 1919), and even through Chuck Jones (*Duck Amuck*, 1953).

– B –

"Bach"—("It's the Arts") Cf. a similar litany of masters, though of the art world, in Eps. 4 and 8 of *FC*. In Ep. 4, the Art Critic (Palin) discusses the painters as he eats the paintings. In Ep. 8, the Art Critic (also Palin) focuses on the "place of the nude" in art, though his slip of the tongue places the nude in his bed. In Ep. 1, of course, the painters and sculptors are listed (by Cleese) as they ride by during a bicycle race.

The composers (their birth and death dates, genre, and country) listed before Johann Gambolputty include: Ludwig van Beethoven (1770-1827; Classic and Romantic, Germany-Austria); W.A. Mozart (1756-1791; Classic, Austria); F. Chopin (1810-1849; Romantic, Poland/France); F. Liszt (1811-1886; Romantic, Austrian-Hungarian Empire); J. Brahms (1833-1897; Romantic,Germany-Austria); R. Schumann (1810-1856; Romantic, Germany); F. Schubert (1797-1828; Classic, Romantic, Austria); Mendelssohn (1809-1847; Romantic, Germany), and J.S. Bach (1685-1750; Classic, Germany).

"bahnwagen"—("Johann Gambolputty . . . von Hautkopf of Ulm") "Bahn" can mean "alley" or "railway," while "wagen" generally means "car." This nonce word could mean automobile or railway car, then. In pronunciation, "eisen-bahn-wagen" seems to run together, perhaps meaning a "railway car."

"BBC Entry"—(link into *It's the Arts*) Two possibilites here. The first is that this is a reference to the Eurovision Song Contest that accepts entries from across Europe and the UK for the annual music competition. Sandie Shaw's "Puppet on a String" won the contest for the UK in 1967. The contest will be referenced again in FC in Ep. 22, and afterwards the Pythons will have to endure a copyright infringement lawsuit over the song "Bing Tiddle Tiddle Bong," sung by Chapman. See notes to Ep. 22 for more. The second (and more likely option) is the Golden Rose of Montreux Festival, where the Pythons submitted a compilation episode in 1971 (losing to an Austrian submission). Gallingly, *The Frost Report* had won in 1967, and *Marty Feldman's Comedy Machine* would win in 1972.

"Bell & Compasses"—("Red Indian in Theatre") An amalgam of pub names like the extant "Bell & Crown" and "Axe & Compasses."

Bishop & Saint—(PSC; "Johann Gambolputty . . . von Hautkopf of Ulm") Gilliam borrowed these figures from the right third of the *Predella of the Pistoia Santa Trinità Altarpiece* (1455-1460), a work created by Francesco Pesellino (fl. 1422-1457). The figures are, most likely, St. James the Great and Mamas, according to the National Gallery. The altarpiece has been on display in the National Gallery since 1937.

Botticelli Lover—(PSC; "Johann Gambolputty . . . von Hautkopf of Ulm") The painting depicted is actually by Bronzino (1503-1572), and titled *An Allegory With Venus and Cupid* (1550). Bronzino was a Mannerist (mentioned in Ep. 4) working for Cosimo in Tuscany. The mistake can be attributed to most of the group writing the script and including the probably generic "Botticelli Lover" entry, and then Gilliam (on his own) finding his own way to represent that idea in animation. Gilliam also hand-tinted the figures of Cupid and Folly, green and blue, respectively.

This is also the painting where Gilliam earlier borrowed the "foot" (Cupid's right foot) for the opening credits to the show. The painting hangs in the National Gallery, London.

"Budapest"—(link into *It's the Arts*) The capital of Hungary, and the administrative center of Budai járás (district) and Pest megye (county). Situated astride the Danube River. The Montreux festival—which this mention is satirizing—is set in Switzerland, and is perhaps being gibed by the Pythons for having the temer-

ity to award the enterprizing David Frost the Golden Rose in 1967.

bus arrives—(PSC; "The Dull Life of a City Stockbroker") This is the "Old 666" bus, and is labeled as covering the Knightsbridge route. This same 1954 London Transport Leyland Titan PD2 RTL1557 bus also appeared in an episode of *The Avengers*, "False Witness" (November 1968) (see theavengers.tv). The driver is Dennis McTighe (WAC T12/1,242).

– C –

"camera"—("Crunchy Frog") This response to Milton's (Jones) "It's a fair cop" once again acknowledges the artifice of the television production, reminding the viewer that a camera is recording actors on a set, etc. Also, seeing that Parrot (Chapman) will address the camera momentarily, perhaps the direct address here is reserved for those in authority. Python regularly reminds the viewer of the constructed nature of the presentation, both in TV and film formats.

In Ep. 7, the avuncular police constable (Chapman) addresses the camera directly with a warm "Evening all," à la George Dixon of *Dixon of Dock Green* fame. Praline (Cleese) will also address the audience during both the "Dead Parrot" (Ep. 8) and "Fish Licence" (Ep. 23) sketches, perhaps looking for moral support in his struggles with the proprietors (both played by Palin).

"Camp, Sandy"—("Red Indian in Theatre") Cf. Ep. 5 where "Sandy Camp, the actor" is harassed by a policeman. This is likely a reference to well-known West End theatrical director Sandy Wilson. See the entry for Wilson in Ep. 31, "Language Laboratory."

"Canada"—("Non-Illegal Robbery") Part of the greater Commonwealth, and a haven for many American draft evaders during and after the Vietnam conflict, when conscription was in place in the United States.

. . . *captions alone*—(captions link into *It's the Arts*) Each week the graphics department at the BBC would provide a written estimate for title work for the upcoming episode. The total captions charge for this episode would come in at £76 (WAC T12/1,088).

The cost factors of BBC television production come into play often in FC, including the sketch "The BBC Is Short of Money" from Ep. 28, where programs are being broadcast from a family's flat due to BBC insolvency. The episodes themselves were being allotted about £4,500 each during this period, and the letters from the Pythons' various agents were already coming in, asking for more money, higher repeat fees, etc. The second series saw a bump to £5,000 per episode, but that didn't stop agent Jill Foster (of Foster & Dunlop Scripts Limited) from writing directly to David Attenborough (Controller, BBC2) and asking for a further budget increase (WAC T47,216).

Chuney, Lon—(PSC; "Johann Gambolputty . . . von Hautkopf of Ulm") Chaney (1883-1930) was known as the "Man of a Thousand Faces," and this particular still photo is taken from the film *The Phantom of the Opera* (1925), specifically the "unmasking" sequence. (Gilliam probably utilized a publicity still, of course, rather than an actual film frame.) Gilliam has tinted this still, as well—the portion of the film it comes from is black and white, though there are significant color sequences in the classic film.

Chartered Accountant—("Vox Pops") Simply an accountant who is a member of a royally chartered organization. Objects of much satire and poking fun in Python's oeuvre (cf. the tax on "thingy," which would make chartered accountancy a "much more interesting" job, Ep. 15), as well as significant mentions in Eps. 2, 8, and 10. Chartered Accountants will also become successful pirates on the seas of international finance in the 1983 Monty Python feature film *The Meaning of Life*.

"chocky"—("Crunchy Frog") Praline obviously uses the term as a slang for "chocolate," but the *OED* gives the spelling variously as "choccy," "chockie," and even "choccky." Colloquially, the term is and has been in fairly common use.

Classical music plays—("It's the Arts") The music beneath the *It's the Arts* title card is Chopin's "12 Etudien Op. 10" (No. 9 in F Minor) performed by Tamas Vasary (WAC T12/1,088).

"cockroach cluster"—("Crunchy Frog") For a similar grotesquerie, see Swift's 1730 poem *The Lady's Dressing Room*, where the "rogue" Strephon steals in to uncover Celia's cosmetic secrets. Strephon produces sweat-stained clothes, filthy combs, "A paste of composition rare, / Sweat, dandruff, powder, lead and hair," as well as grimy towels, scab ointments, and noxious personal items of every purulent kind. It is all enough to turn Strephon's (and our) bowels, and is meant to remain hidden under the lady's made-up façade, just as these "candies" are hiding under tasty chocolate.

In the later *Live at the Hollywood Bowl* stage version of this same sketch, Gilliam plays Parrot, who—after hearing what he's eaten—throws up into his hat.

"Cornish"—("Crunchy Frog") Of or belonging to the Cornwall region, in southwestern England.

"Courtneidge, Cicely"—("Red Indian in Theatre") Sydney-born British actress (1893-1980) of musical

comedy and revue. She would be made a Dame of the British Empire in 1972.

"Cow and Sickle"—("Non-Illegal Robbery") Probably a pub, and created by amalgamating other pub names. There is a "Sheaf & Sickle" on Coventry Road, and a "Cow & Plough" pub in Leicester.

"Cowdenbeath"—("Policemen Make Wonderful Friends") Town in Scotland, northeast of Dumfermline, and north of Edinburgh. The street address is "Masonic Apron Road." Masonry will be lampooned in Ep. 17, "Architect Sketch" and "How to Give Up Being a Mason." Chapman will be photographed wearing a Masonic apron—and little else—for that episode.

credits—(PSC; "Twentieth-Century Vole") All these "Saltzberg" credits are a swipe at the megalomania seen in some Hollywood producers whose name appears throughout a film's credits.

One credit for this episode was penciled out prior to the show being taped, specifically one that suggests Saltzberg is also a drug pusher. Perhaps the "drug pushers" joke might be a bit inflammatory, or just in poor taste (WAC T12/1,087). This elision was probably performed by producer John Howard Davies, though the change isn't attributed, nor is there a memo discussing the change. Such censoring did occur throughout the run of the series, but wasn't profligate. In a later Gilliam animation (in Ep. 19) the word "cancer" will be removed, for example, an elision demanded by BBC higher-ups (see Morgan *Speaks!*).

Cricket Team—(PSC; "Johann Gambolputty . . . von Hautkopf of Ulm") A late nineteenth century (or fin de siècle) photograph of an unidentified cricket team. All of these photos are at least slightly retouched—"animated"—by Gilliam so that the depicted character will "speak" the necessary words.

"crunchy frog"—("Crunchy Frog") Not as unlikely as it may sound—there are popular confections with names like "Polar Bear Paws" and "Jelly Bird Eggs."

Cut to presenter in studio—(PSC; link into "Johann Gambolputty . . . von Hautkopf of Ulm") Though not mentioned in the printed script, the music that comes up under Mr. Figgis' (Chapman) meditation is Elgar's "Nimrod" from his *Enigma* variations, as conducted by Sir Adrian Boult (WAC T12/1,088). The particular orchestra and/or LP is not mentioned.

– D –

"Denison, Michael . . . Dulcie Gray"—("Red Indian in Theatre") Husband and wife, she was born Dulcie

Bailey in Malaysia, and married Denison in 1939. Denison, a Yorkshire native, died in 1998. They acted together on stage and in film, on occasion. Gray would appear in the play *Double Cross* in 1958. Denison's last film appearance was in *Shadowlands* (1993).

Both are also mentioned by the Goons in "The Last Tram (From Clapham)" (23 November 1954), the reference following a protracted and meaningless dialogue between Henry Crun (Sellers) and Minnie Bannister (Milligan) on the subject of a bed Henry is *not* occupying.

"Dial M for Murder"—("Red Indian in Theatre") Frederick Knott's 1954 play would become a Hollywood film in 1954, directed by Alfred Hitchcock and starring Ray Milland and Grace Kelly. The play was a fixture at many UK theatres in the late 1950s being staged, for example, in the Rugby Theatre in 1955.

"Dimitri"—("Twentieth-Century Vole") The " . . . yes, yes, yes . . . " trope is revisited in the "Our Eamonn" sketch in Ep. 31. Perhaps "Dimitri" is Dimitri Tiomkin (1899-1979), the renowned Hollywood composer whose film score credits include *Duel in the Sun* (1946), *High Noon* (1952), and, coincidentally, *Dial M for Murder* (1954), mentioned earlier in this episode. Tiomkin was a resident of London in his later years.

Doctor—(PSC; "Johann Gambolputty . . . von Hautkopf of Ulm") This is a cropped version of Sir Luke Fildes' (1843-1927) *The Doctor*, which was acquired by the Tate and originally exhibited in 1891. The painting was inspired by the death of Fildes' son in 1877, and depicts the boy's caring physician.

"Dorking Civic Theatre"—("Red Indian in Theatre") Dorking is in the Mole Valley, part of Surrey county. Dorking Halls Theatre (Reigate Road) continues to host performances of all kinds, and has been home to the Dorking Dramatic & Operatic Society since 1947. In 1969, this theatre was offering the musical *Call Me Madam*.

"dressing up, yes"—("Vox Pops") Judges in Python are often effete, stereotypically homosexual, or seemingly transvestites—or all three. Cf. the *Dad's Pooves* scene in Ep. 38 (which survives in the printed scripts but not the finished episode), as well as Ep. 21, where two judges effeminately discuss their sexuality (and attraction to "butch" court personnel) as they disrobe, revealing women's underclothing. In Ep. 37, judges participate in a beauty pageant, and several are inconsolable when they lose.

"The Dull Life of a City Stockbroker"—("The Dull Life of a City Stockbroker") This concept of dullness in everyday life in Britain will be visited and revisited in *FC*, and has been discussed at length by one of the

philosophers mentioned often by the Pythons, Søren Kierkegaard. In his "Crop Rotation" chapter in *Either/Or* (1843), the aesthete denounces boredom and describes that purposeful idleness—without yielding to industry or boredom—can be the sensualist's answer to the boring life. Kierkegaard also singles out the English for their prolific boring-ness:

> Boredom is partly an immediate talent, partly an acquired immediacy. Here the English are, on the whole, the paradigmatic nation. One seldom encounters a born talent for indolence, one never meets it in nature; indolence belongs to the world of spirit. Occasionally you meet an English traveller, however, who is an incarnation of this talent, a heavy immovable ground-hog whose linguistic resources are exhausted in a single one-syllable word, an interjection with which he signifies his greatest admiration and *most profound indifference, because in the unity of boredom admiration and indifference have become indistinguishable.* No other nation but the English produces such natural curiosities. (italics added; 231)

So the English City Gent Stockbroker can wander through all manner of fantastic and dangerous situations without noticing or being affected by them in the least, purely because nothing but the unreal, alternate world of the comic book can relieve his boredom.

Kierkegaard will be revisited in Ep. 14, where one of the Piranha brothers' associates named Kierkegaard amuses himself by "biting the heads off whippets," perhaps also to stave off boredom.

– E –

"East Africa . . . plastic surgery"—("Non-Illegal Robbery") Following WWI, Tanganyika was controlled by Britain, and after 1964, parts of East Africa became Tanzania, and continued to be administered by Britain. It seems that extradition treaties were in place, as well, at least by 1968, so that for a British criminal, attempting escape to East Africa may have been a futile undertaking.

Nazi war criminal Martin Boorman was rumored to have endured a botched plastic surgery in South America, but DNA tests in 1999 confirmed that he died, probably by suicide, without leaving Germany.

Ironic, too, that at least originally, when plastic surgery was pioneered (c. 600 BC), it was in India and to reconstruct criminals' noses and earlobes—to assist in the rehabilitation process, and not assist in an escape from justice.

Episode 6—Like most episodes to follow (Eps. 10, 11, and beyond, for example), this episode was *not* given a name/title separate from *Monty Python's Flying Circus*, probably in response to Michael Mills' request for this alternate naming to stop. Mills felt it was confusing viewers and regional programmers alike, making it less likely that the fledgling show would be given a chance outside of London. (See BBC WAC files for the first series for more.) See notes for the entry for "Episode 2" in Ep. 2.

Secondly, the success of the show (probably not in actual numbers, except in London, but in audience letters and surveys) prompted Michael Mills to already (as of 27 November 1969) ask Cleese whether another thirteen episodes could be considered (WAC T12/1,242). In short, the show was beginning to get its legs, and audiences were actually tuning in, looking for *FC*.

Also appearing in this episode are W.F. Fairburn and Dennis McTighe (WAC T12/1,087). (McTighe plays the bus driver in this episode.) The numbers of extras and walk-ons will increase as the series goes on, with upwards of two dozen extras per episode being regularly contracted by the fourth series.

This episode seems to have been shunted off to Golders Green Hippodrome for taping, as happened several times when the studio space at Television Centre was needed for another production (WAC T12/1,087). The theatre setting for "Red Indian in Theatre" also demanded a much larger space, and in this case, one with theatre seats.

All of the music requests for this episode are for some reason found in the records for Ep. 7, in the folder WAC T12/1,088. It may be that there were so few music requests for the two shows that they were consolidated.

– F –

"Figgis"—(link into *"It's the Arts"*) Arthur Figgis is also featured in Ep. 2 as a man (Chapman) who can verify that Mr. Frampton (Jones) does indeed have three buttocks. In neither appearance is he characterized as an accountant. Under this section can be heard the strains of that quintessentially English composer, Edward Elgar, and his "Nimrod" from *Enigma Variations* Op. 36, as conducted by Sir Adrian Boult (WAC T12/1,088).

"fondue"—("Crunchy Frog") Normally, a dish using melted eggs and/or cheese.

"foul the foot"—("Non-Illegal Robbery") A colloquialism meaning a dog defecating on the sidewalk.

Frankenstein monster—(PSC; "The Dull Life of a City Stockbroker") Creature from Mary Shelley's 1818 *Frankenstein* novel, though this iteration looks more like the Boris Karloff version of the creature from the 1931 Universal film *Frankenstein* directed by Englishman James Whale.

"front stalls"—("Red Indian in Theatre") Seats in the orchestra area and/or near the stage.

The music in the background is a section of Ivor Novello's "Vitality" (1951), "Gay's The Word" part two (WAC T12/1,088). The original London cast starred Cicely Courtneidge, whom the Red Indian will mention.

– G –

"Gambolputty"—("Johann Gambolputty . . . von Hautkopf of Ulm") To "gambol" is to frolic, and "putty" is, of course, caulking adhesive, the combination of which almost demands a string of nonce or nonsense words to justify the portmanteau-ing.

garret room—("Non-Illegal Robbery") A room in the uppermost portion of a structure. Under this early part of the scene, a portion of the score from the James Bond film *From Russia With Love* (1963) by John Barry, can be heard (WAC T12/1,088).

Cf. similar gangster "planning" scenes in films like William Wellman's *The Public Enemy* (1931), Robert Siodmak's *The Killers* (1946), John Huston's *Asphalt Jungle* (1950), and perhaps especially Stanley Kubrick's *The Killing* (1956). Cleese (as co-screenwriter) would resurrect this scene in a much later film, *A Fish Called Wanda* (1988), directed by Charles Crichton. Michael Palin acts in this later scene and film, as well, though his part as the stutterer is almost opposite to his smoothly loquacious "The Boss" here in Ep. 6. Palin performed this same service as the planner for the Judean People's Front assault on Pilate's palace in the 1979 movie *LB*. "Reg" (Cleese) was also part of that gang.

"German Baroque"—("Johann Gambolputty . . . von Hautkopf of Ulm") The early Baroque-period (roughly the seventeenth century) Germans were led by the likes of Pachelbel and Froberger, keyboardists both, and both forenamed Johann, coincidentally. Later, organists such as J.S. Bach and Handel led German baroque music through the sacred (Bach's Passions, sonatas, etc.) and more secular realms (Handel's opera, oratorio, and secular cantata compositions). Python's ridiculously monikered hero might be the troupe's erudite jab at the increasing complexity of *music* as written and performed by Germans of the baroque period, as well as of the longer names some of these composers used professionally (i.e., Carl Philip Emanuel Bach).

It also should be noted that of all the composers reeled off by the presenter, Gambolputty is the only Baroque-period name, the rest coming much later, in the Classic and Romantic epochs.

"grumblemeyer"—("Johann Gambolputty . . . von Hautkopf of Ulm") Just might be a play on Ben Jonson's "grumbledory" (an alteration of "drumbledory") in *Every Man Out of His Humour* (1599): "The Goggle-ey'd Grumbledories would ha' Gigantomachiz'd" (5.4).

This list actually reads very much like the alchemical nonsense Jonson conjures up for his charlatans to use against the greedy Puritans in *The Alchemist*:

Subtle: Did you look
O' the bolt's-head yet?
Face: [Within.] Which? on D, sir?
Subtle: Ay;
What's the complexion?
Face: [Within.] Whitish.
Subtle: Infuse vinegar,
To draw his volatile substance and his tincture:
And let the water in glass E be filter'd,
And put into the gripe's egg. Lute him well;
And leave him closed in balneo.
Face: [Within.] I will, sir.
Surly: What a brave language here is ! next to canting.
Subtle: I have another work, you never saw, son,
That three days since past the philosopher's wheel,
In the lent heat of Athanor; and's become
Sulphur of Nature. (Act II)

See the author's *Monty Python, Shakespeare and English Renaissance Drama* (sections on Jonson) for more on Jonson's language, targets of vilification, and the Pythons. The "city comedy" elements are also discussed in the sections on Jonson.

"gutenabend . . . hundsfut"—("Johann Gambolputty . . . von Hautkopf of Ulm") This section is a mangled food order, asking for Nuremberg bratwurst with dog's feet, essentially.

– H –

"Hardy"—("Red Indian in Theatre") In the film and stage versions of *Dial M For Murder*, the character is named Chief Inspector Hubbard, not Hardy. Probably a memorial mistake on the Pythons' part (they'll switch Walpoles in Ep. 33, as well).

"Hautkopft"—("Johann Gambolputty . . . von Hautkopf of Ulm") Can be translated as "skinhead." Skinheads were already appearing in England by this time (late 1960s), especially in depressed areas (mill towns, inner-city neighborhoods).

"heap"—("Red Indian in Theatre") The Red Indian (Idle) probably borrows his phraseology and delivery from early American film Westerns, where Indians rarely spoke in complete English sentences.

"Hemmings, David"—("Twentieth-Century Vole") Actor, star of Antonioni's *Blow Up* (1966) and appearing in the unforgettable *Barbarella* (1968). Cleese made an unbilled appearance in the 1969 Hemmings' flop *The Best House in London*.

"He tells it . . . out of sight!"—("Twentieth-Century Vole") Clichés, all, and a swipe both at Hollywood and American English colloquialisms. The American film industry had exerted a strong—even dominant—influence on the UK since the early days of cinema, causing culture czars in Britain to chafe at the overwhelming presence of things American. The British government had implemented restrictive quotas against foreign (read: Hollywood) films as early as 1927, demanding that a majority of British screens show British films. This led to so-called quota-quickies—domestic films made to satisfy the quotas, quality aside—but British audiences demanded Hollywood films anyway. In fact, most major Hollywood studios merely set up or reconfigured their London offices and operations to make "local" films for the quota market, so American films continued to fill screens.

By 1948, when the BBC laid down the law as to what "quality television" meant in the UK, there were specific warnings against the use of American slangs and colloquialisms. See the entry for "slept with a lady" in Ep. 3.

high street—(PSC; "The Dull Life of a City Stockbroker") In many English towns and villages, the "high street" was the major shopping and dining area, losing some clout only when malls, larger department stores, and big box stores began to build nearer motorway exchanges.

Many towns in the UK, large and small, still boast a "High Street," not unlike the abundance of "Main" streets in the United States.

"himbleeisen"—("Johann Gambolputty . . . von Hautkopf of Ulm") The word "eisen" means "iron," though "himble" seems to be a nonce word (the Germanic spelling would be "himbel" anyway).

"hippy Gestapo"—("Twentieth-Century Vole") Perhaps an allusion to the hippy/flower child influence in the *Springtime For Hitler* production within the film *The Producers* (1968), but also may be inspired by the times themselves, as the early 1960s and 1970s were the heyday of the "hippie" generation and "flower-power" movement. The "Big Cheese" (Chapman) in Ep. 4 dresses as an evil hippy dentist, complete with resplendent flower-power jewelry.

"horowitz"—("Johann Gambolputty . . . von Hautkopf of Ulm") Pianist Valdimir Horowitz (1903-1989) was *not* performing publicly between late 1969 and mid-1974, having performed in Boston in October 1969, then taking a hiatus until May 1974, when he performed in New York. He had performed fairly regularly between 1965 and 1969, and to high praise.

"How to Fling an Otter"—(link into *"It's the Arts"*) Not unlike the later *Blue Peter*-ish sketch "How to Rid the World of All Known Diseases" in Ep. 28 where hosts teach or promise to teach viewers "How to Do It"—how to play the flute, feed the world, and bring peace to Russia and China. The "Fish Club" Adman (Palin) also reminds viewers they've already learned "How to Sex a Pike," and then proceeds to illustrate how to feed a goldfish (with gazpacho and sausage) in Ep. 26. The great British public have prided themselves on their DIY ("Do It Yourself") moxie since at least the privations of the war years. See notes for the listed episodes for more.

– I –

"Indian brave"—("Red Indian in Theatre") Once again, the specter of incongruity—an English-challenged Indian using critical and theatrical idioms—elevates the speaker above his perceived station.

"Intercourse Italian Style"—("Twentieth-Century Vole") There were a series of films produced between 1960 and 1970 with this same genericized title, including *Love Italian Style* (1960), *Divorce Italian Style* (1961, starring Marcello Mastroianni), *Marriage Italian Style* (1964, dir. Vittorio de Sica, starring Sophia Loren and Marcello Mastroianni), and *Adultery Italian Style* (1966). Also cf. the American TV show, *Love American Style*, airing 1969-1974.

It's the Arts—(link into *"It's the Arts"*) This episode was recorded on 5 November 1969, and was broadcast on 23 November 1969. It was actually recorded seventh in the series, but was broadcast after the fifth episode. The title *It's the Arts* does not appear in the script. This is the second (and final) official appearance of the *It's the Arts* sketch format in *FC*.

The title card also features a depiction of Michelangelo's *David* sporting a fig leaf. A full-size replica of this statue has been on display in the Cast Courts at the Victoria & Albert Museum since 1858.

– K –

"kalbsfleisch"—("Johann Gambolputty . . . von Hautkopf of Ulm") Veal.

kirk—("A Scotsman on a Horse") Scottish: "Church."

"kleenex"—(animated link into "The Dull Life of a City Stockbroker") This is actually the proprietary name of the facial wipe, but has become attached to the product inseparably, no matter the maker.

"knacker"—("Johann Gambolputty . . . Hautkopf von Ulm") Can mean things as varied as a lively singer, something that makes a cracking noise, one who buys old horses or houses, a saddle maker, or even testicles, according to the *OED*. Coupled with the following word, "thrasher," "knacker thrasher" could presumably translate into the vernacular "ball buster," to speak in the slang. The term "apple banger" also supports this reading.

Lastly, the intrepid *Private Eye* policeman during this period was Inspector Knacker of the Yard, fashioned after "Slipper of the Yard," or Jack Slipper, the lead investigator on the 1963 "Great Train Robbery" case.

"kurstlich"—("Johann Gambolputty . . . von Hautkopf of Ulm") Perhaps a purposeful Germanicization of "shortly," combining a bad version of "kurz" ("short") and adding "-lich" to fully Germanicize the word. When creating jabberwocky French, the Pythons have also created French-sounding words and phrases (see Ep. 1).

– L –

large African native—("The Dull Life of a City Stockbroker") Later, an American Indian native will be featured in this same episode. Both will be broadly stereotyped, not unlike the City Gent, the Rustic, and the Pepperpot throughout *FC*. This look will return in the "Our Eamonn" sketch, when Eamonn (Chapman), in full tribal kit, appears at his home after a stay in Dublin (Ep. 31).

"lavatories"—("Crunchy Frog") This "direct address" moment makes it seem as if the preceding performance were some sort of Public Service Announcement (PSA). Cf. Ep. 7, where the policeman (Chapman again) interrupts the sketch to remind viewers to report all alien sightings before sending them back to the exciting story.

"Leatherhead Rep"—("Red Indian in Theatre") Leatherhead Theatre is located at 7 Church Street, Leatherhead, Surrey, and was receiving significant Arts Council grants/subsidies between 1963 and 1967, according to files at the V&A. Filmmaker Mike Leigh (b. 1943) got his start as a stage assistant at Leatherhead Rep.

"love story . . . frontal nudity . . . comedy"—(Twentieth-Century Vole") Seemingly pell-mell genre mixing here, with identifiable semantic elements listed in this rant including: a setting in nature ("snow"), Hollywood A-list stars (Hudson and Day), physical passion ("kissing" and "Intercourse"), naughty foreign film ("*Intercourse Italian Style*"), Brit-film (Hemmings, who had also appeared in *The Wednesday Play* and *Dixon of Dock Green*), counterculture art film ("hippy"), WWII-film ("Gestapo officer"), adult film ("frontal nudity"), as well as a "family picture" and a "comedy." Frankly, with the dramatic inroads being made into Hollywood's hegemony by television, inflation, and several years of unwatchable films thanks to changing studio fortunes and leadership, many films of this period were assaying into any genre or subject matter that might bring audiences back into theaters. This may be a comment on films like *Where Eagles Dare* and *Ice Station Zebra* (spoofed later in Ep. 23), featuring all-star casts, pretty girls, intrigue, etc.

– M –

"Masonic Apron"—("Policemen Make Wonderful Friends") Part of the Freemasons' official ceremonial dress. Cf. Ep. 17, both the "Architect Sketch" and "How to Give Up Being a Mason," where Chapman's character is standing in a bus queue wearing an apron.

"massacres"—(link out of "Red Indian in Theatre") Possibly an oblique reference to the experiments underway in live theater in the late 1960s, that is, the radical "Happenings" theatre (c. 1966-1968), where events and activities take the place of plot and action.

More specifically to this reference of a "massacre" at Dorking during a performance, Richard Schechner's "Environmental Theatre" comes to mind. Schechner—a lifelong New Theatre practicioner—attempted to erase the line between performer and audience, between performance and life, even. Schechner defined the six axioms of environmental theatre: (1) "the theatrical event is a set of related transactions"; (2) "all the space is used for performance," and "all the space is used for audience"; (3) "the theatrical event can take place either in a totally transformed space or in 'found space'"; (4) "focus is flexible and variable"; (5) "all production elements speak in their own language"; and (6) "the text need be neither the starting point nor goal of production—there may be no text at all." A fascinating quote from Schechner illustrates the free-for-all potential that a Happenings or Environmental Theatre "performance" could allow: "Unlike the performers, the spectators attend theatre unrehearsed. . . . Thus unprepared, they are difficult to mobilize and, *once mobilized, even more difficult to control*" (italics added; *TDR* 12, no. 3: 41-65). It's easy to see how the Pythons could

take such a statement of possible chaos and adapt it to their satiric ends.

More sobering might be an allusion to the infamous massacre of English women and children by (East) Indians in the so-called Great Revolt in 1857. When news reached England, the outrage was so pervasive that even churchmen called for retaliatory massacres. For a contemporary account, including a call for calm to both the combatants and the hostile English press, see an article by Charles Creighton Hazewell in *The Atlantic Monthly*: "The Indian Revolt" 1, no. 2 (Dec. 1857): 217-22.

Medieval Couple—(PSC; "Johann Gambolputty . . . von Hautkopf of Ulm") This is a version of the Flemish van Eyck's *The Arnolfini Portrait* (1434). Jan van Eyck's (1390-1441) figures are here given animation by Gilliam, as the bridegroom pushes like a button the stomach of his seemingly pregnant bride. This painting also hangs in the National Gallery, London.

"mittler-aucher"—("Johann Gambolputty . . . von Hautkopf of Ulm") In the taped version, this is pronounced more as "mittel raucher," which might translate into "middle smoker."

"Mona Lisa"—(PSC; "Johann Gambolputty . . . von Hautkopf of Ulm") Iconic painting by Leonardo da Vinci (c. 1503-1506), which now hangs in the Louvre, Paris. Gilliam pored through art books for his animations, utilizing works both well known and obscure. He has slightly tinted the figure, and removed the background, replacing it with an incongruous alpine valley scene, so that it looks more like a Mannerist painting.

Modernist artist Marcel Duchamps (1887-1968) had applied a painted mustache to the "Mona Lisa" in 1919, both solidifying the da Vinci work as an icon, and also emphasizing the unquestionable change Modern Art was inflicting on the old masters, classical representation, and "authenticity."

"monosodium glutamate"—("Crunchy Frog") Abbreviated MSG, it has been used as a food flavor enhancer since 1908, and is originally from Japan. The assertion by Mr. Milton (Jones) earlier that no "preservatives or additives of any kind" are used in Whizzo chocolates, then, is a misstatement. Glucose, the most common sugar in nature, is also a key ingredient.

"more exciting"—("Vox Pops") This robbery quickly becomes a Vox Pops moment, one of Python's regular motifs, and a well-used linking item. The "man-on-the-street" interviews were characteristic of TV and radio during this and earlier periods, including the very popular *The Dick Emery Show* (1963), Peter Watkins' *Culloden* (1964), and his film *The War Game* (1965). The perverse excitement of illegality is also discussed in Ep. 2, the "Mouse Problem" sketch.

"motion-picture history"—("Twentieth-Century Vole") Not only is this the longest line of dialogue given to Gilliam in the run of the series thus far, but it's also a nod to obsequiousness à la "The Emperor's New Clothes," where no one save a child wants to disagree with the king over the beauty or even reality of his new "clothing."

The infiltration of fairy tales and fairy tale tenets can perhaps be attributed to Palin, Jones, and Idle, who worked together on a children's television show prior to *FC* (*Do Not Adjust Your Set*, 1967) as well as Jones' interest in and publication of fairy tales himself. For a somewhat fractured children's story time in *FC*, see Ep. 3, where Idle reads from a naughty storybook.

– N –

National health specs—(PSC; "Johann Gambolputty . . . von Hautkopf of Ulm") The NHS came about as part of the sweeping social change called for in the Aneurin Bevan (1897-1960) report, "In Place of Fear," and was officially instituted in 1948. The "specs" are the standard glasses provided by National Health, and would have been those provided to the Pythons as youngsters' had they needed them. The bespectacled man stands next to a light-green panel van (lorry) that bears the BBC's (royal) crest.

"Nelson"—("A Scotsman on a Horse") Nelson is found in Lancashire, northern England, though there is also a Nelson in Caerphilly, Wales. Both are a long distance from either Dorking or Leatherhead (both in Surrey).

newsagents—("The Dull Life of a City Stockbroker") These are often very small shops selling newspapers, magazines, candy and soda, and sundry items, and are typically squeezed into narrow spaces along busy city streets, but can also be corner shops. Cleese buys a paper in and then walks out of one as the "Silly Walks" sketch begins on Thorpebank Road. (This same corner store is no longer extant, having been replaced by a home in the same space.)

According to BBC records, this newsagent shop was located at the corner of Brighton Road and Liberty Lane, Addlestone, Surrey, and was utilized on 22 October 1969 (WAC T12/1,242). Several Vox Pops segments were also recorded here.

newspaper—(link out of "Red Indian in Theatre") The newspaper where he reads about the theatre massacre is a copy of the *Daily Standard*.

"Nicaragua"—("Non-Illegal Robbery") The British formed alliances with local Miskit Indians as early as the seventeenth century, and even treated the Mosquito Coast region as a "dependency" between 1740 and 1786. In 1969, however, the radical, "popular front party" Sandinista National Liberation Front was active in Nicaragua, opposing the Somoza dictatorship, rendering Nicaragua as an unlikely hiding place for a British non-criminal.

"no time to lose"—("Non-Illegal Robbery") This phrase will later propel much of Ep. 38, but is used here as just a tossed-off phrase.

"not at all well"—("Crunchy Frog") Cf. *HG*, where the plague cart man refuses to take a victim who's "not dead yet."

– O –

"over six feet tall"—("Policemen Make Wonderful Friends") This could be either a height requirement, as many professions demand (fighter pilot, submariner, runway model) or just a personal preference. This height precludes most women, of course, so the hint of homoeroticism in the constabulary is evident again. There are no longer any height restrictions in the British police forces. See the note for "policemen . . . friends" below.

– P –

"Pawnee"—("Red Indian in Theatre") North American Plains Indians.

"pen friend"—("Policemen Make Wonderful Friends") A pen pal, exchanging letters.

"piddles"—("Twentieth-Century Vole") Urinates.

pig—(PSC; "Johann Gambolputty . . . von Hautkopf of Ulm") Cf. Ep. 1 for the earlier pig appearances. This photo is of a multi-teated sow. A boar appears later in the episode.

Just prior to this photo there appears a photo of a policeman leaning over some kind of apparatus, though this photo is not listed in the printed scripts. The PC wears the traditional bobby's uniform, including the tall helmet (discussed in some detail in Ep. 43).

"pinko"—("Twentieth-Century Vole") Primarily an American slang word for a Communist sympathizer ("pink" meaning not completely "red"). By using the sobriquet Larry (Chapman) is suggesting that the writer is an agitator.

One of the darkest periods in American cinema was the heyday of the House Un-American Activities Committee and the attendant ferreting out of suspected Communists or Communist-sympathizers, primarily from among the artists (and especially screenwriters) of Hollywood. Those who were called before the various committees to testify and name names were summarily blacklisted if they didn't cooperate to the committee's satisfaction (including the "Hollywood Ten": Alvah Bessie, Herbert Biberman, Lester Cole, Edward Dmytryk, Ring Lardner, Jr., John Howard Lawson, Albert Maltz, Samuel Ornitz, Adrian Scott, and Dalton Trumbo). Those who testified were labeled as informants and stoolies for helping the investigations, similarly attacked by those implicated and those who managed to avoid prosecution (i.e., Elia Kazan).

A Cleese character (a commentator) has already erupted into a splenetic over the "red scum" threatening England's sovereignty, perhaps a nod to the racialist leader of Britain's Union of Fascists, Oswald Mosley (1896-1980). In the late 1950s, Mosley had instigated racist riots in West London, where white Teddy boys hunted out darker "others" for beatings and abuse. By 1969, the Cold War was very much alive and well, with the Brezhnev era in the Soviet Union recently under way, and Nixon in the White House, whom many (probably including the Pythons) considered jingoistic.

pitched battle—(PSC; "The Dull Life of a City Stockbroker") This battle in the streets is reminiscent of the gun battle depicted in Lindsay Anderson's film *If . . .* (1968), and must also be at least indirectly related to the evening news depictions of the fighting under way in Vietnam. Perhaps even more significant might be the increasing "troubles" in Northern Ireland, which held the daily headlines in most newspapers of the time, and which featured British soldiers running through British (Irish) streets, armed and fighting.

Anderson (1923-1994) was one of Britain's newer, politically and socially charged filmmakers, and will be discussed in the notes for Ep. 19.

"policemen . . . friends"—("Policemen Make Wonderful Friends") The police force are regularly lampooned in *FC*, from fighting crime with fairy wands and engaging in homosexual liaisons (both Ep. 13), to pretending to be an airplane (Ep. 17), to incompetent-but-film-literate Flying Squad members (Ep. 29). Policemen are just one type of authority figure regularly mocked in the Python oeuvre, joining church leaders, big business, the upper-class, and others.

"praline"—("Vox Pops") A browned almond (or other nut) and boiled sugar confection. Praline (played by Cleese) is a semi-regular character during the show's first series. He will reappear returning a dead parrot in Ep. 8, and will later try to buy a license for his pet fish in Ep. 23.

– Q –

QC—("Vox Pops") A "Queen's Counsel" is a senior barrister in the UK, a position Cleese may have aspired to had he continued work in the law after Cambridge. See Morgan's *Monty Python Speaks!* for Cleese's version of that decision.

queue—(PSC; "The Dull Life of a City Stockbroker") People waiting in line, or "queuing up." This scene was shot in the Australia Road area of East Acton on 20 October 1969, as was the "driverless" taxi scene (WAC T12/1,242).

– R –

"Redfoot"—("Red Indian in Theatre") No such Plains Indian tribe existed, so this could be just a slight racial slur, akin to "redskin." Python uses racially derogatory terms like "darkies" and "wop" occasionally in *FC*. This level of racial insensitivity was fairly common in this period, seen often in cartoons, in the blackface characterization of *The Black and White Minstrel Show* (1958-1978), and, also, the *Goon Show* (where the jokes about bandleader Ellington's skin color were common).

"Reluctant Debutante"—("Red Indian in Theatre") A 1955 play (a comedy) by Edinburgh-born William Douglas-Home (1912-1992), brother to prime minister Sir Alec Douglas-Home (later Lord Home). The play had actually been performed at Leatherhead Repertory Theatre in August 1957.

restoration-fund—("Vox Pops") Donations for church-related restorations, especially older churches listed on historic registers.

"Rio de Janeiro"—("Non-Illegal Robbery") Capital of Brazil, port city, and one of several well-known South American destinations where extradition difficulties could be expected. In the 1947 Jacques Tourneur film noir *Out of the Past*, Jane Greer flees to Mexico, for example, to escape the revenge of her former boyfriend (Kirk Douglas), and his hired detective (Robert Mitchum).

"Rock Hudson . . . Doris Day"—("Twentieth-Century Vole") Quintessential 1960s Hollywood screen couple, appearing together in films like *Pillow Talk* (1960). In *Gilliam on Gilliam*, Terry Gilliam would describe this duo and their movies as the antithesis to his own style of filmmaking.

In *The Goon Show*, the "Who Is Pink Oboe?" sketch (12 January 1959), Eccles (Milligan) will claim to be Rock Hudson to woo a ladyfriend.

"roll the credits"—("Twentieth-Century Vole") Saltzberg is acting the part of the narrative tyrant here, managing to control the end of the episode. This level of awareness isn't given to many Python characters—most are clearly trapped in their fictional worlds while some few others have the ability to demand changes. In Ep. 1, for instance, Mrs. Stebbings is able to ask for and receive the death of Mr. Foster (Chapman) of Guildford ("Famous Deaths"); in Ep. 2 a man (Palin) calling for "a Scotsman on a horse" (Cleese) is granted that wish ("A Scotsman on a Horse"); in Ep. 30, a dissatisfied participant in a sketch (Idle) gets additional chances to find satisfaction in other sketch settings, and even as different characters ("Bus Conductor Sketch").

This is much like more textually or narratively dominant cartoon characters (e.g., Chuck Jones' Bugs Bunny, Tex Avery's Screwy Squirrel) who can manipulate and control their animated worlds because they possess not only a self-awareness of their cartoony natures, but because they also understand the tenets and limits of that fictional world. The Pythons often treat their created world as if it were animated—plastic, pliable, and abruptly reformable.

– S –

safety curtain—(animated link into "Red Indian") A fire-proof curtain that can be lowered to protect the viewing audience from a fire onstage or backstage.

"Saltzberg, Larry"—("Twentieth-Century Vole") A stereotypical portrayal of a Hollywood movie mogul as a Jew. (See Gabler's *An Empire of Their Own: How the Jews Invented Hollywood*.) This man is perhaps modeled closely on producer Harry Saltzman (mixed with a dash of 1930s-era MGM mogul Irving Thalberg), whose film *Battle of Britain* (dir. Guy Hamilton, 1969) was just such an over-the-top kind of superstar production. (Saltzman also produced James Bond films from 1962 to 1974, after which he sold his stake in the franchise.) Saltzman had also been very much in the news at the forefront of the British film censorship debate when he produced controversial Angry Young Men films like *Look Back in Anger* (1959), *The Entertainer* (1960), and *Saturday Night and Sunday Morning* (1960), arguing for greater freedom of sexual and even political expression in British films (see Aldgate).

A few other moments of caricatured Jewishness can be found in *FC*. In Ep. 7, there is a less-than-iconic Jew (Palin), who just shrugs and ends his single sentence on an upward inflection (mock-Yiddish). If the script hadn't identified this character as a Jew, then he may not have been recognizable at all (he's not caricatured). Cf. Voltaire's (Ep. 2) stereotypical characterizations of Jews (Don Issachar, whose two interests are women and banking; and miserly Jews who might swear by Father Abraham while robbing Candide blind in diamond transactions, etc.) in *Candide*. Jewish Hollywood producer Irving Thalberg (1899-1936) is well known for butting heads with big name directors like Eric Von Stroheim, bringing strict, streamlined studio control to Universal and then MGM projects. Thalberg's personal manner, however, is not recorded as blustery and over-the-top, meaning Chapman's portrayal isn't meant to impersonate Thalberg.

The Jew here and elsewhere becomes a stereotypical "other" in the Python oeuvre, joining the host of Others (Indians, blacks, homosexuals, women, Tories, chartered accountants, England's upper class) similarly enshrined. These Others are generally not treated scornfully, but perhaps thoughtlessly and playfully, which seems to have been characteristic for the period. The humorous (satiric and just silly) treatment of "others" (and then the recovery of same) during this period is summed up aptly by Alan Bennett, of *Beyond the Fringe* fame:

> I don't know that we had any intentions—any overall intentions—I think, what it wasn't, it seems to me was "cutting" and "devastating" satire. There were things that were—I mean Peter did a thing, an imitation of a television broadcast of Macmillan which was very funny, *but it was also quite affectionate*. (Audio transcription, *Eyewitness: 1960-69*, "Beyond the Fringe")

Much of Pythons' work fits into their vein—rather than outright scorn, there seems to be a certain level of affectionate nostalgia attached to the lampooning of ridiculous City Gents and Rustics and Tories and Pepperpots.

"Scotsman on a horse"—("A Scotsman on a Horse") The bagpipe music here is not accounted for in the WAC records. The "Scotsman on a horse" motif initially appeared, also as a request, in Ep. 2. The bagpipe music, which plays as the Scotsman rides through gorse and thistle, alternates with a sober harpsichord ("Bonny Sweet Robin") processional whenever there's a cut to the interior of the kirk (WAC T12/1,088).

The stunt rider here is Harry Woodley, and the Bride seen in a moment is played by Bernardine (or Bernadette) Barry (WAC T12/1,083). Others in this scene (shot on 9 July 1969) include Tobin Mahon-Brown (*Dr. Who*), David Billa (*Dr. Who*), Laurie Goode (*The Wednesday Play*), Evan Ross (*Emma*), and

Elaine Williams (*Some Mothers Do 'Ave 'Em*) (WAC T12/1,242).

"she takes off her wrap"—("The Dull Life of a City Stockbroker") The actress playing the Stockbroker's (Palin) unfaithful wife is Miss Eddy May Scrandrett, who will appear in Ep. 17, as well.

"shönedanker"—("Johann Gambolputty . . . von Hautkopf of Ulm") This is a twisted version of "thank you" in German—"Danke schön."

"Sioux"—("Red Indian in Theatre") North American Plains Indians. Perhaps beyond the incongruity of a period-garbed Indian attending the theater is the fact that he is an American Indian who, along with his Sioux tribe, somehow lives somewhere near Leatherhead and regularly attends an English repertory theatre. It's also later offered that a Pawnee tribe (also American Plains Indians) lives in the Leatherhead/ Dorking region, and also attend the theatre.

Instead of wearing a "single strip of hair," as the script calls for—aka a "Mohawk"—the Indian (Idle) wears a long black wig parted in the middle, and a headband. This stereotype looks very much like what may have been seen on American situation comedies and variety shows of the period. American actor Lon Chaney, Jr. (1906-1973) is coiffed very similarly in ITV's *Hawkeye and the Last of the Mohicans* (1957), though Scar (Henry Brandon) in *The Searchers* (1956) may have been the inspiration for Idle's costuming.

"snogging"—(PSC; "The Dull Life of a City Stockbroker") Kissing passionately, noisily, even messily. Cf. Ep. 45, *Most Awful Family in Britain*" sketch, and the character of Valerie (Chapman), a Member of Parliament and "snogger."

"spelltinkle"—("Johann Gambolputty . . . von Hautkopf of Ulm") This could actually be interpreted as a command. In *Beyond the Fringe*, the monologue delivered by Jonathan Miller titled "A Piece Of My Mind (The Heat-Death Of The Universe)," creates similar disparate readings of a single phrase as he discusses his impressions of British Rail bathrooms:

> [. . .]where they have a marvelous and somewhat mysterious unpunctuated motto printed on the wall over the lavatory: 'Gentlemen lift the seat.' Now what exactly does this mean? Is it a sociological description? A definition of a gentleman that I can either take or leave? Or perhaps it's an invitation to upper-class larceny? (Audio transcription, *Beyond the Fringe*)

"spelterwasser"—("Johann Gambolputty . . . von Hautkopf of Ulm") Since "spelter" is a solder containing significant amounts of zinc, the word might mean a drink of sorts containing the solder, like mineral wa-

ter, but not nearly as healthy. There are such things as a spelter-box, spelter-dust, spelter-heap, spelter-maker, and spelter-ore, according to the *OED*, so spelter-wasser isn't terribly far from actuality. The zinc reference above (as in the "zinc stoat of Budapest" award) shouldn't be forgotten here; also, one of the Upperclass Twits of the Year in Ep. 12 is also implicated, one "Simon-Zinc-Trumpet-Harris."

"splunge"—("Twentieth-Century Vole") An archaic American slang term that means literally "to plunge." The *OED* dates the first recorded colloquial usage to 1839. There's no indication of where the Pythons might have come across the arcane word, though it may have been borrowed from a comic book, given the earlier comic book reference, and the fact that such onomatopoeic words populate action comic pages. (Roy Lichtenstein's "Wham!" [1963] is an example of this comic book trope finding its way into high art.) Also, the *OED* mentions that a form of the word appeared in J.A. Froude's *Life of Carlyle* (1884), which certainly might have found its way to an Oxford or Cambridge reading list.

"steel bolts"—("Crunchy Frog") A description not unlike the booby traps and land mines being dealt with in the Vietnam conflict, and which had been much in the news since the mid-1960s. One such device, called a "cartridge trap," is fired from the ground as a victim steps over it, then explodes.

"still on film . . . studio"—("Vox Pops") This mention of the very different formats—film stock versus videotape—reminds the viewer that a created, constructed thing is being watched. The aesthetic differences between the two media are glaringly obvious to the eye, and certainly would have been jolting to the viewer if, say, a dramatic program (not a comedy show) were to fluctuate between media without a similar "heads up" to the viewer. For another reaction to the film/videotape dichotomy, see Ep. 18, "Society for Putting Things on Top of Other Things." Also, see Ep. 8, where the Colonel stops the hermit sketch, even though it's on film, and not in-studio.

"stoat"—(link into "*It's the Arts*") A European ermine. In Ep. 26, a character (played by Gilliam) will appear with a stoat through his head. This violation is certainly a borrowing from the world of cartoons, where characters are regularly dropped, crushed, stretched, minced, and impaled without permanent damage. All sorts of body horrors are inflicted on Python characters, especially in Gilliam's dismembering and re-membering animations, but the impalings of "live" characters indicate perhaps a cultural fascination with the sacrosanctity-versus-violation ethoi. In *FC* characters are skewered by giant nails and floor lamps (Ep. 14), arrows (Eps. 6 and 38), spear gun darts (Ep. 30), tennis rackets and keyboards (Ep. 33), and hunting spears (Ep. 45).

Of the major American animation studios during the Pythons' formative years (Famous Studios, Disney, UPA, Warner Bros.), only Disney—under the direct orders of Walt himself—explicitly forbade any such violation of his characters' bodies. Not so other studios. Tex Avery's Nazi Wolf (produced while at MGM) is riddled by bullets (so that light can shine through him) in *Blitz Wolf* (1942), and Daffy Duck loses his beak more than a dozen times in the trilogy *Rabbit Fire* (1951), *Rabbit Seasoning* (1952), and *Duck! Rabbit, Duck!* (1953). There are also myriad explosions throughout WB and MGM cartoons, explosions that leave the victim looking much like the "It's Man" when he is handed a cartoony "anarchist's bomb" in Ep. 8. The Pythons (like the Goons previously) seemed to draw heavily and consistently from these more violent, aggressive, and frenetic cartoons throughout the run of *FC*.

Superman-type—(animated link out of "The Dull Life of a City Stockbroker") Cf. Ep. 3, "Bicycle Repair Man" sketch, for an earlier Superman reference.

"swag"—("Vox Pops") *OED*: "A thief's plunder or booty; gen. a quantity of money or goods unlawfully acquired, gains dishonestly made." Dennis Moore's (Cleese) bag loaded with reapportioned goods in Ep. 37 is labeled "Swag," but with the pound sign (£) in place of the "s," thus spelled "£wag."

"sweetmeat"—("Crunchy Frog") The *OED* identifies the term as primarily archaic, and referring to virtually any kind of sweetened (sugary) cake or tart or filling.

– T –

tab—("Red Indian in Theatre") A "tableau curtain," one that is either drawn up or to the sides as the show begins.

"thrasher"—("Johann Gambolputty . . . von Hautkopf of Ulm") Can mean one who threshes.

Three Naked Ladies—(PSC; "Johann Gambolputty . . . von Hautkopf of Ulm") Gilliam's "naked lady" photos come from a large collection of Victorian and Edwardian "boudoir" photographs given to him in the mid-'60s by comedian Ronnie Barker. The images appear hundreds of times in *FC* episodes. See *Gilliam on Gilliam* (1999).

Thrills and Adventure—("The Dull Life of a City Stockbroker") An actual DC Comics title from the 1960s. The music beneath this portion of the film is

from Jack Shaindlin's "March of the Insurgents." Shaindlin is one of many light music composers who—during the 1940s through 1960s—penned music specifically for programmed music needs on radio and then TV (WAC T12/1,088). This type of music was used by a wide variety of shows, and was available on LPs (records). This particular music is also heard in the "Bicycle Repair Man" sketch of Ep. 3.

"ticolensic"—("Johann Gambolputty . . . von Hautkopf of Ulm") A "tico" is a Costa Rican. "Ticolens" is a medical term having to do with oral microbiology and immunology, and may have been contributed by Chapman, the troupe's only medical doctor.

"time for that later"—("Twentieth-Century Vole") Another allusion to the moral price of Hollywood-style fame and success. Cf. the rustic (Cleese) in Ep. 4 who, after having his rustic monologue interrupted, resolves to not "sleep" with another producer.

"tin"—("Vox Pops") In the Scotsman's previous appearance (also Palin, in Ep. 5), he was made "entirely of wood."

"treble"—("Crunchy Frog") Triple, threefold.

"12/6D"—(link into "It's the Arts") Monetary figures in the UK are given as "pounds, shillings and pence" (£.s.d.). The "D." stands for the Latin *denarious*, or penny. The shilling disappeared only after the contentious 1971 move to decimal coinage. Since this episode was written in 1969, the Pythons would be expected to still use the term. Also since 1971, the pound has equaled 100 new pence (*OED*). "New pence" (the newly valued pence, post-1971) is mentioned in Ep. 27.

"Twentieth-Century Vole"—("Twentieth-Century Vole") Play on the name of the American film studio Twentieth-Century Fox, which was established as Fox Studios by William Fox in 1913. This trademark is followed by another animated trademark, this time the Metro Goldwyn Mayer (MGM) "roaring lion" design. (MGM, another storied Hollywood studio, was formed in 1924 by Louis B. Mayer from Metro Pictures and Goldwyn Studios.) In the lion's place, however, is a mangy, weedy-looking vole. (A vole is a short-tailed field mouse, and has been mentioned in Eps. 2, 3, and 5 already.) The "Ars Gratia Artis" ("Art for Art's Sake") part of the trademark is left unchanged.

The music underneath the celebrated logo is Jack Shaindlin's "Spectacular," one of the many bits of program music written and/or performed by Shaindlin, Eric Coates, Ron Hamer, and Keith Papworth, and others, and created for television, radio, and low-budget film use in the 1940s and beyond. Most of the musical score for the Pythons' feature film *Holy Grail* came from such music, specifically the DeWolfe collection.

Two Dancers—(PSC; "Johann Gambolputty") This appears to be a photograph of any one of myriad two-man vaudeville/music hall song-and-dance acts, and could be from either a publicity still or captured from a film.

– U –

"Ulm"—("Johann Gambolputty . . . von Hautkopf of Ulm") A city in southwestern Germany on the Danube River and opposite the Bavarian town of Neu Ulm. This entire "name" sketch is reminiscent of the "John Jacob Jingleheimer Schmidt" children's song, as well, the origins of which are quite obscure.

– V –

vicar—("Vox Pops") This vicar steals from his own parishioners, while other churchmen already presented have or condone bizarre sexual practices (Ep. 2) and are suspected of being smugglers (Ep. 5). Later, in Ep. 13, a vicar will be an ignored entrée at a trendy restaurant.

The pilfering vicar insert was shot at Holy Trinity Church, Lyne Lane, Chertsey, Surrey (WAC T12/1,085).

Viking—("Johann Gambolputty . . . von Hautkopf of Ulm") The Viking character appears several times in *FC* as a linking element, often speaking just a single word on the way to other links or the next sketch. Gilliam often plays the Viking, though the part gets spread around to other Pythons, as well (Palin and Cleese, for example). The identification of the linking item is also a significant aspect of Python upsetting the agreed-upon conventions of TV, including hiding such links in the quest for smooth, invisible continuity.

– W –

weedy—("Johann Gambolputty . . . von Hautkopf of Ulm") A tall, lanky, and weak man or boy. Cf. the "weedy" and also bespectacled lance corporal (Jones) in Ep. 1, who easily succumbs to the funniest joke in the world.

"We present 'The Dull Life of a City Stockbroker'"—("The Dull Life of a City Stockbroker") The background music that swells beneath this scene is a popular light classical music piece from the "London Suite" entitled "Knightsbridge (March)" by Eric Coates (WAC T12/1,087). This is essentially "city" music, composed with the bustling Knightsbridge shopping area of London as its inspiration.

This long sketch begins at the front door of 49 Elers Road, near Lammas Park Road, Ealing, where portions of "The Funniest Joke in the World" were also filmed (WAC T12/1,087). The initial exterior shots for "City Stockbroker" were shot at 49 Elers (in the front yard), while the kitchen interior was also inside this address (fairly unusual, as location interiors are harder to secure and then even harder to light properly) (WAC T12/1,242).

"whizzo"—("Crunchy Frog") *OED*: "An exclamation expressing delight," and "excellent, wonderful." Whizzo Butter was a product mentioned in Ep. 1. A *Private Eye* ad (13 May 1966) offers the following confection advertisement:

> For the appallingly greedy.
> Chocolates filled with gnat's pee.
> Stuff these black gobbets into your
> maw and you'll be the envy of
> other snobs. Send 88gns. for
> illustrated catalogue to:
> Boris Chocolates, Bumhole St. W8. (Ingrams 133)

Women's Institute applauding—(PSC; link out of "A Scotsman on a Horse") This is the first time that the WI footage has been officially requested in the weekly copyright clearance requests for film footage and musical clips (WAC T12/1,088).

"write it"—("Twentieth-Century Vole") All Larry's (Chapman) lines are delivered with an exaggerated American accent, characterized by very hard [r] sounds. All the writer characters in this scene attempt, with varying degrees of success, American accents.

Episode 7

abacus—(PSC; "Science Fiction Sketch") An ancient calculation tool, and right at home in this rustic Scottish "men's wear shop" as conjured by the Pythons. This is perhaps akin to ethnographic filmmaker Robert Flaherty's insistence that Eskimos depicted in his 1922 film *Nanook of the North* put away their twentieth-century accoutrements (rifles, utensils, etc.) in favor of the more romantic, traditional tools like spears and whale bone knives. An outdated abacus in this Scottish men's wear shop—rather than an adding machine or calculator—would be just such an item to instantly denote rusticity, backwardness, Scottishness, etc.

absurdly sexy—(PSC; "Science Fiction Sketch") The woman-as-attractive-prop is also endemic to the sci-fi genre. The characterization here seems more like Altaira (Anne Francis) in *Forbidden Planet* (1956), Irish Ryan (Naura Hayden) in the unintentionally funny *Angry Red Planet* (1960), or the intelligent but marginalized (and ogled) Pat Medford (Joan Weldon) in *Them!* (1954). Perhaps the best (or worst) example is the mute Nova (Linda Harrison) in *Planet of the Apes* (1968).

"allay suspicion"—("Science Fiction Sketch") The detective may be playing the role of skeptic here, or naysayer, the one who tries to explain away the fantastic in purely rational or reasonable terms in many sci-fi and fantasy films. In *The Thing From Another World*, Dr. Carrington (Robert Cornthwaite) sees the creature only as a superior being, while in *Forbidden Planet* Dr. Morbeus (Walter Pidgeon) refuses to believe that it is his own subconscious creating the killer monster. Both, of course, suffer for their shortsightedness.

"a lot faster"—("Science Fiction Sketch") Perhaps an allusion to the reduction of some cricket match lengths in the UK in the 1960s from five days to just one day, a move brought about by sagging attendance and what was considered overly defensive play. One-day cricket began as early as 1962 in county play in England, in the "Midlands Knock-Out Cup" (where Northamptonshire won), and where rules were also adjusted to encourage faster play, more careful bowling, and aggressive batting. League one-day cricket would begin in 1969 in England.

American Voice—(PSC; "Science Fiction Sketch") Meant to send up the very popular U.S. science fiction cinema of the 1950s, from classics like *The Day the Earth Stood Still* (1951) and *The Thing From Another World* (1951), to marvelous cult-flops like *Plan 9 From Outer Space* (1959). The sober, authoritative narrator (Cleese with an exaggerated American accent) was certainly one identifiable semantic element of the sci-fi genre syntax. This allusion continues to illustrate the significant effect that film, and especially Hollywood genre film, had on the Python troupe.

"And this . . . in the final"—("Science Fiction Sketch") So the alien blancmanges can win Wimbledon but that win won't be recognized because they aren't human. Therefore, the invasion will have been unsuccessful. In sci-fi/horror the invading creatures' "Achilles Heel" is often something just that simple, a tiny backdoor waiting to be discovered by the intrepid scientist or the open-minded civilian (it's almost never the military in these films). In *War of the Worlds* (1953), the Martian invaders succumb to a common human virus; in *Forbidden Planet* (1956), the death of one man (Dr. Morbeus and his Id) is enough to destroy the marauding creature; in *The Blob* (1958), teenager Steve discovers the creature's simple temperature sensitivity, and passes the information on to a grateful world. In this *FC* episode, the blancmanges will be undone by the fact that they're not human, so a technicality would keep them from winning Wimbledon anyway, as well as the fact that they're both edible and quite tasty to humans.

Similarly, in Ep. 35, people living in high rises created by Mystico (Jones) can remain safely there as long as they simply believe in the buildings—the moment they doubt, the tower blocks begin to fall.

animation—(PSC; animated link out of "You're No Fun Any More") As the animation finishes (members of an Indian brass band move up and down like piano hammers to music), two of the members disappear, with one man saying to the other that they have to "stop meeting like this." The other answers with this episode's catchphrase, "You're no fun any more." This is yet another homoerotic moment, and one that will be followed closely by an image of two naked men cuddling in Ep. 8. The implication seems to be that if there is an all-male band, then there must be some sodomitical activity going on.

The quick scenes that follow continue the at least homosocial subtext, including a whipping on a nineteenth-century Royal Navy ship, and a Dracula figure (Chapman) who loses his teeth when confronted with the exposed neck of a pretty woman—both scenes end with the "You're no fun any more." Incidentally, it wasn't until after the publication of the Wolfenden Report in 1957 that the depiction of homosexuality became possible in British film and on stage, and then only as long as there were no embraces, for instance (Aldgate 128-29).

"**. . . ate his wife**"—("Science Fiction Sketch") Not unlike similar moments in American gangster films like *Scarface* (1932) or *Asphalt Jungle* (1950) where an authority figure (newspaper editor, police chief) lectures both the diegetic and film audience regarding the evils of criminality, to disabuse listeners of any romantic notions of crime, and to reinforce the "crime doesn't pay" mantra. In the science fiction genre, these moments are reserved for the surviving participants to lament man's recklessness as he dabbles with the powers of God, as Dr. Frankenstein says himself in *Frankenstein* (1931), and Captain Abrams (Leslie Nielsen) reminds us in *Forbidden Planet* (1956).

"**Australia**"—("Science Fiction Sketch") Australia, of course, by 1970 had a rich tradition of international tennis success, including Norman Brookes, John Bromwich, Tony Roche, and many others. The fact that Australia was a part of the Commonwealth but not English allowed them to be rendered here (and elsewhere in *FC*) as Other. The successful Aussies will reappear in Ep. 38, as respected penguin scientists dressed as (and named for) tennis players.

"**be gentle with me**"—("The Audit") See Ep. 5, the "Erotic Film" sketch, where this line is actually spoken by a female character. Here in Ep. 7, though, there is a curious cutaway here to the Bishop (Jones) seated at the table, who leers in a rather unseemly way, as if he's responding in a sexual way to the accountant's (Palin) last line. It doesn't seem to be a moment for the audience (they don't respond to the insert). This sexual moment would fit Python's normal questioning of the libidinal capacities of authority figures in *FC*, churchmen and otherwise. In Ep. 20, three bishops will attack the gowned gong girl (Chapman) on the set of *Take Your Pick*.

"**Berwick-on-Tweed**"—("Science Fiction Sketch") A slightly shortened version of Berwick-upon-Tweed, a town in the northernmost portion of England, in the Scottish borderlands. Historically a part of Berwickshire, Scotland. Dr. Johnson traveled through Berwick-on-Tweed, according to Boswell, on his way to Edinburgh on his tour to the Hebrides (*Life of Johnson* 276).

"**Big Business**"—("Science Fiction Sketch") Like "You're no fun any more," this is another catchphrase. These kinds of phrases were at least partly discouraged in *FC*, probably since they had been (and continued to be) staples of other comedy shows on British radio and TV. The next person who utters the phrase, the Bishop (Jones), will end up tied to a railroad track (in the Feltham Marshalling Yards) for "pinching" the phrase, then lying about it. Later, another phrase will emerge, this time in reference to the afflicted Scotsmen under alien attack. See the entry for "destinies" below.

"**billion**"—("Science Fiction Sketch") "Billion" is certainly an American term, comparable to the older English term "thousand millions" (or even "milliard"), and hence fits better in this American sci-fi film spoof. The terms mean a one followed by nine zeroes (or noughts or ciphers). See Schur. "Billion" was one of the Americanisms insinuating its way into British culture during this period. Interestingly, the postwar debt owed to the United States may have helped this increased usage along. In 1945 the British government owed the United States and allies about "£4,000 million," or £4 billion. The United States would have kept count in billions, of course, and the newspapers and government memos went back and forth between the terms as the debt was discussed and serviced (Wilson, *After the Victorians* 507).

bishop bound and gagged and tied across a railway line—("You're No Fun Any More") The lack of respect accorded members of the Anglican clergy in *FC* is partly attributable to the anti-authority zeitgeist of this period anyway, but there's certainly more. In *Postwar* Judt notes a pan-European groundswell of antiauthoritarianism thanks to a perceived collusion between the power of the state and the will of the church:

> The spiritual authority of the Protestant pastor or the Anglican vicar was by convention offered not as a competitor to the state, but rather as its junior partner . . . [and] the distinction between church and state as arbiters of public manners and morals became rather blurred. The late forties and early fifties [when the Pythons came of age] thus appear as a transitional age . . . where the modern state was beginning to to displace church and even class as the arbiter of collective behavior. (229)

Henceforth in these episodes churchmen will appear as thieves, drunkards, and sexual perverts, as well as in very close proximity (as in this sketch) to members of the ruling power and class.

"black pudding"—("Man Turns Into Scotsman") Traditional Scottish fare, it is sausage made with blood and suet (solid fat).

"blancmange"—("Science Fiction Sketch") A boiled milk and gelatin sweetmeat. A dessert, then, is attacking the Earth and turning men into Scotsmen. In the production notes for this series, Terry Jones was scheduled to have played the blancmange (WAC T12/1,088). The blancmange will be mentioned again very late in the series, in Ep. 41 as a possible food for ants ("Michael Ellis"), and will elicit a healthy laugh of recognition from the audience.

The BBC Radio show *The Goon Show* (1951-1960) had earlier created a sketch where Old Age Pensioners are being attacked at the seaside by "hurled batter puddings" ("The Dreaded Batter Pudding Hurler," 12 October 1954), as well as an episode where Neddie, Moriarty, Bluebottle, Gryptite Thynne, and Bloodnok must track and trap the "most savage part" of the "International Christmas Pudding" (15 November 1955) running amok in Africa. There, the pudding is consumed in the end, as well.

Similar diminutions (lofty purpose/stakes, trivial object/means) have occurred in English literature, of course, with the "mock epic" leading the way. Swift in *Gulliver's Travels* (c. 1725), for example, created wars and rebellions based on which end of an egg should be broken first (part I, ch. IV), and it was a single lock of hair that caused nearly fatal familial strife in Pope's *Rape of the Lock* (1712).

Finally, in describing the kind of Britain that the Angry Young Men were rebelling against in the 1950s, novelist Edward Pierce inadvertently points up the incongruity the Pythons created when employing their "fatal blancmange" image:

> Having heard from parents, mostly, about pre-war agitation, read the books in school—the Old Left book publications—having faint memories of the war and the cause it was all about, and then everything having settled in to a sort of *blancmange*-like existence: common sense, tolerance, and a sort of half-a-grain-change as it were, and being resentful that life was less exciting. (Audio transcription, *Eyewitness 1950-59*, "Angry Young Men II")

"Buenos Aires"—(link into "Science Fiction Sketch") Capital city of Argentina, and nowhere near Thaxted.

"But I must"—("Science Fiction Sketch") Angus says this as if making a fool of himself *is* his ultimate destiny as a Scotsman, a destiny over which he has no control. Refer back to the beginning of the sketch, where it was pointed out that Scotsmen have no control over their own destinies.

"Butley Down"—("Science Fiction Sketch") If a legitimate reference, then it could be a misspelling of either "Bewley Down" (200 miles southwest of London) or "Butley Town" (20 miles southeast of Manchester). She clearly pronounces "Butley" as "Bucky," however.

– C –

"caber"—("Man Turns Into Scotsman") *OED*: "A pole, or spar . . . used in the Highland athletic exercise of throwing, tossing the caber." Probably here must also be recognized for its sexual connotations, as the lament has been that real men don't/couldn't turn into Scotsmen—these three Scotsmen aren't man enough to even have their own caber/penis. Conversely, in Ep. 37 in the "Ideal Loon Exhibition" there is a Scotsman attracting significant Pepperpot attention in the "Nae Trews" exhibit.

"calling it doubles"—("Police Station") So playing with five players in a doubles match is all right, but *calling* it doubles is the problem. As is so often the case in the Python oeuvre, names and naming become a crucial issue, and the power of language is such that simple words can have significant textual power (e.g., "Ni!" in *HG*), and attributed names also can transform a person or situation into something or someone entirely different. In Ep. 36 a police inspector becomes Sir Philip Sidney simply because he is called by that name; in Ep. 37, a dull customer becomes a funny bus passenger and then a music hall straight man, etc. In Shakespeare's world Richard and Henry both name and transform in *Richard III* and both *1 Henry IV* and *2 Henry IV*, creating and re-creating their worlds/friends/enemies to suit their purposes. See Chapter 6 in the author's *MPSERD* for more on this subject.

"camel spotting"—("Camel Spotting") A play on the pastime of trainspotting, where the train enthusiast watches for and notes trains and their numbers passing any given point. (The author has seen these hobbyists along the Paddington-Swansea and York-St. Pancras lines, for example, taking notes on each and every passing train.)

centre court—("Blancmanges Playing Tennis") Centre Court, Wimbledon is where the finals of the men's and women's singles matches are played. Scheduling of centre court assignments certainly also depends on the television appeal of the participants.

Monty Python's tennis scenes seem to have been shot at the Lammas Park tennis courts (Ealing), which is very near BBC Television Centre, and just down the street from Ealing Studios.

"Chairman yet"—("The Audit") Almost a tried-and-true punchline, but it's completely ignored by the other characters, perhaps because he's about to be "outed" as an embezzler.

"CID"—("Police Station") Criminal Investigation Department. See Ep. 3, where the Inspector Dim sings about another, more desirable profession outside of CID, that of a window cleaner.

"civilization"—("Science Fiction Sketch") This can be directly connected to H.G. Wells' *War of the Worlds* (1898), which also takes place in a small English town, Woking, and features aliens from outer space bent on global destruction and domination. The American radio and film adaptations of the novel are set in the United States The campiness of the writing and production value owe a great deal to Ed Wood's cult masterpiece *Plan 9 From Outer Space* (1959), called by many the worst film ever made, but also the myriad low-budget sci-fi coming from both the United States and UK during this period. The UK-based Planet Film Productions, for example, produced camp classics like *Devils of Darkness* (1965), *Island of Terror* (1966), and *Night of the Big Heat* (1967), fun sci-fi/horror/exploitation schlock, all.

collage—(PSC; "Science Fiction Sketch") A collection of filmed and often juxtapositionally edited shots; elsewhere in *FC* this process has been referred to as "montage," which is actually a more accurate term than collage, since mixed media isn't being used here.

"Covent Garden"—(caption link into "Science Fiction Sketch") Originally a convent garden, Covent Garden was laid out as per the design of Inigo Jones (see below), and was the first such residential square in the city. It was also London's principal fresh fruit, flower, and vegetable open market for three centuries (finally moving in 1974). It's also the site of the Covent Garden Theatre established by John Rich in 1732, which could

account for the "7.30", "Saturday (near Sunday)" and "afterwards" quips. The eighteenth-century theatre-going custom was for a show, then refreshments afterwards at local inns or pubs. See Pepys and Evelyn for more on London's theatre history as experienced in the seventeenth century.

credits—(PSC; closing credits) Under the closing credits an unidentified Scottish tune plays, not the customary "Liberty Bell," something of a nod to the significance of the Scottishness of the episode.

cricket blazer . . . fussy print dress—(PSC; "Science Fiction Sketch") Mr. Brainsample (Chapman) wears a "cricket blazer," which is a light jacket, often brightly colored, along with "grey flannels"—trousers made of flannel and to be worn for boating or cricket (*OED*). (Chapman's character Reg will wear very similar attire as he delivers Mr. Wentworth's message in the "Spanish Inquisition" sketch, even though the scene is set in 1911; he will there be able to move into another, more contemporary sketch when the "Spanish Inquisition" sketch sputters to a halt, at least for his character. See Ep. 15.)

Mrs. Brainsample's (Idle) "carrier bag" is simply a handled paper shopping bag (it does look as if the Brainsamples have just gotten off the train from a day in the city).

Mr. Potter (Palin) sports the "briefcase and pinstripes" which, as has been seen, comprises portions of the typical attire/uniform of Pythons' City Gent. In this case, he is leaving the train station for home after work somewhere in London's financial district, probably the City of London.

All these clothing details are meant to create the "typical" characters employed by the Pythons by using already well-known and identifiable items. It's only the seventh episode (sixth, as recorded), and these codes are firmly in place. She's a Pepperpot, and he's one of the rarely seen Pepperpot husbands. Also, as in most sci-fi films, the events center around normal, everyday folk, like the young boy and his parents in *Invaders From Mars* (1953), the wandering orphan girl in *Them!* (1954), or the small-town doctor in *Invasion of the Body Snatchers* (1956). In a more local science fiction story, John Wyndham's 1957 novel *The Midwich Cuckoos* (which would be filmed as *Village of the Damned* in 1960), an entire normal, unexceptional English village becomes involved in an alien invasion.

"crofter"—("Science Fiction Sketch") *OED*: "One who rents and cultivates a croft, small holdings especially in the Highlands and Islands of Scotland." In Ep. 37, Queen Victoria will be characterized as a "simple crofter's daughter" who became queen; when Neddie (Secombe) becomes PM in *The Goon Show*, he is also characterized as a "crofter's son." *Private Eye* has also used a version of the sobriquet to describe PM Macmillan (see notes to Ep. 37). Macmillan had been born in Chelsea of well-to-do parentage.

"Czechoslovakia"—("Science Fiction Sketch") Tennis in Czechoslovakia—in 1970 a Soviet-controlled satellite following the 1968 "Prague Spring" invasion—had produced Wimbledon champions like expatriate Jaroslav Drobny in 1954, and his coach (also a former player) Karel Kozeluh. (See wimbledon.org.)

– D –

"debenture preference stock"—("The Audit") *OED*: "A bond issued by a corporation or company (under seal), in which acknowledgement is made that the corporation or company is indebted to a particular person or to the holder in a specified sum of money on which interest is to be paid until repayment of the principal." In a Wimbledon connection, debentures are available for the acquiring of seat options around center court. The Pythons are probably just throwing finance jargon around here, as well.

"destinies"—("Man Turns Into Scotsman") Cf. the sign in the boardroom, "There's no place in big business for sentiment" earlier in this same episode. This point, that the Scots have no control over their own destinies, is significant as the issues of sovereignty and self-rule are broached within the Commonwealth.

It won't be until the late 1970s when Scotland will gain some independence from England (and primarily based on the increasing importance of Scottish oil reserves, following North Sea oil discoveries in 1969), including an assembly with limited legislative and executive power. Harold Wilson's Labour government of the 1960s had taken the paternal approach and attempted to bring Scotland into the modern age by updating its economy and industry, perhaps a rather heavy-handed (and less than successful) way to keep Scotland from having control over its own destiny. Wilson's moves were also meant to quell a rising autonomy movement within the country (*ODNB*). This point is almost missed in the rapid-fire Python delivery, but salient and sensitive political issues of the 1960s and 1970s were regularly broached.

"Deutschmark"—("The Audit") The West German unit of currency, officially instituted in 1948.

"Dimples, The"—(link into "Science Fiction Sketch") There is a Dimples in Lancashire, near Garstang. In this citation, the Pythons have indicated that "The Dimples" has some sort of geographic significance, like a dell, glen or knoll, or the like. In D.H. Lawrence's

Sons and Lovers (1913), the location of the colliery worker homes is known as "The Bottoms"; in fact, "The Bottoms" are the first words of the novel (1). Also, cf. the vacation spot known as the Wisconsin Dells, for instance. There is also a Dimples Lane in Garstang, Preston.

"dinna"—("Science Fiction Sketch") Scottish slang for "do not," as "wilna" is for "will not."

"do that to a man"—("Science Fiction Sketch") This same question is a rephrased version of similar hyperbolized and fear-ridden questions in *Them!*, *Forbidden Planet*, *The Blob*, and many other sci-fi films, asked when the full power and destructiveness of the "it"—giant ants, alien invaders, monsters from the Id—is finally, fully realized.

"Dr Finlay"—("Man Turns Into Scotsman") Character on a Scottish TV series (*Dr Finlay's Casebook*) that ran from 1962-1971 on BBC, and based on Archibald Cronin's stories. *Flying Circus* director Ian MacNaughton was working for the *Dr. Finlay* show, which he termed a "very turgid drama" and "too dramatic," when he was given the chance to move over to BBC Light Entertainment and Spike Milligan's *Q5* (Morgan, 1999, 32).

Dr. Finlay's Casebook ("Sundays on BBC1") is the cover feature on the BBC's 8 March 1969 *Radio Times*.

"dromedary"—("Camel Spotting") Also known as the Arabian Camel, the one-humped Dromedary is found in northern and eastern Africa (*EBO*). The silliness of this sketch (including and especially the ending) echoes the Ogden Nash poem, "The Camel":

> The camel has a single hump;
> The dromedary, two;
> Or else the other way around,
> I'm never sure. Are you? (*Bad Parents' Garden of Verse*)

(Incidentally, a camel can have either one or two humps.) A camel will also appear a number of times in the "Albrecht Dürer" sketches in the first episode of *Fliegender Zirkus*.

"dull"—("Camel Spotting") Cf. the "dull. Dull. *Dull.* My God it's dull" life of a chartered accountant in the "Vocational Guidance Counsellor" sketch in Ep. 10.

"Dunbar"—("Science Fiction Sketch") Located about fifty miles east of Edinburgh. The photo used here is pointedly rustic and Scottish—a humble cottage with thatched roof in a windswept countryside populated by sheep—befitting the backwardness the Pythons demand of their northern neighbors. It looks like a crofter's cottage, of course, and not a men's wear shop. The photo is not listed in the requests for this episode (WAC T12/1,088).

– E –

"earnest"—("Science Fiction Sketch") A downpayment, made so as to indicate that the deal is imminent, and being done "in good faith."

Episode 7—This episode was recorded sixth on 10 October 1969, and broadcast on 30 November 1969. Also appearing in this episode: Donna Reading (*Softly Softly*), Constance Starling (*Dig*), Sandra Setchworth, J. Neill, and Flanagan (Eps. 11, 12; *Benny Hill*).

Flanagan, by the way, is the same Maureen Flanagan who was during this period a personal friend of the infamous Kray twins, East End gangsters who will be featured pseudonymously in Ep. 14 (as the Pirhana Brothers). See notes to Ep. 14 for more. There is no indication that Flanagan (also a former *Sun* "Page Three Girl") had any qualms with the Pythons spoofing her notorious friends.

Incidentally, in this episode Cleese's voiced "Monty Python's Flying Circus" line (to finish It's Man's utterance) is not included in the printed script, but is heard on the show as recorded. By the tenth episode, the Pythons will clearly be tiring of the "same old, same old" structure for opening the show. See notes to Ep. 10.

"everything depends"—("Blancmanges Playing Tennis") In *Planet of the Apes* (1968), the fate of what's left of humanity rests on Charlton Heston's broad, suntanned shoulders; in *The Day the Earth Stood Still* (1951), a boy must show the alien that Earth has some value, or humanity is doomed; in *Metropolis* (1927), only young Freder's actions will bring change; and in *Doctor Who* (1963-1989) the earth is saved countless times by the title character (often with some assistance, as Podgorny will receive from the Brainsamples).

– F –

fangs fall out—(PSC; "You're No Fun Any More") Since *Dracula* was at least partly a tale of perverse sexual profligacy (the vampire only "satisfied" when he is [en]gorged with blood), the loss of fangs is a sign of sexual impotency or at least inadequacy, especially when the woman's response—that he's "no fun any more"—is noted. Also significant is the fact that the troupe's only homosexual—Chapman—is portraying this emasculated, incapable vampire.

"Fields, W.C."—(link into "Science Fiction Sketch") This is a play on (1) the name of the well-known American vaudeville and film comedian, (2) the British use of the term "fields" in addresses, like St.-Martin-in-the-Fields, and (3) the meaning of "WC" in regional jargon—"water closet."

Film of . . . along street—(PSC; "Man Turns Into Scotsman") Typical shots of the "wasteland effect" of alien invasion, or, in this case, aliens turning normal people into Scotsmen and the infected Scotsmen leaving for Scotland. Similar shots can be seen in *The Day the Earth Stood Still*, for example. Once again, the Pythons are aware of the generic conventions of sci-fi and can either use them faithfully or undercut them, or both.

This sci-fi set-up is most likely borrowed from the very popular Richard Matheson novel *I Am Legend* (1954), wherein a bacterial pandemic has wiped out humanity (at least in Los Angeles), turning most into vampire-like creatures. The first film version of that novel, *The Last Man on Earth*, starring Vincent Price, appeared in 1964.

"Finchley"—("Science Fiction Sketch") Finchley is a London suburb, northwest of the metropolis. The character Bluebottle (Peter Sellers) of *The Goon Show* hails from East Finchley, and is constantly bemoaning his plights on the playgrounds there.

"five people"—("Police Station") The policeman (authority figure) here is more interested in the specter of uneven teams in tennis than in the portent of worldwide destruction. See the police officer in *The Blob* (1958), who spends much of his time making sure Steve McQueen and friends don't drive recklessly, as well as the misguided scientist Dr. Arthur Carrington (Robert Cornthwaite) in *The Thing* (1951) who only sees the scientific marvels of the marauding creature, not the imminent threat. The guards at the door of Swamp Castle as well as inside Herbert's room in *Holy Grail* are also more concerned with the trivia of their duties, and most end up skewered by Lancelot.

"Flight Lt."—(link into "Science Fiction Sketch") "In the Royal Air Force a flight lieutenant ranks below a squadron leader and above a flying officer" (EBO).

football stadium—("Science Fiction Sketch") Stadium where club soccer teams regularly play. This stadium appears to be the Brentford Football Club Ground in Ealing, just a few miles southwest of Television Centre.

Contrary to what the printed script calls for, the play is already in progress when we cut to the scene, the spectator is standing with his noisemaker, and *then* the player scores and celebrates. Most of these are extreme long shots, emphasizing the emptiness of the stadium. (In shooting *Omega Man* in 1970-1971, producers utilized downtown Los Angeles on weekends, when virtually no citizens visited the inner-city streets, and captured a handful of extreme long shots showing almost no human activity.) There is no slow pan around the stadium—also called for in the script—the long shots of the player and referee accomplish this task.

These directional specifics, again, may have been provided by Jones, who was more interested in the camera movement and frame composition than the others (excepting, perhaps Gilliam) seemed to have been. Jones will go on to help edit much of the series (see McCabe; Morgan, 1999), as well as co-direct *Holy Grail*, and direct *Life of Brian* and *Meaning of Life*.

"frog trampling"—(link into "Science Fiction Sketch") In the Python bestiary, frogs and toads appear quite often. One of the discussed names for the show originally was *The Toad Elevating Moment* (which would become a link in the episodes), and Idle mentions a band named "Toad the Wet Sprocket" in a Monty Python album sketch. In Ep. 14, the *Panorama*-type show exposing the Piranha brothers is called *Ethel the Frog*. There is also a "five frog curse" (like a five-car pile-up) occurring in Gilliam's animations in Ep. 17, crunchy frogs are eaten in Ep. 6, and "S. Frog" (Idle) is being fired for ruining an advertising firm in Ep. 24.

This reference is also heard earlier, prior to *FC*, in an episode of *At Last the 1948 Show*, when Joan Shock mentions "Dr. Bartle's Frog Trampling Institution."

– G –

"Galaxy of Andromeda"—("Science Fiction Sketch") A spiral galaxy in fairly close proximity to Earth.

"Gonzales, Pancho"—("Blancmanges Playing Tennis") Gonzalez (1928-1995) was an American tennis player of the 1950s and 1960s who won multiple singles championships. Gonzalez would play his famous 112-game match at the Wimbledon Championships in 1969, finally defeating Charlie Pasarell—he was, in fact, playing as well as he had ever played (as described the announcer [Idle]). Gonzalez won 22-24, 1-6, 16-14, 6-3, 11-9. The match was played 25 June 1969. (See wimbledon.org.)

– H –

Hackforth, Norman—(PSC; "Science Fiction Sketch") Hackforth (1908-1996) was a broadcaster, biographer, and songwriter. Hackforth's character (voiced by Jones) here acts like a game show host, speaking to audience members watching the show. Hackforth played the "mystery voice" on *The Twenty Questions Murder Mystery* (1950)—what the Pythons probably borrowed for their purposes—and earlier was a writer for *Halesapoppin* (BBC 1948).

The traditional game show format for "clue"-type games is employed here, where the audience gets to see the answers before the contestants. It is rather in-

congruous to insert this format into a sci-fi sketch, of course.

"He . . . left them"—("Science Fiction Sketch") Sort of a "meanwhile, back at the ranch" scenario used in serialized dramas in the early days of film, then television.

"He's right you know"—("The Audit") The character Norman echoes this on the *Monty Python Live at the Theatre Royal Drury Lane* LP, in the sketch called "Election Special," and the sketch just fades away. Ron Vibbentrop (Chapman) will say the same thing to potential National Bocialist Party voters, though with a bit of a German accent, in Ep. 10.

– I –

"inadequate brain capacity"—("Man Turns Into Scotsman") Typical sophomoric jab at the Scots, displaying Pythons' penchant for both high and low comedy.

"incidental music"—("Man Turns Into Scotsman") In film, TV, and radio this music tends to be connected to the "incident" at hand (the setting), and can be either diegetic or extradiegetic, meaning created in the world of the film (where the characters can hear it or even create it) or beyond that world. In this scene the characters actually hear the extradiegetic music, which isn't usually the case, and the girl is simple enough to think it's the doorbell ringing. The conventions of the sci-fi genre, then, are being both upheld *and* undercut at a dizzying pace. Also, the traditional separation of the score or musical sound effects (extra-diegetic sound) from the world of the film (the diegesis) is played with, reminding the viewer of the artificiality of the production.

The incidental music used throughout "Science Fiction Sketch" is not accounted for or even mentioned in the surviving papers held at the BBC's WAC records. This is unusual, as virtually every other episode in the series (and file in the WAC) contains such copyright clearance pages. This one may simply have gone missing in the intervening forty years.

"Inigo Jones"—(link into "Science Fiction Sketch") Jones (1573-1652), a renowned British painter, architect, and designer, is credited with founding the English classical tradition of architecture. Jones designed the Queen's House, the Banqueting House at Whitehall, and the Queen's Chapel at St. James' Palace (cf. Ep. 40, when George III [Chapman] wants to schedule a banquet at the palace). Jones is not known to have designed any fish emporia.

"Institute"—("Science Fiction Sketch") The presence of science and scientists—either as megalomaniacs fooling with the powers of God, or as the only answer to the alien threat—appear as necessary semantic elements in many sci-fi films. Charles (Chapman) is the type of scientist who did not create the global or cosmic disaster, but who is poised to (a) uncover the plot of the aliens or reasons for the disaster and (b) possibly offer solutions, thus saving the Earth. Later Charles will discover the aliens' insidious plot, but the invasion will only be countered when seemingly ordinary folk (the Brainsamples) take on the blancmange invaders.

"It's British sir"—("The Audit") Perhaps not the answer the Board Member was looking for, as he (Cleese) looks back to his notes, though the sketch keeps going. Could be a reference to "British sterling," but that's not entirely clear.

– J –

Jewish figure—(link into "Science Fiction Sketch") This character isn't dressed in any caricatured style, actually, so the viewer may not comprehend the racial/ethnic gist. Not sporting a hooked nose or rubbing coins together, this rather vague caricature might be missed by viewers, unless the upward inflection of the character's voice is recognized. Again, this is a shorthand way for Python to identify racial Others. The character is also, of course, concerned with rising costs, which might also be a hint at his stereotyped Jewishness.

"Jocasta"—("Science Fiction Sketch") The name is of nominal interest, as Jocasta is both the odd-woman-out in the doubles match, and, in literature, the widowed queen in Sophocles' *Oedipus the King* (c. 427 BC).

– K –

"ken"—("Science Fiction Sketch") Scottish vernacular for "understand" or "recognize."

"King, Billie Jean"—("Blancmanges Playing Tennis") Female American tennis player King (b. 1943) helped bring women's tennis into the public eye with the creation of the women's professional tennis tour. King was named "Outstanding Female Athlete of the World" in 1967, and had also beaten Ann-Haydon Jones (mentioned again in Ep. 22) for one of her six Wimbledon titles that same year.

knight in armour—(PSC; "You're No Fun Any More") The knight in armour appears in several other *FC* episodes, and was usually played by Gilliam. If the punchline delivered happened to be off-color, pur-

posely unfunny, or an acknowledged and hoary chestnut the knight would appear. This rather obvious visual gag from the music hall and television stage, will soon disappear and not return to *FC*, especially as the Pythons' writing acumen sharpened.

– L –

"Lady Chairman"—("The Audit") There are no women present, and the Chairman is played by Chapman.

"lager and limes"—("Science Fiction Sketch") Light (pale) beers with lime or lime juice added. This could also be a cockney rhyming scheme, where "lager and limes" has replaced a more common word that would rhyme with "limes," and might be built on the near-rhyme with "spine" earlier. See Schur's *British English, A to Zed*, 424-25. Ringo orders this drink for himself and his mates in *Help!* (1965).

"Laver"—("Blancmanges Playing Tennis") Rod Laver (b. 1938), successful Australian tennis player, won four singles championships at Wimbledon (1961-1962, 1968-1969). He is also mentioned in the "Australian Wine" sketch for the Python album *Monty Python's Previous Record* (1972), performed by "Wine Expert" Eric Idle:

> . . . the Australian Wino Society thoroughly recommends a 1970 Coq du Rod Laver, which, believe me, has a kick on it like a mule: 8 bottles of this and you're really finished. At the opening of the Sydney Bridge Club, they were fishing them out of the main sewers every half an hour. (side 2)

The "Laver Institute" is mentioned in Ep. 38, where penguins are being studied by tennis players, including Bartkowicz, Ken Rosewall (b. 1934, Australia), and Jack Kramer (b. 1921, United States). See the entry for "Stolle, Fred" below, as well as Ep. 38, for more.

"leave your radio on during the night"—(link into "Science Fiction Sketch") As television programming would halt at night (and during the war, cease entirely), radios were often left on through the nights to hear civil defense news, warnings, evacuation announcements, etc.

"license fee"—(link into "Science Fiction Sketch") This is the mandatory fee paid annually by all TV and radio owners, and which funds the BBC. The subject of the requisite television license fee appears often throughout May 1969 in political cartoons. The license fees as of 1 January 1969 are displayed in Ep. 20, as the credits roll.

The "Jewish Figure" (Palin) seems less concerned about the rising fee than for the quality of the broadcast material it's paying for.

"lira"—("The Audit") Italian denomination, indicating this corporation does business (and/or has a business presence) internationally.

"London Road, Oxford"—(link into "Science Fiction Sketch") London Road actually runs through Oxford, approximately east-west to/from Headington, which at least the Oxfordians of the troupe (Jones and Palin) would have known, and probably very well.

The "silly address" motif will reappear throughout *FC*, and is a response to the BBC's (and other local networks' and even newspapers') policy of airing letters from patrons. See entry for "viewer's letter" in Ep. 5, as well as the entry for "East Grinstead" in that same episode. (*Private Eye* also published mostly farcical letters made to look like ones sent to the BBC and *Daily Mirror*, etc. They did publish one or two proper letters of complaint from angry readers, as well, which were just as funny.) The BBC often went out of its way to promote regional viewership by catering to those more provincial areas.

". . . look after yourselves"—("Police Station") The very picture of the paternal, all-embracing police or government presence in postwar Britain—powerful enough to interrupt BBC broadcasts, funny and perhaps chilling at the same time. This type of policeman harks back to the warm, avuncular PC Dixon (see Morgan below), and the "direct address" mode is borrowed directly from the beginning and ending of the beloved *Dixon of Dock Green* television episodes. Also, the postwar welfare society instigated and expanded by consecutive Labour (Attlee, 1945-1951) and Conservative (Churchill, 1951-1955; Eden, 1955-1957; Macmillan, 1957-1963) governments posited a similar warm embrace, but at the national level (e.g., cradle to grave health care, nationalized industries).

In *Britain Since 1945*, Kenneth Morgan characterizes the postwar English police force this way:

> In no country did the unarmed police enjoy a more natural respect, with the folk imagery of the 'bobby on the beat', later to be given support in the film *The Blue Lamp* [1950] and later still in the highly popular television serial *PC 49* [BBC Radio and TV, 1947-1953]. The policeman was less a custodian of order . . . than a servant of the community who retrieved lost dogs and helped old ladies across the road. (60-61)

So this is the type of police force the Pythons would have all grown up with, and had reinforced in myriad TV and film depictions. For more on this topic, see notes to Ep. 29, under the "Evening all" entry, or earlier, in Ep. 5, under "All right!"

– M –

"Mary"—("Science Fiction Sketch") A most Catholic name choice (in a most Popish country), just as Angus might be the stereotypical Scottish male name of choice. In Ep. 22, Mary, Queen of Scots will be murdered (in two eerily similar radio drama episodes).

McWoolworths—("Man Turns Into Scotsman") Satirizing the frequent Scottish use of the prefix "Mc" or "Mac" in front of their proper names. (The prefix "mac" or "mc" is Gaelic for "son," and can be properly McDonald, MacDonald, Macdonald, etc.) This is, then, another typal instance, a shorthand way to identify or apply Scottishness in humor, and especially satire. This is the very type of belittlement that the Pythons will not employ in regard to the Irish, who won't be mentioned at all except in the "Our Eamonn" sketch. See notes to Ep. 31 for more on this conspicuous absence.

Woolworths is the proprietary name of a chain of department stores in Great Britain and the United States and founded in 1878.

"mebbe . . . gi'"—("Science Fiction Sketch") More Scottish colloquial spellings for Podgorny's approximate pronunciations. His accent is much thicker than even these special spellings indicate. A word like "has" is pronounced "hah," for instance.

mid-shot—(PSC; "Science Fiction Sketch") Medium camera shot, generally from the waist to just above the top of the subject's head. This is one of the few instances where camera directions, especially camera-to-subject-distance, are mentioned in the written scripts. It could be that Terry Jones, who always had an interest in the actual direction and editing of the program, influenced this inclusion.

moor—("Science Fiction Sketch") Unenclosed wasteland, essentially, often covered in heather or gorse, depending on the latitude. A "moor" is often used symbolically or poetically to depict loneliness and distance from civilization, and is, for example, typically a Sir Walter Scott novel setting (Ep. 38).

"Mr. Llewellyn"—("Man Turns Into Scotsman") This gets a big laugh, perhaps because the specter of a Welshman turning into a Scotsman is even more outrageous than an Englishman doing the same. A well-known referent might be Richard Llewellyn (1907-1983), a Welsh-born novelist, and author of *How Green Was My Valley* (1939).

"mummy"—("Man Turns Into Scotsman") British slang for "mommy." The *OED* notes "mummy" as a childish version of "mommy," which would fit the already infantile, pouty, and obviously sexual depiction of the girl in this scene, a "Lolita" figure (Nabokov novel, 1954; Kubrick film, 1962).

music rises—(PSC; "Science Fiction Sketch") The sweating and rising creepy music are also significant generic components of the sci-fi and horror film genres, building tension for the inevitable surprise moment. See entry for "incidental music" above for more.

– N –

New Pudsey—("Science Fiction Sketch") Pudsey is a city in the Yorkshire area, near Leeds. There is no "New Pudsey" in the UK, just as there is no "North Malden" as depicted in Ep. 27, just a "Malden" and an "Old Malden." The joke is probably that the viewer couldn't imagine anyone wanting to found a New Pudsey, given the obscurity of the original.

newspaper—("Man Turns Into Scotsman") Actually, this is just a sandwich board–type sign with a handwritten headline under the *Daily Gazette* banner. These boards are still seen on London streets advertising the day's headlines.

"nip"—("Science Fiction Sketch") *OED*: "To move rapidly or nimbly."

"no fun any more"—("You're No Fun Any More") An admission that the "comic misunderstanding" characteristic of Renaissance comic history (where, for instance, a commoner is confused with a king) is necessary for the structure of Python humor to stand in this instance (see *MPSERD*, 132). Once the absurdity of the situation is noticed or identified by one of its participants, the narrative must move on to something else, some other constructed absurdity. Cf. the sketch where members of "The Society for Putting Things on Top of Other Things" realize how silly their society really is (and all other similar societies)—they halt the meeting and disband—only to discover they are trapped on film as opposed to video, and a new silliness begins.

– O –

oil lamps etc.—(PSC; "Science Fiction Sketch") The cottage interior seems as rustic as it can get, missing only any visible sign of the oats (or perhaps grazing animals) that both Dr. Johnson and Python would have connected inseparably with a tatty Scottish household.

In his *Dictionary* Johnson defines "oats" as a "grain which in England is generally given to horses, but in Scotland supports the people." Johnson's biographer Boswell, a Scot himself, would later note: "It was pleasant to me to find that 'oats,' the 'food of horses,' were so much used as the food of the people in Dr. Johnson's own town" (*Life of Johnson*, v. 1). Here the interior of the purported "men's wear shop" (a studio set) is made to match the rustic exterior (a photograph), a crofter's cottage surrounded by gorse.

" . . . ought not to go, Angus"—("Science Fiction Sketch") Foreshadowing, or the prescience that characters often display in sci-fi and horror films that something nefarious, creeping, unforeseen, or calamitous is about to happen. In *Invasion of the Body Snatchers* (1956), Wilma (Virginia Christine) knows that her uncle isn't her uncle anymore, but can't prove it before she, too is "changed"; in the even earlier *The Invisible Man* (1933), Flora (Gloria Stuart) begs Griffin (Claud Rains) to stop experimenting, that it will destroy him. Usually, though, these are the characters that survive, while those who ignore such warnings almost inevitably die. Again, since Mrs. Podgorny (Jones) herself will soon be consumed, Python is undermining audience expectations of the genre.

over the head—("Man Turns Into Scotsman") Just one of many examples where females (actual females, not cross-dressed males) in *FC* are treated with violence that is less cartoon-like. See also the art critic (Palin) strangling his wife (Ep. 8) and the shooting of Brian (Cleveland) in "The Lost World of Rouirama," Ep. 29.

– P –

"pelote"—("Man Turns Into Scotsman") Any of a number of ball games played in France, Spain, Mexico, the Philippines, etc.

photo—(PSC; link into "Science Fiction Sketch") This quick photo of a somewhat grizzled farmer-type, coupled with the voiceover reminding viewers to leave their radios on during the night, elicit a laugh from the audience—perhaps as a result of the incongruity of the moment.

This also follows the "license fee" reference, and radios were also subject to license fees until 1971, as a result of the Wireless Telegraphy Act of 1904 (licensed by the Postmaster General).

"pinches"—("You're No Fun Any More") Steals, purloins.

pitch—("Science Fiction Sketch") Usually associated with cricket, but any playing field or surface can be called a pitch. In this case, the players are moving onto the tennis court.

plainclothes man—(PSC; "Police Station") Policeman not wearing a uniform. This is unusual for *FC*, since this out-of-uniform policeman isn't instantly recognizable, and therefore more difficult to identify as a type. In this scene, then, the policeman (Idle) must identify himself by personality and actions. His anger (he slaps Angus) at being mistaken for a lowly sergeant—"Detective Inspector!"—only happens because he isn't uniformed, and Mr. Podgorny (Palin) can't rely on visual cues to determine rank and status.

"plucky"—("Blancmanges Playing Tennis") *OED*: "Characterized by pluck; showing determination to fight or struggle; brave, courageous, daring." This usage is also probably somewhat paternalistic and meant to diminish, as these Englishmen note the tenacity of even the lowly Scots. "Pluck" was the general character trait of many figures in the Ealing comedies of the postwar era, including *Passport to Pimlico* (1949), and *The Man in the White Suit* (1951), all brimming with English eccentricity and pluck. The rueful joke was that these characters had little else in the postwar years of austerity and rationing.

"Podgorny"—("Science Fiction Sketch") Another name in the news at the time of this episode's writing was Nikolay Viktorovich Podgorny, a well-known Soviet statesman and Communist Party official. Podgorny traveled significantly, and was involved in a much-publicized power struggle for Soviet leadership—viz, the eventual overthrow of Nikita Khrushchev—along with Leonid Brezhnev in the mid-1960s. See Ep. 20 for a still photo and another mention of Podgorny. Curious that Angus would have such a non-Scots name, too, unless there is also a subtextual reference to the "them" of the Communist conspiracy of the period.

"Potter, Harold"—("Science Fiction Sketch") This could be an oblique reference to Harold Potter, the author of the substantially soporific *The Principles and Practice of Conveyancing* (London, 1934). "Harold Potter" is also the name of a hoist company in existence in Nottingham (East Midlands) since 1921.

The name itself, "Potter," may be significant: *OED*: "Trifling action or (in Scott) talk. Also, a gentle stroll or saunter." Harold Potter, as underplayed by Palin, does fit these descriptions nicely.

Potter's front gate—(PSC; "Man Turns Into Scotsman") The appropriately bad flying saucer scenes (looking every bit as accomplished as those found in Ed Wood's acclaimed *Plan 9 From Outer Space*) were shot in the BBC's puppet theatre at TV Centre.

The backdrops in the puppet theatre are composited (retouched) still photos of the central London area. Portland House (a very rectangular, International Style skyscraper built in 1963) can be clearly seen in the distance in the first photo, before Mr. Potter is changed. The second photo (when the aliens' "changing beam" fires down from the bouncy, dangling little ship), is also at least partially of the central London area, but appears to be even more of a composite photo, with a Lincoln Cathedral–type structure looming in the distance over London-area rooftops.

"Provost of Edinburgh"—("Science Fiction Sketch") Historically, provosts collected taxes and fines, and served as military leaders and judges. A very curious outburst, this might be an oblique reference to an incident described in Sir Walter Scott's novel *The Antiquary* (1816):

> "Alarm?" said Edie, "troth there's alarm, for the *provost's* gar'd the beacon light on the Halket-head be sorted up (that suld hae been sorted half a year syne) in an unco hurry, and the council hae named nae less a man than auld Caxon himsell to watch the light. Some say it was out o' compliment to Lieutenant Taffril,—for it's neist to certain that he'll marry Jenny Caxon,—some say it's to please your honour and Monkbarns that wear wigs—and some say there's some auld story about a periwig that ane o' the bailies got and neer paid for— Onyway, there he is, *sitting cockit up like a skart upon the tap o' the craig, to skirl when foul weather comes*." (italics added; chapter 43)

Roughly translated, the final sentence describes the man as sitting proudly (cockit) like a cormorant (skart) on the top or point (tap) of the crag (craig). (The heavily pleated kilt was actually known to have often helped turn aside spear and sword thrusts.)

Sir Walter Scott will be mentioned significantly later, in Ep. 38, the "*A Book at Bedtime*" sketch, where multiple cast members attempt to read aloud excerpts from Scott's novel *Redgauntlet* (1824).

– R –

railway line—("The Audit") This is a comic variation of the stereotypical silent gag (from early Biograph films—Griffith's *The Lonedale Operator* [1912], for example) of the "lady in distress" lying across a railroad track. Also popularized in the cartoon world of Bill Scott and Jay Ward, *Rocky and Bullwinkle and Friends* (1959-1967), where heroic Dudley Do-Right saved Nell more than once from a similar fate. These American cartoons were very deft social and especially political satires, deflating the Cold War powers, the space and arms race, Middle Eastern contentions and contenders, TV and advertising, and on, poking at many of the same targets the Pythons would drawn down on a few years later.

"Rayners Lane"—(link into "Science Fiction Sketch") Rayners Road runs through Putney, a London suburb.

red coat—("Science Fiction Sketch") An oily compère, usually played by either Idle or Palin. Here, Palin takes the role. Probably just a well-known type here, but the Butlin's Holiday Camps employed ubiquitous Red Coats as camp directors. The scene is shot at the Staines Recreation Ground (WAC T12/1,086).

"refreshment . . . collector"—("Camel Spotting") All parts of a normal passenger train operating in the UK to this day. The restaurant car serves full meals, the buffet is for lighter fare, and the ticket collector simply ensures that all passengers are ticketed. This fixation on trains and train travel is something of a British national mania, probably due to the indelibly scored images of and experiences with train travel so important to the UK since the mid-nineteenth century.

"rhetorically"—("Man Turns Into Scotsman") Here Charles is speaking rhetorically, a moment of higher thinking, while just two lines before he is extremely literal as he responds, "Hello mummy." Cf. the RSM in the "Self-Defence" sketch, who can teach his students about the dangers of fresh fruit one moment, and react in horror the next when one of those same students mentions a fruit by name.

"Riley"—("Police Station") "Doghouse Reilly" is the fake name Marlowe offers to the flirtatious Carmen Sternwood in Raymond Chandler's novel *The Big Sleep* (1939).

Rise and Fall of the Roman Empire—("Police Station") At the time of the writing of this episode, there were no extant books featuring this specific title. What the Pythons may have been referring to was the quite old *Reflections on the Causes of the Rise and Fall of the Roman Empire*, by Montesquieu (1689-1755), first published c. 1725. The book seems to have been fairly popular, being republished in both London and Scotland in the nineteenth century, probably for university library use.

Not an authoress, Googie Withers (b. 1917) was an actress, one of the many "plucky" Ealing Studios starlets of the postwar period (appearing in the comedy horror film *Dead of Night* in 1945, for example). She had not appeared in a feature film since 1956, taking up the craft again in 1971.

Runs to stop and puts out hand—("Man Turns Into Scotsman") This scene was shot on Bloemfontein Road at the corner of Australia Road, W12, near the White City Stadium (WAC T12/1,088), and not far from Television Centre.

– S –

"Saturday (near Sunday)"—(link into "Science Fiction Sketch") Perhaps an oblique reference to the title of the film *Saturday Night and Sunday Morning* (1960), starring Albert Finney and directed by Karel Reisz. This Saturday night to Sunday morning stretch of time is also key to the conflict in part of Cunegonde's tale in *Candide*, wherein she is being shared by the Jew and the Inquisitor. Also, see the entry above for "Covent Garden."

Scotsman—(PSC; "Man Turns Into Scotsman") The implication here is that a Scotsman isn't a man to begin with. This carries on the age-old, Dr. Samuel Johnson–led assault on all things Scottish, assaults happily countered and reported by his biographer Boswell. Johnson admitted to Boswell that he purposely tried to "vex" the Scots people by his definition of oats in his *Dictionary*. A good example of Python's Other characterizations—anything non-English is suspect.

Perhaps the Pythons' penchant for drawing down on Scotsmen and Scotland (Scotsmen on horses, Scotsmen wearing no underwear, Scotsmen as inept skyjackers, Scotsmen with inadequate brain capacities, Scotsmen as kamikaze bombers, etc.) can be traced back to their comedy heroes the Goons. The Scotsman is for the Goons a consistent target, whether just the use of an outrageous Scots accent, or the setting/subject matter of an entire episode, including "The Treasure of Loch Lomond" (28 February 1956) and "The Curse of Frankenstein" (27 January 1958). The almost complete absence of *Goon Show* references to the Irish or Ireland is also worth mentioning—a very similar lack seen in *FC*. More on this structuring Irish absence in the notes to Ep. 31, the "Our Eamonn" sketch.

Seventh Seal—(PSC; "Man Turns Into Scotsman") A 1955 Swedish film written and directed by Ingmar Bergman. The Pythons were well aware of both European art films and Hollywood fare. The latter would have been available through the first-run movie houses across the country; during the postwar years Hollywood films were far outpacing British films on British screens. The Oxbridge university settings of the period happened to house the target audiences for filmmakers of the French New Wave (1959-1967), Das Neue Kino (1962-1982), and even Akira Kurosawa's internationally influential years (1950-1985). The famous shot from Bergman's masterpiece isn't quite realized here—the distance from subject and the position of the sun don't allow for the proper silhouette effect Bergman was able to create.

The high seriousness, artsy-ness, and Dark Ages setting of *Seventh Seal* would help inspire *Monty Python and the Holy Grail* almost two decades later.

"shareholders"—("The Audit") Owners of stock (shares) in a company or corporation. The Pythons are/were, themselves, shareholders in *FC* and the films and merchandise that have followed.

"shilling"—("The Audit") *OED*: "A former English money of account, from the Norman Conquest of the value of 12d., or of a pound sterling." The shilling would disappear in 1971 with the new monetary system. See the entry for "12/6D" in Ep. 6.

"shivers"—("Science Fiction Sketch") A response generally reserved for the horror genre, though in the 1950s hybridizations of the horror and sci-fi genres occurred (see *The Beast From 20,000 Fathoms*, *Them!* and *Tarantula*), creating more frightening technology-spawned creatures.

"sixpence"—("The Audit") Obsolete monetary unit equal to six pennies. Mr. Pewtey has mentioned the sixpenny bottle in which he and his lovely wife save money during the "Marriage Guidance Counsellor" sketch in Ep. 2.

"Sol"—("Science Fiction Sketch") The sun personified. The starscape background used in the opening portion of this sketch was 35mm stock film secured from Technicolor (WAC T12/1,088).

"Sopwith"—(PSC; "Camel Spotting") The Sopwith Camel, designed by Sir Thomas Octave Murdoch Sopwith (1888-1989), was Britain's premier fighter plane during WWI. The comic character Snoopy flew this "plane" (his doghouse), as well, as he portrayed the World War I Fighter Ace in "Peanuts."

"sporrans"—("Science Fiction Sketch") The "kilt" reference is self-explanatory, but a "sporran" is a bit more specialized: "A pouch or large purse made of skin, usually with the hair left on and with ornamental tassels, etc., worn in front of the kilt by Scottish Highlanders" (*OED*).

spotting gear—(PSC; "Camel Spotting") The camel spotter is wearing hunting cap, plaid coat, etc., and uses binoculars. He could be a bird or train spotter, easily.

"Stolle, Fred . . . Haydon-Jones"—("Blancmanges Playing Tennis") More than just a list of great British tennis players, this is a current sports page featuring the best players from around the world at that time. Fred Stolle (b. 1938) was the undefeated Australian Wimble-

don Champion in 1966; Tony Roche (b. 1945, Australia) was a world Top Ten tennis player between 1965 and 1971; Charlie Pasarell (b. 1944, Puerto Rico) was U.S. Singles Champion in 1967; Cliff Drysdale (b. 1941, South Africa) was founding president of the Association of Tennis Professionals and credited as the first player to use the two-handed backhand swing; and Jane "Peaches" Bartkowitz (b. 1949, US)—misspelled by the Pythons "Jane 'Peaches' Bartcowicz"—was one of the founders of the women's tennis tour in 1970. Bartkowicz will appear (played by Palin) in Ep. 38, the "BBC Programme Planners" sketch. (Also, Bartkowicz was playing a tournament in the middle of May 1969 in Athens, and winning, when the Pythons were writing/recording these episodes.) Finally, Ann Haydon-Jones (b. 1938, Birmingham) was a Brit who won Wimbledon (in 1969) as the first female left-hander. Haydon-Jones' husband's name was actually P.F. Jones. (See wimbledon.org.)

– T –

"Thaxted"—(link into "Science Fiction Sketch") Thaxted is found in Uttlesford, and in the county of Essex.

"Them!"—("Man Turns Into Scotsman") Title of a 1954 sci-fi classic about atomically mutated ants in the southwestern United States In *Them!*, a little girl survives her family's massacre by marauding mutant ants, her first words upon emerging from catatonia being "Them! Them!" In the mock sci-fi case here, the "them" are the blancmanges, and by association the "othered" Scotsmen.

"There is no place for sentiment in Big Business"—("The Audit") According to *Private Eye*, this was an oft-repeated Heath-ism during his years in the leadership of the Tory Opposition (*PE* 4 December 1970: 17).

"They"—(Man Turns Into Scotsman") Throughout the episode the female character has not been and will not be given a name at all, rather identified by her gender, "She." Grammatically, then, this puts her into the same category as "they," the aliens. "She" is singular nominative, while "they" is plural nominative ("them" being plural objective). So the text categorizes her really only different in number from the blancmanges—she is an Other with "them."

thrilling chord—(PSC; "Man Turns Into Scotsman") Generic to the horror/sci-fi genre(s). Also used by Python to announce the appearance of the Inquisitors in Ep. 15. Used again in *Holy Grail* to accompany shocking moments like the appearance of the killer rabbit.

"throw them under a camel"—("You're No Fun Any More") The phrase "you're no fun any more" has itself been pinched (and slightly rephrased) from Ep. 1, where the Nazi officer tells his uncooperative British captive, "Ah . . . you're no fun." Such intertextuality is characteristic of the Python oeuvre; they, like Shakespeare, quote themselves often, creating afresh history and texts. See the "dull" note above.

"toon"—("Science Fiction Sketch") *OED*: "Northern dialect for town." Palin, from the north, would have been quite familiar with the local accents, and often took on the northern parts. See Morgan *Speaks!*.

"tough abrasive look"—("Camel Spotting") Again, the no-holds-barred approach to journalism à la interviewer Robin Day, the declining "refinement" characteristic of much of the TV documentary tradition in British broadcasting of the period. See Ep. 1, *It's the Arts* sketch.

"trainspotter"—("Camel Spotting") One who, as a hobby, looks for, identifies, and often notes trains (numbers, styles, names). This hobby has moved well beyond the purview of just young boys, and is enjoyed by many of all ages.

"Tristram and Isolde"—(link into "Science Fiction Sketch") A play on the characters Tristan and Isolde (but also spelled Tristram and Tristrem, and Iseult, Isolt, or Yseult), a medieval love-romance based on Celtic legend, itself based on an actual Pictish king. Matthew Arnold wrote *Tristram and Iseult* (1852), a three-part poem; *Tristram and Isoud* is Malory's fifth of eight *Works*; and Swinburne published his *Tristram of Lyonesse* in 1882, a poem in heroic couplets.

twizzles—(PSC; "Science Fiction Sketch") Rotates rapidly.

"two goes"—("Science Fiction Sketch") Two trips. The comment here may be that even though the Scotsman Angus isn't terribly bright, his industry, dedication, and work ethic are laudable. He will also figure prominently in overcoming the alien invasion by defeating the blancmange at Wimbledon. The Pythons' trope will become obvious: they will jab and attack, then ultimately recover their target. The Scots are a backward and rustic people, but they alone will be able to defeat the global threat. Pepperpots, homosexuals, even Conservatives—all are skewered and embraced, skewered and embraced. This paradigm runs throughout *FC*. See Larsen's *MPSERD*.

– W –

"wasna"—("Science Fiction Sketch") Contraction/conflation of "was not," part of Palin's continuing take on "Scottishness." "Na" is a variation of "nay."

"Waterloo"—("Camel Spotting") Railway station in Lambeth, London. Heavily damaged in WWII, then rebuilt. Now part of this station serves as a terminus for the Channel Tunnel service.

weird electronic music—("Man Turns Into Scotsman") Again, as with all of the music heard in this episode, this electronic composition is not accounted for in the WAC records for this episode (WAC T12/1,088).

Popularized in sci-fi films by Bebe and Louis Barron in the 1956 movie *Forbidden Planet*, electronic music (tonalities) is a twentieth-century art form made possible by the creation of early synthesizers, which began to appear as early as 1909. RCA created its Electronic Music Synthesizer in 1955, releasing albums of electronic music (music made without musical instruments) soon thereafter.

"Who are Them?"—("Man Turns Into Scotsman") This scene, where the hero (scientist, military man, or normal citizen) thinks aloud, is also a staple of the sci-fi genre. It's also an example of the genre's tendency to be overly and overtly expository.

"Wimbledon"—("Science Fiction Sketch") City located about eight miles southwest of London, and is site of the annual All-England Championships, known as the Wimbledon Championships.

"Wimbledon fortnight"—The two-week run of the Wimbledon Championships. In 1969, Wimbledon began 23 June 1969, and the Pythons had begun meeting and writing by late May 1969. They continued to work, together and in teams, through June and July 1969, with a 24 August deadline set up by BBC. This episode was taped 30 November 1969.

It's clear that the significant presence of Wimbledon figures and news in the press and on TV during this period accounts for the genesis of this sketch. This isn't an isolated example for the Pythons—writing about or being influenced by current events—as will be seen in Ep. 28, *Life of Tschaikowsky*," where the hysteria over the Apollo missions is sent up.

"win Wimbledon"—("Man Turns Into Scotsman") Certainly a reference to the recent paucity of homegrown players (read: English) at the Wimbledon Championships. English tennis player appearances in the final rounds and championship games dropped dramatically in the Python's formative years. No English male had won the men's singles since 1936 (when F.J. Perry won); during that same period, just two English women (Ann-Haydon Jones, 1969, and Angela Mortimer, 1961) had won the ladies' singles championship. So the reference to aliens on Wimbledon's courts is a very real complaint that it had been more than thirty years since an Englishman had won Wimbledon—the winners were aliens, all.

At the Wimbledon final in 1961, Rod Laver (Australia) beat Chuck McKinley (USA), but that's as close as England would come to a men's single's championship. Laver would be celebrated as "British" thereafter, just as Sir Edmund Hillary had been after he conquered Everest (he was from New Zealand).

– Y –

yardarm—(PSC; "You're No Fun Any More") Part of a square-rigged ship, the yard is "a wooden (or steel) spar, comparatively long and slender, slung at its centre from, and forward of, a mast and serving to support and extend a square sail which is bent to it" (*OED*). A yardarm is either end of that yard, then.

"Yes . . . she was . . . yes"—("Police Station") The entire police station exchange is perhaps an allusion to the light and airy banter—liberally spread around to the principal characters, male and female—found throughout *The Thing From Another World* (1951).

"yeti"—("Camel Spotting") The Tibetan "abominable snowman," a mythical creature. Buddhist monk-wannabe and former plumber Cyril Hoskins (in the guise of Rampa Lobsang) claimed to have encountered a yeti in his Himalayan travels. See notes to Eps. 4 and 29 for more on this diverting character, whose bizarre tales may have provided the Pythons with significant creative inspiration.

– Z –

"zillion"—("Science Fiction Sketch") A large, hyperbolized number, meant to suggest an unfathomable amount.

Zoom through the galaxy—("Science Fiction Sketch") The atmospheric music used underneath this set-up is not accounted for in the WAC records for this episode. In fact, all the music requests that eventually appear in Ep. 6 are part of the Ep. 7 file. The episodes were recorded in reverse order.

Episode 8

anarchist's type bomb—(PSC; "It's Man" link into opening credits) This bomb is a duplicate version of those seen in cartoons (especially Warner Bros. and MGM during the Chuck Jones and Tex Avery tenures) for many years—round, with a lighted fuse on top. The fact that it's labeled makes the cartoon connection even stronger. It's more a recognizable icon than a threat, of course.

"Apart from that he's perfectly all right"—("Buying a Bed") Here Mr. Verity (Idle) admits that he's at least aware of Mr. Lambert's (Chapman) perceptual shortcomings, but not his own. So again there are several levels of reality working at once in these sketches, and successful communication or transaction means navigating these levels.

"armoured division"—("Army Protection Racket") A division consisting of tanks and supporting equipment and men. The British Army's Third Division fits this description.

Art Critic—(PSC; "Art Critic—The Place of the Nude") This is the Art Critic's second appearance in *FC*. We first met him eating paintings and getting Vermeer all over his shirt in Ep. 4. Here he is leering at the painting, attempting to get a better view of the Rubens-like nude from angle-on. (The "Rubens-like" nude was requested in the production files, and was created for the episode.) This type of angle would work very well for the Hans Holbein (1497-1543) work *The Ambassadors* (1533), wherein the anamorphic (oblique) skull created by the artist can only be viewed in its lifelike form from a skewed angle. Holbein's *The Ambassadors* has been on display in the National Gallery since 1890.

"bag"—("Hell's Grannies") *OED*: "A disparaging term for a woman, esp. one who is unattractive or elderly." "Rat bag" is also thrown about a few times in *FC*, especially directed at loud, unattractive Python women (like the vulgar and incontinent Mrs. Equator [Jones] in Ep. 9).

"Barbara"—("Vox Pops") As early as Ep. 1 (during the bicycle race sketch), male characters are given female names. The use of this practice in this situation does lend a sodomitical air, of course, and the moment Barbara (Jones) leans his head on Man's (Chapman) shoulder underlines the point.

"barley cross fingers"—("Army Protection Racket") Kind of a "safe" or "time-out mode" in children's play.

bikini—(PSC; "It's Man" link into opening credits) Prototypical depiction of women as objects in *FC*, with the added element of lethality (a femme fatale notion) borrowed from American pulp cinema (film noir) and novels. See Ep. 22 where both the Announcer (Cleese) and the It's Man (Palin) wear similarly sexy attire which undercuts, at least momentarily, the objectification process, since both men make profoundly unattractive bathing beauties.

"blimey"—("Army Protection Racket") Shortened form of "blind me" or "blame me."

"blue in the mouth"—("Dead Parrot") Generally phrased as "blue in the face," meaning talking until one runs out of breath and turns blue. As will be demonstrated in his later memorable appearances in Eps. 19 and 23, Praline (Cleese) is just the type of character to conjure these kinds of portmanteau sayings. In Ep. 31, another character (Chapman) will further mangle the phrase, saying "blue in the breast."

"Bolton"—("Dead Parrot") Bolton is in Greater Manchester, Lancashire. Bolton is also reportedly home to a Mrs. Teal's lover as exposed on the air during the *"Blackmail"* sketch in Ep. 18.

"boo" ("The Flasher") The expectation is that the man is "flashing" those on the street, exposing himself. The payoff of the sign around his neck—"boo"—is a direct borrowing/steal from the 1945 Warner Bros. cartoon featuring Daffy Duck and Elmer Fudd, called *Ain't That Ducky* (dir. I. Freleng). In the cartoon, Daffy and Elmer attempt to see what's inside a valise being held by a young duck—who cries every time he looks inside, yet violently refuses the others even a peek. The payoff (from the valise) is a title card reading "The End." The influence of American animation on the Pythons and especially their use of speed, violence, and gaggery can be seen throughout *FC*, and will be noted where it appears.

"bother"—("Army Protection Racket") *OED*: "To give trouble to; to pester, annoy, worry." Here, though, Dino pronounces the word as "bovver," which the *OED* identifies as appearing in relation to the disturbances created by skinhead (or "crophead") gangs of the late 1960s. The Pythons are thus hybridizing the age-old mafia-type violence and threats with the more recent skinhead phenomenon, conflating images from their collective past knowledge and contemporary experience.

Botticelli Venus—(PSC; link into "Dead Parrot") Sandro Botticelli (1445-1510) was a Florentine Renaissance painter who worked for the de Medici court. He painted this most famous painting (*Birth of Venus*) in about 1485. This image of Venus is used often by Gilliam as part of his animations, including a recurring facial image in the opening credits. The cut-out image here eventually falls into the fish tank on the pet shop set, completing the transition between scenes.

The music underneath is "Gonna Get a Girl" by Harry Bidgood and his Broadcasters (Fox Trot) (WAC T12/1,089).

"bracken"—("Hermits") Dead undergrowth. Arthur and his knights must bring shrubbery to the Knights Who Say "Ni" in *Holy Grail*; and in the later feature film made by Palin and Gilliam, *Time Bandits* (1981), the heroes will be God's shrubbery and bracken makers.

"British Rail"—("Dead Parrot") Britain's national railway system, publicly held since passage of the Transport Act of 1947, and which at its largest employed almost 500,000 and operated trains on as many as 17,500 miles of tracks.

– C –

Cartoon rubbish entitled 'Full Frontal Nudity'—(PSC; animated "Full Frontal Nudity" link into "Vox Pops") The five Pythons not involved in the animation process regularly had no idea what Gilliam was producing during their week of rehearsing and taping, just that he would fill the allotted time slot with often thematically contiguous animated images: *"Cartoon rubbish entitled 'Full Frontal Nudity': Written, created and conceived off the back of a lorry by a demented American"* (Ep. 8).

Incidentally, "rubbish" is producer John Howard Davies' description of the early episodes, on more than one occasion, in BBC memos. See the BBC Written Archives Collection for the first series.

The music Gilliam uses underneath this animated segment is Mantovani's "The Most Beautiful Girl in the World" by Rodgers and Hart (WAC T12/1,089).

Chartered Accountant—("Vox Pops") Cleese wears the recognizable uniform of a City Gent here. Chartered accountancy is implicated often in *FC* as dull, so it's no surprise that a chartered accountant might be looking for any kind of stimuli.

"chastise"—("Hermits") This element of self-flagellation (whether emotionally or physically) still indicates hermit-types in seclusion for religious purposes, seeking an ascetic lifestyle in the wilds—a sort of a John the Baptist, locusts-and-honey life. There is a significant scene in Bergman's *The Seventh Seal* (cf. Ep. 7, "Science Fiction Sketch") depicting medieval flagellants. Living with other hermits, of course, makes this more like the suburbs than the wilderness, and closer to some *monastic* lifestyles, where self-chastisement and self-flagellation were employed for penance.

"closing for lunch"—("Dead Parrot") See Ep. 4, where the entire sketch involving international dental intrigue comes to a halt when lunch break is called. Like the wolf and sheepdog characters in Warner Bros. cartoons, when the whistle blows, the day's work is over and characters drop their business personas and go their separate ways. In *HG*, the historical epic itself will be stopped by the appearance of the modern constabulary, and a hand over the camera lens.

colonel—("Army Protection Racket") London gangster Ronnie Kray's nickname was, ironically, "The Colonel." For more on the Kray brothers see notes to Ep. 14.

"Commission"—(end credits) Actually, picking at nits, it was announced at the beginning of the show that a piece of wood would serve as David Hemmings for the show, meaning Hemmings himself wasn't even appearing. The last voiceover might have more accurately said, then, "The piece of wood portraying David Hemmings appeared by permission of the National Forestry Commission."

"crochet"—("Hell's Grannies") A needlework hobby, and often associated (at least iconically) with sedate, harmless older women. So it's an addiction to crochet instead of heroin or hashish; the grannies have a "habit," and they steal to support that habit. This turnabout—the young feeling responsible for how their elders turned out—is an incongruous reversal of the expected, but might be explained by the distance created between generations after the war years. Many more young people left home for school and work than had prior to the war, making their own way in the world, meaning that as the parent generation aged, the traditional structure of child assuming responsibility for parent was more alien, more strained.

"cuttlefish"—("Dead Parrot") A cuttlefish is a relative of the octopus and squid. In the audio (LP, CD) and live versions of this sketch, Cleese often replaces "cuttlefish" with "banana." The Pythons would have encountered cuttlefish as a food item on trips to Spain, undoubtedly, especially the coastal (resort) areas.

– D –

Davies, Rita—(PSC; link out of "Hell's Grannies") Davies appears in *FC* occasionally (see Eps. 19, 27, and 29), and also plays the murdered historian's wife in *HG*.

"demised . . . late parrot"—("Dead Parrot") This begins the thesaurus portion of the sketch in earnest. The phrases "passed on," "no more," and "ceased to be" are all euphemisms for death, as are "expired," "gone to meet its maker," and "late parrot." "Stiff" is an irreverent reference to a corpse, accounting for the rigor mortis (stiffening) which sets in to a dead body hours after death. As Praline tried to demonstrate earlier the parrot's condition, this stiffness was apparent. In Ep. 26, Man (Cleese) will bring his dead mother in a bag into a funeral home, where she will immediately be identified as a "stiff."

The thesaurus sketch format will return in "Fish Licence" (Ep. 23), "Cheese Shop" (Ep. 33), and "What the Stars Foretell" (Ep. 37).

department store—("Buying a Bed") The store is a John Sanders. There is no record in the BBC archives of the Pythons getting permission to shoot near or in the store (as they had for the F.J. Wallis store in Ep. 1). The camera is set up well across the street, so permissions may not have been needed.

"didn't have to say it"—("Buying a Bed") "It's my only line" is now the false safe haven for transgressing female characters. Once again, it is the female who is treated more contemptuously and with less latitude than any male character. This is the same response the Art Critic's wife gives in Ep. 4 and earlier in Ep. 8.

"dog kennels please"—("Buying a Bed") The bride and groom are certain that they've mastered the language, logic, and in-references necessary to function in this strange mattress-buying world, though they will fall short, as will be seen. Cf. the difficulties of communication as exhibited in the conversation between policemen in Ep. 12, where frequency and volume are the keys to communication, or in *Life of Brian*, where the Centurion (Palin) and Jailer (Gilliam) can't seem to communicate at all without comic misunderstandings.

In this reliance on miscommunication, the Pythons echo many Modernist authors, including and specifically T.S. Eliot, whose *The Waste Land* (1922) mourned the futility of communication—Man's ability to communicate with Man, and even God—after WWI.

"doing all right"—("Army Protection Racket") A euphemism for "making good money" or being successful in business, and is a way for mafioso to justify the collection of protection money.

"done over"—("Army Protection Racket") Beat up, roughed up.

"don't they"—("Army Protection Racket") Dino's (Jones) Cockney accent is especially thick, pronouncing "fings" for "things" and "dunnay" for "don't they." It used to be that a Cockney accent indicated growing up within earshot of the bells of St. Mary-le-Bow in Cheapside, in the City of London proper, meaning this accent is both regional and, more specifically, urban-centered. (See Ackroyd, *London*.)

– E –

Episode 8—"Full Frontal Nudity" was the eighth installment in the first series. It was recorded eighth on 25 November 1969, and broadcast on 7 December 1969. Kathja (also "Katya") Wyeth (Ep. 4; *The Avengers*), Jean Clarke (Ep. 39), and Rita Davies appear as extras in this episode (WAC T12/1,089).

"Full Frontal Nudity" is also a variation of contemporary (1969) phraseology used by the MPAA (Motion Picture Association of America) to categorize at least one reason for giving a "mature" or "for adults only" rating to a film. The standards were fairly new at the time of the episode's creation, having been instituted just the year before (November 1968), and were probably still new enough to be in the news.

"Esher"—("Vox Pops") Located approximately thirty miles southwest of London. This also must be something of an incongruous moment, as there are probably few African natives in tribal dress living in any part of Esher. Esher will be mentioned again, this time as a haven for orgiastic middle-class couples (Ep. 36), and Eps. 28 and 44.

"eyeties"—("Army Protection Racket") A slang reference to Italians. Originally used by the military as a disparaging remark. Python also employs racially derogatory terms like "dago," "wop," "darkie," etc.

– F –

"fifteen bob"—("Army Protection Racket") The Colonel reacts to the silliness, yes, but may also be offended by the cut-rate price the Vercottis are demanding—just fifteen shillings a week to protect an entire modern army base. This currency system was done away with in 1971.

"five bob"—("Army Protection Racket") The haggling motif will reappear in *Holy Grail*, where the "Knights Who Until Recently Said 'Ni'" demand and then plead for additional offerings; in *Life of Brian* as Brian (Chapman) first tries to buy a beard, then sell a gourd. In Ep. 35 ("Bomb on Plane" sketch), the bomber (Idle) demands £1,000 for the location of the bomb, then realizing he'll be blown up, too, asks for just £1. Eventually, he pays the pound himself.

The Colonel is again acting as arbiter of good taste, and also—as a replacement for a punchline or a traditional link—he is a transitionary tool. His outbursts remind the viewer of the constructedness of the performance, of its artificiality, and of the fact that it can be directed and re-directed by characters and elements within the diegetic world. This narrative chicanery is the Pythons' tilting at Auntie BBC—the ancien régime of Light Entertainment to be rebelled against—and will come to characterize the narrative structure of *Flying Circus*.

"fjords"—("Dead Parrot") Glaciated valleys (steeply V-shaped) inundated with seawater, fjords are found throughout northern Scandinavia.

four or five of them—("Hell's Grannies") This is an absurd, incongruous moment, where the specter of aged grannies (dressed typologically, again, in black dresses and caps) knocking about younger people is as ludicrous as the image from Ep. 17 of the tough-looking Bishop (Jones) and his vicar henchman clearing their own path along busy city sidewalks.

There may be an earlier television inspiration for this sketch. A Salada Tea commercial from the late 1960s features a motorcycle gang of senior citizens (à la *The Wild One*) roaring into a diner for tea (see Ellsworth).

This sequence was reportedly shot near the rear entrance to Walpole Park, Lammas Park Road, Ealing on 20 October 1969. Lammas Park is just south of Walpole Park in Ealing. Also, the scenes where the Grannies are knocking about pedestrians, stealing the telephone kiosk, and dropping the sociologist (Idle) into the coal hole were shot on or near Lammas Park Road. All the park scenes were shot in Walpole and Lammas Parks. (See WAC T12/1,242.)

Fourth Hermit—("Hermits") It is by this time obvious that these hermits have retired from the world, but are living as a community. This qualifies them technically as "cœnobites," and not religious ascetics, or "eremites." So what the Pythons constructed perhaps as a joke of incongruity—reclusive, even misanthropic hermits living together, chatting, etc.—is actually historically accurate. Certain "common life" hermits did live together in communities separated from the rest of the world, leading to institutionalized monasticism. See entries in the *OED* and *EBO*.

– G –

"general inspection"—("Army Protection Racket") Daily fallout for inspection of troops, barracks, arms, etc.

"get out of it"—("Hell's Grannies") Chapman as the authority figure again, this time as a policeman. In Ep. 14, Chapman plays another policeman, Hawkins, and plays him as a drag queen in police gear and makeup prior to a sort of "gay police" revue. He camps it up until they exit the dressing room and enter the street, then he's all business, the stoic authority figure again. The implication, then, is that prior to any appearance onscreen or on the street as the sober authority figure, all manly and no-nonsense, Chapman is an outrageously poncing and campy homosexual, only assuming the role of straight policeman for the narrative, and the general public. Perhaps this is a not-so-unconscious allusion to his real life as a gay man in a still very straight world.

"giveaway"—("Art Critic—The Place of the Nude") This same phrase used in *HG* when Chapman (as King) calls Palin (as beggar) a "bloody peasant." To "giveaway" is to reveal, perhaps unconsciously, one's true intent or meaning. In this flavoring it's not unlike the Freudian "faulty action," where an unintended thought/word escapes, causing an embarrassing social situation.

"goat"—("Hermits") The goat is, of course, an ancient symbol of lechery, and fits right into this same-sex hermitage.

"grim"—("Hermits") An escape from the luxuries of the world was certainly a part of the hermit lifestyle. Grimness could be described as a necessary element of the truly ascetic lifestyle. The most noted English hermit was Roger Crab (1621-1680), who wrote *The English Hermite* and moved to Uxbridge, selling his worldly possessions. He was actually sought out for many years for his views on health, diet, and spiritual issues (*ODNB*).

This sketch may also have been at least partly inspired by the less than grim lifestyle of the Maharishi Mahesh Yogi, with whom The Beatles studied Transcendental Meditation (TM) in 1967-1968 and to whom they may have eventually been expected to contribute a sizeable portion of their incomes for the maintenance of his enlightened lifestyle.

– H –

"ha, ha, ha"—("Buying a Bed") Understanding the rules of a Python situation can allow for navigation through that situation. The rules, however, may only function at the level of the sketch, and not at the level of the particular episode, the *FC* show in general, or especially the real world. In "The Argument Clinic" one can argue successfully without realizing an argument is under way; in the "Silly Job Interview," responding in a silly way scores points, and honest, sober answers are marked down, etc. In the "Buying a Bed" sketch here in Ep. 8, it's a matter of mathematics and avoiding a certain very potent word: "mattress" (cf. the entry for "mattress"). Cf. the police station sketch in Ep. 12 where each policeman responds to a different speaking voice (high or low pitched, slow or fast paced, etc.), and the man reporting a crime must speak differently to each to be understood. The policemen already speak each other's languages, of course, and don't recognize or comment upon the phenomenon during the sketch.

"Han"—("Hermits") This can be a feminine term of address/endearment, which would add to the level of aberrant sexuality in this scene (effeminate and "butch" men living together, loincloths, absence of female sexual companionship, etc.).

"happen to it"—("Army Protection Racket") These cryptic allusions are characteristic of media portrayals of mafia-types, especially Hollywood movies like *The Killers* (1946) and *Capone* (1959), Ealing comedies like *The Ladykillers* (1955), and dime pulp novels featuring underworld figures and lower-class elements.

"healthy outdoor sketch"—(link into "Hermits") Interesting that the Colonel is able to direct even the settings of the sketches, it seems, though he has little control over their content or eventual outcome. It's as if his sketch starts out well, grows unruly, and ultimately gets away from him. The Colonel is also acting the part of the Greek or Elizabethan "chorus," narrating action, qualifying actions, and moving the scenes along to his (and perhaps the authors') inevitable conclusions.

Hell's Grannies—("Hell's Grannies") A play on "Hell's Angels," the infamous American motorcycle gang. This may have provoked at least some concern at the BBC, especially since the episode was first broadcast less than one day after the infamous events at Altamont (near San Francisco, California), the Rolling Stones concert appearance on 6 December 1969, where a young black fan, Meredith Hunter, was stabbed to death by Hell's Angels "security" personnel hired to police the show. The proximity of the two events might have precluded anyone involved at BBC, including the Pythons, from being able to do anything about the broadcast of what might have been seen as a tasteless, thoughtless comedic reference to a tragic death. (The episode had been recorded on 25 November, and would be broadcast on 7 December 1969.) Perhaps, though, the much less violent persona of the UK Hell's Angels chapters as opposed to their U.S. cousins was the source for this humor, and the rest was an unfortunate coincidence.

"Hemmings, David"—("Full Frontal Nudity") A film actor, director, and producer, Hemmings (1941-2003) was best known during this period for his role as the photographer Thomas in Michelangelo Antonioni's *Blowup* (1966). (Antonioni will be referenced later, in Ep. 29.) Significantly, the film received an X-rating in the UK, and was released unrated in the United States Hemmings' characterization of the wandering photographer has been described by some as "wooden." Hemmings is also mentioned in Ep. 6, and appeared six times on *Dixon of Dock Green* early in his career.

"hermit"—("Hermits") He is one who has chosen to live in solitude, and the choice can be for religious or just anti-social reasons. A hermit who is a social butterfly, then, would be incongruous, and a perfect Python character. See the entries for "grim" and "Fourth Hermit" for more.

Peter Ackroyd has noted the significance of the hermit in the history of the city of London, identifying them as elements of continuity and touchstones for the city masses. They are "lonely and isolated people who feel their solitude more intensely within the busy life of the streets" (*London* 41). The Pythons have merely transported these hermits and their tendencies into the wild, an outcrop populated entirely by like souls.

Noted Modernist poet W.B. Yeats' work must also have inspired this back-to-nature setting, especially his paean to the hermetic life, "The Lake Isle Of Innisfree" (published 1893):

I WILL arise and go now, and go to Innisfree,
And a small cabin build there, of clay and wattles made:
Nine bean-rows will I have there, a hive for the honey-bee,
And live alone in the bee-loud glade.

And I shall have some peace there, for peace comes dropping slow,
Dropping from the veils of the mourning to where the cricket sings;
There midnight's all a glimmer, and noon a purple glow,
And evening full of the linnet's wings.

I will arise and go now, for always night and day
I hear lake water lapping with low sounds by the shore;
While I stand on the roadway, or on the pavements grey,
I hear it in the deep heart's core.

Yeats would later say that the poem arose from his homesickness for the wilds of Ireland, especially as he found himself lost on the crowded streets of London, where he self-pityingly "planned out a life of lonely austerity, and at other times mixed the ideals and planned a life of lonely austerity mitigated by periodical lapses" (Yeats, *Four Years*). The Python hermits also coveniently mix hermetic austerity with the "lapses" of conversation, gossip, and camaraderie, meeting Yeats' goal of the truly balanced life.

high street—("Buying a Bed") *OED*: " . . . a highway, a main road, whether in country or town; now, very generally, the proper name (High Street) of that street of a town which is built upon a great highway, and is (or was originally) the principal one in the town." In many towns and cities in England, High Street tends to be a main business street today.

hop off—("Buying a Bed") This hopping indicates that even another level of reaction has been reached, beyond singing en masse in the tea chest, and that such consequences could continue to build and expand as transgressions continue. The groom is quick to join in, as well, and the bride (the sole female) is left out of the solution for her verbal "mattress" transgression.

– I –

"in his room"—("Hell's Grannies") Both of these young men are dressed as "toughs," wearing black leather biker gear (Second Young Man, played by Chapman) and a biker jacket (Third Young Man, played by Jones). In other words, they're dressed as if *they* should be the ones causing the crime, and hence the subject of just such a crime documentary. The type of decorated helmet worn by the Jones' character can be seen in a still image in the 1968 film *Yellow Submarine*.

Beginning in the 1950s with the antics of the Teddy Boys, there was great concern in the UK (England, Scotland, and Northern Ireland) with the rise in teen violence, gang activity, delinquency, and a general disaffection among the youth for the traditions of British paternal, familial culture. Blame was placed on both the scarcity and plenty of the postwar rationing years, the move away from child labor to child leisure time, rock and roll music, and the appearance of a bored younger generation flush with discretionary income (*Eyewitness: 1950-59*, "Teenagers" and "Teddy Boys").

"innit"—("Dead Parrot") Vulgar form of "isn't it."

"Inter-City Rail"—("Dead Parrot") Government-run rail service serving Britain's major cities, part of the larger British Railways, or British Rail (see note above) system.

"Ipswich"—("Dead Parrot") Ipswich is a North Sea port town north and east of London, in Suffolk, while Bolton is north and west, well across the country, from London. This would have been quite a time-consuming (and illogical) ruse for Praline (Cleese) to fall for.

"irrelevant, isn't it"—("Dead Parrot") Not surprising that Praline would acknowledge the porter's meanderings, since Praline has already made a habit of addressing the camera (effectively breaking the fourth wall) on several occasions, and will continue to do so in his later appearances in Eps. 18 and 23.

"It's dead, that's what's wrong with it!"—("Dead Parrot") According to Cleese in *Monty Python Speaks!*, this sketch began as a used car sketch written by Palin prior to *FC*. Like the earlier "Mouse Problem" sketch (Ep. 2), this idea was updated and rewritten for Python's needs and *FC*. A few sketches from pre-Python days (from *The Frost Report*, *At Last the 1948 Show*) also made the transition to the Monty Python collection, primarily as part of the various LP recording sessions (e.g., "The Bookshop," *At Last the 1948 Show*, 1.3).

This sketch has entered the cultural lexicon like almost nothing else from *Monty Python's Flying Circus*, and has enjoyed memorialized popularity since its initial broadcast. In 1990, for instance Prime Minister Margaret Thatcher—subject of the Pythons' pokes and jabs on several occasions—included in a political speech a comparison between the Liberal Democrat Party "flying bird" symbol and Python's "Dead Parrot." (Her speechwriters were quite certain she was the only one within earshot who had no idea what the reference actually meant.) Just two years later a former "Thatcherite minister" compared the demise and attempted resuscitation of the Maastricht Treaty to a dead parrot being re-nailed to its perch (Larsen 23-24). The acculturation to Englishness can be measured, John Diamond would write in 1995, by an appreciation of, for one, the "Dead Parrot" sketch, and being able to respond appropriately to a Spanish Inquisition reference (21, 26). The "Dead Parrot" comparison has been used as a reference (by journalists, politicos, et al.) literally hundreds of times in the intervening years (see *MPSERD*).

– J –

"Jerusalem"—(PSC; "Buying a Bed") Popular Church of England hymn, with text by Blake. Cf. Ep. 4 for another extended usage of the hymn. This version of "Jerusalem" is arranged by Blake-Parry, and performed by the Royal Choral Society and Philharmonia Orchestra (WAC T12/1,089).

– K –

keep left signs—("Hell's Grannies") This scene was shot in the Australia Road area in East Action on 20 October 1969, as were the exterior shots for the council house interviews in "Hell's Grannies" (WAC T12/1,242).

"Keep Left" was also the name of a proposal penned by Michael Foot (b. 1913) and other democratic socialists as a third way to deal with Europe—without allying Britain to either the USSR or U.S. demands for foreign policy collusion. Between 1945 and 1951 the left in the Labour movement vociferously used the slogan to remind voters (and party leaders) of the need to stay true to the ideals of the welfare state, as well as set a course left of the United States (*Eyewitness: 1950-59*).

"kiosks"—("Hell's Grannies") Red telephone booths. This one is stolen from Lammas Park Road, which is not far from BBC's Television Centre, and just down the street from where "The Funniest Joke in the World" (Ep. 1) and parts of "Dull Life of a City Stockbroker" (Ep. 6) were shot.

"kipping"—("Dead Parrot") *OED*: "To go to bed, sleep. Also, to lie *down*."

– L –

"Lancs."—(PSC; "Dead Parrot") Short for Lancastershire, or Lancashire.

"leaving you cold"—("Hermits") This conversation might as well be taking place over a brick fence separating row house yards in any London suburb, including the earlier mentioned Esher. Note, though, that there are no female hermits, and that the males we hear from the most have affected, somewhat effeminate accents and mannerisms. Discovering that Mr. Robinson and Mr. Seagrave are "lodging" together adds to the homosocial and even homoerotic subtext already present.

"look after"—("Army Protection Racket") Not unlike the avuncular policeman (Chapman) in Ep. 7 reassuring the viewing public that Her Majesty's government was watching after everyone. Here the paternalistic, patriarchal Mafia "godfathers" (Jones and Palin) offer similar protection and peace of mind, and for a sliding scale price. In 1965 the Kray brothers were arrested and charged with running just such a protection racket in North London. Specifically, they were charged with "demanding money with menaces" from local businesses.

– M –

Mafia—(PSC; "Army Protection Racket") "Mafia" has become the generic name for Italian American crime organizations based around family structures in the United States Organized crime was also a significant problem in Britain (see "Vercotti" below, and "Piranha Brothers" entries in Ep. 14). In 1962, Genovese crime family member Joe Valachi turned state's evidence, for the first time exposing the structure and influence of organized crime in the United States. His memoirs, published in 1968, became a bestseller.

Python's Mafia types dress very much like those in Seijun Suzuki's popular gangster films of this period, *Tokyo Drifter* (1966) and *Branded to Kill* (1967).

"mattress"—("Buying a Bed") One of the miraculous, totem-like words in the Python world. The young married couple here have transgressed the laws of the sketch world—she's mentioned the unmentionable word—and all participants must endure even more elaborate rituals to set things right. This also exhibits once again the power of language and the presence of shibboleths in Python's oeuvre. Use (or abuse) of even a single word can send Python narratives off in wildly different directions, or can immediately "out" an interloper like a woman or anyone who doesn't understand the internal logic of the situation.

In an animation for Ep. 2, for example, Rodin's "Thinker" disappears when his thought bubble ("I think, therefore I am") is popped—he can't exist without those words. See the power of "Ni" in *Holy Grail*, or of Brian's badly memorized but beatific phrases in *Life of Brian*, or even the power of assuming Brian's name at the end of the film, when a man is saved from crucifixion just by saying, "I'm Brian!"

military music—(PSC; link into "Army Protection Racket") More musical selections culled from the vast BBC archives, as were literally hundreds of items—from newsreel stock to publicity stills to sound effects. In particular, this music is "Roll Out the Barrel," performed by the Band of the Scots, from "Music of the Two World Wars" (Part I) (WAC T12/1,089).

The military stock footage here is VISNEWS footage of the British Army, and "British Movietone News" footage of a peacetime army drill (WAC T12/1,089).

"miss"—("Dead Parrot") The Shopkeeper (Palin) actually notices that he's been referred to by a feminine title, which is unusual for Python. In Ep. 7, the Chairman (Chapman) doesn't react at all when he's referred to as "Lady Chairman," for example. In Ep. 8 Praline claims a cold made him say "Miss" instead of "Sir" or "Mr.", and later the Shopkeeper will account for his misspeaking by claiming to have meant a "pun," and then a "palindrome" ("Notlob" for "Bolton"). Again, the miscommunication issue comes to the fore, as will be seen throughout Monty Python's works.

"Monty Python's Flying Circus"—(titles) This iteration of the tagline is delivered by Cleese in his "silly" (affected) voice. Earlier episodes featured Cleese speaking the title in a more sober, BBC announcer-type voice, which of course belied—purposely—the absurdities about to be presented.

"moving in"—("Hell's Grannies") This kind of structure and tone is usually reserved for stories about gang infiltration into neighborhoods, drug use, racial tension, etc. Shows like *Panorama* (1953-2000) treated these topics during this period. Interviewer Robin Day (Ep. 2) worked for *Panorama* beginning in 1967, delivering hard-hitting reports on myriad social and political problems until 1972. Topics tackled by lead interviewers Day (1923-2000) and Richard Dimbleby (1913-1965) included the Suez Crisis, the hydrogen bomb, drug abuse, the Cuban missile crisis, and the first on-camera interview with a member of the royal family, the Duke of Edinburgh (1961).

Thematically, this could be a verbatim pseudo-copy of any period BBC or ITV documentary (or exposé) on the Teddy Boy, punk, and/or skinhead movements in London and the larger industrial cities.

mustache—(PSC; "Dead Parrot") In the sketches where Palin and Cleese play Frenchmen, they share a mustache, taking turns speaking and wearing the mustache (Eps. 2 and 14). In the department store section of the "Michael Ellis" episode (Ep. 41), the salesman attempts to hide his identity by donning a large "fu manchu" mustache. This often suffices in the cartoony Python world to disguise the individual completely, but not in this case.

"my only line"—("Art Critic—The Place of the Nude") Carol Cleveland uses this same line in the next sketch. This also takes us back to the "Watteau, dear?" joke in Ep. 4, and the acid response from the Art Critic. Equally bad puns from the male Pythons don't generally elicit such vitriolic responses (perhaps a chicken on the head).

The Goons offer puns (primarily through characters played by Milligan and Sellers) without apology, and with much gusto, including:

Moriarty: The sky over England is leaking, and that's why the rain is getting in.
Seagoon: Wait! You two men claim the sky is leaking. What proof do you have?
Moriarty: Water proof! (from "Queen Anne's Rain," 22 December 1958)

– N –

"nirvana"—("Hermits") *OED*: "In Buddhist theology, the extinction of individual existence and absorption into the supreme spirit, or the extinction of all desires and passions and attainment of perfect beatitude." Another hybridization, this time of certain Christian ascetic practices and Buddhist universalism. The Hermits here are, of course, not extinguishing their individual selves, instead forming another community away from the one they've all left behind.

"Norwegian Blue"—("Dead Parrot") This is probably funny just because of the incongruity between the dark, frozen north of Norway and the colorful, tropical bird that supposedly lives there. Cf. the end of Ep. 40, where the Norwegian Party is given time on British television for a party political broadcast.

Specialized animals occur throughout Pythons' work, including Dinsdale's enormous hedgehog (Ep. 14), a dangerous, swimming llama with a beak for eating honey (Ep. 9), pantomime horses and geese (Ep. 30), flying sheep (Ep. 2), moping cats (Ep. 5), fish terriers and tucked Airedales (Ep. 10), and a killer rabbit (*HG*). Gilliam also provides numerous animated examples of dismembered and re-membered animals throughout.

"Notlob"—("Dead Parrot") Later in this same episode, when the Announcer (Idle) is surprised that the camera has come back to him, "Notlob" is mentioned again. This is a demonstration of a sort of cross-fertilization—from the acknowledged fictional worlds (sketches) and the acknowledged "real" or documentary worlds (news sets, which can also be called the often unacknowledged fictional worlds), as the newsreader accidentally uses a nonsense palindrome from the preceding sketch. Cf. Ep. 13 for a reappearance of this backward name.

nudges him—(PSC; link out of "Dead Parrot") The Colonel (Chapman) also has no compunction regarding entering the fictional worlds created via sketches and nudging them away from silliness, never surrendering his military character persona, either. He and Praline (Cleese) exhibit certain levels of narrative control in this regard. The Pythons are also, perhaps unconsciously, acknowledging the real-world influence of such a character representing the established authority system (a military-industrial complex operating with tacit government support). The Colonel may be a fuddy-duddy, but he is certainly able to force the narrative at least in the general direction he feels will be more redemptive, and less silly and "long-haired."

– O –

"on film"—("Hermits") Perhaps an acknowledgment of the permanence of the filmed as opposed to the taped image. (Many early television concerns like the BBC regularly cleaned house by "wiping" expensive, reusable video tape, which is why so many episodes and even entire series of significant television shows no longer exist.) Also, this is an acknowledgment of the different media used in the *FC* episodes. The Colonel notes that the media matters little to the audience, which may or may not be true (like the world of a Turner or Constable landscape, it's a choice), depending on the purist sensibilities of particular viewers. However, if an audience is schooled on mixed media (from film to tape to film without acknowledged breaks in continuity), then they are less likely to be bothered by the image quality fluctuations.

"ours"—("Hermits") This first person plural possessive pronoun (as opposed to any singular pronoun like "mine" or "yours") should be a major clue that the standard hermit lifestyle is being sent up here.

– P –

"pacifist"—("Army Protection Racket") This term is especially significant during the Vietnam War years,

when the numbers of pacifists or conscientious objectors rose dramatically in the United States in response to the ever-widening Selective Service draft. In the UK, the period of National Service (1948-1960) saw many applicants for conscientious objector status, but relatively few were granted. Watkins (Idle) could have served as a non-combatant, of course, but the terms (and fairness) of National Service meant that, one way or another, service was going to happen.

"pad out"—("Dead Parrot") *OED*: "To extend or increase." Again, reminding the viewer that this is a show, a play, a constructed thing. In Ep. 10, characters will wait around on-set for the "walk on" part actor to arrive, making the show longer than it should have been. In Ep. 33, the show actually runs short, and the "padding" is purposely clumsy, with Cleese in Conquistador uniform and sword (seen again later in Ep. 36) at the seashore apologizing and explaining why some shows run short.

In "The Choking Horror" episode of *The Goon Show*, the "padding out" of the show is mentioned, as well, and called "filling-in-time type dialogue" (14 February 1956).

"pall"—("Hell's Grannies") This kind of gloomy language was heard during WWII, for example, especially during the Battle of Britain. The *Beyond the Fringe* group painted newscaster Alvar Liddell as one who, on the regular evening newcasts on BBC Home Service, "brought us news of fresh disasters" from the warfront ("Aftermyth of War").

"pension day"—("Hell's Grannies") The day that Old Age Pensioners (OAP) pick up their government checks, rather than drugs, alcohol, or lottery tickets, which might be expected in other such documentaries on a *Panorama*-type show.

"people, chat, gossip"—("Hermits") The balance of the sketch is comprised almost completely of people, chat, and gossip—the very ills of society from which these hermits are allegedly escaping.

"permissive society"—("Vox Pops") The phrase "permissive society" was oft-used in the media of the period to describe the eroding morality seen by many as typifying especially London life. The "mod" movement; the increased availability, use, and abuse of marijuana and psychedelic drugs; and the advent of the birth control pill in 1960 all contributed to this perceived explosion of hedonism, and all played a significant role in the so-called satire boom of the late 1950s and into the 1960s. For more on the "permissive society" and its effects on the entertainment industry in the UK, see Aldgate's *Censorship and the Permissive Society*.

This element of televised sexuality is a response to religiously and politically conservative anti-pornographer figures like Mary Whitehouse, who campaigned for stricter standards on television in Britain beginning in 1964. Whitehouse formed the "Clean Up TV" campaign in 1964, and in 1965 created the National Viewers and Listeners Association (NVLA). The Pythons would later have to face Mrs. Whitehouse in response to the public outcry over the "decency" and blasphemic elements of *LB*, especially as the film might offend Christians. See Hewison's *Monty Python: The Case Against*.

"pining"—("Dead Parrot") To pine is to waste away, physically or emotionally. The use of a word like "pining" instead of something of more modern usage is an indication that this is indeed one of Cleese/ Chapman's "thesaurus" sketches, where they may have literally consulted a thesaurus as they wrote. See Morgan's *Speaks!*. Literary precedents also exist for the usage. See Gerard Manley Hopkins' (1844- 1889) *Felix Randal*:

Felix Randal the farrier, O he is dead then? My duty all ended,
Who have watched his mold of man, big-boned and hardy-handsome,
Pining, pining. (No. 53, stanza 1)

"public relations"—("Hermits") A rimshot moment, in music hall terms, it is the payoff for this sketch, the punchline, even, and the Colonel interjects just as the sketch is about to move off somewhere else, or even conclude on its own. This is curious, in that he rarely lets the sketch reach a punchline status.

"pun"—("Dead Parrot") A pun is a play on words, and in this usage is a good example of Python's oft- employed catachresis (using words improperly, abus- ing metaphors or tropes). Cf. Ep. 29, when "great ex- pedition" is punned into "Great Exhibition," complete with a photo insert of the Crystal Palace. (The Pythons' comedy forebears, the Goons, employed puns often, and without apology.)

– Q –

Queen's Park Rangers—(PSC; "Hell's Grannies") The corrugated metal fence behind the policeman (Chap- man) features some existing graffiti that identifies the actual location for this shot. Earlier, the announcer told us we were in Bolton, but the spray-painted scrawl tells us the local football team is clearly the Queen's Park Rangers, who play in a stadium just around the corner from Television Centre, at Loftus Road (London W12). QPR have been a football club since 1882.

The graffiti painted by the Grannies reads, "Make tea not love," a play on the then-fashionable anti-Vietnam War sentiment, "Make love not war."

This scene was shot in the Australia Road, East Ac- ton area, just a few blocks northwest of Television Cen- tre, on 20 October 1969 (WAC T12/1,242).

– R –

"right out"—("Dead Parrot") A common British collo- quialism, used emphatically to mean "no." Cf. *HG*, where a section from the Book of Armaments is being read aloud, and the number "five is right out."

– S –

"senile delinquents"—("Hell's Grannies") A simple wordplay on "juvenile delinquents," and probably something of an oxymoron, since delinquency requires at least a modicum of deliberate action, which might not be possible for someone suffering from senility or diminished mental capacity due to advanced age. So- cial psychologists in this period (including Oxford's John Michael Argyle) noted the troubling increase of juvenile delinquency, calling it one of Britain's "most pressing problems" (see *Psychology and Social Prob- lems*), meaning the discussion would have been much in the news, as well.

There were also a number of films and television programs produced on the subject of teen delinquency, including the narrative cinema verité–type *Bronco Bullfrog* (1969), to which the Pythons may be referring indirectly, or *Cosh Boy* (1953), which paints a picture of menacing teens (which the Pythons adapt into menac- ing grandmothers), not outcast anti-heroes. The skin- heads had been sort of "officially" recognized in Sep- tember 1969 by being so named in the *Guardian*, and *Bronco Bullfrog* was released not long after.

"shagged"—("Dead Parrot") Generally meaning weary, exhausted. To say both "tired" and "shagged out" might seem a bit redundant, though the the- saurus nature of this sketch will soon become appar- ent, and the redundancy more acceptable. The word "shag" also has copulative connotations, of course, which might account for the laugh from the studio au- dience at its use.

"silly line"—("Army Protection Racket") The military authority figure as played by Chapman often com- ments on and even stops sketches in *FC* when he deems they've reached a certain unbearable level of silliness. He is often used as a linking element between sketches in this manner, a sort of purposeful narrative transition. See Ep. 4 for earlier appearances of the character, and later in Ep. 8 in the "Hermits" sketch.

"small part"—("Vox Pops") The genital reference is intended, certainly.

"sociologists"—("Hell's Grannies") This is a kind of usual suspects list of occupations that have been and will be lampooned in *FC*—usually as insipidly dull—or occupations that tend to attract those with some sort of perverted proclivity, and who hide behind the façade of dull respectability. The City Stockbroker in Ep. 6 must escape into the fictional life of superhero comic books, for example, and vicars tend to be thieves or sex deviants, etc. The sociologist's implication is that the older generation feels it has failed to raise its children properly, in that they've chosen such gainful but perhaps emotionally tepid employment. Incidentally, these are some of the occupations the Pythons avoided by entering the world of show business.

"Sound of Music"—("Hell's Grannies") A Rodgers and Hammerstein musical, filmed in 1965 by Robert Wise and starring Julie Andrews and Christopher Plummer. The implication is that classic Hollywood musicals are the favorite films of senior citizens, especially older women (which was demographically accurate). The cast of the *Sound of Music* will appear in Ep. 42, as a show-jumping obstacle.

"stopping it"—("Army Protection Racket") There are various levels of awareness here. The Colonel (Chapman) is stopping the sketch, but he is still in character as the Colonel, thus on some level the sketch continues. So he is not an actor playing a colonel acting in a sketch, he is a colonel acting in a sketch, and without any funny lines. Below it will be seen that he knows enough as a colonel to identify the TV milieu ("telecine," "director," "close-up," etc.), yet he isn't just an actor. Both Vercottis (Jones and Palin) have fallen out of character, as well, as has Watkins (Idle), but not the Colonel. Note the similar levels of reality as he later stops the hermits, and the "keep left signs" silliness in mid-sketch.

St. Peter's Square—(PSC; "Buying a Bed") These clips are of St. Peter's Basilica, which is in the heart of Rome. This is once again BBC stock footage, and the assembled Roman Catholic crowd is most likely not singing the Anglican hymn "Jerusalem." This footage was *not* on the weekly request list for this episode.

"strangle his wife"—(link out of "Art Critic—The Place of the Nude") The retribution for such a bad joke on her part is obviously death. The implication is that the critic will also, once his wife is dead, be able to move on "to pastures new." The music beneath (which

is almost inaudible) is a portion of Debussy's "Jeux de Vagues" (WAC T12/1,089).

– T –

"tart"—A colloquial name for a prostitute. This mention could be explained away as just a malapropism, like most everything Dogberry utters in Shakespeare's *Much Ado*. Also, see Arthur Figgis' "panties" slip-of-the-tongue as he lists significant composers in Ep. 6. These so-called Freudian slips (Freud's "faulty action" or *"Fehlleistung"*) would have been "discovered" popularly and entered the cultural lexicon between the wars, when Freud's work found its way into the mainstream media.

"telecine"–("Army Protection Racket") The broadcasting of filmed images. The countdown (see "film leader" note in Ep. 2) runs a normal 7, 6, 5, and 4, but then a still photo (a passport or identification photo) of a blonde, *clothed* woman is inserted by Gilliam for just a few fleeting frames. The photo may be Maggie Weston, a makeup artist for *FC*, who would later become Gilliam's wife.

"that's as maybe"—(link into "Army Protection Racket") A variation on the "and now for something completely different," and isn't very different from such diverse and purposely misleading elements like giving titles to episodes that have no connection to the contents of that episode ("Whither Canada?"), providing random episode numbers (this episode is subtitled "12B"), and offering conflicting information between voiceover narration and provided captions, etc. This 1943 wartime intro might have fit the "Funniest Joke" sketch in Ep. 1, but here leads into a decidedly unheroic military shakedown sketch by London mafia members. This is as misleading as the elaborate introduction to Ep. 25, the *Black Eagle* film credits, which goes into the episode, and not the promised film.

"toddle"—("Hermits") To take a leisurely walk, meaning he's not on his way anywhere in particular, and that the hermit's life is often one of pleasant idleness.

"travel, sir"—("Army Protection Racket") This description fits some of the television commercials and print ads of the time period that depicted glamorous ports of call, camaraderie, and excitement as the whole of military life. The U.S. Army's slogan during the 1960s, for example, was "Fun, Travel, Adventure." The specter of the Vietnam War, which was raging through 1969 and would continue until at least 1973, provided news fodder of the fighting and the dying and would have certainly undercut the benign, even playful commercial images.

– U –

"unisex"—(link out of "Hell's Grannies") Anything (especially fashions) that can be utilized by both males and females. The term came into vogue in the late 1960s.

– V –

"valid"—("Vox Pops") The implication, then, is that this policeman would appear in a nude scene if it was, indeed, valid (probably meaning the nudity was somehow organic to the plot, and not "gratuitous"). This has been a moral maxim used by many actresses, especially, to account for their appearances in various states of undress on camera. In Ep. 4 of *FC*, Chapman plays a nude man in a discussion on censorship.

And nudity is also valid, in Python's oeuvre, whenever it can shock or be considered incongruous. However, the full frontal nudity moments are reserved for female figures, not male.

"Vercotti"—("Army Protection Racket") Probably based at least loosely on Ronnie and Reggie Kray, London's infamous gangsters born ten minutes apart in October 1933, Reggie being the older. They dressed in this slick, dapper way, spent most of their time together, and participated in criminal shakedowns—either together or separately—on a regular basis into the 1960s. There were other brothers in London's underworld, including Greek brothers (Tony and Chris Lambrianou), as well as Sicilian mobsters, including Charles "Darby" Sabini. A conflation of these characters might have created the Vercottis. See Thomas Jones' *The Kray Brothers* at "The Crime Library," as well as entries in the *ODNB*. See notes to Ep. 14 for more on the Krays, and their similarities to Python's Piranha brothers, as well.

"Verity"—("Buying a Bed") *OED*: "Without article. Truth, either in general or with reference to a particular fact; conformity to fact or reality." Mr. Verity's "conformity to fact or reality" is at the heart of this bit.

The Pythons had requested name labels be created for "Mr. A. Lambert" and "Mr. F. Verity"—but those do not appear in the episode as recorded (WAC T12/1,086). These names are obviously borrowed from an actual man named Verity Lambert, producer of *Dr. Who* episodes (1963-1966), and the *W. Somerset Maugham* series (1969-1970) on BBC2.

vox pops—("Full Frontal Nudity") Reoccurring "voice of the people" or "man on the street" sound bites. These were earlier staples of *The Dick Emery Show* (BBC, 1963-1981), a sketch and character comedy show, and were also found in far more serious works, including Humphrey Jennings' documentary *Listen to Britain* (1942).

– W –

walking aggressively—(PSC; "Hell's Grannies") The music dubbed to this film is an orchestrated section from the James Bond film *Thunderball*, by John Barry. Cf. the use of the "Peter Gunn Theme" to accompany strutting vicars and "The Bishop" in Ep. 17.

"waterskiing"—("Army Protection Racket") There are a number of similarly themed recruitment posters extant, including a WWI-era British poster declaiming, "The Army Isn't __All__ Work" that depicts three versions of one soldier: one in full combat kit, one wearing cricket togs and carrying a bat, and one sporting football gear and a ball. A more contemporary reference can be found in a recruitment cartoon made for the U.S. Navy in the early 1960s. The cartoon promotes the exotic ports and good money and, of course, depicts happy seamen waterskiing near a pristine beach: "Like action? On water, on land, under the sea? Like to travel? To have adventures in the far corners of the world? Join the Navy!"

"wattles"—("Hermits") *OED*: "Rods or stakes, interlaced with twigs or branches of trees, used to form fences and the walls and roofs of buildings."

"what's all this about"—("Army Protection Racket") The Colonel doesn't understand the brothers' shakedown language, and the brothers continue to verbally dance around their actual threats and demands. As a military figure representing order and strict regimentation, the Colonel is much more literal, characteristically, tending to interrupt when puns, satire, or double entendres begin to crop up, prodding the show toward more sober, straightforward themes.

– Y –

yoghurt—(link into "The Flasher") Just a variant spelling of "yogurt."

It's worth pointing out in this scene that this assumedly professional BBC announcer-type is flustered when addressing the camera, and with what must be a common broadcast snafu—the unexpected "back to the studio" moment—while the average citizen Praline seems to feel perfectly comfortable in his numerous asides to the camera and viewing audience. Clearly there is a demarcation here between the acknowledged world of the news set as separate and distinct from the audience, and the acknowledged world of Praline, where "crossing over" is possible, and even necessary. The fictionality of the sketch world as opposed to the "real" news set world is essential in this demarcation, and is displayed often in *FC*. Both, however, are contrived and operate by agreed-upon paradigms that the Pythons consistently attempt to undermine. Cf. the manipulation of these structures via the filmed insert of the announcer (Idle) taken for questioning, then returned, and the on-set announcer then goes in his place in Ep. 5, "Newsreader Arrested."

Episode 9: "The Ant, An Introduction"

— A —

Ada's Snack Bar—(PSC; link into "Kilimanjaro Expedition [Double Vision]") The sign is one provided by or in cooperation with a soft drink corporation seen on many older cafés, in this case advertising Barr's soft drink. Barr has been making soda drinks in the UK since 1875, including such popular drinks as Irn-Bru and Tizer. (Tizer is also mentioned on the sign, and will be discussed at some length in Ep. 34 by Jeremy Pither [Palin].)

animated sequence—(link into "Homicidal Barber") The animated sequence is preceded by a lonely shot of an empty, old football stadium, most likely the same stadium seen in Ep. 7, Brentford Football Ground, home at that time to the Brentford Football Club. The animation itself features a manipulated version of Francisco del Cossa's *Saint Vincent Ferrer* (1477-1478), which has been part of the National Gallery's collection since 1858.

"Arthur Wilson"—(PSC; "Kilimanjaro Expedition [Double Vision]") Idle is here called "Arthur Wilson," in spite of the fact that the script as printed has been calling him "Bob" from the outset. (For an earlier instance of this conflict between the written script's character identification and the character's professed identification—noting, of course, that both names would have been written by the script writers, building in the confusion at the written textual level—see Ep. 5. There, "Stig" sits down for an interview, only to give his name moments later as "David Thomas" ("Silly Job Interview"). In both cases, the textual confusion would be apparent at the level of the *reader*, not the *viewer*. This structure makes for a far more writerly text (borrowing Barthes' term), demanding that the reader of the scripts perform some cognitive gymnastics as he/she tries to keep separate the written text from the performed text.

Perhaps, however, there are actually two of these men—Bob and Arthur Wilson, both played by Idle. This is another example of the "in-joke" level of the printed scripts, where information that never ends up on screen is included. The viewing audience, then, wouldn't know that the script had already named this character "Bob," and would accept the name he gives as his own, "Arthur Wilson." Perhaps at the *printed* textual level, then, the presence of two personalities is a given, but not at the *visually recorded* textual level. Later, after Arthur Wilson leaves in a huff, someone else (Bob?) is still in the room with Head.

Note the use of the "Arthur" name again, as was common in the early episodes and will continue throughout *FC*.

— B —

"bang"—("Kilimanjaro Expedition [Double Vision]") In this instance, to do something forcefully, namely, trashing the application.

BBC microphone—(PSC: link into "Kilimanjaro Expedition [Double Vision]") This is an angular, stand-mounted (on desk) microphone, and is probably bidirectional in capacity. The Announcer, Cleese, is dressed in DJ ("dinner jacket") evening attire, the uniform of the "old-fashioned" BBC announcer.

"bells are ringing"—("The Visitors") A Christmas song in this most un-Christ-like setting. The carol is known as both "Ding Dong Merrily On High" and "Hosanna in Excelsis."

"Bevis"—("Lumberjack Song") Cf. Ep. 5, where the Bevis featured there also is a sexually dysfunctional male, preferring to show metaphoric films to his underwear-clad girlfriend instead of engaging in actual intimacy.

"bird"—("The Visitors") Slang for a woman or girl. Cf. other instances in *FC* where women are referred to pejoratively as bits of "tail" (Ep. 33, "Biggles Dictates a Letter").

"blasting their heads off"—(link into "Hunting Film") The characters (Customer and Barber) have descended from leading status to linking elements. The transition away from them is one used as early as Ep. 2, where the camera zooms in on a still photo, then there is a dissolve to film footage of that scene. In this case, the photo is of a country house. The following sketch will end with another "photo freeze," and the camera will pull back into the new scene. This type of transition can be seen in the popular Ealing comedy *Kind Hearts and Coronets* (1949), with a transition from a still photo of a manor house to a live shot of the actual house.

"Blenkinsop"—("Kilimanjaro Expedition [Double Vision]") John Blenkinsop, b. Yorkshire (1783-1831) invented the first practical locomotive (*ODNB*). The more likely reference is to Ernie Blenkinsop, born in Cudworth (1900-1969), who was a successful footballer for Sheffield Wednesday, compiling a 58 percent lifetime winning percentage. The fact that Ernie died within months of this episode would have put him in the news, and make him a more likely candidate for Python's name borrowing.

"Bletchley"—("The Refreshment Room at Bletchley") Town located in Buckinghamshire, since 1967 Bletchley has been a part of greater Milton Keynes.

"botanists"—("Kilimanjaro Expedition [Double Vision]") Botany is the study of plant life, and thus an interesting inclusion for a midwinter volcanic mountain assault, where precious little flora can exist. Beyond about 12,000 feet above sea level the scarce rainfall, thinner atmosphere, and very porous volcanic soils discourage most plant life.

"brace"—("Kilimanjaro Expedition [Double Vision]") A matched set, often referring to dueling pistols.

braces—(PSC; "Gumby Crooner") Braces are suspenders, but the key here is that the "Gumby" moniker hasn't found its way indelibly into the written scripts. The character still must be described by his appearance. The braces were also to become a significant part of the uniform of the "hard mods," soon to be known as skinheads (emerging in the late 1960s). See notes to Ep. 8 for more on the juvenile delinquent fears of the period.

"British Columbia"—("Lumberjack Song") The westernmost Canadian province, BC became a "crown colony" in 1849.

"Brown, Arthur"—("Kilimanjaro Expedition [Double Vision]") Two very real possibilities here: The first is Arthur Brown, a musician, born in Yorkshire (as Arthur Wilton) in 1942, who would later appear in *Tommy* (1975). Brown had released a very popular album, *The Crazy World of Arthur Brown*, in 1968. The other reference possibility is the Arthur Brown (1914-2003) who was an Oxford-educated, well-published local labor history scholar. Brown taught at the Colchester Royal grammar school for many years, and published books on the working class in the Essex area.

"Buddha"—("The Refreshment Room at Bletchley") Means "awakened one," and represents the founder of Buddhism, the predominant religion in much of Asia. As an allusion, this is perhaps a nod to the pseudonym assumed by Beat poet Allen Ginsberg (1926-1997), "Rabbi Buddha Whitman/Ginsburg."

– C –

"change the record"—("The Visitors") Mr. Name (Idle) takes the more romantic record off and replaces it with an American march (see entry for "Washington Post March" below). This is perhaps worth mentioning because it's a Dudley Moore recording that's being replaced—"I Love You Samantha" from the album *Genuine Dud* by the Dudley Moore Trio (WAC T12/1,090). Moore, of course, was part of the immediately preceding generation of university wits that includes fellow *Beyond the Fringe* castmembers Peter Cook, Alan Bennett, and Jonathan Miller, a generation that also included Marty Feldman. The Pythons would replace the *Fringe* comedians (and the satire movement in general) at the forefront of British comedy.

Compère—(PSC; "The Refreshment Room at Bletchley") This character is played by both Palin and Idle in *FC*, but here is much more salacious and unctuous than depicted before. Cf. the introduction to "Restaurant Sketch" (Ep. 3) and "Science Fiction Sketch" (Ep. 7) for previous appearances. These figures are meant to resemble the ubiquitous redcoats of the Butlins Holiday Camps, where many cost-conscious Brits spent their bank and school holidays.

"crème de menthe"—("The Visitors") A syrupy liqueur. The *OED* offers two citations wherein this type of drink is matched to a gender or sexuality:

> 1903 *Daily Mail* 11 Sept. 3/3 Crème de menthe, with its strong peppermint flavour, is the one almost exclusively favoured by ladies. 1930 E. WAUGH *Labels* 26 Shady young men in Charvet shirts sit round the bar repairing with powder-puff and lipstick the ravages of grenadine and crème de cacao. (*OED* 2003)

crooning—("Gumby Crooner") Cf. the chanting monks in *HG*, who hit themselves in the foreheads as they walk. These self-flagellants are depicted in Bergman's *Seventh Seal* (1957), though they are there actually whipping themselves.

– D –

"down there"—("Kilimanjaro Expedition [Double Vision]") This language betrays what was a fairly pervasive "them" mentality, especially shared by those who might have had vested interests in Britain's far-flung colonial holdings, including the British Raj in India (1858-1947). One of the deformations expected with long-term colonialization would be the assumption that the colonizers' language (in this case, English) would always be sufficient to get along in-country, especially in government, business, and the courts. African countries Kenya and Tanzania, for example, had only been independent since 1963-1964.

– E –

Episode 9—"The Ant, an Introduction" was transmitted ninth but recorded tenth. The date of recording was 7 December 1969, and the date of broadcast was 14 December 1969. As for the title, ants aren't mentioned at all in this episode. The ant won't become a key narrative figure until Ep. 41, "Michael Ellis."

This is the last episode to be subtitled, probably as a result of Michael Mills' 29 July 1969 memo request that such additional titling was confusing to both programmers and audiences alike (WAC T12/1,242).

Also appearing in this episode are: Fanny Carby (*Dixon of Dock Green*), Connie Booth, Fred Tomlinson and his Singers ("I'm a Lumberjack"), with Jennifer Partridge on piano. The extras are Joanna Robbins (*Emma*), Hunter Clark, Jean Dempsey, and Tricia Peters; walk-ons include Clive Rogers (*Plateau of Fear*), Mike Briton (*Dr. Who*), Tina Simmons (*Dr. Who*), and Maxine Casson (*Z Cars*) (WAC T12/1,090).

– F –

"film society"—("The Visitors") Weekly or monthly gatherings where the latest art films or classic films could be discussed. Film clubs arose in France, Great Britain, and elsewhere across Europe not long after WWII, and flourished during the heyday of Nouvelle Vague movements like Italian Neo-Realism, the French New Wave, Das Neue Kino (West Germany), and Britain's Free Cinema. All of these movements had significant impact upon Python's writing, stylizations, and parodic structures/targets.

There are and have been film societies across Britain, including, for example, the extant Swindon Film Society (est. 1947). The umbrella organization British Federation Film Societies (BFFS) was established in 1925.

The bothersome, prattling, and thick-skinned intruder Arthur Name (Idle) must also be a comment by the Pythons on the "types" who frequent such local film societies.

"Fink, Harry"—("The Refreshment Room at Bletchley") The name, of course, doesn't fit the superlatives that have just been uttered, much like "Tim" doesn't seem the normal name for a powerful enchanter (see *HG*). Harry Julian Fink was an American TV writer (*Ben Casey* and *The Dick Powell Show*, both 1961), and went on to write for Rock Hudson, John Wayne, and Clint Eastwood. Fink wrote with Peckinpah on *Dick Powell*, and Peckinpah will later be satirized in *FC* (cf. "Cheese Westerns" and "Sam Peckinpah's *Salad Days*," Ep. 33).

"forget all about it"—("Homicidal Barber") Often in lurid tales of the period the impulsive killer or rapist will regret his actions and loathe himself for giving in to his depravities—but will go on anyway until he is stopped. The character in Robert Wiene's *The Cabinet of Dr. Caligari* (1919) is haunted by words and images telling him he is Caligari, and that he must become Caligari ("Du muss Caligari werden!"); the Peter Lorre character in Fritz Lang's chilling 1931 film *M* also wants to be able to stop killing, but cannot, and will do so whenever the voice tell him that he "muss"; and Mr. Craig (Mervyn Johns) in *Dead of Night* (1945) finds that he cannot escape his dreamed destiny of becoming a killer again and again, giving in to the urge to kill each time he dreams a certain dream.

This barber/serial killer character is most likely based on Sweeney Todd, the so-called Demon Barber of Fleet Street, made famous by a number of lurid stories and theatrical productions beginning in the mid-nineteenth century. The barber-killer may have actually lived at the end of the eighteenth century, and his exploits lived on in music halls for many years. There was even an early film based on the characters, *Sweeney Todd: The Demon Barber of Fleet Street* (1936).

frail ... rebel maid—(PSC; "Lumberjack Song") Played by Connie Booth, an American and John Cleese's second wife (married 1968-1978), and his partner in *Fawlty Towers*. She is dressed to resemble Nell (Fenwick), the heroine from the American *The Dudley Do-Right Show* cartoons (Jay Ward Studios, 1969-1970), as well as myriad "meller-drammers." The Mounties are dressed in typical RCMP attire, and just like Dudley, as well. "Mountains" [*sic*] films were somewhat saccharine, innocuous late-Weimar (thus post-expressionist) films produced in Germany between the wars (and even during WWII), such as *Die Blaue Light* (1932), starring Leni Riefenstahl, and *Die Weiße Hölle vom Piz Palü* (1929).

The "rebel maid" allusion is based on the character Lady Mary Trefusis, the titular character in the light opera *The Rebel Maid* (music by Montague Phillips; lyrics by Gerald Dodson; libretto by Alexander M. Thompson and Gerald Dodson). The opera premiered in 1921 at the Empire Theatre in London, and had been produced as recently as 1957 by the St. Albans Operatic Society in St. Albans, Hertfordshire.

– G –

"ghastly place"—("The Visitors") A snap judgment rendered by Mr. Freight (Gilliam) as he scans Victor's (Chapman) home, this fulfills the social stereotype of homosexual men being meticulous in personal habit and uncannily adept at interior design.

"Giant redwood . . . scots pine"—("Lumberjack Song") This list of varying trees is an answer to the Barber's (Palin) hated sameness found in barber college. The giant redwood is only found in California, and only in portions of the northern Sierra Nevada mountains (so, not as far north as British Columbia). The larch—previously featured in Ep. 3—is found in Canada and much of North America. The Douglas fir tree is found throughout the mountain regions of Oregon and British Columbia. The scots pine is also called a fir in Great Britain, and is the only native British pine, hence not endemic to the British Columbia region. (See *EBO*.)

"glacier"—("Kilimanjaro Expedition") Of the peaks at Kilimanjaro, only Kibo features a year-round snowcap (*EBO*).

goat—("The Visitors") Both a sign of lechery and just plain animal filth, the goat fits right in with the rest of the group converging on Victor and Iris. The goats used in *FC* (see Ep. 27, as well) came from Animal Kingdom (WAC T12/1,242), and will reappear—eating revolutionary pamphlets—in the Sartre apartment in Ep. 27.

"Golders Green"—("Llamas") Portions of episodes 8 and 9 were recorded at the Golders Green Hippodrome (on Sunday 19 October 1969) (WAC T12/1,090). Golders Green is located in North London, near Finchley, Hendon, and Hampstead. The Hippodrome (est. 1913) was acquired by the BBC in the late 1960s and converted to a television recording studio. Taping of the *FC* episodes occurred primarily on Stage 6 at BBC-TC, but other shows could and did force the Pythons

and crew to move—to TC Stage 8, to Ealing Studios, and to Golders Green on this occasion. The Hippodrome is located on North End Road in Golders Green, London, W13.

"go much"—("The Visitors") Obviously a sexual allusion, as it's voiced to Iris (Cleveland) by the lecherous Mr. Equator (Cleese). Cf. the "Nudge, Nudge" man, who asks "knowingly" whether the gent's wife is "a goer" (Ep. 3). See the *OED* for the sexual connotations of the phrase in literature.

"Good questions"—("Kilimanjaro Expedition [Double Vision]") Note the pluralizations that are creeping in: "Yes, *we* are leading. . . ."; "And what routes will you *both* be taking?", etc. Arthur Wilson (Idle) is figuring out the rules of this seemingly illogical man (Sir George Head) and setting, and is able to communicate effectively once those rules are followed.

"Gumby, Prof. R.J."—("Gumby Crooner") Cf. Ep. 11, where Prof. *R.J.* Canning unsuccessfully attempts to narrate a Black Plague documentary. This use of initials for academics (and casting Gumbys to represent them) lampoons the luminaries and eminent scholars the Pythons would have read in school, such as A.J.P. Taylor (satirized in *HG*, as well), G. Wilson Knight, L.C. Knights, C.S. Lewis, and perhaps especially E.M.W. Tillyard, the progenitor of the well-known "Elizabethan world picture" thesis (1943).

Additionally, there may be a built-in reference here to the older tradition of "Gentlemen vs. Players" in cricket matches at Lords, where forename initials were used to distinguish between professional and amateur players.

– H –

hand-held camera—(PSC; link out of "Llamas") This simply means that the camera is not mounted on a tripod or "gyrocam" support, thus the image often appears bouncy, unsteady, more frenetic. The techniqie was used often in foreign film of the time, especially as an answer to Hollywood's fluid, flowing cameras mounted on tracks and dollies.

"Hitchcock, Psycho"—("Homicidal Barber") The director and his trendsetting 1960 horror film, starring Janet Leigh and Tony Perkins, and for the first time in a major Hollywood film conflating sexuality, disturbed pathology, scopophilia, and violence into a popular and controversial hit.

The film features significant moments of cross-dressing, voyeurism, and violence—all of which would become essential to Python's métier. In *Psycho* Norman (Perkins) dresses as his dead mother and kills "naughty," transgressing women he's guiltily spying upon. In the Python sketch, the Barber has perhaps killed someone (there's plenty of blood as circumstantial evidence) as a result of his mother's negative influence, and will cross-dress once he's happily a lumberjack. See the entry for "mother" below for more on the negative maternal influence.

"Hurst"—("Homicidal Barber") Geoff Hurst scored a celebrated hat trick in the 1966 World Cup final win over Germany. Hurst began playing for West Ham in 1960 as a nineteen-year-old wing half, but was soon moved to a striker position, where he stayed. Hurst replaced Jimmy Greaves in the '66 Cup during the knock-out phase, allowing for the four-goal performance. (Greaves name is flashed in a film leader in Ep. 2.) The audio account of the thrilling final seconds of the match can be heard on the BBC's *Eyewtiness: 1960-69*, "1966 World Cup."

– I –

"I keep falling off"—(link into "Gumby Crooner") This is a moment of extreme literality, when this comment actually refers back to the "permissive society" moments mentioned in Ep. 8, and the "full frontal nudity" theme. Also, cf. the appearances of Mary Whitehouse-types who tilt at the liberal society in *FC*, as in the "Tory Housewives" sketch in Ep. 32. The Goons employed a multitude of such "literal" jokes.

This is also a straight-ahead joke—set-up and payoff, and could fit into a stand-up routine. There are very few of these in the Pythons' oeuvre, and fewer still that aren't undercut or punished. Here, the following title card points up the lameness of this joke, as it is Britain's entry into a Eurovision- or Montreux-type contest for jokes. The Pythons will be invited to enter a cobbled-together episode into the Golden Rose of Montreux contest in 1971, where they'll come second. WAC information for the reshooting of that episode can be found in WAC T12/1,413.

into the fire—(PSC; "The Visitors") Another instance where cats are made the object of violence in Python. Cf. the cat choking to death on lupins in Ep. 33, the cat as doorbell and another being ironed flat in Ep. 45, and the cat being dust-banged against a wall in *IIG*.

"inviting them along"—("The Visitors") The simple plot is beginning to resemble Dr. Seuss' children's book, *The Cat in the Hat* (1957), where an uninvited guest (the cat) appears and causes all manner of havoc as the children try to keep the house in shape for mother's imminent return. Several of the Pythons (Gilliam, Idle, Jones, and Palin) did work together on a

children's show (*Do Not Adjust Your Set* [1967-1969]) prior to *FC*, and also cf. the use of a Richard Scarry book in Ep. 3. This sketch, of course, takes a much more sexual, devious, and lethal turn than Theodor Geisel's works.

In walks . . . necklace—(PSC; "The Visitors") Mr. Freight (Gilliam) looks very much like a glam-rocker of the period. Glam-rock (also glitter rock) featured men dressed effeminately and outlandishly, with the "suggestion of sexual ambiguity or androgyny" (*OED*). The sexual ambiguity issue is key, since Equator (Cleese) mentions that his friend's wife has just died, then Freight shows up with a male companion (Palin), and is called a "great poof." His behavior is also stereotypically gay (a lisping, effeminate voice and poncing, affected posture, etc.).

According to A.C. Hamilton, most "antique and Renaissance" works featuring bisexual figures utilize an effeminate male as representing androgyny, which may have influenced Python's choice here. British glam-rock artists included David Bowie (as Ziggy Stardust), Gary Glitter, and members of Slade, among others. See *EBO*.

Gilliam will dress like this again in Ep. 33, as "Ginger," and be quite offended when it's implied that he might be gay.

"Islam"—(link into "Jug Dancing" animation) The Muhammadan religion established in the seventh century. Islam is monotheistic and follows strict religious practices. In the animation, neither character appears characteristically Islamic (either by race or dress, etc.). This and "Buddha" seem to be used here as just recognizable and silly throwaway names.

The name "Brian" has been and will continue to be utilized in *FC* and beyond, like the name "Arthur," and starting back as early as Ep. 2 (see notes to Ep. 2 for more on these myriad nominal appearances). "Bruce" will also appear again, especially in the "Drunken Philosophers" sketch, where everyone except the new faculty member is named Bruce.

"It's . . .—(PSC; titles) The voiceover "Monty Python's Flying Circus," voiced by Cleese in his "silly" voice, is not noted in the written script.

– J –

jug band music—(PSC; "Jug Band Dancing" animated link out of "The Refreshment Room at Bletchley") A jazz sound characterized by simple, even homemade instruments, like a whiskey jug, washtub, etc., as well as typical jazz combo instruments. Most of this music would have been culled from the BBC's massive archives, and used gratis. This particular piece of music is called "Banjerino," and is a jug, washboard, and kazoo composition (WAC T12/1,090).

– K –

"Kilimanjaro"—("Kilimanjaro Expedition [Double Vision]") Found in Tanzania (near the Kenyan border), it features the highest point(s) on the African continent, and was first climbed in 1889. Head's idea to build a bridge between the two summits of Kilimanjaro isn't as farfetched as the text would have us believe, as Kilimanjaro is actually a three-peak volcanic massif, with cones called Kibo (the highest), Mawensi, and Shira, from east to west (*EBO*). Head could have been thinking, then, of building a bridge between two of the cones, as unlikely as that might be (discounting his double vision, of course). Much like the intended incongruity of hermits living in happy communal groups in Ep. 8, this intended silliness has a basis in reality.

– L –

Letter—(link out of "Lumberjack Song") Letters of this type can be found in many period newspapers and periodicals, including both actual and created ones in *Private Eye*, and in *Spectator*, many responding to previously published letters:

> Sir: Is Sir Richard Acland (21 June) thinking of W.B. Yeats's saying: 'Science is the religion of the suburbs'?
>
> *T.A.M. Jack*

Preston-next-Wingham, Canterbury, Kent (5 July 1969)

This same type of "letter to the editor" is still characteristic of major newspapers to this day, and this format will appear throughout *FC*. (See Eps. 5, 10, and 11 for more letters.)

"Llama"—("Llamas") A relative of the camel, and native to South America. Mutated as it becomes a part of Python's bestiary, the llama does not have a beak, nor does it eat honey (it is a ruminant), have fins, or pose much of a threat to humans. Llamas will later figure prominently in the "silly" opening titles for *Monty Python and the Holy Grail* (1974).

low sexy lighting – ha ha—(PSC; "The Visitors") The "ha ha" is certainly another in-joke, here indicating the remote possibility of achieving mood lighting on this particular stage set with the available light technology. With the entire show working on a very thin budget and on the least choice of available TC sets (usually TC

6, to this point, but perhaps Golders Green), the lights available would have been those most often used for news sets and the like, meaning bright, broad illumination from 5K and 10K overhead lights. More than that, Martin Kempton indicates that TC 6 was the *only* studio space not gifted with a new light control package in 1969 (a dimmer control called a "Thorn Q-File"), which allowed all the other Television Centre studios significantly more control over light levels (see *An Incomplete History of London's Television Studios*). Finally, mood lighting would require not only lights capable of lesser, manipulable illumination, but in-studio cameras that could successfully capture clear video images in such a low light environment.

It's clear that on many of the exterior shoots (on film) to gather inserts and the like the troupe traveled with even less complicated lighting packages, demanding lots of shooting in full daylight. For the kitchen sequence in "Dull Life of a City Stockbroker," however, the show actually used a kitchen in a council house in the Australia Road, East Acton area, which was unusual, as it would have demanded at least some onsite, indoor lighting.

– M –

"Machin"—("Kilimanjaro Expedition [Double Vision]") Richard Harris played Frank Machin, the coal miner who tries to escape to football (rugby) stardom in Lindsay Anderson's tragic "Angry Young Man" film *This Sporting Life* (1963). See notes to Ep. 2 for more on the movement and film, and notes to Ep. 19 for more on Anderson.

Another Machin, Arnold (1911-1999), designed the most recognizable and oft-used effigy of the Queen to be used on British stamps from 1966 onward; and noted English author G.I.T. Machin (*The Catholic Question in English Politics, 1820 to 1830*, published in 1964) could have also prompted this name.

"Mama"—("Lumberjack Song") Cf. the "mother" issues discussed above. Here, rather than castration anxiety, the Barber-cum-Lumberjack seems to have castration envy.

Marseillaise—(PSC; "A Man With a Tape Recorder Up His Brother's Nose") Fitting for Python that the French national anthem would play in this instance where a finger is up a nose. This rendition is performed by the Band of the Grenadier Guards (WAC T12/1,090). The BGG also performs the version of "Liberty Bell Suite" used in the show's credits.

"Matrons"—("Kilimanjaro Expedition [Double Vision]") The *OED* notes that there is a class-specific definition for the term "matron," and it fits the "Sir George Head, OBE" and later "Upperclass Twit" theme nicely: "A married woman, usually with the accessory idea of (moral or social) rank or dignity." But then the dictionary goes on to distinguish between Roman and British matrons, defining the British matron thusly: " . . . jocularly taken as the representative of certain social prejudices and rigorous notions of conventional propriety supposed to be characteristic of married women of the English upper middle-class."

moorland—(PSC; "Hunting Film") Land that has not been cultivated, fenland, etc. This looks to be the same Bournemouth area used in earlier episodes.

moped—(PSC; "Llamas") A "motorized pedal cycle," and used to be called an autocycle. Mopeds are also featured in Ep. 29, the *"Erizabeth L"* sketch.

"mother"—("Homicidal Barber") Perhaps the Customer (Jones) is also a victim of his mother. The images of razors and scissors also invoke the specter of Freud's castrating mother figure, especially as the figurative emasculation renders Norman (Tony Perkins) incapable of natural sexuality, and prevents the Barber (Palin) from successfully cutting hair. None of these three, then, have entered the "genital phase." It seems that all three men (Norman, the Barber, and the Customer) are far too involved with their mothers to achieve sexual normalcy elsewhere. Later, after the Barber has refused/failed to cut the Customer's hair, the presence of an offscreen domineering, castrating mother is confirmed when he laments his mother forcing him into barber school, forcing him to cut hair, which repulses him.

Mounties—("Lumberjack Song") Members of the Royal Canadian Mounted Police (RCMP), Canada's federal peace force, and here wearing their recognizable red jackets and peaked hats, another Python shorthand to remind the viewer that the plot is moving into Canadian territory.

Most of the Mounties here are actually members of the Fred Tomlinson Singers, semi-regular musical guests on *FC* (Ep. 22).

– N –

"Nairobi"—(Kilimanjaro Expedition [Double Vision]") Capital of Kenya. Nairobi is approximately 150 miles north and west of Kilimanjaro. Kenya had been much in the British newspapers and public consciousness during the earlier Mau Mau uprisings, when British settlers were attacked and often killed, some quite gruesomely. See the entries for "armed communist uprising . . . " (Ep. 31) and "Mau Mau" in Ep. 43 for other references.

"Name by name but not by nature"—("The Visitors") A Dudley Moore character—Mr. Spigot, a one-legged actor auditioning for a Tarzan role—introduces himself as "A spigot by name but not by nature" (*Beyond the Fringe*, "One Leg Too Few").

– O –

"OBE"—("Kilimanjaro Expedition [Double Vision]") Stands for Officer of the British Empire, and is one of the "Most Excellent Order of the British Empire" honors, though *not* an admission into knighthood.

The orders were instituted by George V in 1917, made available to many who served the empire during the Great War, including women and foreigners. This broadened application of royal recognition could be part of the reason the Pythons created the perceptually challenged Head—just about anyone could be considered for OBE status. The Order was in the news at this time, as well, when the Chapel for the Order was dedicated in 1969 at St. Paul's, the Queen and the Duke in attendance. The "affected" depiction of Head might be attributed to the fact that the easily targeted Duke of Edinburgh (the Queen's husband, Prince Philip) has been and remains Grand Master of the Order.

Noteworthy Order members of this era include other explorers like Sir Earnest Shackleton, CVO; Sir Edmund Hillary, KG, KBE; yachtsman Sir Francis Chichester, KG; as well as TV actress Violet Carson (*Coronation Street*). Chichester—who circumnavigated the globe solo—was knighted in 1967 on national TV, and with the Queen wielding Sir Francis Drake's sword. Cleese himself would decline the CBE in 1996.

"Odeon"—("The Visitors") The Odeon would have been one of cinemas built by Oscar Deutsch in Great Britain in the 1920s, then purchased by J. Arthur Rank and greatly expanded in the 1930s. He may be referring specifically to the Odeon at Leicester Square, an Art Deco movie palace.

"old days"—("Gumby Crooner") Reflecting the "Yorkshire Gentlemen" sketch where four northern gentlemen sit about and swap hyperbolized stories of childhood privation and hardship, and generally agree that the older days were far more challenging. That sketch was originally written and performed on *At Last the 1948 Show* by Chapman, Cleese, Tim Brooke-Taylor, and Marty Feldman.

"One stain could be the mark . . . "—(PSC; "Homicidal Barber") Here again the script addresses the reader, not the viewer, mentioning that one of the blood streaks seen on the barber's clothing could have been caused by a "hand slipping downward." This isn't clear at all in the performance itself—the Barber just looks blood spattered.

"Only make believe . . . "—("Gumby Crooner") Lyrics from "Make Believe," from the Broadway musical *Showboat* (1927) by Jerome Kern and Oscar Hammerstein. The entire stanza:

Only make believe I love you,
Only make believe that you love me.
Others find peace of mind in pretending,
Couldn't you? Couldn't I? Couldn't we?
Make believe our lips are blending
In a phantom kiss, or two, or three.
Might as well make believe I love you,
For to tell the truth I do.

The musical was restaged on Broadway several times, as well as a celebrated 1966 version staged at Lincoln Center, New York. *Showboat* would be brought to the UK in 1971, and enjoyed a record run of more than 900 shows.

"only one"—("Homicidal Barber") West Ham United Football Club (est. 1895) was a Division One team between 1958 and 1978—to date West Ham have won no Premiership titles or league championships, but can claim three FA cup wins.

"on the carpet"—("The Visitors") This sketch is becoming a precursor to the troupe's final episode, wherein "The Most Awful Family in Britain" is profiled (Ep. 45). The squalor and debauchery here are certainly examples of Python's stated attempts to shock its audience. Mr. Cook (Palin) will change only slightly and reappear in Ep. 12 as Ken Shabby (also Palin), equally vile and debased.

– P –

"Palace"—("Homicidal Barber") Crystal Palace Football Club was formed in 1905, and was named for the glass Crystal Palace the team originally occupied (built for the 1851 Great Exhibition). The team was promoted to Division One by 1969 on the heels of beating Fulham, which is when the Customer (Jones) would have been watching them. An illustration of the Crystal Palace will be seen in Ep. 29, "The Lost World of Rouirama."

Part 2—(titles) One of the many misleading introductory numbers used by Python in *FC*. Cf. episodes 2, 3, 4, and 8 for similar meaningless mis-numberings.

"poof"—("The Visitors") Slang for homosexual. Used often in *FC* (variations "pooftah," "poove"). Here the poof is acknowledged, welcomed, and accepted by the assembled crowd. In Ep. 33, Biggles will kill Alvy (Palin) when he admits his homosexuality. Ginger (Gilliam) then ponces in and is offended at being mistaken for a poof. The popular BBC television show *Dad's Army* (1968-1977) will be lampooned in Ep. 38 (printed script version only) as *Dad's Pooves*, and feature prancing, cross-dressing sadomasochists.

"press wild flowers"—("Lumberjack Song") The practice of "pressing" flowers into books, albums, etc., is listed here probably because it might be considered an artistic, effeminate pastime. The following line then cements the effeminization motif. This specter of effeminization—on the stage and among the audience—is just the vice the anti-theatricalists were railing against at the height of the Tudor and through the end of the Stuart monarchies. Significant anti-theatricalist literature was produced by the likes of Gosson, Stubbes, Northbrook, and Prynne. There was a fear that acting on the stage and watching such play-acting prompted men to become effeminate and more likely to violate sumptuary laws (dressing above their station), as well as indulge in ingles, catamites, and all manner of sodomitical practices. In this sketch Palin's character disdains the "natural" love of his obviously willing female companion in favor of transvestism and even homosexuality, and is willing to play the less-dominant female part of some male-male relationship generated from a bar visit. See Stephen Gosson's *Schoole of Abuse* (1579) and Philip Stubbes' *The Anatomie of Abuses* (1583), both Puritan attacks on the falseness of the stage; see also William Prynne's *Histriomatrix* (1632). (For more on the subject see *MPSERD*, chapter 6.)

This is also a somewhat rare example in Python wherein the transvestism is not only noted textually, but takes on a sexual and even licentious tincture. Usually, cross-dressers (like Pepperpots) are textually treated as female figures (albeit ugly, dowdy, shrill, etc.). In Ep. 14, an admitted "female impersonator" (Cleese) will be gangster Dinsdale Piranha's object of affection.

– Q –

"quadruped"—("Llamas") Any creature employing four-legged locomotion. Here, at least, the Pythons are correct.

– R –

"Radio Times"—(letter link out of "Lumberjack Song") The BBC's programming magazine has been in publication since 1923. The publication would feature *FC* on the cover only once, in 1974, when the final, abbreviated series was about to debut. Cleese appears on the 11 January 1969 cover of the *Radio Times*, but for *I'm Sorry I'll Read That Again* (1964-1983).

"rat-bag"—("The Visitors") *OED*: "A stupid or eccentric person, a fool; an unpleasant person, a troublemaker. Also . . . stupid, idiotic, uncouth." In Renaissance terms, "baggage" could mean a worthless woman, as well. The term will be used again in Eps. 21, 27, and 37.

"rather sharply"—("Kilimanjaro Expedition [Double Vision]") Actually, since Kilimanjaro is made up of three volcanic cones, unlike an Alpine formation the summit topography here is much more gentle, with a saddle at the 15,000-foot level connecting cone rims, and a gradual slope (influenced by past flows) leading to the plateaus below the formation. No mountaineering equipment is necessary to climb even the tallest peak (*EBO*). In a later episode (Ep. 33), the Pythons will attempt to climb the north face of the Uxbridge Road. There is also an aborted mountaineering sketch in Ep. 26, and in Ep. 31 Mt. Everest is climbed by hairdressers.

The description of the summit as tending to go up and up and then to "slope away rather sharply" is silly, yes, but this is very much like Sir Edmund Hillary described the summiting of Everest in one of his earliest recorded accounts of the ascent:

. . . at first glance it was most impressive, and even rather frightening. *Great* cornices—which are *great* overhanging masses of ice and snow—thrust out to the right, and hung over the two-mile drop of the Kan Chung face. If you held too far to that side it would be disaster. . . . I levered my way backwards up [an ice] chimney, praying the cornice would stay in place. . . . Beyond each stretch of the ridge there was always another one curving away beyond it, until we finally realized that the ridge ahead, *instead of rising, dropped sharply away*. (Audio transcription, *Eyewitness: 1950-59*, "The Conquest of Everest")

It should be noted that both Hillary and Richard Dimbleby—who was reverently describing the new Queen's coronation as Everest was being conquered—employ very similar phraseologies (a cornucopia of "great" moments) in their accounts. The more hushed and reverential Dimbleby will be parodied in Ep. 23, beginning in the "Fish Licence" sketch.

"real entertainment"—("Gumby Crooner") This is probably a belief shared by many of the generation. The advent of television did nearly cripple feature filmmaking, causing Hollywood to streamline and in-

novate to survive. Television also replaced radio and newspapers, to a great degree, as the source of news and entertainment for the postwar generations. Evening programming would have also kept more folk at home, and away from the cinema, a stroll, the pub, the musical revue, etc. As early as 1961 the head of the U.S. Federal Communications Commission (FCC), Newton Minow, had called television a "vast wasteland."

Red Indian—("Hunting Film") Another appearance by an American Indian in Britain (cf. Ep. 6), this time also played by Idle. Like the City Gent and Pepperpot, the character is iconicized and reduced to a visual stereotype. In this instance, however, there is no opportunity for the character to overcome that liminalization, as he just plays the part of startled game and scampers off. The Pepperpots are allowed, often, knowledge and narrative control well beyond their appearance and station, and the previous appearance of the Red Indian revealed a literate theatregoer very much up on modern, British theatrical performance. The marginalization created by stereotypical behavior, dress, and speech can be trespassed by certain of these characters, perhaps finding its ultimate realization in the depiction of Dennis (Palin), the uppity peasant in *Holy Grail*.

See entries in Ep. 2 for "city gent," as well as "Pepperpots" in Ep. 1.

"Rubber Mac Award"—(link out of "Lumberjack Song") A rubber mac is a rubber or synthetic material raincoat, as worn by Praline in the "Dead Parrot" sketch in Ep. 8. For the award, cf. the titles to Ep. 6, for the BBC's Eurovision- and Golden Rose of Montreux-like "entry for the Zinc Stoat of Budapest." For information on the Eurovision Song Contest, see entries in Ep. 22.

This image of a battered trophy may be a reference to the infamous "lost" World Cup trophy, which went missing in 1966, the year England won the celebrated title. The trophy was later discovered by a dog in a suburban home garden in South London.

runs out—("The Visitors") P.G. Wodehouse actually used the film term "iris out" (meaning the use of an iris action to leave a scene) as an interesting way to exit characters from a scene. From *Plum Pie* (1966): "After a terrific struggle the hood called it a day and irised out" (177). In the Python sketch, Iris (Cleveland) puts up with as much as she can, then quickly exits.

– S –

"So are we"—("Kilimanjaro Expedition [Double Vision]") There is the implication here that we as an audience now share Head's pathology—we can see the other side of the doubled world that only he has seen until this point. The influence and nominal significance of supernatural author Arthur Machen (1863-1947) can't be overlooked here. In his novella *The Great God Pan* (1894), Machen describes a world beyond or behind the perceived world:

> Look about you, Clarke. You see the mountain, and hill following after hill, as wave on wave, you see the woods and orchard, the fields of ripe corn, and the meadows reaching to the reed-beds by the river. You see me standing here beside you, and hear my voice; but I tell you that all these things—yes, from that star that has just shone out in the sky to the solid ground beneath our feet—*I say that all these are but dreams and shadows; the shadows that hide the real world from our eyes. There is a real world, but it is beyond this glamour and this vision, beyond these 'chases in Arras, dreams in a career,' beyond them all as beyond a veil.* I do not know whether any human being has ever lifted that veil; but I do know, Clarke, that you and I shall see it lifted this very night from before another's eyes. You may think this all strange nonsense; it may be strange, but it is true, and the ancients knew what lifting the veil means. They called it seeing the god Pan. (chapter 1; italics added)

In the sketch, Python seems to have given Head (Cleese) the ability to see this other world, which in the novella is only accessible by surgically altering the gray matter with a "slight lesion," according to Dr. Raymond. Upperclass folk, in Python's world, do tend to suffer from brain maladies, as exhibited by the actions and unintelligible (requiring subtitles) speech patterns (Ep. 12), and even brain shifting, requiring a sharp jostle to realign the tiny, off-center brain ("*Mortuary Hour*," Ep. 35).

"somehow"—("Kilimanjaro Expedition [Double Vision]") At this moment, it seems that the absurdity has been controlled by the introduction of a character who—dressed like a credible mountaineer—assures Bob/Arthur Wilson (Idle) in something of an aside that everything's going to be fine. It takes just moments, though, for that calming effect to disappear as the guide (Chapman) climbs the walls, furniture, etc. A later example of this phenomena can be seen in Ep. 43, where Hamlet is accosted by a series of doctors, each saying that the one before was not a real doctor, only for the new scenario to quickly unravel with the appearance of the next "real" doctor. It's this "no safe ground" idea (where the proverbial rug of reality can be pulled out over and over again)—the fact in Python there is not a return to normalcy, just a new absurdism—that keeps their comedy from being precisely termed "Brechtian." In *MPSERD* the author notes:

Kristin Thompson points out in "Sawing Through the Bough: *Tout va Bien* as a Brechtian Film" (*Wide Angle* 1:3, 1976), that Brecht separated himself from the Dadaists and surrealists and their interpretations of alienation. Ben Brewster's article "From Shklovsky to Brecht: A Reply" (*Screen* 15:2), quotes Brecht: "Their objects do not return from alienation" (Thompson 30). Brecht saw those practitioners essentially paralyzing the function of their art, so that "as far as its effect is concerned, it ends in an amusement" (30). Much of Python's work (especially the *Flying Circus* episodes) is explicitly created to undercut any return, to deny any progress other than that which leads to a comedic, shocking and often open-ended end. In other words, to end in an amusement. (311)

sportin' gentlemen dressed in huntin' tweed—("Hunting Film") The printed script offers this vernacular spelling ("huntin'") throughout the scene description. This is an allusion to a character type created by Arthur Conan Doyle, the blustery Lord John Roxton, an ambitious big game hunter looking to bag a dinosaur in *The Lost World*:

> A sportin' risk, young fellah, that's the salt of existence. Then it's worth livin' again. We're all gettin' a deal too soft and dull and comfy. Give me the great waste lands and the wide spaces, with a gun in my fist and somethin' to look for that's worth findin'. I've tried war and steeplechasin' and aeroplanes, but this huntin' of beasts that look like a lobster-supper dream is a brand-new sensation. (chapter 6)

The music beneath (dubbed to the film) is a lively version of Melodious Brass' "Waltzing Trumpets" by the Fairey Band (WAC T12/1,090).

"stage with him"—("The Refreshment Room at Bletchley") This is not unlike some of the serious prologues written for Restoration or eighteenth-century dramas, especially in their hyperbolic praise; also see the tongue-in-cheek version offered by H. Scriblerus Secundus (Fielding) as the "Preface" to his *Tom Thumb (The Tragedy of Tragedies)* (1731).

"Strong, Arthur"—(letter link out of "Lumberjack Song") Note the connection between the girl's misunderstanding about "rugged" appearances equaling heterosexual virility, and the name and title/rank of the letter-writer. The implication that manly, uniformed, and/or titled men mask "swishy" personas is a consistent Python trope (fairy policemen, campy soldiers, swishy judges). The inclusion of "Mrs" also indicates that even protesting, letter-writer Arthur Strong may share some of the Barber's proclivities.

"Swahili"—("Kilimanjaro Expedition [Double Vision]") More accurately "Kiswahili," since "Swahili" are the Bantu peoples themselves. It is the principal language of the entire region, though hundreds of tribal dialects are still spoken, as well as English. See the entry above for "down there" for more on English colonial expectations, deformations, etc.

swish—(PSC; "The Refreshment Room at Bletchley") Slang for an effeminate man, or a homosexual, but here used to describe a posh, upscale club. See *OED*.

sync—("A Man With a Tape Recorder Up His Brother's Nose") Out of synchronization, which would actually mean that rather than two channels where the sound is divided (voice, instrumentation, etc.), there are two perhaps mono recordings being played back almost simultaneously.

Following this performance, there appears a filmed shot of a single spectator, in long shot, in an otherwise empty football stadium. (This shot is not indicated at all in the written scripts.) The fan is clapping, and obviously taking the place in this instance for the stock Women's Institute footage, but not in stereo. The shot is part of the footage used in Ep. 7, where the lone spectator watched a single player and referee during the blancmange invasion. The stadium appears to be the Brentford Football Ground, Ealing.

— **T** —

tape recorder—(PSC; "Homicidal Barber") The intermediary that prevents actual contact or normal intimacy, here the tape recorder performs the role of a hole in a wall, a mask or role-playing mechanism, or even a peeping camera—in this case allowing the Barber the distance he needs from the actual act of hair cutting (from performance, from intimacy). Cf. the 1960 Michael Powell film *Peeping Tom*, where the 16mm camera performs a similar function, and the killer even uses the camera's tripod as his penetrating weapon/ phallus.

"**this week**"—(link out of "Hunting Film") Perhaps an unconscious indication that the days of the armored knight and chicken were numbered. Gilliam (in the armor) will appear later in the episode in a significantly flamboyant part, and his out-of-armor appearances will increase into the second series. The slapstick knight character will appear only twice more, in Eps. 13 and 35, an indication that Python's writing prowess has gone well beyond the need for such a stock continuity figure.

"**tins of beans**"—("The Visitors") Cf. the Gilliam character (Kevin) in the Garibaldi family in Ep. 45 ("*Most Awful Family in Britain*"), who lays on the couch throughout the sketch, eats beans, passes gas, and screams for more beans.

Mocking the editorial and advertising commingling in the *Daily Express, Private Eye* (on Friday, 6 August 1965) ran a mock news story headlined "The Biggest News of the Day" in the *Daily Getsworse*, which was a "full-page colour ad" for Loosebowl's Baked Beans, a product that has "carried the good name of Britain all over the world" (Ingrams 120). The story is penned by "Squire Barrowboy," a *Private Eye* pseudonym for the powerful *Express* publisher Lord Beaverbrook.

"**Totnes**"—("Homicidal Barber") A town in Devon on the Dart River, essentially due west of the beachside resort town Paignton. A significant portion of the exteriors for the second series were shot in and around Paignton.

"**two men**"—("Kilimanjaro Expedition [Double Vision]") It appear that Head's dictionary was either written by him, or the visual (and, eventually, cognitive) malady afflicts Head and his entire class, including authors of dictionaries. This kind of shared class affliction will reappear in more virulent terms in the "Upperclass Twit" sketch (Ep. 12). The class consciousness is also apparent in the consistent anti-Conservative bent the *FC* program takes, including aligning the Tories in Britain with Germany's National Socialist party, also in Ep. 12.

— **V** —

very small bird—("Hunting Film") This hunting film is structured like a Keystone silent comedy, or the musical montage segment of a show like *The Monkees* (NBC, 1966-1968), but perhaps especially the contemporary (and naughty) *Benny Hill Show*. Hill had been on the air since 1955 (for BBC, ATV, and Thames), and was obviously an inspiration to the Pythons as they attended school and began work in the TV industry. Hill moved to Thames TV in 1969, and would spend the next twenty years there.

The images of the landed gentry blasting everything in sight is also reminiscent of the hunt sequence in Jean Renoir's scathing *Rules of the Game* (1938), a rich criticism of France's disinterested and disintegrating social elite in the pre-war years.

See the entry for "sportin' gentlemen dressed in huntin' tweed" above for more on the literary inspiration for this depiction.

— **W** —

"**Washington Post March**"—("The Visitors") Actual title "The Washington Post," this is a march written by American John Philip Sousa (1854-1932) in 1889, and was culled from the BBC's audio archives (WAC

T12/1,090). The tune had been used previously by Cleese for *At Last the 1948 Show*, the "I've Got a Parrot Up My Nose" song.

Welsh miners—(PSC; "The Visitors") The Welsh miners will reappear in Ep. 26, the "Coal Mine" sketch. Most of them here are the Fred Tomlinson Singers, who have appeared on the show previously, and will again. They will sing their version of "Summarizing Proust" in Ep. 31. Singers in female Welsh national costumes along with a Welsh harpist will appear in *"The Money Programme"* in Ep. 29.

"wet 'em"—("The Visitors") Incontinence jokes also characterize the Garibaldi family sketch in Ep. 45, including references to flatulence and bowel regularity.

winces—("Homicidal Barber") A typical Hitchcock motif, the use of a particular word or sound to remind the protagonist and the viewer of an event, and usually a crime. In *Blackmail* (1929), it's the image of and word "knife," since the heroine (Annie Oondra) had earlier used a knife to kill the artist (Cyril Ritchard) who attacked her.

"with an L"—("The Visitors") There is, of course, no "L" anywhere in his name. Perhaps the "L" can stand for latitude, in relation to the equatorial reference? Also, cf. Ep. 19 where the character "Raymond Luxury Yacht" announces that his name is actually pronounced "Throatwobbler Mangrove," no matter the spelling.

– Y –

"your honour"—("Homicidal Barber") Reading this as a so-called Freudian slip (or "faulty action"), it would appear that the Barber is at least subconsciously thinking about the consequences of his alleged crimes, and an appearance before a magistrate, and/or this is proof that he's perhaps committed a similar atrocity before.

The Art Critic (also Palin) exhibits a similar response in Ep. 8 when the woman catches him trying to get a better look at a Rubens nude, calling her, among other things, "Your honour."

Episode 10

– A –

"Adapt . . . round table"—("Bank Robber [Lingerie Shop]") "Adopt, adapt and improve" is, indeed the motto of the Round Table organization, founded in 1927 by Louis Marchesi. The goal of the organization was to give eighteen- to forty-five-year-old men a place to gather, and provide service, initially, for the citizens of Norwich. The motto for the Round Table was derived from a speech made in 1927 at the British Industries Fair by the Prince of Wales (later Edward VIII):

> The young business and professional men of this country must get together round the table, *adopt* methods that have proved so sound in the past, *adapt* them to the changing needs of the times and wherever possible, *improve* them. (Round Table National Association)

"Airedale"—("Pet Conversions") Short for "Airedale terrier." "Putting a tuck in" may mean somehow seaming or hemming the dog. "Let out" usually refers to letting down hems or opening pleats to increase length or girth on a garment. These alterations are essentially verbal descriptions of what Gilliam's dismembering and re-membering animations accomplish with photos of humans, animals, landmarks, etc.

"American . . . violence"—("Arthur Tree") Cf. the duck, cat, and lizard *not* discussing affairs in Ep. 5. Also probably satirizing the propensity for such entertainment shows to invite celebrities to talk about significant topical issues, including David Frost's own *Frost on Saturday*, *Frost on Sunday*, etc. (See entry at "David Frost type" below for much more.) There were many BBC, ATV, ITV, Granada, and Thames TV shows of a similar nature, including the BBC's flagship panel discussion show *The Brains Trust* (1955-1961).

Anchovy—("Vocational Guidance Counsellor [Chartered Accountant]") Saltwater, schooling, herring-like fish. This characterization by Palin is very much like the nebbish Arthur Pewtey, seen earlier in the "Marriage Guidance Counsellor" sketch.

applause over—(PSC; "Arthur Tree") The forest, then, as the audience for this tree/wood show. But perhaps this is also an intentional double entendre, as the "block of wood" mentioned earlier can also be taken as not just a piece of wood, but as a block (an area, a portion of land) of trees, hence the photo of the forest.

shot of a forest—The color transparencies used here are called "In the Lael Forest" and "Easter Ross" (WAC T12/1,242). Easter Ross is a lush area in the highlands east of Ross, Scotland, while the Lael Forest is in the Ullapool area of Highland, Scotland. Some of the exterior work for series one and two were shot in the Oban and Glencoe areas of Scotland.

"as near as dammit"—("Pet Conversions") Used here as a comparative phrase. The *OED* offers this citation: "1961 *Guardian* 24 Apr. 9/7 'The score standing as near as dammit at two.'"

"Attendants"—("Trailer") Cf. the *Up Your Pavement* TV show featured in Ep. 42. All three of these shows feature less-than-noteworthy characters as the shows' foci, an example of the "leveling" aspects of Python's satire. See chapter 5 of *MPSERD*, as well as Dekker's *Shoemakers Holiday* (1599).

Aztec—(PSC; "Strangers in the Night") Central American Indian culture, and known as such since c. AD 1100. The printed script reveals its own level of textual meaning when it gives similes and metaphors (read: examples) for the reader only, and specifically the production design team charged with costuming the show. This "Aztec" character is supposed to resemble Christopher Plummer (b. 1929) as he appeared in *Royal Hunt of the Sun* (1969), according to the script. *Royal*

Hunt of the Sun actually depicts Incan culture and chief Atahualpa (Plummer) as they interacted with the Spanish explorer Pisarro (Peter Shaw). Plummer also appeared in *Battle of Britain*, also in 1969.

And rather than the sketch being curtailed due to the husband's wandering off, the script mentions that Vera cuts the Aztec off "owing to lack of money," referring to the cost of speaking actors versus mute walk-ons. This is yet another tidbit for the reader(s) only. See Ep. 28, where the fiscal health of the BBC is in question, and speaking roles are discouraged (and the shows are being broadcast from a nice couple's home).

– B –

"bally froggie"—("Strangers in the Night") Slang for "bloody Frenchman," probably originally from RAF-types during World War I. Biggles (Chapman) comes in here as if he's saving the damsel in one of his many adventures. See "Biggles" entry below.

beach—("The First Man to Jump the Channel") These scenes were filmed at the beaches beneath the cliffs of Covehithe. Most of the (beachside) Ron Obvious sketch was shot in the Covehithe, Southwold, and Saxmundham areas of Suffolk (WAC T12/1,083). Portions in the city were shot at the Brighton Road and Liberty Lane intersection, Addlestone, Surrey on 22 October 1969 (WAC T12/1,242).

bedroom of a middle-aged—("Strangers in the Night") The music beneath this introduction into the bedroom scene is "Creepy Clowns" from the Crawford Light Orchestra, by Ronald Hamer (WAC T12/1,091).

"Biggles"—("Strangers in the Night") Based on the aviator character James Bigglesworth created by author Captain W.E. Johns, and who appeared in ninety-six books. Chapman plays Biggles in Ep. 33 as well, while Jones takes the Biggles part in the "Spanish Inquisition" sketch in Ep. 15.

"Algy"—Full name Algernon Montgomery Lacey, Biggles' best friend and companion in his adventures. Ginger, the third member of their team, isn't mentioned here, but will appear in Ep. 33, in the "Biggles Dictates a Letter" sketch, where he's a glam-rock poof. The script notes that Ian Davidson is playing the Algy part, but Davidson clearly enters moments later as the leader of the Mexican band. The actor playing Algy may be Barry Cryer, who was contracted a handful of times by the BBC to warm up the studio audience during this initial series.

Lastly, "Braithwaite" is not Algy's last name (and Biggles is given an incorrect first name, as well in the scene), but Ginger's last name was similar: "Hebblethwaite."

"big jump"—("The First Man to Jump the Channel") This is all perhaps an allusion to the hype and hysteria promulgated by boxing promoters of the time for lightning-rod fighters like Muhammad Ali, but is more certainly connected to the daredevil grabbing headlines in the western deserts of the United States, Evel Knievel. By 1967 Knievel (b. 1938) was jumping lines of cars and buses in very popular events, including the well-documented Caesar's Palace jump/crash that left him with multiple fractures and in a coma for nearly a month. While this *FC* episode was being created, Knievel would have been promoting his greatest jump ever, a Grand Canyon rocket cycle jump. He never received permission for this jump, opting for the spectacularly flawed Snake River attempt in 1972.

Knievel didn't have a Vercotti figure—he was his own promoter, though just as dangerous.

Boring old It's Man—(PSC; link into "Walk-On Part in Sketch") By Episode 10 it appears that some of the new and incongruous elements Python created for their show have begun to wear thin. Cleese would later complain that by the middle of the second series, he felt as if the troupe had already exhausted its originality (see Morgan's *Speaks!*). Note also the *"Animated titles as per usual"* note just below—conspicuously absent are the expected witty rejoinders from the scriptwriters in regard to Gilliam's work. This element of boredom and staidness would be addressed with a "ratcheting-up" of the satire, grotesqueries, and shock value of the writing in some of the following episodes and later series.

"bricks"—("The First Man to Jump the Channel") There is no comment here on the absurdity of carrying anywhere between fifty and fifty-six pounds of bricks during a sporting activity. Ron (Jones) will also be carrying a passport with him—in hand—as he jumps, as seen later.

It is possible that this incident is based on the American astronauts' penchant for taking trinkets along for short space rides in the 1960s—including Gus Grissom (dimes, figurines) and Alan Shepherd (golf balls)—for use as novelty gifts or sale/auction later.

buttress—("The First Man to Jump the Channel") It's not clear that Obvious is biting anything but a wall of the cathedral. And since this isn't actually Chichester Cathedral, but Holy Trinity Church, there are no buttresses to bite, anyway.

– C –

"cabaret . . . New Forest"—("Arthur Tree") Cabaret is generally a floor show, often at a dining establishment. The New Forest refers here specifically to newly planted forests, or reforestations, but also can mean the new forests (frontiers) of America, where Frost was keen to make a name for himself. New Forest is also an area southwest of Southampton.

"Caesar's Christmas show"—(link out of "Pet Conversions") The precedent for performing holiday (holy day) shows for royalty or the powerful goes well back in England. Theatres at Oxford, Cambridge, and the Inns at Court were in operation since the sixteenth century, with Christmas revels going back into the fifteenth century (Cox and Kastan 59-76).

During the English Renaissance period troupes were "owned" and allowed to operate by the Queen, the Lord Admiral, the King, etc. (The Queen's Men, e.g.), with some of their performances expected to be at court, and others in theatres licensed by the state where the sovereign could appear, if she/he chose, for a royal performance. This official performance structure would continue after the Interregnum and well into the eighteenth century. See Gurr, Larsen.

"Calais"—("The First Man to Jump the Channel") Across the English Channel from Dover, essentially, and is France's main cross-Channel port for both passengers and mail. The Goons had made for Calais in their "Napoleon's Piano" sketch (11 October 1955) for *The Goon Show* (1951-1960).

camply—("David Unction" link out of "Bank Robber [Lingerie Shop]") In a campy way.

"Channel"—("The First Man to Jump the Channel") The English Channel separates the British Isles from mainland Europe, and is at its narrowest in the Dover-Calais area, about twenty-one miles. The Channel has become an enduring symbol of Britain's separation from the rest of Europe, acting as a defensive moat, essentially. The Pythons shot this on a shale beach in the Covehithe area, however, quite some distance north of Dover and the white chalk cliffs. Ron would have been jumping at least ninety miles to cross the Channel if he started at Covehithe.

Competitors had been swimming the Channel since 1875, when Captain Matthew Webb completed the swim, leaving from Admiralty Pier in Dover (see Sprawson's article on Webb in the *ODNB*). Webb would later be killed as he attempted to swim below Niagara Falls in 1883, a very Ron Obvious–like stunt. Perhaps more appropriately for this Ron Obvious attempted crossing, the first recorded *attempt* to swim the Channel came in 1872, when J.B. Johnson made it one hour and three minutes into the Channel before giving up. See The Dover Museum Online Exhibition for more.

"Chichester Cathedral"—("The First Man to Jump the Channel") Located in Chichester on West Street, be-

tween Chapel and Tower streets. This location, however, is actually Holy Trinity Church, Lyne Lane, Chertsey, Surrey (WAC T12/1,086 16 November 1969).

The Chichester Cathedral photo is borrowed from *English Cathedrals in Colour* by A.F. Kersting, page 89, originally published in 1960 by Batsford.

"Chippendale"—("Arthur Tree") Thomas Chippendale, b. Yorkshire (1718-1779), English furniture designer (*ODNB*).

"Chippenham"—("The First Man to Jump the Channel") Located in Wiltshire, between Bath and Swindon. Chippenham did have significant brick manufacture going on in its vicinity to provide brick for a boom in new housing in the nineteenth century.

"Chipperfield"—("Vocational Guidance Counsellor [Chartered Accountant]") Chipperfield is a city in Hertfordshire, near Watford.

Cincinnatti—(PSC; "Letters to *Daily Mirror*") Misspelled in the text and taped version, this should read "Cincinnati," which is located in Ohio. These spelling errors can apparently be blamed on the Pythons themselves, since they almost always appear in the writers' requests to the graphics department for captions and title cards, and the captions folk simply create the cards precisely as requested.

As for the mining reference, in 1963 geochemical explorations of Baffin Island revealed enormous deposits of iron ore; natural gas was discovered in the North Sea in 1965; and the Deep-Sea Drilling Project gets under way around the world in 1965-1968. And perhaps most closely linked to this reference is the discovery of oil in the North Sea in 1969. The relatively expensive exploitation process (extracting, delivery, refining, distribution) of North Sea gas and oil kept Britain dependent on foreign sources well into the 1980s, when higher prices worldwide made North Sea reserves more affordable. See the notes for the "New Cooker Sketch" in Ep. 14 for more on this transition.

Coelocanth—(PSC; link out of "Strangers in the Night") This animated figure looks much more like a northern right whale. The *OED* notes that the right whale has been applied to the Bible's "great fish" that swallowed Jonah, making its inclusion in Gilliam's animation (where each animal is eaten in turn) quite apropos. The word is actually misspelled, as well, in the printed scripts, and should read "coelacanth," which is a primeval fish thought to have been extinct until one was caught off the coast of Madagascar in 1938.

conga—(PSC; "Strangers in the Night") Latin American dance.

"cut motor taxes"—("Letters to *Daily Mirror*") This phrase (and topic) found its way onto bumper stickers, window decals, and into political cartoons of the day, and was much-discussed in newspapers' op-ed pages (see the British Cartoon Archive). A £35 motor tax (a "Road Fund" fee) had been proposed by the Wilson Labour government, a tax flamboyant Conservative MP Gerald Nabarro fought against in the press and on the stump. See Keith Waite in *The Sun* (6 February 1969), as well as David Langdon's panel strip in the *Sunday Mirror* on 6 April 1969.

– D –

David Frost type—(PSC; "Arthur Tree") The Pythons would satirize Frost more than once in *FC* (here portraying him as wooden as a tree), including the rather scathing "Timmy Williams" sketch in Ep. 19. Frost's high-pitched laugh, his "super, super" and "can't be bad" quips are part of Idle's spot-on impersonation here. The fact that most of the Pythons had worked with and for Frost at some point prior to *FC* is also significant—familiarity breeding, perhaps, contempt. Cleese wrote for *That Was the Week That Was* (1962); Chapman, Cleese, Idle, and Palin appeared on/wrote for *The Frost Report* (1966-1967); and Chapman and Cleese wrote for *At Last the 1948 Show*, which Frost executive produced in 1967. By 1970 Frost was the pre-eminent television personality among Oxbridge grads, and wasn't afraid to toot his own horn, according to most of his (perhaps a mite jealous) contemporaries. (See McCabe, Morgan [1999] and Wilmut for more on Frost's relationship with the Pythons.)

And it wasn't just the Pythons who took shots at Frost, *Private Eye* featured mock coverage of the ubiquitous, self-promoting presenter on a number of occasions (Ingrams 11, 242-43, and 271). See notes for "Hounslow" in Ep. 2 for much more on Frost and his ambitions.

Davidson, Ian—(PSC; "Strangers in the Night") A mistake in the printed script, as Davidson won't enter the scene as "Algy" but moments later as the "Mexican," asking directions to Vera (Jones). Davidson's name does not appear in the WAC records for this episode. Davidson is a writer, producer, and actor who appears in small roles on *FC* in Eps. 6, 10, 18, 19, and 26. He does not appear in any episode in either the third or fourth seasons of *FC*.

At this same time (1970-1971) Davidson was writing for other television shows, including *The Two Ronnies* and *The Kenneth Williams Show*. He had also helped produce *Do Not Adjust Your Set* in 1967, where he probably worked with the future Pythons for the first time. Davidson had also worked under Barry Took (notes to Ep. 4) on *Comedy Workshop: Love and Maud Carver*

(1964), and may have been brought into the *FC* world through Took.

"dead butch"—("David Unction" link out of "Bank Robber [Lingerie Shop]") The implication, of course, is that the "manly" Vikings were just as prone to at least homosociality and probably homosexuality as the campy David Unction (Chapman). "Butch" generally implies tough characters and/or mannish lesbians, the second of which implicates the Viking's aberrant sexuality, and by his own admission. The *OED* cites the usage of both "fairy" and "butch" in the same instance, where a gay male could be both a fairy and look butch, or tough. This seems to be the point being made by Unction—that the tough-as-nails Vikings were actually mincing queens.

dolly bird—(PSC; "Strangers in the Night") Colloquially, a pretty girl. The *OED* cites "dolly" as emerging during London's swinging days in the mid-1960s, likely on the same wave that brought in The Beatles (and the Merseybeat), the Mods, and the new, free sexuality.

This particular "dolly bird" is identified as Carolae Donaghue in BBC records (WAC T12/1,091). The word "dolly," meaning handsome or attractive, was also part of the London "gay underworld" slang vocabulary, where—not unlike in Cockney rhyming slang—sexual words or phrases that could betray partakers in/of illegal sexual acts were substituted for by slangy terms. (The hairdresser figure [Palin] in Ep. 28 speaks a similarly slangy and affected language.) The underground language was called "Polari," and would have been fading out of vogue in the 1960s and 1970s, having both been co-opted by straight groups and deemed increasingly demeaning by members of the emerging political gay community. Other terms from this vocabulary included "drag" (meaning to dress like a woman), "fruit" (homosexual), and "mince" (to walk suggestively). "Mince" will be mentioned in Ep. 33 when Biggles, Alvy, and Ginger are working out their sexuality.

"Dull"—("Vocational Guidance Counsellor [Chartered Accountant]") Once again chartered accountancy takes it on the chin in *FC*, and will continue to do so through the last Python work, *The Meaning of Life* (1983), where high-spirited pirate-accountants are eventually destroyed by reality. See Gilliam's *The Crimson Permanent Assurance* featurette appended to *ML*. Also, see the description below of an accountant's qualities. Perhaps if the "tax on thingy" mentioned in Ep. 15 were to be instituted, Mr. Anchovy (Palin) wouldn't be looking to switch jobs. The Pythons do seem to make an effort to increase the excitement level of chartered accountancy, including sex taxes and pirate dreams.

"dung"—("Trailer") Cf. Ep. 9 where Arthur Name (Idle) tells a dung joke, and Ep. 19, where "Book of the Month Club" membership comes with buckets of dung. Excretory humor is also present in Eps. 9 and 45, and significantly in *HG*, where the best way to identify a king is by the fact the he doesn't have "shit all over him."

This fascination with the body and especially its elemental/excremental functions in *FC* is indicative of a sort of Ovidian cultural fixation on the body as impure and a locus of change and degradation, rather than the sacred vessel of the spirit. This is the period of the emergence of women's reproductive rights—sexual permissiveness, the birth control pill in 1960, calls for more liberal abortion legislation in the 1950s and beyond—as well as sex change surgery, which began in 1969 in the United States, and major organ transplant surgery beginning in 1967 in South Africa. There is also a childish, sophomoric element to this type of humor—giggling at naughty words and bodily functions—that the Pythons (and many comedians, artists, and literary types of this period) embraced as an answer to the seemingly impenetrable veneer created by High Art and Culture. This then is a return to the carnivalesque humor of the Middle Ages, and the delightful indelicacies of the "grotesque." (See Bishop's "Bakhtin, Carnival and Comedy: The New Grotesque in Monty Python and the Holy Grail," and the author's chapter 5 in *MPSERD*.)

– E –

"East Grinstead"—(letter link out of "Gorilla Librarian") In Ep. 5, another letter is addressed to East Grinstead, that time to the BBC. East Grinstead is in West Sussex.

"eat ants"—("Vocational Guidance Counsellor [Chartered Accountant]") This sort of transmogrification of beasts will be revisited later in the episode in the "Pet Conversions" sketch. In that case, animals will actually be modified to physically resemble other animals.

"Englishmen . . . nations"—("The First Man to Jump the Channel") Indicating the Britishness of the farthest inhabitants of the Empire, as well as the long reach of colonialism and imperialism.

Episode 10—Episode 10 was recorded ninth in order during the first series, but broadcast in the tenth position, swapping places with Episode 9. Episode 10 was recorded on 30 November 1969, and was broadcast 21 December 1969.

Also paid for appearing in this episode: Carolae Donaghue (the "dolly bird"; *Holidays on the Buses*), Sheila Sands (*Troubleshooters*), Des McGovern (studio

guitarist who may have been a friend of Idle's), Stuart Gordon, Gordon Turnbull, Barry Cryer (*Doctor in the House*), Betty Martin (lady in library sketch), and a dog named Phoebe ("Gorilla Librarian" sketch). *Flying Circus* crew members George Clarke and Roger Last appear as themselves in the lingerie shop sketch.

"exploiting Ron for your own purposes"—("Tunnelling From Godalming to Java") These Guinness-type stunts are ironically aligned with the inspiration for the Guinness Book of World Records itself. In 1955 the Guinness (stout) company came up with its own initial publicity stunt, creating a trivia book for each pub in the UK. The book was meant to settle bar bets, and was compiled by Norris and Ross McWhirter.

– F –

"Fin de Cross-Channel"—(PSC; "The First Man to Jump the Channel") The banner they are holding in Calais translates "End of Cross Channel" jump, essentially. Some of the Frenchmen waiting for Obvious to complete the jump include Mike Seddon, John Howard Davies (*FC* producer), and Peter Kaukus (*Dr. Who*). Seddon was a comedy writer well known to the Pythons for his work on *It's Marty* (1968) and *Joint Account* (1969) (bbc.co.uk). Chapman, Cleese, Gilliam, Jones, and Palin had all contributed to *It's Marty* (for Marty Feldman), while Michael Mills (BBC Light Entertainment) produced the latter show. Peter Willis, a BBC cameraman, may also have participated in this short scene. In the WAC records for the episode, these characters are termed "froggies" (WAC T12/1,083).

Floor Manager—("Bank Robber [Lingerie Shop]") George Clarke, Python's actual floor manager, also appears in Ep. 19.

french loaf—(PSC; "Strangers in the Night") These two items—the beret and the bread—typify the character as a Frenchman; he's wearing a "French costume" in the Python world (including "continental nylon mac"). In Ep. 27, when Mrs. Premise (Cleese) and Mrs. Conclusion (Chapman) go to France to meet with Jean-Paul Sartre, most of the folk seen around them are similarly/iconically dressed.

– G –

"get the job"—("Gorilla Librarian") This is a turnabout on the "Silly Job Interview" set-up from Ep. 5, where the Interviewer has deceived the interviewee, Stig/David Thomas (Chapman).

"give generously"—("Vocational Guidance Counsellor [Chartered Accountant]") More like a plea for donations for starving children or abused animals seen on late night television. Chartered accountants, then, aren't capable of helping or saving themselves, and an interdiction must be arranged. (In Ep. 45, a similar plea for very rich people is broadcast.) The inability to do anything beyond chartered accountancy also seems to be a symptom of the disease. The emphasis on "young people" nudges this plea toward a substance abuse message for those dabbling in recreational drug use—use that can have lifelong residual effects. "The Mouse Problem" in Ep. 2 also plays on this theme (there for sexual deviances).

"Godalming"—("The First Man to Jump the Channel") Located in Surrey, south of Guildford. The filming location is, more precisely, just outside of Saxmundham, Surrey.

"great impetus"—("The First Man to Jump the Channel") A sort of mind-over-matter scenario also used in the "Amazing Mystico" sketch in Ep. 35, where tower blocks will remain standing as long as occupants believe in them. As soon as doubt emerges, however, the buildings begin to fall.

"grotty"—("Walk-On Part in Sketch") A shortened, slangy form of "grotesque." George Harrison's character "George" in The Beatle's film *A Hard Day's Night* (1964) appalls a mod teen fashion consultant with his take on hip clothing: "I wouldn't be seen dead in them. They're dead grotty." The out-of-touch consultant Simon (Kenneth Haig) has to ask what the term means.

– H –

"Harold Splinter"—("Chippendale Desk" animated link out of "Arthur Tree") A play on the name of Harold Pinter (b. 1930), noted English playwright and screenwriter who tackles themes of class consciousness, social alienation, and gender issues. Pinter is most likely included because his name happens to rhyme with a wood product, though his creative work tends to poke the Establishment—identifying and enervating sexual, political, social, and class hypocrisies in contemporary British culture. Pinter was part of the "permissive society" cultural malaise so feared by Mary Whitehouse, the NVLA, and others. Cf. Ep. 2 for more on Pinter and his importance not only to this period, but to the Pythons' worldview, as well.

"Harrods"—("Vocational Guidance Counsellor [Chartered Accountant]") Major British department store founded in 1849. Harrods is still on Brompton Road in fashionable Knightsbridge.

Hartebeest—(link out of "Strangers in the Night") South African antelope.

"Heath, Edward"—("Chippendale Desk" animated link out of "Arthur Tree") Prime Minister and leader of the Conservative Party in Great Britain, 1970-1974. As a very visible, even iconic Conservative, Heath is a consistently easy target for the more liberal Pythons. Gilliam uses Heath's image in his animations on many occasions. The "hello sailor" is an equally easy attack on Heath (who was unmarried), calling into question his sexual orientation, and is a phrase used throughout *FC*. Cf. Ep. 14, *"Face the Press"* and "New Cooker Sketch," where other government leaders are similarly portrayed.

On the covers of the 13 February and 22 May 1970 issues of *Private Eye*, Heath's ability to have any kind of sexual relationship with a woman is called into question.

"hedgehog"—("Strangers in the Night") Curious term of endearment—the hedgehog is also utilized by Python as the giant nemesis of Dinsdale Piranha in Ep. 14, and as newsman Robin Day's pet in Ep. 1.

"Hill, Lord"—("Walk-On Part in Sketch") Lord Hill of Luton, Charles Hill (1904-1989) was Chairman of the BBC from 1967 to 1972. Hill did not, of course, write and sign every letter to every walk-on participant for all BBC shows. It was reported (by the BBC) that he usually communicated with BBC Director-General Hugh Greene (1910-1987) through a secretary, and not personally.

Hill had been in charge of the Independent Television Authority, the body making policy for Britain's commercial television networks, and he was, according to Cockerell, brought in by PM Wilson to reign in the permissiveness of programs and programmers, to "humiliate BBC senior ececutives," and, most importantly, to hopefully force then-Director General Greene to resign (qtd. in Freedman 28). Clearly, if Hill had been the man making the final decisions on programming in 1969, *Flying Circus* would likely have never seen the light of day. (For more on Wilson's antagonistic relationship with Greene and the BBC, see notes to Ep. 28, and Freedman's informative article "Modernising the BBC.")

For a photo of Lord Hill, see the cover of the *London Times* evening edition for 11 July 1969.

"howl a bit"—("Pet Conversions") This is another "gross-out" sketch meant to shock, not unlike the proposed eating of "gammy"-legged sailors or freshly dead corpses in Ep. 26. Cleese comments on that diminishing shock value in Morgan (1999). See notes to Ep. 26.

– I –

"in a skin"—("Gorilla Librarian") This "dressing as an animal" routine will be revisited in Python's final feature, *The Meaning of Life* (1983). In the "Zulu Wars" episode, two men (Palin and Idle) have been caught wearing a tiger suit, after making off with an officer's leg.

"It's a Tree"—("Arthur Tree") Yet another "It's" title. Cf. *"It's the Arts"* (Eps. 1 and 6), and *"It's Wolfgang Amadeus Mozart"* in Ep. 1. The connection can be traced back to the It's Man, as well, since for many episodes he appends the word to the title of the show. See similarly titled shows on British TV, like *Yes, It's the Cathode Ray Tube Show* (1957, Peter Sellers); *It's a Square World* (1957, Ronnie Barker); *It's a Man's World* (1962); *It's a Woman's World* (1964); *It's Sad About Eddie* (1964); *It's Dark Outside* (1964-1965); *It's a Knockout* (1966, Eddie Waring); *It's a Long Way to Transylvania* (1967); and *It's Only Us* (1968). See Vahimagi for more on these shows.

The impact of radio should also be noted, with the very popular Tommy Handley show *It's That Man Again* (1939-1949) preparing the way, thematically, for both *The Goon Show* and the Pythons (see Grafton and Wilmut's *The Goon Show Companion*).

The music used here to introduce this David Frost–type show and character is "By George," the "David Frost Theme" (WAC T12/1,091).

– J –

"Jack and the Beanstalk"—(link out of "Pet Conversions") A well-known fairy tale (and especially Christmas pantomime show in the UK) featuring a boy, a giant, and a beanstalk. Like many fairy tales, this one includes moments of a graphic nature and/or grisly violence (implied or otherwise), such as "grinding" victims' bones to make food for the giant. So in perspective, the somewhat horrific images conjured up by Python involving cannibalism, pet mutilation, and maulings by wild animal librarians aren't far at all from many children's stories.

"Jacobs, David"—("Letters to *Daily Mirror*") A radio and TV personality born in London (1926), hosting *Juke Box Jury* (1959-1967), and prior to that appearing on *The Golden Disc* (1958). In 1969 Jacobs was hosting *It's Sunday Night*, but the Pythons would have undoubtedly known him from his many years as a radio disc jockey.

"Janson, Hank"—("Gorilla Librarian") Pseudonym for English pulp gangster novelist Stephen Frances, whose licentious work brought charges against him under the Obscene Publications Act in 1954. Covers to his novels featured scantily clad women in provocative poses, and were regularly censored in the UK. It was the 1959 update of this Act that prompted Penguin to publish Lawrence's *Lady Chatterley's Lover* for the first time in the UK. Penguin was charged and taken to court for the obscenity, but were able to now argue the literary merit of the book, and win the case.

For more see Holland's *The Mushroom Jungle: A History of Postwar Paperback Publishing*, as well as Holland's *The Trials of Hank Janson*.

"Java"—("The First Man to Jump the Channel") A Malaysian archipelago island. Tunneling under such a large body of water might have seemed ridiculous until the completion of the Channel Tunnel in 1994. Plans for such a tunnel had been discussed since at least Napoleon's time.

– L –

lady with a pince nez—("Gorilla Librarian") The third member of the interviewing panel is Betty Martin (WAC T12/1,091).

"larch"—(link out of "Vocational Guidance Counsellor [Chartered Accountant]") Cf. Ep. 3, which prominently featured the larch.

"Last Exit to Brooklyn ... or ... Groupie"—("Gorilla Librarian") The works in question: *Last Exit to Brooklyn* (1964), written by Hubert Selby, and *Groupie* (1969), written by Jenny Fabian. *Brooklyn* features sexuality and language unparalleled for the time, and was set in Brooklyn's seedy lower-class tenements. *Groupie* is a depiction of the real-life exploits of a nineteen-year-old rock groupie in the late 1960s, where the author's described escapades include a "pulling" session with a noted musician, and where depictions of the London counterculture abound. Both books would have been relegated to "locked shelf" status, or not carried at all by many public libraries in the UK and United States. The panel members are obviously just interested in whether such sexually charged books would be available should the gorilla become librarian, and are willing to risk the potential wild animal attacks to have such titles in circulation.

"learning to read"—("Arthur Tree") Probably satirizing the instances of celebrities who toot their own horns on such shows, especially their "unpublicized" charity work and philanthropic efforts. This could be a specific jab at the recent *David Frost Presents ... Frankie Howerd* (February 1969), made for American television, meaning Frost was already successful on both sides of the Atlantic.

lingerie shop—("Bank Robber [Lingerie Shop]") Even at such a feminine place, where one would naturally expect female employees, Python provides only a male assistant, though one obviously familiar with the feminine wares he sells.

"lions"—("Vocational Guidance Counsellor [Chartered Accountant]") In an unusual twist, for *FC* and Python in general, the Counsellor here is actually asking very rational, reasonable questions, and not demanding that the supplicant before him jump through absurd hoops. Cf. the job interview in Ep. 5 where Cleese's character antagonizes Chapman's character without mercy, and without real reason. The "Vocational Guidance Counsellor" sketch ends up being fairly straight-faced satire, without slouching toward absurdity for shock.

The photo with which the Counsellor frightens the applicant is listed as a color print, "Animals 2548 Roaring Lion" L.404 by N. Myers (WAC T12/1,242).

"London, SW3"—("Vocational Guidance Counsellor [Chartered Accountant]") This address actually exists (Lincoln House on Basil St.), located near the junction of Sloane and Brompton roads, and just up the road from Harrods. This isn't terribly far from the actual headquarters of The Institute of Chartered Accountants in England & Wales, found at the corner of Gt. Swan Alley and Copthall Ave., in the City of London.

Long John Silver—("Chippendale Desk" animated link into "Arthur Tree") Another popular Christmas pantomime character looming large in the Pythons' collective nostalgia. Cf. Ep. 5, the "Confuse-a-Cat" sketch, the Long John Silver Impersonators football club (Ep. 23), as well as Ep. 32, where the interviewer (Cleese) transforms into a Long John Silver figure as the interview progresses.

– M –

"man's life"—("Vocational Guidance Counsellor [Chartered Accountant]") Cf. the "copyrighted" Army slogan "It's a man's life in the modern army" used and abused throughout Ep. 4. The balance of Anchovy's (Palin) ebullient description supports this sloganeering: "Banking, travel, excitement, adventures, thrills, decisions affecting people's lives." Watkins (Idle) fell for this kind of line in Ep. 8, joined the army, then asked to be released before his portion of the sketch was identified as "silly" and halted.

"Melton Mowbray"—("Pet Conversions") Located in Leicestershire, northeast of Leicester. Cf. the "Dead Parrot" sketch in Ep. 8 for a precursor to this pet shop set-up. That sketch also featured Palin and Cleese.

Chapman attended Melton Mowbray Grammar School before entering Cambridge.

"Mercury"—("Tunnelling From Godalming to Java") Planet closest to the Sun. Just prior to the period when the Pythons were creating these epiosdes, the Mercury space program (pre-lunar flights) had been very active, and much in the world news.

"Mexican rhythm combo"—("Strangers in the Night") The music played live is a portion of the "Mexican Hat Dance" (WAC T12/1,091).

"*Mirror* View"—("Letters to *Daily Mirror*") Section of the *Daily Mirror* newspaper where letters from and to readers were posted. The *Mirror* has been a UK tabloid newspaper since the late 1930s, and is later mentioned in the printed script for Ep. 25.

"Motspur Park"—("The First Man to Jump the Channel") Near New Malden, in Greater London. The University of London Athletics Ground (featuring a track) is found there, as are the BBC Sports Ground, the Sir Joseph Hood Memorial Playing Fields, and the Manor Park Recreation Grounds, all within blocks of each other.

The Pythons will film in Motspur Park for Ep. 40, "The Golden Age of Ballooning," when the "least talented Zeppelin brother" Barry (Jones) attempts to fly balloons in the shadow of the enormous gas collection tanks.

"Mrs. Brando . . . *Wild One*"—("Walk-On Part in Sketch") Marlon Brando (1924-2004) starred in this 1954 film directed by László Benedek, which, due to its violence and political undertones, wasn't screened publicly in the UK until 1968. By 1954, though, Brando had already risen to international stardom with *Viva Zapata!* (1952) and *A Streetcar Named Desire* (1951). According to imdb.com, Brando did work briefly as an elevator operator prior to stage and screen fame. His mother was Dorothy Brando, of Nebraska.

"Mrs. Newman . . . *Sweet Bird of Youth*"—Paul Newman (b. 1925) starred in the 1962 film directed by Richard Brooks. Newman was also well known by this time, having starred in *Cat on a Hot Tin Roof* (1958) and *The Hustler* (1961) prior to 1962. Also according to imdb.com, young Newman labored in the family sporting goods store and sold encyclopedias door-to-door before taking to the stage. His mother was Theresa Newman, of Ohio.

– N –

"Neaps End"—("The First Man to Jump the Channel") There are a few "Neap" locations in the UK, though most are located in Shetland. There is a Neap Ho (or Neap House) in Lincolnshire.

"nickel"—("Letters to *Daily Mirror*") A chemical element (Ni), and ferromagnetic metal. There are nickel deposits on the Isle of Skye, for instance, and there had been significant mineral and petrochemical discoveries in and around the UK during this period. See the entry for the misspelled "Cincinnatti" for more.

There had been a significant nickel investment scheme making banner economic headlines in some of the major UK newspapers (as well as the more bold *Private Eye*). Poseidon NL company had announced the discovery of impressive nickel deposits in Wandarra, Australia, in September 1969, and these reports bolstered the value of Poseidon stock from 20s all the way to £120, with City investors buying in as much as they could. Other nickel-mining companies also shot up in value, based on announced finds across Australia, but inflated estimates of the value of the deposits soon toppled all these mining concerns, and Poseidon fell, as well (*Private Eye* 6 November 1970: 5). For about a year the skyrocketing values of nickel (and other war-related minerals) kept the London stock market busy, before confidence was outpaced by miserly returns and the headlines turned sour.

"Nixon"—("Letters to *Daily Mirror*") Richard M. Nixon was in the first year of his first administration (beginning January 1969) at the time of this episode's writing and broadcast. He appears often in UK newspapers of the time in regard to the escalating war in Vietnam, relations with China and the Soviet Union, etc. He was also decidedly unpopular with the Pythons and members of the left everywhere as a right-leaning conservative Republican.

Nixon is probably also very significant because as vice president to Eisenhower (depicted in Ep. 44) he was the face and voice of the U.S. government overseas. Between 1953 and 1961 Nixon toured the world at the behest of his president, becoming especially visible in appearances with "enemy" countries, including volatile talks with Nikita Khrushchev in 1959, and bloody, protest-filled visits to Central and South American countries agitated by Communist activists.

Jonathan Miller had described the far left-ness and liberality of Britain's political middle, especially as compared to the United States, in the *Beyond the Fringe* sketch "Home Thoughts From Abroad":

> Cook: Of course one thing you'll notice about America is that it is a very young country, rather like Ghana in that respect.
> Miller: Except for the fact that they have inherited our two-party system.
> Moore: And how does that work?

> Cook: Well they have the, um, the Republican Party which is the equivalent of our Conservative Party, and the Democratic Party which is the equivalent of our Conservative Party.

No surpise, then, that a truly conservative American politician like Nixon with international influence and perhaps Monroe Doctrine and gunboat diplomacy designs on portions of what had been the British Empire would not be a popular face with the UK Left, except as a target.

"No, sir"—("Bank Robber [Lingerie Shop]") The Robber's success rate here is an echo of the available books at the book shop in Ep. 4, the lack of cats at a pet shop (Ep. 10), and the unavailability of fish licenses (Ep. 23), and will be almost repeated in Ep. 33, where the customer tries to buy cheese at a cheese shop. In fact, very few transactions are successfully completed in *FC* shops, probably an ongoing comment on not only customer service in British society, but the specter of scarcity and limited choices for consumers in specifically *postwar* Britain, ranging all the way to about 1956 (see Morgan's *Britain Since 1945*).

Prior to the "Silly Walks" gent (Cleese) successfully purchasing his newspaper in the newsagent's shop in Ep. 17, the customer (Idle) attempts various unsuccessful transactions, and fails because he is seeking sexually affiliated items, succumbing to understood metaphors ("chest of drawers," "a bit of pram," "pussycat," etc.). In that same episode various chemists fail to dispense their products successfully. In these settings the narrative generally tends to wander off in another direction when the transaction isn't successful.

– O –

"Old Codgers"—("Letters to *Daily Mirror*") Perhaps the last bit of evidence necessary to confirm the age and out-of-touchness of the general readership and ownership of the *Daily Mirror*. This had been the popular paper when the Pythons were growing up, and one that *Private Eye*, for example, had been lambasting since 1961.

"old queen"—("Trailer") Literally, an aging homosexual, and generally affixed to the more effeminate partner in a homosexual relationship. See the *OED*.

This is also an example of what others in the troupe have described as Chapman's "out-ness" in terms of his sexuality. See Morgan's *Speaks!*. There may have been no better way for an admitted, practicing homosexual to hide such an unacceptable lifestyle than to overplay that out-ness in character.

This outré behavior is reminiscent of Quentin Crisp (1908-1999), the flamboyant author of *The Naked Civil Servant* (1968), whose public behavior may have given Python the license to camp up their depictions of homosexuals. Crisp described himself as "one of the stately homos of England" in his above-mentioned autobiography. See Ep. 12 for other Crispian allusions.

"open shelves"—("Gorilla Librarian") Meaning the books are in open circulation, not behind the desk or in a locked case. In *Private Eye*, the editors include this short note of admonition to the Librarian at the British Museum: "In the Reading Room's locked case, reserved for pornography, you will find a copy of *Fire in the Flesh* by David Goodis . . . this is a book about a pyromaniac, and can very safely be placed on the open shelves" (22 May 1970, page 4).

"ordinary . . . jump"—("The First Man to Jump the Channel") The standing long jump, or broad jump. Actually, Obvious takes a running start for his jump, which is the type of jump still a part of international track and field competitions. For comparison, the long jump record for the period was held by American Bob Beamon, and was set in the high altitude of Mexico City in 1968 (29 feet 2 inches).

Oxley, Mel—(PSC; "Trailer") Oxley was an announcer for Southern TV (1959-1961), as well as ATV and ABC Television. He was also a voice announcer for BBC-TV between 1965 and 1972.

– P –

"parrots"—("Pet Conversions") The mention of "parrots" elicits a cheer from the studio audience, obviously attesting to the success of the "Dead Parrot" sketch just two episodes earlier.

In 1999, journalist and broadcaster John Diamond wrote that as teens he and his friends defined themselves as British and part of the "in" crowd in relation to the recognizability factor (and in-joke-ness) of their mutual Monty Python interest:

> I knew I was British because when I met other people who called themselves British we found we had things in common. They would look at the chicken in my fridge and say "This parrot is dead!" and I would come straight back there with "It's not dead it's only resting!" and my, but how we would laugh. For I knew that as I was watching Monty Python, so was every other 17-year-old in the country. I knew I could stand at the door of the sixth-form common room the next morning and shout, "No-one expects the Spanish Inquisition!" and only a boy called Kessler, who didn't have a television, would think I'd found Jesus. ("Once I Was British" 1)

The Pythons' studio audience obviously shared this mutual appreciation, meaning the intertextual references were all the more significant to these true fans who'd "found" Monty Python.

"payments"—(link out of "Strangers in the Night") Perhaps a version of a water cooler discussion that most certainly could have occurred sometime, somewhere during the run of *FC*. The topics broached—originality, topicality, predictability, absurd versus more conventional humor, and public tastes—are those the troupe did hear about from the higher-ups at the BBC, according to people like Barry Took and Cleese. There was concern that "normal" viewers wouldn't understand the absurd or archaic references ("They wouldn't understand that in Bradford"), and that such reactionary or shock humor had to be consistently updated to avoid repetition, or would almost certainly be short-lived. See Morgan (1999); also Wilmut 196.

The "balance of payments" comment refers to buying a TV on hire purchase (cf. Ep. 3), but also to the woeful state of the British economy in relation to its foreign debt and the strength of its currency during the early 1970s.

Pearson—(link into "Gorilla Librarian") Canadian Nobel Peace Prize winner Lester Pearson (1897-1972) had delivered the BBC Reith lectures earlier this same year, in January 1969, his subject being a move away from violence and toward "creative social change." See the CBC Archives. See also the BBC 4 Radio Archives.

"permissive"—("Gorilla Librarian") See earlier instances of Python tilting with the "permissive" society, in Eps. 2, 8, and 9.

Physique magazine—(PSC; "David Unction" link out of "Bank Robber [Lingerie Shop]") One of many men's bodybuilding or health magazines that proliferated in the 1950s and beyond. The brown paper bag indicates that Unction is leering over the magazine, so it must be treated more like pornography—contraband—than a health magazine. (Most of these earlier magazines featured chiseled male models with genitalia discreetly covered—not unlike Gilliam's retouching of the Edwardian photos he uses in his animations.) There was a fine line walked during the 1950s and 1960s as gay men's publications found both readership with interested gay men and attention from government and watchdog groups intent on stopping the purveyance of indecency. See Waugh.

picture—("Gorilla Librarian") The assumption is that the picture was titillating, which, in addition to the Vicar's later preferred book titles, reveals a penchant for perhaps deviant sexuality on the part of this man of the cloth. (It isn't necessarily erotic, of course, but the fact that it's being held discreetly renders it illicit.)

Jones creates the same effect earlier in Ep. 7 when he leers after the plea "Be gentle with me." This continues Python's representation of churchmen as closeted postlapsarians always game for the opportunity to dip into the restoration funds (Ep. 6), to drink heavily (Ep. 36), engage in smuggling (Ep. 5), keep a naked lady (Ep. 15), and even have perverted "mouse" tendencies (Ep. 2).

This transition—from scene to scene via dissolve—is another photo-type linking element, as seen already in "Working-Class Playwright" in Ep. 2 and "Hunting Film" in Ep. 9.

"piece of wood"—("Vocational Guidance Counsellor [Chartered Accountant]") This is like signaling a commercial break. And since the previous sketch was by and for wood products, this may well be a commercial, of sorts. From the earliest days of commercial TV in the UK the government demanded that ITA stations schedule commercials only in "natural breaks" of the narrative action—this intrusion might have prompted letters and calls from angry viewers (see "Modernising the BBC").

pince-nez—(PSC; "Gorilla Librarian") Glasses held to the face on the bridge of the nose rather than over the ears. These are probably used emblematically to imply a stuffy, Victorian librarian type.

"predictable"—(link out of "Pet Conversions") Not really all that predictable, since the Man in the sketch hadn't shown any predilection toward deviant behavior, just the Shopkeeper. It could be that Cleese is commenting on the Pythonesque-ness the sketch has embodied, which by the tenth episode could have already started to become business as usual rather than cutting edge. The punchline is undercut, of course, which may be why the Vox Pops responses are included.

"pulling the birds"—("Arthur Tree") Slang for "picking up" females. See John Lennon's comment in *A Hard Day's Night* (1964; dir. Richard Lester) when, seeing two young women alone, he tells Paul McCartney to try a "pull" with them.

"pussy cat"—("Pet Conversions") What's actually being proposed here is nothing more than what Gilliam does on a regular basis with his polymorphous animations—taking bits and pieces of figures and creating new, often monstrous beings. The earliest iterations of the opening credits feature a wheeled Cardinal Richelieu and a part-man-part-chicken, for example.

– R –

railway track—("The First Man to Jump the Channel") Shot on location at the Feltham Marshaling Yards, Feltham, south of Henslow (WAC T12/1,086).

"razor-sharp claws"—("Vocational Guidance Counsellor [Chartered Accountant]") Cf. Cleese as the Enchanter Tim in *HG*, describing the killer rabbit. The Zulu Wars scene in the film *ML* also features a large predator, whose carnage is there mistaken for first a mosquito and then a virus.

"Renaissance bit"—("Arthur Tree") A Renaissance man is one who learns in many areas, who is multitalented, and the meaning of the term originally emerged from the Italian Renaissance and men like Leon Battista Alberti (1404–1472). Alberti was an architect, musician, and painter, as well as being actively involved in the humanist tradition and contemporary politics.

"Rhodesia"—("Letter to *Daily Mirror*") This is a reference to Ian Smith (b. 1919) and the contentious period when Rhodesia sought white minority home rule. Rhodesia (formerly Southern Rhodesia) declared itself free from Great Britain on 11 November 1965, with Ian Smith and a minority white government in charge. The "Support Rhodesia" slogan would have been in support of this continuation of minority rule, as well as a demand that the UK (and UN) recognize the new state and support Britain's colonial empire. See notes to Ep. 45 for more. Smith was pilloried in the press of the left and right, of course, and appears in caricatured form in the pages of *Private Eye*.

Robber—("Bank Robber [Lingerie Shop]") Dressed in cartoon-like attire, with eye mask, striped shirt, black pants, etc. This same get-up will be used for another robber in Ep. 13. A 9" figure dressed just like this, including holding a gun at arm's length, was commissioned early in the series, and appears on the map table (for no apparent reason) in the "Dobson's bought it, sir" link in Ep. 1 (WAC T12/1,082).

"Robinson, Eric"—("Vocational Guidance Counsellor [Chartered Accountant]") Eric Robinson (b. 1908) was a BBC conductor whose show *Music For You* was a popular radio/TV program. This was a live program airing once a month on Wednesday evenings (often shot in Studio E at Lime Grove studios, where *Blue Peter*, *Steptoe & Son*, *Doctor Who*, *Panorama*, and *Nationwide* were also shot). Robinson and his Orchestra also appeared regularly on *New Faces* in 1947 (BBC), so he would have been a very familiar name to the Pythons by the time they reached maturity.

"rollocking"—("Trailer") Boisterous (variant spelling of "rollicking").

Ron leaps off—("Tunnelling From Godalming to Java") The fanfare beneath this jump is "Fanfare on the RAF Call" by O'Donnell (WAC T12/1,091).

"royalty on the loo"—("Arthur Tree") The practice of procuring illicit photos of celebrities—including royalty—in private, compromising, or just embarrassing situations of all kinds has been alive since the inception of modern photojournalism.

"running-in"—("Letters to *Daily Mirror*") The *OED* notes that running-in refers to "the process of operating a new machine (specifically the engine of a motor vehicle) at reduced power in order to establish proper working." This further supports the supposition that the letter writer is an older man, as he obviously drives slow enough on a regular basis to ask other drivers to pass.

– S –

"Save the Argylls"—("Letters to *Daily Mirror*") Geographic area in Scotland, but also the name of a Scottish regiment much decorated since 1794. The latter is certainly the reference here, since the letter writer appears to be a retired military man. After service in Aden was completed (1967) the Argylls were brought home and told, unexpectedly, that the unit was being disbanded in the wake of budget cuts and slowing recruitment. A grassroots "Save the Argylls" campaign erupted (garnering more than a million signatures), and with the help of promises from opportunistic Tories the Argylls were saved and Labour was out after the next general election (see Chamberlain).

Cf. a similar angry letter from Brigadier Gormanstrop (Mrs) in Ep. 5. Also, see notes to Ep. 26 for more on the trials of the Argylls in Aden.

"seen . . . zoo"—("Vocational Guidance Counsellor [Chartered Accountant]") Cf. Mr. Sopwith as he tries to spot camels, dromedaries, and Yetis ("I've heard about them") in Ep. 7.

"Sicily"—("The First Man to Jump the Channel") Largest of Italy's islands, and obviously used here as the acknowledged birthplace of organized crime, or the Mafia. Mario Puzo's betselling novel *The Godfather* had recently been published (February 1969), bringing the American crime organization into the international spotlight.

"sinks his fangs into their soft . . . "—("Gorilla Librarian") This splenetic is characteristic of Cleese and Chapman's writing, where the careful, proper establishment-type suddenly erupts with a stream of invectives or outrageous behavior. Roger Wilmut calls these scenes "escalation" sketches, and we'll see Cleese fly off the handle similarly in Ep. 24, in the "Conquistador Coffee Campaign" sketch (*From Fringe to Flying Circus* 198).

"Sir Francis . . . Antarctic"—("The First Man to Jump the Channel") All noted English explorers and/or military men:

"Drake"—An explorer and seaman, Drake commanded the phenomenally successful defeat of the vaunted Spanish Armada in 1588, bringing the English navy and England in general into a position of world superpower.

"Captain Matthew Webb" swam the Channel in August 1875, the first person to do so. Webb also swam from Dover to Calais, just as Ron plans to do. See "channel" above for more on Webb.

"Nelson"—In Ep. 1, Admiral Nelson is thrown from the upper floors of a high-rise building in a "Famous Deaths" sequence. See notes to Ep. 1 for Nelson's bio.

"Robert Falcon Scott" reached the South Pole in January 1912, the first Brit to do so, one month after Norwegian Roland Amundsen made the first visit.

Record-breaking may have been in the news, as well, as in April 1969 (when the Pythons were writing the initial episodes) Sir Robin Knox-Johnston (b. 1939) was the first man to sail solo and non-stop around the world.

sleep again—("Strangers in the Night") Once again, we are presented with a Python character who can't see the absurdity going on around him. In Ep. 6, the City Stockbroker (also Palin) goes to work amidst the chaos of societal breakdown, and sees none of it, only diverted by his comic book.

"sponsor"—("The First Man to Jump the Channel") The practice of companies sponsoring athletics is and was found in football, rugby, and especially auto racing, where decals dot both car and driver. American baseball players even promoted cigarettes and alcoholic beverages at one time, carrying and using the products. The official sponsors for the Chippenham Football Club, for example, include a vending machine company. See the entry for "big jump" for more.

"spruce . . . Bole"—("Arthur Tree") Spruce trees are evergreens native to cooler climates like Britain and Holland. Gum trees include any tree that exudes gum, and which would be nonnative, hence "making their first appearance" in Britain. "Scots pine and the conifers" sounds much like a 1960s musical group (cf. Buddy Holly and the Crickets, Gerry and the Pacemakers), with the scots pine (a fir tree) being the only native British pine, and conifers being any cone-bearing tree.

For "Elm Tree Bole," cf. the 1832 Tennyson poem *A Dream of Fair Women* (1832): "Enormous *elmtree-boles* did stoop and lean / Upon the dusky brushwood underneath / Their broad curved branches, fledged with clearest green, / New from its silken sheath" (Stanza 15). Also, see Robert Browning's *Home Thoughts, from Abroad* (1845), which features the prominence of things English, and must have appealed to the Pythons:

> Oh, to be in England now that April's there,
> And whoever wakes in England sees, some
>   morning, unaware,
> That the lowest boughs and the brushwood sheaf
> Round the *elm-tree bole* are in tiny leaf,
> While the chaffinch sings on the orchard bough
> In England—now! (Stanza 1, italics added)

A bole is the trunk of a tree, specifically. In Tennyson's *Mariana*, a poplar tree figures prominently, as well. The Pythons join Tennyson and Browning, as well as such luminaries as Shakespeare, Milton, and Longfellow in utilizing trees as significant textual tools.

Tennyson (played by John Hughman) will reappear in Ep. 41, "Michael Ellis," reading from his "Charge of the Ant Brigade."

starts the sketch—("Vocational Guidance Counsellor [Chartered Accountant]") This acknowledges the artifice of the television medium—here we're seeing the "before" moments—moments which are most often sacrosanctly concealed for the sake of continuity and to facilitate the viewers' suspension of disbelief. This hearkens back to the introductory sketch ("Lingerie Shop") where the actors dressed as characters and on a set waited for the walk-on to arrive. The character before us even participates in the sketch's theme song, breaking down the barrier between the "bookends" (opening credits with theme; closing credits with theme) normally found in the television format.

In a scene that appears in the printed scripts but somehow did not make it into the following video or DVD versions of *Flying Circus*, "Party Political Broadcast" in Ep. 38 offers campy Tory-types rehearsing for their party political broadcast message, as if they were part of a 1930s backstage musical.

"stroppy"—("Vocational Guidance Counsellor [Chatered Accountant]") *OED*: "Bad-tempered, rebellious, awkward, obstreperous, unruly."

– T –

"television license"—("Letters to *Daily Mirror*") Cf. Ep. 20, where the BBC's license fees for 1969 are actually posted and readable. Each television owner (for purposes of viewing broadcast television) must purchase the license, each year, the funds raised going to support the BBC. See also the note for "license fee" in Ep. 7, as well as the entry for "cat detector van" in Ep. 23.

"335C"—("Vocational Guidance Counsellor [Chartered Accountant]") Anchovy reverts to his more natural self, the accountant, more interested (at least subconsciously) with the numbers involved than with the act of lion taming.

tombstone—("Tunnelling From Godalming to Mercury") The "Funniest Joke in the World" (Ep. 1) sketch ended similarly, with a tomb for the "Unknown Joke" somewhere in the Berkshire countryside. This tombstone scene is back at the Holy Trinity Church, Chertsey, used earlier in place of Chichester Cathedral.

"to the camera"—("Strangers in the Night") The same warning given in Ep. 6 by Praline (Cleese) to Mr. Whizzo (Jones), acknowledging the self-consciousness by denying it. Insider comments about the existence of a sketch, pages of scripts, and character reactions also drag the artifice out into the light of the set.

tweedy colonel type—(PSC; link out of "Pet Conversions") This description must have something to do with Chapman's now accepted role as the Colonel, here dressed down in conservative tweed, like a Cambridge don.

– U –

Unction—("Trailer") Probably an indication of his smoothness, oilyness, etc. It's likely no accident that his first name happens to be "David" (as in David Frost), either.

"Upper Science Library"—("Gorilla Librarian") Probably a reference to the Bodleian Library at Oxford, where Jones and Palin studied. The Library features Upper and Lower designations for study rooms, collections, etc.

– V –

"Vercotti, Luigi"—("The First Man to Jump the Channel") Luigi (Palin) has appeared earlier in Ep. 8, with his brother Dino (Jones), there shaking down the Army for protection money; he will also appear in Ep. 13, as owner of the La Gondola Restaurant and purveyor of back-room pornography. See notes to Ep. 8 for the Vercotti brothers resemblance to the real-life Kray brothers.

"very talented"—("Tunnelling From Godalming to Java") One of the catchphrases heard many times during the long run of *The Goon Show* often referred to the earnest but inept Neddie Seagoon (Harry Secombe) character, "He's very good, you know."

vin ordinaire—(PSC; "Strangers in the Night") Simple French wine; table wine.

– W –

"walk-on"—("Walk-On Part in Sketch") Again, this Pepperpot-type is given significant—even technical—

information which her husband does not possess. She's also familiar with the films of Brando and Newman, American actors.

For these walk-on types of roles (often noted as "w/o" in the BBC paperwork), Terry Gilliam, for example, was making £5/5 from the BBC (WAC T12/1,082).

"watch"—("Pet Conversions") The specter of voyeurism, again, as the seemingly respectable customer (Cleese) reveals his disturbing proclivities. Also, once we reach the "Undertaker's Sketch" in Ep. 26, the son of the deceased (also Cleese) is included in the proposed cannibalistic feast. Through and with Gilliam's dis-membering and re-membering animations, too, the audience are watching, eagerly, these types of grotesqueries.

– Z –

"zany madcap humour"—("Tunnelling From Godalming to Java") Cf. the BBC Man (Cleese) in Ep. 15 as he describes *Flying Circus* ("a bit madcap funster . . . frankly I don't understand it myself"). The BBC had similar difficulties characterizing this show for its regional broadcasters and viewers. See notes for the first few episodes, including memo comments from producer/director John Howard Davies regarding the rubbishy qualities of the series.

"Zatapathique"—("Letters to *Daily Mirror*") Perhaps Python's catchall name for any Frenchman. Cf. Eps. 2 and 14, for Jean-Brian Zatapathique, Ep. 22 for Chief Inspector Jean-Paul Zatapathique, and Ep. 23 for Brianette Zatapathique.

Episode 11

– A –

Agatha Christie type—(PSC; "Agatha Christie Sketch") Christie, born in Torquay (1890-1976) was a noted, prolific mystery writer. The drawing room setting and assembled suspects are a standard Christie motif, and have been seen in St. Martin's Theatre (Trafalgar Square, in London's West End) where *Mousetrap* (1952) has been playing since 1974. The play first took the stage at Ambassadors Theatre, London, in November 1952. An "Inspector" character is also featured in many of Christie's stories.

This particular set-up—wherein a body is discovered in the living room—is reminiscent of Christie's 1954 play *Spider's Web*, which was filmed in 1960. The character names in *Spider's Web* also ring familiar, including "Clarissa and Henry Hailsham-Brown," "Sir Rowland Delahaye," "Miss Peake," "Jeremy," "Elgin," "Pippa," "Hugo," "Mrs. Elgin," "Oliver," and, of course, "Inspector Lord." Cicely Courtneidge (mentioned by the Red Indian in Ep. 6) appears as Miss Peake in the 1960 film.

"albodyduce"—("Agatha Christie Sketch") Cf. the misspeaking in the "Spanish Inquisition" sketch (Ep. 15), as well as various characters who speak beginnings, middles, or ends of sentences or in a roundabout way (Ep. 26), in anagrams only (Ep. 30), who is alternately rude and polite (Ep. 18), or who inserts malapropisms without knowing it (Ep. 36). A significant portion of Python humor deals with the inefficacies of communication.

"all-in cricket"—("Interesting People") No holds barred, like professional wrestling, for instance. All-in wrestling appears in Ep. 2, "Epilogue," when a monsignor and an academic wrestle to determine the existence of God. Colin "Bomber" Harris (Chapman) will famously wrestle himself in live appearances like *Live at the Hollywood Bowl* (1980).

In the 1969-1970 cricket season there were multiple protests and even riots at cricket and rugby matches across England. Protestors were angry that England's ruling sports organizations (including the MCC) had allowed South African cricket and rugby teams to tour the UK. See notes for Ep. 15 for more on the South Africa and apartheid situation. One political cartoon from the period mentions that cricket and rioting together might actually make cricket entertaining (Sidney William Martin, *Sunday Express*, 15 February 1970). See the British Cartoon Archive.

The crowd noise over the all-in cricket match is borrowed from British Movietone News, "Football Crowd Cheering" (WAC T12/1,092).

Animation—("Interruptions") In the printed script, this animated sequence is described for the reader as "beautiful and not zany," meaning they wanted Gilliam to create an intro that seemed more at home in Kenneth Clark's *Civilisation* program, not *Flying Circus*. The more sober and serious the introductory piece, it seems, the more apparent the incongruity of what's to follow.

arrow through his neck—("Agatha Christie Sketch") Cf, Ep. 30, where the pantomime goose kills Terence Rattigan (also played by Cleese) with an arrow through the neck. See notes to Ep. 30 for more on Rattigan.

– B –

"Batley Townswomen's Guild"—("Batley Townswomens' Guild Presents the Battle of Pearl Harbour") Batley is in West Yorkshire, and such "association and mutual interest" guilds are still present in English towns and regions, including the Nene Valley region and Portsmouth.

"Battle of Pearl Harbour"—("Batley Townswomen's Guild Presents the Battle of Pearl Harbour") Significant turning point in WWII, when the Japanese attacked the American Pacific naval forces stationed at Pearl Harbor, Hawaii, in an attempt to both destroy the American Pacific naval fleet and discourage the United States from entering the war against the Axis. What the Battle of Britain was to the English population (and the young Pythons), Pearl Harbor was to Americans.

"Battle of Trafalgar"—("The Battle of Trafalgar") Significant British naval victory (21 October 1805) led by Admiral Nelson (see Ep. 1), and where he lost his life. The battle cemented Britain's naval superiority for many years to follow.

"before his death"—("Interesting People") Perhaps an oblique allusion to Lord Frederick Charles Cavendish (1836-1882), who also lost his life just as he undertook a significant endeavor. Cavendish was murdered by Irish nationalists in 1882, when goodwill for England and England's representatives was at a low point.

"Bignall, Mary"—("Letters [Lavatorial Humour]") Some memorial and spelling mistakes evident here. The Rome Olympics were actually held in 1960; the 1964 Games were played out in Tokyo, Japan. Mary D. (Bignal) Rand took the gold in the same event in 1964 at the Tokyo Games; Brit Sheila Sherwood took a silver medal in the long jump at the 1968 Mexico City games. Rand's winning jump was 6.76 meters, or 22 feet-2 1/4 inches. Rand (b. 1940) is credited as the first British athlete to win an Olympic gold medal in track and field (*EBO*).

The film footage is of Mary Bignal Rand, and was requested from BBC archives (WAC T12/1,092). Her name (Bignal) is misspelled in the archives, as well.

"The Black Death . . . plague"—("Interruptions") The Black Death pandemic afflicted Europe between 1347 and 1351, and both bubonic and pneumonic types were rampant. It is estimated that roughly twenty-five million died worldwide. The Pythons will revisit the plague theme in the later *Holy Grail* feature film.

"Bologna"—("Literary Football Discussion") Bologna FC was formed in 1909, and would win the Italian Cup in 1969-1970.

"boutique"—("Literary Football Discussion") This perhaps betrays the actual footballer the Pythons are satirizing, George Best. Irishman Best (1946-2005) was considered by many to be the best footballer of his generation, and played primarily for Manchester United, winning the Football League Championship in 1965 and 1967, and the European Cup in 1968. During

his peak in the late 1960s, Best acted and spent money like a rock star, including opening several unsuccessful boutiques and even a nightclub.

Friends of the Pythons, The Beatles had also opened a boutique in 1967 in Baker Street in London, to much media fanfare. "Apple," as the trendy boutique was called, would close not long afterward.

BP—("The Battle of Trafalgar") Back projection screen. Used often on news or current affairs type sets in *FC*. The same set-up can be seen anytime the actual *Nine O'Clock News* (1970-) or *News at Ten* (1967-) sets are depicted. The first news set is seen in Ep. 30, and the latter in Ep. 13, when the Queen has reportedly switched over to watch the evening news.

"Brian"—("Literary Football Discussion") Perhaps a reference to English sports commentator and interviewer Brian Moore (b. 1932 in Kent). The effete and intellectual timbre of the interview/er, however, point more toward a critic who will be directly lampooned in Ep. 33, Philip Jenkinson (b. 1935). See notes to Ep. 33 for more.

"Buzzard"—("Literary Football Discussion") Character name brought to the group by Cleese, who had earlier created an imaginary football front line of "Bunn, Wackett, Buzzard, Stubble and Boot." (See Morgan, 1999, 26.) *FC* Episode 3 had been known by this longer title through most of its pre- and production life in BBC communications.

"By jove"—("Agatha Christie Sketch") An epithet used by, for example, Tommy (among many other Christie characters) in *The Secret Adversary* (1922):

> "Lost her memory, eh?" said Tommy with interest. "By Jove, that explains why they looked at me so queerly when I spoke of questioning her. Bit of a slip on my part, that! But it wasn't the sort of thing a fellow would be likely to guess." (chapter 18, "The Telegram")

This was Christie's second novel. Coincidentally, and perhaps subconsciously conflated on the Pythons' part, the Pickering featured in another play, Shaw's *Pygmalion*, also utters the "By Jove" epithet.

– C –

"Camp on Blood Island"—("Batley Townswomen's Guild Presents the Battle of Pearl Harbour") Title of 1957 film from England's Hammer Studios, directed by Val Guest, and depicting a Malaysian POW camp run by the Japanese in the closing days of the war.

"Canning, Prof. R.J."—("Interruptions") Cf. the reference to R.J. Gumby and Canning in the notes to Ep. 9, and the allusion to noted historians of the time, including the *FC*-referenced A.J.P. Taylor, who after 1950 made regular appearances on the BBC, and Kenneth Clark, famous by this time for the immensely popular *Civilisation* series first appearing on BBC, then PBS in America.

There is also an R.J. Canning, Ltd. company in Berkshire.

"cat sat on the mat"—("The Battle of Trafalgar") This, of course, sounds very much like a line from a Theodor Geisel learn-to-read book, and may well be a comment on the real-world knowledge of such learned academics.

"clearly not written by the general public"—("Letters [Lavatorial Humour]") This is the first example in the series where the façade of reality over the letter-writing trope is removed/acknowledged, and it's given to an imagined viewer to write in and identify the "man behind the curtain," as it were. Generally, once the sent-up material (parody) is itself sent-up (acknowledgment of parody), the effectiveness and appearance of that material diminishes. Silly letters will continue to be a part of a number of *FC* episodes (as they were during this period in the pages of *Private Eye*), most of which purport to be from actual viewers.

Colonel Pickering—(PSC; "Agatha Christie Sketch") Name of a character in G.B. Shaw's play *Pygmalion* (1913), specifically, the man who bets Henry Higgins that he cannot properly refine Eliza Doolittle. No explanation is given here as to why he's appearing in an Agatha Christie–type sketch, nor is his name mentioned by any of the characters.

contemporary picture . . . Trafalgar—(PSC; "The Battle of Trafalgar") This still—"La Gloria Di Trafalga No. 942: 1805 Trafalga"—is from the Colour Plate BBC Reference Library (WAC T12/1,092).

– D –

"Dorking"—("Interesting People") A theatre massacre (by Red Indians) occurred at the Dorking Civic Theatre in Ep. 6. Dorking is in Surrey, south of London, and just south of Leatherhead, also mentioned in the "Red Indian" sketch. East Grinstead (mentioned earlier) is southeast of Dorking.

– E –

"Elementary"—("Agatha Christie Sketch") Sherlock Holmes' signature word, and usually spoken to Watson. The characters were by Englishman Sir Arthur Conan Doyle (1859-1930). It's now obvious that Python is mining a number of more well-known British authors, rather than parodying Christie alone.

"entire Bible"—("Interesting People") Later in the episodes there will be an attempt to summarize

Proust, as well (Ep. 31). All of Ron Obvious' attempted sporting feats in Ep. 10 are also impossible, including jumping the English Channel and tunneling to Java.

Episode 11—This episode was recorded on 14 December 1969, and broadcast just two weeks later, on 28 December 1969. Note that mention of the Announcer is omitted from this episode's script, as is the standard "It's" utterance (at least in print). This is just one episode after the "It's Man" was termed "boring" in the printed script itself.

Also scheduled to appear in this episode, according to BBC records: Flanagan (Ep. 12; *Benny Hill*), Sheila Sands (Ep. 10; *Troubleshooters*), Alan Fields, Nigel Tramer, Anton Morrell, Kurt Muller, Beulah Hughes (Eps. 12, 33, 34; *Hands of Orlac*), Susan Marchbanks, Kay Baron, June Collinson, Bernadine Barry (Ep. 6; *Dr. Who*), Perrin Lewis (*Wednesday Play*), Joe Santo (*Dixon of Dock Green*), Dennis Balcombe (*Timeslip*), Leslie Weekes (*Z Cars*), Alan Troy (*Target*), and Peter Robinson (his appearance was eventually cancelled, according to surviving pay records) (WAC T12/1,092).

"existentialist football"—("Literary Football Discussion") This theme of philosophical football will be approached later by Python in a more lengthy and visualized way, via "The Philosopher's Football Match," where German and Greek philosophers face off on the football pitch. This sketch will be introduced in the second *Fliegender Zirkus* episode (September 1971), then reappear in the Pythons' *Live at the Hollywood Bowl* performance in 1978.

– F –

"fellow historians"—("The Battle of Trafalgar") This is a rather clever ridicule of the then-current academic debate surrounding Taylor's book *The Origins of the Second World War* (1961) examining the reasons behind and responsibilities for World War II and the infamous Western (read: English) appeasement of Nazi aggression. Here, then, all historians are equally "thick," and equally misinformed on even the facts of history (and certainly the then-culled historical facts).

fling her—("Interesting People") Eighteenth-century English novelist Tobias Smollett used such an image to describe the size of his hero Humphrey Clinker's London quarters: " . . . pent up in frowsy lodgings, where there is not room enough to *swing a cat*" (*The Expedition of Humphrey Clinker*, vol. II).

– G –

"German . . . fleet"—("The Battle of Trafalgar") Drake was involved with the defeat of the *Spanish* Armada in

1588, and had been dead since 1596. His naval skirmishes were primarily against Spanish vessels and holdings, not German.

gravediggers . . . surfboarder—("Undertakers Film") Like a clown car at a circus, this resembles any of a number of similar *Benny Hill* scenes, as well as *The Monkees* (1966-1968) on American television. Cf. Ep. 9 for more on Hill's "silly" influence on the Pythons.

Gumby . . . handkerchief, etc.—("The Battle of Trafalgar") Here the script concretely (and for the first time in *Flying Circus*) identifies both the costume characteristics of the Gumby characters, and also attaches the "Gumby" name to the description. The appellation "Gumby" didn't even appear until Ep. 9, affixed to Chapman's "Gumby crooner" (Prof. R.J. Gumby).

– I –

"I'm off"—("Interruptions") Like the historian lecturing in *HG*, Canning is cut short by other narrative elements. In this case the interruption is simply an annoyance. In *HG* the historian is killed by a marauding knight as he attempts to control the narrative by his own descriptions and proscriptions.

"Inspector Tiger"—("Agatha Christie Sketch") Almost certainly at least a reference to Scotland Yard inspectors in general (as visible authority figures), but may also be a nod to the many television and film iterations of "Inspector" and "Detective Inspector." For instance, see the cast of the 1962 British TV series *Z Cars*. (*Z Cars* is one of the several shows—along with *Dr. Who*, *Softly Softly*, and *Dixon of Dock Green*—casting from the same talent pool for extras with *FC*.) In the 1947 film *Whispering City* there is an "Inspector Renaud" (loosely translating to "fox"), giving rise to "Inspector Fox." (The instance of "Renaud" as an early variation of "Reynard" is taken from the fourteenth-century epic poem *Sir Gawain and the Green Knight*. See the *OED*.)

Also, veteran English actor Michael Bates (*Patton*; *Battle of Britain*) played Inspector Mole in the 1964 TV series *Cluff*. Bates' inspiration to the Pythons is even more cemented when it's noted that he also appeared in *The Rise and Rise of Michael Rimmer* (1970), co-written by Chapman and Cleese (and others), and co-starring Cleese in a small role.

In Ep. 29, finally, Cleese plays Inspector Leopard (who has changed his name from "Panther"), and Idle plays both Inspector Thompson's Gazelle and Inspector Baboon, and Chapman plays Inspector Fox.

"interesting sport"—("Interesting People") This film footage of various sports is from "Sportsview" (WAC T12/1,092). *Sportsview* (Eps. 35 and 39) appeared on the BBC beginning in 1957, and was hosted by Ken Wolstenholme (Ep. 21), Peter Dimmock, and Brian Johnston (Eps. 20, 21), among others.

"Ivor Bigbottie"—(letter link into "Literary Football Discussion") *Ivor the Engine* was an English children's show about a Welsh train, 1958-1963, made for Associated-Rediffusion. In Ep. 13, Eric (Idle) is a child being interviewed, and he mentions that Raquel Welch has a "big bottom."

– J –

"Jarrow"—("Literary Football Discussion") Working-class town northwest of Sunderland, on the Tyne, and featured in Ep. 15 as the setting for "The Spanish Inquisition" sketch. East Jarrow United football club (a Catholic school league) was part of Jarrow & District League. See the entry for "smart interviewer and footballer" below.

– K –

"Kantian"—("Literary Football Discussion") Of or pertaining to the works of philosopher Immanuel Kant (1724-1804). The sheer level of thinking exhibited by the names mentioned overwhelm the "midfield cognoscento" Buzzard, who may know football, but not nineteenth- and twentieth-century philosophy. The Interviewer (Idle) is just doing what many such interviewers and critics do—overanalyzing what Buzzard (Cleese) knows is nothing more than the kicking of a ball into a net. And if the Interviewer thinks Buzzard is, indeed, an "arch-thinker," then the Interviewer's state of mind must also be called into question.

Private Eye ran a regular short column called "Pseuds Corner" where readers could submit clippings from various respected British newspapers, clippings that featured the cream of euphuistic pretentiousness. One such entry from the 31 January 1969 issue, discussing the recent Leeds United versus Manchester United match:

Leeds United 2   Manchester Utd 1

The bitter malevolence that erupted in the funeral dolorousness of the first half was blessedly relieved, although never expunged in the more intense legitimate conflict of the second.

ARTHUR HOPCRAFT
Observer (qtd. in *Private Eye* 31 January 1969, 4)

A similarly florid description of a cricket match in the offing appeared just a short while later in *The Times*:

It was a hot, hazy, sometimes steamy day, the kind of day to win the toss. The Edgbaston field looked lovely, with its broad strips of dark and light green, rippling *crepe de chine* rather than velvet. The drab scar of the concrete wicket was unbearably poignant.

ALAN GIBSON
The Times (qtd. in *Private Eye* 22 May 1970, 4)

And finally, the cake is taken by one Brian Chapman writing for the *Guardian* as he gushes over an epic cricket match:

Middlesex beat Yorkshire by three wickets at Lords yesterday with only one ball of the final 20 overs remaining. A match that for two days had dragged its leaden feet rose in the end to heights of drama. Reluctant heroes on both sides buckled on Homeric armour. The lotus-eaters, in Tennysonian idiom, rose from their soporific banks of Amaranth and gave battle.

BRIAN CHAPMAN
Guardian (qtd. in *Private Eye* 14 August 1970, 4)

Given these actual splendiferous rehearsals of sporting events, Idle's Interviewer sounds rather tame, even understandable.

"Kendal . . . Westmorland"—("Interesting People") Kendal is in the county of Westmorland, at the edge of the Cumbrian Lake District.

"Keith Maniac"—("Interesting People") Perhaps a reference to the then-rising paranormalist star Uri Geller (b. 1946), who by 1969 was becoming known for his highly publicized "abilities" to practice telekinesis (spoon-bending, watch-starting) and foresee the future.

In Ep. 35, a character played by Jones (Mystico) and dressed/acting in a similarly strange fashion is able to build high-rise housing simply by hypnosis.

Lastly, *Private Eye* had labeled longtime BBC presenter Jack de Manio "Mr. de Maniac," mock-lauding him for his "amazingly high standard of childish patter day after day," as well as for his performance in dog food commercials (*PE* 1 January 1971, 11).

kitted out—(PSC; "Interesting Sport") Wearing the complete cricketer's gear, including padding and sweater, etc.

– L –

"Lobotomy"—("Agatha Christie Sketch") Radical surgical procedure where parts of the brain's frontal lobe are removed. The surgery hasn't a history of being used for treating confusion, rather schizophrenia and depression. This type of caption is also used often in

FC as a means of ellipses, or the removal of time. Cf. Ep. 29, where "dead unjugged rabbit fish" and "rat tart" are consumed during the ellipses.

"Lookout"—("Agatha Christie Sketch") Like Python's humor in general, this sketch, rather than resolving itself, continues on to the next absurdity, in this case the next appearance of an authority figure who also happens to be stuck in a literal mode.

This continuing reference to "So and so of the Yard" is a reflection of the ubiquitous presence of police shows like *Dixon of Dock Green*, but must also be connected to Jack "Slipper of the Yard" Slipper (1924-2005), Detective Chief Superintendent of the Metropolitan Police during this period. "Slipper of the Yard" hounded the "Great Train Robbery" gang for many years, and in several countries. Slipper was tall and sported a pencil mustache, the latter copied by the Pythons as various inspectors burst into scenes throughout *FC*. See the various detective entries in Ep. 29 for the "type."

"Lord Hill"—(link into closing credits) Previously a radio doctor, Charles (later Lord) Hill (1904-1989) of Luton led the BBC (as chairman 1967-1972) during this period, and enjoyed a close relationship with Labour Party PM Harold Wilson (1916-1995). Wilson was PM from 1964 to 1970, and also 1974-1976. It was even reported (by the BBC's Peter Scott) that Hill was appointed by Wilson just to force political foe Director-General Hugh Greene out of the BBC, though Greene held firm until 1969 (allowing, for example, the Pythons a shot at a television contract).

See the entry on Lord Hill in Ep. 10, where he personally invites a walk-on to appear in a BBC sketch.

– M –

masculine voice—("Eighteenth-Century Social Legislation") Generally, if Python is going to abrogate a female's speech or presence she is either presented as a mute sexual object, or given facile, dimwitted dialogue that marginalizes her narrative significance (cf. Episodes 4 and 7). In this case, her own voice is muted and replaced with a voice representing the patriarchy, but she is still able to "perform" her feminine role as the sexual object (writhing in orgasmic pleasure). This might be characterized as a somewhat disturbing hermaphroditic moment, or just another attempt at a new shock value level.

"Men of Harlech"—("Interesting People") A martial song characterized as an unofficial anthem of Wales. Harlech Castle is in northern Wales, and was originally designed to play a part in the subjugation of the Welsh. The castle was built in 1283 under

Edward I. The music became well-known after its use in the film *Zulu* (1964), the heroic story of an undermanned Welsh detachment fighting in the Zulu Wars in 1879. See the website data-wales.co.uk/harlech.htm. The Pythons will revisit this film and setting in the feature film *ML*, the "Fighting Each Other" section.

"Municipal Baths, Croydon"—("Interesting People") Outer borough of London, in Surrey. The only public outdoor pools/baths in Croydon were (they have since closed) Wandle Park and Purley Way Lido. Indoor baths were built in 1926.

– N –

"Nazi War Atrocities"—("Batley Townswomen's Guild Presents the Battle of Pearl Harbour") These came to complete light during the Nuremberg Trials just after WWII. In Ep. 12, a fully uniformed Hitler, Himmler, and Von Ribbentrop (here renamed Hilter, Bimmler, and Ron Vibbentrop) will attempt to win a by-election in North Minehead. Hitler has already been lampooned in Ep. 2 (he is admittedly an easy target), and was a consistent target during WWII for cartoonists (like Tex Avery, Walt Disney, and Chuck Jones) across the Allied world.

"notice me"—("Interesting People") Like Ellison's character in *Invisible Man*, Mr. Walters notices that he is not noticed. In 1958 Incorporated Television had created a thirteen-episode series *HG Wells' The Invisible Man*, which may have inspired the Pythons. In that series, the title character tries to fit into society as he seeks a cure for his own invisibility, helping police solve crimes and friends in distress. Idle's characterization here of the "problems of the Invisible Man at home" aren't, then, far from television reality.

– O –

oilskins . . . sou'westers—("Interesting People") These bell ringers are all wearing yellow rain gear, much like Vicky (Idle) in Ep. 1. The hat is the "sou'wester," and the coat is the "oilskin." The costuming will reappear in Ep. 33, in the "Lifeboat" sketch.

"old one like that"—("Agatha Christie Sketch") Inspector Theresamanbehindyer (Jones) is the only inspector character so far not suffering from extreme literality. Each of the other inspectors treats his own name as either a command or a threat, and responds violently when hearing it.

out of frame—(PSC; "Eighteenth-Century Social Legislation") This "linkman from on high" seems to be at least a somewhat derisive comment on the elevated status of intellectuals like the fictional Canning, and especially the very real A.J.P. Taylor (1906-1990) and colleagues (including C.S. Lewis, 1898-1963) at Oxford, Cambridge, etc. The implication is clear: Inspiration comes from the hand of God to men like Taylor and Canning.

"out of the yard"—("Agatha Christie Sketch") An example of a character's literality. She assumes he's giving her a command, rather than his name, and he has obviously never heard a pun on his own very punnable name. Cf. Mr. Smoke-Too-Much in Ep. 31, who finally "gets" the double meaning of his name, long after the "getting" can be funny.

This "of-the-yard" trope may be at least partly attributable to Harry Secombe's character in *Down Among the Z Men* (1952), "Bats of the Yard," and will reappear in myriad episodes throughout *FC*.

– P –

pile of dead policemen—("Agatha Christie Sketch") The dead policemen, including Ian Davidson, when he hits the top of the pile, also include Lesley Weekes, Dennis Balcombe, Peter Roy (*Englebert with the Young Generation*), and Alan Troy (WAC T12/1,092). (See the note above for "*Episode 11*" for more on these other actors.) This pile of bodies is yet another visual moment drawn from the cartoon world.

"plain wrapper"—("The Battle of Trafalgar") Perhaps this image of the eminent historian and BBC personality as seductive siren is a comment on the allure of the "flavor-of-the-month" new theories in history. It seems to be a look at the splash that new historical readings and revelations can often make—especially when an event as fresh and raw as Nazism is the subject—before the newness wears off thanks to the next reading, a mis-reading, or even a discrediting of the previous "find" that sets the table anew.

See the entry for "sparked a wave" below for more on this revisionism.

"plastic arts"—("Literary Football Discussion") Art forms that utilize some kind of malleable medium, including sculpture, woodworking, ceramics, even painting and sometimes film, etc. The use of the term itself identifies the interviewer as something of an effete intellectual.

"poison"—("Agatha Christie Sketch") The daughter of a surgeon and a WWI nurse herself, Agatha Christie included significant uses of poisons in her mysteries. The three means of murder (poison, arrow, gunshot) are also each characteristic of Christie's novels.

"programme"—("Interruptions") Professor Canning doesn't seem to mind the irreverent comedic takes on historical events depicted, treating them quite respectfully, just the interruptions he has to endure.

"Proustian"—("Literary Football Discusssion") Of or pertaining to author Marcel Proust (1871-1922), a prominent literary figure whose work is mentioned several times in *FC*. Proust is best known for being the author of the seven-volume *À la recherche du temps perdu* (1913–1927; *Remembrance of Things Past*). In Ep. 31, there is a contest to determine who can summarize the entire novel set, and in Ep. 23 Praline nearly comes to blows with a man who hints that Proust might be a "loony."

The "Proustian memory" trope is significant to this discussion and this annotated work in general, since the Pythons clearly draw on "involuntary memory" throughout *FC*. The "recovery of the past" so important to Proust allows for a more structured reading of the seemingly random and chaotic *Flying Circus* world, where university reading lists and cherished historical figures and cartoon violence and contemporary, topical faces and foibles come together in a sort of noisome ever-present. This is why long-dead figures like Mozart or Julius Caesar can share screen space and time with Gumbies and Pepperpots, and why a "throes of orgasm" lady can discuss eighteenth-century social legislation in a man's voice—rather than treating time as an uninterrupted line, the Pythons stack discrete events/ people into one jumbled "now."

psychedelic flowers—("Undertakers Film") A nod to the "flower generation," or hippie culture prevalent as a subculture in the United States and UK during the 1960s and early 1970s. Such displays were often visual symbols of the "peace" movements opposed to the war in Vietnam, or British imperialism in Africa, etc.

The music under this change is a sped-up version of "There's No Business Like Show Business" from *Annie Get Your Gun* by Irving Berlin, as performed by Werner Muller and His Orchestra (WAC T12/1,092).

– R –

"Regius Professor"—("Eighteenth-Century Social Legislation") This is a professorship established by royalty in the older British universities, like Cambridge, Oxford, Dublin, Edinburgh, etc. Hugh Trevor-Roper, for example, was the Regius Professor of Modern History at Oxford (probably over Jones, specifically) between 1957 and 1980.

"Rijksmuseum"—("Eighteenth-Century Social Legislation") This famous "state museum" hasn't been in The Hague since the museum's contents were moved to Amsterdam in 1808. The Hague is the seat of government of The Netherlands, and Amsterdam is the official capital city. Many of Rembrandt's best known works can be found at this museum, including *Portrait of Willem Bartholsz Ruyter* (c. 1638), mentioned in the notes to Ep. 2 earlier.

"roomself"—("Agatha Christie Sketch") The Constable (Palin) also responds *literally*, mimicking Inspector Tiger as precisely as he can.

"Royal Philharmonic Orchestra"—("Letters [Lavatorial Humour]") The London-based orchestra was founded in 1925 by Sir Thomas Beecham, and resides at the Royal Albert Hall. None of the recordings during the run of the show were created by the RPO.

– S –

"shirty"—("The Battle of Trafalgar") Ill-tempered.

"Shut up!"—("Interesting People") Cleese's characters often try and control their environments by resorting to this (shutting off or shouting down opposition), including the nervy interviewer (Ep. 1), the ex-RSM (Ep. 4), the psychiatrist (Ep. 13), Praline (Ep. 18), Jim the TV commentator (Ep. 20), and on.

On *The Goon Show*, "Shut up, Eccles!" had become a catchphrase, while Minnie Bannister and Henry Crun often shouted "shut up" to each other.

side of the head—("Agatha Christie Sketch") Cf. Ep. 35 where the Attendant (Cleveland) must jar the Peer's (Palin) brain back into position, otherwise His Grace just stammers without end.

"Sir Gerald"—("Agatha Christie Sketch") One of several references to Sir Gerald Nabarro (1913-1973), who was a Tory MP standing for South Worcestershire. Nabarro is also mentioned in Eps. 19, 21, and 23 (twice), and in the notes for Eps. 15, for example. In the mid to late 1960s Nabarro was also a fixture in the political cartoon panels across the Empire, with many hinting not-so-subtly that he, not PM Harold Wilson, was in charge.

Nabarro was a noted old school Conservative, who at different times, according to Joan Sutherland, "opposed Europe, the abolition of capital punishment, drugs, students, pornography and pop music. He supported Enoch Powell on immigration and white rule in Rhodesia [see notes to Eps. 10 and 45]. If he could have, he would have stopped the calendar at 1959" (*Guardian* 27 December 1999). He would have been a ripe target for Python, of course, and his fall from grace following a compromising auto accident with his female secretary—there were conflicting reports as to who was at the wheel, etc.—made Nabarro even more vulnerable.

Smart interviewer and footballer—(PSC; "Literary Football Discussion") The Pythons are more than likely skewering the still-current tradition of analyzing and overanalyzing athletic contests, this time comparing international league football to existential philosophy of the nineteenth and twentieth centuries. They will return to this subject in a very effective short filmed sketch, "The Philosophers' Football Match," which appears in one of the German episodes (*FZ*), and later in *Live at the Hollywood Bowl*, where Greek and German philosophers (and one actual footballer, Franz Beckenbauer) face off.

Jarrow can't boast a significant national or international football reputation, meaning the "Stadium of Light, Jarrow" (see below) mention is obviously a swipe at this working-class town. (The actual Stadium of Light, Estádio da Luz, was built in 1954 and was home to SL Benfica in Lisbon, Portugal.) Jarrow has a number of school-age teams (Catholic, public, etc.) that have been in place since the late nineteenth century. There are and have been popular professional football clubs in the region, however, including teams in Sunderland (est. 1880) and Newcastle (est. 1892).

The supposedly obsolete "catenaccio" defensive system was quite feared for many years on the continent—it involved an additional defensive man, a "sweeper," behind four defenders—and had been pioneered by an Austrian coach in the late 1930s. The system was employed contemporarily (and run very well) by Helenio Herrera's Inter Milan in the late 1960s, to which the Pythons probably allude by mentioning "Signor Alberto Fanfrino's Bologna FC" squad (see Motson and Rowlinson; Gray and Drewett).

The Pythons may have been indirectly referring to the rather storied 1967 European Cup, described by Andy Gray and Jim Drewett as:

> . . . the biggest clash of footballing styles you could . . . imagine . . . a meeting of two teams who inhabited opposite ends of the tactical spectrum. Jock Stein's Celtic played in the traditional Scottish way with two out-and-out wingers and a basic philosophy of all-out attack while Helenio Herrera's Inter Milan, the pioneers of *catenaccio* . . . defending, with four man markers and a sweeper, excelled at grinding out 1-0 wins. For many this game was more than a battle for the European Cup, it was a kind of good versus evil contest with Celtic on some kind of crusade to save free-flowing attacking football from extinction. (*Flat Back Four*)

Celtic won the match 2-1, incidentally, which was held in Lisbon's National Stadium. There was also, of course, no Jimmy Buzzard on the team, just Simpson, Craig, Gemmell, McNeill, Clark, Johnstone, Auld, Murdoch, Lennox, Wallace, and Chalmers. Real Madrid (Spain) won five straight European Cups (1956-1960), and then again in 1966, which may have felt like a stranglehold to UK fans. And when Real Madrid wasn't winning, AC Milan (Italy) took the prize twice in that decade (1962-1963 and 1968-1969).

The fact that a British team (Jarrow/Celtic) could go on the offensive and overcome the staid entrenchment of defensive continental football (Bologna/Internazionale) is a celebration of Britishness, of course, but it's worth noting that the Jarrow winners (and the Pythons) are employing the works of continental philosophers such as Kant and Proust, so it must also be a victory of new, enlightened thinking over the old.

"Positivism" stressed immediate experience as opposed to more structured (abstract, formalist) approaches to experience put forth by Idealists, and was very much in line with the "creative force" of nature and the emerging/exploding technologies of the nineteenth and twentieth centuries. The "obsolescent" Idealism was being overthrown on the fields of (philosophical) play as Kant (1724-1804) wrestled with the "deficiencies" of Rationalism and Empiricism in his three "critiques."

The "thrusting and bursting" is also "an almost Proustian display" of the formative significance of the "creative energies of past experience" formerly lodged in the unconscious emerging to affect the expression of the artist (Drabble, 1985, 794). The significance of Proust (1871-1922) to the Pythons and their generation of university wits can't be overstated, as he and/or his works are mentioned and mimicked throughout *FC* and even their feature films. See the entry for "Proustian" above for more on Proust's "involuntary memory."

"social betterment"—("Eighteenth-Century Social Legislation") The lecturer here ventures from English social legislation to Dutch matters, employing a German as opposed to a more proper Dutch accent, and he leaves the eighteenth century in favor of the fifteenth century, before abandoning the lecture altogether.

"sparked a wave of controversy"—("The Battle of Trafalgar") The specter of revisionist history and revisionist historians shadowed this period, with the first significant Holocaust denials (or emendations) appearing in the 1960s, this on the heels of revisionist looks at Japanese and German atrocities committed during WWII, as well as the Allies' "real" reasons for going to war in the first place. David Hoggan's *The*

Myth of the Six Million was published in 1969, and a firestorm erupted over the book's factual soundness, neo-Nazi point of view and support, and anti-Semitic slant. This was a period when many shared national "myths" were taken to task by historians, and careful re-examination of neglected, new, or just ignored records cast long-held and often much-cherished beliefs into doubt. By casting dimwitted Gumbies as these learned men of letters, the Pythons belittle the entire revisionist undertaking, even though they themselves participate, at least comedically, in this type of revision.

"Stadium of Light, Jarrow"—("Literary Football Discussion") This may be a clever passing allusion to the Nationwide *Festival* of Light organized by anti-permissive society campaigners Malcolm Muggeridge and Mary Whitehouse, among others. One of the stated goals of the event(s) was to counter the rising incidence of sex and violence in the media in the UK, which may be directly connected to the Interviewer's (Idle) "thrusting and bursting" descriptions of Jarrow's play. The first gathering was in Westminster, and regional meetings followed in fall 1971.

"Stools"—("Interesting People") Medical terminology for human feces.

"Superintendents 9"—(link out of "Agatha Christie Sketch") Cf. the scorekeeping in Ep. 1, where the results are based on equally fatal acts: "Pigs 9 - British Bipeds 4."

– T –

"Taylor, A.J.P."—("Eighteenth-Century Social Legislation") Taylor (1906-1990) is the English author of *English History 1914-1945* (1965), the final volume from the Oxford History of England, as well as the very controversial *The Origins of The Second World War* (1961), where Germany was blamed for the war, but where both France and England also came under fire for "vacillation" and appeasement policies. The reception of the book's thesis led to "a mixture of international obloquy and acclaim" for Taylor, according to Thompson (*ODNB*). See notes to Ep. 9 for more.

Also, for an example of perhaps some kind of shared mindset between Taylor and the Pythons, note just the title of Taylor's 1956 work: *Englishmen and Others*. Taylor's painting of all Conservatives and any conservative thought or policy with a negative, socially regressive brush betrays his own politics, and may actually be quite in line with those of the Pythons.

Tchaikovsky piano concerto—(PSC; link into "Letter [Lavatorial Humour]") This is Tchaikovsky's "Piano Concerto No. 1 in B Flat Minor, Op. 23," performed by Julius Katchen with the London Symphony Orchestra conducted by Pierino Gamba (WAC T12/1,092). Cf. this same concerto used in Ep. 28, where a concert pianist (Jones) plays the piano as he escapes a chained bag.

"Tiddles"—("Interesting People") Cf. Arthur Waring and his musical mice in Ep. 1 for similar animal treatment. "Bing Tiddle Tiddle Bong" is the name of the song performed at the end of Ep. 22. Cats continue to be the household pet that suffers the most in *FC*, and will be ironed and inserted into a wall in Ep. 45, and beaten against a wall (to shake out the dust, presumably) in *Holy Grail*.

"tie"—("Literary Football Discussion") *OED*: " . . . a match played between the victors in previous matches or heats."

"Tired of life?"—(link out of "Interruptions") Spoofing the television medium again, this like a commercial for bath oils, suicide, or just imminent, blissful death.

"Toovey"—("Interesting People") Roy Tuvey is a British TV comedy writer (*Up the Front*; *Whoops, Baghdad!*). The latter show was produced by John Howard Davies, a director and producer for *FC*.

torchy music—(PSC; "Eighteenth-Century Social Legislation") This "torchy music" is "Night Train" from the album *David Rose and his Orchestra play "The Stripper" and other fun songs for the Family!* (WAC T12/1,092).

"tuts"—(PSC; link into "Letters [Lavatorial Humour]") *OED*: "An ejaculation (often reduplicated) expressing impatience or dissatisfaction with a statement, notion, or proceeding, or contemptuously dismissing it."

– U –

undertakers—("Undertakers Film") Most of these sketches—interruptions—are staged to be similar to silent comedy film routines. When the undertakers carry the coffin between the "Agatha Christie Sketch" and "Literary Football Discussion," the music utilized is from the Lansdowne Jazz Series Traditional Parade, "Oh, Didn't He Ramble" by Terry Lightfoot & his New Orleans Jazzmen. Bits of "The Dead March" are also used in other links (WAC T12/1.092).

– V –

very mad way—("Interesting People") The treatment of foreigners (here "Ali Bayan") continues to be somewhat one-dimensional, and will be later replicated on the short-lived BBC series *Whoops, Baghdad!*, produced by John Howard Davies in 1973. Ali Bayan is actually a city in Iraq.

Voice—(PSC; "Interesting People") Not credited in the scripts, but Jones provides the voice characterization for Mr. Stools. Some of this type of voice work may have been parceled out on the fly as the episode was being staged, then recorded.

– W –

"West Hartlepool"—("Interesting People") In the county of Durham on the North Sea coast, and just north of North York.

"West 12"—W12 covers the Hammersmith and Fulham areas, the area surrounding BBC Television Centre.

"what it's like being invisible"—("Interesting People") Perhaps a reference to the 1952 novel *Invisible Man* by Ralph Ellison, about the invisibility of the black man in a white world. The "Dull Stockbroker" (Palin) depicted in Ep. 6 isn't invisible, though catastrophic events around him have no effect on him, and he scurries through life missing and getting missed by everything. This is certainly a look at the impersonal, dehumanizing effect of modern industrial society, and the fact that "dull" types get marginalized, or just aren't interesting enough to be featured on shows like *Man Alive* (Ep. 26) or *Tomorrow's World* (Ep. 20).

Wife—("Interesting People") The voice characterization is delivered here by Chapman, though he's not credited in the written text.

Winn, Anona—("Agatha Christie Sketch") Anona Winn (d. 1994) was an Australian-born actress who appeared in the 1934 film *On the Air*, as the Chambermaid, and participated in the radio shows *Just a Minute* and *Twenty Questions*.

World of History—("Interruptions") The music behind the titles and introductory graphics is "Music for Vive L'Oompa" Funeral March by Chopin, played by The London Brass Players (WAC T12/1,092).

"woven in the woof"—("The Battle of Trafalgar") Cf. Thomas Gray's 1757 poem "The Bard":

> Weave the warp, and weave the woof,
> The winding sheet of Edward's race.
> Give ample room and verge enough,
> The characters of hell to trace. (2.1.1)

Perhaps the real question is whether Python is saying that such eminent historians are "characters of hell" in their quest for academic and popular acclaim. The evidence seems to support such scornful treatment.

– Y –

"Yorkshire"—("The Battle of Trafalgar") Describing, really, a central aspect of *FC* itself. Almost nothing was shot "on location," with areas in and around London (and especially Ealing and Acton) standing in for far-flung and exotic locales. The actual Cudworth is northeast of Barnsley (where the coal mining son went "poncing off" to in Ep. 2) in South Yorkshire.

"You Jane"—("Agatha Christie Sketch") Reference to the stilted dialogue spoken by Tarzan, the Ape-Man, an Edgar Rice Burroughs (1875-1950) character, in the Hollywood movie version of the story.

– Z –

"zoom in"—("Interruptions") Canning is aware of both the medium's capabilities and the "meaning" of such a camera movement—the zoom creates more of an intimacy, but is also more intrusive. Holding the long shot, then, would have been less threatening, allowing Canning to exit without "following" him and without preemptive action from him. Chapman's Colonel character also exerts narrative authority as he commands the camera (and the switcher board in the studio) in Ep. 4 earlier.

Episode 12

"121 . . . SE21"—("Police Station [Silly Voices]") Dulwich is located in the Greater London area, not far from Wimbledon and Crystal Palace. Dulwich is a part of the SE21 zip code. There is no Halliwell (Street, Road, Lane, etc.) in the SE21 postal code area. The nearest Halliwell Road is near Brixton Prison in the Lambeth area of Greater London.

127th—("Upperclass Twit of the Year") Indicating that Upperclass Twits as a definable, contesting group have been recognized since about 1842. This could be a reference to the changing times signified by the rise of the Conservative Robert Peel to the PM position in 1841. The Opium War also ended the following year, leaving Britain in control of significant Chinese territory (China ceding Hong Kong and opening other ports to British trade) and cementing its reputation as a gunboat diplomacy nation. These types—"Eton, Harrow and the Guard"—would have been just the fellows to fill the plum military and civil service positions both at home as well as abroad in the far-flung British Empire.

– A –

ANIMATION (possibly incorporating falling)—(PSC; link into "*Spectrum*—Talking About Things") The fact that the Pythons writing the episode (all except Gilliam) didn't know what their animator had planned wasn't unusual, his work generally happening while the others rehearsed and blocked the week's show. More than likely, the writing team had told Gilliam of the falling sketch, without giving too many details, and the animator went from there. See Morgan *Speaks!*, and *Gilliam on Gilliam* for more.

"annex Poland"—("Mr. Hilter") Hitler's Nazi forces overran Poland in a matter of days beginning 1 September 1939, which was part of Hitler's systematic efforts to control all of Prussia, and even all of Europe and Soviet Asia.

"Arabella Plunkett"—("Upperclass Twit of the Year") Arabella Fermor was the name of the young woman whose hair was snipped by an impulsive suitor, unleashing bad blood between aristocratic families and providing the inspiration for young Alexander Pope's *The Rape of the Lock*. The poem is itself an indictment of the propensity for the elevation of a trivial matter to the heroic, tragic level—such elevations are, of course, part and parcel of Python's satire.

"Armstrong-Jones"—("The Minehead By-Election") Tony Armstrong-Jones (officially Snowdon, Antony Armstrong-Jones, 1st Earl of) was Princess Margaret's husband from 1960 to 1978, and is an award-winning photographer and filmmaker. Armstrong-Jones' photos appeared on the set of the 1958 John Cranko revue *Keep Your Hair On*, a disastrous London revolution epic set in a hairdresser's shop. Perhaps this bizarre juxtaposition inspired the Pythons to place Hitler planning his own revolution in Minehead. A photo of Armstrong-Jones appears in Ep. 30.

Additionally, the 23 March 1969 *Sunday Times* published the results of an opinion poll asking readers to gauge the "relative popularity" of members of the royal family. *Private Eye* also published the poll results, but wondered why Lord Snowdon had been left off the list, even though it was discovered he'd scored a 20. (The Queen came first at 63, then Philip at 55, the Queen Mother at 48, etc.) Snowdon would have come eighth, after Princess Anne (26) but before his wife, Princess Margaret, who was only able to score 2. The Duke of Kent (satirized in Ep. 30), managed a dismal -4. *Private Eye* pointed out that Snowdon happened to be a contributor to the *Sunday Times*, coincidentally, hence his mysterious omission from the list (Ingrams 227).

attacked by a bear—(PSC; link into "Falling From Building") Signal boxes have long been points of social, political, and just plain criminal attention, including acts of violence. In the pre-WWI era, suffragettes claimed or were accused of myriad railway and signal box bombings; in the 1920s, it was the "troubles" in Northern Ireland that led to similar attacks; in the later 1920s organized labor caused considerable unrest on railway lines in attempts to bring attention to their cause; and finally, anarchists in the pre-WWII days planted numerous bombs and fired shots in and around railway buildings and trains.

During WWII, the Luftwaffe targeted Britain's railways often, especially in the early days of the conflict, and significant damage was recorded.

"Axis Café in Rosedale Road"—("The Minehead By-Election") The primary Axis powers during WWII included Germany, Italy, and Japan. There is no Rosedale Road in Minehead. The closest such road is located in Bristol, near where Cleese grew up.

This café is actually Dens Café on the corner of Crabtree Lane and Rainville Road, Fulham, London W6 (WAC T12/1,094).

– **B** –

bear—(PSC; link into "Falling From Building") Another entry into the Python bestiary, this bear is obviously a man (perhaps Gilliam) in a bear costume. Why a bear would be in a Hove signal box isn't addressed. Cf. the librarian in the gorilla suit (Ep. 10), or the equally out-of-place Pantomime Goose and Pantomime Horses (Ep. 30).

Incidentally, the Pythons asked for a polar bear costume in the original costuming requests, but obviously had to settle for a brown bear (WAC T12/1,093).

"Bed-Sitter"—(PSC; link into "How Far Can a Minister Fall?") The printed script identifies this shot as a "corner of a bed-sitter." A room that serves a dual purpose—bedroom and sitting room, and here simply used as a transition from one sketch to another. The *OED* notes that this usage is considered university slang, which might account for Python's usage. The actress in the scene is Flanagan (Eps. 11-13, 22).

"Bell and Compasses"—("Mr. Hilter") A fictitious pub already mentioned in Ep. 6 where the Indian tribe often relax after seeing a stage show.

"Bideford"—("Mr. Hilter") In Torridge, Devon, on Bideford Bay. Bideford is south and west of Minehead, across Exmoor, and would be at least a forty-mile hike as the crow flies. Following a prescribed trail would certainly be significantly longer.

As Cleese hails from Weston-Super-Mare, not far north of this area, much of this rather precise geography could be attributed to his influence.

"board meeting"—("Falling From Building") In the aftermath of Black Tuesday and the onset of the Great Depression, gallows humor flourished, not surprisingly, and one running joke became the specter of distressed, bankrupt brokers and business types leaping to their deaths from tall buildings.

"Bobby . . . Peters"—("Mr. Hilter") Both men were on the 1966 England World Cup team. Bobby Charlton (b. 1937) played for Manchester United, and Martin Peters (b. 1943) for West Ham United. Mr. Bimmler (Palin) is merely displaying his credentials as a true Englishman.

Fittingly, England had beaten Germany 4-2 in the 1966 Cup, meaning Bimmler had to pretend to be happy that his "native" country had lost.

brown mackintoshed—(PSC; "Ken Shabby") Wearing a brown "mac" overcoat. The black, opaque "rubber mac" is the outerwear of choice for Praline in the "Dead Parrot" sketch in Ep. 8, as well as "Fish Licence" in Ep. 23. This same type of brown, soiled mac will be part of the costume for the wild rapists in the first *Fliegender Zirkus* episode.

"brush"—("Ken Shabby") Another veiled punchline, delivered without retribution or even comment. Rosamund's father (Chapman) doesn't even react to the news, but then he also doesn't notice that Mr. Shabby (Palin) is a sex-starved shambles who gropes his precious "English rose" (Connie Booth) and gobs on the carpet.

budget—(PSC; "How Far Can a Minister Fall?") Yet another instance where the script's "personal" side is exposed, where text meant for the reader only (in this case, the director, Ian MacNaughton) is included: "*He thumps on the desk and he falls through the floor. (Yes Mr Director you did read that right: he fell through the floor and added a fortune to the budget).*" Moments later, the camera has to be turned upside down, as well—another challenge to the normally straight-ahead, three-camera set-up the Pythons (and most of the BBC) employed. This note from the Pythons also implies that a trap door didn't exist early in the show's run, at least in a studio space normally available to them. Perhaps this scene was eventually shot in a neighboring studio featuring a trap door, such as Ealing or even Golders Green (or one of the more elaborate TC studios). Such trap doors were fairly typical on British television stages, being holdovers from similar devices used in major theatre spaces like the Rose and the Globe and beyond. Cf. the TV stage trap door (at the Hammersmith Odeon) used to elevate Paul's Grandfather onto the soundstage in the penultimate scene of *Hard Day's Night* (1964). By Ep. 30, a trap door is obviously in place for the Merchant Banker (Cleese) to get rid of Mr. Ford (Jones) who is soliciting donations.

"by-election"—("The Minehead By-Election") Any parliamentary election held off-year, or outside of a General Election. Very often the sitting government will lose some of its seats during these off-year elections, which is why Hilter and friends may have chosen to run during this election period, hoping to pick up disaffected voters.

– C –

"cake hole"—("Mr. Hilter") A British military slang term for "mouth," and picked up by children after the war. Sellers' *Goon Show* character Grytpype-Thynne uses the term in "The Sale of Manhattan" episode (29 November 1955).

The Pythons would revisit this type of banter in Ep. 42, the "RAF Banter" sketch. This might also serve to reassure the assembled folk that these three are as English as they claim to be.

"Camber Sands"—("Police Station [Silly Voices]") Camber Sands is located in East Sussex, north of Hastings and Bexhill.

"cat's boil"—("Visitors From Coventry") This in the category of "more information than absolutely necessary," another example of a Python character treading beyond accepted social boundaries, and another character (Idle's Mr. Johnson) not seeming to notice. Perhaps Johnson's forthcoming loquacity is his own version of that same social boundary violation, since the Landlady (Jones) seems to put up quite pleasantly with his account of their trip to her home. Cf. Ep. 27 where Mrs. Conclusion (Cleese) admits casually to trying to bury her still living cat, as well as Ep. 4 where priceless art is destroyed and even eaten without guilt or recriminations.

"conservative then?"—("The Minehead By-Election") Aligning Britain's Conservative Party with the Nazis (the National Socialist party in Weimar and WWII Germany) is no surprise considering the Pythons' left-of-center politics. Even purportedly impartial historians like the eminent A.J.P. Taylor spouted similarly veiled anti-Conservative biases in works such as *Englishmen and Others* (1956).

In the 1966 elections, Somerset North retained its Conservative seat by about 2,300 votes, as would Weston-Super-Mare (where Cleese was born and raised).

In June 1970, the third-party Liberals under Jeremy Thorpe (mentioned repeatedly in Ep. 45) would lose half their seats to the Conservatives under Edward Heath in a political downturn for both Labour and the Liberals. This would have been a bit of a surprise to the Pythons, as well, as all opinion polls indicated a comfortable Labour victory in 1970.

"coons"—("The Minehead By-Election") Pejorative term for blacks, but also used to describe members of the Whig party in the United States. See *OED*. This possible (but oblique) double meaning is interesting, since the reference can work both ways. The Nazis would have been anti-black, certainly, since the blacks aren't part of the Aryan race, but also anti-Whig, which translates into anti-Liberal.

Here the offensive term is delivered in what would be considered a racist (or racialist) way, but the sting is quickly removed as the woman (Jones) admits she's "a bit mental."

couple—(PSC; "Visitors From Coventry") Perhaps this description more than any other betrays the Pythons' general take on contemporary English society and politics, and just where they might be found on the political spectrum. Words like "typical" and "bourgeois" are the giveaway terms, and are used as both clues to the production design team (for costuming purposes) as well as handy "type" descriptions for the actors themselves, hinting at expected performance, for example. The couple will prove to be as dim or bright as anyone else, however, when they, too, are unable to realize that they are interacting with three infamous and allegedly long-dead Nazis.

Mrs. Johnson is played by Gillian Phelps, according to BBC records (WAC T12/1,093). She will also appear in Ep. 25.

"Coventry"—("Visitors From Coventry") This is actually one of the few times that the Pythons carefully laid out directions from one place to another—this Coventry-to-Minehead route explained by Mr. Johnson (Idle) is spot on. Such accuracy is unusual for the troupe, who lean toward memorialized directions and history-off-the-cuff, meaning memory or factual errors can and do creep in. In the first episode, for instance, Picasso's cycling race route traced out by Eddie Waring and others does not follow such a clear path, nor does Head's proposed Kilimanjaro route in Ep. 10. Coventry lies east of Birmingham on the M6, in Warwickshire, and the distance from there to Minehead is about 132 miles.

"M5 . . . Droitwich"—The M5 runs between Bromsgrove and Worcester, and through Droitwich, in Worcestershire.

"before Bridgwater"—The A38 leaves the M5 corridor at Bridgwater, heading west to Williton, where it becomes the A39 to Minehead. There does appear to be a potentially major traffic situation where the A39 and A38 meet in the north part of Bridgwater (Bristol and Bath roads meet to become Monmouth Street).

"A372 . . . Stogumber"—Taunton is south of Bridgwater, and the A358 runs northwest out of Taunton. Both Crowcombe and Stogumber are small towns off of the A358, and don't appear to be potential traffic generators, to any great degree. The possibility that the small towns of the region empty toward the seaside on holidays and weekends may be what Mr. Johnson is talking about, or the very real possibility that penny-pinching weekenders from the north (like the Johnsons) crowd into this resort area on a regular basis.

current-affairs-type music—(PSC; "*Spectrum*—Talking About Things") Other shows of this nature from the period include *Nationwide* (1969) and *Panorama*, and given the name similarities, *Spectrum* might have been Python's direct adaptation of *Panorama* (1953-). Robin Day (1923-2000) appeared on *Panorama* between 1967 and 1979 (Ep. 1). Another connection to the Pythons is the presence on *Panorama* of Michael Barratt (b. 1928), who also appeared in *The Magic Christian* (1969) as a TV commentator, to which Cleese and Chapman contributed material (and in which both appeared). Alan Whicker also appeared in this film (cf. Ep. 27) as a TV commentator.

The music used for this section is the "Prelude to Richard III" from Walton's "Shakespeare Film Scores for Henry V, Hamlet, Richard III", with Sir William Walton conducting the Philharmonia Orchestra (WAC T12/1,093).

– D –

debs—("Upperclass Twit of the Year") "Débutantes" are young women who have just emerged into high society. These three young women are played by Beulah Hughes, Ciona Forbes, and Sue Marchbank, according to BBC paperwork (WAC T12/1,093). This may be a bit of an anachronism by 1969, as the day of the young society woman's official visit to the court seems to have been waning by the late 1950s, according to former deb Fleur Hansen:

> The real question is what's the point of it? Of course it means you're "out"—I'm not quite sure what coming out entails, except that it's okay to be seen at a night-club, although that's a doubtful advantage, too. Of course it gives point to the season. I suppose the season of dances and dreary all-female tea parties will go on. But without being presented at court it won't be as exciting, and it is exciting, now there won't be any anymore. I know debs are supposed to be silly and pam-

pered and so on, but to be invited by the Lord Chamberlain to curtsy alone to the Queen of England, the latest of a line of monarchs going back for over a thousand years is an invitation I have no hesitation in saying I was deeply honored to accept. (*Eyewitness 1950-59*, "Life in the Fifties")

– E –

"Earth's crust"—("How Far Can a Minister Fall?") Perhaps just a literal depiction of the "fall" of various political parties or politicians. In the Pythons' lifetimes, administrations and coalitions had fallen from time to time, including Churchill's rousting in the 1945 General Election, Macmillan's landslide election in 1959 (a majority of more than 100 seats), the rather sound thrashing that the Conservatives later took from Labour in 1964, and then Harold Wilson's Labour government was about to be voted out in the June 1970 elections in a surprise turnabout of political fortunes. Wage controls, the devaluation of the pound, the ever-diminishing British influence overseas, the embarrassment of/in Suez and Rhodesia, and rising taxes were all precursors to this fall, rendering the Pythons somewhat prescient in their satire.

All things considered, however, the stiff minister (Chapman) handles the situation surprisingly well, another example of the Pythons attacking, bloodying, but then recovering their target. Over and over again the Pythons will send up characters and points of view and, with perhaps the exception of actual women and the upper-class (in this episode, especially), they eventually re-embrace those characters. See Larsen, chapter 6.

This may also be directly referencing the precipitous fall of John Profumo (Ep. 2), who toppled from the highest levels of government as a Cabinet member to actually cleaning toilets at an East London charity house. See notes to Ep. 2 for more on the scandal.

"eating . . . Picadilly line"—("Mr. Hilter") A mishmash of Englishness which Himmler recites rather badly. "Fish and chips" are of course a noted English food; a "toad in the hole" is sausage baked in a batter, as well as a name for at least two children's games; "Dundee cakes" are rich fruit cakes covered with split almonds; "Piccadilly" is the well-known London tourist mecca, where such food items could have been bought and consumed.

This could be a play on the WWII-era practice (by American POWs, often) of identifying an enemy plant via his knowledge of American cultural trivia, specifically sports figures and World Series winners.

"Elsmore, Mrs."—(link out of "Ken Shabby") Philip Elsmore (b. 1937) is an English actor, born about the same time as the Pythons, in Worcestershire. Elsmore performed many linking and continuity duties for ABC and then Thames TV during this period. In 1969 Elsmore was narrating for *Two in Clover*.

The following narrated name, "Doug," is accompanied by a photo of a large sow, a still also used in Ep. 6. The inclusion of the sow photo may reflect back on Elsmore, as *Two in Clover* was a comedy set on a farm, where two city boys try and make it in rural life (read: lots of manure, farm machinery, and livestock jokes).

English rose—(PSC; "Ken Shabby") The phrase appears in describing the pink-skinned, blonde-haired English beauty as early as 1902 (according to the *OED*). Ironically, this "English rose" is portrayed here by the American Connie (or Constance) Booth, who earlier played the "rebel maid" in Ep. 9, the "Lumberjack" sketch. Booth and Cleese were married 1968-1978.

Episode 12—Recorded on 12 December 1969, and broadcast on 4 January 1970. In the WAC records, the dates for the entire episode (broadcast demands, costume requirements, etc.) are given as 4 January 1969, not 4 January 1970, a typo that seems to have gone unnoticed.

Also, official references (meaning beyond the walls of the BBC) to the program seem to have begun as early as January 1970 (when this episode aired), when an Ulster Unionist MP, Rafton Pounder, asked for a copy of a *Flying Circus* script so that he could use portions of it in his debate on accountants in the House later in January. The BBC sent him the copy straight away, though it's not indicated in the WAC files the precise episode requested (WAC T12/1,242). More than likely, however, the description of the dull life of a Chartered Accountant and efforts to "save" same in Ep. 10, "Vocational Guidance Counsellor," was the sketch remembered by the MP.

"extraordinary personal magnetism"—(link out of "Ken Shabby") This moment launches a soap opera–type narrative that had previously been employed by the Goons in the "Silent Bugler" episode (23 February 1958). In a "the show so far" scenario, a Goon character rehearses what has gone before (none of which, of course, actually did go before):

> Narrator (Sellers): Helen Lovejoy, beautiful heiress to the Halibut millions, has been jilted at the altar by Villian de Paprikon, son of Louis the XIV. Peter, Villian's Eton boating friend, has heard this, but being in Tibet has embarrassed Mary, his fiancée, who being the only cousin of Sir Ray Ellington has passed the title on to Baron Geldray, also heir to the Halibut millions. Now read on . . .

These "show so far" moments often have little or nothing to do with the show at all, for both the Goons and the Pythons. In Ep. 33, however, the "show so far" moment will be accurate, up to and including the assault by giant cartoon hammer of the narrator (Jones).

"extraordinary way"—("Vox Pops" link into "Upperclass Twit of the Year") In other episodes where they appear, these Upperclass Twits often have to be subtitled, their speech is so affected. They are treated as Other by the Pythons, as much as actual foreigners, and their speech (and affectations) is often the giveaway. See *MPSERD*, chapter 6.

– F –

"Fiver?"—("Falling From Building") There is a slight pause here as the line of impropriety is considered, then quickly crossed. Up to this point, the behavior has been within expected—if cynical—parameters, but with the wager on someone's death, the threshold into black humor is broached. The "rooting" to follow just ups the ante. Cf. a similar pause during the journey between normalcy and black comedy in Ep. 26, when the character (Cleese, again) is considering whether or not he should eat his recently deceased mother.

"Frampton Cottrell"—("Visitors From Coventry") Actually spelled "Frampton Cotterell," this village lies northeast of Bristol.

"frothing and falling"—("*Spectrum*—Talking About Things") This paragraph owes much to the Modernist writers Gertrude Stein and Virginia Woolf, as well as Lewis Carroll, where words aren't chosen for meaning, necessarily, but for sound, for how well they fit in with the previous word and the following word and the entire sentence. The Pythons' willingness to create nonce and nonsense words ("zalling" and, later, "Dibbingley") and stream-of-consciousness sentences and paragraphs is a direct reflection of the Modernist literature and even art they'd grown up reading and experiencing.

"Führer"—("Mr. Hilter") Typical title and respectful means of address for Hitler, especially after he became Chancellor of Germany in 1934. It means "leader," and is the less formal version of the official *Führer und Reichskanzler* (*OED*).

Later, Bimmler will call Hilter "Führer cat," mimicking the "Mod"-speak heard in swinging London and the "London hipster" films of the 1960s. His later "Soon baby" is another nod to the younger generation.

"fun in Stalingrad"—("Mr. Hilter") Referring to the German army's miserable siege of Stalingrad (now Volgograd) which lasted seven months in 1942-1943 and, thanks to the tenacity of the Russian people and the especially harsh winter, turned the tide of war against the Nazis. Almost two million people (military and civilian) are believed to have lost their lives during the battle.

– G –

"Gervaise . . . basket"—("Upperclass Twit of the Year") The name Gervaise Brook-Hampster might be an oblique reference to Tim Brooke-Taylor, who worked with various Pythons on *At Last the 1948 Show* (1967), *Marty* (1967), and *How to Irritate People* (1968).

"gobbed"—("Ken Shabby") Slang term. To gob is to spit a clump of slimy substance—in this case, probably phlegm. In the earlier appearance of the Shabby-like Mr. Cook (also Palin) in Ep. 9, it was the goat that "did a bundle" on the carpet.

"God himself is made of"—("How Far Can a Minister Fall?") Perhaps a swipe at the "enthusiastic" reporting being provided by American (and British) television news personalities as the Apollo 11 lunar mission results were discussed—including the importance of soil samples from the Moon's surface providing clues to the origins of not only the Moon, but the Earth, Solar System, and even the universe. (The BBC had created and broadcast some twenty-seven hours of coverage over the ten-day period in July 1969.) The cover of the 28 July 1969 Late London Edition of *The Times* carries a story entitled "Rocks of Moon a Puzzle," and the subject was covered numerous times in other period newspapers, television reports, editorial pieces, and cartoon/comic panels. (See the British Cartoon Archive as well.)

It also looks as though Third Robert (Cleese) is made up to appear to be upside down, just as the Minister (Chapman) was earlier.

goes back to wrestling with bear—(PSC; link into "Falling From Building") Cf. the film *HG* where a hairy beast reaches in to the "Book of the Film" section to snatch away the maiden's hand.

Elizabethan crowds enjoyed (and officials tolerated) bull- and bearbaiting, public performances which often outdrew even the most significant plays of the period, and were performed in "bear gardens." Producer Hounslowe even seems to indicate that he might have made more profits from such staged events than from producing plays (Gurr).

"going to die"—("Mr. Hilter") This is precisely the same structure we saw when the façade dropped completely in Ep. 4, the "Secret Service Dentists" sketch.

"Goswell Road"—("Falling From Building") North of the Thames in London, between Farrington and City roads. High-rise buildings dot the road.

gramophone—(PSC; "The Minehead By-Election") Alluding to the manufactured crowds, enthusiasm, and support for the Nazi party in Germany prior to and even during the war. The 1934 Nazi Party Congress, for example, was a staged, theatrical event designed to impress and embolden Germans (as seen in Leni Riefenstahl's *Triumph of the Will* [1935]), and strike fear and respect in the rest of the world.

The music being played is the German national anthem "Deutschland Uber Alles," this specific recording by the Band of Grenadier Guards, and conducted by Harris (WAC T12/1,093).

"gremlins"—("How Far Can a Minister Fall?") According to the *OED*, this was originally an RAF term, which might explain the minister's (Chapman) usage as well as his character's military background.

– H –

"Hardacre"—("*Spectrum*—Talking About Things") Paul H. Hardacre is the author of *The Royalists During the Puritan Revolution* (1956).

"'Hearts of Oak'-type music"—("Ken Shabby") Music written by William Boyce (1711-1779), with lyrics by renowned actor David Garrick (1716-1779) in 1759. The song is a chest-thumping English naval hymn:

> Come cheer up, my lads! 'tis to glory we steer,
> To add something more to this wonderful year;
> To honour we call you, not press you like slaves,
> For who are so free as the sons of the waves?
>
> Heart of oak are our ships, heart of oak are our men;
> We always are ready, steady, boys, steady!
> We'll fight and we'll conquer again and again. . . .
> (contemplator.com/folk2/heartoak.html)

The "hearts of oak" phrase was adapted from a Rabelais work, *Gargantua and Pantagruel* (1548).

The music actually used for this transition is "The Rose"—Selection Myddleton, by the Band of Grenadier Guards, conducted by Harris (WAC T12/1,093).

"Henley"—("Upperclass Twit of the Year") On the Thames in South Oxfordshire (Oxfordshire). Henley also boasts Stonor Park, the ancestral home of Lord and Lady Camoys and the Stonor family for more than 800 years, and to whom the Python's may have been referring when creating the Nigel Incubator-Jones character.

The Goons had already employed this seemingly out-of-place rhyming word in their "Junk Affair" episode (7 October 1957), when Milligan's character says: "See you later, incubator."

"Hilter"—("Mr. Hilter") By simply rearranging/replacing letters in their names (Hilter, Bimmler, and Ron Vibbentrop) these characters are able to live and work openly (even dressed as Nazis) in North Minehead without fear of detection.

This is not unlike the Elizabethan stage practice of breech roles or the donning of flimsy disguises that rendered the character completely unrecognizable, even to lovers, spouses, and close family members. In those cases, the disguise was often used to elicit more emotionally honest responses from others in the play, who felt more free to speak, etc. Cf. Benedick's disguise (and the soothsaying results) as he discusses himself with Beatrice in *Much Ado*. Actually, the Nazis in this sketch also tend to reveal more about themselves even in disguise, though the rather dim townspeople never seem to quite catch on. The Rustic on the street, however, doesn't seem to be taken in, nor are the children terribly impressed. The Conservative Vox Pops responders take to the message, of course.

Lastly, and most sinister, former Nazis determined to escape war crimes tribunals changed their names and appearances, and eventually fled Europe after the war. None of the biggest names in the Nazi party made it to any kind of postwar freedom, of course, but infamous others—including former doctors Josef Mengele (who later died in Brazil) and Aribert Heim, who disappeared into hiding in 1962, and Eichmann's former aide Alois Brunner—lived (or are living) long lives in concealed freedom.

"Hitler . . . Ribbentrop"—("Mr. Hilter") Adolf Hitler (1889-1945) was, of course, the leader of the Third Reich during the reign of the National Socialist Party in Germany (1933-1945). Hitler would commit suicide in a bunker in 1945 as the Russians closed in on Berlin.

Heinrich Himmler (1900-1945) was Hitler's right hand, especially during the war, leading all Nazi police forces, including the feared SS. Himmler would commit suicide the night before his Nuremberg trial was set to begin.

Joachim Von Ribbentrop (1893-1946) was a pseudo-aristocrat and Nazi foreign delegate who orchestrated the German-Soviet Nonaggression Pact of 1939, providing the way for the attack on Poland in September 1939. He was foreign minister 1938-1945, and was hanged as a war criminal after Nuremberg.

The *Private Eye* writers had created an exclusive in their 3 January 1969 issue, leading with the headline: "Hitler Arrested in Torquay." The article goes on to say that Hitler has been living in this sleepy resort town since the end of the war, that his neighbors just think he's a nice foreigner, and that both Goebbels and Mussolini were visiting friends (Ingrams 212).

Hitler ranting in German on a balcony—(PSC; "Mr. Hilter") The physical affectations, and especially the crossing of the arms and slight hunch, are borrowed from the surviving film footage of Hitler's address given at the Sportpalast in 1938, where he didn't have a podium to lean on or stand behind.

"Hove"—(link into "Falling From Building") Seaside town just west of the resort town Brighton, both in Sussex.

"Hunt Ball Photograph"—("Upperclass Twit of the Year") A hunt ball is a ball given by those organizing a fox hunt. The photograph would be the traditional pre- and/or post-hunt posing for cameras. The photo with the young ladies would have been one destined for a Kensington reader's newspaper society page.

"Hurlingham Park"—("Upperclass Twit of the Year") In the Greater London area (Fulham) on Hurlingham Road, SW6. Much of Eps. 11 and 12 were shot within a few square miles of this part of greater London. The park does feature a large grassy area, as well as a track, as depicted in the episode. The park is about six miles southeast of BBC TV Centre, and is one of the few times that a specific location is both named in the episode and then actually used as a setting.

In several of the camera angles facing northeast, the looming Battersea Power Station can be seen over the houses, well in the distance. The interior of the power station will be used for the "Find the Fish" sketch location in *Meaning of Life* (1983).

– I –

"Ilfracombe and Barnstaple"—("Mr. Hilter") Barnstaple is at the junction of the A39 and A361, and Ilfracombe is north of Barnstaple, at the mouth of the Bristol Channel. Both are in Devon.

in a very deep voice—("Police Station [Silly Voices]") This is much like the "Buying a Bed" sketch in Ep. 8, where the young couple have to speak and even listen differently, depending on the salesman they are confronting.

All these characters (Mr. Lambert, Mr. Verity et al.) have learned to communicate among themselves, leaving only the Man to get up to speed, like the audience. The importance (and, often, difficulty) of communication in *FC* is a significant trope. In Ep. 14, the Minister delivers his answer in his "normal voice, and then in a kind of silly, high-pitched whine." Other characters only speak parts of words, so that only in a group can they utter complete sentences; one character speaks in anagrams; and one insults the listener with every other sentence, etc. In a nicely visual twist on the trope, in Ep. 30, gestures are offered to denote "pauses in televised talk."

Incidentally, the poet T.S. Eliot titled the first two sections of his epic modernist poem *The Waste Land* "He Do the Police in Different Voices," a quote from Dickens' *Our Mutual Friend* (1864-1865).

Iron Cross—(PSC; "Mr. Hilter") Prussian military award instituted in 1813, and reinvigorated in 1939 by Hitler. Von Ribbentrop received his Iron Cross for service in WWI, as did Hitler.

– J –

"Johnson"—("Falling From Building") A "Johnson" may have been the man who actually jumped from the board meeting earlier, rather than Parkinson. The First Man (Idle) has already bet that Parkinson would jump next, while Second Man (Cleese) bets against Parkinson. They then cheer for or against "Parky," and even after the letter writer falls, and Second Man celebrates (that it's Parkinson), Second Man calls out, "Johnson!"

– K –

"Kensington and Weybridge"—("Upperclass Twit of the Year") Part of Greater London, Kensington lies west of London, and is home to Kensington Palace, which still acts as a private residence for royals. Kensington and Chelsea have been home to kings, queens, royalty of all kinds, and "people of quality and note" since at least the fifteenth century, and remained the home of the fashionable upper class into the Pythons' era. Weybridge is in Surrey, directly south of Heathrow Airport, and is home to the annual Royal Regatta.

"Kicking the Beggar"—("Upperclass Twit of the Year") A game that the more socialist-minded might attribute characteristically to more conservative folk. In other words, the monied upper class ignoring or even harming the poor, or anyone outside of their class.

"Know what I mean . . . "—("Ken Shabby") In this case, the character of the father (Chapman) does not seem to appreciate Shabby's intentions. This is another example of a sketch wherein the characters can't see (or refuse to see) the absurdity of the situation, much like in an upcoming episode (Ep. 14), where the Minister (also Chapman) is cross-dressed, and a patch of liquid is allowed to "argue the case against the government." Shabby (Palin) will also use very clear sexual euphemisms throughout, much like the "Nudge, Nudge" man in Ep. 3, but Rosamund's father will miss those, as well.

– L –

"Lady . . . Smith"—("Upperclass Twit of the Year") Cf. Ep. 18, where the names of candidates for the various parties are recited including: "Tarquin Fin-tim-lin-bin-whin-bim-lin-bus-stop-F'tang-F'tang-Olé-Biscuitbarrel." Actual names obviously generated this reference, names from the peerage (like Eustace Gervais Tennyson-d'Eyncourt, and Kenneth Oliver Musgrave St. John et al.) that also graced the society pages during this period.

"lampshade time"—("Mr. Hilter") Probably a euphemism for death, meaning to cover or diffuse the light (life). Sounds like a borrowing from a pulp fiction novel, perhaps. For Tex Avery, a lampshade on the head (and a bulb in the mouth) of the temporarily stunned Wolf is used as a blackout gag, a payoff before the next set-up (see *Red Hot Riding Hood*, 1942). Noting the Pythons' awareness and use of cartoon elements (and Hitler's admitted fondness for Mickey Mouse cartoons, as well), this is a possible, glancing referent.

Lancet—(link out of "Ken Shabby") Significant British medical journal founded in 1823. The Gumby Brain Specialist (Cleese) is looking in vain for his copy of *The Lancet* in Ep. 32.

"Leeds University"—("*Spectrum*—Talking About Things") Located in Leeds, Yorkshire, the university is one of the "new" schools, and was officially established in 1904.

"leg-before-wicket"—("Mr. Hilter") Cricket terminology. The batsman can defend the wicket with his leg or any part of his body, but can also be dismissed for same for not using his bat. The French guard (Cleese) who taunts Arthur and his knights in *HG* also disparagingly uses this phrase to taunt the "silly English 'kuh-niggets'."

"Local Government Bill"—("How Far Can a Minister Fall?") The extreme localization indicated here was part of the reason that the Conservatives were in trouble in 1962 as they approached defeat by Labour in 1964, a defeat that would end thirteen years of Tory rule. The international reputation and trading power of Britain had suffered under the Conservative government, and the former colony, the United States, had risen to superpower status in the interim; Britain found itself having to consult with the United States before embarking on any kind of significant monetary or military endeavor, which was quite galling to many (*Eyewitness 1950-59*).

London-Brighton train journey—(PSC; link out of "*Spectrum*—Talking About Things") The signal box where the episode began near Hove is near Brighton. There is no indication in the WAC records for this episode that this "stock film" was hired, so it may actually have been shot by BBC/Python personnel on the trip to Brighton.

Additionally, this film clip is reminiscent of the short live-action section of George Dunning's *Yellow Submarine* (1968), where filmed images and still photos are manipulated to appear as if the camera is racing through/over them.

– M –

"Mainwaring"—("Upperclass Twit of the Year") Captain George J. Mainwaring was the lead character in the popular television show *Dad's Army* (1968-1977). The show was a fictional treatment of a small seaside town (not unlike Minehead) and its WWII Home Guard unit, the local voluntary militia.

Many of the names chosen for the "Upperclass Twit" sketch are straight from the list of the most gentrified families in the UK. There are currently more than sixty "Mainwaring" entries at peerage.com, for example, as well as myriad families named "Brooke," "Smith" and "Smythe," "Harris," "Jones," and "St. John."

"McGoering"—("Mr. Hilter") Here Hermann Goering is cast as a Scotsman. The actual Goering (b. 1893) committed suicide at Nuremberg in 1946, and had been the rather flamboyant head of the Luftwaffe (Nazi air forces) during the war.

"Meinhead" ("The Minehead By-Election") Note the Germanic spelling of the first syllable, which now connotes possession ("my"), and probably meant to refer to Hitler's prewar magnum opus, *Mein Kampf* (1925).

"Minehead, Somerset"—("Visitors From Coventry") On the Bristol Channel, Minehead's principal industry is, not coincidentally, tourism.

"Mr. and Mrs. Phillips"—("Visitors From Coventry") Gilliam plays Mr. Phillips, and Connie Booth plays Mrs. Phillips.

"Mr. Farquar's"—(link out of "Ken Shabby") At this point, a still from *The Phantom of the Opera* (1925; Lon Chaney) appears. The same still was used in Ep. 6. Gilliam used a number of photos and cutouts over and over again, whether for familiarity or just time considerations. The balance of the narration reads like an update to a long-running soap opera.

– N –

The Naked Ant—(PSC; captions for "Signalbox" link into "Falling From Building") Cf. Desmond Morris'

1967 book *The Naked Ape*, a poster of which is seen in Ep. 4 in the bookshop. See notes to Ep. 4. Also, the allusion to the openly gay Quentin Crisp's 1968 autobiography *The Naked Civil Servant* can't be overlooked, especially when the "poncing" campiness of Python's homosexual or effeminate characters are discussed. See David Unction (Chapman) in Ep. 10 for such behavior.

Napoleon—(link out of "Ken Shabby") This is a black and white portrait of Napoleon. It is a photocopy of "The Emperor" by Meissomer, and was borrowed from *The Life of Napoleon Bonaparte* by S. Baring-Gould (Methuen & Co., First Edition 1896, Second Edition 1908—Abridged), according to BBC archives (WAC T12/1,093).

"National Bocialist"—("The Minehead By-Election") Again, a single letter replaced or misplaced and the meaning is lost completely. In Idle's harangue as a potential tourist in Ep. 31 he also replaces the letter [c] with [b], as in "Hotel Bontinental," "bolor supplements," and the eventually censored "silly bunt."

"Nigel . . . stockbroker"—("Upperclass Twit of the Year") These first three competitors—Simon, Nigel, and Gervaise—also all share the seeming inability to form and keep normal familial/fraternal relationships. Simon's spouse is a piece of furniture, Nigel has a tree for a best friend, and Gervaise acts as a waste receptacle for his father.

If there is a modicum of scorn meted out by the Pythons, it's often doled out along class lines, with the upper crust male getting the lion's share. This could simply be a matter of sour grapes, as none of the Pythons came from anything but working-class backgrounds, though each would have rubbed shoulders (or noses) with such upper-class types at Cambridge and Oxford.

Nixon—(PSC; "Vox Pops" link out of "Police Station [Silly Voices]") Perhaps thanks to Gilliam's American background, Nixon appears several times, and may have been alluded to earlier as a Nazi ("Dickie old chum"). Also, Nixon's international presence during his term as vice president to Eisenhower put him in the British news (and the political cartoons) of the period regularly.

"Nürnberg"—("Mr. Hilter") City where the postwar Nazi war crimes trials were held. Himmler didn't actually make it to the trials, having committed suicide (by poison) after falling from Hitler's grace as the war wound down. Von Ribbentrop was found guilty on all four charges brought against him, and was sentenced to death. He was hanged soon thereafter.

– O –

"old men"—("How Far Can a Minister Fall?") Likely a swipe at the Conservative Party, seen as the stodgy party of the status quo, representing the landed, monied, titled interests, etc. This treatment also indicates that such politicians have trouble functioning without carefully written scripts, and that minor technical difficulties can prevent the delivery of the party message. (See the printed script version of Ep. 38 for a rehearsed, choreographed party political broadcast.) Labour's Harold Wilson was in his late forties when he took office in 1964; Edward Heath is fifty-four when he assumes the post in 1970. Harold Macmillan was the nearly-retirement-age of sixty-three when he took office in 1957, and wouldn't retire until he was sixty-nine. The Pythons were part of the rebellious postwar generation, of course, all between about twenty-four and thirty-one years old in 1970, so anyone over forty must have seemed quite ancient and out of touch.

"Oliver . . . twit"—("Upperclass Twit of the Year") "Harrow" is a public (independent) school attended by such notables as Robert Peel, Henry John Temple (Lord Palmerston), Richard Brinsley Sheridan, Lord Byron, John Galsworthy, Lord Shaftesbury, and Winston Churchill. Rather than simply producing Conservative graduates, Harrow was considered to be a nursery for the cultured elite, as indicated by the list above.

"The Guards" refers to the Queen's Household Cavalry Mounted Regiment (Life Guards, Blues and Royals), and this progression—from a school like Harrow or Eton through the Guards and into country life retirement—was the chosen path for many aristocratic young men. This ideal progression is embodied in Oliver here, and he is characterized as the "outstanding twit" of the year.

As for "Mollusc," there is a mollusc documentary acted out in Ep. 32.

"Oxfam"—(link out of "Ken Shabby") *OED*: "An organization for the distribution of food, funds, etc., in disaster areas and to poor countries."

– P –

"Pagoda"—(link out of "Ken Shabby") Asian temple or spiritual building.

"Parkhurst"—("Police Station [Silly Voices]") Parkhurst Prison is located in Parkhurst on the Isle of Wight.

"Parkinson"—("Falling From Building") Perhaps an allusion to noted British television presenter Michael Parkinson (b. 1935). Parkinson had also appeared on

World in Action (1963), *Cinema* (1964), and *The Morecambe & Wise Show* (1968).

"Party Political Broadcast"—("How Far Can a Minister Fall?") Party political broadcasts involve television (and/or radio) airtime allotted to the major parties prior to elections. The "Wood Party" probably wouldn't have qualified for the time, though may be connected to other "wooden" characters like Arthur Tree and his guests (Ep. 10), David Hemmings (Ep. 8), and certainly the stuffy old Conservatives like former PM Macmillan and his successor, Alec Douglas-Home, who was sixty when he became PM. Other parties were extant but generally not allowed TV time (inclusion of parties was based on a certain level of performance at previous elections, number of seats contested and won, etc.). Participating parties have included Whigs, Workers (socialist), Conservatives (Tory origins), Labour, Liberal and Social Democrats, etc.

Conservative, Labour, and Liberal would have been the three parties seen and heard on most party political broadcasts during the Pythons' lives, but in the 1966 General Election the increasing political spectrum in Britain was acknowledged. Broadcasts including the Communist, Scottish National, and Plaid Cymru (Wales) parties were offered.

"Peterborough, Lincolnshire"—("Mr. Hilter") The real Von Ribbentrop actually spent some time in Canada prior to WWI (1910-1914), selling wine. Ron Vibbentrop is obviously flustered, since Peterborough is actually in Cambridgeshire, not Lincolnshire.

"piledriver"—("Upperclass Twit of the Year") *OED*: "A very strong or powerful hit, stroke, kick, etc., in various games; something of great strength or power." It has also become known as a professional wrestling move, which may be more apropos in this setting.

"polecat"—("Ken Shabby") A weasel, essentially. Playwright John Gay also speaks of killing polecats in his *What d'ye call it* (1714).

"pluck"—("Upperclass Twit of the Year") *OED*: "The heart as the seat of courage; courage, boldness, spirit; determination not to yield but to keep up the fight in the face of danger or difficulty." This term is often heard when the character of the (mostly common) British citizenry is being lauded, especially as they conducted themselves during the war years.

– R –

"racialist"—("The Minehead By-Election") Cf. the Gumby (Cleese) in Ep. 5 who rails against foreigners and any Englishman who might leave the country, and who also swore he wasn't a "racialist." Conservative MP Enoch Powell had made similar claims in his infamous "Rivers of Blood" speech, also discussed in the notes for Ep. 5.

Coincidentally, the British fascist leader Sir Oswald Moseley (1896-1980) was also active during this period, having returned from self-imposed exile in France to contest Kensington North in 1959 and 1966, hoping to capitalize on the smoldering sentiments after the race riots in Notting Hill. He was unsuccessful in both races.

"rallies"—("The Minehead By-Election") A reference to the National Socialist rallies and party congresses where hundreds of thousands of Germans celebrated their new leader, Hitler. These gatherings began as early as 1921, when Hitler rose to power in the party and scores or hundreds would gather, and would culminate, in the early years, at enormous rallies in places like Nuremberg (1927). Leni Riefenstahl's 1934 film *Triomph den Willen* "documents" the 1934 Nazi Party Congress in Nuremberg.

The Pythons create an audience for Hilter and friends out of several children, a Rustic (Jones), and bemused onlookers. This balcony scene was staged at a building near the corner of Greswell Street and Stevenage Road, just across from the Fulham FC grounds (WAC T12/1.094). This is just around the corner from the "Axis Café" location seen in a previous shot.

rapid montage—(PSC; link out of "How Far Can a Minister Fall?") The fact that many of these characters hail from earlier episodes illustrates the careful preparation not only each episode but the entire series demanded. It means that they were planning the end of Ep. 12 much earlier. These characters are, in order of appearance: Second Robert (Idle), Third Robert (Cleese), Switchman (Jones), Bear (who shakes his head), Second Sergeant (Chapman, singing), Sergeant (Cleese, low register), Pepperpot (Idle), Stockbroker (Cleese), Gumby (Jones), Cassowary (animated), Gumby (Jones again, but no "no"), Fairy (Idle), City Gent (Chapman), Pepperpot (Jones), Gumby (Palin), Twit (Cleese, who struggles to say "no"), Ron Vibbentrop (Chapman), Hilter (Cleese) and Bimmler (Palin), an animated right whale, Madd (Chapman's foaming-mouth City Gent), and finally the *Spectrum* Presenter (Palin).

This last character is crushed by the cartoony sixteen-ton weight created by the BBC Property department for the show. Palin's head clearly breaks the top of the primarily Styrofoam prop, and a request to have the prop fixed can be found in the archival material. The prop will be broken again on 2 July 1970, while taping portions of Ep. 15, though, curiously, the scene where the

weight is used (and clearly again broken) won't appear until Ep. 16, as a "Vox Pops" insert.

"Reginald"—("Mr. Hilter") So his assumed name is Reginald Bimmler, and below we see that Hitler is actually Richard (or Dick) Hilter. It shouldn't be surprising that Python would choose these names—Reginald and Dickie—for their Nazis' pseudonyms. The "Reginald" is certainly an allusion to Reginald Maudling, the much-lampooned Tory MP and Cabinet member. His sometimes arch-Conservatism made him a Python target, of course. Maudling's "naughty bits" are pointed out in Ep. 22, for instance.

The "Dickie" can be none other than Richard Nixon, then president of the United States and consistent target of Britain's Left-leaning press and socialist government members. Nixon is also mentioned or depicted a number of times throughout *FC*, including later in this same episode during a Vox Pops section. Nixon had figured prominently in the international public eye since the early 1950s, when he served as Dwight Eisenhower's vice president (1953-1961), traveling widely throughout the world.

"Rosamund"—("Ken Shabby") Rosamund the Fair (de Clifford), 1140-1176, was Henry II's mistress/concubine whom the king kept safely hidden away in a garden bower in Woodstock, Oxfordshire, near Blenheim Palace. The Pythons describe their Rosamund as an "English rose" (meaning fair-skinned and attractive), and period descriptions of the historical Rosamund agree: "A sweeter creature in this world / Could prince never embrace" (see Somerville). Artists Rosetti and Waterhouse painted famous images of Rosamund in 1861 and c. 1905, respectively. (See Drabble's *Oxford Companion to English Literature* 846.)

Taken together, these descriptions of Fair Rosamund and the romantic historical and royal atmosphere of the story make the presence of Ken Shabby—and his "haven't had it for weeks" intentions—all the more incongruous.

"Rt. Hon. Lambert Warbeck"—(PSC; "How Far Can a Minister Fall?") The title "Rt. Hon." is described in the *OED*: "Right Honourable is applied to peers below the rank of Marquess, to Privy Councillors, and to certain civil functionaries, as the Lord-Mayors of London, York, and Belfast, and the Lord Provosts of Edinburgh and Glasgow; sometimes, also, in courtesy, to the sons and daughters of peers holding courtesy titles."

Here it's the titled authority figure Python renders ridiculous. The sight of a proper, Conservative gentleman hanging upside down on national television sends up not only the Tories but the entire political process. In the 1951 party political broadcast, Lord Samuel (Labour) delivered a wooden, made-for-radio address that ran boring and long and may have helped inspire this sketch. The 1955 party political broadcasts saw gaffes that fit the new medium of television to a tee: the Conservative candidate (Harold Macmillan) fumbled through prop malfunctions and blown lines; the Labour candidate (Clement Attlee) interviewed much shorter than expected, flustering his interviewer.

As to the name "Lambert Warbeck," in 1491 Perkin Warbeck, a Flemish merchant, infamously posed as a prince of the House of York (as Richard, the younger son of Edward IV), and claimed the English throne held by Henry VII. Warbeck was eventually executed in 1497. (A previous claimant to the same throne, coincidentally, had been one "Lambert Simnel." He was deposed and—considered harmless—allowed to work for the king.) Python's use of the name might be a subtle comment on the "pretender" political parties vying for airtime and parliamentary seats during the late 1960s and early 1970s. "Lambert" was also the name of the afflicted mattress salesman in Ep. 4, also played by Chapman.

"running sores"—("Mr. Hilter") Himmler here is not unlike the cat whose boil was being attended to as the sketch began. There is no record of Himmler having suffered any physical malady that might keep him from military service; in fact he briefly served in a Bavarian regiment at the end of WWI.

As alleged WWII Nazi war criminals were tracked down and brought to justice many years after the war ended, one of the consistent (and pitiful, but not pitiable) defenses espoused by many was their unfitness for trial, their infirmity due to advanced age.

– S –

"sap"—(link out of "Ken Shabby") Generally considered a pejorative term, the *OED* reports that in Eton College slang a "sap" is one who studies a great deal. This is another script-only comment, and wouldn't have been available to the viewers, and reads:

> *"Cut to strange PHOTO CAPTION SEQUENCE (to be worked out with Terry 'the sap' Gilliam) (if he can find the time)."*

The seeming impatience and frustration implied in the commentary may be attributable to the fact that this piece would have to have been created in addition to Gilliam's normal contributions (interstitial animations), and his time and energies (and patience) may have been stretched thin.

"Shabby, Ken"—("Ken Shabby") This character seems an adaptation of an earlier Palin character appearing

in Ep. 9, Mr. Cook, whose goat fouls the carpet, and looks forward to the street dwellers from *"Up Your Pavement"* in Ep. 42. Shabby is the lower-class figure thrust into upper-class society, and is reminiscent of G.B. Shaw's *Pygmalion* scenario, and especially including Eliza's father, whom Shaw describes as

> an elderly but vigorous dustman, clad in the costume of his profession, including a hat with a back brim covering his neck and shoulders. He has well marked and rather interesting features, and seems *equally free from fear and conscience*. He has a remarkably expressive voice, the result of a habit of giving vent to his feelings without reserve. His present pose is that of wounded honor and stern resolution. (2.196-99; italics added)

Shabby is just as out of place in fair Rosamund's world as Alfred is in Higgins'. These clashes of culture (ever more apparent in a class society like Britain's) are utilized to humorous ends throughout *FC*. See the entry for "Rosamund" above. G.B. Shaw (played by Palin) will be later featured in Ep. 41, the "Poetry Reading (Ants)" sketch, fending off the verbal barbs of both Whistler (Cleese) and Wilde (Chapman).

signalbox—("Signalbox" link into "Falling From Building") Small buildings where railroad switching levers are located. Trainspotters and locomotive enthusiasts in general would (and still do) take/swap/discuss photographs of such boxes, and surviving photos of Somerset-area boxes look remarkably like the box depicted in this episode. Most of these boxes were built by Saxby & Farmer.

The BBC released *Engines Must Not Enter the Potato Siding* in 1969, a collection of short railway films including *Signal Man*, which looked at life and work at "one of the loneliest and busiest jobs on the railway line," and which also happens to be set in Northern England. (Also, the Goons prominently feature the Pevensey Bay signal box in "The Pevensey Bay Disaster" [3 April 1956], where a bomb is being planted to derail the Hastings Flyer.)

The signal box in Minehead had been removed by British Rail in 1966, and the next year would see the closing of the Crowcombe signal box. These closings and consolidations—which prefaced a great deal of local consternation, given the number of rail enthusiasts—may account for the inclusion of this somewhat bizarre section in *FC*.

There are today signal box web pages across the Internet, dedicated entirely to the signal boxes, past and present, of particular regional railways in the UK.

"Simon . . . lamp"—("Upperclass Twit of the Year") This character's name sounds like a Cleese creation, much like his "Bunn, Wackett, Buzzard, Stubble and Boot" football line from pre-Python days. Simon Harris was a character (a doctor) on the American daytime drama *The Doctors* (1963-1982), which may have been known by at least Cleese from his work in NYC; Gilliam, an American; and perhaps even Chapman, a doctor himself. Both Cleese and Chapman wrote for a doctor television show in 1969, as well. The "Simon Harris" character appeared in 1968. The "zinc" reference may qualify that chemical element as Python's favorite, already mentioned in Eps. 2, 3, and 6.

The hyphenated or just plain silly name tropes are also seen in English literary tradition, including "Catsmeat Potter-Pirbright" and "Gussie Fink-Nottle" in Wodehouse's *The Code of the Woosters* (1938). The Pythons' immediate comedy predecessors, the Goons, created the oddly monikered Hercules Grytpype-Thynne, Bluebottle, and the Frenchman Count Jim Moriarty, among many others.

"Somerset"—("Mr. Hilter") Somerset—home to Minehead—is where Ron Vibbentrop says he was born, denying the Düsseldorf address. Von Ribbentrop was actually born in Wesel, Niederrhein, though both Düsseldorf and Wesel are in North Rhine, Westphalia.

"Stock Exchange"—("The Minehead By-Election") Again, a representative of the Conservative class, the established and monied elite here supports the fascistic policies of a growth-spurred government. The fact that Enoch Powell, for example, remained a staunch Conservative infuriated many in the party (who saw him as a dividing demagogue), while it bolstered others who feared the Lib-Lab approach to immigration policy would lead to a tidal wave of "colour" into Britain in the 1950s and 1960s.

This may also be a reference to the significant support the National Socialists enjoyed in the 1930s in the UK (including the British Union of Fascists, banned in 1940), especially among people of note, many admiring the Nazi government's ability to drag Germany out of its financial straits and toward full employment and unmatched industrial production in the late 1930s.

– T –

tatty—(PSC; "Visitors From Coventry") Somewhat neglected or run down.

"Television Doctor"—("Mr. Hilter") This reaction is probably a tongue-in-cheek allusion to doctor shows in general, and specifically the show *Doctor in the House*, for which Chapman (a non-practicing doctor himself) and Cleese wrote the pilot episode in 1969. (See Wilmut 187-88.) The show was produced by Humphrey Barclay, and ran through several iterations. Wilmut reports that Chapman and Cleese used actual names of friends and real people for characters, something they would continue to do as Pythons (187).

Though neither Himmler nor Hitler were actors, nor were they alive when commercial television was pervasive, archival footage from various Nazi rallies and addresses was used regularly in films and on TV. Significant Himmler/Hitler footage appeared in the 1956 TV presentation, *The Twisted Cross*, and they "acted" (as themselves) in Leni Riefenstahl's films *Der Sieg des Glaubens* (1933) and *Triumph of the Will* (1934).

This mention may have emerged from the Nuremberg trials, as well, since there was a special section of the proceedings set aside for doctors who had participated in human experiments, executions, etc., and much was made of the "missing" doctors, including the infamous "Der Weisse Engel" Josef Mengele.

Noteworthy television doctors from this period include Chapman himself from *Doctor in the House* (1969), Dr. Finlay (mentioned in Ep. 7), and Dr. Kildare. Lastly, the earlier-mentioned Lord Charles Hill was the well-known (and sexually saccharine) "Radio Doctor" in the 1950s, hosting a staid, rehearsed teenaged chat show ostensibly about sex, but focusing more on morality (*Eyewitness 1950-59*, "Sexual Attitudes").

3.48 seconds—(PSC; "Signalbox" link into "Falling From Building") The printed script mentions that the signalman (Jones) "wrestles [the bear] for 3.48 seconds," a comment meant for the reader only, of course. The "wrestle" actually lasts a little over 12 seconds.

"Tiddles"—("*Spectrum*—Talking About Things") Also the name of the cat in Ep. 11, and would become the name of a cat living in a ladies' bathroom at Paddington Station just months after this episode aired for the first time.

"Twit of the Year"—("Upperclass Twit of the Year") If comedy comes from below, as has been said, then so might certain population controls. This type of "eugenics" might also have its inception in the lower or middle classes, in the Python world, as opposed to the ruling class attempting to manipulate the physical and racial makeup of Man (well, Poorer, Lower-Class, and Third World Man). The significance of eugenics for many Modernists—at least, before ethnic cleansing became practicable and then brutally practiced in the twentieth century—was the promise of social elevation, the reduction of congenital disease and genetic weakness, and just a better world.

Success in this "Twit" competition, then, is defined as eliminating the Upperclass Twit (more specifically, the upper-class males) from society, and erasing the flawed bloodline from the English genetic pool. Gumbies and Pepperpots and even Ken Shabby can live and procreate, but not the upper class. Twits Simon

(Jones) and Nigel (Cleese) will also prove successful at taking their own lives, joining Gervaise (Palin) in "winning."

– U –

"Uberleben muss gestammen . . . "—("The Minehead By-Election") The German used here is a mixture of actual German and mangled English-German as has been used before in Ep. 1 ("The Funniest Joke in the World") and like those for French (Ep. 2, "Flying Sheep") and Spanish (Ep. 9, "Llamas"). This jabberwock concoction of German and English is also used—and is perhaps where the Pythons were inspired—in WWII-era cartoons lampooning Hitler, including *Blitz Wolf* (1942, MGM), and *Daffy the Commando* (1943, WB). Various British (and American) radio comedians also employed the "Germlish" language in comedy broadcasts lampooning Hitler and the Nazis.

The pseudo-German of Python is used again here, including Germanicized English words like "schneaky." Essentially, Hilter here is telling the people of Minehead that they have a historical claim on the Taunton region. Taunton is southeast of Minehead, along the A39, then A358, and seems to be of little strategic value, except as a tourist destination. Hitler made similar claims on much of Central Europe in the years leading up to WWII, including the Rhineland, which he flooded with German troops in 1936, claiming Germany's historical right to the area.

"Und . . . Somerset"—("The Minehead By-Election") Rough translation: "And Bridgwater is the last desire we have in Somerset." In other words, appease us with Taunton and Bridgwater, and there will be peace, Hilter assures his listeners. (Bridgwater is north and a bit east of Taunton.) This is of course what Hitler and Germany claimed in regard to the Sudetenland prior to the eruption of WWII. From Hitler himself, in 1938:

> I hope that in a few days the problem of the Sudeten Germans will be finally solved. By October 10 we shall have occupied all the areas which belong to us. Thus one of Europe's most serious crises will be ended, and all of us, not only in Germany but those far beyond our frontiers, will then in this year for the first time really rejoice at the Christmas festival. It should for us all be a true Festival of Peace. (From Hitler's address of 5 October 1938 at Sportpalast, Berlin)

These filmed speeches were played over and over again during the Pythons' young lives, as propaganda for the war effort, and later as propaganda for a strong England in the face of the specter of expanding international Communism, for example.

"Upperclass Twit"—("Upperclass Twit of the Year") A particular target of the Pythons, these characters will be ridiculed at unprecedented length in the fully narrated sketch. These representations might be built on literary precursors like Bertram "Bertie" Wooster in the P.G. Wodehouse (1881-1975) book series featuring the exploits of the foppish upper-class Wooster and his clever man, Jeeves. The first of this series was *The Man with Two Left Feet* (1917). Python, employing the "rules" of satire, distorts the "amiable, vacuous" Wodehouse characterization with their almost unmitigated scorn of the Upperclass Twits (Drabble, 1985, 1084). Also, Agatha Christie's Captain Hastings character (*The Disappearance of Mr. Davenheim* [1924]) might be an early reference.

These twittish upper crust characters may also be updated versions of the fops so essential to Restoration and eighteenth-century comedy, including Sir Fopling Flutter (from Etherege's *The Man of Mode*) and Lord Foppington (from Vanbrugh's *The Relapse*, Sheridan's *A Trip to Scarborough*, and Cibber's *The Careless Husband*). See Nettleton and Case, *British Dramatists from Dryden to Sheridan* (1939) for more on this character. The pages of fashionable mags like *The Tatler* and *Country Life* are also replete with such characters, posing for photos at mansion galas, debutante balls, cricket and fox hunting outings, and receiving the myriad "orders" (OBE, DSO) from HRH.

According to BBC records, this portion of the show was shot on 3 December 1969 at Hurlingham Sports Ground, Hurlingham Road, W6 (WAC T12/1,094). See the entry above for "Hurlingham Park" for more on this location.

– V –

"verges"—("Visitors From Coventry") The grassy areas bounding the roadway might here be squeezed between road and some structure, like the hospital he mentions, for instance.

via the miracle of cueing—(PSC; "Police Station [Silly Voices]") This acknowledges that the timely entrance of the detective inspector isn't serendipitous, but carefully planned and staged for the maximum comedic/dramatic effect. Such "cues" are meant to be invisible in most Western theatrical practices, and only become evident when there is a mistake in the transition, or the more modern/postmodern theatrical standards are applied. The Pythons are certainly commenting on the artifice of the production, the acknowledged practices of the television format, and are aligning themselves with the more overtly barefaced and theatrical stage conventions in vogue at the time. This is also another bit of information (an aside) that is only for the reader of the scripts, not the viewer.

"Vivian . . . chemo-hygeine"—("Upperclass Twit of the Year") Vivian Anthony Stanshall (1943-1995) was the lead singer for the Bonzo Zip Dog Doo-Dah Band, the "house band" for the Jones/Palin/Idle 1967 show *Do Not Adjust Your Set*.

An "O-level" ("ordinary level") is one of the standardized exams administered to students in UK secondary schools, the other being the "A-level" ("advanced level"). Respective scores for these exams are asked of Mr. Bee (Jones) in the "Job Hunter" sketch in Ep. 24.

– W –

"warm and wet"—("Visitors From Coventry") Idle's characters tend to spout many of these idiomatic aphorisms. Cf. Arthur Name in Ep. 9 ("Name by name but not by nature"); or Ep. 3, where Norman tells the Gent that "a nod's as good as a wink to a blind bat" in the "Nudge, Nudge" sketch. In *HG*, Cleese's Lancelot is very concerned with utilizing the proper idiomatic expressions and behaviors for his character, including manly escapes and knightly speeches.

"Was . . . bewegen"—("Mr. Hilter") Probably supposed to be interpreted as "What's the word for hike?", especially when the answer is taken into account. Python's dubious command/application of the German language renders the question almost meaningless, however. "Hiking" would more likely be translated as "Wanderung." "Rückreise" could be what they meant, meaning "return journey," which would have ironically fit Hitler's yearning for a return to power.

"window cleaner"—("Mr. Hilter") Himmler actually studied agriculture before joining right-wing organizations prior to allying himself with Hitler and the National Socialists (finding time to be a failed poultry farmer, too); Von Ribbentrop was a sparkling wine salesman in Canada; and Hitler was, of course, a failed painter.

"wouldn't have had much fun in Stalingrad"—("Mr. Hilter") Actually, it isn't at all clear that the Landlady (Jones) could be capable of making such a subtle historical-political reference, and since she doesn't really seem to appreciate that the leaders of the Third Reich are in her drawing room, the possibility is even more remote. (She also could be referring to contemporary Stalingrad, which may have been equally bleak under the current General Secretary, Leonid Brezhnev. In 1961 the name of the city had been changed to Volgograd, incidentally.) On the other hand, it's the seemingly common character (like the plumber/narrator later in "The Montgolfier Brothers" sketch) who is able to make the salient comment, the clever and illusive connection, and the historical or political allusion in the Python world.

"writing to complain"—(PSC; "Falling From Building") The printed script uses this "falling" ellipses format shown in the letter itself, as well. It's a simple but effective visual complement to what happened with the Voice Over (Chapman) voice as he "falls" off-screen. The structure isn't unlike the recently named "concrete" or "shape" poetry, where the poem's text can be shaped and arranged to assist/comment on the "meaning" of the verbal images.

This is also a moment built into the script for the reader only, of which there would have been very few (the other Pythons, the production team, and a handful of BBC higher-ups, perhaps). Cf. the "Beast of Aaarrrrggh" scene in *HG*, where the last words/moans of Joseph of Arimathea are reportedly inscribed on the cave wall.

– Y –

"Yes that's better"—(animation link into "Ken Shabby") The music used behind a portion of this animation is a version of "Hallclujah" (from Handel's *Messiah*), performed by the London Philharmonic Choir with the LP Orchestra conducted by Susskind (WAC T12/1,093).

yokel—(PSC; "The Minehead By-Election") This yokel is played by Jones and is dressed just like the man in Constable's *The Hay Wain*, as seen in Ep. 25, the "Art Gallery Strike" sketch. Also, see the "real rustic" depicted in Ep. 2, there played by Chapman. The Village Idiots are dressed similarly in Ep. 20.

Episode 13

– A –

"abuse you"—("Restaurant [Abuse/Cannibalism]") Reference to the notion that waiters (especially at upscale restaurants) can be rude and condescending, especially toward more obviously petit bourgeois or provincial couples.

This is probably a Sartrean conceit at its core (from *Being and Nothingness*), and builds on the Homicidal Barber who actually wants to be a Lumberjack (Palin) in Ep. 9. In that case, the Barber chooses to act on his total freedom, not allowing social class or breeding (or his mother) to determine his life choices, and he launches into his "Lumberjack Song," accessing and embracing those freedoms. To Sartre, the obsequious or surly waiter (or barber or a porter [Ep. 8]) escapes into "bad faith" when the total freedoms of the world create anxiety, and the waiter then blames and abuses others for his situation, for his inability to act. The Butcher (Idle) in Ep. 18 also abuses his customer, though he is alternately rude and polite, as if still on the cusp of his Sartrean decision—freedom or bad faith. In this "Abuse/Cannibalism" episode, however, the Head Waiter will likely continue in his bad faith ways, as he laments arriving late to a wife-swapping party (and getting a bad second wife), he still wets his bed, still defers to his old Headmaster, etc.

"Albania"—("*Probe-Around* on Crime") Ex-King Zog (1895-1961) was also referenced in Ep. 4. See notes to Ep. 4.

"albatross"—("Restaurant [Abuse/Cannibalism]") Reference to Samuel Taylor Coleridge's use of the metaphor in *The Rime of the Ancient Mariner* (1798): "Instead of the cross, the albatross About my neck was hung" (2.14). Likened to a millstone here, and representative of the way the husband has been treating the wife throughout this sketch.

Cleese will actually wear an albatross around his neck as he tries to sell albatross later in this episode, and popularly at various Python live shows, including *Live at the Hollywood Bowl* (1980). The albatross is the largest of sea birds, and will be mentioned later as the only type of refreshment he has for sale, though as soon as he sells one, he offers "gannet on a stick" (a gannet is a type of goose).

"All men are the same"—("Restaurant [Abuse/Cannibalism]") A common epithet heard among the more radical elements of the women's liberation movement of the period. The husband (Cleese), Head Waiter (Palin), and Headmaster (Chapman) in this scene would have been described as blinkered "male chauvinists" (a term in the 1960s appropriated from its more nationalistic heritage), or men who treat women as less than equal. See *EBO*.

"all sorts of lines in here"—("Restaurant [Abuse/Cannibalism]") Sounds very much like the atmosphere in Rick's café in *Casablanca* (1942), or the group settings in a John Ford Western (*Stagecoach*; *My Darling Clementine*). This also could be a comment on the unpredictable nature of *Flying Circus* itself, where interloping characters or animations can propel the narrative in different directions at any time.

"almost human"—("Restaurant [Abuse/Cannibalism]") An interesting paraphrase of a sentiment from a Robert Lowell (1917-1977) poem, *To Mother* (1977): "It has taken me the time since you died / to discover you are as human as I am . . . / if I am." Earlier, in 1964, Saul Bellow had expressed a similar sentiment: "I am simply a human being, more or less" (*Herzog*). Taking these readings into account, the husband's assessment of his wife as "almost human" is almost an affirmative.

"anyway"—("Restaurant [Abuse/Cannibalism]") This last line spoken as an aside to the camera. The suggestion is here, as well, that there might be something more devious going on out of sight, like the Barber (Palin) who happens to be homicidal in Ep. 9, or the funeral parlor workers who eat corpses in Ep. 26.

"arrive late"—("Restaurant [Abuse/Cannibalism]") These last few lines, delivered in fairly detached manners, signal an end to any cohesion the scene may have had. This line as spoken by the Head Waiter (Palin) is also by definition a one-liner, as is the previous retort from the wife, both of which are somewhat uncharacteristic of the Python's writing style, and run counter to their "tyranny of the punchline" credo. This entire scene, however, is more cynical and glib than most of their work in *FC*.

Similarly, in *Private Eye*, columnist "Jolly Sooper" wrote of meeting her "second husband at a wife-swapping party given by his third wife" (Ingrams 238).

"Attila the Hun"—("Mr. Attila the Hun") King of the Huns, he died in 453. Ep. 20 will begin with a spoof of American situation comedies called *The Attila the Hun Show*, and, in *HG*, it is St. Attila who has left instructions as to the operation of the "Holy Hand Grenade of Antioch."

– B –

back on—("Mr. Attila the Hun") Another "man-behind-the-curtain" moment, when a bit of costuming (here a mustache) is noted as such, and the artificiality of the construct is acknowledged. Jones also seems to be attempting to keep the mustache in place—it's popping off as he speaks—and he eventually pulls it off and pops it into his hat.

Ballantyne, David—("Restaurant [Abuse/Cannibalism]") This actor plays both the Prologue and the waiter who announces the dead bishop. The dead bishop scenario will appear in Ep. 29, the "Salvation Fuzz" sketch. Ballantyne, incidentally, was paid £42 for his work in this episode (WAC T12/1,094).

David Ballantyne was something of a minor singing sensation on the UK pop music charts, releasing "I Can't Express It" and "Love Around the World" in 1966. He may have been brought into the Python mix by Idle, a musician himself and very connected to the London music scene during this period.

"Beryl"—("*Probe-Around* on Crime") Beryl Reid (1920-1996) starred in the 1968 television series *Beryl Reid Says Good Evening*. She also appeared in the *Before the Fringe* series, which, as its name implies, predated the *Beyond the Fringe* iteration. Both Ronnie Barker and Cicely Courtneidge appeared in the *Before . . .* series. Barker worked with the Pythons on *The Frost Report*,

and Courtneidge is mentioned prominently in Ep. 6 by the Red Indian (Idle).

"botherkins"—("*Probe-Around* on Crime") Pronounced "bodkins," and is an oath derived from "God's dear body." As spelled in this episode, the word doesn't appear in the *OED*.

breath test—("Mr. Attila the Hun") A test administered by law enforcement officials to determine a suspect's blood alcohol level. The test, using a "breathalyser," made its debut in the UK in 1960.

This image of a breathalyzer that can "out" certain people is earlier seen in a political cartoon panel from 1968. The *Daily Express* published a cartoon by Michael Cummings depicting PM Harold Wilson kicking out a female figure labeled "The Conscience of the Left." She is carrying a breathalyzer labeled: "Moralyzer test—Racialist breath turns crystals white" (British Cartoon Archive.) The Wilson government's favorable policies toward continuing military sales to the apartheid government of South Africa was treated regularly in the daily news across Britain during this period. For more on the South Africa situation, see notes to Ep. 15.

"bunches of five"—("Psychiatry—Silly Sketch") Cf. Dylan Thomas for an earlier appearance of this imagery, in the poem "The Hand That Signed the Paper" (1936):

> The hand that signed the paper felled a city;
> Five sovereign fingers taxed the breath,
> Doubled the globe of dead and halved a country;
> These five kings did a king to death.

burglar's outfit—(PSC; "Quiz Programme—*Wishes*") The cartoonish, visually iconic representation of a burglar in *FC*, and could have been lifted right out of an early Mack Sennett film. (Python Frenchmen, interestingly, are given very similar dress.)

– C –

"Cardinal . . . Clark"—("Historical Impersonations") This revisits a moment from Ep. 3, where Palin played Richelieu in a courtroom setting, using what appears to be the same handheld microphone. This very short scene may even have been shot for the earlier episode, then held for an opportune moment later in the series (many links would have been shot, catalogued, and archived for upcoming episodes).

Petula Clark (b. 1932) was a very popular singer/actress whose career spanned five decades. "Don't Sleep in the Subway" was written by Tony Hatch, and reached well into the top twenty most popular songs in both the United States and UK in 1967. Clark is also mentioned later in Ep. 37. This particular recording is from the album *These Are My Songs*, and is arranged and conducted by Ernie Freeman (WAC T12/1,094).

"care about me"—("Restaurant [Abuse/Cannibalism]") Cf. the Catholic mother in *ML*, who gives birth while doing housework (the baby drops to the floor), adding to her scores of children. This is also the period of the so-called zero-population move (a term coined by Kingsley Davis), when groups were calling for a worldwide zero growth policy to save the planet's resources for future generations.

"Chelsea . . . Scrubs"—("Advertisements") Carefully chosen prison-related restaurant sites, mingling Vercotti's underworld activities and the dining experience. Chelsea is actually a flower show to which Leyhill Prison has contributed for many years, though this may also be a slighting reference to the posh neighborhoods of the Upperclass Twits (see Ep. 12); Parkhurst is on the Isle of Wight, site of Parkhurst Prison; Dartmoor Prison is in Devon, and is located in Princetown near Plymouth; and "the Scrubs" is actually Wormwood Scrubs Prison in west London.

"choc-ices"—("Albatross") *OED*: "A brickette of ice-cream covered with chocolate."

"Cockfosters"—(link out of "Albatross") Cockfosters is a part of Greater London, and is northwest of London proper.

"come back to my place"—("Come Back to My Place") Homosexual activity between even consenting adults had been a criminal offense in the UK since passage of the "Offences Against the Person Act" in 1861. The Wolfenden Report (released 1957) recommended decriminalizing such acts between those over 21, leading to the passage in 1967 of the "Sexual Offences Act." The Wolfenden Committee had convened after a number of high-profile men were arrested and convicted of criminal activity in the early 1950s as a result of their active homosexuality.

The Goons refer to the report in the episode "Spon" (30 September 1957), noting that Bloodnok has secured "the film rights of the Wolfenden Report," and they're certain that "Walt Disney will never forgive him" for the intrusion.

"court order"—("Operating Theatre [Squatters]") Referencing the invocation of the Forcible Entry Act of 1381, which demanded a court order prior to any eviction in Britain. Without proof of a *forcible* entry, police were unable to prove a crime, and proper names of those being indicted had to be secured, as well, which was no easy task. Further, the law provided that once

peaceable entry was undertaken, a squatter could place his own lock on the dwelling door(s), thus making it illegal for even the building's owner to enter and evict. Squatters were able to have owners then prosecuted for forcible entry violations into their own buildings. (See Andrew Friend, squat.freeserve.co.uk/story, chapter 14.) The continuing lack of affordable housing for many in Britain, especially in the urban areas (and made all the worse in the postwar years), certainly fueled both the emboldened squatters and the law's reluctance or even inability to deal harshly with displaced persons in an era of elevated social liberality. The charity Shelter estimated that as many as three million British citizens were in desperate need of better housing in 1969 (see "1969: Shelter Exposes Slum Homelessness" at news.bbc.co.uk).

During 1970-1972 the laws would begin to swing back toward actual owners, easing the process for eviction, news of which would have made the papers and other media, and on into the Python's written grist-to-the-mill. See the entry for "squatter" below for more.

– D –

"diamante"—(PSC; "Quiz Programme—*Wishes*") *OED*: "Material to which a sparkling effect is given by the use of paste brilliants, powdered glass or crystal, etc." The Minister for Home Affairs (Chapman) will wear a diamante necklace in the following episode, where housing (see "Operating Theatre [Squatters]" sketch for more) will also be the subject.

Dick Barton—("Quiz Programme—*Wishes*") Titular character in a BBC radio serial and several films, including *Dick Barton Strikes Back* (1949) and *Dick Barton at Bay* (1950), the music written by Rupert Grayson and Frank Spencer. Barton was a post-WWII radio hero fighting foreign criminals and femmes fatale.

This music ("Devil's Gallop" by Queen's Hall Light Orchestra, directed by Charles Williams) is also used in other "chase" moments, including the hurried climax of the "Spanish Inquisition" sketch in Ep. 15. The Goons also employ this same recognizable, even iconic tune in the wrap-up to their episodes "The Plasticine Man" (23 December 1957) and "The Whistling Spy Enigma" (28 September 1954).

"Do Not Open 'Til Christmas"—(PSC; "Quiz Programme—*Wishes*") A typical cartoon moment—a large wooden box and the affixed signage—one that continues the cartoonish feel of the short film. This same gag was used in myriad Warner Bros. cartoons, for example, including an ur-Bugs Bunny short, *Prest-O Change-O* (1939).

Dr Kildare *theme*—("Psychiatry—Silly Sketch") Dr. Kildare is the titular character in an American TV series (NBC and MGM-TV) which was broadcast 1961-1966, as well as a number of feature films from the 1930s and 1940s. Lionel Barrymore and Lew Ayres appeared in many of the feature films, while Richard Chamberlain starred in the TV series. Dr. Kildare is mentioned a number of times in American cartoons, including Tex Avery's *Blitz Wolf* (1942), where the Nazi wolf calls for him as he's about to die.

The theme here is played by Johnnie Spence and His Orchestra (WAC T12/1,094).

Dr. Larch—(PSC; "Psychiatry—Silly Sketch") The larch (a pine tree) is featured prominently in Ep. 3. There was a character Dr. Lench (played by James Edwards) on *Dr. Kildare* in 1965.

"ducks and drakes"—("Psychiatry—Silly Sketch") A continuation, in a sense, of the thesaurus nature of the sketch already introduced by the Cleese psychiatrist. This phrase is possibly adapted from the Mother Goose rhyme:

> A duck and a drake,
> And a halfpenny cake,
> With a penny to pay the old baker.
> A hop and a scotch
> Is another notch,
> Slitherum, slatherum, take her.

"Ducks and drakes" is also an idiom that fittingly means "messing or playing about with," etc., as well as a stone skipping game. See the *OED*.

– E –

Episode 13—Not titled in the script version, this episode was recorded on 4 January 1970, and was broadcast one week later on 11 January 1970. This was the final episode of the first series, and the Pythons wouldn't resume recording (the second series) until July 1970.

An "Audience Research Bulletin" taken on Sunday, 11 January 1970, 11:15-11:45pm, BBC 1, estimated that 4.8 percent of the UK were watching *Monty Python's Flying Circus*, and the 104 respondents rated the show as follows: A+ (21%); A (37%); B (26%); C (7%); and C- (9%). The respondent comments ranged from "load of rubbish" to "inspired lunacy" (WAC T12/1,094).

Also appearing in this episode, according to the repeat fee schedule: Flanagan, Pat Prior, Beulah Hughes (all three playing Judges), Neil Fraser, Matthew Gray, Sheila Sands, and Rosemary Lord.

"Euphemism"—("Me Doctor") The Doctor (Idle) isn't speaking euphemistically or metaphorically, but simply rattling off words and names that start with a "you" sound.

– F –

"Flight . . . (Mrs)"—(letter link into "Psychiatry—Silly Sketch") Many letters to the program are from military personnel, retired and active, and many are WWII veterans. In this instance, "Lieutenant" is pronounced the British way "lef-tenant," and his name is borrowed from Mary Shelley's fictional doctor, Frankenstein, who created a monster/man from salvaged body parts. It also seems that many times it is actually the spouse of the writer who pens these letters "(Mrs)", though the voiceover is usually performed by one of the male cast.

"Florence . . . London"—("Historical Impersonations") Florence Nightingale (1820-1910) was considered to be the founder of modern nursing, and she did gain international fame serving during the Crimean War.

Brian London (b. 1934) was an English boxer (fl. 1955-1970; record: 37-20-1) who in the recent past (1959 and 1966) had been knocked out by Floyd Patterson and Cassius Clay, respectively. In this section, long-dead historical figures are reaching forward in time to impersonate still-living personalities like Hill, Waring, and London.

folk songs—("Psychiatry—Silly Sketch") Often acoustic, guitar-based music that was very popular during the "hippie" generation times, and which wouldn't have included Bacharach-penned tunes (those being pop music). Acts like Peter, Paul and Mary; Bob Dylan; Woody Guthrie; the Kingston Trio (and Julie Felix, in the UK) were particularly well known. Many of the songs were socially progressive and reactionary, railing against war, hunger, capitalism, corporate greed, etc., and would have been the antithesis of what most of the WWII generation felt music and patriotism should be.

In an advertisement for a new poetry anthology in *Private Eye*, "Doves for the 70s," Julie Felix (a David Frost favorite) is highlighted as a special musical guest at the anthology's publication party on 30 December 1969 (19 December 1969, 8).

"formica"—(Restaurant [Abuse/Cannibalism]") "Formica" is the proprietary name for a man-made counter-top material. But it is also a play on the "heart of gold" saying. This is a good example of one of Python's negative portrayals of a female, especially in relation to her husband, who is portrayed as quite affable. The wife is also allowed to ramble without much interference or even notice by others, until the husband apologizes and, later, bemoans his marital fate.

Four undertakers—(link into "Intermissions") The music clip used under this funereal moment is, specifically, the London Brass Players performing Music for "Vive L'Oompa" Funeral March, by Chopin (WAC T12/1,094). The scene looks like a carryover from Ep. 11, where funeral sketches abounded. No music cue is mentioned in the printed script, but the snippet was obviously requested anyway.

– G –

"giveaway"—("Restaurant [Abuse/Cannibalism]") The "slip of the tongue" (or faulty action, to Freud) appears quite often in *FC*. David Unction (Chapman) wants to be thought of as an "Old Queen" (Ep. 10), the Art Critic (Palin) mentions naughty bits when discussing art (Ep. 8), and the Interviewer (Jones) can't help but notice (and comment on) his subject's enormous teeth (Ep. 24). The word chosen here, "giveaway," is characteristic of Palin's work, and used by the Art Critic in Ep. 8, and Dennis the Peasant in *HG*.

Golden . . . Torremolinos—("Advertisements") The Golden Palm is a merit award of the Cannes Film Festival, which has been held in France since 1946. Films including *If* (1968, Lindsay Anderson), *Blowup* (1966, Michelangelo Antonioni), *Signore & Signori* (1965, Pietro Germi), *Un homme et une femme* (1966, Pierre Uytterhoeven), *Knack . . . and How to Get It* (1965, Richard Lester), *Umbrellas of Cherbourg* (1964, Jacques Demy), and *The Leopard* (1963, Luchino Visconti) had won the award in the recent past. Of these, the Pythons make references in *FC* to *If*, David Hemmings (the star of *Blowup*), director Antonioni, and both Visconti and *The Leopard*. Torremolinos is a resort city in southern Spain.

Grace—(animation in "Historical Impersonations") W.G. Grace (1848-1915) was considered one of the finest cricketers to ever play the game. He is credited with popularizing cricket around the world (at least within the Commonwealth countries). His bearded image will also be used in *Holy Grail*, where he, probably appropriately, plays God.

"Great, A.T."—("Mr. Attila the Hun") Alexander was referenced earlier in this same show, attacking and bisecting a sales assistant at Freeman, Hardy and Willis.

– H –

Harley Street—("Psychiatry—Silly Sketch") The Harley Street surgeons carried this vaunted reputation for many years according to A.N. Wilson:

The British Medical Association was holding its annual meeting in its headquarters in Tavistock Square. This was a building where clerical staff, as late as the 1930s, were *instructed that they must vacate the lift, rather than share it with the frock-coated, top-hatted consultants who had arrived from Harley Street* to conduct business. Deference towards doctors in the great hospitals rivalled the reverence shown towards the higher clergy in Rome. (italics added; *After the Victorians* 510)

The Surgeon (Chapman) plays a gramophone record for effect as he soliloquizes, with the music being "The Dr. Kildare Theme" as played by Johnnie Spence and His Orchestra (WAC T12/1,094).

Historical Impersonations—(PSC; "Historical Impersonations") This sketch is a direct relation to the "Famous Deaths" sketch from Ep. 1, where Mozart (Cleese) hosts a show featuring the deaths of historical figures. Most of the series would have been written within a several-week period, making the appearance of similarly themed sketches understandable, and even expected. The practice was not to get rid of such similarities (or variations on a theme), but pepper the sketches throughout the run of the series, so they don't jumble one atop another in a single episode.

hits him over the head—("Me Doctor") The novelty of this type of ending/transition is wearing thin by Ep. 13, perhaps at least partly due to the live audience's lack of response to the Knight and chicken. In this case, there is almost complete silence after the gag. Other recurring characters, like the Gumbies or Praline or Cardinal Ximinez get appreciative, recognizing laughs when they appear. Not so with the Knight. The woman (Idle) complaining about a lack of "proper punchlines" earlier in the episode seems somewhat less annoying and more prescient, perhaps, by this time.

"how's it work?"—("Mr. Attila the Hun") Cf. the Holy Hand Grenade section of *HG*, where King Arthur (Chapman) is able to understand the significance of the weapon that is the Holy Hand Grenade, but when it's in his hand he has no idea how to work it, nor does Lancelot (Cleese). They consult the scriptures and figure it out. Arthur then throws the hand grenade, destroying the killer rabbit. This later feature film scene benefited significantly from the comedic structure in the above "breathalyser" section.

"Hun, Norman"—("Mr. Attila the Hun") A combination of conquerors—the Huns and the Normans—that could produce an ideal warrior, though this nebbish-like, Pewtey-ish man (also played by Palin) belies that potentiality.

– I –

"I'll never fall in love again"—("Psychiatry—Silly Sketch") A 1969 number one hit written by Burt Bacharach (b. 1929) and lyricist Hal David (b. 1921) for the Broadway musical *Promises, Promises*. Not really a folk song, of course, but certainly more at home on the easy listening (and pop) AM dial of the period.

"Imagine . . . construe"—("Restaurant [Abuse/Cannibalism]") A jabberwock take on the Prologue from Shakespeare's *Henry V*, where the Chorus asks his audience to imagine "vasty" fields, prancing horses and men at arms:

> But pardon, gentles all,
> The flat unraised spirits that hath dar'd
> On this unworthy scaffold to bring forth
> So great an object. Can this cockpit hold
> The vasty fields of France? Or may we cram
> Within this wooden O the very casques
> That did affright the air at Agincourt? (1.1.8-14)

Idle's character (Prisoner) in Ep. 3 has already launched into a Laurence Olivier–like speech on freedom, mentioning the "owl of Thebes" then, as well.

"I'm sorry"—(PSC; link into "Psychiatry—Silly Sketch") The full line in the printed script reads: *Cut to letter (as used for* Xmas night with the stars *after pet shop. I'm sorry . . . as not used in* Xmas night with the stars*")*. This seems more like a marginal comment than a part of the finished script—a very first person moment as the script/sketch writer takes the time to not only write something in error, but then keeps that error and adds a rejoinder. These are comments available to the reader only, meaning a very limited audience prior to the 1989 publication of the scripts.

There is no letter inserted after either pet shop setting, in Ep. 8 or 10, as seen on *A Christmas Night With the Stars* or any other show, of course. Scenes, links, and inserts were often changed and rearranged, put in or elided as the shows came into shape during the writing and then taping processes.

"into consideration"—("Mr. Attila the Hun") This to perhaps gain some leniency in sentencing. Cf. Ep. 29, where the father (Idle) asks the Church Police (Palin and Gilliam) to take the three dead bishops by the bin "into consideration," as well.

"Irish agriculture"—(link out of "Operating Theatre [Squatters]") The *Radio Times* (official publication of the BBC) had originally described *FC* as a "show to subdue the violence in us all."

"ironing"—("Mr. Attila the Hun") In this episode alone, policemen have been characterized as homosexual, transvestites, and effeminate (often assuming female roles). The publication (it became an instant bestseller) of the so-called Wolfenden Report, *Report of the Departmental Committee on Homosexual Offences and Prostitution* (3 September 1957), certainly put homosexuality and its illegality and social stigma into the public eye. The image later of the policeman (Cleese) agreeing to a homosexual encounter with a citizen (Palin) may be a very boldfaced acknowledgment of the changing public perception of homosexual relationships between consenting adults in the UK. See more at the "come back to my place" entry above.

"Ivan . . . Willis"—("Historical Impersonations") Ivan IV (1530-1584) was the first Russian monarch to assume the "czar" title. "USSR" stood for the Union of Soviet Socialist Republics, the name given Russia (and its satellite countries) in 1922.

"Freeman, Hardy and Willis" sounds like a fictional law firm, but sales assistants would be more at home in a men's wear shop or department store. The following sentence in the episode describes the setting as a shoe store. The "Freeman, Hardy and Willis" reference may be a manipulation of a company name like Marks and Spencer Life Assurance (Marks and Spencer was established in 1884).

– J –

"Janet"—("Restaurant [Abuse/Cannibalism]") Hopkins is speaking to a male waiter. The male presenter played by Idle in Ep. 1 is called "Vicky," and Jones plays "Barbara" in "Full Frontal Nudity" in Ep. 8. Neither are characterized as drag performances.

"jelly babies"—("Operating Theatre [Squatters]") Nickname for marijuana or hashish cigarettes. Also, though, these are the type of candies that schoolboy Bluebottle (Peter Sellers) often asks for in return for his services in *The Goon Show* from BBC Radio (1951-1960).

"John . . . Hill"—("Historical Impersonations") John the Baptist was, of course, the biblical prophet who "prepared the way" for the coming of Christ. Charlton Heston had recently portrayed John the Baptist in *The Greatest Story Ever Told* (1965); John had been played by Mario Socrate in Pier Pasolini's 1964 *The Gospel According to St. Matthew*; and even earlier by Robert Ryan in *King of Kings* (1961), meaning the image of the Baptist's severed head on a platter would have been a familiar one to the Pythons and their audience by 1970.

Graham Hill (1929-1975) was the British winner of multiple Grand Prix events, as well as the Indianapolis 500.

"Julius . . . Waring"—("Historical Impersonations") Both Caesar and Waring have appeared in *FC* before. Caesar (Chapman) appeared as a closet mouse in the "Mouse Problem" sketch (Ep. 2), as well as a quick Vox Pops moment in Ep. 10. A Waring-like figure (Idle) played the scorekeeper during the "Famous Deaths" sketch in Ep. 1. Eddie Waring was a well-known, oft-imitated television sports broadcaster in Britain. See notes to Ep. 1.

– L –

"Lazarus"—("Psychiatry—Silly Sketch") Cf. the Biblical account of Lazarus who was raised from the dead by Christ.

"light show, baby"—("Operating Theatre [Squatters]") The Squatter sounds very much American, like a Haight-Ashbury district (San Francisco) hippie or flower child. (A cartoon panel from 17 September 1969 features squatters borrowing a cup of sugar from Buckingham Palace, while a newspaper headline nearby reads "Hippie Squatters Move In Near Palace" [Mac *Daily Sketch*].) The lights would be "showy" if the Squatter is experiencing an "acid trip," or the effects of ingesting the psychedelic hallucinogen LSD. See the many cartoons poking fun at squatters and the squatters' movement at the British Cartoon Archive.

As he continues, the Squatter (and friends) spout many of the well-known terms/maxims of the period, including "groovy," "bread," "great scene," "baby," "fuzz," "man," and "fascist." All of these connote a certain membership status, as well as articulating just who the "others" are as opposed to the counterculture movement. If you're in the groove and part of the scene (recreational drug use, no acknowledgment of property rights, "tuning out" of the status quo culture), then the terms of endearment apply; otherwise, you're a fascist and uptight.

Timothy Leary's "Tune in, turn on, drop out" mantra certainly applies here. (Remember, a subtitle for the first episode was included in the show's paperwork, but not in the show itself: "A new comedy series for the Switched On." Perhaps this was the Pythons' aborted attempt to connect with their younger, more "hip" viewers?) In November 1970, the *Listener* noted that "thought of a traditional kind . . . is the recognised enemy of the counter-culture," so it is the status quo being rebelled against here (622-23). Interesting that in this era of blossoming freedoms, including a woman's right to control her own body, the Pythons are suggesting that even one's body (albeit a white male's body) isn't something over which personal control can be exercised in the welfare state environment of 1960s Great Britain.

– M –

"Marceau, Marcel"—("Historical Impersonations") Marceau (b. 1923) was an internationally famous French mime performer. Marceau's name will reappear in Ep. 27, where he lives in the same apartment as Jean Genet and Jean-Paul Sartre.

"medium-sized intermission"—("Intermissions") The music here is again Steiner's theme from *A Summer Place*, as played by the Percy Faith Strings (WAC T12/1,094). See the entry "seven seconds" below for more. The music is used again for the "whopping great intermission" later.

model of a burglar—("*Probe-Around* on Crime") This model prop was requested much earlier, and is seen in Ep. 1, during the "Funniest Joke in the World" sketch, but not used or acknowledged there (WAC T12/1,082).

"muggins"—("Restaurant [Abuse/Cannibalism]") A fool, a simpleton.

– N –

Napoleon—("Psychiatry—Silly Sketch") Jones earlier dressed as Napoleon in Ep. 2 (as a closet mouse) and earlier in this episode (as the R101 disaster). See notes below for more on that infamous crash.

"no money"—(Restaurant [Abuse/Cannibalism]") A reference to the fading practice of the bride bringing a dowry into the new marriage, and which was often provided by the bride's father.

"Notlob"—("Psychiatry—Silly Sketch") Like the "Rottingdeans" reference earlier in this same episode, mentioning "Notlob" is a Python intertextuality, a moment of self-reference that loyal viewers tend to pick up on and enjoy. It is, again, Bolton spelled backward, and mentioned in Ep. 9 by the Shopkeeper (Palin) and Praline (Cleese).

"Nova"—("Operating Theatre [Squatters]") A popular and trendy women's art, fashion, and photography magazine for/from London and the UK, published 1965-1975. From a contemporary listserv wherein an oral history of the magazine and its cultural significance is currently under way:

Nova employed cutting edge writers, designers and editors who mixed an enthusiasm for sex, fun and fashion with editorial issues such as gender equality, contraception, and racism in a way that challenged the idea of what a woman's magazine 'should' be. Alongside the importance of its editorial legacy *Nova* is now seen as a style bible for a new generation of designers, stylists and musicians. (Alice Beard)

One issue of *Nova* from 1967, for example, included articles on Ossie Clark and Quorum (popular fashion designer and his shop), Barry Fantoni (comic artist for *Private Eye*), inflatable houses, and Terence Rattigan (Ep. 30).

"'Nuff said?"—("Restaurant [Abuse/Cannibalism]") An American colloquialism meaning enough information has been given, and in this case, it takes the place of a "know what I mean?" phrase. Often shortened to "N.S." The phrase appeared in Al Capp's *Li'l Abner* comic strip, which was published regularly in newspapers from 1934.

"Nurse me"—("Me Doctor") Patterned after classic vaudeville-type patter, such as the "Who's On First?" (Abbott and Costello) routine. Also, this is another moment of a character's extreme literality, where a question ("Me, Doctor?"). can be perceived as a statement ("Me Doctor.") It's as if the Doctor cannot appreciate either the upswinging pitch of the questions as questions, and/or he isn't understanding the comma (pause) between "me" and "doctor." Again, simple miscommunication leading to complete misunderstanding, a Python trope.

– O –

Ouija board—("Quiz Programme—*Wishes*") OED: "A proprietary name for a board having the letters of the alphabet and other signs used for obtaining messages and answers in spiritualistic séances and in the practice of telepathy."

– P –

"padre"—("Restaurant [Abuse/Cannibalism]") Probably a chaplain gone missing from the grammar school setting, the man who had formerly controlled the boys. The implication later—that the boys had descended into, perhaps, masturbation or homosexuality—signals the absence of a consistent authority figure. The Headmaster's (Chapman) speech here is cryptic and scattered, at best, so conclusions are difficult. Notice that he doesn't answer the Head Waiter's (Palin) question to begin with, continuing on in his own unilateral monologue.

In Ep. 18, *Seven Brides For Seven Brothers*" sketch, the Padre (Palin) is late arriving for his role in the school production of *Seven Brides for Seven Brothers*, and his "wrestling with Plato" excuse is taken as a sexual metaphor ("What you do with your private time is written on the vestry wall").

Panorama—("*Probe-Around* on Crime") Very popular and long-running (1953-present) interview and reporting television show. Cf. Ep. 2, "The Mouse Problem" sketch, for notes on the show.

The "*Panorama*-type" music behind this transition is Rachmaninov's "Symphony No. 1 in D Minor Op. 13," "Allegro Con Fuoco," as played by the USSR Symphony Orchestra, with Yevgeny Svetlanov conducting (WAC T12/1,094).

"part-time notice board"—(letter link into "Psychiatrist—Silly Sketch") A comment on the uselessness of the WWII veteran generation? The specter of aging men reminding the younger generation of the sacrifices they made during the war, and the unspoken debt owed to the war participants by subsequent generations, is a subject that surfaces often in letters and even sketches throughout *FC*.

In *Hard Day's Night*, the grumpy establishment-type City Gent on the train reminds the young Beatles that he had "fought the war" for their type, and Ringo wonders aloud whether he's sorry he won. It's conceivable that the Pythons and their peers could have grown weary of hearing these "Yorkshire gentlemen" dressings-down, and these same veterans and their spouses were obviously in the editorial pages of the period, lamenting the changing values in the 1960s and 1970s.

Lastly, the letter writer claims to have spent the war in India, which means he would have been serving in a colonial capacity (helping rule the colonies), a trainer for Indian regiments, or busy with the supply and logistical aspects of the war. In any case, he probably didn't actually fight. These types of letters from retired career military and/or WWII vets can be found throughout the pages of traditional UK newspapers of the era, as well as in *Private Eye*.

"Pearls for Swine"—("Advertisements") Reference to the biblical mentioning (Matthew 7:6) of giving precious things to those ill-prepared for such. Here used as a means of insulting an audience in a movie theater. Gilliam, at least, was obviously unhappy with the current cinematic offerings in and around London, and especially the "dank" theatres themselves, it seems.

"pill"—("Restaurant [Abuse/Cannibalism]") Birth control pill. Introduced in 1960 by G.D. Searle, the pill (called Enovid)—as a birth control tool—would have been disallowed for Catholics, among others, meaning the couple here are probably Anglican, if they're churchgoers at all.

The Lambeth Conference of the Church of England (1930) had agreed that contraception was allowed when abstinence was "impractical," while that same year the Pope (Pius XI) reaffirmed the Catholic Church's position against such measures. Just months before the Pythons gathered to create *Flying Circus*, Pope Paul VI had underscored (in 1968) via his encyclical letter *Humanae Vitae* ("Human Life") the Catholic position against all forms of contraception, with the exception of "total abstinence, and the unreliable rhythm method" (see "rhythm method" entry below).

This somber and sweeping papal decree set off a firestorm of not only public and private debate, but had a concussive effect on the flock. In the words of the BBC's *Eyewitness: 1960-69* (written by Joanna Bourke and narrated by Tim Pigott-Smith), "the Catholic Church imploded," and many, many British Catholics simply continued using the pill and attended confession on a weekly basis (*Eyewitness: 1960-69*, "Humana Vitae" parts 1 and 2).

The Wife (Idle) in this sketch doesn't take the pill simply because it's "nasty," and not—presumably—because it's forbidden by church edict. Cf. the lecture given by the Protestant husband (Chapman) in *ML* as to the significance of contraception and its relationship to personal and religious freedoms.

"pinny"—(*Probe-Around* on Crime") A colloquialization of pinafore.

"pith . . . marrow"—("Psychiatry—Silly Sketch") Cf. Ep. 3, the defendant's Olivier-like soliloquy.

pixilated motion—(PSC; "Quiz Programme—*Wishes*") Adjusting the speed of the film as it travels through the camera. In this case they are probably exposing a single frame or two, then the grouped actors move forward, then another exposure, and on. The amount of light available for each shot varies (thanks to moving clouds, rotation of the earth, etc.), betraying the pixilation technique, as well. Cf. Ep. 5, where the same technology is used to create the performance for the confused cat, as well as Ep. 7, where Englishmen are turning into Scotsmen. Fellow Brit and television funny man Benny Hill employed this technique often on his *The Benny Hill Show* (1955-1968), and it was pioneered by Canadian filmmaker Norman McLaren in *Neighbors* (1952).

"Portnoy . . . Piccadilly"—(link out of "Albatross") Piccadilly is a historic section of London known for many years as the location for those seeking "casual sex" (Ackroyd, *London: The Biography*). (Not unlike Times Square in New York City, the Piccadilly area has more recently become a tourist mecca for shopping, dining, and entertainment.) The fact that a dank cinema featuring suggestively posed models is connected to the area is fitting. The nearby Charing Cross Road (on the edge of Soho) area used to be the home to many sex shops (adult bookstores, novelties, etc.), which Jonathan Miller mentions in his "Porn Shop" monologue for *Beyond the Fringe*.

"profits"—(link out of "Albatross") Fairly accurate, actually, as theatre owners—especially of single or just a few screens—paid (and still pay) very high rates for the rental of feature films, and tend to make their profits on concession sales alone.

projector and film—("Advertisements") The viewing medium of choice, during this period, for non-theatrical pornographic film exhibition. The term "8mm" refers to the size of the film stock.

prologue—(PSC; "Restaurant [Abuse/Cannibalism]") From the Greek, meaning "before speech." Shakespeare's Prologue in *Henry V* speaks often, begging the audience be patient in watching the unreal stage version of action and reality. Chaucer's prologue to his *Canterbury Tales* is also significant. Here in the restaurant, of course, the characters see prologue as a nuisance, adding misinformation (the waiter's hissed "No, it doesn't!"), not illumination to the scene.

David Ballantyne plays the Prologue character, and also plays the "Indian Head" later, in the squatter sketch. See the entry for "Ballantyne, David" above for more on this actor/musician.

"proper punchline"—("Restaurant [Abuse/Cannibalism]") So Shirley (Idle) supports the staid, formulaic mode of comedy writing that Python came out against from the initial episode, but they still slouched into whenever the opportunity for a zinger presented itself.

– R –

"R101"—("Historical Impersonations") The R101 was a British-built airship that crashed near Beauvais, France, on 5 October 1930, killing everyone aboard. Cf. Ep. 40 for an entire episode devoted to airships (not balloons). The music behind the stunt is "Le Marseillaise" as played by the Band of the Grenadier Guards (WAC T12/1,094).

"Rainwear Through the Ages"—(link out of "Albatross") Perhaps a reference to the "dank" nature of some cinemas referred to in this link, or the seemingly constant need for rainwear in the London area, but may also be a slap at the international cinema of the period. Many recent "New Wave" films dealt with seemingly trivial or pedestrian or overtly oneiric (and therefore more personal) subjects and people, no longer focusing on kings and exciting historical events and larger-than-life Hollywood figures. Resnais' *Last Year at Marienbad* (1962) examines memory and desire in long, slow, undramatic (and for many, unwatchable) takes; Truffaut's *Jules and Jim* (1961) focuses on three normal young folk looking for sex and love; and Godard's 1967 film *Weekend* is as disconnected and narratively nontraditional a film as had been seen outside of the avant garde movements of the 1920s and 1930s.

Rainwear appears often in *FC*, which shouldn't be surprising considering the climate in and around London. Occasionally, rainwear figures into a character or sketch significantly. Cf. Eps. 8 and 23, where Praline (Cleese) wears a rubber mac, or Ep. 33, where the crew of a lifeboat find themselves in Mrs. Neves' (Jones) kitchen.

"rhythm method"—("Restaurant [Abuse/Cannibalism]") Spoken directly to the camera. The rhythm method is a method of birth control (or to gauge fertile periods) using a woman's menstrual cycle to pinpoint ovulation. It is said to be the preferred method of pregnancy prevention even among those opposed—for religious reasons—to artificial forms of birth control.

This inflammatory subject had sparked quite a bit of controversy on the David Frost show *Not So Much a Programme, More a Way of Life* in November 1964, when a birth control sketch was featured. *NSMP* was a follow-up to Frost's popular *TW3*, which had been taken off the air as General Elections approached in 1964. Ned Sherrin (Ep. 5) again produced the show, but it seems none of the future Pythons contributed any material.

"Rottingdeans"—("Come Back to My Place") Rottingdean (not "Rottingdeans") is south and east of Brighton, on the seashore. It's also not far down the coast from Hove, mentioned as the location of the "bear attack signalbox" in Ep. 12. It's perhaps fitting that the activity following is happening in a resort area.

This is also an intertextual moment, as there is no "Rottingdeans" in the UK, only in the Python world of Ep. 9, from which Sir George Head (Cleese) embarked to Africa: "The A23s through Purleys down on the main roads near Purbrights avoiding Leatherheads to the A231s entering Rottingdeans from the north. From *Rottingdeans* we go through Africa." The Pythons create the world of action, and then reference that same world, much as Shakespeare "quoted" himself (see Bergeron and/in Larsen's *MPSERD*).

Just before the transition to the policeman being propositioned by the man there is a filmed image of the Queen with accompanying music, "Great Britain: God Save the Queen" by National Anthems of the World, Band of the Grenadier Guards (WAC T12/1,094).

– S –

"salt of the earth"—("Restaurant [Abuse/Cannibalism]") Phrase also used by Biggles (Chapman) to describe Ginger (Gilliam) in Ep. 33. This is also an indication, again stereotypically, that the wife (Idle) is overly attached to her mother.

"second form"—("Restaurant [Abuse/Cannibalism]") English school vernacular. *OED*: "One of the numbered classes into which the pupils of a school are divided according to their degree of proficiency. In English Schools the sixth form is usually the highest; when a larger number of classes is required, the numbered 'forms' are divided into 'upper' and 'lower', etc." Previous mentions of the levels of school include "Upper Science library" (ep. 10) and, later, lamentations over stock deals going on in "big school" (Ep. 28).

second interviewer—("*Probe-Around* on Crime") Narrators usurping narrators is something of a Python staple, and is probably a comment on the competitive nature of the modern media. Cf. the "Whicker Island" sketch in Ep. 27, the documentary figures attacking each other in Ep. 30, the "Rival Documentaries" segment in Ep. 38, and even the killing of the Learned Historian (John Young) in the feature film *HG*. The power of the narrator is paramount—the controlling, leading voice, the forwarded point-of-view, the support or undercutting of the status quo, etc., all figure into this control—and lethal means are often used to secure such a privileged position of communication and power.

The adversarial and confrontational interviewing (almost interrogating) style of Robin Day, for example, so new to British television, is a significant influence here (see notes for Ep. 1 for more).

"second wife"—("Restaurant—Abuse/Cannibalism") Cf. Euripides' characterization of a second wife as a hateful viper (*Alcestis*, line 309).

"seen it and seen it"—("Psychiatry—Silly Sketch") Commenting on the kind of narrative and/or structural predictability in the television medium that the Pythons sought to parody, lampoon, and overthrow in *FC*. Actually, the sketch has already subverted expectations by not only allowing us to see the "out-of-character" exchange between the Receptionist (Cleveland) and Psychiatrist (Cleese), but giving us another out-of-character reaction by the Napoleon figure (Jones)—this kind of subversion had already come to be Python's signature in *FC*. Reacting against tradition—the hallmark of Modernism—works well until the reaction becomes traditional, then constant subversion is required.

Thus entrenched, the Pythons were trapped by their own demands for new approaches and the subsequent normalization/codification of those new moments. Audiences would have by now been tuning in and requesting live tickets to see more of this anarchic brand of humor, fully expecting to see more of the *same*. The subversive moments become the norm, and another predictable structure is created—an interesting paradox confronted by all things new in art. This is part of the reason, Cleese admits, that he left the show after the third season, and earlier why Michael Bentine (1922-1996)—one of the original Goons—left *The Goon Show* show after just two increasingly successful seasons. See Wilmut and Grafton. For the remaining Pythons, the fourth series would be new by virtue of the episodes' thematic continuity, building on the success of Ep. 34 and Pither's "Cycling Tour," as well as the absence of Cleese's influence/presence, and the minimal use of outside writers, including Douglas Adams (1952-2001) and David Sherlock. See notes to the fourth series for more on the structural and tonal changes brought on by this increased attention to a single, overarching theme, as well as the new creative personnel.

seven seconds of (slightly) speeded up Mantovani—(PSC; "Intermissions") The music that fills this spot is actually Percy Faith's version of the theme from *A Summer Place* by Max Steiner, and not Mantovani (WAC T12/1,094). The show's theme music follows immediately.

Mantovani—Called Monty by friends, Mantovani was a first-chair-violinist-cum-light-orchestra-conductor, and a naturalized Englishman. His music is heard in other episodes (Montreux compilation episode; Eps. 3, 16, and 35), but not this one.

Other music heard during the animated and live action "movie theatre" filmed sections include: Robert Hartow in "Sunday Night at the Palladium" by the London Palladium Orchestra, conducted by Cyril Orandel; "On the Button—Quick Mover" by The Studio Group, directed by Keith Papworth; "Happy Harp" from Johnny Teupen and His Harp; "Sweet & Singing" by Gene Herrmann and His Orchestra; Musical Boxes 1-8; and from "TV & Radio Commercials," "Mother & Baby," and "Bossa Nova Beat" (WAC T12/1,094).

"sherry"—("Restaurant [Abuse/Cannibalism]") Originally, a Spanish fortified wine. Cf. the "Sherry-Drinking Vicar" sketch in Ep. 36, as well as the besotted Old Lady (Chapman) in Ep. 40.

"Shirley"—("Rastaurant [Abuse/Cannibalism]") The wife's first name first uttered at this point. Later the husband will be identified, as well—"Douglas." Shirley Douglas (b. 1934) is an actress who appeared in Kubrick's *Lolita* (1962) as the piano teacher. Peter Sellers also appeared in the film, as Clare Quilty, which may have provided Python's link to the "Shirley" and "Douglas" names.

"Sicilian delicacies"—("Advertisements") The balance of this narration will deal in double entendres, making the link between food and sexuality utilized in many works, from the fourteenth-century Spanish work *Libro de buen amor* through more contemporary filmmakers Von Stroheim, Bunuel, Fellini, Godard, and beyond.

Popular and controversial Nouvelle Vague film director Jean-Luc Godard would bring food, sex, politics, and death together in 1967 in the film *Weekend*, where pre-Pythonesque absurdities include rape, cannibalism, and Marxist political speechifying accompanied by a live drummer. *Weekend* was called "a film found on a dump" in one of the film's intertitles, which the Pythons will spoof directly in Ep. 23, "French Subtitled Film," shooting the episode on a rubbish tip. See notes to that episode for more on the significance of this film, filmmaker, and the various New Waves in general to/on the Pythons.

"sixteen stone"—("Historical Impersonations") About 224 pounds. It's not clear what Cardinal Richelieu actually weighed. Another Python referent, Hilaire Belloc (Ep. 2), wrote a biography of Richelieu published in 1929.

"slit you up a treat"—("Operating Theatre [Squatters]") A colloquialism meaning to cut him "extremely, excessively." See *OED*, "treat," entry 5b. The Piranha brothers will be "slit up a treat" in Ep. 14 when they attempt to strongarm the MCC.

"Soho"—("Advertisements") Soho is a district in the West End of London, known for many years for its population of foreigners, ladies of the night, and restaurants, and "latterly for its night clubs, striptease shows, [and] pornography shops" (*OED*). It's fitting that Mr. Vercotti would set up a restaurant here, then, and that all sorts of questionable activity could be taking place in the back rooms. Another period description of the parish mentions the sordid but colorful world of Soho:

> "Untidy, full of Greeks, Ishmaelites, cats, Italians, tomatoes, restaurants, organs, coloured stuffs, queer names, people looking out of upper windows, it dwells remote from the British body politic." (Qtd. in Ackroyd, *London* 526)

One of the female "models" is astride one of the cars in the advertisement, much like a pub sign described by Ackroyd in *London*:

> A once famous inn known as the Mischief, in Charles Street, had as its sign a drunken courtesan straddling a man's back while holding a glass of gin with the legend "She's Drunk as a Sow" inscribed by her. (527)

Ackroyd concludes that it was the very "foreignness" of the area that allowed for such significant (illegal) sexual activity, and the Pythons, by employing Vercotti and his restaurant's "delicacies" and "specialities," acknowledge and even embrace and celebrate that foreign influence many years later.

"smile, a conquest, and a dagger up your strap"—("Historical Impersonations") Perhaps a nod to the old comedic "rule of threes." Julius Caesar was stabbed to death on 15 March (44 BC) in the senate house in Rome. Caesar (Chapman) also appeared in Ep. 2 as a closet mouse, and in Ep. 10 in relation to his Christmas show. The moment Caesar gets a dagger up his strap is re-enacted in Ep. 15, the *"Julius Caesar* on an Aldis Lamp" sketch.

"squatter"—("Operating Theatre [Squatters]") A "squatter" is someone who occupies lands or property without legal ownership, and this is originally an American term. Portions of the counterculture movement of the 1960s in the United States adopted a sort of aboriginal notion of property rights, claiming the earth belonged to everyone, and that ownership wasn't allowed by/in Nature. This was primarily a sociopolitical argument, as most of the hue and cry happened to be against corporate, big business and big money entities/persons.

In England, conversely, the London Squatters Campaign of the 1960s was fueled by the critical housing shortage experienced after the end of WWII, and squatting en masse became a familiar practice, especially in London. Each sitting and hopeful government (Labour and Conservative alike) promised more council houses, year after year, but demand far outpaced the government's ability to build affordable (and livable) homes for all qualified citizens. (This problem led to some of the ill-advised tower estates built in the 1960s; one of these collapsed in 1968, and the entire right-headed but shoddy endeavor is satirized by the Pythons in Ep. 17, and *Private Eye* in 1968 and 1969 issues.)

Andrew Friend characterizes the years 1969-1977 as the high water point in London squatting, a time when the "adroit use of the law by squatters [had] frequently delayed evictions and provided time for organisation and negotiation." Later in the sketch, the Surgeon (Chapman) confesses that he can't remove the squatters without a court order. According to Friend, the squatter in England benefited from the fact that under English law squatting was trespassing, which was not a criminal act, meaning police found themselves a bit powerless to enforce property rights if the squatters were in situ. The sketch plays on that notion throughout. (See the entry for "court order" above.)

For more on the housing problem and the adequate/inadequate governmental response to the situation in postwar Britain, see the entry for "build . . . houses" in Ep. 14.

sticking pins—("*Probe-Around* on Crime") A voodoo practice of the West Indies, where the intended victim is pained by the pins inserted into his/her likeness. The doll seen here was ordered very early in the production of the series, perhaps because the scene was intended for earlier broadcast (WAC T12/1,082). See the entry for "model of a burglar" above for more on this curious prop.

strops—(PSC; "Operating Theatre [Squatters]") Meaning to sharpen a blade on a razor strop.

– T –

"television"—("Restaurant [Abuse/Cannibalism]") Blaming the media for the crumbling of whatever society she pictures, Shirley is glumly, unattractively espousing the Mary Whitehouse line. A conservative, moralistic media watchdog group, Whitehouse's National Viewers' and Listeners' Association (NVLA) tilted long and loud against England's "permissive society," and especially the potential damage done by loosened moral standards on television, in films, and in books and magazines. See notes to Ep. 32, "Tory Housewives," for more.

test card—(link out of "Operating Theatre [Squatters]") *OED*: In "television, a diagrammatic still picture transmitted outside normal programme hours and designed for use in judging the quality and position of the image on any particular screen." Test cards have disappeared almost completely from today's television, as programming tends to run on around the clock, even on local stations.

theatre audience—("Quiz Programme—*Wishes*") Stock footage of an applauding opera audience (simply termed "Opera Audience"), with the camera positioned at stage left looking out into the house (WAC T12/1,094).

thesaurus—("Psychiatry—Silly Sketch") A self-deprecating comment on the type of sketches written, often, by Chapman and Cleese, and eventually parodied by others in the troupe. See Ep. 33, "Cheese Shop," and Ep. 37, "What the Stars Foretell."

"These hands . . . German bands"—("Psychiatry—Silly Sketch") For the spirit of the entire speech, cf. the structure of the soliloquy given by John of Gaunt to the Duke of York in Shakespeare's *Richard II* (1595):

> This royal throne of kings, this sceptred isle,
> This earth of majesty, this seat of Mars,
> This other Eden, demi-paradise,
> This fortress built by Nature for herself
> Against infection and the hand of war,
> This happy breed of men, this little world,
> This precious stone set in the silver sea,
> Which serves it in the office of a wall,
> Or as [a] moat defensive to a house,
> Against the envy of less happier lands,
> This blessed plot, this earth, this realm, this England.
> . . . (2.1.40-50)

In Ep. 3, the defendant's soliloquy, Python also waxes Shakespearean, and the psychoanalyzing of the character Hamlet will comprise most of Ep. 43.

"Tota . . . Hull Kingston Rovers"—("Historical Impersonations") Translation: "Gaul (or France) is divided into three parts, Wigan, Hunslett and Hull Kingston Rovers."

The first portion of the quote is actually from Julius Caesar, writing in regard to the justification for the sacking of Gaul: "Gallia est omnis divisa in partes tres" (*Comentarii De Bello Gallico*, I.1).

"Wigan"—The Wigan rugby league (Greater Manchester area) is still active.

"Hunslett"—A misspelling of Hunslet, the Hunslet Rugby Club being formed in 1883, in South Leeds, Yorkshire.

"Hull Kingston Rovers"—Hull Kingston Rovers rugby team began in 1882, and won the Yorkshire Cup in 1966-1967, and 1967-1968. A noted matchup between Wigan and Hull occurred in May 1959, when Wigan beat Hull 30-13. Wigan also defeated Hunslet in May 1965 by a score of 20-16. Both matches were played at Wembley. See notes for Wembley below.

"two bricks"—("Historical Impersonations") In Ep. 9, the Gumby Crooner (Chapman) sings a song while hitting himself in the head with two bricks, and later Ron Obvious (Jones) attempts to jump the Channel carrying a load of his sponsor's bricks (Ep. 11), and Ken Maniac (also Jones) puts a brick to sleep in Ep. 10.

– V –

"vegetarian"—("Restaurant [Abuse/Cannibalism]") Vegetarianism generally means eating only fruits and vegetables, and avoiding animal flesh of any kind. This, of course, seems to run foul of the obvious fact that the restaurant serves human flesh, which might be a comment on the place of humans in relation to animals in the eyes of the more fervent animal rights activists.

The "smug" comment is perhaps a slap at the animal rights activists and/or vegetarians of the time who may have assumed self-righteous attitudes about their life choices as opposed to those who disagreed with them. The early 1970s saw the beginnings of Greenpeace (to combat over-whaling) and a significant rise in the number and activity of anti-vivisectionist groups.

Vegetarianism was in the news at this time, as well. (Keith Waite had produced a cartoon in April 1969 for *The Sun* showing a vegetarian gone begging. See the British Cartoon Archive.) In October 1969 the two long-competing societies in the UK, the Vegetarian Society and the London Vegetarian Society, had publicly joined forces to become The Vegetarian Society of the United Kingdom Limited.

"Vercotti, Luigi"—("Advertisements") Cf. Vercotti's equally oily appearances in Eps. 8, 10, and 14, each time as a shady underworld businessman with something or someone to sell. The Vercottis are loose, comedic versions of the real-life Kray brothers, East End gangsters who dealt in racketeering, prostitution, drugs, influence, and all manner of illegal activity, and who were sentenced to long prison terms in December 1969.

vestibule—(PSC; "Restaurant [Abuse/Cannibalism]") In the coat check room, the actress Flanagan (*Groupie Girl*) can be seen. She also appears in Eps. 7, 11, 12, and 22. A "vestibule" is a transitional entrance area.

vicar sitting thin and unhappy in a pot—("Restaurant [Abuse/Cannibalism]") Believe it or not, there is a *direct* reference for this scene. Harold Davidson (1875-1937), the Rector of Stiffkey, Norfolk, had been leading a double life. In addition to his work as the vicar of the small coastal town of Stiffkey, he also visited the Soho district in London to minister to the prostitutes there, where he was eventually arrested and charged with illicit activities unbecoming his position. It was never satisfactorily proven that he actually did anything untoward with the soiled doves of London, but the publicity cost him his position, reputation, etc. In either a fit of pique, a paroxysm of mental stability, or just to point up the absurdity of his arrest and conviction, he climbed into a barrel on the Blackpool Pier and stayed there for a year, on display. Fittingly, Davidson would eventually die as a result of a lion attack on stage in a freak show (*ODNB* and *Eyewitness 1930-39*, "The Rector of Stiffkey" and "The Return of the Rector of Stiffkey").

– W –

"wafers"—("Albatross") A good question, since ices would be commonly served with wafers. Ice cream sandwiches also consist of ice cream sandwiched between wafers.

"Warner . . . Cuppa"—("Restaurant [Abuse/Cannibalism]") "Warner House" and "Badger House" would be residence halls in Eton or Harrow-type schools (for Upperclass Twits), or even a school like the Pythons themselves had attended. Badger is located in Shropshire, and a Badger House is found there. The "headmaster" would be principal master of such a school.

The Pythons school backgrounds make such references quite understandable:

- Chapman attended Melton Mowbray Grammar School in Leicester
- Cleese boarded at Clifton College in Bristol, where the individual houses included Oakley's, North Town, Watson's, and Wiseman's (Cleese lived in North Town)
- Idle attended the Royal Wolverhampton School (Wolverhampton), where the houses are called Dartmouth, Rogers, and Victoria
- Jones attended the Royal Grammar School, Guildford, where the houses are called Austen, Beckinghan, Hamonde, Nettles, Powell, and Valpy
- Palin was enrolled at Shrewsbury School in Liverpool, where the individual houses include Churchill's, Ingram's, Moser's, Oldham's, and Rigg's.

"Second Cuppa"—The interval (halftime) during cricket matches gives players and umpires the opportunity to rest and enjoy tea and cucumber sandwiches, with a "second cuppa" being possible only if there's sufficient time.

"Welch, Racquel"—("Quiz Programme—*Wishes*") Actually spelled "Raquel." Hollywood starlet who appeared in *Fantastic Voyage* and *One Million Years B.C.* (1966), and, perhaps most significantly, *The Magic Christian* (1969), where she played the Priestess of the Whip. Chapman and Cleese contributed written material to this Peter Sellers film.

Wembley—(PSC; "Historical Impersonations") Sports stadium located in Wembley, Greater London. The stadium was the site for both the British Empire Exposition of 1924-1925 and the 1948 summer Olympics. Wembley is home to the FA Cup Finals, has hosted many European cup finals, the 1966 World Cup, and Rugby League Challenge Cup Finals. The footage is from a "Cup Final" film (WAC T12/1,094).

"We're All Going to the Zoo Tomorrow"—("Psychiatry—Silly Sketch") According to BBC records, this Julie Felix song is titled "Going to the Zoo" and performed here by The World of Harmony Music (WAC T12/1,094). Julie Felix's songs were also heard on various David Frost programs during the 1960s—in short she was very high profile during this period.

"wet my bed"—("Restaurant [Abuse/Cannibalism]") The barefaced honesty displayed by Shirley's (Idle) rantings, along with Donald's (Cleese) assessments of his wife's qualities, seems to have allowed the Head Waiter (Palin) to speak more freely than usual.

"without a pudding"—("Restaurant [Abuse/Cannibalism]") Interestingly, most puddings would have been made using animal entrails and animal stuffing, meaning this restaurant wouldn't have served them (unless they substituted human or vegetable ingredients).

– X –

'Xmas night with the stars'—(PSC; link out of "Mr. Attila the Hun") *Christmas Night With the Stars* (1958-1994) was a long-running television special in the UK, starring, among others, Ronnie Barker (1929-2005). Here the script writers reference this show, then admit the reference may be wrong, but leave the entire passage in the script anyway.

– Y –

"Yew Tree . . . U Thant"—("Me Doctor") Yew trees are found throughout Europe and Asia, and often planted in churchyards. Utrecht is a town in Holland. (Cf. the mention of the Treaty of Utrecht in Ep. 2.) Utrillo is an artist—also mentioned elsewhere in *FC*—his paintings among those eaten by the Art Critic (Palin) in Ep. 4. Burmese diplomat U Thant (1909-1974) was the Secretary-General for the U.N. between 1961-1971.

This passage is very much reliant on the sounds of the words as opposed to any meaning or interconnectivity they may share or create. In this the Pythons are referencing the works of Modernist writers including T.S. Eliot (Ep. 28), James Joyce, and especially Gertrude Stein. Stein's ability to write for sound as opposed to meaning is manifest in many of her works, and exhibits the "modern" removal away from word signification toward less symbolic associations based on sounds. This decreased dependence on what words (or images, in art) "mean" was indicative of the Modernist period, where virtually all closely held truths of art and representation were called into question, upended, turned inside-out, or ignored altogether. From Stein's "Melanctha," from *Three Lives* (1909):

> Every day now, Jeff seemed to be coming nearer, to be really loving. Every day now, Melanctha poured it all out to him, with more freedom. Every day now, they seemed to be having more and more, both together, of this strong, right feeling. More and more every day now they seemed to know really, what it was each other one was always feeling. More and more now every day Jeff found in himself, he felt more trusting. More and more every day now, he did not think anything in words about what he was always doing. Every day now more and more Melanctha would let out to Jeff her real, strong feeling. (394)

Idle characters will often fall into this kind of "Stein meditation," where the outside world/narrative seems to have little or no influence on the phraseology being uttered, and the recitation can be repetitive, but actually builds and builds on previous lines. (See Ratcliffe for this discussion in relation to Stein.) The Pythons clearly embraced the linguistic and referential freedoms made possible by Modernist poets, novelists, and artists.

Episode 14

– A –

a foot thick—(PSC; "The Ministry of Silly Walks") No character wears such shoes in the film clip. "Little Tich" is the stage name of Harry Relph (1867-1928), a Cudham-born music hall and pantomime performer. Tich's 28-inch (in length) boots are on display in Cudham today.

"Air Chief Marshal"—(link into "New Cooker Sketch") During this period, this would have been the second-highest ranking for an RAF officer. Other noted Air Chief Marshals included ACM Charles Portal (1893-1971), and ACM Sir Norman Howard Bottomley (1891-1970).

"Forster"—The character mentioned ("Air Chief Marshal Sir Vincent 'Kill the Japs' Forster") is yet another WWII-era veteran who obviously served in the Pacific Theatre and who, in 1969-1970, could very well have written the kind of angry/obtuse letters mentioned earlier. The depiction here, though, is likely based on the infamous head of RAF Bomber Command during WWII, Sir Arthur "Bomber" Harris (1892-1984), who engendered both respect and infamy for his advocacy of carpet, seemingly indiscriminate bombing on civilian targets like Cologne in 1942 and Dresden much later in the war.

There was also an actual General Forster, though he was head of the German Luftwehr (Air Defense) during WWII.

"Allied Bomber Command"—(link into "New Cooker Sketch") WWII-era organization in charge of the (primarily) American and British bomber squadrons operating out of Britain. Britain's Bomber Command merged with fighter forces in the late 1960s, its demise covered extensively in the news.

"Anglo-French"—("The Ministry of Silly Walks") The British and French have endured rocky relations for centuries, going from outright war to uneasy peace by the nineteenth and twentieth centuries. Recently, Britain's attempted entry into the EEC (European Economic Community) had already been vetoed twice by this time by deGaulle (rebuffing Macmillan and Wilson separately), and it wouldn't be until 1973 (and under a Tory government) that Britain would finally join the continental organization. In political cartoons of the period, the phrase is often found in panels lampooning the failed Anglo-French foreign policy endeavors in North Africa, the Middle East—especially in relation to the oil-rich states of the Gulf—the touchy EEC issue, the Concorde SST (Ep. 2), and of course the Channel Tunnel. The reinvigorated concept of the Channel Tunnel (c. 1957-1963) had become an enormously expensive (publicly and bi-laterally funded) and cooperative undertaking with the French, as the Concorde program had been. In an Abu Abraham panel, de Gaulle and Macmillan meet in the tunnel under the Channel, just to thumb their noses at each other (*Observer* 22 September 1963). See the British Cartoon Archive for this cartoon and many more.

"argh!"—("Tobacconists [Prostitute Advert]") At the mention of the possibility of giving blood, the shabby man offers a subtle hand/arm gesture to indicate sexual penetration. Blood is "often synonymous with sexual passion," according to Henke in *Courtesans and Cuckolds*.

as she opens the door—(PSC; "New Cooker Sketch") As usual for the series, the props and set decorations of these interior sets are carefully composed and chosen to reflect the typical—in this case middle-class—British Midlands home. (Most of the Pythons' references and influences and settings emerge from the Midlands, interestingly, from London northward to York, the "middle" of the country where the working class are the representative population.)

Behind her, on the far wall are framed prints of paintings, including Thomas Gainsborough's portrait *The Marsham Children* (1787), and an unidentified landscape. The décor of the room (set in a "G-Plan," see below) includes what appears to be a mass-produced, drop-shoulder version of a "Devon" 1940s fireplace (Art Deco, cream-grey tile), and inside that a faux-Edwardian copper or brass stove (probably coal-burning).

– B –

backyard of terraced house—(PSC; "New Cooker Sketch") This location is not the Thorpebank Road house, since the backyards are much smaller. This long backyard is located behind a home on Goodhall Street, very near the Willesden Junction Station, less than two miles north of the Thorpebank Road location (WAC T12/1,416).

"Baldwin, Stanley"—("The Piranha Brothers") Baldwin (1867-1947) was a Conservative British Prime Minister 1923-1924, 1924-1929, and 1935-1937. It's no surprise that the sexuality of a Tory PM would be called into question by the Pythons. Also, as Baldwin died in 1947, Dinsdale would have been under eighteen when this alleged affair took place.

This consistent blurring of past and present in *FC*—here the mention of a political figure now dead for twenty-three years—reminds us that, as Judt mentions in *Postwar*, the Pythons had been reared in a time as Edwardian as modern, living through a postwar "suspended time" where "daily life . . . would have been thoroughly familiar to men and women of fifty years earlier" (226). The Victorian and Edwardian emblems were everywhere: the almost total dependence on coal for power and heat and the concomitant blackened fog shrouding London; the popularity of Terence Rattigan's throwback plays and Ealing Studios' quirky "nineteenth-century" comedies; and the dance halls and "working-men's clubs" (226-27). This is the ancien regime the Pythons' both reveled in and rebelled against, and the war had merely extended the period's lease in the British public's collective conscience.

"Bath Chronicle"—("The Piranha Brothers") Both of these papers—the *Bath Chronicle* and the *Bristol Evening Post*—are still being published. Bath is southeast of Bristol, on the River Avon. The *Western Daily News* is also extant.

"BBC2"—("The Piranha Brothers") The second publicly owned channel began broadcasting in 1964, and produced shows including the groundbreaking documentary series *Civilisation* (1964-), *Late Night Line-Up* (1965-), and *The World About Us* (1967-). BBC2 would also pioneer color television in the UK in 1967, a move which benefited the Pythons and *Flying Circus* greatly.

Ben Hur—(PSC; "New Cooker Sketch") A 1959 biblical epic starring Charlton Heston and directed by William Wyler, and based on the popular 1880 Lew Wallace novel. The title is, indeed, made to look like letters chiseled from enormous stone blocks. Gilliam would revisit this look in the titles for *Life of Brian*, another "biblical" epic.

The music used for these impressive titles is the programmatic music "Epic Title" by Jack Shaindlin (WAC T12/1,417).

Putting such a seemingly simple and mundane bit of modern life—the new cooker—at the center of an epic presentation (worthy of "artistic" treatment) has an earlier context, interestingly. British painter Spencer Gore's *The Gas Cooker* (1913) is a quiet work celebrating both the artist's wife and her work in the modern kitchen. The painting has been part of the Tate's collection since 1962. Moving away from the strictures of classical art, modern art and artists often examine the everyday, the mundane, and find those subjects as compelling as any hero, myth, or legend. W.P. Sickert's commentary from this period and his own motivations for common subject matters and settings is illuminating:

> The more our art is serious, the more will it tend to avoid the drawing-room and stick to the kitchen. The plastic arts are gross servants, dealing joyously with gross material facts. They call, in their servants, for a robust stomach and a great power of endurance, and while they flourish in the scullery, or on the dunghill, they fade at a breath from the drawing-room. (From Sickert's "The Idealism News" in *A Free House! Or The Artist as Craftsman; Being the Writings of Walter Richard Sickert*, ed. Sitwell.)

Being the center of the typical English home, the kitchen is the center of not only many so-called kitchen sink dramas of the postwar British stage and screen, but in the parodic versions of that world created by the Pythons. See the Man and Wife (Palin and Jones) discussing a walk-on BBC part over breakfast (Ep. 10), the couple (Davidson and Jones) discussing the Indian massacre at Dorking theatre in Ep. 6, the "Salvation Fuzz" sketch with "Strawberry Tart" in Ep. 29, and *"The Most Awful Family in Britain"* in the final episode. In the feature film *The Meaning of Life*, a man will donate his liver on his own kitchen table, and the delights of sex for enjoyment will be discussed over the morning's eggs and toast.

"Binkie"—("The Piranha Brothers") Certainly a reference to Hugh "Binkie" Beaumont, the noted West End theatre impresario who produced plays for Terence Rattigan (Eps. 24, 30) and Noel Coward (Ep. 35).

"Birmingham"—(link into "New Cooker Sketch") Large city in Warwickshire, called England's "second city," the BBC maintains studios in Birmingham at Pebble Mill. Much of the action and people described in the Tourist's tirade in Ep. 19 center on the greater Birmingham area, where Idle grew up and went to school.

"bit of pram"—("Tobacconists [Prostitute Advert]") A play on the phrase "bit of tail," mentioned in several episodes, and refers to, again, the female pudendum. Cf. Ep. 33, where Biggles calls his secretary a "bit of tail."

"bless him"—("The Piranha Brothers") This affectionate, nostalgic look at very real gangsters as portrayed by the Pythons would be reinforced in life. From the time of the Krays' arrest and convictions there were demonstrations for the brothers' release (they were folk heroes to many East Enders), and latterly by the presence of an estimated 100,000 funeral procession attendees for Reggie's 2000 funeral, "standing six deep along Bethnall Green Road," according to Jones, and this quote from a local female onlooker: "It's an East End event," said a woman. "I think they were a legend. The public liked them. They were gangsters, fun" (see Jones' article at "The Crime Library," and entries for the Krays in the *ODNB*).

"Block . . . Voice"—(PSC; "The Piranha Brothers") These two speeches aren't credited in the printed scripts, but are delivered by Jones and Palin, respectively.

"boot in the groin"—("The Piranha Brothers") Reggie Kray developed a favorite assault mode, as well, formulating a sucker punch that reportedly broke many unsuspecting jaws. See Jones, chapter 3. Again, the Pythons are staying fairly close to actuality as they tell the tale of their fictional Piranha brothers. The Pythons were also likely emboldened by the fact that the Krays had very recently been handed lengthy prison sentences, as well as that the editors of *Private Eye*—who had "outed" the brothers in the national press for the first time—had not themselves suffered physical retribution.

"born on probation"—("The Piranha Brothers") The Krays were born in 1933, not 1929, in Hoxton, Hackney,

Greater London, in the heart of the crime-rich East End. At the turn of the twentieth century philanthropist/ researcher Charles Booth (1840-1916) would describe the area as "the leading criminal quarter of London, and indeed of all England" ("Poverty in England").

"boxer"—("The Piranha Brothers") Both Kray boys and their older brother, Charlie—not their mother— became accomplished amateur boxers in the East End.

"Boys' Clubs . . . Household Cavalry"—("The Piranha Brothers") Ronnie Kray was an admitted and practicing homosexual, and was said to have had a fondness for younger men of any color. See Jones.

As for "household cavalry," these are the troops specially assigned to protect the sovereign, and favorites of the royal family generally fill these positions. These are the kinds of organizations that the Upperclass Twits also represented in Ep. 12.

"Bristol Rep"—("The Piranha Brothers") Bristol is also across the Severn from Cardiff, but almost due east. "Bristol Rep" probably refers to a smaller regional theatre, like the Dorking Civic Theatre mentioned in Ep. 6. This also may be a reference to the prestigious Bristol Old Vic, the renowned local repertory company, or the Rapier Players, another repertory group in the area. Cleese grew up in this area.

"build . . . houses"—(*Face the Press*) The subject of housing comes up again and again in post-WWII Britain, and these shortages led to documentaries (*Housing Problems*, 1935, directed by Edgar Antsey and Arthur Elton), prefabricated housing movements, so-called New Town constructions, as well as a significant squatters' movement. The 1951 Conservative government, for example, back in power after losing leadership in 1945, promised to build 300,000 new houses every year. Election-year promises aside, during 1950-1954 there were actually just 912,805 local authority houses (not including private-built homes) constructed in England and Wales (Cook and Stevenson, *Modern British History* 171-72). Cf. Ep. 13 for more on the squatters' movement, which was quite active in postwar London, especially. Leading up to the 1964 election, both Labour and the Tories promised more and more houses, with the announced Labour number reaching 500,000 (*Labour Manifesto*). See notes to Ep. 35 for more.

According to the "London Housing Unit—History of Social Housing," more than four million homes were built in England and Wales in the two decades following WWII. Additionally, the pre- and postwar emphasis on local control for new housing led to supply bottlenecks and many fewer houses being built

than had been optimistically announced/planned
(K. Morgan, *Britain Since 1945* 39). By 1947, however,
these difficulties were being overcome, according to
Morgan, and houses were being built at the rate of
about 200,000 per year (40). Between 1952 and 1956,
more than 939,000 homes were built under the Conservative government (elected 1951), and 1956 saw the
beginning of the move toward high-rise housing.
(Morgan points out that it was the Labour government
of the 1940s who designed and built terraced council
estates "homes," while it was the Conservative government of the 1950s primarily responsible for the
high-rise "projects" of the 1950s and 1960s [39–40].) By
1969, 400 high-rise blocks had been built in the Greater
London area, but the Ronan Point disaster in 1968 signaled the end of enthusiasm for such structures (until
very recently), and by the end of the century, they were
being demolished in many towns. These same high-
rise blocks are mentioned in Ep. 17 ("Architect
Sketch") and Ep. 35, where such structures are created
thanks to Mystico's imagination. In Ep. 17, the satire is
such (a high-rise model like Ronan Point bursts into
flames) that the Pythons felt they had to perhaps protect themselves from prosecution by highlighting the
satirical bent of the sketch. See notes for Ep. 17. For
more on Greater London government-subsidized
housing, see lhu.org.uk/history.htm, as well as "New
Housing" on the *Eyewitness: 1950-59* collection.

"buy a fruit machine"—("The Piranha Brothers") The
real Krays were charged in March 1965 with attempting to extort protection money from a Soho club
owner, offering him doormen (bouncers) for a hefty
percentage of the club's receipts (*ODNB*).

   "fruit machine"—A "fruit machine" is a coin-
operated slot-type machine, and would have been a
machine installed as a profit-making device for the
Krays/Piranhas, not the club owner. The easing of
postwar rationing, as well as the legalization of gambling, had opened new vistas for corruption and
shakedowns in the London underworld.

– C –

"Cardiff"—("The Piranha Brothers") Jones was born
in Colwyn Bay, on the northern coast of Wales (near
Liverpool and Manchester). Cardiff is in southern
Wales, south and east across the Mouth of the Severn
from Weston-Super-Mare, Cleese's birthplace. Crossing the geographical borders of England for the wilds
of Wales or Scotland had been practiced by those on
the lam for centuries.

"Cartesian dualism"—("The Piranha Brothers") René
Descartes' dualistic belief in "the physical world [ex-

ternal] as mechanistic and entirely divorced from the
mind [internal world], the only connection between
the two being by intervention of God." See *EBO*. In
other words, the "intervention" or presence of God
might be what Mrs. Simnel (Palin) sees as the problem
with youth of her day.

"case against"—(*"Face the Press"*) This is a prime example of Python's "fair play" rule, since the case
against the obviously Conservative government is to
be argued by a stain, in essence. The normally Conser-
vative-bashing Pythons here put the more socially progressive Labour and/or Liberal parties into the seat of
derision, as well. This follows, for example, The Beatles' naming of both parties—Heath's Conservatives
and Wilson's Labour—as responsible for perpetuating
the onerous tax burden in "Taxman" (1965), and by
Private Eye's by then eight-year bash against any silly
or thick government figure, policy or party.

   More specifically to the housing crunch in the late
1960s, the razing of derelict housing tracts and factories and the building in their place of new housing facilities was a major plank in the Labour Party's platform as early as the 1930s, thanks to the 1930
Greenwood Act. See "build . . . houses" note above.

   Also, *Monty Python: The Case Against* is the title of
Hewison's book on Python's struggles with censorship and obscenity charges.

"Chamberlain, Richard"—("The Piranha Brothers")
Richard Chamberlain (b. 1935) appeared in many television mini-series, and would have been known to the
Pythons thanks to his famous role as Dr. Kildare (ABC,
1961). The music for *Dr. Kildare* will feature prominently in Ep. 26.

   "Peggy Mount"—Peggy Mount (b. 1918; Essex) is a
veteran character actress, appearing in *Oliver!* (1968).

   "Billy Bremner"—Billy Bremner was a star football
player for Leeds United and Scotland, and died in 1997
at the age of fifty-four. In 1970, Bremner was a mid-
fielder for Leeds.

"cheque had bounced"—("The Piranha Brothers") A
notorious slum landlord in the Notting Hill area, Peter
Rachman (1902-1962), had attempted to pay the Krays
the first installment of protection money with a bad
check. Instead of waiting around for the thugs to return
and demand payment, Rachman went underground,
and eventually found a way for the Krays to make
money from investments he was connected to, without
having to succumb completely to the brothers' thuggery
(*Eyewitness: 1960-69*, "Rachmanism 1" and "Rachmanism 2"). See also the entry for Rachman in the *ODNB*.

   The Kray brothers' trial was the longest in English
legal history, and perhaps the trial that garnered the
most (and mostly salacious) attention.

"chest of drawers"—("Tobacconists [Prostitute Advert]") Volpone employs this same double entendre stratagem in Jonson's *Volpone* (1606), continuing a long tradition of sexual double entendres in English theatrical performance. Drawers is, of course, slang for underwear.

"Chief Constable"—("The Piranha Brothers") The Krays were known for attempting to bribe police officers, and for providing fringe benefits in their clubs for same. They even finagled publicity photos with "Nipper" Read and Lord Boothby (much like American gangster John Dillinger had posed, smiling, with his captors/prosecutors), pictures that were attempts at either legitimacy or blackmail, whichever worked out.

city gent leaves the shop—(link into "The Ministry of Silly Walks") This was a corner store called Pickfords, and was used on 25 May 1970. The permissions for the location usage cost the show £10, and the address was 107 Thorpebank Road (WAC T12/1,242). Period phone books give the owner as an "R. Pickford," and the space is listed as a newsagent's shop (precisely: "Pickfords, Nwsagts, 107 Thorpebank Rd W12 . . . 01-743 5752"). (See the British Telephone Archives.)

Cleese will walk out onto and across Thorpebank Road, then continue west on Dunraven Road. The corner store has since been converted into a single-family home.

"Clerkenwell"—("The Piranha Brothers") Neighborhood in the borough of Islington in Greater London, and where St. Bartholomew's Hospital—where *Doctor* Graham Chapman interned—is located. More appropriately, Clerkenwell has been the site of a prison (or a series of prisons) for several hundred years. Islington is also the area where Black Power leader and some-time-terrorist Michael X was attempting to set up a peace commune, of sorts.

The school used in this interview scene is actually St. Hubert's School. There is no record in the WAC material for this episode that permission was either requested or received to shoot so near the school. St. Hubert's Secondary School is located at Mellitus St., Shepherds Bush W12.

"clip joint"—("The Piranha Brothers") A bar or club that charges excessively, and just the kind of establishment that the Krays were known for running. The term is used often in gangster and film noir (see *Detour* [1946]; *Asphalt Jungle* [1950]).

"colour supplements"—("The Piranha Brothers") Portions of the newspaper with added color. See the entry for Harry "Snapper" Organs below for more on the significance of the colour supplements. Cf. the "Travel Agent" sketch in Ep. 31, where "bolour supplements" are mentioned.

"completely different"—(titles) Cleese and Palin (It's Man) are in zoo cages here, shot at Chessington Zoo, Epsom Road, Chessington, Surrey (WAC T12/1,416). Cleese continues to deliver the tagline "And now for something completely different" in the BBC's received pronunciation, typical of BBC announcers.

The title tagline, however, is delivered in Cleese's "silly" voice, a change from the very sober kind of southern (read: London) "received pronunciation" earlier in the series, and employed whenever a BBC announcer is depicted. Palin will later take over this tagline duty.

"cooey"—("New Cooker Sketch") A call originally used by Australian aborigines, then adapted by British colonists as a way to bring attention to the caller. See *OED*. Jones is the only one who uses the term in the show (see Ep. 27).

"CookEasi"—("New Cooker Sketch") Probably a fictional proprietary name. The appliance used in the sketch looks to be a New World "Solaire"-type Gas Cooker.

"creosote"—(*Face the Press*) *OED*: "A colourless oily liquid, of complex composition, with odour like that of smoked meat, and burning taste, obtained from the distillation of wood-tar, and having powerful antiseptic properties."

"crimes of violence"—("The Piranha Brothers") Even though the Krays were known to have engaged in money laundering, drug dealing, terrorism (especially against immigrant families), racketeering, intimidation, multiple assaults, illegal gambling, and a laundry list of felony charges, they were only brought to trial and eventually convicted for murder. See Jones, chapters 16 and 17.

– D –

"Deptford"—("New Cooker Sketch") In Lewisham, a part of Greater London, and key to London's shipping industry for many generations. Peter Ackroyd reports in *London: The Biography*, that the Deptford area in the nineteenth century was described as "the worst part of the great City's story," and that it was "muddy," melancholy," and "empty" (543). The enormous buildings of industry—including sprawling warehouses and dockside quay houses—contributed to this dehumanizing effect.

"Dinsdale"—("The Piranha Brothers") Dinsdale Landen (b. 1932; Margate, Kent) was an English character actor who appeared in shows like *Dr. Who* and *The Guardians*. Dinsdale is also a well-known area in Darlington, where the Pythons shot portions of Ep. 25 for the second series.

"Doug"—("The Piranha Brothers") Of the twins, Ronnie may have been notably unpredictable, but Reggie was the heartless killer, according to Jones. Reggie was the lethal enforcer when Ronnie might only want to threaten and harm.

"drag"—(PSC; *Face the Press*) A man dressed as a woman; transvestitism. From the very first episode when Pepperpots were interviewed on the street, Python has eschewed the typical notion of casting women, or even including a woman in the troupe (Cleveland somewhat excepted), in favor of dressing the parts themselves. This is definitely a holdover from their revue days at Cambridge and Oxford, where there were few females either writing or performing, and men consistently took on female roles. (Cambridge actually had a sort of ban on women performing with Footlights, according to Idle.) This practice is also a significant throwback to the male-only Elizabethan stage practices. What is unique about this particular instance is that the man in drag is actually acknowledged, textually, which doesn't happen often in Python's oeuvre. Usually, a man dressed as a woman (e.g., a Pepperpot), is treated/perceived as a woman. Transvestitism is acknowledged twice in this episode, and again in Ep. 33, where Biggles (Chapman) admits that he sometimes dresses as his wife.

– E –

"Eastend"—("The Piranha Brothers") The eastern end of London, known for its immigrant population, rough living and working conditions, and high crime rates. Major employment prior to WWII was located in the "London Docklands." Specifically, the East End is located "east of Shoreditch High Street, Houndsditch, Aldgate High Street, and Tower Bridge Approach. It extends eastward to the River Lea and lies mainly in the Inner London borough of Tower Hamlets, part of the historic county of Middlesex" (*OED*). See Ackroyd's *London* for more on the "perilous region's" troubled history.

"Egernon Road"—("New Cooker Sketch") No such street exists anywhere in the UK, though there is an "Egerton Road" just off of Stamford Hill, and an "Egerton Crescent" in SW3. This is unusual for the Pythons, as they commonly choose existing street names then set them in different towns, probably culling such names from memory. Perhaps also it is a

particular pronunciation of "Algernon," though the spelling in the scripts doesn't support this.

The frontal exteriors of this sketch were actually shot on Thorpebank Road, which intersects Uxbridge Road, London, W12. Because of its proximity to Broadcast Centre, this neighborhood was used many times for exterior shooting, including the opening section of the "Silly Walks" sketch.

"English"—("The Piranha Brothers") Reggie Kray purportedly "excelled" in English at Daniel Street School (Jones chapter 2).

Episode 14—This episode was the first episode recorded for the show's second series, and is known throughout WAC records as "Series 2, Ep. 1." It was taped on 7 July 1970, and was the fourth episode recorded, but the first aired. It was broadcast on 15 September 1970.

Other actors scheduled to appear in this episode, according to WAC records, included so-called Tourists, other period credits given where available: Paul Lindley (*Dixon of Dock Green*), Raymond St. Claire (sound, *Ginger*, 1971), Eric Lindsay (*Play For Today*), Cy Town (*Dad's Army; Star Wars*), Jonathan Gardner (*Warship*), Elizabeth Broom (*Dixon of Dock Green*), Deborah Millar, Philip Howard (*Dixon of Dock Green*), Michael Channon (Southampton FC), Moyra Pearson, Daphne Davey (*The Troubleshooters*), Paul McNeill (folk singer), and Morris Terry (WAC T12/1,242). David Ballantyne, Stanley Mason, and John Hughman (each appearing in the "New Cooker Sketch" in Mrs. Pinnet's [Jones] front room) were also scheduled to appear in small roles (WAC T12/1417).

exterior of police station—("The Piranha Brothers") This was one of the pick-up shots recorded while the troupe and personnel were on the coast, here specifically recorded on 12 May 1970 at the Paignton Police Station (WAC T12/1,416).

"extroverted suicide"—("The Piranha Brothers") Chapman makes an earlier appearance as this same kind of borderline psychiatrist character in the "Mouse Problem" sketch in Ep. 2, where perverted, masturbatory "mouse tendencies" are reinforced, not discouraged.

– F –

"Face the Press"—(*"Face the Press"*) Perhaps inspired by similar shows like *Face to Face* (1960), an interview-format show hosted by John Freeman and directed by Hugh Burnett. Freeman was also a presenter on *Panorama*. On American television, NBC's *Meet the Press* has been a news/talk staple since 1947.

The music behind the description of the Minister's (Chapman) dress is "Warm Hands," performed by the Watt Peters Orchestra (WAC T12/1,417).

"family of sixteen"—("The Piranha Brothers") The Kray twins had an older brother, Charles, Jr. (1927-2000), also an accomplished boxer and repeat felon, who spent most of his adult life in prison as well.

"February 22, 1966"—("The Piranha Brothers") The specific date doesn't seem to be significant to the Krays, though on 8 March 1966, a gun battle between gang members resulted in a Kray cousin's death, setting the Krays on the path to murder. For the Krays, it would be when the brothers graduated from strong-arm tactics to gangland murders that would demand police "take notice."

Also, there is the very real possibility that the in-depth reports on the Krays and the criticism of the lethargic police investigation into the Kray empire appearing in the pages of the non-Fleet Street publication *Private Eye* actually spurred/shamed authorities into action.

"female impersonator"—("The Piranha Brothers") One of the rare occasions in *FC* where a cross-dressed character is identified as such. Another is in the opening sketch (*"Face the Press"*) of this same episode.

Fifth Gas Man—("New Cooker Sketch") Not credited in the script at this point, this is David Ballantyne, who also appears in Eps. 13 and 17. The Sixth Gas Man is Gilliam (misidentified as the Fifth Gas Man in the script), and the Seventh Gas Man is actor John Hughman. Hughman also appears in Eps. 17, 27, 28, and 41. The Eighth Gas Man is also unnamed in the script at this point—he is Stanley Mason (Ep. 17).

"film producers"—("The Piranha Brothers") The Krays attracted significant celebrity attention during the early 1960s, cavorting with both American and British entertainment and crime figures.

"fiver"—("Tobacconists [Prostitute Advert]") A five pound note. See *OED*.

"four hundred years"—("The Piranha Brothers") The Kray twins went on trial officially (at the Old Bailey, seen at the end of the "Spanish Inquisition" sketch) in January 1969, and were sentenced to life in prison in March 1969. Jones notes that "life" at the time generally meant ten to twelve years, but that the judge in the case demanded actual sentences of not less than thirty years for both Krays. Reggie was sent to Parkhurst Prison (mentioned in Eps. 12 and 13), and Ronnie went to Durham Prison.

Gilliam—(PSC; "New Cooker Sketch") This is incorrect, as Gilliam does not speak this particular line, though he will appear, with many others. This line is spoken by David Ballantyne, who also appeared in Ep 13 as Prologue, a waiter, and an Indian Head. Gilliam is the Sixth Gas Man, mentioned above.

"giveaway"—("The Piranha Brothers") The Krays did lay low after the two murders, traveling on the continent and avoiding the limelight, as "Nipper" Read and his men tracked their movements and painstakingly built a solid case against them (Jones).

"Gloucester . . . Lear"—("The Piranha Brothers") Character in Shakespeare's play *King Lear*. Gloucester is blinded by Regan and Cornwall for supposedly supporting Cordelia. Organs' (Jones) other characterizations include:

A "pork butcher"—This still shot was taken in the tobacconist's shop seen earlier in the episode. The sexualized "chest of drawers" is just behind him.

"Blind Pew"—Evil character in Stevenson's *Treasure Island*, Pew will be mentioned again in Ep. 32. *Treasure Island* and its characters are mentioned often in *FC*, probably based on the familiarity of the Treasure Island Christmas pantomime, both live and on the BBC. See entry for *"Long John Silver"* in Ep. 5 for more.

"Ratty . . . Toad Hall"—*Toad of Toad Hall* was a 1946 television production based on Kenneth Grahame's popular novel *The Wind in the Willows* (1908). "Ratty" was the character Water Rat.

"Sancho . . . *La Mancha*"—Sancho is Don Quixote's servant in the book (1605, 1615) and Broadway play (1965). (The film version would not appear until 1972.) Notice, also, that all of Organs' roles are supporting, not leads.

It was noted by many pundits of the period that the high profile inspector "Nipper" Read was as much playing for the cameras and press as he was performing his job. *Private Eye* would satirize him as the intrepid "Knacker" of the Yard.

"go"—("Tobacconists [Prostitute Advert]") Cf. the Idle-penned "Nudge, Nudge" sketch in Ep. 3, also filled with double entendres of familiar words given sexual connotations ("go," "sport," "games"). See *Shakespeare's Bawdy* for more on this rich allusiveness. D.H. Lawrence uses the term "go" similarly in *Lady Chatterly's Lover* (1928), a scurrilous text that pushed the boundaries of decorum in publishing as late as 1960, when Penguin Books was sued for obscenity. Penguin would win the case (see notes to Ep. 10, "Gorilla Librarian," for more). Lawrence figured prominently in Ep. 2 in relation to the "working-class" sitting room (borrowed from *Sons and Lovers*) and the coal mining family life.

goat with a hat—("New Cooker Sketch") The goat was obtained from Animal Kingdom for the taping (WAC T12/1,417). Animal Kingdom Ltd., Animals For Hire, was located at 179a High Street, Uxbridge.

"good condition"—("Tobacconists [Prostitute Advert]") Referring to the "bit of pram" he'd like to have, this would mean young and free from sexually transmitted diseases, in the shabby man's (Idle) estimation.

"Government"—(*Face the Press*) Meaning the sitting government. When this episode was recorded, the Tories (Conservatives) were in power, having won a majority in the 18 June 1970 elections. When the episode was written, however, Labour would have still been seated, so the "small patch of brown liquid" mentioned later would have been representing the Conservative Party.

G-plan type—(PSC; "New Cooker Sketch") A "G-plan" means a home designed/built on the design of Messrs. E. Gomme, Ltd., including the mass-produced utility furniture so prevalent in postwar Britain (and Europe, to a certain extent). Along with food and fuel, a nationwide shortage of industrial products (wood, plastic, metal) after the war (c. 1945-1954) meant that furniture designed for the thousands of new homes and apartments had to be as spare as possible, but without completely sacrificing attractiveness and comfort.

The G-Plan, introduced in 1952, featured modern style furniture that could be affordably purchased by British consumers into the 1970s. There were a limited number of items to choose from, and consumers could buy in a "modular" way for individuality. Houses became coordinated from room to room. This would have been the furniture that the Pythons grew up with (mixed in with handed-down antiques), building on the Utility Scheme furniture of the war and postwar years, and which the BBC prop department obviously carried in quantity. (The Utility Scheme had been instituted by the government during the early years of the war to make the best use of limited raw materials— furniture, appliances, and even toys fell under its rubric.) There were a number of other manufacturers of modern (even minimalist) furniture of the period, including Avalon and Meredrew.

See Attfield's *Utility Reassessed* (1999) for more on the various government utility programs during and after WWII.

gravestone—("The Piranha Brothers") This gravestone scene was one of the pick-up shots taken while the troupe was in Torquay (WAC T12/1,416).

– H –

"Hawkins"—("The Piranha Brothers") Jim Hawkins is the young boy's name in *Treasure Island*, the novel-cum-Christmas pantomime that obviously so fixated the young Pythons they refer to it over and over again in *FC*.

"Hello Sailors"—(link into "New Cooker Sketch") The clarion call of the homosexual or effeminate male in *FC*. Cf. the swishy David Unction (Chapman) in Ep. 10, as well as the title of Tom Jack's book in Ep. 3. The phrase can probably be attributed to "working girls" at dockside calling to newly disembarked sailors.

"help me"—("Tobacconists [Prostitute Advert]") What follows is a characteristic Idle sketch where double entendres and misunderstandings rule. Here the shabby character (Idle) misinterprets harmless posted adverts for sexual enticements. After some back-and-forth between the customer and proprietor, the façade is dropped and the advert the customer seems to have been searching for is presented. Cf. the "Pornographic Bookshop" in Ep. 36 where a Tudor storefront masks a pornographic bookstore.

"Hockney, David"—("New Cooker Sketch") Hockney (b. 1937, Bradford) is a Pop Art and photography-inspired painter, printmaker, and stage designer who would have been something of a flamboyant peer of the Pythons. Ironically, Hockney was a conscientious objector, meaning he expressed a fundamental opposition to fighting in WWII, and performed his National Service in a hospital, instead.

Hockney spent much time in the United States in the 1960s, in the company of people like Andy Warhol, and may have come to Cleese's and/or Gilliam's attention there. (His public profile was elevated enough by this time, however, that he was appearing in newspapers, and being covered on TV and radio, etc.) He painted images of showers and swimming pools, so the utility/facility aspects of his work might have inspired the Pythons to name him as a bomb designer.

Also, the acknowledged homoerotic content/context of his work (including *Man Taking Shower in Beverly Hills* [1964]) would have made him a perfect target. On the Sir Forster set (with Cleese and the attendant fan boy) there is a chaise lounge, which also appears in Hockney's painting *Three Chairs with a Section of a Picasso Mural* (1970).

"Home Affairs"—(*Face the Press*) The Home Affairs Committee stands as the examiner of the Home Office, including administration, policy, and expenditures.

– I –

Intercom Voice—("The Ministry of Silly Walks") This woman (who will appear with the tray in moments) is Daphne Davey (*The Troubleshooters*).

– K –

"Kierkegaard"—("The Piranha Brothers") Søren Kierkegaard (1813-1855) was a Danish religious writer and thinker, who argued, among many other things, that truth was finally subjective. His name will be mentioned again in the following sketch. The "Kierkegaard's Journals" title is a reference to the approximately 7,000 pages of journals Kierkegaard produced during his lifetime. There are twenty-three volumes of the journals.

Kierkegaard is obviously important to the Pythons' *weltbild*, and is discussed at length in notes to Ep. 28 and 42.

– L –

"Lauderdale"—("The Piranha Brothers") Police Constable Lauderdale was a character on the long-running British police television show *Dixon of Dock Green* (1955-1978). Richard "Dickie" Attenborough played RSM Lauderdale in the 1964 film *Guns at Batasi*. Attenborough is satirized at length in Ep. 39, the "*Light Entertainment Awards*" sketch. In that same film, Jack Hawkins played Colonel Deal.

line of gas men—(PSC; "New Cooker Sketch") These brown-coated men snaking down Thorpebank Road included the following, according to BBC records: Bernard Egan (*Plague of the Zombies*), David Grinaux, Eric Kent (*Doctor in the House*), Tony Maddison (*Dr. Who*), David Joyce (*Dr. Who*), Scott Andrews (*Tiffany Memorandum*), Anthony Mayne (*Z Cars*; *Play For Today*), Lesley Parker (*Softly Softly*), Ron Gregory (*Dixon of Dock Green*), Willy Bowman (*The Wednesday Play*), Michael Earl (*Dixon of Dock Green*; *Doctor in the House*), Norton Clarke (*UFO*), Walter Henry (*Public Eye*; *Dr. Who*), Alex Hood (*Play For Today*), Brian Nolan (*Paul Temple*; *Z Cars*), Garth Watkins (*The Guardians*), Neville Simons (*Dr. Who*), Harry Tierney (*Dr. Who*), John Caesar (*Paul Temple*), Derek Chafer (*Dr. Who*; *Softly Softly*) (WAC T12/1,242).

"Luton"—("The Piranha Brothers") Mentioned often in *FC* as a representative bastion of middle-class values (and home to the BBC's Lord Hill, for example), Luton is northwest of London. The London Luton air-port is located there. Cf. the Tourist's reference to Luton in his rant in Ep. 19.

– M –

"MCC"—("The Piranha Brothers") Acronym for the Marylebone Cricket Club, which just continues (to the absurd) the brothers' (Kray and Piranha) penchant for attempting to subjugate all sport betting activities. The MCC is and has been the home of English cricket, and is located at Lord's Cricket Ground in St. John's Wood, well out of the Piranhas' (or Krays') actual sphere of influence. That the brothers were "slit up a treat" indicates that they were unable to take over by force the MCC; the oldest and stodgiest of establishment fixtures are too much for such lower-class types.

The tough reputation of the MCC, however, can also be attributed to the group's resolute stance in favor of continued play with South Africa's cricket teams, and completing a tour of South Africa in 1968-1969. There are myriad political cartoons depicting very old MCC types in full cricket gear threatening long-haired protesters and politicians into submission, including one from Jak (Raymond Jackson) in the *Evening Standard* on 21 Jan 1970. The depicted cricketers, with bats ready, are asking the hippie demonstrator—whom they're about to execute—if he wants to go "fast, medium, or slow off-spin." The controversial tour was eventually cancelled.

"Minister . . . Ola Pola"—(link into "New Cooker Sketch") In the taped version, "Minister" is actually pronounced "Ministerette," an additional and diminutive emasculation of the armed forces/government personnel. The "-ette" suffix is usually appended to a name or title to indicate a female, or in this case, an effeminate male in "outrageous drag."

By the 1960s, the UK was struggling to maintain its air forces amid aircraft manufacturing slowdowns and the U.S. military taking key NATO roles for defense of Europe against the Soviet Union. The celebrated failure of a missile system (Blue Streak) and the early retirement of the V-Bombers (in the face of elevated Soviet AA missile technology and deployment) weighed heavily on the Air Ministry and its funding future.

The Ministry of Aviation itself was formed in 1959, at the height of the Cold War, but by 1967 the control of aircraft was transferred to the Ministry of Technology, and the Board of Trade assumed other of Aviation's duties.

The British military participated in a northern Norway NATO exercise termed "*Polar* Express" in 1968, at least partially meant to discourage the Soviets—who had recently rolled tanks across Czechoslovakia—to flex NATO's military muscle within shouting distance of the Soviet sphere of influence.

Ministry—(PSC; "The Ministry of Silly Walks") Name given to areas of British government, such as the Ministry of Food, Ministry of Information, Ministry of Health Economics, and the Ministry of Agriculture, Fisheries and Foods. The phrase "Ministry of Silly Walks" has become something of a catchphrase in Britain when government mismanagement and pork-barrel spending are discussed. See notes to *MPSERD*.

"mother"—("The Piranha Brothers") It's unclear here whether Vercotti (Palin) is actually talking to his mother—and she's just ordered a Chinese prostitute—or to a client whom Vercotti calls "mother" to belay suspicion. There is a pause after he says "bye-bye," as if the "mother" is an afterthought.

"Mr Pudey"—("The Ministry of Silly Walks") Arthur Pewtey (also Palin) appeared in Ep. 2, and this type of characterization from Palin appears many times throughout *FC*, including the similarly mannered Mr. Pither in Ep. 34, "The Cycling Tour."

Mrs Pinnet's house—(RSC; link out of "Tobacconists [Prostitute Advert]") This outdoor location (corner of Thorpebank and Uxbridge roads, London, W12) was seen earlier in the episode. The "Silly Walks" sketch will begin at the other end of Thorpebank Road, just north of this corner.

– N –

"nailed to the floor"—("The Piranha Brothers") There is a Kray story involving a victim being stabbed so violently that the knife impaled him to the floor. This is one of the murders for which the Krays were eventually prosecuted (Jones).

"National Service"—("The Piranha Brothers") In effect between 1939 and 1960, National Service included either active participation in the armed forces or commensurate service outside of military duties. (Artist David Hockney [mentioned above] performed hospital duties, for example.) All able-bodied young men were to serve in active duty for eighteen months (later two years), and then as reserves for an additional four years. Both Reggie and Ronnie were dishonorably discharged from the Army after spending significant time in military stockades for desertion, insubordination, and all manner of violence against fellow conscriptes and their guards (*ODNB*).

None of the Pythons performed National Service.

"No fear!"—("*Face the Press*") Idiomatic expression, used now as an exclamation.

– O –

"Operation, The"—("The Piranha Brothers") The Krays' crime organization was known as "The Firm." Also, Peter Cook's satirical club (Greek Street, Soho) was called simply and ironically "The Establishment," a term that had been recently coined by *Spectator* columnist Henry Fairlie to refer to the government and its unseen operations (Carpenter, 2000, 130).

"Organs, Harry 'Snapper'"—("The Piranha Brothers") The policeman who doggedly led the investigation of the Krays from 1964 through their first major arrest and trial in 1965 was Detective Chief Inspector Leonard "Nipper" Read. His nickname—played up in the tabloids of the time—is attributed to a successful boxing career as a youth.

This depiction is certainly also connected to Sergeant Norman Pilcher, who made a number of high-profile celebrity arrests in the late 1960s, and may have followed the movements of these celebrities (including John Lennon, Mick Jagger, Donovan, George Harrison) through their coverage in the "colour supplements" of the tabloids. For more on Pilcher and his star-studded investigations, see the "found on the premises" note in Ep. 5.

"organza . . . tulle"—("*Face the Press*") "Organza" is described by the *OED* as "a thin stiff transparent dress-fabric of silk or synthetic fibre," and "tulle"—"a fine silk bobbin-net used for women's dresses, veils, hats, etc."

"diamante"—This would be a necklace made "sparkly" by adding powdered glass, crystal, etc. See *OED*.

"Bond Street"—Off of Chiswick Common Road, just south of Bedford Park in London. A fashion district, like Harley Street is a medical locus. In Wodehouse's *Code of the Woosters* (1938), it is revealed that the burly, masculine Spode actually runs a fashionable ladies underwear shop on Bond Street, and even makes the underthings himself (297).

"hair is by Roger"—Probably a reference to the then-popular Raymond of Mayfair, the celebrity hair stylist. Raymond will be mentioned by his nickname, "Teasy-Weasy," in Ep. 31.

"Out of her mind"—("The Ministry of Silly Walks") It's not clear here why the minister (Cleese) would conclude this, unless he's responding to her calling him "Mr Teabag." If he is, then her name, "Mrs Two-Lumps," is equally absurd, though she responds to it without question. Perhaps it's in reference to his request for coffee, and her response with a tea-related answer. The woman is Daphne Davey.

outrageous drag—(PSC; link into "New Cooker Sketch") Characterizing the country's leadership—in this case the military—as highly effeminate, and of dubious sexual orientation. Earlier, the police suffered the same treatment, as have upper-class types and authority figures of all stripes. Later in *Flying Circus*, judges will be lampooned in a similar manner, and the effeminization of male (often, but not always, Conservative) leaders serves the satirical purpose of making small by ridicule and derision.

– P –

"Panama Canal"—("The Piranha Brothers") As Organs (Jones) recites the liturgy of his unsuccessful tracking of the Piranhas, he makes a trip back from South America through the Canal. The Krays were known to have looked into both Africa and Latin America for investment opportunities. More to the point, the investigation into the Great Train Robbery defendants led Scotland Yard to Rio de Janeiro, Brazil, where they tried, unsuccessfully to first kidnap, and, failing that, to extradite Ronnie Biggs.

"Piranha, Arthur"—("The Piranha Brothers") Continuing Python's affinity for this first name. The Krays' father was Charlie Kray, their mother, Violet. Arthur Piranha is also characterized as both a "devout Catholic" and often in trouble with the authorities (the real Kray patriarch was a proud WWII deserter and spent years on the run). This conflation can't be overlooked—that of a criminal and practicing Roman Catholic in this Anglican country. The Inquisition (enacted by the Catholic Church) is also a significant topic in this episode. See entries for Ep. 15.

"Piranha brothers"—("The Piranha Brothers") Cf. Ep. 8, the Vercotti brothers (Jones and Palin), for a previous iteration of the gangster siblings milieu. Doug and Dinsdale are certainly characters based loosely on London's most famous crime twins, Ronnie and Reggie Kray. The Krays were born ten minutes apart in October 1933, Reggie being the oldest. Ronnie died in prison in 1995, and Reggie died in October 2000, having been paroled for medical reasons after thirty-two years in prison (*ODNB*). As mentioned in the notes to Ep. 8, the Krays spent all their (free) time together, and participated in various criminal shakedowns and enterprises—either together or separately—on a regular basis into the 1960s.

The Krays had been featured on the cover of the satirical magazine *Private Eye* on 14 March 1969, meaning their private, corrupt lives were becoming much more public. Most conventional (Fleet Street) London newspapers had ignored or buried Kray coverage to this point.

"pussy cat"—("Tobacconists [Prostitute Advert]") "Puss" (in its various forms) has been slang for both the female pudendum and "whore" since at least the seventeenth century, as in Jonson's *The Alchemist* (5.3.38), performed first in 1610. This is probably not a reference to bestiality, but the shabby man (Idle) misinterpreting a real cat for sale for a "sex kitten." This term was first affixed to Marilyn Monroe in the late 1950s, and later to Raquel Welch (Ep. 13), Brigitte Bardot, Anita Ekberg (*FZ*), and others.

– R –

"Reading"—("New Cooker Sketch") Reading is in Berkshire, and is thirty-eight miles west of London. Reading's proximity to the Thames and railroad junctions makes it a good choice for a gas company distribution hub. The BBC's Written Archives Collection is also located across the river from Reading, in Caversham Park. The other locations mentioned in this rant include:

"Cheltenham"—Northeast of Gloucester, in Gloucestershire;

"Hounslow"—In Greater London, near Heathrow Airport, Hounslow will figure prominently in Ep. 28 (in the "Surbiton to Hounslow" trek), and is also the actual location of Slade House, the high-rise apartment building where Lord Nelson leaped to his death in Ep. 1. In the "Mouse Problem" sketch in Ep. 2, the "Hounslow" title card insert was the made-up address of Arthur Jackson, mouse pervert, and was created after the episode aired once (to cover up David Frost's actual address). See notes to Ep. 2, "Hounslow" for more;

"Twickenham"—In Greater London, just southeast of Hounslow; in 1971 Twickenham Station doubled for Hounslow's train station for Ep. 28, along with Twickenham Bridge and multiple locations in the Twickenham area (WAC T12/1,428);

"Holborn"—In Camden (near where Idle lived during this period), Holborn is also part of Greater London, and mentioned later in Ep. 19;

"Hainault"—In Greater London, between Redbridge and Chigwell, and also prominently mentioned as part of Neville Shunt's play title in Ep. 24;

"Southall"—Southall is also in Greater London, near Ealing;

"Peckham"—Part of Greater London, and home to Peckham Rye Station;

"Tottenham, Lewisham, Ruislip"—Tottenham, Lewisham, and Ruislip are also areas within Greater

London. (The map displayed later during the *"Ethel the Frog"* section of this episode depicts this same area, centering—as is often the case—the *FC* action in Greater London.) Tottenham will be mentioned in Ep. 35, "Olympic Hide-and-Seek Final," while Ruislip will be utterly destroyed in Ep. 44, when Mr. Neutron (Chapman) is attacked by a nuclear missile barrage from the United States.

As part of the postwar welfare state reform, the Gas Act of 1948 had nationalized the more than 1,000 natural gas concerns into twelve regional gas boards, controlling the delivery and prices of domestic gas as well as creating the inevitable bureaucratic mess as depicted by the Pythons. Some of the confusion here must be as a result of the alignment and realignment of gas board region boundaries during the 1950s and 1960s, meaning there would necessarily be villages and gas distribution points shifting from one board's purview to another, and oftentimes more than once.

Additional confusion and expense certainly emerged in 1967, when North Sea natural gas was transported onshore to Easington terminal for the first time, sparking a ten-year conversion program that would see the conversion of every gas appliance in the country from "town gas" to the new "natural gas." This conversion involved thirty-four million appliances, eventually, and a reported thirteen million homes. (See gasarchive.org for more.)

"Reverend Smiler Egret"—("The Piranha Brothers") The Reverend is given a name as if he is a gangster, not unlike classical musician Arthur "Two-Sheds" Jackson (also Jones) interviewed in Ep. 1.

– S –

"sarcasm . . . satire"—("The Piranha Brothers") A sophisticated level of humor and observation, sarcasm and satire might not have been possible (or indeed necessary) for the Krays, as at least Ronnie was characterized by a state psychiatrist as below average in intelligence. The subtleties of thought and speech required for a speaker/writer to use such figures of speech as parody, satire, and bathos are incongruous with the Krays' penchant for physical violence and deadly intimidation. These are all tools in Python's quiver, however, and are used throughout their work.

"dramatic irony"—When an audience, for example, knows more about a character's situation and/or fate than the character. This can create a sense of superiority, but also an empathy with and for the character based on the crushing effects of Fate that are certain to come. In the case of the Krays, dramatic irony came into play when they murdered associate James

McVite—the brothers staged a party, had McVite invited, and killed him when he arrived (Jones).

"metaphor"—A common quality between two ideas, thoughts, figures suggested by metaphoric reference ("men are sheep").

"bathos"—Interesting that Vercotti would include this figure of speech, as it is an *accidental* fall from perhaps the sublime to the ridiculous in vain attempts at elevated speech—Dryden's detractors used this claim against him on more than one occasion. Lower-tier or court/occasional poets of the seventeenth and then eighteenth centuries (the latter category including Dryden) tended to fall prey to the bathetic.

"puns"—A pun is a play on words, a deliberate confusing of terms, primarily—for example, a confusing of homonyms and synonyms.

"parody"—The Pythons employ parody often, imitating epic works of art and literature, and especially parodying television shows and the paradigms of presentation and broadcasting in general.

A "litote"—like "no small tempest"—is an indirect affirmation by denial of the opposite, and another rather clever figure of speech (Baldick 142).

"say any more"—(*"Face the Press"*) In Ep. 17, Chapman (playing "Man"), asks Devious (Palin) if he has any more lines to say. When he hears that he is finished, he decides to leave the sketch. In Ep. 15, when Chapman is playing Reg, his questions bring on the Inquisitors. But when that sketch begins to fade, and Reg is out of lines, he agrees to answer the door in another sketch.

"says here"—("New Cooker Sketch") This type of seemingly insignificant bureaucratic mistake—even a misunderstanding—can have lasting, even lethal effects in the Python world. Later in this episode, a man (Chapman) will be assaulted based on a mistaken identity (he's *not* "Clement"), and, further assaulted when he points out the mistake (that he's not Clement). In Ep. 17, "Motor Insurance Sketch" (with *Ben Hur* titles again), the fine print in the Vicar's (Idle) insurance policy clearly states that no claim he makes will ever be paid. In *Meaning of Life*, obtaining an organ donor's card obligates the cardholder (Gilliam) to surrender his liver—even if he's "still using it." And in Gilliam's later feature film *Brazil* (1986), which was co-written by Gilliam, Charles McKeown, and Tom Stoppard, the entire scenario is based on a single typo on a government work order. In a Python bureaucracy, the form's the thing.

"School"—("The Piranha Brothers") The Kray twins attended Woods Close and Daneford Street School (Bethnal Green), and boxed at the Robert Browning Youth Club (Southwark). By age fifteen, however, they had quit school in favor of boxing and their "work."

Pythagoras was a pre-Socratic philosopher best known for his teaching of the transmigration of souls and theory of numbers. This may have been included by the Pythons as a reference to the Krays' much-publicized belief in fortune-telling, and the early predictions that the boys were destined for short, brilliant lives (Jones).

scrambles—(PSC; "New Cooker Sketch") After performing this somewhat tomboy-ish, un-ladylike feat, Pinnet (Jones) carefully straightens her dress, then crawls through the rear window. This is a good example of a crossdressed character not afraid to perform role(s) somewhat hermaphroditically.

Second Policeman—(PSC; "The Piranha Brothers") Not noted in the text, but this actor appears to be actor/singer David Ballantyne, who also appears in Eps. 13 and 14, as well as the 1971 Montreux compilation episode.

"shot silk"—("*Face the Press*") *OED*: "Woven with warp-threads of one colour and weft-threads of another, so that the fabric (usually silk) changes in tint when viewed from different points. Also, applied to mixed fabrics (esp. of cotton and silk), dyed by a process which produces a variegated effect similar to that of 'shot silk.'"

"shtoom"—("The Piranha Brothers") A Yiddish version of the German word "stumm," meaning silent or dumb. This is also a Cockney term, generally meaning "shut it." As with Cockney rhyming slang (and Palani slang), the goal in using these words and phrases was to communicate in public (and especially in front of authorities) without betraying one's intentions. Here, Vercotti (Palin) wants to communicate with the caller without giving away the illicit details of the transaction.

silent movie type—("The Ministry of Silly Walks") The music used behind this black-and-white film is "Cockney Song" from "Silent Film Music" (WAC T12/1,417).

"Silly Walks"—("The Ministry of Silly Walks") Futurist F.T. Marinetti (1876-1944) proposed an avant garde film called *Futurist Life* (c. 1915), where the successful futurist would learn to employ various walks, including "neutralist walk," "interventionist walk," and "the Futurist March." In regard to this last proposed new walk, see the mention of "La Marche Futile" further on in the sketch.

The posted sign here says, "Ministry of Silly Walks," but as requested on the show's "Graphics Requirements" page, it should have read "Ministry of Silly Walkers." There is no indication as to when the requirement was changed (WAC T12/1,417).

"Simnel"—("The Piranha Brothers") Simnel Cake is a fruity Easter cake, which would account for both the woman's last name and "April." Also, Lambaster Simnel was a pretender to the English throne in 1486-1487, and even though he was eventually exposed, he was thereafter employed in the king's kitchens. Cf. Mr. Lambert in Ep. 8. In Ep. 21, an archeological dig at "Abu Simnel" will be mentioned.

This scene is also shot on Thorpebank Road, in front of number 102, and just across the street from number 107, where Pickford's corner store was located.

small ad—(PSC; animated link into "Tobacconists [Prostitute Advert]") The text of this small ad isn't included in the printed scripts, as it was most likely not known at the time of the script's writing (per Gilliam's *modus operandi*). The ad reads: "Vacancy: Pilot Needed to Fly Vintage Model Monarchs." The ad is written by the animator's hand, and is preceded by various royal figure cutouts (including Elizabeth I and Charles II) sporting propellers and flying around.

Monarch Airlines had been in business since 1967, headquartered in Luton, and would have been the type of airline that most British vacationers heading to the warmer continental destinations (Ibiza, Mallorca) would have flown. (See the Tourist in Ep. 19 for more on these package trips.) Monarch's only operating planes during this period were prop-driven Bristol 175s (from the early 1950s), certainly qualifying as "vintage" in the jet age.

"smashing bloke"—("The Piranha Brothers") Even toward the end of the brothers' freedom, police could find very few people who would testify against he Krays, relying on the testimony of one henchman who had cut a deal with prosecutors. Their status as local heroes would be reaffirmed over and over again, with people like Flanagan (Eps. 7, 11-13, 22) lobbying for their release, as well as by their well-attended funerals.

"Social Security"—("The Ministry of Silly Walks") Actually, public spending typically consumed around 40 percent of the British Government's total annual public spending during this period. In 1970-1971, for example, the total came to 42.7 percent of the gross domestic product (GDP). Health spending sat at about 9 percent GDP in 1969; education spending reached about 11 percent in the same year; and defense spending fell to about 13 percent in 1969. Defense spending in the UK had fallen as a percentage of GDP every year since 1955. (See "UK Government Spending".) The demands of the welfare state ("cradle to grave" coverage) precluded spending monies (to any extravagant degree) on areas outside of social security, health, etc.

"Southwark"—("The Piranha Brothers") A borough in Greater London. Historically, since Southwark was south of the City of London and across the Thames, the long arm of the City's royal law didn't reach into its dark recesses. Public playhouses not licensed by the court and many businesses and inns—both nefarious and legitimate—set up shop within sight of London without having to answer to the City's authority. Southwark was also the location of Chaucer's Tabard Inn, where his pilgrims began their journey in *Canterbury Tales*. See Ackroyd.

There is no Kipling Road in Southwark, but there is one not far away in Warwick.

"special delivery"—("New Cooker Sketch") This sketch is evolving into a satire on Britain's postwar socialist bureaucracy, and will soon escalate—a Python trope—into absurdity. The end result is that Mrs Pinnet (Jones) has to agree to a new name (Crump-Pinnet) and even assisted suicide before her stove can be hooked up—notions to which she eagerly accedes. (Cf. the "Live Organ Donor" sketch in the feature film *Meaning of Life*.) The cooker sketch here has no real ending, and it can't, since the bureaucratic labyrinth also has no end. This is made clear later in the episode as "Silly Walks" begins, with the Minister (Cleese) walking past Mrs. Pinnet's home and the long line of brown-coated gas men still waiting in the street. Gilliam (with Palin) will revisit this paperwork scenario in his 1986 film *Brazil*.

"Spiny Norman"—("The Piranha Brothers") Ronnie Kray was prone to fits of manic behavior and prolonged periods of meditation (or catatonia), and lived much of his later life in a prison mental hospital. He is believed to have suffered from undiagnosed paranoid schizophrenia. Cf. the description by Sir Isaiah Berlin in his *Hedgehog and Fox* (1953) of the so-called hedgehog mentality in life, or "those who relate everything to a single central vision." (Originally, from Archilochus: "The fox knows many things—the hedgehog one big one.") The realization of a giant, malevolent hedgehog might account for this vision for Dinsdale.

A few years earlier Soviet premier Nikita Khrushchev had told the *New York Times*: "If you start throwing hedgehogs under me, I shall throw a couple of porcupines under you" (7 November 1963).

Lastly, this name (Spiny Norman) might be an oblique reference to Sergeant *Norman* Pilcher, the man who arrested a number of Python associates, including members of The Beatles and the Rolling Stones on drug possession charges. See Ep. 5 ("Police Raid"), and the entry for "Harry 'Snapper' Organs" (above) in this episode.

"Stoats, Brian"—("The Piranha Brothers") This name seems to be an amalgam of Pythonisms, including the

oft-used first name Brian, and a reappearance of the "stoat," which was mentioned in Ep. 6.

"support"—("The Ministry of Silly Walks") A reference to the massive waste attributed to Whitehall and the government in general and discussed ad infinitum in the newspapers and periodicals of the period. Millions and even billions of pounds were being overspent annually thanks to ineffective oversight policies in the Civil Service, overlapping ministerial areas, and outright fraud. (See Dixon for more.)

"Investment grants" had also become significant sources of easy money for what turned out be—in many instances—dubious business ventures. Also see the editorial in the October 1967 *Management Today* where the real problem blamed on Wilson and his economic policies is termed a "stopped economy" (18).

– **T** –

"tarts"—("The Piranha Brothers") For a thesaurus-like list of other names for prostitutes, see Ep. 33, the "Biggles Dictates a Letter" sketch. Vercotti's (Palin) other work—representing Ron Obvious (Jones) in his ultimately deadly record-setting attempts—he also consistently characterizes as legitimate and above board.

"tatty office"—("The Piranha Brothers") This same type of cheap restaurant/office setting is carried over from Ep. 13, where Vercotti runs a low-end restaurant in Soho, a clip joint with girls and pornographic films in the back. The décor is very similar to a contemporary Margaret Belsky cartoon panel, as well, featuring two Kray-types in an equally tatty restaurant discussing the just-finished Old Bailey trial (*The Sun* 6 March 1969). See the British Cartoon Archive.

"This Week"—(PSC; "The Piranha Brothers") Popular and long-running Associated Rediffusion's and then Thames TV's show *This Week* (AR, 1956-1968; Thames, 1968-1992).

The music is actually not from a TV show, but is a portion of "Karelia Suite Op. II, Intermezzo" by Sibelius, performed by the Danish State Radio Symphony Orchestra" (WAC T12/1,417).

"Times"—("Tobacconists [Prostitute Advert]") *The Times of London* or just *The Times* was the flagship British newspaper, established in 1788. This would have been the paper of choice for many monied Conservatives of the day, including the City Gent type portrayed here by Cleese.

"Trubshawe"—(link out of "The Ministry of Silly Walks") Featuring the return of Zatapathique and Trubshawe as Frenchmen (Cleese and Palin) speaking "rubbish" or jabberwock French. See notes to Ep. 2. Note here that Zatapathique is still a celebrity "poof." The transference of the mustache still gives the bearer/wearer voice, or the floor, as it were.

"tv quizmaster"—("The Piranha Brothers") Perhaps a reference to the scandal-ridden American television quiz show industry after the 1958 revelation that *Twenty-One* (1956-1958) contestant Charles van Doren was provided answers prior to the show.

– U –

usual grey suit and floral tie—(PSC; "The Piranha Brothers") The uniform of the "current affairs" television presenter, and which was common from network to network (BBC, ATV, etc.). This harks well back to the beginnings of the BBC, when Lord John Reith (1889-1971) made sure his announcers wore dinner jackets in the evenings (*Eyewitness 1920-29*, "John Reith Joins the BBC").

– V –

"various well-known London locations"—("The Piranha Brothers") These shots are still photographs that Gilliam would have secured during production of the show, with an enormous Spiny Norman emerging from hiding in each location, calling for Dinsdale. None of the photos was officially requested (meaning copyright/use fees assessed) in the production material for this episode.

The photographed locations are, in order of appearance: Trafalgar Square, the Houses of Parliament, Buckingham Palace, The Strand (with St. Paul's in the distance), and the Chessington Zoo setting where the episode started.

"Vercotti"—("The Piranha Brothers") Himself a shakedown artist from Ep. 8, Vercotti (Palin) here assumes the role of little fish in a big pond, just as frightened of the Piranhas as anyone else. This scenario is also reinforced by Jones as he describes Kray thugs muscling out other thugs in the quest for gangland control of the East End.

– W –

"Welsh accent"—("The Piranha Brothers") Undoubtedly a comment on Jones' own "high-pitched Welsh accent."

"What does that mean?"—("Tobacconists [Prostitute Advert]") The final line links this sketch, structurally, to the "Nudge, Nudge" sketch, both featuring almost identical punchlines. The shabby customer (Idle), then, is only aware of innuendo and connotation, and fails to appreciate the *literal* meanings of the words and phrases. Other characters in the Python world—like Mr. Pewtey (Palin)—miss the literality of words, inflections, and situations, meaning that the most outrageous things can happen to and around him without much effect.

"What's all this then?"—("The Piranha Brothers") Along with "Hello, hello!", this phrase has become the standard cry of an arriving policeman in *FC*. Phrase perhaps borrowed from Wodehouse, among others, in works like *The Code of the Woosters* (1938), where a constable appears as from nowhere to question Bertie (20). The latter ("Hello, hello!") is a borrow from Peter Sellers as he plays a Bow Street Runner in *The Goon Show*, "The Last Smoking Seagoon" (28 January 1960).

Whitehall—(PSC; "The Ministry of Silly Walks") This area is and was home to a number of official offices, including the Admiralty Building, the Minstry of Defence, the Department of Health, and even 10 Downing Street, where the Prime Minister still maintains his official residence.

The Minister (Cleese) is in fact walking along in front of 12 Whitehall, specifically just south of the confluence of Pall Mall, Cockspur, Northumberland, and Strand avenues (just south of Trafalgar Square). Behind him can be seen the Whitehall Theatre (14 Whitehall), the Old War Office buildings complex on the east side of the street, and Big Ben's tower in the distance to the south. Confirming beyond a doubt the location and time, the Whitehall Theatre's marquee can just be glimpsed, advertising the rather scandalous *Pyjama Tops* "nudie" revue that occupied the theatre space 1969-1974.

Though the Pythons often indicate they are shooting in one place and then make do somewhere else (e.g., Norwich Castle for Edinburgh Castle), there are obviously some locations that are so completely iconic that shadow locations won't do. The very recognizable Whitehall is one, and so is Trafalgar Square (Eps. 26 and 35), Television Centre (Ep. 32), and the Houses of Parliament (Ep. 20).

"win 'em all"—("The Piranha Brothers") Chapman here delivers a very campy, stereotypically gay performance, complete with makeup and swishy affectations. The authority figure—here a policeman—is again depicted as a latent homosexual, and more, the indication is that the stern, manly figure he cuts in public is merely a well-staged, costumed, and powdered burlesque.

working-class sitting room—(PSC; "New Cooker Sketch") There is obviously a common picture in the mind of both the Pythons and the production personnel for the show, one so understood that just "working-class sitting room" and "G-Plan" suffice for description in the printed scripts. This understanding indicates a common background—as children, they grew up in the same postwar Britain in the same kinds of housing developments sitting on the same furniture, obviously, and they've even watched the same BBC adaptations and serials. For a more Northern description of this type of setting, see Ep. 2, the "Working-Class Playwright" sketch.

"wrong house"—("New Cooker Sketch") All this visual absurdity—which should, normally, have led into a sketch featuring Pinnet (Jones) and the visitor (Gilliam)—is instead immediately undercut by the announcement she may be in the wrong house. A clever variation on the "wrong number" scenario. This is also a comment—again, along the lines of the housing situation in Greater London and country towns with council housing—on the indistinguishable nature of terraced houses, row houses, and the ubiquitous apartment tower blocks so prominent in the suburbs.

These terrace houses became popular (at least for councils and builders) in the early Victorian period, when myriad textile mills were popping up around the country and worker housing was needed. The homes were nearly identical to facilitate rapid and far-flung construction, allowing for a consistent use of materials and construction methods. The result, of course, was row after row of homes virtually indistinuishable not only from each other, but from similar tracts in neighboring villages and counties. The opening shot of the "Miracle of Birth: The Third World" section in *Meaning of Life* depicts a Yorkshire version of these endless tracts.

Episode 15

– A –

AA sign—(link out of "The Spanish Inquisition") The UK's automotive association. The sign constructed for the sketch is meant to be identical to the recognizable, yellow-and-black AA signs seen on UK roads since the 1930s. See the entry for "AA" in Ep. 1, "Picasso/Cycling Sketch," as well as Mrs. S.C.U.M.'s (Jones) questions about a dreadful post-apocalyptic world without an AA in Ep. 44, the "Mr. Neutron" sketch.

"Aldis lamp"—(*"Julius Caesar* on an Aldis Lamp") A naval signaling lamp employing Morse code signals.

animation—(link out of "The Spanish Inquisition") In this animation Reg's (Chapman) head is removed and used for the setting, and his right iris is eventually "borrowed" (in the animated diegetic world) for use as a cannonball. Gilliam's animations are often built on borrowing—on the dismembering and re-membering of the human figure, specifically. Recognizable faces from the world of politics (Nabarro, Heath), sport or entertainment (W.G. Grace, Greer Garson) are given new, often grotesque bodies and/or abilities in Gilliam's world, and normal, unknown folk from staid family photos also appear. The wholeness of the human body is the expectation, and Gilliam takes every opportunity he can to dismember and make strange and monstrous that formerly sanctified figure. This "body horror" phenomena isn't new to Gilliam or the Pythons, having crept into feature films (Hammer horror, bloody Peckinpah Westerns, George Romero's *Night of the Living Dead*, etc.) and on the nightly news as the color images from the day's fighting in Vietnam was reported.

The music in this particular animation is from Offenbach's "Orpheus in the Underworld" (WAC T12/1,437).

"answer the door in a sketch"—("The Spanish Inquisition") In Ep. 10, Lord Hill (of Luton) has sent a letter requesting Man (Palin) appear as a walk-on in the "Bank Robber (Lingerie Shop)" sketch. Every week as *Flying Circus* episodes were taped and filmed, walk-ons and assorted actors/production personnel were needed.

In BBC records for this episode, additional hires (i.e., speaking or active parts) include Marjorie Wilde, Pat[ricia] Prior (*Dr. Who*; *Softly Softly*), Pam Saire (*Softly Softly*), and Philip Howard (*Softly Softly*; *Dixon of Dock Green*). Walk-ons for the episode—some who would also have significant film and TV appearances elsewhere—were Maurice Quick (*Dixon of Dock Green*; *Softly Softly*), Cy Town (who would go on to play a Storm Trooper in *Star Wars* [1977]), David Melbourne (*Softly Softly*), Eden Fox (appeared with Chapman in *Doctor in the House*), Jim Delaney (*Emma*), Anne Jay, Derek Glynne (*Brett: Investment—Long Term*), and Bill Johnston (WAC T12/1,437). Marjorie Wilde (an actual mature woman) will have the largest part in this episode, playing the Dear Old Lady in the "Spanish Inquisition" sketch.

appropriate film music throughout—(PSC; "The Semaphore Version of *Wuthering Heights*") This sweeping music seems to be a version of "The World Turns" by L. Stevens (WAC T12/1,437).

– B –

"Belsize Park"—("Court Scene [Charades]") Belsize Park is located in Camden, part of Greater London. Idle visited a flat in the Camden area during part of the run of the series, in Camden High Street, specifically, at/above World's End. See notes to Ep. 19 for more.

"Biggles"—("The Spanish Inquisition") Well-known children's book aviator character. Group Captain Biggles is featured in Eps. 10 and 33, in both places played by Chapman. Other obviously significant characters (based on myriad appearances in *FC*) from the Pythons' collective youth include panto characters like Long John Silver, Dobbins, and Puss in Boots.

Black Dyke Mills Band—(PSC; "The Spanish Inquisition") A brass band organized around 1833, and featuring a French horn player who happened to own the Black Dyke Mills, John Foster. The music used here is Liszt's Hungarian Rhapsody No. 2, and it is actually performed by the Black Dyke Mills band (WAC T12/1,437). For more on the mill and band, see the entry for John's father, "William Foster" at *ODNB*.

"borrow your head for a piece of animation"—(link out of "Jokes and Novelties Salesman") This is precisely what Gilliam has been doing since the show's inception, and usually without asking or attribution. (See *"animation"* note above for more.) The BBC's records for the show almost always indicate when a piece of music or photograph or a bit of film stock is used outside of an animated sequence, but *not* when they were to be part of Gilliam's animations. Gilliam would use photocopies from the pages of art and history books, stills from popular and educational films, and even actual photographs of real people, living and dead, and the BBC never seems to have demanded a copyright review for any of these items. Some quite famous (and therefore recognizable) heads seen in *FC* include Venus (from the Botticelli painting), W.G. Grace (of cricket fame), and Queen Victoria.

Gilliam would get into trouble on at least one occasion for including material without permission or attribution, however. In December 1972 the animation company Halas and Batchelor (*Animal Farm* [1955]) complained in writing that an animated sequence in Ep. 35 contained a soundtrack element taken from a German television spot created (and owned) by H&B. The letter asks how and why such a borrowing could have happened (WAC T12/1,413). Rather than contest the matter, BBC higher-ups simply decided to edit the jingle out before it was rebroadcast (WAC T12/1,428).

Breugel—(PSC; link out of "Photos of Uncle Ted [Spanish Inquisition]") The portion of the famous painting depicted here is Pieter Brueghel's (the Elder) *Triumph of Death* (c. 1562), which is in the collection of the Museo del Prado, Madrid, Spain. Brueghel is a Flemish/Dutch Renaissance painter who will be mentioned again when his skating characters cause a "terrible bloody din" in the "Art Gallery Strike" sketch (Ep. 25). The section of the painting depicted is the upper right corner of the large painting.

"bugger"—(link out of "Court Scene [Charades]") A fascinating possibility arises from the inclusion of this invective, beyond its sodomitical context: "Bugger" was actually a specialized term used to describe an Albigenses heretic in the fourteenth century (*OED*). The Albigenses felt that marriage and procreation were grievous sins, meaning sexual intercourse where fertilization is impossible might be more acceptable—buggery, then, becoming the sin of choice, and one that might be on the lips of the Church's Inquisitors.

Used here for the first time in the series (before being heard again in Ep. 21), the word has a long and controversial history in British dramatic production. Over and over again in the late 1950s the term "bugger" and its variations ("buggery," "bogger," etc.) were consistently underscored by the British Board of Film Censors (BBFC) and the Master of Revels for deletion from films and plays, respectively. As late as 1966 and the "British New Wave" film *Saturday Night and Sunday Morning* and the swinging 1960s film *Alfie* (and subsequent staged plays for each) the term was being elided, no matter the eventual rating or venue. It wouldn't be until *Up the Junction* (1967) that the BBFC would allow the use of the term "bugger" in British film and, somewhat coincidentally, full frontal nudity the following year in Lindsay Anderson's *If . . .* (1968).

"burnt at the stake"—("Court Scene [Charades]") This type of punishment hasn't been practiced since the late eighteenth century, and by then only after the victim had been strangled first. Hanging had been the punishment of choice in England since at least the Romans went home in the fifth century, but later boiling and beheading also became popular. England was well-known during the eighteenth century for attaching the death penalty to literally hundreds of offenses, many quite minor (pickpocketing, poaching), so the pseudo-contempt of court charge here ("do you for heresy")—and a religious charge at that—actually isn't out of bounds given historical precedent.

– C –

"Cardinal Fang"—("The Spanish Inquisition") In *Oliver Twist*, Mr. Fang is a blustering magistrate caught up in his own authority and importance. *Fang* was also the name of a publication Gilliam contributed to while attending Occidental College in California.

"cat of nine tails"—("Court Scene [Charades]") Under South African law during this period, corporal punishment was not only legal, but used quite liberally. One popular method was caning, originally reserved for younger offenders, and which was officially administered in 1968-1969 on more than 5,200 separate occasions in South Africa. The cat of nine tails was for adult males, primarily, and was the corporal punishment weapon of choice in the nineteenth century. Public opinion (domestic and international) in the war years led to a reduction in its implementation, and it's believed that 1958 saw its last use, at least officially.

"Central Criminal Court"—("Court Scene [Charades]") Located in the Old Bailey, City of London, which features prominently in relation to the final ("Oh, bugger!") scene of "The Spanish Inquisition."

"chartered accountancy a more interesting job"—("Tax on Thingy") This is one of the few times that accountants—consistent targets in *FC*—are given something to hope for. Earlier iterations of these accountancy mentions feature timid, hopelessly oneiric, sexually frustrated/twisted types. In Ep. 10 there is even a call for intervention to save anyone falling into the inescapable trap of chartered accountancy. The popularity of this good-natured niggling was confirmed when an Irish MP asked for a script for quotation purposes in Parliament. See notes to Ep. 12 for more.

"cheap labour"—("Court Scene [Charades]") There is a typically condemning cartoon (by David Low) in the *Manchester Guardian* (7 May 1954) linking Britain to South Africa economically—as Britain publicly decried the South African policies—through continuing investment and ownership of South African interests, and especially the abundant "cheap labour" available and utilized by British interests. See the British Cartoon Archive.

"comfy chair"—("The Spanish Inquisition") This is perhaps an unintentional irony, since the Pythons were probably meaning to create humor via incongruity—viz., torture by soft pillow and comfy chair. During the days of the various Inquisitions, the term used when identified heretics were turned over (from church) to secular authorities was "relaxed," so that the church would have no blood on its hands (*OED*).

courtroom—("Court Scene [Charades]") This courtroom set-up and the earlier drawing room for the "Spanish Inquisition" sketch are much larger than the usual *FC* sets, which is why much or all of this episode's interiors were shot on the Ealing TFS stages, and not at BBC Television Centre.

"CS"—("Jokes and Novelties Salesman") CS gas is a riot gas invented in 1928 (*OED*). The reference here might be attributable to the very recent discovery (Autumn 1969) of a shipment of CS gas to South Africa—then enduring an arms embargo for its human rights abuses—a shipment that had managed to slip past the Foreign Office before being identified as containing banned items (*PE* 31 July 1970, page 16).

– D –

"Des O'Connor . . . Tom Jones"—(link into "Jokes and Novelties Salesman") These comments indicate the "older" generation of music and performer to which this "arty" type is attracted.

Des O'Connor (1932-) appeared in *The Des O'Connor Show* (1963-1968), and with Morecambe & Wise (beginning in 1961), creating more familiar, traditional comedy and variety shows than the Pythons may have appreciated (and would have been rebelling against), which is why the "arty" BBC man would prefer the genre. O'Connor also appeared on *The Ed Sullivan Show* and in Las Vegas, making a fairly successful ripple across the pond.

Rolf Harris (1930-) starred in *The Rolf Harris Show* (1967), and is a TV presenter, singer, painter, and cartoonist, and also presented animal shows (*Rolf's Amazing World of Animals*), art shows, and children's shows. Again, the family-friendly nature of Harris probably put him on this list of Python TV pablum.

Tom Jones (1940-) is a Welsh-born pop singer and entertainer then and still very popular with adult women and middle-of-the-road-trendy. During the mid-to-late 1960s he sported the fashionable Edwardian look (tight pants, billowy shirts), and appeared in his own very popular TV show *This is Tom Jones* (1969-1971).

This link (the BBC man and Reg) is listed as being shot on 1 June 1970 at 39 Elers Road, Ealing, a continuation of Lammas Park Rd. (WAC T12/1,416).

"Diabolical Laughter"—("The Spanish Inquisition") This "superimposed caption" motif—a graphic intertitle commenting on the narrative action "on the fly"—will be revisited in Ep. 17, when the burning apartment block (made to resemble Ronan Point) image is tempered with a "Satire" caption. This intertitling allows for another level of humor and even meaning, and will appear throughout the series.

Dick Barton music—(PSC; link out of "Court Scene [Charades]") This theme, "Devil's Gallop" performed by Charles Williams, is borrowed from the *Dick Barton* radio and TV shows. The Goons also used the tune occasionally, and the Pythons have already employed its recognizability for Ep. 12. See notes for Ep. 12 for more on the theme.

DJ—(PSC; "Man-Powered Flight") "Dinner Jacket." This was the uniform of the BBC announcer, especially early in the BBC's life under first director general John C.W. Reith (1922-1938). As a BBC Announcer about to be thrown into the sea in Ep. 3, Cleese wears the prototypical DJ attire.

– E –

"emigrating . . . South Africa"—("Court Scene [Charades]") The British empire had assumed control of the Cape in 1806 from the Dutch, and in 1910 the four colonies on the Cape were merged to form South Africa. In 1948 a rightist, anti-British coalition party—the Afrikaner National Party—won the general election, and the fifty years of apartheid policy began. The new regime was repressive by nature and necessity, as well as authoritarian, as the majority black population needed to be kept in check.

By 1970, when this episode was written and recorded, South Africa had become a republic, having left the Commonwealth in 1961. Political, economic, and familial ties and relations remained, of course, sometimes unofficially, between South Africa and Great Britain. So even as England moved away from authoritarian government and criminal punishment at home, South Africa was becoming all the more authoritarian, which would have given judges like Chapman depicts a clear choice between the two.

As early as 1948 political cartoons began appearing in British newspapers regarding the nationalist political agenda in South Africa, and its attractiveness to many hard-line Conservatives in the UK. One such cartoon from the 27 June 1950 *Daily Express* features a prim, Conservative, upper-middle-class woman who laments: "I can tell you that but for the fact that Labour got in by only a *tiny* majority, I should have emigrated to S. Africa." In other words, if Labour had won handily, she was off to the more politically conservative former colony.

Tony Judt reports that in the immediate postwar years (1946-1948) more than 150,000 Brits emigrated to (predominantly white) Commonwealth countries, mostly due to the privations demanded by the austerity programs as the Welfare State struggled through its infancy (163).

Epic film music—("The Spanish Inquisition") According to WAC files, this music is "Aggression" by Eric Towren, as played by the International Studio Orchestra (WAC T12/1,437).

Episode 15—The second show of Series 2 (BBC listing Series 2, Episode 2), recorded on 2 July 1970, and broadcast on 22 September 1970. This episode was recorded third in the second series, but broadcast second. Extras and walk-ons for this episode are listed above in the "answer the door in a sketch" entry.

"Et Tu Brute"—("*Julius Caesar* on an Aldis Lamp") Famous line borrowed from Shakespeare's version of the life and death of Caesar (*Julius Caesar* 3.1.77).

The production that may have gotten the Pythons' minds turning in this absurd direction is the 1970 film production *Julius Caesar* starring Charlton Heston as Marc Antony, Jason Robards as Brutus, and John Gielgud (Ep. 33) as Caesar. The film was directed by Stuart Burge, and received scathing contemporary reviews for its acting, staging, directing, and even poor set construction and sound mix (see Roger Ebert's 1971 review, for one).

– F –

"fanatical devotion to the pope"—("The Spanish Inquisition") The church men who carried out the work of the Inquisition may have less a devotion to the sitting pope—Sixtus IV, who was against the zealousness of the endeavor—than to their worldly sovereigns, Ferdinand and Isabella, and the eradication of any religious dissent within the ranks of the Holy Church itself.

"find something new to tax"—("Tax on Thingy") The income tax rate in the UK was steep—above 90 percent during and just after the war at its highest, with monies going to the creation and support of the welfare state. Just a handful of the national taxation sources in the UK included: Income, National Insurance, Value Added Tax (VAT), Corporations, Fuel, Councils, Business, Stamps and Tobacco, Vehicle, Spirits and Beer/Cider, Inheritance, Capital Gains, Gaming, etc. In the late 1960s and early 1970s the tax pinch would have felt quite strong, with most middle-class incomes disappearing before paychecks could even be cut. (See Her Majesty's Treasury figures for more.)

front door of the house—(PSC; link into "Joke and Novelties Salesman") The location here is 49 Elers Road, situated just across the street from Lammas Park and Walpole Park, Ealing. The Ealing TFS is just a half-mile north and east of this location. This park setting (and surrounding area) has been used previously for portions of "Bicycle Repair Man" (Ep. 3), "Hell's Grannies" (Ep. 8), and "The Dull Life of a City Stockbroker" (Ep. 6). (See WAC T12/1,242.)

– G –

Gentlemen Prefer Blondes—("*Julius Caesar* on an Aldis Lamp") Popular 1953 Howard Hawks film starring Marilyn Monroe.

Gunfight at the OK Corral—("*Julius Caesar* on an Aldis Lamp") A 1957 Hollywood film directed by John Sturges, and starred Burt Lancaster and Kirk Douglas.

Morse code is a dot-and-dash communication method developed first for the electric telegraph, but soon became useful as a silent, sight-only communication method for military purposes. In this scene, the gunfighters use Morse signallers instead of guns, delivering electronic dots and dashes instead of bullets. The means of communications has become the weapon, then, unlike the previous scene from *Julius Caesar*. By the time we transition to the Criminal Court for charades, the code (charades) will be employed for communication again, and not as a weapon.

– H –

"heresy"—("The Spanish Inquisition") *OED*: "Theological or religious opinion or doctrine maintained in opposition, or held to be contrary, to the 'catholic' or orthodox doctrine of the Christian Church, or, by extension, to that of any church, creed, or religious system, considered as orthodox."

– J –

jarring chord—("The Spanish Inquisition") The now-famous "jarring chord" used to herald the appearance of the Spanish Inquisition is from "Openings and Endings No. 2," by Robert Farnon (WAC T12/1,437).

"Jarrow"—(PSC; "The Spanish Inquisition") In Tyne, Jarrow is a northern industrial town, about 300 miles northeast of London. Jarrow had been significant in the strife-ridden, labor-management relationship since at least 1932, when "hunger" marchers left Jarrow for London to protest high unemployment, scarce unemployment benefits, and the "means test," which often further reduced a family's benefits.

The local *Newcastle Daily Chronicle* for 4 January 1912 reports with much chagrin the closing of the nearby Wardley Colliery (*not* the Jarrow Colliery), and notes that the Wardley Village built up around the colliery was already becoming a ghost town. The notice had gone out just two weeks earlier, right around Christmas, which would explain the Pythons placing this scene on New Year's Eve 1911 and New Year's Day 1912. According to *Whellan's 1894 Directory of County Durham*, *all* of the working villagers living in Wardley Village were miners.

– K –

"kids seem to like it"—(link into "Jokes and Novelties Salesman") This is a bit ironic, as Cleese was himself

over thirty by this time (born in 1939), the age over which one became "untrustworthy" to the younger, hipper generation. This may be part of the reason Cleese was keen to move on from Monty Python much earlier than the others, leaving after the third series to prepare for his instructional video work as well as *Fawlty Towers* (1975-1978).

– L –

"life imprisonment"—("Court Scene [Charades]") Capital punishment had been suspended throughout the UK in October-November 1965, for a period of five years. In mid-December 1969, when episodes from Series 1 were still being broadcast, the suspension of the death penalty was made permanent, and executions were abolished for all crimes excepting piracy and high treason. During this same period in South Africa (especially after 1967), death penalty cases were being heard and carried out in record numbers.

"life-size winkle"—("Jokes and Novelties Salesman") A "winkle" is a childish reference to the penis. In this same year, poet Ted Hughes (1930-1998) published this stanza from the epic poem *Crow*:

> O do not chop his winkle off
> His Mammy cried with horror
> Think of the joy will come of it
> Tomorrer and tomorrer
> Mamma Mamma.

Hughes was a West Yorkshire-born poet, coincidentally (see "One on't . . . treddle" below), and attended Pembroke College, Cambridge. Idle also graduated from Pembroke, as did earlier-mentioned folk including Peter Cook, Tim Brooke-Taylor, and Stephen Greenblatt (Ep. 27).

The tiny doll Mr. Johnson (Idle) calls "wicked willy" is also a troll doll, this one a much smaller version than the "naughty Humphrey" (see note below) he held up earlier.

– M –

mechanical wings—(PSC; "Man-Powered Flight") This Victorian inventor-type image was probably culled from actual history, specifically the attempts at man-powered flight (vehicles like the ornithopter) by men like Edward Purkis Frost. Frost's attempts in 1902 were using wings made to resemble a crow's, and were constructed of willow, silk, and feathers, according to the Science Museum of London. One wing of Frost's last ornithopter is on display in the museum, as is a scale replica of the Montgolfier brothers' hot air balloon (see Ep. 40). There are myriad surviving short films capturing failed attempts at early flight, and in Ep. 40 the Pythons offer a fin-de-siècle film piece featuring Barry Zeppelin (Jones) attempting balloon flight.

This flying scene was shot at Seaford Cliffs, Seaford on 9-10 June 1970 (WAC T12/1,416).

"MP . . . nem. con."—("Tax on Thingy") Playing on the governmental affinity for acronyms. "MP" stands for Member of Parliament; "PM" is Prime Minister; "AM" and "PM" are, of course, time indicators (L. *ante meridiem*, before noon, and L. *post meridiem*, afternoon); "LSD" is both an abbreviation for pounds, shilling, and pence, as well as the then-popular psychedelic drug Lysergic acid diethylamide; "PIB" is the Prices and Incomes Board; "PPS" is Parliamentary Private Secretary; "NBG" is "no bloody good"; and "nem. con." is an abbreviation of the L. *nemine contradicente*, "(with) no one contradicting" (*OED*).

This convoluted mess translates rather simply into "more money (or LSD) from the Prices and Income Board is needed."

"My old man said . . . "—("The Spanish Inquisition") The beginning of this song is heard from Gilliam, though without the printed scripts it isn't clear at all what he's saying. The verse is borrowed from the Cockney English music hall song "My Old Man":

My old man said "Follow the van,
And don't dilly dally on the way,"
Off went the van with me 'ome packed in it,
I walked behind with me ol' cock linnet,
But I dillied, I dallied,
I dallied and I dillied,
Lorst the van and don' know where to roam.
And you can't trust the specials like an old time copper,
When you can't find your way 'ome!

The song was made popular by Marie Lloyd (1870-1922), a Cockney English music hall entertainer later lauded by T.S. Eliot and others. She popularized the singing for and about common folk in England, much as Eliot and the Modernists would preach the significance of the mundane, of the everyday.

– N –

"naughty Humphrey"—("Jokes and Novelties Salesman") This appears to be one of the "troll" dolls that became wildly popular in the mid-1960s. Mr. Johnson (Idle) will pull out another, slightly smaller troll doll toward the end of his threshold spiel. The "Humphrey" reference may be a nod to Python chum Humphrey Barclay (b. 1941), who will be mentioned again (by complete name) in Ep. 19. See notes to Ep. 19 for more on Barclay.

Nurse—(PSC; "The Semaphore Version of *Wuthering Heights*") The Nurse is played by Jean Clarke, and the Old Man is played by Albert Ward. Call time for these shots (at Ealing TFS) was 1:30p.m. on 29 May 1969 (WAC T12/1,242).

– O –

"Oh! Heathcliffe"—("The Semaphore Version of *Wuthering Heights*") The dialogue here is not lifted directly from the novel or the film, but is an approximation of the heightened emotionality of the entire story, characters, setting, period, etc. The Pythons play the scene as if it's right out of the overtly melodramatic *East Lynne*, a much-staged (and filmed) nineteenth-century novel and stage play. (The play's oft-quoted line "Dead, and never called me mother" is voiced by The Big Cheese [Chapman] in Ep. 4.)

Lines like "Oh, Catherine" and "hark" do appear, but not in the overly emotional way the Pythons imply, and the following "You've been seeing Heathcliffe" exchange is completely fabricated.

"Old Bailey"—("Court Scene [Charades]") The home of the Central Criminal Courts in London, the Old Bailey is near London's financial district and St Paul's Cathedral. Judges are called "My Lord" (or "M'lud") in this court. Once again, Ximinez—asking for two, then three tickets—has confused his numbers.

These exterior shots were recorded on 3 June 1970 (WAC T12/1,416).

"One on't . . . treddle"—("The Spanish Inquisition") Delivered in a thick northern accent, and obviously not understood by the more affluent, patrician wife of the mill owner. The scene in D.H. Lawrence's *Sons and Lovers* (mentioned so prominently in the production notes and final script for Ep. 2) where a boy from the mine rushes to Mrs. Morel to tell of her husband's mine accident, is staged very much like this one (80-81). As for the accent, cf. one of Morel's very Northern rejoinders as he and his wife argue over his drinking and the constant frittering away of their money:

"Then get out on it—it's mine. Get out on it!" he shouted. "It's me as brings th' money whoam, not thee. It's my house, not thine. Then *ger out on't—ger out on't!*" (21, italics added)

Clearly, the more angry Morel gets, the more "northern" his talk becomes, the façade of being married to a southern woman and yearning to talk like her evaporating with the heat of rage.

In the "Spanish Inquisition" introductory material here, not only does Lady Mountback (Cleveland) not understand Reg's (Chapman) northern accent, once he does translate into "proper" English for her, she still has no idea what the phrase means. It's clear this is a barefaced set-up for the narrative intrusion that is to follow (the Inquisitors), and that perhaps the absent Lord Mountback (ostensibly, the mill owner) was the intended recipient of this message. Yet another example of a failed communication in the Python world, this time—as is often the case—leading to reprisals and narrative punishments.

In a textile mill (cotton, for example), treddles (or treadles) were often foot-operated devices used "to produce reciprocating or rotary motion" (*OED*). Water, steam, and electric power would eventually take most of the treddle work from laborers.

opulent sitting room—(PSC; "The Spanish Inquisition") This room looks as if the BBC designers and propmasters simply watched *The Edwardians* (Granada, 1965), and copied the drawing room depicted in the episode "The Madras." (See Vahimagi's *British Television*.)

A source of significant and ongoing consternation for laborers, unions, and even government figures was the lavish lifestyle often enjoyed by mill and mine owners, especially in relation to the living and working conditions of their employees.

Much of the fire in the bellies of the "Angry Young Men" writers arose from this imbalance they saw in many northern towns. There are photos of many of these managers'/owners' homes and even castles in Colum Giles' *Yorkshire Textile Mills, 1770-1930*.

Finally, the size and layout of this set demanded that the show relocate to Ealing Television Film Studios (Ealing TFS) for most of this episode (WAC T12/1,437).

"our *three* weapons"—("The Spanish Inquisition") This "counting problem" will reappear with King Arthur in *Monty Python and the Holy Grail* (1974).

– P –

"Phelps, Brian"—("Court Scene [Charades]") British diver who won the bronze medal in the 1960 Rome Olympics. In 1970 (when this episode was written and recorded) Phelps was performing in a dive show at the Aquadrome on the Isle of Man. (Another Brian Phelps, also a Brit, won the three-metre springboard in the 1932 Perth Olympics.)

"playing fields"—("Vox Pops") The need for additional playing fields may be a reference to the continuing destruction and vandalism of cricket fields across

England by protestors angry that South Africa cricketers were being allowed to tour in the UK. The protestors would invade the pitches at night, often armed with shovels, and dig holes and furrows, generally destroying the playing surface. See other entries relating to South Africa for more.

"Program Planning"—(link out of "The Spanish Inquisition") The swipes at the mentality and creative acumen of BBC types appear over and over in *FC*. Cf. Ep. 38, where BBC Programme Planners are compared (unfavorably) with penguins and non-English-speaking foreigners. The fact that BBC Man (Cleese) can boast a university degree automatically disqualifies him for BBC creative employment. Later in the episode, the Programme Planner will read a missing punchline and decide to "make a series out of it."

Throughout the run of the first three series, at least, there is constant, simmering unrest over the scheduling for various *FC* episodes, as evidenced in memos in WAC files. The Pythons and their representatives ask for and sometimes demand clarification as to broadcast time slots, broadcast regions, the frustrations of opt-out agreements, and just changes—sometimes week-to-week—in what time slot the *FC* epsiodes would appear.

– R –

"rack"—("The Spanish Inquisition") A frame-and-roller torture device where the vicitm is tied down and stretched, eventually suffering socket dislocation. In this case, of course, it's a dish drying rack. Inquisitor torture methods included water torture and hanging by the wrists. See the *Catholic Encyclopedia*—which offers a very thorough and surprisingly candid section on the Inquisition—for more.

Roman chariot race—(PSC; "*Julius Caesar* on an Aldis Lamp") This film footage is borrowed from P. Jenkinson's *Chariot Race* (WAC T12/1,417). Jenkinson (b. 1935), a film critic, writer (*Marty*), and television presenter, is lampooned by name and depiction in Eps. 23 and 33.

– S –

"Semaphore Code"—("The Semaphore Version of *Wuthering Heights*") Semaphore is a code using differing positions of the arms (sometimes holding flags), with each separate position indicating a particular letter. (There is a very similar scene in Chuck Jones' 1942 cartoon *The Dover Boys of Pimiento U* where boy scouts, within talking distance of each other, use signal flags and semaphore instead.)

The code as delivered by the Pythons is accurate to a certain point, though that accuracy depends on the signaler. Instead of "Oh, Catherine," for example, Heathcliffe (Jones) signals just "Oh," twice, but accurately. Both Jones and Idle (the Husband) can signal with very close approximations to the actual code, erring only in precise placement of the flags, on occasion.

Catherine (Cleveland), however, was obviously just instructed to move her arms and flags as the mood of scene struck her, as her first longer signal translates (letter-by-letter) "e, (incomprehensible signal), t/u, h, j, x, y, i" and a break, and then "o, e, (incomprehensible signal)." (The "incomprehensible signals" are those that represent flag positions used by the actors that are *not* part of semaphore code.) As part of Pythons' consistent "othering" of the female characters this may also be something of a slight—only the men in the scene either knew or learned the code for the sketch. This isn't much of a conjecture, as previous females (actual women, that is) have failed to understand facial cues, aural cues, and metaphoric language (Ep. 7), not been allowed to pun along with the boys (Ep. 8), and punished for uttering the unutterable word "mattress" (Ep. 4).

Continuing along this thesis, the Husband (Idle) fairly clearly signals "Catherine," transposing only a "p" for the "i" in the name, probably due to the speed of the signaling. He also emphasizes the break or stop after/between words (both flags held against the legs, pointing straight down to the ground), as if this were the visualization of yelling in semaphore. Catherine answers, spelling out "p, h (wrong hands again), y/v, r, k, r" and a break. Her husband then, using larger flags, starts her name again, and gets through "c, a, t, h, and e," before there is a cut to the baby crying (signaling gibberish, not "waaaagh"). The Nurse (Jean Clarke) signals "s" (not "sssh"), and the Old Man (Albert Ward) "z" and "h" for sleeping sounds.

The gibberish takes over from here all around. When asking if she's been seeing Heathcliffe, the Husband spells out "y, q, n, e, r, j, h/b, e, u" and a break. But it's Catherine who gets to rant on in meaningless (but entirely watchable) semaphore, for, as she paces around her husband, defending her relationship with Heathcliffe, she clearly spells out "o, q, j, r (break), r, z, h (break), r, j, j, r, r (break), r, f, r, (incomprehensible signal), r, f, r, j, r (break), r, z, r (break), r, j, r, f, r," and on and on. At this point her signaling is so fluid that each incomprehensible signal blends into the next, for complete gibberish, at least at the semaphoric level. It may just be, finally, that emotion wins out, and words (and letters threatening to become words) grow meaning-

less in the presence of such strong feelings, and with such iconic characters.

small hills, in rolling countryside—("The Semaphore Version of *Wuthering Heights*") This looks to be filmed on or near Hookney Tor on Dartmoor, Devon, which is near Headland Warren, the long house where the building scenes were shot for this episode. The show was, according to WAC records, shooting in Devon for this episode (WAC T12/1,437).

"smashing film"—("The Spanish Inquisition") Delivered like a film promo, bringing attention to the entertainment value of this tragic period in history, and reminding the viewer that television—even public television—is aware of and dependent on ratings/viewership. Cf. Ep. 25, where the *Black Eagle* film is triumphantly introduced, then fizzles out.

"something new to tax"—("Tax on Thingy") During this period, there was significant concern over the increasing tax burden in the burgeoning welfare society. Political cartoonist Keith Waite lampooned Chancellor of the Exchequer Roy Jenkins, who was seeking a new series of revenue streams: "Wealth tax; 'Young people have far too much money these days,' says Chancellor, introducing licences for bicycles and tricycles, goldfish and white mice" (*The Sun* 1 January 1969). See the British Cartoon Archive.

"Spanish Inquisition"—("The Spanish Inquisition") Probably working from memory, the Pythons came close to historical accuracy in this introduction. Originally proposed to root out converted Jews, then Muslims, who might stray from the Catholic faith, the Inquisition was instigated in 1478 by Spanish heads of state Ferdinand and Isabella, and was actually opposed by Pope Sixtus IV. Sixtus consistently tried to limit the scope and ferocity of the endeavor, his "let and hindrance" being actively engaged. Eventually, however, all members of the Spanish church were potential subjects to Inquisitors' attentions. Tomas de Torquemada was the first well-known leader of the Inquisition. Why the inquisitors would be in the north of England in 1912 isn't explained. (See the *Catholic Encyclopedia* for more on the period and participants.)

The obvious influence on the Pythons of Voltaire (Ep. 2) and *Candide* may also have an influence here, as Candide describes the auto-da-fé (public trials) of the Spanish Inquisition in great detail and with equally great satire.

Interestingly, recent scholarship had called into question the actual scope and levels of violence perpetrated, with very low percentages of those called before Inquisitors reporting any torture at all. This, of course, wouldn't have prevented the Pythons from beefing up the violent details, anyway.

Lastly, this fixation on the Spanish Inquisition may be attributable to the then-current talk of so-called Spanish practices in industrial settings. Trade unions (the bane of PM Wilson's existence) could promote overstaffed shops, increased overtime, shorter hours, etc., which came to be known as "Spanish practices"— by definition good for the workers and unions, but bad for management. These unions would be accused of "holding to ransom" all of Great Britain by both the Wilson and then Heath administrations, especially as inflation began to erode consumer spending and saving abilities, but certain wages continued to spiral. For the Pythons, (worker) Reg's trouble communicating effectively with (owner) Lady Mountback leads to the appearance of the loud Spaniards, and they intrude (with varying degrees of effectiveness) throughout the episode.

"Stage, The"—("Jokes and Novelties Salesman") *The Stage* is a weekly newspaper published since 1880, and focusing on the entertainment industry (and specifically theatre) in the UK.

Stock . . . mill town—(PSC; "The Spanish Inquisition") This is a still photo of an unidentified industrial concern. The Pythons wouldn't, certainly, have spent much time making certain that their researcher provided them with an actual photo of a Jarrow-area mill, or even a mill at all, so an industrial-looking, turn-of-the-century photo obviously served the purpose. The cooling towers and the four-chimney structure in the background indicate that at least portions of this complex comprised a coal-fired power station, and this *may be* a period photo (1930s) of the Blackburn Meadows Power Station, which was demolished (excepting the cooling towers) in the 1980s. There is no record in the BBC archives for this episode of where the photo was obtained.

– T –

"tax all foreigners living abroad"—("Tax on Thingy") The British colonial empire was, historically, a very effective means of gathering tax monies from, yes, foreigners living abroad. They may have become subjects of His/Her Majesty, but they were never Englishmen. The fact that this taxation request is delivered by a Conservative City Gent type (Jones) is expected. In fact, the City Gents and businessman types in this Vox Pops section are primarily concerned with (1) increasing Britain's colonial presence and profit, (2) sexuality and taxation, (3) capital punishment and the profiteering possible in that business, and (4) getting rid of the body's naughty bits—these Pythonesque Conservative types are, as ever, a strange and twisted lot.

"tax . . . thingy"—("Tax on Thingy") Technically, since prostitution behind closed doors and where no third party is acting as manager or pimp was and is not illegal in the UK, there were many men and women probably at least eligible to pay taxes on their sexual incomes.

As for taxes on pleasure items, there was a joke going around (in cartoons of the day) that if cannabis could just be legalized the government would have a significant new and very reliable tax revenue. See "Jon's" cartoon in the *Daily Mail* for 9 January 1969. Another cartoon lists the recent rise in taxation, addressing the uproar Sir Gerald Nabarro instigated, as well: "New moustache tax / Nab[arro] for PM / Import tax up! / Postage up 6d / S.E.T. [Selective Employment Tax] doubled / Car tax up! / Dog tax up! / Jenkins [Chancellor of the Exchequer] is a jerk / The Pill Tax / Petrol up Whisky up Every bloody thing up" (Papas, *The Guardian* 4 February 1969). Other items (fictional and not) suggested for taxation or increased taxation in the political cartoons of the day include handlebar mustaches (as the one worn by Conservative MP Gerald Nabarro), land betterment projects, tissue paper, betting, personal wealth, beer, retail sales taxes to pay for new roads in London, death duties, income tax, and capital gains. See the British Cartoon Archive.

As a barometer of the tax burden in the UK, and therefore the significance of its effect on the public conscience, it's worth noting that in the period 1964-1970, the so-called tax freedom day (indicating the number of days in a year it takes to pay the tax burden) lurched forward from April 23 to May 26. Pundits of the period were well aware of this increasing tax burden, and their cries are heard in newspapers, magazines, and interviews.

Many have concluded that this egregious financial burden led directly to Wilson's Labour government being surprisingly ousted by the Heath-led Conservatives in 1970, though a change of government didn't presage a significant change in the economy (and the Tories lost in 1974).

Torchlight dungeon—(PSC; "Photos of Uncle Ted [Spanish Inquisition]") This large and seemingly multileveled set makes it clear the the show is being recorded at Ealing TFS, not back at Television Centre.

– W –

"We are not amused"—(animated link into "Tax on Thingy") Gilliam includes this line in the "Reg's head" animation. The phrase is somewhat apocryphally attributed to Queen Victoria (in *The Notebooks of a Spinster*

Lady, 1919), in several settings and in relation to several possible events. *Private Eye* had picked up on the saying, as it appears in a 7 August 1964 Gerald Scarfe panel cartoon depicting the ailing *Punch* as the central character in Hogarth's *The Rake's Progress* (Ingrams 108).

The phrase and its connection to Victoria return in Ep. 41, when the Queen appears at a department store Victorian poetry reading to complain about ants. There is even dispute as to whether the Queen was employing the royal "we" or merely referring to herself and the ladies of the court. See notes to "We are not . . . amusiert" in Ep. 41 for more.

"week 39.4"—(link out of "Jokes and Novelties Salesman") This week in 1970 would have been the last full week of September, the twentieth through the twenty-sixth. The Pythons were actually in the studio during this week, recording the final version of Ep. 22 on Friday, 25 September. The location sequences (at 49 Elers Road) were shot in May 1970 (WAC T12/1,242).

"Welch, Raquel"—("Vox Pops") Mentioned earlier in Ep. 13, some of the Pythons may have run into Welch on the set of *The Magic Christian* (1969), to which Chapman and Cleese had contributed.

"we're on film"—(link out of "The Spanish Inquisition") Another moment—"It's a link, is it?"—where the artifice of the production is acknowledged. During this period, 16mm film cameras were the primary "out of studio" recording devices for television production, not bulky, more sensitive videotape cameras. (One of these new studio color video cameras,

model EMI 2001, can be seen in Ep. 2, in the "A Man With Three Buttocks" sketch.) These video cameras were used in the studio setting, and the filmed and taped images were then cut into a single episode, obvious picture clarity and medium differences notwithstanding.

Wilde, Marjorie—(PSC; "Photos of Uncle Ted [Spanish Inquisition]") The "Dear Old Lady" Wilde (1902-1988) is an actual older woman playing that very part, one of the few times the Pythons went this route. Like many of the other extras and walk-ons employed by the troupe, Wilde had appeared in several familiar television shows prior to this appearance, including *Troubleshooters* and *Z Cars*.

– Y –

"You will get expenses"—(link out of "The Spanish Inquisition") The Pythons did employ local walk-ons and extras in much this manner, hiring local actors for location shooting in Bournemouth and Norwich, at least (WAC T12/1,445).

– X –

"Ximinez"—("The Spanish Inquisition") The Grand Inquisitor chosen by Ferdinand and Isabella was Tomás de Torquemada (1420-1498), known as "the hammer of heretics." For more on Torquemada see the *Catholic Encyclopedia*.

Episode 16

– A –

"aeroplane"—("Flying Lessons") Curious, since this was (and is) a word still in very common usage in the UK. It may just be that Anemone (Chapman) is simply picking on Chigger (Jones) for not using the newer, trendier (perhaps more American) "airplane," determining "aeroplane" to be more effete, uppercrust, and old-fashioned.

and an owl—(PSC; link into opening titles) Actually, no lion is visible in this menagerie, but there is a cobra, a rabbit, a boar, and perhaps a monkey visible besides what's listed in the printed scripts. It's the ferret that explodes, not the owl, as indicated in the printed scripts.

Anemone—(PSC; "Flying Lessons") An anemone is both a plant with beautiful flowers or a sea creature, named so for its flower-like appendages. There often seems to be no pattern for the naming of characters, besides the silliness of silly names. Mr. Anemone (Chapman) isn't addressed this way by any of the characters or himself, meaning he is named simply for the amusement of the writers and to differentiate him from Mr. Chigger (Jones).

announcer rises up in front of the window—(PSC; "Girl in the Window" link into opening titles) This sexually suggestive shot seems to have been recorded on 21 May 1970 (WAC T12/1,416). WAC records don't indicate the specific building used for this shot, nor the usual permissions to use a device like the cleaner hoist.

"ask anyone"—("The Poet McTeagle") This continual begging was also the modus operandi of the American cartoon character Wimpy, who appeared in the *Popeye* series. Wimpy always asked for a hamburger, with the promise that he would make good the load the next Tuesday. After its initial run as a theatrical cartoon se-ries, which had begun in 1933, *Popeye* appeared on American TV 1956-1963.

– B –

badly—("Girl in the Window" link into opening titles) This dialogue is dubbed, meaning they may have shot on location without sound equipment, though it's actually dubbed fairly well. (The sound will be recorded live later, as Cleese appears on the hoist.) The script call for bad dubbing may have been an attempt to mimic earnest but poorly made pornographic films of the period (e.g., *I Am Curious Yellow* [1967]), or even some of the more respected (but also technically challenged) Nouvelle Vague films from the neo-realists onward. Hong Kong exports of this era (*Come Drink With Me*, e.g.), were also distributed in the West in badly dubbed versions.

"bally"—("Hijacked Plane [to Luton]") "Bally" is the mild epithet of choice among Python (and jolly RAF) aviator types, hence Zanie (Chapman) here calling himself a "flying man, you know." (Chapman's character's name—but not his characterization—has changed between sketches, from Anemone to Zanie.) This also refers back to the character Captain Biggles, from Ep. 10, and who will be featured again in Ep. 33 (both Chapman). A close look at such RAF banter will be seen later, in Ep. 42.

"BALPA"—("Hijacked Plane [to Luton]") BALPA is the British Airline Pilots' Association, the guild that speaks for most of Britain's pilots. It was founded in Croydon in 1937.

The airline industry had spent a good deal of time on the nation's front (and op ed) pages in 1970, including the much-celebrated and much-poo-poohed arrival of the first Boeing 747 jumbo jet, hijackings to

Cuba and terrorist bombs on European airliners, and a threatened strike by airline unions if British United Airways did not merge with BOAC. See myriad cartoons, for example, at the British Cartoon Archive.

"Basingstoke"—("Hijacked Plane [to Luton]") Basingstoke is at least forty miles southwest of Heathrow, meaning it's probably well in line with a London-Cuba flight path. Basingstoke will be referenced again in Ep. 42, when it somehow becomes part of Westphalia.

"Belpit"—("A Bishop Rehearsing") Not a very common name anywhere in Britain or Wales, there were just a handful of Belpits living, for example, in the Paddington area in London according to the 1891 UK census, and none in the Greater London area in the late 1960s.

big pile of straw—("Hijacked Plaine [to Luton]") This exterior shot (where Zanie [Chapman] falls from the plane) was recorded on 3 June 1970 at the public restrooms at Old Oak Common, Acton. The Pythons were booked for rehearsals into the Old Oak Club in Acton during this series (WAC T12/1,093).

Bishop—("A Bishop Rehearsing") The Bishop (Palin) is dressed much like Terry Jones' character "The Bishop" will be in the following episode. A "mitre" is a bishop's staff. This costume will reappear in Ep. 20, "*Take Your Pick*," when the Bishop (Palin) will assault a cross-dressed game show hostess (Chapman).

"bladder trouble"—("The Poet McTeagle") Cf. "Biggles Dictates a Letter" in Ep. 33 for a similar letter, with similar sentiments.

"bob"—("The Poet McTeagle") A "bob" is one shilling.

"British Psychiatric Association"—("Psychiatrist Milkman") The British Psychiatric Association will be mentioned again in Ep. 43, when a bogus psychiatrist (Palin) is trying to prove his credentials. The British Psychological Society (Tavistock House, South Tavistock Square, WC1) had been overseeing Britain's mental health industry since the early part of the twentieth century. The British Psycho-Analytical Society was also extant, housed at 63 New Cavendish, W1.

"British Sugar Association"—("Psychiatrist Milkman") The British Sugar Corporation was formed by an Act of Parliament in 1936, and was from its inception a nationalized industry. Its corporate headquarters during this period were found at 134 Piccadilly W1.

"building society"—("The Poet McTeagle") According to the *OED*, a building society is "a society in which the members periodically contribute to a fund out of which money may be lent to any of their number for the purpose of building (or purchasing) a house." Technically, then, McTeagle (Jones) shouldn't have been able to use his divvy money for anything but a house purchase or construction.

"buttered scones"—("Flying Lessons") Scones are soft cakes made of barley or oatmeal. The Lumberjack (Palin) sings of having "buttered scones for tea" in "I'm a Lumberjack" sketch in Ep. 9. He also happens to be a transvestite, which may be flavoring Anemone's appraisal of Chigger's flying inabilities in this sketch. In the "Flying Lessons" setting, however, the scones are a symbol of Mr. Chigger's alleged snobbery.

– C –

"Cameron tartan"—("The Poet McTeagle") There are myriad Cameron tartans representing Camerons from different regions in Scotland. Incidentally, McTeagle (Jones) doesn't appear to be wearing a Cameron tartan, either, meaning this particular entry (and many others in these volumes) is performing a service similar to that of both the BALPA spokesman (Idle) and the Highlander (Cleese) in this episode.

This "fact-checking" (to which the Pythons clearly weren't wed) would come back in another form during the following series. For Ep. 33, a 30 September 1971 letter from the Royal National Life-Boat Institution—to whom the Pythons had directed a request to shoot on a lifeboat, and obviously submitted a script of the sequence, as well—granted the request but asked simply if they intended showing a Shoreham life-boat then it should be named specifically, and that the script reference to "Ramsgate" be eliminated, as Ramsgate had "no self-righting life-boat" (WAC T12,1,428). See notes to Ep. 33 for more on the locations and equipment used in this scene.

"certain involuntary muscular movements"—("Hijacked Plane [to Luton]") This sort of narrative devolution—from confident assertion to qualification to equivocation to outright backpedaling—will reappear as Dennis Moore (Cleese) tries to rob a coach in Ep. 37. Idle's Mr. Sopwith in Ep. 7 also goes from spotting all yetis to seeing just one to spotting a little one to seeing a picture of one to just hearing about yetis—all in one dialogic decrescendo of diminution.

Chigger—(PSC; "Flying Lessons") A harvest mite, which fastens itself to the skin, causing irritation.

"Cooper, Tommy"—("Hijacked Plane [to Luton]") Tommy Cooper was a British music hall comedian and sometime magician who died in 1984. Cooper was also a television personality, appearing on many shows and having his own show (twice) on ATV. There is no record of Cooper appearing in any of the many versions of *Sherlock Holmes* produced for television.

"crofter"—("The Poet McTeagle") A crofter is essentially a Scottish tenant farmer or sharecropper. Again, this is the shorthand way to identify the rustic Scottishness of the character, and the Scots in general, in the Python oeuvre. This same approach was used in Ep. 7, when aliens were turning normal Englishmen into alien Scotsmen, and probably can be connected back to Samuel Johnson's similar marginalizing of the Scots even as he enjoyed their countryside and the company of one of their own, his biographer James Boswell.

– D –

"divvy"—("The Poet McTeagle") A "divvy" is a colloquial abbreviation of "dividend," or a payout from a common fund or investment.

"don't anybody move"—("Hijacked Plane [to Luton]") What follows is a sort of postmodern deconstruction of the shopworn movie, TV, and dime novel criminal's phrase "don't anybody move." The point here is that in Python's world (and in this transitionary Modern-Postmodern world in general) no word or phrase (or meaning) is stable, especially those words that may have entered the *cultural* lexicon and come to mean the same thing to everyone—in Python, these most common utterances are the best targets, always already ripe for the cycle of misreading and reinvestment and misreading.

In Ep. 8, the word "mattress" has been connected not to something to sleep on, but to a ritualized set of bizarre behaviors enacted by Mr. Lambert (Chapman) and counteracted by his co-workers, where the "something to sleep on" is to be known as a "dog kennel." Later, in Ep. 38, the phrase "No time to lose" will be worried over until it becomes meaninglessness, completely detached from its context, its connotative and denotative moorings, as Man (Palin) can't even figure out which word or syllable to stress, and the RSM (Jones) doesn't recognize the phrase at all. Successful communication, therefore, continues to evade most person-to-person transactions in the Python world.

"dormice"—("Hijacked Plane [to Luton]") "Dormice" is the (folk) plural of "dormouse," which is a small, hibernating rodent (*OED*). It also can mean a sleepy or dozing person. The Second Pilot's (Cleese) questioning response probably arises from the Hostess' uses of "dormice" rather than perhaps "church-mice." The rodent also makes a sleepy appearance in Lewis Carroll's *Alice's Adventures in Wonderland*, a text and au-

thor the Pythons have often leaned toward in their absurd visual and linguistic constructions.

– E –

Episode 16—Given no specific title in the printed scripts, the episodes wouldn't be titled again regularly until the fourth and final series in 1974. This is the third show of the second series, broadcast 29 September 1970, and recorded fifth on 16 July 1970.

The BBC records for this episode indicate only one official extra or walk-on, Jeanette Wild (*Z Cars*; *Up Pompeii*). She plays Second Secretary in the "Flying Lessons" sketch, and has a very brief speaking part (including a voiceover in the "Hijacked Plane" sketch).

"Eton and Magdalene"—("Flying Lessons") Eton is an ancient college (high-school-aged pupils) founded by Henry VI in 1440, a so-called public school where Britain's elite were and are nurtured. One of Harold Wilson's oppositional complaints about the ruling Tory government between 1951 and 1964 was both the fact that so many blue-blooded Conservatives had attended Eton, and took care of their own, essentially:

> We take the view that everyone should be equal in the matter of selection and yet, well, the last three Prime Ministers have all been to one school, and there are forty-thousand schools in this country. Nearly half the Cabinet comes from that school. I think it still shows I think that the Conservative party is out of touch with the times in which we live. (*Eyewitness 1960-69*, "Macmillan Resigns")

"Madgalene" [sic] is a misspelling of Magdalene (probably just a typo [and pronounced "Maud-lin"]), part of Cambridge University (est. 1542). There is also a Magdalen College in Oxford. All of these schools have been associated with producing the elite, ruling class of Britain for centuries. (Ironic, since five of the Pythons attended these very same institutions.)

The Pythons were able to attend Oxford and Cambridge, yes, but none of them were in the social or financial class for Etonian matriculation. Many of the political and/or society characters lampooned in the series follow this same educational trail, including Ludovic Kennedy (Ep. 37); Liberal leader Jeremy Thorpe (Ep. 45); Prime Ministers William Gladstone (Ep. 2); a Liberal, and Conservative Alec Douglas-Home (Ep. 30); and Lord Snowdon, Antony Armstrong-Jones (Ep. 19).

"exaggerated, violent movements"—("Hijacked Plane [to Luton]") The characters have to put a finer and finer point on the original catchphrase (an absolute: "don't anybody move"), narrowing, refining, and then winnowing out the obvious and the not-so-obvious variations of "movement" as they are identified. A sort of relativism has been broached here, rendering the phrase "don't anybody move" not only moot, but somewhat ridiculous and physically, even cosmically impossible. The solid, knowable days of Modern art (where a pear could still look like a pear) were rapidly being undermined by the Postmodernism of abstraction, nonrepresentation, and metamorphosis—the separation of the signifier from the signified was well under way during this period. Dennis Moore (Cleese) will find this as he attempts to convince his victims that he practices every day, then most days, then whenever he can, etc.

– F –

"fags"—("The Poet McTeagle") "Fag" is a slang term for cigarette. In Ep. 15, the acronym-spouting Politician (Cleese) demands a fag so he won't "go spare."

"Fly Me to the Stars"—("Hijacked Plane [to Luton]") This made-up title is probably a play on the Frank Sinatra standard "Fly Me to the Moon," penned by Bart Howard in 1954, and recorded by Sinatra in 1964.

"fly the plane to Luton"—("Hijacked Plane [to Luton]") A turnabout on the familiar skyjacking destination of Cuba, which many considered a haven for radical Leftist revolutionaries since Castro's forces overthrew the dictator Batista in 1959.

Hijacking (or skyjacking) had become a real danger in the 1960s, with smaller political groups reaping very high public exposure via these essentially low-tech crimes. In September 1969, the International Federation of Airline Pilots' Association was even considering a worldwide strike to draw attention to the hijacking situation.

Political cartoons of the period treat the subject a number of times, with one in particular jabbing at similar targets as the Pythons. Keith Waite in *The Sun* (2 September 1969) is certain that no one would be interested in hijacking any Monarch-like airline (he calls it "Busy Bee") destined for the continent, for example, and in another panel an air hostess tells a gun-wielding hijacker: "We can't possibly fly you to Syria, we're already flying to Cuba." See the British Cartoon Archive for more.

– G –

"Gilbert and Sullivan"—("Psychiatrist Milkman") Noted nineteenth-century English light opera partnership. The Gilbert and Sullivan Society was formed in London in 1924. See the notes for "I want to marry you too sir" in Ep. 19.

glen—(PSC; "The Poet McTeagle") A "glen" is a "mountain-valley, usually narrow and forming the course of a stream," and was initially applied only to such places in Scotland and Ireland, according to the *OED*. A "scar" is a rocky crag or steep, rocky precipice. A "coot" is a swimming/diving bird, and a "moorhen," also called a water-hen, is a bird that favors watery areas. A "tarn" is a small mountain lake, while a "loch" is a lake or inland sea, often land-locked. These are Sir Walter Scott (1771-1832) locations, words, and phrases, really, whose *Redgauntlet* had been very recently produced as a popular eight-part miniseries for Scottish television in January 1970.

The Pythons will read aloud (with great difficulty) from Scott's *Redgauntlet* (1824) in Ep. 38.

Good mornings—(PSC; "Flying Lessons") This entire "arty shot" is elided from the filmed version of the sketch. Ingmar Bergman's 1955 film *The Seventh Seal* was a well-known art film of the recent past, and featured a much-copied silhouette shot of the type described above (and perhaps borrowed by Bergman, as well, from Griffith's *Birth of a Nation* forty years earlier, frankly). In the case of *Seventh Seal*, it was Death personified leading the mortals along the brow of the hill toward their ultimate destination. This same shot/film source is mentioned in Ep. 7, as transformed Scotsmen enter Scotland, and will be revisited in some detail in the Pythons' final feature film, *The Meaning of Life* (1983), where Death leads the motorcars and passengers into heaven.

Most likely, the demands of an "evening" shot (waiting for the right silhouette light, the "golden hour") as called for in the script precluded this scene, given the time and budget constraints the show would have been under, especially on location.

"Gordon"—("Flying Lessons") Possibly a reference to Gordon Campbell, Heath's Secretary of State for Scotland between 1970 and 1974. Heath's Conservative government had replaced the Wilson Labourites after a successful 18 June 1970 General Election.

GPO tent—(PSC; "Flying Lessons") A small fabric or plastic covering for General Post Office employees working in manholes, etc. A portion of the GPO's work includes communications, meaning this tent depicted was probably being used over a manhole where land line work was under way. This same type of tent appears in *A Hard Day's Night* (1964), when the Beatles use it to help sneak into the recording studio (from a vehicle) and away from screaming fans. The GPO was essentially dissolved in 1969, just as the Pythons were writing these initial episodes. The name ("GPO tent") would understandably have remained in consumers' minds long after the dissolution of the GPO.

"gynaecologist"—("The Poet McTeagle") This said as if being a gynaecologist isn't actually being a doctor, and/or that on the side, this woman's doctor examines male patients (and/or that Scottish males aren't men). This will be repeated later in the episode. The latter charge would seem to be refuted by Ep. 37, when in the "Ideal Loon Exhibition" there is a revealing "Nae Trews" exhibit that seems very popular to female visitors.

– H –

"Harpenden"—("Hijacked Plane [to Luton]") Harpenden is another London borough, situated five miles southeast of Luton.

haystack in a field—("Hijacked Plane [to Luton]") This haystack was also shot at Old Oak Common, just as the previous haystack scene, but the restrooms are not visible. A quick jump cut on the gunman's hand as he flags the bus takes us instead to the same area where the "rocky highlands" of the wandering poet McTeagle (Jones) were shot, at Newbridge, Dartmoor on 14 May 1970 (WAC T12/1,425). In one cut the action moves more than 175 miles away, from the London suburbs to Devon.

He is Mr. Boniface—("Déjà Vu") This character's name is never mentioned by another character, but included (and pointed out) in the printed script. In literary tradition, Boniface is the well-known character from Farquhar's *Beaux' Stratagem* (1707), the good-natured innkeeper. In the unsettling *It's the Mind* world sketch, Palin's Boniface struggles mightily to live up the eponymous nature of his name.

"High Chaparral"—("Hijacked Plane [to Luton]") *The High Chaparral* was an American television Western airing 1967-1971, and appeared via the BBC on British TV. *Bonanza* and *Big Valley* were also popular on ITV and BBC, respectively. *High Chaparral* (scheduled for BBC2) is featured on the 22 March 1969 *Radio Times* cover.

highland gentleman—(PSC; "The Poet McTeagle") Here the Pythons employs obvious visual cues to identify a Scotsman. He wears a kilt, as well as a "tam-o'-shanter," which is a circular woolen bonnet originally worn by Scottish ploughmen. He also carries a "knobkerrie," a "short thick stick with a knobbed head, used as a weapon or missile by South African peoples. Also extended to similar weapons used by other peoples, e.g. in Polynesia and Australia." There's no indication in the *OED* that such a cudgel was ever characteristic of Scotland, though there are significant evidences that such cudgels were carried by Irish priests (as they taught rowdy schoolboys), among others. The etymology of the word ("knobkerrie") is even African.

In the 1948 Warner Bros. cartoon *My Bunny Lies Over the Sea* (dir. Chuck Jones), several Scottish-type characters carry similar cudgels as walking canes, including a disguised Bugs Bunny.

– I –

"I am somebody's lunch hour"—(animated link into "Psychiatrist Milkman") The music Gilliam uses in this animation includes the International Studio Orchestra playing the "Flute" Promenade by Eric Towren, and then "Long Trail" from "Far West Suite" by Eddie Warner (WAC T12/1,436).

Ian Mckellan figure—("The Poet McTeagle") Actually spelled "Ian McKellen"—now Sir Ian—he is a respected English stage and screen actor, who in 1970 performed the one-man show *Keats* for the BBC. Born in 1939, McKellen is a member of the Python generation, attending St. Catharine's at Cambridge. McKellen had played Richard in *Richard II*, Edward in *Edward II*, and T.E. Lawrence in Terence Rattigan's *Ross* in 1970, as well, and all for the BBC. The costume chosen by the Pythons for this "Ian Mckellan figure" looks a bit like the one he wore for the *Richard II* production.

"If I could . . . "—("Psychiatrist Milkman") Both the Milkman (Idle) and Milkmaid (Chapman) hold up a warning index finger to the Lady, a joke and gesture that will be seen again in Eps. 17 and 18. The indication, again, is that the "rimshot" joke of the past—the well-known set-up and punchline payoff—is indeed to be left in the past. This "If I could walk that way . . . " joke is a hoary chestnut from music hall and vaudeville days, when verbal comedians would patter through a series of "Doctor, Doctor" jokes in burlesque shows.

These farms scenes were shot on 21 May 1970 in the area around Torquay (WAC T12/1,416).

inspiring Scottish music—("The Poet McTeagle") These selections—heard beneath the various portions of the McTeagle (Jones) scenes—include performances by the Pipes and Drums of the Royal Scots Greys of "Scotland's Pride," "Skye Boat Song," and "Road to Isles" (WAC T12/1,436).

"Inverness pantomime"—("The Poet McTeagle") Inverness' variety theatre during this period was the Empire Theatre, which offered pantomime shows through at least the 1950s and 1960s. (Inverness is in the Scottish Highlands area along the Moray Firth coast.) These pantomimes are children's entertainments featuring well-known fairy or nursery tales, songs, slapstick, and stock characters "such as a pantomime 'dame', played by a man, a leading boy, played by a woman, and a pantomime animal, e.g. horse, cat, goose, played by actors dressed in a comic costume, with some regional variations" (*OED*). A pantomime goose, horse ("Dobbins"), Princess Margaret and Puss, and even Long John Silver make appearances in *FC*, a testament to the entertainment's cultural significance to the young Pythons. (In 1967-1968, for instance, *Aladdin* was the pantomime running in Glasgow's King's Theatre, while in the early 1960s the *Jamie* series [e.g., *A Wish for Jamie*]—pantomimes in full Scottish dress—played to packed houses.)

The "leading boy played by a woman" and the panto animal will both make appearances in Ep. 28, while other pantomime characters including Margaret, a goose, and horses are featured throughout *FC*. See entries for Ep. 30 for more.

"Isn't!"—("Flying Lessons") This meaningless, repetitive argument is much like both the "Dead Parrot" exchange in Ep. 8, especially when the Shopkeeper (Palin) hits the cage, and most of the "Argument Clinic" dialogue found in Ep. 29. The obvious fakery is also present—and equally defended—in the feature film *HG*, where a woman (Connie Booth) has been forcibly dressed up as a witch, complete with false nose and witch's clothing.

It's the Mind—("Deja Vu") The illustration in the opening title sequence for *It's the Mind* is from *Gray's Anatomy*, p. 868, figure 743, and is called "The veins of the right side of the head and neck" (33rd edition, published 1962, and edited by Davies and Davies). The show paid £5/51 for the rights to use the illustration (WAC T12/1,242). The photos used in this title sequence are not acccounted for in the archival material for this episode. This also continues the long tradition on British TV of the "It's" title (see Ep. 1).

The weird music beneath this title sequence (and the reiterations of the titles) is from P. Wilsher and K. Chester's "Eye of Horns" from the "Electroshake" album (WAC T12/1,436).

– J –

"Jeez"—("A Bishop Rehearsing") "Jeez" is a particularly American colloquialism, though neither the character (Bishop) nor the actor (Palin) affect an American accent or delivery. (The Bishop follows this reading with a Scottish and then Japanese version of the phrase.) The word also appears in a "Barry McKenzie" cartoon in the 2 January 1970 edition of *Private Eye* (12).

– K –

"Kirby, Kathy"—("Hijacked Plane [to Luton]") Kathy Kirby never did sing on *High Chaparral*, but did have her own show, several hit records, and in 1963 was voted the top female British singer. She would take second two years later in the popular Eurovision Song Contest, singing "I Belong." See Ep. 22 for the Pythons' version of the Eurovision Song Contest.

– L –

"Lassie O'Shea"—("The Poet McTeagle") Here the Scotswoman (Idle) isn't even given a true name, but simply called "Lassie," meaning a young girl.

"lurex"—("Hijacked Plane [to Luton]") "Lurex" is "the proprietary name of a type of yarn which incorporates a metallic thread; also, fabric made from this yarn" (*OED*). Since proprietary, it could/should have been capitalized in the printed scripts. There is no indication as to what kinds of "fun" the BALPA man (Idle) would be using the dancing tights for, but the uniform and air of authority would point us toward some sexually deviant activity, given the Pythons' previous depictions of such "types." Perhaps the BALPA Man is hinting at the homosocial/homosexual atmosphere with the "chaps at BALPA House."

"Luton"—("Hijacked Plane [to Luton]") Luton, about twenty miles north and west of London, has been and will be mentioned a number of times in *FC*, and was most notably the place where the Pirhana brothers detonated a nuclear device in Ep. 14, specifically at Luton's airport. Luton was also the jumping-off point for many continental package tour excursions, the type that the Tourist blasts in Ep. 19.

The Pythons' ultimate boss, Lord Hill (mentioned in Eps. 10, 11, and 18), the former "Radio Doctor," was created a life peer as Baron Luton, after successfully standing for parliament for Luton in 1950.

– M –

"Mater"—("Flying Lessons") The Latin word for "mother," "mater" was an in-vogue term for British public schoolboys (along with the later-mentioned "pater" for "father") from the nineteenth and twentieth centuries. This tradition of the higher-born boys leaving for boarding school is lampooned by radio comedian Tony Hancock (1924-1968) in *Hancock's Half Hour*:

> Mother: Come along, Anthony; lift your cases down.
> Hancock: Right-ho, Mater, I'm ready.
> Mother: This is the first time you've been away from home, you must be a brave little soldier.
> Hancock: I will, Mater, I will.
> Mother: Promise to write to me every week, study hard and don't get into bad company.
> Hancock: I'll try jolly hard to make myself a credit to you and Pater. (Series 4, Ep. 15, January 1957)

"Maudling"—("Flying Lessons") Yet another reference to Reginald Maudling (1917-1979), Home Secretary under Heath, and much-maligned Conservative figure throughout this period. What it is Maudling wouldn't do for fifty shillings isn't clear, but a reputation for financial promises delayed or not kept (i.e., promises to move from direct to indirect taxation) dogged Heath's government, as did a moribund economy. As early as 1966, however, Maudling's alleged involvement with companies that engaged in kickbacks, bribery, and influence peddling found its way into the press and, obviously, the Pythons' quiver.

During the 1968-1974 period, major newspapers featured 260 political cartoons depicting Maudling and Tory comrades, and Maudling found himself on the cover of *Private Eye* eight times between 1962 and 1974, with his pecuniary improprieties making prime, real news fodder for the satirical magazine.

Mercer, David—(PSC; "The Poet McTeagle") Mercer (1928-1980) was, in fact, a respected playwright, having created *Emma's Time* (1970), *On the Eve of Publication* (1967), *The Parachute* (1967), *In Two Minds* (BBC, 1967), and *Morgan: A Suitable Case for Treatment* (1966) prior to this *FC* episode being written. Mercer contributed often to the "Wednesday Play" TV series, which were commissioned plays presented by the BBC between 1964-1970. (Many *FC* extras also found work during this period on the various "Wednesday Play" productions.) The type of sincere, dramatic performance evinced by both McTeagle and the "Mckellan" character was characteristic of the "Wednesday Play" series.

"milk-float"—("Psychiatrist Milkman") A "milk-float" is a wagon or vehicle for distributing milk products. In this sketch, psychiatry is being dispensed.

In the following episode (Ep. 17), the "Architect Sketch" offers a "deck access"-type apartment block designed by Mr. Wiggins' (Cleese) firm. These elongated developments were given very wide entry decks ("streets in the sky") just so milk-floats could maneuver down them easily, delivering dairy products door-to-door, obviating the need for inhabitants to even leave their apartments on grocery errands. This led many to feel all the more trapped in these intricately planned and efficient but joyless grey structures, and levels of depression, apathy, and crime climbed in most such developments. A psychiatrist milkman would have been most welcome and needed, then, in these oppressive and depressing flats.

Milkman—("Psychiatrist Milkman") Idle often plays the intrusive man-at-the-door, including a nudging pub visitor (Ep. 3), a vicar selling sundries (Ep. 28), an encyclopedia salesman pretending to be a burglar (Ep. 5), and a novelty joke salesman (Ep. 15).

Mr. Chigger follows—(link into "Flying Lessons") The light, jaunty music underneath this long walk is Eric Coates and the Philharmonic Promenade Orchestra playing the "Knightsbridge March" from "London Suite" (WAC T12/1,436). This same music is used in Ep. 41, "Michael Ellis."

"mush"—("Flying Lessons") "Mush" is actually a term of address, though here it may take the more pejorative meaning as found in the phrase "mush-head," or "a person of a yielding disposition; one lacking in firmness" (*OED*). The American usage can mean "idiot," and the Pythons have been known to employ American vernacularisms when necessary.

– N –

"New Guinea"—("The Poet McTeagle") To continue the "correctional" motif of this episode, the practice of lip plate insertion isn't common to New Guinea (an island in the Melanesia chain), but is found in many areas of East Africa (e.g., the Mursi tribe of Ethiopia).

"No. They're all number three"—("Psychiatrist Milkman") In this case, another example of "it's not what you say but how you say it" in the Python world. Often, in the Python world, the correct answer isn't the answer, since the question may change before the answer is provided in the emerging Postmodern world. The "Silly Job Interview" in Ep. 5 is an example of the shifting relationship, again, between signifier and signified, and between expectation and experience.

This is also perhaps a comment on the seeming randomness of psychiatry's standard, subjective, and interpretive diagnoses (the interpretable Rorschach ink blot, for example). The diagnosis is based on the Lady's *need* for dairy products, and is thus perhaps a slap at the then-emerging (the early 1970s) and flourishing books and trends (and fads) in sexuality, gender studies, self-help and self-improvement, etc. See notes to Ep. 2, "The Mouse Problem," for more. Note also that the psychiatrist milkman's diagnosis only confirms the woman's suspicions that he's actually a milkman.

"not in this show"—("A Bishop Rehearsing") The Bishop (Palin) here immediately steps out of the fictional world of the sketch and identifies the setting for what it is, a show. It's not made clear whether he's actually a bishop auditioning/practicing for a part, or an actor dressed as a bishop doing the same. (In an audio sketch created for *The Contractual Obligation* album [1980], the Bishop of Leicester [Palin] reads radio commercial voiceovers—happily taking the paycheck, and quibbling only slightly with the evolutionary nature of the text. The radio personnel [Chapman and Idle] wish aloud that they could have secured the Bishop of Bath and Wells, who's busy doing a frozen peas advert, or the Bishop of Worcester, instead.)

Chigger (Jones) doesn't seem ready or willing (or able) to step out of the fiction, continuing to press the "flying lessons" agenda, even as the Bishop, on another narrative level, can't or won't help him. So there are at least two sketches going on with the Bishop and Mr. Chigger—and they intrude on one another only momentarily. Either way, the "fiction within a fiction" structure—so endemic to Python—emerges again.

The Pythons could have been inspired by the Goons, again, for in "The Great Spon Plague" episode (10 March 1958) a Scottish character (played by Sellers) introduces himself, begins to recite his family history, and then quickly bids the audience good night because he has nothing more to do with/in the episode.

– O –

"'oop"—(PSC; "Flying Lessons") An *initial "h" dropping*, characteristic of a number of English dialects in the UK, including Cockney and what's now known as "Estuary English" (a working-class accent spoken along the Thames). A G.B. Shaw moment, certainly, where one Englishman identifies and pigeonholes another Englishman the moment the other speaks. This is a class-based determination set in "proper" or accepted English pronunciation, often assumed to be centered in London and modeled by the BBC and Oxbridge schools. Here the affected upper-crust accent will re-emerge, with Anemone (Chapman) assuming Chigger (Jones) didn't/couldn't understand his provincial, lower-class pronunciation of "hoop." Anemone also employs the more formal "an," even though Chigger didn't use it himself. The italicized "*h*" is provided in the scripts, as well as being emphasized in the speaking.

Other common characters, like blustering constables, also h-drop with their characteristic "Allo, allo" (or "Ello, ello") as they enter various Python sketches. Palin's First Gas Man in Ep. 14 also clearly h-drops ("'ere" and "'ave"), indicating his working-class status.

"orf to play the grahnd piano"—(PSC; "Flying Lessons") Here the uppercrust accent is indicated by phonetic spelling in the scripts. Such precision is almost never the case in the *FC* scripts.

– P –

"Pancho"—("Hijacked Plane [to Luton]") Pancho (Jones) used to be Mr. Chigger, of course, though his first name may have been "Pancho." The name could be a reference to Pancho Gonzalez, the American tennis player, who is mentioned a number of times in Ep. 7. More likely, however, since "Pancho" in this scene is a co-pilot or sidekick, this is a reference to the character Pancho in the long-running American Western television show *The Cisco Kid* (1950-1956), starring Duncan Renaldo as Cisco, and Leo Carillo as Pancho. *The Cisco Kid* was picked up by the BBC for children's programming in the mid-1950s.

"Pat-a-cake . . . "—("Psychiatrist Milkman") Perhaps this rhyme simply continues the pantomime thematic thread from the previous sketch. The instances of such irruptions into present sketches of previous themes or characters are seen throughout *FC* (see Ep. 27, for example). Also, according to the *OED*: "Hence pat-a-cake *v., nonce-wd.*, to superintend or direct any one's action as the nurse does the baby's hands in this game." The Lady (Chapman) is being directed by the Milkman (Idle) into purchasing his goods or accepting his pat psychiatric diagnoses—and preferably both.

perfectly calm and friendly—(PSC; "Hijacked Plane [to Luton]") This textual comment—that no one seems to notice the potential danger of the hijacking situation—is unusual for Python. Most of the scenes where this kind of absurdity occurs aren't commented upon at all in the stage directions. This same kind of drifting away from the danger at hand into tangential semantics happens often in *FC*, notably later in a similar hold-up scene featuring Dennis Moore (Ep. 37).

pillar box—("The Poet McTeagle") A "pillar box" is a receptacle for receiving mail. Similar boxes will be commissioned throughout Ep. 44, stretching around the world.

"Pim, Mrs."—("Psychiatrist Milkman") Mrs. Pim (Chapman) was previously called Mrs. Ratbag.

posh accent—(PSC; "Flying Lessons") This "imitation posh accent" is used often in *Flying Circus*, especially when one character is deriding the allegedly high-bred manners or speech of another character. See the RSM (Cleese) in Ep. 4. Biggles (Chpaman) uses this type of accent in all his speeches and dictations in Ep. 33.

"pottery"—("The Poet McTeagle") A malapropism or "faulty action." The author may actually be, however, rejecting the "traditional cliches of modern pottery" as he pursues his poetry. As an Art Critic in an earlier episode, Palin also tried to comment on the "place of the nude" in his bed, rather than art (Ep. 8).

pouffe—(PSC; "The Poet McTeagle") A somewhat obsolete usage, a "pouffe" is usually an overstuffed ottoman or seat. In this case, the pouffe is a blue inflatable chair which looks like it belongs on the set of a trendy arts program.

"Puss in Boots" ("The Poet McTeagle") The pantomime *Puss in Boots* is referenced again during Ep. 28, when an adaptation of *Puss in Boots* attempts to take over the show. The female lead there is played by Julia Breck.

– R –

Radio Voice—(PSC; "Hijacked Plane [to Luton]") Not credited in the printed scripts, this voiceover sounds like Jeannette Wild, who appears at the beginning of this episode.

"rejecting all the typical clichés of modern pottery"—("The Poet McTeagle") This rejection places the poet more in line with the unconventional, doggerel verse of the "Mersey Sound" poets, who had actively attempted to bring poetry down from its lofty perch using vernacular language and common, everyday settings and characters. See the entry for "simple, homespun verses" for more on these so-called Liverpool Poets.

"right on my uppers"—("The Poet McTeagle") This is a colloquialism (from "down on my uppers") meaning "down on my luck." Uppers were wrappings worn above the ankles, and could be wrapped around the bottom of the foot as boots wore out. The Scottish poet Burns—though talented and much respected—spent most of his life in dire financial distress, which probably prompted this characterization.

rises up—(PSC; "Girl in the Window" link into opening titles) An obvious sexual element here—"rises up"—this scene with the cleaner's hoist was shot on 5 June 1970.

rocky highland landscape—("The Poet McTeagle") This "rocky highland landscape" depicted means they are clearly far from Basingstoke and Hampshire in general (home to the flatlands around the Basingstoke Canal), and actually filming somewhere in the rougher Devon countryside. The WAC records for this episode confirm this, indicating that these "Scottish" scenes were shot on 14 May 1970 in the Newbridge, Dartmoor area near Ashburton (WAC T12/1,416).

– S –

"scheduled flight to Cuba"—("Hijacked Plane [to Luton]") Interestingly, this is a near copy of an existing political cartoon detailed above in the "fly the plane to Luton" entry.

"Seasons of mists . . . "—("The Poet McTeagle") Drawn from John Keats' *To Autumn* (1819-1920), and titled much like many of Burns' poems. (It's actually "Season" and not "Seasons," by the way.) Keats (1795-1821) toured Scotland in July and August 1818, and the rugged scenery inspired his later *Hyperion* (1820).

"I wandered" is from William Wordsworth's "I Wandered Lonely as a Cloud" (1804). Wordsworth (1770-1850) will be mentioned later (for his "bloody daffodils") in Ep. 17.

For some reason the Pythons also chose epic Restoration poet John Milton (1608-1674) to group here with these Romantic poets. Milton flourished in the mid- to late seventeenth century, creating *Paradise Lost* (1667), among others. Milton's characters (Satan, Eve, Gabriel) will later also appear as crew building a new motorway (Ep. 35).

Second Secretary—(PSC; "Flying Lessons") Though not credited in the printed scripts, this actress appears to be Jeannette Wild. (She is given a credit at the end of the taped performance.)

secretary some yards away—(PSC; "A Bishop Rehearsing") The journey to a flying appointment Mr. Chigger (Jones) and the Secretary (Cleveland) are about to embark upon was quite circuitous—shot in and around the Torquay area (beaches, Dartmoor), as well as in Ealing/Acton comprising a period of about six weeks (WAC T12/1,416).

She starts to undress—("Girl in the Window" link into opening titles) The music swelling beneath the disrobing "busty girl" is Mantovani's "It's 3 O'clock in the Morning" by Robledo/Terriss (WAC T12/1,436).

"Sherlock Holmes"—("Hijacked Plane [to Luton]") Shows starring the Sherlock Holmes character were on British television in many iterations, including a 1951 series, a 1964 installment (eventually starring Peter Cushing by 1968), and then even 1967 in West Germany. The character was created by Sir Arthur Conan Doyle.

"show five"—("A Bishop Rehearsing") Coincidentally, this episode was actually recorded fifth in the second series, but broadcast third. Throughout the

WAC records it is known as "Series 2, Episode 5." Ep. 19 would be recorded as the eighth show of this series, where Palin will also show up as a bishop, but wearing a suit and "dog collar." In Ep. 20, the robe-wearing Bishop played by Palin will finally show up, though he won't mention "Mr. Belpit"—he'll assault a game show hostess with two other (dog-collared) bishops, instead.

"simple, homespun verses"—("The Poet McTeagle") This may be a comment on the still-trendy "Liverpool Poet" movement, a Beat-inspired collection of poets and poems whose inspirations and subject matters were down-to-earth, everyday, contemporary, and often quite playful (see Drabble's *Oxford Companion to English Literature*). The Liverpool Poets Adrian Henri, Roger McGough, and Brian Patten co-published *The Mersey Sound* in 1967. See the entry for "McGough" in Ep. 37 for more on the movement and Idle's relation to these poets/performers.

This is also a reference to fellow Scotsman Robert Burns' penchant for the provincial Ayrshire dialect of the Lowland Scots in many of his works.

"skint"—("The Poet McTeagle") To be "skint" is to be penniless or broke. This is a term used a number of times by the Goons, as well.

stuffed animal which explodes—("Déjà Vu") It is a stuffed rabbit that explodes here. A killer rabbit will be destroyed by the Holy Hand Grenade in the 1974 feature film *HG*. The script calls for a lion, tiger, cow, elk, leopard, two ferrets, and an owl. What makes it into the finished scene are a tiger, cow, elk, cobra, rabbit, monkey, and a boar.

– T –

"Trident"—("Hijacked Plane [to Luton]") The Trident was a de Havilland-built commercial airliner that flew primarily in the 1950s and 1960s. The "vanguard" is the leading edge of an army, just as the middle tine of a trident would lead the way in a thrust. Ironically, the Trident was not an attractive plane to international buyers, and did not have a long life.

Additionally, British European Airways (BEA) and a Trident airplane were in the news in July 1969 when a plane on a passenger route (and with passengers) took part in a commercial aerial display. Several political cartoonists, including Osborn Lancaster for the *Daily Express* (26 July 1969) and Keith Waite for *The Sun* (25 July 1969), satirized the moment of profoundly bad judgment. See the British Cartoon Archive.

trolley—(PSC; "Flying Lessons") A trolley is a tea service cart, and is featured in Eps. 17, 22, and 23, as well.

Other trolleys, aka "gurneys," appear in Eps. 25, 34, and 35.

"two poems"—("The Poet McTeagle") The respected poet Burns wrote to favorite women, as well, including Alison Begbie and Mary Campbell, and a "Mrs. M'Lehose."

– U –

"unique style first flowered"—("The Poet McTeagle") Most likely a two-sided commentary, referring to at least two noted Scotsmen, William McGonagall and Robert Burns. The first was the flamboyant Scottish poet and tragedian William McGonagall (1830-1902), called by many the "worst poet" who ever lived, and who was satirized by the Goons as William J. Mac-Goonigal ("The Tay Bridge Disaster," 9 February 1959). McGonagall asked for and eventually received two guineas (perhaps his only successful poetic transaction) for a short poem meant to sell soap:

> Gentlemen you have my best wishes, and I hope
> That the poem I've written about Sunlight Soap
> Will cause a demand for it in every clime
> For I declare it to be superfine.
> And I hope before long, without any joke,
> You will require some more of my poems about Sunlight Soap.
> And in conclusion, gentlemen, I thank ye-
> William McGonagall, Poet, 48 Step Row, Dundee.

McGonagall would also dress up in full Scottish kit in any public performance, though contemporary accounts say the raucous, booing crowds often led to fights and the throwing of fruit at the earnest poet (see *Scotland on Sunday*, 10 Feb 1991).

But this characterization could also be an oblique, clever reference to the well-regarded eighteenth-century Scottish poet Robert Burns, who utilized careful observation and detailed minutiae of Scottish customs, nature, dialect, and folkways in his poetry. Burns' financial hardships throughout his life—even as a celebrated poet and songwriter—are well known, and perhaps inspired the financial bent of McTeagle's poetry here. As Burns was a lifelong ploughman, the use of the tam-o'-shanter in Python's depiction of their "typed" rustic Scottish poet might be particularly apt. *Tam o' Shanter* was Burns' last major poem, as well.

– V –

"vanguard"—("Flying Lessons") Definitely a bit of an in-joke for the "chaps at BALPA House," the Vickersbuilt Vanguard was a turboprop airliner developed and introduced (in 1959) just before commercial jets took the lead for good in passenger and cargo aviation. Because of the appearance of jets, the Vanguard was never a big commercial success, nor was the Trident, also mentioned by BALPA Man. See "Trident" above for more.

"Project Vanguard" was also the name of the U.S. government's earliest artificial satellite program.

– W –

"walk on the moon . . . hire purchase agreements"— ("Hijacked Plane [to Luton]") Apollo 11 had successfully landed on the moon to great worldwide fanfare in July 1969, prompting the first significant overnight coverage on the BBC.

"Hire purchase agreements" are contracts to buy goods (e.g., appliances) on credit, making regular payments. Mrs. Conclusion (Chapman) will wonder later about anyone being free in a world where "nine installments" are left to be paid on a refrigerator (Ep. 27). These agreements had become very popular after WWII, when thousands of new homes needed new furnishings, and money was tight.

"Whittington, Dick"—("The Poet McTeagle") A familiar panto figure, Whittington is based on the real-life Richard Whittington who would become Lord Mayor of London several times. A song that accompanied this panto character:

Turn again, Whittington,
Once Mayor of London!
Turn again, Whittington,
Twice Mayor of London!
Turn again, Whittington,
Thrice Mayor of London!

Another Dick Whittington was a contemporary comedian and a regular on *Rowan & Martin's Laugh-In* from 1968 to 1969. Both *Laugh-In* and the contemporary rise of stand-up comedy in general were significant influences (from the American side of the pond) on Monty Python.

– Z –

Zanie—(PSC; "Bomb on Plane") "Zanie" is actually the Shakespearean spelling of "zany": "A comic performer attending on a clown, acrobat, or mountebank, who imitates his master's acts in a ludicrously awkward way; a clown's or mountebank's assistant, a merry-andrew, jack-pudding; sometimes used vaguely for a professional jester or buffoon in general" (*OED*). For Shakespeare's usage, see *Love's Labours Lost* 5.2.463 and *Twelfth Night* 1.5.96. Jonson would also spell it this way (see *Every Man in His Humour* 2.3.) In the case of the man entering the cockpit, he seems more of a hanger-on, a parasite, which is the second *OED* entry.

Zanie (Chapman) had been Mr. Anemone just moments before, in the "Flying Lessons" sketch. In the same sketch, Chigger (Jones) becomes Pancho in the transition to the cockpit.

Episode 17

– A –

"abattoir"—("Architect Sketch") Abattoirs were cattle slaughterhouses on the continent. The term didn't enter the common English lexicon until the later nineteenth century (*OED*).

"Aberdeen"—("Chemist Sketch") There is an Aberdeen near Bradford, but the Chemist may also be referring to the Aberdeen much further north, on the Scottish coast.

"Aldrin, Buzz"—("Police Constable Pan-Am") Edwin Eugene Aldrin, Jr., U.S. astronaut and second man to set foot on the moon on 20 July 1969. The photo the Pythons use is Aldrin's official astronaut photo (most likely made available long before to the BBC for Apollo news coverage) taken prior to the Apollo 11 mission in 1969. Aldrin will also figure prominently in the German-language *Fliegender Zirkus*, Episode 2, made for Bavarian TV in 1972.

A version of "The Star-Spangled Banner" can be heard under this image, as well. WAC records only record that the piece is used, and not the performing band, though it sounds like the British Grenadier Guard version.

all-in wrestlers—(PSC; "*The Bishop*") "All-in" means "without restrictions," or anything goes, in wrestling. "Cauliflower ear"—a thickening and disfiguring of the ear tissue—results from repeated abuse in boxing, wrestling, etc. These all-in wrestlers/actors include Anthony Powell (*Softly Softly*) and John Lord (*Dr. Who*) (WAC T12/1,418). All-in cricket (featuring robust beatings and even impalings) will be depicted in Eps. 11, 18, and 45.

American car—(PSC; "*The Bishop*") The car driven by the Bishop and his henchmen appears to be a 1967 Pontiac Firebird convertible, a popular American "muscle

car" of the period. In the Hollywood movies of the day, it was the "tough guys" who drove these muscle cars. The prototypical screen tough for this period, Steve McQueen, drove a fastback Ford Mustang in *Bullitt* (1968). Pontiac Firebirds are featured prominently in *Bullitt*, *Le Clan des Siciliens* (1969), and *Le Cercle Rouge* (dir. Jean-Pierre Melville, 1970). Hamlet (Jones) will drive another big American car in Ep. 43, an obvious betrayal of his deep-seated desire to be a "private dick."

animated item (the Butterfly)—(link into opening titles) The two pieces of music Gilliam includes underneath this opening animation are "Grazing Land" (for the pastoral moment) followed by "Vistavision Title" (when the butterfly emerges), both by stock music composer Jack Shaindlin. The Pythons will continue to employ stock music as linking, mood-setting, and titling material throughout the series. During this period, many British television shows did the same, paying for broadcast rights for stock music rather than employing a composer.

The stock music industry was a thriving one as the BBC (radio and TV) and the British commercial television stations greatly expanded programming after 1955. For the feature film *Monty Python and the Holy Grail*, the Pythons will cull the DeWolfe music archives for most of the film's incidental music.

"Architects Sketch"—("Architect Sketch") Once again the Pythons illustrate their awareness of current events, here referencing the recent revelations regarding the architectural firm John Poulson Associates and the influence of Freemason membership. It seems that Poulson and then Opposition deputy leader Reginald Maudling (majority shareholder and chairman, respectively, of International Technical and Construction Services) were part of an insider deal to award public works contracts to fellow Freemasons, in this case a contract to build Bradford's city center (*Private Eye* 22

May 1970, 19-20). The article lists at least six Freemasons who also happen to be in on the deal in some way, and "would be among those reluctant to give a clear denial that they are complete strangers to the collar, the trowel, and the knotty handshake" (20). Poulson eventually fell prey to tax evasion difficulties, and declared bankruptcy; Maudling would later be forced from office in 1972 (as Home Secretary) in the wake of this influence-peddling scheme.

"Aston Martin"—("Motor Insurance Sketch") British racing car firm established in 1914. The valuable Aston Martin series available during this period (1967-1972) was the "DB" series, named after newer (1947-1972) company owner David Brown.

"avant-garde . . . namby-pambies"—("Nude Man" link out of "Poets") A typical Cleese/Chapman farrago of invectives, in this case aptly illustrating the Pythonesque "attack-then-defend" motif. Here the Pythons attack the more left-leaning point of view that they might otherwise defend, being less than conservative themselves. (In this they follow the stated positions of the *Beyond the Fringe* cast and the creators and contributors to *Private Eye*—any reckless or feckless power, from any point along the political spectrum, can be dangerous and should be tilted at.) Immediately, though, the Pythons undercut the attack by having the position delivered by a nude man and, in reality, a nude gay man (Chapman). These are the kinds of diatribes the Pythons themselves heard (from viewers and media pundits) during the run of *FC*, but especially in 1978-1979 as *Life of Brian* was being produced. (See Hewison's *Monty Python: The Case Against*.) In-house memos will also reveal that by the end of this second series the show was upsetting mid-level BBC managers, who term portions of Ep. 26 "disgusting," "over the edge," and "in appalling taste" (WAC T12/1,469). See notes to Ep. 26 for more.

"Namby-pamby" is a slur attributed to critics (including Carey and Pope) of Ambrose Philips (d. 1749) and his writing style, which some considered childish, though Samual Johnson greatly appreciated the "pleasant" language usage. The term has now come to mean "ineffective" and "wishy-washy." See Drabble (1985) and the "Ambrose Phillips" entry at *ODNB*.

– B –

"BBC TV Action Replay"—("Architect Sketch") Instant replay was first used by the BBC for the Grand National in 1964.

"be a Mason?"—("How to Give Up Being a Mason") The practicing (and antler-wearing) Mason (Chap-man) is offered visual enticements in the animation to surrender his Masonic tendencies—these dangled carrots include photos of nude ladies, to which he eventually says "no," calling into question the sexual preference of this and all Masons (and bowler-hatted City-types, and all authority figures, including Churchmen, etc.).

"behavioural psychotherapy"—("How to Give Up Being a Mason") Clinical attempts to modify behavior via "talking" (Freud) and reinforcement of positive habits, or punishment for negative habits, as seen here.

Bishop's crook—(PSC; "The Bishop") *OED*: "The pastoral staff of a bishop, abbot or abbess, shaped like a shepherd's staff; a crosier." The Bishop wields it here like a weapon, and also uses it as a phone device. The costume used here is similar but not identical to the one worn by Palin's bishop in Ep. 16.

A mitre is the recognizable tall cap, an embroidered head-dress in the Church of England (and the Western Church).

This Bishop also has a Y-shaped scar on his cheek, which could have significance in archaic terms, and wouldn't be beyond the well-read Pythons. The *OED* gives this possibility: "Used for the Greek letter Y (*u psilon*), esp. as a Pythagorean symbol." The dictionary goes on to cite numerous instances where the "spreading branches" symbol is used to indicate the Pythagorean "life on earth is short, but life is eternal" motif, and a "y" is metaphoric for virtue (see below), which is "small at the foot but broad at the top." For more, see the *OED*.

So this tattoo or scar could be the tough Bishop's way to remind himself and others of the divergent ways of God and man, and that "to obtaine vertue is *verie painefull*, but the possession thereof passing pleasant" (Greene's *Morando, the Tritameron of Love* 96).

"Bishop of Woolwich"—("Nude Man" link out of "Poets") This link takes us right back to the crime-fighting character of "The Bishop," and forward to the dual-roled (and very real) Bishop of Woolwich, then Liverpool.

The Bishop of Woolwich during this period (1969-1975) was David Sheppard (1929-2005; Trinity Hall, Cambridge), a former professional cricketer (Cambridge, Sussex, and England) who was named Wisden Cricketer of the Year in 1953. This is a cricketer the Pythons would have grown up with, followed in the news, and perhaps even been able to watch. Sheppard had been ordained in 1955, and played test cricket until 1963. He was called an active "campaigner," as a member of the clergy, for the betterment of inner-city conditions, as well as actively working against the UK participating in apartheid-era South African cricket matches. So Sheppard was a Bishop who could put down his staff and pick up a cricket bat, if necessary, and a ripe influence for the Pythons' crime-fighting clergyman.

See the other entries for *"The Bishop"* sketch and character for more.

"bit the ceiling"—(*"The Bishop"*) Expectedly, the Bishop speaks in TV and film noir clichés, not unlike some of the pot-boiler dialogue from classic pulp films like *Double Indemnity* (1944), *T-Men* (1947), *Pickup on South Street* (1948), and even *Shock Corridor* (1963). Television crime shows like *The Untouchables* (1959) also can be mentioned. "Bit the ceiling" is obviously a variation on "bit(e) the dust": "To bite the dust, ground, sand, etc.: to fall in death, to die; also, to fall to the ground, to fall wounded; to be abased" (see *OED*).

"blinkered . . . ignorance"—(*"Architect Sketch"*) Being "blinkered" figuratively, means being limited in outlook or vision; the term "philistine" can be "applied to persons regarded as 'the enemy', into whose hands one may fall, e.g. bailiffs, literary critics, etc."; and "pig ignorance" means having the characteristics of one so pig-headed (stubborn, obstinate) that nothing new or enlightened can penetrate. See the *OED*. The diatribe rambles on, with Mr. Wiggin (Cleese) carrying off a classic Python splenetic that includes:

"non-creative"—The specter of conformity and uniformity as anathema to youth, the artist, and freedom is a theme that runs consistently through *FC*. It seems that Wiggin is the voice of the Modernist, attacking the Establishment way of seeing art and architecture, and asking that conventional ideas and forms be reimagined. This is also a defining, delimiting comment—the creative types are "us," and the non-creative are "them."

"tinker's cuss"—Historically held in low repute, to be said to do anything like a "tinker" constituted a degrading insult (*OED*).

"toadies"—A toady is a "servile parasite; a sycophant, an interested flatterer" (*OED*). The "hypocritical toadies" comment also connects back to Wiggin's Modernist tendencies. In their design wants the City Gents (Palin and Jones) are clinging to the conventional, the usual, the "simple block of flats" mode of architecture that the Bauhaus group and other Modernist artists had been reacting against since the 1920s. Wiggin's design doesn't look terribly cutting edge, but it's the creative, innovative usage of the building—as a slaughterhouse—that separates him from the norm.

"colour TV sets"—Color TVs were more expensive and the license fees were higher, as well, proving here that perhaps only the (relatively) wealthy could afford such a luxury. It was only in 1969 that BBC shows began to be broadcast regularly in color, which certainly benefited *Flying Circus* a great deal in assuring both its survival (in videotape format) and legacy. (The BBC and other networks regularly "wiped" videotape for re-use, meaning many pre-1970 shows, including those featuring the Pythons, no longer exist in any viewable format.)

"Tony Jacklin golf clubs"—Jacklin (b. 1944) is an English golfer who won the U.S. Open in 1970, the first Brit to claim the title in fifty years. Jacklin had played successfully on the European and American professional golf circuits during the 1960s. Clubs bearing his name, then, would have been quite a status symbol. Jacklin will be mentioned again in Eps. 21 and 28. Jacklin and Ann Haydon-Jones (Eps. 7, 19, 22) had been named Sportsman and Sportswoman of the Year, respectively, in November 1969.

"masonic handshakes"—Secret handshakes of ancient origin used by the Freemasons to identify other members of the order. The Pythons, of course, will later make them appear quite ridiculous.

Freemasonry is a secret, fraternal society with associated rituals, handshakes, signs, knocks, ceremonial apparel, etc. These masons were initially connected to the building trades, including architecture. (Coincidentally, but certainly not lost on the Pythons, the development in which the Ronan Point building was constructed in Newham is called "Freemasons Estate." The other eight blocks were built between 1968-1970, and all are now demolished. There were no other collapse failures in this type of building, partly because concerned councils went back and performed expensive retrofits on the other buildings.)

"blackballing"—*OED*: "To exclude (a person) from a club or other society by adverse votes, recorded by the placing of black balls in the ballot-box, or in other ways." Because membership in the Masonic organization often provided critical business and social opportunities ("It opens doors. I'm telling you."), chapters could be quite selective, even exclusive. Many Freemason chapters have historically employed the black and white ball ballot box, as well.

"purulent"—Having the qualities of pus.

Finally, Cleese and Chapman are known for writing such vitriolic, end-to-end vituperative imprecations (a kind of "escalation" format) for their formerly mild-mannered characters to suddenly spew, with Cleese himself often being cast in this role.

"block of flats"—(*"Architect Sketch"*) *OED*: "A suite of rooms on one floor, forming a complete residence." In this case, a vertical city block of such structures, the type of which can still be seen across the UK (i.e., Barbican Centre, built 1964-1975). These structures (inspired by the Modernist architect Le Corbusier, and Bauhaus principles) were very popular across not only the UK but into Europe, Eastern Europe, and the Soviet Union. The efficiency, locations, and city views offered by these types of buildings were initially attractive, but in the long term building and neighborhood decay tarnished the blocks' image. The 1968 fire and collapse at Ronan Point sealed the public's negative opinion of the structures. See notes below for more, as well as the entry for "milk-float" in Ep. 16.

Wiggin's (Cleese) version of the "block of flats" looks more like a Robin Hood Gardens (Poplar) design, or Park Hill (designed by Lynn and Smith in Sheffield) than a tower block as proposed by Mr. Leavey (Idle). Robin Hood Gardens is a long, low block of flats designed by Alison and Peter Smithson, and was being constructed as these episodes were being written and recorded. Park Hill was finished in 1961.

The magazine *Private Eye* also satirized these monuments to what it called "New Barbarism" in its architectural columns.

(blows raspberry)—(PSC; "Architect Sketch") A raspberry is a derisive sound made using the tongue and lips, also called a "Bronx cheer" (*OED*), and Wiggin (Cleese) employs it in his entreaty to the City Gents (Palin and Jones). Instead of a carefully placed raspberry, though, the original script actually called for Mr. Wiggin to say "sod" (see Morgan's *Speaks!*). BBC censors asked that the word not be used, determining the term to still be too offensive for the British viewing public. (It may be that since the word was being used anatomically rather than adjectivally, it was more offensive.) By Ep. 27 they are able to get away with "Intercourse the penguin!" without much concern. And by the final *FC* episode, Ep. 45, they offered up "get off my sodding wick" without influence or interference of the censors, meaning either that times had changed or it was acknowledged that this was the last show of the series (or both).

– C –

"cement"—("Motor Insurance Sketch") Death by cement is a typical method employed by underworld hoodlums, by whom the Devious (Palin) character seems inspired. The presence of organized crime-types in the building trades, especially as suppliers of material, including cement, has perhaps allowed for the death-by-cement scenario heard so often in film and TV. Generally, though, the victim's feet are placed in cement and then he is dumped into a river, or the body is (allegedly, perhaps even apocryphally) thrown into a new building's cement pour.

See the entry for "Devious" below, and this sketch's relation to the infamous Emil Savundra.

"central . . . concrete"—("Architect Sketch") What the architect is describing here is another Modernist influence, the International Style (what many call "Brutalist") type architecture, Le Corbusier-inspired, and which is often defined by massive, geometric blocks of concrete and very little baroque ornamentation. A "central pillar" (probably of steel and concrete) would have carried the weight of the cantilevered floors, meaning structural support (load-bearing) at the inner ("dividing") and outer walls was deemed unnecessary. The explosion and collapse of the Ronan Point block indicated that this design—pre-cast, reinforced concrete blocks brought onsite and "slotted" into place—left something to be desired, especially as the onsite construction seems to have been substandard.

"chemist"—("Chemist Sketch") British term for "pharmacist." A chemist shop in the UK can provide sundries, as well, including film development (Ep. 19).

cinema—(PSC; "Living Room on Pavement") A large sign can be seen on the front of the cinema (though isn't referred to by the characters or the text itself), actually a marquee advertisement for the Peter Sellers film *Hoffman* (1970), directed by Alvin Rakoff. Peter Sellers and the other Goons (Milligan and Secombe) were admittedly influential to Python and the style and structure of *FC*.

This cinema appears to be the ABC Cinema on Uxbridge Road, and is just down the street from the sidewalk location where portions of *"The Bishop"* were shot.

"C. of E."—(*"The Bishop"*) The Church of England or Anglican Church, the official church of the state since 1534, when Henry VIII separated himself and the country from the Roman Catholic faith.

congregation—(PSC; *"The Bishop"*) Members of the congregation in *"The Bishop"* include Roger Tolliday (*Special Branch*), George Ballantyne (*Emma*), Mary Maxted (*Miss Bohrloch*), Elizabeth Broom (*Dixon of Dock Green*), Elaine Williams (*Studio 4*), Joyce Freeman (*Play For Today*), and Joanna Robbins (*Emma*). These scenes were shot in the larger spaces of Ealing TFS (WAC T12/1,418).

crime-series-type titles, suitable music—(PSC; *"The Bishop"*) The music under these titles is Dave Lindup's "Superperformance (Impact and Action)" (WAC T12/1,431).

– D –

"Devious"—("Motor Insurance Sketch") Devious (not unlike another shady Palin character, Dino Vercotti) sports a couple of facial scars, greased hair, inner-city accent, and here is reading an erotic book, probably from a pornographic series published in Germany or the Netherlands.

This entire incident may be a reference to the notorious Emil Savundra (1923-1976), a Sri Lankan businessman who pioneered the auto insurance fraud industry in the UK in the 1960s. Savundra took in far more premium-paying customers than he could ever hope to service if any number of claims were made, and he was eventually grilled on national television by none other than David Frost on *The Frost Programme* (1967). Idle was working on the Frost program at this time. The encounter helped make Frost's reputation as a dogged interviewer.

"Dibbingley Road"—("Architect Sketch") No such road or street exists in the UK. Just the onomatopoeic appeal of this and similar names—Dibble, Dibley, Dibbingley—perhaps account for their recurring appearances in *FC* (more mentions in Eps. 18 and 19). These all "sound" like silly places and names, not unlike Carroll's fanciful language: . . . "slithy toves / [Could] gyre and gimble in the wabe; / All mimsy were the borogoves, / And the mome raths outgrabe" (final stanza, *Jabberwocky*).

The Modernist author Gertrude Stein—according to Mabel Dodge in her 1913 essay "Speculations, or Post-Impressionism in Prose"—was particular in choosing "words for their inherent quality, rather than for their accepted meaning." The Pythons would even choose their sentences for similar reasons, as was seen earlier, when the Presenter (Palin) launches into his *Spectrum* tirade in Ep. 12. The new and unorthodox word-smithing of Stein and Carroll, of Virginia Woolf and James Joyce are clearly influential throughout *FC*.

"dirty books"—("Motor Insurance Sketch") In the "Tudor Jobs Agency" sketch, Ep. 36, dirty books are the real products for sale in the job agency.

"documentary"—("Living Room on Pavement") One of the major television formats satirized by Python throughout *FC*, the others including TV news, sitcoms, quiz and game shows, commercials, and BBC serial dramas. These kinds of on-the-scene-reporter documentary shows were being produced by *Panorama* during this period.

dog collars—(PSC; "The Bishop") This is a derogatory term for the clerical collar.

"Don't say the text!"—("The Bishop") Each time the Bishop (Jones) intervenes in these filmed segments, it is on behalf of a Church of England clergyman, and as that clergyman is performing one of his sacerdotal (and specifically ordinance) duties. The preaching of a sermon, an infant baptism, a wedding, a bell ringing, and a graveside service are all moments when the Bishop attempts to thwart Italian-looking (hence, Roman Catholic?) thugs from killing C. of E. vicars—and importantly, as the vicars attempt to ritually administer to their respective flocks. The Bishop (Jones) is always too late, of course. When he intervenes on behalf of Reverend Morris (Idle) in Devious' office, though, it is in response to cries for help, as if Morris was trapped in a burning building. The question of where *"The Bishop"* film begins is questionable, eventually, perhaps even Alpha and Omega, without beginning or end.

"do you for heresy"—("Police Constable Pan-Am") A slang phrase, to be "done" here means he'll be arrested for crimes against the church. Generally (in England) this would indicate the Christian Church, but in the case of the text and its reflexivity, is probably referring to the Roman Catholic Church as indicated by the Inquisitor allusion. (Though, of course Elizabeth I had her own inquisitor, Richard Topcliff [see the *ODNB*], who performed very similar functions, but for good Queen Bess, England, and the Anglican Church.)

This is rather ancient form (c. 1000) of "do," as well, according to the *OED*: "To impart to, bring upon (a person, etc.) some affecting quality or condition; to bestow, confer, inflict, to cause by one's action (a person) to have (something). In later use, associated more closely with the notion of performance."

Duke of Edinburgh—(PSC; "Chemist Sketch") The printed script describes Gilliam as walking into the chemist's shop "with hands clasped behind him à la the Duke of Edinburgh." The Queen's husband, Prince Philip (b. 1921), has adopted the "arms behind the back" pose for most of his official career. For two examples, see Illingworth's cartoon published in *The Daily Mail* on 10 November 1969, or Jak's in *The Evening Standard* eight days later. Even today (2007) in political cartoons, he is very often depicted in this characteristic, even iconic pose. See the British Cartoon Archive.

– E –

"East Midlands"—("Poets") The East Midlands region includes the counties of Lincolnshire, Northamptonshire, Derbyshire, Nottinghamshire, Leicestershire, and Rutland. Chapman is from this area, having attended elementary school in Melton Mowbray. This portion of the episode seems to have been recorded on Uxbridge Road, W5, in front of the local ABC Cinema.

Episode 17—This episode was recorded as the ninth episode of this second series on 18 September 1970, and then broadcast on 20 October 1970. It was broadcast as the fourth episode, however. There must have been some confusion or the episode or even sketches were jumbled along the way—the WAC records sometimes refer to actors appearing in this episode as appearing in "Ep. 8," even though it eventually was recorded ninth.

Denton De Gray (*Quatermass II*) and Julie Desmond (*Casanova*, *The Goodies*) also appeared in this episode, though the WAC records don't identify their roles (WAC T12/1,431).

– F –

female Gumbys—(PSC; link out of "Police Constable Pan-Am") These are actually women, and the sounds they make are trilling sounds, not unlike the Arab women during a battle in *Lawrence of Arabia* (1962). Again, the mere presence of a real woman becomes a bit more unusual, especially with so much cross-dressing in *FC*.

Floor manager—(PSC; "After-Shave") One of the on-set TV production team members, the floor manager normally stands between cameras (off-camera), and indicates with hand signals which camera is "hot," etc., and usually is wearing headphones and carrying a clipboard with a shot sheet attached. The show's actual floor manager appears in Eps. 2, 10, and 19. The position has some less significance today, as a director can communicate with on-screen talent directly through hidden ear pieces, and cameras are often remotely controlled.

four henchmen—(PSC; "*The Bishop*") These four toughs/vicars are Michael Stayner (Eps. 17-19; *Billion Dollar Brain*), Brian Gardner (Ep. 18; *The Fabulous Frump*), Bill Leonard (Eps. 18, 19), and Tom O'Leary (Ep. 18; *A Man Called Shenandoah*). These actors were all hired from Cagneys Agency (WAC T12/1,418).

"Frankincense"—("Vox Pops") A pleasant resin for burning. Ximenez (Palin) is appearing again as the Cardinal (in front of the Old Bailey and to audience cheers) after Ep. 15's "Spanish Inquisition" success.

The biblical frankincense-and-myrrh theme is revisited in the opening scene of the Python feature film *Life of Brian* (1979), where the Three Wise Men (Cleese, Chapman, and Palin) accidentally deliver their valuable gifts to the baby Brian, and not Jesus.

"Freemasonry opens doors"—("Architect Sketch") It was generally agreed that such fraternal orders did (and even do) offer members significant networking opportunities in the business world, "opening doors" to promotions and other advancements thanks to the desire for members to help members whenever possible. See the note above to "blackballing" for more.

"f'tang"—("Police Constable Pan-Am") A word borrowed from the Pythons' comedy inspirations, the Goons, which can be heard in the episode "The Call of the West" (20 January 1959) several times in the phrase "Fort F'tang."

furnishings of a bathroom—(PSC; "Living Room on Pavement") In the first, establishing shot of this scene, Alfred, Lord Tennyson is not yet in the tub. He won't appear until Mrs. Potter (Chapman) goes to draw a bath.

– G –

gets script out—("Architect Sketch") This breaking of the illusion of the world of the sketch will become common in *FC*, as well as in the later feature films. When the "Man" (Chapman) asks if he has any more to say, he is reminding the audience they are watching an act, a sketch. The script is consulted on a number of occasions in *FC* episodes, including "Lost World of Rouirama" (Ep. 29) and at the unsuccessful ending of the "Jokes and Novelties Salesman" sketch (Ep. 15).

Participants in the inspirational *The Goon Show* (1951-1960) would on occasion pause and consult the script, or address the audience as audience, or even acknowledge that they are each playing multiple characters. In "The Jet-Propelled Guided NAAFI" episode, Sellers picks up and reads from the script for a moment, moving the sketch from one scene to another (*The Goon Show*, 24 January 1956).

"Grimsby"—("*The Bishop*") The printed script reads "Grimsby," though the video (and eventually DVD) version uses "Gromsby," and includes a hyphen afterward. Gilliam would have produced this title sequence, and the physical disconnect between Gilliam's work/working space and the rest of the troupe probably accounts for this error. Grimsby is a city in Lincolnshire, and in archival sources (genealogy records, for instance) it seems that the Grimsby/Gromsby confusion goes well beyond the Pythons. "Urqhart" is the name of a castle in Scotland, to push the Scottish motif of these titles a bit further.

Gumbys—(link into "Architect Sketch") This could have been a name derived from the boots the characters wear, though the *OED* doesn't mention "Gumby" at all when defining "gum-booted" in its latest edition. Additonally, the Gumbys sport napkins or kerchiefs tied to their heads, wire-rimmed glasses, Hitler-like mustaches, too-small vests, white shirts with rolled-up sleeves, rolled-up trousers, and of course the rubber boots. They characteristically shout everything, and first appeared in the first series' Ep. 5 (see notes there).

Another strange possibility (at least for the nomenclature) has to be the popular American animated character "Gumby," created by Art Clokey, and who began appearing regularly on the children's show *The Howdy Doody Show* on ABC in 1956. *The Gumby Show* then appeared on NBC in 1957, and new episodes appeared sporadically in 1962, and 1966-1967.

– H –

"Halitosis"—("Vox Pops") Foul breath.

hammer—(animated link out of "Architect Sketch") The large hammer, both animated and in prop form, is used often in *FC*, especially to end a sketch or act as a link. This is certainly a cartoony prop, not unlike the sixteen-ton weight and the round, black ("anarchist's") bomb prop. The hammer acts much as the iconic crook did for the music hall/vaudeville stage decades earlier—in this case bringing the act to a close with a resounding "thud." In this way the hammer is both a nontraditional replacement for the purposely avoided punch line, a punishment for the delivery of a punchline, as well as the more traditional linking element so key to the sketch/musical variety show structure. Using the prop in myriad ways insures that the Pythons are able to have their cake and eat it, too.

"Hardy, Thomas"—("Poets") Thomas Hardy (1840-1928) was both a novelist *and* a poet, producing eight volumes of poetry which were somewhat tepidly received during his lifetime, though greatly appreciated since. Hardy's admitted dislike of flowery speech, the "jewelled line," accounts for why the housewife disdains her Hardy and seeks the "garden of love" with Wombat (*MPSERD* 98n).

"Hart, Derek"—("Nude Man" link out of "Poets") Derek Hart (1925-1986) was a respectable member of the news cast for the *Tonight* program (1957-1965) created by the legendary TV producer Grace Wyndham Goldie (1900-1986), and also starring Ned Sherrin (mentioned in Ep. 5), and Alan Whicker (Ep. 27).

"Hendon"—("Architect Sketch") In the borough of Barnet, Greater London, Hendon is a stone's throw northwest of Golders Green, which figures prominently in Ep. 9, and the Pythons recorded studio portions of several episodes at the Hippodrome there. The nearest Masonic hall to Hendon seems to have been in Watford, Hertfordshire, to the northwest.

hoarding—(PSC; "How to Give Up Being a Mason") *OED*: "A temporary fence made of boards inclosing a building while in course of erection or repair; often used for posting bills and advertisements; hence, any boarding on which bills are posted." This appears to be a purpose-built billboard, and is situated next to another billboard with an actual advertisement (for cognac) on it.

"housing problem facing Britain's aged"—("Living Room on Pavement") The subject of adequate housing comes up again and again in *FC*, and the problem is a consistent feature in newspapers of the period.

An example from Birmingham: The local council was building as many as 2,000 new homes every year by 1968, but the waiting list for homes stood at about 60,000, which helped lead to Ronan Point–type buildings. For more on the chronic housing shortage in postwar Britain, see notes to Ep. 14, as well as Morgan's *Britain Since 1945*, Judt's *Postwar*, and Wilson's *After the Victorians*. (Housing shortage was a chronic problem across all of Europe in the wake of the Allies' indiscriminate bombing, and Goebbel's "total war" responses.) By Ep. 43, unscrupulous Python characters (there played by Palin) are advocating the easy removal of the elderly from their homes to make way for businesses and younger, higher-income tenants.

In the political cartoons of the period, the wrangling debate over Britain's support of the United States in Vietnam is tied directly to inattention to domestic matters like inadequate housing (e.g., Illingworth, *Daily Mail* 08 Dec 1969). See the British Cartoon Archive.

humming and harring—(PSC; "How to Give Up Being a Mason") The Gumbies are moving about and muttering to themselves, getting situated for the link. The printed scripts sometimes include these bits of business, but usually not.

hymn is heard—(PSC; "The Bishop") The hymn that ends as the Bishop (Jones) and his cronies approach the church is a version of Blake's "O, Jerusalem," which has been heard earlier in Eps. 4 and 8, and will be featured again in Ep. 29.

– I –

"Ironside and Malone"—("Architect Sketch") Edmund Ironside (c. 993-1016) was king of England for a short period in 1016, and died trying to repel Danish invaders. Also, the American crime drama *Ironside* (1967-1975), starring post–*Perry Mason* actor Raymond Burr, was a current popular hit. A prominent Malone included another Edmund—Edmund Malone (1741-1812)—a noted editor of Shakespeare's corpus. Malone attended Trinity College, Cambridge.

– K –

"Kensington"—("After-Shave") Part of the Royal Borough of Kensington and Chelsea, Greater London, and fashionable home (to the Pythons, at least) of Upper class Twit types.

"kn*ckers"—("Chemist Sketch") Though "knickers" (short pants/underwear) would fit here, this is probably meant to be "knockers," since the word is given twice. The Pythons resort to such bodily/schoolboy (or even "carnivalesque") humor as often as their lofty predecessors Jonson, Swift, and Voltaire (see *MPSERD*, chapter 2.) The Goons also employed vulgar euphemisms, but within the more restrained limitations imposed by the BBC ("Auntie Beeb") of the 1950s. In just moments, another word—"Semprini"—will also be banned based on an assumed sexual connotation. See the entry for "Semprini" below for more.

– L –

"Leviticus 3-14"—(*"The Bishop"*) This is probably not meant to indicate all chapters between and including 3 and 14, though that's how it's written in the printed script. The fourteenth verse of the third chapter of Leviticus reads as follows: "And he shall offer thereof his offering, even an offering made by fire unto the LORD; the fat that covereth the inwards, and all the fat that is upon the inwards" (King James Version).

"lifts"—("Architect Sketch") British term for "elevators."

"longeurs"—("Words Not to Be Used Again") *OED*: "A lengthy or tedious passage of writing. Also in extended use, of music, etc." As the customer (Idle) waits for the Chemist (Palin) there is a rather lengthy passage of time, of dead air, which actually had become fashionable in various New Waves of the recent past. French films, especially, had begun experimenting with "lived" or "perceived" time (inspired by Henri Bergson's musings on *duré*) as opposed to cinematic time, which can be quite elliptical. (See notes for Bergson and his significance to the Pythons in Ep. 20.) See the long and often repeated tracking shots in Alain Resnais' *Last Year at Marienbad* (1961), or the empty pauses in Jean-Pierre Melville's *Le Samourai* (1967). The *OED* also identifies this particular spelling as incorrect, with "longueur" being the accepted spelling.

"lunar module"—("Police Constable Pan-Am") The portion of the Apollo 11 spacecraft that actually landed on the moon's surface, containing Armstrong and Aldrin, was called the "Eagle." Collins orbited in the command module. The U.S. Apollo space missions had been front-page news in British newspapers since the earliest "destination: Moon" flights. Also, in 1969 alone there were almost 120 op-ed cartoons referencing the Apollo missions in British newspapers. See the British Cartoon Archive.

In Ep. 28, an Apollo-inspired three-stage model of Tschaikowsky will be examined during the *"Life of Tschaikowsky"* sketch. Models of the various Apollo crafts were used by BBC presenters during these broadcasts.

– M –

"mainly design slaughter houses"—("Architect Sketch") Peter Ackroyd notes in *London: The Biography* that the designer of the Holloway Prison (opened 1852), James B. Banning, also designed buildings for both the Coal Exchange (Lower Thames Street) as well as the Metropolitan Cattle Market (Caledonian Road, Islington), and utilized similar design principles from building to building (253).

"moderator"—(PSC; *"The Bishop"*) In the Presbyterian churches: A minister elected to preside over any one of the ecclesiastical bodies, for example, the congregation, the presbytery, the synod, the general assembly. In the Scottish church, historically, a Moderator was often appointed to "avoid confusion in reasoning," according to the *OED*.

"mush"—("Architect Sketch") *OED*: "Man, 'chap'; hence also as a term of address."

– N –

"neo-Georgian"—("Architect Sketch") A revival of eighteenth- (and nineteenth-) century British architectural styles, the neo-Georgian look was very popular in the late Edwardian era and into the 1920s. Clearly, the symmetry of Wiggin's (Cleese) design is characteristic of the reinvigorated style. The extant Grosvenor Square Marriott is an example of the neo-Georgian style; Mayfair is also home to a number of neo-Georgian buildings.

Neuk—(*"The Bishop"*) Small town/region of Scotland. The Goons also use the name, in a mention of "Mrs. Violet Neuk of 5 Sussex Road" ("The Last Smoking Seagoon").

"No I'm not"—("Police Constable Pan-Am") Though not identified in the script, this is Gilliam speaking—acting the upper half of the mac—with the diminutive Stanley Mason (Eps. 14, 17, 19, and the Montreux special; *Dr. Who*) below.

"not meant to be luxury flats"—("Architect Sketch") This rather offhand treatment and general lack of consideration for the would-be inhabitants of this structure lends credence to Mr Wiggin's (Cleese) earlier outburst, and even to his assessment of them as "philistine" and uncaring, which was certainly Python's intent. This also goes right along with the general concerns voiced publicly and in government halls after the Ronan Point disaster, when it was thought that local councils and contractors were more interested in getting the more affordable experimental blocks finished and occupied than in the assurance of safe, quality housing.

Nude Lady—("Motor Insurance Sketch") This actress appears to be Mary (Maxted) Millington (1945-1979) who would go on to become a "Page 3" girl in *The Sun*, and star in a number of celebrated "adult" films.

– P –

"Pan Am"—("Police Constable Pan-Am") A U.S. airline, Pan American Airways was formed in 1927, and pioneered the transpacific, transatlantic, and around-the-world flights. Pan Am also purchased the first jet (Boeing 707) for commercial airline use. The citation of a prominent American airline continues the episode's Yankee trend that includes mentions of astronaut Buzz Aldrin and the "Raindrops Keep Fallin' on My Head" refrain from a popular Hollywood movie (*Butch Cassidy and the Sundance Kid* [1969]).

"Peter Gunn Theme"—(*"The Bishop"*) The "Peter Gunn Theme" was composed by another American, Henry Mancini, and the theme originally appeared in 1958. It has become almost generic in its application to crime stories/themes on TV and in film. The theme kicks in when the Bishop and henchmen are walking down the street, knocking everyone aside as they go. This same effect was created in Ep. 8, when the "Hell's Grannies" characters strut down the street to the theme from the James Bond film *From Russia With Love* (1963).

"plumped"—("Motor Insurance Sketch") This means to pay for at once, as well as "to fall for," making a poor choice. See *OED*. Both definitions fit the Vicar's situation as he tries to make a claim on a worthless policy.

"poet in every home"—("Poets") There had recently been socially responsible movements calling for natural gas in every home, a nationwide change to North Sea natural gas, as well as the denial of gas for those living in recently built high-rises (following the Ronan Point disaster in 1968). See entries in Ep. 14 for more on the gas situation in the UK.

The "Poet Jingle" song heard during the short Gilliam animation was composed by Bill McGuffie and sung by Jones and Cleveland (WAC T12/1,431). McGuffie also plays live accompaniment for Cleese and Chapman in Ep. 3 ("Someone Else I'd Like to Be"), and composed songs for Eps. 22 and 25, also in this second series (WAC T12/1,242).

"pox"—("Chemist Sketch") Any venereal disease. Here we can identify sufferers and their complaints by their postures and/or appearances. Note that no one wants to admit to having the transmittable disease, leading to the reticent raised hand (Idle). The man (John Hughman) with the boil on his "botty" is standing, of course; the very busty woman (Julie Desmond) has the chest rash; and the man suffering from flatulence (Jones) is keeping himself as far away from the others as he can.

"Prebendary 'Chopper' Harris"—(PSC; *"The Bishop"*) A prebendary: "The holder of a prebend (portion of the revenues of a cathedral or collegiate church granted to a canon or member of the chapter as his stipend); a canon of a cathedral or collegiate church who holds a prebend"; and "chopper": "One who barters or exchanges . . . in ecclesiastical benefices" and/or "chops logic" (*OED* 1989). This is a character that has both access to the church funds and the ability to divvy out favors and spiritual gifts—so he sounds very much like a combination of both the Pardoner and the Monk from Chaucer's *Canterbury Tales*, for example.

There are several other similarly monikered Python characters, Colin "Bomber" Harris (a wrestler), Harry "Snapper" Organs (a police inspector), and Colin "Chopper" Mozart (a ratcatcher). (This type of nickname was often garnered as a result of a boxing background.)

The character's actual namesake is most likely Detective Chief Inspector Leonard "Nipper" Read, who was instrumental in bringing the Krays to justice. See notes to Ep. 14 for more on the Krays.

– Q –

"quid"—("Architect Sketch") A sovereign, or one pound sterling.

– R –

"raindrops . . . my"—("Police Constable Pan-Am") "Raindrops Keep Fallin' on My Head" was written and performed by B.J. Thomas (b. 1942) for the 1969 film (and fitting there somewhat anachronistically) *Butch Cassidy and the Sundance Kid*. The song went on to become an international hit, crossing over to radio, sheet music, and elevator music fame.

"recessed . . . grooves"—("Architect Sketch") *OED*: "Magnalium": "A light aluminium-based alloy containing some magnesium."

"flange"—"A projecting flat rim, collar, or rib, used to strengthen an object, to guide it, to keep it in place, to facilitate its attachment to another object, or for other purposes."

In lay terms, these are inset walls, ostensibly slotted into (but not affixed to?) the central pillar. This was similar to the construction of the Ronan Point tower which partially collapsed in 1968. See the entry for "SATIRE" below.

rubber mac—(PSC; "Poets") A rubber, dark-but-still-see-through overcoat also worn by Cleese in the "Dead Parrot" sketch and other Praline character appearances, including Ep. 19. The "Mackintosh" is named for Charles Macintosh (1766-1843), who invented the cloth and rubber cement overcoats. More recently, the name "Mackintosh" has been used to designate any type of rain-proof coat, and is very often shortened to "mac."

– S –

"Sandalwood"—("Vox Pops") A fragrant wood often used for perfume. Myrrh and frankincense were also used in perfumes. Chanel No. 5 (not "Rancid Polecat number two") was a very popular and expensive perfume in the early 1970s. Chanel had introduced with great fanfare a No. 19 perfume in early 1970.

"SATIRE"—("Architect Sketch") This inserted caption could be just a slap at the typical, mindless television viewer who wouldn't know satire unless it were captioned. More pessimistically (and perhaps realistically), this could be the Pythons' weak attempt at avoiding any kind of legal action from the building trades, the Freemasons, City Councils, etc., given Britain's rather draconian libel laws in place at the time. The satirical magazine *Private Eye* had already attacked the subject with vigor the previous year, but the *Eye* also had a history of being served with myriad writs, and paid out thousands of pounds in damages, and even accepted donations from readers to help pay for legal fees. As at least nominally a traditional organ of the government, the BBC was quite unwilling to suffer similar exposure.

Specifically, this points back to the Ronan Point disaster of 1968—a relatively small gas explosion destroyed a corner of a high rise in Newham, top to bottom—where at least four died and seventeen were injured (a first-

person acount can be heard on *Eyewitness: 1960-69*, "Ronan Point Tower Collapses"). Charges were tossed about that shoddy building practices were used—since the flats were for public housing—and the segmental design itself was ultimately admitted to be compromised by improper installation. (There were at least 429 such buildings in Birmingham alone, for example, and more than one million people living in these structures throughout Britain.)

The BBC carried the flag on a number of these exposé programs, prompting ministerial calls for a more cautious, less profligate broadcast approach to the topic. The satirical magazine *Private Eye* seemed to apply the pressure early and with consistency, posing some of the toughest questions for those responsible (Ingrams 192-93). In November 1968 a high rise under construction in Sheffield also partially collapsed, bringing calls for increased tower block inspections, review of designs, inspection of already-built structures, and many, many op-ed pieces and biting political cartoons (including a cartoon by Jak, *Evening Standard* 15 November 1968). See the British Cartoon Archive, as well as Pearson and Delatte, and *Private Eye*.

See Hewison's *Monty Python, The Case Against* for more on Python's brushes with the law and the religious orthodoxy, especially after the release of *Life of Brian* (1979).

"saw the light"—("*The Bishop*") Play on the phrase "seeing the light," with an emphasis on the explosion and even heaven's brightness as Reverend Neuk (Chapman) crosses to the other side. Generally, however, to "see the light" means to come to some better understanding.

"scaly"—("Vox Pops") The "Ken Shabby" character is also here making a return appearance, having been introduced in Ep. 12.

"second-hand apron"—("Architect Sketch") An apron worn by Freemasons as part of their ritual clothing, it has certain symbolic meanings in the organization, including the representation of the wearer's soul. Wiggin (Cleese) appears to have bought his used, or inherited it. When Chapman appears in the animation to follow he is also wearing a Masonic apron, and little else.

"Semprini"—("Words Not to Be Used Again") A.F.R. Semprini (1908-1990) was a British pianist who became a fixture on BBC Radio. His *Semprini Serenade* made its debut in 1957 and ran at least through 1969 (on Radio 1 and 2). This reference, of course, could also be an "othering" by Python of a something non-English, in this case an Italian. This would also continue the theme established earlier in *"The Bishop"* film, where Italian-looking gangsters were the threat.

The young woman who appears here and asks, "Semprini?" is actress Sandra Richards.

"shouts out of window at gumbys"—("Architect Sketch") In this exchange there is a cutting back and forth between the very separate and distinct worlds of the videotape and film stock image. The image quality difference of the filmed as compared to the taped image is very evident, though the Pythons make no attempt to hide or even blur the rather obvious transitions. Often, the transition from videotaped to filmed image is a simple cut from inside the studio to the outside, from one sketch to another, but not always. In this case the continuity of the scene might seem to be in jeopardy, but it's likely the viewing audience is quite accustomed to these transitions, as they are clearly evident in earlier BBC shows like *Benny Hill, Do Not Adjust Your Set*, etc. The difference there is, of course, that those shows were all broadcast in monochrome (black and white), meaning the distinct image qualities were less noticeable. In color transmission (which BBC2 pioneered in 1968), the color quality of the 16mm filmed images and the studio-bound videotaped images is quite distinct, but these noticeable, self-conscious transitions continued anyway.

The script also calls for just "two gumbys" outside, but all five (Chapman, Cleese, Idle, Jones, and Palin) are included throughout. Gilliam is missing because this scene was shot in the Greater London area, not in a far-flung Devon or Norwich location—and most likely during the week leading up to the show's taping—when the animator would have been busy with his own contributions to the episode.

"Show 8"—("Architect Sketch") This is of course Ep. 17, the fourth show of the second series, and is called Episode 4 by the folks at Light Entertainment. This episode was recorded ninth, then moved up to fourth in the broadcast line.

"Spanish Inquisition"—("Police Constable Pan-Am") Again, an Ep. 15 reference, but here no one leaps out dressed as an Inquisitor, and none of the characters wait in anticipation. Cardinal Ximinez (Palin) has already appeared in the Vox Pops section of this episode counting off his favorite aftershave lotions. This episode was recorded more than two months after Ep. 15 was completed.

"standing in the garage"—("Motor Insurance Sketch") *OED*: "That remains at rest or in a fixed position." The car, essentially, was parked, legally, then hit by a lorry (delivery truck), seemingly an open-and-shut insurance claim for the Vicar (Idle). The Vicar (Idle) isn't likely to have been the type that Emil Savundra (see the entry for "Devious" above) would have insured, since he doesn't fit the high-risk profile.

"Straight Man"—("Motor Insurance Sketch") This continues the subtitling motif already established, though the actions of these characters also betray their roles. In a comedy sketch, the straight man is the member of the team who sets up the funny lines. Bing Crosby often played straight man to partner Bob Hope, for example. Idle will play a straight man wanting to be a funny passenger in Ep. 30, "Bus Conductor Sketch."

straight through the balsa wood door—(PSC; *"The Bishop"*) The script comments on the particulars of the stunt here, which is rare, and would only have been intended for the other Pythons as readers. The walls of the set begin to fall over, as well, meaning this entire hallway was purpose-built on the studio floor for this one scene.

"strengthening a bit"—("Architect Sketch") All high-rise blocks built to May 1968 and to similar standards as the one which collapsed at Ronan Point were inspected and strengthened in the months following the explosion. Repairs included concrete where, sometimes, only crushed newspaper had been stuffed, and the bolting of slotted pillars (Pearson and Delatte).

"Swinburne . . . Shelley"—("Poets") Algernon Charles Swinburne (1837-1909) was a Pre-Raphaelite poet, a so-called decadent poet, writing of life and love, before easing into middle-aged respectability.

Percy Bysshe Shelley (1792-1822) was called "Mad Shelley" at school (University College, Oxford), where he was a writer of Gothic horrors and politically reactionary (and prescient) works on revolution and reform. See Drabble (1985) and the *ODNB* for more on both poets. Shelley (or "Sherry") will reappear in Ep. 41 in the department store's Victorian poets reading room.

Harness could have found complaint with either of these Victorian and pre-Victorian poets, of course, as he will with Wordsworth's "bloody daffodils."

– T –

Tennyson, Alfred Lord—("Living Room on Pavement") Tennyson (1809-1892) is considered by many to be the father of Victorian poetry; he became Poet Laureate and was the first poet raised to peerage (1884). (See Ricks' article on Tennyson in the *ODNB*.) The Tennyson in the tub (Jones) is reading from *The Princess: A Medley* (1847, 1850):

> The splendour falls on castle walls
> And snowy summits old in story:
> The long light shakes across the lakes,
> And the wild cataract leaps in glory.
> Blow, bugle, blow, set the wild echoes flying,
> Blow, bugle; answer, echoes, dying, dying, dying.

In keeping with the Masonic tendencies of the episode, it's worth noting that Tennyson was a member of the Cambridge Apostles, a secret society at Trinity College, Cambridge (*ODNB*). Tennyson (played by John Hughman) will also appear in the Victorian poets reading room scene in Ep. 41.

"Thank you"—("Architect Sketch") This tirade by Mr. Wiggin seems to have had no effect on the Gents, who sit quite passively, even pleasantly. In fact, it isn't until Wiggin mentions Freemasonry that they seem nonplussed at all.

"third party"—("Motor Insurance Sketch") This means insurance to cover injuries/damages to someone/something not directly involved in the accident.

Threadneedle Street—(PSC; "Architect Sketch") The printed scripts indicate that this is to be shot on a crowded city street "e.g., Threadneedle Street." Threadneedle is a thoroughfare running through the heart of London's financial district; both the venerable Bank of England and the Stock Exchange are located here. This first location may be Wandsworth Bridge Road in Hammersmith & Fulham, very near locations for a number of Series 1 episodes (including "Upperclass Twits"), and where an ABC Drug Store is located (seen behind the hopping gents).

"torch"—("Poets") A flashlight, and in this case one that assumes a sexual connotation for She (Jones).

trolley—("Motor Insurance Sketch") In this case, the trolley is a shopping cart. Tea trolleys and hospital trolleys are seen in other episodes.

"twenty-eight storeys"—("Architect Sketch") Interestingly, these are just the types of public housing blocks that would later be demolished or, as very lately, become fashionable apartments for the new wealthy. The blocks had become centers and symbols of urban blight, drug use, and crime prior to recent renovation and neighborhood change. The Barbican Estate (begun in 1965), for example, features three such buildings, each of which rises to forty-two stories. What many occupants of these concrete behemoths lamented (especially in the New Towns) was the move away from a village setting, where going to the shops or the pub had been such a significant part of the social day (*Eyewitness 1950-59*, "New Housing").

– V –

voice of God—(PSC; "*The Bishop*") Though the voice of God is promised in the credits to "*The Bishop*," it's never heard in this short—and repeated—film.

– W –

WW***—("Words Not to Be Used Again") The use of asterisks (or other symbols) in place of letters is a common practice when objectionable words are displayed in both print and televised journalism.

In 1948 the BBC had produced a lengthy list of "do nots" for its writers, producers, and its television and radio shows in general. The "Variety Programmes Policy Guide for Writers and Producers" became compulsory reading for any hopeful creative type at Auntie Beeb in the decades afterward, and was still in at least nominal effect in 1969. Inappropriate language and social, political, and cultural taboos are very clearly defined in the document. (See notes to "slept with a lady" in Ep. 3 for more.)

"Walton Street"—("Living Room on Pavement") Perhaps the Walton Street in the Brompton (SW3) area, near Brompton Road. Walton Street runs north and eastward toward the Harrod's block, and is near the Egerton streets mentioned in the notes to Ep. 14. During much of this period, the "hard drug" area of West London was centered in Piccadilly.

"wee-wees"—("Words Not to Be Used Again") This nursery word can refer to both the act of urination and the penis itself, especially for children.

"West Country . . . Pennines"—("Poets") The major weather movement over the UK is from the West Country and across southeast England, generally affecting London last before moving out to sea and on toward the continent.

"whatever we happen to have down there"—("Police Constable Pan-Am") Cf. a very similar police reaction in Ep. 5, where the actor Sandy Camp (Idle) is confronted by a constable (Chapman) looking for "certain substances of an illicit nature." He eventually tries to plant the "illicit" substances, but ineptly. See the notes for Ep. 5 for the historical reference connected to this "creative" police work and Det. Robin Constable. (On 6 May 1970, incidentally, Constable would be officially cleared of any corruption charges by an *internal* review board, news sardonically delivered by *Private Eye* in an article entitled "Carry on Constable!" [22 May 1970, 19]).

"What's all this then?"—("After-Shave") This is a reflexive moment, wherein the fiction of the show refers to itself, another fiction. The Chemist character (Palin) here notes that this catchphrase has become synonymous in *FC* with police officials (including constables, detectives, inspectors) as they enter a room. See Eps. 5, 7, and 11 for earlier PC entrances. Python often quotes itself, accessing its own history, just as Shakespeare did in his histories. Falstaff recalls the events of Gad's Hill, Bergeron notes, though, as a fictional character himself, he is actually accessing Shakespeare's version of history as laid out in *1 Henry IV*. See Bergeron, Larsen.

"Wombat"—("Poets") A wombat is a nocturnal Australian marsupial. In Ep. 20, the "News for Wombats" is delivered by the helpful BBC newsreader (Palin).

"Wordsworth"—("Poets") William Wordsworth (1770-1850) was a Romantic-era poet, and eventually made poet laureate of England (1843-1850). His *Lyrical Ballads* (1798), written with Samuel Taylor Coleridge, helped launch the English Romantic movement.

working-class lounge is arranged on the pavement—("Living Room on Pavement") This cinema location is just down the street from the cigarette shop where the Bishop (Jones) and his Vicars stroll like toughs down the crowded sidewalk.

– Y –

"yus"—("Police Constable Pan-Am") Colloquialization/regional variation of "yes."

Episode 18

– A –

Animation—(PSC; link out of "Escape [From Film]") This is one of the very few times that a complete description of the animation is included in the printed scripts. Usually, the animation is being completed as the show is prepared, and Gilliam is away from the rest of the troupe. In this case, however, the matte work necessary for the videotaped versions of the escaping men to blend into the animated world would have required significant preparation, so the animation would have to have been completed earlier than normal. The following animated sequence in the episode is, as usual, not described. See *Gilliam on Gilliam* for more on the animation process in *FC*.

Animation sketch links us to a butcher's shop—(PSC; link out of "*Seven Brides For Seven Brothers*") The music used in the animation is a rough piano version of "Keep the Home Fires Burning" by Ivor Novello.

"Australasia"—("Society for Putting Things on Top of Other Things") Australasia includes Australia, New Guinea, Tasmania, New Zealand, and many other area islands. For this Society, however, it's most likely that "Australasia" refers just to the "white islands" Australia and New Zealand, the rest of the area being far too aboriginal.

– B –

"Babbacombe"—("Linkman" link out of "Documentary on Boxer") Babbacombe is a seaside town in Torbay reached by the main road between Newton Abbot and Torquay. It is about five miles north of Paignton, along the A3022. For this episode and several others shot during this stretch most of the exterior (and filmed) scenes/sketches were actually shot in this re-

sort region. The snack bar interiors were shot on 22 May 1970 (WAC T12/1,416).

Big showbiz music crashes in—("*Blackmail*") The music used in this scene is listed as "Bright Lights" by Sam Fonteyn (WAC T12/1,430). Fonteyn was one of the many stock and light music composers the Pythons would employ for the incidental music during the series, along with Keith Papworth (Eps. 6, 13), Eric Coates (Eps. 6, 42), Trevor Duncan (Ep. 33), and others. See notes to these episodes for more on the light music composers and their significance not only to the Pythons but British television, radio, and film between 1940 and the 1960s.

Bishop in the field—(PSC; link into "*Seven Brides For Seven Brothers*") The Bishop is making an unscheduled reappearance, after having an equally unscheduled appearance in Ep. 16. In both instances he reminds us that he won't be appearing until a later episode, even though he *is* appearing in this episode.

This field and the following school hall exteriors were shot in Torquay (WAC T12/1,430).

"Bolton"—("*Blackmail*") Southeast of Preston, Bolton is earlier mentioned in Ep. 8 and spelled backward, becoming "Notlob."

"Brazilian dagger"—("Accidents Sketch") The fact that this prop is named just means that the owner is a wealthy collector of sorts, as the layout of the room already indicates. The dagger is obviously a prop with a retractable blade.

This set piece is a bit unusual for the Pythons, especially as it plays more like an action-reaction Danny Kay scene (until the deaths) than a Python sketch. At this level, however, it is also what Wilmut characterized as an escalation-type sketch, with the levels of violence escalating as the sketch progresses (in other sketches, the dialogue or anger levels of characters can rise, as well). This is not unlike the favored Tex Avery cartoon structure, as seen in *King Size Canary* (1947) and *Bad Luck Blackie* (1949). In the latter film, a bulldog smitten with increasing bad luck is nearly crushed—in turn—by a sink, a tub, a piano, a steamroller, a plane, a city bus, and a battleship.

The cartoony-ness of *FC* has already been pointed out, including the cartoon props (giant hammer, sixteen-ton weight, anarchist's bomb), as well as the levels of cartoon violence and even the rendering of characters (in this very episode) into cartoon cutouts for animation purposes.

"Bromsgrove"—(*"Blackmail"*) Bromsgrove is in the county of Worcestershire, south of Birmingham, and would have been familiar to Idle, who attended the Royal Wolverhampton School, founded by a noted Freemason (see Ep. 17).

Politically, Bromsgrove had been a Conservative stronghold (and so a natural Python target) since at least the 1951 General Election, when John Higgs held the seat, garnering more than 52 percent of the vote. In 1955, Bromsgrove went even more Conservative with a 55.2 percent win by James Dance, who also won in 1959 with a 58 percent polling. Even in the swing year of 1964 when Labour took the reins of power, Bromsgrove returned their Conservative candidate (Dance) by the largest majority (more than 11 percent) over the Labour candidate. Bromsgrove would remain Conservative in 1966 and 1970, as well.

For all General Election results see Peele University's Election Results website at www.psr.keele.ac.uk.

– C –

"cheeky and lovable Cockney sergeant"—("Escape [From Film]") This scene and "cheeky" character are most directly borrowed from the British POW film *The Wooden Horse* (1950). The character of Peter as played by Leo Genn (1905-1978) in this POW film may be the actual sergeant character the Pythons were referencing. In the book version, however, it's Paul's "cheeky" mouth (not Peter's) toward his German captors that lands him in the cooler again and again. See the note for "horse" below.

"city of London ex-public school type"—(PSC; "Society for Putting Things on Top of Other Things") The printed script calls for a very precise character type, but it is identifiable (and seen as early as Ep. 2, "Flying Sheep"). The "City of London" reference means these are bankers or otherwise financial types—those who wear trilbies, carry brollies, speak with polished accents, and belong to exclusive clubs—these epitomize the "City Gent" for the Pythons. These types are found within the confines of the City of London, a rather small place (about one square mile) that acts as the heart of England's financial industry.

The "public school" reference means these types were educated at the expensive, class-rigid schools like Dulwich, Eton, and Harrow, and not state-supported schools. For many years these public schools had acted as nurseries for leadership positions in the empire, including royalty, Prime Ministers, MPs, cabinet members, colonial sinecures, etc.

All this history and acculturation is summed up—for the Pythons and their viewers alike—with an iconic, recognizable shorthand description ("city of London ex-public school type") that is interpreted by the show's dressers into an equally recognizable costume. This level of cultural awareness would most certainly be missed by the unacculturated (non-English) viewer, and even the native viewer given sufficient passage of time. In fact, the brollie and trilby look was already dated by 1970, meaning the studio audience knew they were seeing a throwback reference to a bygone day, to the City Gent look of the Pythons' youth.

"colour separation"—("Current Affairs") This is a television chroma key process that allows for the combination (usually as a superimposition) of images, and is accomplished by a blue- or green-screen effect.

"cotton head"—("Current Affairs") Something of a misnomer, as the term is usually applied to a dotty elderly person, i.e., an older person who drives too slowly in the fast lane.

"current affairs issues of burning import"—("Current Affairs") This may be a swipe at such newer and trendy news shows including *The World at One*, which made its BBC debut in 1965. The "softer" and flashier format reportedly angered old-timers in the BBC's news organization. The even softer news and current affairs show *Nationwide* also made its debut in 1969, which the Pythons spoof in Ep. 35, "Olympic Hide-and-Seek Final." *Nationwide* is remembered for human- and pet-interest stories often bordering on the silly, including skateboarding ducks, for example.

– E –

Edwardian gentleman—(PSC; animation link out of "Escape [From Film]") This "Edwardian gentleman" is a medical chart type. The usual Edwardian and Victorian images in this series are the female nude postcards that Gilliam uses in the title sequences and animated links. Gilliam collected the images from friend and comic mentor Ronnie Barker in the late 1960s. See *Gilliam on Gilliam* (41).

The Edwardian era dates from approximately Queen Victoria's death (1901) through at least King Edward VII's passing in 1910. The era saw a flourishing of appreciation for the arts and architecture, following the monarch's passions for Continental Europe, entertainment, and travel.

"eighteen . . . weight"—("Documentary on Boxer") Eighteen stone (one stone equals fourteen pounds) comes to about 252 pounds, much heavier than the very thin Cleese, obviously, and much, much heavier than the 112- to 119-pound bantamweight classification.

Episode 18—Not titled in the original scripts. This episode was recorded seventh (on 10 September 1970) in the second series, and aired fifth on 27 October 1970.

As so much of this episode (and Ep. 19, as well) was (1) scheduled to be shot on film, (2) already recorded on film in Torquay in May and June, and (3) scheduled away from BBC Television Centre (on location and at Ealing TFS), the studio time for the two episodes were combined, freeing up a full week of studio time for other shows at the BBC (WAC T12/1,242). As a result, some of the participants in this and Ep. 19 are included in the same WAC file. Curiously, one of the Python's agents, Jill Foster (of Fraser & Dunlop Scripts Ltd., 91 Regent Street, London), complains in a letter dated 20 August 1971 written to "David Attenborough Esq" that because of budgetary constraints the Pythons had to tape two shows in one evening and asks that the budget for the show be raised "because of lack of money." (They were already receiving £5,000/show in late 1971, up from £4,500 the season before [WAC T47/216].) In the memo, Foster neglects to mention the greatly reduced in-studio needs for these two episodes—needs determined by the troupe's writing/compiling for the episode—angling for a raise, instead.

The list of additional, often uncredited participants in this episode, according to BBC files, include: Connie Booth, Denton De Gray (Ep. 24; *Quatermass II*), Corona, Eddie May Scrandrett (Eps. 17, 19), Bill Leonard (Eps. 17-19), Michael Stayner (*Billion Dollar Brain*), Stephanie Marrian (*Benny Hill*), Barbara Smith, Bunny Saunders (likely of the "Bunny Saunders Pop Singers & Orchestra" fame), Colin Skeaping (*Star Wars*), Barbara Lindley (*Benny Hill*), Ian Davidson (and Mrs. E. Toller, Mr. D. Grice, Mr. P. O'Brien, Mrs. G. Dewhurst, Mrs. I. Docherty, and Mrs. Barbara Ball—these last six seem to be the parents for the boys in the "School Prize-Giving" sketch), Neil Innes (studio audience warm-up; *Do Not Adjust Your Set*; later contributor to *FC*), Terry Williams, Reuben Martin (*Carry On Up the Jungle*), and Roy Scammell (stuntman/actor, *Benny Hill*; *A Clockwork Orange*) (WAC T12/1,242).

"Everything seems to be in order"—("Escape [From Film]") The "cheeky" character seems to have been a staple of most of these POW films, from *The Wooden Horse* to *Stalag 17*, so the Pythons' entry in the POW genre couldn't be complete without his appearance.

– F –

finger gesture—("Escape [From Film]") Once again, the punch line is forbidden. In Ep. 17, when this same joke is started and successfully completed, the man who delivers the punch line is immediately arrested and hustled off.

frail and lovely—(PSC; "Documentary on Boxer") The printed script describes Connie Booth in this way, much as her earlier appearance as the "rebel maid" in the "I'm a Lumberjack" sketch for Ep. 9 ("a frail adoring blonde, the heroine of many a mountains film, or perhaps the rebel maid"). Booth was married to Cleese during this period.

"freemason"—(*Blackmail*) Cf. Ep. 17 for a more direct assault on Freemasonry. For the Pythons, such accepted fraternal organizations are natural breeding grounds for sexual deviants.

– G –

gates of a hospital—(PSC; "Documentary on Boxer") This sequence was originally shot (or scheduled to be shot) at Glenfield, Old Torwood Road, Torquay on 22 May 1970 (WAC T12/1,416). WAC records indicate that the scene between Ken (Cleese) and the gesturing doctor (Chapman) was later shot/reshot on 2 June 1970 at Hammersmith Hospital, near Wormwood Scrubs. Old Torwood Road connects to Babbacombe Road, mentioned by the Waitress (Chapman) later in the episode.

"gedderbong"—("Documentary on Boxer") Slang for "gentlemen," this term is also used in Ep. 5, in the "Confuse-a-Cat" sketch.

"germoline"—("Documentary on Boxer") Misspelled here, "Germolene" is the proprietary name for a first aid (antibiotic) ointment still popular in Britain.

gonk—("Documentary on Boxer") A Gonk is actually a proprietary name for an egg-shaped doll that was the rage in the UK from about 1964, meaning the innocent young boxer (Booth) would certainly have collected a few for her bedroom.

"great white hope"—("Documentary on Boxer") *Great White Hope* was a 1970 film starring James Earl Jones and directed by Martin Ritt, depicting the life of boxer Jack Johnson. Johnson (1878-1946) was the first black heavyweight champion of the world, and his various opponents were often called "great white hopes" as they fought and inevitably lost to him.

The British, Commonwealth, and European champion during this period was Henry Cooper, according to the International Boxing Hall of Fame. In March 1970, Cooper had defeated Jack Bodell (featured later in Ep. 37) to regain his British heavyweight crown. (The American and world heavyweight champion during this period was Joe Frazier.) Cooper would also appear on *A Question of Sport* (BBC, 1970-), a sports quiz show very popular during this period.

The "great white hope" moniker is quite fitting for Cooper, as he managed to knock Cassius Clay (who would later become Muhammad Ali) to the canvas in the fourth round of their 1963 fight at Wembley Stadium. Clay would recover in between rounds and go on to win by TKO. Their 1966 rematch was not so favorable for Cooper, with the fight being stopped in the sixth round.

green baize apron—(PSC; "Accidents Sketch") Baize is a coarse woolen material, often used for linings on shelves where clothes were stored.

The "man in the green baize apron" is an emblematic, humble, old man serving figure from a number of sources, including Joseph Conrad's *Arrow of Gold* (1919) and *The Secret Agent* (1907), as well as Virginia Woolf's *The Waves* (1931), and perhaps the most significant Victorian literature source, Dickens' *Bleak House* (1852-1853). The "green baize door" is also used as a literary trope depicting the dividing line between the two sides/levels of the manor house—between the landed family and their domestic help.

Grillomatic snack bar—(PSC; "Linkman" link out of "Documentary on Boxer") In the printed script, the final mention of this snack bar is spelled quite differently from previous iterations. As a matter of fact, the name of the snack bar is spelled severally as "Grill-o-Mat," "Grillomat," and, finally, "Grillomatic" in the printed script. The actual name of this Torquay-area snack bar is not mentioned in the WAC records for the episode or series.

– H –

"horse"—("Escape [From Film]") This is a vaulting horse used for calisthenics, and would seem to have no place in a Royal Society meetinghouse. In the transition to the WWII prisoner-of-war camp setting, however, the horse does actually fit, as a number of POW camp films included sports/calisthenic activities for

the prisoners, including baseball in *The Great Escape* (1963).

Specifically, however, a film set in Stalag-Luft III where the actual "Great Escape" took place, *The Wooden Horse* (1950) is the real basis for this part of the sketch. In Stalag-Luft III the prisoners would carry a large vaulting horse out into the exercise yard nearer the perimeter fence, two men hiding inside, and as the other prisoners exercised, the hidden men would dig an escape tunnel. The hole entrance would be hidden at day's end and the horse returned, men and sand inside, to the barracks, the sand then broadcast around the compound. See Williams' *The Wooden Horse* for a first-person account of this camp, the tunnels, and the eventual mass escape. See the entry for Williams at *ODNB*.

"Humperdinck, Englebert"—("Documentary on Boxer") Two men, actually. The first Engelbert Humperdinck (1854-1921) was a German composer known for his opera *Hansel and Gretel* (1893). The second is an Indian-born popular singer of the same name who was raised in Leicester (as was Chapman) and has sold millions of records. In the late 1960s Humperdinck's records were outpacing The Beatles' albums in sales, and his fans were legion.

– I –

"I'm more of a visual performer"—(link out of "Documentary on Boxer") Cleese is of course being reflexive again, reminding the audience of the already much-loved sketch ("Ministry of Silly Walks") that had aired just a few weeks earlier, on 15 September 1970. Reappearances of non-typed characters—including Ken Shabby and Cardinal Ximinez (both Palin)—elicit applause and sounds of recognition from the studio audience, indicating the show had generated a significant following by this time, less than a year into its existence, and that the home viewers were making efforts to secure tickets and see the tapings live. Contemporary fans like Jeremy Paxman and John Diamond (mentioned in notes to Ep. 8) attest to this cult of familiarity in the teen and twenty-somethings of the Greater London area in 1969-1970.

In subsequent interviews Cleese mentions that he and Chapman (often as writing partners) tended to create the more verbal sketches based on wordplay and escalation of character/setting temperament, while Jones and Palin contributed more surreal, often bizarre sketches. For audience members familiar at all with Cleese's previous work (prior to *Flying Circus*), of course, Cleese had become the picture of a sober, straight-laced type who could be egged into outbursts of splenetic rage, as earlier seen in the "Architect Sketch" (Ep. 17), as well as a talented wordsmith. (See Cleese's work in *The Frost Report* [1966] and *At Last the 1948 Show* [1967], for example.) The "Silly Walks" scene, then, would have been a novel bit of a departure for the sober, respectable former barrister Cleese, which probably accounts for its continuing appeal. See Morgan's *Monty Python Speaks!* and McCabe's *The Pythons*.

– K –

Ken jogging . . . trees—(PSC; "Documentary on Boxer") According to the BBC, most of this footage, including the council houses, streets, and village areas were shot in and around Torquay (WAC T12/1,430).

Ken's house is located at Glenfield, Old Torwood Road, Torquay (WAC T12/1,416). Parts of this sketch were also shot in the Richmond and Norfolk areas.

– L –

Linkman—(PSC; "Live From the Grill-o-Mat Snack Bar, Paignton") This is the first time that a Linkman has been so prominently featured in *FC*, though links are consistently, pointedly, even clumsily pointed out across the series. The linking character is probably something of a holdover from the days of radio, when such transitions were necessary, as there were no graphics or picture transitions available. The Pythons are clearly lampooning the stodgy role of the unctuous or inept linkman—his witticisms forced and puns all bad. Such linkmen in the BBC world are obviously important figures in the Pythons' collective viewing experiences as they grew up—they appear throughout *FC*, often as greasy compères, as well.

"live from the Grillomat Snack Bar"—("Live From the Grill-o-Mat Snack Bar, Paignton") This, of course, would have been recorded on film long before the episode was recorded in the studio on 10 September 1970. This snack bar location (in Torquay) was used on 22 May 1970.

"load them up with cutlery"—("Escape [From Film]") In the "Great Escape" from Stalag Luft III, prisoners used utensils, bowls, and hand-fashioned spades to dig the escape tunnels "Tom," "Dick," and "Harry." See Williams' *The Wooden Horse*.

"Lord Hill"—("Current Affairs") Lord Hill (of Luton) was in charge of the BBC during this period. He is mentioned earlier in Ep. 10, in the "Bank Robber (Lingerie Shop)" sketch, as well as Ep. 11, by the miffed Professor Canning (Chapman). Lord Hill had allegedly inter-

vened not long before as the new, color-format *Newsroom* appeared on BBC, arguing that the sheer number of satellite-spewed pictures from around the world could convince the British public that the world was in a state of "greater ferment" than it actually was. (See the BBC's information on *Newsroom* at news.bbc.co.uk.)

This is the second time that a character has been included in a show where either there is no time for it or he's not scheduled to appear. In Ep. 16 (and later in Ep. 18), the Bishop (Palin) can't answer questions since he's not scheduled to appear in the episode in which he is appearing. Later in this episode (Ep. 18) this same rehearsing Bishop (Palin) will appear as the gentlemen from the Royal Society make their way to the *Seven Brides for Seven Brothers* play. The Bishop is still not scheduled to appear, he tells the gentlemen. In Ep. 19, the Announcer (Cleese) also mentions that he's not scheduled to appear in that episode, and yet there he is (he realizes the irony, however).

– M –

Man Alive—(PSC; "Documentary on Boxer") *Man Alive* aired on BBC2 from 1965 to 1982, and was a hard-hitting current affairs program covering topics including molestation, marriage, and agoraphobia (Vahimagi 138). The show was designed to offer the viewpoint, often, of the common man. In the printed scripts, "camera noise" is mentioned, meaning the sound of the whirring film spools should be heard as the interview progresses.

Man Alive will be mentioned again, by Herbert Mental (Jones), in Ep. 26, as the show he'd hoped would invite him for an interview.

"Maybe it's because I'm a Londoner . . . "—("Escape [From Film]") This recently penned pub song (written by Hubert Gregg in 1946) is the song the men are attempting to sing as they vault:

> Maybe it's because I'm a Londoner, that I love London so.
> Maybe it's because I'm a Londoner, that I think of her wherever I go.
> I get a funny feeling inside of me, just walking up and down.
> Maybe it's because I'm a Londoner, that I love London Town.

A curious choice, since the Stalags and their Allied prisoners were liberated in 1945, prior to the song's composition. Actor/singer Bud Flanagan would popularize the song in a musical revue called *Together Again* that ran for several years on the West End after the war.

Finally, *Dixon of Dock Green* would also use the tune for its titles song. See entries in Eps. 5 and 7 for more on this iconic police show.

"Medwin"—("Escape [From Film]") Michael Medwin (b. 1923) appeared in *The Bruce Forsythe Show* (1967), as well as Lindsay Anderson's *If . . .* (1968), which will be mentioned prominently in Ep. 19. There were also several characters named "Medwin" in the *Doctor at Large* series, for which both Chapman and Cleese contributed at least eight episodes (writing) together.

Mr. Cutler runs up . . .—("Escape [From Film]") Here the characters cement the *Wooden Horse* homage by tapping on the vault (Cleese) and pretending to begin to hide in it, before following Sir William (Chapman) out of the scene.

"my mother"—("Society For Putting Things on Top of Other Things") In Ep. 2, "The Mouse Problem," Dino Vercotti also pretends to have been speaking to his mother on the phone—when actually he was confirming a Chinese prostitute appointment ("the Chinese watch") for that evening.

– N –

"no need for me to interrupt at all"—(link into *"Seven Brides for Seven Brothers"*) But of course he is interrupting as well as creating a link, not unlike Praline (Cleese), whose current affairs show was earlier cancelled, though he appeared anyway, and the rehearsing Bishop (Palin) who appears but is always scheduled for a later show.

– O –

"on film"—("Escape [From Film]") Continuity did not seem to be a problem for British viewers when a TV show switched from video format to film format, even in this kind of interior/exterior match cut, which really doesn't match at all. It is possible that since 1968-1969 was the year that the transition from black-and-white to color broadcasts was undertaken at the BBC—and that in black-and-white broadcast the clarity difference between a filmed and videotaped image is much less noticeable—audiences for *Monty Python* and news shows, for example, would have taken the image dissimilarities as par for the course, as it were.

Portable video cameras were a bulky rarity during this period, with most news field reporting being done on film. The trade-off, of course, is that the graininess, depth and color quality of the 16mm image contrasts greatly to the sharp but shallow video images. Again,

audiences new to color television would have known nothing else for comparison. But the Pythons knew. Cf. Ep. 15, where the linking element of film is mentioned as the Hermits' sketch is stopped and the Major (Chapman) cues the show back to the studio. This acknowledgment of the world of film as separate and distinct from the world of the studio is yet another example of the Pythons not only breaking the traditional barrier between the audience and what goes on behind the scenes of a TV show—in this case, identifying the differing visual formats—but making sure that audiences are aware of these artifices.

The white, portico-and-column exterior shots for this scene were recorded at Thorne House, Ham Common, Richmond on 4 June 1970 (WAC T12/1,416).

– P –

"Paignton"—("Live From the Grill-O-Mat Snack Bar, Paignton") Paignton is in South West England, and is part of the "English Riviera" coast country. Portions of *"Scott of the Antarctic"* (Ep. 23) are shot at the Paignton Pier. The snack bar location is actually in Torquay, according to BBC records (WAC T12/1,430), and was utilized on 22 May 1970.

"piano stool"—("Current Affairs") Praline (and Brooky) will reappear, piano stool in hand, to accompany both the *Seven Brides for Seven Brothers* performance as well as the animated "Hunting Piggybanks" animation that follows.

"poovy po-nagger"—("The Man Who Is Alternately Rude and Polite") These variations on effeminating homosexual insults, including "poofta," "pillock," and "spotted prancer"—appear elsewhere in *FC* as "poove," "wee wee," and "mincing fairy."

This structure—here alternately rude and polite—will be revisited in Ep. 26 with a man who speaks only the middle of words, except every third and fourth sentence where he speaks full sentences.

"population explosion"—("Current Affairs") The Nobel Peace Prize for 1970 was awarded to Norman Borlaug (b. 1914), whose area of study was the population and world food crisis.

Birth control methods in China, for instance, weren't significantly encouraged until the early 1970s, several years after this episode, and China's population (under Mao's encouragement) had been growing prodigiously, reaching a birth rate of about 34.3 in 1970. The *China Statistical Yearbook* (2003) notes that China's population grew from 806.7 million in 1969 to 829.9 million in 1970. (For reference, the population of the entire UK stood at only about 55 million in mid-1970, or about 6.6 percent of China's population.) In 1991, the future date mentioned in the sketch, China's population had reached about 1.16 billion.

Gilliam's animation in Ep. 24 depicts yellow Chinese characters overwhelming a young secretary, with an animated Mao leading the way. The references to China throughout *FC* indicate a mix of fascination and fear in the Western world of this inscrutable, emerging superpower.

"posh talk"—("The Man Who Is Alternately Rude and Polite") Reaffirming George Bernard Shaw's belief that one Englishman will inevitably despise another Englishman the moment he opens his mouth—a maxim based on the level of sophistication of language and diction in "Southern" English (read: London) as opposed to the coarser, earthier Northern dialects. The Gent (Palin) here isn't dressed to the nines, however—e.g., trilby and brollie—but does sound a bit more refined than the average customer ("I'd care to purchase a chicken").

"prep"—("*Seven Brides for Seven Brothers*") The standard thirty minutes of homework in secondary schools, often conducted in a study hall setting before or after classroom instruction (*OED*).

"Preston . . . Lancashire"—("*Blackmail*") Preston in the county Lancashire lies along the River Ribble near the coast of the Irish Sea northwest of London. Preston North and South had gone Labour in the 1964 and 1966 General Elections, but both went Conservative in the 1970 General Election in June. This would have allowed the Pythons to take some solace in the Labour loss when they finally recorded the episode in September, locating their sexual deviants in comfortable Conservative neighborhoods.

"prospective Tory MP"—("*Blackmail*") This man would be someone standing for Parliament for the Conservative Party, as opposed to the Labour, Liberal, or one of the myriad fringe parties. The fact that he is a Tory earmarks him, in the Python world, for sexual deviancy.

There is the very real possibility that this sketch is yet another reference to the still-fresh Profumo sex scandal that essentially toppled the Macmillan government in 1964, and gave Labour its control of the government until 1970. Cf. Ep. 2, "The Mouse Problem" for an earlier, more in-depth treatment of this sex-and-political-intrigue scandal. In the Profumo case of 1963, highly placed and well-respected Conservative politicians—and especially Secretary for War John Profumo—engaged in sexual improprieties (including costumed sadomasochism) and then lied to the House of Commons about their involvement. (The latter was

seen by many as the more egregious sin, by the way.) The government change ushered in the much more liberal Harold Wilson (a so-called New Age Labourite) government, a change always seen as at least indirectly precipitated by Profumo's sexual shenanigans.

– R –

"Reigate"—("Documentary on Boxer") Located in Surrey, near Gatwick airport. This location is actually on Old Torwood Road, Torquay, according to BBC records (WAC T12/1,416).

"Pesticide Research Centre at Shoreham"—Shoreham is in Kent, south of Dartford. There has been a pesticide research center at Silwood Park since 1955, known as the International Pesticide Application Research Centre. Silwood Park is in the Royal Borough of Windsor and Maidenhead.

"Reading"—Reading is in Berkshire, on the Thames west of London. It was mentioned in the "New Cooker Sketch" in Ep. 14. The BBC written archives are also "near Reading," in Caversham Park.

"Bangkok"—Capital and largest city of Thailand. The distance between London and Bangkok is about 6,000 miles.

"Kyoto"—Ancient capital of Japan.

"return of post"—("*Blackmail*") An idiom that can just mean as soon as possible, though more precisely, a response delivered at the next available posting of the Royal Mail.

"Richard, Cliff"—("Documentary on Boxer") British pop musician Richard (b. 1940) had been popular since 1958, and was the type of teenage heartthrob that young girls like Petula (Booth) would have swooned over surrounded by her Gonk collection. Richard's image and record sales had suffered since the appearance of The Beatles (and the Mersey sound, and skiffle groups), but he was still a popular draw, managing high ratings (for "Congratulations") in the 1968 Eurovision Song Contest, for example.

roadside diner—(PSC; "Documentary on Boxer") This scene was shot at the base of the Walton Bridge, on Walton Bridge Road, Shepperton, Middlesex. This is near Walton-on-Thames, where the Pythons were scheduled to shoot portions of this sketch, and had already shot scenes for Eps. 1 and 2 (WAC T12/1,083).

Robin Hood hat—(PSC; "*Blackmail*") The script calls very specifically for a "Robin Hood hat" on this character. The hat's brim is slightly turned up at the back and down at the front. According to one entry in the *OED*, this type of hat made something of a comeback in 1960: "*News Chron.* 11 Apr. 8/4 Gone are the heavy-looking trilbies . . . in their place have come the delta and the Robin Hood." The trilby is the hat of choice for Pythons' stereotyped City Gents (Ep. 17), though the "Eton, Harrow and the Guard" Upperclass Twits (Ep. 12) sport the Robin Hood–type hat.

"rota"—("Escape [From Film]") A "rota" is a rotation of persons or routines, and here is used much like the escape procedures in *The Great Escape* (1963), with some men digging the tunnels, some standing guard, some resting, and some acting as distractions to the prison camp guards. The *Great Escape* motif will be revisited more plainly (including the well-known theme music) in Ep. 28, the "Trim-Jeans Theatre" sketch.

The rota in *The Wooden Horse* (which inspired the inclusion here) included vaulting, initially, then medicine ball, calisthenics, and even running as the long process of digging went on beneath them. See Williams' *The Wooden Horse*.

"Royal Society"—("Society for Putting Things on Top of Other Things") There are myriad Royal Societies, for arts and letters, sciences, husbandry, etc., which is probably why the Pythons could lampoon the idea. Just some include: the Royal Society for the Protection of Birds, the Royal Commonwealth Society, the Royal Agricultural Society, as well as Royal Societies of chemistry, medicine, etc. To qualify as a "royal" society, the group must receive a charter from the sitting monarch. (The BBC, for example, possesses such a charter.) The original Royal Society was found in 1662 during the reign of Charles II, and was designed as a bastion of scientific learning.

Swift satirizes the Royal Society in his *Gulliver's Travels*, specifically in the third book, on the flying island of Laputa.

"rubs gravel into his hair"—("Documentary on Boxer") A bit of comedic overkill here as Ken (Cleese) performs a silly act—rubbing gravel into his hair—and the narrator describes the act as it's being performed for us. This obviates at least one level of possible incongruity, that between the visual and the spoken. Earlier in the sketch, for example, Ken inexplicably runs from his home to the Pesticide Research Centre, but the visuals just offer generic running shots, leaving the viewer to make the connection between the visual and aural suggestions.

Comedian Woody Allen (b. 1935) slips into this same reiterating trap in his early comic film *Take the Money and Run*—when the narrator mentions Orthodox Jews in prison, then cuts to praying Orthodox Jews in a cell—as well as the man having sex with a loaf of rye bread in *Everything You Always Wanted to Ask About Sex But Were Afraid to Ask* (1969). The incon-

gruity of the gags is significantly undercut when the ridiculous payoffs are rendered so concretely.

– **S** –

"Sabine School for Girls"—(*Seven Brides for Seven Brothers*) Turned into "sobbin' women" in the Benet short story, the "Rape of the Sabine Women" is depicted by Livy and Plutarch, among others. The story involves Romulus' Romans abducting Sabine women to become brides. Here the Dibley boys have convinced just two Sabine girls to appear in the stilted performance.

same stupendous sound effects as for all-in cricket—("Documentary on Boxer") An example of the Pythons being reflexive, mentioning the all-in cricket sketch in Ep. 11, and offering the production crew (in this case, the sound team) a quick reference to effects already used and available. The resulting sound effects are, needless to say, hardly stupendous, meaning the direction was glib. This glibness is seen earlier in Ep. 9 when mood lighting is requested ("Ha!") in the printed script, the writers knowing such lighting isn't available.

"Satellite Five"—("Documentary on Boxer") Probably meant to be a play on *Saturn V*, the enormous rocket used by NASA to conduct moon launches for the Apollo program (1967-1973). The proliferation of satellites in the 1950s and 1960s may also account for this reference, with the United States and USSR launching multiple satellites for weather observation, communication, military, and surveillance activities. The UK wouldn't launch its first man-made satellite until 1971.

Schoolmaster—(PSC; "*Seven Brides for Seven Brothers*") This is Palin speaking this line, off-camera, though he is not credited. He will appear in a few moments as the Padre.

"semi-detached house"—("Documentary on Boxer") This location is 67 Broughton Avenue, Ham, Richmond, Surrey, and the interior and exterior footage was shot on 3 June 1970 (WAC T12/1,242).

"Seven Brides For Seven Brothers"—("*Seven Brides for Seven Brothers*") A popular Hollywood film musical from 1954 (dir. Stanley Donen), the significant singing and dancing demands (and large cast requirements) of *Seven Brides* make it an unlikely (and therefore funny) choice for an all-boys school production. The original story was written by Stephen Vincent Benet, and was called *The Sobbin' Women*.

School shows in the UK had been common since at least Shakespeare's youth, when his Stratford Grammar School would regularly perform plays like

Nicholas Udall's *Ralph Roister Doister* (1553), featuring an all-boy cast. The Pythons variously acted in school plays in their grammar school experiences, as well.

"shop where you bought the equipment"—("*Blackmail*") These kinds of sex shops, according to one of Alan Bennett's *Beyond the Fringe* monologues ("The Porn Shop"), were located in the Charing Cross Road area of the West End, London, and were especially pervasive in the 1950s and 1960s.

"Silly! I suppose it is"—("Society for Putting Things on Top of Other Things") There aren't many occasions in *FC* where the character admits to the silliness of the set-up or situation, a sort of "Emperor's New Clothes" scenario where the Emperor's nakedness is pointed out. More often, the silliness is reinforced, then built upon, then undercut or supplanted by yet another silliness, etc.

"Smith Major"—("Seven Brides for Seven Brothers") This is a specialized, public school usage, according to the *OED*, where such a phrase designates "the elder or senior of two pupils with the same surname or the first to enter the school (used especially in British public schools)."

"Smith brothers"—The family name for the brothers in the 1954 feature film *Seven Brides for Seven Brothers* is actually "Pontipee."

"southpaw"—("Documentary on Boxer") A boxer who leads with his/her left hand.

"Staffordshire"—("Society For Putting Things on Top of Other Things") Staffordshire is a West Midlands county south of Manchester. The Pythons continue to find their locus of provinciality in the Midlands regions, which will become irrefutably evident in Ep. 19, when the Tourist (Idle) rants about nightmarish package tours originating in Luton.

stock film . . . blown up—("Accidents Sketch") The post-explosion sequence (where Idle holds the doorknob in a pile of rubble) following the stock film explosion was shot in the London area, according to the BBC (WAC T12/1,430).

– T –

"ten bob"—("Current Affairs") "Ten bob" usually referred to the ten-shilling note, until that note was removed from circulation in 1971, when British currency "went decimal." In 1969-1970, the BBC was paying walk-ons (at least for the *Flying Circus* series) about five pounds and five shillings, according to WAC records (WAC T12/1,082).

"Thames Ditton"—(PSC; "*Blackmail*") This exterior was actually shot in the London area, according to BBC records (WAC T12/1,439). Thames Ditton is in Surrey, South East England, on the Thames near Esher. In the printed script, the writers placed a "(sic)" after "Thames Ditton," though there was no misspelling. This could be an acknowledgment that the scene was not or would not be shot in Thames Ditton, but somewhere closer to home—most likely Ealing or East Acton. (Though difficult to see clearly, the setting looks very much like the 39 Elers Road, Ealing location [near Lammas Park Road], where portions of the first series were recorded.) This is yet another example of a scripted moment available only to other readers, and not the eventual viewer, and is meant to be an in-joke.

Also, the inclusion of "(sic)" could be a reference to the "anomalous or erroneous" (*OED*) use of such a setting as Thames Ditton in the first place, since nearby Esher had remained overwhelmingly Conservative in the 1966 general election, garnering more than 55 percent of the vote. The *Private Eye* editors occasionally included a "(sic)" after a properly spelled word or name, usually to draw unwarranted attention to it.

These exterior scenes were shot on 1 June 1970, according to WAC records (WAC T12/1,416).

tin helmet—(PSC; "Escape [From Film]") This ubiquitous tin helmet was worn in combat, by civil defense workers, and even miners, but is probably most associated with British soldiers serving in Burma during World War II.

Two Girls—(PSC; "*Seven Brides For Seven Brothers*") These girls are Connie Booth and Lynn Idle. Booth was married to Cleese at this time (1968-1978), and Lynn was Eric Idle's wife (1969-1978).

– U –

underneath she wears black corsets—("*Blackmail*") This actress apperas to be Helena Clayton, who also played the Dominatrix in the *Flying Circus* Montreux episode compilation in 1971 (WAC T12/1,413).

– V –

"vestry"—("*Seven Brides for Seven Brothers*") A room in a church setting often adjacent to the chapel, where vestments and church records are kept (*OED*).

"Victoria Station"—("*Blackmail*") Victoria Station is located in Westminster in the heart of London. It is perhaps ironic that blackmail demands for the prospective Tory MP's sexual deviancy should be paid in the station named for the virtuous Victoria, the eponymous representative of Britain's supposedly buttoned-down sexual period.

another interesting portrayal of women for the Pythons, in this case, as an armed, seductive dominatrix bent on humiliation of the submissive male.

– W –

"we're really out this time"—(link out of "Accidents Sketch") If what Sir William (Chapman) is referring to is the fact that they were caught on film, then they are clearly not "out," since this scene is also shot on film. They are out of the Edwardian gentleman's entrails, of course, but that was shot on both videotape and film.

whip—("*Blackmail*") With the whip and black corsets she is obviously playing to the man's domination fetish, commenting on the sexual proclivities of the Conservative types. The Profumo confessions included details of sadomasochistic orgies. This is also

– Y –

"youth organization to which they belong"—("*Blackmail*") Dinsdale Piranha is also described as being fond of such younger groups, including "Boy's Clubs . . . Chorister's Associations . . . [and] Scouting Jamborees" as part of his sexual deviancy. The host (Palin) hints here that the Conservative "Mr. S. of Bromsgrove" is a sexual fetishist who enjoys pederasty and perhaps bondage. Continuing this theme later in the episode, the Butcher (Idle) will castigate his customer (Palin) with all manner of sodomitical epithets, including "pillock," "trollope," and "poovy po-nagger."

Episode 19

– A –

"Additional Material By"—(PSC; "Timmy Williams Interview") This long, fast laundry list of names is a hodge-podge of well-known entertainment and sport figures, lesser-known figures from the same areas, characters/authors from Oxbridge academic reading lists, and assorted people known only to the individual Python who contributed the name.

According to one person so named, Jonathan Ashmore, the bulk of the "unknowns" on the list were "layabouts" at a flat at World's End (in Camden High Street, London) during this period. See the entry for Ashmore below.

"agent"—("Election Night Special") One who represents the candidate, in this case.

"all five of them"—("Registry Office") What begins as a characteristic, Pythonesque misunderstanding between characters eventually becomes a rather sly comment on heterosexual marriage and the volatile sexual liberation movement of the 1960s and 1970s. Homosexuality in the UK had only been (partly) decriminalized three years earlier, but was still quite stigmatized. In fact, sexual acts between consenting men (aged twenty-one and above) had been legalized, but even a third person anywhere in the home recrimininalized the act, so the five Pythons would have still been subject to arrest. See the restrictions of the Sexual Offences Act of 1967 for more.

"Allied Technician's Union"—("Foreign Secretary") The very powerful Trade Union Congress (TUC) was an umbrella organization representing many unions and was quite active in 1970. The pressure applied to management and government in the late 1960s would help bring Wilson's Labour government down (and encumber the incoming Heath government, as well)

with threatened or actual strikes at industrial concerns like Ford Motors, by newspaper publishers, miners, and even a national dock strike. Strike activity was at its highest during the 1970-1974 period in the UK, as the Tories tried to rein in the power of organized labor, and the TUC is referenced more than sixty times in UK newspaper op-ed page cartoons in 1968-1970 alone. See the British Cartoon Archive.

ANIMATION: for a minute or two strange things happen—(animated link out of "The Time on BBC 1") The animated head Gilliam uses in this sequence is a still photo of Wolverhampton MP Enoch Powell (1912-1998), whose "Rivers of Blood" immigration speech (see notes to Ep. 25) had bounced him from Cabinet status but into very high popularity with Conservative voters (and many others who feared unfettered immigration). The fact that Powell was an outspoken and blunt Tory painted him a perfect target for the Pythons. Powell would have been representing Idle's own constituency.

"Applied Mathematics"—("School Prize-Giving") Mathematics used in the sciences, including astronomy, physics, etc.

Arabs—("Foreign Secretary") Stereotypically attired in flowing robes and head coverings, the "Arabs" whoop and leap about as they toss various characters into the river. Between 1967 and September 1970 (when this episode was recorded), the Palestinian Liberation Organization (PLO) along with the Popular Front for the Liberation of Palestine (PFLP) had operated as a militant terrorist organization in Jordan, kidnapping and killing foes and foreigners, and the PFLP eventually hijacking planes and destroying them. A handful of Brits were on the three planes hijacked in September 1970, and were eventually rescued by Jordanian army troops on 26 September (Office for National Statistics).

"Ashley, Len"—("Timmy Williams Interview" credits) Perhaps the sibling of Lyn Ashley, who was Mrs. Idle between 1967 and 1979.

"Ashmore, Jonathan"—("Timmy Williams Interview" credits) Ashmore was at one time a child actor who appeared in the 1955 film *A Kid for Two Farthings*, directed by Carol Reed. Ashmore is more recently Professor Jonathan Ashmore, FMedSci FRS, Department of Physiology, University College London. From Ashmore: "It's just that I happened to share a house c. 1970 in World's End, London with some good friends of Eric Idle . . . some of the other people in those high speed rolling credits were drunks/layabouts/crazies/hangers-on too . . . " (from e-mail correspondence with the author).

"at the rate of knots"—("Election Night Special") A British colloquialism meaning "very quickly."

"Avery, Charles"—("Foreign Secretary") Charles Avery was one of the original Keystone Kops at Mack Sennett's Keystone studio, appearing in (and even directing) scores of early Hollywood knockabout comedies. It is no surprise that the Pythons would offer a bumbling screen comic as the employers' representative in this sketch.

– B –

bank of a river—("Foreign Secretary") These riverbank scenes were shot while on location in the Easton Lodge area, Easton, at River Bank, on 24 August 1970 (WAC T12/1,413). The following day, the crew moved further north to shoot in and around Norwich.

"Barclay, Humphrey"—("Timmy Williams Interview" credits) A friend and employer to the Pythons, Barclay produced several shows involving various members of the troupe, including *Complete and Utter History of Britain* (1969), *Doctor in the House* (1969), and *Do Not Adjust Your Set* (1967). Barclay was also active in the Cambridge Footlights events, writing, directing, and producing.

"Barrow-in-Furness"—("Election Night Special") Situated on the Irish Sea, and west of Lancashire. The entertainer Engelbert Humperdinck never stood for this (or any) constituency, hailing from Leicester. In the General Election of 1970, Albert Booth (the Labour candidate) held his seat in this constituency, and would remain in that position until 1983.

"BBC 2"—("The Time on BBC 1") On 20 April 1964 BBC2 came on the air, quickly earning a reputation for fostering edgier, often more daring programming than BBC1. Hit shows on BBC2 would often then make the jump to BBC1 (especially when any hint of inappropriateness had worn off).

"Beach, James"—("Timmy Williams Interview" credits) Jim Beach was a fellow Cambridge Footlights member with Eric Idle in 1964, an entertainment lawyer who went on to eventually manage the band Queen and produce TV, theatrical performances, and films. Beach also produced the Pythons' "Monty Python at Drury Lane" and "City Center New York" projects.

"Beamish, Adrian"—("Timmy Williams Interview" credits) A graduate of Christ's College, Cambridge in 1962, Beamish would go on to become British ambassador to Mexico, and is now Sir Adrian Beamish.

"Bishop of East Anglia"—("School Prize-Giving") East Anglia was *not* an Anglican diocese during this time, which may be why the Pythons chose the location. East Anglia is an area northeast of London comprising (primarily) the Norfolk and Suffolk regions, and where the Pythons shot some of the location material for the second series. It is so named because it was the easternmost part of the ancient kingdom of Angliæ.

The Idiots later (Ep. 20) will be trained at the University of East Anglia (Norwich, Norfolk), one of the oft-maligned "new" universities set up as a result of the government's Robbins Report released in October 1963. See entries for the "Idiot" sketch for more.

"Bloggs, David"—("Timmy Williams Interview" credits) Probably a nonsense name, since "Joe Bloggs" (and sometimes "Fred Bloggs") is a British place-holding name, like "John Q. Public" in the United States. The character is played here by John Hughman (Eps. 14, 17, 28).

"Board of Trade"—("Foreign Secretary") This episode was recorded in October 1970, just when the major alterations in the Board of Trade were front-page news. Created in 1761, the Board of Trade had gradually changed functions by 1970. In October 1970, the Department of Trade and Industry was formed from remnants of the Board of Trade and the Ministry of Technology.

Roy Mason (b. 1924) and then Michael Noble (1913-1984) were presidents of the Board of Trade in 1969 and 1970, respectively, just before the Board was reformulated.

"Book of the Month Club"—("Dung") Concern founded in 1923, where "outstanding" books are chosen monthly and provided to paying subscribers. Accompanying items are usually limited to tote bags and the like, not dung or dead Indians.

Gilliam will use a copy of a Book of the Month Club ad (featuring titles like *The Rise and Fall of the Third Reich*, *The Naked Ape*, etc.) in his animation "The Spot" later in this episode.

"Bradshaw, Elizabeth"—("School Prize-Giving") Dressed in a trench coat and hat, Inspector Bradshaw looks very much like the prototypical Scotland Yard official whom often breaks in on *FC* sketches. The use of the female first name for a male character is also, of course, a Python trait of diminution for authority figures.

"breach of promise"—("Registry Office") Under British law, engagements had been treated as enforceable contracts until almost the twentieth century, meaning a woman—after accepting a man's proposal of marriage—could seek damages if he backed out. Part of the consideration was that the woman could lose her virginity (and, hence, her future marriage value) in such a breach. (In *Hard Day's Night* [1964], Paul mentions that his philandering grandfather has cost the family "a fortune in breach of promise cases.") The twist for this scene, of course, is that British law did not recognize a homosexual marital relationship, and the injured party (the Registrar) couldn't technically have demonstrated breach.

"Brian!"—("Timmy Williams Interview") This actor appears to be David Kempton (WAC T12/1,434).

"Bristols"—("Election Night Special") "Bristols" is a word of rhyming slang: "Bristol cities" becomes "titties" (breasts), hence "Bristols." This reference elicits quite a laugh from the studio audience. Similarly, "Jethro Q. Walrus*titty*" was the Silly candidate for Leicester earlier in the sketch.

"buzzing noise"—("Election Night Special") Sending up the "earpiece" news flashes and off-camera direction broadcasters receive while on air. The buzzing itself would have been interference or microphone feedback, and newscasters often have to remove the earpiece if the noise or director's messages get too jumbled and distracting.

– C –

"charabanc"—("Timmy Williams Interview") A kind of motor coach, and one that might even be open to the air. The openness of the vehicle seems to fit Timmy Williams'/David Frost's need for being in sight at all times (as if he's royalty on parade). Also, traveling with the Timmy Williams/David Frost entourage would seem to demand such a vehicle.

"chemist's"—("*If*—A Film by Mr. Dibley") Drugstores were the primary drop-off point for undeveloped film (including still film and 8mm and 16mm motion picture film), and is where Dibley's film was evidently being developed.

Coffee Time—("Timmy Williams Interview") The intimation now is that the entire "chance" encounter between Timmy and Nigel was all part of the Timmy Williams schedule of shows and events. In just a four-year period Frost himself appeared on *The David Frost Show* (1969), *Frost on Saturday* (1968), *Frost on Sunday* (1968), *David Frost Presents* (1967), *The Frost Programme* (1966), and *The Frost Report* (1966). He was also executive producer for *The Rise and Rise of Michael Rimmer* (1970), *The Ronnie Barker Playhouse* (1968), and *At Last the 1948 Show* (1967), and during the same period. He also appeared twice on *Rowan & Martin's Laugh-In* in 1968. It wouldn't be surprising if the Pythons' unflattering treatment of Frost didn't smack of at least a modicum of professional jealousy—Frost was, after all, the face of popular British TV at this time.

"Coleman, George"—("Timmy Williams Interview" credits) George Coleman (1935-) was an American saxophone player who appeared with the likes of Miles Davis and Herbie Hancock during the 1960s, and may have been known to Idle, who mingled in the popular London music scene.

Compère—("It's a Living") A TV host figure, usually sequined and brashy in *FC* episodes.

"complete with silly walk"—(link out of "Dead Indian") This photo Gilliam has chosen to manipulate for this silly walk moment is a Civil War photo, likely from the Union side.

(could they be soldiers?)—(PSC; "School Prize-Giving") This is an in-joke moment for the readers of the script only, and is probably just an example of the Pythons finding ways to make the writing and communicating process (between themselves and the production personnel for the show) more interesting. There are comments about boredom and tediousness peppered throughout the printed scripts, especially in relation to the repeated appearances of characters like the "It's Man," for example.

"council estate"—("Registry Office") Local municipal councils are responsible for planning and building homes for their citizens, and have included rowhouses, semi-detached homes, and even tower blocks (as in Birmingham).

– D –

Dead Indian—("Dead Indian") This Dead Indian appears to be played by Ian Davidson, who is noted as having appeared in (and been paid for) this episode in the BBC records (WAC T12/1,242).

"Dibley"—(*"If*—A Film by Mr. Dibley") "Gwen Dibley's Flying Circus" was a name floated early on as a possible title for the show, and was the name of the boys' school in Ep. 18, the *"Seven Brides for Seven Brothers"* sketch. The name allegedly came from an obituary. Versions of Dibley—including Dibbingley, Dibble, and even Richard Dimbleby—appear throughout the series. Dibley is not a terribly unusual name, however, appearing more than a dozen times in the 1968 edition of the Greater London area phone book (*British Phone Books*).

"Driffield"—("Election Night Special") Situated in the Yorkshire Wolds, east of York and north of Kingston upon Hull. This report originated at Harpenden, but somehow moved to the village of Driffield in the middle of the delivery.

In the 1964 General Election, nearby Bridlington remained Conservative, easily, and even gained a few percentage points in the 1970 election.

"due to the number of votes cast"—("Election Night Special") Said in jest, but at least partly true. With the voting age dropping to eighteen for the first time in a general election (thanks to the Representation of the People Act 1969), turnout dropped to the lowest rate since 1935, by percentage of possible votes. A larger turnout would have assured Labour the win, historians seem to agree (Clarke 318).

"Dulwich"—("Registry Office") A city in Greater London, Southwark, south of Westminster. In the 1970s, the once sleepy town where Dickens' and Wodehouse's characters could grow up and grow old had become a destination for the new rich, and probably more open to "special" marriages like the one depicted here. Conversely, ultra-conservative PM Margaret Thatcher bought a home there in one of the most upscale developments, Hambledon Place, Dulwich Common.

"dung"—("Dung") Interesting that it's with a third book order that dung is merited, which may be a comment on the Fowles' novel (though *French Lieutenant's Woman* was a very popular book, selling millions of copies).

There were dung delivery attempts being made right around this time, but they were from angry National Farmers' Union (NFU) farmers (demanding higher subsidies) delivering loads of offal to ministerial offices in London. *Evening News* cartoonist "Gus" depicted the protests in a cartoon on 21 March 1969. See the British Cartoon Archive.

– E –

"Elstree"—("Dead Indian") Elstree Studios is located in Elstree (and Borehamwood), Hertfordshire, and was a fixture in the British film industry for many years, producing, among many other titles, the *Star Wars* films.

"Emerson, Ralph"—("Timmy Williams Interview" credits) Ralph Waldo Emerson (1830-1882) was an American philosopher and poet. Emerson had significant contacts with Python favorites Coleridge, Wordsworth, and Carlyle. This reference also connects back to Dame Irene's Emersonesque (via John Oxenham) poem mentioned in the "Foreign Secretary" sketch.

"Eyes down"—("School Prize-Giving") A bingo term, meaning to look down at the card at the start of a game; here it could be meant more literally (and deviously), meaning attendees should look away as the "Chinaman" steals the school prizes. Bingo (or "Housey Housey") had swept through Britain in the postwar years, becoming a socially appropriate leisure activity for, especially, women (*Eyewitness: 1950-59*, "Popular Culture").

The appearance of Chinese references—all threatening—indicate that as of 1969 the first sweeping Cultural Revolution had come to an end, that Mao was at least nominally in control with his zealous young Red Guard (and People's Liberation Army) cadres causing civil chaos, and foes like Deng Xiaoping purged into ineffectiveness. The escalating border confrontations with the Soviets in 1968 and beyond had forced China's leadership to bury a few hatchets and take a more vocal, united approach to both foreign and domestic affairs, meaning the PRC would have been much more in the public eye during this period.

– F –

"faulty cooker"—("Dung") In Ep. 14, Mrs. Crump-Pinnet (Jones) is convinced that she can get the best gas company service if she's first overwhelmed by fumes—murdered—from a faulty cooker. The faulty cooker syndrome plagued Britain for years, with gas build-ups causing explosions or near-explosions in high rises (1968-1969), leading to the outlawing of gas cookers in such buildings. A David Langdon cartoon from the *Sunday Mirror* published 17 November 1968 depicts faulty gas cookers being tossed from a high rise and at a Gas Board lorry (British Cartoon Archive).

Finian's Rainbow—(*"Finian's Rainbow*—Starring the Man From the Off-Licence") A very late (1968) and somewhat clunky and self-conscious Warner Bros. musical (starring an aging Fred Astaire) directed by the very young Francis Ford Coppola as part of a multi-picture arrangement with WB-Seven Arts.

The "her" Mr. Dibley mentions as being essential to a quality film is the character Sharon McLonergan, played in the original film musical by Surrey-born Petula Clark (b. 1932). Clark is also mentioned in *FC* in Eps. 13 and 37.

"first result"—("Election Night Special") In the actual BBC coverage of the 1970 General Election, Cliff Michelmore, Robin Day, David Butler, and Robert McKenzie led the way. The location for these scenes appears to be the St. Mary's Wing of the Whittington Hospital, Highgate Hill, London N19, and were shot on the night of 15 September 1970 (WAC T12/1,242).

"Fitzjones, Brian"—("Timmy Williams Interview" credits) Brian Fitzjones contributed to the "television discussion program" *London: A New Look* (1960), including a filmed segment, according to the NFA Catalog at BFI.

"flog back"—("It's a Living") Slang, meaning the prize can be sold for cash rather than kept, probably avoiding the significant tax bite on the value of the item.

"Forbes Minor"—("School Prize-Giving") Based on the school reference ("Smith Major") in Ep. 18, it's likely this is a similar reference to the younger boy named Forbes enrolled in this "old school." Filmmaker Bryan Forbes will be mentioned later (Eps. 20, 36), and is also witheringly satirized in the pages of *Private Eye* (17 July 1970, page 5).

"Foreign Secretary"—(link out of *"Finian's Rainbow—Starring the Man From the Off-Licence"*) A Secretary of State, since 1945 this position has been responsible for foreign as opposed to domestic relations. In 1970, the Foreign Secretary was Sir Alec Douglas-Home (from 20 June, under Prime Minister Edward Heath). During this period, secret negotiations were under way for Britain's entry into the Common Market and the eventual adoption of the euro, the resumption of arms sales to South Africa and the controversial South African cricket team tour of the UK, as well as the escalating troubles in Northern Ireland, making the position of Foreign Secretary a significant flashpoint for controversy. Cabinet members Douglas-Home (known as "Baillie Vass" in the pages of *PE*) and "Reggie" Maudling were the lightning rods for the Opposition during this administration.

There seem to have been no attempts on the life of Britain's foreign secretary during this period, but there were several unsuccessful attempts made to assassinate King Hussein of Jordan by Palestine Liberation groups in 1970.

"Frankel, Dennis"—("Timmy Williams Interview" credits) Dennis Frankel appears in the period London phone books living at 1 Northwood Gardens N12 (*British Phone Books* 1159).

Frost, David—(PSC; "Timmy Williams Interview") The script mentions that this may slightly resemble David Frost, but Idle carries off a spot-on impersonation and even caricature of Frost, so much so that the studio audience reacts uproariously to the rather acid-toned spoof. The audience are clearly enjoying the jokes at Frost's expense as the sketch unfolds.

Frost was a one-time collaborator, then employer for several of the Pythons, especially on shows like *That Was the Week That Was*, and they'd been at least familiar since their Oxbridge days, when Frost managed to get a secretary job with the Footlights. His aggressive personality was apparent even then.

Just two years earlier (September 1968), The Beatles had also taken Frost down a notch or two as guests on his own show, *The Frost Programme*. As Frost tries to introduce the band and be convivial, Paul, George, and especially John ignore him, needle him, and fret with their instruments as Frost vamps nervously, struggling to regain control.

By mid-1970, *Private Eye* is calling him "the odious Frost OBE," pillorying Frost's stepping backward into fame and fortune at every turn (17 July 1970, page 4). Frost interviews "Lassie the Wonderdog" in this same *PE* issue.

"fully motorized pig"—(PSC; "Dead Indian") The printed script mentions that Gilliam is expected to create this insert. The motorized pig is reminiscent of the flying transport sheep in Ep. 2.

"Fyffe-Chulmleigh" ("School Prize-Giving") Chulmleigh is a small town found in Devon (where the Pythons shot significant location footage), while Fyffe Robertson was a presenter/reporter for *Tonight* on BBC. Robertson would work with other BBC types mentioned in *FC*, including Alan Whicker (Ep. 27) and Derek Hart (Ep. 17).

– G –

"gastroenteritis"—("Election Night Special") An inflammation of the intestinal tract that can exhibit itself in vomiting and diarrhea, which is certainly what Gerald (Cleese) is referring to when he mentions the "very messy" possibility spreading across the countryside. Palin's "auntie" (in Australia, by then) will be mentioned again in Ep. 31.

"German television"—("Timmy Williams Interview") Bavarian television officials also approached the Pythons about creating two shows, which eventually were written and recorded in German and English as *Der Fliegende Zirkus*.

"Gilbert, James"—("Election Night Special") Gilbert (b. 1923) was a producer and director, producing various shows that included Python members as writers, including *Idle at Work* (1972), *The Two Ronnies* (1971; director and producer), *The Frost Report* (1966), and *Not Only . . . But Also* (1965). He would become head of BBC Comedy in 1973, while the Pythons were still on the air. Gilbert also worked with Sydney Lotterby (from the "Timmy Williams Interview" credits list) on *Me Mammy* (1969-1971). Gilbert also won several BAFTA awards in the 1960s.

Gone . . . Woman—("Dung") *Gone With the Wind* was published in 1936 by Margaret Mitchell, and also garnered a Pulitzer prize; Hugo's *Les Miserables* was published in 1862; and *The French Lieutenant's Woman*, by John Fowles, was published in 1969. Of the three, the first two are admitted classics, while the third is the only one by a British author, and the most likely, being a contemporary novel, to be part of a Book of the Month Club listing. Also, however, the parodic structure of the Fowles novel, wherein a nineteenth-century plot and characters (and the novel itself) are examined in a very twentieth-century way, offers much in comparison to the Pythons' similar parodic re-examination of television and historical and political figures.

According to a 1943 *Time* article on the burgeoning Book-of-the-Month Club market, popular "Club authors include Pearl Buck, Sylvia Townsend Warner, Sinclair Lewis, Ernest Hemingway, [and] Willa Cather," not to mention that year's most popular author and book, William Saroyan's *The Human Comedy* (15 March 1943).

"Goschen, David"—("Timmy Williams Interview" credits) David Goschen is also "one of the gang" with and around Idle in 1970 London, then in 1972 established Florian Studios (in Saxmundham, Suffolk) to create decorative tiles.

"Gosse, Edmund"—("Timmy Williams Interview" credits) Gosse (1849-1928) was also an early Modernist poet (like Hovey, below) who worked as a librarian to the House of Lords, wrote academically on English poets Gray and Congreve, and for the *Sunday Times* (*ODNB*).

"Gowers, Michael"—("Timmy Williams Interview" credits) Michael Gowers was the TV critic for the *Daily Mail* during this period, and wrote and produced for ITV.

"Granville Cup"—("School Prize-Giving") There is a Granville Cup in which Bishop Vesey's Grammar School (Birmingham) participates.

gray suit and purple stock and dog collar—(PSC; "School Prize-Giving") According to the *OED*, a stock is "an article of clerical attire, consisting of a piece of black silk or stuff (worn on the chest and secured by a band round the neck) over which the linen collar is fastened." A "dog collar" is a colloquial, derisive term for a priest's neckwear. The Bishop's suit is actually dark blue or black, or perhaps charcoal gray. In short, the character is meant to portray the padre or headmaster (or both) of a public school, both figures seen earlier in Ep. 18, in the *"Seven Brides for Seven Brothers"* sketch.

"Grimwade Gynn"—("School Prize-Giving") Peter Grimwade (1942-1990) was a writer and director, working on *Z Cars*, and especially *Dr. Who*. The Pythons and *FC* shared extras and walk-ons with both of these shows, almost on a weekly basis, between 1969 and 1974.

"Gulf of Amman"—("Foreign Secretary") In 1969-1970, Egypt embarked upon a series of border conflicts with Israel, during which negotiations for a cease-fire were sought by British interests. Fighting in Amman, Jordan drew U.S. warships (for Israel) and Soviet tanks (for the PLO) into the region. The strife in the region was the subject of myriad op-ed pieces and political cartoons across the UK.

– H –

"Harpenden"—("Election Night Special") The Pythons give Harpenden to the Sensible Party by a single vote. The Hitchin & Harpenden electorate remained a Labour stronghold through the 1970 General Election, with Shirley Williams (Labour) garnering 48.53 percent, R. Luce (Conservative) at 44.18 percent, and the Liberal candidate, T. Willis, claiming 7.29 percent of the vote. Williams and Labour had earlier won the seat in 1964.

"Harris, Reg"—("Foreign Secretary") Reg Harris (1920-1992) was a world champion cyclist, Olympic medalist, and World Amateur Sprint Champion in 1949-1952 and 1954. He was also awarded an OBE and named Sportsman of the Year, and would have been the premier English cyclist during the Python's formative years.

"Haydon-Jones, Ann"—("Election Night Special") Ann was an English tennis player and has already been mentioned in Ep. 7, when the blancmanges played at Wimbledon. She was named UK Sportswoman of the Year in 1969. See notes to Ep. 7. Haydon-Jones will also be mentioned in Ep. 22.

"heap dizzy"—("Dung") Standard Hollywood Indian-speak from hundreds of serial and feature westerns, and used by the Pythons in Ep. 6, the "Red Indian in Theatre" sketch. The Dead Indian is played by Ian Davidson, though he's uncredited in the printed scripts. Davidson will also appear in Eps. 18, 20, and 26 during this series.

He is dragged down by an unseen hand—("School Prize-Giving") The appearance of the Mao-jacketed character (Chapman) indicates this is a send-up of the recent internal struggles in China as a result of Mao's Cultural Revolution. By 1967 Mao was publicly encouraging mid-level Party leaders and members (and even workers and military men) in the larger cities to regularly denounce counter-revolutionary activities and figures. The paranoia spread into the central leadership, with many embracing the CR as an opportunity to rid themselves of political enemies, since denouncement led to inevitable and quite often fatal purgings. The following years' struggle between Mao and Lin Biao (1907-1971)—where assassination attempts went both ways, each trying to supplant the other in the peoples' hearts and minds—only ended when, after a failed armed revolt, Lin died in a plane crash as he tried to flee the country.

The constant mention of Chinese political and military activity in international newspapers and newscasts probably accounts for the Pythons' seeming fixation on the subject. In larger UK newspapers there were, for instance, more than 200 political cartoons poking fun at the Chinese political situation published between 1967 and 1970 alone. See the British Cartoon Archive for more.

"held Leicester"—("Election Night Special") In the (18 June) 1970 British General Election, Conservatives took 330 seats to Labour's 288 (with six seats going to the Liberals and six to Others, including the Communist Party, Plaid Cymru, Scottish National Party, and the Republican Labour Party). The Scottish National Party scored its first General Election seat in 1970, a triumph of a fringe party obviously not lost on the Pythons.

In the Derby-Leicester area, for example, a higher-than-average swing vote to the Conservative side was achieved, with two seats—formerly held by Labour fixtures George Brown and Jennie Lee—going "Conservative for the first time at a general election since the war" (see Butler and Pinto-Duschinsky's *The British General Election of 1970*). This trend toward Conservatism (a 4.7 percent boost to Conservatives between 1966 and 1970 in by-election races) would certainly have alarmed the left-leaning Pythons, and would certainly have flavored this sketch as a result. This swing followed a 7.0 percent swing to Labour during the preceding inter-election years, 1959-1966. In fact, according to Butler and Pinto-Duschinsky, suburban and rural areas like those around Luton and Leicester were Conservative's strongest areas by 1970, where they regained many of the seats they'd recently lost.

"Herbert, George"—("Timmy Williams Interview" credits) Herbert (1593-1633) was a noted English poet, and a Trinity College, Cambridge graduate. Another George Herbert was a character name in H[erbert] G[eorge] Wells' *War of the Worlds* (1898), and yet another George Herbert financed Carter's King Tut archaeological digs between 1907 and 1922. Lastly (and most likely the source of this reference), George Herbert was a local British actor appearing in such memorable cult films as *The Secrets of Sex* (1970) and TV shows like *Boy Meets Girl* (1967). A number of extras appearing in *FC* also appeared in *Secrets of Sex*.

"He's not dead!"—("Dung") This exchange will be famously revisited in the feature film *HG*, in the "Plague Cart" scene.

"Holborn"—("Timmy Williams Interview") Just outside the City of London, near the British Museum. There were a number of very fashionable, Italian-type coffee shops in this area in the 1960s.

"hot up"—("Election Night Special") Variation of "heat up." The BBC broadcast of this particular (1970) election was also quite overheated, especially as the returns clarified the shocking turn-of-political-fortunes for the two major parties.

Noted BBC personalities covered the election—Cliff Michelmore, Robin Day (Ep. 2), Desmond Wilcox, Alf Garnett, David Butler, Alan Watson, and Bob McKenzie were in-studio as returns came in, while out among the constituencies were David Dimbleby (in Huyton), Michael Charlton (in Bexley), Keith Kyle (in Wolverhampton), Dennis Tuohy (in Guildford), and James Burke (Ep. 35) in Cheltenham. There were on-air BBC personnel reporting from many other cities, as well. Cutting back and forth between the studio, the graphics, and live shots made for a hectic night, especially as the swingometer registered the surprising results—a Conservative victory. Opinion polls had predicted a comfortable Labour win. (Ian Jones provides an enlightening play-by-play of that tumultuous evening at offthetelly.co.uk.)

Lastly, Michelmore at one point mentions that the races are "warming up" (Jones).

"Hovey, Richard"—("Timmy Williams Interview" credits) Richard Hovey (1864-1900) was an American Modernist poet and playwright. Hovey also wrote the Dartmouth Song "Men of Dartmouth," which connects him to another anthem-writer mentioned in this list, John Stamford (see below).

"how big a swing"—("Election Night Special") Election night commentator McKenzie (see entry for "swingometer") was during the broadcast guessing a

Conservative gain of about 6 percent, which was, technically, off the chart.

"Hughes, Geoffrey"—("Timmy Williams Interview" credits) Geoffrey Hughes (b. 1944) is an actor who contributed Paul's voice in the animated film *The Yellow Submarine* (1968), and appeared on the wildly popular *Coronation Street* for a decade. He also guest-starred on *Dad's Army*, *Doctor Who*, and *Up Pompeii* in the 1960s, and produced Frost's *The Frost Programme* (1966).

"Humperdinck, Engelbert"—("Election Night Special") British singer born Arnold George Dorsey in India, Humperdinck (played by Chapman) is identified as Ken Clean-Air Systems' (Cleese) manager in Ep. 18. Humperdinck was raised in Leicester (as was Chapman). *The Engelbert Humperdinck Show* appeared on British television in 1969.

– I –

"ICI"—("Foreign Secretary") ICI is "Imperial Chemical Industries," founded in 1926 to produce paints and specialty chemical products. ICI was considered a top company in Britain for many years.

"If"—("*If*—A Film by Mr. Dibley") Lindsay Anderson's 1968 film is correctly printed *If....*, and featured an assistant editor named Michael Ellis, whose name will figure prominently in Ep. 41, which is entitled "Michael Ellis." (All the episodes in the fourth and final series were given titles, and several were even monothematic.) The film starred Malcolm McDowell (b. 1943), and was deemed so controversial it was given an "X" rating in the United States.

"if . . . 2001 . . . Midnight Cowboy"—("*If*—A Film by Mr. Dibley") These three films form a significant portion of the core of "new wave" films emerging from the United States and UK in the late 1960s, some ten years after the advent of France's Nouvelle Vague. These would have been just the type of cutting-edge films that astute cinephiles like the Pythons (and their university and workplace pals) would have frequented in the many London-area cinemas offering international fare. Other foreign new wave films and filmmakers mentioned in *FC* include the Italian directors Visconti and Antonioni (Ep. 29), American Sam Peckinpah (Ep. 33), and they clearly satirize the films of Frenchman Jean-Luc Godard in the "French Subtitled Film" sketch (Ep. 23).

"I get so bloody bored"—("The Time on BBC 1") The BBC employed myriad announcers and linkmen to introduce shows, lay out programming for the evening, etc.—they were ubiquitous before the days of pre-

recorded sound bites. In Ep. 30, in the "Neurotic Announcers" sketch, the BBC announcer (Cleese) works through his confidence problems with the help of an announcer friend (Palin) and his wife (Cleveland), all on the air.

The reference to dullness and being "bloody bored" has already been broached in Ep. 6 with a look at "The Dull Life of a City Stockbroker"; in Ep. 7, when Sopwith (Idle) admits that camel spotting is "dull"; and Ep. 10, where the Chartered Accountant (Palin) wants to become a lion tamer because his work is "desperately dull and tedious and stuffy and boring." Philosophers referenced often by the Pythons in *Flying Circus*—including Schopenhauer and Heidegger (*FZ*), and especially Kierkegaard (Eps. 2 and 14)—all point to boredom in the Industrial Age as a particularly affecting malady. In Kierkegaard's "Crop Rotation" essay, boredom is the fundamental reason humans exist, and seems to define the world of the Pythons quite accurately:

> So all people are boring. The word itself indicates the possibility of a subdivision. "Boring" can describe a person who bores others as well as one who bores himself. Those who bore others are the plebeians, the mass, the endless train of humanity in general. Those who bore themselves are the elect, the nobility; and how strange it is that those who don't bore themselves usually bore others, while those who do bore themselves amuse others. The people who do not bore themselves are generally those who are busy in the world in one way or another, but that is just why they are the most boring, the most insufferable of all. . . . The other class of men, the select, are those who bore themselves. As remarked above, generally they amuse others, outwardly occasionally the mob, in a deeper sense their fellow initiates. The more profoundly they bore themsleves, the more powerful a means of diversion they offer others, when boredom reaches its zenith, either by dying of boredom (the passive form) or (the active form) by shooting themselves out of curiosity. (*Either/Or* 230)

It is for this reason—the ineluctable boredom of modern life—that characters like the Waiter (Jones) in Ep. 13 can (or must) go off and commit suicide, but "not because of anything serious." Clearly, the "busy in the world" people defined as "most insufferable" by Kierkegaard are the chartered accountants and city stockbrokers and City Gents that populate the Python world, and they end up killing themselves not out of curiosity (see the Upperclass Twits in Ep. 12), but because they are too addled to do anything else. However they die, though, it's a blessing.

For his part Heidegger would write: "For if life, in the desire for which our essence and existence consists, possessed in itself a positive value and real content, there would be no such thing as boredom: mere existence would fulfill and satisfy us" (from *What is Metaphysics?* [1929]). Well, in the twentieth century—and especially in the Python world where "positive value and real content" are replaced with a postmodern pastiche of nostalgia and cultural malaise and television-encouraged consumerism—the simple joy of "mere existence" is *not* enough, and the Python character (and narrative) tends to be adaptive and elusive, to become and become and become, constantly undercutting and reinventing itself.

ignore him—(PSC; "Foreign Secretary") Again, absurdities playing out for the audience while most of the characters miss them entirely, or treat them as matter-of-fact.

"impostor"—("School Prize-Giving") Ep. 43 will feature several impostor psychiatrists, each seeking sexual details from Hamlet (Jones) about his relationship with Ophelia.

"interesting undergarments"—(link out of "Dead Indian") This is a fin-de-siècle advertisement page for "Madame Dowding" corsets. Madame Dowding's was located at 17 Charing Cross Road.

"interrupt"—("Interruption" links out of "The Time on BBC1") This series of interruptions is a jab at the characteristic interruptions of programming by BBC announcers and the like, which also happens in Ep. 7, where the constable (Chapman) interrupts the sci-fi sketch to reassure viewers at home. These narrative interruptions emerge often in *FC*, including the Major (Chapman) interrupting and prodding the show in different directions in Ep. 8, and the city of North Malden and two Pepperpots (Chapman and Cleese) repeatedly interrupting "Njorl's Saga" in Ep. 27. The sanctity of the fictional televised world is one of the medium's pillars, and one that the Pythons undercut on a regular basis.

"in toto"—("It's a Living") Latin phrase indicating totality, completeness.

"Israeli embassy"—("Timmy Williams Interview") As part of *The David Frost Show*, Frost had already interviewed many noteworthy world leaders, including Israeli PM Golda Meir and Defense Minister Moshe Dayan (both July 1969).

It's a Living—("It's a Living") Reminiscent of many show titles from British television over the years (*It's a Knockout*; *It's a Square World*; and *Yes, It's the Cathode-Ray Tube Show!*), and is often satirized on *FC*, including several *It's the Arts* programs. The "It's Man" (Palin) himself was created by the Pythons to represent the hoary chestnuts of such show names and obvious links (he's haggard, frayed, and worn out).

"I want to marry you too sir"—("Registry Office") The comic misunderstanding used so often in Python, and which is earlier seen in Shakespeare, Dekker, and Jonson (see *MPSERD*), where, in this case, the literality of one character almost renders impossible successful communication. Another noted English stage comedy team, Gilbert and Sullivan (mentioned earlier in Ep. 16), fell into this music hall prattle, as well, including the following exchange in *The Pirates of Penzance* (1879):

> General: I ask you, have you ever known what it is to be an orphan?
> King: Often!
> General: Yes, orphan. Have you ever known what it is to be one?
> King: I say, often.
> Pirates: Often, often, often. (Act I)

– J –

"Jones, Alan"—("Election Night Special") A well-known Welsh cricketer, Jones scored more than 40,000 runs for Glamorgan between 1957 and 1983. England's selectors overlooked him for the series until 1970, which may account for Python's inclusion of his name in this sketch.

– K –

"Kerr, Malcolm"—("Timmy Williams Interview" credits) A noted Islamic student and scholar of the period, expatriate-American Kerr could have been known to the Pythons for several reasons. His wife attended Occidental College, where Gilliam had also been a student. Kerr would also later take a post-doctoral position at Oxford. Kerr's publications centered on the Arab political situation (having been raised in Beirut), and may account for Python's recurring use of the Arab motif in this episode.

"Kubrick, Stanley"—("If—A Film by Mr. Dibley") Kubrick (1928-1999) was an American expatriate director who spent most of his career in the UK. Kubrick's first UK-based film was *Lolita* (1962). Like *If. . . .*, Kubrick's *2001: A Space Odyssey* also came out in 1968, though to significant audience puzzlement, then cult and critical acclaim, before finding its honored place in film history.

– L –

Late Night Line-Up—("It's a Living") *Late Night Line-Up* debuted in 1964 as simply *Line-Up*, then in September

1964 became *Late Night Line-Up*, and ran through 1972. The show offered "slots for films, books, jazz, folk and progressive rock music," according to *British Television* (Oxford, 1996). The original cast included Dennis Tuohy, Michael Dean, Nicholas Tresilian, and Joan Bakewell. Terry Jones contributed material to the show in the mid-1960s.

The day after the final episode in the second series (Ep. 26) was broadcast, 23 December 1970, the "TV Weekly Programme Review" team met at Television Centre to perform its regular post-mortem on the week's broadcast. Bill Cotton (Head of Light Entertainment) complained that the Pythons' unscheduled (or just unannounced) appearance on *Late Night Line-Up* in December had just exacerbated concerns about the vulgarity of the later *FC* episodes (WAC T47/216). See notes to Ep. 26 for more.

"Latin Elegaics"—("School Prize-Giving") Misspelling of "elegiac." These are (often structural, as in coupleted) elegies written in Latin, and covering a wide range of subjects. A well-known English elegy is Thomas Gray's "Elegy Written in a Country Churchyard." Gray dwelt at Cambridge for several years, though not as either a student or professor.

Latin elegists include Tibullus, Catullus, Sulpicia, and Ovid. For a later reference to the Pythons' more Ovidian approach to sensuality, see notes to Ep. 36.

"Leicester . . . Luton"—("Election Night Special") Leicester (Chapman's birthplace) is a northern city by geography, lying northeast of Birmingham in Leicestershire. Tom Boardman was elected MP for Leicester SW at a by-election in 1967. Luton is a borough in Bedfordshire. Luton figures prominently in many *FC* episodes, but especially as the hiding place for Spiny Norman, Doug Dinsdale's enormous imaginary tormentor. Dinsdale eventually explodes a nuclear device at the Luton Airport (Ep. 14).

In the 1970 General Election, Luton and all districts of Leicester turned out more than 70 percent of their constituencies. Luton-area MPs in 1970 included Sir D. Madel (for then-South Bedfordshire). Will Howie (Labour) lost his seat in Luton in 1970, held since 1963. Luton East went to Labour (from Conservative) in the following 1974 General Election.

Lastly, Lord Hill, head of the BBC (1967-1972) during much of the Pythons' tenure there, was also from Luton.

"Lord Mayor, Lady Mayoress"—("School Prize-Giving") The Lord Mayor is played by Evan Ross, while the Lady Mayoress is played by Eddy May Scrandrett (WAC T12/1,242).

"Lotterby, Sydney"—("Timmy Williams Interview" credits) Lotterby (b. 1926) is a British producer and comedy director, who by the time of this episode's writing had created *Up Pompeii* (1970) and *The Liver Birds* (1969). Lotterby was living at 55 Watchfield Ct., Sutton Court Road, Hounslow during this period (*British Phone Book* 2129).

"Luton Town Hall"—("Election Results") These night shots of the silly election results were all shot on the night of 12 May 1970, which would have made for a very long day. Also shot that day were the scenes for the All Blacks football match for the "Derby Council vs. All Blacks Rugby Match" sketch for Ep. 23. The following day portions of the "French Subtitled Film" sketch were shot, as was the soccer match between the gynecologists and Long John Silvers, all in the Torquay area. They also shot at Anstey Cove for Ep. 25 footage (see notes to that episode for more). They would keep shooting in the area until at least 22 May 1970, then take a week or so off before resuming the more local location work back in Ealing on 1 June (WAC T12/1,416).

"Luxury Yacht, Raymond"—("Raymond Luxury Yacht") This character also appears in Ep. 22, where, instead of being a "leading skin specialist," he is seeking plastic surgery for his oversized false nose. The "false nose" bit will reappear in the feature film *HG*, when a medieval village mob puts a false nose on a woman (Connie Booth) to make her look like a witch.

"Lynn, Johnny"—("Timmy Williams Interview" credits) Jonathan Lynn, a Cambridge alum, contributed to the *Stuff What Dreams Are Made Of* writing at the Cambridge Footlights in 1964, during Idle's time there.

– M –

"Mail"—("Timmy Williams Interview") Refers to the *Daily Mail* newspaper, a conservative tabloid often termed the "*Daily Hate Mail*" by *Private Eye*, and one the *PE* editors take to task for:

> its slavish adherence to every tiny fluctuation in the Conservative Party line, its progression of vacillating editors, its third-rate staff and fourth-hand ideas . . . all contributed to what is undoubtedly the dullest and most amateurish product that Fleet Street has ever known (barring only the *Daily Sketch* and the *Evening News*). Nothing can be served by prolonging the grisly farce of the *Mail*'s continued existence any longer. (Ingrams 285)

man—("Timmy Williams Interview") This "Man," as he's referred to in the printed script, is David Ballantyne, who also appears in Eps. 13, 14, and 17 in this series. At one point he's paid £42 for his scheduled appearances (BBC WAC T12/1,094).

"Mangrove"—("Raymond Luxury Yacht") Though an unusual name, Mangrove is not completely made up. Graham Chapman writes of a young man he knew named Buzz Mangrove, who was a junior warden with passkeys to residence halls in London, where young medical students could billet (McCabe 92). There are no surviving phone records indicating that a "Mangrove" (using this spelling) actually lived in the Greater London area, however. There was also a restaurant in the Kensington area at 8 All Saints Road, W11, during this period called "Mangrove Restaurant."

Mao jacket and cap—(PSC; "School Prize-Giving") The plain "uniform" worn by Chairman Mao Tse-Tung (1893-1976), at this time the (ailing) leader of the People's Republic of China, and standard wear for Chinese men (and many women) during Mao's tenure. This character is also wearing the white "dog collar" under his Mao tunic, probably to indicate that he's purporting to be the Bishop of East Anglia.

In Ep. 30, a Chinese man (Chapman) will portray the English ambassador to Russia, complete with pidgin English and an overstated knowledge of the Cornish countryside and English leisure customs.

"Marwood, Reginald"—("Timmy Williams Interview" credits) Reginald Francis Cheese was John Cleese's father, who would change the family name to "Cleese," while John's middle name was "Marwood."

"Massinger, Thomas"—("Timmy Williams Interview" credits) This name could be an accidental conflation of the Jacobean playwrights and writing partners, Thomas Dekker (or Thomas Middleton) and Phillip Massinger.

"Matherson, Ian"—("Timmy Williams Interview" credits) There was an Ian Matheson living in Hounslow during this period, at 20 Northcote Avenue, W5 (*British Phone Book* 345).

"M4 motorway"—("Dead Indian") The M4 stretches some 200 miles from London to Wales, and was fairly new at this period. The section of whatever roadway they've chosen for this scene seems to be near completion but not yet open. Construction on the actual M4 was under way in this period.

"Milk Marketing Board"—("Dung") MMBs are regional controlling entities for the selling of milk products in the UK, and they were originally created in the early years of the Great Depression. Many MMBs have since been disbanded, allowing for competition in the milk production and distribution industries in the UK. "Single cream" is cream with a manipulated low fat content.

"Millichope, Ray"—("Foreign Secretary") Millichope was the film editor for *FC*, as well as *Not Only . . . But Also* and *The Two Ronnies*.

Mix through—(PSC; link into "If—A Film by Mr. Dibley") Television term for moving from one shot to another, in this case involving a cut from the live color film to a TV-produced filmed image of the same battle scene.

Muted music and sophisticated lighting—("Dung") Actually, the lighting looks as even and featureless as ever—the Pythons quipped about the lack of lighting control in their studio space as early as Ep. 9, in "The Visitors" sketch. (The Pythons tended to share sound-stage space with news and game shows, meaning the installed lighting packages in these stages were only minimally manipulable.)

As for the muted music, the background music seems to be "Late Night" by Roger Webb (WAC T12/1,434).

Muted trumpet plays a corny segue—(School Prize-Giving") This snippet of badly played music is "Comic Bugle Call" by Alan Langford (WAC T12/1,434).

– N –

"Nabarro"—(PSC; link into "School Prize-Giving") The character portrayed by Chapman is called "Nabarro" in the printed script. Sir Gerald Nabarro was a South Worcestershire MP until his death in 1973. Nabarro is also mentioned prominently in Ep. 23, where he is noted for having a pet prawn called Simon, and Ep. 21, by name only. Nabarro was one of the old Conservatives that the Pythons and the Left loved to hate, and he appeared on the cover of the satirical journal *Private Eye* on 14 February 1969.

A prominent and often lightning rod politician, Nabarro tweaked the nose of the government—including his own party—more than once (e.g., the Motor Tax issue mentioned in Ep. 10). Nabarro is mentioned more than 200 times in political cartoons in UK newspapers between 1968 and 1974, and he would have been quite recognizable to *FC* thanks to his impressive trademark mustache.

"Negus, Arthur"—("Election Night Special") Negus (1903-1985) was an antiques expert and a broadcaster. He came to BBC television in 1966 on *Going for a Song*, where he valued antiques for an audience. Negus won the Sir Ambrose Fleming Memorial Award in 1967 for service to television in the Bristol area (see entry for "Bristols" above for more), where he may have come to the young Cleese's attention. Negus will be mentioned again in Ep. 21, in the *"Archaeology Today"* sketch.

"new cooker"—("Dung") This harks back to the "New Cooker Sketch" from Ep. 14, though there Mrs. Crump-Pinnet (Jones) doesn't get the free dead Indian. This man (Chapman) is wearing the same uniform that Cleese wore as the East Midlands Poet Board man in Ep. 17.

"New Haven . . . Continent"—("Foreign Secretary") Crossing point for tourists over the English Channel to France.

"Nigel"—("Timmy Williams") John Cleese would sometimes write under the pseudonym Nigel Farquhar-Bennett, while Terry Jones' older brother is Nigel Jones (Ep. 27).

No reaction . . . guests—("School Prize-Giving") Again, this non-reaction is a moment in the Python world where characters ignore completely the outlandish goings-on, just adding to the absurdity of the scene.

The Mayor is played by Evan Ross (*Emma*; *Dad's Army*), and the Mayoress by Eddy May Scrandrett (Ep. 17); others at the table include Peggy Scrimshaw (*Yes, Honestly*), Hazel Cave (*Upstairs, Downstairs*), Brian Gardner (Ep. 17; *The Fabulous Frump*), Tom O'Leary (Ep. 17), Michael Stayner (Eps. 17-18; *Billion Dollar Brain*) and Bill Leonard (Eps. 17-18). The soldiers are played by Gordon Winter and David Melbourne (*Softly Softly*; *Z Cars*). The row of boys watching the awards (not mentioned at all in the printed script) include Robert Toller, Brian Ball, Garry O'Brien, David Docherty, Nigel Grice (*Oliver!*), and Keith Dewhurst (*Z Cars*) (WAC T12/1,242). The boys' parents (mothers, primarily) are noted as being on the set, as well, during filming.

"Nought"—("Election Night Special") The forty-seven parties standing candidates for the 1970 General Election each received some votes, though at least eighteen scored a statistical nil (0.00 percent) of the total vote, with six more registering just 0.01 percent each. Peele University figures indicate that 408 candidates forfeited their £150 deposits in 1970, failing to garner the requisite minimum votes. The Anti-Abortion Party received the fewest votes, claiming just 103. The Liberal Party lost many of the seats (7 of 13) won in the by-election years. Welsh and Scottish nationalists also fared very poorly in 1970, and the Communists were only able to claim 1.2 percent of the vote (see Peele; Butler and Pinto-Duschinsky).

The "lost deposit" embarrassment will be revisited in Ep. 45, where the Liberal Party candidates (the Pythons themselves) will, in the closing credits, all forfeit their deposits.

– O –

"off-licence"—("If—A Film by Mr. Dibley") A licensed liquor store in the UK that sells alcohol for consumption off the premises (as opposed to a pub or tavern).

"old school"—("School Prize-Giving") For the schools attended by the Pythons, see notes to Ep. 13. This "Nabarro" fellow is obviously referring to a public (fee paying) school, where Britain's elite are trained. Most of these schools keep and promote lists of celebrated graduates, and do invite those grads back for these annual award-giving ceremonies.

ordinary interview set—("Raymond Luxury Yacht Interview") The music beneath this transition is Gerry Mulligan's "Jeru" (WAC T12/1,434).

– P –

"Pennycate, John"—("Timmy Williams Interview" credits) His last name actually spelled "Penycate," John Penycate (b. 1943) is a BBC reporter and producer who began as a researcher for *The Frost Programme*.

"people have drawn comparisons between your film"—("If—A Film by Mr. Dibley") During the 1960s, AIP (American International Pictures) kept up a steady stream of very low budget and often salacious knock-off films, including *Angel Unchained* (1970), which drew its inspiration from Kurosawa's *Seven Samurai* (1954), and *Strawberries Need Rain* (1970) from Ingmar Bergman's *Seventh Seal* (1957).

"phone to America"—("Timmy Williams Interview") The awful Garibaldi family will also be making a deal with American film/TV people in Ep. 45, and American film producers make a trans-Atlantic call to the idiots' banker (Chapman) in Ep. 20. Clearly there is an equating here of moronic, self-absorbed behavior with American entertainment, as well as a new level of success if the lucrative American market can be broached. Many British musicians and performers, including Cliff Richard, Frankie Howerd, and The Beatles set their sights on success in the States—and only The Beatles managed to accomplish this success.

Frost himself had been commuting (often on the Concorde, no less) between New York and London since 1963 when his *TW3* produced a very popular tribute to John F. Kennedy, and he became a known face in America. The American version of *TW3* increased that high profile, and subsequent interview shows with President Richard Nixon, for example, elevated Frost to international celebrity status. One of the concerns voiced by many who knew him during this period was that he tried to be everywhere, do everything, and have some kind of relationship with everyone in the world of television in both the UK and United States (see Morgan's *Speaks!*, as well as the introduction to Ingrams' *The Life and Times of* Private Eye for more).

"Picksley, Frank"—("Timmy Williams Interview" credits) Frank Pixley (1867-1921) was, like Hattie Starr below, an early American composer. Pixley had co-written *King Dido*, a musical comedy that premiered in 1902. Pixley was also a member of the Royal Geographical Society in London. The misspelling (of his name, albeit phonetically) is characteristic of the show, where faulty memorial misspellings occurred in original material submitted to the graphics department as well as subsequent mistakes on the title cards.

"polling's been quite heavy"—("Election Night Special") Voter turnout in the 1970 General Election reached almost 72 percent, down about 3 percent from the 1966 General Election.

"polystyrene"—("Raymond Luxury Yacht") Most of the props used in *FC*, and especially the larger ones (the sixteen-ton weight, for example) are made from polystyrene, according to the requisitions and constructions forms extant in the WAC collection for the show.

"Portman, Lord"—("Foreign Secretary") Character in Anna Austen Lefroy's book, and mentioned by Jane Austen in 1814 letters to Anna concerning suggestions for editorial work on the manuscript.

In life, the actual Lords Portman had been members of the peerage since Henry VIII's time, with Edward Henry Berkeley Portman, ninth Viscount Portman occupying the title in 1969-1970. The Lords Portman would have been peers in the House of Lords, having less political power than their elected counterparts at this time (and significantly less today).

"pyramid"—("Foreign Secretary") According to WAC repeat fee records, these three performers are Terry Williams, Colin Skeaping (stuntman, *Star Wars*), and Bunny Saunders. The script calls for each to be wearing shorts, but they are clearly dressed in business attire, which adds to the incongruity.

– **R** –

"Raymond, Paul"—("Timmy Williams Interview" credits) Paul Raymond (b. 1925) was a publisher of erotic magazines and producer of "nudie" revues, the latter (Raymond called it "Vaudeville Express") of a type Idle describes in his biography section of *The Pythons* (McCabe). Raymond also produced the theatrical show "Pyjama Tops"—a live, all-nude farce—in the Whitehall Theatre, the marquee for which can be glimpsed in the "Ministry of Silly Walks" sketch (street scene) in Ep. 14.

Rear Window—("*If*—A Film by Mr. Dibley") Feature film directed by Hitchcock in 1954 and starring James Stewart and Grace Kelly. Incidentally, Hitchcock's last "silent" film was *Blackmail* (1929), which was initially shot as a silent, then partially reshot and dubbed for sound release.

"repeat fee"—("*It's a Living*") Fees generated for the actors whenever the episodes are rebroadcast. By February 1971, the Pythons were commanding £80 per BBC repeat. Many of the memos and letters surviving in WAC records discuss repeat schedules and fees, and careful cast lists were compiled by the BBC primarily to make sure repeat fees were distributed properly.

"Report on Industrial Reorganization"—("Foreign Secretary") In 1969 a number of "white paper" proposals were being considered for the formation of an Industrial Reorganization Corporation during the Harold Wilson Labour administration. The 1969 white paper "In Place of Strife: A Policy for Industrial Relations" created by Employment and Productivity Secretary Barbara Castle for the Labour government called for strict controls of unions (the bane of Wilson's existence during this period), but never did become law. Castle and Wilson were demonized by union leaders for this attempt at big labor control.

With the passage of the Monopolies and Mergers Act of 1965 there was also much public focus and discussion on/of any industrial reorganization that involved two or more UK companies, especially if gross assets of the target company exceeded £5 million or a monopoly (approximately one-third control of a market) could emerge from the union (Pickering 123).

"result for Leicester"—("Election Night Special") There were four Leicester voting districts in the 1970 General Election, with Labour taking two and the Conservatives taking the other two. Both parties held their seats. The fringe parties Anti-Immigration, National Democrat, and National Front all registered votes in Leicester, with Anti-Immigration leading the way at 5.25 percent (Keele).

"Returning Officer"—("Election Night Special") This official conducts the various elections and reports the results (*OED*).

ripple effect—(PSC; "Interruption" link into "School Prize-Giving") An electronic transitional tool in television production—a dissolve, actually—where under a "rippling" transitional effect the scene "dissolves" from the Nabarro character shot to the shot of the boy playing the trumpet.

"rumourlette"—("Timmy Williams Interview") This appears to be a word created here by/for Timmy Williams, and characteristic of the way "Frostie" himself talked.

– S –

Samurai warrior—("Foreign Secretary") The samurai class were Japanese feudal warriors attached to great lords and houses in ancient Japan. The proliferation of internationally known Japanese films featuring samurai—including *Yojimbo* and *Sanjuro* (Kurosawa, 1961 and 1962), *The Loyal 47 Ronin* (Inagaki, 1962), and *Seppuku* (Kobayashi, 1962)—would have firmly planted this figure in the public's consciousness. The continuing references to international film and art movements and figures throughout *FC* attests to the Pythons' awareness of these foreign filmmakers (see Eps. 23 and 29 for more on current, referenced French and Italian filmmakers).

"Savage, Richard"—("Timmy Williams Interview" credits) There are two Englishmen of note who could have been on the Pythons' minds. Richard Savage, the eighteenth-century poet discussed by Dr. Johnson in his *The Lives of the English Poets*, and who was the author of *The Wanderer* (1729) and *The Bastard* (1728). The other, more contemporary Richard Savage wrote the novel *Stranger's Meeting* in the late 1950s, which was made into a 1958 film.

"Schlesinger, John"—("*If*—A Film by Mr. Dibley") British filmmaker Schlesinger (1926-2003) directed one of the quintessentially American films of the late 1960s, *Midnight Cowboy* (1969). In the film, Ratso Rizzo was played by Dustin Hoffman (b. 1937).

"semitic"—("Raymond Luxury Yacht") Characteristic of a Semite, or Python's shorthand way of identifying a "Jewish-type" nose, a "hooknose." The only other script-identified "Jewish" character appears for a moment in Ep. 7. His only identifying trait was the spoken inflected upswing—Yiddish-like—at the end of his sentence. There are also several references to "kosher" car parks, a phrase that also can be heard in *The Goon Show*. In Ep. 37, there is an unmentioned but visual reference to Jewishness, when the "Chairman of the Amalgamated Money TV, Sir Abe Sappenheim" (Chapman) is depicted with a larger-than-normal nose.

"sensible constituency"—("Election Night Special") Luton (home to Lord Hill, the Pythons' boss) was a narrow Conservative gain in 1970, with C. Simeons taking 50.99 percent of the vote, followed by the Labour candidate W. Howie (48.04 percent) and Communist candidate A. Chater (0.98 percent).

"Shand, Neil"—("Timmy Williams Interview" credits) Shand was a writer for various BBC shows, including Spike Milligan's *Q5* (1969), and *The World of Beachcomber* (1968).

"Shaw, Joe"—("Timmy Williams Interview" credits) Shaw (b. 1928) was a star defender for Sheffield United between 1948 and 1966—through all of Palin's (a Sheffield native) formative early life.

"silly"—("Election Night Special") Used here in the northern (or Scottish) sense, since Leicester is the setting, which would mean a person "deserving of pity, compassion, or sympathy," and one who is "weakly, feeble, sickly, ailing."

The sheer number of parties eligible to participate in elections in the UK during this period merits the "silly" appellation. In 1970, votes were registered for at least forty-seven separate parties, including the well-known major parties, as well as these smaller vote-getters (some with platform definitions, where necessary): Anti-War, Anti-Common Market, Anti-Election, Anti-Immigration, Anti-Labour, Anti-Party, Anti-War Radical, Unity (Irish nationalists), Independent, Communist, Protestant Unionist (Northern Ireland unionists), Republican Labour, Independent Labour, Independent Conservative, Democratic, National Democratic (right-wing extremist), National Front (extremist, anti-immigration), National Democrats, Vectis National (seeking Isle of Wight freedoms), Independent Liberal, World Government, Mebyon Kernow (seeking Cornwall freedoms), British Movement (British neo-Nazi), Independent Progressive, Socialist Party (Marxist), Young Ideas, Ratepayers, and British Commonwealth. (Peele University maintains a complete record of the General Elections results in the UK.)

"silver cup"—("School Prize-Giving") Representative of the various trophies and other awards given by public schools in England, including, for example, the Gold Duke of Edinburgh Award at the Bromsgrove Upper School, as well as the Tony Limbert Trophy, Paul Sawtell Trophy, Ben Showell Memorial Rose Bowl, and various Headmaster prizes also given at Bromsgrove and similar schools. The schools the Pythons attended would have had their own prizes to be annually awarded. Palin's school, Shrewsbury, for example, offers multiple academic and related scholarship awards for its third and sixth form students.

"skinhead"—("Dead Indian") Youth gang members characterized by heavy boots and workingman's clothing, the skinheads were known to cause significant troubles during this period, especially in poorer neighborhoods and at sporting events (*OED*). Aggressive youths do appear in *FC*, including leather-wearing "Teddys" (Ep. 8), but never a skinhead, perhaps because the movement was (a) fairly new at the time and (b) the Pythons were too old to have gone through the skinhead phase themselves.

The skinhead phenomenon had been profiled in the 3 September 1969 issue of the *Daily Mirror*, and appeared as subject in more than a dozen political cartoons in major UK newspapers in 1969-1970. (Many of the cartoons, incidentally, were comparing the Conservative government to the violent, bovver-booted skinheads.) See the British Cartoon Archive.

"Smith, Arthur J."—("Election Night Special") The Sensible Party candidate and his agent both wear a green rosette (ribbon). The Silly Party candidates wear yellow rosettes. Indicating party affiliation, red rosettes have been worn by Labour candidates, and blue by Conservative. The rosettes can be as elaborate as the candidate desires.

"Smith, Sidney"—("Timmy Williams Interview" credits) Probably meant to be "Sydney Smith," a well known cricketer. Smith (1881-1963) was born in Trinidad but would eventually play in England, notably for Northamptonshire, and be named as a Wisden Cricketer of the Year in 1915. The Pythons will exhibit a fan(atic)'s knowledge of English cricket and cricketers throughout the series. Northamptonshire borders Leicestershire, home to Chapman.

"Smith, Simon"—("Timmy Williams Interview" credits) Simon Smith was a barrister in London, his office located in the Queen Elizabeth Building, Temple EC4 (*British Phone Books* 3157).

"Snowdon"—("Timmy Williams Interview") Lord Snowdon (Antony Armstrong Jones, b. 1930) was a respected portrait photographer in the 1950s, creating portraits of the royal family before marrying the Queen's sister, Princess Margaret in 1960. A 1970 *Time* magazine article notes that Snowdon was well known for his own "wicked" impersonation of David Frost (6 July 1970).

Armstrong-Jones attended Jesus College at Cambridge, where he studied architecture, while Frost attended Caius College, Cambridge.

"Something Silly's Going to Happen"—("Foreign Secretary") This title heralds the now-expected Python version of the "set-up and payoff" comic formula, where the mundane and normal quickly turns absurd. The Pythonesque undercutting of traditional humor structures would eventually need to be undercut if the Pythons were to continue exploring their medium. (The subversive, tradition-usurping Modern Art movements active since the turn of the century suffered from similar demands for the "new and fresh"—creating the need for perpetual turnover, constant renewal, perpetual undercutting.) This consistent need for change and reevaluation would send Cleese shopping for something new as early as the second series. See Morgan's *Speaks!*.

"Special Branch Speech Day Squad"—("School Prize-Giving") There will be a special branch investigating foreign film directors in a later episode (Ep. 29). The "Special Branch" section of the Criminal Investigation Department (CID) is generally involved with political security.

In UK public schools, "Speech Day" is the day at the end of the school year when prizes (and commencement speeches) are given. The influence of Lindsay Anderson's 1968 film *If. . . .* is already apparent by this point. See notes for *If. . . .* above.

"Spike"—("Election Night Special") Spike Milligan (1918-2002), the comedic idol of the Pythons, seems to have been watching during this evening's taping somewhere off-camera. Milligan will later appear with the Pythons in the feature film *Life of Brian* (1979).

"Spoon"—("School Prize-Giving") Perhaps an ironic award, since at Cambridge it was the student who performed worst in math who was awarded a wooden spoon, and later any academic or sport contestant/team could be eligible for such an honor. The sometimes very large spoons were last officially awarded in the early twentieth century, but live on unofficially at the Oxbridge schools and in public life (and are especially favored by UK consumer affairs gadflies).

At Cambridge, for example, "Sir William Browne's Medals" are awarded annually for best Greek Ode and Greek Elegy, Latin Ode and Latin Elegy, Greek Epigram and Latin Epigram; the "Montagu Butler Prize" goes to the best Latin Hexameter Verse; and there are also dissertation and translation prizes for Greek and Latin subjects.

"Spot, The"—(animated link into "Election Night Special") Subject of one of the few real censorial dilemmas faced by *Flying Circus*, this animated cancer spot originally narrated by Carol Cleveland was ordered changed by BBC higher-ups so as not to offend or disturb cancer patients, victims, and their families. Instead of dying of "cancer," the young prince pictured dies of "gangrene." The new word was dubbed, and badly, by someone—and with a male voice, to boot—other than the Pythons, perhaps John Howard Davies or Ian MacNaughton.

In Hogarth's *Marriage a la Mode* (1743), "The Inspection," both central figures bear prominent black spots, both suffering from sexually transmitted diseases. In the painting (displayed in the National Gallery since 1824) the afflicted are being treated by a quack healer. Hogarth significantly paved the way for the Pythons, examining theatrical convention and the joy and misery of everyday life in his work, satirizing the French and Catholicism, and displaying a fascination with London's low and prurient lifestyles and neighborhoods.

"Stamford, John"—("Timmy Williams Interview" credits) John Stamford was the editor and founder of the *Spartacus International Gay Guide*, a gay travel guide, which began publishing in 1970.

"Starr, Hatty"—("Timmy Williams Interview" credits) Hattie Starr was a Tin Pan Alley singer and songwriter in the 1890s, and later a Theodore Dreiser character from the novel *Titan* (1914), where she was "plain Hattie Starr, the keeper of a more or less secret house of ill repute" (chapter 40). See the entry for "Frank Picksley" for more.

"Stoat, Dame Irene"—("Foreign Secretary") This may be an oblique reference to Dame Irene Ward (1895-1980), a Pepperpot-type Conservative politician representing the Tyne and Wear area in the 1940s and into the 1970s, serving thirty-eight years. Not a noted poet, there is a collection of her own poems included in her manuscripts and papers held at the Bodleian Library at Oxford.

The lowly stoat continues to be a favorite in the Python bestiary, and will be mentioned again in the very long name of the Very Silly candidate in the "Election Night Special" sketch later.

"Stop-Press"—(link out of "Dead Indian") A printing term. A "stop press" in the printing run of a newspaper is an interruption in the run for the insertion of last-minute material. The presses had to actually be stopped, the material inserted, then the presses were restarted. Usually, this meant that the papers that had already been printed would have been destroyed.

"straight fight"—("Election Night Special") A "straight fight" is an election where there are just two candidates vying for the office. This happened somewhat rarely during this period in the UK, though there were many races where the fringe candidates lost their deposits by polling well below the minimum percentage.

"Super, super!"—("Timmy Williams Interview") Apart from being just an admitted Frostian characteristic, this repetitive phraseology can be found in a number of British period films, including Jack Clayton's "Angry Young Man" film *Room at the Top* (1959), where it's used quite sardonically.

swingometer—("Election Night Special") An actual BBC device used during the 1970 election broadcast, it had to be "extended" to account for the unexpected results toward the Conservatives. The BBC version featured a background of the British Isles (in green) and a red and blue (Labour and Conservative, respectively) pendulum track. Robert McKenzie operated the swingometer during this broadcast, and correctly predicted the Heath and Conservative win at 11:43 p.m. GMT. The BBC website offers video clips from the 1970 British General Election.

"swong"—("Election Night Special") Both "swong" and "swang" are certainly meant to be silly variations of "swing," but they also both have meaning. "Swong" means "thin, lean," while "swang"—in Northern dialect—is a marshy bog (*OED*).

– **T** –

"that's the game"—(*"It's a Living"*) In Ep. 37, an interview show about the necessity of a fourth TV channel (BBC 4) is settled when the four panelists issue single word answers, and the show is over.

"the book"—("School Prize-Giving") Though it sounds silly, this could actually be a reference to any Church of England *Clergy List* (of which there are many) including *Kelly's Clergy List*, which made available the information for each member of the Anglican Clergy in all the British Isles, as well as the Colonies and in military service anywhere.

"three-cornered fight"—("Election Night Special") A "three-cornered" contest is one where two similar candidates can draw significant vote percentages while a third, more distinct candidate can actually win the election. In 1966, for instance, the Scottish National Party (SNP) contested its most seats ever (twenty-three), and took 14.3 percent of the votes in those races. In the following by-election (November 1967), SNP candidate Winnifred Ewing was able to win the Hamilton seat by effectively splitting the Conservative and Labour vote (see *Westminster Target Seats* at alba.org.uk/nextwe/snp.html). Labour had won the seat in the previous election by a convincing majority.

"Fin-tim-lin-bin"—("Election Night Special") There have been and continue to be a fair number of longer-than-average-named candidates in any UK election. In the 1970 General Election, just a few include Sir Frederic Mackarness Bennett, Norman St. John-Stevas, Sir Brandon Rhys Williams, and Christopher Brocklebank-Fowler. The longer names tend to be from those whose families come from older money, which also makes them certain targets for the Pythons.

Following are explanations of some of the less gibberished sections of these candidate names (though in toto the names are meant to read as Lewis Carroll–like nonsense):

"lin-bus"—Idle actually pronounces this "limbus," separating it from the following "stop." "Limbus" means "limbo," or a place for the unbaptized.

"Biscuitbarrel"—Not a nonce word, "biscuit barrel" is actually a purpose-made barrel for, especially, biscuits.

"Bong"—Perhaps a drug paraphernalia reference, but also looks forward to the song "Bing Tiddle Tiddle Bong" sung by Inspector Zatapathique in Ep. 22, and for which the Pythons were sued for copyright infringement. See Ep. 22 notes for details. As for the name Phillips-Bong, the number of hyphenates in the 1970 General Election were myriad, including Robin Chichester-Clark, Sir Alec Douglas-Home, and Sir R. Grant-Ferris, and others.

"Tarquin . . . lin"—Certainly a phonetic game, where words are chosen in a Modernist, Gertrude Stein kind of way (for how well they sound together, not what they mean), but several of these words/utterances also have their own meanings. A "fin" is both a fin-like appendage on an animal or vehicle, as well as a five-dollar note (U.S.); "tim" is variously an insult word (used by English Renaissance playwright/poet Ben Jonson), and "a Protestant nickname for a Roman Catholic [and especially] a supporter of Glasgow Celtic football club" (*OED*). "Lin" means to leave off or desist from; "bin" is of course a container of sorts, and is also short for loony bin, which fits well here; "whin" is both a gorse-type shrub as well as (in Northern dialect) short for whinstone. A "Bim" is slang for a Barbados resident. Lastly, Tarquin Olivier is the son of actor Laurence Olivier. Tarquin appeared as a child actor in *Eagle Squadron* in 1941, and the name is also mentioned in Ep. 4.

"F'tang"—Used here as part of a nonsense name, but also found in several episodes of *The Goon Show*, including "The Call of the West." "Tang" can mean the sting (or bite) of an insect or snake, and may be the source of this variation, and the word as used threateningly in Ep. 17 by Constable Pan Am (Chapman).

Finally, the editors of *Private Eye* create a faux "Letter to the Editor," making fun of their own long-standing penchant for such names, offering a writer complaining about the use of long names for a "so-called joke." The letter is signed: "KAISER-BILLY B'UNTER-DEN-LINDEN-BAINES-JOHNSON'S-BABY-POWDER-ROOM-FOR-THREE-MORE-STANDING-INSIDE-STORY-OF-MY-LIFE-BY-ALAN-HERBERT-GUSSETT" (20 November 1970: 13).

"three drinks at the BBC"—("*It's a Living*") The cast-members of the BBC satire show *That Was the Week That Was* acknowledge that there was indeed a set up for drinks not unlike the one described here, and that because they were working for the "news" section and not "light entertainment," they were able to have drinks and food catered by a Mrs. Reynolds after the tapings. See Carpenter (2000) for more.

"Three hundredweight"—("Dung") A hundredweight can actually vary from 100 to 120 pounds.

trumpeter—(PSC; "School Prize-Giving") This young trumpeter is Garry O'Brien, one of the schoolboy aged extras hired for the day (WAC T12/1,242).

"turkish bath"—("Timmy Williams Interview") The Ironmonger Row baths are found just northeast of Holborn (where Woppi's is supposedly located) in Islington.

"*TV Times*"—("Timmy Williams Interview") An ITV publication that made its debut in 1955, *TV Times* was a weekly listing of the ITV broadcast schedule, as well as media stories and advertising.

– U –

"unable to appear in the show this week"—("Interruption" link into "School Prize-Giving") In Eps. 16 and 18, the character (played by Palin) rehearsing for the Bishop's part (or perhaps he is a Bishop rehearsing for some other part) also says that he doesn't appear in those particular episodes, though he obviously does appear in both.

Also, the vague way which the script refers to this link (*"announcer in a silly location"*) indicates it was one of the many pick-up shots made during location shooting, and would later be inserted wherever it might fit. WAC records indicate that inserts and pick-up shots (including "It's Man," Vox Pops, and the Announcer bits) were on location shooting "to-do" lists.

This particular insert was filmed in the traditional blacksmith's shop at Heydon Village, a privately owned village (owned by the Bulwer-Long's since 1640) in Norwich. WAC records note that permission to shoot in the village was granted by a "Captain W.M. Bulwer-Long," and most of the filming was completed on 25 August 1970 (WAC T12/1,242).

"Unseen Translation"—("School Prize-Giving") Common course/exercise in preparation for examinations in UK schools, where passages (in Latin, Greek, French, etc.) are given to students for translation, sight unseen. Entire courses are structured to prepare students for the exam.

– V –

Vatican crowds—("Foreign Secretary") The shot is of a crowd in the vast St. Peter's Square in front of the Basilica in Rome. The footage is from the BBC Library, and was originally only scheduled for use in Ep. 22 (WAC T12/1,242).

"Velly solly"—("School Prize-Giving") Standard Pythonesque (or, honestly, most period comedy television) shorthand characterization here, with Chapman squinting his eyes and adopting an "l" for "r" Chinese accent. See notes for Ep. 30 for more on this, as well as Ep. 34, where Jeremy Pither (Palin) is accosted by myriad Chinese characters pretending to be British diplomats. This "accent" was also typical of most Hollywood films of the sound era whenever a Chinese character was depicted.

"Very Silly candidate"—("Election Night Special") This is certainly silly, and well over the top, but there have been a number of candidates whose lengthy names almost defy belief. Just a handful who contested the 1966 General Election included Labour MP Arthur Leslie Noel Douglas Houghton, Baron Houghton of Sowerby (1898-1996), Conservative MPs Hugh Charles Patrick Joseph Fraser (1918-1984) and Alfred George Fletcher Hall-Davis (1924-1979). Hall-Davis was educated at Clifton College, where Cleese also attended.

Since the names chosen for this spiel might be just off-the-top-of-the-head, the following are approximations of where the references may have begun:

"Umbrella Stand"—In Ep. 20, the Third City Idiot (Chapman) acts as a "wastepaper basket" for his father.

"Jasper"—Ann Jasper was a designer for Cambridge Footlights in 1961-1962.

"Wednesday"—*The Wednesday Play* premiered in 1964 (and ran through 1970), and many of the *FC* extras/actors also found acting work in that series.

"Stoatgobbler"—Literally, one who consumes stoats, a favorite Python animal reference, also appearing or being mentioned in Eps. 5, 6, 26, and 30.

"Harris"— Richard Harris was a Cambridge Footlights member in 1966, and participated in the show *This Way Out*.

"Mason"—In 1965, John Hope-Mason was the revue director for the Cambridge show *My Girl Herbert*.

"Fruitbat"—This reference would find its way into *HG*, as the Book of Armaments passage is read aloud.

"We'll Keep a Welcome"—A traditional Welsh song composed by Mai Jones:

We'll keep a welcome in the hillside.
We'll keep a welcome in the Vales
This land you knew will still be singing
When you come home again to Wales.

This land of song will keep a welcome
And with a love that never fails,
We'll kiss away each hour of hiraeth
When you come home again to Wales.

"Raindrops Keep Fallin' On My Head"—B.J. Thomas song from the 1969 film *Butch Cassidy and the Sundance Kid*. By January 1970, the song had reached number one on the Billboard Hot 100, and would win the Academy Award for Best Original Song. At the time of this taping, however, the Pythons would have known the song for its place in the popular film, and probably as a single on the radio.

"Don't Sleep in the Subway"—Petula Clark hit from 1967, reaching number 5 on the U.S. charts. A Cardinal Ximinez figure (played by Palin) sings part of the song in Ep. 13.

"Mannering"—Col. Guy Mannering is Sir Walter Scott's titular character from the 1815 novel *Guy Mannering*, as well as the name of an immigrant ship. The character/novel will be mentioned again in Ep. 38.

– W –

"Waring, Guy"—("Timmy Williams Interview" credits) Guy Waring is a character in Grant Allen's (1848-1899) novel *What's Bred in the Bone* (1898), and his first appearance is, coincidentally, at an inn in Holborn (see the entry for "Woppi's").

"What's all this then?"—("Dead Indian") The catchphrase for many of Python's constabulary, and even mentioned reflexively by the Naughty Chemist (Palin) in Ep. 17.

"Whitehouse, Mary"—("Election Night Special") Founder of the "Clean Up TV Campaign" in 1964, which became the National Viewers' and Listeners' Association (NVLA) in 1965, with the goal of raising standards on television in the UK. Upon the announcement of the filming of *Life of Brian* (1979), she turned her cannons on the Pythons, sending EMI (studio that funded the film) running for cover. Ex-Beatle George Harrison would step in and help finance the picture. See *Monty Python: The Case Against*.

"Who shall . . . eternal gain"—("Foreign Secretary") Reminiscent of portions of Emerson's *Celestial Love*, and even William Cowper's (1731-1800) work, but this snippet is actually taken from the much more obscure John Oxenham's post-Edwardian poem "Profit and Loss," first printed in the collection *Bees in Amber: A Little Book of Thoughtful Verse* (American Tract Society: New York, 1913). Oxenham (born W.A. Dunkerley) was a native of Manchester, a novelist, journalist, and by WWI a successful poet.

Oxenham's work was included in numerous anthologies of the period—such as *The Oxford Book of English Mystical Verse* (1917)—as he wrote across genres and themes.

"Wonderful Mr. Williams, The"—("Timmy Williams Interview") During this period (1969-1972), Frost was hosting and producing the very popular *The David Frost Show*, interviewing celebrities and world leaders.

"won you in a police raffle"—(link out of "Dead Indian") In the 6 August 1965 edition of *Private Eye*, female readers can win Conservative opposition leader Ted Heath, a weekend with Reginald Maudling, or a "lifetime with Enoch Powell" (Ingrams 121).

"Woppi's"—("Timmy Williams Interview") Probably a racial slur (based on "wop") as the printed script describes the setting as an "expensive looking coffee shop, Italian style." This also could be a reference to the restaurant chain "Wimpy's," popular in the UK for many years. There is a Wimpy restaurant in Holborn, in Kingsway Street.

The advent of the Italian-style coffee shop in London neighborhoods began as early as 1953 with the opening of Gina Lollabrigida's "The Moka," and the trendy coffee shops spread throughout the metropolitan area over the next two decades.

"wrench"—("Registry Office") In this case, "wrench" means an unforeseen twist.

"Wright, Bill"—("Timmy Williams Interview" credits) Billy Wright (1924-1994) was a talented footballer for Idle's Wolverhampton Wanderers, later a manager for Arsenal, and a presenter for *Youth Sportsview* (BBC, 1957-62).

"writing a book on me"—("Timmy Williams Interview") Author Willi Frischauer (Austrian by birth) was preparing a book on Frost at this time, having, ironically, already published books on Nazis Hermann Goering and Heinrich Himmler, as well as the Aga Khans. Part of the reason the Pythons (and other Oxbridge grads) may have been unenthusiastic about Frost is just the fact that such celebrity biographies were under way less than a decade into Frost's very public entertainment career. *David Frost* would be published by Michael Joseph in 1972.

– Z –

"Zeigler, Anne . . . Webster Booth"—("Foreign Secretary") "Zeigler" is a misspelling of "Ziegler." Anne Ziegler (1910-2003) and Webster Booth (1902-1984) were a popular British vocal duo. Teamed in the 1930s, their signature song was "Only a Rose." Ziegler also appeared in three postwar feature films. Booth was a tenor who began his career with an opera company in the mid-1920s. The fact that several characters in this series (Eps. 21, 22) have signature songs may account for this couple's inclusion. Several studio audience members (probably of the younger generation) applaud at the sight of the hampers containing Ziegler and Booth being tossed into the river, meaning the Ziegler-Booth duo probably appealed more to their parents' generation.

Episode 20

"agricultural subsidies"—("Secretary of State Striptease") The long-standing policy of government support for farm product prices in the UK had reached a crisis level in mid-1969 when the National Farm Union (NFU) staged protests for higher prices for meat and wheat, as well as protections against lower-priced imports. A farmers' protest was held in Newton Abbot, Devon (just north of Torquay and Paignton) in December 1969, where the Pythons would shoot much of the early second series. Farmers and their families also marched outside the Ministry of Agriculture along the Strand, and across Waterloo Bridge. These fears would only escalate over the next few years, of course, as the Conservative government pushed and pulled the country closer to EU membership.

What the stripping minister is saying, essentially, is that a balance must be achieved between artificial (meaning government-inflated) support for local goods/prices and the need for consumer-friendly prices that imported products could provide. In essence, he is promising the Commonwealth countries that they will continue to receive MFN or Most Favored Nation status in trade matters.

This subject found its way onto op-ed pages across the country in 1969-1970 (see the British Cartoon Archive).

"Agricultural Tariff"—("*Today in Parliament*") Import fees attached to foreign agricultural products designed to protect domestic (UK) farmers and producers. See the "agricultural subsidies" note above.

"Alaric . . . Ostrogoth"—("*The Attila the Hun Show*") The Visigoths invaded Roman lands at the end of the fourth century, taking Spain. Vandals were Germanic and also invaded Western Europe during this period.

Ostrogoths are "Eastern Goths" who conquered Italy in the late fifth century (*EBO*).

Here the Pythons are generally accurate historically: The Visigoths were led by Alaric (370-410) between 395-410 (even allying with the Romans against the Huns at one point); the Vandals by Genseric (c. 390–477, aka Gaiseric); and the Ostrogoths, by "Theodoric" (c. 454-526), not "Theodoris." Several of the Pythons read in history (including Jones, who has written texts in history since), and they probably depended on their collective memories as they wrote this scene.

"Allen, Gubby"—("Test Match") Sir George Oswald Browning Allen (1902-1989) was another well-known cricketer, though born in Australia. Allen captained England in three series, with his Test debut in the England vs. Australia match at Lord's, 2nd Test, 1930. The "'32" reference indicates, rightly, that Allen participated in the infamous "Bodyline" tour of 1932-1933, when fast bowling aimed at the batters upset the Australian cricket team, officials and fans, and even caused a diplomatic incident.

American-living-room-type set—(PSC; "*The Attila the Hun Show*") The printed script describes the room (for the production designers), and the layout seems to fit the larger living rooms seen in the single-family homes typical of the suburban United States (as opposed to the council estate rowhouses in the UK). As a set, the room would have been larger than a typical living room, anyway, and missing the fourth wall, as seen in period Hollywood sitcoms like *I Love Lucy*, *The Honeymooners*, and *The Debbie Reynolds Show*.

ANIMATION: *perhaps even mixed with stock film*—(PSC; "Killer Sheep") Again, at the time of the script's writing, the rest of the Pythons had little idea what Gilliam would be creating weeks or months later for the in-studio taping of the show. They do know, however, that rather than a linking element, this animation serves as a proscribed bridge in the story, so clues were obviously provided that Gilliam then had to follow with his "fevered mind."

In the animation, the sheep rob the Westminster Bank Limited, blow up and rob the Midland Bank Limited, then make good their escape in a 1930s-era convertible to the music "Banjo in the Hollow" from The Dillard's 1963 album "Back Porch Blue Grass" (WAC T12/1,433). (The London-area bank photos are obviously vintage, since by 1968 Westminster Bank had been merged out of existence, becoming part of National Westminster Bank.) Also, Gilliam did not follow the scriptwriters' call for a "sheep with machine-gun coming out of its arse, etc." as he created his animation.

The WAC records actually note that the banjo song used by Gilliam is by a "D. Allard," a slight typo.

"Armchairs!"—(*"Take Your Pick"*) This type of "bad answers to easy questions" scenario will be revisited in Ep. 22 ("Burma!"), as well as the feature film *HG*, where Sir Bedivere (Jones) asks what floats in water, and the peasants guess everything from bread to small rocks and churches.

"Arthur X"—("Killer Sheep") Most likely a reference to the Trinidad and Tobago-born Michael X (born Michael de Freitas, 1933-1975), a revolutionary and sometime civil rights voice in London of the 1960s. Michael X had lived in the racially volatile Notting Hill area since 1957, and had initially been a drug dealer and even a thug for slumlord Peter Rachman (see "cheque had bounced" entry in Ep. 14), before taking up the black power revolutionary banner. He would be hanged for murder in 1975.

At the time this episode was being created, Michael X was trying to set up a commune in Islington, according to Joan Didion ("Without Regret or Hope," *NY Times Review of Books*, 12 June 1980).

"ate . . . eucalyptus leaves"—("The News for Wombats") The Pythons have confused their Australian marsupials here. Wombats actually eat grass, roots, and bark. Koalas eat the eucalyptus tree leaves.

– B –

"back benches"—(*"Today in Parliament"*) These would be the lower-ranking members of either party in Parliament, and thus perhaps more likely to be such discontented rabble rousers, in the Python oeuvre.

"Baxter, Ray"—("Ratcatcher") Raymond Baxter's (b. 1922) 1965 show *Tomorrow's World* introduced new technology developments on film and in studio reports. It was called a "science-future" show, and was initially transmitted live (see Vahimagi's *British Television*).

"beautifully not done anything about"—("Test Match") This is certainly a purposeful irony, since Colin Cowdrey was anything but a timid or unaccomplished batter during his long career. What this could be a reference to is the hold on a particular run that Cowdrey endured on the way to his maiden century in 1954. His Wisden obituary remembers Cowdrey's "wonderful maiden century . . . [where he] was becalmed on 56 for 40 minutes." This seeming eternity could certainly have elicited the Pythons' barb—"a superb display of inertia"—in the sketch.

"Bergson, Henri"—(*"Take Your Pick"*) Frenchman Bergson (1859-1941) was a philosopher influenced significantly by Spencer, Mill, and Darwin, and who then based his career on opposing their "rationalist" systems. He won the Nobel Prize for literature in 1927. In his 1900 work *Laughter*, Bergson developed a theory of comedy and laughter which seems to have been an influential work on the Pythons, and perhaps especially Cleese. In doing so, the respected Bergson elevated the study of comedy to a more academic level, worthy of study in works looking at aesthetics and philosophies of art forms.

Being au courant of Bergson and his theories seems to have been quite fashionable during this period—and certainly when the Pythons were attending university. Cleese's Announcer character is discussing his "Bergsonian theory" of humor in Ep. 35 as the show begins.

bike crashing off camera—(PSC; "Attila the Nun") Taken from the opening moments of David Lean's epic 1962 film *Lawrence of Arabia*, when Lawrence is killed after a harrowing motorcycle ride and crash. The rider here appears to be Jones, though he's not credited in the printed script. This scene was shot in picturesque Heydon Village, Norfolk, where they were gathering filmed material in late August 1970 (WAC T12/1,430).

bishops—(*"Take Your Pick"*) These rambunctious bishops are played by Ian Davidson, Palin, and Gilliam. Palin is dressed in the full attire (mitre and robes) he's worn before when practicing the "Mr. Belpit" line (see Ep. 16). The others are wearing black clerical outfits and "dog collars."

blacked up like Rochester—(PSC; "The Attila the Hun Show") In black-face, as was the tradition for playing performing blacks in U.S. vaudeville and UK music hall performances, etc. The BBC still offered the very popular *The Black and White Minstrel Show* (1958-1978), featuring singing and dancing black-face performers, this following the long-standing tradition of such shows on BBC radio and the fin-de-siècle music hall stages. See the article on the show by Sarita Malik at the Museum of Broadcast Communications for more.

As for the "Rochester," reference, Eddie Anderson (1905-1977), television personality Jack Benny's sidekick for twenty-seven years, was a black man, and not "blacked up." *The Jack Benny Show* was a spin-off of Benny's popular radio show, and ran for almost fifteen years on American television.

"Black Rod"—("Vox Pops on Politicians") The "Gentleman Usher of the Black Rod" (he carries a black wand with a golden lion) is the usher to the House of Lords and part of the royal household (*OED*). The position of Black Rod in 1970 was occupied by George Holroyd Mills (18 June 1963 through 1 September 1970), followed by Frank Roddam Twiss. See Bond's *The Gentleman Usher of the Black Rod*. So at the time of this episode's writing, Mills would have been Black Rod, and the object of Second Girl's (Chapman) affections.

"blow on the head"—(*"Take Your Pick"*) The prompting for this type of game show may have come from the very popular *It's a Knockout* (1966), a rough-and-tumble contest show where contestants performed fairly pointless physical feats (building giant hamburgers, running obstacle courses, etc.) as quickly as possible. Eddie Waring (Ep. 1) was one of the show's commentators. The shows will be spoofed again in Ep. 30, where a successful anagram quiz contestant (Jones, again) is bludgeoned with a giant hammer.

"bollard"—("The News for Parrots") A "bollard" is a traffic island post. The *Beyond the Fringe* cast created an entire sketch (and song) around a fictional cigarette with the brand name "Bollard."

"Bosanquet, Reginald"—("Ratcatcher") An original *News at Ten* newsreader (ITN, 1967-), Bosanquet (1932-1984) also contributed to *Dateline* (ITN 1961-1967). *News at Ten* was ITV's (Independent Television) first half-hour newscast. Bosanquet himself will appear briefly in Ep. 26 of *FC*.

"Brando, M."—("The Idiot in Society") American actor Marlon Brando is also mentioned in Ep. 10. Mr. Brando (Chapman) stands in front of what is purportedly a branch of the Northwestern Provincial Bank, which would put this "idiot's bank" outside of London, of course, in the East Midlands or Lancashire area—the rustic north. Most of the footage for this sketch was shot in and around Heydon Village, Norwich.

Brezhnev, Podgorny and Kosygin—(PSC; "The News for Parrots") Many historians name these three men among the moving force behind Nikita Khrushchev's rise to power in 1958 as well as his eventual ouster in 1964.

Leonid Ilyich Brezhnev (1906-1982) is actually in the middle of the trio as they stand on the reviewing stand, probably watching a recent annual celebration of the famed October Revolution. Brezhnev was Soviet leader from as early as 1964 to his death in 1982. Nikolai Podgorny (1903-1983, on the left), who helped Brezhnev to power, was ceremonial head of state, but was himself replaced by Brezhnev as President of the Presidium of the Supreme Soviet of the USSR in 1977. (In Ep. 7, the plucky Scots tailor [Palin] is named Angus Podgorny.) Aleksei Nikolaievich Kosygin (1904-1980) was another fellow anti-Khrushchevite who supported Brezhnev's ascendancy, and became Chairman of the Soviet of Ministers USSR. The solidarity among these leaders during this period (and among the highest government bodies in general) was quite unprecedented in Soviet history. See Rigby for more on this period.

– C –

Canned laughter—(PSC; *"The Attila the Hun Show"*) "Canned" laughter is a prerecorded laugh track (and often applause) that is laid over/under the live or animated action of a TV show, ostensibly to give the illusion of a live studio audience. Many sitcoms utilized canned laughter and applause, as did almost all Hanna-Barbera and Filmation cartoons of the 1960s and 1970s.

The Debbie Reynolds Show (1969-1970) was a thinly veiled rip-off of the very successful *I Love Lucy* (1951-1957), where a live audience reacted well to the real laughs in the weekly filmed episodes. The fact that Reynolds' version followed *Lucy* by more than a decade may account for the staleness of the idea and forced delivery as performed by the Pythons. The producers of the Reynolds' version of the show probably realized very quickly that their product was short on laughs, as well as hopelessly quaint, forcing them to add post facto laughter and applause. In the *Attila* case canned laughter and applause are purposely over-the-top, and being used to send up the Hollywood sitcom genre.

"Cartesian dualism"—(*"Take Your Pick"*) Philosopher Bertrand Russell (1872-1970) characterized Descartes' "method of systematic doubt" as an attempt to doubt everything that couldn't be proved, that his doubt proved only his own existence, thus leading him to only believe in his own existence (*Problems of Philosophy* 18-19). Descartes therefore could build a philosophical world based on this "duality." Opponents of the theory argue that mental events cannot cause or effect physical events, an immaterial effecting the material.

See the note on Descartes (referenced in a Gilliam animation) in Ep. 2 for more.

cashier—("The Idiot in Society") This character is played by Eddy May Scrandrett, who also appeared in Ep. 19 (WAC T12/1,242).

"Charles Crompton, the Stripping Doctor"—("Secretary of State Striptease") A clever and fluid Pythonesque transition here, starting with Chapman's character (Crompton) acting the part of a doctor who appreciates/encourages stripping, and metamorphosing into Cabinet ministers who strip while mouthing government policy.

Charles Crompton contributed to the Marxist-Leninist publication *The New International* in the late 1930s.

Chief Commissioner of Police—(PSC; "Killer Sheep") The body in the drawer is supposed to have been played by Leslie Noyes (*Dad's Army*; *Z Cars*), according to WAC documents (T12/1,418), but the actor looks very much like Ian Davidson. Several times the official BBC records—especially for casting—indicate one actor in a particular role when it is obviously someone else entirely by the time they taped the show.

city gents in their own clothes—(PSC; "The Idiot in Society") This stock film footage is also from the BBC Library (WAC T12/1,242). This is also a wry comment on the "look" and clothing of both the Idiot and the City Gent. The Pythons have clothed the Idiots for this scene and then let them "work"; the City Gents don their recognizable costumes themselves and go shoulder-to-shoulder off to work.

"civil servants"—("Vox Pops on Politicians") Government employees, especially those who serve in civilian capacities of the public administration, including the diplomatic corps, post office and communications, state-run educational institutions, the collection of revenues, etc. The term was originally only applied to employees of the East India Company (*OED*). This definition doesn't seem to necessarily include MPs, however.

Cleveland, Carol—("The News for Parrots") This portrayal of a nurse who "parrots" with everyone else is an example of Cleveland getting in on the comedy, increasingly on equal footing with the boys. She is still used often for her more feminine attributes, but as the series moves on she more and more is allowed to display her comedic talents, as well. Cleveland had appeared in the earliest (1969) publicity photos with the rest of the troupe, but was never a named writing partner or material contributor to the show.

"coach party"—("The Idiot in Society") Generally a tour group traveling by bus, or motor coach. In this case, the tourists would have been actual visitors to scenic Heydon Village, where most of this sketch was filmed.

"Common Market"—("Secretary of State Striptease") An on-again, off-again initiative to join with Europe as trading partners in a "common market" had existed in the UK for many years. Two areas of contention from as early as 1962 included the agreements on agricultural price parity and the gutting of internal tariffs (and, additionally, that England was not "European enough" to satisfy de Gaulle). See the entry for "agricultural subsidies" above. The British Parliament would approve Britain's application for Common Market membership in 1972, and in 1975 voters approved the move by a two-thirds majority.

"Council Ratcatcher"—("Ratcatcher") This is actually a position in many boroughs in the UK, including, for example, Doncaster and Stokes St. Milborough. There is a small display in the Chobham Museum of very old rat tails as caught by the Chobham municipal ratcatcher. The museum is on Benham's Corner, West End, London.

In Ep. 21, Colin Mozart (Palin), a ratcatcher, will be featured. His famous father has pushed him into the more respectable job of ratcatching, and away from the shameful world of composing.

"Cowdrey"—("Test Match") Michael Colin Cowdrey (1932-2000) was a popular right hand bat and employed a "leg break" bowling style. "Leg break" is a pitch that is thrown almost like baseball's "screwball," and breaks into a batter's body off the bounce, from the batter's "leg" side. (See *Dictionary of Cricket Terms*.) Cowdrey played mainly for Kent, Oxford University, and England, with his Test debut coming at the England vs. Australia at Brisbane, 1st Test, 1954/55. Cowdrey was Wisden Cricketer of the Year in 1956. It's said that his father loved cricket, and chose his son's initials (MCC) appropriately. In retirement he was a noted cricket administrator. Cowdrey also participated in the "England and the Rest of the World XI" Test in 1970 (*ODNB*).

"crops go gey are in the medley crun"—("The Idiot in Society") This provincial, northern version of English can be heard earlier in *At Last the 1948 Show*, specifically show five in the first series

Cut through to a Cruikshank engraving of London—(PSC; "The News for Parrots") Not a Cruikshank engraving, the print looks much more like the early- to mid-eighteenth-century work of John Maurer, Sutton

Nicholls, but perhaps especially John Fairbairn, whose perspectival (location of POV, etc.) renderings of London's squares match this print. This print is not accounted for in the WAC records for the episode, meaning no copyright clearance was requested, and no royalty had to be paid for its use.

The graphic over the projected print, "London 1793," is off significantly. The events being depicted in *A Tale of Two Cities* involving Darnay, Lucie, and her father occur in 1780-1781, according to Dickens. This is yet another probably memorial mistake on the Pythons' part, as these events occur prior to the French Revolution in Dickens' tale. The events of the novel actually conclude sometime in mid- to late 1790.

– D –

"darkies"—("Test Match") In the past, a popular colloquial term in the United States for African Americans. The British public would have been introduced to the term through over-the-counter products, interestingly, like "Darkie" toothpaste, and the black-face images on Gollywog-brand jam. In this specific case, the cricketing reference indicates that "darkies" are members of teams representing West Indies, Pakistan or India.

Debbie Reynolds Show, The—(*"The Attila the Hun Show"*) Appeared on American television (NBC, Tuesdays) 1969-1970, with twenty-six episodes recorded. Produced by an *I Love Lucy* writer, the show was based on that show's premise and situations. The show's musical theme was written by Jack Wilton Marshall, and was sung by Reynolds herself over the closing credits. The show appeared on BBC 1 in January 1970, and ran for all twenty-six episodes.

The theme that plays beneath the titles is *The Debbie Reynolds' Show* theme, here Mike Leroy's version of "With a Little Love" by T. Romeo (WAC T12/1,433).

"Did he have his head all bandaged?"—("Ratcatcher") This may be an oblique reference to writer/presenter Raymond Baxter being injured in a punch-up between drivers Graham Hill and Jim Clark as Baxter covered the 1964 European Grand Prix held at Brands Hatch. *Private Eye* TV critic "George Millais" mentions that Baxter "suffered incurable brain damage in the pits at Brands Hatch" that day, though this didn't stop him from participating in what Millais derisively terms *Man Half-Alive* (actually, *Man Alive*, see notes to Eps. 18 and 26 for more) (Ingrams 168).

"don't know"—("Killer Sheep") Again, playing on the moment in many sci-fi and horror films when the scientist or military figure(s) attempt to explain the deadly phenomena. This is usually an expository moment for the audience more than anything else. This same sort of helpful moment endemic to the sci-fi genre is also employed in Ep. 7, the "Science Fiction Sketch."

"Dorset"—("Wainscotting") A rural county at nearly the southernmost tip of England. Dorset was the inspiration for the bucolic setting "Wessex," central to Thomas Hardy's pre-industrial revolution England in many of his novels.

– E –

Episode 20—This episode was recorded 2 October 1970, and broadcast 10 November 1970.

"Epsom"—("The Epsom Furniture Races") Epsom Downs is in Surrey, and is the racecourse where the Derby is run. The actual film location, however, is not Epsom, as they most likely would not have been granted permission to film there (just as in Ep. 7, when a local tennis court park had to stand in for Wimbledon Centre Court). The former Alexandra Palace Race Course is the actual setting here (WAC T12/1,430), which closed officially in 1970.

"Eton, Sandhurst and the Guards"—("The Idiot in Society") This has been the standard trajectory for important British diplomats and military men in the past. Eton is the largest ancient English college, founded by Henry VI on the Thames opposite Windsor; Sandhurst is the Royal Military Academy at Sandhurst; and "the Guards" refers to various members of the Household Cavalry, or troops employed to guard the monarch.

Exciting crime-type music—(PSC; "Killer Sheep") The music used by Gilliam in the early portion of the animation is Westway Studio Ensemble's "Woodland Tryst" by C. Watters (WAC T12/1,433).

– F –

"Farmer Ambushed in Pen"—(PSC; "Killer Sheep") This headline is placed on an altered copy of the Friday, 4 September 1970 edition of *The Daily Courier*.

"Merino Ram in Wages Grab"—This headline replaces the headline for the Friday, 18 September 1970 *The Daily Echo*, a Dorset-area newspaper.

The printed script also calls for "eerie science fiction music" during this transition, but there is none in the finished film.

fast bowler—(PSC; "Test Match") A bowler who uses speed to overpower batsmen, as opposed to a spin bowler.

"Figgis, Arthur"—("The Idiot in Society") Not perhaps a completely fabricated name or person, as there was at least one "Arthur Figgis" listed in the Greater London telephone books of this period. Figgis is also mentioned in Eps. 2 and 6, and is, in the pages of *Private Eye*, the ancient librarian of the maligned (and equally ancient) *Punch* magazine.

French Revolution type music—(PSC; "The News For Parrots") This music is a portion of the Orchestra of Amsterdam's performance of Berlioz's "Symphonie Fantasie, Fourth Movement" (WAC T12/1,433).

"front-bench"—(*Today in Parliament*) In both houses of Parliament, the front seats are where the most influential members (often spokesmen) sit. There are front and back benches for both the party in power and the opposition.

The Front Bench Spokesman for the opposition between 1964 and 1970 (when the Conservatives were in the minority) was Margaret Thatcher, mentioned in Eps. 21, 22, and 30.

– G –

"get a-head"—("The Attila the Hun Show") A purposely bad pun perhaps borrowed from a Hat Council (UK) ad slogan for 1965, "If you want to get ahead, get a hat" (*ODMQ* 8). The Pythons are clearly lampooning the broad, less-than-deft comedy writing (and delivery) characteristic of most American television sitcoms of the period.

"get your hand off my thigh, West"—("Test Match") There is no indication that Peter West (see below) ever "hit on" one of his broadcast partners, but the jovial, bon vivant atmosphere in the cricket broadcast booths certainly created a sense of companionship for and with listeners/viewers.

Groupie—("Vox Pops on Politicians") This look and just the inclusion of these types may have been influenced by the recent (both August 1970) open air pop festivals in London and on the Isle of Wight, where Jimi Hendrix, Joan Baez, and many others performed, and "hippie"-types attended in droves.

– H –

"Headingley"—("Test Match") Headingley (Leeds) has been the home of the Yorkshire CCC since 1891. Brian Close (b. 1931), who will be mentioned later, played for Yorkshire.

"Home Secretary and mother won the Derby"—(link out of "The Idiot in Society") The Home Secretary is the Secretary of State for Home Affairs in the UK. The colloquial "Derby" (pronounced "darby") is the oldest horse race in the country, founded by the Earl of Derby in 1780, and run at Epsom. The fact that the mother figure could be referred to as a "horse" is reminiscent of the term "war-horse," which can mean a strong-willed woman. The Epsom racecourse will be the supposed site of the later "Epsom Furniture Race," and is actually shot at the Alexandra Park course, according to WAC records. The Fourth City Idiot's (Jones) mention of the Derby isn't out of place—this type of horse race has been supported by the gentry in England since at least the end of the eighteenth century.

"Hunlets"—("The Attila the Hun Show") A play on pop music names of the period, including the Ronettes (Veronica Bennett, Estelle Bennett, and Nedra Talley).

"Huns"—("The Attila the Hun Show") A fifth-century Asian tribe that, under Attila—the scourge of God—invaded and terrorized Europe.

Attila the Hun lived c. 406-453, was king of the Huns (c. 433-453), and was characterized as cunning and ambitious, even unpredictable. In the feature film *HG*, the young monk (Palin) reads from the Book of Armaments about St. Attila and the Holy Hand Grenade.

– I –

"Iceland"—("Test Match") Iceland has no history of cricket, meaning England is now struggling to beat even the non-cricket-playing nations. This pessimism was well founded in 1970. The South African Test tour was cancelled, and MCC had to scramble to put together cricket for paying audiences for the year. In June-August of 1970, the "England and a Rest of the World XI" series of matches were played in the UK, pitting an English team against an international squad comprised of players representing South Africa, Australia, West Indies, India, and Pakistan. England eventually lost 4-1.

As of 1970, there were only seven recognized Test-status cricket nations: England, Australia, South Africa, West Indies, New Zealand, India, and Pakistan.

"ICI have increased . . . "—("The Idiot in Society") ICI is Imperial Chemical Industries, in 1970 one of the largest and most successful UK companies. This is one of the companies that Mr. Brando (Chapman) will term as a "big industrial combine," where a "really blithering idiot" can be found.

idiot gear with BA hoods—("The Idiot in Society") The "BA hood" is part of the recognizable academic regalia, and traditionally worn with a cap and gown. The Pythons, as Oxbridge grads, would have worn prescribed clothing underneath their regalia, as well, and the "idiot gear" with the academic kit seems a comment on that strict dress code. The majority of the poking-fun, however, is obviously reserved for these graduates of the "new" and certainly more plebeian university system, where virtually any "idiot" could complete a degree and call himself a university graduate.

"Is the third test in here?"—("Ratcatcher") The difficulties surrounding the South African cricket team's tour of the UK in 1970 are covered in notes to Eps. 14 and 17. In short, the increasingly separatist and racist policies of the South African government toward its majority black population led to calls for boycotts of all but essential trade with South Africa, as well as bans on international sporting cooperation with Springbok teams. At one point, protestors were damaging playing fields in England so that matches could not be held, leading to rescheduling efforts (officials trying to find suitable alternate sites), and finally the cancellation of the tour.

It was also earlier this same year (in April 1970) that there had arisen a significant row over England's cricket team making a trip to South Africa, with the result that a broadcaster like John Arlott at BBC decided to not make the trip in protest of the regime's oppressive racial policies. Arlott explains himself in an open letter found in *The Guardian* on 17 April 1970, mentioning prominently the play of English cricketer Graeme Pollock with a West Indian team the previous summer, and what a marvelous experience it was (see *Guardian Century 1970-1979*).

The cricketers behind Cleese include walk-ons David Aldridge (*Dr. Who*), Steve Smart, David Gilchrist (*Dad's Army*), Jim Haswell (*Dr. Who; Z Cars*), and George Janson (*Mystery and Imagination*) (WAC T12/1,433).

– J –

Jenny and Robin—("*The Attila the Hun Show*") On the Reynolds' TV show, the couple had no children, but the "two child" family was right for the American sitcoms of the period, as exhibited by both *I Love Lucy*, with children Desi, Jr. and Lucie; *The Adventures of Ozzie and Harriet* (1952-1966), with sons David and Ricky; and *Leave it to Beaver* (1957-1963), with Wally and the Beaver.

"Joey Boy"—("The News for Parrots") Name of a 1965 British film set during WWII, but also a traditional name for a parrot.

– K –

"killer"—("Killer Sheep") As early as Ep. 2 (recorded first, however), sheep have been portrayed incongruously as clever by the Pythons, contrary to the popular (and literary) belief that they're quite dumb. Marianne Moore, for example, in her 1959 poem *The Arctic Ox (Or Goat)*, calls camels "snobbish" and sheep "unintelligent" (stanza 9). In Ep. 2, Harold the Sheep was teaching other sheep to fly, and planning an escape from the rustic shepherd (Chapman).

"Knightsbridge"—("*Today in Parliament*") Located in the city of Westminster, and home to Harrods, Knightsbridge is probably mentioned due to its proximity to Parliament and the seat of government.

knitting—("Ratcatcher") She's actually stuffing a chicken with what appears to be stuffing. She (Palin) then wears the chicken on her right hand throughout the scene.

– L –

"Licence Fees"—(PSC; link out of "*Take Your Pick*") On 1 January 1969, the mandatory license fee—the annual fee paid by all television and radio owners in the UK—had been increased by £1. This fee helps fund the BBC.

"Little bastard"—(link out of "Vox Pops on Politicians") Kind of an oxymoronic statement, since both the Groupie's parents are there, but typical for the Pythons. This is an interesting parody of the then very topical "rebellious generation" syndrome, where flower children and the hippie generation sought something beyond their parents' ken. The satire rests in the fact that these young people are actually interested in politics and politicians, rather than "turning on and dropping out." This same turnabout can be seen in the upended "Angry Young Man" drawing room scenario in Ep. 2, "Working-Class Playwright."

"little joke"—("Ratcatcher") As he puts on his workingman's hat Mr. Ames' (Chapman) posh, obviously patrician, and MCC-appropriate accent changes to a much more rustic accent.

"lobbying"—("Vox Pops on Politicians") Originally, this was an American term for the (legal) act of influencing political figures, legislation, etc. It seems to have appeared in the UK around 1894, as the term was used in the 4 April 1894 *Yorkshire Post* with quotation marks around it, as if it were a newer, less familiar, even specialized term (*OED*). The groupies seem to be using it in a sexualized way, of course.

One recent bit of lobbying had led to the Representation of the People Act of 1969, wherein the vote was given to those over the age of eighteen in the UK, meaning these groupies might have just recently achieved some measure of influence and access to their representatives. Some pundits have connected this expansion of suffrage to the distinct drop in voter turnout in the 1970 General Election, leading to the subsequent loss by Labour.

Lastly, *Private Eye*'s mention of Westminster's lobbyists is nothing short of bracingly scornful, employing the words "clowns," "deceiving," and "toadying," before concluding that "these drunks, toadies and geriatrics are as guilty by default as the politicians are for all the ills which beset our punk little, drunk little island" (*PE* 1 September 1970, 17).

"Look of fear!"—("Killer Sheep") This is identified by the Professor (Idle) as another "strange line," this time because the line actually reads more like a stage direction than dialogue. The line could also be read as a shot sheet entry for the overacted reaction shot seen in many science fiction and horror films.

Lords cricket grounds—(PSC; "Test Match") They did shoot at the gates of Lords for this intro, but the cricket match itself was shot much earlier at the Norfolk County Cricket Ground (WAC T12/1,430). Lords is the home of English cricket, and is located in exclusive St. Johns Wood, and would likely have not welcomed the Pythons onto their pitch for the scene.

– M –

macs—(PSC; link into "Secretary of State Striptease") Mackintosh overcoats. Most shabby Python characters wear such a coat, though Praline's (Cleese) is always rubber. These same extras also appear in the "Killer Sheep" sketch as cricketers, and include David Aldridge, Steve Smart, David Gilchrist, Jim Haswell, and George Janson. The music played for their "observation" is "The Stripper" by Rose, as played by the Concert Band of Her Majesty's Lifeguards (WAC T12/1,433).

"maintain consumer prices"—("Secretary of State Striptease") The Labour government rode this horse into the 1970 General Election, with sitting PM Harold Wilson sounding very much like a stripping Minister as he blasts the opposition's economic proposals:

> Conservative policies are deliberately designed to raise prices. To raise food prices by abolishing the food subsidies which protect the housewife and imposing levies—food taxes—on the food we buy from abroad. To raise almost all other prices by their Value Added Sales Tax. To raise rents, by getting rid of our present system of housing subsidies. By ending the protection which Labour's Acts of Parliament give to the householder in the face of rising council house rents. They would scrap all the controls we operate to restrain price increases. . . . The Conservatives have made it clear that they would scrap all we are doing. (transcribed from the "Labour Party Election Broadcast, 1970")

The Conservative position (voiced by Edward Heath) also touched on prices and social programs, but in the party political messages in 1970, neither party spent much time talking up agricultural subsidies or the Common Market—meaning, perhaps, that the bleak domestic situation outweighed foreign issues in the minds of potential voters.

The party election manifestoes for Labour and the Tories in 1966 also touch on the strength of the UK as part of the Commonwealth and an arm's-length participant in the Common Market (thought the Conservative platform calls for a more active Common Market cause). (See the various manifestoes for recent UK elections at psr.keele.ac.uk.)

maybe they're brown coats—(PSC; "The Epsom Furniture Races") These men look like the line of gasmen depicted in Ep. 14, as part of the "New Cooker Sketch." Again, the writer(s) of this scene could have easily erased the "white coats" reference in the printed scripts and penciled in "brown coats," but the asides to the reader continue.

"Merino"—("Killer Sheep") A merino is a type of sheep quite prized for its wool in the UK.

"Minister of Pensions and Social Security"—("Secretary of State Striptease") The Ministry of Social Security was set up in 1966, and the Department of Health and Social Security followed in 1968. The Labour minister for this position (until June 1970) was Richard Crossman. Crossman was replaced in 1970 by Sir Keith Joseph, who would remain in the post until the Conservatives lost the 1974 General Election.

"Minister of Technology"—("The News for Parrots") Tony Benn (b. 1925) was Minister of Technology (Labour government) from 1966 to 1970. On 19 June 1970, Geoffrey Rippon took the position for the newly elected Conservative government. The photo included by the Pythons is of Benn. Benn is also remembered for losing his House of Commons seat after a by-election win from Bristol South-east in 1960 because he was Anthony Wedgwood-Benn—he had inherited an unwanted viscountcy. He would go on to press the cause of those who would renounce their titles to seek Commons seats, realized in the Peerage Act of 1963.

"Minister without Portfolio"—(*"Today in Parliament"*) A government minister not in charge of a specific department of state, and perhaps relegated to the back benches.

"Shadow Minister"—Member of the opposition party (the party not in the majority in Parliament) nominated to be counterpart to the sitting minister. In late 1970, Labour assumed the shadow posts, having lost badly (and unforeseenly) in the summer General Election. See the entries for "Election Night Special" in Ep. 19 for more on that surprising change of power.

It's worth noting that in this monologue the Pythons are skewering *both* sides of the political aisle, front and back benchers, Conservative and Labour, at least. (Liberals will be lampooned in Ep. 45.)

modern box—(PSC; "Test Match") The script calls for the commentators to be sitting in a "modern box," which appears to be nothing more than a standard broadcast booth loaded with alcohol.

"M1"—("The News for Parrots") The M1 is the major London-to-Birmingham motorway, which opened in 1959.

– N –

"*naturally* mad . . . I don't use any chemicals"—("The Idiot in Society") English poet A.C. Swinburne (mentioned in Ep. 17) would comment in *Testaments* (1590) on the "naturall foole" who is idiotic by nature (meaning birth). The Upperclass Twits fit nicely into this category.

The "chemicals" reference is a pertinent comment during a period when experimentation with myriad drugs was rampant, including among the Pythons (see McCabe). In sports, the increasing use of performance-enhancing drugs (e.g., steroids, doping) is also significant. (The first drug disqualification in Olympic history came in 1968 when a Swedish modern pentathlete tested positive for "excessive" alcohol.) As early as the mid-1950s the Soviet weightlifting teams were being given testosterone injections, and the U.S. squad allegedly followed suit in the following Oympic games, spurring the East German sports machine into the fray, etc., opening the floodgates for drug use in myriad Olympic sports.

"new strain"—("Killer Sheep") This is one of the foundational semantic elements of the 1950s sci-fi film genre, viz., the mutation of an existing species by either Man's or some unknown—often alien—interference. For example, see the mutated ants in *Them!* (1954), a tarantula and other animals in *Tarantula* (1955), *The Giant Gila Monster* (1959) mutant, and even mutated humans in *The Incredible Shrinking Man*

(1957). These sheep begin to perform very human acts, all criminal, of course, which may also be a vague allusion to the human-like HAL 9000 computer in *2001: A Space Odyssey* (1968), and the Colossus computer in *The Forbin Project* (1970). The reason for the sheep's mutation is never made clear, unlike the more complete sci-fi sketch in Ep. 7, where it's revealed that alien blancmanges are attempting to win Wimbledon.

"nobody does that anymore"—("The Idiot in Society") Certainly at least an oblique comment on the transition the Pythons were very much associated with—the move away from the traditional, music hall-ish Frankie Howerd or *Morecambe and Wise*–type (gag-rich, set-up-and-rimshot-payoff) school of television comedy.

"none surpassed . . . cruelty"—(*"The Attila the Hun Show"*) This claim is supported by many sources, including (and not surprisingly) *The Catholic Encyclopedia*: " . . . plundering and devastating all in his path with a ferocity unparalleled in the records of barbarian invasions and compelling those he overcame to augment his mighty army" ("Attila").

"Northants"—("Test Match") Short for Northamptonshire.

Northwest Provincial—(PSC; "The Idiot in Society") The sign behind Mr. Brando at the bank reads "Northwest Provincial," placing this scene in the Merseyside, Manchester, Lancashire, Cumbria, and Cheshire region. (It was actually shot in Norfolk, well across the country to the east, but still well north of London, and civilization.) Simply put, anywhere north of London can be considered provincial, which has been the bias of southerners for generations.

"not so many of them"—("Ratcatcher") There were four into-camera newsreaders for the 1967 *News at Ten* (ITN) debut: Alastair Burnet, Andrew Gardner, Bosanquet, and George Ffitch; four foreign correspondents (John Edwards, Alan Hart, Richard Lindley, and Sandy Gall); and Gerald Seymour in the ITN studio, among others (see Vahimagi).

"Notts"—("Test Match") Short for Nottinghamshire.

"now it's the North East's turn with the Samba"—("Test Match") A direct reference to the popular BBC show *Come Dancing* (1949-1995) which the Pythons obviously were aware of as they grew up. The broadcast dance show began to promote competitions between regions in 1953, which accounts for the "North East" reference (Vahimagi 25). The mention during cricket coverage is also significant—cricket commentator Brian Johnston appeared on *Come Dancing* as a presenter. *Come Dancing* will also be mentioned in Ep. 39, where it will be known as *Come Wife-Swapping*, though still hosted by Peter West (Idle).

– O –

"off stump"—("Test Match") "Stumps" are the upright sticks behind the batsman, and the two "bails" laid on top of them complete the "wicket." The "off stump" is the stump to the keeper's far right, the "leg stump" is nearest the batsman's leg, with the "middle stump" in between.

"O'Nassis"—("The Idiot in Society") Certainly a reference to the then in-the-news Onassis family, including Aristotle and wife Jacqueline Kennedy Onassis. With the apostrophe, the name is Gaelicized (specifically, to an Irish name).

outside loo—(PSC; "Vox Pops on Politicians") The script indicates that he is standing in front of the door to an "outside loo," which is an outdoor privy. However, when he turns to go in the door, the following match cut is the interior of his home (which may, of course, be a comment on the typical council estate home of the period).

– P –

"parrots"—("The News for Parrots") The happy Commonwealth theme is carried on here, with animals native to distant but Commonwealth-member countries—parrots (Australasia, India), gibbons (the Indian Archipelago), and wombats (Australia)—being offered culture-friendly and species-specific news from the BBC.

This is also a play on the BBC's myriad broadcast offerings for specific regions/peoples like Devon and Wales, the Middle East, and all the far-flung corners of the former British Empire. One such offering, Persian Radio, has already been mentioned by Arthur Frampton (Jones) in Ep. 2. In the film *Hard Day's Night* (dir. Richard Lester, 1964), the TV director bemoans his fate after The Beatles' less-than-perfect taping session, certain that his next stop is the *News in Welsh* backwater.

Lastly, proto-BBC (then known as "2LO") broadcaster Arthur Burrows (1882-1947) was known to deliver the newscast twice, consecutively—once at a normal clip, and once "exceptionally slowly" (*Eyewitness 1920-29*, "Early Broadcasting"). Burrows was also known as "Uncle Arthur" on the BBC's *Children's Hour* for many years. See Burrows' entry at the *ODNB* for more.

patriotic music—(PSC; "Vox Pops on Politicians") The music played beneath this shot is the first march of the "Pomp and Circumstance Marches" composed by archetypal English composer Edward Elgar in 1901. Also known as "Land of Hope and Glory," it became a sort of unofficial anthem of the Conservative Party, hence its inclusion here. It has since become associated with graduations, sporting events, and upper-crust pomposity in both the UK and United States.

"Peephole Club"—("Secretary of State Striptease") Certainly modeled after one of the many clip joints and nudie clubs in the Soho area of the West End of London. The Soho neighborhood has been the center of London's sex trade for at least two centuries (Ackroyd, *London* 527-28).

"Pennine Gang"—("Killer Sheep") Pennine sheep are special in that they are "hefted," meaning they remain in a particular territory (on a hill or moor, for instance), and thus don't necessarily need to be herded or even fenced. This becomes ironic as we see the Pennine Gang breaking out of their territoriality to rob and pillage. The name is a play on the "Barrow Gang" of Clyde Barrow and Bonnie Parker (et al.), and the "pickin'" music used in the sequence supports that reading. Also, the printed script mentions "Basil Cassidy and the Sundance Sheep," whose real-life inspirations led the "Hole in the Wall Gang" (or the "Wild Bunch Gang"). *Bonnie and Clyde* was released in 1967, followed two years later by *Butch Cassidy and the Sundance Kid*.

"Peter"—("Test Match") Peter West (1920-2003) joined the BBC in 1947 and became the voice of cricket coverage for a generation. He also starred on BBC's *Guess My Story* quiz show (1953-1954); he earlier presented for the BBC's *Come Dancing* (1949-1995). Brian Johnston presented in the early 1960s on this latter show. (See the note above for "now it's the North East's . . . " for more on the show.)

"Brian"—Brian Johnston (1912-1994) almost took the City Gent route (Eton, Oxford, and the Grenadier Guards) but joined the BBC instead in 1946, where he would work for almost fifty years. He covered cricket from the beginning, on both radio and TV, joining the Test Match Special team in 1970. Pictures indicate that he did have a rather large nose, and in several he is posing with glass conspicuously in hand. The request for the polystyrene prosthetic nose to be built can be found in the surviving WAC records.

"Naughton"—This could be a reference to Naunton Wayne (1901-1970), actually, a British actor who portrayed a cricket enthusiast in at least eleven films (several times partnered with Basil Radford), including Hitchcock's *The Lady Vanishes* (1938). Naunton died in November 1970.

"Knott"—Cricketer Alan Knot (b. 1946) played for Kent, Tasmania, and England, appearing on the national cricket scene in 1965 when he was considered the best young cricketer in the country. By 1967 be was a Test player, and in 1970 was the Wisden Cricketer of the Year. His first test was played, incidentally, at *Nott*ingham.

"Newton"—Harry Newton (b. 1935) played for Sussex and England, participating nationally in 1966. Another Newton—Harold Newton (b. 1918)—was actually born in and would play for Northamptonshire (Northants).

"postcards for sale"—(*"Today in Parliament"*) Probably "naughty" Edwardian erotic postcards such as those Gilliam utilizes in his animations. The following "who likes a sailor, then" adds credence to the sexualized nature of the reference. Again, the straight-laced (and especially Conservative) MP-types, in the Python world, are more likely to be sexual profligates and deviants than simple public servants.

– R –

rampaging bun—("Attila the Bun") In this animated sequence, it's worth noting that the figure on the dining room table who eventually consumes the rogue bread is labeled "BBC."

"rhubarb"—(*"Today in Parliament"*) Both a vegetable often used in English summers as a fruit, as well as a canted word used by radio actors to imitate the sound of a large gathering—the Goons often "Rhubarb! Rhubarb!" heartily in their characterizations of Lords and Ministers in Parliament chambers, for instance. Here the rhubarb seems to be hinted at as a possible sex toy, as well, along with a dachshund.

"rodental"—("Ratcatcher") The word is actually "rodential."

– S –

"said it again"—("Wainscotting") This gag is repeated to great effect in the second "Knights Who Say Ni" appearance in *HG*, reinforcing the power and significance of *words* in the Python world.

"Secretary . . . Affairs"—("Secretary of State Striptease") This minister would have been in charge of relations with members of the Commonwealth, many former colonies now elevated to trading partner status. The striptease may be a comment at the ridiculous façade many saw Britain attempting to shore up as its international presence and influence continued to shrink in the postwar era. In many cases, Common-

wealth members were flourishing even as Britain ebbed into international ineffectiveness.

In 1970, the Secretary of State for Foreign and Commonwealth Affairs was Sir Alec Douglas-Home. Members of the Commonwealth (with Britain) in 1970 included: Australia, Canada, New Zealand, India, Pakistan, Sri Lanka, Ghana, Malaysia, Nigeria, Cyprus, Sierra Leone, Jamaica, Trinidad and Tobago, Uganda, Kenya, Malawi, Malta, Tanzania, Zambia, Gambia, Singapore, Barbados, Botswana, Guyana, Lesotho, Mauritius, and Swaziland.

"Selfridges"—("Killer Sheep") A UK department store chain in business since 1909. Its Oxford street store has been the site of numerous protests and demonstrations (anti-fur, anti-Israel, etc.) since at least 1967.

The BBC had broadcast *The Great Store Robbery* in 1970, a program looking at retail theft, and Selfridges was one of the establishments featured prominently. See the BFI Film and TV Database website for program information.

"self-taught idiot"—("The Idiot in Society") The past decade had been a significant transitioning period between the few, elite (or very intelligent) students finding their way successfully through university, and the realization of higher education for just about anyone with the building of myriad universities and upgrading of technical colleges after WWII, and especially in the 1960s. These "New Universities" were often derided (especially by those who'd attended the Ancient Universities) as places where the great unwashed could pretend to higher learning. In late 1963, acceptance of the findings of the Robbins Report led to plans for multiple "plate glass" universities across the country, including the mentioned Univerity of East Anglia in Norwich, which entered students beginning in 1963.

This was also the period when the "University of the Air" (and later "Open University") was under discussion, and political cartoonists were having great fun taking jabs at this radical, long-distance learning concept. See notes to Ep. 41 for much more on Open University.

Lastly, it was primarily during the Pythons' young lives that the significant transition from the apprentice to the university (or arts college) system was gathering steam. Filmmakers, animators, television personnel, and plastic artists and performers of all types were graduating from degree programs and entering the marketplace, rapidly replacing the "self-taught" types in the arts and entertainment fields. The Pythons themselves were certainly a result of this transition.

This Idiot's (Idle) "ooh arh" is the stereotyped Yorkshire accent heard much earlier in Ep. 2, from the Rustic (Chapman) in the "Flying Sheep" sketch.

sexily dressed girl . . . strikes a small gong—("*Take Your Pick*") The gong ringer for *Take Your Pick* was actually Alec Dane, a more-than-middle-aged man. This gong moment will be revisited in Ep. 25, the "Court (Phrasebook)" sketch.

"sheep poison"—("Wainscotting") There is no such thing, of course, though there is rat poison, which is often strychnine.

"simple country girl"—("Attila the Nun") A Joan of Arc (c. 1412-1431) or even Bernadette of Lourdes (1844-1879) type of description, excepting the "brutality." Both Joan and Bernadette were simple country girls when they received their visitations and took up their various vows.

soft breathy jazzy music—(PSC; "Secretary of State Striptease") The music beneath the stripping Secretary (Jones) is very muted, and is another "stripper"-type song, of which there are many. This song is not accounted for in the WAC records.

"Southcott, Joanna"—("The Epsom Furniture Races") Southcott (1750-1814) was a Devon-area religious fanatic who wrote verse prophecies, and gathered quite a large following. Her "box" supposedly contained prophetic material necessary for Britain when a time of great crisis appeared, and was to be opened in the presence of all the sitting C. of E. bishops (*ODNB*). In the 1960s and early 1970s there were organized groups demanding that Southcott's wishes be followed and the box at last opened, which is why the bishops in the following sketch are screaming for "the box" to be opened.

"Spam"—("*Take Your Pick*") American pressed lunch meat referenced again in Ep. 25, and very popular in Britain after WWII, when food rationing meant a limited supply of meat. SPAM wasn't one of the rationed items, meaning Britons could buy it, eat it, and even store it whenever it became available, without ration cards.

"Speaker"—("Vox Pops on Politicians") The Speaker of the House of Commons in 1970 was Dr. H. King (1965-1971), and afterwards J. Selwyn Lloyd (1971-1976). This position is chosen by the House of Commons—and the party in power—and is charged with representing the Commons and presiding over debate—choosing those who will speak, among other duties.

stock film—(PSC; "The *Attila the Hun Show*") There were at least three color feature films available by 1970 for this pillaged footage, including *La Regina dei tartari* (1961), *Tharus figlio di Attila* (1962), and the big-budget Anthony Quinn/Sophia Loren vehicle *Attila* (1954).

The WAC records indicate that the film stock used was called *Attila the Hun*—no mention of where it came from, which probably means it was already somewhere in the BBC collection (WAC T12/1,242).

stock film of fast moving Huns—(PSC; "The *Attila the Hun Show*") The music underneath this stock footage is "Episodes From the Bible" by Derek Laren, and is played by the International Studio Orchestra (WAC T12/1,433).

"strange, strange line"—("Killer Sheep") Commenting on the often hypertrophic dialogue and situations of the sci-fi genre, science fiction films are well known for offering arch, often over-the-top dialogue that, generically, could have no home in another genre. See entries for the "Science Fiction Sketch" in Ep. 7 for more on the Pythons' sci-fi genre acumen.

This is also a very self-conscious moment, of which there are many in *FC*. Period sci-fi films (featuring mutated creatures) that the Pythons might be lampooning include *Tarantula* (1955; rodents and arachnids grow to enormous killers), *Them!* (1954; killer ants), *It Came From Beneath the Sea* (1955; a giant octopus), *Beginning of the End* (1957; mutated grasshoppers), and perhaps especially films like *The Giant Gila Monster* (1959). Most of these films share the incongruous plot structure—formerly docile or just "too small to be real threats to humanity-type" creatures are mutated and run amok.

– T –

Take Your Pick—(PSC; "*Take Your Pick*") Quiz show (1955-1968) produced by Arlington Television and Radio, with Michael Miles (1919-1971) as host. The printed scripts describe Miles as a "grinning type monster." Not unlike the Python version of the show, the studio audience members for *Take Your Pick* would shout "Open the box!" to the contestant if they felt the proffered money wasn't sufficient.

Tale of Two Cities—("The News for Parrots") Novel by Charles Dickens, published 1859.

"Test Selection Committee"—("Ratcatcher") "Test" is short for Test Match, "an official two-inning match between two accredited national teams, usually spread over 5 playing days (30 hours)" (see *Dictionary of Cricket Terms*). Results of the Rest of the World in England, 1970 include England XI vs. Rest-of-the-World, played at Lord's, London on 17, 19, 20, and 22 June 1970 (a three-day match). The result: Rest-of-the-World won by an inning and eighty runs. See the "Association of Cricket Statisticians and Historians." There were four other England XI vs. Rest-of-the-World matches in 1970, played at Nottingham, Birmingham, Leeds, and The Oval (in Kennington).

The Test Selection Committee would have been in charge of selecting players to represent England in the planned international tests.

"third test"—("Killer Sheep") Cleese is in black-face, and speaks with a vague Jamaican/West Indies accent in this appearance. (This is the second blacked-up character in the episode, following Rochester [Idle] in the "*Attila*" sketch.) The Jamaican cricket team played four matches in England in 1970: against Glamorgan at Swansea, 25-28 July 1970; against Lancashire at Manchester, 8-11 Aug. 1970; against Sussex at Hove, 15-18 Aug. 1970; and against Essex at Leyton, 19-21 Aug. 1970. See the Association of Cricket Statisticians and Historians records for more.

Cricket was very much in the news during this period. MCC bore the brunt of national and international concern as the South African cricket team prepared to tour the UK in 1969-1970. Protests included the destruction of cricket pitches across the country, meaning teams had to play in different stadia or cancel matches. The South African tour was eventually cancelled due to this uproar.

This is Your Life—(PSC; "Killer Sheep") The printed script calls for a bit of the show's theme music. *This is Your Life* was a radio series created by Ralph Edwards in the late 1940s. It led to a U.S. television series that ran on NBC from 1952 to 1961. The British version appeared on the BBC 1955-1964, then moved to Thames TV in 1969.

The snippet of music played as the Commissioner is rolled out is not from *This Is Your Life*, as requested in the printed script, but is instead the theme for the very popular *Sunday Night at the Palladium* (1955), a weekly musical variety show.

Today in Parliament—("*Today in Parliament*") A BBC Radio program that has covered political proceedings at the Houses of Parliament since 1945, and had been broadcast from Westminster.

"tonight's star prize"—("*Take Your Pick*") Michael Miles did offer a "star prize" on *Take Your Pick*, though the prize was more likely to be a lounge suite, as seen later in the "Communist Quiz" sketch (Ep. 25).

Turkish music—(PSC; "Secretary of State Striptease") The music here is borrowed from an LP and is performed by the Concert Band of Her Majesty's Lifeguards, featuring John Leach. The track is called "Arabian Belly Dance" (WAC T12/1,433).

"Ty Gudrun and Nik Con"—("*The Attila the Hun Show*") Nik Cohn (b. 1946, Ireland) is a rock journalist whose works pioneered the critical appreciation of the rock music industry. By late 1970 he had published *I Am Still the Greatest Says Johnny Angelo* (1967), *Pop* (1969), *Awopbopaloobop Alopbamboom* (1970) and *Market* (1970). His magazine article "Tribal Rites of the New Saturday Night" led to the hit movie *Saturday Night Fever* (1977).

"Ty Gudrun"—The Baader-Meinhof Gang was active in Germany during this period (firebombing department stores, for example), and leader Gudrun Ensslin could have inspired the other name chosen here.

– U –

"Uncle Tom"—("*The Attila the Hun Show*") Titular character in Harriet Beecher Stowe's *Uncle Tom's Cabin* (1851-1852), but also used allusively and derogatively for any servile black man, or even as a catch-all term for any black man.

"University of East Anglia"—("The Idiot in Society") In Norwich, the university was set up in 1963, one of many new universities chartered as the Robbins Report was surfacing. The university's motto is "Do Different," which may account for the Pythons' placing of the idioting degree at UEA. The motto comes from the old Norfolk saying, "People in Norfolk do things different." It was also the first English university to adopt the modular, semester system.

Much of the location work for this part of the second series was shot in and around Norwich, meaning the Pythons' proximity to UEA could also account for its inclusion here.

University scarves—(PSC; "The Idiot in Society") Scarves that indicate a particular school matriculation. The fact that UEA also sits adjacent to Norfolk, seen as the best-preserved medieval English town in the country, is also significant as the sketch discusses the transition between ancient village life and the modern world. See UEA's website for more.

This dancing scene was shot at Stanford Training Area, West Tofts Camp, Norfolk (WAC T12/1,242).

University setting—(PSC; "The Idiot in Society") This setting—where the Vice-Chancellor is awarding degrees to the Idiots—was filmed at Elm Hill, Norwich (WAC T12/1,242).

– V –

Viking—("Killer Sheep") Various Pythons dressed as Vikings act as transitional (linking) or just interruptive elements throughout the series. Perhaps a nod to the

Viking culture's history as marauders and plunderers up and down England's seacoasts and rivers, but more likely the Viking get-up just looks appropriately incongruous.

There is also a similar, perhaps ur-*Monty Python* moment in the popular Ealing comedy *I'm All Right Jack* (1959), where, at a television studio, two actors dressed as Vikings walk casually (and obviously) through the shot, then stop and stare.

"village idiot"—("The Idiot in Society") This term may be no older than the Pythons' parents' generation, actually. "Village idiot" seems to appear in print first in G.B. Shaw's play *Major Barbara* (1907), so he's at least English, if not medieval. There are significant mentions of idiots in smaller villages and towns, in both American and British literature, but the term "village idiot" seems of more recent coinage.

The attire chosen for the village idiot here is identical to that chosen for the Rustic (Chapman) in Ep. 2, and later the Hay Wain (Jones playing yet another rustic) depicted in Ep. 25. The idiot's name, Arthur Figgis, was also used in Ep. 2.

Continuing their interest in English poets, this idiot motif might also be drawn from Wordsworth's *Lyrical Ballads* collection, specifically "The Idiot Boy" (1798), wherein a retarded child is sent into a village to fetch a doctor.

– W –

"wainscotting"—("Wainscotting") Formerly, imported oak used for paneling, though now referring just to the paneling itself, whatever the wood type. The exteriors for these cutaways to the "little Dorset village" were shot in Heydon Village, where much of the "Idiot in Society" sketch was shot (WAC T12/1,242).

"Warner, Plum"—("Test Match") Truly a "Grand Old Man" of English cricket (though not as early as 1732), Sir Pelham Francis Warner (1873-1963) was both a player and later administrator, founding *The Cricketer* magazine (now *Cricketer International*). Warner was also a batsman and Captain for Oxford University (Championship in 1920) and England, where he was captain for the successful 1903-1904 Ashes tour. He would go on to become a Test selector and Chairman of the Test selectors, as well as occupying various leadership positions in the MCC until his death. See the *ODNB* for more.

"WC Pedestal"—("The Epsom Furniture Race") A water closet (bathroom) sink and pedestal.

Westminster—("*Today in Parliament*") Westminster is the home of the Palace of Westminster (including the Houses of Parliament) and Westminster Abbey.

"What do penguins eat?"—("*Take Your Pick*") This seemingly simple and innocent question elicits a barrage of wrong answers from Mrs. Scum (Jones), including:

"Cannelloni"—Rolls of pastry or pasta filled with cream or meat. The word "cannelloni" does sound like a sea creature, however.

"Lasagna . . . with cheese"—Moussaka is a traditional Mediterranean meat and potatoes dish, while lobster thermidor is a haute cuisine sauce-and-cheese, in-shell dish. The latter is also mentioned in Ep. 25, during one of the Spam menu recitations.

"Brian Close"—The cricket references continue. Dennis Brian Close (b. 1931) is a cricketer who played for Yorkshire, Somerset, and England; he was a left hand bat. Close was Wisden Cricketer of the Year in 1964, and will be referenced again in Ep. 21.

"Brian Inglis, Brian Johnson, Bryan Forbes"—Brian Inglis wrote significantly on the Irish situation, especially in the 1950s and 1960s; Brian Johns(t)on was a longtime host of BBC's *Sportsview*; and Bryan Forbes (b. 1926) is a British actor/director/writer who appeared in *The Guns of Navarone* (1961) and wrote *King Rat* (1965). Forbes also directed *The Madwoman of Chaillot* (1969), which will be mentioned in Ep. 23. Johnston will be mentioned again in Ep. 21, and is castigated by the editors of *Private Eye* in late 1970.

"Nanette Newman"—Newman (b. 1934, Northampton) appeared in the 1970 film *The Raging Moon* for director Bryan Forbes (see above), which probably accounts for their proximity/inclusion here.

"Reginald Maudling"—Home Secretary under Heath's Conservative administration (1970-1974). Maudling is a consistent Python target, and will be mentioned again in Eps. 22 and 30.

If this were the portion of *Take Your Pick* known as the "Yes/No Interlude," where the contestant had to answer questions over a sixty-second period without saying either "yes" or "no," then Mrs. Scum performs very well. Most contestants (drawn from the studio audience) couldn't last more than a few seconds with Miles.

wide-shot of Lords—(PSC; "Test Match") This footage of a match at Lords is drawn from the BBC Library's own collection of classic cricket film stock (WAC T12/1,242). Lords cricket ground is located at St. John's Wood, Greater London, and is named after founder Thomas Lord (1757-1832). It is the headquarters of the Marylebone Cricket Club (MCC), mentioned as being the only organization able to withstand the Piranha brothers in Ep. 14. The Pythons identify Lords as one of the pillars of the "idiot in society" world.

"Wildeburg Bo"—("Test Match") Bo *Wideberg* (1930-1997) was a Swedish director of the period, most notably directing *Elvira Madigan* in 1967.

"wild slogging"—("Test Match") A vernacular term for aggressive (or even overly aggressive) batting in cricket. The term is not covered in Lord's *Laws of Cricket*. The "boundaries" indicate both the edges of the playing area and the scoring possibilities while batting (when the ball touches or goes over the boundary, or the fielder touching the ball does same, for example). Boundaries are discussed in Law 19 of the *Laws of Cricket* published by MCC (pages 42-45). The term "innings" (always plural when used in this way) indicate when one side is "in" or at bat, and/or any one batsman during his turn at bat. An "over" is a sequence of six balls bowled by one bowler from one end of the pitch.

"wolf's clothing"—("Killer Sheep") Playing on the Aesopian and biblical allusions to the wolf in sheep's clothing (Matt. 7:15). In *HG*, it is a harmless white bunny that kills many knights, and has to be destroyed by the Holy Hand Grenade. In many Warner Bros. cartoons the smallest, least harmful-looking characters (chicken hawks, gremlins, chicks) often packed the biggest punch, which may have informed this *FC* scenario.

Episode 21

– A –

"abolished hanging"—("Judges") In the UK, the death penalty was replaced by life imprisonment by the Murder (Abolition of Death Penalty) Act of 1965, with the exception of acts of high treason and piracy. See notes to Ep. 15 for more on previous mentions of capital punishment.

"Abu Simnel"—("*Archaeology Today*") The site of the Temple of Abu *Simbel* in Egypt built during the reign of Ramses II, where four large, seated statues still guard the entrance. This site was much in the news during this period, which may account for its inclusion here. The building of the Aswan Dam (1960-1970) and the creation of Lake Nasser would have inundated the site, and between 1963 and 1968 the entire temple was with great fanfare disassembled and moved to higher ground.

In Ep. 14, a Mrs. April *Simnel* (Palin) reminisces fondly about the young "boot-in" Piranha brothers.

"Annaley . . . Softee"—("Trailer") A great example of scriptwriting without checking for spelling or factual errors, this rider's name is actually "Anneli Drummond-Hay," and her mounts were Merely-a-Monarch and November Rain, among others. Drummond-Hay won the Burghley Three Day event in 1961, the Great Badminton in 1962, etc., and was a well-known rider of the period.

"Mr. Softee" was an award-winning Northern Ireland show jumping horse that competed in the 1968 Summer Olympics, and was ridden by David Broome. The show jumping theme will return to *FC* in Ep. 28, "The BBC Is Short of Money," when Mrs. Kelly's flat is being used for studio space, as well as Ep. 42, the "Show Jumping (Musical)" sketch.

archaeological dig—(PSC; "*Archaeology Today*") The Middle-Eastern atmospheric music used in the transition to the dig site is the London Studio Orchestra's version of "Casbah" by Keith Papworth (WAC T12/1,429).

"*Archaeology Today*"—("*Archaeology Today*") An allusion to the show *Chronicle*—a fifty-minute, monthly program on BBC2 that took to the air in 1966, and focused on archaeology and history. Glyn Daniels (Cambridge archaeology lecturer) and Magnus Magnusson introduced the show. See notes below for "Silbury Dig."

"Arnold, P.P."—("Leapy Lee") Born Patricia Ann Cole in Los Angeles, P.P. Arnold was "discovered" by Tina Turner, then by Bill Wyman and Charlie Watts, and she was off to a singing and acting career in England in 1966.

"awful bore"—("Mr. and Mrs. Git") The obviously atrocious first names aren't noticed by the Gits, just their unfortunate last name, a structure of misunderstanding employed by the Pythons and English Renaissance dramatists Shakespeare, Jonson, and especially Dekker (see *MPSERD*). This is perhaps an allusion to the well-known "Ima Hogg" appellation from American (Texas) history. The last name was unfortunate enough (to the hearer), but when coupled with the choice of first names, American folkloric history was created. Ima's brothers were more carefully named William, Michael, and Thomas.

– B –

"Bailie"—("Judges") Derivation of "bailiff," a bailie is now "a municipal magistrate corresponding to the English alderman" (*OED*). Used more in Scotland, according to the *OED*, which fits the Glaswegian allusions of this sketch.

"Baldwin, Mrs. Stanley"—("Mrs. Thing and Mrs. Entity") Stanley Baldwin (1867-1947) was a Conservative

MP and later Chancellor of the Exchequer, then PM in 1923 when Bonar Law resigned due to ill health. He had married Lucy (Mrs. Stanley Baldwin) in 1892.

See the entry for Baldwin in Ep. 14, where he's mentioned in regard to an alleged sexual relationship with Dinsdale Piranha. Baldwin and his Conservative government will again be mentioned in Ep. 24, when the stripping (and wearing ladies underclothes) Ramsay MacDonald appears.

"bent"—("Judges") The term often means corrupt or venal, but here it's given the obviously more British meaning of gay or effeminate.

"black cap"—("Judges") *OED*: "That worn by English judges when in full dress, and consequently put on by them when passing sentence of death upon a prisoner."

"body stocking"—("Judges") A full body leotard, often worn in place of undergarments and, often, to give the illusion of nudity. The Lycra-based product appeared in about 1965, and quickly became fashionable.

brothers standing on a tank—(PSC; "Mosquito Hunters") This shot was taken at the main gate, Army School of Transport, Longmore, Liss, Hampshire (WAC T12/1,413). The Tory Housewives will also pose on the tank here for Ep. 32.

"bugger"—(end credits) Slang, meaning someone who participates in sodomy, or "buggery." This is the last word used, as an invective, in Ep. 15, as Cardinal Ximinez (Palin) fails to reach the Old Bailey in time.

"butch"—("Judges") Originally an American slang, the *OED* defines "butch" as "a tough youth or man; a lesbian of masculine appearance or behaviour." In this scene the usually effeminate men are describing their more masculine moments using the term, especially a more "mannish" voice.

– C –

camp—(PSC; "Poofy Judges") A slang word meaning "ostentatious, exaggerated, affected, theatrical," and in this case stereotypically homosexual (*OED*). The Pythons often "camp it up" when depicting effeminate men—an affectation borrowed from the music hall, the Goons and Benny Hill, among others, and which has become one of the hallmarks of Monty Python's over-the-top-ness. All the troupe members take it in turn "swanning about," including Gilliam as the flamboyant glam-boy in Ep. 9 and the equally poofy Algy in Ep. 33, Chapman as a policeman in makeup (Ep. 14) and as David Unction (Ep. 10), and all as gay army personnel (Ep. 22). Here, as elsewhere in *FC*, a stuffy or

authority-type figure is undercut by lampooning or questioning (or outing) his sexuality, a technique used by screenwriter Terry Southern (a Python mate) in the 1964 satirical film *Dr. Strangelove*, as well.

"catarrh"—("Mr. and Mrs. Git") Essentially, fluid from a runny nose (and eyes).

characters are in twenties' clothes—(PSC; "Archaeology Today") The costuming requests for this sketch describe Cleese's Eversley costume as "a Mortimer Wheeler type" (WAC T12/1,429). Sir Mortimer Wheeler (1890-1976) was an eminent English archaeologist who did significant work in the London area, and brought archaeology to the general public via radio and television shows including *Animal, Vegetable, Mineral?* (1952) and *Chronicle* (1966; with Magnus Magnusson). The young Pythons would have grown up with the dapper Wheeler as their image of a proper archaeologist, certainly.

"cheeky"—("Poofy Judges") Common British colloquialism, meaning to be insolent or audacious. It's adapted from "cheek," meaning to talk insolently.

"Chopper"—("Colin Mozart [Ratcatcher]") Could just refer to Colin's chosen killing technique, but also is slang for a machine gun, or one who operates such a gun. (A machine gun will figure in later in the sketch.) This term also means a fine, strapping child. This is probably also yet another intertextual reference to Detective Chief Inspector Leonard "Nipper" Read, responsible for arresting many celebrities during this period (see notes to Ep. 14).

"Close, Brian"—("Trailer") Wisden Cricketer of the Year in 1964. See notes to Ep. 20 for more on Close.

cocktail party—("Mr. and Mrs. Git") In this scene the camera first focuses in on a book being read by one of the partygoers: *Raising Gangsters For Fun & Profit*. The title is probably a reference to F.G. Ashbrook's *Raising Small Animals for Pleasure and Profit* (1951), or even a galley (or UK) version of Paul Villiard's book *Raising Small Animals for Fun & Profit*, which was eventually published in the United States in 1973.

The two featured extras in this scene are Patricia Prior (*Troubleshooters*) and Barbara Lindley (*Benny Hill*). Lindley also appears as the bride in the "Registrar (Wife Swap)" sketch.

"Coleman, David"—("Trailer") Coleman (b. 1926) was a presenter of the World Cup Final in 1966, where Wolstenholme supplied commentary, for BBC1. See the entry for *Grandstand* below.

"Common Market"—("Mrs. Thing and Mrs. Entity") A reference to the much-debated common pan-European trade market, where duties on trade were, ideally, either reduced or done away with altogether, creating a large, powerful trade zone able to compete with, for example, the exploding and rapacious postwar U.S. market. In the late 1950s France, West Germany, Italy, Belgium, Luxembourg, and Holland formed the consortium, with France (and specifically anglophobe President De Gaulle) tweaking Britain's nose by refusing to admit England into the group.

Many in Britain resisted membership for many years (see Marwick's comment about Britain's xenophobia in *British Society Since 1945*, page 133), but it was Conservative PM "Mr. Heath" (1970-1974), ironically, who was instrumental in bringing the country to the CM table in the early 1960s. Full membership for the UK would come in 1973.

"Compton, Denis"—("Trailer") Denis Charles Scott Compton (1918-1997) was a cricketer, and played for Middlesex, Holkar, Europeans (India), and England. His first Test appearance was in 1937, and two years later he was named Wisden Cricketer of the Year (*ODNB*).

– D –

Danielle joins in—(PSC; "*Archaeology Today*") The dig has become much like a Hollywood musical from the 1930-1960 period, where characters can un-self-consciously break into song at any moment to swelling, extradiegetic music. In critical terms, this would qualify as a fairy tale musical (see Altman), where "sex as adventure" and "sex as battle" are played out through song and dance. Here, the adventure is the dig and discovery, and the battle is between Sir Robert (Cleese) and his romantic interest Danielle (Cleveland), and the Interviewer (Palin) and his fawning "partner" Kastner (Jones). The melodramatic nature of the Silbury Dig itself (huge egos looking in vain for bits of history) certainly contributed to this sketch, as the Silbury dig was carried out in front of BBC cameras and a watchful nation. See notes for "Silbury Dig" below for more on the media event.

"Davis, Joe"—("Trailer") Called the world's greatest snooker player, Davis (1901-1978) was a fourteen-time world champion before retiring, unbeaten, in 1946. Davis was awarded the OBE in 1963. See the *ODNB* for more on Davis.

"Day, Robin"—("Registrar [Wife Swap]") A noted TV interviewer (*Panorama*), Day is characterized as helping usher in the more pointed, combative style of modern journalism. See notes to Ep. 2 for more, as well as the *ODNB*.

"deed poll"—("Registrar [Wife Swap]") This means that Mr. Git's (Jones) name change attempt would be "made and executed" by just one party (*OED*).

"dirty version"—("Mr. and Mrs. Git") This piling on of crudities is a precursor to the "*Most Awful Family in Britain*" sketch that will appear later in Ep. 45, the final original episode broadcast for the show.

"dolly sentences"—("Judges") Actually a cricket (and gaming) term meaning easy, soft. In Ep. 15, the Judge (Chapman) was also complaining about the lack of real teeth in criminal case punishments, and was off for the more corporal South Africa the very next day.

Dulwich—(PSC; "Mr. and Mrs. Git") The city setting is only mentioned in the script, and not by any of the characters (or by subtitle). Dulwich is a city in Greater London, south of Westminster. Dulwich is characterized as a well-to-do, perhaps even Tory-friendly area, boasting, among others, Margaret Thatcher's residence. See notes to Ep. 19 for more.

Durante, Jimmy—(PSC; "Colin Mozart [Ratcatcher]") Durante (1893-1980) was an American vaudeville, film, and television entertainer. An accomplished musician, Durante also played in jazz bands for many years.

"I'm the guy that found the lost chord"—This is a multi-layered reference, to be sure. Firstly, light opera composer Arthur Sullivan (of Gilbert and Sullivan) wrote "The Lost Chord" as a serious work to offset his well-known lighter pieces. The gist, according to Sullivan, is the elusiveness of that "perfect" chord, found and then inevitably lost, which can only be reclaimed upon crossing the veil into the afterlife. Jimmy Durante later sang of finding that same chord as he sat at the "pianer . . . improvisin' symphonies." "Bing! Bing!" and he has the chord, then just as quickly—"Bong! Bong!"—and the chord is lost. Try as he might, he cannot find the chord again, remembering, lastly and ironically, that he normally plays "by ear" (Schroth). This entire Beethoven/mynah bird/ratcatcher scene then, is based on this "lost chord" idea; if Beethoven truly played by ear, his deafness would have finished his composing career (it did not, of course).

This recording is from Jimmy Durante's *Schnozzles* record album (WAC T12/1,429).

– E –

"Egyptian tomb paintings"—("*Archaeology Today*") If they are truly in the studio to discuss El Ara, then a scholar like Kastner is out of place. Abu Simbel is a temple site, not a burial site, and features bas-relief works and carved statues.

Episode 21—Recorded as the eighth show of the second series on 9 October 1970. This episode was broadcast 17 November 1970.

Also appearing in or working for this episode are Barbara Lindley (*Benny Hill*), Pat Prior (*Dr. Who*), and Bill McGuffie (*Softly Softly*; *Dr. Who*) and his orchestra. Extras (uncredited) in this episode include Troy Adams (*Upstairs, Downstairs*), Gary Deans (*Dr. Who*), Barry Ashton (*Dr. Who*), Derek Hunt (*Z Cars*), Constance Carling (*Softly Softly*; *Z Cars*), and Jean Sadgrove (*Z Cars*).

"Eversley, Robert"—(*"Archaeology Today"*) Loosely based on Prof. Richard Atkinson, leader of the Silbury Dig. See "Silbury Dig" notes below.

There also may be a reference to an earlier explorer of the Abu Simbel site, Giovanni Belzoni (1778-1823), who reportedly stood 6' 7" tall. The *Catholic Encyclopedia* reports that Giovanni performed in pantomime and music hall–type performances in London to support himself and his English wife earlier in his life, which may account for the musical references the Pythons include. Belzoni is credited with removing the sand from around the temple in the early nineteenth century, and reportedly removed most of the portable artifacts from the dig.

– F –

fairly rough country location—(PSC; *"Mosquito Hunters"*) Much of this scene was shot in the Easton, River Bank and Ringland Woods area. The exterior work for *"Attila"* (Ep. 20) and Dame Irene (*"Foreign Secretary,"* Ep. 19) was also photographed in this area, all on 24 August 1970 (WAC T12/1,413).

"fifth dynasty"—(*"Archaeology Today"*) The Fifth Dynasty (2490-2330 BC) in Egypt is characterized as a period of relative decline, with smaller pyramids being built. Mentioned later, the Fourth Dynasty (2613-2494 BC) in Egypt was characterized by more significant pyramid construction. The Silbury Mound is thought to have been built c. 2750 BC. This proximity probably meant that news coverage of the Silbury Dig period highlighted the more familiar Egyptian dynasties for BBC viewer reference.

The Hittites were non-Semitic peoples in Asia Minor who flourished from approximately 1900 to 700 BC (*OED*).

first few notes of the fifth symphony—(*"Beethoven's Mynah Bird"*) Historically, there doesn't seem to be any indication that Beethoven struggled with these well-known notes, nor that he ever married (so that his wife could constantly disturb him). His deafness was progressing rapidly as this symphony was being composed (1804-1808).

Flick Colby Dancers, Pan's People—(PSC; *"Trailer"*) Dance troupe formed by BBC dancer/choreographer Flick Colby, as was the Pan's People troupe. The dancers appeared regularly on BBC's *Top of the Pops*. These dance troupes would perform to a well-known song when the song's performer was unable to appear.

"four corners"—(*"Archaeology Today"*) An image of the measure of creation attributed to Coverdale's version of the Old Testament.

"funny he never married"—(*"Mrs. Thing and Mrs. Entity"*) Heath (1916-1992) never did marry, but there doesn't seem to have been any real evidence that Heath favored men, according to his biographer John Campbell (1993). Mrs. Entity and Mrs. Thing seem to be positing a relationship between Heath's bachelor status and his unwillingness to hop into bed with France and the rest of Europe.

– G –

"Galsworthy, John"—(*"Trailer"*) Galsworthy (1867-1933) was a Nobel-prize winner (1932), an actor and playwright/novelist. This reference is undoubtedly connected to his epic *Forsyte Saga* that premiered on BBC in 1967 starring Nyree Dawn Porter—it was a critically hailed and very popular twenty-two-hour miniseries.

"Git"—(*"Mr. and Mrs Git."*) A slang term meaning a worthless or useless person. Originally from Scotland and northern England, "git" is a derivation of "get," and specifically refers to a bastard, or a brat (*OED*). The term will reappear in Ep. 29 as part of the "Abuse" section of the oft-quoted "Argument Clinic" sketch.

gobs—(PSC; *"Mr. and Mrs. Git"*) Usually meaning "spits," but here she nearly throws up. Ken Shabby (Palin) earlier "gobbed" on Rosamund's Father's (Chapman) carpet in Ep. 12.

Grandstand—(*"Trailer"*) Billed as the longest-running live sports series, *Grandstand* took to the air in 1958 (BBC), and was hosted by David Coleman until 1968. The *Grandstand* tune was penned by Keith Mansfield, but the tune actually used in this transition (and just a snippet at that) is Burns' "Saturday Sport" (WAC T12/1,429).

– H –

"had"—(*"Judges"*) Meaning he "had" him sexually, it would seem. This is an Old English usage, but certainly familiar to the Pythons.

Hammond organ accompaniment—(PSC; *"Archaeology Today"*) The cheesy organ accompaniment to Eversley's obviously dubbed song is provided by the song's composer, Bill McGuffie, and members of his orchestra.

"Harrods"—("Registrar [Wife Swap]") Giant, upscale department store in Knightsbridge, London, originally established in 1849.

"hen"—("Judges") A diminutive term of affection, like "love" or "dear." Idle's floor director character will also use it in Ep. 12 as the minister (Chapman) hangs upside down.

"Hittite"—("*Archaeology Today*") An ancient Iron Age civilization centered in what is today Turkey.

"Sumerian"—The Sumerian culture existed long before the Hittites in the ancient Near East.

"Hutton, Sir Len"—("Leapy Lee") Leonard Hutton (1916-1990) was a cricketer who played for Yorkshire and England. His Test debut came in 1937; he was named Wisden Cricketer of the Year in 1938, and knighted for "services to cricket" in 1956. The continuing mentions of cricket legends like Hutton, Compton (see above), and W.G. Grace, among others, indicate the singular importance of cricket in the Pythons' collective youth. English football players also get this kind of star treatment in *FC*.

– I –

"I didn't like the colour"—("Registrar [Wife Swap]") The Pythons' rather ambivalent attitude toward women is perhaps no better represented than here, where a wife's/woman's place as commodity, an article of trade, is reinforced. Elsewhere in *FC*, actual females are most often included for their physical attributes, with Carol Cleveland only occasionally being allowed a fair share in the funmaking. And if they're not being ogled, the female in *FC* is often the target of abuse, both verbal and physical.

– J –

"Jacklin, Tony"—("Trailer") Internationally known British golfer, not a television announcer. Those who own Jacklin's "golf clubs" are excoriated by the architect (Cleese) in Ep. 17.

Jacklin had been named Sportsman of the Year in 1969, and appeared in February 1970 on the very popular *This Is Your Life* (1955-), significantly, as the Pythons prepared to write the scripts for the second series of *Flying Circus*.

Jewish accent—(PSC; "Colin Mozart [Ratcatcher]") It's unclear why the Pythons would give Mozart—born

and raised as a German-speaking Austrian—a Jewish accent, except that it's a noticeable incongruity. See the note for Mendelssohn below for a more practicable usage of such an accent. Idle's portrayal of Shakespeare is also Jewish-accented, for perhaps the same reasons.

"JP's"—("Judges") Semi-offical shorthand for Justice of the Peace, so-called "inferior magistrates" for county or town legal enforcement. As representatives of the establishment, JPs are natural targets of the Pythons' ridicule, in this case by calling into question their sexual orientations.

– K –

"Kant"—("Colin Mozart [Ratcatcher]") The list of occupants in this star-studded apartment include:

"Mr. and Mrs. Emmanuel Kant"—Kant (1724-1804) was an eminent philosopher whose belief in the *a priori* nature of certain, necessary, and determinable truths guided much of the trajectory of twentieth-century philosophy, and included the bridging of the Materialist and Idealist modes of philosophical thought. His belief in "things as we experience them" seems key to the Pythons' created world, where experience of a situation or reaction often flies in the face of the expected.

"Frau Mitzi Handgepäckaufbewahrung"—Roughly translates into "Mrs. Mitzi Carry-on Luggage Storage." For their Bavarian episodes, Connie Booth will play Princess Mitzi Gaynor in "Schnapps With Everything," the second *Fliegender Zirkus* episode.

"Mr. Dickie Wagner"—Given the "great man" motif employed thus far, this is most likely Richard Wagner (1813-1883), the nineteenth-century German composer.

"K. Tynan"—Kenneth Tynan (1927-1980) was a flamboyant, effete British theatre critic seemingly devoted to smoking, sadomasochism, and regularly upsetting the status quo. Tynan was the drama critic for *The Observer* during the Angry Young Men heyday, and helped champion the movement. He also was the first person to use the word "f**k" live on the BBC—quite matter-of-factly, too—bringing upon himself the rage of myriad Conservative *and* Labour politicians, Mary Whitehouse, and many in Britain's "moral majority" of the period. He was seen by many as the flagbearer for the so-called permissive society (Eps. 8 and 32), and a downward-trending moral barometer.

Tynan attended Magdalen, Oxford, and his in-your-face literary, sexual, and public style made him the ideal Python hero figure, especially as they chafed against the restrictions of the BBC and the television medium in *Flying Circus*. For more on Tynan, see the *ODNB* and the many references to the critic in the pages of *Private Eye*.

"Mr. and Mrs. J.W. Von Goethe"—Johann Wolfgang von Goethe (1749-1832) was a German Romantic writer. As for a "Mrs." Goethe married Christiane Volpius late in life, in 1806.

"Herr E.W. Swanton"—E.W. "Jim" Swanton (1907-2000) was a legendary cricket broadcaster who's already been mentioned earlier in this episode. See notes to Ep. 20 for more on Swanton, as well as *ODNB*.

"Mr. and Mrs. P. Anka"—Paul Anka (b. 1941) is a Canadian pop singer and prolific songwriter and lyricist. He wrote the lyrics for Frank Sinatra's "My Way." Anka had appeared on *The Ed Sullivan Show* in 1969, and had toured the UK in the late 1950s at the height of his teen idol fame. "Mrs. Paul Anka" was Anne De Zogheb, whom he married in 1963.

"Mr. and Mrs. Ludwig van Beethoven"—The lifespan is correct (1770-1827), but Beethoven was never married, though he seemed to have involved himself in a number of tempestuous romantic relationships, often with involved women.

This same kind of laundry list of celebrity names reportedly living in a nondescript apartment will be revisited in Ep. 27, when Mrs. Premise (Cleese) and Mrs. Conclusion (Chapman) travel to Paris to visit Jean-Paul Sartre.

There is something of a German theme to this particular apartment setting, supposedly the home of composer Beethoven (Bonn) and fellow Germanics Kant (born in East Prussia), Wagner (born in Liepzig), and Goethe (Frankfurt).

"Kastner, Prof. Lucien"—(*"Archaeology Today"*) Seems to be loosely modeled after Magnus Magnusson (b. 1929, Iceland), host of *Chronicle* and former reporter for *Tonight*.

– L –

"Laker, Jim"—("Trailer") James Charles Laker (1922-1986, Yorkshire) was a noted Test player who also appeared in the cricket-themed film *The Final Test* (1953), written by Terence Rattigan. (Rattigan will be mentioned again—killed, actually—in Ep. 30.) Laker played primarily for Surrey, Essex, and for England. His Test debut was 1947-1948, and he was named Wisden Cricketer of the Year in 1952 (*ODNB*).

Laker may also have been the model for the "Jim" character (played by Cleese) in the "Test Match" sketch in Ep. 20.

"Leapy Lee"—("Leapy Lee") Comedian/singer whose real name is Lee Graham (b. 1942), Leapy had a close relationship with Ray Davies and the Kinks, and formed a backup group for himself called the Peppers in 1968. Davies wrote "King of the Whole Wide World" for Lee in 1966. Lee was appearing on *Beat Club* (German TV) in 1968-1969.

"Little arrows that will"—Lyric from the song called "Little Arrows" released in 1968-1969, and sung by Leapy Lee. The song was reissued three more times in the following years.

The boxer who appears and floors Leapy Lee (Idle) is played by Gilliam, who from the beginning of *FC* has taken on small walk-on roles as needed during taping. He has also played the ubiquitous Knight, a Viking, and a man with a stoat through his head in the early episodes. According to BBC records, Gilliam was paid stipends by the appearance for these roles.

"Lockheed Starfighter"—("Mosquito Hunters") The F-104 was the state-of-the-art fighter/bomber built by the United States in the mid-1950s and part of the West German, Belgium, Japan, and Netherlands air forces well into the 1980s.

"Lulu"—("Trailer") A British pop singer, Lulu (born Marie MacDonald McLaughlin Lawrie in Scotland, 1948) sang the theme song for the film *To Sir With Love* (1969) and became an immediate sensation. Lulu will appear in Ep. 28, with Ringo Starr and the It's Man (Palin), and she is featured on the *Radio Times* cover on 29 March 1969.

– M –

"Mao Tse Tung"—("Leapy Lee") Leader of the People's Republic of China. Mao is also mentioned prominently in Eps. 19, 23, 24, and 25. See notes in those episodes for more on the international presence of China during this period.

"Maudling, Mrs. Reginald"—("Mrs. Thing and Mrs. Entity") Maudling was a Conservative MP and Cabinet secretary, and is mentioned/ridiculed perhaps more than any other living politician in *FC*. "Mrs. Reginald Maudling" was Beryl Laverick Maudling, and they were married in 1939. A favorite lightning rod for the Pythons and the Left, then-Home Secretary Maudling appeared on the BBC (news, election coverages, current and political affairs shows) more than 200 times in the late 1960s and through the course of the run of *Flying Circus*. See the BBC Programme Catalogue for more. Also, confirming Maudling's status as a recognizable face of the Conservatives, just between 1969 and 1974 Maudling is lampooned in at least 275 political cartoons in newspapers of every kind in the UK. See the British Cartoon Archive.

"Mein Lieber Gott"—("Beethoven's Mynah Bird") Beethoven's German expressions of frustration translate as: "My dear God" and "God in Heaven."

"Mendelssohns"—("Beethoven's Mynah Bird") Felix Mendelssohn (1809-1847) was born into a Jewish family, but later converted. He wasn't alive when Beethoven was composing his Fifth Symphony. Mendelssohn became friends with Goethe in 1821 (see note for Goethe). Mendelssohn's wife was Cecile Jeanrenaud, and they would have five children.

"Michelangelo"—("Michelangelo" link into "Colin Mozart [Ratcatcher]") Michelangelo (1475-1564) was an Italian Renaissance painter, poet, and sculptor, and preferred men to women, at least romantically.

"Mozart"—("Colin Mozart [Ratcatcher]") Presumably Wolfgang Amadeus Mozart (1756-1791), he also appears in Ep. 1, as the host of "Famous Deaths." W.A. Mozart did have two sons (with Konstanze Weber), Karl Thomas (b. 1784) and minor composer Wolfgang Franz Xaver Mozart (b. 1791).

Wolfgang and Constanze had six children together, two of whom lived into adulthood, and both children pursued music-affiliated careers.

"Mrs. Thing"—(PSC; "Mrs. Thing and Mrs. Entity") Probably a reference to philosopher Nietzsche's work on the impossibility of a "thing-in-itself," and the importance of "relationships" and "actions" (see *The Will to Power*).

– N –

"Nabarro, Sir Gerald"—("Leapy Lee") A rather flamboyant Conservative MP, Nabarro is mentioned and lampooned in *FC* more than once. See notes to Ep. 11 and 15. Nabarro will also be mentioned by name in Ep. 23.

"National Trust"—("Silly Vicar") The National Trust was founded in the nineteenth century to preserve the UK's historic buildings and places. This type of publicized appeal isn't uncommon. In the late 1920s there was a concerted effort on behalf of the National Trust to save Stonehenge, for example, including newspaper advertisements and broadsides.

– O –

"Off-Spin Bowling"—("Trailer") A cricket bowling term, this is a spin that moves the ball from the off side and toward the leg side. See Rundell's *The Dictionary of Cricket* (1995).

Old Bailey—(PSC; "Poofy Judges") "Old Bailey" is mentioned here as a setting, and not in dialogue. Home of the Central Criminal Court, the Old Bailey

features prominently in Ep. 15 and the "Spanish Inquisition" sketch.

"Old Man of Hoy"—("Trailer") A prominent sandstone sea stack landmark about 137 meters high, found in the Orkney Islands. The Old Man had been climbed in 1967, and BBC cameras were there. See notes to Ep. 31 and 33 for more on this media event.

ono—(PSC; "Trailer") This is an acronym included in the printed script, "o.n.o.", "or near(est) offer," and is a note to the Pythons themselves and the show's researcher. In other words, in the case of a needed photo of the Flick Colby Dancers or Pan's People, any contemporary dance troupe picture would do, and the Pythons weren't sure what their researcher would be able to find in the interim.

"Owzat"—("Trailer") A colloquialism used in cricket, meaning "How's that?"

– P –

"Panorama"—("Trailer") Long-running (1953-) BBC current affairs program. See notes to Ep. 2, the "Mouse Problem" sketch.

Party Hints—("Leapy Lee") This could be a reference to the popular and long-running morning talk show *Girl Talk* (1963-1970), where the female hosts covered topics ranging from the Cold War to celebrity gossip to health and home issues.

"pikelets"—("Beethoven's Mynah Bird") A pikelet is a Western and Midland name for a kind of tea-cake, refocusing the Python frame of reference on the areas north and west of London, where most of them grew up, and firmly placing the Beethovens in the provincial middle-class.

"Pitt the Elder, Mrs. William"—("Mrs. Entity and Mrs. Thing") William Pitt the Elder (1708-1778) was the first Earl of Chatham. Pitt had married Lady Hester Grenville in 1754, and probably never had to go truffle hunting, especially with her snout. Female pigs were commonly employed to sniff out the buried tubers.

"Polynesian influence"—(*Archaeology Today*) Explorer Thor Heyerdahl spent the better part of his long career proving that aboriginal peoples did indeed have the technological expertise to build rafts that could cross oceans successfully. Heyerdahl's crafts, Kon Tiki, Ra, and Ra II are mentioned in Ep. 28.

"Porter, Cole with Pearl Bailey and Arthur Negus"—(*Archaeology Today*) American singer Bailey (1918-1990) released the composer Porter (1891-1964) cover album *Pearl Bailey Sings the Cole Porter Songbook* during this period. Arthur Negus (1903-1985), already mentioned prominently in Ep. 19, "Election Night Special," was a popular antiques expert and television personality. He had recently appeared on *The Jimmy Logan Show* in 1969.

"Porter, Nyree Dawn"—("Trailer") Porter (1936-2001) was a New Zealand–born actress who starred in the 1967 BBC2 staging of Galsworthy's twenty-two-hour *The Forsyte Saga*.

– Q –

"QC's"—("Poofy Judges") "Queen's Counsel," meaning in the service of the queen. Not called so because of Elizabeth, but thanks to the very long reign of Queen Victoria, and the appellation stuck. As one trained in the law, Cleese would have been very familiar with this world.

"Queen's evidence"—("Judges") Play on the double meaning of the term "queen," of course. *OED*: "To turn King's (Queen's, State's) evidence (formerly also to turn evidence), said of an accomplice or sharer in a crime: to offer himself as a witness for the prosecution against the other persons implicated." Secondly, in Ep. 10, David Unction (Chapman) calls himself "an old queen" as he's caught reading a male physique magazine.

Quiet party type music—(PSC; "Mr. and Mrs. Git") This light, vibraphone-type music is from the Franco Chiari Jazz Quartet, and is called "Romantic Theme" (WAC T12/1,429).

– R –

"rat-bag"—("Beethoven's Mynah Bird") Originally Australian and New Zealand slang, the *OED* defines it in terms ranging from "stupid" to foolish and even "uncouth." Used in Eps. 10, 16, 27, and 37 as well.

ratcatcher—("Colin Mozart [Ratcatcher]") Cf. Ep. 20 for an earlier appearance of a ratcatcher.

Registrar—(PSC; "Registrar [Wife Swap]") The Registrar is the local official who keeps records for marriages, births, deaths, etc. (*OED*). The Registrar wouldn't actually perform the wedding ceremony.

Roy Spim—(PSC; "Mosquito Hunters") Idle plays this character as a one-armed Australian big game hunter. This may be a reference to Alan John "Jock" Marshall (1911-1967), an eminent, larger-than-life Australian academic and zoologist who was a Reader at St. Bartholomew's Hospital, where Chapman studied.

– S –

"Scottish Assizes"—("Judges") Assizes are periodic courts held throughout the United Kingdom since the twelfth century, but especially in England and Wales. The long-running joke of the well-endowed Scotsman is employed here, as well, as elsewhere in *FC* (including Ep. 37, the "Nae Trews" section of the "Ideal Loon Exhibition").

Shakespeare washing up at a sink—(PSC; "Shakespeare" link into "Colin Mozart [Ratcatcher]") What the Pythons are doing here is moving away from the "Great Man" approach to history, at least as it's usually pursued. The Pythons would have grown up with the historical approach of Thomas Carlyle (1795-1881) and undoubtedly read the *Encyclopedia Britannica Eleventh Edition* (1911), both of which focused on the noble and heroic endeavors of the greatest men in/on "History." History could be read and accessed, then, only through the exploits of such great men.

The Pythons are clearly responding to (1) the New Criticism rejection of biography in favor of close textual reading, (2) the French New History movement of the late 1960s, and (3) they are anticipating fellow Englishman Stephen Greenblatt's (Ep. 27) New Historicist movement, the second and third of which are more interested in the influence and deformative effects of culture and society on history. Also, the seemingly less significant events of history—ignored by the Great Man theorists—become much more visible and effective in such histories, where Shakespeare can participate in the housework; Beethoven can compete with his wife, household pets, and a sugar bowl; and Michelangelo can play wetnurse to his own brood. This is the elevating of the domestic to the (ig)noble, and where the Pythons spend a great deal of their time and energies in *FC*.

"Silbury Dig"—("*Archaeology Today*") In 1967 an enormous archeological dig was begun to determine the makeup and reasons for existence of Silbury Mound (or Silbury Hill, Avebury, Wiltshire), the largest man-made prehistoric mound in Europe. The mound had previously been explored at least three times, in 1732, 1776-1777, and sometime in the nineteenth century, the remnants of which were found in the 1967-1969 dig. BBC2 shot hours of documentary footage for its *Chronicle* program, and viewers by the millions tuned in to watch the findings. (Mortimer Wheeler was attached to this show. See the entry for "characters are in twenties" above for more on Wheeler.) By October 1969, the excavation was ceremonially filled in, leaving more questions than answers. Prof. Richard Atkinson led the dig, and the BBC's Paul Johnstone headed up the footage compilation. Dr. John Taylor was the mining engineer. Many saw the whole thing as a major embarrassment and boondoggle, since a much hoped-for burial site was not unearthed.

snooker cue—(PSC; "Trailer") A stick (like a pool cue) used in this billiard table game that combines pool and pyramids. Televised snooker is and has been a fixture on British TV for many years.

Snooker will be mentioned again by Mrs. Thing (Chapman) as she and Mrs. Entity (Idle) discuss the non-drudgery of married life, especially for wealthy Conservatives like Mrs. Reginald Maudling.

"sod"—("Beethoven's Mynah Bird") An insult generally meaning one who practices sodomy. In this case, the term is used as a crude invective, essentially meaning "screw the sugar bowl." This same word was earlier censored by a nervous BBC before the taping of Ep. 17, in the "Architect Sketch," and was replaced (by Cleese then, too) with a "raspberry." The viewing audience's toleration of such crudities seems to have reached new levels by this time, and the word made it through.

"Stolle, Mrs Fred"—("Leapy Lee") Pat Stolle is the wife of British tennis player Fred Stolle (b. 1938, Australia) mentioned in Ep. 7. Stolle is winner of eighteen grand slam titles.

street with old-fashioned shops—("Colin Mozart [Ratcatcher]") The music that creeps in under this transition is Mozart's "Eine Kleine Nachtmusik" (G-dur KV525) (WAC T12/1,429). This is the Rondo: Allegro movement.

This scene is shot at Elm Hill, Norwich, where a large number of early sixteenth-century Tudor homes and buildings can still be found (WAC T12/1,413).

"Swanage"—("Mr. and Mrs. Git") A Dorset coastal village south of Bournemouth, where the Pythons performed significant location shooting.

"Swanton, E.W."—("Trailer") "Jim" Swanton (1907-2000) was a longtime cricket writer for the *Daily Telegraph*, and a former player for MCC. He was also part of the first radio broadcasts of international cricket matches in the late 1930s, and made the transition to television cricket commentating (*ODNB*).

– T –

take the name—(PSC; link out of "Registrar [Wife Swap]") Referees in football (soccer) take names of those charged with infractions, keeping a record of the game and allowing for punitive action (i.e., disqualification) if additional penalties are incurred by the particular player. Those substituting must also be named

with the officials. This moment continues the sporting theme of the episode.

"Talk of the Town"—("Trailer") A very popular, trendy restaurant and cabaret (and general performance space) in London's Hippodrome that opened in 1958. The Talk of the Town billed itself as "the world's most modern theatre restaurant," and hosted the best dance troupes and bands. Also a valuable recording and performing space, The Temptations, for example, would record a live album at the club in the summer of 1970.

tense music as they worm their way forward—(PSC; "Mosquito Hunters") This mood music is Ronald Hanmer's "Elephant Country" followed by bits of "Heroic Saga" (WAC T12/1,429).

"Thatcher, Margaret"—("Leapy Lee") Idle does actually look like Thatcher here. Now Lady Thatcher (b. 1925), she was in 1970 a leading Conservative politician, first elected to the House of Commons in 1959 as Member for Finchley (*ODNB*). She was a vocal frontbencher 1964-1970, in the opposition, and in 1970 in the Heath government was appointed secretary of state for education and science. Thatcher would have been the archenemy to Pythons' liberality during this period, and is often derided (usually in Gilliam's pictorials) as a heartless Tory.

theme and film titles as for a Western—(PSC; "Archaeology Today") The "Western-type" theme music here is "Overland to Oregon Part 1" (WAC T12/1,429).

"third dynasty"—("Archeology Today") (c. 2686-2575 BC) Representing the first part of the Egyptian "Old Kingdom," the Third Dynasty covers about six rulers and about seventy-five years. Pharaohs in this dynasty were the first to construct pyramids (step) as shrines to themselves. Imhotep was born during this dynasty.

"Today I hear the robin sing"—("Archaeology Today") This song was written by Bill McGuffie, who received £20 for this and another composition heard in Ep. 17 (WAC T12/1,242). The script indicates that McGuffie plays a Hammond organ as accompaniment. McGuffie also plays accompaniment for Cleese and Chapman as they sing in Ep. 3.

"too sharp"—("Judges") Meaning here too keen, too brisk, and too forward, even.

"treacle"—("Silly Vicar") Variously a molasses-type syrup, and, anciently, a pharmacological concoction.

"trench"—("Archaeology Today") Miss Vanilla Hoare (Cleveland) acts in a trench (and has acted previously in a furrow and syncline) in Ep. 23. The significant height difference between members of the troupe was the subject of some conversation, reportedly, and here finds its way into the final staged product. There is also the real possibility that what the Pythons are lampooning are the academic reputations of archaeologists diminishing as a result of Silbury-like frustrations, leaving other archaeologists "taller" in the profession.

"Truss"—("Silly Vicar") Probably not a misprint, and the clever assumption would be that the Pythons meant to equate the work and value of the landmark-saving National Trust (est. 1895) with that of a hernia appliance. See the entry for "National Trust" above for more. Trusses will be mentioned again (and depicted) in Ep. 26, when the "Hercules Hold-Em-In" is pitched prior to *Fish Club*.

"two thousand years before"—("*Archaeology Today*") A memorial mistake here, as the young Tut ruled about a thousand years before the temple at Abu Simbel was even built. Ramesses II commissioned the temple to commemorate his own rule, and it was completed in about 1264 BC.

– U –

"used to have to get up at midnight"—("Mrs. Thing and Mrs. Entity") This oneupsmanship structure is reminiscent of the "Four Yorkshire Gentlemen" sketch first seen on *At Last the 1948 Show* in 1967.

– W –

"waggled"—("Poofy Judges") Cf. Wodehouse's usage of the word in *The Code of the Woosters*, where its coquettish possibilities are highlighted: "She *waggled* her chin, like a girl who considers that she has put over a swift one" (192). Just a few pages later, this same character (the charming and scheming "Stiffy"),

"*wiggled* from base to apex with girlish enthusiasm" (206).

"Washington Post March"—(PSC; "Beethoven's Mynah Bird") Composed by John Philip Sousa (1854-1932). Cleese had written lyrics for this tune for the *At Last the 1948 Show*, and called it "Rhubarb Tart." He also performed the song. The *FC* theme song is a version of another Sousa composition, "Liberty Bell."

"Watutsi"—("*Archeology Today*") Actually spelled "Watusi," they are a minority racial group historically in Rwanda and Burundi (*OED*). The Interviewer (Palin) probably means the Maasai tribe, who often grow to more than six feet tall.

"well-hung"—("Judges") Another sexual play on words. A hung jury is one that cannot agree on a verdict, while a well-hung man is one who possesses larger-than-average genitalia.

"West, Peter and Brian Johnston"—("Trailer") Both mentioned prominently in the previous episode. The significant presence of cricket in Eps. 20 and 21 certainly indicates the high media saturation level that Test cricket was enjoying as England played host to "Rest of the World" in the summer months of 1970. Johnston was called "the voice of cricket," and Peter West was also a much-loved cricket broadcaster. See notes to Ep. 20.

Women's Institute—(PSC; "Leapy Lee") Stock black-and-white footage of women applauding. See notes for "Women's Institute" in Ep. 2.

"Wostenholme, Kenneth"—("Trailer") Kenneth *Wolstenholme* (1920-2002) was a sports broadcaster, his credits including the monumental and memorable 1966 World Cup final at Wembley. He also appeared on *Sportsview* with David Coleman, and hosted *Match of the Day* on BBC1 and BBC2.

Episode 22

"Abbos"—("Bruces") A derogatory abbreviation of "aborigine," and in this period more commonly spelled "abos" (*OED*). The plight of the aboriginal people would have been much discussed in relation to the Queen's most recent visit to Australia, certainly. Aborigines had been enfranchised only recently, beginning in 1963, and in 1967 were included for the first time in legislative and census decisions and activities.

"And so on and so on and so on . . . "—(link out of "The Man Who Contradicts People") Cleese's acknowledment of the familiarity and repetitive (and even tedious) nature of this interrupted sketch points up a growing disaffection for both the material and structure, as well as the difficulty the Pythons were already encountering (well into the second series) in generating afresh the "Pythonesque" elements. In this they are struggling as all Modern Art types struggle—with the constant need for new outrages, new definitions, new reactions.

a penguin . . . sits contentedly looking at them in a stuffed sort of way—(PSC; "*The Death of Mary Queen of Scots*") Once again, the penguin appears as a source of incongruous humor. There's no rational reason for the penguin to be atop the TV, which is probably why they've included him, and just as little reason for it to explode later. Also, the printed script is once again creating in-jokes—references for the other *readers* only.

"Barley sugar"—("Cut-Price Airline") Doses of barley sugar sweets have been known to help diabetics get the "sugar injection" they may need before stressful activities, and has been a traditional treatment for upset stomachs and sore throats for many years.

It might be just coincidental that Man (Idle) also crosses his fingers in a "barley cross" gesture, essentially indemnifying himself from whatever he's just averred. The barley cross fingers motif was earlier mentioned in Ep. 8, "Army Protection Racket," there also by Idle.

BEA, TWA, Air India, BOAC—(PSC; "Cut-Price Airline") BEA began as BEAC (British European Airways Corporation) on 1 August 1946, the European division of the British state airline, BOAC. In 1947 fourteen British airline companies were merged under BEA's control. TWA was Trans World Airlines, an American airline created as "Transcontinental & Western Air" in 1930. TWA was formed after a forced merger of regional airlines, as well. Air India began operations in 1948. BOAC was British Overseas Airways Corporation, and was Britain's state airline from 1939-1974.

The introduction of the new airline consortium Airbus in 1970 had something to do with the genesis of this sketch. There was a general fear of mongrelization from many in the UK as the Common Market became more and more real, and forced cooperation with the French and others loomed large.

"Birmingham . . . Burnley . . . Barclay's"—("Eurovision Song Contest") Birmingham is a large northwestern city near Idle's old stomping grounds, while Burnley is much farther north in Lancashire, not far north of Bolton. Barclay's has been in the banking business in the UK since the seventeenth century.

"bit crook"—("Bruces") Australian and New Zealand slang for bad or unpleasant.

"blank verse"—("The First Underwater Production of *Measure for Measure*") Unrhymed verse, which was introduced by the Earl of Surrey in the early sixteen century. The line of dialogue heard seconds later—"Servant ho!"—is found nowhere in *Measure for Measure*, incidentally.

"Board of Trade"—("Cut-Price Airline") Very much in the news at this juncture, the Board of Trade ceased in some ways and continued unabated in others in the fall of 1970 as its duties were subsumed into the Department of Trade and Industry.

"both bodies flown back"—("Cut-Price Airline") This treatment of the airline industry is probably generated by the instability of that industry in the late 1960s and early 1970s (see the "BEA" note above), as well as the still-recent crash of an Ariana Afghan Airlines 727 at Gatwick Airport, where fifty people died. Also, the number and frequency of hijackings continued to escalate, further discouraging Britons from air travel.

"Brandt, Willi"—("Batley Townswomen's Guild Presents the First Heart Transplant") West German Chancellor "Willy" Brandt arranged and attended the first postwar German-German summit; his counterpart was the East German Prime Minister, Willi Stoph. The summit was held in the East German town of Erfurt in March 1970. East German crowds reportedly chanted "Willy!" in support of the visiting leader.

"Bronowski"—("Exploding Penguin on TV Set") Dr. Jacob Bronowski (1908-1974) presented the popular BBC series *The Ascent of Man* (1973), but prior to that he appeared on *The Brains Trust* (1950), where the young Pythons most likely first encountered him.

"Brussels . . . Cromer"—("Cosmetic Surgery") Brussels, Liege, Antwerp, and Asse are all cities in Belgium. Cromer is actually the name of a series of geologic features—freshwater deposits featuring abundant fossils, specifically—found at the coast of Cromer, Norfolk. The Pythons shot much of their second series location footage in the Norwich, Norfolk region.

– C –

"Camp Square-Bashing"—("Camp Square-Bashing") "Square-bashing" is military slang for marching, drilling. In the feature film *Meaning of Life*, recruits who don't want to go "marching up and down the square" are allowed to beg out for piano practice, family time, the cinema, etc. "Bashing" can also carry a masturbation association, which fits the sexualized nature of the send-up.

"classical philosophy"—("Bruces") Referring to noted ancien regime philosophers, including those who will later play on the Greek football team (Plato, Socrates, Aristotle et al.) against the more "modern" Germans (Liebnitz, Wittgenstein, Heidegger et al.) in the

Philosophers' Football Match created for the second *Fliegender Zirkus* episode.

"colour sergeant"—("Camp Square-Bashing") A non-commissioned rank in the British Army infantry regiments.

"come on a camping holiday"—("Cosmetic Surgery") This same type of alleged professional relationship (in this case, a simple doctor-and-patient two-set), followed by the pay-off of an aberrant (read: incongruous) sexual relationship is earlier explored with a policeman (Cleese) and victim (Palin) in Ep. 13, the "Come Back to My Place" sketch.

"confusion"—("Bruces") The implication here, then, is that nonconformity is the cause of confusion, not conformity.

"Coronation Scot"—(PSC; *"The Death of Mary Queen of Scots"*) This theme (from the BBC's *Paul Temple* radio series) is performed by the Queens Hall Light Orchestra, and is by Vivian Ellis (WAC T12/1,432). *Paul Temple* was a crime novel detective show heard on British radio between 1938 and 1968, and in 1969 made for German TV, as well.

"crack the tubes"—("Bruces") A "tube" is an Australian colloquialism for a beer can. The phrase simply means to open the cans of beer.

– D –

"Derbyshire Light Infantry"—("Camp Square-Bashing") The term "light" is probably meant to signal a sort of "light in the loafers" connotation, meaning to be light on one's feet, originally, and later a prancing, poncing man.

There is an Oxfordshire and Buckinghamshire Light infantry unit in existence, among others, while light infantry units were often termed "irregulars," the othering being significant in this usage.

dog-collar—(PSC; "Bruces") Clerical collar slapped on by the padre. See notes to Ep. 19.

"ducky"—("Camp Square-Bashing") A term of endearment.

"duty-free"—("Cut-Price Airline") Most international airports have duty-free shops, where items can be purchased with no customs or excise taxes collected.

– E –

"eccles cakes"—("Cut-Price Airline") Small, grape-filled cakes, originally, and supposedly named after the town of Eccles, Salford.

eight soldiers—(PSC; "Camp Square-Bashing") The four in the back row clearly are Pythons, while those in the front rank are actual dancers, as they are much more fluid in their movements. These dancers were hired specifically for this episode, and are (in no discernible order) Roy Gunson (*The Avengers*), Ralph Wood, Alexander Curry, and John Clement (*Diary of a Sinner*) (WAC T12/1,432).

"elevenses"—("Bruces") Light refreshment taken at about 11:00 a.m., also called "elevens."

Episode 22—Recorded 25 September 1970, then broadcast on 24 November 1970. It was the tenth episode recorded, and the ninth broadcast. Previously unnamed walk-ons for this episode include Karen Kerr, Nick Moody, Malcolm Holbrooks, and John Freeman (*Adam Adamant Lives!*) (WAC T12/1,432). They each seem to have posed for "Naughty Bits" still photos, and were brought in from the Jaclyn Model Agency (WAC T12/1,432).

Eurovision—(PSC; "Europolice Song Contest") A very popular Pan-European song contest. On 24 March 1969, in Madrid, Spain (at the Teator Real), sixteen countries competed. Representing the United Kingdom was Lulu, singing "Boom Bang-a-Bang." (The Pythons would later be nearly sued for perceived infringement of copyright in relation to this song and their publication *Monty Python's Big Red Book* [see Hewison's *Monty Python* 29-30].) In March 1970 the contest was won by Ireland's Dana singing "All Kinds of Everything." The presenter in 1970 was Willy Dobbe, and the show was hosted by the Netherlands.

Eurovision girl—("Europolice Song Contest") The presenter in the 1969 Eurovision Song Contest was Laurita Valenzuela (b. 1931), a possible source for Pythons' Girl (Idle) host, but the 1968 host, Brit Katie Boyle (whom Idle seems made-up to resemble), is the more likely target here. See notes to Ep. 38 for another mention of Boyle, there as a possible "loony."

– F –

"fairly butch"—(*"The Death of Mary Queen of Scots"*) To be described as "butch" is to be perceived as either an aggressive, masculine woman, a tough youth, or, more appropriately for the Pythons, a non-mincing gay man.

"first heart transplant"—("Batley Townswomen's Guild Presents the First Heart Transplant") The world's first heart transplant took place in Groote Schuur Hospital in South Africa. Professor Christiaan Barnard performed the surgery on 3 December 1967. The recipient lived eighteen days with the new heart.

Also, Barnard was pictured on the cover of the satirical magazine *Private Eye* on 6 June 1969, and there are more than thirty mentions of the historic operation in the political cartoon pages of UK newspapers. The editors of *PE* follow the exploits of Barnard for a few issues, cataloging the deaths of his patients, his publicity stunts, and the general furore over the "miraculous" new technology (that seemed to signal a death sentence for each and every patient).

"flying philosopher"—("Bruces") Perhaps referring to the dream of the philosopher Chang Tzou (c. fourth century BC), where he becomes the butterfly, or the butterfly becomes him. The "butterfly dream" has found its way into Western philosophy, as well.

Also, when the Queen visited Australia in 1963 she toured the *Flying Doctor* Service base in Alice Springs. Pictures of that particular visit can be found in the National Library of Australia. The Flying Doctor Service brought modern medicine and physicians into contact with outback dwellers and aborigines alike.

"Formula 2"—(link out of "The First Underwater Production of *Measure for Measure*") An auto race circuit introduced in 1947 for those drivers who could not qualify for the Formula 1 circuit, and acted as a sort of minor league for the faster, more expensive, and more exclusive Formula 1 level.

Fred Tomlinson Singers—(PSC; "There's Been a Murder") The PCs in the drawing room sketch behind Sgt. Duckie are Tomlinson's singers, with accompanist Jennifer Partridge somewhere offscreen.

"F.R.S"—("Cosmetic Surgery") Most of the acronyms on this rather long list are actual appellations, as follow:
"F.R.S."—Fellow of the Royal Society
"F.R.C.S."—Fellow of the Royal College of Surgeons
"F.R.C.P."—Fellow of the Royal College of Physicians
"M.D.M.S. (Oxon)"—Doctor of Medicine, Master of Science from Oxford University ("Oxon" indicates Oxford University, and is only used in titles)
"M.A., Ph.D., M.Sc. (Cantab)"—Master of Arts, Doctor of Philosophy, and Master of Science, Cambridge University (the last indicating Cambridge University, and also used only in titles)
"Ph.D. (Syd)"—Doctor of Philosophy, University of Sydney
"F.R.G.S."—Fellow of the Royal Geographical Society
"F.R.C.O.G."—Fellow of the Royal College of Obstetricians and Gynecologists
"F.F.A.R.C.S."—Fellow of the Faculty of Anaesthetists of the Royal College of Surgeons
"Birm"—Degrees from University of Birmingham
"M.S. (Liv)"—M.S. degrees from University of Liverpool ("Liv"), Guadalajara University ("Guadalahara")

in Mexico, the University of Karachi ("Karach") in Pakistan (originally part of pre-British India, and then the British Raj), and the University of Edinburgh ("Edin")

"B.A. (Chic)"—Bachelor of Arts, University of Chicago

"B.Litt."—Bachelor of Literature, Bachelor of Letters

"D.Litt"—Doctor of Letters

"Ottawa"—University of Ottawa, Ontario

"Medicine Hat"—In Alberta, Canada. There is also a Medicine Hat College, incidentally

"B.Sc."—Bachelor of Science

Chapman's training and qualification as a medical doctor were undoubtedly referenced as this sketch was created.

– G –

gorgeous lovelies in bikinis—(PSC; link into *"How to Recognize Different Parts of the Body"*) These actresses/models include—in approximately this order—Flanagan (Eps. 7, 11-13, 20; *Benny Hill*), Beulah Hughes (Eps. 29, 33, 34; *Hands of the Ripper*), Marie (erotic model of the period, Marie can also be seen in posters advertised in *Private Eye*), Barbara Lindley (Ep. 18; *Benny Hill*), and Sandra Richards (Ep. 17) (WAC T12/1,242).

"great socialist thinkers"—("Bruces") This would certainly include at least the Structuralist school so popular in the 1960s and 1970s in Europe, including luminaries such as Ferdinand de Saussure, Claude Levi-Strauss, Lacan, Foucault, and Althusser.

The seminal importance of language and linguistic structures as the foundation of contemporary philosophy cannot be overstressed, especially for its influence on the Pythons (and the arts in general during this period). The fact that the speaker is now structured by his speech resonates throughout *Flying Circus* and the feature films, allowing peasants to banter with kings, words like "it" to carry cosmic significance, and things to simply be or not be by mere invocation.

– H –

Harley Street—(PSC; "Cosmetic Surgery") Center of the high-end medical establishment in London, it will be mentioned again in Eps. 32 and 37.

"Haydon-Jones, Ann"—(link into *"The Death of Mary Queen of Scots"*) Popular tennis player Haydon-Jones has already been mentioned in Eps. 7 and 19. See notes to Ep. 7 for more.

"Hegelian philosophy"—("Bruces") G.W.F. Hegel (1770-1831) was a post-Kantian German idealist who posited that "the rational alone is real."

"Hollowood, Bernard and Brian London"—(*"The Death of Mary Queen of Scots"*) Bernard Hollowood (1911-1981) was a writer and editor, publishing in the 1950s and 1960s in literary magazines including *Lilliput*. Hollowood also edited *Punch* magazine (1957-1968) and was resident pocket cartoonist for same. Hollowood's cartoons have been donated to the British Cartoon Archive at the University of Kent. Hollowood had published the book *Cricket on the Brain* in 1970.

Private Eye satirizes Hollowood in a Gerald Scarfe cartoon in the 7 August 1964 issue, where he is depicted being knighted as a wanna-be cricketer (Ingrams 108).

Brian London has already been mentioned (Ep. 13), and was an English boxer (fl. 1955-1970). See the entry for Brian London in notes for Ep. 13.

"How to Recognize Different Parts of the Body"—(*"How to Recognize Different Parts of the Body"*) Reminiscent of the sketch *"How to Recognize Different Types of Trees From Quite a Long Way Away"* from Ep. 3. These may be references to the myriad WWII-era public information films created for the homefront on both sides of the Atlantic, including *Recognition of the Zero Fighter* (1943). It's also reminiscent of the various "how to"–type (now "DIY") shows on British television, and lampooned by the Pythons in Ep. 26 (*"How to Feed a Goldfish"*) and Ep. 28 (*"How to Rid the World of All Known Diseases"*).

– I –

"Inspector Zatapathique"—("Eurovision Song Contest") Brian Zatapathique (Palin) is presented in Ep. 2 as a "French Lecturer on Sheep-Aircraft," and again in Ep. 14.

"intercourse the penguin"—("Exploding Penguin on TV Set") Rather than say "sod," "intercourse" is used in this phrase, though Cleese still manages to nearly laugh aloud at the mention. They had tried "sod" back in Ep. 17, and had to replace it with a raspberry sound. BBC higher-ups would regularly view the episode, make a listing of potentially offensive words/scenes/references, and suggest changes (*Monty Python: The Case Against* 38-39). In the LP versions of many of these sketches, the more graphic curse words are kept in place.

– K –

Kamikaze—(PSC; "Cut-Price Airline") This actor is Vincent Wong (*Dr. Who*), who will also appear in Ep. 43 as a Japanese business man.

– L –

like this one—(PSC; link into "Batley Townswomen's Guild Presents the First Heart Transplant") Similar to Python's "deflating" announcements in other episodes, including the *"Black Eagle"* intro of Ep. 25.

"logical positivism"—("Bruces") The school of philosophy emerging from the Vienna Circle in the 1920s and 1930s, and set against, primarily, the metaphysical (and ultimately all speculative) approaches to philosophical questions.

lyrical film . . . frolicking in the countryside—(PSC; "Cosmetic Surgery") This location footage looks as if it were shot in the same area where the nature scenes for *"The Attila the Hun Show"* (Ep. 20) were photographed.

– M –

"Machiavelli . . . Benaud"—("Bruces") Why the new Bruce (Jones) in the Philosophy Department will be teaching political science isn't clear, but the confusion with eminent cricketers quickly moots the point anyway.

"Machiavelli"—An Italian Renaissance philosopher and writer, Niccolo Machiavelli (1469-1527) wrote on republicanism and realist political theory, citing "force and prudence" as the basis for a successful government.

"Bentham"—Jeremy Bentham (1748-1832) was a noted English philosopher and social reformer (*ODNB*).

"Locke"—John Locke (1632-1704) influenced Bentham, but this Englishman would oppose Hobbes' "state of nature" with a "will of the people" approach to legitimate government.

"Hobbes"—Earlier English philosopher Thomas Hobbes (1588-1679) published *Leviathan* in 1651, proclaiming the social contract theory of political/social philosophy.

"Sutcliffe"—Probably meant to be Herbert Sutcliffe (1894-1978), an English (not Australian) cricketer whose best years came in the 1920s and early 1930s, long before the Pythons' births. The English team did enjoy a very successful tour of Australia in 1928-1929, where Sutcliffe batted with talented teammate Jack Hobbs (1882-1963). (See cricinfo.com for more complete statistics.)

"Bradman"—Australian cricketer Don Bradman (1908-2001) was a Wisden Cricketer of the Year in 1931. During the 1930s and 1940s, most considered Bradman to be the greatest cricketer in the world.

"Lindwall"—Ray Lindwall (1921-1996) was also an Australian cricketer, and was named Wisden Cricketer of the Year in 1949.

"Miller"—Australian Keith Miller (1919-2004) partnered with Lindwall, and was named Wisden Cricketer of the Year in 1954.

"Hassett"—Lindsay Hassett (1913-1993) followed Bradman as captain of the Australian team, and was named Wisden Cricketer of the Year in 1949.

"Benaud"—Richard Benaud (b. 1930) came much later than any of the abovementioned cricketers, captaining the Australian team in 1958-1959 against England. Benaud was named Wisden Cricketer of the Year in 1962.

Bradman, Lindwall, Miller, and Hassett played together against England at Kennington Oval in London in 1948, winning 4-0. The young Pythons—aged between about five and nine at this time—may have been uniquely aware of England's poor showing in this 1948 match.

Mary is getting the shit knocked out of her—(PSC; "The Death of Mary Queen of Scots") This is one of the very few places where the Pythons include an actual curse word—one of those generally not allowed on broadcast television—and not just a crudity. Granted, the word only appears in the printed text, and a nonspoken portion at that.

Contemporary reports indicate that it took at least three blows of the executioner's axe to sever Mary's head, and—going along with the Pythons' "No I'm not" from Mary—she was still alive and perhaps even conscious after the first two strokes. See the *ODNB* for more on Mary.

"Mary, Queen of Scots"—(*"The Death of Mary Queen of Scots"*) Mary (1542-1587) was the eldest daughter of Henry VIII, and a devout Catholic. Serialized dramas on the royal families (Plantaganets, Tudors et al.) were common on BBC radio and then television, including *An Age of Kings* (1960), which covered five Shakespeare history plays in fifteen parts.

There was a feature film in production at this time, *Mary, Queen of Scots*, starring Vanessa Redgrave and Glenda Jackson, which would be released in 1971.

"Maudling, Reginald"—("Naughty Bits") Oft-jabbed (by the Pythons) Conservative politician Maudling (1917-1979) was the embattled Home Secretary during this period. A lightning-rod figure to many, during the initial run of *Flying Circus* (1969-1974), Maudling is mentioned (lampooned) in more than three hundred political cartoons in UK newspapers, and was a regular in the pages of *Private Eye*, especially for his alleged financial improprieties and influence peddling.

"Measure for Measure"—("The First Underwater Production of *Measure for Measure*") Shakespeare's 1604 play was performed first at King James' court. This was Shakespeare's last comedy, and was followed by a series of tragedies. These seaside scenes were shot on 9-10 June 1970 near Seaford Cliffs, Seaford (WAC T12/1,416).

mincing—(PSC; "Camp Square-Bashing") To walk or act in a dainty or effeminate manner.

"Monaco is the winner"—("Europolice Song Contest") Monaco did compete in 1970, placing eighth.

Muffin the Mule—(PSC; "There's Been a Murder") Muffin was a popular and long-running marionette puppet character (fl. 1946-1955) on early British TV children's programs. The character had been on TV since the mid-1930s, but not named "Muffin" until 1946.

This is yet another example of the printed script proffering information to which the intended audience—namely, viewers at home—had no access. The name "Muffin the Mule" isn't spoken in the scene, nor is it included in a caption—it was included for the Pythons themselves.

– N –

"Nolan, Sydney"—("Bruces") Sidney Nolan (1917-1992) was perhaps the best-known Australian artist of this period, and his work often focused on life in and the people of Australia. Sir Kenneth Clark (Eps. 25 and 37) had "discovered" Nolan in 1949, and provided the means for his introduction to London and the art world (*ODNB*).

"no pooftahs"—("Bruces") Not an unusual or even bigoted statement, certainly, since same-sex sexual activity ("buggery") wouldn't begin to be decriminalized in Australia until 1975. The Campaign Against Moral Persecution (CAMP) was formed in 1970 in Australia, with gay and lesbian demonstrations appearing in the following year.

– P –

"padre"—("Bruces") Generally referring to a chaplain, a padre also appeared in the big school production, *"Seven Brides for Seven Brothers"* sketch in Ep. 18.

"parcel post"—("Cut-Price Airline") Simply the branch of the UK postal service that deals with posted (mailed) packages.

"perhaps it comes from next door"—("Exploding Penguin on TV Set") In the Python world, such things can, in fact, be just next door. In Ep. 32, it turns out that Lake Pahoe is found at 22A Runcorn Avenue (*not* 22 Runcorn Avenue), the "Argument" office is just one along from "Abuse" (Ep. 29), and in Ep. 33, Mrs.

Neves (Jones) steps out her kitchen door and onto the deck of a lifeboat.

picture of the cabinet at a table—(PSC; "Naughty Bits") Conservative Ted Heath's cabinet in late 1970 (he was elected in June) included: Home Secretary—Reginald Maudling; Lord Privy Seal—Earl Jellicoe; Lord Chancellor—Lord Hailsham; Chancellor of the Exchequer—Iain Macleod, then Anthony Barber; Secretary of State for Foreign and Commonwealth Affairs—Sir Alec Douglas-Home; Secretary of State for Defence—Lord Carrington; Secretary of State for Scotland—Gordon Campbell; Secretary of State for Social Services—Sir Keith Joseph; Secretary of State for Education and Science—Margaret Thatcher; Secretary of State for Trade and Industry and President of the Board of Trade—John Davies; Minister of Housing and Local Government—Peter Walker; Minister for Public Works—Julian Amery; Secretary of State for Employment—Antony Barber, then Robert Carr; Secretary of State for Wales—Peter Thomas; Minister of Agriculture Fisheries and Food—James Prior; Minister for Housing and Construction—Julian Amery; Minister of Overseas Development—Richard Wood; Minister of Technology—Geoffrey Rippon, then John Davies et al.

In the photo provided by/for Gilliam for this "Naughty Bits" sequence, Heath, Barber, Maudling, Jellicoe, Douglas-Home, and Thatcher are clearly visible. The photo is grainy enough that others in attendance can only be guessed. Heath sits at the center on the right side of the table.

Most of these names and faces appear fairly regularly in the pages of *Private Eye*, where their various exploits (primarily involving cuts in services, government waste, and personal peccadilloes) are tracked.

"plastic surgery"—("Cosmetic Surgery") Cosmetic (as opposed to reconstructive) plastic surgery of the nose—to approve appearance—was a relatively young practice at this time, having appeared at around the turn of the century.

"pommy bastard"—("Bruces") Actually an affectionate term in Australian English, its use even ascribed to the Queen on the cover of the 8 May 1970 issue of the satirical magazine *Private Eye*. The story covers the Queen's return from her extended (two-month) visit to Australia, and the cover shot gives her a balloon quote: "Greetings to all youse loyal pommy bastards!"

To be from "pommie land" means to be from England. This is probably a slangy reference to the potato-eating stereotype of the UK population (from *pomme de terre*).

"pooftah"—("Bruces") An Australian slang term for an effeminate male, or a homosexual. Other derivatives heard in *FC* include "poof" and "poove."

Pope—("Naughty Bits") The Pope in 1970 was Pope Paul VI (fl. 1963-1978).

"Prime Minister"—("Bruces") The Australian PM in 1970 was the Rt Hon. John Grey Gorton (January 1968 to March 1971). The Queen had recently visited Australia, in March-May 1970, and before that in 1963 and 1954.

"pull"—(link into "Camp Square-Bashing") To "give a pull" is to attempt to hit on, romantically/sexually; the term is used by John Lennon in the train buffet car scene in *A Hard Day's Night* (1964).

– Q –

"quid"—("Cut-Price Airline") A sovereign (one pound sterling).

– R –

"Radio 4"—(*"The Death of Mary Queen of Scots"*) One of the four extant BBC radio stations, BBC 4 came on the air in September 1967.

In 1970 all four radio stations were in the process of major revamping, with the goal being a clearer portrait of each channel as its own, discernible entity. The BBC's policy paper "Broadcasting in the Seventies" was the roadmap for this change, and was, in a way, exploding the somewhat confused and often overlapping areas of interest the four radio channels had been operating with, some since WWII.

"ratty"—("Camp Square-Bashing") Here meaning irritated, angry.

"Raymond Luxury Yacht"—("Cosmetic Surgery") Cf. Ep. 19 for the earlier appearance of this character.

"re-enactment"—("Batley Townswomen's Guild Presents the First Heart Transplant") An example of Python's self-reflexivity, their references to their own corpus, in this case, footage from a muddy pasture where Pepperpots bash each other with purses. The audience usually reacts quite appreciatively when these moments appear, meaning the studio audience (at least by the second series) is made up of those who also watch the show on TV at home.

– S –

"safe as houses"—("Cut-Price Airline") A British and Australian idiom meaning worry-free.

"Second Armoured Division"—("Camp Square-Bashing") Ironically, this is the division that Elvis Presley

trained under during WWII. The division was quite active during the early part of the war (December 1939-May 1941), but after most of the division were captured in Libya by the Nazis, the unit was disbanded. This ill-gained notoriety may account for Pythons' mention of the division in this campy setting.

"sheepdip"—("Bruces") A place where sheep are washed, or the fluid in which they are washed.

"Sheila"—("Bruces") A colloquialism for a young woman or girlfriend, and primarily used in Australia and NZ.

The Queen is also credited by these Bruces with not being "stuck up," which means to put on airs and be pretentious, or a "sticky beak," which is to be nosey. Her Majesty's lengthy 1954, 1963, and 1970 visits went quite favorably, and featured hospital openings, art exhibitions, opening of sports and government buildings and even an airport terminal. These very positive, even glowing images were played up on television back home in the UK.

"sherry"—("Bruces") A high alcohol content wine commonly made in Spain. Cf. notes for Ep. 36, the "Sherry-Drinking Vicar" sketch, as well as the Victorian woman (Chapman) in Ep. 41.

show eleven—(PSC; "Batley Townswomen's Guild Presents the First Heart Transplant") See notes to Ep. 11 for more on this footage.

"someone gets stabbled"—(PSC; "There's Been a Murder") The printed script clearly spells the word "stabbled," not "stabbed." Probably a misprint, though there is such a word—to "stabble" means to tramp dirt around, as on a clean floor (*OED*).

"springbok"—("Batley Townswomen's Guild Presents the First Heart Transplant") A nickname for a South African, but also referring to an antelope of the region. The term is used almost exclusively in the sports pages, political cartoons, and op-ed pages in English newspapers of the period when referring to South African white males, primarily, and especially those representing sports teams. See the entries for Eps. 14, 15, 19, and 20 for more on the South African references.

"Stewart, Michael"—("Batley Townswomen's Guild Presents the First Heart Transplant") Referring back to Foreign Secretary Michael Stewart (later Lord Stewart of Fulham) who spoke for Harold Wilson's Labour government as he justified their support for interfering with Biafra's attempts at independence in the late 1960s. The Christian Biafrans had been struggling for independence from Muslim Nigeria since the country won its freedom from the UK in 1960.

swanning about—("Camp Square-Bashing") "Swan" is actually a military term, meaning "an apparently aimless journey; an excursion made for reconnaissance or for pleasure." Here the men are swanning about in a very effeminate, campy way.

"Sydney Harbour Bridge"—("Bruces") This bridge was erected in 1932, and is a single-arch bridge. There are retail and/or historical establishments in several of the four brick piers, incidentally, meaning a "Sydney Harbour Bridge Room" is possible.

– T –

"Thatcher, Margaret"—("Naughty Bits") A cabinet member in Heath's 1970-1974 Conservative government, Thatcher (b. 1925) was already perceived as the "Iron Lady" of the Tories, meaning she was a consistent Python target.

"Thirty bob"—("Cut-Price Airline") Thirty shillings. A shilling was worth 1/20 of a pound sterling, and was phased out of the British monetary system with the adoption of the decimal system in 1971, not long after this sketch first aired.

track along this name plate—("Cosmetic Surgery") The stirring music underneath this extended tracking shot is "National Anthems (Eire)" as played by the Band of the Royal Engineers (WAC T12/1,432).

"Triumph Herald"—("Cut-Price Airline") This small car was produced between 1959 and 1971 in the UK, with the original model featuring a 948cc engine that generated about 50 bhp. Luxury car manufacturer Rolls Royce was well known for producing both prop-driven and jet engines.

"two hundred each on the plane"—("Cut-Price Airline") This is actually the ceiling for the number of cigarettes that could be brought into the UK by travelers—any more and there was a potential arrest for smuggling. See the note for Ep. 5, "Vox Pops on Smuggling" for an earlier mention.

– V –

Venus de Milo—(PSC; *"How to Recognize Different Parts of the Body"*) Famous parian marble statue found at De Milo, and dated to about 120-130 BC. An image of this statue will also be used in Ep. 25, "Art Gallery Strike," where she is the only statue to abstain in a "show of hands" vote.

– W –

"Waltzing Mathilda"—("Bruces") Unofficial Australian national anthem written by Andrew "Banjo" Paterson (1864-1941), a bush poet and ballad writer. This arrangement is from Peter Dawson's album *My Life of Song*, and is arranged by Patterson-Cowan and Thomas Wood (WAC T12/1,432).

"wattle"—("Bruces") The golden wattle (or acacia) is an indigenous Australian tree, as well as the official flower/tree of Australia.

"Woolamaloo"—("Bruces") Probably a misspelling of "Woolloomooloo," which has been a working-class, docklands area of greater Sydney. During her 1963 visit to Australia, the Queen had toured the University of New South Wales, and opened two schools on campus. She was also a visitor at the University of Western Australia and Australian National University on this trip.

This university-in-the-bush setting may be another nod to the eminent Australian zoologist Alan "Jock" Marshall, who taught at St. Bart's (London) for more than a decade and then joined the faculty at Monash University in 1960. See the entry in Ep. 21 for "Roy Spim."

Episode 23

"Aldermen"—("Derby Council vs. All Blacks Rugby Match") Aldermen are ward officers, not unlike city council members. They can and do wear such official regalia in the course of their duties. Much of the aldermanic tradition would be done away with in 1972 with the passage of the Local Government Act.

"All Blacks"—("Derby Council vs. All Blacks Rugby Match") The national rugby team from New Zealand. These All Blacks are actually Torquay Rugby FC members (WAC T12/1,416).

"Anka, Paul"—("Fish Licence") Canadian pop singer and songwriter Anka was known during this period for the number one song "Diana," as well as hugely popular songs written for Buddy Holly, Johnny Carson's *Tonight Show*, and Tom Jones. Anka (and his wife) have already been mentioned in Ep. 21.

"Ataturk, Kemal"—("Fish Licence") Mustafa Kemal Ataturk (1881-1938) fought for and founded the Republic of Turkey, becoming its first president. Ataturk led the successful fight against the combined and ill-fated British and ANZAC forces at Gallipoli in 1915.

The fictional book mentioned ("*Kemal Ataturk, The Man*") is supposed to have been written by E.W. Swanton, the noted English cricket broadcaster already mentioned (and pictured) in Ep. 21.

– B –

"blood goes pssssssssssshhh in slow motion"—("*Scott of the Antarctic*") The success of Akira Kurosawa's pulpy samurai film *Sanjuro* (1962)—with its shocking and celebrated "fountain of blood" ending—led many younger filmmakers to ratchet up the blood and gore content in their own films. This level of blood and violence wouldn't reach Hollywood screens (due to the lingering effects of the Production Code) until the late 1960s, when Arthur Penn's *Bonnie and Clyde* (1967) and especially Sam Peckinpah's *The Wild Bunch* (1969), among others, made their debut.

"breakdown in communication in our modern society"—("French Subtitled Film") In a nutshell, this defines *Flying Circus*. There are very few examples in the series of a *successful* communication or transaction. In most cases, the message is misunderstood, delivered improperly, or perceived incorrectly. A man who wants an argument gets abuse, complaints, and "being hit on the head lessons"; a man who wants to report a burglary has to speak louder, then lower, or he won't be understood; a visit to the doctor becomes a homosexual tryst; a man who seeks advice from a marriage counselor loses his wife to the counselor in the transaction, etc. In the *FC* world, successful transactions (robbing a lingerie shop, buying a converted pet, returning a dead parrot, buying cheese) are nearly impossible.

The communication issue is key for the Pythons, and is based on the recent interest in semantics and semiotics, the growing awareness that meaning isn't just "there," it is imbued by and for society/culture, and that meaning can and does fluctuate depending on *context*. The separation of a word from its "meaning" allows for new meanings and even multiple meanings to be temporarily affixed to a word—there now exists the possibility of "wiggle room" in the world of language. Modernist authors like Joyce, Stein, Pound, Woolf, and Eliot pushed this separation, this interchangeability, and the Pythons came along at just the right time to explore that new ambiguity in the television format.

"Bullock, Alan"—("Fish Licence") Bullock (1914-2004) was an Oxford grad, a British historian, and author of the influential *Hitler: A Study of Tyranny* (1952).

"But soft . . . "—("Fish Licence") Oft-used Elizabethan dramatic phrase, and used as a transition or link in the speaker's thought pattern or attention (as when something/someone unseen is overheard), and found in Shakespeare's history plays *Richard II* (5.1), *1 King Henry IV* (1.3), *Richard III* (1.3), comedies *The Taming of the Shrew* (4.5), *The Comedy of Errors* (2.2; 3.1), *A Midsummer Night's Dream* (4.1), *The Merchant of Venice* (1.3), *Much Ado About Nothing* (5.1), and even his tragedies *Cymbeline* (4.2), *Titus Andronicus* (5.3), *Romeo and Juliet* (2.2; 3.4), Julius Caesar (1.2), and even *Hamlet*, when the ghost approaches Horatio in act one. Praline uses the phrase similarly to move from one grille to the next, hoping for success in attaining a fish license.

– C –

"Cardiff Arms Park"—("Derby Council vs. All Blacks Rugby Match") The home stadium of the Welsh rugby union, and named after a pub nearby. These scenes were actually shot on 12 May 1970 at the Torquay Rugby Football Ground, with the All Blacks played by members of the Torquay RFC (WAC T12/1,416).

"cat detector van"—("Fish Licence") In the UK, a license must be purchased if a TV is going to be viewed in the home or business. This licensing fee helps fund the BBC (and local radio/TV), and has been bringing money to the BBC coffers since 1904 (initially, just for radio broadcast). To help encourage compliance with these mandatory fees, special "detection vans" had been patrolling British streets with the stated ability of detecting whether a TV in a particular home/office is receiving broadcast transmissions. Using a master address list of license holders, the detectors can allegedly identify if the address is legally watching TV. One license fee per single-family household covers all TVs in the home.

Conger—("*Scott of the Antarctic*") A conger is a type of eel found in the coastal regions of the UK (and caught for food), the mention of which may be a comment on this type of BBC coverage of these Hollywood superproductions, including the recent *Ryan's Daughter* (1970) and especially the painfully unfunny *Casino Royale* (1967), which J. McGrath (see entry below) actually directed.

Conger's wardrobe cues are listed as "like Tony Bilbow, almost Regency" in the wardrobe requests for the episode, while Gerry Schlick is described as "Ameri-

can, like Marcel Hellman" (WAC T12/1,435). Bilbow (b. 1932) was writing for the show *Mind Your Own Business* in 1970 (and would later appear with Idle in *Rutland Weekend Television*), while Romanian-born Hellman (1898-1985) had produced a version of *Moll Flanders* for the big screen in 1965. The "Regency" (historically, between "Georgian" and "Victorian" in England) comment means Conger is to look a bit of a dandy, and very concerned with the neatness of his appearance.

cos lettuce—(PSC; "French Subtitled Film") Lettuce from the island of Cos, the lettuce is named in the script. See entry for "Webb's Wonder" below.

"crumb bum"—("*Scott of the Antarctic*") A term used, appropriately, by the prostitute ("Sunny") Holden visits in Salinger's *Catcher in the Rye* (1951). She calls him a "crumb-bum" when he pays her five dollars instead of ten.

– D –

"Derby"—("Derby Council vs. All Blacks Rugby Match") A city in the East Midlands. These scenes were shot in Torquay, which is much farther south.

"Derby Council XV"—("Derby Council vs. All Blacks Rugby Match") The "XV" indicating that this is rugby *union* football, where fifteen players per team are involved, as opposed to thirteen players for rugby *league* football. In the episode as filmed, however, there appear to be only eleven All Blacks and about twelve Derby Council players on the pitch.

"Derry and Toms"—("Derby Council vs. All Blacks Rugby Match") An upscale department store initially founded in 1920 when two companies merged, then came into its own in 1932 with the building of its lavish, garden-topped headquarters in Kensington High Street. It will be mentioned again in Ep. 37. The Derry and Toms concern would close just months after the broadcast of this episode, in 1972.

"Devonshire resort will be transformed"—("*Scott of the Antarctic*") Typical of the money-saving practice for many Hollywood (and bigger-budget foreign) films. D.W. Griffith's *Birth of a Nation* (1915) was shot in southern California (not the deep South); *55 Days at Peking* (1963) was shot in Spain; and parts of the *Lawrence of Arabia* (1962) sand dunes were also shot in California. The Hollywood blockbuster film that at least partly inspired the *Scott of the Antarctic* spoof here, *Ice Station Zebra* (1963), was shot entirely in sunny southern California, even though it is set entirely in the frozen Arctic.

"disappointing result"—("Derby Council vs. All Blacks Rugby Match") In fall 1970 the fifth Rugby League World Cup was held in Great Britain. Played in late October and early November, the British team was strong and impressive early, but surprisingly lost 7-12 to an Australian team that had struggled to even qualify for the final match.

"Distel, Brian"—("French Subtitled Film") Sacha Distel (1933-2004) was a French-born singer and guitarist who had many hits during the 1960s and 1970s, as well as television specials and even his own show. Idle's penchant for including music folk into his writing should probably be credited for Distel's sideways mention. "Brian," of course, is, along with "Arthur," one of the catch-all first names given to Python characters throughout not only *FC*, but into the feature films.

"Brianette Zatapathique" is a bit of silliness that keeps appearing in *FC*, with the name Zatapathique being mentioned prominently in Eps. 2, 17, and 22.

– E –

"edited highlights of the match"—("Long John Silver Impersonators v. Bournemouth Gynaecologists") A reference to the practice of the BBC's popular *Match of the Day* since the 1960s, when edited highlights of Division One football (soccer) matches were shown on Saturday evenings to millions of viewers. David Coleman (Ep. 21) was the main presenter during this period.

"electric penguin"—("*Scott of the Antarctic*") This bit of silliness is most likely a reference to the 1961 adventure film *Voyage to the Bottom of the Sea*, where a giant octopus attacks the intrepid submarine and crew. (Actually, it's a normal-sized octopus photographed in close-up and with miniature props.) That film also starred young and beautiful Barbara Eden (b. 1934), cast to attract the young male audience, not unlike Miss Vanilla Hoare (Cleveland).

The music played beneath this oft-seen fowl (at least in *FC*) is from The Machines, "Electronic Screams" by Eric Peters (WAC T12/1,435).

enters shot—(PSC; "French Subtitled Film") The Nouvelle Vague filmmakers drew attention to the formal elements of cinema, in this case acknowledging the cinematographic frame, its existence and role as "divider" of photographed space. The fact that the boom mic drops into the shot is also a comment on the movement's inattention to some of the "finished" details of film, more interested in the visceral experience of the cinematic moment. Also, lower-budget films tend to suffer more continuity problems, as reshoots are more expensive than can be justified.

Episode 23—Recorded 2 July 1970, and broadcast 1 December 1970. This episode was actually recorded second in the second series, but aired as the final episode of the season. This episode was also recorded on the same evening (2 July 1970) as what eventually would be known as Ep. 15, meaning there were fewer in-studio shots/scenes than usual.

"'E's an 'alibut"—("Fish Licence") An example of class differentiation even among the middle class, the Post Office Worker (Palin) doesn't understand Praline's (Cleese) "common" English, his dropping of the initial "h," and Praline must speak more precisely: "He is an halibut."

"Exeter Amateur Operatic Society"—("Derby Council vs. All Blacks Rugby Match") There is and has been an Exeter Operatic Society, and there exist many amateur societies, including the Barnstaple Amateur Operatic Society. Both of these are in Devon.

– F –

fanfare of trumpets—(PSC; link out of "Fish Licence") The fanfare is "Aggression" from Eric Towren, one of Britain's many light music composers whose work could be heard on British TV and radio throughout the 1950s and 1960s, and in countless low-budget films (WAC T12/1,435).

first of two grilles—(PSC; "Fish Licence") The name plates under these grilles are "Miss McCheane," "Mr. Balfour," and "Mr. Last." Mary McCheane is a producer's assistant on the show, James Balfour is a cameraman, and Roger Last is one of the show's floor managers.

In a sidenote, McCheane (*Top of the Pops*) and sometime *FC* musician/composer Bill McGuffie (1927-1987) were husband and wife. McCheane died in 2002.

"Fromage Grand, Le"—("French Subtitled Film") French, literally "The Big Cheese." In Ep. 4, Chapman plays the part of "The Big Cheese," a Blofeld-type villain who intervenes into the "Secret Service Dentists" sketch. Ring Lardner (American novelist and screenwriter) is credited with bringing the phrase into common parlance in his hard-boiled small-town fiction from about 1914 (*OED*).

– G –

"geological syncline"—("*Scott of the Antarctic*") A syncline is a downward-curving fold, which can create basins—meaning Miss Hoare (Cleveland) could certainly act in one.

Girl—(PSC; *"Scott of the Antarctic"*) Not named in the script, this is Lyn Ashley, Idle's wife at this time.

– H –

hand-held camera—("French Subtitled Film") One of the characteristics of the French New Wave (Nouvelle Vague) was a conscious move away from classical, prestige-film Hollywood aesthetics in favor of more genre-influenced styles. The manipulation of classical form included taking the camera off of the tripod and especially the dolly, where steady, beautiful shots had created a hallmark of Hollywood cinema. Hand-held camera work (inspired by documentary films and especially the combat footage of WWII), black-and-white film stock, elliptical editing and storytelling, sex and sexuality as integral to the narrative and characters, and topicality characterized the movement. Godard's 1959 film *Breathless* is a terrific example of these formal concerns.

– I –

Intercut . . . plane—(PSC; "French Subtitled Film") Jean-Luc Godard used stock documentary footage of student demonstrations, riots, and police and military actions in his 1968 compilation film *Cinétracts*. Much of this stock footage is culled from the BBC's own film archive. This particular shot isn't accounted for (by name) in the WAC records.

The live-action (starring the Pythons) insert portions were all shot in the Torquay city area; the few interiors were shot at Ealing TFS (WAC T12/1,435).

"I rewrote it"—("Scott of the Antarctic") Joseph McGrath is credited (unofficially) with significant rewrites of the *Casino Royale* (1967) script, as were many other directors who had contact with the troubled project. See entry for "McGrath" below.

– J –

"John the Baptist"—(*"Scott of the Antarctic"*) Cousin to Jesus, there is no indication in any surviving record that John was ever married or had a daughter named for him, meaning Vanilla (as Miss Evans) could be talking about a particularly bold casting move for the John the Baptist story in a previous film. It also could be that since she is playing against gender as a female Evans (both of the "Evans" participants on the actual

Scott expedition were men) that she is merely continuing this intriguing casting, having played female versions of John the Baptist, Napoleon, Alexander Fleming, and the astronomer Galileo in what in the film industry were known as "biopics."

Fleming (1881-1955) was a Scotsman credited as discovering penicillin, and who won the Nobel prize in 1945.

Significant Hollywood biopics the Pythons are referencing include Pual Muni's *The Story of Louis Pasteur* (1935), *The Life of Emile Zola* and *Juarez* (both 1937), as well as the star-studded *Becket* (1964).

– L –

Lawrence of Glamorgan—(*"Scott of the Antarctic"*) A play on the very popular David Lean film (also a biopic) *Lawrence of Arabia* (1962), starring Peter O'Toole. Glamorgan is a traditional county in Wales, and is home to Cardiff, Caerphilly, and Swansea.

Bridge Over the River Trent—This title adapted from Lean's *Bridge on the River Kwai* (1957). The River Trent runs through cities like Burton and Nottingham, and generally through the Midlands to the Humber Estuary.

The Mad Woman of Biggleswade—Reference to the *The Mad Woman of Chaillot*, a play (and then film) written by Jean Giradoux. The film, directed by Bryan Forbes, premiered in 1969, and starred Katharine Hepburn. Forbes has already been mentioned in Ep. 20, *"Take Your Pick,"* and is also unflatteringly referenced in *Private Eye* (17 July 1970, 5). Biggleswade is actually in Bedfordshire, north of London.

Krakatoa, East of Leamington—Another spoofed title, this time of the disaster film *Krakatoa, East of Java* (1969), starring Maxmilian Schell. Leamington Spa is in Warwickshire.

lid slams on his hands—("French Subtitled Film") This stock film footage sequence is reminiscent of the recent and somewhat celebrated BBC-sponsored Tony Palmer film, *All My Loving* (1968). Palmer employed music of The Beatles and images of filmed violence from the twentieth century, eliciting rave reviews from the major newspaper critics of the day. *Private Eye*, of course, is the exception, blasting the film as nothing more than a vanity piece from "Tony Palmerlotofsensationalfilmclipsonthepublicandtryandpretenditissomething-significant" (Ingrams 204). The images used are fairly standard—Vietnam, burning monks, student protests, concentration camp footage, etc.

"Longueur, Jean Kenneth"—("French Subtitled Film") Probably a portmanteau name comprising directors Jean-Luc Godard and Ken Russell (Eps. 29 and

31). A "longueur" is a tedious or lengthy passage or thing. Critics and viewers alike have complained that Godard's political agenda often outpaces and overwhelms his artistic accomplishments. The famous traffic tracking shot in *Week End* (1967) lasts at least eight minutes, well longer than most audiences expect, and demands that the viewer begin to think not only about the content but the shot itself.

"Lord Mayor"—("Derby Council vs. All Blacks Rugby Match") Part of the joke here, of course, is that the smallish East Midlands city (so awarded by the Queen much later, in 1977) Derby is not one of the cities in the UK to have a Lord Mayor.

– M –

McGrath, J.—(PSC; *"Scott of the Antarctic"*) The printed script actually mentions that this besotted character "McRettin" is supposed to resemble Scottish director "J. McGrath," a writer, director, and producer well known to the Pythons. Joseph McGrath produced television's *Not Only . . . But Also* (1965, starring Peter Cook and Dudley Moore), and directed the feature film *The Magic Christian* (1969, starring Peter Sellars, with writing contributions by Chapman and Cleese). McGrath also directed the TV version of *The Goon Show* in 1968. He was born in Glasgow, Scotland in 1930 and, like *FC*-director Ian MacNaughton, is depicted as a bit of a drinker.

McGrath also co-directed *Casino Royale* (1967), a cult film known for its frenetic, frantic production, including outbursts from stars Peter Sellers and Woody Allen, and ongoing friction between Sellers and mercurial Hollywood star Orson Welles. The Pythons may well have been drawing on the much-publicized on-set shenanigans of *Royale* for their portrait of the confused, besotted McRettin.

"Ministry of Housinge"—("Fish Licence") The Ministry of Housing and Local Government was established after World War II (January 1951) and was headed by Anthony Crosland in 1969-1970.

miserable attempt to capture joy and togetherness—(PSC; "French Subtitled Film") Again, the ennui of modern life tends to be the focus of much New Wave film, meaning "joy and togetherness," if ever realized, will inevitably be crushed by the weight of the real world. In *Breathless*, the Bogart-wannabe "hero" (Jean-Paul Belmondo) has a series of meaningless physical relationships before being gunned down by the police in the street, never achieving his goal of a solid relationship with the pretty American girl (Jean Seberg); in *400 Blows*, Truffaut's alter ego escapes from reform school, only to realize there's nowhere to run; in *Jules et Jim* (1962), the fantastic prospect of a successful and lasting ménage à trois runs smack up against conventional morals and the crushing weight of fate. In other words, most of the New Wave films—from France, Italy, Poland, Hungary, West Germany—offer characters who reach for the brass ring, but eventually fall and are destroyed. (Frenchman Truffaut's characters, at least, can and do experience significant joy in the early stages of the narrative—making the inevitable fall all the more poignant.)

"Miss Evans"—(*"Scott of the Antarctic"*) In the 1948 version of the film starring John Mills as Scott, the only significant female figure is Scott's wife, Kathleen, played by Diana Churchill. There are two actual people named Evans in the Scott story, Petty Officer Edgar "Taff" Evans and Lt. E.G.G. "Teddy" Evans, and Conger seems to pick up on this discrepancy when, upon being introduced to Evans, he repeats her name as if surprised to hear the "Miss."

montage of scenes of destruction—(PSC; link out of "Long John Silver Impersonators v. Bournemouth Gynaecologists") These filmed images of explosions and warplane strafing runs are not accounted for in the WAC records for the episode.

"Morgan, Cliff"—("Derby Council vs. All Blacks Rugby Match") Morgan (b. 1930) is a Welsh-born former Cardiff RFC player, then sports analyst and enshrinee into the International Rugby Hall of Fame. The printed script even indicates that Morgan is to have a Welsh accent, an unusual (and textually rare) bit of direction considering the many variations of English spoken throughout *FC*, most of which aren't identified except by the speaker's dress or the accent itself. Morgan was a commentator on *Rugby Special* during this period.

– N –

"Nabarro, Sir Gerald"—("Fish Licence") Conservative minister and cabinet secretary who was typically seen as a bit loony to the Pythons and the more liberal Left. Nabarro has already been mentioned by name in Eps. 11, 15, and 21. His very recognizable and prominent handlebar mustache is used occasionally in City Gent Vox Pops characterizations, especially by Chapman.

"New Zealanders"—("Derby Council vs. All Blacks Rugby Match") The New Zealand All Blacks handily beat the Welsh team in May and June 1969 in New Zealand; in the previous season they'd toured Australia and Fiji and gone undefeated in twelve games, many shutouts; and in 1967, the All Blacks had toured the UK, and gone 16-0-1. In short, they had trampled across most of the Commonwealth rugby fields and teams in the very recent past, and would probably have had little trouble, actually, defeating Derby Council.

– O –

"Olympic pole vaulter"—("*Scott of the Antarctic*") Using a well-known athlete here is not unlike American footballer O.J. Simpson making guest appearances on American TV shows such as *Dragnet 1967*, *Here's Lucy*, and *Medical Center* in the late 1960s, and Super Bowl hero Joe Namath appearing in three films in 1970, including *C.C. and Company*, *The Last Rebel*, and *Norwood*.

The presence of retired American football star Jim Brown in films like *Ice Station Zebra* (1968) must also have fueled this parody, with Kirk Vilb (Palin) here playing the virile and hirsute Rock Hudson part. Also, the casting of NFL quarterback Roman Gabriel and lineman Merlin Olsen in the John Wayne 1967 film *The Undefeated*—which also features Rock Hudson—is certainly a target.

"oranges"—("Derby Council vs. All Blacks Rugby Match") Eating slices of orange is a long-standing halftime tradition in rugby and football throughout the Commonwealth. The oranges were seen as a quick energy food. (Recent studies have indicated that the mango is the best fruit for such replenishment, and many teams and coaches have switched.)

organ music—(PSC; link out of "Fish Licence") This organ music played under the narrated "fishy exemption" section is by Helmut Walcha on the Church of Capperl Schritger Organ, and is the "Prelude & Fugue, D Major BWV 532" by J.S. Bach.

– P –

"Paignton"—("*Scott of the Antarctic*") Resort city on the English Channel, south of Exeter. Nearby Torquay is actually termed the "Queen of the English Riviera." Most of the location work for the second series was actually shot in this area.

"Palethorpe, Dawn"—("Fish Licence") Dawn Penelope (Palethorpe) Wofford (b. 1936) competed for the British Show Jumping Olympic team in 1956 and 1960. In 1956 Palethorpe was riding Earlsrath Rambler. Later in the rugby match section of this sketch, Palethorpe will be riding a horse named Sir Gerald (referring to Tory MP Gerald Nabarro).

Paris riots and clubbing—(PSC; "French Subtitled Film") Obviously supposed to be film from the fairly recent May 1968 riots in Paris, when students took up a revolutionary cause and stormed various French universities. One of the leaders of the student movement, Daniel Cohn-Bendit, would later visit London in an attempt to urge English students into similar acts of civil disobedience, but managed only a few, relatively quiet appearances.

This section of film stock (and the remainder of the war-related footage in this scene) is not accounted for by name in the WAC records.

penguin is close to the camera in the foreground and appears huge—(PSC; "*Scott of the Antarctic*") This is a standard special effects composition for low-budget films of this period. Using a lens (with plenty of lighting) that both can focus on an object close to the camera *and* deeper in the shot, the illusion of a looming element can be achieved. Meaningful interaction between the two objects is the real trick, of course, and this is where most of these films show their seams, as the Pythons indicate when the script calls for the film to "intercut a lot of phoney reverses." The two separate objects never truly can interact or share the same space, even, so the illusion is often spoiled. The Pythons will re-employ this illusion in the feature films *Holy Grail* and *Life of Brian*, where miniature castle and city sets, respectively, are placed on small hills in the background.

pimply youth—("French Subtitled Film") Played by Idle, the critic isn't pimply, but does affect a "swishy" tone and delivery. Identified as "Phil" in the scripts, there is the possibility that he is modeled on Philip French, a regular BBC contributor since 1960, and columnist for the *Observer* and *New Statesman* during this period.

More likely, however, he is Philip Jenkinson (b. 1935), who has earlier been mentioned in both the *FC* episodes and WAC notes, and who was, among other things, a writer for *Marty* (1968) and film reviewer for the BBC's *Radio Times*. Jenkinson also hosted *Film Night* beginning in 1970 (where Tony Bilbow also appeared), which is the context the Pythons give him in these appearances. Often lampooned by the Pythons (see his brutal murder in Ep. 33), Jenkinson was obviously a friend—he would appear in Idle's *Rutland Weekend Television* in 1975, and occasionally provided film clips from his own collection for later *Flying Circus* episodes.

"played by your very own lovely Terrence Lemming"—("*Scott of the Antarctic*") The nominal Brit in the main *Ice Station Zebra* cast was Patrick McGoohan (b. 1928), playing David Jones.

post office—(PSC; "Fish Licence") The printed script calls for a "real" post office after the backward mailing animation, but this is actually a redressed Market Street Methodist Hall in Torquay (WAC T12/1,416).

Praline—(PSC; "Fish Licence") One of the few *named* recurring characters in *FC*, Praline first appeared as a policeman in Ep. 6, then in the "Dead Parrot" sketch (Ep. 8), and as the host of a mysteriously canceled talk show in Ep. 18.

Proust, Marcel—("Fish Licence") Proust (1871-1922) is one of the most influential (certainly to the Pythons) writers of the twentieth century, his *Remembrance of Things Past* or *In Search of Lost Time* (*À la recherché du temps perdu*) seen by many as the most significant novel ever written.

Proust has already been mentioned in *FC*, in Ep. 11, and will figure prominently again in the "Summarize Proust" competition in Ep. 31. Proust's interest in time and memory, and the essentiality of experience (the "essence" of the madeleine cookie) is obviously important to the Pythons as their characters experience the modern, nostalgic, and pastiche world.

– R –

reverent voice over—(PSC; "Derby Council vs. All Blacks Rugby Match") In this voiceover Cleese mimics the earnest but soft delivery (loaded with "greats" as well) of Richard Dimbleby (1913-1965), longtime interviewer and reporter for *Panorama*. Cleese is specifically channeling Dimbleby's well-known hushed, reverential broadcast description of Queen Elizabeth II's coronation on 2 June 1953, broadcast live from Westminster Abbey:

> Here in the Abbey Church of St. Peter in Westminster, a great congregation of seven thousand, come from every part of the world, awaits the arrival of Her Majesty. And we'll see very shortly the procession as it passes right up the great church. (*choir and organ begin*) As the choir begin their lovely anthem . . . there come into sight all the splendors of the great officers and their regalia. Behind the heralds, the scepter with the cross carried by the Master of the Royal Air Force, the Viscount Portal of Hungerford . . . Saint Edward's staff, borne by the Earl of Lancaster. . . . (Audio transcription, *Eyewitness 1950-59*, "Coronation 2")

On the *Goon Show*, Peter Sellers had also impersonated the mellifluous Dimbleby in several play-by-play-type commentaries in several episodes, including "The Starlings" (31 August 1954) and "The Last Tram" (23 November 1954).

"revolutionnaire"—("French Subtitled Film") In French New Wave filmmaker Jean-Luc Godard's *Le Vent d'est* (1969), there is a character named simply "La révolutionnaire." In Godard's 1967 film *Week End*, the estranged couple find cannibalistic revolutionaries in the woods. The events of May 1968 helped push Godard and other left-leaning artists into more overtly political artistic expression.

rubbish dump—("French Subtitled Film") This setting is reminiscent of French New Wave director Jean-Luc Godard's film *Week End* (1967), where two garbage men rant about contemporary politics and the state of the capitalist world, and the film's somewhat self-aware heroes, Roland (Jean Yanne) and Corrine (Mireille Darc), argue about sex, cigarettes, traffic, and the lousy film they're having to slog through. The entire sequence in this "French Subtitled Film" sketch is obviously a parody of Godard's (and Chabrol's, and Resnais' et al.) often political, often overt, and certainly preachy and indicting French films of the late 1960s and early 1970s. A number of New Wave–type films from this period include garbage dumps as evidence of the detritus of modern capitalist society, including Luis Bunuel's *Los Olvidados* (1950) and Andrzej Wajda's *Ashes and Diamonds* (1957), where our "heroes" die ignominiously among the other trash.

A mention must be made of an older, more mature (and therefore, assumedly, more conservative) filmmaker, Akira Kurosawa, whose remarkable 1970 film *Dô dese ka den* is set entirely on a vast rubbish dump. Rather than making an overt political (meaning anti-West, anti-capitalist, anti-U.S.) statement, Kurosawa looks at the lives of society's lost people, the slum dweller, and tries to find nobility there.

The actual setting for the "French Subtitled Film" scene is a rubbish tip in Torquay, specifically the Lawsbridge Refuse Depot, and was shot on 13 May 1970 (WAC T12/1,416).

– S –

Scott of the Antarctic—("Scott of the Antarctic") There is a 1948 British film called *Scott of the Antarctic* starring John Mills and Diana Churchill.

The sweeping music heard underneath this sketch is from Sir Adrian Boult and the London Philharmonic Orchestra's "Sinfonia Antartica," selections from the First, Third, and Fifth Movements by Vaughn Williams (WAC T12/1,435). The music cues are not mentioned in the printed script, just in the WAC records.

Scott of the Sahara—("Scott of the Sahara") The music played during this sequence includes the International Studio Orchestra playing "Aggression" by E. Towren, as well as "Pride of the Ride" and "Nathan le Prophete" by Edward Michael (WAC T12/1,435).

She is walking in a trench—("Scott of the Antarctic") A jab at the well-known Hollywood practice of using camera angles, carefully chosen actors/extras, and "apple boxes" and trenches to make stars taller or shorter, including such diminutive A-list stars as Alan Ladd and Humphrey Bogart. In *Shane* (1953) for example, the (reportedly) 5'5" Ladd had to hold his own—compositionally—against Van Heflin (6') and Jack Palance (6'4"), so trenches were dug and apple boxes employed to negate the height differences.

Shot of a Spitfire—(PSC; "French Subtitled Film") This bit of film stock is called the "RAF Style Dog Fight," and is from VizNews, film number 13774 (WAC T12/1,428). This is one of the very few sections of stock film in this scene actually accounted for in WAC records.

"Sir Gerald"—("Derby Council vs. All Blacks Rugby Match") Yet another reference to Sir Gerald Nabarro (1913-1973), the flamboyant Conservative politician. Obviously a popular and polarizing figure, Nabarro is mentioned/lampooned in more than one hundred political cartoons during this period.

sixteen-ton weight falls on him—(PSC; link out of "Long John Silver Impersonators v. Bournemouth Gynaecologists") The large prop was clearly broken in this shot (recorded 2 July 1970), and a request for it to be either repaired or replaced is found in the WAC records (WAC T12/1,242).

"Sixty quid"—("Fish Licence") See the entry for "cat detector van." The most expensive license fee as of January 1969 (for color TV and radio) came to just £11.

"sort it out on the floor"—("*Scott of the Antarctic*") Meaning, they'll fix the problem in the editing room later. Filmed flubs or just bad or extra takes end up on the proverbial "floor" of the editing room.

"Stafford"—("Fish Licence") Sir Richard Stafford Cripps (1889-1952) was the (Labour) Chancellor of the Exchequer in 1947-1950 under PM Attlee, and would have been much in the news during the Pythons' formative years.

Stig—("French Subtitled Film") This character is wearing a tight shirt, wide belt, and scarf, almost identical to a character ("Man in Farmyard," played by Michel Cournot) standing in a farmyard in Godard's *Week End* (1967). Stig (Jones) will also wander out of shot, just as characters do in *Week End*—one of the garbage men, for example, is normally offscreen, yet still rants on.

The character Stig, not mentioned by name by any of the characters (but named in the printed scripts), may be based on an actual Stig, one Stig Dagerman (1923-1954). Dagerman was a Swedish existentialist, who immersed himself and his plays and novels in the despair and anxiety of the movement. After losing his

marriage and suffering a nervous breakdown, Dagerman committed suicide in 1954. Dagerman was also attracted to the Syndicalist movement—where workers would control factories—a famous reference to which will apear in *Monty Python and the Holy Grail*.

– T –

"Town Clerk"—("Derby Council vs. All Blacks Rugby Match") The Town Clerk was often the senior administrator in towns and villages, and would have merited regalia befitting this high office.

"try"—("Derby Council vs. All Blacks Rugby Match") A "try" in rugby is a grounding of the ball over the opponent's goal line (a "touch-down"). The Lady Mayoress (Cleveland) will end up scoring both tries in this match.

The "set-pieces" the New Zealanders are going to struggle with in the second half would include the "scrum," "line-outs," and "restarts."

– U –

"US furlong"—("*Scott of the Antarctic*") A U.S. furlong is 660 feet, or 220 yards.

– W –

"Watford"—(link into "Long John Silver Impersonators v. Bournemouth Gynaecologists") Watford is a town in Hertfordshire, and Bournemouth is on the South Coast in Dorset.

"Wayne, John"—("French Subtitled Film") Wayne (1907-1979), the iconic Hollywood actor, had most recently appeared in *True Grit* (1968), *The Undefeated* (1969), *Chisum* (1970), and *Rio Lobo* (1970). None are particularly bloody, especially when compared with the newfound penchant for sex, violence, and gore in the films of Sam Peckinpah (Ep. 33; *The Wild Bunch*) and Arthur Penn (*Bonnie and Clyde*; still used in Ep. 33). The cast of *The Undefeated* featured, coincidentally, retired American football players Merlin Olsen and Roman Gabriel, as well as the rugged, hirsute, and Kirk Vilb–like Rock Hudson.

"Webb's Wonder"—("French Subtitled Film") Actually "Webb's Wonderful," a crisp lettuce, which (significantly) is a cultivar that originated from France. This went to graphics not as "Webb's Wonder," but as "Cos Lettuce," before someone changed the request (WAC T12/1,435).

"What about China?"—("Derby Council vs. All Blacks Rugby Match") In 1970, Mao Tse-Tung was probably ailing, and Lin Biao (also Lin Piao; 1907-1971) had tacitly assumed power in China with the support of the military. Biao would die mysteriously a few months after this episode aired, however, when Mao probably began to fear his subordinate's rising influence. Liu Shaoqi (Lin Shao Chi) was considered quite powerful and perhaps even the heir apparent to Mao, but was purged in the late 1960s. The "second-half" hope Zhou Enlai (Chou Enlai; 1898-1976) was premier in China from 1949 to 1976, and considered the third most powerful man in China during this period.

Mao and China are mentioned significantly in *FC* a number of times, illustrating the increasing international presence the Communist country and regime were enjoying in the late 1960s and early 1970s. See notes for Eps. 24 and 25 for more.

To get one's "finger out" is a British naval term meaning to uncover the powder so a cannon can be touched off (*OED*). Colloquially, it means to get a move on. In the 5 April 1963 edition of *Private Eye*, the spread cartoon from "Timothy" depicts a hip new Britain under Tory leadership, and includes Prince Philip and the Queen on a float. Philip, in his customary hands-behind-back position, is whispering: "Ie must gette my bloodye finger out before she notices!" as if he's caught himself in an unseen Chinese finger trap (Ingrams 80-81).

"wingers"—("Derby Council vs. All Blacks Rugby Match") A winger is a forward whose place is on the back row of the scrum.

Episode 24

ANIMATION: An elderly secretary . . . —(PSC; animated link out of "Job Hunter") This is one of the few occasions where a Gilliam-rendered animated link is included in its entirety in the printed script. And even though it is included and reads like a traditional sketch, it's not given its own title.

"anytime free men anywhere waver in their defence of democracy"—(animated link out of "Job Hunter") This gunboat diplomacy (or Monroe Doctrine) foreign policy practice meant that during the 1950s and 1960s there were significant and ongoing U.S. efforts in Asia, Africa, and perhaps especially Latin America (being so close to home) to support any administration that would fight Leftist insurgencies. Consequently, militaristic and often brutal Right-wing regimes were at least tacitly supported by U.S. funding and advisors, often through the CIA. This subject will be revisited more specifically in Ep. 33, the "Storage Jars" sketch.

Archbishop Shabby—(PSC; "Crackpot Religions Ltd.") Ken Shabby (Palin) has already appeared in Ep. 12, and Mr. Nudge (Idle) has also appeared, in Ep. 3. Both characters are greeted affectionately by the studio audience, indicating home viewers of the show were making efforts to get tickets and watch the show in person. Gumby characters are also recognized throughout the series.

Arnold, Malcolm—("Repeating Groove") Arnold (b. 1921) is a composer who scored, among many other works, *The Bridge on the River Kwai* (1957) and was awarded a CBE in 1970. The "travelogue music" that the script mentions in relation to Arnold includes *Royal New Zealand Journey* (1954), a documentary on the Queen's trip to NZ that year. There were six such

films made on the subject of the Queen's half-year visit to Australasia.

The music being played beneath the scene here is not from Arnold, but is a selection from "Overtures from Fingal's Cave" by Mendelssohn as played by the Vienna Philharmonic Orchestra (WAC T12/1,414).

"Arsenal's 1-0 victory"—("Interview in Filing Cabinet") Arsenal FC is a football club which called Highbury home in 1970, and would win the FA Cup in the 1970-1971 season, defeating Liverpool 2-1.

"Baldwin, Stanley"—("Ramsay MacDonald Striptease") Already mentioned in passing in Eps. 14 and 21, Baldwin (1867-1947) was the Conservative PM chosen by George V, 1923-1924, then reclaimed the office 1924-1929. Ramsay MacDonald (1866-1937) led the Labour government (and the country as PM) both before and after Baldwin.

"battle against Caractacus"—("Film Director [Teeth]") There is no evidence that Julius Caesar and Caractacus met on the battlefield (they were separated by a number of years). Claudius was Caesar when Caractacus was captured.

beach huts across to beach and sea—("*How Not to Be Seen*") This idyllic beach scene is shot in the Broadsands Beach area 11-13 May 1970 (WAC T12/1,416).

"Bishop of Dulwich"—("Crackpot Religions Ltd.") There is no Bishop of Dulwich, of course, an area of London in the Southwark region, south of the Thames and therefore, anciently, out of the influence of the monarchy and haven to all sorts of illegal activity. On the other side of criminality (but still suspect, in the

Pythons' eyes), Conservative leader Margaret Thatcher owned a home on Dulwich Common.

"bishopric in a see of your choice"—("Crackpot Religions Ltd.") The granting of sinecures is as old as such valued religious posts have existed. The Pythons will revisit one such arrangement in Ep. 28, "Trim-Jeans Theatre," Thomas Becket's placement as the Archbishop of Canterbury in 1162, ostensibly to be Henry II's ecclesiastical rubber stamp.

"Bishop's Stortford"—("Crackpot Religions Ltd.") Yet another pun (see "North See Gas" below), Bishop's Stortford is a smaller town in Hertfordshire. On the old road between Cambridge and London, Chapman, Cleese, and Idle may have passed through the town in their student years.

"novice"—A "novice" is a person who's in probationary status in a religious order, a new entrant. The allusion here is that this "diocesan lovely" is anything but inexperienced.

bleak landscape—(PSC; animated link out of "Job Hunter") Staged very much like a Shell Oil commercial from 1964 titled "Mojave Run," which featured side-by-side cars driving across a barren desert. The oil additive being touted in these commercials was "Platformate."

"Bonetti, Peter"—("Crackpot Religions Ltd.") Bonetti (b. 1941) is a retired footballer for Chelsea and England.

"Bradshaw, Mr. E.R."—(*How Not to Be Seen*") Jones has played Inspector Elizabeth Bradshaw in Ep. 19, in the "School Prize-Giving" sketch.

– C –

"Chabrol stops at nothing"—("Mr. Neville Shunte") Claude Chabrol (b. 1930) was a significant French New Wave film director of this period. Directing films in Italy and France, Chabrol had produced *Les Biches* in 1968, a daring look (for its time) at bisexuality, and a film that most likely had many more conservative types asking if he would stop at anything, indeed.

"Charlton, Jackie"—(*Yummy, Yummy*") Jack Charlton (b. 1935) wasn't a frontman for a pop group, but a star defender for Leeds United. He played for England between 1965 and 1970, and was part of the successful World Cup team in 1966.

Chinese for Business Men—(PSC; "Conquistador Coffee Campaign") The book cover reads "*Chinese for Advertising Men*," while the printed script called for "*Chinese for Business Men*." Silly as it may sound, BBC

Publications offered the very similar *Introduction to Chinese: A BBC Radio Course in Spoken Mandarin* (1966) by David Pollard, which was a companion piece to a BBC Radio program.

The continuing presence of China and Chinese references in *FC* indicate the expanding Chinese presence in the international community during this period, and most probably reflects the very real anxiety felt by many as China's population and economy boomed. This is the era of Chinese-American saber rattling and then diplomacy, with President Nixon's much-celebrated visit to China in 1972 affirming the growing significance of China in the First World of global politics, and eventually economics. See entries for Eps. 23 and 25 for more.

"cholera . . . athlete's head"—("Conquistador Coffee Campaign") "Cholera" is a diarrheal illness caused by bacteria; "mange" is a skin condition caused by burrowing mites (often in pets); "dropsy" is soft tissue swelling due to excess water; "the clap" is a sexually transmitted disease; "hard pad" is a form of distemper in dogs; and "athlete's head" is a silly version of athlete's foot (*tinea pedis*, mentioned in Ep. 25), a fungal skin infection.

coastline—(PSC; "Repeating Groove") This entire scene was shot above Broadsands Beach, South Devon, on 13 May 1970 (WAC T12/1,416).

"Conquistador Coffee"—("Conquistador Coffee Campaign") A wry comment on the presence of European conquerors ("conquistadores") in Central and South America from the fifteenth century and beyond, introducing and then controlling the production and distribution of coffee for many years thereafter.

"Crelm"—(animated link into "Agatha Christie Sketch [Railway Timetables]") Probably intended to sound like the proprietary and popular "Crest" toothpaste brand name, which had introduced its fluoride additive "Fluoristan" in 1955. See more on Crelm and early British TV advertising in notes to Ep. 26.

"cross the Atlantic on a tricycle"—("Crossing the Atlantic on a Tricycle") This is likely a reference to the recent and celebrated crossing of the Atlantic by explorer Thor Heyerdahl on papyrus rafts (Ra I and Ra II). Heyerdahl and his exploits will be covered in much more detail in Ep. 28, "Emigration From Surbiton to Hounslow."

Also, Brit John Fairfax had recently rowed alone across the Atlantic, and had been featured on *This Is Your Life* in early 1970 for his troubles.

"crumpet over sixteen"—("Crackpot Religions Ltd.") A "crumpet" is a slang term for a sexually available woman, in this case of legal age.

– D –

Daily Mirror—("Crackpot Religions Ltd.") The *Daily Mirror* was by this time competing (and badly) with Rupert Murdoch's *The Sun*—candid photos like this one of Bishop Sarah appeared regularly in both papers, and obviously appealed to the reading audience.

"deliberate ambiguity, a plea for understanding in a mechanized world"—("Mr. Neville Shunt") This very concern fueled much Modern Art in the late nineteenth and early twentieth centuries. The dehumanizing effects of the Industrial Revolution found their way into the man-machine sculptures of Epstein, the horrors of the more efficient and gruesome slaughter in WWI, the antiseptic architecture of Gropius and the Bauhaus movement, the restless cacophony of Eliot's *Waste Land*, the cinematographical poetic images of Ezra Pound and Vachel Lindsay, and that same filmic influence in Duchamps painting and sculpture, among many others.

In a number of works "the beast" embodied the heartless, relentless machine, and even earlier, of course, that mechanical marvel the train had been known as "The Iron Horse."

The "deliberate ambiguity" has also been a staple of avant garde film since the 1920s, and then New Wave film in the 1950s and 1960s, a reaction to the spot-on narrative clarity ("this means this") of most traditional (read: classical narrative) film. See Bordwell and Thompson for more.

"diagram of a tooth"—("animated link out of "Job Hunter") This is the same image Gilliam used—his own smile—in the previous episode for the "Conrad Pooves' Dancing Teeth" animation.

Different Voice Over—(PSC; animated link into "Job Hunter") Uncredited in the printed script, this is Idle.

"Domino Theory"—(animated link out of "Job Hunter") Gilliam's narrator (Gilliam himself) describes this theory fairly accurately. Much U.S. foreign policy in this period was aimed at supporting anti-Communist governments, forces, or even rebels around the world, both covertly and, where necessary, in full view on the world stage, as in Vietnam.

– E –

"Ecce homo"—("Mr. Neville Shunte") Latin, the phrase translates to "behold the man" (John 19:5).

Episode 24—Recorded as Episode 6 (Series 2, Episode 6), and broadcast eleventh in the series.

Also appearing in this episode, and uncredited, are Dilys Marvin (*Omnibus*), Lewis Alexander (*Dr. Who*), and Len Kingston (on film; *Play For Today*). The David Agency (located at 6 Holborn Viaduct EC1) provided Willy Bowman (*The Troubleshooters*), George Feasey, and Philip Webb (*The Wednesday Play*), while the Blyth Agency sent over Marvin, Dorothy Watson (*Z Cars*), and Pat Dooley for small roles.

Exchange & Mart—(PSC; "Job Hunter") A long-standing buying and selling publication for all sorts of goods (cars, appliances, real estate), which now has a significant online presence in the UK.

– F –

"film's won a prize"—("Conquistador Coffee Campaign") The worldwide film festival phenomenon came to life during the Pythons' formative years, with the major festivals—including those held annually in Cannes, Berlin, Moscow, and San Francisco—being established in the 1950s. It was at these festivals that many of the so-called New Wave films and filmmakers appeared for the first time, and the film festival became a very important venue for non-traditional (meaning outside the Hollywood studio or approved national film systems worldwide) films to find both a critical and then commercial audience. Filmmakers who obviously influenced the Pythons—including Truffaut, Godard, Pinter, and Antonioni—were discovered at such festivals.

"Football Special"—("Agatha Christie Sketch [Railway Timetables]") Often an additional train put on just for days a football match is in the offing. This way, fans of a particular team can travel together and begin their merrymaking before reaching the stadium. (The author experienced this firsthand, watching as two Chelsea supporters consumed significant quantities of vodka—"hidden" in sports drink bottles—between Hammersmith/Fulham and Cardiff. Incidentally, a celebration was in order, as Chelsea beat Arsenal 2-1, and won the FA Community Shield.)

– G –

"get knotted"—("Mr. Neville Shunte") A *New Society* article reported in 1963 that "get knotted" was an emerging phrase, and that younger people were using it to mean, essentially, "go to hell."

"GLC 9424075"—(animated link into "Agatha Christie Sketch [Railway Timetables]") Shell gasoline was advertised in 1954 with the new additive "ICA"—"Ignition Control Additive." Closer to home,

"GLC" was the then fairly new acronym for the Greater London Council, an administrative authority for public works in Greater London, and which the Conservatives controlled in 1970.

Also, "942" was the telephone prefix for New Malden in 1968. See Ep. 27 for more on Malden.

"gradient signs"—("Agatha Christie Sketch [Railway Timetables]") These are ground-level signs posted along railroad right-of-ways indicating the grade (up or down, ending or beginning) along the track ahead. The signs usually feature an upward or downward arrow and a number.

– H –

holds up a card saying 'joke'—(PSC; "Conquistador Coffee Campaign") Returning here to the time-honored cartoon tradition seen in Warner Bros. cartoons of the 1940s and beyond, and especially in the self-conscious, gag-ridden cartoons of Tex Avery. These asides to the television (not studio) audience rather abruptly take the sting off particularly pointed barbs, or those just in really poor taste. In Ep. 17, the "Architect Sketch," captions ("Satire") are used to the same effect.

holidaymaker in braces, collarless shirt . . .—(PSC; *"How Not to Be Seen"*) Though quite a long way from the camera, the man (Chapman) doesn't appear to be dressed much like the costume description provided by the printed script.

"Holidaymaker Special"—("Agatha Christie Sketch [Railway Timetables]") A train destined for a holiday spot, probably the southern coast, and likely making fewer stops along the way. These also could be additional trains put on during bank holidays, when pilgrimages are made south to the beaches.

"Hornchurch"—("Agatha Christie Sketch [Railway Timetables]") As in the "New Cooker Sketch" in Ep. 14, the Pythons reel off a slew of locally known place-names, including:

"Hornchurch"—Located about fifteen miles north and east of Charing Cross, there is not a train station in Hornchurch. The nearest main line is located at Upminster.

"Basingstoke"—South of Reading, in Hampshire.

"Caterham"—Both Caterham and Chipstead (both in Surrey) are on the Caterham and Tattenham Corner Services line and part of the Southern Railway.

"Lambs Green"—There is a Lambs Green in Dorset and Sussex, both well away from the Caterham and Chipstead line.

"Swanborough"—In Swindon (see below), it seems that Sir Horace's beloved railway has in fact been dis-

mantled. The portion of the line that ran between Stanton Fitzwarren and Hampton (through Swanborough) is no longer in service.

"King's Cross"—Still a major hub in northeast central London, King's Cross is in Camden.

"Swindon"—Located in the southwest of England (Wiltshire), Swindon is also mentioned in Ep. 26.

"Wisborough Junction"—Wisborough Green is in West Sussex.

"Gillingham"—There is a Gillingham in both Kent and Dorset.

"Bedford, Colmworth"—Both in Bedfordshire.

"Fen Ditton"—Just outside Cambridge in Cambridgeshire, this station should have been well known to at least the two Cambridge alums, Chapman and Cleese.

"Sutton"—Also located in Bedfordshire.

"Wallington"—In the London Borough of Sutton, on the Southern rail line. The jumbled directions these stops would require indicate that the Pythons grabbed names from their collective hats as they wrote this sketch—the joke being the attention to detail the characters like Tony (Palin) and Lady Partridge (Chapman) exhibit for their beloved railway timetables.

"Hainault"—In the London Borough of Redbridge, Hainault lies at the very edge of Greater London, north and east of the City. Hainault was originally on the loop line to Ilford.

As in other sketches where directions or precise details are included, the Pythons tend to rely on memory as well as plainly contrived information, meaning the overall point here is the fixation Neville Shunt (Jones) exhibits for railway timetables, and not the specifics of the timetables themselves. The BALPA Spokesman in Ep. 16 (played by Idle), would disagree, of course, arguing the point for accuracy, as did a number of letter writers to *TC*.

– I –

"I inherited this religion from my father"—("Crackpot Religions Ltd.") Almost certainly a slighting reference to the radio preachers Herbert and Garner Ted Armstrong, a father and son associated with the Worldwide Church of God. Beginning as the Radio Church of God in the 1930s, the organization grew rapidly with the rise of its medium, with the broadcast being named "The World Tomorrow" on the eve of WWII. Similar to Arthur Crackpot's church, the Worldwide Church of God solicited donations (tithes) of its membership, and was seen by many Christian pundits as a cobbled-together (and very profitable) cult:

Small wonder that the church's annual income is estimated at around $55 million. Or that Founder Armstrong zips round the world to visit such leaders as Japan's Prime Minister Eisaku Sato or India's Indira Gandhi in a Grumman Gulfstream jet that gobbles up at least $1.5 million a year. Former W.C.G. members charge that the Armstrongs live like kings while members often live in poverty in order to pay their tithes. They maintain that each of the two Armstrongs has elegant homes in Texas, California and England; that Herbert sports a $1,000 watch and bought a $2,000 set of cuff links and tie tack for a Jerusalem trip. (*Time* 15 May 1972)

The church operated a university in St. Albans, as well, and could claim chess champion Bobby Fischer (Ep. 35) as a sympathetic friend.

The son, Garner Ted, had taken over as the voice of the media church in the 1960s, but a power struggle came to a head in May 1972, and the church's inner politics became front-page news. The "devilish" animation provided by Gilliam reflects the charge presented by Herbert to the church faithful in May 1972—son Garner was "in the bonds of Satan," and had to be reined in. See the balance of the contemporary article in *Time* on the church, its history, finances, and its internecine strife (15 May 1972).

"in our Durham studios"—("Crossing the Atlantic on a Tricycle") The BBC had regional offices and studio space in Midlands cities like Norwich and Birmingham, where regional material could be put together and eventually broadcast. These were the areas that often decided to "opt out" of broadcasting *Flying Circus*, especially during the first series, in favor of more local programming. For the Durham area, the BBC regional offices are located in Newcastle upon Tyne.

"inside the distance"—("Crackpot Religions Ltd.") A sports betting term from both racing and boxing, allying the work of Crackpot's bishops and archbishops with that of the influence-peddler and illegal gaming industries.

"international Chinese Communist Conspiracy"—(animated link out of "Job Hunter") Chinese historian Elizabeth Perry writes of the then-rabid Chinese Communist conspiracy talk, especially virulent in the United States in the 1960s. (And since this is an animated link, it's not surprising that the troupe's lone American, Gilliam, would broach the subject.) Those active in the anti-Chinese movements included men like Robert DePugh, founder of a militia in California, whose beliefs included the alleged presence of an enormous and hostile Chinese Communist army massing on the Mexican side of the California-Mexico border, according to Perry. This over-the-top American paranoia is the subject of the following animation, as well. DePugh had been arrested after being on the run for more than a year in New Mexico in 1970, which

probably kept both him and his beliefs in the public eye during this period.

Additionally, the threat of Chinese communism in 1970-1971 (before Nixon's celebrated trip to China in 1972) is clear in speeches/writings from the White House where SEATO and pan-Asian interests are discussed, and any mention of China is conspicuously absent (see "Building for Peace: A Report by President Richard Nixon to the Congress, 25 February 1971"). The goal was to strengthen a buffer zone around China, hopefully preventing a "domino theory" scenario across the Asian diaspora.

"It All Happened on the 11.20 from Hainault . . . "— ("Agatha Christie Sketch [Railway Timetables]") The Hainault to Redhill via Horsham and Reigate route (all in the Greater London area) demands quite a bit of backtracking, not surprisingly. And while Carshalton, Tooting Bec, and West Croydon are more or less on the way, Malmesbury is well west in Wiltshire.

"I've been in the sea for thirty-three years now"— ("City Gents Vox Pops") This beach scene was shot at Broadsands Beach on 13 May 1970 (WAC T12/1,416).

– J –

"John the Baptist had the most enormous . . . dental appendages"—("Film Director [Teeth]") This may be a rather clever comment on the very popular film theory of the period, the "auteur" theory. Propounded by French New Wave writers-cum-filmmakers like Godard and especially Truffaut in the pages of *Cahiers du Cinema*, then expanded and championed by American critic Andrew Sarris in 1968, the theory essentially argues that the director of a seemingly generic film produced by the studio system can still exert significant and ultimately identifiable "personality" on/in that film, so much so that his body of work can be examined for those influences. Directors mentioned by these theorists include Howard Hawks, Orson Welles, Fritz Lang, Sam Fuller, etc.

The fact that all Curry's characters feature large teeth, like Curry, is significant for the auteur theory, as well. For Truffaut, his own autobiographical experiences tend to emerge over and over in his films, including *400 Blows*, creating personalized films that reveal as much, allegedly, about the director as the subject or time in which the film was created. For Hawks, his depictions of relationships—especially older and younger male, the homosocial benefits of the male group, and male-female—provide a commonality from film to film, across the many genres he attempted.

– L –

Labienus—(PSC; "Film Director [Teeth]") Titus Labienus, known as "Caesar's Lieutenant," lived c. 100-45 BC.

"La Fontaine's elk"—("Mr. Neville Shunte") This may be an oblique reference to Jean de la Fontaine, the seventeenth-century beast fabulist.

"Lambert, E.V."—(*How Not to Be Seen*) Verity Lambert (b. 1935) has already been mentioned in Ep. 8, the "Buying a Bed" sketch. Lambert was a producer for *Dr. Who* episodes.

late-night line-up—("Film Director [Teeth]") The two-chair set-up was characteristic of many discussion-type shows of this period. Already mentioned in Ep. 19, "It's a Living," *Late Night Line-Up* (1964-1972) was a popular television discussion program whose cameras showed up at a *FC* taping (probably Ep. 26), much to the consternation of the BBC hierarchy (WAC T47/216).

"lead piping"—("Crackpot Religions Ltd.") Lead products used in construction in the UK—including piping, gutters, and roofing tiles—have for generations been stolen for resale on the street (lead melts down and is reformed very easily), especially by low-end criminals and drug addicts looking for quick money.

Lennon, John—(PSC; "Crackpot Religions Ltd.") Python contemporary and friend John Lennon (1940-1980) and Yoko Ono (b. 1933) had staged a very publicized "sleep-in" (or "bed-in") in 1969 in an attempt to bring awareness to the misery going on in Vietnam.

"level crossing"—("Mr. Neville Shunte") Simply an intersection on the same level of either a road and a railway, or two railways (*OED*). The trainspotting subculture would have appreciated this reference, along with "bogies" and "shunt," for example.

"lists her hobbies as swimming, riding, and film producers"—("Crackpot Religions Ltd.") The gist here is, of course, that Bishop Sarah is engaging in sexual affairs with film producers—visiting the "casting couch"—to secure acting parts.

"Lord Langdon"—(*How Not to Be Seen*) A character from a "Biggles" adventure, *Biggles Sorts It Out* (1967). Biggles has already been mentioned in Eps. 10 and 15, and will figure significantly in Ep. 33, where he (played by Chapman) will dictate a letter and shoot his best mate Algy (Palin).

"Lower class—I can't touch it"—("Crackpot Religions Ltd.") Again, as Crackpot (Idle) earlier admits that paid church membership will bring prizes, here he is refreshingly candid as to the preferred level of income his parishioners need to have reached for participation. In Ep. 26, the undertaker (Idle) is also quite honest with the man (Cleese) who's brought his dead mother to the funeral home, describing the nastiness of both cremation and burial, and then admitting she's "quite young" enough to be "an eater." The undertaker then good-naturedly invites the man to join in the feast. In both instances, the characters are defying the common language of a transaction by admitting their levels of self-interest.

– M –

"MacDonald, Ramsay"—("Ramsay MacDonald Striptease") The image of a respected, sober, and even grave man-of-the-people wearing women's undergarments is the deflation-by-ridicule approach employed by the Pythons throughout *FC* and the feature films. And MacDonald (1866-1937) was not the monied, cultured elite, either—he was of illegitimate birth and a working-class Labour politician—not the City-Gent-closet-pervert type the Pythons usually jabbed.

"Manchester and the West Midlands, Spain, China"—(*How Not to Be Seen*) Not surprising anymore to see the conflation of two Midlands areas, both destroyed here by nuclear attack, along with two of the most notably dictatorial regimes in existence, Franco's Spain and Mao's People's Republic of China. Franco had been in power since 1939; Mao since 1949, or much of the collective Pythons' lives.

"Millar, Gavin"—("Film Director [Teeth]") A writer, actor, director, and editor, Millar (b. 1938) co-authored (with filmmaker Karel Reisz) *Technique of Film Editing* (1968), and created documentary profiles on big-screen luminaries including American Busby Berkeley, Brits Powell and Pressburger, and Frenchman Jean Renoir. Millar was also the film critic for *The Listener* for many years, beginning in 1970, also contributing to periodicals like *Sight and Sound*, etc.

Miss Johnson—(PSC; link out of "Job Hunter") Though not credited in the printed script, this voice seems to have been provided by Carol Cleveland.

"Most Popular Religion Ltd."—("Crackpot Religions Ltd.") By sheer numbers worldwide, this would clearly be the Roman Catholic faith, though in Britain, Anglican Church membership exceeded Catholic figures.

Mr. Frog comes in—(PSC; "Conquistador Coffee Campaign") Though not mentioned in the printed script,

Frog (Idle) enters through the window, not the door. This may have been a last-minute change to the scene, as most such moments (even the silliest ones) are noted in the printed scripts as written prior to tapings. The backdrop outside the window makes it clear that the office is supposed to be at least one floor above street level, as well. As the Pythons move into the second and third series, especially, the standard set of television practices—including entrances and exits and transitions of all kinds—are more and more altered, done away with, or made visible to the viewing audience, bringing a self-consciousness to the show that fed on itself, reflexively, from week to week, and then from series to series.

– N –

"narrow traction bogies"—("Agatha Christie Railway Sketch [Railway Timetables]") A bogie is the wheel-and-axle configuration beneath train cars and engines. The newest bogie introduced during this period had appeared in 1963.

"nasty, greedy, cold hearted, avaricious, money-grubber . . . *Conservative*"—("City Gent Vox Pops") In short, the Pythons' definition of the enemy during this period, the Tories. They tended to poke fun at politicians and authority types in general, irrespective of political affiliation, but the real barbs and low blows are always reserved for more conservatives types (Heath, Thatcher, Maudling, Nabarro et al.).

A similarly themed cartoon appeared in the pages of *Private Eye* and features two City Gents, one saying to the other: "It's simple really—pensions for the over 80's, then the Euthanasia Bill . . . " (17 July 1970, 5).

Nesbitt—(PSC; *"How Not to Be Seen"*) A name used several times (see Eps. 26 and 37, as well) for the prototypical Pepperpot. "Nesbitt" is also used by Peter Cook in his "Sitting on the Bench" sketch for *Beyond the Fringe*.

"Harlow New Town" is in Essex, and is one of the "new towns" designed and built after the war in the surge for adequate housing for the displaced millions.

"nine out of ten small countries"—(animated link out of "Job Hunter") A play on the toothpaste advertising slogan of the period, "4 out of 5 dentists surveyed," it was actually true that scores of countries around the world were benefiting from the somewhat paranoid foreign policy of the United States, and enjoying the proffered money, CIA presence, and trade deals. This may also be a comment on the continuing presence of American military forces in Europe and Asia since the end of WWII.

"no names no pack drill"—("Crackpot Religions Ltd.") A "pack drill" is a military term for a punishment that includes forced marching with a heavy pack. The phrase means he's not naming names. Arthur Crackpot (Idle) further asserts that most religions demand such spiritual and temporal activities from adherents, and promises that his religion will not.

"North See Gas"—("Crackpot Religions Ltd.") One of those topical, very contemporary puns that can become illusory over time, Britain was in the late 1960s still fairly new to the dependence on North Sea gas (then North Sea oil in the 1970s), meaning petroleum products were finally coming from British sources, not overseas suppliers. The phrase "North Sea Gas" was appearing regularly in newspaper headlines and stories during this period.

"North Walsham, Norfolk"—("Crossing the Atlantic on a Tricycle") North Walsham is some twenty-five miles north of Norwich, already mentioned in this episode, and the location for much spring and summer location shooting for the Pythons.

"Norwich City Council"—("Crackpot Religions Ltd.) A significant mention only because the Pythons had shot a good deal of location and insert footage in the Norwich area, hiring local actors where necessary, etc.

"Not for sale, what does that mean?"—("Job Hunter") Cleese will later play a Merchant Banker who has no understanding of charity, giving, or the meaning of "inner life" (Ep. 30). These are the same kinds of character traits that will also be seen in the "Argument Clinic," where each man only understands his own specific area of expertise—"abuse," "complaints," arguing, and "being-hit-on-the-head" lessons (Ep. 29).

Number 10 Downing Street—(PSC; "Ramsay MacDonald Striptease") Official residence of the PM since the eighteenth century, though many PMs have used it only as an official residence (more like an office), and actually lived elsewhere.

– O –

"O Levels"—("Job Hunter") This is the "ordinary level (of the General Certificate of Education examination)" (*OED*). An "A Level" is the "advanced level." These General Certificate of Education exams were introduced in 1951, just when the young Pythons would have been encountering their rigors in school. Performance on the A-Level exam often indicated whether or not a student was an acceptable candidate for university.

– P –

"Paddington"—("Mr. Neville Shunte") Major departure and arrival station for train travel west and south of London.

"Public Service Film No. 42"—(*How Not to Be Seen*) These public service films did, in fact, exist, and included titles like *Litter Defence Volunteers* (1968), showing how children can band together to clean up Britain; and *Teenagers Learn to Swim* (1972).

– R –

"Rio Tinto"—("Crackpot Religions Ltd.") Rio Tinto is an international mining corporation, and would have been a solid investment for the "Most Popular Religion" priest/investor. "Allied Breweries" disappeared in a 1978 merger, but had been a large UK-based distillery corporation. The priest also appears to be reading a copy of the *Financial Times*, the voice of the marketplace and modern investor, and certainly meant here to take the place of a Holy Bible.

Rio Tinto was unwillingly in the news during this period when it was leaked that a secret uranium mining deal had been reached between the UK government's Atomic Energy Authority and Rio Tinto in South West Africa, an unofficial colony of South Africa (*Private Eye* 31 July 1970, 16-17). All above board business dealings with the apartheid state had become news fodder, forcing such deals into backrooms and out of the public eye.

– S –

"SE5"—(*How Not to Be Seen*) The postal code SE5 is in the Camberwell area of Greater London. There is only one Black Lion Road in the UK, and it's in Wales.

"S. Frog, sir"—("Conquistador Coffee Campaign") The use of the initial can be seen as an attempt by Mr. Frog to ally himself with the more respected academicians, athletes, and highly placed social and political figures of Britain's nineteenth and twentieth centuries. Most noted nineteenth-century cricket players were known throughout their careers by initialed names, like "W.G. Grace," for example. Life in academe also merited such respect, including A.J.P. Taylor (referenced in Ep. 11 and *HG*) and E.M.W. Tillyard, to name just two.

Secondly, this may be yet another reference to the tradition of "Gentlemen vs. Players" in Lords cricket matches. There, forename initials were used to distinguish between the professional and amateur players. In this case, S. Frog (Idle) wants to be clustered in with the "Gentlemen" as opposed to the more plebeian "Players" in the world of competitive advertising. See the note for "Gumby, Prof. R.J." in Ep. 9.

"Shrill"—(link into "Agatha Christie Sketch [Railway Timetables]") Shell Oil is a British-Dutch oil and gas consortium in business since the late nineteenth century. The word "shrill" (meaning a loud, strident sound) may also refer to the way in which the Shell Oil TV (and much American TV) commercials were delivered/perceived in the period.

Commercial television didn't appear in the UK until 1954, when ITV came on the air, and competition with the BBC was finally in place.

The "Shrill" Man (uncredited) is Palin.

"Shunt, Neville"—("Agatha Christie Sketch [Railway Timetables]") An appropriate name for this train-obsessed playwright, as a "shunt" is a British railway term for "switching" individual cars into connected trains. Shunt is spelled "Shunt" and "Shunte" in the printed scripts.

This is certainly a reference to the writer Nevil Shute (1899-1960), an aeronautical engineer-turned-author whose works often centered on the very technical. For example, his novel *No Highway* (1948) sets a fictional narrative within a discussion of aircraft structural integrity and design. It's reported that Shute's books were often on grade school required reading lists, where the young Pythons may have found them, and judged them exceedingly pedantic.

"Slough"—(*How Not to Be Seen*) There are a number of Leighton Roads in the UK, not surprisingly, though none in Slough, which is north of Windsor and south of Gerrards Cross.

"Smegma"—(*How Not to Be Seen*) A secretion from the sex gland areas of mammals, and here a rather sophomoric "naughty" word. A Mr. Glans (Cleese) appeared in the previous episode.

There is a "Belmont" in the very same area of Llanelli, Carmarthenshire as Black Lion Road. See the entry for "SE5" for more.

"soft-sell"—("Conquistador Coffee Campaign") Advertising that attempts to be subtly persuasive, as opposed to loud and aggressive (*OED*). American television of the period was *not* considered to be a bastion of the soft-sell approach (see the entries for "Crelm" and "Shrill").

stock film of Ramsay MacDonald—(PSC; "Ramsay MacDonald Striptease") The stock film used here is nine seconds of MacDonald footage from VisNews. Ramsay MacDonald (1866-1937) was twice Prime Minister and the first Labour PM—in 1924, and then 1929-1935. See the entry for MacDonald above.

stock film of a small house—(PSC; *"How Not to Be Seen"*) The stock film of explosions is not accounted for in the WAC records for the episode, excepting a ten-second section from the Bond film *Goldfinger* (actually from a 1964 news report *about* the upcoming Bond film) from British Movietone "Goldfinger" E. 9536 (WAC T12/1,414).

"stopping train"—("Agatha Christie Sketch [Railway Timetables]") In the UK, a "stopping train" is one that makes stops at smaller stations between larger cities. The express trains race right past most of these smaller stations.

– T –

"today's diocesan lovely"—("Crackpot Religions Ltd.") This presentation is meant to mimic the well-known nude and semi-nude "Page 3 Girls" feature of the tabloid *The Sun*, introduced by owner Rupert Murdoch in 1969. This same set-up is earlier used in the courtroom scene of Ep. 15, where Miss Rita Fang is introduced.

"Tom Jones"—("Mr. Neville Shunte") "Tom Jones" is of course (1) the titular character from the 1749 Henry Fielding novel, and (2) the more contemporary Welsh-born (b. 1940) pop singer. British director Tony Richardson (1928-1991) had produced a very popular film adaptation of the Fielding novel in 1963. In 1969-1971, the singing Jones was starring in his own very popular *This is Tom Jones* TV show, airing on ABC and ITV.

"tonight's star prize"—("Crackpot Religions Ltd.") Yet another game show reference, this to the popular *Take Your Pick* (1955-1968), where the "star prize" could have been a lounge suite, home organ or appliance, etc. *Take Your Pick* has already been satirized in Ep. 20.

This reference is certainly at least a jab at the emerging evangelical broadcasting phenomenon which would sweep across the Bible Belt of the United States in the 1970s, as well as the "older" churches (Roman Catholic; Church of England) long-established practices of offering sinecures, forgiveness, absolution, and even guaranteed escape from damnation with appropriate contributions to the cause. What the Python characters seem to actually be doing—in barefacedly asking for contributions and aknowledging the quid pro quo nature of the modern church(es)—is pulling back the veneer of respectability to reveal a perfectly understandable business arrangement that can satisfy both parties. In this they propose and even make likely a *successful* transaction—a rarity in the Python world. They will revisit this particular area of spiritual hypocrisy in their controversial feature film *Life of Brian*.

trendy pop-music set—(PSC; *"Yummy, Yummy"*) This set is probably meant to look like *Top of the Pops* (1964-2002), which in 1970 was setting trends by highlighting current pop acts to an audience of millions.

"Turkish Champions FC Botty"—("Interview in Filing Cabinet") The Turkish football champion in 1969-1970 was Fenerbahçe SK, and in 1970-1971 was Galatasaray SK.

"Twelve Caesars"—("Film Director [Teeth]") Perhaps a reference to the 1968 Granada TV television series (six episodes) *The Caesars*, directed by Derek Bennett, and starring Freddie Jones.

– V –

various atom bombs and hydrogen bomb—(PSC; *"How Not to Be Seen"*) A number of these film clips of mushroom clouds were already quite well known, many having been used in the closing credit sequence of the 1964 Kubrick film *Dr. Strangelove*.

"Vespasian"—("Film Director [Teeth]") Vespasian was emperor of Rome from 69 to 79 AD.

– W –

waterbutt—(PSC; *"How Not to Be Seen"*) A receptacle for gathering rainwater. In this case, it is a large barrel, and it's apparently where Ken Andrews is hiding before he's blown up.

"West End hit"—("Agatha Christie Sketch [Railway Timetables]") London's West End has been the center of theatregoing in London for many years. There are multiple theatrical houses in this area that have featured everything from Christie's long-running *Mouse Trap* to Terence Rattigan works to revivals to the most contemporary hits from playwrights including Harold Pinter (Ep. 10) and David Storey (Ep. 28).

"white card . . . black card"—(animated link into "Agatha Christie Sketch [Railway Timetables]") In the late 1950s and early 1960s Crest ran a commercial where half a school class reportedly brushed with Crest while half used ordinary toothpaste, with the Crest half displaying shining white teeth.

white flannels and boater—("Agatha Christie Sketch [Railway Timetables]") This is the uniform (for the Pythons) of the "jolly upper class," and includes creased pants ("white flannels") and the straw hat ("boater"). This same uniform will be used in Ep. 33, "Salad Days," and was earlier seen in the "Undressing in Public" sketch (Ep. 4) shot on the Bournemouth beaches for the first series.

wide-boy type—(PSC; "Crackpot Religions Ltd.") A street tough, essentially, one who lives by his wits, criminality, etc. A "respray job" would be repainting a stolen car prior to selling it on the street. The printed script calls for Palin to also be dressed in a "small moustache and kipper tie," but he's instead dressed as a vicar, and just "acting" shady.

"Worplesdon Road"—("*How Not to Be Seen*") There is a Worplesdon Road in Guildford, Surrey. "Ivy Cottage" is a very common place/home name, not unlike "The Dells." "Hull" (or Kingston upon Hull) is located in Yorkshire. Hull was first mentioned in Ep. 1, where Mrs. Violet Stebbings requests the death of Bruce Foster (Chapman), and will be mentioned again in Ep. 39 by the Eddie Waring character, played by Idle.

– Y –

"you won't catch the 3.45"—("Agatha Christie Sketch [Railway Timetables]") This fixation on and fascination with railway timetables has some precedent in life, actually, as Peter Ackroyd points out in *London: The Biography*: "It [the railway, during the nineteenth century] became the great conduit of communication and of commerce in a world in which 'railway time' set the standard of the general hurry" (581). By 1849, Ackroyd continues, the enormous impact of the burgeoning railway system in and around London led to "the whole country" being "transfixed by the idea of rail travel." Mr. Shunt, mentioned above, is certainly one of those so transfixed.

Among more noted poets (than Shunt), Alfred, Lord Tennyson would also "draw poetic images" from the railway in some of his work during the bustling nineteenth century (see Drabble's *For Queen and Country*, 116-17).

Philip Scowcroft has written an interesting piece on the history of railways and trains in music, which includes mentions of songs and even suites composed for train lovers, and in response to train experiences (musicweb.uk.net/railways).

"Yummy, Yummy, Yummy"—("*Yummy, Yummy*") This cover version is from an album called *Autumn Chartbusters*, and the original song is written by Arthur Resnick and Joey Levine (WAC T12/1,414).

Episode 25

"28th day of May 1970"—("Dirty Hungarian Phrasebook") During most of May 1970 the Pythons were shooting location, insert, and pick-up material (all on film) in the Torquay area. Between 22 May, when they shot "Ken Clean-Aire Systems" and the snack bar (both Ep. 18), and 1 June 1970, when they were back on Elers Road, Ealing, they must have scheduled something of a break (WAC T12/1,416). This in-studio section (where Yahlt [Palin] is on trial for publishing the dirty phrasebook) would be shot nearly a month after this stated date, on Thursday, 25 June 1970.

– A –

"acceptable legal phrase"—("Court [Phrasebook]") At Gray's Inn (see "Gray's Inn" note below) dining sessions, "permission to smoke" or even permission to leave a room must be obtained from the most senior barrister present, meaning even a bathroom break could be put off almost indefinitely.

Adventure music as for buccaneer film—(PSC; *"The Black Eagle"*) The musical snippet used here is called "Battle at Sea," and is penned by J. Pearson (WAC T12/1,416).

"Afro-Asian Nations"—(link out of "Court [Phrasebook]") These would have generally been Third World nations with existing Commonwealth or potential trade status with Britain, including South Africa, India, Pakistan, etc.

"A horse . . . a horse"—("Hospital for Over-Actors") From Shakespeare's *The Tragedy of Richard III* (5.4.7). The part of Richard has been for generations played in a rather arch style, and Shakespeare himself contributed to this over-the-top-ness by giving Richard a hunched back and something of a cripple's manner that may have been completely fictional.

"All we bloody want is a little bloody consultation"—("Art Gallery Strike") Probably a call for more equitable consultation in the NEDC, the National Economic Development Council, where government, trade unions, and management were supposed to be able to talk amicably. The return of "reformism" with the new Heath administration in 1970 meant that trade unions had become burdensome throwbacks, a more free market economy (and Thatcherism) was on the horizon, and labor unrest would only escalate with increasing global competition (falling prices, runaway production, etc.). This ongoing attempt to wrest control of production from wealthy, often distant owners to workers (via unions) is the same "anarcho-syndicalist" movement mentioned later by the peasant Dennis (Palin) in *Holy Grail*.

An unattributed TUC announcement after the Conservatives came to power in 1951 made it clear this crucial "consultation" would continue to be during the Tory years:

> The range of consultation between both sides of industry has considerably increased, and the machinery of consultation has enormously improved. We expect of this government that they will maintain the full practice of consultation (qtd. in Unit 20 *Britain: 1950-1990*).

It seems that by 1970, what workers still wanted (and weren't getting from their union leaders) was just a bit of "bloody consultation."

It's also probably no accident that in this episode—where recognizable communist leaders attempt to compete on a game show (and then two of them "snog")—there is a significant left-leaning, up-with-labor presence. In the UK, at least, the British Communist Party was inextricably intertwined with workers and trade unions, at least by empathy and influence, if not number of elected representatives.

ANIMATION: sketch leading to . . . —(link out of "Communist Quiz") The painting used by Gilliam for his "little joke" with Madonna and child (eyes open, eyes shut, eyes open, etc.) is Giovanni Bellini's *The Madonna of the Meadow* (c. 1500), which has been a part of the NG collection since 1858.

At one of the "TV Weekly Programme Review Meetings" held regularly after the broadcast week, BBC executive Oliver Hunkin (of Religious Affairs) complained that he found this particular image objectionable (WAC T47/216).

"Assizes at Exeter"—("Court [Phrasebook]") Assize courts were criminal courts held around England (and Wales) until 1972 (replaced by the Crown Court), where judges traveled from city to city, region to region, hearing cases and rendering judgments. Assizes were held regularly in Exeter, with cases heard including those charged with murder, religious heresy (including being a Quaker), witchcraft, etc. Having spent so much time shooting in the Devon area, it's no surprise that the Pythons mention Exeter (since Devon County assizes were typically held at Exeter).

"Aussies certainly know a thing . . . "—("Court [Phrasebook]") Probably a reference to Australian-born Rupert Murdoch (b. 1931), owner and publisher of the rival to *The Daily Mirror*, the equally salacious tabloid *The Sun*.

- B -

"baked beans"—("Spam") The "traditional English breakfast" as advertised on café and restaurant sandwich boards around London to this day consists of (primarily) the following: eggs, bacon, sausage, baked beans, mushrooms and tomato, and bread.

"beautiful lounge suite"—("Communist Quiz") This was just the type of fabulous "star prize" offered on the popular game show hosted by Michael Miles, *Take Your Pick*.

Black Eagle—("The Black Eagle") Other pirate movies include *Captain Blood* and *Treasure Island* (which will figure prominently in this episode). There is a Western of the same name filmed in 1948, and directed by Robert Gordon, as well as a silent Indian film (1931) and a 1965 South Korean film.

The title here seems to be taken directly, however, from the 1942 swashbuckling film *The Black Swan*, based on the Rafael Sabatini novel and starring Tyrone Power and Maureen O'Hara.

"Blighty"—("*Ypres 1914*—Abandoned") British armed forces slang term for "home."

Blue Eagle, The—("*The Black Eagle*") A 1926 film based on an O. Henry short story, directed by John Ford and starring George O'Brien and Janet Gaynor.

Noted author Sabatini (1875-1950) penned books that inspired the popular swashbuckling movies *The Sea Hawk* (1924), *Scaramouche* (1923), and *Captain Blood* (1924). Of Italian birth, Sabatini lived much of his later life in Wye, on the border of England and Wales. He did not write *The Blue Eagle*, but he did write the color-named stories/novels *The Red Mask* (1898), *The Red Owl* (1900), and *The Black Swan* (1931), etc.

"breach of the peace"—("Dirty Hungarian Phrasebook") A legal term indicating a violation of the public peace by affray, riot, or similar disturbance (*OED*).

"Bristol . . . Molineux"—(link out of "Communist Quiz") The Bristol Rovers are the team Cleese grew up admiring.

"Molineux" is the home stadium of Idle's team, the Wolverhampton Wanderers.

"British Empire . . . ruins"—("*The Black Eagle*") By 1970, the British empire had changed drastically since even Queen Victoria's day, and even since the end of WWII. Australia, Canada, and New Zealand were granted "Dominion" status in 1926 (translating to autonomy in the Empire), followed in 1947 by Pakistan and India being granted a peaceful independence. Many others, including Cyprus, Zambia, the Seychelles, Zimbabwe (Rhodesia [Ep. 45]), and Malaysia also were separated (forcibly, often) from the British Empire in the twentieth century. So in the short lifetimes of the Pythons, the British Empire had indeed diminished in size and international significance.

This "devolution" figured prominently in election after election, with both major parties arguing time and again that each other were to blame. See Morgan's *Britain Since 1945* and Marwick's *British Society Since 1945* for more. The political cartoons of the era are also replete with the pundits' take on the British Empire's precipitous decline in both scope and influence. See the British Cartoon Archive.

In economic terms, the UK's inflation rate was up but not dramatically—reaching 6.4 percent in 1970, after a steady three-year rise. Though still relatively low, the inflation rate was the highest it had been in the UK since the very bleak days of 1952, and the depths of postwar paucity. And "tomorrow" won't be any kind of salve for the Pythons and the UK—by the last season of *FC*, in 1974, inflation will reach a burdensome 16.0 percent. Needless to say, Labour took full advantage of the Conservative's bad luck with the economy during 1970-1974, whipping the "staggering economy horse" to a Labour victory in the 1974 General Election. Myriad labor strikes (including the first national dock strike since 1926) and trade union and worker unrest also helped fuel the "British Empire in ruins" fires in the early 1970s.

See the various pertinent entries in *Eyewitness: 1970-79* for more on this economically depressed era, when both Tory and Labour candidates shouldered significant voter blame, and the Liberals (and fringe parties) picked up many disaffected voters.

"Bromley"—("Spam") Part of Greater London, and located south of the City.

"Brueghels"—("Art Gallery Strike") Pieter Brueghel (or Bruegel) (c. 1525-1569) has been called the "greatest and most original Flemish painter" of his period, and his centers of interest were the "activities of man," especially in village and communal settings. Weddings, harvests, dances, group meals caught his attention, and ice skating is significant in at least three paintings—*Winter Landscape with a Bird Trap* (1565), *Numbering at Bethlehem* (1566), and *Winter, Hunters in the Snow* (1565).

Brueghel employed satire and humor in his work and, significantly, Brueghel "chooses the peasant, whom he sees as an uncomplicated representative of humanity; a member of society whose actions and behavior are open, direct, and unspoiled by the artificial cultural gloss that disguises, but does not alter, the city-dweller's natural inclinations" (Gardner's 619). Monty Python's commoners (Rustics, Pepperpots, middle-class couples) are similarly open and straightforward, cutting through social niceties and mores without shame, pause, or self-consciousness. Python goes the step further, too, acknowledging the characters' postmodern surroundings, by "complicating" their peasants to such a degree that they can stand toe-to-toe with their betters in virtually any setting. It's also worth noting that myriad Flemish artists of this period included similar characters in their work, as there are skaters and laborers and shopkeepers in abundance in these paintings.

Interesting, too, that Brueghel would often be commissioned to paint people *into* existing landscapes/monument portraits by other artists. In the Monty Python world, those same characters are now walking out of some of these same paintings.

"Brentford Football Ground"—("Art Gallery Strike") Extant stadium on Griffin Park, Braemer Road, Brentford. The Brentford Football Club still plays at this site. This is the site where portions of Ep. 7 were recorded for the first series.

"Bridge at Arles"—("Art Gallery Strike") The Dutch Post-Impressionist Vincent Van Gogh (1853-1890) painted multiple versions of the *Bridge at Arles* motif, most in 1888.

British Tommy—(PSC; "*Ypres 1914*—Abandoned") The British WWI infantryman. Short for "Thomas Atkins," or "Tommy Atkins," the typical private soldier, the name worked its way into official and unofficial military parlance by the early nineteenth century.

– C –

"canteen's open upstairs"—("*Ypres 1914*—Abandoned") In the BBC's studios in Shepherd's Bush, the canteen is actually located on a floor above the studio spaces.

cherub—(PSC; "Art Gallery Strike") This figure is not in the original Titian painting, and has been placed there by Gilliam for the purposes of the narrative. (See the entry above for Brueghel—he would do the same thing for certain prestigious clients.) In fact, with the inclusion of the cherub, it seems that the focus of the adoration has moved from the Father and Son, who sit atop the painting, to the foregrounded cherub.

"Chichester Festival"—("Spam") This theater was founded in 1962 under director Laurence Olivier, featured a thrust stage (no proscenium), and played host to virtually all Shakespearean actors of repute. The artistic director through the late 1960s and into the 1970s for Chichester was John Clement. There were no productions of *Richard III* between 1962 and 1972 at Chichester. (See the festival's website for more.)

"ChromaColour"—("*The Black Eagle*") Probably meant to refer to the many early film color processes (Technicolor, ComiColor, CineColor, Brewster Color, etc.), since this is a film reference, but it is also a reference to the 1969 introduction of the Zenith "Chromacolour," a new television picture tube that greatly increased the color saturation of the picture. In other words, this is a TV picture tube that would have been much talked-about at the BBC and elsewhere.

"Clarke, Sir Kenneth"—("Art Gallery Strike") This might be a bit of a doubled reference. The Sir Kenneth *Clark* (1903-1983) who would appreciate the state of the work of art had created *Civilisation* (1969), the groundbreaking TV series looking at art and history. The other possibility (homonymically, but also by profession) is Python contemporary Kenneth Clarke (b. 1940), a Cambridge graduate and lawyer. Clarke contested Mansfield in 1964 and 1966 but lost, then took the Rushcliffe seat in 1970 from Labour. His focus in his early political career was industrial relations, making him a perfect fit for this sketch.

During his Cambridge years, Clarke offended many by inviting—in his capacity as chairman of the Cambridge University Conservative Association—the "fascist, Oswald Mosley, to speak there, provoking a near riot and the resignation of his contemporary, Michael Howard" (*The Observer* 5 August 2001). Chapman, Cleese, and Idle may have known Clarke in school, and he was certainly the rising star in labor relations during this period, and would have been rather high profile.

"Colwyn Bay"—("Spam") Located in northern Wales, Jones was born in Colwyn Bay in 1942. The Jodrell Lecture Theatre, however, is located in Kew Gardens in London.

crash zoom—(PSC; "*Ypres—1914*") A rapid camera zoom in on a character or object. As the lens movement is very self-conscious, the shot has been little-used since the 1970s. Crash zooms can be seen in abundance in myriad Hong Kong cinema action pictures, however.

"Cup Final in 1949"—("Communist Quiz") The Wolverhampton Wanderers (also called the Wolves) did win the 1948-1949 Football Association Cup on 30 April 1949, beating Leicester 3-1, with Arsenal winning the 1949-1950 FA Cup by beating Liverpool, 2-0.

Idle grew up in the Wolverhampton area, attended the Royal Wolverhampton School, and followed the Wanderers closely, which is probably why this fact is memorialized correctly.

– D –

"Déjeuner Sur L'Herbe"—("Art Gallery Strike") A fitting choice to instigate a strike, as this painting is credited with breathing to life the Modernist movement in the arts. The painting was created by Edouard Manet (1863; Galerie de Jeu de Paume, Paris), who actually predates the Impressionist movement, and is known as a Realist. The painting features a classical setting and figures—a nude woman sitting with clothed men in a pastoral scene—but the facts that each of the figures depicted were actual people and not mythological characters, and that Manet utilized nudity unconventionally, outraged many.

Manet's "lot" might have been Gustave Courbet, Jean François Millet, and Honoré Daumier, and this group inspired the later Impressionists such as Monet, Renoir, and Manet himself. The Impressionists both associated with these Realists, as well as exhibited with them, according to *Gardner's* (760). Critical response to Realism was fairly harsh, and the public struggled to appreciate the limited palettes and bold use of paint.

"De Vere, Dino"—("*The Black Eagle*") The surname is perhaps a reference to animator Alison De Vere (1927-2001), who had been working for TV Cartoons as *The*

Yellow Submarine progressed in 1967-1968. An example of a Python-rendered agglomerate name, "Dino" may be a reference to noted film producer Dino De Laurentis (b. 1919). De Laurentis was producing *Waterloo* (1970) during this period, and had produced the critically acclaimed Italian films *Bitter Rice* (1949) and *La Strada* (1954) from directors De Santis and Fellini, respectively.

– E –

"English portraits"—("Art Gallery Strike") These would include Hogarth, Gainsborough, Joshua Reynolds, Thomas Lawrence, John Constable, George Romney, and others. All of these artists' works are featured in the National Gallery's collections.

Episode 25—Recorded as Ep. 1 (Series 2, Episode 1) on 25 June 1970, and broadcast 15 December 1970. The Pythons (in consultation with Ian MacNaughton, John Howard Davies, and studio bosses like Michael Mills and Duncan Wood) would go through the scripts and the recorded shows and decide which were the strongest, and those would be placed at the start of the season. In September 1972 Wood watched and ranked the first nine episodes of the third series, then hinted very strongly that they should be broadcast in the order he suggested (WAC T12/1,428).

"Esher"—("Court [Phrasebook]") The home of this sexually active judge has also been the alleged setting for "Confuse-a-Cat" and "The Dull Life of a City Stockbroker," meaning it was the epitome of Greater-London-middle-class-dom for the Pythons. In Ep. 36 an orgy is supposed to have occurred in the city. Python friend and later financier George Harrison lived in Esher during this period.

Esher is mentioned often elsewhere in *FC*, including Eps. 9, 28, 31, and 44.

– F –

famous statues—("Art Gallery Strike") The statues depicted include: Michelangelo's *David* (1501-1504; Galleria dell Accademia, Florence), and *Moses* (1513-1515; San Pietro in Vincoli, Rome); the Venus de Milo (130-120 BC; Louvre); Rodin's *The Thinker* (1880; Metropolitan Museum of Art), and *The Kiss* (1886; Musee Rodin, Paris); and the *Discus Thrower* by Myron (c. 485 BC-c. 425 BC); and *Laocoon* (Vatican Museum), among others.

"fisties"—("*Ypres—1914*") Child's game, also called "rock, paper, scissors."

"Flemish school"—("Art Gallery Strike") Includes names like Jan van Eyck, Rogier van der Weyden, Hieronymous Bosch, Pieter Brueghel, Peter Paul Rubens, Frans Hals, Rembrandt van Rijn, and Jan Vermeer, and covers the end of the fourteenth through the seventeenth centuries. Van Eyck, Bosch, Brueghel, Rubens, Rembrandt, and Vermeer are all well represented in the National Gallery in London. It's clear that in writing the sketch, the Pythons were basing their choice of paintings on those held by the National Gallery, and equally clear that Gilliam (working apart from the others) felt free to pick from whatever paintings struck his fancy, and were available in the art books Gilliam had at hand.

Floor Manager—(PSC; *"Ypres 1914*—Abandoned") The actual floor manager for *FC* during this period was George Clarke.

"Foreign Nationals"—(*"The Black Eagle"*) These are foreign visitors (and perhaps potential immigrants), many with the intent of seeking permanent UK residency. This mention follows the much-publicized "Rivers of Blood" speech given by Conservative Cabinet member Enoch Powell (and which would cost him his position in the Heath opposition government). See the notes to Ep. 5 for much more on Powell and the inflammatory racial issue in late 1960s Britain.

– G –

"Gainsborough's Blue Boy's"—("Art Gallery Strike") Thomas Gainsborough (1727-1788) actually preferred landscape to portraits, though he worked in both. His "Blue Boy" is actually titled *Jonathan Buttall: The Blue Boy* (c. 1770).

"German woodcuts"—("Art Gallery Strike") Most notably, the German woodcuts of Albrecht Dürer, who will be prominently featured in the first of Python's German episodes in 1971, *Monty Python's Fliegender Zirkus*. Other later German woodcut artists include Max Beckmann (1884-1950), and Franz Eichenberg (1901-1990).

"Gray's Inn"—("Court [Phrasebook]") One of the four Inns of the Court (with Middle Temple, Inner Temple, and Lincoln's Inn) where English lawyers are called to the bar. Cleese, at least, would have been familiar with both the terminology and the profession, having read law at Oxford.

"Grin and Pillage It"—("Spam") "Grin and Bear It" was an internationally syndicated cartoon panel originally drawn by George Lichtenstein, as well as the title of a 1954 Donald Duck cartoon short from Disney.

group of famous characters from famous paintings—(PSC; "Art Gallery Strike") These protesting characters include Venus, Rembrandt (his 1669 self-portrait), Arnolfini, Margarita, Mr. Andrews from Gainsborough's *Mr. and Mrs. Andrews* (1748-49; National Gallery), and "La Goulue" from Toulouse-Lautrec's *La Goulue Arriving at the Moulin Rouge with Two Women* (1892). See the entry for "various famous paintings" below for more.

This strike action send-up may also have been suggested by the ongoing strike by ITV personnel that came to be known as the "Colour Strike." Technicians at all ITV companies refused to use the colour recording or broadcast equipment in 1970-1971, forcing dozens of newly colorful shows to go back to glum black and white for the duration.

– H –

"Hammers"—("Communist Quiz") Nickname for the West Ham United football club, formerly the Thames' Ironworks club, hence the nickname.

"Coventry City"—Coventry would not even be involved in an FA Cup Final until 1987, when they would beat Tottenham Hotspur 3-2 at Wembley. This is probably a bit of a pranging from Idle, at least, toward a perennial also-ran in English football.

"FA Cup"—The Football Association's Challenge Cup was instituted in 1871 when fifteen teams vied for the small trophy cup, with the Wolverhampton Wanderers (Idle's hometown team) winning. More recently, 600 teams a year try for the FA Cup, with Manchester United leading the way with ten championships, followed by Arsenal and Tottenham Hotspur (eight apiece).

"Hay Wain" *by Constable*—(PSC; "Art Gallery Strike") John Constable (1776-1837) was one of England's most celebrated and prolific landscape painters of the late eighteenth and early nineteenth centuries. His *The Hay Wain* was painted in 1821, and was part of Constable's abiding interest in the English countryside and rural people.

And while it's clear the Pythons are using their memories of this painting to conjure this rustic image, even peering closely at the painting in the National Gallery it's impossible to tell what the haymaker standing near the hay wain is actually wearing. The haymakers in the far background actually look to be wearing at least the same colors as Pythons' version of the man. There is even a similarly clad figure in Constable's *The Cornfield* (1826).

Two other works in the National Gallery feature more prominently figures like this "bumpkin": Hart's

A Rustic Timepiece (1856) features a smocked boy, and John Robertson Reid's *A Country Cricket Match* (1878) also features similar rustic costuming. The Pythons' continuing use of "normal folk" in *Flying Circus* indicates a similar (albeit comedic) interest in the English common man shared by these nineteenth-century landscape artists.

Lastly, a copy of Constable's famous painting will be used as set decoration in Ep. 39, in the Zambesi home.

He claps his hand to his mouth; gong sounds—(PSC; "Court [Phrasebook]") This game show "gong" moment (delivered by the Clerk) is a reference to the gong sounding if a character says either "yes" or "no" during Michael Miles' barrage of questions (the so-called Yes/No Interlude) on *Take Your Pick* (1955-1968). Alec Dane was in charge of the gong on *Take Your Pick*.

"Hepworths"—("*The Black Eagle*") Meant to invoke the fashionable designers and design houses who worked for the major Hollywood studios in the 1930s and 1940s, including "Adrian" (1903-1959), who designed costumes for Rudolph Valentino films, and for Cecil B. DeMille and MGM studios.

"Horton Terrace"—("Court [Phrasebook]") There is a Horton Terrace in Halifax, near the intersection of Halifax Road and Denholme Gate Road.

"Hughes, Norman"—("*The Black Eagle*") A Lecturer then Fellow at Queen's College at Cambridge between 1952 and his retirement in 1985, Hughes (1918-1994) may have been a professor remembered by the Cambridge Pythons (Chapman, Cleese, and Idle) as they wrote this episode and cast about for names. Hughes was a palynologist, or one who studies plant microfossils—and primarily pollen and spores. Hughes was characterized as "outrageously authoritarian" by many who knew him, which may also account for his memorability to the Pythons.

– I –

"Impressionists"—("Art Gallery Strike") Includes artists like Monet, Pissarro, Renoir, and Degas who depicted scenes from contemporary life and landscapes, and whose preoccupation with the immediacy of the moment actually sent them out-of-doors to paint in the elements (as opposed to eighteenth- and early nineteenth-century landscape artists like Constable and Turner who would paint from sketch books back in their studios). The Impressionists' fascination with light and its coloring effect on landscapes and structures characterized much of their work. Monet, for example, painted twenty-six different views of Rouen Cathedral.

The Impressionists are especially significant to the Pythons due their collective rejection by the "Academy" of classical art in France—this snubbing signaled the beginnings of Modern Art, paving the way for non-traditionalists in the other artforms, including literature, comedy, and television, eventually.

"Industrial proletariat"—("Communist Quiz") Marx's partner in ideology Frederick Engels (1820-1895) wrote *The Condition of the Working Class in England* in 1845, a significant section of which (chapter 3) is entitled "The Industrial Proletariat." And as has been pointed out by a number of historians, Marx consistently discussed the condition of the industrial proletariat only in relation to a nineteenth-century capitalist paradigm, so applying his work to Maoism or even Leninism (or Trotskyism), for example, would be, to many, as silly and unsupportable as Marx appearing on a game show.

"In 1914, the balance of power lay in ruins"—("*Ypres 1914—Abandoned*") This phrasing is a bit of a giveaway that the source of the material is actually World War I–era history and period writings. The term "balance of power" seems to have been used quite a bit to describe the European situation, as well as justify attack or retreat at the outset of the war. One noteworthy example: In economist John Maynard Keynes' *The Economic Consequences of Peace* (1919), he writes of the devastating results of the recently concluded war, seeing very little to celebrate. Keynes (1883-1946)—a Cambridge man who ran in the same intellectual circles as Russell and Wittgenstein (both Ep. 32)—was especially concerned about the long-term effects the Versailles Treaty reparations would have on Germany and the world:

> England had destroyed, as in each preceding century, a trade rival; a mighty chapter had been closed in the secular struggle between the glories of Germany and France. Prudence required some measure of lip service to the "ideals" of foolish Americans and hypocritical Englishmen, but it would be stupid to believe that there was much room in the world, as it really is, for such affairs as the League of Nations, or any sense in the principle of self-determination except as an ingenious formula for rearranging *the balance of power* in one's own interest. (80; italics added)

By Ep. 37, the Pythons will be very nearly quoting historian Trevelyan as they write about the European wars for "Dennis Moore."

"International Court in the Hague"—("Court [Phrasebook]") The International Court of Justice was created after WWII, and is connected to the United Nations. This "judging" theme will be revisited at the conclusion of Ep. 37, where judges who finished out of the money are consoled by mothers, spouses, etc.

"Italian Masters of the Renaissance"—("Art Gallery Strike") See entry for "Renaissance School" below.

– J –

"Johnson, Teddy and Pearl Carr"—("Communist Quiz") Husband-and-wife contestants in the 1959 Eurovision Song Contest, Carr (b. 1923) and Johnson (b. 1920) performed "Sing, Little Birdie." Carr and Johnson came second in the contest, which features songs/singers from European countries. The contest began in 1956, and has already been featured at the conclusion of Ep. 22.

"jurisprude"—("Court [Phrasebook]") A clever play on words, a "jurisprudist" (a somewhat archaic term) is one knowledgeable in the law, while a "jurisprude" adds a sexual connotation to the legal definition. In the Python world the conflation of illicit sex and legal figures (judges who wear female underwear beneath their robes, for example) has become something of a given. In Ep. 15, the accused judge (Jones) keeps a mistress in Belsize Park, while the sitting judge (Chapman) allegedly has a "Chinese bit" at "8a Woodford Square," the divulging of which leads to a capital punishment sentence, even though the death penalty's been abolished since 1965. Also, in Ep. 27, the judge (Jones) can't wait to get out of the courtroom and attend his Gay Lib meeting.

– K –

King Rats—(PSC; "Hospital for Over-Actors") King Rat is a character in the "Dick Whittington" pantomime. Panto characters obviously loomed large in the Pythons' collective youth—Dobbins, Puss, Principal Boy, Goose, Ratty, and Long John Silver (and the Pantomime Princess Margaret) appear throughout *FC*.

The Nurse in this scene is a walk-on part played by Barbara Shackleton (*Dixon of Dock Green*). In the BBC records the King Rats (and the others in this scene) are simply described as "9 male water rats," and they are: J. Neil, Neil Crowder, Donald Groves (*The Wednesday Play*), James Haswell (*The Wednesday Play*; *Dr. Who*), Roy Brent (*Some Mothers Do 'Ave 'Em*), Les Bryant (*The Wednesday Play*), Stuart Myers (*Dr. Who*; *Star Wars*), Aubrey Danvers-Walker (*Dixon of Dock Green*), and Alistair Stuart-Meldrum (*Brett*) (WAC T12/1,242). The scene was shot at Ealing TFS on 27 May 1970 (call was at 8:30 a.m., incidentally).

– L –

"Landseer, Edward"—("Art Gallery Strike") This is a memorial mistake, as Landseer's first name is "Edwin." The Pythons do often write from memory, without checking for specifics.

Sir Edwin Henry Landseer (1802-1873) was an English animal painter. Many of his works were made into engravings, and he was very popular and much copied. The Tate Britain features many Landseer paintings; the National Gallery, none. His work depicted here, *Stag at Bay*, was created in 1846.

Long John Silver—("Hospital for Over-Actors") Silver is a character from Robert Louis Stevenson's novel *Treasure Island* (1883). The book was filmed by the Walt Disney Company in 1950, starring Robert Newton as the Long John Silver character, and then re-filmed in half-hour episodes for television. The Pythons mention the character several times in *FC*, including Eps. 5, 10, 23, and 32. Long John Silver's annual, seemingly unforgettable presence in the popular Chritmas pantomime (also broadcast on the BBC) probably accounts for his constant inclusion in *FC*.

– M –

man . . . mouth—(PSC; "Art Gallery Strike") This character is meant to look very much like the Rustic (Chapman) character from Ep. 2; he is clearly a visual "type" borrowed from Rembrandt, Constable, and the Pythons' oeuvre, as well. See notes to Ep. 2 for more on the Rustic "type."

"Marx, Karl"—("Communist Quiz") Similarly, a 1966 newspaper cartoon by Cummings features a David Frost interview show with guests Charles de Gaulle, Lyndon Johnson, Alexei Kosygin, Mao Tse-Tung, and Adolph Hitler (23 November, *The Times*). See the British Cartoon Archive.

Marx was a German-born resident of London (after 1849) when he penned one of his most famous works, *Das Kapital* (1867). Marx (1818-1883) was the ideological inspiration for many in the later Russian Revolution of 1917, and his writings would be trumpeted (and reinterpreted) by followers of Lenin, Trotsky, and Stalin. Marx would live in England for almost thirty-four years, plenty of time for him to actually appreciate the exploits of various English football teams.

"Lenin"—Famed leader of the October Revolution in Russia in 1917, the figure of Lenin (1870-1924) is here played by Eden Fox (*Doctor in the House*, contributed to by Chapman and Cleese), who will also appear sawing a woman in half in "Art Gallery Strike."

"Che Guevara"—Latin American political activist, Guevara (1928-1967) would have been fresh news fodder during this period, after he was captured and executed in Bolivia. Gilliam takes this role.

"Mao Tse-tung"—Leader of the People's Republic of China, Mao is played by actor Basil Tang (*Doctor Who*). Mao seems a favorite reference point for the Pythons, having been mentioned previously in Eps. 19, 23, and 24, all in the second series.

Lastly, it shouldn't be a surprise by this time to see this jumble of historical figures in an incongruous setting, as the Pythons are clearly what French film maker Jean-Luc Godard would call "children of Marx and Coca-Cola," or a product of the pastiche, aggregate culture that was the late 1960s, the beginnings of the Postmodern period.

Miles, Michael—(PSC; "Communist Quiz") The prototypically unctuous and effusive host, Miles has already been mentioned by name—and called "a grinning type monster"—in the printed script for Ep. 20. The leering, often violent Michael Miles–type host/Priest also appears in Ep. 24, also played by Cleese, when Mrs. Collins (Palin) tries to win the star prize (of the Norwich City Council).

" . . . my bum"—("Dirty Hungarian Phrasebook") Again, miscommunication is the fillip for the scene, with the unusual additional element being that here the miscommunication is textually acknowledged. Generally, the Python characters will push on through a scene—usually attempting some sort of communication or transaction—without mentioning the miscommunication at all (cf. the "Police Station" in Ep. 12). This may be an indication of the transition in various episodes during this series from the self-aware-but-silent Modernist approach (where Joycean dialogue, for example, can be delivered and responded to without any character batting an eye) toward the more brazen self-aware-and-trumpeting-the-fact Postmodernist approach to the artificiality of the constructed scene. The fact that the oft-used "Women's Institute" film clip has already been mentioned by a character acknowledges the artificiality (the "television-ness") of the setting.

"my company does publish"—("Dirty Hungarian Phrasebook") This structure—repeating the question in the form of an answer—was typical of the *Take Your Pick* game show, specifically the "Yes/No Interlude" hosted by Michael Miles. As long as the contestant did not use the words "yes" or "no" in their answer, the game went on, with questions coming one on top of the next. Miles and *Take Your Pick* are mentioned in Eps. 20 and 24.

– N –

"National Gallery"—("Art Gallery Strike") It was decided as early as 1824 that an art collection for the nation was needed, and Parliament funded the purchase of John Julius Angerstein's private collection (for £57,000), and even used his house on Pall Mall to display the paintings. Trafalgar Square was later chosen as the designated site for the purpose-built gallery, intended to be accessible to the wealthy and commoner alike. From the outset, the National Gallery has also encouraged students to use the Gallery, where the field-tripping, school-blazered Pythons in their grammar school years may have traipsed.

newspaper like the **Mirror**—(PSC; "Court" [Phrasebook]") The *Daily Mirror* is a sensationalist and (often) lurid daily tabloid published in London since 1903, and which adopted the tabloid layout in the late 1930s. The Pythons have already lampooned letters to the *Mirror* in Ep. 10, as well as the pin-up girl photos and commentary in Ep. 24. Another period tabloid newspaper "like the *Mirror*" is Rupert Murdoch's *The Sun*, discussed in the notes to Ep. 24.

Nimmo, Derek—(PSC; "Dirty Hungarian Phrasebook") The printed script gives the only hint that this is an impersonation of an actual person. Nimmo (1930-1999) was a British character actor who by 1971 had appeared in the TV shows *All Gas And Gaiters* (1966); *The Bedsit Girl* (1966); *Blandings Castle* (1967); *Sorry I'm Single* (1967); and *Oh Brother!* (1968-1970). He had also appeared in small roles in the feature films *A Hard Day's Night* (1964) and *Casino Royale* (1967).

Nimmo is featured on the BBC's 17 January 1970 *Radio Times*, advertising a new series of *Oh Brother!* (1968-70).

– O –

"over the top"—("Hospital for Over-Actors") Playing a scene melodramatically, or "chewing the scenery," as the theatrical stage saying goes. The villains in the blood tragedies of the Elizabethan and Jacobean stage were often written for just such bombastic, snarling, over-the-top-ness—audiences accustomed to bear-baiting and cockfights reveled in the Tamburlinian carnage.

A contemporary review of a *Richard III* production staged in Nottingham starring Leonard Rossiter (*Oliver!*) as the renowned king celebrates this over-the-top-ness: "Mr. Rossiter assumes the stance of a maimed hero; he stalks about, lurches, and jerks his head bird-like from side to side. He is often quite still, and occasionally erupts into dangerous rages" (Frank Marcus, *Sunday Telegraph*, 1971).

In April 1970 Norman Rodway (1929-2001) was playing Richard in the Royal Shakespeare Theatre.

– P –

"Phillips . . . pen"—(*"Ypres 1914"*) Certainly a schoolboy's complaint, and perhaps even indicative of the young Pythons growing up in the immediate postwar years. Since "Phillips" is a fairly English name, the complaint that he is a "German" must also be an attempt at an insult (and would have been, certainly, when the Pythons were growing up in the shadow of the Second World War). If the child's nationality was not known at the time, this kind of betrayal could have landed him and his family in one of the British government's internment camps set up just before the war to protect the homefront from acts of sabotage (*Eyewitness: 1940-49*, "Internment").

The "yah boo" reference finally cements the origin of the invective, being an oft-heard English prep school witticism the Pythons would have known well. (Several legitimate letters to the editor in *Private Eye* also employ the word, accusing the editors of being priggish.)

A derivation of this phrase—"yarooh" ("hooray" spelled backwards)—was the catchword for Billy Bunter, the schoolboy literary creation of Charles Hamilton (as Frank Richards), published 1908-1940. See the entry for "Bounder" in Ep. 31 for more on Billy Bunter and friends.

"Privateers"—(*"The Black Eagle"*) Sir Francis Drake (1540-1596) was one such privateer, meaning a ship, captain, and crew commissioned by the sovereign to prey on foreign shipping. Drake (or "Dlake") will be mentioned in Ep. 29, in the "Erizabeth L" sketch.

– Q –

"QC"—("Court [Phrasebook]") Queen's Counsel. Here used primarily to rhyme slyly with "cutie."

– R –

"radiator"—("Art Gallery Strike") According to the National Gallery's Technical Services team, in 1836 there were a number of fireplaces scattered about, as well as hot water pipes running under the floors for heating, with water supplied from a central boiler. Two additional central boilers and ventilation were installed in 1876, with the heating for the building's

wings *always* being provided centrally (with the exception of the individual fireplaces). Thus, individual radiators were never a part of the National Gallery's heating system.

"Renaissance School"—("Art Gallery Strike") The Renaissance period is seen as a revival of arts and letters built upon the influence of classical models, and is the dividing era between the so-called Dark Ages and the modern world. Significant names in the Italian Renaissance School of art would be Giotto, Duccio, Donatello, Angelico, Botticelli, Da Vinci, Michaelangelo, and others. (Other European countries also had their various Renaissance periods, mostly in the fifteenth and sixteenth centuries.) Titian was a sixteenth-century Venetian artist, part of the later "High Renaissance," and was considered by many to be the father of modern painting. He was often imitated and had many followers, meaning his position as a shop steward for the paintings' union was an apt choice by the Pythons.

"Richard III"—("Hospital for Over-Actors") Last of the Plantaganet monarchs, Richard maneuvered his way to the throne, reportedly, over the bodies of friends, kinsmen, and enemies. This crippled, hunched, overtly evil figure is probably a dramatic creation of Shakespeare based on earlier (and also literary as opposed to historical) works by Holinshed and Thomas More. Many productions of the play have taken up this "crippled" standard, as it makes for better visual, metaphoric drama—the hunch and unsteady gait play well to the back rows.

round corner and down another street—(PSC; "Dirty Hungarian Phrasebook") This running section (with Chapman) starts and finishes in the same Thorpebank Road area where "Silly Walks" (Ep. 14) began and Mrs. Crump-Pinnet lived (Ep. 14). The stadium lights for the Queens Park Rangers facility can be seen in the background of several of these shots.

– S –

"Schlack, Joseph M."—(*"The Black Eagle"*) Probably a reference to the noted Hollywood producer Joseph M. Schenck (1878-1961), who headed studios such as United Artists in the 1920s and Twentieth Century-Fox later, and was instrumental in bringing to market the Todd-AO widescreen process. Schenck produced many of Buster Keaton's most notable films, among others.

A younger, hipper, and more unctuous Hollywood producer-type of a similar name—Gerry Schlick (Idle)—is featured in Ep. 23, "*Scott of the Antarctic*." Both "Schlick" and "Schlack" sound like Yiddish-type cousins to what the Pythons might really be intending—"schlock," or shoddy (movie) goods.

scudding clouds—(PSC; *"The Black Eagle"*) Essentially, being driven by the wind with little or no sail. A phrase used in various forms by such varied authors as Edgar Rice Burroughs, Leo Tolstoy, Bram Stoker, and Herman Melville.

Sheikh, a Viking warrior . . . Greek Orthodox priest—(PSC; *"Ypres 1914—Abandoned"*) In the BBC studios, there would have been multiple comedy and game shows in production during this period, so there actually could have been colorfully costumed extras available. Dramas, however, would mostly have been shot in separate studio spaces.

For this particular sketch, the Sheik is played by Ishaq Bux (*Dixon of Dock Green*), the Viking Warrior by Steve Kelly (*Barlow at Large*), the Male Mermaid by Cy Town (*Dr. Who*; *Star Wars*), the Nun by Gillian Phelps (Eps. 12, 32, 39; *Microbes and Men*), the Milkman by David Melbourne (*Softly Softly*; *Z Cars*), and the Greek Orthodox Priest by Andrew Andreaus (*Dr. Who*). The Spaceman who appears momentarily is played by Fred Clemson (*Softly Softly*) (WAC T12/1,416).

"shore of England"—(*"The Black Eagle"*) That treasure had been coming home to England since at least 1588, when Drake defeated the Spanish Armada, signaling the beginning of the end of Spain's worldwide domination.

slowly and silently toward the shore—(PSC; *"The Black Eagle"*) This extended faux-intro scene was shot on the night of 13 May 1970 at Broadsands Beach, near Torquay (WAC T12/1,416). The pirate landing boat was hired from G. Dyer in Brixham (WAC T12/1,242).

Solomon—(PSC; *"Art Gallery Strike"*) In the printed script, the character played by Chapman is named "Solomon." The two figures at the top of the painting are actually, however, the Father and the Son, with the Holy Ghost depicted as a dove. King David, bearing a harp, is also depicted toward the bottom of the painting, but not Solomon.

"Sotheby's"—(*"Art Gallery Strike"*) Fine art auction house founded in London in the mid-eighteenth century.

"spam"—(*"Spam"*) Pressed, canned meat product from Hormel that appeared in 1937. The UK has been the second-leading consumer of SPAM for many years, according to Hormel. The Pythons may have included the reference due to SPAM's very significant presence during the food rationing postwar years in England, when the tinned product would have been much more available than other meats—if it could be found to buy,

it could be eaten without worrying about ration restrictions.

Interestingly, only two weeks after this episode was first broadcast, on 15 December 1970, *Private Eye* included a short, familiar passage in their 1 January 1971 issue that betrays the almost instantaneous cultural influence of *Flying Circus* by the end of the second series. An article describing the attractions of Neasden includes the "adventure" of eating out:

> Try the Fiesta (Tesco Road) just by the station. Specialities: Egg and chipps [*sic*] 3s 9d. Egg, chips and peas 4s 6d. Egg chips sausage and peas 5s 6d. Egg chips sausage bacon and peas 6s 9d. Egg chips sausage bacon tomato and peas 7s 11d. Egg chips sausage bacon tomato beans and peas 8s 9d. Eggs chips sausage bacon tomato beans fried bread and peas 12s 6d. (*"Off the Beaten Track* with Cyril Lord David Cecil B De Mille," *PE* 1 January 1971, 13)

"Spanish Main"—(*"The Black Eagle"*) This is what English traders (and pirates) called parts of Spain's holdings in the New World, including the northern coast of South America to the Caribbean Islands. It's actually a shortened version of "Spanish Mainland," which originally referred to what is now Columbia and Venezuela.

The Spanish empire had actually reached its height during the reign of Philip II (1556-1598), followed by a steady decline. During the eighteenth century, Spain fought a series of unsuccessful wars for territory (the Americas, Minorca, etc.) with Great Britain, and by 1742 (the date mentioned in the show) was greatly diminished in international significance.

"starter for ten"—(*"Communist Quiz"*) A phrase used in the quiz show *University Challenge* (see *University Challenge* entry below).

stock film of goal being scored—(PSC; *"Communist Quiz"*) The music under the closing credits of "Communist Quiz" is Johnny Scott's "News Titles" (WAC T12/1,416). This stock film footage is not accounted for in the WAC records.

– T –

"Tesler"—(*"Court [Phrasebook]"*) The name "Abigail Tesler" is most likely a creation of the Pythons, though she may be a namesake of Brian Tesler (b. 1929), producer of *The Benny Hill Show*. Featuring a plethora of historical impersonations, television send-ups, and off-color humor in general, *Benny Hill* was clearly an influence on the Pythons and the structure of *FC*.

"Thank you very much for the change"—(*"Dirty Hungarian Phrasebook"*) The stiltedness of this delivery and the common dress (Fireman) of the character may be a reference to the similarly stilted "normal" folk who appeared often on British TV. Myriad "vox pops" type moments featured people on the street answering questions, offering opinions, even reading lines—all with varying degree of clumsiness and earnest stammering. In Peter Watkins' 1965 British docudrama *The War Game*, on-the-street interviews asking shoppers about emergency preparedness and the possibilities of nuclear attack produce some very self-conscious moments. Palin does a similar turn as a walk-on in Ep. 10, and as the "whiskery old porter" Hargreaves in Ep. 29.

"There'll Always Be An England"—(PSC; "*Ypres 1914*") This overtly patriotic song is employed here anachronistically, as it was later penned by Ross Parker and Hughie Charles, becoming a beloved World War II anthem. The Band of the Irish Guards plays this version (WAC T12/1,416).

"Tinea Pedis"—("*The Black Eagle*") The medical term for athlete's foot. Probably offered by the troupe's only doctor, Graham Chapman.

"Titian"—("Art Gallery Strike") Venetian painter Tiziano Vecellio (c. 1485-1576) was known as "Titian." This mocked-up version seems to be after either the Titian work *Gloria* (1551-1554, Museo del Prado, Madrid, Spain), or more likely of a painting done "after Titian" (perhaps in a workshop setting) which is part of the National Gallery's collection, called *The Gloria*, and probably produced after 1566.

Titian was perhaps the greatest painter in sixteenth-century Venice, and his influence was also pervasive, as his work affected such luminaries to follow as Michelangelo and Raphael, as well as Rubens, Velázquez, Rembrandt, Delacroix, and even the Impressionists, many of whose work is involved in this painting strike. In their praise, then, the art critics in the scene are correct—if slightly unctuous—as they laud the work.

"height of his powers"—Painted late in his career, about 1554, this painting would have indeed been Titian at his best.

"Trondheim"—("Spam") A major port city in Sør Trøndelag, Norway, Trondheim was the point of departure for many Viking expeditions.

TV Centre—(PSC; "*Ypres 1914*") The BBC's broadcast headquarters at Shepherd's Bush, west of London. The building opened in 1949, and was designed in the shape of a question mark to fit its triangular plot of land.

When the Padre (Cleese) is carried out on the stretcher, he is taken to a waiting ambulance from BBC main reception, then along the Westway to Hammersmith Hospital (near Wormwood Scrubs) (WAC T12/1,416).

– U –

University Challenge—(PSC; "Communist Quiz") Very popular quiz show that pitted teams of university students, the show made its debut on TV in the UK in 1962. Cambridge finally won in 1970, after three years of public universities (Sussex and Keele) taking the crown from Oxford in 1966. Either Cambridge or Oxford teams would win the next seven *University Challenge* contests.

– V –

various famous paintings whose characters suddenly disappear—(PSC; "Art Gallery Strike") These characters walk out of their various paintings in Gilliam's initial animation section: Venus from Sandro Botticelli's *The Birth of Venus* (c. 1482); the child Margarita from Velazquez's *Las Meninas* (1656); the white-frocked citizen (who flies away) from Francisco Goya's *The Third of May* (1808); Mona Lisa (who puts on a hat to leave) from Leonardo da Vinci (c. 1503-1505); the groom (after patting his bride's hand) from Jan van Eyck's *Giovanni Arnolfini and His Bride* (1434; National Gallery, London); the man (probably John) holding the Christ figure from Caravaggio's *The Deposition* (1604); Charles I from Anthony Van Dyck's *Charles I Dismounted* (c. 1635); and the dead Marat (who goes down the drain of his tub) from Jacques Louis David's *The Death of Marat* (1793). Most of these paintings aren't found in the National Gallery collections.

In the weekly postmortem discussion of BBC broadcast shows, this sequence was mentioned by several as being "unfortunately" offensive, specifically the animation where Christ is dropped (WAC T12/1,416).

"VC"—("*Ypres 1914*—Abandoned") The Victoria Cross is a decoration for Army and Navy personnel awarded for exceptional personal valor, and was instituted in 1856.

"Vermeer's . . . Window"—("Art Gallery Strike") The picture is not shown here, and there is no Vermeer painting of that title, though he did paint many female figures standing near a window, some writing, some just posing. Johannes Vermeer (1632-1675) was a skilled painter of genre scenes, landscapes and allegories, and was mentioned in Ep. 4, the "Art Gallery" sketch (when the Art Critic [Palin] gets Vermeer all over his shirt).

Two Vermeer "lady at window" paintings are in the National Gallery: *A Young Woman Standing at a Virginal* (c. 1670); and *A Young Woman Seated at a Virginal* (c. 1670), the previous painting a part of the collection since 1892.

The painting here is sold for "two bob," or a single shilling.

– W –

"walk-out"—("Art Gallery Strike") A labor strike where workers put down their tools and leave the factories, essentially. Labor in the UK has a long history of union activity and strikes, including the infamous 1926 General Strike, where up to three million railwaymen, transport workers, printers, dockworkers, and iron and steel workers struck on 3 May 1926. The Conservative Baldwin government had prepared for the strike, however, and was able to keep supplies and transportation flowing fairly well, undermining the effectiveness of the strike.

More significant for the Pythons may have been the French general strike of 1968, where a reported ten million people took to the streets in major French cities to demonstrate against poverty, high unemployment, and the stultifyingly conservative government. Bus strikes in the UK came in 1950, 1954, 1955, 1957, and 1958, according to the UK's Public Record Office, and crippling rail strikes occurred in 1955 and 1962. A glance at the op-ed pages of contemporary British newspapers—overflowing with political cartoons and opinion pieces discussing trade union activity—indicate the cultural and political significance of Big Labor in postwar Britain. See the British Cartoon Archive.

The Pythons will revisit this topic in Ep. 26, when Welsh coal miners will call a strike based on management's ignorance of classic temple architecture construction.

"watch out for sharks, Abigail!"—("Court [Phrasebook]") These fairly wretched double entendres were the stock-in-trade of the tabloid pin-up sections, probably delivered tongue-in-cheek, acknowledging the cheesecake aspects (but reveling in the naughtiness, nonetheless) of the "Page 3 Girl" sections.

"WCA System"—(*The Black Eagle*) Meant to indicate a manufacturer of sound and equipment systems for film, and is probably an amalgam of RCA and Western Electric.

"Welles, Thornton . . . Laurent F. Norder"—(*The Black Eagle*) As seen before (Ep. 19), and as will be seen later (Ep. 27), these "lists" are generally a mix of

identifiable individuals, made-up names, silly names, etc., created in much the same way as seen in the pages of the satirical magazine *Private Eye* since 1961. At least a portion of the list of individuals thanked in the "Timmy Williams" sketch include Idle's flatmates and friends of the time, for example.

"Thornton Welles"—This may be an amalgam of noted filmmakers/playwrights Thornton Wilder and Orson Welles.

"Wembley"—("Art Gallery Strike") Stadium built in 1922 where FA Cup matches would be played (first game—April 1923).

"England beat Spain"—Another reference to the World Cup football matches held at Wembley Stadium. In 1966 England hosted and won (4-2) the World Cup at Wembley Stadium. The World Cup in 1970 featured Brazil beating Italy 4-1 in Mexico City.

"whence they sailed on May 23rd"—("Spam") On 23 May 1970, the Pythons were most likely in transit back from Torquay to London, having wrapped location shooting the day before.

"women applauding"—("Court [Phrasebook]") This is the first acknowledgment (in the diegetic world of the narrative) of the oft-used "Women's Institute" footage. In Ep. 29, a color insert of the Crystal Palace will also be noted by the characters, even though they are in no position to see the insert.

"workers control of factories"—("Communist Quiz") The following snippets voiced by the Michael Miles type (Idle) and Marx (Jones) are lifted from various Marxian writings and attributions, most of which had entered the cultural lexicon after the success of the October Revolution in Russia.

The "development" phrase is found in Marx's *The Class Struggles in France, 1848-1850*: "The development of the industrial proletariat is, in general, conditioned by the development of the industrial bourgeoisie" (chapter 1: "The Defeat of June, 1848").

The "struggle of class against class" discussion is also found in the above work, but is most clearly voiced in Marx and Frederick Engel's *Manifesto of the Communist Party* (1848): "But every class struggle is a political struggle" (10).

The "workers' control of factories" and the "struggle of the urban proletariat" are also discussed in the *Manifesto*. The phrase "urban proletariat" is also characteristic of Lenin's later phraseology, including *The Proletariat and the Peasantry*: "the common struggle of the rural and the urban proletariat against the whole of bourgeois society" (231-36).

World Forum—("Communist Quiz") Granada Television had been producing the respected on-the-scene current affairs program *World in Action* since 1963, which quickly gained a reputation for taking alternate (non-status quo) editorial stances, while the BBC had been producing the studio-bound *Panorama* since 1953.

– Y –

young major—excruciatingly public school—(PSC; "*Ypres 1914*") The "public school" sobriquet means the major is from a name family, and attended an upper-crust academy like Eton, Winchester, or Harrow. He's not one of the "blokes," he never will be, and it's no surprise that the Pythons consistently give him the shortest straw, nor that he consistently finds a way to wriggle out of being chosen.

"Ypres"—("*Ypres 1914*") The Battle of Ypres took place in Belgium, and was the first battle where the Allies (England, France, Belgium et al.) stopped the German force on its "Race to the Sea." The battle began in October 1914, and lasted through November 1914 when both sides dug in, and trench warfare that would endure for the next three and a half years began. During the Second Battle of Ypres, in April 1915, the Germans would use poison gas for the first time. Britain would lose 908,400 in WWI, and 2,090,200 would be wounded.

Though staunchly against Britain's involvement in the war, Labour party leader Ramsay MacDonald (lampooned in Ep. 24) had visited Ypres in 1914.

Episode 26

– A –

"abacus"—("Coal Mine [Historical Argument]") *OED*: "Arch. The upper member of the capital of a column, supporting the architrave; in the Tuscan, Doric, and ancient Ionic orders, a square flat plate."

Following are the balance of the rattled-off architectural terms:

"triglyphs"—The triglyphs are a simple pattern of three vertical lines located between the metopes.

"frieze section"—The frieze section is located above the columns and the architrave, and has simple patterns.

"entablature"—"The upper part of an order, consisting of cornice, frieze and architrave. Essentially the beam which spans between columns. Literally it means something laid upon a table, i.e. flat" (*Conservation Glossary*).

"classical Greek Doric temples"—The least ornamented type of Greek temples, and includes the Parthenon.

"metope"—The Foreman (Idle) and the Fourth Miner (Ian Davidson) are correct. The metope (plain, smooth stone section) is found between the triglyphs on Doric temples. The abacus is located below the frieze section, atop the column shaft, and helping to support the architrave.

"aechinus"—Spelled "echinus" in the *1911 Edition Encyclopedia*, it is the convex molding that supports the abacus in a Doric column. It's uncertain whether the Pythons knew that in Greek it could translate as "hedgehog."

"capital"—The abacus is the uppermost member of the capital of the column, and simply provides a larger support surface for the architrave. The capital is the top portion of the column.

"All Through the Night"—("Coal Mine [Historical Argument]") A Welsh lullaby that became associated with laborers in the UK's heartlands. This performance is from the Treorchy Male Choir from the album *The Pride of Wales* as arranged by Robinson (WAC T12/1,415).

"Argylls ate in Aden"—("Lifeboat [Cannibalism]") The Argyll regiment spent about three years in Aden (1964-1967), though they apparently never had to eat Arabs. There was a protracted stalemate between local "terrorists" and the British forces, as the lawless area known as the "Crater" was surrounded, cut off, and eventually stormed and retaken by British forces. The Argyll regiment has already been mentioned by one of the Old Codgers types who write to the *Daily Mirror* in Ep. 10. Also, a "Scottish" regiment will be recommended by the Brigadier (Cleese) in his lecture to the "Well-Basically Club" in Ep. 35.

as per **Eamonn Andrews Show**—(PSC; "Man Who Says Things in a Very Roundabout Way") Andrews (1922-1987) was both a television presenter and, later, a broadcasting administrator. His most recognized shows included *What's My Line?* (1951), *This Is Your Life* (1955), *Pantomania: Babes in the Woods* (1957), and *The Eamonn Andrews Show* (1964), the latter referenced here in the printed scripts. *The Eamonn Andrews Show* ran from 1964-1969 for ABC-TV, and was preceded in 1956-1957 by a same-titled show running on BBC-TV. The formats for both were "late night medley(s) of talk and music," with Andrews entertaining up to five guests at once (Vahimagi 125).

In Ireland, he also acted as television's first Chairman in the governing body, the RTE Authority. See Andrews' entry in *ODNB* for more.

"Avril"—("Girls' Boarding School") Probably a nod to Avril Stewart—wife of Cambridge alum and budding mathematician Ian Stewart. Avril would later appear as Dr. Piglet in *Holy Grail*.

333

– B –

Babycham animal—(PSC; "How to Feed a Goldfish") An advertising deer character created for the Babycham drink product in the 1950s, the studio audience reacts appreciably to this obviously recognized character.

Babycham was initially a clear sparkling drink made from pears, and was test marketed in the Bristol area (where Cleese grew up). The drink was bottled in the trademark "baby champagne" bottles in 1950, and was launched nationally in 1953. This is approximately when the deer image became associated with the drink. This was also a drink marketed primarily to women.

"BBC wardrobe department"—(link out of "Insurance Sketch") This BBC department holds more than two million items, and was raided regularly by the Pythons to create their historical sketches.

"binomial theorem"—("Coal Mine [Historical Argument]") This is another example of commoners exhibiting knowledge well beyond their seeming grasp or ken (cf. virtually any Pepperpot sketch, or the "Mollusc Documentary" sketch, or much of the feature film *Holy Grail*). The Pepperpots in Ep. 27, for example, will argue the finer points of Sartre's existential philosophies. The binomial theorem is an algebraic formula discovered by Newton (*OED*).

"Blue Danube"—("Exploding Version of 'The Blue Danube'") "The Blue Danube" is a popular waltz composed by Johan Strauss (1825-1899) in 1867.

"Bradshaw, P.F."—("The Man Who Collects Birdwatcher's Eggs") The Bradshaw name has been popular during the latter part of this second series, appearing in Eps. 19, 24, and now 26.

– C –

Carmarthen—("Coal Mine [Historical Argument]") Llanddarog is in Carmarthen, Carmarthenshire, in south Wales, and was a rugged town at the end of the rail line.

Coal mining in Great Britain may go back as far as Roman times, and perhaps earlier (even the Bronze Age), but exploded in the nineteenth century to fuel Britain's burgeoning industry and empire. Entire cities and towns were built up around these mines, and these same settlements suffered as the mines later suffered. Most ore and metal mines in the UK had closed by WWI, as seams ran out or just became harder to follow, meaning it became much cheaper to import coal and metals from South America, the United States, etc.

Much of the labor unrest during this period centered on either diminishing returns, like in the mines, or in heavy industry where newer, more efficient, and less manual labor–intensive machines were needed to maintain profitability. Both meant reduced employment figures, of course, and the trade unions fought the changes.

There does not seem to have been a pit head like the one described here in Llanddarog, though there would have been surface or near-surface mining works throughout the area, meaning collieries would have dotted the countryside.

"cave"—("Girls' Boarding School") English public school slang meaning "hide, the headmaster (or butch mistress, in this case) is approaching."

"coal face"—("Coal Mine [Historical Argument]") The face of the coal seam where workers/machines remove coal, following the seam.

The coal mine and the coal town have been settings for many British films and novels, from novelists D.H. Lawrence (*Sons and Lovers*) and David Storey (*This Sporting Life*) to filmmakers Lindsay Anderson (*This Sporting Life*) and even Hollywood film legend John Ford (*How Green Was My Valley*)—most of which examine the stultifying effects of the mines and mining town life. The Pythons have already treated a scene from *Sons and Lovers* in Ep. 2, "Working-Class Playwright."

"cold consommé"—("How to Feed a Goldfish") A strong, clear soup. The other items and organizations mentioned include:

"gazpacho"—A cold Spanish vegetable soup.

"spring greens"—Leaves of young cabbage plants.

"RSPCA"—The Society for the Prevention of Cruelty to Animals was created in 1824, though didn't achieve royal recognition until 1840.

"treacle tart"—A filled pastry. In the UK, treacle is the thick, dark residue left over in the sugar refining process, or "molasses" in the United States.

"breadcrumbs . . . pheasant"—Actually, goldfish are quite happy with some kinds of non-fish-food, including fresh foods like Romaine lettuce, cucumber, grapes, oranges, and spinach, as well as cooked peas, eggs, and even earthworms and insect larvae.

"collecting butterfly hunters"—("The Man Who Collects Birdwatcher's Eggs") This unexpected incongruity—a man who collects those who collect—is a borrow from Tex Avery's cartoon visual gags, like a short phone for local calling and a tall phone for long distance, a short waitress for regular cigarettes and a very tall girl for "king size" cigarettes, etc.

colonial governor's helmet—(PSC; "Coal Mine [Historical Argument]") The character is dressed as if he is a ranking official in colonial India or Malaya, with the subtext being Wales depicted here as a Third World, colonized pit to be mined for its natural resources.

These coal mines were nationalized in 1947, following the costly war and even more despairing postwar malaise, and even though there was significant power in the hands of miners and their unions between 1947 and 1970, as Kenneth Morgan indicates, there was still a noticeable, even shocking difference between, for example, the homes built by the government for mine management (villa style, often), and the terraced rowhouses built by the same government for the miners themselves (*Britain Since 1945* 62).

The significance and relative impressiveness of official headgear is also discussed at length in Ep. 43, "Police Helmets."

"Crelm"—("Commercials") Already mentioned in Ep. 24, where Gilliam parodies the very visible Crest and/or Colgate toothpaste commercials of the period, while the plot (cars racing across the landscape) is very much like an Esso (gasoline stations) commercial from the late 1950s, where the car running on clean Esso petrol runs farther, faster, than competitors. In this episode, the dragon who brushes with Crelm gets (to eat) all the girls.

Incidentally, the first commercial on British television in 1955 was a toothpaste ad, for Gibbs SR toothpaste (see whirligig-tv.co.uk for more).

– D –

"Dagenham"—(link out of "Coal Mine [Historical Argument]") East London location of a Ford Motor Company plant where labor strikes, slowdowns, and absenteeism curtailed production on a number of occasions during the 1960s and early 1970s. This plant was much in the news during the Pythons' lifetimes, making hundreds of appearances on op-ed pages and in political cartoons since the 1930s, almost all relating to labor actions, and with a disproportionate number appearing in 1968-1970. See the British Cartoon Archive.

deerstalker and tweeds—(PSC; "Man Who Collects Birdwatcher's Eggs") A Sherlock Holmes–type hat and tweed jacket, with pants. This is the uniform, obviously, of the Pythons' version of a birdwatcher.

Dr. Kildare—(PSC; "Hospital Run by RSM") Long-running and very popular ABC-TV show starring the young Richard Chamberlain (b. 1934). The show was a fan favorite in the United States and UK, providing stiff competition for *Dr. Finlay's Casebook*, mentioned in Ep. 7 as a source of deforming Scottishness. The theme music is performed by the Johnnie Spence Or-

chestra, and written by Jerry Goldsmith (1929-2004) (WAC T12/1,415).

Chamberlain's smiling face graces the cover of the 11 March 1966 *Radio Times*, and he has already been mentioned by the Pythons in Ep. 14.

"dump ... Thames"—("Undertaker's Sketch") Historically, of course, the Thames and its tributaries (some now gone completely or controlled, like the rivers Fleet and Tyburn) were dumping grounds for the detritus of the metropolis, including a number of murdered young prostitutes in the late 1950s and into the 1960s by a man dubbed by the press as "Jack the Stripper" (*Time* 8 May 1964). Up to the nineteenth century, at least, the bodies of those executed at Wapping were consigned to the waters of the Thames, as well (see Mailik). Earlier, when London Bridge boasted houses and businesses, every bit of sewage and refuse from those establishments emptied into the river (Ackroyd 331). In fact, it wasn't until the 1860s that purpose-built sewers were constructed to keep raw sewage out of the river, and that only after the so-called Great Stink of 1858, when many had to flee the city—the stench was that overpowering.

There is also a rather sardonic poster on the Thames seen in a *Quatermass* television episode that reminds Londoners: "It is forbidden to dump bodies in the river."

"Dunfermline"—("Man Who Speaks Only the Middle of Words") The historic capital of Scotland, where Robert the Bruce is buried.

– E –

Episode 26—Recorded 16 October 1970, and broadcast 22 December 1970.

Also scheduled to appear in this episode were semi-regulars Ian Davidson and John Hughman, as well as Willi Bowman (*The Wednesday Play*; *Z Cars*), Eddie Connor (*The Wednesday Play*), Paul Fraser (*Half Hour Story*), Barry Kennington (*Dr. Who*; *Des O'Connor*), Troy Adams (*Upstairs, Downstairs*), Maurice Berenice, and Neville Bourne (WAC T12/1,415). Berenice and Bourne were brought in from Oriental Casting (239 Lancaster Rd. W11).

"equerry"—("The Queen Will Be Watching") One of the Queen's "men," or servant/representative. In 1970 the Queen's Equerry was Lt. Commander Jock Slater, LVO Royal Navy (b. 1938).

"Essex"—("Man Who Speaks Only the Beginnings of Words") A county in the east of England, and an area not mentioned much in *FC*. The bulk of the regional references are apportioned to the Midlands and Greater London.

"everybody out"—("Coal Mine [Historical Argument]") Another labor strike (remember the painting subjects who went out on strike in Ep. 25), this time in an understandable place, a working coal mine, but for very odd reasons. The general strike-worthy complaints of the miners and their union included a shorter working week, reduced working hours, higher wages, better housing and health care, and improved safety in the mines.

This period (1958-1979) in the UK was particularly active in antagonistic labor relations, with multiple strikes against Ford Motor Company (in 1968, 1969, 1970, and 1971), for example, over pay scale grades, equal pay for women, and parity with Ford workers at other plants in the UK (*Socialist Review* 243, July/August 2000). Miners, dockworkers, and transport unions also struck. During this period successive governments—including Macmillan's Conservatives and Wilson's Labour—reached out to big labor, seeing it as a rather vibrant and politically powerful body. Heath's Tories saw organized labor as a threat, and acted peremptorily on that perception.

– F –

Feldman—("Insurance Sketch") Certainly a nod to the Pythons' friend, inspiration, and sometime writing and performing partner, Marty Feldman (1933-1982). Chapman and Cleese appeared/wrote with Feldman in *At Last the 1948 Show* (Rediffusion, 1967), and Chapman, Cleese, Jones, and Palin contributed to his 1968 show, *Marty* (BBC-2, 1968-1969).

First Butch Voice—("Girls' Boarding School") This silliness actually has some grounding in television reality. In 1947, BBC broadcast *The Happiest Days of Your Life*, a wartime farce wherein the Ministry has accidentally placed boys and girls together in a boarding school setting.

"floods . . . pneumoconiosis"—("Coal Mine [Historical Argument]") Coal mines (and other deep pit/tunnel mining operations) fight the battle against incoming groundwater for as long as the mines are in operation, while cave-ins are also a constant hazard, especially as large, rich seams are hewed out.

"English criminal law"—This is probably just a Python swipe at the alleged in-born criminality of the Welsh in general, like saying all Scotsmen have a "diminished brain capacity" in Ep. 7, or indicating that all white Rhodesians think like Ian Smith (Eps. 31 and 45).

"Carbon monoxide"—A colorless, odorless gas that can kill by replacing oxygen in the bloodstream. Ca-

naries were used by miners to determine when the mine's air supply began to dwindle or sicken. Two canaries had been employed in each pit in the UK since 1911, finally phased out in 1986.

"Pneumoconiosis"—Also called "coal miner's disease," or "black lung," pneumoconiosis is a lung disease brought on by the inhalation of coal dust or other mineral/metallic particles.

"14th Marine Commandos"—("Girls' Boarding School") Probably referring to the West Yorkshire Regiment, also known as "The Prince of Wales' Own," which may be a comment on the young prince (about 22 at this time), as well.

"Fractured tibia sergeant"—("Hospital Run by RSM") There is actually a kind of precedent for this juxtaposition of the military and convalescing patients. When Victoria's son "Bertie" (Edward VII) decided to close most of his mother's beloved Osborne House on the Isle of Wight in 1903, he replaced the royal tenants with naval college cadets in training, and retired officers in convalescent settings (Wilson, 2005, 5). Also, in the Humphrey Jennings' documentary *A Diary For Timothy* (1945), the pluck of the wounded British military man demands that he can't wait to get back to fighting the enemy—the fighter pilot is even trying to get back into his cockpit, still bandaged and limping.

– G –

"gaffer"—("Coal Mine [Historical Argument]") The foreman of a work gang.

"gammy leg"—("Lifeboat [Cannibalism]") An injured leg, especially with the wound becoming infected.

"great grey suit"—(link out of "Insurance Sketch") This cadence (and the overuse of "great") is very much a spoof of revered British broadcaster Richard Dimbleby, as already spoofed by Cleese in Ep. 23 as the All Blacks play the Derby Town Council in rugby. Dimbleby famously covered the Queen's ascension in 1953 with such reverence.

The traditional grey to black suit is worn by the Pythons whenever a character is meant to disappear, to blend away, to act the faceless, spineless salaryman, such as Arthur Pewtey (Palin, Ep. 2) or James (Cleese, Ep. 34). Artist Gerhard Richter wrote of grey in regard to his 1966 painting, *Two Greys Juxtaposed*: "Grey is the epitome of non-statement, it does not trigger off feelings or association . . . for me grey is the welcome and only possible equivalent for indifference, for the refusal to make a statement, for lack of opinion, lack of form" (comments included with the painting, National Gallery).

British version of the capitalist system precludes full employment, frankly.

– H –

"Henry III was a bad king"—("Coal Mine [Historical Argument]") Henry of Winchester (1207-1272) was a Plantagenet king who fought expensive wars, kept close ties to Rome, and eventually had to acknowledge the rule of law as his nobles consolidated their own power (*ODNB*). Dante even includes Henry in his *The Divine Comedy*, an ignoble accomplishment at best.

The silliness of this demand—"thirteen reasons why Henry III was a bad king"—as a plank in the strikers' platform is actually indicative of the damage done by such unofficial or uncoordinated strikes, or even by the fact that a strike in and of itself is often a public relations nightmare for the coordinating union. The rash of strike activity during the early 1970s in the UK certainly contributed to this inclusion.

"Her Majesty the Queen"—("The Queen Will Be Watching") Queen Elizabeth II, who had occupied the throne since 1952.

– I –

identical hard-boiled eggs—(PSC; "The Man Who Collects Birdwatcher's Eggs") A comment on the English penchant for collecting/recording what might be considered odd things, such as the phenomena of trainspotting (cf. Ep. 7), photographing switching houses, or bottle collecting (Ep. 2), etc.

"Insurance Sketch"—("The Insurance Sketch") This is the precise set-up used earlier (Ep. 24) for the "Conquistador Coffee" sketch (desk, window, etc.). That sketch didn't properly conclude, either.

"iron foundry at Swindon"—("Hospital Run by RSM") A significant iron foundry was located in Swindon, connected to the booming rail industry (and the Great Western Railway) in the region in the nineteenth and twentieth centuries.

This may also be a swipe at successive postwar governments' attempts at "full employment" (what Beveridge [of NHS fame] would characterize as 3 percent or lower unemployment), schemes that always seemed to culminate in unwieldy, overheated economies, inflation, higher interest rates, balance of payment problems, etc. The promise also has a place in most party platforms approaching every election in the UK during this period, but the realities of the

– K –

"kosher"—("Lifeboat [Cannibalism]") "Kosher" food is food that is certified (rabbinically) to be fit for consumption by those of the Jewish faith. A human corpse would, of course, fly in the face of that striving for purity, whether he/she were "properly" killed or not.

The Pythons have also mentioned kosher car parks and kosher parking spaces in earlier episodes.

– L –

lifeboat—("Lifeboat [Cannibalism]") Certainly a reference to the popular Hitchcock film *Lifeboat* (1944), but also to the wreck of the Dumaru during WWI (1918, off Guam), where survivors resorted to eating two of the dead sailors in the open boats. The men of the Dumaru were adrift for a total of twenty-four days. *The Wreck of the Dumaru* was a popular book written by Lowell Thomas in 1930, which sensationalized the event.

– M –

management man arrives—(PSC; "Coal Mine [Historical Argument]") The music used in this pompous entrance is from the Band of Corps of Royal Engineers, "National Anthems" (WAC T12/1,415).

Man Alive—("Man Who Collects Birdwatcher's Eggs") *Man Alive* was a public affairs program that ran from 1965 to 1982 on BBC2, and at least initially looked at ordinary people in "situations that shaped their lives." *Man Alive* did take on more serious subjects as time went on, including child molestation, psychological phobias, and the inadequacies of Britain's public institutions (Vahimagi 138).

"Mature, Victor"—("Commercials") Hollywood actor Mature (1913-1999) starred in scores of films, including *My Darling Clementine* (1946), and became the embodiment of the screen *man* (and not at all the type to have to wear a surgical garment). Mature had starred in *The Egyptian* (1954), as well, which may account for the "sail down the Nile" comment from the Adman.

In a classic *Beyond the Fringe* sketch "Porn Shop," Jonathan Miller talks a great deal about "curious" Charing Cross Road shops that sell these "rupture appliances."

"Maudling"—("Lifeboat [Cannibalism]") Another of the many references to Gerald Maudling, Heath's Home Secretary during this period, who was one of the Pythons' (and the editors of *Private Eye*) favorite whipping boys. See the entry in Ep. 16, the "Flying Lessons" sketch for more.

"McGuffie . . . report"—(link into "Hospital Run by RSM") Probably named for sometime house composer Bill McGuffie, who was married to *FC* show assistant Mary McCheane.

Reports from special commissions were often the first public step toward change in the National Health Service (and any other publicly held organization), with White Papers and Green Papers functioning as findings/proposals from these inquiries.

In 1970, the *Daily Telegraph* notes that one particularly cantankerous issue was the fundamental, flawed structure of health care in the UK: "Doctors are divided over the second Green Paper on the future structure of the National Health Service ["National Health Service: The Future Structure of the NHS in England," London: HMSO, 1970] put forward for discussion, [which] proposes the scrapping of the present hospital boards and committees" (10 April 1970). This well-publicized discussion may have been the impetus for this sketch.

"North London hospitals" during this period would have included North London Nuffield Hospital, University College Hospital, St. Bartholomew's Hospital (where Chapman had worked before deciding on a career in television), Middlesex Hospital, Royal College of Physicians of London, St. Mary's Hospital, Northwick Park Hospital, etc.

motors and asdic—(PSC; "Submarine") These are simple "submarine sounds" as called for by the printed script, including sonar pinging ("asdic"), communication, and engine noises. The sound crew's job would have been to gather these effects from the BBC's sound archives based on this simple request.

– N –

National Anthem—("Insurance Sketch") This version is played by the Band of Corps of Royal Engineers (WAC T12/1,415).

Nationwide—("The Man Who Collects Birdwatcher's Eggs") Called a "populist current affairs" program, *Nationwide* (BBC1, 1969-1984) was an evening program that tried to reach every region of BBC TV, covering such topics as the "miners' strikes, hot pants fashions and glitter rock" (*BT* 176). It was presented by Michael Barratt and Frank Bough (and later Richard Dimbleby). Bough will be caricatured in Eps. 35 and 39.

"Naughtiest Girl in the School"—(PSC; "Girls' Boarding School") The printed script mentions that this character is to be played "by one of us," when in fact oft-extra John Hughman takes the part. This still photo was taken by Joan Williams (WAC T12/1,416).

News at Ten—(link out of "Insurance Sketch") The first ITV extended news program (thirty minutes), it replaced the previous twelve-minute format program that had aired at 8:55 p.m. At its inception in 1967, the newsreaders were Alastair Burnet, Andrew Gardner, Reginald Bosanquet, and George Ffitch.

Reggie Bosanquet (the real one)—Newsreader Bosanquet (1932-1984) helmed *News at Ten* from 1967 to 1979, and was also mentioned in Ep. 20, in the "Ratcatcher" sketch. He was the son of noted cricketer Bernard Bosanquet.

– O –

"Oakdene . . . Science"—("Girls' Boarding School") The Oakdene girls' school in Beaconsfield (Bucks) closed in 1992, having been in operation since 1911, while the same-named school in Gloucestershire remains open today.

"ones that are really ill do sport"—("Hospital Run By RSM") The music here (not identified in the printed script) is "Saturday Sport" by Burns (WAC T12/1,415).

"only the ends of words"—("Man Who Speaks Only the Ends of Words") A sketch about miscommunication once again. In this case, using their various idiosyncratic modes of speech, these guests are able to understand each other perfectly, as has been the case in earlier sketches, including "Police Station (Silly Voices)" (Ep. 12).

"O.W.A. Giveaway"—(link out of "Lifeboat [Cannibalism]") Meaning "Oh what a giveaway."

– P –

panto geese—("Girls' Boarding School") The Pantomime Goose—of Christmas pantomime tradition in the UK—has made several appearances in *FC*, most recently in Ep. 30.

pastoral music—(PSC; "Commercials") These selections are from Neil Richardson, and are titled "Open Air" and "Fresh Breezes" (WAC T12/1,415).

pit head—(PSC; "Coal Mine [Historical Argument]") The top of the mine pit, an entrance and exit, for workers, ore, and detritus.

pompous music—("The Man Who Says Things in a Very Roundabout Way") This "pompous" tune is "Culver City Title" (from "Signature Tunes and Titles") by Jack Shaindlin (WAC T12/1,415).

– R –

racing pigeon fanciers—(link out of "The Man Who Collects Birdwatcher's Eggs") These outdoor scenes in this "open field" were shot in the Ashburton and New-bridge areas of Dartmoor on 14 May 1970 (WAC T12/1,416). The music that appears when they switch to Trafalgar Square is Elgar's "P&C March" again, the same version as used in the opening credits.

"rat's bane"—("Girls' Boarding School") Rat poison, arsenic.

"Rhondda"—("Coal Mine [Historical Argument]") A city in South Wales that is home to coal mining, and specifically the Powell Duffryn Coal Company (est. 1864), the company that ran, owned and operated many mines in Wales, employed thousands, and essentially owned the towns that sprang up around its works. The coal mining industry bottomed out in the area during the Pythons' lifetimes, with steep declines between 1946 and 1971 that were never reversed, and multiple strikes and well-publicized labor unrest characterizing miners' struggles against the loss of their livelihood.

A "typical bleeding Rhondda" might be a miner from the big city, if you will, who sees himself as more erudite and sophisticated (and better politically connected) than miners from smaller, end-of-the-railroad-line towns like Llanddarog. This seems to indicate that there's not equality even at the coal face.

"Royal . . . cannibalism"—("Undertaker's Sketch") The evidence for cannibalism in the Royal Navy is scant, though Sir John Franklin's disastrous expedition into the Northwest Territories between 1819 and 1822 may have involved murder and cannibalism. The occurrences of tribal cannibalism encountered by James Cook and *Endeavour* in the eighteenth century—and Cook's reported indifference to the practice, seeing it as indigenous custom and not savagery—might also be significant here (see Salmond and the *ODNB*).

– S –

"senior . . . All Souls"—("Coal Mine [Historical Argument]") All Souls College has been part of Oxford since 1443, and was created to serve postundergraduates who would "take Orders and . . . engage in higher studies," according to the College's own history. The school was becoming a known research institution for Visiting Fellows in the 1960s when the Pythons were Oxbridge students. The senior common room would have been a comfortable gathering spot for advanced students.

soap powder—(PSC; "Commercials") In the United States, "laundry detergent." This late 1950s period saw the British TV ad wars for various laundry detergents, including White Tide ("Get your clothes clean. Not only clean but deep-down clean") versus Surf ("Hold it up to the light. Not a stain and shining bright!") versus Domestos ("Killing all known germs in one hour"), all claiming to clean better that any competitor. (See "1950's Commercials," whirligig-tv.co.uk/tv/adverts/commercials.htm.)

"something decent . . . it's disgusting"—("Undertaker's Sketch") There were letters, calls, and voiced complaints about *Flying Circus* after this particular episode aired on 22 December 1970, with the weekly review board (made up of heads of other BBC departments) leading the way (WAC T12/1,415). Several on the review board felt that the show had become crude for crude's sake, essentially.

"specimen"—("Insurance Sketch") Some insurance policies require rigorous medical examinations, blood and urine samples, etc., before the policy will be enacted, especially life insurance policies. This scene suggests something a bit more nefarious.

Spiny Norman—(PSC; link out of "Man Who Collects Birdwatcher's Eggs") The giant hedgehog who appears in Ep. 14 to terrorize Dinsdale Piranha. The studio audience applauds enthusiastically, obviously recognizing the character from the earlier episode. Clearly by this time (the last episode of the second full season), the show had garnered a loyal audience who not only watched at home, but who came to the live tapings of the show. (The BBC WAC records include several ticket requests, most of which seem to have been quickly honored.)

St. Martin-in-the-Fields—(PSC) Spiny Norman appears above this church in the short animation. Designed by James Gibbs in 1726, it is a parish church. It was originally surrounded by fields where livestock belonging to Westminster Abbey grazed, hence the name, and it is now on the east side of Trafalgar Square. (Note: Its columns are Ionic in design, not Doric, and thus would not have been part of the coal miners' argument earlier in this sketch.) This photo is not accounted for in the WAC records for this episode. Most of the photos utilized by Gilliam were not included in the copyright request portions of the paperwork for the episodes.

Stalin . . . Gandhi—(PSC; link out of "Girls' Boarding School") The images included here for this "documentary time" include Gandhi, Hitler, Mussolini, bomb-ravaged wartime London, Churchill's "V-sign" hand, a Nazi swastika flag, a sheep, a nuclear mushroom cloud, a wing of the White House, Neville Chamberlain and his infamous treaty (Ep. 1), a burning U.S. battleship at Pearl Harbor, and British General Montgomery. There is no record in the WAC archives of where these images were obtained.

"St. Bridget's"—("Girls' Boarding School") St Bridget's Catholic Primary School is found on St Bridget's Lane in Egremont, Cumbria.

"St. Gandulf's"—("Hospital Run by RSM") Gandulf (or Gundulf) was the bishop of Rochester in the late eleventh and early twelfth centuries. Chapman's hospital was St. Bartholomew.

Most of these shots were made, however, nowhere near a hospital, but (fittingly) at the Stanford Training Area, West Tofts Camp, Norfolk (WAC T12/1,413).

"St. Pancras"—("The Man Who Collects Birdwatcher's Eggs") A "High Victorian" train station built 1864-1868, and designed by engineer William Henry Barlow in conjunction with R.M. Ordish.

string vest and short dibley haircut—(PSC; "Girls' Boarding School") The string vest is a mesh undershirt, often worn by military men, while the "dibley" haircut is a short, effeminate bob. In 1956 the British Ministry of Supply and War Office had commissioned a study of the military string vest in both hot and dry conditions. Results of that study are available in the National Archives. Mr. Bee (Jones) wears (and eventually barters away) his string vest in Ep. 24.

"Surrey"—("The Man Who Collects Birdwatcher's Eggs") Terry Jones moved to this area with his family at a young age. Surrey is a county in southeast England, just south and west of greater London, and includes the *FC*-mentioned cities of Leatherhead, Reigate, Epsom, Esher, Walton-on-Thames, Godalming, Weybridge, Guildford, Surbiton, New Malden, and Purley.

"Surrey hedgerows"—These are planted hedges that grow into walls, dividing properties from one another, and providing wildlife corridors throughout the Surrey Hills area.

– T –

teleprinter—(PSC; "Coal Mine [Historical Argument]") Generates printed material for television display.

"Thirty Years War"—("Coal Mine [Historical Argument]") Fought between 1618 and 1648 in the central European portions of the Holy Roman Empire, this was primarily a religious war between Protestants and Catholics. See the "Treaty of Westphalia" note below.

"Battle of Borodino"—Fought 7 September 1812, it was part of the Napoleonic Wars (1803-1815) with Napoleon commanding a force of some 600,000. Borodino was an indecisive, bloody battle that set the stage for Napoleon's unsuccessful and ultimately disastrous Russian campaign.

"tiger's bum"—("Coal Mine [Historical Argument]") The relative tightness of a kangaroo's rectum is the subject of one scene in the first of two *Fliegender Zirkus* programs produced for Bavarian television in 1971.

"titles"—("The Queen Will be Watching') The music underneath is Elgar's "Pomp and Circumstance March" in D Major played by the London Symphony Orchestra (WAC T12/1,415).

"total cashectomy"—("Hospital Run by RSM") Recent economic difficulties were forcing the Tory government to consider some very unpopular budget cuts in the welfare state, including Margaret Thatcher's adjustments to the elementary school milk program, and, more to the point of this sketch, Chancellor of the Exchequer Anthony Barber's proposed cuts to medical benefits coupled with increased charges for "free" medical services. Hospital beds were being considered for so-called hotel fees, for example, so that taxes wouldn't be raised, just fees.

traditional expanding square—(PSC; "Commercials") An electronic "wipe" (a transition in television broadcast) that originates in the center of the screen as a tiny square, then "opens" to reveal the following scene.

Trafalgar Square—(PSC; link out of "Man Who Collects Birdwatcher's Eggs") A very busy square that was, at the time of *FC*, a congested one-way traffic area, as well. Home to the National Gallery (cf. Eps. 4 and 25), St. Martins-in-the-Fields church (see above), Canada House, South Africa House, and Admiralty Arch, etc., the Square as pictured has traffic flow all around the area where the Lord Nelson statue stands. Today, the National Gallery is connected to the Square by a pedestrian mall.

The Square was designed (1829-1841) to be a place where the commoner (from South London) and the wealthy (from the West and North) could mingle. Nelson's Column was built in honor of Admiral Nelson after his victory in 1805 at the Battle of Trafalgar (cf. Ep. 1, where Nelson dies a "Famous Death"). The Column was designed by John Nash in the 1830s, and is 185 feet high, and supports a seventeen-foot high statue of Nelson. The lions around the base were added later, and designed by Landseer (mentioned in

Ep. 25). The "Olympic Hide-and-Seek Final" sketch will commence at the foot of the column in Ep. 35.

"Treaty . . . 1713"—("Coal Mine [Historical Argument]") This is not so simple as it seems. The Treaty was signed 11 April 1713 by France, Great Britain, Prussia, Savoy, Portugal, and the Netherlands, and then later by Spain (July 1713 and June 1714 and Feb. 1715), then even later by others, even until 1725, when all parties seemed to be in agreement, including the Holy Roman Empire. See Trevelyan.

"Treaty of Westphalia"—The treaty (or series of treaties) that ended the Thirty Years War on 24 October 1648, a conflict between Catholic and Protestant forces.

"Trevelyan, page 468"—("Coal Mine [Historical Argument]") Fairly close, really. In both the 1926 and 1952 editions of George Macaulay Trevelyan's *History of England*, the Treaty of Utrecht is first discussed on page *486*, only a slight transposition. See Trevelyan's *History of England*. G.M. Trevelyan (1876-1962) was an eminent Harrow-then-Cambridge historian; he'll be nearly quoted by the Pythons in Ep. 37.

"tuck in"—("Lifeboat [Cannibalism]") Colloquialism meaning to dig right in and eat.

"tuck shop"—("Girls' Boarding School") A pastry or sweet shop, often in proximity or even connected to a school, and catering primarily to schoolchildren. Many secondary schools in the UK still have such shops. There would have been similar shops in Oxford and Cambridge, catering to the university population, including "The Tuck Shop" and now "The Alternative Tuck Shop" in Oxford.

– U –

"uncompromising hell of one mile under"—("Coal Mine [Historical Argument]") The subject of mine safety may have been a very sore one, this just three years after the infamous Aberfan disaster, where tons of an unstable coal waste tip slid into and over the mining town of Aberfan, Wales, killing 144, most of whom were children in the local elementary school (*Eyewitness: 1960-69*, "The Aberfan Tragedy").

"unofficial strike committee"—(link out of "Coal Mine [Historical Argument]") The Solidarity Federation (the current publication of the British Section of the International Workers' Association) has noted that a very high number of strikes in the UK during the postwar period have been so-called wildcat strikes—where single unions or even segments of unions (hence "unofficial") have struck without consulting national union leadership—diminishing the effectiveness of the concerted strike effort a trade union promises, and undermining the members in general, especially as such strikes were often painted negatively in the press. Striking for a definition of an architectural term, or for reasons why a monarch is "bad" probably qualify as less-than-useful strike actions, at least to the Pythons.

– V –

"Virginian, The"—("The Queen Will Be Watching") American Western-themed TV series that ran from 1962 to 1971, starring James Drury, Lee J. Cobb, and Doug McClure. *The Virginian* was featured on the cover of the BBC's *Radio Times* on 22 March and 1 November 1969.

The satirical magazine *Private Eye* reported (on its 7 November 1969 cover) that the Queen had decided to give up television, fearing "over-exposure."

– W –

Wales—(PSC; "Coal Mine [Historical Argument]") Python Terry Jones was born in Colwyn Bay, in northern Wales, and would early in life be moved to Surrey (see Herbert Mental later in the episode).

"War of Spanish Succession"—("Coal Mine [Historical Argument]") Fought 1702-1713, the combatants were from across Europe, and the struggle was to ensure that France and Spain would not merge as a result of the succession of Louis XIV's grandson Philip V to the Spanish throne. The Treaties of Utrecht and Rastatt ended the war in 1713-1714. The portion fought in North America was termed "Queen Anne's War."

"Whacko the diddle-oh"—("Girls' Boarding School") An Australian colloquialism, thus a bit out of place at an English girls' boarding school, unless it's a reference to/from the very popular Jimmy Edwards' show *Whack-O!*, appearing 1956-1960.

Episode 27

– A –

"Alitalia"—("Court Scene [Viking]") Italian airline company, founded in 1947. Perhaps there is a focus on airlines here (and "Cut-Price Airline" in Ep. 22, and the "Bomb on Plane" sketch in Ep. 35) thanks to the dramatic increase in airliner hijackings between 1967 and 1976, with the 1968-1969 period being the worst years.

"And now for something completely trivial"—(PSC; link into "Court Scene—Multiple Murderer") This is one of the handful of asides offered directly to the reader, interestingly, as if the Pythons were considering the script as something that might be studied, as well as something that would be eventually performed (not unlike Ben Jonson, the Elizabethan-Jacobean dramatist—see *MPSERD*). This also may signal the waning interest that the Pythons (and especially Cleese) had begun to experience as the show continued into its third season, and with the standard (now-Pythonesque) openings, transitions, endings, and narrative structures, etc.

See the entry for "he looks identical" below for more on the Pythons' seeming collective disenchantment with the series.

"Assaulting a police officer!"—("Court Scene [Viking]") This may be a reference to a much-publicized case of alleged police brutality going through Criminal Court in Croydon in 1971 and 1972, involving a man who says he was brought in for questioning, then assaulted by police officers before being charged with a crime (see *R v. Inwood* 23 February 1973). The increasing use of police force since the student riots of 1968, then through and including the abolishment of the Irish Parliament in 1972 and the implementation of emergency powers in Ireland must also be considered.

In the late 1960s the Nottting Hill and North Kensington areas (and establishments like the Mangrove and the Metro) endured literally hundreds of race-instigated arrests, harassments, and incidents during this period as the hippie culture and the burgeoning civil rights movement (and immigrant unrest) attracted constant police attention (Vague, chapter four). Police blotters and newspapers of the period are full of these events, with "assaulting a police officer" becoming the sort of catch-all justification for arrest and detention in myriad cases, and thus could be chorused by the jury in this courtroom setting. The fact that the police (Chapman and Palin) are able to enter into evidence "the big brown table down at the police station" and "bouncing around in his cell" indicate trumped-up charges, or at least less-than-reliable probable cause.

Private Eye had covered the allegations of brutal, lying policemen in its 1 November 1963 issue, remarking that since there is no racial discrimination in Britain, everyone "stands an equal chance of being beaten up by bent coppers who later give perjured evidence . . . and are subsequently, having for once been very properly sacked, reinstated in the police force" (Ingrams 96).

– B –

"BEA"—("Mrs. Premise and Mrs. Conclusion Visit Jean-Paul Sartre") British European Airways, founded in August 1946, it was in operation under this name until 1974.

Birchenhall, Mr.—(PSC; "Court Scene [Viking]") This may be a reference to Python contemporary Chris Birchenhall, a Cambridge graduate who went on to become a computational science academic. This BBC executive will be sentenced to five years, while the mass

342

murderer was released without punishment earlier, from this same court. In the printed script, Birchenhall (Chapman) is only named in the description of the scene; after the scene begins, he is simply "Man."

"Bjornsstrand"—("Icelandic Saga") Perhaps a reference to one of Ingmar Bergman's favorites from his stable of actors, Gunnar Bjornstrand (*The Seventh Seal*, 1957). Bergman's film was previously mentioned in the script for Ep. 7.

"bland garbage"—("Court Scene [Viking]") Available shows on British TV in 1972 included such diverse entertainments as *Clochmerle* (BBC2; lavatorial humor), *Crown Court* (Granada; dramatic serial), *The Frighteners* (LWT; suspense), *Lord Peter Whimsey* (BBC1; sleuthing miniseries), and *Love Thy Neighbour* (Thames TV; crude comedy). Very vocal supporters of the BBC during this period (including Mary Whitehouse's NVLA organization) were adamant that Auntie Beeb not lower herself to the level of established and emerging commercial TV in Britain.

"bonus incentive schemes for industrial development"—("Icelandic Saga") These are tax and even environmental regulation breaks of many kinds that invite larger businesses to relocate to business-friendlier climes, especially near smaller towns in less-developed areas.

"breed in the sewers"—("Mrs Premise and Mrs Conclusion Visit Jean-Paul Sartre") Fashionable and long-lived urban legend that flushed pets somehow manage to live and thrive underneath major cities. In London, there are significant sightings and even photographic documentation of pigeons riding the underground, getting on at one stop, and getting off at another. There have also been reports of snakes and rats using plumbing fixtures and pipes for transport, but not budgies.

In Thomas Pynchon's *V.* (1963), Benny hunts alligators in the sewers of Manhattan, this based on the report of an eight-foot alligator found in these same sewers in 1935.

bucketful of water—("Stock Exchange Report") This is a tried-and-true TV variety show or, earlier, music hall (vaudeville) gag, usually to "cool off" an overheating (sometimes sexual, sometimes bombastic) character, or to end a sketch without the traditional spoken punch line. The Pythons usually employ such gags quite self-consciously, like the knight carrying the rubber chicken, and the hammer or sixteen-ton weight on the head, though here the drenching water seems to be used quite traditionally.

The animated character that appears immediately following this scene is actually the one who dumps the water, giving some narrative control to an animated figure, Mrs Cut-out, which is unusual.

"Budapest"—("Mrs Premise and Mrs Conclusion Visit Jean-Paul Sartre") This grubby laundromat seems an incongruous place for international phone directories (Paris and Budapest), but so is the discussion about the real meanings of Sartre's masterworks carried on by its denizens. Again, these are common folk who, in the Python world, often hold the store of cultural knowledge not given to the upper class.

"budgie"—("Mrs Premise and Mrs Conclusion Visit Jean-Paul Sartre") This is a colloquial abbreviation of "budgerigar," a small Australian parrot or parakeet, and a very popular cage animal in the UK.

– C –

"cheesed off"—("Court Scene [Viking]") Even the *OED* is unclear as to the etymology of this phrase, though it has been in use since at least the 1940s, and means "to be upset."

chuffed—(PSC; "Court Scene—Multiple Murderer") Counsel (Cleese) is embarrassed, pleased, and even blushing with the defendant's praise.

crashing chord—(PSC; "Icelandic Saga") The stirring music here is from Quatorze Esquisses Pittoresques pour Orchestra, "Au Fil de L'eau" (side 2, track 1), by Edward Michael (WAC T12/1,426).

Cut to a courtroom. Severe atmosphere—(PSC; "Court Scene—Multiple Murderer") This set-up is very much modeled after the courtroom setting in the 1957 film *Witness for the Prosecution*, directed by Billy Wilder and starring Charles Laughton, Marlene Dietrich, and Tyrone Power. Even the repeated "calling off" for a new witness (here rendered "Call Erik Njorl!") is heard often in the earlier feature film.

– D –

does a Dickie Attenborough—(PSC; "Court Scene—Multiple Murderer") A reference to Sir Richard Attenborough (1923-), now President of the Royal Academy of Dramatic Art, who will appear in an extended, weeping performance (by Idle) in Ep. 39, "Grandstand," as the host of a British film awards show. These moments harken back to both Attenborough's emotional appearance as the host for the 1971 "British Screen Awards: A Gala Night for Television and Film," as well as his turn as the mass murderer John Christie in the 1971 film *10 Rillington Place*. So Idle is not so much caricaturing Christie as he is the later performance(s) of Attenborough, pointing up the somewhat chilling similarities between the depictions. See the Attenborough entries in Ep. 39 for more.

– E –

"elfin glades"—("Icelandic Saga") Elves (and other supernatural beings) are part of some of the Icelandic sagas, but secondary to the family histories and noble deeds of valorous men and women. Runic inscriptions in Iceland (of the medieval period) tend to mention elves and trolls and the like more often, which just indicates that the influence of the Norse gods and beliefs continued even after the introduction of Christianity. The Pythons, then, are mixing runes and saga literature, and may well be mixing in the more recent and popular J.R.R. Tolkien creations (which make significant use of the Icelandic sagas).

Episode 27—Recorded 14 January 1972, and broadcast 19 October 1972. This represents almost fifteen months between recording sessions for the series, with Ep. 26 being completed back in October 1970. (In the interim, two *Monty Python's Fliegender Zirkus* episodes for Bavarian TV were written and recorded in Germany.)

Also appearing in this episode, according to WAC records: (in-studio) Rita Davies, Connie Booth, and Lyn Ashley (see "First Juryman" note below). The Clerk "Maurice" is played by the recognizable Frank Williams (*Z Cars*; *Dad's Army*). Nigel Jones (Terry Jones' brother) plays one of the Constables in the scene, and doubles for Njorl.

Extras in this episode: Maureen Nelson (*Softly Softly*), Margo Henson, Pat Quayle (*Bedtime Stories*), Gary Dean (*Dr. Who*), Donald Campbell, Michael Hamilton, Tony Hamilton, Tony Allen (*Rossiter Case*), Michael Buck (*Dr. Who*), Terence Conoley (*Fawlty Towers*), Julia Breck (Ep. 28; *Q5*); (and appearing on film) Peter Kodak, Tony Christopher, Jonas Carr, Jay Neil, Roy Brent, Graham Skidmore, Julie Desmond, Arthur Brooks, David Ewing, Fred Wilkinson, George Wade, John Brunton; and David Stevenson, Neill Bolland, Les King, and P.R. Monument (these last four are locals cast in Norwich) (WAC T12/1,426). Many of these London-area actors will appear as walk-ons in multiple episodes in the third series. See "*Episode*" entries in eps. 36, 37, and 38 for more.

Erik comes into the dock—(PSC; "Court Scene [Viking]") This idea will be revisited in the feature film *Holy Grail*, where the star(s) of a medieval epic (King Arthur, Bedivere, Lancelot) are chased and then arrested for crimes committed in the here and now,

namely, the killing of the Learned Historian. In Ep. 3, Cardinal Richelieu (Palin) appears as a character witness in another modern-day trial. Throughout their work, the Pythons manage to tear down the barriers that separate time and place, allowing for historical and ahistorical characters to interact, and for anachronisms like a Viking warrior wandering the streets of a Greater London town. See the discussion of Shakespeare's Falstaff and the Pythons' historical imprecisions in Larsen's *MPSERD*.

"Erik Njorl . . . Hangbard the Fierce"—("Icelandic Saga") Annotations for this entire naming recitation follow:

"Frothgar"—Probably a play on the name "Hrothgar," the legendary king of the Danes (found in *Beowulf*), whom Beowulf saved from the fiend Grendel and his mother.

"Hangar"—Scandinavian and Anglo-Saxon personal names were primarily formed by combining two common words, e.g., Hrothgar (which became Roger), meaning "fame-spear." In *The Tale of Ragnar's Son*, one of the principal characters is named "Agnar," while his brother's name is "Eirek."

"Thorvald"—Fairly common name, though perhaps here in reference to Eirik the Red's father, Thorvald (son of Asvald) (see *Erik the Red's Saga*). The name Thorvaldr also appears twenty-eight times in the annals of the *Landnámabók* (c. twelfth century).

"Gudleif"—Gudleifr appears just a handful of times in the *Landnámabók*, though spelled not with a medial [d] but with a [∂] (called "edh" and pronounced like the "th" in "this"). Changing it to a [d] is a common typographical mistake.

"Thorgier"—Spelled "Thorgeir," he is a character in *Njal's Saga*, and found in section 146, "The Award of Atonement with Thorgeir Craggier."

"Ljosa water"—See "Ljosa" entry below.

"took to wife Thurunn"—This name (Thórunn) also appears in the *Landnámabók* a total of thirty-four times, and is a feminine name. This name begins, actually, with a þ, called a "thorn," and not with a "Th," which has become customary.

This genealogical recitation can also be found in actual Icelandic epics (see note below), but also in better-known works like the Bible. The book of Samuel begins with this recitation: "Now there was a certain man of Ramathaim-zophim, of mount Ephraim, and his name was Elkanah, the son of Jeroham, the son of Elihu, the son of Tohu, the son of Zuph, an Ephrathite:/ And he had two wives; the name of the one was Hannah, and the name of the other Peninnah: and Peninnah had children, but Hannah had no children" (verses 1-2).

Other portions of the Old Testament also offer such litanies (see Numbers et al.), which the Pythons will further satirize in *Holy Grail*, when portions of the Book of Armaments are read aloud.

"Thorkel Braggart"—"Thorkell" appears a total of fifty-eight times in the *Landnámabók*, and appears to have been a fairly common name. The Thorkell Eyolfson mentioned in *The Laxdaela Saga* is reported drowned at the age of eighty-four, in AD 1026, and a Thorkel is also noteworthy in *Erik the Red's Saga*. Attesting perhaps to its common nature, "Thorkel" is spoken again in this recitation, just below.

A "braggart" is one who brags, and is not necessarily an Icelandic or Scandinavian name. Here "braggart" is used adjectivally, like the following "powerful," "brave," and "fierce." The Pythons will revisit this nominal fun in *HG*, with Lancelot the Brave, Galahad the Pure, Sir Robin the Not-So-Brave-as-Sir-Galahad, etc. In the *Laxdaela Saga*, Thorkell Braggart may be, however, one Thorkell Goat-Peaks, who allowed an ambush to occur without interference, and was later described this way:

> Thorkell has behaved evilly in every way in this matter, for he knew of the ambush the men of Laugar laid for Kjartan, and would not warn him, but made fun and sport of their dealings together, and has since said many unfriendly things about the matter; but it seems a matter far beyond you brothers ever to seek revenge where odds are against you, now that you cannot pay out for their doings such scoundrels as Thorkell is. (chapter 52, *Laxdaela Saga*)

This Thorkell was then led out of his house and killed most unceremoniously.

"slayer"—According to *Njal's Saga*, section 145, Gudmund survived the great battle at the Thing, brokered a peace, exiled various combatants, and returned home laden with rewards.

"Howal"—An uncommon first name, but also the name of an industrial concern founded in 1969, Howal GmbH, in Karlsruhe. The Pythons spent a good deal of time in 1971 in neighboring Bavaria, shooting two *Fliegender Zirkus* episodes, and may have found the name there.

"Arval"—There is a very interesting note in the text of the *Landnámabók*, where the nineteenth-century translator, Loptsson, discusses Arval not as a name, but as part of the ceremony surrounding funereal practices in Nordic lands anciently:

> I may here add the following note on Arvals and Arval in their Cumberland acceptation (Ice erfi). It is given also in my volume on *Lakeland and Iceland*, published by the English Dialect Society. "Arvals is used of meat and drink supplied at funerals. Arval is anything connected with heirship or inheritance; used chiefly in reference to funerals. The friends and neighbours of the family of deceased were invited to dinner on the day of the inter-

ment, and this was called the Arval dinner, a solemn festival to exculpate the heir and those entitled to the possessions of deceased from the mulets or fines to the lord of the manor, and from all accusation of having used violence. In later times the word acquired a wider application, and was used to designate the meals provided at funerals generally." (Part 2, page 4)

See the *OED*, as well, for more on this entry.

"Sochnadale"—An Anglicized version of "Soknadale" or "Sunnudal," the birthplace of Thorstein Staff-Struck, found in the saga *Thorstein Staff-Struck*. Today spelled "Sokndal," the city is located in Rogaland County in southern Norway.

"Norway"—There is a significant Norwegian and Scandinavian presence in Iceland during this period, with the language being primarily Nordic. These Northerners had come to Iceland about AD 900 looking for more and better farmland than they had in Norway, and by the fourteenth century, Norway would come to rule the island.

"Gudreed"—Gudrid Thorbjarndottir was a world traveler c. AD 1000, making the voyage to Greenland, the New World, even Rome. Several Gudrid characters are mentioned in *Erik the Red's Saga*, as well, including the well-known traveler. In fact, many believe the tale could be more accurately called *Gudrid's Saga*, since she figures so prominently.

"Kettle-Trout"—Made-up name, but there is the name Ketilbjörn which appears in the *Landnámabók* a few times. There is also a male nickname used in the *Landnámabók* of "aurridi" (with medial [ð], not [d]) which means "salmon-trout."

"Half-troll"—An actual nickname also from the *Landnámabók*, and spelled very similarly: hálftröll. It actually means "half-troll."

"Ingbare"—There are a number of period names that begin with "Ing-," including Ingjaldr, Ingolfr, Ingileif, Ingvöldr, etc. These can often be references to Englanders, England, etc.

"Ingbare the Brave"—Compare this to characters in *Njal's Saga*, including Wolf the Unwashed, Harold Greyfell, Harold Fair-hair, Eric Bloodaxe, Gizur the White, Thorolf Bladder-skull (from *The Laxdaela Saga*), and Valgard the Guileful.

"Isenbert"—It's recorded that one Isenbert, a master of schools for the town of Saintes, was recommended by King John in AD 1201 to build a stone bridge across the Thames, and that any edifices erected on the bridge would be taxed for bridge maintenance.

"Gottenberg"—Göteborg is in Sweden, on the Göta Älv.

"Hangbard the Fierce"—Inspired by well-known Northern European and Norse epics like *Beowulf* (c. eighth century) and histories/travel accounts like *Book of the Icelanders* (c. AD 1122-1133) and the *Book of Settlements*

(c. twelfth-thirteenth century), but more specifically by other Icelandic sagas, including *Njal's Saga* (aka *Burnt Njal*), the titular character himself being a lawyer. Other significant period sagas include *Egil's Saga* (a Viking warrior-poet), *Laxdaela Saga* (starring contentious foster brothers), and the fantastical *Eyrbyggja Saga*. Most Icelandic sagas were written between the twelfth and thirteenth centuries, and most were written anonymously, documenting either "the lives of specific people or whole communities" ("Icelandic Sagas," phwibbles .com/sagas/).

A passage from *Njal's Saga* (section 20) will illustrate the structure of the Icelandic writing, and why the Pythons might have enjoyed the prolix style:

> There was a man whose name was Njal. He was the son of Thorgeir Gelling, the son of Thorolf. Njal's mother's name was Asgerda. Njal dwelt at Bergthorsknoll in the land-isles; he had another homestead on Thorolfsfell. Njal was wealthy in goods, and handsome of face; no beard grew on his chin. He was so great a lawyer, that his match was not to be found. Wise too he was, and foreknowing and foresighted. Of good counsel, and ready to give it, and all that he advised men was sure to be the best for them to do. Gentle and generous, he unravelled every man's knotty points who came to see him about them. Bergthora was his wife's name; she was Skarphedinn's daughter, a very high-spirited, brave-hearted woman, but somewhat hard-tempered. They had six children, three daughters and three sons, and they all come afterwards into this story. She was the daughter of Lord Ar the Silent. She had come out hither to Iceland from Norway, and taken land to the west of Markfleet, between Auldastone and Selialandsmull. Her son was Holt-Thorir, the father of Thorleif Crow, from whom the Wood-dwellers are sprung, and of Thorgrim the Tall, and Skorargeir. (Sunsite.berkeley.edu)

And from the opening paragraph of "Hrafnkel the Priest of Frey":

> It was in the days of King Harald Fairhair, son of Halfdan the Black, son of Gudrod the Hunting King, son of Halfdan the Freehanded but Foodstingy, son of Eystein Fret, son of Olaf Woodcutter the Swedish king. (from *Eirik the Red and Other Icelandic Sagas* 88)

What's more, even the critical writing *about* the sagas sounds Pythonesque, as displayed by this passage from *The Cambridge History of English and American Literature* (1907–1921):

> Many of the persons and events mentioned in *Beowulf* are known to us also from various Scandinavian records, especially Saxo's *Danish History*, Hrólfs *Saga Kraka*, *Ynglinga Saga* (with the poem *Ynglingatal*) and the fragments of the lost *Skiöldunga Saga*. Scyld, the ancestor of the Scyldungas (the Danish royal family), clearly corresponds to Skiöldr, the ancestor of the Skiöldungar, though the story told of him in *Beowulf* does not occur in Scandinavian literature. Healfdene and his sons Hrothgar and Halga are certainly identical with the Danish king Hafdan and his sons Hròarr (Roe) and Helgi; and there can be no doubt that Hrothwulf, Hrothgar's nephew and colleague, is the famous Hrólfr Kraki, the son of Helgi. Hrothgar's elder brother Heorogar is unknown, but his son Heoroweard may be identical with Hiörvar[char]r, the brother-in-law of Hrólfr. (Volume I: "From the Beginnings to the Cycles of Romance"; Section III: "Early National Poetry"; § 3. "Beowulf: Scandinavian Traditions; Personality of the Hero; Origin and Antiquity of the Poem; the Religious Element")

Finally, the look and presentation of this type of sketch/saga must have been inspired by the many period dramas on British television and available to the young Pythons. These include: *The Black Arrow* (BBC, 1950-1951); *Robin Hood* (BBC, 1953); *The Three Musketeers* (BBC, 1954); *The Adventures of Robin Hood* (ABC, 1955); *The Adventures of the Scarlet Pimpernel* (Towers of London Prod/ITP, 1955); *The Children of the New Forest* (BBC, 1955); *The Adventures of Sir Lancelot* (Sapphire Films, 1956); *The Buccaneers* (Sapphire Films, 1956-1957); *The Count of Monte Cristo* (Vision Prod/TPA, 1956); *The Adventures of Long John Silver* (ITV, 1957), and many, many more.

Erik riding through a bleak landscape—(PSC; "Icelandic Saga") The music has changed here, from the Edward Michael (Njorl's signature tune) piece to "Monegasque" by Primo di Luca. When Erik reaches North Malden, the tune changes distinctly to the well-known light music composer Wally Stott (now Angela Morley), formerly of *The Goon Show*, and his composition "Rotten Row" from London Souvenir. The International Studio Orchestra's "New World—Man of Destiny" by Sam Fonteyn will also be heard (WAC T12/1,426).

"Essence"—("Mrs Premise and Mrs Conclusion Visit Jean-Paul Sartre") The characters here seem to be named after literary and even philosophical terms. In Sartre's *Being and Nothingness* (1943), he discusses the basics of his philosophical system, where "existence is prior to essence." Mrs. Essence does turn out to be practically useful, though, as she somehow knows Sartre's Paris phone number by heart.

"Exchange Telegraph"—("Stock Market Report") Prominent UK company that introduced the ticker tape in 1872.

– F –

"Faversham"—("Icelandic Saga") Faversham is located northwest of Canterbury in Kent. There is a

Westbrook Avenue found in Kent, but it is quite a ways from Faversham.

film of Whicker plane—(PSC; "Whicker Island") This stock footage is "*Whickers World*" (K1418) and "Coral Islands" (SKRP65) (WAC T12/1,426).

First Juryman—(PSC; "Court Scene—Multiple Murderer") These three jurists are all women wearing mustaches, suits, and men's wigs. None of the three is credited in the original scripts. The First Juryman is Lyn Ashley, Australian-born actress, usually credited as "Mrs Idle" (in the closing credits), who was married to Eric Idle from 1969 to 1975; the Second Juryman is Connie Booth (1944-), who was married to John Cleese at this time, and would later co-write/co-star with Cleese on/in *Fawlty Towers* (1975-1979); and the Third Juryman is Rita Davies. Ashley also appears in episodes 18, 23, 32, and 35; Connie Booth also appears in episodes 9, 12, and 18, as well as *FZ* (1972), *Holy Grail* (as The Witch), and *And Now For Something Completely Different* (1971); Rita Davies also appears in episodes 8, 19, and 29, as well as in *HG* as the Historian's Wife.

"fortnight"—("Mrs Premise and Mrs Conclusion Visit Jean-Paul Sartre") Two weeks, or "fourteen nights."

"freedom"—("Mrs Premise and Mrs Conclusion Visit Jean-Paul Sartre") Typically incongruous and deflating transition here, from small animals interrupting excretory performance to the freedom of the individual in a modernist (and approaching postmodern) world. What less auspicious way to introduce the man considered to be the father of modern existentialist thought, Jean-Paul Sartre, then via talk of bowel movements and pet euthanasia?

"Frelimo"—("Mrs Premise and Mrs Conclusion Visit Jean-Paul Sartre") Acronym for the "Front for the Liberation of Mozambique," begun in 1961 with guerrilla activity against the Portuguese colonial rulers in Mozambique. By 1964, the group controlled much of northern Mozambique. In 1974, Portugal would grant independence to the country.

And while Sartre may not have been directly associated with this cause, he was known for his support of the cause of Algerian freedom from France, supporting this "War of Independence" by signing the "Manifesto of the 121," for instance.

French accordion music—(PSC; "Mrs Premise and Mrs Conclusion Visit Jean-Paul Sartre") This is Georgia Brown's version of the "Theme from *Roads to Freedom*" by James Cellan-Jones and Herbert Kretzmer. *Roads to Freedom* was a 1970 television adaptation of the Sartre masterwork.

front door of an apartment block—(PSC; "Mrs Premise and Mrs Conclusion Visit Jean-Paul Sartre") This was also shot at Elm Hill, Norwich, with the extras being predominantly from local casting calls (WAC T12/1,426). This location was earlier used in the "Colin Mozart (Ratcatcher)" sketch in Ep. 21, as well as some of the "Idiot in Society" and "Hospital Run by RSM" scenes.

"full penalty of the law is hardly sufficient"—("Court Scene—Multiple Murderer") Probably a comment on Britain's lack of capital punishment, meaning life in prison was the most any criminal could expect in 1971. As early as Ep. 15 a Judge (Chapman) is lamenting the few punitive resources available him, and announces he's off to South Africa where real justice (executions, whippings, canings, etc.) can still be judiciously meted out. Capital punishment had been abolished in the UK in 1965. The mass murderer that this character is meant to represent, John Christie, was hanged in 1953.

– G –

"Gay Lib"—("Court Scene [Viking]") Gay Liberation is a movement spawned in the 1960s to bring awareness to issues of homosexuality and to give a voice to the gay community. The Gay Liberation Front was officially founded in July 1969 in New York City. The first official Gay Lib Front meeting in the UK took place at the London School of Economics (LSE) in October 1970 (*Eyewitness 1970-1979*, "The Gay Liberation Front"). That the Pythons would attach the judge—an authority figure representing the legal establishment and by association the government—to such a fringe organization is right in line with their "Poofy Judges," gay policemen, and sexually/mentally challenged Upperclass Twits.

"Genet, Mr. and Mr."—("Mrs. Premise and Mrs. Conclusion Visit Jean-Paul Sartre") Jean Genet (1910-1986) was a homosexual French novelist, playwright, and poet who would have spent his life in prison for theft but was released thanks to the efforts of Sartre and others. Genet supported himself in the 1930s as a male prostitute and thief. Genet's works are peopled by homosexuals, prostitutes, thieves, and outcasts doing self-destructive things, often in confined locations. See Drabble (1985).

"Gildor"—("Icelandic Saga") Character in J.R.R. Tolkein's *Lord of the Rings* fantasy/adventure series (*The Hobbit* was published in 1937; the *Lord of the Rings* trilogy in 1954-1955). In Tolkien's world, Gildor Inglorion is an elf of the House of Finrod.

Here we see the casual historical mixing that the Pythons so often employ, writing not from a single source, but from a combined (and probably memorial) handful of heteroglossic chains reaching back across history, fantasy, literature, etc. Shakespeare, of course, would feel the same liberty in his deployment of the ahistorical Falstaff amid the very real characters of English history. See Bergeron and Larsen for more.

"Girl From Ipanema, The"—("Mrs Premise and Mrs Conclusion Visit Jean-Paul Sartre") Ubiquitous "waiting" song heard in elevators and outer rooms around the world, this bossa nova classic was written in 1962, won a Grammy in 1965, and had obviously already reached iconic status less than a decade later.

Glencoe—(PSC; "Icelandic Saga") In central Scotland, on Loch Leven. Parts of the feature film *Holy Grail* would later be filmed here, as well. The Pythons were shooting location footage and insert material for the third series in the Glencoe area in October 1971. These particular shots were made very near the Kings House Hotel in the Glencoe, Ballachulish, Argyll area.

"Gudmund"—("Icelandic Saga") Spelled often as Gudmundr, but again with the medial [d] (actually [ð]). Here the Pythons are fixing their own error with yet another error. Gudmund the Powerful appears in section 139 of *Burnt Njal*. The "Pedigree of Gudmund the Powerful" is set out in section 112 of *Burnt Njal*, and reads very much like the episode being considered here:

> Einar was the son of Audun the Bald, the son of Thorolf Butter, the son of Thorstein the Unstable, the son of Grim with the Tuft. The mother of Gudmund was Hallberg, the daughter of Thorodd Helm, but the mother of Hallbera was Reginleifa, daughter of Saemund the South-islander; after him is named Saemundslithe in Skagafirth. The mother of Eyjolf, Gudmund's father, was Valgerda Runolf's daughter; the mother of Valgerda was Valbjorg, her mother was Joruna the Disowned, a daughter of King Oswald the Saint. The mother of Einar, the father of Eyjolf, was Helga, a daughter of Helgi the Lean, who took Eyjafirth as the first settler. Helgi was the son of Eyvind the Easterling. The mother of Helgi was Raforta, the daughter of Kjarval, the Erse King. The mother of Helga Helgi's daughter, was Thoruna the Horned, daughter of Kettle Flatnose, the son of Bjorn the Rough-footed, the son of Grim, Lord of Sogn. The mother of Grim was Hervora, but the mother of Hervora was Thorgerda, daughter of King Haleyg of Helgeland. Thorlauga was the name of Gudmund the Powerful's wife, she was a daughter of Atli the Strong, the son of Eilif the Eagle, the son of Bard, the son of Jalkettle, the son of Ref, the son of Skidi the Old. Herdisa was the name of Thorlauga's mother, a daughter of Thord of the Head, the son of Bjorn

Butter-carrier, the son of Hroald the son of Hrodlaug the Sad, the son of Bjorn Ironside, the son of Ragnar Hairybreeks, the son of Sigurd Ring, the son of Randver, the son of Radbard. The mother of Herdisa Thord's daughter was Thorgerda Skidi's daughter, her mother was Fridgerda, a daughter of Kjarval, the Erse King. (Section 112, *Burnt Njal*)

– H –

" . . . harsh uneconomic realities of life in the land of Ljosa . . . "—(link out of "Court Scene [Viking]") This harks back to the complaint voiced earlier about what viewers really want. The not-so-subtle invasion of commercialism into a BBC program—as North Malden promotes itself in an Icelandic saga—was the very fear of many viewers, politicians, and social welfare types in the decade following the introduction of commercial television in the UK in 1955. By 1956, the regional broadcasters including Granada, Associated Rediffusion, ATV, and others, were also up and running, bringing commercial television to the entire country.

" . . . he looks identical to the way he did in that deceased classic of our time 'And now for something completely trivial'"—(PSC; opening credits) This comment is for readers of the scripts only, and further indicates the tiredness with which the Pythons must have been approaching this new series, and especially some of the hoary visual chestnuts from the first series. Cleese indicated early that he was less than excited about another go, and the entire troupe took more than one year off from the BBC version of the series. In 1971 they completed the Bavarian *Fliegender Zirkus* episodes, as well as the feature film (reprising highlights of the first two seasons) *And Now For Something Completely Different*.

Each of the Pythons also worked on individual projects in this 1970-1971 period, including *The Ronnie Barker Yearbook* (Cleese and Chapman), *The Magnificent Seven Deadly Sins* (Chapman), *The Two Ronnies* (Palin), *Ronnie Corbett In Bed* (Idle), *Marty Amok* (Jones), and *The Marty Feldman Comedy Machine* (Gilliam).

"He wants to sit down and he wants to be entertained"—("Court Scene [Viking]") This idea of TV as entertainment is especially pertinent in this era when commercial television was gaining a strong foothold in Britain. Many viewers felt that the BBC should maintain some sort of high ground in this entertainment-versus-education/culture debate, and not go the way of all commercial television.

The idea of TV entertainment coupled with education is again broached in the "Mollusc Documentary" sketch in Ep. 32, where a documentary program comes into a couple's home, but has to be "sexed up" to be of any interest.

horse—(PSC; "Icelandic Saga") Horses (and not necessarily banners/posters) *had* been a significant part of Iceland's culture since Vikings brought sturdy Nordic horses to Iceland between AD 874-930.

"Hotel Miramar"—("Mrs Premise and Mrs Conclusion Visit Jean-Paul Sartre") Cf. Idle's loudmouthed tourist (Mr. Smoke-too-Much) in Ep. 31, who bemoans the hopelessly vanilla and ubiquitous hotels of this type catering to penny-pinching British tourists ("Hotel Miramars and Bellevueses and Bontinentals").

"Huddinut"—("Icelandic Saga") A nonce name, probably meant to sound Icelandic, but actually can mean the husk ("hud" or "hood") of a nut. The fact that Huddinut (Palin) is a local solicitor—an attorney—is significant in that it directly connects him to the actual titular character from *Njal's Saga*, himself a skilled lawyer.

"Humber . . . Mersey"—("Court Scene [Viking]") The line that historically has divided the north of England from the south.

– I –

"Ibeezer"—("Mrs Premise and Mrs Conclusion Visit Jean-Paul Sartre") Colloquial mispronunciation and misspelling of "Ibiza," another popular British tourist destination off the eastern Spanish coast in the Mediterranean. Mallorca and Manorca are nearby. Biggles (Chapman) will have recently visited "Ibitha" (closer to the Castilian pronunciation) as mentioned by his secretary (Nicki Howorth) in Ep. 33.

"Iceland 1126"—("Icelandic Saga") Iceland circa 1126 had been settled by Vikings, Celts, and a significant mixture (as the mitochondrial DNA of modern Icelanders would later attest) of Northern and Southern Europeans. This was an active period in early self-governance (without a monarchy) and Icelandic literature, as other annotations will explain.

There is also a more contemporary reason that the Pythons might venture into Icelandic sagas. In 1971, just months prior to this episode's creation, Denmark began a much-celebrated giving-back of Icelandic literature to Iceland, specifically to the Arni Magnusson Institute.

"Icelandic Saga Society"—("Icelandic Saga") There were all sorts of literary/historical societies in the UK at this time, including: The Society for the Promotion of Roman Studies (1910-); the Society for the Promotion of

Hellenic Studies (1910-); The (Samuel) Johnson Society of London (1928-); the Viking Society for Northern Research (1892-), and on. Perhaps most significantly to this sketch was one of the newer societies—the Tolkien Society was founded in 1969.

Icelandic seashore—(PSC; ("Mrs Premise and Mrs Conclusion Visit Jean-Paul Sartre") Chosen as a location due to the rocky beach and visible cliffs, probably, this scene was actually shot on the beaches of Oban Bay (WAC T12/1,428).

Many of the beaches around the UK are so-called shingle beaches, meaning the grain size is between 1 and 200 millimeters (up to about 7.8 inches), so the rocks that are evident in the shot qualify. Icelandic beaches would tend to be volcanic in origin, so often black, and fairly fine-grained.

"ICI"—(PSC; "Icelandic Saga") Imperial Chemical Industries is a British chemical conglomerate formed in 1926, and has large paint plants near a number of rural towns like Stoke Poges and Stowmarket. ICI has already been mentioned as a promising investment by the Village Idiots, in Ep. 20, "The Idiot in Society."

"If any of you at home have any ideas . . . "—("Icelandic Saga") Coincidentally, when in July 1970 Reginald Maudling was asked for his ideas to bring the "Irish situation" to a successful conclusion, he replied that he had none: "No, not really. If anyone's got any ideas, perhaps they will let me know." *Private Eye* included Maudling's name and direct address for postcards from readers willing to offer solutions (17 July 1970, 5).

"I meant"—("Icelandic Saga") This is the second time this motif has appeared in this episode. Another miscommunication, this time based on the varying meanings of a single word, "terrible," in various contexts. Later, in the feature film *Life of Brian* (1979), the Jewish Official (Cleese) and an onlooker (Palin) will be stoned to death for committing blasphemy by uttering "Jehovah," but in the context of a court proceeding, where they should be safe.

– J –

"Joe Public doesn't want . . ."—("Court Scene [Viking]") "Joe Public" is an American vernacularism, originally describing theatrical viewing audiences, and here indicating that the long-term presence and influence of American commercial television (active since at least 1940) on the BBC is being keenly felt in the early 1970s. The advent of British commercial TV in 1954-1955—closer to the American version, but perhaps a bit more refined—must also have caused a stir at Auntie Beeb, where it didn't used to matter how many households were tuned in—she was the only game in town.

Jones, Nigel—(PSC; end credits) Nigel (b. 1940) is Terry Jones' older brother, and appears in the courtroom scene, as well as doubling for Njorl.

– K –

"kicked"—("Court Scene [Vikings]") Perhaps no coincidence that police brutality is treated here, as 1972 was the bloodiest year in Northern Ireland to date. The Public Record Office attributes 500 dead, 5,000 injured, 2,000 explosions, and more than 10,000 shootings in 1972 alone to the "Troubles." And though the Irish question is almost never directly addressed in *FC* (notably excepting Ep. 31, in the "Our Eamonn" sketch), the accounts of police beatings, deaths of demonstrators, mysterious abuses/deaths of Irish prisoners in British custody, and the ultimate approval of arrest and internment without trial (introduced in 1971) filled newspapers across the UK, and must have been in the Pythons' minds as they worked. This was also the year that rule of Ireland from Westminster began.

"King"—("Icelandic Saga") Presumably Njorl's still in Iceland (though he could be in the Faroe Islands, or he crossed into the realm of the fantastic altogether), and one of the peculiarities of medieval Iceland was its lack of a centralized monarchy. Farmers tended to hold most of the power, with many having left Scandinavia to escape oppressive monarchs, a defined aristocracy, and taxation. So, there would have been no King Gildor type in Iceland, but perhaps a wealthy landowner. This may also be the intrusion of the Tolkein-like fantasy involving the sagas, not unlike North Malden will continue to keep its "investment" foot in the BBC's door as the saga moves on.

"dukes"—The aristocracy, as such, was less developed in Iceland of this period, with the powerful men being those not necessarily with titles (as there was no monarch), but with lands.

armoured knights—(PSC) A mixed bag of costuming and prop choices. The Viking-era shield would have been made of wood, not metal, while the helmets the Pythons chose here appear accurate, as do the swords.

"chest . . . letters"—Instead of letters, such warriors would, if they were wearing any insignia or uniforms at all, wear heraldic emblems (dragon, lion, family crest, etc.) on their chests, shields, banners, etc.

The small lake Erik pauses at when the dukes attack is "Hospital Loch" above Glencoe Hospital, and the Forestry Commission had to give approval for ther film crew to set up there (WAC T12/1,428).

– L –

"Larches, The"—("Icelandic Saga") Regional pet name for bed and breakfast–type establishments, housing developments, even country homes in the UK, especially the counties around Greater London. There is a "The Larches" in West Sussex, and also in Bromley.

"Le . . . chose"—(Mrs Premise and Mrs Conclusion Visit Jean-Paul Sartre") "Capitalism and the Bourgeoisie are the same thing."

"letters of their dread name"—("Icelandic Saga") The men playing these roles are: Peter Kodak (*Dr. Who*), Tony Christopher (*Some Mothers Do 'Ave 'Em*), Jonas Card, Jay Neil (*Some Mothers Do 'Ave 'Em*), Graham Skidmore (*Dixon of Dock Green*), and Roy Brent (*Some Mothers Do 'Ave 'Em*) (WAC T12/1,428). They will also play background Pepperpots in the Mrs. Entity and Mrs. Conclusion "Laundromat" scene.

"Ljosa waters"—("Icelandic Saga") Literally, "good waters," or light waters, etc. (see *Grimm's Teutonic Mythology*). The Old Norse word for light is "ljós." Ljosa is also part of the nearby (to Iceland) Faroe Islands.

"London Borough"—("Court Scene [Viking]") The London boroughs (areas of London surrounding the oldest part of the city) include: (north of the Thames) The City, Hounslow, Ealing, Brent, Hillingdon, Harrow, Barnet, Hammersmith, Kensington and Chelsea, Westminster, Camden, Haringey, Enfield, Islington, Hackney, Tower Hamlets, Waltham Forest, Newham, Redbridge, Barking, and Havering; and (south of the Thames) Richmond, Kingston, Wandsworth, Merton, Sutton, Lambeth, Croydon, Southwark, Lewisham, Bromley, Greenwich, and Bexley. Most of these boroughs are mentioned at least once in *Flying Circus*.

Counties surrounding the boroughs are Berkshire, Buckinghamshire, Hertfordshire, Essex, Kent, and Surrey. The Maldens are actually in the county of Surrey, and not part of the London Boroughs at all.

"loo"—("Mrs Premise and Mrs Conclusion Visit Jean-Paul Sartre") Toilet. The term perhaps is derived from a collation of "Waterloo" and water closet, perhaps as they are put together by Joyce in *Ulysses*, page 556 (1922).

"Lufthansa"—("Court Scene [Viking]") German airline company, originally (1926) "Deutsche Luft Hansa Aktiengesellschaft" (and renamed "Lufthansa" in 1933). Chapman played Constable Pan Am in Ep. 17.

– M –

Marty Feldman's Comedy Machine—(PSC; animated link out of "Court Scene [Viking]") A fourteen-episode

ATV comedy show starring and written by Marty Feldman, with whom the Pythons had worked (severally) in the past. Gilliam contributed animated sequences to Feldman's show during the Python hiatus in 1971, so this is a very topical reference.

"Marxist"—("Mrs Premise and Mrs Conclusion Visit Jean-Paul Sartre") One who supports the views/writings of Karl Marx in relation to economic systems and their political attributes. Marx himself has appeared on a *University Challenge*–type quiz show in Ep. 25.

Sartre explored his view of Marxist thought and commitment (what some called his "Sartrian Socialism") in *Critique of Dialectical Reason* (1960), and found that a lack of personal freedom (in the Soviet Union, for example) precluded a true Marxist dialectic, and that forcing an individual into a political system would never work to achieve freedom.

"Match of the Day"—("Icelandic Saga") Originally, the show offered scheduled portions of a football match recorded by BBC cameras and run the same day on BBC2 (1964-1966). When it moved to BBC1, the televising of football was legitimized, and it has been a staple since.

"merde"—("Mrs Premise and Mrs Conclusion Visit Jean-Paul Sartre") Literally, "shit." Often used just as an expression of annoyance or exasperation (*OED*). For the Pythons, though, this was most likely an opportunity to swear without the BBC higher-ups forcing a change.

"Mills, Mr."—("Icelandic Saga") This is a reference to Michael Mills, Head of Comedy, Light Entertainment at BBC in the early years of the show.

"modern suburban shopping street"—("Icelandic Saga") Milletts Leisure can be seen behind Erik, which means this footage of the Viking riding through North Malden was actually shot in George Street in Oban, Argyll. Much of the exterior and location work for the third series was filmed in and around Glencoe, Oban, and Duror, all in western Scotland.

"Mrs Conclusion"—("Mrs Premise and Mrs Conclusion Visit Jean-Paul Sartre") Mrs Premise and Mrs Conclusion are aptly named here, as they both begin and end this entire narrative thread, and even have the ability to overcome the narrative tyrannies that have been and will continue to plague this episode.

"Mrs Cut-out"—("Mrs Premise and Mrs Conclusion Visit Jean-Paul Sartre") Further proof that the boundaries between sketches and storylines aren't sacred in this episode, or almost anywhere in the Python oeuvre, as an animated character from the animated world can take solid form and "walk" through the live-action world.

"music of repeat fees"—("Whicker Island") As early as February 1971 the Pythons were each getting about £80 per episode for their own repeat fees on the first series (WAC T12/1,082).

– N –

"new pence"—("Mrs Premise and Mrs Conclusion Visit Jean-Paul Sartre") There were "New Pence" coins stamped in 1971, when decimalization was introduced, which even had "New Pence" stamped on the flip side. On 15 February 1971, the very familiar pound (£), shilling (s), and pence (d) coins began to be phased out in favor of pound units of ten, including half, one, two, five, ten, and fifty pence denominations.

"Sixty new pence for a bottle of Maltese Claret"—The man at the off-licence would of course know this (see entry below for "off-licence"). This somewhat strange rejoinder may be a complaint on Premise's part regarding the reliability of the man at the off-licence, especially if he overcharges for claret. She may also be complaining about the valuation of the new pence in relation to the old coins, since the old penny and new penny were valued differently, and many during this period complained that the currency exchange rate favored the government, and not the individual.

Also, the better clarets (originally yellowish or light red wines) would not have come from Malta but from France, specifically the Bordeaux region, and would have been "mixed with Benicarlo or some full-bodied French wine" (*OED*). This may be a comment on Premise's lack of sophistication, though she seems to understand modern philosophy fairly well. It's later revealed that Sartre also drinks "vin ordinaire" (and not some expensive premium wine), and lives in a ratty apartment kept clean by a goat, putting all of these characters on a similar social standing.

Njorl's Saga—("Icelandic Saga") Cf. *Njal's Saga*, in the "Erik Njorl" entry above for more.

"North Malden"—("Icelandic Saga") There is and has been both an Old Malden and a New Malden, and even a Malden, but not a North Malden. The various Maldens are located on the edge of Greater London and Surrey, about 6.5 miles north of the M25, and just 1.8 miles from Thames-side docking. Oban, Argyll, Scotland stood in for North Malden for this episode.

"not at all well"—("Mrs Premise and Mrs Conclusion Visit Jean-Paul Sartre") This phraseology is used a few times in *FC*, including Ep. 29, when the jugged rabbit fish has been "coughin' up blood" just the night before, and later in *HG*, when the old plague victim complains that he's "not dead yet." The man carrying him (Cleese) rejoins: "You'll be stone dead in a moment."

"not the way the BBC works"—("Icelandic Saga") As early as 1957 shows *were* being broadcast on British television just to sell products, though perhaps not by the BBC. *Jim's Inn* (A-R, 1957-1963) was just such a show, where characters actually discussed products and prices in a homey, fictional setting. By 1963, this so-called Admag format—a television program created around commercials—was made illegal by order of Parliament. Other titles included *About Homes and Gardens* (ATV, 1956), *What's in Store* (ABC-TV, 1956), and *Slater's Bazaar* (ATV, 1957-1959). See Gable's *The Tuppenny Punch and Judy Show—25 Years of TV Commercials*, as well as entries in Vahimagi's *British Television* for more on the admag phenomenon.

This same indirect-sell approach will be used later in *FC* with the "Trim Jeans" weight-loss pants sketch. During the period when the *FC* shows were being written (1969-1974), these same concerns were being voiced about children's programming and advertising, but in the United States, and specifically in relation to Saturday morning cartoons being made to sell breakfast cereal and toys.

– O –

"off-licence"—("Mrs Premise and Mrs Conclusion Visit Jean-Paul Sartre") A shop where alcohol is sold that can be legally consumed off the premises; a liquor store. In Ep. 19, it is the man from the off-licence (Palin) who lamely stars in Mr. Dibley's version of *Finian's Rainbow*.

"Oui"—("Mrs Premise and Mrs Conclusion Visit Jean-Paul Sartre") Yet another Monty Python monumental narrative build-up that leads almost nowhere, in diminution, as in the *"Black Eagle"* sketch (Ep. 25), the *"Is There?"*-type panel discussion sketches about life after death (Ep. 36), and the proposed new BBC television channel (Ep. 37). This deflation takes the place of the usual payoff punchline, sending the narrative slouching into the following scene. The denouement for the feature film *The Meaning of Life* also ends very anti-climactically, with the Lady Presenter (Palin) reading from a card: "Try and be nice to people, avoid eating fat, read a good book every now and then, get some walking in, and try and live together in peace and harmony with people of all creeds and nations."

– P –

"Pan Am"—("Court Scene [Viking]") An American airline company, Pan American was founded in 1927, and was originally meant to serve the entire Americas—North, South, and Central—at affordable prices. In 1970, Pan Am was one of the largest airlines in the world.

Chapman's version of PC Pan Am appeared in Ep. 17, in the "Chemist Sketch."

Part III—("Court Scene [Viking]") Actually, this is attempt number three to start *Njorl's Saga*, though it fails to materialize at all, instead moving into a modern-day courtroom setting. The narrative tyrannies continue.

There is also no sign of a crest above the judge in this courtroom setting—this may or may not be a Crown Court, and could be a Magistrates Court.

"personal possessions"—("Mrs Premise and Mrs Conclusion Visit Jean-Paul Sartre") Perhaps a better fit is found in Sartre's *Being and Nothingness* (1943, trans. 1965), section 2, "Doing and Having": "Generosity is nothing else than a craze to possess. All which I abandon, all which I give, I enjoy in a higher manner through the fact that I give it away. . . . To give is to enjoy possessively the object which one gives."

"popularity is what television is about"—("Court Scene [Viking]") There has been a long-standing debate in and around the BBC as to what role a state-owned broadcaster should adopt—purveyor of education or entertainment, straight-ahead news or "managed" news, etc. The fact that the BBC is and has been funded by license fees attached to each television and radio sold gives the people of the UK—shareholders, essentially—a significant voice in the discussion. So Mr. Birchenhall (Chapman) is merely arguing the shareholders' case for a more responsive BBC.

"press is here"—("Court Scene [Viking]") Meaning, they are being watched, and if they fail to follow exact courtroom procedure, the snafu will end up in the tattle pages of the newspapers. This hints at a deeper collusion, of course, between the law enforcement and judicial entities of England, a suspicion that many in the UK entertained during this period.

"proposed M25"—("Icelandic Saga") This is an "orbital" roadway that encircles London, and is approximately 117 miles in circumference. This orbital road around London was first proposed in 1937, then again in the "Abercrombie Plan" of 1945 (a five-road proposal), which eventually became the Greater London Development Plan, which included the M25 ring.

Construction would begin three years after this episode aired, in 1975, and it is essentially a city by-pass road.

– R –

"Rainiers"—("Mrs Premise and Mrs Conclusion Visit Jean-Paul Sartre") Essentially the King of Monaco and his wife, Grace Kelly. Officially, he was Rainier III, Rainier Louis Henri Maxence Bertrand Grimaldi (1923-2005), and was the hereditary Prince and Head of State of the Principality of Monaco. He married the American actress Grace Kelly (1929-1982) in 1956.

"Randall, Michael Norman . . . Felix James Bennett"—("Court Scene—Multiple Murderer") Following are as many identifications of these listmembers as possible, with the usual acknowledgment that some of the names on such Python lists are invariably made up, while others denote actual (often obscure) persons, some even close acquaintances of the particluar writer. The long list of closing credits for "Timmy Williams" in Ep. 19 is an earlier example of this structure:

"Charles Patrick Trumpington"—The Trumpington name figures prominently into the history of Cambridge University and its environs. There is a Trumpington Hall and a Trumpington Road at Cambridge, thanks to Crusader namesake Sir Roger de Trumpington (d. 1289).

"Marcel Agnes Berstein"—There is a single "M. Berstein" in the London phone book of 1971.

"Lewis Anona Rudd"—Lewis Rudd was an executive producer for the children's program *Magpie* in 1968, a Thames TV production that ran through 1980.

"John Malcolm Kerr"—A "Malcolm Kerr" is introduced by Cleese's character in the "Theatre Critic" sketch from *The Frost Report* (1967).

"Nigel Sinclair Robinson"—There is a "Nigel Robinson" listed by BT as living in southeast London in 1971.

"Norman Arthur Potter"—Norman Potter wrote *What Is a Designer: Education and Practice, A Guide for Students and Teachers* (1969). There is also a "Norman A. Potter" living in southwest London in 1971, according to period telephone directories.

"Felicity Jayne Stone"—There is a "F.J.F. Stone" listed as living in Kingston Upon Thames in 1971.

"Stephen Jay Greenblatt"—A very real person. Cambridge-educated Greenblatt (b. 1943) would have been a contemporary of the Pythons, graduating from Pembroke College (where Idle matriculated) with his A.B. in 1966 and M.A. in 1968. Greenblatt was a Renaissance scholar at UC Berkeley (1969-1997), thence at

Harvard (1997-), publishing prolifically, and is responsible for the flowering of New Historicism in the United States. He was already well-published and his work much talked about as early as 1969, and certainly by 1972. Greenblatt also took advanced degrees from Yale, and was a Fulbright scholar and Guggenheim fellow.

"Karl-Heinz Muller"—Luftwaffe Unteroffizier shot down in a new type of plane, the Jul88, near Hemley, in Suffolk on 15 October 1943. Muller was actually mortally wounded by the hostile British fire, and was pushed out of the crippled plane, with open parachute, in hopes that he might live. Two others were taken into custody by a local police constable.

"Belinda Anne Ventham"—There are two "B.A. Ventham" listings in southwest London for 1971. Actress Wanda Ventham appeared in contemporary shows *Dixon of Dock Green*, *Z Cars*, *Dr. Who*, and *Doctor at Large*, the same shows where the Pythons cast many of their own extras. Wanda also appeared, coincidentally, in Idle's *Rutland Weekend Television* in 1975.

"Lord Kimberrley [*sic*] of Pretoria"—Sir John Wodehouse, Fourth Earl of Kimberley (1924-2002), and his then wife Margaret Simon (he was six times married, five times divorced) would have been Lord and Lady Kimberley in 1972, though neither of them died at the hands of a mass murderer. The Earl (known as Johnny Kimberley) was much in the news during this period, sleeping around, spending millions of pounds, and getting sacked from the House of Lords, as both his memoirs and obituaries tell. The fourth Earl's grandfather—John Wodehouse, first Earl of Kimberley (1826-1902)—was significantly involved in colonial affairs, becoming Secretary of State for the Colonies, and after the great diamond discovery in South Africa, the town of Kimberley was named after him.

"The Right Honourable Nigel Warmsley Kimberley of Pretoria"—To be termed "Right Honourable" is an entitlement for Privy Council members, Barons and Earls, some Lords Mayors, etc. A number of the Kimberleys qualified.

"Robert Henry Noonan"—Robert Noonan was the pen name of Robert Tressell (1870-1911), a fin-de-siècle painter and socialist novelist, producing the well-respected *Ragged Trousered Philanthropists* (1914), which, after it became quite popular in the 1930s, may have helped Labour win the General Election in 1945. Noonan also spent a number of years in South Africa, working in/on union affairs.

"Felix James Bennett"—There are several "F.J. Bennett" listings in the period phone books for the Greater London area. Felix Bennett was also a popular reggae band sax player in this period, and may have been known by Idle.

"ratings conscious"—("Court Scene [Viking]") This would not have been even a factor when BBC was the only TV network available (1936-1955), but after the appearance of ITV (Independent Television) in 1955, and its offshoots (including Granada in 1956, serving the north and west of England), viewing choices were possible. In 1968, ITV was reviewed and broken into regional broadcasters, including Thames TV, London Weekend TV, Yorkshire, Granada, and ATV.

BBC Light Entertainment would itself gather and peruse a weekly audience survey report, looking at estimated audience size, audience opinions of the target episode (everything from "fresh" and "brilliant" to "rubbishy" and "offensive"), and audience responses to the performers themselves (WAC T12/1,428).

"Revisionist"—("Mrs Premise and Mrs Conclusion Visit Jean-Paul Sartre") Generally, a revisionist is a historian who reinterprets accepted, institutionalized history in the wake of, for example, new eras/theories like post-colonialism, feminism, queer theory, etc. History can be experienced as one thing, then retold as another, with the goals being the challenging of events as they "actually" occurred and/or challenging the "authoritative" interpretations of that history (in history books, for example).

Mrs Conclusion's (Chapman) somewhat vehement response is actually a bit curious here, given that Sartre himself was attempting to revise Marxism as it was then practiced in most so-called Marxist countries, and he may have been comfortable with either being called a Marxist, or entertaining visitors who were similarly revision-minded.

Apropos of the Sino focus of a number of Python sketches, it's relevant that Mao and the Communist Party of the People's Republic of China appropriated the term "revisionist" during the Cultural Revolution to define themselves in opposition to the Soviet Union. PRC official Lin Biao (already mentioned in Eps. 19 and 23) had the following to say in 1967, addressing a Peking Rally commemorating the October Revolution:

> The modern revisionists, represented by Khrushchev and his successors, Brezhnev and Kosygin and company, are wildly opposing the revolution of the people of the world and have openly abandoned the dictatorship of the proletariat and brought about and all-round capitalist restoration in the Soviet Union. This is a monstrous betrayal of the October Revolution. This is a monstrous betrayal of Marxism-Leninism. It is a monstrous betrayal of the great Soviet people and the people of the whole world. . . . It is our good fortune that Comrade Mao Tse-tung has comprehensively inherited and developed the teachings of Marx, Engels, Lenin and Stalin on proletarian revolution and the dictatorship of the proletariat. (6 November 1967)

This is the type of rhetoric that defined Sino-Soviet relations for this period, so it's no surprise that Mao, Lin Biao, the PRC, and the Russians Khrushchev, Kosygin, and others make their presence felt in *Flying Circus* episodes.

"rickety rackety roo"—("Stock Exchange Report") The respectful, staid delivery of this business information (which would have occurred on BBC radio and TV everyday) devolves/evolves into Seuss-ian nonsense by the end, becoming more infantile. This also may be a comment on the silliness not only of the straight-ahead delivery of most BBC presenters, but also on the types of commodities that are traded in stock markets, including tin, canola, and frozen concentrate orange juice futures. See Idle's appearance as the reader in the *Book at Bedtime* in Ep. 38 for more bedtime story nonsense.

Roads to Freedom—("Mrs Premise and Mrs Conclusion Visit Jean-Paul Sartre") A series of novels published 1945-1949, in *Roads* Sartre argued that freedom did have a purpose, and that since the subject of literature had always been "man in the world," the writer "must show the reader his power to make, or to unmake, in short to act—for man is to be reinvented every day." And what was the task of the writer? Certainly "to struggle in favor of the freedom of the person and of socialist revolution." So action is essential, meaning the Pepperpots must make their trip to Paris, and confront the author himself.

"Rotter"—("Mrs Premise and Mrs Conclusion") Julian Rotter (1916-) is a psychologist who coined the phrase "locus of control" in the 1960s, which here coincides neatly with Conclusion's and Premise's disagreement about Sartre's intentions regarding man's freedom and action.

Rotter looked at people and their ways of defining *control* in their world. He asked questions about agency and power, and whether we (a) take credit for the "good" things that happen to us, or (b) blame some outside force for the "bad" things, etc. Rotter's "Locus of Control" test was designed to help determine whether the examinee was an "internaliser" or an "externaliser." His "Locus of Control Scale" was published in *Psychological Monographs*, Volume 80, 1966. He also published *Social Learning and Clinical Psychology* (1954), where he showed that an individual *and/in* his environment were essential in shaping the individual.

The fact that it was Rotter who placed the whoopee cushion under Sartre might reflect the degree of control and free will that he felt, and would fit well into Sartre's world of man answering to himself and within his own sphere of action/influence, and not some higher power.

"Rues à Liberté"—("Mrs Premise and Mrs Conclusion Visit Jean-Paul Sartre") *Roads to Freedom*, Sartre's trilogy written between 1945 and 1949.

– S –

"Sartre, Jean-Paul"—("Mrs Premise and Mrs Conclusion Visit Jean-Paul Sartre") Sartre (1905–1980) was a French philosopher, essayist, playwright, and novelist. He lived with but never married Simone de Beauvoir (1908-1986). He was awarded the 1964 Nobel Prize, but declined, saying he did not want to become an institution.

Sartre embraced and redefined the existentialist movement in the postwar years, building on Husserl's phenomenology and Kierkegaard's version of man's existential being. Sartre believed in a world without God, where man's ultimate responsibility and condemnation is his freedom, his ability (and sentence) to choose. In the Python group, Cleese seems to be the one most sympathetic to Sartre's ethos. (See Cleese's comments in both Morgan's *Monty Python Speaks!* and the more recent *The Pythons* by McCabe.)

shot of a modern road sign: "North Malden—please drive carefully"—(PSC; "Icelandic Saga") This is an example of what would have been called an "unnatural break" in early commercial TV in the UK. From very early in the life of commercial TV in Britain, viewers, regulatory personnel, and Members of Parliament lodged complaints regarding just what constituted a "natural break," or the proper place for a commercial during a broadcast show on ITV, for example.

"so many people"—("Court Scene—Multiple Murderer") This character, Michael Norman Randall (played by Idle), is certainly a reference to the recent UK mass murderer John Reginald Haliday Christie who was blamed for at least eight murders between 1943 and 1953. Christie would be executed in 1953 for at least one of those murders.

These murders were made even more memorable when the film *10 Rillington Place* was released in 1971 (and starring Richard Attenborough, not coincidentally), just months prior to this episode being written. See the entry for "does a Dickie Attenborough" for more on this conflation of real and re-enacted life.

"Sorrento"—("Mrs Premise and Mrs Conclusion Visit Jean-Paul Sartre") A popular southern Italian resort city situated on the Sorrento Peninsula, overlooking the Bay of Naples. This is the type of nearby yet still exotically foreign resort town that beckoned to flocks of postwar British travelers who couldn't travel far due to spending money restrictions (see Morgan's *Britain Since 1945*).

"spirit . . . original text"—("Icelandic Saga") Most of the Icelandic sagas were written in plain, unforced language, without much description or flowery verbiage, but with clipped descriptions of *actions* (and not necessarily *intents*). In this way, the North Malden version is somewhat more like the original texts—heroic men and deeds, and careful descriptions of commerce and industry.

Stock shot of Eiffel Tower—(PSC; "Mrs Premise and Mrs Conclusion Visit Jean-Paul Sartre") This film footage is from Elstree Studios, "World Backgrounds," and is titled "Eiffel Tower" and "French Street" (WAC T12/1,426).

"string remained confident"—("Stock Market Report") To this day traded commodities on the stock markets are often anthropomorphized, as if they have a life and sentience of their own as they rise and/or fall. Commodities and the market itself can be "strong" or "weak," "safe" or "volatile," etc., as the market allows.

– T –

"Thameside docking facilities"—("Icelandic Saga") The facilities nearest the Maldens are yachting-type facilities (to the west), for the most part, and not industrial. As larger roadways like the M25 came into use in and around Greater London, however, and lorry transport replaced river/canal transport, the desirability of such docking facilities—except for leisure use—diminished considerably.

– U –

" . . . um"—("Icelandic Saga") If this is actually Eric Njorl reading his own account, then the narrative hijacking begins very early in this episode, and remains the strongest motif of the show. The next time Eric Njorl appears, he is played by Jones, and his name is spelled "Erik."

There is a saga from this same period called *The Tale of Eirek the Traveller*, wherein Eirek is also called "Eirek the Norwegian." See earlier entries in this episode for much more on the sagas. The "Online Medieval & Classical Library" hosted by the University of California, Berkeley graciously offers translations for these and other sagas. See sunsite.berkeley.edu.

"usher"—("Court Scene [Viking]") An officer of the court. The usher works under the direction of the Court Clerk, normally. The "card" the usher carries would have the oath written down on it, so that a witness being sworn in could read along, hand on the Bible, and affirm to tell the truth.

– V –

"Vadalesc"—("Icelandic Saga") This is probably a misspelling, but if not, then the fact that here it is spelled without the medial "l" (in the original recitation it was "Valdalesc") may account for the textual revision. Jones' voiceover contains no other change or emendation from the original recitation by Idle's character other than the new *spelling*.

"vin ordinaire"—("Mrs Premise and Mrs Conclusion Visit Jean-Paul Sartre") "Ordinary wine," French wine for everyday use.

Voice—(PSC; animated link out of "Court Scene—Multiple Murderer") The "Voice" (singing "which nobody can deny") sounds like and probably is Gilliam, who continues on with the animation.

– W –

"waterfall"—("Icelandic Saga") This backdrop appears to be a waterfall at Glencoe, West Highlands, Scotland, where there are a series of falls leading into Loch Achtriochtan and the River Coe.

"We'll ask him"—("Mrs Premise and Mrs Conclusion Visit Jean-Paul Sartre") Just that simple, like the "Man from the Hay Wain" walking up to a Titian painting and being able to talk to the Father/Solomon figure. Woody Allen will borrow this set-up in his 1977 movie *Annie Hall*, where he is able to pull television critical studies professor Marshall McLuhan (1911-1980) from out of nowhere to back up a point of discussion on broadcast theory.

Whicker's World—("Whicker Island") Alan Whicker (b. 1925) hosted his travel/interview shows around the world, working for the *Tonight* program in the 1950s, then producing such shows as *Whicker Down Under*, *Whicker on Top of the World*, *Whicker Down Mexico Way*, and at least six more similarly titled shows by 1972 (see note for end credits just below). *Whicker's World* appeared in 1959, and ran consistently through 1988. Whicker also appeared in the Peter Sellers' film *The Magic Christian* (1969), for which Chapman and Cleese provided material.

"Windsor, Duke and Duchess"—("Mrs Premise and Mrs Conclusion Visit Jean-Paul Sartre") The tenants in this Paris apartment are as incongruous as the rest of this scene:

Former King Edward VIII (1894-1972) and his American wife Wallis Simpson (1896-1986) did have a Paris villa, near the Bois de Boulogne, where she lived until her death in 1986. Edward had abdicated his throne in 1936 to marry Simpson, and had gone to Paris to escape the press and to allow his younger brother (George VI) the full spotlight as the new king. During the war, the couple lived abroad in the Bahamas, where they were known as the Duke and Duchess of Windsor. After WWII, they returned to France.

"Yves Montand"—Montand (1921-1991) was a French actor. The Pythons here are probably pulling out names of French personalities, as this is an eclectic bunch only connected by their celebrity. Montand's films of this period were *Tout va Bien* (Jean-Luc Godard; 1972), *La Folie de Grandeurs* (1971), and *Le Cercle Rouge* (1971).

"Jacques Cousteau"—Cousteau (1910-1997) was an underwater adventurer, inventor of the SCUBA system, and well-known television personality by this time. His *The Undersea World of Jacques Cousteau* ran on American TV from 1966 through 1973. Cousteau will be mentioned again in Ep. 30, wrestling for documentary film broadcast rights and repeat fees.

"Jean Genet and Friend"—See note on Genet above. Incidentally, Genet's longtime "friend," Abdallah Bentaga, had committed suicide in 1964. Three years later, Genet would attempt to take his own life. He spent the rest of his life championing radical political and social causes (the Black Panthers, for example) around the world, sneaking across the Canadian border into the United States after being repeatedly denied a visa as a "sexual deviant." It wouldn't be until 1974 (well after this episode is written and broadcast) that Genet would start a new, long-lasting relationship.

"Maurice Laroux"—*Leroux* (1923-1992) was a composer for such films as *Le Ballon rouge* (1956), *Le Salaire du péché* (1956), *Les Mistons* (1957), and the Godard film *Le Petit Soldat* (1966). That Godard's name continues to show up isn't coincidental, as he was a prolific and highly controversial political filmmaker, and whose sometime pretentiousness the Pythons had already deflated (see the "French Subtitled Film" in Ep. 23).

"Marcel Marceau . . . Ltd."—Marceau (1923-) was a French mime, whose most recent film appearance had been, interestingly enough, *Barbarella* (1968). Marceau performs whiteface mime, and his character's name is "Bip." His trademark is his very subtle and believable "walking against the wind" routine.

"Indira Gandhi"—Gandhi (1917-1984) was Prime Minister of India from 1966 to 1977 and again 1980-1984. Educated at Oxford, there seems to be little reason for her to be living in this Paris flat, except that it's silly, and she would have been quite topical.

– Y –

"you were wilfully and persistently a foreigner"—("Court Scene [Viking]") The level of xenophobia in the UK seems to have been elevated during this period, with immigration acts passing into law in 1962, 1968, and 1971. Conservative Opposition Cabinet member Enoch Powell would lose his post after speaking his mind about the perceived threat in 1968 (Eps. 5 and 12), when thousands of Kenyan Asians were *legally* entering Britain, many finding their way onto the welfare rolls.

In general, immigration acts passed by Conservative governments tended to tighten immigration policies (i.e., including a demand for employment vouchers), which limited immigrant numbers, while Labour government immigration acts (as in 1968) tried to ease those restrictions, amending the more draconian elements of the Commonwealth Immigrant Act of 1962, for example, The Wilson government did, however, try and stem the legal flow of Commonwealth immigrants, which caused a stir when this hypocritical tack was outed in the press. See the Commonwealth Immigrants Act of 1968 for specific amendments, emendations, and limitations. In Ep. 25, the foreign nationals wandering the streets of London are Hungarian, and thus not strictly affected by the various Commonwealth immigration acts.

Episode 28

– A –

"AA book"—("Emigration from Surbiton to Hounslow") Motor guide book from the British Automobile Association. The location of a handy AA office—in the case of nuclear attack—is of great concern to Mrs. S.C.U.M. in Ep. 44, "Mr. Neutron."

"abbatoir"—(*"Life of Tschaikowsky"*) A slaughterhouse. Mentioned prominently earlier in Ep. 17, in the "Architect Sketch."

"Abide-A-Wee"—("Emigration from Surbiton to Hounslow") A play on a Northern phrase meaning to stay awhile ("bide-a-wee"), to "wait a bit." The Norris' home even sports a sign that reads "Abide-a-Wee," though it's not highlighted; it's not clear whether the propmaster put up the sign, or the homeowner has actually named his dwelling. Walter Scott employs the phrase in several of his novels, including *Rob Roy* (1829) and *Old Mortality* (1816). Scott and his works will be featured in Ep. 38.

"Absolve all those you have excommunicated"—("Trim-Jeans Theatre") Other than the attackers, only Edward Grim witnessed this murder firsthand, and he recorded the following in *Vita S. Thomae, Cantuariensis Archepiscopi et Martyris* (c. 1170-1177):

> The knights came back with swords and axes and other weapons fit for the crime which their minds were set on. . . . The knights cried out, 'Where is Thomas Becket, traitor to the King?' Becket . . . in a clear voice answered, '*I am here, no traitor to the King*, but a priest. . . . I am ready to suffer in His name . . . be it far from me to flee from your swords.' Having said this, he turned to the right under a pillar . . . and walked to the altar of St. Benedict the Confessor. . . . The murderers followed him; '*Absolve*', they cried, '*and restore to communion those whom you have excommunicated and restore their powers to those whom you have suspended.*' He answered, '*I will not*

absolve them.' 'Then you shall die,' they cried. (italics added)

The Pythons borrow from the Eliot play *Murder in the Cathedral* for their source (see Eliot note below). The play premiered in November 1935. The text as Eliot wrote it for the stage is as follows (original playscript structure not retained), and it's easy to see how Python adapted the scene for their "Trim Jeans" admag infomercial:

> Thomas: I am here. No traitor to the king. I am a priest.
> A Christian, saved by the blood of Christ,
> Ready to suffer with my blood.
> This is the sign of the Church always,
> The sign of blood. Blood for blood.
>
> First Knight: Absolve all those you have excommunicated.
> Second Knight: Resign the powers you have arrogated.
> Third Knight: Restore to the King the money you appropriated.
> Fourth Knight: Renew the obedience you have violated. (2.2)

all in trim-jeans—(PSC; "Trim-Jeans Theatre") Contemporary, local productions of *Murder in the Cathedral* are myriad. A December 1970 production by the Brize Norton Theatre Club in Brize Norton, Oxfordshire; in 1971, the Studio Theatre Club (Salisbury) also performed the play; there is also record of performances in 1955 and 1972 of the play at Brockenhurst County High/Grammar School (meaning other secondary educational institutions, especially Catholic ones, would also have performed the play), the production value of which may have given the Pythons ideas about their own version. The Pythons themselves, as students, *may* have performed in such a play, as well, though the secular nature of the subject matter makes it unlikely.

Becket (Chapman) is the only one on stage not wearing the product, signaling his otherness.

"And now . . . "—(link out of "Emigration From Surbiton to Hounslow") The setting for this series' "And now . . . " moments (with Cleese at the announcer's desk) looks to have been filmed in Thetford, where the Pythons stayed during Norwich-area location shooting in October 1971. The Bell Hotel—where the Pythons and crew were billeted—can be seen over Cleese's shoulder, on King Street, Thetford, Norfolk (WAC T12/1,428).

"Anton Chekhov can certainly write"—("Trim-Jeans Theatre") Clever marketing ploy here, giving weight loss credit not to the product, but to the writer and production. This might be seen as a way to avoid litigation if the product proves defective or unable to fulfill its promises (though Sauna Belt's many days in court would seem to belie that possible protection).

Apollo-type monograph—(PSC; *"Life of Tschaikowsky"*) The backdrop flat is made to look like an Apollo news coverage set from the BBC's extensive coverage of the U.S. space program.

"arrogated"—("Trim-Jeans Theatre") The fact that there is rhymed verse perhaps unintentionally echoes the affected, alliterative poetic speech used by the critic/hairdresser (Palin) earlier. Unless they are singing or staging portions of a rhymed play, the Pythons tend to avoid rhymed speech. There are multiple versions of this death scene (from Grim through Tennyson and Eliot), with the Pythons choosing the rhyming Eliot version.

"Ascot water heaters"—("Vicar/Salesman") There exist Ascot hats, dresses, ties, etc., all suitable for wearing to the Royal Enclosure at Ascot. The Ascot Gas Water Heater was a smaller, often single-tapped water heater prevalent in starter homes, council and student housing, etc. They would, perhaps, have been small enough to sell door-to-door.

"biros"—Generically meaning a ballpoint pen.

"noddy dog"—Dog figurine with a bouncy head.

– B –

bare light bulb—(PSC; "The BBC Is Short of Money") The darkened set is a reference to the nationwide power shortages experienced by the UK in December 1970, brought on by work-to-rule strikes across the country. Power would be reduced as much as 40 percent in many areas, with hospitals being forced to use candles and flashlights (see *Guardian Century Year 1970*).

There is a remarkably similar political cartoon by Stanley Franklin in the *Daily Mirror* (4 November 1966) depicting BBC Director-General Hugh Greene (1910-1987) in a bare office, reading the news under a single light bulb. The cartoon is titled "BBC Plan Economy Cuts." Between 1964 and 1969, at least, the Wilson government saw the BBC, under Greene, as something of an enemy (identifying the BBC as "anti-Labour," specifically):

> Labour had an uneasy relationship with a BBC in the throes of the "Greene revolution," the Director General's successful attempt to modernise the corporation and to compete more effectively with ITV. In opposition Labour had benefited from the BBC's new-found dynamism as the latter sought to shrug off its stuffy image. A programme like the notorious *TW3* was "anti-pomposity, anti-sanctimony, anti-snob and—blatantly—anti-Conservative." The problem was that it was only a fine line between being anti-Conservative and being anti-government, *any* government. (Freedman 25)

(Ironically, Tory Winston Churchill had always seen the BBC as a Leftist bastion, and in conversation, opined for a chance to shut the medium down.) As a result, license fee changes, structural reorganizations, and even threats of license revocation were whacked about like political shuttlecocks. One of the more challenging ordeals was PM Wilson's reluctance or refusal to raise the license fee, since he saw the BBC as biased in favor of the political right, leading to cutbacks in BBC production and availability in 1966-1967. (Alternately, Wilson seemed "comfortable" with the bosses at ITV, which made many feel his bias had to be personal against Greene and the BBC [28].)

"BBC are short of money"—("The BBC Is Short of Money") The Goons (*The Goon Show*) had already questioned the financial stability of the BBC more than a decade earlier. In one of the show's introductory sections, the BBC announcer is taking tips (or handouts) whenever he speaks, and in another, Harry Secombe announces that the BBC have been sold for ten shillings. In another episode, the performers admit that the BBC have agreed to save money by combining sound effects (a car and a bagpipe will make the same sound to cut costs, for example). The fact that the BBC relied on the license fee (affixed to every radio and TV set sold in the UK) meant that as consumer discretionary spending went, so went the fortunes of the BBC, and the postwar era is known as a very challenging time for the British economy.

By 1969, Lord Hill and Harold Wilson's Labour government were preparing to trim the ranks at BBC, including hiving off significant Radio 3 orchestra personnel. The newspapers of the period (including articles, op-ed pieces, and political cartoons) covered the story and public and union outcry from about May through at least September 1969. A cartoon from "Jon" for 25 September 1969 depicts a BBC radio newsreader about to offer a repeat of the previous day's news to save money (*Daily Mail* 25 September 1969). See the British Cartoon Archive for more.

"BBC has to pay an actor twenty guineas if he speaks"—("The BBC is Short of Money") There were precise amounts affixed to walk-on and extra roles, with speaking parts generating more in payment than others. In the Goons' "Tay Bridge Disaster" episode, one of the band members speaks (with an alarmingly bad Scots accent), and Seagoon (Secombe) comments: "There he goes folks, he and a speaking part fee of two guineas" (9 February 1959).

"BBC Publications"—("Trim-Jeans Theatre") Companion (printed) publications offered to many BBC shows, the BBC Publications office was located at 35 Marylebone High Street, London during this period. In the late 1960s and early 1970s, BBC Publications released titles that included Roger Fiske's *Chamber Music* (1969), Whitting and Bryer's *Byzantium* (1968), and Richard Hooper's *Colour in Britain* (1965). *Byzantium*, for example, was the companion text for a twelve-part BBC Radio broadcast in 1968.

"Becket, Thomas"—("Trim-Jeans Theatre") Becket (1118-1170) was a clerk, Chancellor, and eventually became Archbishop of Canterbury during Henry II's reign. He had been rather hedonistic and even thug-like prior to his appointment to the deaconship, riding with Henry into battle and enjoying the pomp and fruits of power. He was a great friend to Henry (who was twelve years his junior), and his change surprised, confused, and eventually angered the monarch (not unlike Shakespeare's Prince Hal becoming Henry, and leaving old pal Falstaff dumbfounded and dejected). When Becket began to show more allegiance to God than his king (Henry saw it as betrayal and popery), the end was set for Thomas.

big liner sinking—(PSC; "World War One") This is a miniature special effect shot featuring a model labeled "Titanic." The WAC records indicate that Movietone Library footage from *Titanic* was utilized here, including images A17702-126, A17654-1076, A17709-126, and A17636-1073 (WAC T12/1,427).

The *Titanic*, of course, wasn't sunk by hostile fire. There were a number of passenger ships lost to German attacks during WWI, including the *Lusitania*, *Arabic*, *Sussex*, and *Laconia*.

"Big School"—("How to Rid the World of All Known Diseases") Generically, the next level of schooling (i.e., secondary school for an elementary pupil).

Blue Peter—(PSC; "How to Rid the World of All Known Diseases") Long-running children's television program (BBC1, 1958-), *Blue Peter* was a children's television magazine show originally presented by Christopher Trace and Leila Williams, followed by Valerie Singleton and Peter Purves (and John Noakes). The show did have a dog, Petra, after 1962 (Vahimagi 70).

"box girder bridge"—("How to Rid the World of All Known Diseases") A bridge composed of linked iron boxes, with the four corners of each box connected by angle-irons.

– C –

"capitalist dog"—(animated link into "World War One") Mentioned in Mao Tse-Tung's writings and speeches often, with Mao characterizing any anti-revolutionary element as "Imperialist running dogs" and the like. For example: "The imperialists and their running dogs, the Chinese reactionaries, will not resign themselves to defeat in this land of China" (from Mao's "Address to the Preparatory Committee of the New Political Consultative Conference" [15 June 1949], *Selected Works* 4:407).

"People's Republic"—The People's Republic of China was established in 1949 by Mao Tse-tung and his Red Army, with Mao installed as the chairman of the central government council.

The fact that China had little or nothing to do with the WWI events and combatants depicted in this animation exhibits the significant contemporary threat (or at least fascination) that Mao's China must have represented, at least for/to Gilliam—here the contemporary Chinese can impose themselves on historical events in which they had no historical part.

"car-swapping belt"—("Emigration From Surbiton to Hounslow") A kind of regional appellation, like the "Bible Belt" across America's deep south. Some car enthusiasts in the UK practice car-swapping during road rallies, changing cars as clues are discovered. This is probably meant to be a joke, since few would find swapping into a Ford Popular much of a thrill.

cathedral interior—(PSC; "Trim-Jeans Theatre") Historically, Canterbury Cathedral was where Thomas was murdered. This scene was staged in Ealing TFS, where larger set needs could be fulfilled (see "School Prize-Giving," "The Bishop," and "Accidents Sketch," e.g.).

Others in this scene include Priests John Hughman, Ian Elliott (*Paul Temple*; *Dr. Who*), and Paul Lindley (*Dixon of Dock Green*), and Waiting Ladies Elizabeth Broom (*Dixon of Dock Green*) and Naomi Sandford (WAC T12/1,428).

"chartered accountancy"—("Emigration from Surbiton to Hounslow") This dull, uninspired, and wholly inoffensive man is the prototypical Python "type" for a chartered accountant, played often by Palin, and seen earlier in Ep. 2 ("Marriage Guidance Counsellor") and Ep. 10 ("Vocational Guidance Counsellor"). In the featurette "The Crimson Permanent Assurance" prior to *Meaning of Life*, it is the old and beaten-down accountants who swashbuckle their way to financial glory.

"chemists"—("Emigration from Surbiton to Hounslow") A film developer, often in a pharmacy setting. Boots the Chemist has been popular in the UK for many years, as was the ABC Pharmacy chain, and Harts before that.

Chinese Fish—(animated link into "World War One") This is a bit of an anachronism, as the Chinese during WWI were not part of the Kaiser's war effort (internal political turmoil occupying China's factions), and it wouldn't be until WWII and after when Mao and the Communists would figure significantly into world politics. The Chinese Fish is characterized by stereotypical slanted eyes, buck teeth, and is colored yellow—stereotypes not unlike the traditional WWII-era cartoons featuring Axis characters.

"choice"—("Trim-Jeans Theatre") The freedom to choose and define oneself is perhaps the most significant theme of existential thought. In the Python world, choices have consequences, and they are often fatal. If you ask to see a neighbor die, he will (Ep. 1, "Famous Deaths"); if you agree to attack the self-defense instructor with a banana, you will be shot (Ep. 4, "Self-Defence"); if you choose to see "a Scotsman on a horse," he'll appear (Ep. 2); if you choose to believe in the fantasy block of flats in which you're living, they will remain standing (Ep. 35, "Mystico and Janet"); if you choose to answer honestly that you are, indeed, a "fairy," you will also be shot (Ep. 33, "Biggles Dictates a Letter"); and if you choose blue as your favorite color, then change your mind to yellow, you'll be catapulted to your death (*Holy Grail*).

clips a face—(PSC; animated link into "Farming Club") This looks very much like a cut-out photo of then-FBI director J. Edgar Hoover, who ran the FBI for forty-eight years. This episode was recorded in January 1972, and Hoover would die in May of the same year.

"Cobbley, John"—("Farming Club") Cobbley was a tenor horn player who, with his G.US Footwear Band Quartet, won the British Open Quartet Championships in Oxford 1966-1968. He may have been known to the Oxfordians (Cleese and/or Palin) in the troupe. The other members of the quartet were John Berryman, David Read, and Trevor Groom.

"Musical . . . Director"—George Solti (1912-1997) was the musical director for the Royal Opera House, Covent Garden from 1961 to 1971. Colin Davis (1927-) became musical director there in 1971.

"Covent Garden"—Area in London (near Trafalgar and Leicester squares) where fruit and garden markets had historically been located, as well as the Royal Opera House. The site had been the abbot of Westminster's convent garden when Charles II established the area in 1671.

"complete photographic record"—("Emigration from Surbiton to Hounslow") No spouses made the Kon Tiki or Ra expeditions—no women at all, actually—so the photographic record was fairly shared by whomever was holding the camera at any particular time. It is possible that Heyerdahl's wife shot some photos of her own as Ra II left its Moroccan port, but she clearly remained behind. Crew member Carlo Mauri shot 16mm film of the Ra II journey, while Heyerdahl notes that even the ship's cook took photographs en route.

"Coover, Gary"—("Trim-Jeans Theatre") Gary Coover is an actor featured in actual Trim Jeans TV and print advertisements of this period.

"Cup final tickets"—("Vicar/Salesman") There is an English Cup final played at Wembley every year, and a World Cup series of matches played internationally every four years.

– D –

"duckety-poos"—(*Life of Tschaikowsky*) Probably a term of endearment, based on "ducky." The following affected alliterations can be read as elevated, effeminized verse, and correspond well with the hairdresser, his "drag queen" voice and bright costume. All of these indicators coalesce to form the "type" the Pythons (and many on TV during this period, including *Laugh-In*'s Alan Sues) project as "gay":

"semi-Mondrian"—Piet Mondrian (1872-1944), an abstract painter—a neoplasticist—Mondrian eschewed naturalism in favor of angular shapes and primary colors. He was very influential for the later Bauhaus and International Style groups. Since Mondrian was only twenty-one when Tchaikovsky died, and it wasn't until 1910 that Cubism could influence him away from naturalism, the possibility of Tchaikovsky living in a house reminiscent of Mondrian's later work or influence is, well, impossible.

"Lily life"—Also, note that much like the Second Presenter (Cleese) just above who speaks aloud his parentheticals, Maurice (Palin) seems to be doing virtually the same thing—he's saying aloud what could be left in parentheses, and essentially adding merely alliterative words that don't necessarily modify the words that follow them. The sentence reads quite straightforwardly with the words removed: "Here Tschaikowsky wrote some of the most super symphonies you've ever heard in the whole of your life."

The "not-parentheticals" are also all just fairly common first names: Robin, Harry, Tammy, Sammy, Henry, Lily, Sally, Patsy, Adrian, Conny, Vera, Peter, and Fanny. These are followed in his last speech below by "Dickie," "Colin," "Patsy," "Gertie," and "Percy." This is not unlike Ep. 12 wherein the policemen characters must speak/shout in different registers, tempos, even pitches to be properly understood among each other. This type of mis-communication is a Python trademark, with characters having learned or having to learn the particular speech idiosyncrasy before communication is possible.

Lastly, speech-language pathologist Caroline Bowen, Ph.D., gives a quick rundown of what it might mean to "sound gay," and it's as if the Pythons read the primer, then wrote these flamboyant characters. Bowen identifies the subtle prolonging of /l/, /s/ and /z/, the emphasizing and increased aspiration of final stop consonants, lisping, upward inflections, prolonging vowels ("extraooordinary") and consonants ("Ssssammy sssuper sssymphonies"), pursing lips at word initiation, rising voice pitch, and "breathing through sounds." Finally, she identifies the use of vocabulary and expressions that have been culturally flagged as "gay" (the critic/hairdresser refers to Tchaikowsky as "she"), as well as "the adopting of a high camp demeanor." Language, expression, and appearance, then, continue to be oft-used tools as the Pythons construct ready-made types for quick audience identification. See Bowen for more.

– E –

"EBW 343"—("Emigration from Surbiton to Hounslow") License plate number of the Ford Popular, and probably a play on the designations "Ra I" and "Ra II," etc.

"Eliot, T.S."—("Trim-Jeans Theatre") Thomas Stearns Eliot (1888-1965) was a poet, essayist, and playwright, whose interests moved from the desolation of *The Waste Land* (1922) to religiosity and even some hope for the salvation of humanity, as exhibited in his 1935 play *Murder in the Cathedral*.

Eliot was influential to the Pythons as he focused on two major themes in much of his work: primitive and metropolitan life—which the Pythons also explore and satirize throughout *FC* and beyond, into the feature films. (See Crawford's *The Savage and the City*.) Eliot's portrait of London in *The Waste Land* is also compelling, as is his use of nontraditional language and imagery.

"encyclopedias"—("Vicar/Salesman") This gag is also found in the magazine *Private Eye* (July 1962), and was first broached in *FC* in Ep. 5, when an encyclopedia salesman poses as a burglar just to get into a home and make a sale.

Episode 28—Recorded 28 January 1972, and broadcast 26 October 1972.

These people were scheduled to appear at Television Centre 6 (TC6) on 28 January 1972 for extras work: Julia Breck (*Q5*), Graham Skidmore (*Dixon of Dock Green*), Jeremy Higgins (*Doctor in Charge*), Frank Menzies (*Dr. Who*), Eric Kent (*Doctor in the House*), Terence Sartain (*Dr. Who*), Chris Hodge (*Softly Softly*), Geoffrey Brighty (*Emma*), Keith Ashley (*Doctor in the House*), Harry Tierney (*Dr. Who*), Douglas Hutchinson, Freda Jeffries (*Z Cars*), and *FC* semi-regular John Hughman (WAC T12/1,428).

"escape from a sack"—("*Life of Tschaikowsky*") It is possible that since pianist Richter (1915-1997) was a Soviet citizen and not free to travel without permission (or collateral), he may have been seen as an escape artist of sorts as he performed in the West. In fact it took significant time and convincing of Soviet authorities to allow Richter his first trip to America. As with other artists (dancers, musicians, filmmakers) from the Soviet Union, the international goodwill potential for the Communist state often outweighed the possibility (and actuality, sometimes) of a defection. (Celebrated dancer Rodolf Nureyev, for example, defected in 1961.)

The visual symbols of chains and a suffocating bag would have been eminently recognizable to those in the West who were living with the fears of the so-called Red menace and the Cold War.

"handcuffs"—This leans more toward a Harry Houdini feat than Richter, but the incongruous combination of the two seems about right for Python. Refer back to a government minister performing a burlesque dance while citing foreign agricultural trade policy in Ep. 20.

"exeat form"—("Schoolboys' Life Assurance Company") A permission slip, essentially, to leave the school's premises.

"extremely naughty for his time"—("*Life of Tschaikowsky*") Referring to Tchaikovsky's homosexuality, of course, which troubled him throughout his life—some scholarship even claiming it was the reason behind his death by suicide. For more, see entry for "Glenda Jackson" below.

– F –

"Farming Club special, the life of Tchaikowsky"—("*Life of Tschaikowsky*") The very popular radio show *The Archers* (1950-) had begun as a sort of Ministry of Agriculture mouthpiece, where listeners could be reminded of postwar rationing limits, the "English way" of doing things in the face of the thriving European market, and agricultural tips for gardens and farms. It was an organ of the government, designed to make postwar scarcity and thrift more palatable.

first piano concerto—(PSC; "Farming Club") This is not, in fact, Tchaikovsky's first concerto, which will be heard later in the episode as the pianist Sviatoslav Richter (Jones) escapes from chains.

The track being used here is a portion of the first movement of Tchaikovsky's "Symphonie Pathetique," his sixth symphony ("Adagio—Allegro non troppo" section), his final and most poignant work. The symphony was written after he turned fifty, and as he struggled with failing health and what he feared was an evaporating musical gift; he wrote to his nephew that he was suffering "torments" (Orlova). This was the "tortured old ponce" the Pythons were treating here, and someone in the troupe picked the appropriate musical work for the moment. Tchaikovsky would die just a few days after the symphony's premiere.

This specific performance is by the USSR Symphony Orchestra ("Symphony No. 6 in B Minor Allegro non Troppo") (WAC T12/1,427).

"foot and mouth"—("Farming Club") Also called FMD (foot and mouth disease, or "hoof and mouth"), the disease is less rampant than it was, but is still usually fatal (meaning animals must be quarantined and destroyed).

"Ford Popular"—("Emigration from Surbiton to Hounslow") Ford automobile built in the UK between 1953 and 1959, the Popular was a very basic car, with few amenities, and designed for the "austerity" period after WWII. There were more than 150,000 produced during this period for the eager postwar buyer.

"Forty minutes . . . Brentford"—("Emigration from Surbiton to Hounslow") The Richmond-to-Hounslow leg is actually about a sixteen-minute train ride, and traveling via "Clapham, Fulham and Chiswick" (well east of Hounslow) would take the Norrises well out of their way, unless they were headed for Ealing. As indicated in the "Railway Timetables" sketch in Ep. 24, of course, finite accuracy isn't the benchmark the Pythons often attempt, rather humor.

The Brentford Football Ground was where various works of fine art gather to take a strike vote (Ep. 25), and where the Pythons shot the apocalyptic football sequence for Ep. 7.

"four knights"—("Trim-Jeans Theatre") These are the four knights who acted on Henry II's rash cry for Becket's life. Becket was allegedly stabbed and hacked to death in the cathedral itself on 29 December 1170. The knights by name: Hugh de Morville, William de Tracy, Reginald Fitz Urse, and Richard Le Bret.

Fox, Paul Jnr—(PSC; "Emigration from Surbiton to Hounslow") Paul Fox (b. 1925) was at this time Monty Python's boss, essentially, and a generation older, at least. Fox was, with Bill Cotton, head of BBC Light Entertainment, which oversaw *FC* and other comedy programs. Fox will actually be lampooned later in the episode ("The BBC Is Short of Money"), played by a made-up Jones.

The Pythons had clashed with Fox at the beginning of the broadcast run of the second series, when their time slot was slated for an "opt out" slot in most regions, and most regions were opting out and not carrying the show (WAC T12/1,418). Opt-outs allow for regional or even local programming in place of national shows.

The bad feelings didn't just go away, obviously, as a September 1972 memo from Duncan Wood to Ian MacNaughton (then in Bayern, Germany for the *FZ* shooting) asks if the continued use of a cut-out image of Paul Fox in the animations is really a good thing, or just "an in-house joke gone too long" (WAC T12/1,428).

"Francis, Kevin"—("Trim-Jeans Theatre") Francis was a production manager for the Python film *And Now for Something Completely Different* (1971), which the Pythons shot while on hiatus between series two and three of *FC*. Jones and John Hughman play the part in the "Trim-Jeans Theatre" sketch.

"Fritz"—(animated link into "World War One") Shortened version of Friedrich, and used as a nickname for German soldiers in World War I. The epithet "Jerry" was used more in World War II. It's not entirely clear why this sketch is set in/called "World War One," except that the ship being sunk may be a *Lusitania*-type passenger liner, several of which fell prey to German U-boats in WWI.

– G –

"GDBDMDB"—("Emigration from Surbiton to Hounslow") Probably a play on early computer lingo

("GDB," "MDB"), part of the jabberwock language often spoken by Python characters.

"excess . . . tamping"—Again, silly speak, since a "wopple" is actually a bridle lane and "tamping" means to pack a blast hole above the charge. This is symptomatic of Idle's consistent playfulness with words and language, as heard in the "Stock Exchange Report" in the previous episode.

General panic and dramatic music—(PSC; "World War One") The dramatic music as the ship sinks is from Theme Suites, Vol. 11, "Under Full Sail" by Johnny Pearson (WAC T12/1,427).

"generated independently"—("Emigration from Surbiton to Hounslow") Heyerdahl had originally gone to the Marquesas Islands in 1937-1938 to study the transoceanic flora and fauna, finding that it was far more reasonable to assume that ancient travelers had made their way to the South Pacific with the help of the strong currents, and began to debunk the reigning theory that Southeast Asian ancients had found a way to struggle against the currents to reach the islands. So it was a similarity and commonality in plant and animal life that first piqued Heyerdahl's interest, *then* the search for human-made similarities would begin.

Heyerdahl's work was published in 1941 and 1952. In the Galapagos (1952) and Easter Island (1955-1956) expeditions, Heyerdahl's discoveries include Incan and pre-Incan tools and instruments (including navigational instruments), and stone carvings similar to those found in Peru, further supporting his theories.

"Gielgud, Sir John"—("Trim-Jeans Theatre") Gielgud (1904-2000) was a well-respected British actor and, co-incidentally, portrayed Louis VII in the 1964 film about Thomas, *Becket*. The role of Becket was played by Richard Burton, while Peter O'Toole played Henry.

Golden Egg or Wimpy—(PSC; "Emigration from Surbiton to Hounslow") Golden Egg was a chain of low-priced restaurants (owned by Philip Kaye and family) where drinks, coffee, or a meal could be had. Begun in the 1950s, they were described as "colourful, cheap and homogenous: the same layout whether you were in Dover or Dundee" (from "Designing Britain"). Golden Egg franchise outlets were originally located in Aberdeen, Bath, Birmingham, Bournemouth, Brighton, Colchester, Coventry, Great Yarmouth, Norwich, and Liverpool.

The "Wimpy" name came from J. Wellington Wimpy of *Popeye* fame, and was a high street restaurant franchise begun in the UK in 1954 (imported by J. Lyon).

In the film it's clear that they are dining in a restaurant called "Egg Nest," with some slightly garish red lighting inside. This is most likely the Egg Nest then located at 132 High Street, Hounslow. This means the Pythons have located their characters at the end of their journey (Hounslow) before it even has begun (supposedly, in Surbiton).

Great Escape, The—(PSC; "Trim-Jeans Theatre") Hollywood feature film based on a true story of the escape of seventy-six prisoners from Stalag Luft III in 1944, directed by John Sturges, and starring Steve McQueen. The signature music was composed by Elmer Bernstein for the film. The book was written by Paul Brickhill, who was himself an escapee of Stalag III. This film/book was referenced earlier in Ep. 18, "Escape (From Film)." This escape footage was shot in the Oban area while the Pythons were shooting in Scotland.

The signature music is performed by Geoff Love and Orchestra, from the album *Big War Movie Themes*, and was composed by Elmer Bernstein (WAC T12/1,427).

– H –

"Hello Pianist"—(*Life of Tschaikowsky*) The title of "Hello Sailor" (same homosexual connotation) was used in Ep. 2, and later spoken in a very effeminate manner in Ep. 14, the "New Cooker Sketch" (by a flamboyantly gay cross-dresser). As seen in earlier episodes, this is the clarion call of the poofy presenter, the academic, the politician, even the historical icon—in short, the sexual orientation of any establishment type is immediately in question in the Python world.

Horse of the Year Show—("Puss in Boots") Britain's yearly indoor equine event, the show includes showing, jumping, and stunt and trick riding.

"Hounslow"—("Emigration From Surbiton to Hounslow") South and west of the City, in Greater London, near Heathrow Airport. The Egg Nest restaurant where Mr. and Mrs. Norris (Palin and Chapman) dine was found in Hounslow.

"Hounslow 25 Miles"—("Emigration from Surbiton to Hounslow") Surbiton and Hounslow are only about eight miles apart, so Mr. Norris (Palin) was obviously already well off course. Later, Mr. Pither (also Palin) will find Soviet Russia on his tour of Cornwall (Ep. 34).

How to Do It—("How to Rid the World of All Known Diseases") A spoof of the 1966-1981 Southern TV children's show *How*, offering "facts and fun" for the younger viewer. The hosts were Bunty James, Fred Dinenage, Jack Hargreaves, and Jon Miller (see Vahimagi *British Television* 148).

The happy music played beneath these titles is from the Theatre Orchestra Light Intimations, "Days Work," by Mike McNaught (WAC T12/1,427).

Hughman, John—("Trim-Jeans Theatre") It almost never happens that an extra is mentioned by name in the scripts, but Hughman's tall, very gaunt frame was just what the Pythons were thinking when they wrote the "after" character for this Trim-Jeans promo image. A bit actor, Hughman appears in several *FC* episodes, including Eps. 14 and 41, and later in *Whoops Baghdad!* and *Time Bandits*. Hughman also poses for the "Naughtiest Girl in the School" photo (in string vest and skirt) in Ep. 26, has appeared in a bit speaking part as a Gasman (Ep. 14) and an embarrassed Chemist customer (Ep. 17), and will finally play Tennyson in Ep. 41.

– I –

"Italian Grand Prix at Monza"—("Schoolboys' Life Assurance Company") A car race event initiated in 1922, this Formula One series event in 1971 featured the fastest average speed in the history of the race, a record that still stands. Peter Gethin won this 1971 race, and Emerson Fittipaldi would win the 1972 event.

In 1972 Fittipaldi became the youngest driver (age twenty-five) to win a Formula One championship, a possible reason for the inclusion of the race in the Python sketch about youngsters doing adult things.

It's—("The BBC Is Short of Money") There were a number of shows beginning with "It's" on British TV, including *It's a Knockout* (1966), *It's a Square World* (1960-1964), and *It's Only Us* (1968). See notes for Ep. 2 for more uses in *FC*.

– J –

"Jackson, Glenda"—("Trim-Jeans Theatre") Born in 1936, Jackson is an actress who played an uncredited bit part in the early Angry Young Man film *This Sporting Life* (1963), she played both Elizabeth I and Mary Queen of Scots in 1971, and appeared in Ken Russell's *The Music Lovers* (1971). This was Russell's version of the tumultuous life of Tchaikovsky, and the inclusion/mention of Jackson connects this Becket sketch back to the Tchaikovsky sketch seemingly finished earlier.

jolly music of Edward German—("Fish-Slapping Dance") One of the few times in the printed scripts that the Pythons are so specific in their incidental music cues. Edward German (1862-1936) was perhaps the first professional British film music composer, and his orchestral works obviously inspired this inclusion. The WAC records for the episode do not mention German, meaning the music used was found elsewhere (perhaps more affordably), and the Pythons were likely referring to German's "Seasons" or "Merrie England" compositions for the needed "jolly" jauntiness.

Jolly showbiz music—(PSC; "Trim-Jeans Theatre") The music used under the opening titles of this infomercial is Anthony Mawer's "Theatre Overture" (WAC T12/1,427). The Pythons would go back to Mawer for some of the incidental music for the feature film *Holy Grail*, using a portion of his composition "Countrywide." The serene theme can be heard in *HG* when the opening credits change to the more sedate mode, prior to the producers being "sacked" again.

– K –

"Kierkegaardian moment"—("Trim-Jeans Theatre") Thomas must choose between his longtime friend Henry and the friendship they once knew, and the responsibilities of leading the Church and serving God. Philosopher Søren Kierkegaard (1813-1855) writes in the "Equilibrium Between the Aesthetic and the Ethical" chapter of *Either/Or*:

> But the reason why it can seem to an individual that he could constantly change yet remain the same, as if his inmost being were an algebraic entity that could stand for whatever it might be, is to be found in the fact that he has the wrong attitude; he has not chosen himself, he has no conception of doing so, and yet even in his lack of understanding there is an acknowledgment of the eternal validity of personal existence. For someone with the right attitude, on the other hand, things go differently. He chooses himself, not in a finite sense, for then this "self" would be something finite along with other finite things, but in an absolute sense. And still he chooses himself and not another. This self he thus chooses is infinitely concrete, for it is himself, and yet it is absolutely different from his former self, for he has chosen it absolutely. The self did not exist previously, for it came into existence through the choice, and yet it has been in existence, for it was indeed "he himself." (517)

This "choice" made by Thomas—to abandon the reprobate person he was and follow God—means he has become, by choice, a new and distinct self, a new Thomas. Henry is upset because the Thomas he knew and loved is gone forever, essentially betrayed and even destroyed by the new Thomas. Shakespeare demands that young Prince Hal make this same choice when he "grows up," abandons Falstaff and his old tavern acquaintances, and becomes "Henry," his father's kingly son. Falstaff feels betrayed, like Henry II, but cannot act to crush the betrayal.

For the Pythons, choice can and does bring into existence all sorts of things, as mentioned above in the "choice" entry. In Ep. 9, a "straight man" (Idle) wants to become more funny, and his choice leads to him becoming the butt of all the following jokes. Perhaps even more interesting is the appearance of Bob's twin (both characters played by Idle) after Sir George Head (Cleese) wills him into existence for the viewer—the new Bob is "absolutely distinct from his former self," so much so that he is very much ready to embark on the trip his twin has just refused.

"Kingston by-pass"—("Emigration from Surbiton to Hounslow") Built in the 1930s to reduce the traffic congestion on old Portsmouth Road.

"Kon-Tiki"—("Emigration From Surbiton to Hounslow") A modern "primitive" log raft built and sailed in 1947 by explorer/archaeologist Thor Heyerdahl. His goal: to prove his own thesis that ancient South Americans first settled Polynesia, and could have sailed from Peru to the Tuamotu Archipelago, part of French Polynesia. Heyerdahl wrote a very popular book about the voyage, called *Kon Tiki*, which was released in 1950.

– L –

"left at Barnes"—("Emigration from Surbiton to Hounslow") Barnes is in Greater London, Richmond Upon Thames, and these are confused directions, at best. The A308 does run west, but from Hampton Court west, while Norbiton is actually north and east of Surbiton, so Mr. Norris (Palin) would be well off course going that route. Directions have been confused in *FC* since the first episode, when Picasso tried to paint while competing in a bike race, and continuing through Sir George Head's attempts to get from London to Africa in Ep. 9, and Neville Shunt's railway timetable plays in Ep. 24.

"*Life and Loves of Toulouse-Lautrec, The*"—("Trim-Jeans Theatre") There was a Brazilian TV film from 1963 called *Moulin Rouge, A Vida de Toulouse Lautrec*, written and directed by Geraldo Vietri, as well as a 1939 German film called (in its U.S. release) *The Life and Loves of Tchaikovsky*. Toulouse-Lautrec was previously mentioned/shown in Ep. 1.

"London Electricity Board"—("The BBC Is Short of Money") A formerly government-owned (nationalized in 1947) utility that has since been privatized. Many of the nation's most critical industries were brought into central control during or after the war, in the hopes of controlling production, security, and prices.

Long Day's Journey into Night—("Trim-Jeans Theatre") Eugene O'Neill (1888-1953) play written and presented to his wife in 1941, but not produced until

1956, three years after his death. Sir Ralph Richardson (mentioned elsewhere in this scene) appeared in the acclaimed 1962 film version directed by Sidney Lumet.

"Lose inches . . . abdomen"—("Trim-Jeans Theatre") In 1970-1971, the Trim-Jeans product and company (Sauna Belt, Inc.) were the focus of a lawsuit alleging false advertising, misrepresentation of the product's effectiveness, safety, etc. The California court would find on 20 January 1971 that the complainants failed to prove sufficiently the charges against Sauna Belt, and that Sauna Belt had already altered its advertising claims to ameliorate the situation.

In October 1972, however, a further proceeding reversed the earlier decision, and found for the complainants, ordering "remedial" steps be taken against Sauna Belt, Inc. for false advertising, obtaining money through the mail fraudulently, etc. The full text of the proceedings can be found on the usps.com/judicial website.

Perhaps the fact that the Sauna Belt company was under such intense scrutiny gave the Pythons license, they felt, to openly satirize the company and its products and pitch techniques. English libel and slander laws were/are known for favoring the plaintiff, meaning the Pythons certainly could have gotten into trouble for this possible defamation (as the editors of *Private Eye* did, regularly), but the extant legal troubles for Sauna Belt probably kept their attention off the Pythons.

Lulu—(PSC; "It's") Pop singer and actress born in 1948 in Glasgow, she appeared in the movie *To Sir, With Love* (1967), and sang the title song, as well as co-winning the Eurovision Song Contest in 1968 with the song "Boom Bang a Bang."

"lying like a silver turd"—("Emigration From Surbiton to Hounslow") The Thames has been poetically treated in literature for centuries, and even in the squalor of the modern, industrial city, T.S. Eliot can ask "Sweet Thames, run softly, till I end my song" (which is itself a borrow from Spenser), and much of *The Waste Land* is dedicated to this artery of the city.

The Thames had, of course, been the dumping ground for the city's human garbage, industrial waste, medical waste, offal, abbatoir dumpings, and on and on—and provided drinking water all the while—until well into the nineteenth century, meaning, by composition, the Thames was very much "like a silver turd." Ackroyd points out that Spenser, Herrick, Pope, and Drayton all described the Thames with the "silver" epithet, meaning the Pythons would have found the simile in their classical readings (*London* 532-33).

– M –

"married to Vern Plachenka (Julie Christie) but secretly deeply in love . . . "—(*"Life of Tschaikowsky"*) This thumbnail sketch of the plot sounds very much like a spoof of the recent hit film *Dr. Zhivago* (1965), starring Omar Sharif and Julie Christie.

"Metropolitan Railway"—(*"Emigration from Surbiton to Hounslow"*) Britain's national rail service for the Greater London area, and including the underground sections. The Metro Railway opened in January 1863.

This station is in Twickenham, and permission for what looks like early morning shooting had to be obtained from British Railways. These shots were made on 4 November 1971 (WAC T12/1,482).

"Minister for Overseas Development"—(*"Mrs Nigger-Baiter Explodes"*) The Ministry for Overseas Development was set up in 1964 as a separate ministry to develop and oversee colonial economic matters. This ministry was a combination of the Department of Technical Cooperation, as well as "the overseas aid policy functions of the Foreign, Commonwealth Relations and Colonial Offices" ("DFID Historical").

By 1970, though, the ministry was again dissolved and its functions transferred to the Secretary of State for Foreign and Commonwealth Affairs, with the overseas work then under the aegis of the Overseas Development Administration (ODA).

During the period this sketch was written/performed (1971-1972), the man filling this ministerial position was the Right Honorable Richard Wood (1970-1974). There is no indication that Wood lived with his aged mother in this way, but he was in the news as he traveled to Pakistan after a particularly devastating cyclone in December 1970, ostensibly to bring millions of pounds in relief and aid packages, but instead disingenuously proffering already-promised funds with significant interest and restrictive quid pro quo trade agreements attached (*Private Eye* 187 December 1970, 22).

"Ministry"—(*"Farming Club"*) In this case MAFF, the Ministry of Agriculture, Fisheries and Food. James Prior was the minister in place 1970-1972.

Mother Goose—(*"Puss in Boots"*) One of the well-known pantomimes performed during Christmas in Britain, others include *Peter Pan, Sleeping Beauty, Dick Whittington, Aladdin,* and *Snow White*. All feature audience participation, cross-dressing (ugly sisters played by men), pratfalls, song, and broad humor. Python employs the pantomime goose a number of times in *FC*, as well as pantomime horses, and even a pantomime Princess Margaret (see Eps. 29, 30).

"Mrs David . . . Number 3"—(*"The BBC Is Short of Money"*) Atalanta 3 was a chestnut born in 1948, and had a career including seventy-six starts, twenty wins, seven places, and ten shows. David Barker rode North Flight at the Tokyo Olympics in 1964.

– N –

naked sailor—(PSC; *"Life of Tschaikowsky"*) This photo (shot by Robert Broeder) was used earlier, in Ep. 2 (WAC T12/1,427). One of the more pernicious rumors of the period was that Tchaikovsky's intimate relationship with a nobleman's son may have led to the composer's suicide (or even murder) by poisoning.

Nazi Fish—(PSC; animated link into *"World War One"*) These three voices are not identified in the written scripts but are as follows: Nazi Fish—Terry Jones; Britisher Fish—Michael Palin; Chinese Fish—Graham Chapman.

"Nelson's Column"—(*"Life of Tschaikowsky"*) Found in Trafalgar Square, the column is 185 feet tall, with a seventeen-foot statue of Nelson atop.

News at Nine—(*"The BBC Is Short of Money"*) Fashioned by the Pythons after ITV's *News at Ten* (ITN, 1967-), which had originally aired in a twelve-minute format at 8:55 p.m. *News at Ten* was one of the top twenty-ranked shows on British TV in 1970-1972. *News at Nine* and anchor Richard Baker will be prominently featured again in Ep. 30, as well as Ep. 33.

"Nigger-Baiter"—(*"Mrs Nigger-Baiter Explodes"*) Literally, the term used here means one who "baits" or taunts, jabs, or calls out a black. (But, if this is being used as the terms bear-baiting and bull-baiting were utilized in Elizabethan times, then the term actually means "the action of baiting a black with dogs." Neither is a particularly attractive option.) It should also be noted that even in the press of the Pythons' youth these terms were ubiquitous. In a *Time* magazine article from 1941 detailing FDR's actions against wildcat strikers, the columnist identifies "the noisy nigger in the strike woodpile" (16 June 1941). In this article the term is used as an inoffensive colloquialism, and not intended as a bit of inflammatory speech (the magazine's white, upper-middle-class readership acknowledged). By the 1960s the level of sensitivity had increased somewhat, at least in the popular press, and the "nigger-baiter" term is often printed as "race-baiter," instead. (A number of these characters appeared in films looking at American soldiers in WWII, becoming almost a type, or stock character.)

The level of racial insensitivity during this period on British television programs has to be looked at in the context of the times, as the Pythons (and others) felt free to use terms like "Nip," "Jap," "Wop," and "Darkie" without apology and, importantly, without censure. Just a generation earlier the Goons had used black bandleader Ray Ellington as the butt of myriad jokes focusing on his skin color, many of which Ellington himself initiated (at least textually). The cartoons the Pythons (and their viewers and employers) grew up with were also quite racially insensitive, with the major American studios (including Warner Bros., MGM, and Disney) producing countless images of shiftless, lazy, shuffling black characters throughout the 1930s and 1940s. See WB's *Inki and the Mynah Bird* (1943), directed by Chuck Jones, for instance. (See Bogle's *Toms, Coons, Mulattoes, Mammies, & Bucks* for more on the subject, and it becomes disturbingly clear just what cinematic and television depictions of blacks the Pythons could draw from.) Hispanic characters suffered the same stereotyping in the "Speedy Gonzalez" cartoons, as well. There isn't any indication in the WAC records for the show that the BBC higher-ups—who complained liberally about depictions of Christ and cannibalism and the royals, etc.—ever lodged an official complaint in regard to the depiction of any foreigner, race, or use of racially charged term.

It is worth pointing out, however, that the character with such an offensive name ("Nigger-Baiter by name, Nigger-Baiter by nature"?) is immediately destroyed in the text, as if suffering instant karmic retribution. In the feature film *Meaning of Life* (1983), the charwoman (Jones) cleaning up after Mr. Creosote (also Jones) is textually punished immediately after she admits she's glad she doesn't work for Jews. The "grinning type monster" Michael Miles character (Cleese) in Ep. 20 is not punished, however, for disliking "darkies," so the Pythons clearly pick and choose their moments.

"not Church people"—("Vicar/Salesman") This is usually a response to door-to-door evangelizing, but in this case potential converts are actually potential customers, and they're not going to *buy* a product because they don't happen to be members of the Church of England. This equating of organized religion and boundless greed is seen earlier in *FC*. In Ep. 24, the Pythons offer Arthur Crackpot as the unapologetic money-grubber in the guise of an organized religious leader, while in Ep. 6, the vicar is clearly stealing from the donation box.

"not religious"—Again, its not what's for sale, per se, but the fact that something is being sold by a man of the cloth. Here the selling of traditional door-to-door items is equated with the selling of salvation by representatives of the church (ostensibly the Church of England), and of religion in general.

– O –

"old poof"—("*Life of Tschaikowsky*") Tchaikovsky was in fact a closet homosexual, and spent much of his life fighting against his inclinations, at least publicly. He did even marry, disastrously, and eventually (some scholars have asserted) took his own life rather than be publicly revealed as a practicing homosexual (see Orlova).

"Omalley"—(The BBC Is Short of Money") Misspelled here in the printed scripts. Harvey Smith placed third on "O'Malley" in the 1963 European Show Jumping Championships.

– P –

"Panorama report"—("Schoolboys' Life Assurance Company") *Panorama* is a long-running interview/presentation program on BBC-TV (1953-) featuring interviewers Robin Day and Richard Dimbleby, and others. The Pythons often use the *Panorama* "style" for their documentary and interviewing spoofs.

"Parsons Green"—("Emigration from Surbiton to Hounslow") In Hammersmith, south and west of the City of London. This is not far south of BBC Television Centre in Shepherd's Bush.

"Pasteur"—(link out of "Vicar/Salesman") Dr. Louis Pasteur (1822-1995) was a renowned French chemist who pioneered work in bacteria, Pasteurization, and vaccines. For many, the idea of inoculation (introducing a virus into the host to stimulate antibody production, thus protecting the host) did promote skepticism, even as late as Pasteur's era. So, the Doctor (Chapman) is merely mimicking this treatment regimen, though with dynamite, and more lethal results.

"people explode everyday"—("Mrs. Nigger-Baiter Explodes") Spontaneous human combustion was much in the news in the UK in the mid-1960s, especially after the publication of a paper entitled "A Case of Spontaneous Combustion" by Dr. David Gee of the University of Leeds. Previously thought to be quite supernatural, the phenomena of people exploding in flames was in 1965 gifted with a critical, academic explanation, and was much-discussed in the contemporary media.

photo of two ballet dancers—(PSC; "Trim-Jeans Theatre") These still photos were taken by Joan Williams, who also contributed photos to Eps. 22 and 26 (WAC T12/1,415).

picture of Tschaikowsky—(PSC; "*Life of Tschaikowsky*") This photo of the composer is borrowed from the Mansell Collection (WAC T12/1,427).

pigs appear on the screen—(PSC; "Farming Club") These stock pig photos (AG3131 and AG6256) were taken by Thomas A. Wilkie (WAC T12/1,427).

poofy presenter—("*Life of Tschaikowsky*") This could be a lampoon of film critic Barry Norman (1933-), host of *Film* (BBC1) from 1972 to 2002, or even another jab at Philip Jenkinson, who was spoofed in Ep. 23, and who will be dealt with rather violently (and gleefully) in Ep. 33.

"Port of Spain"—("Puss in Boots") In Trinidad and Tobago, on the Gulf of Paria, in the Caribbean. Venezuela ships iron ore through this port regularly.

"Potato Marketing Board"—("Farming Club") One of many agricultural products marketing boards meant to raise awareness of a domestic product via advertising and information, keeping prices high and providing subsidies for domestic production in the face of international competition.

The Egg Marketing Board had made the news very recently, being scrapped in 1971 due to inefficiency. Overall, these boards as presented by the Pythons seem like a combined "traditional English breakfast" marketing board.

principal boy—(PSC; "Puss in Boots") The principal boy is the leading actor in a pantomime, and traditionally is played by a girl/woman. This role here was originally intended for Beulah Hughes (*The Hands of Orlac*), Carol Cleveland, or Diana Quick (*Complete and Utter History of Britain*), all mentioned by name in notes for the episode, but is instead played by Julia Breck (see WAC T12/1,427 and T12/1,428). Breck appeared with Spike Milligan in his *Q* series, as well as in the controversial Andy Warhol play *Pork* (1971) in its London debut at the Roundhouse.

"Purley and Esher"—("Emigration from Surbiton to Hounslow") Esher is a residential suburb of London in Surrey, and is often mentioned (interchangeably with Purley) in *FC* as the backwater of the Commonwealth. Purley is south of London along the A23.

"Putney Public Library"—("Emigration from Surbiton to Hounslow") This library is currently located at 5/7 Disraeli Road SW15 2DR.

– Q –

quayside—("Fish-Slapping Dance") This scene was shot at Teddington Lock, Richmond upon Thames, just a few miles from Broadcast Centre.

– R –

"Ra 1 . . . Ra 2"—("Emigration from Surbiton to Hounslow") The 1970 Heyerdahl expedition on a reed boat from North Africa to the New World was called "Ra 1." This boat began to take on water very near the end of the voyage, and had to be abandoned, though the crew felt it could have continued successfully.

"Ra 2"—One year after the Ra 1 failure, the redesigned Ra 2 set sail, making the voyage successfully, proving that such trips, even anciently, were possible, and that there could have been cross-cultural influences between ancient civilizations long thought to be mutually isolated. A documentary film and book followed the celebrated journey.

Red Indians—(PSC; "World War One") The stereotypical outfit from myriad Hollywood films and television shows, including feather headdress, face paint, and buckskin leggings.

"Remaindered"—("Emigration from Surbiton to Hounslow") This means the store is selling the book at a reduced price to be rid of it.

"Renaissance courtier . . . Borgias"—("World War One") The Borgias were Italians (via Spain), descendants of Pope Alexander IV, and very powerful figures in Italy, attracting poets and artists alike. Lucrezia Borgia (1480-1519) and her brother Cesare (1476-1507) were noted members of the family, and led the Italian (Roman) Renaissance-era court and culture.

The Medicis were Florentine socialites and behind-the-scenes political leaders from the fifteenth century to 1737. The family produced three popes and two queens of France.

A "Renaissance courtier artist" look may have been borrowed from or at least inspired by several paintings in the National Gallery, including *Portrait of a Gentleman* (1550s) and *Knight with His Jousting Helmet* (1530s), both by Giovanni Battista Moroni. (The headdress/hat doesn't match at all, however, especially the tassels.) Raphael's (1483-1520) *Self-Portrait* (1506) and *Self-Portrait With His Fencing Master* (1518) don't fit this look at all, and Leonardo Da Vinci's *Musician* (1470s) shows a young Italian artist wearing a simple felt cap and undershirt, tunic and vest. (There probably wasn't a uniform for courtiers or artists, though, so the Python's "impression" approach actually makes some historical sense.) Stibbert's 1914 book offers significant period illustrations, including "Young Venetian Gentlemen of the 15th Century," none of which precisely match the Python version (*Abiti E Fogge Civile E Militari Dal I Al XVII Secolo*).

There are examples in the mid-fifteenth century of hats much like the one the sailor sports in the episode, but most of the wearers are French aristocrats. (See Jules Quicherat, *Histoire du costume en France*, Paris, 1875.) Stibbert offers at least one example of a young Flemish man (occupation/status unknown) wearing a costume much like the one in the episode, in a print labeled "15 Century Flemish Dress."

Finally, the costume shop request for this week's episode called for Idle to be dressed in, simply, a "medieval outfit," so it's rather interesting to see what they came up with, and how "medieval" became "Renaissance" (WAC T12/1,427).

"Richardson, Sir Ralph"—("Trim-Jeans Theatre") Richardson (1902-1983) was a noted stage and screen actor and, also coincidentally, appeared in the film version of *Long Day's Journey Into Night* (1962).

"Richmond and Isleworth"—("Emigration from Surbiton to Hounslow") These cities lie just across the Thames from each other. The bridge(s) in this shot are the Twickenham Rail Bridge and Twickenham Bridge. The Rail Bridge is in the foreground. These scenes were shot in October 1971, according to a memo from crewmember George Clarke. They also shot some of the Norrises driving scenes on Arlington Road, Chertsey Road, and St. Margaret's Road in East Twickenham (WAC T12/1,428).

"Richter, Sviatoslav"—("*Life of Tschaikowsky*") Famed concert pianist (1915-1997) born in the Ukraine who performed Haydn, Rachmaninoff, Schubert, Prokofiev, Schumann, Mussgorsky, Beethoven, and others, and was considered the finest Russian pianist of his generation. There is no record of Richter performing (in public) any Tchaikovsky piece after 1960. He performed the piece in December 1940 and January 1941 (in Russia), February 1942, March and May 1950, May 1954, November 1957, February 1958, December 1960 (see "Sviatoslav Richter Chronology," at trovar.com).

Richter first performed in London at the Royal Festival Hall July 1961, then again in January and February 1963, June 1966 and June 1967, October and November 1968 (Royal Festival and Goldsmith's Hall, respectively), October and November 1969, etc.

ripple—(PSC; "Puss in Boots") Traditional TV special effect that has come to signify an approaching dream sequence, or that a flashback is about to be recounted. The Pythons, of course, draw attention to the usually invisible transition by not completing the transition, and forcing the narrative to go on anyway.

"Round Table"—("Emigration from Surbiton to Hounslow") An actual discussion group of similarly minded enthusiasts, the Round Table organization was formed in Norwich in 1927 by Louis Marchesi. See Ep. 10 for more on Round Table.

Royal Albert Hall—(PSC; "*Life of Tschaikowsky*") Located across from Hyde Park on Kensington Gore, in London, and opened in 1871. Richter first played the Royal Albert Hall in 1961.

"Russell, Ken"—("*Life of Tschaikowsky*") Film director Russell (1927-) had already created TV films on Prokofiev, Elgar, Bartok, Debussy, and Tchaikovsky, and was in production on a film about Gustav Mahler in 1971. Being "born in a Ken Russell film" would refer to Russell's penchant for squalor—inner and outer—where characters like Dante Alighieri (*Dante's Inferno*, 1967) struggle with psychosexual problems in the detritus of the postlapsarian world. Tchaikovsky would very much have been one of these tortured characters. Also, Russell's 1970 film *The Music Lovers* (about Tchaikovsky) would have been many viewers' introduction to the composer, meaning he was "born" to them in that Ken Russell world.

Russell will be mentioned again in Eps. 29 and 33, his repeated appearances indicating he was something of a front-pager at this time.

Other references in this fictional film cast include:

"Leo McKern"—Actor McKern (1920-2002) had most recently appeared in the David Lean epic *Ryan's Daughter* (1970), and had also appeared in *A Man For All Seasons* (1966), *Help!* (1965), and *The Running, Jumping and Standing Still Film* (1959). He had also played Third Knight in the 1952 film version of *Murder in the Cathedral*—based on the death of Thomas Becket—directed by George Hoellering. (See the "Trim Jeans" notes below for more on this connection.) As a "freelance bishop," this character would be a Bishop somehow not affiliated with any organized religion, or perhaps one who is available to move from see to see. The C of E does not have celibacy vows as part of its dogma, so this Bishop could have been married.

"Julie Christie"—Actress Christie (1941-) was by this time internationally known for playing Lara in *Dr. Zhivago* (1965) and Bathsheba Everdene in *Far From the Madding Crowd* (1967).

"Shirley Abicair"—Australian-born actress/singer Abicair (1930-) came to the UK to break into TV performance, playing her zither and singing folk and contemporary songs. She appeared on children's shows, variety shows, and in a few films. She also appeared later on the *Eurovision Song Contest* show.

"Madame Ranevsky"—Character in Chekhov's *The Cherry Orchard*, she has fled Paris for the safety of her home, though the tragedy there and the fate of the orchard combine to prevent her from escaping into her nostalgic memories. Chekhov will be mentioned prominently later, also in the "Trim Jeans" sketch.

"Norris McWhirter"—Co-founder of the Guinness Book of World Records, McWhirter (1925-2004) also appeared for many years on the *Record Breakers* TV show which appeared in 1972. The fact that the Pythons cast a man into a woman's part shouldn't be surprising, nor was it terribly rare. Leo McKern, for example, had played the role of Duchess in the 1966 *Alice in Wonderland* adaptation for BBC1.

"Eldridge Cleaver"—Eldridge Cleaver (1935-1998) was an American black revolutionary, a "minister of information" for the Black Panthers Party in the late 1960s. Cleaver had appeared in the *Black Panther* documentary in 1969 with fellow members Huey Newton and Bobby Seale, as well as *Eldridge Cleaver, Himself* in 1970, the latter an Algerian documentary. Cleaver's book, *Soul on Ice*, was published in 1968 after he was released from prison. Cleaver had been in exile (in Algeria) since 1969, and would not return to the United States until 1975. (The Algerian exile may tie Cleaver to the earlier Sartre reference, the French philosopher very much sympathetic—and vocally so—to the Algerian cause.)

"Moira Lister"—Lister (1923-) is a South African-born actress who had appeared in 1968 on *The Eamonn Andrews Show* (mentioned in the script for Ep. 26). Lister is characterized as playing a "posh lady," which would seem to be the Pythonesque counterpart for Eldridge Cleaver and a character named Stan the Bat. Lister is mentioned, then featured, respectively, on the covers of the 17 and 24 May 1969 *Radio Times* for her appearance in *The Very Merry Widow* (BBC1 Friday).

"Stan the Bat"—This could be a reference to Stan Musial, superstar American baseballer elected to the Hall of Fame in 1969. It also could be "Stan the Bat" is just a silly name along the lines of childrens'-show characters "Muffin the Mule" (Ep. 22) or "Basil Brush" (see notes for "Boom boom!" in Ep. 30). There's even the possibility it's an oblique reference to Stan McCabe (1910-1968), the Australian batsman who stood up so well against the infamous English fast-leg bowlers in the Body-line series in 1932. (See notes to Ep. 20 for more on this memorable series.) Lastly, and most likely, there are rumblings of a somewhat fearsome table tennis player in the UK who called himself "Stan the Bat," aka Stanley Battrick (1931-1998), an Essex player who excelled in veteran's play. Battrick's passing is noted in the *Essex Gazette* (14 December 1998).

"Omsk"—Major industrial city/region in Western Siberia; Russia, also a home for political prisoners beginning in the nineteenth century, including Fyodor Dostoevsky. Omsk has already been mentioned in passing by the Newsreader (Cleese) in Ep. 3 as he's being stolen from TV Centre.

"Eddie Waring"—British TV and sporting news personality, Waring (1910-1986) is first mentioned in Ep. 1, in the "Famous Deaths" sketch. Waring also appeared in episodes of *The Goodies* (1973, 1975) and *It's A Knock-*

out (1966). In this sketch Eddie is portraying the entire city/region, it seems.

"Anthony Barber"—There is also a prominent Australian television personality of this name, and very active during this period, but this is more clearly a reference to the Right Honourable Anthony Barber (1920-2005), a front-page Conservative politician and Cabinet member. Barber will be mentioned again and his picture shown (as a potential "loony") in Ep. 38. Barber had beeen named Chancellor of the Exchequer by Heath in 1970, meaning he was the focus of the British public's anger and frustration during the economic malaise of the early 1970s, especially as National Health Service cutbacks and charges were introduced.

"Russians and the Chinese"—("How to Rid the World of All Known Diseases") During this period, the nuclear and conventional saber rattling between the Russian and Chinese governments was at its highest following a series of nasty border wars in 1969. See the notes for "Revisionist" in Ep. 27.

– S –

"sceptical about my work"—(link out of "Vicar/Salesman") A reference back to Heyerdahl's difficulty convincing established academicians as to the worth of his theses, viz., that ancient maritime technology was sufficiently advanced for trans-Atlantic journeys, and/or that allegedly less-advanced peoples could make such a perilous trip at all.

school . . . caps—(PSC; "World War One") This is the same schoolboy outfit Chapman will wear in Ep. 29 ("Salvation Fuzz") when he announces he's found another "dead bishop on the landing."

scrubland—(PSC; "Trim-Jeans Theatre") This looks to be on the premises of a BBC transmission tower, and is likely the Booster Station near Gallanach (WAC T12/1,428). These scenes were recorded in October 1971. In the first two series, location shooting was completed by summer, for the most part, meaning that by the time the Pythons got around to shooting these scenes it was quite a bit colder, especially further north in Scotland.

"scuppers"—("Puss in Boots") The opening on a ship's deck that allows water to drain from the surface of the deck.

"Seagull . . . Chekhov"—("Trim-Jeans Theatre") Anton Chekhov (1860-1904) was a Russian dramatist and short story writer. The Moscow Art Theater produced his play *The Seagull* in 1898. He died of tuberculosis at age forty-four in Germany.

semi-detached house—("Emigration from Surbiton to Hounslow") Two houses joined together (built as one, duplex-style), and originally identical on either side. Using the conveniently placed light pole as divider, the shot mentioned here makes it look as if they've created a split-screen effect, when in fact it's a non-process shot. This scene was actually shot in Hounslow (WAC T12/1,428).

"sent to Moscow"—("*Life of Tschaikowsky*") Tchaikovsky moved to Moscow in 1866 to teach at the Moscow Conservatory, after three years teaching privately in the St. Petersburg Conservatory.

"Shazam"—(PSC; "Mrs Nigger-Baiter Explodes") "Shazam" is the magic word spoken by Billy to become Captain Marvel, and first appeared in Whiz Comics in 1940.

Showbiz music—(PSC; "It's") The music is "Theatre Overture" by A. Mawer, which has become a popular cell phone ring tone recently.

"Sleeping Beauty . . . Fanny forte"—("*Life of Tschaikowsky*") All Tschaikovsky compositions. *Sleeping Beauty* composed 1875-1876; "Pathetique" (Symphony No. 6) composed 1893; the "1812 Overture" composed 1880. He composed myriad pieces for the pianoforte (the instrument that replaced the harpsichord and clavichord), as well as several for piano and violin.

Slightly eerie music—(PSC; "Puss in Boots") The accompanying music underneath the Captain's (Jones) scary story is from "Theatre Overture Dramatic and Horror," "String Suspenses" by Paul Lewis, while the (unsuccessful) transitional music is from Harp Solos, "Descending Glissando," by Gareth Walters (WAC T12/1,427).

"small rat"—("Puss in Boots") Presaging the small white rabbit that will wreak so much havoc in the cave scene of *Holy Grail*.

"Smith, Harvey"—("The BBC Is Short of Money") Famous Yorkshire showjumper of the 1960s and 1970s, Smith also competed in the 1968 Mexico City Olympic games with his horse Madison Time. Fellow Brit David Broome competed, as well, on Mr. Softee. Smith also competed in the 1972 Olympics on Summertime.

"Smith, Pat Hornsby"—("The BBC Is Short of Money") Hornsby-Smith (1914-1985) was a Conservative representing Chislehurst, and serving in the House of Commons 1950-1966, and 1970-Feb. 1974, and then in the House of Lords 1974–1985. She was named Dame Commander of the British Empire (DBE), and granted a Life Peerage in 1974. She also held these offices: Parliamentary Secretary, Ministry of Health (1951-1957), Joint Under-Secretary of State, Home Office (1957-1959), and

Joint Parliamentary Secretary, Ministry of Pensions & National Insurance (1959-1961).

South . . . state—("PSC; "World War One") Later this "South American" country is named as Venezuela, but during this period (early 1970s) the so-called police states in South America might have included Chile (under Pinochet), Paraguay (under Stroessner), Uruguay (under Bordaberry), Bolivia (under Suárez), Ecuador (under Lara), and Brazil (under Silva, then, ironically, Gen. Emilio Garrastazú *Médici*).

Venezuela during this period was moderately stable thanks to a president (Raúl Leoni [1906–1972]) who utilized coalition governments to keep many ideologies (left, right, and center) happy and represented.

Starr, Ringo—(PSC; "It's") The former Richard Starkey (b. 1940) makes his only appearance on the show, and would have been an ex-Beatle by this time. The Pythons had working and personal relationships with The Beatles during this period. In Ep. 24, Idle dresses as John Lennon for a vox pop moment, and after *FC*, he would form the mock Fab Four group The Rutles. Another ex-Beatle, George Harrison (with Denis O'Brien) would, in 1978, assist the Pythons in obtaining financing and distribution for their controversial *Life of Brian*, through Handmade Films.

"statement . . . six"—("Mrs Nigger-Baiter Explodes") The Rhodesia question had been front and center since at least 1953, when calls for independence began to be acknowledged by the British government. Rhodesia's white minority would declare unilateral independence in 1965 under Ian Smith (b. 1919), causing concern and consternation to both Conservative and Labour administrations. Cf. Ep. 45 for much more. The Son (Cleese) is preparing to speak in the House of Commons, the lower, elected house of Parliament—such speeches tended to be in favor of finding a way to deal with Smith, to cajole him out of minority rule, and do postcolonial damage control on the international stage (*Eyewitness: 1960-69*, "Rhodesia Unilateral Declaration of Independence 1965").

Stirring music—(PSC; "Emigration from Surbiton to Hounslow") The music here and later in this film is from New Concert Orchestra, Background Music, "Sinfonia Tellurica" and "Homines" by Trevor Duncan (WAC T12/1,427).

"Storey, David"—("Trim-Jeans Theatre") David Storey (1933-) is a playwright and novelist who first came to attention in 1963 for his working-class, "Angry Young Man" novel *This Sporting Life*, which would then quickly become a movie, as well, directed by Lindsay Anderson. (See notes to Ep. 2 for more on this working-class film/play/novel movement.)

Storey's play *Home* (1970) won the New York Critics Best Play of the Year Award, and became something of a surprising star vehicle for Richardson and Gielgud, who were by this time middle-aged.

Lastly, there is a different take possible when this line is listened to/performed, and not read from the script. It sounds as if Gielgud and Richardson are losing inches as they "act" in Storey's home (house), lending a more sexual interpretation to the moment, and perhaps commenting on at least Gielgud's homosexuality (Richardson was married, and father of one child), and/or even Storey's work in *Radcliffe*, featuring a sexual relationship between a gay man and a married man. (Gielgud had been arrested, coincidentally, for "cottaging" in Chelsea Mews in 1953, meaning he was visiting a public lavatory for the purposes of casual homosexual sex. These bathrooms were designed to look like cottages, or small homes.)

stuffed cat—(PSC; "Puss in Boots") Could be Puss from *Puss-in-Boots*, but could also represent the cat from *Dick Whittington*, another very popular pantomime.

"Surbiton"—("Emigration From Surbiton to Hounslow") Further south and still west of London than Hounslow, as well, and very near New Malden. As if the set-up for this sketch isn't absurd enough, there is and has been a London United (bus service) route, number 281, that runs from Hounslow to Tolworth via Surbiton.

"Swan Lake"—("Trim-Jeans Theatre") Another Tchaikovsky mention, *Swan Lake* is his 1875-1876 ballet.

– **T** –

tannoy—(PSC; "World War One") Loudspeaker system.

"tassles"—("World War One") Misspelled version of "tassels." There doesn't seem to have been a precedent for tasseled hats in either Flanders or Italy during the fourteenth to sixteenth centuries, though embroidered chevrons were part of much Renaissance sewing practice during the period.

"fitted doublets"—A tight-fitting garment worn about the shoulders and chest, a kind of early jacket, and could be sleeved or sleeveless. Common between the fourteenth and eighteenth centuries throughout Europe.

"This is BBC 2"—(link out of "Puss in Boots") As early as 1966, PM Wilson was threatening to de-fund and starve to death BBC2, seeing it as an expensive drag on the government, and not a little superfluous: "I don't see why we need to increase licence fees to pay for a programme that no one wants to see—and

many can't see even if they wanted to" (Freedman 30). *Flying Circus*, of course, would be one of these little seen BBC2 shows just four years later.

"Thor . . . Hillary"—("Emigration From Surbiton to Hounslow") Thor Heyerdahl (1914-2002) was an anthropologist and explorer who studied and then physically attempted to prove the thesis of ancient peoples performing intercontinental travels. Heyerdahl was from Norway.

Sir Edmund Hillary (1919-2008) was probably the first (in recorded history) to reach the summit of the tallest mountain in the world, Mt. Everest, on 29 May 1953, with his guide/companion Tenzing Norgay, a Nepalese Sherpa. Hillary was a New Zealander. More on Hillary and the climb in Ep. 31.

"three-stage model"—("*Life of Tschaikowsky*") This "Tchaikowsky XII" set-up is fashioned after the often quite enthusiastic Apollo mission coverage on both UK and U.S. television networks. The Apollo XII mission was carried out in November 1969.

In the UK, ITN carried *Man on the Moon* (21 July 1969) and BBC presented *Apollo 11-Man on the Moon* (BBC2), both of which offered live reports and live coverage of the first moon landing. The BBC's coverage stretched from 15 July through 24 July. For the BBC, it was James Burke (b. 1936; Ep. 35) who handled the plastic mock-ups of the Saturn V rocket and lunar module/command ship that could be broken down into constituent parts as the mission proceeded.

"tighter, firmer, neater"—("Trim-Jeans Theatre") In an extant print ad version of this advertisement, Coover is credited with saying "tighter, firmer, and 10 1/2 inches trimmer." Gary is also shown standing casually, and wearing a dark T-shirt and leather sandals, just like the Pythons in the sketch. The company in the print ad is listed as "Sauna Belt Incorporated," with headquarters in San Francisco, California. There was no London home office for the company during this period.

"Tooting"—("Emigration from Surbiton to Hounslow") Part of Greater London, just east of Wimbledon. Tooting is mentioned by the narrator in Neville Shunt's play *It All Happened . . .* in Ep. 24.

"transmissions for this evening can be continued as planned"—("The BBC is Short of Money") It was actually reported that in mid-December 1970 the BBC was actively pursuing what might be termed "innovative" means of prolonging the broadcast day in the face of national power shortages:

Last Monday, the day on which the first power cuts struck the nation, the BBC commissionaires set off round the TV Centre instructing all typists to turn their office lights out. It was explained to the girls that if they all switched off there might be just enough power for *Panorama* to go out that evening. (*Private Eye* 18 December 1970, 6)

"Treasure Island"—("Trim-Jeans Theatre") See notes to Ep. 25 for more on *Treasure Island* and Long John Silver (and the Pythons' repeated reference to them).

"Trigorin"—("Trim-Jeans Theatre") He is a writer, and a prolific one, whose lament is that he *must* write, finishing one story and immediately starting another. He calls it "a dog's life." This may have been how the Pythons began to feel as the show moved on, especially Cleese, who had wanted to explore new ideas and especially venues as early as during the second series. By summer 1971 Cleese was indicating to his agent that he was interested in exploring something other than Monty Python episodes the following year. (The nature of British TV during this period was for more shows and shorter runs, which is why the Pythons could work for so many different shows before and even during *FC*.) The BBC's Duncan Wood had tried to start contract negotiations (via letters to agents) with the troupe for a fourth season (a minimum of six shows) on 20 August 1971 (WAC T12/1,428). Cleese would eventually opt out of this new contract.

Trim Gentlemen of Verona, The—("Trim-Jeans Theatre") *The Two Gentlemen of Verona* (c. 1592-1598) is seen by many as a minor Shakespeare comedy.

trim-jeans—(PSC; "Trim–Jeans Theatre") An actual line of weight loss products (c. 1967), the identification of which—by actual name—is unusual. Normally, the Pythons will alter the name and just mimic the sales pitch (as in Whizzo Butter, Crelm Toothpaste, FibroVal Soap Powder), perhaps to avoid litigation, copyright problems, etc. See notes for "lose inches" above for more on the Trim-Jeans phenomena.

"Trim Jeans Theatre Presents"—("Trim-Jeans Theatre") In the early days of British and U.S. radio and TV, individual shows often were directly sponsored by advertisers like Palmolive, Colgate, Bell Telephone, Texaco, etc. (*The Flintstones* and *I Love Lucy*, for example, were both sponsored by tobacco companies, and the characters smoked the product in title sequences or commercial breaks.) The products may have been mentioned in these slots, but weren't often featured as part of the fictional world of the production. Here the line is certainly crossed as actors wear the Trim Jeans, not unlike the previous episode (Ep. 27) where North Malden inserted itself into an Icelandic saga.

There were also so-called Admag shows on early British TV, where products and services were pre-

sented by characters in a fictional world, like a sales documentary. See notes to Ep. 27 for more on this phenomenon.

"Tschaikowsky"—("Farming Club") Peter Ilyich Tchaikovsky (1840-1893) was a Russian composer known for numerous operas, concertos, symphonies, and songs. He used European rather than overtly nationalistic Russian "forms and idioms," setting himself apart from his Russian colleagues.

"Tschaikowsky's . . . Minor"—(*Life of Tschaikowsky*) Tschaikowsky's first piano concerto in B Flat Minor (officially the "Concerto for Piano and Orchestra in B flat minor, op. 23") was composed in the winter of 1874-1875 for pianist Nikolai Rubinstein, who hated it after playing it through once. The composition, however, became famous in Europe and the United States very quickly, and even Rubinstein would later work the piece into his performance repertoire for many years.

– U –

"unit-trust . . . facilities"—("Schoolboys' Life Assurance Company") This scheme represents an investment trust where units can be bought by participants, with the value of these units based on the value of investments. Units can be sold back to the trust, as well. The boys, then, acting as portfolio managers of the trust, were selling more units (ostensibly to other classmates at big school) than they could reasonably buy back at any time.

– V –

Voice From Back—(PSC; "Puss in Boots") Not credited, but this voice is Idle. The Second Guard is also Idle, and uncredited. The Third Guard, also uncredited in the printed scripts, is Palin.

– W –

warning signs—(PSC; animated link into "Farming Club") These same kinds of warning/directional signs have been used in many cartoons, including *Inki and the Minah Bird* (Chuck Jones, 1943), and the *Rabbit Fire* (1951), *Rabbit Seasoning* (1952), and *Duck, Rabbit, Duck* (1953) series from Jones. Dante even employed a warning sign over the entrance to Hell: "Abandon hope, all ye who enter here" (*Divine Comedy*).

"sprocket holes . . . view"—This is a very self-conscious moment where the medium is acknowledged, and the artificiality and limitations of the cinematic world are foregrounded. This is not unlike the self-reflexive cartoon *Duck Amuck* (1953), where Daffy is confronted with the artificial and plastic nature of his ink and paint world, or many of Tex Avery's cartoons (at Warner Bros. and MGM). In one Avery cartoon (*Screwball Squirrel*, 1944), Screwy Squirrel lifts the edge of the frame he's in to see what's going to happen to him next, for example, and in *Duck Amuck*, Daffy ends up getting in a fight with an adjoining frame's version of himself. These cartoons, with their hyperviolence, speed, and reflexivity, obviously had a profound influence on the Pythons and the often cartoony world they would later create for television.

"Weldon, Huw"—("The BBC Is Short of Money") BBC Managing Director for Television during this period. The Pythons even joked in internal memos that perhaps Weldon (1916-1986) himself might appear on the episode, playing Paul Fox, if he were asked politely. There is no record that Weldon was actually officially queried about such an appearance (WAC T12/1,428).

well-choreographed . . . toward her—(PSC; "Puss in Boots") The group knows how to react to and perform with this principal boy character, as the rules of the pantomime world are known to them. From the pantomime *Snow White*, the following is a representative scene:

> Wicked Queen: I am the fairest of them all.
> Audience: Oh no you're not!
> Queen: Oh yes I am!
> Audience: Oh no you're not!

The Pythons have created another level of diegetic reality here as the actors shift from their initial roles into roles as pantomime audience members, allowing one narrative to overtake a previous narrative thread. This new reality will also be overthrown when the performance is interrupted by Mrs. Kelly (Palin) and the set is shut down—the characters becoming unemployed actors at that moment.

"Williams, Dorian"—("Puss in Boots") Show jumping broadcaster and commentator, born in 1914.

"women and children first"—("World War One") Though treated comically here, of course, Peter Clarke points out that during the early part of the twentieth century, it was the working man in the British household who received most of the food and money, and virtually all of the meager meat portions of the family diet. Women and children were, as indicated comically in this sketch, put to the back of the line because they were not wage earners, and were therefore somewhat expendable. Both women and children were also far more susceptible to tuberculosis and premature death, primarily because of their poor diets. (See *Hope and Glory: Britain 1900-1990*.)

"'Wrong Way' Norris"—("Emigration from Surbiton to Hounslow") Douglas "Wrong Way" Corrigan (1907-1995) had in 1938 piloted his small plane mistakenly from New York to Ireland, rather than the planned New York to California. His mistake made him quite the celebrity during the hard-bitten times of the Great Depression, and when he arrived back in the United States, the *New York Post* even printed a banner headline—"Hail to Wrong Way Corrigan"—backward on its front page. It's thought by many that Corrigan—who had applied many times for permission to fly nonstop from NY to Ireland, and been denied every time—finally made the trip without permission, and blamed a faulty compass and clouds (David Onkst, U.S. Centennial of Flight Commission).

– Y –

"Yes (successfully)"—("Emigration from Surbiton to Hounslow") Perhaps a comment on achieving the bottom of the hour (8:30 a.m.), but more likely a sexual double entendre.

Episode 29

– A –

"afters"—("Salvation Fuzz") The course that follows the main course in a meal (*OED*). In the time period perhaps being depicted (WWII-era), "afters" were a thing of the past, as shortages and rationing reduced most Britons' diets to subsistence levels.

"Akwekwe"—("Jungle Restaurant") Kwekwe is a town founded on the African gold rush in 1902 in Zimbabwe, Africa.

These "jungle" scenes were shot on film at Ealing TFS on 27 and 28 October 1971 (WAC T12/1,428).

"Alliveldelchi Loma"—("Fraud Film Squad") "Arrivederci Roma," a song written for the 1958 Hollywood musical *Seven Hills of Rome*; the music is by Renato Ranucci, and Italian lyrics by Pierre Garinei and Sandro Giovannini. Perry Como made the song famous in 1966 on his album *Perry Como in Italy*.

"And did these feet in ancient times . . . "—("Salvation Fuzz") From the hymn "Jerusalem" (lyrics by William Blake), used several times in *FC* episodes, including Eps. 4 and 8.

"annex . . . Russia"—("Salvation Fuzz") "Gerald" (Sir Gerald Nabarro, again) calls for precisely what Hitler did, in fact, prior to WWII. Tory MP Nabarro has been mentioned in Eps. 11, 15, 21, and 23, and it's no surprise that since he's a Conservative, the Pythons would align him with Hitler and the National Socialists. The "Norman" mention that follows probably continues the right-bashing reference. See "Norman" below.

There were many on both sides of the political aisle (Labour and Conservative) who either allied themselves with the views of the successful National Socialists prior to the war, or who bent over backward to appease the Nazis up to and including the infamous Munich Agreement. Fear of another world war trumped the rights of certain Europeans in the Sudetenland, for example.

"Antonioni, Michelangelo"—("Six More Minutes of *Monty Python's Flying Circus*") Born in 1912, filmmaker Antonioni's major works were released in the 1960s, including *Blow-Up* (1966), starring the "wooden" David Hemmings (Ep. 8). The films of the various European New Wave directors were very available in the London area, and especially in the West End, meaning the Pythons would have had ample opportunity to see these films.

"argument please"—("Argument Clinic") The implication here is, of course, that anything can be purchased, and that there are such places in the modern UK for any kind of person/malady. At this clinic one can also purchase abuse, complaints, and lessons about being hit on the head.

This is one of the Python sketches that owe a debt to both the music hall stage and, latterly, radio (and more specifically the Goons), as it demands little or no visual accompaniment, and could (and does) play well with just the audio alone. This same kind of dialogue-rich and language-driven sketch will be revisited in Ep. 33, in "Cheese Shop," as well as *Holy Grail*, where two castle guards (Chapman and Idle) are being told to guard the prince (Jones). The camera is essentially locked down for the bulk of this "Who's on first?" kind of scene.

"argument . . . proposition"—("Argument Clinic") Quoted almost verbatim from the *OED*, which defines an "argument" as: "A connected series of statements or reasons intended to establish a position." In Ep. 37, the Pythons will very nearly quote from historian G.M. Trevelyan, specifically from the 1952 edition. See notes to Ep. 37 for more.

"ask the team"—("Salvation Fuzz") As Man (Idle) and Woman (Jones) listen to the radio in the tatty kitchen, the show is a play on the *University Challenge* game show (1962-), which was earlier lampooned by Cleese and Chapman on *At Last the 1948 Show* (1967). The Radio Voice actually sounds like Tim Brooke-Taylor, a member of the *1948 Show* team, though WAC archives offer no confirmation of the actual speaker.

Another Voice—(PSC) Not credited, but this is Michael Palin, and, as "Gerald," he may be another appearance of/reference to Sir Gerald Nabarro; "Norman's Voice" is also uncredited, but this sounds like Cleese, using a "swishy" voice; finally, the "Man's Voice" is Terry Jones.

– B –

"Bailey, Betty"—("Jungle Restaurant") Betty Bailey was a professional diver in the 1930s, as well as the name of a popular dress-up doll in the early 1900s.

"Barclaycard"—("Jungle Restaurant") This line is very hard to hear, meaning the studio audience misses the joke. Barclay's Bank created Barclaycard in 1966, and was the UK's first credit card. By 1972, there may still have been a number of places that did not take this newer card, especially overseas.

"Bath and Wellsish"—("Salvation Fuzz") This is asked and answered as if Bishops can be identified by the diocese they administer. Located in Somerset, the first Bishop of Bath and Wells was appointed by the Pope in 1244. It was during Henry VIII's reign that the diocese became Anglican.

The Bath and Wells bishop may have been mentioned here by virtue of the long-standing tradition (from Richard I) whereby Bath and Wells assisted on the left hand of the new monarch during coronation, with the Bishop of Durham on the right. Richard Dimbleby's hushed, dulcet tones and stream of "great" qualifiers (see notes to Ep. 23) transmitted over the BBC rendered the images vivid and permanent (*Eyewitness 1950-59*, "The Coronation").

blacked up—(PSC; "Six More Minutes of *Monty Python's Flying Circus*") Made up in black-face, as was done in music hall and vaudeville shows (and early films). Hiring performers who were actually black was quite rare in the early days of film and vaudeville. In Ep. 20, "The Attila the Hun Show," Rochester (Idle) is blacked up, as well, even though his namesake was a black man. See notes to Ep. 20.

"British Explorer's Club in the Mall"—(The Lost World of Rouirama") The Explorer's Club was incorporated in 1905, and its London chapter is located at Victoria Court, Knightsbridge. The Traveller's Club (est. 1819) is actually located at 106 Pall Mall.

"Bulldog Drummond"—("The Lost World of Rouirama") Series of films (and a play, and novels) begun in earnest in 1929 and twice starring Ronald Colman (1891-1958) as a British WWI officer-turned-detective. The character as he appeared in novels was quite brutal, racist, and even fascistic, lending credibility to Python's mention of him here as an example of Britain's failed colonial policies.

– C –

Cronaca Di Un Amore—("Six More Minutes of *Monty Python's Flying Circus*") Antonioni's (see bio above) first film was actually *Gente del Po* (1943), which was followed by eight other films before his 1950 film, *Cronaca du un amore*. The Pythons would have perhaps been much less aware of Antonioni's earlier films, as these were more influenced by the tenets of neo-realism, so less reactionary and more stylistically conservative. The descriptions provided by the Pythons are fairly accurate for each film, meaning they've spent significant time watching foreign film.

"colour"—Antonioni's first color film was *Red Desert* (1964), and starred Monica Vitti and Richard Harris.

Crystal Palace—(PSC; "The Lost World of Rouirama") The Crystal Palace was built for the Great Exhibition of 1851, inspired awe in thousands of spectators, and eventually burned down. It's clear from the studio audience's non-reaction to the joke (the "Great Expedition" comment prompting an image of the "Great Exhibition" site) that either they did not hear the prompting phrase, or, more likely, the Crystal Palace wasn't nearly as recognizable as the Pythons thought.

Also, the image of the Crystal Palace would have to be viewed in the studio setting on a television monitor (or even BP screen), meaning the studio audience may have had to look away from the filmed segment to see the insert, and just missed it.

"curlicued"—("*The Money Programme*") Fantastically curled or twisted, while "filigree copperplating" simply means intricately worked plating on a particular coin.

– D –

"dead bishop on the landing"—("Salvation Fuzz") This is primarily funny because it's incongruous—church police, dead bishops, rat tarts—and this also continues the theme visited in Ep. 28, where Thomas Becket's murder was lampooned.

"Du-Bakey"—("Argument Clinic") A misspelled reference to Michael Ellis De Bakey (1908-), who was prominent in world news at this time (he was featured on the cover of *Time* magazine on 28 May 1965). De Bakey in 1966 had implanted the first completely artificial heart into a human. Taken in context with the mention of Barnard below, another heart specialist of the period, the reference seems certain. The later episode entitled "Michael Ellis" (Ep. 41) may also have been named in relation to this man.

"Barnard"—A reference to Dr. Christiaan Barnard (1922-2001), the South African heart surgeon who completed the first human heart transplant in 1967. (Barnard was featured on the cover of *Time* on 15 December 1967.) Barnard has already been mentioned in Ep. 22, where the Batley Townswomen's Guild re-enact the first heart transplant. In 1967 and 1968 Barnard found his smiling face in the pages of *Private Eye*, but only as a target for vilification, especially as his much-celebrated patients deteriorated and died, and Barnard carried on famously.

– E –

ecclesiastical accoutrements—(PSC; "Salvation Fuzz") These appear to include a navy blue or black Latin cassock, white clerical collar, purple gloves (with gold crosses), a green and gold chasuble and stole (without white alb), a cross pendant, and bishop's crook. He looks to be a cross between a Metropolitan policeman and a vicar, naturally.

Elizabethan music—("PSC; "*Erizabeth L*") This bit of music is from The Early Music Consort of London and the Morley Consort—Two Renaissance Dance Bands playing "Passe & Medio & Reprise le Pingue," "Basse Danse," and "Bergeret sans Roche" (WAC T12/1,445).

Elizabethan palace—(PSC; "*Erizabeth L*") This somewhat dilapidated "Elizabethan palace" is actually more a Jacobean house, as construction on what is known as Felbrigg Hall, Norwich, Norfolk began in 1624. The house is shown at such an odd angle because it is attached, on the (viewer's) right side, to another wing built in the classical style some fifty years later. (The inscription above reads, "Gloria Deo In Excelsis.") The Jacobean portion of the house was designed by John Wyndham—twenty-one years after the death of Elizabeth, and one year after James I's death.

As for the actual Tudor palaces and homes, this could be set at any one of about sixty that Henry VIII built, remodeled, or inhabited—including Hampton Court, Windsor Castle, and Nonsuch Palace—during his reign, and that his daughter paid to keep up.

This outdoor shot was recorded on 12 November 1971 (WAC T12/1,428). The interiors are all recorded at Ealing TFS.

"empire building"—("Six More Minutes of *Monty Python's Flying Circus*") A comment on the depictions of Britain's benignly magnanimous empire in British films of the period, and in this case the focus on the travails of white British explorers in black Africa, where all black characters are either toadying or threatening. It makes sense that the African director Akawumba (pretending to be Italian director Antonioni) would be aware of the falseness of these colonial or post-colonial depictions, and decry the "shit."

This fits here in this particular episode, as well, since the conquest of the Spanish Armada in 1588 led to England's rise to international dominance, when empire building could begin in earnest.

Episode 29—Recorded 4 December 1971, but not broadcast until 2 November 1972. This was actually the first episode recorded for the third series, and it was broadcast fourth.

Light Entertainment head Duncan Wood screened recorded episodes 1-9 in September 1972 as they were preparing for broadcast of the third series, and suggested this order for the strongest schedule: Ep. 7 (Ep. 28), 5 (Ep. 27), 1 (Ep. 29), 9 (Ep. 31), 6 (Ep. 32), 4 (Ep. 33), 10 (Ep. 34), 11 (Ep. 35), and 8 (Ep. 37) (WAC T12/1,428).

Also appearing in this episode, according to BBC records: Fred Tomlinson and Singers, Sheila Bromberg (harpist); (as trumpeters and courtiers) Cy Town (*Colditz*), Ron Tingley (*Dr. Who*), Roy Pearce (*Dr. Who*); (as the gorilla) Reuben Martin (*Carry On Up the Jungle*); (as Africans) Omo Ade, Ajibade Arimoro, and Kyesi Kay; and Peter Kodak, Tony Christopher, Jonas Carr, Jay Neil, Roy Brent, Graham Skidmore, and Robyn Williams (see "*Episode*" entries in eps. 36, 37, and 38 for more on these seven); Chet Townsend (*Man About the House*), Frances Pidgeon (*Softly Softly*; *Dr. Who*), Nicholas Ward, Tony Adams, Raymond George (*Secrets of Sex*), Julie Desmond (*Casanova*), Sally Anne, Jean Clarke (*The Borderers*), Jill Lamas, and Daniel Jones (*Asylum*) (WAC T12/1,445).

"Erizabeth L"—("*Erizabeth L*") The BBC had just produced (and then sent to American television screens) the very popular *Elizabeth R* in February-March 1971, starring Glenda Jackson (mentioned in Ep. 28) as the Virgin Queen. The Pythons clearly modelled their costuming demands on this recent and much-watched series.

"Evening all"—("Argument Clinic") Standard greeting of the title character from the long-running folksy

BBC police show *Dixon of Dock Green* (1955-1976), starring Jack Warner (1896-1981) as PC/Sgt. George Dixon. The character first appeared in the 1950 film, *The Blue Lamp*. See notes to Ep. 7 for more on the helpful, genial policeman figure.

The Pythons may be including PC Dixon for sentimental reasons, of course, but the fact that TV clean-up campaigner Mary Whitehouse had given *Dixon of Dock Green* her tacit approval as wholesome television might figure into these depictions. See notes to Ep. 32 for more on Whitehouse and her campaign to clean up British TV.

– F –

"festering gob . . . tit"—("Argument Clinic") "Gob" is northern dialect slang for mouth, and a "tit" in this context would mean a fool.

"toffee-nosed"—One who is snobby. The slang is of British military origin (and according to the *OED*, specifically the Women's Auxiliary Air Force).

"filming us"—("The Lost World of Rouirama") An acknowledgment of the artifice that has become more and more prevalent as the shows have progressed. Part of the troupe's dissatisfaction with the third series was this growing dependence on displaying the man behind the curtain, as it were, the postmodern upending of any narrative track, instead of where they began in 1969—strong gag and character writing, and a healthy dose of irreverence for the television medium. The obvious knowledge of international cinema of the period (Visconti, Antonioni) betrays the troupe's interest in and perhaps influence from the various New Waves sweeping the film world, and those filmmakers' movement away from traditional narrative structures.

"fins"—("Salvation Fuzz") A "rabbit fish" (a rabbit with fins) is an animal more like Gilliam's animated creations. In Ep. 10, the shopkeeper (Palin) will offer to do pet conversions (dog to cat, dog to parrot, etc.).

"Fraud Film Director Squad"—("Fraud Film Squad") There has been a Special Operations Fraud Squad at Scotland Yard for many years, listed as "SO6." The Pythons also couple their inspectors with Flying Squad–type capabilities—officers who respond to crime situations quickly—allowing for trench-coated inspectors to burst through doors and catch folk red-handed, leading to "Flying Fox of the Yard."

– G –

"Gardening Club for 1958"—("Apology for Violence and Nudity") *Gardening Club* made its debut on the BBC in 1955, and ran under that title until 1967, when it became *Gardening World* (Vahimagi 49). Ken Russell's version of *Gardening Club* would, of course, involve more nudity and psychosexual themes and situations. See the entries for Russell in Ep. 28.

Gardening Club music—("*Ken Russell's Gardening Club*") The theme for *Gardening Club* was adapted, here by the Folk Dance Orchestra, and was originally "The Shrewsbury Lasses" by Thompson (WAC T12/1,445).

gorilla tear a man from his table—(PSC; "The Lost World of Rouirama") The gorilla is played by Reuben Martin (1921-1993), who also played a gorilla in several of the *Carry On* films.

"Götterdämmerung epic"—("Fraud Film Squad") A reference to Wagner's "Ring" cycle, and means a sort of apocalyptic or disastrous series of events leading to utter destruction. Visconti's film *The Damned* certainly qualifies in this regard.

– H –

"He has oldeled the whore freet into the Blitish Channer"—("*Erizabeth I.*") England's fortunes were indeed all ventured in this gambit, and the victory became a jumping-off point for the spread of English rule around the globe.

The more contemporary reason for the Pythons' inclusion of a sketch ostensibly about the Spanish Armada is the Christmas-time 1969 broadcast of a *Chronicle* (notes, Eps. 19, 20 and 21) episode called, "The Fate of the Armada," which was introduced by Magnus Magnusson (note, Ep. 21).

"horsefeathers"—("*Erizabeth L*") This is much later (post-Elizabethan), originally U.S. slang meaning "rubbish" or "nonsense."

huge hand descends—(PSC; "Salvation Fuzz") This hand appears to be a blown-up version of the hand of God from the ceiling of the Sistine Chapel, by Michelangelo. It was most likely xerographed at Gilliam's request. The same type of hand appears and strikes dead a high-strung general (Chapman) in *Meaning of Life*. Gilliam's own hand has been pictured a number of times throughout *FC*, continuing the tradition of early animation where the creator was figuratively represented in relation to his character (McCay, Blackton, Fleischer et al.).

– I –

"I don't think you're Luchino Visconti at all"—("*Erizabeth L*") This impostor sequence—especially in its crude audacity (note Visconti's Japanese accent)—is perhaps inspired by the celebrated case of Lobsang Rampa, author of *The Third Eye*. (See notes to Ep. 4, "Secret Service Dentists" sketch, for an earlier reference to this impostor.) Rampa, a self-proclaimed Tibetan monk, published his autobiography *The Third Eye* in 1956; it became a strong seller, but in 1958 he was discovered to be one Cyril Hoskin (1910-1981), originally from Plympton, Devon. The revelation caused something of a furore, but Hoskin continued to write and publish strange books (one dictated to him telepathically from his cat) into the 1980s (*ODNB*).

A poster for Rampa's eleventh book, *Beyond the Tenth* (1969), is seen in the bookshop in Ep. 4.

– J –

"jugged"—("Salvation Fuzz") Food that has been stewed or boiled in a jug (*OED*).

jungle drums—(PSC; "Jungle Restaurant") The drum track is from Guy Warren of Ghana, "African Drums" (WAC T12/1,445).

"just now"—("Argument Clinic") Here, the Man (Palin) tries to restart the original argument and, in true contradictory form, Mr. Vibrating (Cleese) takes him along another path, frustrating him as he searches for an argument while, ironically, having an argument.

– L –

"Leicester"—("Salvation Fuzz") The Bishop of Leicester during this period was the Right Reverend Ronald R. Williams. Chapman was born and raised in Leicester.

"ligging around"—("Erizabeth L") Slang term meaning to sit around, to "sponge" (*OED*).

"Light Entertainment"—("Argument Clinic") Arm of the BBC charged with developing and broadcasting comedy shows, especially, that would please without offending.

"lolly"—("There is Nothing Quite So Wonderful as Money [Song]") Slang term for money, and probably short for "lollipop" (*OED*).

"London Brick Company"—(PSC; "The Lost World of Roiurama") Located in Bedfordshire, the London Brick Company by the mid-1930s had become the largest manufacturer of bricks in the world, and 135 chimneys punctuated the Marston Vale skyline.

The filmed image is culled from BBC SKP 1879-1880 or BBC SKP 1816-9 (WAC T12/1,428).

long corridor—("Erizabeth L") This dark wood, square-paneled construction is typical of the Tudor and then Elizabethan-era palaces, and then even homes, and can still be seen in places like Hampton Court (especially in the older, Wolsey-built sections of the palace, begun as early as 1515) and the dining room at Hardwick Hall, Derbyshire (built 1591-1597), Haddon Hall, etc. The long gallery was a significant room in both the castle and manor of the Elizabethan period, with many stretching more than 100 feet.

This scene was shot at Ealing TFS, using some of the same sets as were seen in Ep. 18, "Accidents Sketch."

– M –

"Marxist ways . . . phase"—("There is Nothing Quite So Wonderful as Money [Song]") Rather prescient, as in 1972 the demise of Communism as a practical political/economic/social tool wasn't at all certain. The Brezhnev era had officially begun earlier in 1971, and the Soviet economy (including wages, crops, and factory output) was on the up, at least according to the speeches given at the twenty-fourth Congress of the Communist Party of the USSR in March 1971.

Money Programme, The—("The Money Programme") Made its debut on BBC2 in 1966, when David Attenborough was in charge, and is by now the BBC's longest-running business and market program. *The Money Programme* was created (from an idea by Harman Grisewood; see notes to Ep. 3) to explain the British market to everyday folk, and especially to make sense of au courant terms like "balance of payment" and "devaluation," both thrown around in the media during this economically difficult time. See the *ODNB* entry for Grisewood for more.

The theme music for the actual *Money Programme* is the familiar "Jimmy Smith Theme" (also known as "The Cat") from "The Carpet Baggers" by Bernstein (WAC T12/1,445).

"Monty Python's Flying Circuses"—(PSC; credit link out of "There is Nothing Quite So Wonderful as Money [Song]") This is the first time in the series that Palin is performing the title, though he's not credited in the printed script.

– N –

native guide—(PSC; "Jungle Restaurant") A black character is in this case actually played by a black actor, which is unusual for Python. The black actors in this scene are Omo Ade (who plays the guide), Ajibade Arimoro, and Kyesi Kay (playing a "pygmy") (WAC

T12/1,428 and T12/1,445). A black man appears in another non-speaking role in Ep. 7, as a jazz musician who becomes a Scotsman. When it comes time in the scene for a black character to speak, however, Jones and Palin, both in black-face, take the roles.

The gorilla in the scene is played by Reuben Martin (*Carry On Up the Jungle*) (WAC T12/1,428), who played a gorilla in several other films, as well.

"nicked"—("Argument Clinic") Interesting colloquial use here, since the word, according to the *OED*, had come to mean "stolen," and not "arrested."

"Nip"—("*Erizabeth L*") WWII-era slang for a Japanese person. Short for "Nippon" (or "Nipponese") the Japanese name for Japan. According to the *OED*, the Royal Air Force was an early employer of the term.

"wop"—U.S. slang for a person of Italian descent, used especially in East Coast cities.

Norfolk jacket and plus fours—(PSC; "The Lost World of Rouirama") "Our Hero" is described as wearing a "Norfolk jacket," a sporting jacket made popular by the Prince of Wales in the nineteenth century, and "plus fours," pants cut four inches below the knee that were also popularized by the future King Edward VII.

This sequence looks and feels very much like a classic nineteenth-century melodrama, complete with over-the-top acting, amateur cast, and very obvious stage makeup. The characters in this and the earlier "Lumberjack Song" sketch were clearly drawn from the "Hearts and Flowers" world of the "mellerdrammer" plays like *East Lynne* ("Gone, and never called me mother!").

"Norman"—("Salvation Fuzz") This somewhat swishy and affected delivery may be a reference to Tory MP Norman St. John Stevas (b. 1929) who never married, loves cats, and appeared on the Ned Sherrin-produced *BBC3* in 1965. Found on BBC1, *BBC3* was essentially a follow-up to Frost's *Not So Much a Programme*. . . . The mention of Sir Gerald Nabarro in the previous question probably confirms the anti-Conservative bias in this sketch.

"Notte, La"—("Six More Minutes of *Monty Python's Flying Circus*") The 1961 Antonioni film starring Marcello Mastroianni, Jeanne Moreau, and Monica Vitti (1931), who also appeared in Antonioni's *L'Eclisse* (1962) and *L'Avventura* (1960).

– O –

"One hundled and thilty-six men of wal"—("*Erizabeth L*") There were actually about 130 warships and merchant ships converted for the fight, so it's possible to call all of them "man of war" ships, since all were armed.

Organ music—(PSC; "Salvation Fuzz") As Klaus (Idle) is accused by the hand of God, a very short section from Bach's "Fantasia & Fugue in G minor" (BWV 542) is used, and was performed by Helmut Walchive (WAC T12/1,445).

"Ossessione . . . 1951"—("Fraud Film Squad") *Ossessione* (1943) is Visconti's neo-realist film, and for many, it is the movement's first installment. *La Terra Trema: Episodio del mare* (1948) is another neo-realist text that looks at the lives of poor fisherman.

The balance of Leopard's (Cleese) arrest explanation also mentions the following:

"*I Bianche Notte*"—The 1957 Visconti adaptation of Dostoyevsky, starring Marcello Mastroianni and Maria Schell.

"Dostocvsky"—Actually, Russian author Fyodor Dostoevsky had died in 1881; his 1848 novel *White Nights* was adapted by Suso Cecchi d'Amico and Visconti for this 1957 film.

"Boccaccio 70"—1962 film directed by Vittorio de Sica, Federico Fellini, and Visconti.

"*The Leopard*"—Big-budget 1963 Visconti film examining the collapse of the aristocracy in nineteenth century Sicily and the rise of Italian unification, and starring Burt Lancaster and Claudia Cardinale.

"Risorgimento"—Meaning renewal or renaissance, the Risorgimento in Italy led to the unification of the country in 1870, with Rome becoming its capital.

"Somerset House"—Home to the General Register Office from 1836 to 1970, where all public records were housed and created. Construction on Somerset House began in 1547. This sprawling building is located on the Strand at the Waterloo Bridge.

"*The Damned*"—*The Damned* is a film very much as described here by Inspector Leopard, though Berger's (b. 1944, Austria) character isn't so much a transvestite as a pedophilic sociopath, and Charlotte Rampling (b. 1945, UK) is anything but curvaceous (she is decidedly thin).

"Dirk Bogarde"—Born in Hampstead, Bogarde (1921-1999) was christened Derek Jules Gaspard Ulric Niven van den Bogaerde, and began his career on the stage before moving to motion pictures.

"elderly poof what expires in Venice"—The plot for Death in Venice does involve the death of a homosexual older man in Venice. It is considered by many (including Bogarde himself) as the actor's finest performance.

– P –

polar expedition . . . pass him—(PSC; "The Lost World of Rouirama") The stuffed expedition described in the script is more of an exotic menagerie when it's presented to viewers, and includes what looks to be a stuffed bear, a llama, a dog or two, and perhaps a flamingo. The group of winter-dressed explorers "Our Hero" (Jones) has been sitting with also includes one dead man, seemingly frozen.

"primeval creatures"—("The Lost World of Rouirama") This was the supposition of various stories about this tepui and others (in Brazil, for example), that prehistoric creatures would be found in this remote, unexplored environment. (The small, hopeless frog *Oreophrynella* is one such creature not discovered until 1898, but in existence for millions of years.)

The subject was in the news recently in the UK. In 1971, a British expedition to the North Ridge of Mount Roraima was undertaken, and a filmed version of the event was shown on the BBC's *World About Us*, and called "To Catch an Orchid." New species of frogs were discovered, but no prehistoric beasts.

– R –

"rabbit fish"—("Salvation Fuzz") Given the WWII-era radio topic (National Socialist policy) and the available food—"rabbit fish" and "strawberry tart"—this scene references the difficult war and postwar years in Great Britain. Rationing (from January 1940) was a part of life in the UK for many years, with coffee, meats, sugar, butter, bacon, etc. all diminished as the war pushed on—remaining scarce in the frugal postwar years, until at least 1954. Beginning in 1940 each family registered with the local government and were given coupons for precisely what they deserved, by age and number of family members, and no more.

In the larger cities especially, where there was less chance of growing a useful garden, Brits had to scrounge and resort to illicit sources for all sorts of items, from cigarettes to tea and, eventually, even bread. Londoners reported many days when bread and milk were the only meals, when housewives had to travel outside the city to buy black market vegetables and dairy products from small farms, and when virtually any kind of small animal could be justified as a meal (*Eyewitness: 1940-49*, "Wartime Austerity"). Fresh strawberries would have been virtually unknown, of course, and strictly controlled if there were any about.

One of the austerity-inspired dishes created under the auspices of the Ministry of Food was known as "Woolton Pie," a vegetable dish meant to be available from non-rationed home garden ingredients, including potatoes, cauliflower, turnips, carrots, rolled oats, and spring onions. Meat would not have been one of the recommended ingredients, rat or otherwise. (Horseflesh became available in some areas, though many refused to buy it.)

"Reichstag"—("Salvation Fuzz") Located in Berlin, it is the nominal seat of German representative government.

"Roiurama"—("The Lost World of Roiurama") Misspelled, but Mt. Roraima is in Venezuela, on the border with Guyana and Brazil, and is a flat-topped mountain (tepui) left unexplored into the nineteenth century. It is said to be the inspiration for Sir Arthur Conan Doyle's *The Lost World*, which became a film in 1925.

"thrown up . . . movements"—Actually, the tepuis are sandstone massifs, and have most likely emerged as a process of erosion over millions of years, not upward thrust.

The image used here of the Roraima Plateau is called "South American Expedition," and is from David Bromhall, Dept. of Zoology, South Park Rd., Oxford (WAC T12/1,428).

"Russell, Ken"—("*Ken Russell's Gardening Club*") Born in 1927, Ken Russell had just finished *The Devils* in 1971, starring Vanessa Redgrave and Oliver Reed. (Most contemporary critics skewered the orgiastic film.) See the entry for Russell in Ep. 28.

The audience would certainly have recognized Russell's name. *The Devils* was only allowed for release with an "X" rating after very significant editing, in accordance with the British Board of Film Classification demands. It also received an "X" rating in the United States.

– S –

sings to piano accompaniment—(PSC; "There is Nothing Quite So Wonderful as Money [Song]") The song "Money, Money, Money" is sung live by Idle, and accompanied by the Fred Tomlinson Singers and harpist Sheila Bromberg. The music was written by Fred Tomlinson, with lyrics by John Gould (WAC T12/1,445).

"Slit Eyes Yakamoto"—("Fraud Film Squad") Fairly run-of-the-mill Python use of racial slur to refer to a person of Asian descent, in this case structured like a gangster's name.

"smell of the rain-washed florin"—("*The Money Programme*") This build-up sequence is written very much like the introduction to the "I'm a Lumberjack" song from Ep. 9, though the earlier song was written by Jones, Palin, and McGuffie.

"society is to blame"—("Salvation Fuzz") The idea of a "permissive society" was quite prevalent at this time, with more conservative elements in the UK (e.g., Mary Whitehouse) certain that the tolerant liberality of these so-called permissives was to blame for the younger generation's immorality, drug use, disrespect of values and tradition, etc. Whitehouse and friends targeted the media, particularly. Contemporary psychiatrists and sociologists were often using "society" (obviating personal choice and accountability) as the hook upon which to hang the blame for troubled teens, seeing, essentially, a lost generation. (See Aldgate's *Censorship and the Permissive Society*.)

There is a quote in the 1952 film *Europa '51* directed by Roberto Rossellini that echoes this sentiment: "If you must blame something, blame our postwar society."

"Spare-Buttons"—("Jungle Restaurant") Mr. Spare-Buttons is perhaps a quip at the long-standing use of personal attributes, occupation, or area of origin to name Englishmen—for example, Chapman (meaning "merchant"), Norton (meaning "north town"), etc. Also, this may be in reference to colonial native populations naming their new white friends by virtue of their skin color, hair color, or even apparel or accoutrements they carry.

steamy tropical jungle—("Jungle Restaurant") The mood music is from Dave Lindup, "Elephant Herd," as well as the New Concert Orchestra playing "Background Music 'Stings'" by Alan Langford (WAC T12/1,445). These "Stings" are used when the explorers are seeing shocking images of the volcano, Rouirama, the brick factory, and Crystal Palace.

Stock film of Houses of Parliament—("The Lost World of Rouirama") This is from the BBC's own archives, BBC 3SKP20 (WAC T12/1,428). The music is Elgar's "Pomp and Circumstance March," which is used at least a dozen times in *FC* (and at least once leading to a threatened lawsuit by Elgar's executors).

"Suffragan or diocesan?"—("Salvation Fuzz") A suffragan is a bishop "considered in regard to his relation to the archbishop or metropolitan, by whom he may be summoned to attend synods and give his suffrage" (*OED*), while a diocesan is a bishop of a diocese, and more often considered in relation to that diocese.

"sullearist"—("Erizabeth L") This may be Yakamoto's betrayal of his impersonator status, as Visconti was *not* known for employing surrealist elements (as Bunuel, Fellini, and even Godard were, in this period). The bulk of the surrealist films appeared in the 1920s and 1930s, from Antonin Artaud, Salvador Dali, Louis Bunuel, Rene Clair, Man Ray, and Jean Cocteau, for instance. Elements of surreality in films thereafter are often confined to dream sequences, drug-induced hazes, or other "altered" points of view. Disney's "Pink Elephants on Parade" sequence in *Dumbo* (1941) is a fine example of the surrealists' impact on feature filmmaking—where the narrative justifies the surrealist escapade via the characters' accidental inebriation.

The Pythons will revisit this surrealist world in their final feature film, *Meaning of Life*, specifically in the "Find the Fish" sequence.

– T –

"Tattooed on the back of his neck"—("Salvation Fuzz") As if the Church would exercise its ownership of bishops by indelibly marking each, much the way the First Pepperpot (Chapman) argues that zoo animals are stamped on the bottom of their feet at birth (Ep. 22).

Though tattooing has a long tradition in the British Isles, as early as 787 AD the Holy Church banned body marking of any kind as a pagan practice. Later adventurers in the Orient and the South Pacific brought tattooing back into Britain's public consciousness, and it became almost de rigueur for the highest and lowest classes, interestingly, including the two royal princes Albert Victor and George Frederick Earnest Albert, both tattooed while serving in the royal navy on HMS *Bacchante* in 1879 (*ODNB*).

Perhaps this is also an idea borrowed from the low-budget sci-fi movie *Invaders From Mars* (1953), where the aliens surgically marked each of their human zombies on the back of their necks. (This isn't really a stretch, considering the Pythons portrayal of church-types throughout *FC*.)

"tosh"—(link into "One More Minute of *Monty Python's Flying Circus*") A vague epithet that can have little intended derogatory meaning, according to the OED, almost a filler word.

three trumpeters play a fanfare—(PSC; "Erizabeth L") This is Spencer Nakin's "Trumpet Calls" from the album *Towers & Spires*. These three actors pretending to play horns are Cy Town (*Colditz*; *Star Wars*), Ron Tingley (*Dr. Who*; *Z Cars*), and Roy Pearce (*Z Cars*; *Dr. Who*), who also play courtiers in the following scene (WAC T12/1,445).

two nuns run in—(PSC; "Ken Russell's Gardening Club") The subject matter for Russell's *The Devils* is religious and sexual hysteria, with most of a nunnery participating in graphic, carnivalistic sexual activity with each other, bones, crucifixes, etc. The basis of the story is Cardinal Richelieu (Eps. 3 and 13) attempting to quash a political rival in Father Grandier.

– V –

"Visconti, Luchino"—(*"Erizabeth L"*) Italian film director influential in the neo-realist movement of the postwar era. He then moved into a more realist and even romantic period.

"volcano of Andu"—("The Lost World of Roiurama") Perhaps referring to portions of the Flinders Range in South Australia, which would continue this batch of shows' references to Australia. The photo is from the BBC collection, BBC SKP 2812A-6 (WAC T12/1,428).

"Vo-oorale"—(*"Erizabeth L"*) "Volare," a song made famous by Dean Martin.

– W –

Welsh . . . costume—(PSC; "There is Nothing Quite So Wonderful as Money [Song]") The female Welsh national costume (tall black hat, long skirt, white apron and a shawl) was popularized as such in the nineteenth century by figures such as Lady Llanofer.

Welsh harpist—A Welsh Harp is a triple-strung harp (here a Challen Upright 74947), and is played for this sketch by Sheila Bromberg. This sketch was recorded on 4 and 5 December 1971 at TC6 (WAC T12/1,428).

"we must to Tirbuly—(*"Erizabeth L"*) Tilbury was the site where Elizabeth spoke to her troops prior to the land battle that most feared would follow the naval engagement.

Episode 30

– A –

"anagrams"—("The Man Who Speaks in Anagrams") An anagram is the purposeful transposition of letters in a word or name to make a new word or name. The character here is actually not making real words (except by accident, occasionally, as will be shown), he's most often merely jumbling the letters.

See the entry for "Peter Scott" below for another anagram mention.

"anagram version"—("The Man Who Speaks in Anagrams") There have been and continue to be multiple versions of Shakespeare plays—in modern dress, in non-Anglo cultures, supporting or attacking one political persuasion or another—The Bard's are perhaps the most adapted theatrical pieces in the history of staged spectacle (see Dollimore and Sinfield's *Political Shakespeare*). In *FC* there is an underwater production of Shakespeare (Ep. 22) as well as Hamlet brought onto a contemporary psychiatrist's couch (Ep. 43).

This kind of soft subject was the caliber of topic seen on the earlier episodes of *Man Alive*, before "they got all serious" according to Herbert Mental (Jones) in Ep. 26, that or a regional report on the equally fluffy *Nationwide*.

"art . . . revival"—("Mary Recruitment Office") William Morris (1834-1896) was a Victorian-era art and architecture luminary whose work led to the Arts and Crafts Movement. The twentieth-century Art Nouveau movement was inspired by Morris' exploration of the medieval and Arts and Crafts movements.

– B –

backdrop of a circus ring—(PSC; "Army Captain as Clown") The music in the background is "Acrobats" by Keith Papworth from the album *The Big Top* (WAC T12/1,442).

Baker, Richard—(The News with Richard Baker [Vision Only]") Baker was the presenter for the first BBC news broadcast in 1954, and he continued in that position until 1982.

Nine O'Clock News—BBC TV's *Nine O'Clock News* went on the air on 14 September 1970.

The Pythons were able to convince two prominent contemporary newsreaders—Baker and Reginald Bosanquet—to bring their sober and respected on-air credentials into the service of *FC* via these bits of self-deprecating, reflexive humor. *Rowan and Martin's Laugh-In* (1968-1974) had plied these waters earlier with the appearances of President Richard Nixon, newscaster Hugh Downs, sports broadcaster Vin Scully, and uber-presenter David Frost, for example, and even earlier The Goons several times welcomed BBC newsreader John Snagge (before whom Walt Greenslade would truckle). Baker plays the gesticulating character straight, as does Bosanquet in his earlier appearance, effectively underscoring the incongruous silliness.

beat the clock—(PSC; "Anagram Quiz") There was an American TV game show called *Beat the Clock* (1969-1974) where couples attempted to perform feats within certain time constraints.

Bols Story, The—(PSC; link into "Gestures to Indicate Pauses in a Televised Talk") This title has absolutely nothing to do with the piece that follows it, precedes it, or appears anywhere in the episode—which is becoming more the case in *FC*. Bols is an Amsterdam-based spirits company, established in 1575. It may be that Mr. Orbiter-5 (Palin) fully intends to talk about Bols, but he speaks around the topic before being cut off completely.

The music beneath this intro is De Sik's "The Windmill Song" from the *Greensleeves* album (WAC T12/1,442).

"Boom boom!"—("Bus Conductor Sketch") This was the signature line for the glove puppet character Basil on *The Basil Brush Show* (BBC1, 1968-1980), a children's show.

– C –

carnivorous house—(PSC; animation link out of "Life and Death Struggles") Gilliam uses sections from the songs "Prairie Vista" by Dudley Simpson and "Bright Lights" by Roger Webb in this animated link (WAC T12/1,442).

cartoon-type hammer—(PSC; "Anagram Quiz") Again acknowledging the influence that cartoons had on the Pythons, an influence which has been evident to this point, but not stated outright in the printed scripts.

"Champion"—("Merchant Banker") Horse ridden by Gene Autry (1907-1998), star of dozens of TV and film Westerns. Autry also wrote and performed dozens of songs, including "Here Comes Santa Claus." Champion died in 1990.

"Trigger"—A horse ridden by another American "singing cowboy," Roy Rogers (1911-1998). Trigger died at the age of 33 in 1965. Rogers and Autry appeared in films and TV shows together, as well.

CHAMRAN KNEBT—(PSC; link into "Merchant Banker") The jaunty music beneath this unscrambling is "Droopy Draws" from the album *Selling Sounds* by Barry Stoller (WAC T12/1,442).

"chum"—("The Man Who Speaks in Anagrams") One of the few words that Man (Idle) actually renders anagrammatically. The others are "sit" from a mispronunciation of "that's it," "mating" from "taming," and "thing" from "night."

City Gent—("Merchant Banker") This is one of the first times that a type known as "City Gent" has been allowed to participate in a sketch to a significant degree. City Gents have generally appeared in Vox Pops segments, blathering ultra-Conservative comments or just plain blathering. In this case, the City Gent (Cleese) is allowed to continue his traditional rightist, upper-middle-class, profit-at-any-cost litany in a sketch setting. The result is the same, however: the City Gent is by the Pythons indicted (or self-indicted, really, by his own admissions of his obscene wealth, his detachment from the common man, etc.).

In this indictment that the Pythons have pressed throughout the series, they continue to build on the Modernist artists who so often shared and promoted this anti-establishment cause, but just as often with venality, not humor. Artists like George Grosz (1893-1959)—who survived WWI and was forever changed—were certain that the evils of the capitalist machinery that led to the war hadn't becalmed after the bloody saturation, leaving this disillusioned painter to see, especially in his native Germany, that Berlin (and the capitalist world) was still "owned by four breeds of pig: the capitalist, the officer, the priest and the hooker, whose other form is the socialite wife" (Hughes 75-78). While not giving in to despair or outright loathing, the Pythons clearly target these same "pigs" in their typological humor, satirizing the City Gent, the "What's All This Then?" Policeman and martinet Colonel, any Church representative, and women in general throughout *Flying Circus*.

collage of photos appear—(PSC; "The News With Richard Baker [Vision Only]") The photos appearing in the green screen circle behind Baker (as appearing in the printed script) include:

"*Richard Nixon*"—Seen earlier in Ep. 5, and mentioned again in the feature film *Holy Grail*, this American vice president and president was a consistent target of left-leaning artists and activists, and it must have been immeasurably galling that he was able to be elected not once but twice during this tumultuous period. Nixon had traveled widely in his capacity as vice president, as well, meaning he had been in the worldwide public eye for a generation by this time.

"*Tony Armstrong-Jones*"—Antony Armstrong-Jones, first Earl of Snowdon (b. 1930) was a professional portrait photographer and, most notably here, Princess Margaret's husband—he's already been mentioned by Timmy Williams (Idle) in Ep. 19 as "the lovely Snowdon." Armstrong-Jones was an Eton and Cambridge grad.

"*the White House*"—Just a standard shot across the front lawn. The opening shot of this newscast, where the title is featured, is a 16mm film clip of New York City, and specifically the United Nations building. These shots are probably included to mimic a typical evening newscast of the period, though the Princess and Lord Snowdon did make an unofficial visit to the LBJ White House in November 1965.

"*Princess Margaret*"—The younger sister to the Queen, Margaret (1930-2002) married Armstrong-Jones in 1960, and they were divorced in 1978. The Pantomime Princess Margaret will appear later in this episode, as well as in a cameo role in Ep. 33. Baker may be miming the mixing of a drink when Margaret's picture is shown, but it's not clear, and the rumors of her profligate lifestyle seem to have not been confirmed. See Margaret's various obituaries, including comments from Margaret's "friend," who tries to separate her reputation from reality (*Observer* 17 February 2002). According to WAC records, this very popular costume/prop was first requested for construction on 23 September 1971 (WAC T12/1,445). The unhappy couple appear on the 14 August 1970 cover of *Private Eye*, and are given equally unflattering dialogue balloons:

She: What's all this about us rowing in public?
He: Shut up you fat bitch and keep smiling!

"parliament"—Standard upriver shot of the famous building, and there's no obvious connection between the photos displayed yet. This juxtaposition may be an allusion, though, to Margaret's attempts to marry Air Force pilot Peter Townsend in 1955. Townsend was much older than Margaret, and had been divorced, and it seems that the Queen was advised to discourage the match, including threatening Margaret's place in the succession, etc. Even at the time there were knitted brows over just who controlled the rights to succession, with Britain's left-leaning *New Stateman and Nation* arguing that it was not Canterbury or the Queen, but Parliament alone, and everyone else should clear off:

It raises sharp constitutional issues. The Princess declared that she has been "aware that, subject to my renouncing my rights of succession, it might have been possible for me to contract a civil marriage." This seems to imply that a civil marriage could have been possible only if the succession were renounced. But who has made her "aware" of any such thing? Is it even true? The right of succession is *peculiarly a matter for Parliament*. (qtd. in *Time* 14 November 1955)

With this very public and increasingly acrimonious debate still warm, the juxtaposition of Margaret and Parliament makes more sense.

"naked breasts"—This partial nude may be Karen Burch, who signed a "partial nude" (or "use of skin") appearance contract and posed on 18 November 1971 (WAC T12/1,445).

"a scrubbing brush" followed by *"a man with a stoat through his head"*—The serious news has given way to the oddball, or perhaps human interest, the famous stoat appearing or being mentioned in Eps. 5, 6, and 26. Gilliam sported the stoat in Ep. 26.

"Margaret Thatcher"—Back to the hard news, with the Iron Lady perhaps considered an archenemy of the more liberal Pythons. The fact that her image follows the man with a stoat through his head and precedes a toilet indicates just where the Pythons would rank the high-ranking Tory. Thatcher (b. 1925) would have been

front-page news at this time. In the summer of 1971 she endorsed an end to the free milk program for schoolchildren over the age of seven, part of an enormous cuts package (including health and public services) pushed by the Conservative government and approved in September 1971.

"a lavatory"—A standard toilet, the photo was probably taken right there in Television Centre.

"a Scotsman lying on his back with his knees drawn up"—Chapman will assume this position as the "Unexploded Scotsman" in Ep. 38. This photo was probably taken in Norwich, where the Pythons shot location footage for part of the third series, including the exterior work for "Kamikaze Scotsmen" at Norwich Castle.

"a corkscrew"—Taking the previous photo into consideration (a supine, spread-eagled Scotsman), it's probably safe to assume the corkscrew may be included for its sexual connotations.

"Edward Heath"—Conservative Heath (1916-2005) had been PM since the surprising June 1970 General Election, but the economy had been in the doldrums before and since, meaning he was something of an unpopular figure by this time. The recent drastic cuts in government spending (including the milk reductions mentioned above) were also weighing heavily on consumer/voter confidence in 1971-1972. The recent 1971 Industrial Relations Bill, meant to hamstring big labor, had also created a very hostile environment between 10 Downing, Parliament, and the TUC.

"a pair of false teeth in a glass"—The juxtaposition here may be that Heath is too old and out of touch to do the country any good. (He would have been fifty-five at this time—younger than many former PMs, but old enough to be untrustworthy to the younger generation of the late 1960s.) Heath had surrounded himself with a sort of "usual suspects" gang of Cabinet members and influential Ministers, probably reeking of cronyism to young liberals like the Pythons and the editors of *Private Eye*.

Without dialogic comment, these juxtaposed images are not unlike the famous pictorial experiments performed by Lev Kuleshov's workshop in the 1920s. Kuleshov and his students juxtaposed the unchanging image of a man's face with separate, unrelated images to determine how an audience "reads" these juxtapositions. In this case, the Python audience is asked to read images of well-known politicians and public figures intermixed with images of everyday items and silliness, with a third element being Baker's mimes that also "comment" on the images.

"consequently bad television"—("Life and Death Struggles") An acknowledgment that even in documentary filmmaking—where a realistic representation of life is the supposed hallmark—there must exist an entertainment factor if the viewer is going to stay tuned in. Mr. Birchenhall (Chapman) in Ep. 27 went to jail arguing this very point—that viewers won't stand for evenings of straight ahead televised documentaries, they want entertainment. With this in mind, documentary filmmakers like Cousteau, Scott, and Seilmann have to pick subjects with viewability in mind—among other considerations—then capture images that they hope will be editable into compelling television. One of the often misunderstood elements of documentary film is this very selective, very objective-driven editing process where the "story" of the characters is revealed (or coaxed, coerced, and often created). The specter of aggressive male versus aggressive male, of competition within an ecosystem, of, yes, life and death struggles in the animal world, is the focus of many of Seilmann's and Cousteau's documentaries of this period.

In the end, of course, they aren't arguing about point of view or subject matter or potential maipulation or observational technique—they're brawling over profits, which clearly makes for good television.

"Cousteau, Jacques"—("Life and Death Struggles") Already mentioned in Ep. 27, where he is found living in Paris in the same building as Jean-Paul Sartre, Cousteau was the pre-eminent name in televised nature documentaries. See notes to Ep. 27 for more on Cousteau.

credits roll—(PSC; end credits) They managed a few anagrams from the names and titles in the closing credits, but the bulk are just jumbles. The successful anagrams include: "Rice" for "Eric," "Lied" for "Idle," "Lapin" for "Palin," and the brilliant "Torn Jersey" for "Terry Jones," They also are able to create another very believable name from Gilliam's first and last names—"Marty Rigelli."

" . . . crreoct"—("The Man Who Speaks in Anagrams") "That is correct." (Translations are provided herein—the taped version offers no subtitles.) This is a very different sketch from "The Argument Clinic," because the text as delivered almost demands that there is a reader, and not just a listener. Most of the jumbles are difficult if not impossible to decipher without a printed script, so the payoff has to be the fact that the guest (Idle) leaves in a huff, and not in comprehension of the dazzling mis-speak that Idle employs.

"Cumberland"—("The Man Who Speaks in Anagrams") One of the northernmost counties of England, situated along the Scottish border. Cumberland is in county Cumbria.

– D –

dinky little set—("Blood, Devastation, Death, War and Horror") The uncredited music behind the Interviewer's introduction is from the Lansdowne Light Orchestra, "Newsroom" by Simon Campbell (WAC T12/1,442).

Dobbin—(PSC; "The *Pantomime Horse is a Secret Agent* Film") There are several possibilities here. Besides the well-known pantomime horse figure, Dobbin was a coach horse fondly eulogized in *The Post Boy* in April 1699; "Dobbin" is also the name of a traditional rocking chair (with horse head and reins) still available in the UK; finally, a Dobbin is traditionally a steady old horse, a work horse, a horse gentle enough for a child, etc. This last meaning is found in a poem by Walter De La Mare (1873–1956), and others, especially those poems set in the bucolic English countryside of the recent past. In short, "Dobbin" as the name for a recognizable horse figure seems an easy choice.

"does gardening"—("Blood, Devastation, Death, War and Horror") The emphasis for this sentence as spoken by Palin is on the word "does," for some reasoning, which elicits quite a laugh from the studio audience. Perhaps the juxtaposition of a gardener—quite a common sight on British TV—with such a bloody-themed show is the reason.

dog fight . . . blazing—(PSC; "Blood, Devastation, Death, War and Horror") The order and variety of these shots as shown is slightly different from the printed script: (1) Head-on train wreck (silent film footage); (2) 1930s car crash and burn (probably from a gangster film); (3) train falling from a trestle bridge (special effects footage from a silent film); (4) exploding volcano; (5) burning, sinking ship (this is the *Torrey Canyon*); (6) and forest fire footage. There is no "RAF" or "Spanish hotel" footage used in the film.

The sources for these photos/film stock is as follows (some footage was used, some was not): trains crashing (Philip Jenkinson, *Casey Jones*), hotel blowing up (Movietone E9536 [1040]), volcano erupting (BBC CL 45072), car crashing and exploding (BBC SP1891 or EMI E1740 [red sports car]), train on collapsing bridge (P. Jenkinson), and forest fires (BBC NPA 6688) (WAC T12/1,428).

"Douglas-Home, Sir Alec"—(*"The Pantomime Horse is a Secret Agent* Film") Formally, Sir Alexander Frederick Douglas-Home, fourteenth Earl of Home, Baron Home of the Hirsel of Coldstream (1903-1995). Douglas-Home sat in the House of Commons, was a parliamentary undersecretary to Neville Chamberlain, an undersecretary of state for foreign affairs for Churchill, and became Prime Minister in 1963. Home (pejoratively called "Baillie Vass" in *Private Eye*) is certainly one whom the Pythons would have seen as a "teeth-in-the-glass" Tory. A Conservative (and thus a Python target), his tenure was dogged by a very poor economy and the shrinking of the Empire, and he was succeeded in 1965 as party leader by Edward Heath, who would later become Prime Minister.

"Duke of Kent to the rescue"—(*"The Pantomime Horse is a Secret Agent* Film") The Walton "Orb and Sceptre" piece, originally written for Elizabeth's coronation in 1953, is heard as Rattigan and the Duke of Kent arrive in the open car.

The fact that it is the Duke of Kent (b. 1935) who saves the day may be due to his position as President of the Royal National Lifeboat Institution (RNLI), an organization featured in Ep. 33, but the fact that he was also serving in active duty in Cyprus in 1970 and then Northern Ireland in 1971 would also keep him much in the news. There was some real concern that the Duke would be either killed, or—worse—kidnapped and used as leverage by IRA forces in Northern Ireland.

"Durham Light Infantry"—("Mary Recruitment Office") Created in 1881, the DLI served in Gibraltar, the Boer War, WWI, and beyond.

"orange"—The Durham Light Infantry color is green, primarily, with some white and tan.

– E –

"*edge* of the sailor's uniform, until the word 'Maudling' . . . "—("Gestures to Indicate Pauses in Televised Talk") Once again, with "Hello Sailor" being the clarion call for the gay male on the hunt in the Python world, Reginald Maudling—a noted Conservative and Cabinet member to Heath—is painted with the "sexual deviancy" brush so often used in *Flying Circus*.

"Edward VII"—("The *Pantomime Horse is a Secret Agent* Film") In Ep. 1, King Edward VII is an unseen contestant in "Famous Deaths," where he achieves the lowest score. Edward VII (1841-1910) was Queen Victoria's eldest son, and was a man of great appetites in women, entertainment, food, and all pleasures of the flesh. His hunt clothing favorites (Norfolk jacket and plus fours) have been featured in the previous episode.

"effeminate"—("Mary Recruitment Office") Most depictions of the military in *FC* begin in earnest, then move to humor and eventually brutality or effemi-

nization (or both), including soldiers who "camp it up" in close-order drills (Ep. 22), and the lecturing Brigadier (Cleese) in Ep. 35, etc. Some depictions are more swishy from the get-go—like Air Chief Marshal Sir Vincent "Kill the Japs" Forster (Cleese) in Ep. 14, who's flaming (cross-dressed, campy, effeminate) right out of the gate.

"dead butch"—An expression meaning *not* homosexual, in this context.

Episode 30—Recorded 11 December 1971, and broadcast 9 November 1972. This episode was recorded second and broadcast fourth.

Also included on the later "repeat cost" lists: Richard Smith (*Van Der Valk*), Brian Codd, Frank Lester (Ep. 40; *Dixon of Dock Green*), Desmond Verini (*Dr. Who*), Mike Reynell (*Dr. Who*), and Jane Cussons (*Nine Tailors*).

Lastly, Steve Peters (*Daleks' Invasion Earth*), Anthony Hamilton, Gerry Alexander (*Z Cars*), Reg Turner (*The Goodies; Z Cars*), Barry Kennington (*Dr. Who*), Clive Rogers (*Z Cars*), and Fred Davis (*It's the Bachelors*) were brought in on 25 October 1971 to play the Coolies, Panto horses, a Panto goose, etc. at Black Park (Fulmer, near Slough, Buckinghamshire). This location was also used on 3 November 1971 (WAC T12/1,428).

exciting chase—(PSC; "*The Pantomime Horse is a Secret Agent* Film") The music beneath the love scene in the boat is "Love in Slow Motion" by Reg Tilsley and the International Studio Orchestra; beneath the car chase scene is "Devil's Gallop" by the Queen's Hall Orchestra; and beneath the rickshaw chase sections is "Viet Theme" by Roger (WAC T12/1,442).

– F –

fish down the trousers—("Bus Conductor Sketch") Yet another of the tried-and-true vaudeville and music hall gags, with the following bucket of whitewash and finally the custard pie as the coup de grâce. (The original ending of Terry Southern-penned *Dr. Strangelove*, of course, was to have featured an all-in custard pie fight in the War Room, but the scene did not make the final cut.) It would generally have been the authority figure getting this kind of ridiculous treatment, though here a befuddled straight man works just as well.

On American television in this period, *Rowan and Martin's Laugh-In* (1968-1974) had been recycling these music hall gags with gusto (and go-go dancers) to great audience and advertiser delight almost two years before *Flying Circus* aired for the first time.

– H –

"harsh and bitchy world of television features"—("Life and Death Struggles") The music selections underneath the complete documentary sequences include: "The Rite of Spring" by Stravinsky, performed by L'Orchestra de la Suisse Romande; "Coach and Pair" and "Camel Team" by Merrick Farran; "Orb and Sceptre" by Walton, performed by the Royal Liverpool Philharmonic Orchestra; "Theme and Variation" by R. Tilsley; Today's World "Walk Tall" by Keith Papworth; "Gong Sinister" by J. Gunn; "Waterbuck Koala" by Sam Sklair from "Cartoon Capers"; and "Hearts and Flowers" by Czibulka, W. Warren, performed by the London Symphony Orchestra (WAC T12/1,442).

"has not been able to announce since our youngest, Clifford, was born . . . "—("Neurotic Announcers") Not to put too fine a point on it, but Jack may be suffering a loss of confidence due to his wife's sexual unavailability since childbirth, not an uncommon situation, and one that renders Jack "impotent" and unable to perform before the BBC microphone.

– I –

"I don't understand"—("Merchant Banker") The Merchant Banker as depicted here (and perhaps especially by the somewhat leftist and mercurial Cleese) is incapable of understanding pity, empathy, even charity—he is the prototypical heartless, money-grubbing City (of London) Gent Conservative. The Merchant Banker is certain that orphans are a viable developing market, that Mr. Ford (Jones) wants a loan and not a gift, and that said gift must be just a clever way of avoiding taxes. They are on completely different wavelengths, communication-wise, a situation not uncommon in the Python oeuvre, and might as well be speaking/hearing at different pitches ("Silly Voices," Ep. 12).

"I know I'm pausing occasionally"—("Gestures to Indicate Pauses in Televised Talk") Palin does a masterful job of precisely stepping back from actually beginning his presentation with every refinement he attempts to communicate. First "we" are going to talk, then he qualifies that to "I," then from the future tense ("I *am* going to . . . ") to the present ("I *am* talking about it . . . "), then to clarify he hasn't begun actually talking about the subject, but he is still talking, and on and on.

The structure here is very much like the convoluted, qualifying, clarifying, and even extirpating narrative structure in Sterne's *Tristram Shandy*, which spends page after page attempting to relate the facts surrounding Tristram's birth, but digressions abound and overwhelm the narrative thread—and the novel and characters know it. It is Volume III before we reach the (somewhat) blessed event. Mr. Orbiter-5 (Palin) never does get to talk of Bols, however.

"I'm not unusual"—("Mary Recruitment Office") Adapted from the Tom Jones' 1965 hit song "It's Not Unusual." Jones has already been referenced in Ep. 24 by the fast-talking Art Critic (Cleese).

"Inniskillin . . . Regiment"—("Mary Recruitment Office") An Irish regiment that came to contemporary prominence in 1965 when they were trapped in a blockaded Rhodesia after Ian Smith declared independence (*Eyewitness: 1960-69*, "Rhodesia Unilateral Declaration of Independence 1965"). The Anglian Regiment was formed in 1964 from several existing regiments.

"I stom certainly od. Revy chum so"—("The Man Who Speaks in Anagrams") Translation: "I most certainly do. Very much so."

" . . . Wersh"—"Yes, yes—that is correct. At the moment I'm working on *The Taming of the Shrew*." *Shrew* is Shakespeare's 1593-1594 comedy.

"Nay"—It's not clear why he uses "nay" here, since it's not anagrammatic (except for "any") or even jumbled, though perhaps it is a nod to the Elizabethan English found in the plays being discussed, and not therefore jumbled at all.

" . . . Venice"—*Two Gentlemen of Verona, Twelfth Night, The Merchant of Venice*." All Shakespeare plays, *Verona* was written/produced in 1592-1593, *Twelfth Night* in 1601-1602, and *Merchant* in 1596-1597 (see Evans' *Riverside Shakespeare*).

" . . . nestquie"—*Hamlet*. 'To be or not to be, that is the question.'" *Hamlet* was produced in 1600-1601.

"thrid"—Another perhaps accidental anagram here, as "thrid" is an obsolete version of both "third" and "thread." *Richard III* was written/produced by Shakespeare in 1607.

"shroe"—An obsolete word for "shrew" (*OED*), so this would qualify as an anagram, though perhaps unintentionally. This quote is from Shakespeare's *Richard III* (5.4.7), which has already been quoted in Ep. 25, the "Hospital for Over-Actors" sketch.

– J –

James Bond style opening titles—(PSC; "The Pantomime Horse is a Secret Agent" Film") Gilliam would have provided the titles, which look very much like those he created for Ep. 17, "*The Bishop*."

– K –

kicking . . . shins—(PSC; "Pantomime Horses") Perhaps at least partially inspired by the painters Rubens (*A Lion Hunt*, 1616), Gericault (*Race of Riderless Horses*), and perhaps especially Delacroix (*Arabian Horses Fighting in a Stable*, 1860), whose paintings featured horses in violent scenes, and many of which were available in the National Gallery. *The Lion Hunt* had been on display there since it was purchased in 1871. Here, of course, the Pythons have deflated the nobility of the act in favor of silliness.

"King Haakon of Norway"—("The *Pantomime Horse is a Secret Agent* Film") King Haakon VII (1872-1957)—formerly Christian Frederik Carl Georg Valdemar Axel—married the youngest daughter of Edward VII, and Haakon became newly independent Norway's first king in 1905.

"Corpse-Haakon Production"—Implying that Douglas-Home is the "Corpse" or lifeless partner in this partnership (though Haakon had been dead and buried for more than a decade by this time), which fits the Pythons' generally anti-Conservative bent.

– L –

"limpet"—("Life and Death Struggles") *OED*: "A gasteropod mollusc of the genus Patella, having an open tent-shaped shell and found adhering tightly to the rock which it makes its resting-place."

The film footage in this sequence is from the following sources: Sea lions fighting (BBC Bristol 8917); limpets ("Seashells," Educational Foundation for Visual Aids or "Animals of the Rocky Shore" [Rank 5689222]); "wolf" (static shot, thirty-four seconds long), a slide from Windrose Dumont Time; and "honey bears" from Phillip Ware (WAC T12/1,428).

"sprightly opponent"—Neither limpet is actually doing much of anything in these shots, which adds to the incongruity.

loony get up—(PSC; "The *Pantomime Horse is a Secret Agent* Film") This insert was shot in the Glencoe area, when the Njorl scenes were being recorded for Ep. 27. The Pythons would record enough outdoor material for the entire season (or more) at a single location, including links, inserts, and exterior continuation shots, saving money and travel time.

– M –

"Maudling"—("The News With Richard Baker [Vision Only]") Referring once again to Sir Reginald Maudling. See entries in Eps. 12, 16, 20-22, 26, and 36 for more on Maudling and his recurring presence in *FC*, as well as the pages of newspapers and satirical organs like *Private Eye*.

"merchant banker"—("Merchant Banker") One who engages in credit and financing for businesses, as opposed to individuals.

music hall comedian—(PSC; "Bus Conductor Sketch") Probably meant to reference comedians like Arthur Askey (1900-1982) and George Robey (1869-1954), both active during the Pythons' formative years.

– N –

nuns—(PSC; "Mary Recruitment Office") A nun reference again, this after the previous episode where Ken Russell's salacious treatment of the world of Cardinal Richelieu and nonconforming priests and nuns in *The Devils* is highlighted (in the "*Ken Russell's* Gardening Club" sketch). In early 1971 producers of the film were advertising heavily in *Private Eye*, taking out half- and full-page ads.

– O –

"off we go again"—("Pantomime Horse") Another nod to the constructed nature of the performance, this link is much more artificial and visible than if it had been announced as a link. Again, with Cleese involved, the façade is almost cynically broached, and the theatrical corner-cutting becomes more and more blatant.

Orbiter-5—(PSC; "Gestures to Indicate Pauses in a Televised Talk") The Lunar Orbiter 5 was a NASA-created orbital moon vehicle launched on 1 August 1967. The Orbiter was sent to photograph the moon's surface, assess meteoroid impact data, and measure radiation in preparation for manned lunar missions. Orbiter-5 was the last of the unmanned Lunar Orbiter missions to the moon.

– P –

"pantomime horse"—("Pantomime Horse") Significant figure in English pantomime tradition, along with various barnyard animals (e.g., geese). Pantomimes are performed regularly at Christmas in the UK, both live and on TV.

pantomime music—(PSC; "Pantomime Horses") The bit of music used here is Reg Wale's music hall riff from the *Looney Tunes* album, a so-called walk on, walk off selection (WAC T12/1,442).

"pantomime Princess Margaret"—("Life and Death Struggles") This larger-than-life figure will appear again in Ep. 33, and is often played by Cleese.

Margaret (more fully, HRH The Princess Margaret, Countess of Snowdon, 1930-2002) was the younger sister of Elizabeth, and was frequently in the news thanks to her lifestyle and love life. She was even called "that wayward woman" by noted anti-monarchists of the day, and her dalliances with younger men, divorced men, other women, drug use, and high society in general kept her a tabloid favorite for many years. One prominent author/critic, Richard Hoggart (b. 1918), described the cultural paucity of the period using Margaret as the plinth of mediocrity:

> Society in the fifties was a sort of feeble continuation of society before the fifties, with little, tentative innovations . . . it was a lukewarm or less than lukewarm bath, artistically, of such things as the plays of N.C. Hunter [*A Day By the Sea*, 1955], and the late, watered works of Noël Coward. It was a period when the great, infashionable, smart drink was mateus rosé, and *Princess Margaret was a leader of society and fashion, and almost passed for an intellectual*. . . . (Audio transcription, *Eyewitness: 1950-59*, "Fifties Society")

Margaret was also prominently featured (as a young woman) on the first BBC news broadcast in 1954 as she visited Lancashire for charitable purposes.

She was most likely included in this sketch, however, thanks to her well-documented appearances in Windsor Castle pantomimes as a child, where she played "Aladdin," for example, during the war. These broadcasts were made available to the besieged British public.

"punch-up"—("Life and Death Struggles") A fight, a brawl.

– Q –

"Queen Juliana of the Netherlands"—(*"The Pantomime Horse is a Secret Agent* Film") Juliana (1909-2004) became the monarch in 1948, and showed herself as a pacifist, so this rather bloodthirsty action-adventure film might not have been her first choice, were she a film director. By the 1960s, she looked very much like a prototypical Pepperpot with her print dresses, neat hats, and clutch handbag. Juliana retired from the throne in 1980.

– R –

RAF—(PSC; "Blood, Devastation, Death, War and Horror") The Royal Air Force took the upper hand from the German Luftwaffe during WWII in sustained aerial attacks on German bombers, buzz bombs, and fighter planes.

rather tatty revue—(PSC; "Bus Conductor Sketch") The music hall tradition thrived 1850-1960 in the UK, with public houses across the country creating space for the variety performances. London featured the most and largest such houses, but towns like Leeds, Bradford, and the Isle of Man boasted their own purpose-built music hall spaces. A smaller venue like Collins Music Hall in Islington Green, London may be the "rather tatty" type the script describes.

"Rattigan, Terence"—("Life and Death Struggles") Mentioned earlier in the notes to Ep. 1, Terence Rattigan (1911-1977) was a playwright and screenwriter, contributing the screenplay for *Goodbye Mr. Chips* in 1938. He was schooled at Harrow (on scholarship), then Trinity College, Oxford. Rattigan was homosexual, and may have given the Pythons their inspiration for the Pepperpot character from his "Aunt Edna" creation.

Rattigan is even earlier mentioned by the Goons in their episode "The Flea," when Bluebottle (played by Peter Sellers), quips: "Well, we've given them enough Terrance Rattigan-type dialogue." The dialogue had been particularly bland and silly, of course, up to that point—featuring Bluebottle's somewhat successful attempts to humiliate Eccles.

For more on Rattigan, see notes to Eps. 1 and 32.

"redundancy scheme"—("Pantomime Horse") The Redundancy Payments Act of 1965 requires certain employers to pay a lump sum to dismissed employees. Called "severance pay" in the United States.

"repeat fees"—("Life and Death Struggles") Schedule of payments if a TV show is picked up for foreign distribution, or just rerun on domestic TV. The BBC keeps very accurate records of just who appeared in what show for the purposes of calculating and paying repeat fees.

"Rothwell, Talbot and Mirielle Mathieu"—(*"The Pantomime Horse is a Secret Agent* Film") Rothwell (1916-1981) was a principal writer for the popular TV series *Up Pompeii* (BBC, 1969) and many installments in the *Carry On* motion picture series (1963-1983). Both of these shows were more like the standard situation comedies the Pythons had created *Flying Circus* to react against, so this is probably not an homage to or flattering mention of this writer.

Mathieu (b. 1946) is a French singer who rose to prominence in the early 1960s, and by 1965 her first album was well on its way to the one million sales mark. She appeared on *Toast of the Town* in 1966. She would have been featured prominently on British radio during this period.

"RSM"—("Mary Recruitment Office") Regimental Sergeant Major. The character in the "self-defence" sketch in Ep. 4 was an RSM (played by Cleese), and the hospital in Ep. 26 is run by RSM types.

– S –

"school fees"—("The Man Who Makes People Laugh Uncontrollably") Many schools in the UK charge significant tuition for attendance and/or boarding, ranging into the tens of thousands of pounds annually. These fee-paying schools are distinct from the state and county schools, which are supported by public means (taxation). This jeremiad from the City Gent (Jones) is a familiar one in the UK of this period, when many lower- and middle-class families scrimped and saved so that their children could at least try and have the same experience as the children of the elite.

"Scots Guards"—("Mary Recruitment Office") A regiment in the British army originally formed in 1642 by Charles I.

"Scott, Peter"—("Life and Death Struggles") Sir Peter Markham Scott (1909-1989) was a naturalist, artist, author, adventurer, and filmmaker. His interests tended toward ornithology, primarily, and he made a number of TV docs on the subject around the world. One of the films the Pythons may have been referring to is titled *To the South Pole with Peter Scott* (BBC and Time-Life Films, 1967), a self-narrated journey from Cape Crozier to McMurdo Base at the South Pole. Scott was the son of Capt. Robert Falcon Scott, who successfully made the Pole trip in 1912.

In keeping with the anagram theme begun earlier, it is interesting to note that Scott is also remembered for later naming the Loch Ness monster so that it could be registered as an endangered species. The scientific name he chose—*Nessiteras rhombopteryx*—means "the wonder of Ness with the diamond shaped fin," but also happens to be a clever anagram of "Monster hoax by Sir Peter S." (See *Word IQ Dictionary* entry for Peter Scott.)

"Sielmann, Heinz"—("Life and Death Struggles") Writer, director, and noted host of animal documentaries, including *Masters of the Congo Jungle* (1960), *Galapagos: Trauminsel im Pazifik* (1962), *Wonderen van het Afrikaanse woud* (1968), and *Mystery of Animal Behavior* (1969). Sielmann (b. 1917) was born in Germany.

"Slater Nazi"—("Merchant Banker") Equating bloated capitalists with bloodthirsty fascists is commonplace in more leftist fare, and is employed throughout *FC* whenever Conservatives (City Gents, specifically) are depicted. This man can't even remember his own name—his profession has overtaken his personality and identity.

The "Slater" mentioned here may actually be based on the now legendary UK investor Jim Slater (b. 1929), whose Slater Walker Securities (a secondary bank) turned £2000 to £200 million in just eight years (1965-1973), only to see it all crumble by 1974. The "Walker" was Peter Walker (b. 1932), the oft-satirized (in *Private Eye*) Conservative MP and Cabinet member at this time. Walker is credited with creating the PEG, or "price earnings to growth ratio," a formula which looks at projected prices and expected earnings, and is based significantly in speculation. This financial rigamarole fits well with the Merchant Banker's spiel as the skit began.

"some kind of a sign, like this" (*makes a gesture*)—("Gestures to Indicate Pauses in Televised Talk") The problem here and in Ep. 33 when Captain Biggles (Chapman) attempts to dictate a letter is literality—characters in the Python world (perhaps not unlike Sterne's Uncle Toby) can be so literal that they cannot appreciate double meanings, inflections, etc., leading to the camera cutting away here, and Biggles' secretary to type what he's *not* dictating. The Marriage Registrar (Idle) in Ep. 19 also suffers from the literalness. Again, mis-communication fuels many of the Python scenarios, indicating how significant communciation or the lack of communication—between generations, from seats of power to the masses, between the sexes, etc.—loomed in this period.

"split hairs"—("The Man Who Speaks in Anagrams") Putting a fine point on it, the presenter (Palin) hasn't worried about the guest's "jumble" as opposed to anagram usage thus far. This is clearly a way to get out of the sketch without a proper punchline, as the arrests at the end of the previous episode claimed. More and more sketches will just end—abruptly and trailing off—as the series continues.

"spoonerism"—("The Man Who Speaks in Anagrams") *OED*: "An accidental transposition of the initial sounds, or other parts, of two or more words." The *OED* credits Oxfordians in the late nineteenth century for promoting its usage. "Ring Kichard" is a spoonerism. Not a surprise that it's one of the troupe's Oxfordians, here Michael Palin, who identifies the spoonerism masking as an anagram.

Stock colour film—(PSC; "Blood, Devastation, Death, War and Horror") All the clips are actually in black and white.

– T –

"timber ant"—("Life and Death Struggles") Probably referring to the carpenter ant, which tunnels through wood but doesn't eat the wood.

Torrey Canyon—(PSC; "Blood, Devastation, Death, War and Horror") The *Torrey Canyon* was a bulk oil carrier that ran aground on the Seven Stones Reef between Lands End and the Islands in March 1967 with 120,000 tons of Kuwaiti oil aboard. The Wilson government decided to set the oil ablaze rather than just let it drift into coastal areas. In all, forty-two bombs were dropped on the wreck, and the oil was eventually burned away. The fact that roughly 25 percent of the bombs missed the target was fodder for the newspapers and the opposition party in the following weeks.

This stock is from a Navy newsreel film (WAC T12/1,428).

turning his back on city gent—(PSC; "The Man Who Makes People Laugh Uncontrollably") Since before (but notably including) Pope and Jonson, derision and scorn of the powerful and mighty via laughter has been the stock-in-trade of the poet, playwright, and librettist, and here the Pythons have to do nothing more than objectify their oft-seen City Gent to disarm him as a symbol of power. He cuts a ridiculous figure, of course, in costume and erect, but if it's considered that his presence renders others powerless to act in/on their own control, then the City Gent could conversely be re-read as an incredibly powerful symbolic figure, one well beyond the slings and arrows of satire. The fact that his boss "collapses in helpless mirth" underscores the latter reading, which may actually be a(n unconscious) Python comment on the inevitability (and power) of such figures and sociopolitical constructions in the modern world.

"turn the paper over"—("Gestures to Indicate Pauses in Televised Talk") These types of "fold-ins" appeared at the back of every issue of *Mad Magazine* since 1964.

"typical . . . documentaries"—("Life and Death Struggles") An acknowledgment of the artifice, this type of self-conscious moment is not unusual in *FC*, where the nuts and bolts of television are often revealed. Also, "these documentaries" would include the similar docs and nature films being released during this same period from others like Jacques Cousteau (*World Without a Sun* [1964]) and Walt Disney Studios (*Yellowstone Cubs* [1963]).

– V –

Voice Over (John) **(German accent)**—(PSC; "Life and Death Struggles") Not credited in the printed scripts, but this is voiced by Cleese in a very Dr. Strangelove–type nasal voice, à la Peter Sellers. The German accent is most likely meant to mimic the voice of documentary narrator Heinz Sielmann, discussed above. The narrators with these types of accents used by Sielmann included Dutchman Herman Niels (*Lords of the Forest*, 1959) and German Ernst Zeitter (*Lockende Wildnis*, 1962).

– W –

waiting to answer his phone—(PSC; "Merchant Banker") By this time in the course of *FC*, the acknowledgment of the artifice becomes common, becomes the norm, and it even appears, occasionally, that the actors are a bit bored with the convention of "pretending" to answer the phone, talk to someone offscreen, create the illusion of offscreen space, etc. This is particularly true for Cleese, who embarked on the third season with some reluctance. See McCabe and Morgan (1999).

"weak ending"—("The *Pantomime Horse is a Secret Agent* Film") For much of *FC*, the necessity of having an ending at all was eschewed in favor of upsetting the traditional "sketch format comedy show" structure. Most of the episodes just end without much fanfare at all. The lack of ending, then, becomes the structure, and yet another rigid parameter is constructed. Constantly reacting to such restrictions fueled the show, at least through the first two series. The ending of Ep. 41 is actually chosen by the characters, after they run through a list of possible endings. See Morgan (1999) for more comments from the Pythons as to the structure of *FC*.

"What's the Welshman doing under the bed?"—("Bus Conductor Sketch") A well-worn music hall joke revisited by The Goons, as well. The leek is a national emblem of Wales.

"Women's Royal Army Corps"—("Mary Recruitment Office") Formed in February 1949, the green-uniformed WRAC members occupied primarily administrative and support positions for most of the organization's life.

"work for one of our announcers"—("Neurotic Announcers") Announcers and interludes (stock shots with music between shows) were common on the BBC, especially during the 1950s when much of the broadcast material was live. These announcers tended to stick to what had just been watched, what was immediately following, and what was to be expected later in the broadcast day (and sometimes what was on over on the other BBC channel). Announcers continued to be used for transitions well into the 1980s, and can still be heard today, though the practice of showing the BBC World symbol and just hearing the announcer didn't take hold until the 1960s. (See Crisell [2002] and Vahimagi for more.)

As technology improved, fewer announcers were of course needed, since an announcer could both announce and run his/her own sound board, work which may be what Jack (Cleese) is lamenting as "a bit thin." (See Crisell [2002].)

Episode 31: "The All-England *Summarize Proust Competition*"

– A –

"A La Recherche du Temps Perdu"—(*"Summarize Proust Competition"*) Literally, *In Search of Lost Time* (c. 1913-1927), the work is a seven-novel epic, three of which were published posthumously. Many believe the novel(s) to be the finest example of narrative fiction ever produced. And as has been and will continue to be seen throughout *Flying Circus*, the Pythons themselves expend a great deal of energy and time searching out, dusting off, and examining closely the remembrances of their own collective pasts, from their Pepperpot mothers to Gumby working fathers to cricket and football heroes and the Great Men of English history.

As fanciful as the subject of summarizing Proust might seem, future *Beyond the Fringe* co-creator Alan Bennett, while at Exeter College, Oxford, had written a satirical cabaret that included references to Proust, and had even jotted a poem (lifted from a cabaret lyric) into the Exeter College Junior Common Room "suggestions book," which was saved and eventually bound for the Bodleian Library:

Marcel Proust had a very poor figure,
He hadn't the chest for sexual rigour.
He lay with Albertine tout nu;
Ce n'est seulement le temps qu'il a perdu. (Qtd. in Carpenter, 2000, 26)

It is certainly possible that either or both Jones and Palin, while at Oxford just after Bennett, had read the inscriptions or seen/heard about the revue, and filed the idea away for future use.

This is also the book that Praline (Cleese) is ready to fight for with Man (Palin) for a perceived slight in the "Fish Licence" sketch in Ep. 23. In that sketch, the sickly Proust is well enough to have his own hobby—he keeps a haddock.

"All-England"—(*"Summarize Proust Competition"*) There are myriad "All-England" sporting and music competitions, from badminton and billiards to dancing and (horse) show jumping.

animated sketch—(PSC; animated film out of "Everest Climbed by Hairdressers") This amorous photo couple appear to be Greer Garson and Errol Flynn from *That Forsyte Woman* (1949), directed by Compton Bennett and based on the John Galsworthy book (already mentioned in Ep. 21). Flynn and Garson play Soames and Irene Forsyte in the film version.

"armed communist uprising near your home when you're having a party"—(*"Party Hints* with Veronica Smalls"*) This sounds very much like an actual account given by the "respectable" Mrs. Dorothy Raynes Simpson, who, along with supper guest Mrs. Kitty Hesselberger, fought off a band of armed Mau Mau terrorists in the front rooms of her home in Kenya, January 1953. As Joanna Bourke writes (and Tim Pigott-Smith narrates), "Englishness" during this period became identified by order and structure, with "the British media represent[ing] the colonial war in Kenya in terms of guarding English domesticity against an alien other." "Domestic order," Bourke continues, "was an increasingly important marker of Englishness." The sedate, sober account of the attack and defense of home as recounted orally by Mrs. Simpson is both chilling and oddly funny; the smaller, seemingly insignificant details (e.g., "sweets," "a nut") color the telling, as if Veronica Smalls (Idle) were narrating:

Mrs. Hesselberger and I were in the sitting room, and I was having a light supper in the sitting room, and Mrs. Hesselberger had just turned on the wireless at nine o'-clock to hear the BBC news. And after she had turned it on and got the signature tune she came over to the table where I was having sweets. She took a nut off the table and cracked it when the houseboy came through rather hurriedly—made us a little bit suspicious—we looked up, and I said, "They're here." There was a number of figures in the room, all strangers. I leapt out of my chair, and luckily, I had my revolver next to me, and I shot at the first boy that was coming towards me, and then I heard Mrs. Hesselberger saying "Be careful." I turned to her, and I saw one of the boys on top of her [here it seems Mrs. Simpson shoots the boy and her own dog, who is intervening—DL] . . . it was all over in a matter of seconds. When Mrs. Hesselberger was free, we dashed out, and there was, so it seemed, another attack was coming towards us, and in the darkness Mrs. Hesselberger fired, and shot another boy. (audio transcription, *Eyewitness 1950-59*, "Kenya")

According to State of Emergency accounts regarding the incident, the ladies killed at least three of the machete-wielding invaders, and wounded at least one other, successfully putting down the uprising, at least for the evening. The Mau Mau uprising continued to terrorize settlers and the British reading public alike for many months.

"Arthur"—("*Summarize Proust Competition*") Yet another Python character given the name Arthur, a fallback name used so often in the first and second series. In the very popular *Beyond the Fringe* (1961) satirical revue, several of the mentioned (but unseen) characters are named "Arthur," including Arthur Tinty and Arthur Grodes.

– B –

"Bagot, Harry"—("*Summarize Proust Competiton*") Perhaps accidental, but there was an extant Harry Eric Bagot, Seventh Earl Bagot (1894-1973). There is also the possibility that the fact he was living helped the BBC decide that "masturbation" was not an acceptable hobby for Bagot (Chapman), badly inserting the dubbed "strangling animals and golf" after the fact.

There is a precedent for such possible action, of course. When the Cobham family complained that Shakespeare's beloved but ignoble character John Oldcastle (from whom the Cobhams descended) was demeaning to their family name and heritage, Shakespeare made the change to "Falstaff." Interesting, then, that Falstaff the fictional character would be able to enjoy such narrative and even historical control as a created character, where Oldcastle would have certainly been more tied to history and appropriate behavior. See Bergeron and Larsen for more.

"Balleys of Bond Street"—("Theory of Brontosauruses by Anne Elk [Miss]") There is a "Bally" of Bond Street, offering fine shoes since it opened in 1881. The original building there on Bond Street was completely refur-

bished in 1965, which may account for Bally being prominently mentioned here.

"brogue"—A more country or sports type shoe, as opposed to a formal dress shoe.

"Bedser, Alec and Eric"—("*Summarize Proust Competition*") Alec Bedser (b. 1918) was the Wisden Cricketer of the Year in 1947, and was eventually knighted for his contributions to cricket. Eric Bedser was Alec's twin brother, and also played for Surrey. Both were right hand batters.

The other panelists include the following:

"Stewart Surridge"—Stuart Surridge (1917-1992) was a Surrey right hand bat, and Wisden Cricketer of the Year in 1953.

"Omar Sharif"—Sharif (b. 1932) is an Egyptian actor who had most notably appeared in the David Lean epic *Dr. Zhivago* (1965) and the later *Funny Girl* (1968). The detailed plot outline offered by the Art Critic (Cleese) in Ep. 28 was at least partially borrowed from *Dr. Zhivago*.

"Laurie Fishlock"—Fishlock (1907-1986) was a Surrey left hand bat, and Wisden Cricketer of the Year in 1947.

"Peter May"—May (1929-1994) was a Surrey right hand bat, and Wisden Cricketer of the Year in 1952. It seems clear that these men would have been the sports heroes for at least some of the Pythons in their youth, perhaps especially Jones, who lived in Claygate, Surrey for almost fifteen years (McCabe 45).

"Yehudi Menuhin"—Menuhin (1916-1999) was an American-born violinist who became a British citizen, peer, and knight. His Yehudi Menuhin School was established, perhaps not coincidentally, in Surrey in 1962. Menuhin also has at least a distant connection to the Pythons' generation in that he was one of the first paying members of the Peter Cook satirical club "The Establishment," set up on Greek Street in Soho, London in 1961 (Carpenter, 2000, 131). There's no indication as to whether or not he actually went to the club, or that any of the Pythons actually met/saw him there.

Clearly, Surrey-ite Jones contributed a great deal to this sketch, with a number of semi-autobiographical references. For Idle's version of this favoritism, centered instead on the West Midlands, see the "Travel Agent" sketch, as well as notes below.

"Bingley"—("*Summarize Proust Competition*") Bingley is in West Yorkshire County.

"Birmingham"—("Travel Agent") Industrial city of the English West Midlands, Birmingham is the second-largest city in England. Idle would have known this area and its people very well, having gone to boarding school just west of Birmingham, at the Royal Wolverhampton School, West Midlands. This entire venting is replete with references to West Midlands locations and personalities, betraying Idle's participation in the sketch's creation, as well as the perhaps nostalgic significance of the Pythons' various backgrounds to their comedy and to *Flying Circus* specifically.

"bitching in the tents"—("Everest Climbed by Hairdressers") Not just a joke, the reports of personal/personnel conflicts in the Himalayas have significant historical support. The 1971 expedition led by Norman Dyhrenfurth and including climbers from more than a dozen countries ran into "oneupsmanship, personality conflicts, and organizational problems" (everestnews.com). The climb was split into at least two groups, and a rescue party was to be dispatched when a storm paralyzed the climbers. One man died as a result of exposure.

"bodega"—("Travel Agent") Typically, a wine cellar/shop in Spain, where the Tourist (Idle) would have seen and loathed the ubiquitous symbol of Great Britain's fading (now corporate) empire—the Red Barrel. See the entry for "Watney's" below for more. Cultural maven Richard Hoggart makes this same sort of elitist argument as he describes the social wasteland of 1950s England, where a vulgar common man's drink—the Portugese bulk wine mateus rosé —served as mock evidence of high culture (*Eyewitness: 1950-59*, "Fifties Society").

"bog"—("Travel Agent") A vulgarization of "boghouse," meaning a privy or toilet.

"bolour supplement"—("Travel Agent") The "colour supplements" were mentioned earlier by Harry "Snapper" Organs (Jones) in Ep. 14. These supplements are colored pages in newspapers, often indicating advertising sections. A typical color supplement from the *Radio Times* advertised holiday trips to places from Paignton to Ulster to Colwyn Bay (Carpenter, 2003, 4). Similar color supplements (tipped-in to the magazine) can be found in period *Private Eye* issues, as well, also advertising trips to exotic but affordable continental locales.

"Bolton Choral Society"—("*Summarize Proust Competition*") There was a Bolton Catholic Amateur Operatic & Dramatic Society (so named in 1962) that had been functioning in various capacities since 1925. There are also literally hundreds of choral societies up and down the UK, from Bath to Wimbledon, and from Bristol to Wokingham.

"Bounder of Adventure"—("Travel Agent") In the very popular "Billy Bunter" magazine, comic, and film series there was a character named Herbert Vernon Smith, who was known as the Bounder. The "Billy Bunter" character appeared in hundreds of stories (1908-1940), then comics (1940-), and finally television

episodes (1952-1961). These same characters even appeared in a few Christmas stage performances. (See Vahimagi.) Sir Gerald Nabarro also confessed to being a bit of a "bounder" (or a loveable cad) in his military life, politics, and business ("Nabarro," *ODNB*).

"Bournemouth"—("*Summarize Proust Competition*") Located on the south coast in Dorset. The Pythons shot most of their location footage in this area for the first series, including dune-area scenes for "Famous Deaths" and "The Funniest Joke in the World" (Ep. 1), and "Undressing in Public" (Ep. 4).

"Boys' Brigade"—("Our Eamonn") A UK organization founded in October 1883 by William Smith, designed to give boys discipline and self-respect in a structured environment, and was influential to Baden-Powell's later Boy Scout organization. Their motto was "Sure and Steadfast," and their credo: "The advancement of Christ's Kingdom among Boys and the promotion of habits of Reverence, Discipline, Self-Respect, and all that tends towards a true Christian Manliness" (*ODNB*). Mervyn of course sees them as useless, since they aren't firefighters.

"Briddock, I.T."—("*Summarize Proust Competition*") Dave Briddock was a character played by Simon Cuff (*Z Cars*) on the popular *Doctor in the House* (1969-1970), for which Bill Oddie, Chapman, Cleese, and David Sherlock (Chapman's life partner) contributed material.

"British Shoe Corporation"—("Travel Agent") Established by Charles Clore (1904-1979), and in the early 1960s expanded into multiple countries with additional manufacturing plants ("Clore," *ODNB*).

"Brixton"—("Everest Climbed by Hairdressers") There are a number of Brixtons, including one in Greater London, and one in Devon near Plymouth. The Pythons spent a good deal of time shooting in the Plymouth area for previous shows.

"brylcreem"—("Travel Agent") Trademarked name of a hair gel patented in 1929 (in Birmingham, UK, incidentally).

"bungalow"—("Our Eamonn") Perhaps also a nod to the artificial nature of these sets, since there would not have been a second floor in the studio. In Ep. 17, the "Chemist Sketch," the characters discuss the actions involved when a character runs off camera, pretending to either "nip down to the basement" or out of the chemist's shop after a "fishy requisite," revealing the nuts and bolts of the creative geography employed by the television medium.

One-story bungalows were built by the thousands during and after the war, including more than 150,000 pre-fabs between 1944 and 1948, and were much-desired as single-family homes. The housing crunch forced local councils to opt for semi-detached, rowhouse, and tower block projects, however, all providing more living space and occupying less open space.

– C –

"calamares . . . two veg"—("Travel Agent") If "meat and two veg" is an idiom for a traditional (in this case, probably unimaginative, too) English meal, then "calamari and two veg" (fried squid and two vegetable side dishes) must be the Majorcan equivalent whipped up for the British tourists crowds.

"Charlie George Football Book"—("Our Eamonn") Charlie George (b. 1950) played for the Arsenal Football Club from 1969 to 1975, he became so popular that there were songs written about him, and even a café named after him. Arsenal had won the FA Cup in the 1970-1971 season.

"chiropodists"—("Everest Climbed by Hairdressers") One who treats corns and bunions. There were and are all sorts of climbers who make the Everest attempt, including trained mountaineers (Ep. 9), wealthy businessmen, extreme sports types, and just groups of interested outdoor enthusiasts.

"cornplaster"—Popular treatment for corns. Worrying about corns was less a concern than equipment like shoes, tents, and oxygen gear wearing out or malfunctioning on the subzero slopes.

"Dr. Scholl"—A UK foot doctor, it was Scholl's nephew William Howard Scholl who pioneered fashionable orthopedic shoes, especially the very trendy "Dr. Scholl's clog" (a sandal, of sorts) in the mid-1960s.

"cloth caps . . . cardigans"—("Travel Agent") The "cloth cap" is known as a "flat cap," and was very popular in both the UK and United States, but was particularly associated with the British Northern working-class man in the twentieth century. There are innumerable photos to document the cap's popularity, with one in particular depicting a smithy in Slaidburn (photo number BU04734A, Bertram Unné, Unnetie Digitisation Project). The smithy and his co-worker and customer all sport the same cap.

A "cardigan" is a sweater that zips or buttons down the front.

"cotton sun frocks"—Similar to the simple, flowered outfits the Pythons dress themselves in as Pepperpots, probably colorful and thin enough for the hot Mediterranean days.

Competition—("*Summarize Proust Competition*") There had indeed been celebrated attempts to summarize Proust's masterwork, including a three-word summary by Gérard Genette in *Figures III* (Paris: Seuil 1972): "Marcel devient écrivain" ("Marcel becomes a writer"). See tempsperdu.com.

"constitutional settlement"—("Our Eamonn") This is one of only a handful of instances in all of *FC* that the "troubles" (violence perpetrated by Protestant and Catholic combatants) in Northern Ireland are really broached. (The others include: Ep. 32, where a minister is busily engaged in "dealing with the Irish situation," and the other is in Ep. 41, when Reverend Ian Paisley types are lecturing about Irish sovereignty at a department store counter.)

There is a conspicuous absence in *FC* of pointed jabs at Ireland or Northern Ireland, especially as both Scotland and Wales take it on the chin regularly. It may be that since so many deaths were associated with the struggle in Northern Ireland (for the better part of the century), the issue had become politically taboo, especially in the Light Entertainment division. More routinely, the Poet-Reader-cum-Weatherman (Palin, Ep. 17) mentions that a front is arriving from Ireland, the Ian Paisley types talk to themselves in Ep. 41 (the audience seems to miss the allusion), and the *Radio Times* had early described the nascent *Flying Circus* program as a "history of Irish agriculture"—that's the extent of Ireland and the Irish in *FC*.

Even the BBC found significant opposition to a planned "in-depth" program on Northern Ireland in December-January 1971, with various ministers warning (and even threatening) BBC Director-General Lord Hill that such a program could only damage prospects for peace in the region (reported in *The Times*).

The *Northern Ireland Constitutional Proposals* would be published in March 1973 (after this episode was written and broadcast), and were an attempt to define the problem in Northern Ireland relative to the monarchy and the quest for a free Northern Ireland (rejoined with the Republic of Ireland). A poll was held in early March 1973, with electors voting 591,820 to 6,463 in favor of Northern Ireland remaining a part of the United Kingdom.

These constitutional reforms were undertaken in an effort to stop the intimidations, bombings, assassinations, and executions that had become part of everyday life in Northern Ireland since the "troubles" began. In January 1972, for example, an IRA bomb blast in Belfast killed fifty-five people.

Perhaps also built into the structure of the sketch is the fruitlessness of the ongoing talks in Northern Ireland, as Eamonn (Chapman) here tries unsuccessfully and for the third time to explain conditions in Dublin, and as various phone conversations go nowhere (and the futility spreads to other sketches, as well). Eamonn never does get to anything beyond the possibility of a "constitutional settlement" in his interrupted answers, and the sticky subject is both commented on and ultimately avoided.

contrapuntally, in madrigal . . . until they rallentando—(PSC; "*Summarize Proust Competition*") Tomlinson's singers are essentially combining their melodies and rhythms in counterpoint, though they don't really rallentando (begin to slow down) as much as they are cut off by the fifteen-second gong.

"Cuba Libres"—("Travel Agent") A lime juice and rum drink, sometimes topped with iced Coca-Cola, probably something the Tourist (Idle) would dislike, as well.

Cut to stock film of people actually climbing Everest—("Everest Climbed by Hairdressers") This BBC film stock is only accounted for by number: K26544, K26545, and K26546, which may mean that it's all actually K2 footage, and not Everest (WAC T12/1,441).

– D –

"dago"—("Travel Agent") Slang for someone of Spanish, Portuguese, or Italian origin, one of the many such slang terms employed by the Pythons.

"bandy-legged"—Legs that curve inwardly, perhaps indicating dietary deficiencies.

"dead"—("Our Eamonn") Mervyn (Cleese) doesn't comprehend metaphoric or allusive language, a trait seen later in Mr. Wensleydale (Palin) in the "Cheese Shop" sketch in Ep. 33. This also could be a reference to Cleese's stated preference for wordplay sketches, where characters would generally be expected to use such euphuistic language with ease.

Devils, The—("Language Laboratory") Film directed by Ken Russell, who had also directed a film version of Sandy Wilson's *The Boy Friend*, a version Wilson reportedly detested. *The Devils* (1971) depicts the rise to power of Cardinal Richelieu, and the priest who stands in his way, the latter portrayed by Oliver Reed. Parts of the film—especially its attempts at historically accurate production design—were obvious inspirations for the later *Monty Python and the Holy Grail* (1974).

Russell has already been mentioned in Ep. 29 ("Ken Russell's *Gardening Club*") and will be mentioned again in Ep. 33, "Sam Peckinpah's *Salad Days*." See entries to those episodes for more on Russell, *The Devils*, and his attraction for the Pythons.

"doctor encouraged me"—("Summarizing Proust Competition") Summarizing Proust, then, acts like a trip to the mineral water spa or a drier climate, and must also

be equated with "strangling animals, golf, and masturbating," as those are also Bagot's (Chapman) hobbies.

ducks-on-wall house—(PSC; "Our Eamonn") A metaphor meaning "cheaply decorated," the phrase will be found in a Kinks' song just three years later. The phrase is meant to be a shorthand from the Pythons for the set designers and property masters, who will then scour the BBC prop collections for the proper decor.

In the 17 July 1970 issue of *Private Eye*, the phrase is invoked. After PM Wilson (called "Wislon" by *PE*) lost to Heath, it was rumored that Mrs. Wilson was slow to move out of 10 Downing Street:

> For over a fortnight after the Grocer's [Heath] election triumph she kept coming back for bits and pieces left behind. . . . The situation so exasperated Anthony Royle, one of Baillie Vass's [Alec Douglas-Home] stooges at the Foreign Office that he was heard to remark: "If that woman isn't out of here by tomorrow, I personally will come and shoot the f***ing ducks off the wall." (14 August 1970, 5)

– E –

"Enterovioform"—("Travel Agent') An anti-diarrheal medication now banned in the United States due to its connection to nerve damage in many patients.

Episode 31—Recorded 24 April 1972, and broadcast 16 November 1972. This episode was recorded ninth and broadcast fifth.

The music gathered for this episode included the following, according to WAC records: (in-studio) "Stage Struck" by Jack Parnell; "World Trip for Big Orchestra No. 1, Pizzicata Milanese" by H. Kressling; New Concert Orchestra playing "Pistons" section from *Crankcraft* suite by Trevor Duncan; music dubbed to film: London Philharmonic Orchestra playing "Sinfonia Antarctica" by Vaughn Williams; "Theme From Glorious West"; London Studio Group's "Inner Reflections Gentle Touch" by Reg Wale; International Studio Orchestra playing "Military Preparation" by Hugo de Groot; "Culver City Title" by Jack Shaindlin; and "Dramenasuspence No. 5" by R. Sharples (WAC T12/1,441).

This does not mean that each one of these pieces was eventually used in the particular episode. Occasionally, two episodes' worth of music cues and even actors (extras) are combined in a single episode file; also, at times the music cue is asked for (by the Pythons in the script) but is either not found or is found to be prohibitively expensive, and a similar, generic piece of music replaces it. This last reason is why there is a surfeit of British light music in these shows (from composers Reg Tilsley, Trevor Duncan, Keith Papworth, Reg Wale et al.)—the music was available and affordable for quick acquisition, mostly from LPs already in the BBC collection.

– F –

fire engine—(PSC; "Fire Brigade") Rather than bring in equipment for the set or shoot in a firehouse somewhere on location, they employ a rear screen projection of a firehouse interior, and add appropriate costumes.

fire engines skidding out of the fire station—(PSC; "Our Eamonn") These fire engine locations scenes were shot in Jersey with the Jersey Fire Brigade in March 1972 (WAC T12/1,428).

"five principles"—("Language Laboratory") There were "five principles" (plus one later) outlined by the British government in 1965, designed to lead Rhodesia to majority rule, and are as follows:

1—Unimpeded progress to majority rule must be maintained and guaranteed.
2—There must be guarantees against retrogressive amendment to the constitution.
3—There must an immediate improvement in the political status of the black population.
4—There must progress towards ending racial discrimination.
5—The constitutional proposals must be acceptable to the people of Rhodesia as a whole.
6—There must be no oppression of the majority by the minority or of the minority by the majority.

The sixth principle was added in 1966. Ian Smith (Ep. 45) and the minority white government in Rhodesia declared unilateral independence in 1965, leading to international sanctions. See more at "Smith," who will also be mentioned by Mr. Smoke-Too-Much (Idle) later, as well as in Ep. 45. There, Mrs. S's son (Cleese) is on his way to the Commons to deliver an address on Rhodesia when Mrs. Nigger-Baiter (Palin) explodes.

Fourth Booth—(PSC; "Language Laboratory") Not credited in the scripts, this actor is Gilliam. The Fifth Booth actor is also left uncredited—he is probably a Fred Tomlinson Singer. Others in the booths include Fred Tomlinson and his various singers.

"Franco"—("Travel Agent") Generalissimo Francisco Franco (1892-1975) and his fascist government ruled Spain from 1939 to his death in 1975. Franco assumed power after the Spanish Civil War, after having served in military positions on the Balearic Islands between 1931 and 1933.

"from this cinema"—(animated link out of "Everest Climbed by Hairdressers") There was significant local advertising in both UK and U.S. movie theatres during this period, with adverts shot on film and run prior to the feature film. The ads were directed at both local villagers and urbanites, and were primarily from local merchants. One such title card, from an American drive-in theatre c. 1960, asked viewers to "patronize the following leading merchants for quality merchandise and expert service," then offered a series of ads for local stores and services. After a significant hiatus, this kind of local advertising in movie theatres is returning.

– G –

"Glasgow . . . Choir"—("Everest Climbed by Hairdressers") The Glasgow Orpheus Choir was active for a half century under the direction of Sir Hugh Robertson. The name chosen by the Pythons may have been an amalgamation of the Glasgow choir combined with the Grimsby and Cleethorpes Orpheus Male Voice Choir, begun in 1949.

Separate groups of Danes, French, Englishmen, Americans, Norwegians, Chinese, Russians, etc. made various unsuccessful assaults on the world's tallest mountain from the 1920s through the early 1960s. Some of these groups had permission, some did not; some had state-of-the-art equipment for the period, others came down nearly dead, if they came down at all. Legitimate sponsoring groups for these expeditions included the Alpine Club, the Royal Geographic Society, the Swiss Foundation for Alpine Research, the National Geographic Society, etc.

"greengrocer"—("Travel Agent") Simply, one who deals in fruit and vegetables. In other words—a common, working man. The satirical magazine *Private Eye* had been calling Conservative leader Edward Heath "Grocer Heath" or just "The Grocer" since 1962. (Heath represented Bexley, southeast of London, not Luton.)

– H –

"Hillary, Sir Edmond"—("Everest Climbed by Hairdressers") Hillary (b. 1919) is mentioned in passing in Ep. 28, the "Emigration from Surbiton to Hounslow" sketch.

"Sherpa Tensing"—Tenzing Norgay (1914-1986) was a Nepalese Sherpa who led Hillary on the first successful climb of Everest in 1953, and who had made a number of reconnoitering climbs in the decades prior to reaching the summit.

"Hoddesdon"—(*"Summarize Proust Competition"*) Located in Hertfordshire, just north of Greater London near Hertford.

– I –

"I can't get the fire brigade Mervyn"—("Fire Brigade") Not just an incongruity, relations between No. 10 Downing Street and labor had become so strained that even fire brigade unions had gone on strike during Heath's Tory administration, along with other critical care-type professions, many striking for the first time in history.

"Industrial Relations Bill"—("Our Eamonn") There are two references that inform this mention. The first is the Industrial Relations Act of 1946 that set labor and wage policy for, specifically, Northern Ireland's industry. The act was revisited and revised over the years. Secondly, various industrial relations bills considered during this period had primarily pitted the sitting governments (Wilson, then Heath) against the TUC (Vic Feather, Clive Jenkins et al.), the political significance of which is represented by well over 200 surviving political cartoons (see the British Cartoon Archive). Most recently, the Conservative government's Industrial Relations Bill of December 1970 had created a firestorm of protest from trade union activists, leading to strike actions and labor unrest across the nation. Heath addressed the significance of the industrial relations changes in a 6 December 1970 speech:

> Within six months of coming into office, we have introduced the most important and the most far-reaching part of our legislative program, the Industrial Relations Bill. And already, as we expected, it has raised a storm of ill-judged protest. But I want to promise you this: that your government is not going to bow before this storm. (*pause for applause and "Here, here!" calls from the assembled audience*) We will persevere and we will come through it. We shall win the arguments, and we shall win the votes, and the bill will become law. This is the storm before the calm. (Audio transcription, *Eyewitness: 1970-79*, "Industrial Relations Bill 1971")

This was immediately followed by the passing into law of the Industrial Relations Act (1971), which greatly curtailed the powers of the trade unions.

"Instamatic . . . *Daily Express*"—("Travel Agent") Kodak's first Instamatic brand-name camera was sold in 1963, and the ensuing versions sold millions through the late 1980s. It would have been a typical, affordable tourist's camera of this period.

Dr. Scholl's "exercise sandals" sold in the millions as well in 1968, the success of which may be the reason the Tourist mentions them here; this also accords with the mention of the sandals being fit for chiropodists climbing Everest earlier in the episode.

The *Daily Express* was a Conservative paper started by the future Lord Beaverbrook, and by the 1930s had become the nation's highest-circulating newspaper. No surprise here that the Tourist's targets would be clutching this paper, an icon of Englishness in the remnants of the shrinking postcolonial Empire.

interior of hairdresser's salon—("Everest Climbed by Hairdressers") This beauty shop is located on Moore Street in Jersey, and was used with permission from K. Moser (of Charles of Switzerland). The salon location was used 28 March 1972.

– J –

"Jenkins, Clive"—("Language Laboratory") Welshman Jenkins (1926-1999) was a white-collar union activist who spoke for and led the Association of Scientific, Technical and Managerial Staffs to huge membership numbers and industry prominence. He was a darling of the Labour Party, and represented the new left of big labor for many years. Jenkins is depicted dozens of times (usually antagonizing the Tory government somehow) during this period in political cartoons. See the British Cartoon Archive.

"Jensen"—("Language Laboratory") Cars manufactured in West Bromwich, West Midlands, near Birmingham.

Jersey—(PSC; "Everest Climbed by Hairdressers") One of the Channel Islands off the coast of France, and perhaps 100 miles south of Weymouth, the States of Jersey is much closer to France (only fourteen miles offshore) than to the UK. The entire cast and crew set up shop here for location shooting 19-29 March 1972. Most of the exterior footage for the latterly episodes of the third series is recorded on the island.

– K –

"Keble Bollege Oxford"—("Travel Agent") Keble *College* Oxford was founded in 1870. The two Oxfordians in the troupe attended Brasenose (Palin), and St. Edmund's (Jones) colleges. Python mate and author Humphrey Carpenter (1946-2005) graduated from Keble.

"K2 . . . Vidals"—("Everest Climbed by Hairdressers") K2 (the second peak surveyed in the Karakorum range) is the second-highest peak in the world at 28,250 feet, and is found on the China-Pakistan border.

It was first climbed successfully in 1954. Annapurna is actually a massif of the Himalayas, with two major peaks, Annapurna I and Annapurna II. Annapurna I was first climbed in 1950 by a Frenchman named Maurice, coincidentally.

"Vidal" would be Vidal Sassoon, the very influential hair stylist of the 1960s and beyond. See the entry for "Teasy-Weasy" for more. Vidal's head office during this period was in New Bond Street in London.

"Kettering and Boventry"—("Travel Agent") Kettering and *Coventry* are within a few miles of each other, and both east of the larger city of Birmingham, and both within Idle's sphere of influence as he grew up—the West Midlands being the locus for much of this rant.

– L –

lady with enormous knockers—(PSC; *"Summarize Proust Competition"*) This is Julie Desmond (*Casanova*), who was one of several actors to sign the "use of skin" clause demanded by the BBC for permission to exhibit "more" of themselves on camera (WAC T12/1,445). The others signing such contracts during the third series included Sally Anne, Reuben Martin, and Karen Burch.

"la maladie . . . chose"—(*"Summarize Proust Competition"*) The translation for this phrase reveals the typical jabberwock the Pythons often offer as spoken French: "The imaginary invalid of recondition and of all surveillance is soon one and the same." Providing this translation, Professor Daryl Lee (Brigham Young University French & Italian Dept.) also points out that the phrase "malade imaginaire" is most likely drawn from Moliere's play of the same name, and perhaps reminds us of the frail physical condition of Proust.

"Leicester"—(*"Summarize Proust Competition"*) Chapman's home town, Leicester is in Leicestershire, and is north and east of Birmingham, and well north of London. It was the Bishop of Leicester who was discovered, in Ep. 29, on the landing in the "Salvation Fuzz" sketch. Leicester (the city, the bishop, and the diocese) is mentioned in eleven separate episodes.

"local Roman ruins"—("Travel Agent") There are a number of surviving Roman sites on these islands, including burial sites, an amphitheatre, a bridge, and the sites around ancient Pollentia. Tour companies made regular pilgrimages to these sites, ushering tourists from ruin to ruin as quickly as possible.

loony leans into the camera—(PSC; "Everest Climbed by Hairdressers") The printed scripts give no indication as to who this might be (though Gilliam often takes

these kinds of roles), but WAC records indicate that Frank Lester took the part this time (WAC T12/1,441). The audience response (mostly silence) indicates that there's an uncertainty as to how to respond to the odd interjection, perhaps partly because he is interacting with a projected image, and the studio audience misses the "effect" witnessed by the viewing audience at home.

"Luton"—(*"Summarize Proust Competition"*) Approximately thirty-two miles from London, Luton is home to an international airport, and the site where Dinsdale Piranha set off a nuclear weapon in Ep. 14. Luton is mentioned again below, by the Tourist (Idle), as he rambles on about boorish West Midlands tourists on the continent, where it is cited as the example of a typical, middle-class north-of-London city producing benign, self-absorbed Englishness in its citizenry.

"Luton airport"—("Travel Agent") Opened in 1938, by 1969 Luton was handling a full one-fifth of all "package tour" flights to the continent, was the "most profitable" airport in the UK by 1972, and would have been the place the Tourist or even Idle himself (and family) might have embarked on such a vacation. (See London-luton.co.uk.) The shorter runways at the Birmingham International Airport (closer to home for the "adenoidal typist" and others) did not allow for larger planes—its smaller planes servicing Scotland, Ireland, etc., instead—meaning Luton became the international (and certainly Mediterranean) hub in the 1950s and 1960s for the entire West Midlands.

– M –

"Majorcan"—("Travel Agent") Of or from Majorca. The larger of the Balearic Islands chain (Majorca is also spelled "Mallorca"), Menorca, Ibiza, and Formentara are also major islands in the chain. In Ep. 33, Biggles (Chapman) will be reminded that he recently took a Spanish holiday (like so many of his fellow countrymen) in Ibiza, though he'll counter that such a visit doesn't count as a trip to Spain. It seems that the more familiar the destination becomes, and the more English-tourist-friendly, the less it becomes an exotic destination—it is essentially colonized and co-opted, and can be dismissed. This, of course, is much the reason the Tourist (Idle) seems so worked up—he travels to a foreign land and only to encounter his unliked neighbors in every queue, his own culture pasted into Mediterranean streets.

"Malaga"—("Travel Agent") Coastal city of Andalucia, Spain, and obviously the destination point of the flights carrying package-tour tourists originating at Luton.

"Maybe It's Because I'm a Londoner"—("Travel Agent") Written by Hubert Gregg late in the war (1944-1945), during the last months of the V-rocket blitz:

> Maybe it's because I'm a Londoner, that I love London so.
> Maybe it's because I'm a Londoner, that I think of her wherever I go.
> I get a funny feeling inside of me, just walking up and down.
>   Maybe it's because I'm a Londoner, that I love London Town.

The jolly British POWs in Ep. 18 begin to sing this refrain as the "Escape (From Film)" begins. See the entry in Ep. 18 for more on the traditional song that wouldn't become a hit until after the war.

"Memorial Baths, Swansea"—(PSC; *"Summarize Proust Competition"*) Swansea is in Wales on Swansea Bay. This is probably modeled after the celebrated War Memorial Swimming Baths in Windsor, opened by the Queen in 1963. (*Private Eye* had earlier reported a Miss Neasden contest originating from the "Stafford Cripps Memorial Baths, Neasden" [4 December 1970, 13].)

This is a curious moment. Generally, the printed scripts' decriptive sections do not try and participate in the obfuscation—there can be quips and asides to the other Pythons, but when a setting is announced, it's usually fairly accurate. Example: just a bit later in the episode the description tells us that the setting is a garden in Jersey, which is exactly where the Pythons shot the scene. In the case of the "Summarize Proust" sketch, however, the description tells the reader the setting is Memorial Baths, Swansea, while the spangly Mee (Jones) announces they're in the Arthur Ludlow Memorial Baths in Newport. There is also no indication in the WAC records that the Pythons did any shooting—location, studio, or otherwise—anywhere but the following areas: Devon, Norfolk, Greater London, Scotland, and Jersey. (In actuality, they likely shot this in Television Centre, as it's recorded on tape. With the exception of the occasional bumps to Golders Green and Ealing TFS, the Pythons didn't shoot on tape outside of TC.)

"Mervyn"—("Our Eamonn") Perhaps drawn from Terence *Mervyn* Rattigan, and just continuing their slighting references to the well-known playwright begun in Ep. 30—Mervyn here is depicted as fairly dim.

"Milo"—("Everest Climbed by Hairdressers") A chocolate drink from Nestlé (introduced in 1933), and often served warm for breakfast.

"Mt Everest. Forbidding. Aloof. Terrifying."—("Everest Climbed by Hairdressers") This is yet an-

other Python skewering of an English sacred cow, in this case the sixty-year quest by the British government to reach the world's highest mountain before any other nation. Gordon Stewart discusses the significance to "Empire" that Everest represented between 1890 and 1953, and the serendipitous fact that Hillary's ascension coincided neatly with Elizabeth's ascension propped up—at least in newspapers and the public imagination—Britain's continuing presence as a superpower and a real player in world politics. Stewart notes that Everest was a watershed moment:

> In Britain the Everest triumph was viewed as a symbolic event which revealed significant things about contemporary British culture, about the values which had been conventionally associated with Britain's rise to world power in the nineteenth and early twentieth centuries, and about the British identity in the modern world. (170)

As with earlier ridiculing references to Elizabeth I, Drake, Shakespeare, Nelson, and others, the Pythons undercut the Everest expedition by belittling and deriding it, toppling Empire-building (or Empire-shoring-up) at a single stroke.

The Goons had also rendered silly the Everest adventure, with Seagoon (Seacombe) certain that if he manages to eat the highest peak in the world Hollywood will come calling, and he'll be rich and famous ("The Mountain Eaters," 1 December 1958). The Goons had also performed an episode entitled "The Ascent of Mount Everest" on 28 April 1953, and this was reworked as *Telegoons* episode in 1963, as well.

Music starts, continuity-type music—(PSC; *"Summarize Proust Competition"*) This brief snippet of music is from World Trip for Big Orchestra No. 1, "Pizzicata Milanese" by H. Kressling (WAC T12/1,441).

– N –

"never thought about that"—("Travel Agent") There is a significant audience laugh at this point, indicating that something's been edited out. In the audio version of this sketch, and in the original script, the Tourist (Idle) finishes by saying, "What a silly bunt." "Bunt," of course, stands in for "cunt" here (continuing the initial "b" and "c" switching trope), and when Duncan Wood (then Head of Comedy at BBC) screened the first nine episodes in September 1972, he specifically demanded that the line be removed. (The line has also been elided from the printed scripts.)

Interesting that the clumsy removal of the word "masturbating" (also demanded by Wood in his Sept. 1972 memo) at the beginning of this episode has been cited many times since as an example of the BBC's censorship practices, but the excision of this second, veiled crudity often goes unmentioned.

"new theory about the brontosaurus"—("Theory on Brontosauruses by Anne Elk [Miss]") Beginning in about 1964, the scientific community and then the public imagination were caught up in this excitement as new discoveries changed the way dinosaurs were perceived. The discovery and identification of deinonychus in 1964 (by John Ostrom) meant that the pantheon of enormous, lumbering, cold-blooded dinosaurs had to make room for the more bird-like, warmer-blooded hunters like the raptors. (See one of Ostrom's many articles on the subject—"*Archaeopteryx*: Notice of a 'New' Specimen"—in *Science* 170.3957 [30 October 1970]: 537-38.)

"North Col"—("Everest Climbed by Hairdressers") Discovered and climbed by George Mallory (1896-1924) and his team in September 1921, and became the key to making the northern ascent. Mallory would die on the slopes of Everest, his body not discovered until 1999.

– O –

"our Eamonn"—("Our Eamonn") Probably borrowed from the popular *The Eamonn Andrews Show* (1964-1969) on BBC-TV, which starred Eamonn Andrews. Andrews (1922-1987) became known for not only presenting shows such as *What's My Line?* (1951-1963), *This is Your Life* (1955-1987), and *Crackerjack* (children's show; 1955-1964), but also for his off-the-cuff non sequitur linkings that made no sense, and which Python would satirize over and over again in *FC*. Andrews has already been referenced in Ep. 26.

"Dublin"—Eamonn Andrews was born in Synge Street in Dublin, Ireland, and became the first head of the state-run RTE Authority in 1961, which governed television in Ireland.

– P –

panning shot across mountains in CinemaScope format—(PSC; "*Party Hints* with Veronica Smalls") Cinema-Scope is a widescreen process utilizing an anamorphic lens to project 35mm film at a 2.66:1 aspect ratio. This effect was used primarily as a means to combat the rise in television's influence on American viewers, ideally bringing audiences back into movie theaters for spectacular visual effects not available on TV. Other widescreen processes used in Westerns from other studios included Todd-AO (*The Alamo*), Super Panavision 70 (*Cheyenne Autumn*), and VistaVision (*The Searchers*).

This particular title sequence is actually inspired, however, by the *Cinerama* uber-Western-film *How the West Was Won* (1963), directed by the troika of Henry Hathaway, John Ford, and George Marshall, and starring everyone from Henry Fonda and Karl Malden to Jimmy Stewart, John Wayne, Debbie Reynolds, and Spencer Tracy—twenty-four name stars in all. The Cinerama widescreen technology is fundamentally different from those mentioned above. The process involves three separate filmed images connected, side to side, for an unprecedented and not a little disconcerting widescreen effect—the "forced" perspective draws attention to itself—especially in a panning move, or if a character moves into the foreground or background of the shot.

The music underneath is the "Theme From Glorious West," and the film stock is borrowed from EMI, and called *Cowboy Western* (WAC T12/1,441).

"permanent strike"—("Travel Agent") As part of the student- and worker-led strikes sweeping across France, air traffic controllers at Orly joined other trade unions and originally went out on strike in May 1968. Afterward and to this day, strikes have been used whenever working conditions demanded it, often shutting down transportation systems and entire cities across France, and having a ripple effect across Europe. (As perhaps a nudge to the Pythons in writing this sketch, TUC took its coal miners out on strike in January 1972, their first such walkout in half a century. By mid-February, lights were being turned off across the country to save power.)

photo of Everest—(PSC; "Everest Climbed by Hairdressers") The stock photo is from the Alfred Gregory Camera Press, "Nepal 161A" (WAC T12/1,441). The superimposed dots graphic motif is borrowed directly from the BBC's celebrated coverage of an Old Man of Hoy climb in 1967, and would have been quite familiar to this studio audience.

"Powell, Enoch"—("Travel Agent") Powell entered Parliament in 1950 as a Conservative from Wolverhampton (Idle's home), and would champion ultra-conservative and rigidly nationalistic policies throughout his stormy career. Powell (1912-1998) was born and raised in Birmingham, taught university in Sydney, and studied Urdu in his early quest to become the Viceroy of India (*ODNB*).

Both Powell and Ian Smith are mentioned in this sketch as exemplars of what the Pythons must have seen as Britain's last attempts at colonial control in a rapidly changing world. Both are depicted as ideologues or "racialists" (see Ep. 5, "Vox Pops") who want to transplant or resuscitate the British way of life and authority into/onto Third World countries.

"pretty bad there"—("Our Eamonn") This episode was recorded in April 1972, and followed close on the heels of the infamous "Bloody Sunday" (30 January 1972), where twenty-seven civil rights demonstrators were shot by British soldiers in Derry.

The fact that Eamonn (Chapman) is completely decked out as an African warrior is perhaps a reference to the wildness, the other-ness with which Northern Ireland was perceived by many Englishmen during this period. Admittedly, if he *were* dressed as an identifiable Irishman, the BBC and Television Centre may have become a target for IRA reprisals.

"Proust"—(*Summarize Proust Competition*") Marcel Proust (1871-1922) was a sickly youth who spent a great deal of time recuperating and writing. See the note for *"A La Recherche . . . "* above for more.

"Proust's novel . . . intemporality"—(*Summarize Proust Competition*") The quick summary by Harry Bagot (Chapman) is quite accurate, the Pythons betraying their appreciation of this significant Modernist work.

"Pules"—("Everest Climbed by Hairdressers") "Pule" actually means to whimper or whine, which works well with the poncing nature of the characters here. The highest permanent structure in this area (below Everest base camps) is most likely the Rongbuk Monastery, at about 20,900 feet above sea level.

– R –

"rabbitting"—("Travel Agent") Shortened colloquialism meaning to talk on and on incessantly, and deriving from the rhyming slang "rabbit-and-pork," meaning "having a conversation."

"Rhyl"—("Travel Agent") Located on the north coast of Wales, Rhyl is a beach town just a few miles up the coast from Colwyn Bay, where Jones was born.

– S –

"Saxones"—("Our Eamonn") Perhaps the common Latin term for the collection of locals (Angles, Saxons, Frisians, Jutes, Germans) found in Britain during the Roman occupation. It's not clear what kind of question she (Jones) might be answering at this point, though she may be having to identify her ancestry. Venerable Bede (673-735) uses the term to describe a portion of the peoples of the British Isles, part of the larger *Anglii* culture (*ODNB*).

"shooting anyone under nineteen"—("Travel Agent") Spanish dictator Franco's policies were quite oppressive, as he outlawed even political parties and raised the Catholic Church to the status of a state religion, complicit with and even perpetuating his fascistic policies. There were approved Francoist youth movement organizations, including the Phalange. All other groups were outlawed, though there seemed to have been a number of such groups, including active but hidden cadres of more politicized Boy Scouts.

Showbiz music, applause . . . —(PSC; *"Summarize Proust Competition"*) This music is Jack Parnell's "Stage Struck" (WAC T12/1,441).

"sodding"—("Our Eamonn") A vague epithet, here almost equivalent to "damn." The term will be used again with more of its sexual connotation in place in Ep. 45. Earlier, in Ep. 17, Cleese's "sod" was replaced prior to taping with a voiced raspberry; standards have changed, clearly, with the increased popularity of the show.

"soldering a crystal set"—("Fire Brigade") A radio (often homemade) that employs a crystal detector. Crystal radios were very popular hobby store items during the Pythons' younger years.

"South Col"—("Everest Climbed by Hairdressers") "South Col" was the route used by Hillary and Norgay in 1953. It is the site of the highest camp before making the summit—Camp IV, at about 26,000 feet.

"Lhotse Face"—A wall of glacial blue ice that must be traversed when using the southeast approach.

"North Ridge"—They'd be way off course here. After Lhotse Face, the stops and/or landmarks traditionally are Yellow Band, Geneva Spur, South Col, Southeast Ridge, South Summit, Cornice Traverse, Hillary Step, and finally the Summit.

"Smith"—("Language Laboratory") Referring to Ian Smith, nominal and controversial leader of Rhodesia during this period, who led the unilateral independence movement of Rhodesia from Great Britain. See below for more.

"Smith, Mr."—("Travel Agent") Two real possibilities here. Sir Dudley Smith was a Tory MP who represented Warwick and Leamington, a West Midlands parliamentary constituency, during this period. Idle would have grown up hearing and reading about Dudley Smith, and his conservatism may have appealed to the Tourist's take on the ignorant British tourist.

But given the following mention of Enoch Powell (see entry above), the "Smith" reference probably actually refers to Ian Smith (b. 1919), who had taken Rhodesia under white minority control in 1965 (and held it until 1979)—perhaps the Tourist is hoping Smith can do the same for Spain and her islands, and then even Britain. These policies reflect the hopes and promises of the British Union of Fascists, though BUF hadn't been an effective political concern since the 1930s, and was actually banned in 1940. (See the recorded entries on British fascism as part of *Eyewitness 1930-39*, beginning with "Fascism in Britain.")

"Spanish tummy"—("Travel Agent") A colloquial, catch-all (and less alarming) way to refer to stomach and intestinal problems associated with visits to Spain and the Continent. In 1664-1665, it was the bubonic and pneumonic plague that resurged in London, killing as many as 70-100,000 (of a total population of less than 500,000) before giving way to the cleansing destructiveness of the Great Fire in 1666. London's great cholera epidemics actually occurred in the nineteenth-century, killing thousands, then hundreds, and then dozens in successive outbreaks. The last great London cholera epidemic ravaged the city in 1854, and was blamed on a contaminated well in Broad Street.

"Guardia"—A quasi-military police force in Spain, originally formed in 1844, and used by General Franco to enforce the government policies in Fascist Spain. See entry for Franco.

stock film of Everest—(PSC; "Everest Climbed by Hairdressers") The film stock here is BBC film stock, and titled "K26544, -45 and -46", and may actually be of K2, and have been taken of a 1965 expedition (WAC T12/1,441).

"strangling . . . masturbating"—("*Summarize Proust Competition*") This latter word was actually edited out of the broadcast, leaving the studio audience to seemingly respond (with belly laughter) to the audibly mangled "golf and strangling animals." Duncan Wood of BBC Light Entertainment had a meeting with several of the Pythons, telling them that the term "masturbating" was not going to pass muster. This is one of the few times that a finished episode was actually edited/censored for content on BBC brass demand. See Morgan (1999) and McCabe for more.

Along a similar vein, noted British philosopher Bertrand Russell mentions that as a lonely adolescent his keen interests in "sex, mathematics and religion" kept him from suicidal thoughts (see *The Autobiography of Bertrand Russell*, 38-39). Russell admits that masturbation allowed him to survive between ages fifteen and twenty, when he finally fell in love. See Ep. 32 for more on Russell—as a curmudgeonly, free-thinking, sexually obsessed scientist/philospher/activist/gadfly, he probably very much appealed to the Pythons.

Sunday Mirror—("Travel Agent") Popular Sunday edition of the *Daily Mirror* (Eps. 10, 24) founded in 1915, and became the *Sunday Mirror* in 1963. Seen as a "paper of the people," appealing to a broad middle-class English readership, which is why Idle's Tourist would denigrate it. See notes to Eps. 10 and 24 for more on the *Daily Mirror*, its readership and features.

– T –

"Teasy-Weasy"—("Everest Climbed by Hairdressers") "Mr. Teasy-Weasy" was Raymond Bessone, aka "Raymond of Mayfair," the owner/operator of a hair salon in posh Mayfair that claimed a long list of celebrity clients. Bessone was the most popular hair stylist of 1950s London, and gave the young Vidal Sassoon his start in the business.

The reference to celebrity hairdresser "Roger" in Ep. 14 ("*Face the Press*") is likely a nod to Raymond, who was by this time popular enough to go by just his given name. His salon was located at 18 Grafton Street W1.

thirties routine—("Language Laboratory") Meant to indicate a 1930s-era Hollywood musical number, like those found in the films *Golddiggers of 1933* or *42nd Street*, both produced by the American studio Warner Bros., and both choreographed by Busby Berkeley.

Thrust—("Theory on Brontosauruses by Anne Elk (Miss)") Meant to mimic probing and/or current affairs news shows like *Panorama*, then airing on BBC1 since 1953. *The World About Us* (BBC2; 1967-1986) was also running, but this show focused on natural history. The combination of current affairs and natural history actually seems quite apropos as Anne Elk (Cleese) discusses her unusual brontosaurus theory.

"Timothy White's suncream"—("Travel Agent") Skin protection cream popular during the Pythons' youth, the company (Timothy Whites and Taylors Ltd.) had been acquired by chemist giant Boots in 1968, so this is probably a bit of a nostalgic reference. There were still many Timothy White stores (more than thirty) in the Greater London area in 1969.

Tomlinson, Fred—("*Summarize Proust Competition*") Tomlinson and his singers appear in Eps. 22, 25, 26, 29, 36, and 37. They will also appear later in this episode in the "Language Laboratory" sketch.

"transistor radios"—("Travel Agent") To listen to their favorite BBC shows, news, and perhaps especially sport, rather than the local media. Much of this diatribe reads like a postcolonial antagonism, wherein the speaker blasts the vestiges of British imperialism carted along with tourists like so much essential baggage.

"Transworld International"—("CinemaScope" link into "*Party Hints* with Veronica Smalls") The broadcasting arm of the U.S. sports marketing group IMG, run by Mark McCormack (1930-2003), TWI was set up in the 1960s to tape and broadcast golf, initially.

Keeping in mind the Python penchant for mixing real Mortimers with fake ones (the debt to Shakespeare acknowledged), the other entries in this list of fanciful credits include:

"Nimrod Productions"—A biblical figure purported to be a great hunter, "Nimrod" has also become a pejorative term, perhaps thanks to Bugs Bunny's usage in reference to Elmer Fudd in several Warner Bros. cartoons.

"Arthur E. Ricebacher"—A European-sounding (and most likely Jewish) name for a typical Hollywood movie mogul, like Larry and Irving R. Saltzberg in Ep. 6.

"David A. Seltzer Production"—A play on the name of film producer/studio owner David O. Selznick (1902-1965), producer of such films as *Gone With the Wind* (1939) and *Spellbound* (1945).

"Hasbach Enterprises"—A municipality in Germany, though there has also been a Hasbach GmbH (performing industrial sanitary services) in operation in Datteln, Germany since 1928. This could have been a name the Pythons picked up during their time in Bavaria shooting the first of two German episodes of *Fliegender Zirkus* in 1971. There is a noticeable gap in the *FC* recording dates for the 1972 season, with no activity noted in February or March—they were in Germany during most of this period. Upon their return to BBC in late March or early April, the Pythons went back to recording, with episodes 37 and 31 recorded in April 1972.

"Pulitzer Prizewinning Idea"—The Pulitzer Prize is awarded every year (since 1917) for achievement in journalism, drama, poetry, photography, etc.

"Daniel E. Stollmeyer"—No certainty here, but there were Stollmeyers who played cricket for the West Indies in the 1950s and 1960s, Jeffrey and Vic. Jeff Stollmeyer (1921-1989) was captain of the team, and the West Indies won the first two Tests (of five). This series may have been a memorable one for the youngish Pythons as it featured incidents of fan violence, official team complaints about rulings, substitutions, etc., and generally caused lots of friction between the countries. See Wisden. (Incidentally, there are no "Stollmeyer" entries in any extant London-area phonebook between 1965 and 1975.)

"from Robert Hughes's Novel"—Hughes (b. 1938) is a Sydney-born art critic and historian who has been publishing *non-fiction* since 1966, and has been art critic for *Time* magazine for many years. He is perhaps now best known for his influential book and TV series *The Shock of the New*, which looks at modern art in the age of commercialism.

"Louis H. Tannhauser"—This (and the "Vernon D. Larue" that follows) sounds much more like the made-up names from earlier lists ("Juan-Carlos Fernandez," "Thor Olaf Stensgaard") picked for how they sound, and not as a direct reference to any historical person. The name Tannhauser has a significant Cambridge connection, however, as occultist Alisteir Crowley (1875-1947) matriculated there (Trinity College), and would go on to write his own version of the Tannhauser story as a sort of "progress of the soul." This was also the name of a Wagner opera of 1845.

"Selzenbach-Tansrod Production"—A sort of half-hearted jumble of Seltzer-Hasbach and Tannhauser-Nimrod, though not unlike some of the co-named production companies of the day, including "Prodimex," a company used by Roger Corman (*Little Shop of Horrors*) for Spanish- and Italian-language exploitation pictures in the 1970s. Another portmanteau-ish example: the home that Mary Pickford and Douglas Fairbanks shared was called "Pickfair."

"Victor A. Lounge"—Though this is likely to be a reference to Victor Mature (mentioned earlier in Ep. 28), husband-and-wife Charles and Ray Eames had made a film in 1956 called *Eames Lounge Chair*, an experimental film looking at their newly designed and very popular piece of Modern Art furniture.

"Rolo Nice Sweeties"—A Nestle chocolate-and-caramel candy. This is a certain return to actual references to actual people/products—the balance of the list is documentable.

"Fison's Fertilizers"—A proprietary name for a weed killer and fertilizer available in the UK in the 1950s and beyond.

"Time Life Innit-For-The-Money Limited"—The *Time-Life* company has been in business since 1961, and had been packaging books with records (LPs) since 1966. This crawl, then, is directly inspired by the 1963 film *How the West Was Won*, which proudly proclaimed on its lobby posters: "Suggested by the LIFE series!" The serialized story *How the West Was Won* appeared in *LIFE* magazine in 1959. See "panning" note above for more on this film.

"Trustees of St. Paul's Cathedral"—The Cathedral was designed by Christopher Wren, and built between 1675 and 1708. The trustees would have been in charge of any and all decisions regarding use or upkeep of the property, and continue to do so today.

"Ralph Reader"—Broadway choreographer (1903-1982) who also produced *The Gang Show Gala* (1970), which starred Peter Sellers. His early *Gang Show* productions were amateur variety shows.

"Ralph Nader"—American consumer activist and author, Nader (b. 1934) was during this period campaigning for better safety equipment in American automobiles, including seatbelts. His influential report was called "Unsafe at Any Speed," and appeared in 1965.

"The Chinese Government"—Included because China was emerging on the world stage in a very big way during this period. See entries for some of the many other Mao and China/Chinese references in Eps. 18, 19, 21, 23-25, 28, and 34.

"Michael's Auntie Betty in Australia"—Palin did have an Auntie Katherine (Palin Greenwood).

– U –

usual late-night line-up set—("Theory on Brontosauruses by Anne Elk [Miss]") *Late Night Lineup* (BBC2, 1964-1972) starred Joan Bakewell (Ep. 5), Denis Tuohy, Michael Dean, and Nicholas Tresilian. The "usual set" was a simple two-chair interview set, with backdrop. The show ran as many as six and seven nights per week, and looked at current trends in television, film, literature, music, etc. *Late Night* also featured a section called *Plunder*, where the vast BBC archives were raided for amusing pre-1955 TV clips, very much as Python would do when they had access to those same archives (Vahimagi 129).

The music underneath this exchange is Trevor Duncan's New Concert Orchestra playing "Pistons" from *Crankcraft*, a suite written about trains (cf. the "Neville Shunt" section of Ep. 24). British composer Duncan's (1924-2005) light orchestra music can also be heard in Eps. 28 and 45.

– V –

Voice Over (John)—(intro link into "The All-England *Summarize Proust Competition*") This is a mistake in the script, as Palin has by this time essentially taken over the "*Monty Python's Flying Circuses*" recitation chore.

– W –

"wallop"—("Language Laboratory") A colloquialism for "mild beer," perhaps Australian, and used by Orwell in *1984* (1949), and earlier by J.B. Priestley in *Three Men in New Suits* (1945).

"wasp farm"—("Theory on Brontosauruses by Anne Elk [Miss]") *Wasp Farm* was the title of a fairly popular book published in 1963 by Howard Ensign Evans of Cornell University. The book looked at the lives and activities of, especially, the solitary digger wasps.

"Watney's Red Barrel"—("Travel Agent") Catering to British tourists, this Spanish shop sells English food and the English drink, Watney's Red Barrel. A pale lager brewed by the sprawling Watney's Brewing empire during the 1960s and 1970s, the quality of this mass-produced beer was always in question, and the CAMRA organization (Campaign for Real Ale), founded in 1971 to combat the disappearance of individual breweries in the UK, was certainly helped along by Red Barrel's pedestrian infamy.

"Well I'll go . . . Ee ecky thump. Put wood in 'ole muther"—("Language Laboratory") Traditional or stereotypical Yorkshire sayings and accent, as delivered by northerner Palin. "I'll go to the foot of our stairs" is a Northern exclamation of surprise, not unlike "Well I'll be," while "Put wood in 'ole, muther" means "shut the door, mother," both delivered in the heaviest of Yorkshire Dales dialect.

"Thump" is a Yorkshire festival, but can also be a feast or wake, and "Eckythump" (Lancastrian martial arts) would become a classic *Goodies* episode (1970-1982). This phrase may have been borrowed from Python colleague Bill Oddie (b. 1941 in Lancashire), star of *The Goodies* (1970-1981). Oddie worked with several of the Pythons (Chapman, Cleese, Idle) on *At Last the 1948 Show* (1967), and attended Cambridge, knowing Chapman, Cleese, and Idle there.

Whistling wind, stirring music—(PSC; "Everest Climbed by Hairdressers") This music seems to be borrowed from Vaughn Williams' "Sinfonia Antarctica," probably the Epilogue section (WAC T12/1,441). This is the musical score from the 1948 film *Scott of the Antarctic*, which the Pythons spoofed in Ep. 23. The performance here is by the London Philharmonic Orchestra.

Wilson, Sandy—("Language Laboratory") Wilson (b. 1924; educated Harrow, Oriel College, Oxford) was a composer and lyricist of what has been called "lighter" theatrical fare. Wilson may have come to the Pythons' attention when he wrote music for Peter Cook's various revues, including *Pieces of Eight*.

Episode 32

"Aberdeen versus Raith Rovers"—("The Silliest Interview We've Ever Done") Aberdeen FC competes in the Scottish Premier League, and was formed from multiple Aberdeen-area clubs in 1903. Raith Rovers FC was formed in 1883, and play in Stark Park in Fife, Scotland. The Rovers are part of Bell's Scottish Football League Division 1.

Ambulance racing—("Gumby Brain Specialist") This film footage is listed as reference numbers NP/NT73292 and NP/NT65980 (WAC T12/1,446).

armoured vehicle—("Tory Housewives Clean-Up Campaign") This is the same tank and location used in Ep. 21, "Mosquito Hunters," and is located at the main gate, Army School of Transport, Longmore, Liss, Hampshire (WAC T12/1,430).

art gallery exterior—(PSC; "Tory Housewives Clean-Up Campaign") The location for this shot appears to be the columnar façade of the Tate Britain, on Millbank in London.

art gallery interior—(PSC; "Tory Housewives Clean-Up Campaign") In January 1970, police entered the London Arts Gallery and removed lithographs by/of John Lennon and Yoko Ono, citing the Obscene Publications Act of 1959, and following filed complaints.

London's museums had also been much in the news in 1971-1972, with the sweeping implementation of admission fees to formerly free national museums and galleries, as well as the imminent arrival of the "King Tut" exhibit to the UK. See the British Cartoon Archive.

"arthropods"—("Molluscs—'Live' TV Documentary") Arthropods are, indeed, the largest phylum of animals.

"Badger"—("The Silliest Sketch We've Ever Done") Badger (Idle) will appear again, in Ep. 35, as a would-be hijacker ("Bomb on Plane"), there offering to *not* interrupt the show for various small sums of money.

"Batley"—("Minister For Not Listening to People") Home of the earlier-mentioned Batley Townswomen's Guild and their famed and muddy historical re-enactments (see Eps. 11 and 22). Batley is in West Yorkshire.

"battle like bingo boys"—("Tory Housewives Clean-Up Campaign") "Bingo boys" is actually slang for a heavy drinker, especially of brandy, which is a purposely ironic appellation for the Victorian-throwback Tory housewives (*OED*).

This could also be a slight and even purposeful misspeaking, and Idle could have been referring to the "Biff Boys." These were "stewards," or hired muscle, used by noted British fascist Sir Oswald Mosley in the early 1930s to protect the meetings of his New Party, an ultra-conservative nationalist party separate from any established party or platform. Mosley, who actually stood successfully for the Conservative party in Harrow (1918), would become disenchanted with the government's handling of the Irish situation and switch first to independency and then Labour in the early 1920s. Still dissatisfied with the sitting government, Mosley studied fascism and switched again. His New Party candidates would have no success in the 1931 elections, and he would go on to form the British Union of Fascists in 1932. (See *ODNB* and *Eyewitness 1930-39* for more.)

"Bell's whisky"—("The Silliest Interview We've Ever Done") In 1970, Bell's was the leading whisky brand in Scotland, and had been in business in Scotland since the 1840s.

"big bad rabbit"—("Tuesday Documentary/Children's Story/Party Political Broadcast") This same "bad-tempered rodent" will appear in the feature film *Holy Grail*, and will be destroyed by Holy Hand Grenade of Antioch. The "killer rabbit" character—as silly and absurd as it seems in the hearing—may be traced to a marvelous sequence in Modernist novelist D.H. Lawrence's *Women in Love* (1921), where a pet rabbit reacts to being handled by Winnie and Gudrun:

> They unlocked the door of the hutch. Gudrun thrust in her arm and seized the great, lusty rabbit as it crouched still, she grasped its long ears. It set its four feet flat, and thrust back. There was a long scraping sound as it was hauled forward, and in another instant it was in mid-air, lunging wildly, its body flying like a spring coiled and released, as it lashed out, suspended from the ears. Gudrun held the black-and-white tempest at arms' length, averting her face. But the rabbit was magically strong, it was all she could do to keep her grasp. She almost lost her presence of mind.
>
> . . . .
>
> Gudrun stood for a moment astounded by the thunderstorm that had sprung into being in her grip. Then her colour came up, a heavy rage came over her like a cloud. She stood shaken as a house in a storm, and utterly overcome. Her heart was arrested with fury at the mindlessness and the bestial stupidity of this struggle, her wrists were badly scored by the claws of the beast, a heavy cruelty welled up in her. (chapter 18)

As early as Ep. 2, in the "Working-Class Playwright" sketch the Pythons display their knowledge of the England of D.H. Lawrence.

"black spot"—("Expedition to Lake Pahoe") In *Treasure Island*, those that are meant to suffer or die are given or "marked with" a black spot. The captain fears his mutinous crew is preparing a spot for him, as they want his chest. When Jim asks the captain what a black spot might be, the captain merely answers: "That's a summons, mate. I'll tell you if they get that" (13). When Blind Pew does slip the black spot into the captain's hand, the captain dies immediately.

A black spot will figure prominently in a censored Gilliam animation in Ep. 19. See notes for "The Spot" in that episode.

"Blenheim Crescent"—("Expedition to Lake Pahoe") There are at least fourteen Blenheim Crescent roads in the UK. In London, it can be found between Elgin Crescent and Cornwall Crescent near the Notting Hill area (W11). There is also a Runcorn Place just a block or so south and west of this same Blenheim Crescent.

British director David Lean (1908-1991) was born in Blenheim Crescent, Croydon. A Lean-like director (Ross, played by Chapman) appears in Ep. 1.

"Blind Pew"—("Expedition to Lake Pahoe") An evil, wounded pirate character in Stevenson's *Treasure Island*, Pew seeks the map and treasure. Jim describes Pew in their first painful encounter: "I never heard a voice so cruel, and cold, and ugly as that blind man's. It cowed me more than the pain, and I began to obey him at once" (15).

"Squire Trelawney"—The character in Stevenson's *Treasure Island* (1883) who finances the treasure hunt, and who also inadvertently gives away the plan to the bad guys.

These are just the latest of the many references to this obviously seminal text in *FC*, probably as a result of the novel having become a very popular Christmas pantomime years earlier.

"boy's bedroom"—("Tuesday Documentary/Children's Story/Party Political Broadcast") A do-it-yourself moment (DIY), which a number of British cultural observers have identified as particularly English, including Jeremy Paxman in a 1998 *Sunday Times* article (see the author's *MPSERD* 22).

"British"—("Tory Housewives Clean-Up Campaign") Interesting reference to the entire colonial empire, or at least the islands of the United Kingdom, as being "British" (of greater Britain) and not "English." Perhaps, though, Whitehouse and her Conservative allies were trying to refashion the "British" empire into an "English" one, excluding or transforming the darker, foreign-born, other-tongued interlopers and their white enablers and apologists.

"British Common Market"—("Tory Housewives Clean-Up Campaign") The tongue-in-cheek term for the proposed European Common Market (or European Economic Community, as it was called), which Britain would join in January 1973, and then reaffirm at the polls two years later (June 1975) via national referendum. Heath and the Labour Party had led the way for Britain's place in the Market, with France's de Gaulle being against Anglo membership in overriding votes in 1963 and 1967. One of the concerns closely held by many Gaulish EEC members was that English would immediately become the de facto language of business in the EEC, and that Britain would never be "European enough."

burning books—(PSC; "Tory Housewives Clean-Up Campaign") There seems to be no evidence that Mary Whitehouse actually destroyed books or films, being more focused on television depictions of sexuality during this period, and setting her sights on the BBC and its "permissive" director, Hugh Greene (and his underlings, including the pictured Robert Robinson).

"Bertrand Russell"—Russell (1872-1970) was a British mathematician and philosopher, and an outspoken liberal and critic of nuclear arms and the Vietnam War. Russell would also have angered the conservative Christian world with his comments in *Why I Am Not a Christian: And Other Essays on Religion and Related Subjects* (1927). Russell has been mentioned in the notes to Ep. 30, in relation to one of his early hobbies—masturbation. See entry for "Jean . . . Genet" below for more on Russell.

"Das Kapital"—Karl Marx's seminal work would have made the list for its godless, stateless Marxism (he's appeared as a gameshow contestant and in a homosexual encounter with Che Guevara already).

"The Guardian"—This has long been a left-of-center British newspaper, supporting the State of Israel in 1948, for example.

"Sartre"—See the notes to Ep. 27 for reasons the Tory Housewives would disapprove of the French existentialist.

"Freud"—Father of modern psychoanalysis Sigmund Freud's translated writings on sexuality and the unconscious had become part of the popular culture mélange between the wars, and, coincidentally, his books were also burned by Nazi stormtroopers in 1933 Germany.

On the side of the pile is a paperback copy of the infamous Kim Philby's *My Silent War* (1968). Philby was the high-ranking MI6 man who reported secrets to the Soviets for many years before defecting in 1963.

(Incidentally, this book burning image/theme may be what prompts the inclusion of Irish author Edna O'Brian later in the show. See below.)

The final two books pulled from the pile before being consigned to the flames are titled *Plato* and *Two Gentlemen Sharing*. Perhaps the Pythons are painting Plato and Socrates with the same broad brush, since Socrates was found guilty of corrupting the youth of Athens and was executed. The last (and almost unreadable) title is *Two Gentlemen Sharing*, a 1963 book by David Stuart Leslie (which would become a 1969 film) that posits a white, uptight advertising type having to share a flat with a Jamaican cricketer. The title implies a homosexual relationship, but the novel is more about race relations in restrictive middle-class London.

"Business is booming"—("Tory Housewives Clean-Up Campaign") For a very enlightening look at the *economic* impact of Modernist art(s) and literature(s) see Laurence Rainey's article "The Cultural Economy of Modernism" in *The Cambridge Companion to Modernism*, edited by Michael Levenson. Briefly, this was the period when *ars gratia artis* reigned, and modern artists enjoyed gala showings and equally impressive sales to private collectors. See Hughes' *The Shock of the New* for more on the cultural temblors in commercial/fine art during this period.

"But it's an ordinary house"—("Expedition to Lake Pahoe") Organizations including the Greater London Industrial Archaeology Society, HADAS (The Hendon & District Archaeological Society), the London Underground Railway Society, the City of London Archaeological Society, the London Museum, and myriad university-affiliated archaeological societies in Greater London have for many years conducted digs in and under the houses, buildings, and streets of Greater London, so the prospect of an expedition coming to a basement apartment in the Notting Hill area isn't unusual at all. In 1972 in Morville St., E3, for example, an archaeological dig produced Roman pottery in burial pits and ditches dating to the first and second centuries.

This underwater shot was made in a pool at Butlins Holiday Camp, Bognor on 18 October 1971. The Pythons and the show's crew are chided in extant communications from local safety officials about not preparing adequately for scuba gear use, improper safety personnel, etc. (WAC T12/1,428).

"by-elections"—("Tuesday Documentary/Children's Story/Party Political Broadcast") Regional interim elections that can often foretell the voting public's approval or disapproval of the sitting government's policies and accomplishments, but most often are based on more local issues and personalities. Part of the reason Labour was surprised by their 1970 loss to the Conservatives was based on a lack of identifiable dissatisfaction in the electorate in recent by-elections. Wilson confidently then scheduled the June 1970 election to cement the Labour mandate, but a seemingly insignificant downward-trending economic forecast in May and early June swayed voters back to the Tories (*Eyewitness 1970-79*, "General Election, 18 June 1970").

– C –

Camera pans across a bleak landscape—("Apology [Politicians]") These scenes, as well as the background for the following sketch, were shot while the cast and crew were in the Glencoe, Scotland area.

"cannibalism . . . British Navy"—("Expedition to Lake Pahoe") An 1845-1850 expedition led by Sir John Franklin ended, it seems, in cannibalism and starvation for the 134 men on HMS *Terror* and HMS *Erebus*. The men had been looking for the Northwest Passage, and had probably lost their ships to crushing ice. A letter from one explorer who followed Franklin's trail a decade later wrote back to the Admiralty: "From the mutilated state of many of the corpses and the contents of the kettles, it is evident that our wretched countrymen had been driven to the last resource—cannibalism—as a means of prolonging existence" (John Rae, cited in *The Times* [23 Oct 1854]; see "Franklin, Sir John" in *ODNB*). See entries in Ep. 26 for more on this same subject.

carrying a plywood flat with portion cut out to represent TV—("Molluscs—'Live' TV Documentary") There were initially a number of competing (and often impoverished) regional independent television entities to bring commercial TV to the British viewer, including Associated-Rediffusion and Associated Television (for London), Associated Television and ABC Television (for the Midlands), and Granada and ABC Television (for the North) (Crisell, 2002, 85). These groups tended to lose money between 1955 and 1957, when viewership began to increase dramatically, eventually exceeding the BBC in audience by as much as 3 to 1.

In the case of Zorba (Cleese) having to come into the Jalin's home and entertain, the Pythons were likely pointing up the BBC's struggles to keep viewers where those viewers had a choice between ITV and the Beeb.

Children's Story—("Tuesday Documentary/Children's Story/Party Political Broadcast") There was a popular and long-running children's show *Jackanory* (1965-1996), where limited budgets meant that storytellers of all kinds took center stage—like Idle's direct-address used here—and not re-enactments. Both Spike Milligan (*The Goon Show*; *Q5*) and Alan Bennett (*Beyond the Fringe*) were readers for *Jackanory* during its early years.

"chlorpromazine"—("Expedition to Lake Pahoe") Also known as Thorazine, chlorpromazine is a low-potency anti-psychotic drug, often used to treat delusions and hallucinations.

"Classic Serial"—("Tuesday Documentary/Children's Story/Party Political Broadcast") *Classic Serial* and the more general radio serialization of classic works have run on BBC Radio since at least 1938, according to Robert Giddings, author/presenter of the lecture "Dickens and the Classic Serial" at a Staff Research Seminar, School of Media Arts and Communication, Bournemouth University (15 November 1999). Giddings speaks of growing up listening to these serials, and the effect they had as they were interwoven into the fabric of British life. For more see Giddings' and Keith Selby's *The Classic Serial on Television and Radio*.

This nostalgic, state of an ever-present, stream-of-consciousness effect is seen in the Python text, as well, as the various radio and TV stories weave in and out of the textual foreground.

"Clermont-Ferrand"—("Tuesday Documentary/Children's Story/Party Political Broadcast") Home of Blaise Pascal, French mathematician and philospher mentioned in Ep. 1 during the "Whizzo Butter" sketch.

"council"—("Expedition to Lake Pahoe") This referring to the local housing council, where such complaints (water damage, infestations) would have been reported. In the 14 August 1970 edition of *Private Eye*, editors contribute a biting exposé on the shoddy building standards in Britain's council housing tracts. Specifically, the article "Condensation St." looks at the new building standards that reduced or eliminated venting in the homes (block flats and bungalows) and especially near the furnaces, leading almost immediately to elevated humidity levels, then dripping and running condensation, then mold and rot, etc. It was estimated that 97 percent of new homes being built during this period featured inadequate ventilation and suffered from "the damp" (16-17).

"Cunningham, Sir John"—("Expedition to Lake Pahoe") Sir John H.D. Cunningham was Admiral of the Fleet 1946-1948.

– D –

"D'Arcy . . . man"—("Tuesday Documentary/Children's Story/Party Political Broadcast") A borrowing from *Pride and Prejudice*, when Darcy reveals to Elizabeth in the famous letter that Wickham isn't as pure as might have been imagined or hoped for. A version of this oft-staged classic appeared on the BBC in 1967.

David—("Tory Housewives Clean-Up Campaign") There has been a *David* cast replica of the original statue housed at the Victoria & Albert museum since 1857 (when it was called the South Kensington Museum). The V&A website reports that upon receiving the unannounced gift, Victoria was so shocked by the nudity she commissioned a fig leaf to be made, and ordered that it be installed before any royal visit. It seems the Pepperpots and Mary Whitehouse may have had something of a patron saint in their Queen Victoria.

Desdemona . . . Othello—("Tory Housewives Clean-Up Campaign") Othello is, of course, a Moorish character, and cavorting with a white woman.

This depiction of the Conservatives as the party willing to "whiten" Britain is interesting, especially as it's remembered that Harold Wilson's Labour government worked just as hard in the later 1960s to stem the tide of Asian immigrants from Kenya, for example, responding to calls from constituencies being flooded with refugees, essentially. See notes to Ep. 27 for more on this convenient double standard.

"Dorset"—("The Silliest Interview We've Ever Done") Dorset is in Dorchester on the southwestern coast of England, known as "Thomas Hardy country," near where the Pythons did significant location shooting for the first series.

Dr. Kildare—("Gumby Brain Specialist") "The *Dr. Kildare* Theme" here is played by John Spence and Orchestra, as composed by Jerry Goldsmith (WAC T12/1,446). *Dr Kildare* was a long-running and very popular BBC drama, starring the young Richard Chamberlain. The show was featured on the cover of *Radio Times* in October 1961 and October 1963, and the Pythons borrow the music at least once in each of the four series.

– E –

"endless overtime"—("Tory Housewives Clean-Up Campaign") Continuing unrest in British labor and a moribund economy kept the Heath government from governing as successfully as Heath had envisioned, as his foreign endeavors seemed to bear fruit while domestic policy and support withered on the vine. In the weeks leading up to the devastating January 1972 coal strike, miners had actually refused overtime in their dispute over the government's refusal to raise wages more than 7.9 percent, a sort of work-to-rule tactic.

Episode 32—Recorded 21 January 1972, and broadcast 23 November 1972.

Additional cast members and extras for this episode: Lyn Ashley (also known as Mrs. Idle), John Scott-Martin (*Wednesday Play*; *Crimson Permanent Assurance*), George Ballantine (*Emma*); (appearing on film) Frank Lester (the "looney" in Ep. 31), Desmond Verini (Ep. 30; *Dr. Who*), Mike Reynell (Ep. 30; *Dr. Who*), Bruce Guest (*Aftermath*), Harry Tierney (*Dr. Who*), Terry Leigh (*Dr. Who*), Johnny Champs, Danny Sinclair, Cy Town (Ep. 29; *Z Cars*), Laurence Rose, Bill Leonard (first series), Bill Hewitt (*Play For Today*), David Freed (*Dr. Who*), Stephen Cass, Dennis Balcombe (*Timeslip*), Michael White, Pippa Hardman (*Hair*), Marion Park (*Law and Order*), Geoffrey Brighty (*Emma*), Chris Holmes (*Softly Softly*), Wolfgang von Jurgen, Ian Elliott (*Paul Temple*; *Emma*), John Hughman (Eps. 14, 28, 41; *Whoops Baghdad*), Rosemary Lord (*Softly Softly*), Jay Neil (*Softly Softly*), Roy Brent (*Some Mothers Do 'Ave 'Em*), Robyn Williams (*Jackanory*), Terence Denville (*Play For Today*; *Dr. Who*), Jack Dow, Jack Campbell, David Peece, Milton Cadnam, Peter Desmond, Nicholas Coppin (*Omega Factor*), Isobel

Gardner (*Sutherland's Law*), Desi Angus (*Omega Factor*) (WAC T12/1,446).

"Euthymol toothpaste"—("The Minister For Not Listening to People") Toothpaste that would have been around when all the Pythons were growing up after the war. Now manufactured by Pfizer.

– F –

"feet clean"—("Tory Housewives Clean-Up Campaign") This long-running joke has British tourists certain that the bidets they encounter on visits to the continent are actually for foot-washing.

– G –

"Gastropods! Lamellibranchs! Cephalopods!"—("Molluscs—'Live' TV Documentary") There are actually nine classes of mollusca, with the largest group being gastropoda.

"Glencoe vox pop"—(link out of "Molluscs—'Live' TV Documentary") One of the inserts shot while on location (for shooting the "Njorl's Saga" scenes) in and around Glencoe, Scotland, in October 1971 (WAC T12/1,428). This is one of the very few times that the location of the shot is mentioned—perhaps here to make sure the production team looks in the right place for the film.

"Grable, Betty"—("Expedition to Lake Pahoe") Pin-up girl Grable (1916-1973) had made her name in Hollywood musicals, but was perhaps better known in the 1960s for her television commercials for Playtex girdles.

All three of these Hollywood starlets mentioned in the "Expedition to Lake Pahoe" sketch—Grable, Jane Russell, and Dorothy Lamour—were pin-up girls during the war years, their posters decorating barracks in many countries.

"Grenville"—("Tuesday Documentary/Children's Story/Party Political Broadcast") There is a Lord Grenville character in Powell and Pressburger's *The Elusive Pimpernel* (1950). *The Elusive Pimpernel* was also a 250-minute miniseries aired on BBC in 1969.

– H –

Harley Street—(PSC; "Gumby Brain Specialist") Harley Street has been a locus of dentists, physicians, and surgeons, as well as a number of hospitals for many years.

Heath, Edward—(PSC; "Tory Housewives Clean-Up Campaign") Leader (Prime Minister) of the Conservative Party 1970-1974, after the Tories defeated Wilson's Labour government in the 1970 elections. Heath had championed EEC membership since at least 1963. He was replaced as PM by Harold Wilson when, after the 1974 elections (and myriad labor strikes and economic setbacks at home as well as strife in Northern Ireland), he failed to create a coalition government.

The film stock found for Heath was acquired from the documentary TV series *Omnibus* (WAC T12/1,446).

"Hegelianism"—("Tory Housewives Clean-Up Campaign") The product of Hegel's life work (not usually meant to include Hegel [1770-1831] himself, but responses to him), he may be rejected by the Tory Housewives for his obscurantism—he's just too complicated for comprehension. Also, the fact that he's a foreigner would render him suspect for the PP brigade.

"Liebnitz [*sic*] to Wittgenstein"—Ludwig Wittgenstein (1889-1951) had trained under Bertrand Russell, whose books the ladies were burning earlier, and his homosexuality and left leanings might explain his mention here. It seems that Gottfried *Liebniz* (1646-1716) would have been preferred by these Housewives, as he included deity in his "Principles": "God assuredly always chooses the best," though he was still a "nasty continental" (Loemker 311).

"Home Office"—("The Minister For Not Listening to People") The building housing the department of the Secretary of State for Home Affairs, which is located in 2 Marsham Street, London. The much-maligned Reginald Maudling was the current Home Secretary, his office embroiled in a restriction of immigration from Commonwealth countries imbroglio during these months. Maudling would resign and be replaced by Robert Carr in July 1972, just four months after this episode was recorded.

"Houses of Parliament"—("The Minister For Not Listening to People") Iconic building on the Thames River in the City of Westminster, London, where the House of Commons and House of Lords conduct parliamentary business. The buildings are in the shadow of the tower containing the bell, Big Ben. Part of the structure dates from the eleventh century, while most of the buildings were rebuilt in the mid-nineteenth century in the Gothic Revival style.

The photo is BBC 3SKP20 (WAC T12/1,428), and is one of the standard shots of the structure seen in myriad evening newscasts of the period.

"hunger marches . . . 1931"—("Tuesday Documentary/ Children's Story/Party Political Broadcast") The

Labour government under Ramsay MacDonald resigned in 1931 under intense economic pressure, thanks to the effects of the Great Depression, including massive unemployment and civil unrest ("Ramsay MacDonald" in *ODNB*). Hunger marches began as early as 1932, most often in response to attempted governmental change in social programs meant to combat the effects of the Great Depression. Many of the labor marches began in coal mining towns in Wales and the north of England, including Jarrow (see entry below), which were particularly hard hit by the Depression.

Rather than resign, MacDonald would abandon his party and create a coalition government consisting of Labour, Conservatives, and Liberals, and would win the next election by a wide margin. This may be the reason behind the inclusion of MacDonald as a closet transvestite in Ep. 24—on the outside he appeared to be a staunch defender of the working man, but he would refuse to support militant strikers or even his own party. See the BBC's coverage of these events in "A History of Labour," at bbc.co.uk, and Miller's "British Unemployment Crisis of 1935," and the "MacDonald" entry below.

– I –

"increased productivity"—("Tory Housewives Clean-Up Campaign") There were significant grumblings during this period about the surge in economic prosperity of countries on the continent (including the economic miracle in the defeated and rebuilding Germany), even as Great Britain continued to see decreases in productivity, and huge increases in inflation, taxation, and government spending to support the welfare state.

A 9 January 1972 coal miner strike—four months before this episode was recorded, and the first massive coal walkout in half a century—was a devastating blow to Heath's promises of increased productivity and lower prices.

"Irish situation"—("The Minister For Not Listening to People") The second and final mention of the "troubles" in Northern Ireland. See notes for Ep. 31 for more. The other oblique reference (lost on today's viewers) to the Irish problems is the depiction of versions of the vociferous Reverend Ian Paisley in Ep. 41. See those notes for more.

– J –

"Jarrow"—("Tuesday Documentary/Children's Story/ Party Political Broadcast") Unemployed workers marched from Jarrow to London in 1936 to meet with Prime Minister Stanley Baldwin, who essentially turned them away. Jarrow was experiencing unemployment rates as high as 65 percent during this period, with many already out of work for eight years and longer (*Eyewitness 1930-39*, "The Jarrow March"). This same year would see riots in the East End of London, including the Battle of Cable Street, sparked by fascist group(s) marches and their mostly Jewish opponents mentioned in the "bingo boys" note above. There had been an unsuccessful general strike in 1926, as well, pitting the Trades Union Congress (TUC) against the sitting government, with the hopes that coal miners' wages and standard of living could be increased. (See Morgan's *Oxford History of Britain*.)

The stock film footage used here is called "Jarrow Marchers" (K22514/5) (WAC T12/1,446).

"Jean . . . Genet"—("Tory Housewives Clean-Up Campaign") Bertrand Russell and Jean-Paul Sartre co-organized a tribunal in 1966-1967—the Russell Tribunal—to bring to light what they saw as the United States' war crimes in Vietnam.

That their works of art might make good kindling is no surprise. Sartre was, of course, both an atheist and French, more than enough to condemn him for Whitehouse and others; Russell's *Marriage and Morals* (1929) advocated sex outside of marriage and "compatibility" marriages—he was a lifelong anti-Victorian, essentially; Genet was a homosexual, and his writings trumpeted both homosexuality and criminality.

– L –

"Lake Pahoe"—("Expedition to Lake Pahoe") The mountain lake found in the Sierra Nevadas in the United States is called Lake Tahoe, and there is also a Lago Pahoe, a glacial lake in the Chilean Highlands. The expedition is also referencing the 1969 one-man sub dive into Loch Ness by Dan Taylor, and more contemporarily the Academy of Applied Science Expeditions begun in 1972, which included the use of sonar machines in the fabled loch. Both expeditions went into the water looking for "hitherto unclassified marine life," as Sir Jane (Chapman) indicates. There have been calls for many years for the Royal Navy to conduct an extensive Loch Ness survey, as well.

"Lamour, Dorothy"—("Expedition to Lake Pahoe") Lamour (1914-1996) starred with Bob Hope (Ep. 28) and Bing Crosby in the celebrated "Road" pictures (*Road to Bali*, 1952), and during this period was making guest appearances on American TV shows like *Love, American Style* and *Marcus Welby, M.D.*

"Lancet"—("Gumby Brain Specialist") An international, independent medical journal published in New York and London.

Long John Silver jacket—(PSC; "Expedition to Lake Pahoe") Again, one of the Pythons' favorite characters reappears, having already shown up in Eps. 5, 10 (in animation), 23, 25, and 28.

– M –

MacDonald, Ramsay—(PSC; "Tuesday Documentary/ Children's Story/Party Political Broadcast") Prime Minister for the Labour government, Ramsay (1866-1937) was PM in 1924, and again 1929-1935. His years at the head of the government during the Great Depression were the most trying, and he was faced with constant civil unrest, both at home and in Ireland. A working-class man by birth, Macdonald was first elected from Leicester in 1906.

The "stock film" used here is "Ramsay MacDonald," film reference "BBC News WPA16133/A" (WAC T12/1,446).

"Magna Carta"—("The Silliest Interview We've Ever Done") The 1215 legal document that outlined the rights and responsibilities of the king, landed barons, and even the church in England.

man-trap—(PSC; "Expedition to Lake Pahoe") These types of traps have been illegal in England since the nineteenth century, and is more the type seen in cartoons than used for hunting or poaching deterrence.

Match of the Day—("Tuesday Documentary/Children's Story/Party Political Broadcast") By this time a fixture on BBC 2, *Match of the Day* was first broadcast 22 August 1964, a football match introduced by Kenneth Wolstenholme. Liverpool beat Arsenal 3-2 on that day, and there were approximately 20,000 viewers, according to bbc.co.uk.

"Molluscs . . . Cephalopods"—("Molluscs—'Live' TV Documentary") The nature documentary begun in earnest in Ep. 30—where bull limpets face off on a rock—but which falls into disarray as characters and producers get into a fist fight, indicates that the world of television documentaries might indeed be unwatchable without something extra. (This was also broached in Ep. 27, when BBC man Mr. Birchenhall [Chapman] complains that primetime viewers don't want documentaries, just entertainment and sport, like they were getting from the commercial networks.) In this case, the sex lives of the documentary subject is the only thing that keeps the Jalins watching (and offended, but still watching).

This may be a response to the much-ballyhooed introduction of a graphic sex education documentary film (showing a married couple engaging in intercourse) for UK schools in 1970. The film was written and directed by Dr. Martin Coles, Aston University. Also, in May 1971 a radio broadcast of a portion of a schools' sex education film, *Growing Up*, that described the masturbation process for boys and girls was decried as unnecessarily graphic and titillating by Mary Whitehouse and NVLA. There were calls for increased ministry control of the radio broadcast for schools program thereafter.

– N –

"nasty continental shows"—("Tory Housewives Clean-Up Campaign") After the introduction of BBC2 in 1964, the possibility of increased foreign programming reaching British households became much more likely. The Government worked to keep the BBC ahead of the independently owned (commercial) stations by placing quotas on foreign programming, and even specifying generic appropriatness in purchased foreign shows (Museum of Broadcast Communications). In 1965, the suddenly very conservative (and perhaps xenophobic) Labour government allowed that just 2 percent of programming could come from the Continent (14 percent from the United States; 1.5 percent from the Commonwealth) (MBC).

naval-lib badge—("Expedition to Lake Pahoe") A play on the au courant terms of social and sexual protest, including "Gay Lib" (see the Judge's complaint in Ep. 27), and "Women's Lib," among others. It seems that ratings like Dorothy Lamour (Idle) want to liberate the navy from hair cuts, rank discipline, and the taboo against cannibalism.

"navy's out of sight man"—("Expedition to Lake Pahoe") By this time, the absence of conscription powers and the cessation a generation earlier of National Service meant that the British armed forces were relying on enlistment, and standards necessarily suffered. One visible accoutrement of the hippie genration—long sideburns (or sideboards)—were a constant source of consternation to career military men and those who'd "fought the war."

Also, news footage from the United States would have presented the loud, slangy, hip reaction to the unpopular Vietnam War, with soldiers being interviewed who just wanted to go home. There was also a case of two U.S. soldiers on a gunboat (described as "hippies" by their comrades) who mutinied and deserted, seeking asylum in Cambodia.

Newsreel footage—(PSC; "Tory Housewives Clean-Up Campaign") The music beneath this footage is "Queen of the Fleet" by George S. Chase (WAC T12/1,446).

newsreel voice—(PSC; "Tory Housewives Clean-Up Campaign") The cadence and jocular word choice is characteristic of the wartime newsreels presented to Britain's beleaguered population, the commentators ever-positive and spinning the news in favor of a rosy outcome. In one such newsreel, combat motorcyclists are pictured going through camouflage-draped maneuvers:

> The one-time footsloggers have turned kickstart pushers. . . . The left right, left right folks have got both feet off the ground at the same time. They are part of Britain's mighty mobile mountain. All keen welcomers of Adolf when he drops in for a cup of tea and a cream bun. (qtd. in Wilson, 2005, 403)

"Nine O'Clock News"—(link into "Molluscs—'Live' TV Documentary") The men of *Nine O'Clock News* (including *FC*-participant Richard Baker) were featured on the cover of the BBC's *Radio Times* in late 1970.

Nurse—("Gumby Brain Specialist") Played by Lyn Ashley, or Mrs. Idle, as the credits sometimes refer to her (WAC T12/1,446).

– O –

"O'Brien, Edna"—(link into "Molluscs—'Live' TV Documentary") There is a photo of the transplanted Irish writer Edna O'Brien (b. 1930) included with her mention, but the audience doesn't verbally respond to the image. She was known somewhat dubiously at this time for having all her books banned in her native country. It may be that she wasn't as well known as some of the other celebrities mentioned in *FC*, though she may have been known to at least Idle for her participation in the Peter Whitehead documentary on "Swinging" London's night scene, *Let's All Make Love in London Tonight* (1967). Also appearing in that documentary were David Hockney (mentioned in Ep. 14) and Julie Christie (Ep. 28).

In many of her works, O'Brien's frank protrayals of sexuality in (and outside) marriage, and from a woman's point of view, led to her books being sometimes banned and even burned, and perhaps merits her mention by Monty Python in relation to a mollusc documentary that only gets interesting when deviant sexuality is introduced.

– P –

Party Political Broadcast—("Tuesday Documentary/ Children's Story/Party Political Broadcast") Party Election Broadcasts began in 1951, with Lord Samuel delivering the first speech. Both major parties were given equal time on BBC air and radio waves. Printed texts for many of these broadcasts are available online through Keele University's UK Elections website. A choreographed Party Political Broadcast from the Conservatives is the first sketch in Ep. 38, though only in the printed scripts.

"Penrose, Roland"—("The Minister For Not Listening to People") Penrose (1900-1984) was a British surrealist painter credited with bringing surrealism to Britain. His coterie of associates included fellow artists Picasso, Miró, Man Ray, Ernst, and Tapies. A number of Penrose's works are currently in the Tate Modern in London.

pepperpots—("Tory Housewives Clean-Up Campaign") All are reading copies of the *Daily Telegraph*, which has been derisively called the "Daily Torygraph" for its fairly consistent Conservative editorial positions.

"permissive society"—("Tory Housewives Clean-Up Campaign") The postwar society of television, where many (like Mary Whitehouse) saw the erosion of traditional morals and values being caused by permissiveness in entertainments like TV and film, novels and plays, and even art shows. Increases in drug use, the appearance of the birth control pill, the public visibility of homosexuality and promiscuity, all were part of this permissive society, and all could be blamed on television's negative influence. See Aldgate's *Censorship and the Permissive Society*.

picketing with slogans—("Tory Housewives Clean-Up Campaign") *"Fair Pay"*—In the mid-1960s the Seamen's Union struck for pay increases, less hours, and a "fair deal"; teachers at Durham School went out over wage stagnation and a demand for smaller class sizes; in 1970-1971 it was nurses, postal workers, British European Airways employees, and even farmers demanding higher subsidized agriculture prices. During this period strike actions (whether official strikes or just work-to-rule actions, wildcatting, demonstrations, etc.) kept either party from claiming big gains in employment and monetary policies—there were just too many labor fires to put out.

"Less Profits"—There have been demands for curtailed (or just better shared) profits from industry since the earliest days of the Industrial Revolution. Many strike placards in the 1955-1975 period ask for a more fair division of the corporate spoils.

"Parity"—This variably meant prices set at reasonable levels, and job pay also fine-tuned for comparability between regions, trades, etc. One political cartoon of the period (depicting Dagenham Ford strikers in 1971) offers workers opining for parity—as a result of their next big strike—with entertainer Tom Jones (Eps. 24, 30). This cartoon is from Bernard Cookson, and originally appeared in the *Evening News* (2 February 1971). See the British Cartoon Archive.

"No Victimization"—Referring to the worker as the scrap of food between hungry dogs. As early as 1955 British newspaper cartoonists like Michael Cummings were depicting big labor *and* big government as well-dressed bullies with equally menacing clubs (*Daily Express* 25 November 1955). See the British Cartoon Archive.

Certainly the biggest concern during this period leading up to Britain's entry in the Common Market were the great unknowns about the pending too-close-for-comfort relationship with the historically untrustworthy Continental. In a 5 July 1971 article in *Time*, the London correspondent summarized the common fears:

> The average Briton is still afraid of the EEC's high food prices and fearful of losing British sovereignty to the Brussels-based Eurocracy. Britain's most powerful trade union leaders are dead set against the EEC. The pressures already are so great that the Labor Party may soon be forced to take an anti-Market position.

pictures and statues—(PSC; Tory Housewives Clean-Up Campaign") Referring to the presence of exploitative sex and sexuality on TV, Whitehouse is quoted as saying, "I object to having strange male nudes in my living room." The Pythons here have merely extended this objection to male nudes in art galleries and museums. Chapman plays just such a strange male nude in Ep. 17, where he is being interviewed by Derek Hart (Cleese) and blasting the slumping morals of television.

"plastic arts"—("Tory Housewives Clean-Up Campaign") Art that involves a medium that can be physically molded, shaped, formed, etc., like sculpture and painting.

"POLITICIANS . . . PROGRAMME"—("Apology [Politicians]") The continuing unfavorable opinion of Ministers of Parliament and the Government (and Shadow Government) in general is also a carryover from other comedy/satire shows like *The Goon Show* (1951-1960) and *Beyond the Fringe* (1961). In the first instance, a Minister Without Fixed Address (played by Harry Secombe) often wanders about getting into mischief, and in the latter, there are scathing impersonations of Harold Macmillan, the then sitting Prime Minister, as well as Cabinet members bumbling through a nuclear deterrent lecture, and instead of convincing a Russian to praise Macmillan, the man raspberries instead. The questionable antics and ethics of government men like Reginald Maudling, Alec Douglas-Home, and Peter Walker (all mentioned or referenced earlier in Ep. 30), among others, probably increase the ferocity of this roller caption.

The music heard underneath the apology roller is Elgar's "Pomp and Circumstance" played by the London Symphony Orchestra, the use of which led to a bit of a punch-up. The trust that controls Elgar's music complained that "P&C" had been used illegally, in a slanderous way, and asked for damages. The BBC legal department countered that since the music had been used straight and without editing or manipulation, that it was in no way defaming Elgar or the music, and told the trust to shove off, essentially (WAC T12/1,446).

"Porky"—("Tuesday Documentary/Children's Story/Party Political Broadcast") A reference to the Warner Bros. cartoon character Porky Pig, but the story being told sounds more like Disney's 1933 cartoon *The Three Little Pigs*, which would also be satirized a decade later by Tex Avery in the MGM cartoon *Blitz Wolf* (1942). The cartoony violence employed by the Pythons indicates a significant cartoon influence on the troupe.

Idle, Jones, and Palin had all written for and acted in the children's show *Do Not Adjust Your Set* (ITV, 1967), just prior to coming together to form Monty Python.

P.P.—(PSC; "Tory Housewives Clean-Up Campaign") "Pepper Pot." The image here is, of course, meant to be reminiscent of other fascist groups (Hitler's SS troops, Mussolini's Black Shirts, even Britain's own British Union of Fascists) wearing identifying armbands.

– R –

rating—(PSC; "Expedition to Lake Pahoe") The script identifies the man about to eat the leg as a "rating," which is a naval term for an enlisted man. It is normally confined to plural usage (*OED*).

"Rattigan, Terence"—("The Minister For Not Listening to People") The previous-generation playwright already mentioned in Eps. 1 and 30, Rattigan (1911-1977) wrote serious, dramatic plays like *The Winslow Boy* (1946) and *The Browning Version* (1948), though his plays would fall out of favor when the Angry Young Men types stormed the scene in the late 1950s. Rattigan became a target of more progressive elements and was labeled an outdated Conservative trapped in an imagined past, which may account for his several appearances in *Flying Circus* (see especially Ep. 30, "The Pantomime Horse is a Secret Agent Film" sketch).

Red Devils—(PSC; "Tory Housewives Clean-Up Campaign") A memorial mistake (but see below for more on that). The Red Devils were an Army aerial acrobatic team, by this time performing organized *parachute* jumps at air shows around the UK. (John Bilsborough wrote a poem entitled "Albert and the Red Devils" in 1971 about the team, featuring his recurring character Albert Ramsbottom.)

The planes shown in this clip are actually Korean War–era jets (perhaps American F-86A-5 Sabres, FJ-4 Furies, or even British Lightnings) flying in formation. This footage may be an example of the proper or needed photo/film clip not being located in time for the show, and the show going on anyway.

What the Pythons intended to include here was not "Red Devils" but "Red Arrows," the Royal Air Force's acrobatic team—they didn't jump out of their planes, opting for close formational flying. The footage reference number is "BBC News Southampton 458" (WAC T12/1,446).

"Regent Street"—(PSC; "Tuesday Documentary/Children's Story/Party Political Broadcast") Major shopping street and thoroughfare in London's West End, connecting into Piccadilly Circus. The area is a magnet for visitors during the Christmas season. The stock film footage is from the BBC vaults, and is called "Christmas Lights" (74630) (WAC T12/1,446).

Religion Today—("Tuesday Documentary/Children's Story/Party Political Broadcast") Significant religious programming has been and continues to be available on the BBC radio and TV outlets, including the BBC's *Songs of Praise* (1961-), and myriad discussion-type shows.

Robinson, Robert—(PSC; "Tory Housewives Clean-Up Campaign") This is one of those moments in *FC* where the viewer (especially today's viewer) would be hard-pressed to identify the humor or topicality behind the photo reference. A writer and presenter, Robinson (b. 1927) is perhaps best remembered for the satirical show *BBC-3* (BBC, 1965-1966), and for enduring the use of the "f-word" on this same show by author/critic Kenneth Tynan (broadcast 13 November 1965), the first time that word had been uttered on British television. Robinson and the show immediately became targets of Mary Whitehouse and her organization. See bbc.co.uk/comedy for more on the show and controversy.

"Robson, particularly, in goal"—("The Silliest Sketch We've Ever Done") Probably a nod to Bryan "Pop" Robson (b. 1945), who in 1971 had signed what was then an enormous contract to play for West Ham. Robson had earlier played for Newcastle United.

"Russell, Jane"—("Expedition to Lake Pahoe") Hollywood film actress famed for her voluptuousness, Russell

(b. 1921) appeared in Howard Hughes' racy Western *The Outlaw* (1943) and *Gentlemen Prefer Blondes* (1953). The latter film is mentioned in Ep. 15, in a smoke signal version.

Later in her life (primarily after her movie career) Russell appeared in Playtex bra commercials, while fellow pin-up Grable (see above) appeared in girdle ads for the same company. By the early 1970s these former starlets were perhaps all better known for their small-screen work (TV ads and guest appearances), and only vaguely remembered for their luminous movie careers.

– S –

"selling them again"—("The Minister For Not Listening to People") There was a very active black market both during the war and afterward, through the years of rationing, when shortages of essentials were rampant, and ration books necessary until 1954.

"Shadow Minister"—("The Minister for Not Listening to People") A minister representing the political party not currently in power. During this period (1970-1974), Labour would have provided the shadow government. Typical (and actual) Shadow Ministerial titles include Shadow Minister for Northern Ireland, Shadow Minister for Social Security, and Shadow Minister for Defence, Foreign and Commonwealth Affairs.

"Shiver me timbers"—("Expedition to Lake Pahoe") This phrase is borrowed from Robert Louis Stevenson's famous pirate in the book *Treasure Island*. See the entry for "black spot" above for more.

short sequence of footballers in slow-motion kissing—(link into "Apology [Politicians]") The romantic music here is from the well-known Mantovani Orchestra playing "Charmaine," by Rapee and Pollack (WAC T12/1,466).

"sneaky second channel"—("Tory Housewives Clean-Up Campaign") BBC2, brought on-line in 1964, went to full color in 1967. BBC2 broadcast more serious and challenging fare from the beginning, and has been a proving ground for new shows before they migrate to BBC1. The more frank depictions of sexuality and violence upset Whitehouse's group from the channel's inception, and, ironically, the first show to be broadcast by BBC2 was the children's program *Playschool* (1964-1988).

The men in control of BBC2 during this period—and who would have been on the receiving end of the NVLA and Clean Up TV campaign attentions—were: Michael Peacock (1964-1965); David Attenborough (1965-1969); and Robin Scott (1969-1974).

"spotty continental boys"—("Tory Housewives Clean-Up Campaign") Referring to the fact that a number of very young and even pimply "agitators" plaguing various sitting governments in the UK had actually been foreign nationals, including Daniel Cohn-Bendit (b. 1945), a French-born German-Jew and student in France at the University of Nanterre. Cohn-Bendit, 23, had almost single-handedly organized the student revolts that would eventually ripple across France, creating a general strike that nearly toppled the de Gaulle government. After being expelled from France in late May 1968, Cohn-Bendit came to Great Britain on 11 June 1968 on a twenty-four-hour visa, and ended up staying a fortnight. He arranged and led a sit-in at the BBC's Television Centre in Wood Lane, and visited Karl Marx's grave. He would later become a German citizen. See news.bbc.co.uk/.

"stirring music"—("Gumby Brain Specialist") The music being played underneath is "Main Titles and Openers: Wide Screen Title" by Jack Shaindlin (WAC T12/1,446).

"sub-aqua head"—("Expedition to Lake Pahoe") Following the mass production of scuba gear (co-created by Jacques Cousteau [Ep. 30]), "sub-aqua clubs"—essentially, diving clubs—began to appear throughout the UK in the early 1960s.

– T –

"tatty, scrofulous old rapist"—("Molluscs—'Live' TV Documentary") The lamellibranch (scallop) is characterized as scruffy ("tatty") and morally corrupt ("scrofulous")—scallop are hermaphroditic, which may account for the species' "depravity" as described by Zorba (Cleese). The term and characterization "rapist" is used twice by the Pythons—one in this episode, and once in *FZ* where the joke is stretched into a sketch—indicating that the sensitivity and public reaction surrounding the term was either diminished or just ignored during this period. There are no mentions of public or in-house reaction to the term's usage, for example, in WAC records. This kind of "insensitive" humor (racial epithets, sexist language and depictions), then, can be helpful as this period is studied, hinting at cultural biases, perceptions, allowances, etc.

"firm-breasted Rabelaisian"—Like author O'Brien mentioned earlier, François Rabelais (1494-1553) also had most of his books banned, though in France, but also because of the books' licentious, satiric treatment of monasticism.

"Fanny Hill"—Title character in John Cleland's scandalous 1749 novel, Fanny becomes a prostitute, a mistress, and just plain sexually active to survive in a man's world. The book was eventually banned in the UK and United States alike.

"like a dead Pope"—This comparison may also be two-edged, as there were a number of popes who behaved in questionable ways, including offering sinecures, soliciting murder, currying political favor, and engaging in bacchanalian sexual depravity—their dissolute lives might have shamed someone like Fanny Hill, actually. Also, in the "Cadaver Synod" (897 AD), nine-months-dead Pope Formosus was exhumed, put on trial, found guilty, his corpse desecrated and dumped into the Tiber. His dead body was then rumored to have performed miracles. Thus, a dead Pope could have been surprisingly active and vital, not unlike Fanny herself.

"whelk"—Another gastropod whose only fault might be its carnivorousness, the characters here crush it because of its alleged homosexuality. In Ep. 33 Algy (Palin) will be killed when he boldly admits his same-sex attraction. Again, the insensitive humor (killing women or homosexuals simply because they are female or homosexual) wasn't insensitive for the period, the genre, the medium, or there might have been more of a recorded reaction.

The words are quite large and easily readable . . . —(PSC; "Apology [Politicians]") One of the few very obvious directorial/technical elements included in the scripts, this command is obviously intended for whomever will be physically turning the roller caption machine (still cranked by hand during this period).

"Timothy Whites"—("Minister For Not Listening to People") A chain chemist's shop found in Midland-area towns like Preston (Lancashire), Seaham (Durham), and Bromsgrove (Worcestershire). Timothy Whites is also mentioned by the ranting Tourist (Idle) in Ep. 31 (see notes). This particular chain store seems to have found its way into the hearts and memories of many in the Midlands; this is obviously the name of the chemist that most of the Pythons grew up with, as "Timothy Whites" is mentioned at least twice in *FC*, and Boots the Chemist isn't mentioned at all.

Today in Parliament—("Tuesday Documentary/Children's Story/Party Political Broadcast") Radio 4 has produced this show since 1945, offering insights on the comings and goings in Britain's legislative bodies.

"Tory Tours"—(PSC; "Tory Housewives Clean-Up Campaign") The Conservative Party has carried the nickname "Tory" since c. 1830, when "Conservative" became the name of choice. "Tory" had been in use since about 1689 to refer to royalists. The term can be used both affectionately and in a more derogatory manner, depending on the user.

"Trade Practices Bill"—("The Minister For Not Listening to People") Standard bit of legislation before Parliament in the area of international trade. There would be a significant Restrictive Trade Practices Act drafted in 1976, following others in 1974, and a Trade Descriptions Act 1968 which made it "an offence for a trader to apply, by any means, false or misleading statements, or to knowingly or recklessly make such statements about services." Similar bills and acts can be found making their way through former Commonwealth members India and Australia during this same period.

"Tuesday Documentary"—("Tuesday Documentary/Children's Story/Party Political Broadcast") A BBC weekly TV show, featuring titles like "Christians at War," "The Price of Violence," and "Last Night Another Soldier," all about the continuing slaughter in Northern Ireland. These episodes were broadcast 5 October 1971, 14 November 1972, and 4 December 1973. *Tuesday's Documentary* is featured on a late 1969 cover of the BBC's *Radio Times*.

"two-up, two-down house"—("Tuesday Documentary/Children's Story/Party Political Broadcast") More likely this is describing what the ordinary English worker lives in, a terrace house set in rows of other terrace houses. Enormous, soulless housing blocks were actually being built around Paris (Sarcelles) after the war to deal with the population boom, and the burgeoning migration to the capital.

– U –

undercrank—(PSC; "Tory Housewives Clean-Up Campaign") The film camera would be "cranked" (actually run by an electric motor) slower than twenty-four frames per second, meaning the projected image would appear to move faster than usual.

– V –

V-sign—(PSC; "Expedition to Lake Pahoe") The "palm-back V-sign" offered by the woman (Jones) is an insult meaning "up yours," and has been used in the UK for generations.

– W –

"war against pornography"—("Tory Housewives Clean-Up Campaign") Drawing parallels between the militant campaign of NVLA and the armed, fascistic military campaigns being waged around the world at that time, probably including at least the Israel-Egypt Six Days War (1967), Vietnam, and the still-stinging Suez Crisis (1956), where British gunboat diplomacy was effectively humbled, and her second-tier world power status was confirmed (*Eyewitness: 1950-59*, "Aftermath of Suez").

"weetabix"—("Expedition to Lake Pahoe") UK cereal company founded in 1932.

Whitehouse, Mary—(PSC; "Tory Housewives Clean-Up Campaign") A strident defender of public morality, Whitehouse (1910-2001) was the founder and president of the National Viewers and Listeners Association (NVLA), a public television and radio morals watchdog group. The first public meeting she addressed took place in Birmingham, coincidentally, and her target was the "permissive" BBC and its director Sir Hugh Greene. It's been reported that thirty-seven coachloads of supporters accompanied her. Whitehouse (a native of Wolverhampton, like Idle) would later lock horns with the Pythons over the "blasphemous" film *Life of Brian* (1979).

"windmills"—("Tory Housewives Clean-Up Campaign") A reference to the character Don Quixote de La Mancha from Cervantes' novel *Don Quixote* (1605, 1615), and fairly typical of the kind of pop-allusive language used in these newsreels. It also indicates that these ultra-conservative crusaders aren't in their right minds, at least to the Pythons.

– Y –

"young people"—("Tory Housewives Clean-Up Campaign") In Ep. 31, the Tourist alluded to General Franco's mistrust and mistreatment of young people in postwar Spain, and that theme is carried over here, to Whitehouse and her Clean Up TV campaign. One of the well-known posters created during the May 1968 student demonstrations in France depicted a young person with his mouth being covered by a sinister adult (a silhouette of de Gaulle) from behind, and the caption: "Sois Jeune et Tais Toit" ("Be Young and Shut Up").

– Z –

Zorba—(PSC; "Molluscs—'Live' TV Documentary") Probably drawn from Anthony Quinn's memorable depiction of Zorba in *Zorba the Greek* (1964). The presenter's name is never spoken, so this is yet another moment lost on the viewer, but available to the reader.

Episode 33

– A –

"accoutrements"—("Climbing the North Face of the Uxbridge Road") All necessary components for rock climbing during this period, and many would have been carried by the intrepid hairdressers climbing Everest in the previous episode. "Carabino" is actually "carabiner" (or even "karabiner"), and is a device for connecting looped ends of ropes or for hooking onto a piton, which is a spike driven into a rock fissure.

"Algy"—("Biggles Dictates a Letter") Algernon Montgomery Lacey, Biggles' close friend in the W.E. Johns' adventures. See entries below for "Biggles" and "Johns" for more.

ANIMATION: television is bad for your eyes—(animated link into "The Show So Far") The music used under this link is from the International Studio Orchestra, "Sea Music," "Ripcord" by Julius Steffaro (WAC T12/1,444).

"Ark Royal"—("Lifeboat") The only really modern aircraft carrier in the Royal Navy at the outbreak of WWII, *Ark Royal* was in service 1938-1941, when she took a U-boat torpedo hit and sank off Gibraltar (see *Ships of the World*). The film stock used in this sequence is "*Ark Royal* NP78078" (WAC T12/1,444).

– B –

"bad for your eyes"—("Bad For Your Eyes" animation) During this animation sequence, a fairy godfather figure appears, claiming to be from "Program Control." The face Gilliam used here is of Paul Fox, BBC Controller, a man the Pythons crossed swords with more than once in regard to regional time slots and repeat airings for the episodes. Duncan Wood (Head of BBC

Comedy through the third series) had asked in a September 1972 memo (somewhat rhetorically) whether it wasn't time to put away the Paul Fox bashing in the animations, seeing it by the third series as a kind of reflexive "joke gone too long" (WAC T12/1,428). (The editors of *Private Eye* also lament Fox's continuing presence at the BBC [18 December 1970, 5].)

In Ep. 28, the naughty book Mr. Norris (Palin) is reading, *The Lady With the Naked Skin*, is authored by "Paul Fox Jr."

"BBC cameras"—("Climbing the North Face of the Uxbridge Road") In 1966, the BBC did cover an assault on the Old Man of Hoy, giving over much of the broadcast day to the climb, and popularizing both the sport of climbing and the climbing of the various "stacks" in Scotland. Another similar BBC broadcast followed in 1967.

"Biggles"—("Biggles Dictates a Letter") Actually James Bigglesworth, he was a character created by author W.E. Johns (see below) in 1934 for the long-running series of flying adventures books. Palin admits to reading the books as a youngster, fascinated by the books' exotic foreign settings (McCabe).

"Biggles Flies Undone"—("Biggles Dictates a Letter") A play on actual Biggles titles such as *Biggle Flies Again*, *Biggles Flies East*, etc.

"Biggles, Mary"—("Biggles Dictates a Letter") Biggles did fall in love with Marie Janis in the story "Affair De Coeur" in *The Camels Are Coming* (1932), a romance retold in the later book *Biggles Looks Back* (1965).

"bouzouki"—("Cheese Shop") A Greek mandolin instrument, the bouzouki is being played by Alan Parker, who has continued to play bouzouki (and Oud) gigs to this writing. The song is "Grecian Nights" (WAC T12/1,444).

Buckets of blood burst . . .—(PSC; "Sam Peckinpah's *Salad Days*") The blood flows generously in this sequence, of course, as has been specifically requested by director Ian MacNaughton. In a note to the production design team, MacNaughton emphasizes that the vast quantities of blood "cannot be overdone" (WAC T12/1,445).

– C –

Capote, Truman—("Philip Jenkinson on Cheese Westerns") Mercurial, eccentric novelist (*In Cold Blood*), Capote (1924-1984) was also flamboyantly, even stereotypically gay. His birth name was Truman Streckfus Persons. During this period (1971-1972), Capote was serializing portions of a forthcoming novel, *Answered Prayers*, in *Esquire* magazine, angering and alienating his socialite friends by outing their lavish and debauched lifestyles.

"Cheese Westerns"—("Philip Jenkinson on Cheese Westerns") There were straight-ahead Hollywood Westerns like *Shane* (George Stevens, 1950), and *My Darling Clementine* (John Ford, 1946), Noodle Westerns including Akira Kurosawa's *Yojimbo* (1961) and *Sanjuro* (1962), and even Spaghetti Westerns—Sergio Leone's memorable *A Fistful of Dollars* (1964), *For a Few Dollars More* (1965), and *The Good, The Bad, and the Ugly* (1968).

"courtesan"—("Biggles Dictates a Letter") Not in the original sense of the word, she's not. "Courtesan" actually means a lady of the court. Here it is clearly used to mean a prostitute.

"Crippen"—("Climbing the North Face of the Uxbridge Road") "Doctor" Peter Hawley Harvey Crippen (1862-1910) of 39 Hilldrop Crescent, Camden Town, London killed his wife, Belle Elmore, in 1910, dismembering and burying her beneath the house, and then took his secretary and tried to escape to America. Crippen would be caught by use of Marconi wireless telegraph as he and his secretary (disguised as a boy) sailed across the Atlantic. He was found guilty and hanged in 1910. Crippen was the subject of a 1962 film called *Dr. Crippen*, starring Donald Pleasance in the title role. Finally, Crippen is also mentioned by the Goons in the "Lurgi" episode.

The mention of this name and the following lines are stumbled over badly in the film (significant traffic noise and ambient sound), and the audience probably misses the historical allusion, as there is little or no reaction.

Cut to the deck of a lifeboat—(PSC; "Lifeboat") The structure here has acquired a sort of stream-of-consciousness, with the dream state (the illusion earlier of a lifeboat deck) becoming reality as Mrs. Neves (Jones) exits her home to the deck of that same lifeboat. The illusion was originally denied by Neves, as she claimed there was no lifeboat "out there," but then confirmed as she entered that world, seemingly without noticing any disruption. This reality will continue until a new one replaces it.

The "Elizabethan Pornography Smugglers" sketch (Ep. 36) will follow a similar progression, crossing between real and imagined worlds and across time, in that case, until a sort of revolving-door-ever-present is possible. Several of the sketches in the latter series attempt these more sophisticated structures, playing with time and space, and move away (at least temporarily) from the gag-laden bits.

– D –

"do you have any cheese at all?"—("Cheese Shop") Coincidentally, cheese was something of a headline item at this time. After Britain had managed to finagle the necessary votes to gain entry into the European Common Market (yes, after de Gaulle was out of the way), an unforeseen hurdle presented itself. According to a *Time* magazine report from 5 April 1971, the whole deal was about to go sour because Commonwealth member New Zealand demanded guarantees that its dairy farmers could continue to sell the bulk of their cheese (and butter) to the UK, by far their biggest market. Other European countries with dairy interests complained that protectionism was just what the Common Market was trying to overcome, and it took an eleventh-hour deal to keep both the negotiations and the cheese flowing ("Common Market: Breaking Out the Bubbly," *Time* 5 July 1971).

– E –

"Ee I were all hungry like"—("Cheese Shop") Communication difficulties, again, but this time based on class, upbringing, and regionalization. An elementary school teacher in an urban Lancashire classroom (c. 1905) noted that since children had no access to a cultural clearinghouse like BBC radio, meaning no real aural or verbal contact with the rest of England, they had no idea anyone spoke any differently than they did. The teacher describes having to consciously switch from her London-based English to a broad Lancashire accent in order to be understood on even the simplest terms, a process that steepened the learning curve significantly, and set these children well behind others (*Eyewitness 1900-09*, "Education in a Slum School").

"eels"—("Biggles Dictates a Letter") Eels have been a part of many Englanders' cuisine for generations; jellied eels can still be bought from street vendors in East London.

Episode 33—Recorded 7 January 1972, and broadcast 30 November 1972. This episode was recorded fourth and broadcast seventh.

In-studio taping was performed on 7 January 1972 at TC6, and the following guests and extras were called in: Richard Baker (*News at Ten*), Nicki Howorth (*Not Tonight Darling*), and Alan Parker (musician); extras included: Clinton Morris (*Z Cars*), Steve Ismay (*Softly Softly*), Roy Pearce (Ep. 29; *Dr. Who*), Ron Tingley (Ep. 29; *Dr. Who*; *Z Cars*), Ken Halliwell (*Z Cars*), Terry Sartain (Ep. 28; *Dr. Who*), and David Waterman (*Dr. Who*).

On film for this episode: Pippa Hardman, Marion Park, Beulah Hughes, David Wilde, Richard de Meath, Jean Clarke, Elaine Carr (*Fashion Time*), Francis Pidgeon, Alan Hutchinson, and Richard Baker (WAC T12/1,444).

"explosion . . . Lords"—("The News with Richard Baker") By this time, there had been more than 100 explosions of various devices planted by various factions in the fight for control of Northern Ireland. A bomb planted in the Post Office tower in London was detonated in 1971, with no injuries. The early 1970s saw elements of the IRA taking its fight for independence out of Northern Ireland and into the streets of London, especially with bombs and mortar attacks.

Much earlier, the Gunpowder Plot of 1605 was an attempt to blow up the Houses of Parliament, kill James I, and bring Catholicism back to England, all in one fell swoop. The plot was discovered, the gunpowder removed, and the conspirators tortured and executed (*ODNB*).

– F –

First World War fighter planes in a dog-fight—(PSC; "Biggles Dictates a Letter") The film footage here is "Dog Fight" VisNews 2266 (WAC T12/1,444). The "[h]eroic war music" is from the Royal Liverpool Philharmonic Orchestra, and is William Walton's "Spitfire Prelude & Fugue" (WAC T12/1,444).

– G –

"Ginger"—("Biggles Dictates a Latter") The third member of the comrades-in-arms group in the Biggles books, Algy and Biggles meet Ginger after the war and eventually form an air transport company. There is no indication that any of the three were homosexual, at least in Johns' characterizations. Here the Pythons have taken homosociality and elevated it to homosexuality, simply because it's funnier.

"Greek rebel leader"— ("Storage Jars") Greece had, in fact, undergone significant political turmoil and change in recent months and years. A military junta had seized power from the monarchy in April 1967, and King Constantine II was forced into exile. The military leader who took control was Colonel George Papadopoulos, who would eventually try to legitimize and even soften his rule by surrendering his military post to become prime minister, then president. Unsuccessfully trying to quash cultural embellishments like long haircuts and miniskirts, Papadopoulos would be ousted in a coup just a year after this episode was broadcast (November 1973). See Papadopoulos' obituary in the *London Times* (July 1999), and the article "The Poly-Papadopoulos" in *Time* (3 April 1972).

guerrilla leader . . . gun—(PSC; "Storage Jars") This is a still frame (or, more likely, a publicity still) of Warren Beatty as Clyde Barrow from the Warner Bros' 1967 film *Bonnie and Clyde*. This is the kind of "new Hollywood" film of the late 1960s and early 1970s—darker, edgier, bloodier, more sexualized—that the Pythons spoof in the "*Salad Days*" sketch, as well as when Jenkinson (Idle) is gleefully shot later in this same episode.

"*Gunfight at Gruyère Corral*"—("Philip Jenkinson on Cheese Westerns") A play on the Western film title *Gunfight at the O.K. Corral* (1957), directed by Preston Sturges and starring Burt Lancaster and Kirk Douglas. Gruyère is a salty cheese from Switzerland.

"*Ilchester '73*"—A play on the western film title *Winchester '73* (1950), directed by Tony Mann and starring Jimmy Stewart. The Ilchester Cheese Company creates cheeses blended with beer and spices.

"*The Cheese Who Shot Liberty Valance*"—A play on the film title *The Man Who Shot Liberty Valance* (1962), directed by John Ford and starring Jimmy Stewart and John Wayne.

It's not surprising that so many Hollywood genre films of the 1940s and 1950s (Hollywood's "Golden Age") are mentioned in *FC*. During the war years, film imports fell off dramatically in the UK and across Europe. It wasn't until 1946 that the flood of backlogged Hollywood films could burst into European theatres, providing comedies, Westerns, historical epics, gangster pictures, musicals, and love stories for a war-weary audience. The young men who would become the leaders of the French New Wave, for example, watched all these films one on top of another—cinephiles in the UK would have done much the same.

"guttering"—("Climbing the North Face of the Uxbridge Road") A play on some of the standard but perhaps unfamiliar rock climbing jargon that would have been part of the 1966-1967 BBC broadcasts of the Hoy assault. This refers to terms like "barn-dooring" (swinging out from the rock like a barn door), "edging" (moving along a narrow edge) and "scumming" (a crack-climbing technique).

– H –

"Haakon"—("Biggles Dictates a Letter") King Haakon is earlier mentioned in Ep. 30 as producer (with Sir Alec Douglas-Home) of the film *The Pantomime Horse is a Secret Agent*. It's curious again to have mentioned Haakon here, as he had died in 1957. See notes to Ep. 30 for more. Haakon's last state visit to the UK took place in 1951, followed by a state visit from Queen Elizabeth to Norway in 1955.

"hardship . . . glove"—("Climbing the North Face of the Uxbridge Road") This may be based on the post-trek accounts of these types of adventurers, who would give interviews and write books and articles about the reasons behind the climb, the journey, the sacrifice, etc. Sir Edmund Hillary's book was *High Adventure* in 1955, and Thor Heyerdahl's were *Kon-Tiki* (1950), and *The Ra Expeditions* (1971). (See notes to Ep. 28 for more on both Hillary and Heyerdahl.) The publication of all three followed close on the heels of the actual events depicted.

This sketch may also have been influenced by the appearance in 1971 of a popular and very serious climbing book, *The Black Cliff: Clogwyn du'r Arddu* by Crew, Soper, and Wilson.

"HMS Defiant"—("Lifeboat") Not an active or even recently active royal naval vessel. *HMS Defiant* is the title of the 1962 film starring Alec Guinness and Dirk Bogarde, and is set during the Napoleonic wars. Bogarde was mentioned earlier for his virtuoso performances for director Luchino Visconti, including his swan song in *Death in Venice* (Ep. 29). *Defiant* is also the name of a wooden sailing ship converted to a Royal Navy torpedo training vessel in about 1899.

"HMS Eagle"—("Lifeboat") *Eagle* was commissioned in October 1951, and was part of the Audacious-class of carriers. *Eagle* was decommissioned as part of the Royal Navy downsizing in 1972—just when this episode was being written, recorded, and broadcast—and ultimately scrapped in 1978.

Howorth, Nicki—("Biggles Dictates a Letter") A model and actress, Howorth appeared in *Not Tonight Darling* (1971) and *Are You Being Served* (1977), as well as appearing in the erotic Pirelli calendar in 1973. She is one of the few actual females to appear on *FC* in a speaking role, along with Carol Cleveland, Connie Booth, Marjorie Wilde, Rita Davies, and Julia Breck.

– J –

Jenkinson, Philip—("Philip Jenkinson on Cheese Westerns") Born in 1935, Jenkinson was a writer for the TV series *Horne A'Plenty* and *Marty*, both in 1968, and would later appear on *Rutland Weekend Television* (1975). Jenkinson also interviewed Alfred Hitchcock for the BBC in 1966. In 1971-1972 Jenkinson was hosting *Film Night*, as well as working behind the scenes on Ken Russell's (Ep. 28) film *The Boyfriend*. See the BFI website for a more complete list of Jenkinson's credits.

The Pythons would access various stock film footage titles from what appears to be Jenkinson's collection throughout the run of *Flying Circus*. See the entry for "pederast vole" below for more.

"Johns, Captain W.E."—("Biggles Dictates a Letter") Johns (1893-1968) wrote almost 100 Biggles books between 1932 and 1970 (the character being created for an earlier *Popular Flying* magazine), himself a veteran of the Gallipoli, Suez, and Salonika campaigns, and he later joined the Royal Air Force. (See *ODNB* for more on Johns.)

"Julian Slade's *Salad Days*"—("Philip Jenkinson on Cheese Westerns") Born Julian Penkivil Slade (1930-2006; Eton and Trinity College), Julian Slade was a musical writer of some accomplishment, and began composing musicals and incidental music for productions at Cambridge.

Salad Days is a Slade musical that premiered at the Bristol Old Vic (Ep. 2) in 1954, then moved to the Vaudeville Theatre in London on 5 August of that year. It ran for more than 2,280 performances. *Salad Days* is mentioned here because of what it was not—a messy, contemptible, violent bloodbath of a production. It was instead a breezy, "whimsical" musical, seen by many as just the type of British musical that might nudge the popular American musicals off of British West End stages ("Julian Slade Obituary").

– K –

"Kup Kakes"—("Lifeboat") This was a trademark brand name from the J. Lyons company (est. 1887), a baking interest in Hammersmith, London. Lyons catered events at Buckingham Palace, Windsor Castle, London's Guildhall, Wimbledon, etc. By 1972, Lyons was stretching across the globe with packing plants, frozen food plants, even hotel chains. The difficult 1970s (oil shortages, recession) would hit Lyons hard, according to Peter Bird, as Lyons was heavily overextended just when interest rates skyrocketed worldwide. Easy to see how the Pythons could put a Lyons-type shop on a lifeboat, then, given Lyons' ubiquitousness during this period.

There was a Lyons Teashop at 54 Uxbridge Road during this period, just down the street and around the corner from Television Centre.

– L –

lifeboatmen—("Lifeboat") The men who eventually fill Mrs. Neves' (Jones) kitchen include Clinton Morris (*Z Cars*), Steve Ismay (*Softly Softly*), Roy Pearce (*Dr. Who*), Terry Sartain (*Emma*), Ron Tingley (*Play For Today*; *Z Cars*), David Waterman (*Dr. Who*), Ken Halliwell (*Play For Today*; *Z Cars*) (WAC T12/1,444).

"loopy brothel inmate"—("Biggles Dictates a Letter") What follows is a now typical Python trope of listing, and in this case the use of metaphoric or poetic terminology for a sexual object. Miss Bladder (Nicki Howorth) is a "loopy brothel inmate," "not a courtesan"; she is a harlot, "paramour, concubine, *fille de joie*," and a "bit of tail." But rather than be one-sided about this stereotypical name-calling, the Pythons turn the tables on the "men" in the conversation. Miss Bladder is allowed to interject and then go on the offensive, calling Biggles a "demented fictional character," then Algy a "fairy," a "poof," and finally a "mincing old RAF queen." All of these later appellations, in the world of the sketch, turn out to be accurate, by the way, giving the narrative power to Miss Bladder—a true female, purposely and actually attractive—which is unusual for the Pythons. Even more unusually, she is not punished, textually, for her cheek.

The allusive language continues, with terms like "old fruit," "ginger beer" (rhymes with "queer," see note below), a "terrible poof," and finally Biggles' celebration of England's regained masculinity in his sort of "John of Gaunt" speech (see "salt of the earth" below for more).

– M –

"Major Dundee"—("Philip Jenkinson on Cheese Westerns") 1965 Sam Peckinpah film starring Charlton Heston.

"*Wild Bunch* and *Straw Dogs*"—The hyperviolent anti-Western *Wild Bunch* (1969) brought Peckinpah to international acclaim, and the equally disturbing rape-and-revenge film *Straw Dogs* (1971) cemented

that reputation. Peckinpah often said that he wanted to make Westerns the way Akira Kurosawa made Westerns, obviously being very influenced by Kurosawa's over-the-top violence in *Yojimbo* (1961) and especially *Sanjuro* (1962), which Peckinpah's films tend to resemble, as well as Sergio Leone's influential "spaghetti Westerns" *A Fistful of Dollars* (1964), *For a Few Dollars More* (1965), and *The Good, the Bad, and the Ugly* (1966).

Mousebender—("Cheese Shop") Perhaps a reference back to the "bent" character Cleese portrayed in Ep. 2's "The Mouse Problem" sketch, who felt more comfortable dressed as a mouse. Mr. Mousebender's name is never mentioned by the characters in the sketch, which is often the case in *FC*, remaining a sort of lifelong in-joke for the script writers and readers. A "mouse bender" could also occur, of course, if a mouse happens to get loose in a cheese shop.

Finally, "Mousebender" might also be an oblique reference to the then-prominent psychic and kineticist Uri Geller (b. 1946), a so-called mindbender who demonstrated a mental utensil-bending ability on various TV shows and public appearances between 1969 and 1972.

Mrs Pinnet type—("Lifeboat") References the character, also played by Jones, who appeared back in Ep. 14, in the "New Cooker Sketch." She is essentially a Pepperpot, but not nearly as fussy, more like a sweet mother type. The Pythons here have gone a step further in their reflexivity, their self-referentiality—they've moved from a clear, long-held British TV (and literary) type (the fussy, middle-aged woman), to referencing one of their own refinements of that type, "Mrs. Pinnet." Production designers could then easily access the generic construct "Mrs. Pinnet," greatly facilitating wardrobe, makeup, and even prop and set dressing decisions.

– N –

naked quartet—(PSC; titles) The single chord played by this fright-wigged quartet is borrowed from "String Quartet in G minor" by Debussy (WAC T12/1,444).

"never even been to Spain"—("Biggles Dictates a Letter") Perhaps because by this period, travel to the Spanish coast wasn't really considered international travel by the English tourist, it had become so traditional.

"Ibiza"—A Spanish Mediterranean island mentioned previously in Ep. 27 as the vacation spot where Mrs Premise (Cleese) and Mrs. Conclusion (Chapman) met Jean-Paul Sartre and his wife (Palin), Betty-Muriel. See notes to Ep. 27.

"Newhaven"—("Lifeboat") The Newhaven Lifeboat Station was founded in 1803 to serve England's south coast. It is located sixty miles west of Dover, the area where the Pythons were shooting exteriors for this series. The Pythons and crew shot with the crew of Newhaven Lifeboat on 20 Oct 1971, all for a £20 donation to the Newhaven branch of the RNLI (WAC T12/1,444).

"no better than you should be"—("Biggles Dictates a Letter") A phrase taken from various sources, including Beaumont and Fletcher's *The Coxcomb* (act 4, scene 3; perf. 1612), and Henry Fielding's *The Temple Beau* (also 4.3; perf. 1730). In the first, the young lady in question is being accused of being a thief and perhaps more, and in the latter she is an unsavory match for a monied young man based on her "flaw"—alleged sexual libertinism. In both, the meaning is clear: Once a sullied woman, always a sullied woman—and the sullied woman will ever act the part.

Also, this phrase appears in Joyce's *Ulysses*, coming from Deasy as he is regaling Stephen about foot and mouth and the curse of the Jews:

> I have put the matter into a nutshell, Mr Deasy said. It's about the foot and mouth disease. Just look through it. There can be no two opinions on the matter. . . . May I trespass on your valuable space. That doctrine of laissez faire which so often in our history. Our cattle trade. The way of all our old industries. Liverpool ring which jock-eyed the Galway harbour scheme. European conflagration. Grain supplies through the narrow waters of the channel. The pluterperfect imperturbability of the department of agriculture. Pardoned a classical allusion. Cassandra. *By a woman who was no better than she should be*. To come to the point at issue. (*Ulysses*, Episode 2—"Nestor"; italics added)

(And yes, the above does sound very much like the topics and even cadence of the "Farming Club" and "*Life of Tschaikowsky*" sections of Ep. 28. The influence of Modernist writers like Joyce and Stein and Eliot on the Pythons has been pointed out and discussed. See notes to Eps. 1, 12, 13, 17, 23, 25, and on.)

In the Biggles sketch the Secretary sits "provocatively" and wears a short, form-fitting dress, emblematic of her "should be-ness." She is very much a biological, sexualized woman in this raving cast of transvestites (Biggles when he's dressed as his wife), homosexuals (Algy), and flamboyant glam-rock cross dressers (Ginger). This "type" casting is typical of Python, and has been seen with other types, including City Gents, Rustics, Pepperpots, etc.

"No longer used in the West"—("Storage Jars") This is often the case in developing countries. In Cuba, for instance, big American cars of the 1950s were used for many years as "new" cars—none were being imported from the United States, so those abandoned when Bautista's government fell in 1959 had to be made to last.

– O –

"one of my favourite film directors, Sam Peckinpah"—("Cheese Westerns") Jenkinson had interviewed another American Western filmmaker, John Ford, in 1971 for *Listener* (12 February 1970).

– P –

Pantomime Princess Margaret—("Biggles Dictates a Letter") Pantomime Princess Margaret has appeared in Ep. 30, as well, where she harpooned her breakfast tray, then stomped the tea service to death. Cleese is playing the part in this scene (WAC T12/1,444).

Peter Ackroyd notes that a German visitor to England for the coronation of George IV recorded that the king "was obliged to present himself, as chief actor in a pantomime" (*London* 146). It is also mentioned earlier that the young girl Margaret performed in pantomime for Christmas broadcast during the war, though admittedly not as a "dummy." See notes to Ep. 30. The Pythons' massaging, then, of Princess Margaret from royal to player to "pantomimetic royal person" is not as ridiculous as it may have seemed.

"Peckinpah, Sam"—("Philip Jenkinson on Cheese Westerns") Peckinpah (1925-1984) was indeed born in Fresno, California, and would die as an expatriate in Mexico, after living and working abroad in England, as well.

pederast vole—(PSC; "Cheese Shop") These comments comparing Philip Jenkinson to a hybrid Truman Capote/pederast vole would have been for the other Pythons only, really, and those who had to prep the script for the taping of the show. It's interesting that these textual comments were never excised from the printed scripts, as they may have represented actionable slander under UK law. Perhaps it is because the scripts weren't originally intended for publication. It also could be that since the comments in question occur in the scenic directions and aren't voiced by any character, printed on the screen, or visually/aurally depicted in any way, the hallmark for slander wasn't reached? Or, the characterization could have been a good-natured joke among friends. Whatever the reason, the Pythons comparing their contemporary Jenkinson to a gay, pedophilic rodent has remained in the *FC* printed scripts since 1972.

"phone up"—("Apology") In *That Was Satire, That Was* Humphrey Carpenter (1946-2005) reports that BBC viewers have a long tradition of making their feelings known via phone and mail, with significant complaints lodged over especially satirical shows like *That Was the Week That Was, Benny Hill,* and *FC* later. The British Board of Film Censors (BBFC) and the Lord Chamberlain's office also fielded hundreds of calls and mail items in regard to controversial filmed productions from this period, including *Look Back in Anger, Room at the Top, Billy Liar, A Taste of Honey,* and on. Both the BBFC and the Lord Chamberlain's Office (for theater) were quite considerate about responding—and civilly, respectfully—to all such complaints. See Aldgate.

As a sort of sideways testament to this careful viewer attention the BBC enjoyed, there are a number of letters (and telegrams) from *Flying Circus* viewers in the WAC records for the show, asking for tickets, offering jokes and new characters and funny storylines, showering congratulations and clucking tongues alike. By sheer number, most letters are offering written material, which the producers kindly and thankfully decline, saying the troupe writes all its own material. Many BBC comedy shows accepted outside material, meaning the practice was fairly usual, if the material was worthwhile (see Carpenter).

"puzzle her"—("Biggles Dictates a Letter") Perhaps he is referring to the use of "Saxe-Coburg" rather than "Windsor," if he is talking about Margaret's immediate family. Both are adopted surnames, anyway.

– R –

"Red Leicester"—("Cheese Shop") A cheese originally made in Leicestershire. This section of the sketch seems to be a ready-made in-joke, poking fun at Cleese's propensity for writing wordier, even encyclopedic sketches. It is also the "most failed transaction" of all of Pythons' myriad failed transactions in *Flying Circus.* This "list" scenario will be revisited in Ep. 37, and has become legendary (even by 1972) thanks to the success of the "Dead Parrot" sketch in Ep. 8.

Of all the cheeses mentioned, thirteen are from the UK; twelve from France; four from Italy; three from Switzerland; two each from Holland, Denmark, and Czechoslovakia; and one each from Norway, Austria, and Germany. Remarkably, "Venezuelan Beaver Cheese" seems to be the only "made-up" cheese in the entire spiel. In most lists ("Timmy Williams," *"The Black Eagle,"* "Court Scene—Multiple Murderer") there

are a few names that are clearly real, and then many just as clearly cobbled together from multiple sources. The cheese list itself isn't meant to be funny—real cheeses, proper pronunciations—it's the sheer length of the list and the willful persistence of the participants where the humor emerges. In Tex Avery's *Blitz Wolf* (1942), the new secret weapon meant to destroy Nazi Germany and Fascist Japan simply looks like a big cannon—it's not funny until the camera "pans" along the barrel for a full thirty-one seconds, and it seems as if it's never going to end. (The Pythons will revisit this "waiting" structure of humor in *Holy Grail,* when Launcelot [Cleese] runs toward Swamp Castle's front gate numerous times.)

At last this sketch may be about optimism—the customer (Cleese) is content to push on through the cheese list on the real possibility that the shop actually sells cheese, and the proprietor (Palin) good-naturedly allows the customer his full range of ordering potentiality, knowing from the outset that there is no cheese to be had. In the end, both seem to agree that the gunshot is an acceptable ending to the failed transaction.

"Rhyming slang—ginger beer"—("Biggles Dictates a Letter") "Ginger beer" is a Cockney rhyming slang phrase for "queer." It's said that so-called Cockneys created this secret rhyming language so they could converse about their nefarious affairs in front of anyone, including a constable. This would have lasted only as long, of course, as it took the authorities to learn the slang.

In Ep. 7 the Compère (Palin) uses another Cockney rhyming slang, "lager and lime," slang for "spine," in that case.

"rock buns"—("Lifeboat") Simple drop cakes made of flour, butter, sugar, dried fruit, eggs, and milk.

"Rogue Cheddar"—("Cheese Shop") This short film sequence is borrowed from EMI's *Cowboy* C2 859 (WAC T12/1,444).

"Rogue . . . Walpole"—("Cheese Shop") Actually, *Rogue Herries* (1930) was written by *Hugh* Walpole (1884-1941), part of his Cumberland family saga. *Horace* Walpole (1717-1797) lived much earlier, and nearly single-handedly created the Gothic novel genre with *The Castle of Otranto* (1764), and was the son of Robert Walpole, the former first Prime Minister.

And speaking of lists, Horace Walpole had set up a printing concern at his Strawberry Hill estate, publishing, among other things, catalogs and list-like materials, including *Catalogue of Royal and Noble Authors of England* (1758), *Anecdotes of Painting in England,* and *A Catalogue of Engravers* (1762-1771).

– S –

"salt of the earth"—("Biggles Dictates a Letter") Borrowed from the New Testament, Matthew 5:13. The balance of the declamation is perhaps Biggles' version of John of Gaunt's stirring "this realm, this England" assessment of the English character in *Richard II*, that, or Henry's "Once more unto the breach" speech on the eve of St. Crispin's Day and the Battle of Agincourt depicted in *Henry V*. Algy soon joins his worthy English predecessors in noble death, of course.

"stout fellow"—Guest star Valentine Dyall uses this phrase several times in *The Goon Show* episode "The Giant Bombardon" (17 November 1957), there describing the essence of British military manhood, Colonel Splun.

"Saxe-Coburgs"—("Biggles Dictates a Letter") Name taken from a German duchy, and was the royal house for a number of European monarchies, including the Wettins (now called Windsors). For the English portion of this large royal family, the German surnames and titles were dropped during the First World War, for obvious reasons, and "Windsor" was adopted. This family name will be mentioned again in Ep. 36, in the "Tudor Jobs Agency" sketch.

"canasta"—A card game (of Uruguayan origin) combining portions of both rummy and pinochle (*OED*).

"self-righting models"—("Lifeboat") Lifeboats that were designed to right themselves even after being overturned in heavy seas came into regular service in the UK as early as 1881, and would have been standard by the 1970s.

show-off angles—("Cheese Shop") This form—still photos shot "artily"—was used by French "film essayist" Chris Marker in his landmark 1962 film *La Jetee*, as well as hundreds of school films and slide show presentations of the period.

This is also clearly a reference to the early Cleese and Gilliam collaboration in a 1968 *Help!* magazine panel story (*fumetti*), wherein a man (Cleese) falls in love (and eventually has relations) with his daughter's Barbie-type doll. *Fumetti*, or photo novels, are laid out like a comic book set-up, complete with thought balloons, speech bubbles, and written sound effects. For "Cheese Shop," just the arty photos are employed.

silver stars—(PSC; "Biggles Dictates a Letter") Gilliam's flashy attire here is a throwback to the transgendered "Mod" crowd of the 1960s, but more precisely to the more current fashions in the Glam Rock movement popular in the UK. Note the title of a Tyrannosaurus Rex album from this period: "My people were fair and had sky in their hair but now they're content to wear stars on their brows." Gilliam here looks very much like Marc Bolan of T-Rex fame, circa 1972.

sou'wester—(PSC; "Lifeboat") A large, waterproof hat (formerly made of oilskin).

Spanish soldier's outfit—(PSC; "Seashore Interlude Film") This is a shot recorded during the shooting of the seaside portions of the soon-to-be-aired Ep. 36, where Sir Philip Sidney (Palin) fights Spanish porn merchants. These exterior, on-location shots were generally done in one or two goes, at the beginning and middle of the various seasons, then parsed out as needed for each episode. The "lemon curry" inserts were shot in the Glencoe locations in October 1971, for instance, then held for Ep. 33.

"strife-torn Bolivia"—("Storage Jars") According to the *Columbia Encyclopedia*, Bolivia has endured at least 190 coup attempts since 1825, with the 1960s and 1970s being particularly uneasy. There was an overthrow in 1964, another in 1969, and widespread nationalizations of essential industries in between. A rightist junta overthrew the 1969-inaugurated government in 1970, but was only able to keep power for a single day, when a leftist coup assumed control. This leftist government was itself unseated in 1971 by a U.S.-friendly government, and on and on.

The still photo is from the Colour Library International, "G.V. La Paz" 60914 (WAC T12/1,444).

– T –

"Tee Hee"—("Sam Peckinpah's *Salad Days*") This is the Pythons enjoying the sight of one of their targets "getting his," while at the same time perhaps covering themselves in case Jenkinson actually is offended by the depiction. (See the entry for "pederast vole" above for more on this curious and potentially actionable slander.) If the latter case, the subtitle acts as the "SATIRE" subtitle in Ep. 17 ("Architect Sketch") and the "A Joke" flashcard in Ep. 24 ("Conquistador Coffee Campaign") where the seriousness of the on-screen depiction of a Ronan Point–type disaster (Ep. 17) is undercut by satiric humor that is also carefully underscored.

"terpsichorean muse"—("Cheese Shop") Terpsichore is the muse of dancing.

"thank you, love"—("Old Lady Snoopers") This could be a comment on the media watchdogs seen earlier in Ep. 32, Mary Whitehouse and her friends at the National Viewers and Listeners Association (NVLA). More simply, it could just be a send-up of the typical nosy neighbor scenario.

"Thurmond Street"—("Cheese Shop") There is a cheese shop, Bloomsbury's, very near Broadcast House, on the corner of Leigh Street and Judd Street, WC 1.

– U –

urgent documentary music—(PSC; "Storage Jars") This "urgent" music is P. Gerard's "Riot Squad" from the Standard Music Library (WAC T12/1,444).

"Uxbridge Road"—("Climbing the North Face of Uxbridge Road") This main road is found in Shepherd's Bush, W12, just near BBC Production Centre; however, according to Palin, the scene was actually shot on South Ealing Road, W5. This is not far from Lammas Park (both the park and the adjacent road), where portions of the "Bicycle Repair Man" sketch were shot for Ep. 3. Due to budgetary constraints, most of the neighborhood exteriors for *FC* were shot with a ten-mile radius of BBC Television Centre, Shepherd's Bush.

– W –

"what about that"—("Biggles Dictates a Letter") The dangers of (mis)communication are illustrated here again, as in Ep. 30, where pauses in televised speech have to be precisely described and delineated from actual or finished speech.

– Z –

Zabriskie Point—("Sam Peckinpah's *Salad Days*") Michelangelo Antonioni's 1970 film looking at late 1960s America and the emerging youth culture. Antonioni and his films are discussed at length in Ep. 29. It's worth noting that even though the Pythons are sending up Peckinpah and American excess in film, they are asking that the scene be shot in the manner of a noted Italian director, which may just mean that stylistically Peckinpah had yet to leave a memorable visual signature to be copied.

slow motion—This is the same kind of violence being asked for by the American producer (Idle) in Ep. 23, in the "*Scott of the Antarctic*" sketch. This level of violence, and the "geysers of blood," had really begun with the influence of the final sequence in Kurosawa's anti-heroic samurai Western *Sanjuro* (1962).

Episode 34: "The Cycling Tour"

– A –

"agent in the town"—("Trotsky") After he was expelled from Russia, Trotsky was fairly consistently a target for assassination. He was exiled in 1927 to the far-flung remoteness of eastern Russia, then had to flee to Istanbul, several locations in France, Norway, and finally Mexico, according to his own work and that of biographers. (Trotsky wrote seemingly non-stop throughout his lifetime.) There was either political pressure everywhere he went, viz., Stalin and supporters pressing local governments, or agents to watch and report on Trotsky's movements and associations. It was 1940 when agents with orders to kill were finally sent, and sent successfully.

– B –

"Bakewell's tart"—("Bingo-Crazed Chinese") Long-popular English confection.

"bloodstained shadow of Stalinist repression"—("Jack in a Box") Trotsky had said—when favorable comparisons were being made between Lenin and Stalin after Lenin's death—that a "river of blood" (1927) separated the two men, as it separated Stalinism from Bolshevism.

Trotsky and his Left Opposition group were all expelled from the Communist Party in November 1927, and he was deported in 1929 to Istanbul and then France. He would eventually be assassinated in Mexico.

"Bovey Tracey"—("Mr. Pither") Small town in Devon north of Newton Abbot on the B3387 and the A382.

Brief film clip of rioting Chinese—(PSC; "Bingo-Crazed Chinese") The film stock here is "Red Guards" 1376/67, 961/67 from VisNews (WAC T12/1,440).

Brun, M.—(PSC; "Trotsky") "Brun" simply means "brown," and is probably meant to indicate a kind of standard surname. This could be a reference to the noted electronic music composer and performer Herbert Brun (1918-2000), who was internationally active in 1972.

"Bude"—("Clodagh Rogers") One of the few locations mentioned by Pither that is actually in Cornwall, Bude is a coastal town.

"Budleigh Salterton"—("Mr. Pither") City on the coast a little north and west of Bovey Tracey in Devon, Pither would have had to cross the Exe (or navigate the Dawlish Marshes) to reach this site, a distance of about twenty-six miles.

"bugged or unbugged"—("Smolensk") The Soviet Union of the Cold War era (c. 1949-1989) employed clandestine intelligence-gathering both at home and abroad, as outlined in, for example, the KGB's "Annual Report" for 1967, where the installation of "electronic monitoring devices" in at least thirty-six foreign buildings is discussed. The goal of such monitoring was identified as "improvement of counterintelligence work inside the country . . . so as to ensure more efficient struggle with military, economic and political espionage." Hotels in the Soviet Union frequented by foreign visitors (especially Western foreign visitors) were regularly bugged and guests photographed.

The crossed-out pictures behind the Clerk include Robert Baden-Powell (1857-1941), founder of the Boy Scouts. Powell may be here because he represents what many in the Sino-Soviet bloc during this period saw as a "sleeper" paramilitary organization—the Boy Scouts—or because he was a member of the British secret service during his military career.

Secondly, the middle picture seems to be of St. Tikhon of Moscow (1865-1925), the Russian Orthodox

432

Church Patriarch from about 1917 to his death. Tikhon would spend time in prison/house arrest for speaking and writing against the excesses of the Soviet government.

"Bulganin"—("Jack in a Box") Nikolai Bulganin (1895-1975) was a Soviet soldier, secret police member, WWII general, and eventually Prime Minister of Russia when he and Khrushchev toured the UK in the late 1950s. He was a Marshal during and just after WWII.

"Charlie" was the name of Edgar Bergen's ventriloquist doll. This image—a powerful military or political figure with a ventriloquist's dummy—was a common sight in political cartoons of the period, including a 1962 cartoon from Fritz Behrendt featuring Khrushchev with Janos Kadar (Hungary) and Mao with Enver Hoxha (Albania). Both dummies are screaming epithets at the other, while their manipulators look away (*Observer* 2 December 1962). See the British Cartoon Archive.

Burgess and Maclean—("Jack in the Box") These names appear on a poster in Pither's Moscow cell. Guy Burgess (1911-1963) and Donald MacLean (1913-1983) were British diplomats when they disappeared in 1951, only to reappear in Moscow in 1956, and their careers of spying for the Soviet Union became banner headlines.

The U.S. government's extensive files on Burgess, MacLean, and the rest of the so-called Cambridge Five spy ring are now available from the FBI.

– C –

Camera pans very slightly—("Mr. Pither") Pither is the type of character who sees the world in his own way. He never takes offense, even when offense is intended; he misses facial and body cues that signal the end of conversations or the subtle discomforts of another; he is also invincible, seemingly protected by the hands of God (not unlike Harry Langdon's character in his early Frank Capra–directed films for Columbia). In the Python world, this type of character will survive and even flourish in spite of himself.

What Smollett wrote of his character Roderick Random (from *The Adventures of Roderick Random*) fits Pither quite well:

> [In creating and presenting the character Roderick] I have attempted to represent modest merit struggling with every difficulty to which a friendless orphan is exposed, from his own want of experience, as well as from the selfishness, envy, malice, and base indifference of mankind. (*Letters* 8)

See the entry for "Tobias Smollett" in the *ODNB* for more on the author and his picaresque characters.

chemist's shop—("Mr. Pither") The sign on this pharmacy clearly reads "West Park Pharmacy" and "Cheapside Post Office," meaning these scenes were shot on location in the St. Helier area, Jersey, along with most of the exterior work for these later third series episodes. This shot appears to be taken at 3 Pierson Road, where West Park Pharmacy still operates today.

"Compton, Denis"—("Clodagh Rogers") Compton (1918-1997) was both a cricketer (for England) and footballer (Arsenal), setting records in the immediate postwar years. He has earlier been mentioned in Ep. 21.

"continue in English"—("Jack in a Box") An acknowledgment of the standard practice in British and American films (and TV) of having all central characters—no matter their native tongue—speak English (but with an accent) to approximate a foreigner.

Cook, Peter and Dudley Moore—("Jack in a Box") Listed on a jail cell poster as appearing in the Moscow Praesidium, Peter Cook (1937-1995) and Dudley Moore (1935-2002) had been performing together since the early 1960s, when they joined Alan Bennett and Jonathan Miller in *Beyond the Fringe*. The show's satirical edge and wordsmithing were clear influences on the Pythons. In 1972 when this episode was being produced, Cook and Moore were on tour together in Australia, incidentally.

"crunchie"—("Jack in a Box") According to Cadbury, the Crunchie bar was first sold in the UK in 1929. The "Mars bar" (from Mars, Inc.) mentioned earlier appeared in 1936 in the United States.

"Cycling Tour"—("Mr. Pither") After thirty-three hodge-podge episodes, where central characters come and go seemingly at random, this nearly unilinear narrative follows Mr. Pither from start to finish, perhaps signaling a change in mood for the Pythons. They have never attempted to maintain interest via a single character's storyline, and this episode may have been a chance to test the writing chops—and certainly served to shake things up generally—as they create this sort of picaresque journey for the unflappable Mr. Pither (Palin).

Pither is very much crafted in the vein of earlier celebrated peripatetic literary characters, including Cervantes' Don Quixote, Fielding's Joseph Andrews and Tom Jones, Smollett's Humphrey Clinker, and even Sterne's Uncle Toby (who doesn't go very far but does talk a good deal of his experiences). Astride his Rocinante, a rickety ten-speed, Pither moves from experience to experience, living out the empiricist theory (à la Locke) as he observes the natural world, "senses it," and then reflects upon those observances and sensations for himself, the viewer, and anyone who'll listen during his journeys.

And Pither is a sensory being, certainly, as will be seen, especially as he repeatedly falls from his mount, then describes in very real and tactile language the results of those experiences—after a crash his lunch has "grit all over it" and "small particles of bitumen in the chocolate kup kakes" from the "tarmacadam surface" of the roadway, etc.

This episode ends up being one of the oddest but also most philosophically centered in all of *FC*, as the Pythons—perhaps unconsciously—create a classically inspired picaresque, neatly adorned with the twentieth-century philosophies that so influenced them.

– D –

Dawlish Road—("Mr. Pither") The Dawlish Road runs south from Exeter in Devon, where the Pythons shot location footage for the first series.

Devon countryside—("Mr. Pither") These outdoor scenes were actually recorded on the island of Jersey.

District Hospital—("Clodagh Rogers") The depictions here also keep the text close to Tobias Smollett's world, especially with the treatment of the hospital as the last place one would go when sick or injured. In volume one of *Humphry Clinker*, Bramble writes to Dr. Lewis that the waters of Bath can't possibly be a cure-all, and that the man who subscribes to the myth of Bath "sacrifices his precious time, which might be employed in taking more effectual remedies, and exposes himself to the dirt, the stench, the chilling blasts, and perpetual rains" (23). See also Bramble's lengthy complaint to his doctor when he arrives in Bath, calling it a "national hospital," and then enumerating its unhygienic and even dangerous faults (33-35).

This entire episode is a cleverly updated version of the picaresque-type novels of eighteenth-century England, including *Tom Jones*, *Joseph Andrews*, *Humphrey Clinker*, and *Roderick Random*.

"Dr. Wu"—("Clodagh Rogers") There has been concern and discussion for many years in the UK regarding the quality of doctors and critical-care nurses in regional and especially rural National Health Service facilities. Based on the views expressed in hundreds of letters to various newspapers and now websites and blogs, it's still assumed by a large portion of the British public that the NHS struggles to entice the highest-qualified medical personnel into less lucrative and seemingly provincial state service—and it gets worse the further one happens to be from London. Example: In Webster's *The National Health Service: A Political His-*

tory, figures indicate that the Southwestern region (Devon and Cornwall) had consistently run well beneath fiscal allocation goals between 1963 and 1975. Over this same period, however, the Metropolitan regions (Greater London) consistently ran above the allocation goals. A series of government Green Papers on the subject (briefly mentioned earlier in Ep. 26) had been in the public forum since 1970.

Though backhanded, this reference to an Asian doctor in a slap-dash rural hospital might be a hint at this still-smoldering issue in UK healthcare. When the doctor (played by Cleese) appears, of course, it's clear he isn't Asian, nor even "acting" like one, which Chapman will do later in the episode.

– E –

Episode 34—This nearly single-narrative episode was recorded 4 May 1972 and broadcast 7 December 1972. It was the tenth episode recorded, and the eighth broadcast, with most of the exterior work accomplished between March and May 1972.

Walk-ons for this episode include: Ron Gregory (*Dixon of Dock Green*; *Z Cars*), John Beardmore (*Softly Softly*; *Colditz*), Charles Saynor (*Blue Lamp*; *Man in the White Suit*), Desmond Verini (*Day of the Daleks*), Aldwyn Francis Davies (*Under Milkwood*), Peter Brett (Eps. 38, 45; *Dixon of Dock Green*), Pat Cleveland, Beulah Hughes (*Hands of the Ripper*), Charlotte Green; (as Maoists) Arnold Lee (*Dr. Who*), George Laughing-Sam, Kelwin Sue-a-Quan and C.H. Yang (both findable in period Greater London–area telephone directories), Jack Tong, Ken Nazarin (*A Casual Affair*), Carey Wilson, Richard Gregory (*Paul Temple*) (WAC T12/1,440).

– G –

"Gulliver"—("Mr. Pither") Well-known character from Swift's *Gulliver's Travels*, it's no surprise that this character name appears in this episode so clearly indebted to eighteenth-century literature and philosophy. Lemuel Gulliver was a traveler, to be sure, but his encounters being termed by Swift as the "great foundation of Misanthropy" were not the ends sought by the Pythons. Gently satirizing the cheerful, dopey English traveler as well as Communist fervor is perhaps shooting fish in a barrel, but it's the incongruity of a jangling Pither meeting Clodagh Rogers, Trotsky, Chinese insurgents, Soviet Communist party members and executioners, and others, and blissfully living through it all that drives the narrative.

Once Mr. Gulliver (Jones) joins Pither on his adventures, the tale takes on a sort of *Humphrey Clinker* feel to it, with the letter-writing Matthew Bramble and Humphrey on the road through rural Britain. Bramble is gouty and complaining, of course, and shackled with a lovesick niece and a maiden sister, so he's no Pither, who is the picture of blind optimism.

Smollett's focus on illness, medicine, and healing in *Humphry Clinker* is also borrowed by the Pythons here. Pither will be nearly injured as he consistently falls from his bike, he'll visit a doctor in a rural town who can only give him directions, his travel partner Gulliver will be injured and go to a very dangerous hospital, as well as undergo several personality changes, Pither will nearly be executed, etc. Part of the Pythons' satire here must be the inadvisablity of traveling into Britain's provinces, where both hospitality and hospitals fall well short of reasonable (southern, as in London?) expectations. Smollett would have agreed with this, certainly.

Gulliver dashing through the trees—("Clodagh Rogers") Very much a Swiftian character trait, in Chapter I of "A Voyage to Brobdingnag," Lemuel Gulliver confesses to being "condemned by Nature and Fortune to an active and restless life" and leaves his wife and children for yet another maritime adventure (63).

– H –

"Hackney Star"—("Bingo-Crazed Chinese") The Hackney Empire Theatre had been an early television studio before becoming a bingo hall in 1963.

The "Top Rank Suite" theater in Doncaster, for example, hosted first-tier concerts including Pink Floyd (1971), Ziggy Stardust (David Bowie, 1972), and The Velvet Underground (1972).

Heath, Ted—("Eartha Kitt") In November 1972, following power shortages, mine and general labor strikes, big business struggles, an unpopular Industrial Relations Bill, and the consistent fumbling of the economic ball, Heath and government had instituted a wage and salary freeze, cellaring their already-low opinion ratings among working families. The Conservatives would be not-so-politely ushered out of office in 1974, to Wilson's Labour coalition. See Morgan's *Britain Since 1945* for more.

This particular speech was most likely delivered in late 1971 or early 1972, when the government had given concessions to coal miners.

hospital—("Clodagh Rogers") This exterior location is the General Hospital found on Gloucester Street, in St. Helier, Jersey.

"Housey! Housey!"—("Bingo-Crazed Chinese") This was a kind of alert call from street vendors in Hong Kong (and India) announcing a game of "tambola," a lotto-type game. The postwar craze for bingo in an otherwise impoverished, rationed, and grey Britain is discussed in the "Popular Culture" section of *Eyewitness: 1950-59*.

"How do you know so much about cycling?"—("Mr. Pither") Pither has intricately connected his food experience and appreciation with his cycling avocation, meaning it becomes difficult to see where one leaves off and another begins. In the same vein the "Trim Jeans" users losing pounds and inches in performance owe their weight loss to the writing abilities of Chekhov, according to the announcer (Palin), and not necessarily exercise or even the Trim Jeans product.

– I –

"I'd be happier with a bugged one"—("Smolensk") Curious, unless it's considered that the likelihood of home invasion from authorities in a totalitarian state is probably greatly reduced if that authority knows exactly what's going on in the home. In the science fiction film *THX-1138* (dir. George Lucas) released in 1971, most men of this future (and stiflingly oppressive) society choose the certain, comfortable safeties of oppression over the unknown waiting "out there." For the Soviet citizen under Stalin (and perhaps even Brezhnev, in 1972), a bug meant nothing controversial is ever discussed, therefore no need for special attentions from the state.

"Iddesleigh"—("Mr. Pither") In West Devon.

"I decided to check . . . "—("Smolensk") This is a very interesting moment, narratively, what Gérard Genette would call a "narrative metalepsis," and what sets this episode apart from most of the previous thirty-three. Pither for the first time in the narrative speaks to "us" (or his own narrating voice) when he thanks the Military Man (Idle) for providing directions just when he needs them; the voiceover (Pither) then continues to the "all the way from Monte Carlo" line, and the Military Man interrupts, helpfully again, to which Pither (on his bike) says "thank you" again. With that thank you, the "live" Pither continues on with "I decided to check . . . ," only to be interrupted by the voiceover Pither saying the same thing. Here we have multiple levels of possible narration and story progression tripping over one another for a brief, fascinating moment. These progressions of course are always flowing, at the diegetic and metadiegetic levels, at least, but we generally only hear from one at a time to avoid such confusions. Genette notes such "second-degree narratives" in *Tristram Shandy* and *Manon Lescaut*, and "in

[Brontë's] *Wuthering Heights* (Isabella's narrative to Nelly, reported by Nelly to Lockwood, noted by Lockwood in his journal), and especially in *Lord Jim* [Joseph Conrad], *where the entanglement reaches the bounds of general intelligibility*" (*Narrative Discourse* 232-33; italics for emphasis added). The Pythons merely slip their toe into these less-fathomed waters, then allow the ever-gracious Pither to bow out and let his voiceover self continue the exciting narration.

"Ilfracombe"—("Clodagh Rogers") A fairly small Devon town in the North Devon Coastal area.

Imperial music—(PSC; "Bingo-Crazy Chinese") The music used here is "Pomp and Circumstance" by Elgar (from Marches No. 1 in D major) (WAC T12/1,440).

– J –

"Jack in the Box"—("Clodagh Rogers") This particular recording of the song is from "Unaccompanied Artists" and was written by David Myers and John Worsley (WAC T12/1,440).

– K –

"Kerensky"—("Clodagh Rogers") Alexander Fyodorovich Kerensky (1881-1970) was an anti-Tsarist revolutionary instrumental in toppling the Russian monarchy. He was a major figure in the coalition government(s), before being himself unseated when the Bolsheviks (under Lenin) seized power. He would later live out much of his life in exile in the United States, and is buried in England. One of the handful of active early Soviet figures still alive in the 1960s, Kerensky had recently published *Russia and History's Turning Point* in 1966.

"Kitt, Eartha"—("Jack in a Box") Born in 1927, Kitt is an American singer who came to prominence in the 1950s. She is perhaps included here because in 1968 she had offended the White House with anti-war remarks, and her American bookings dried up. She went to Europe and successfully continued her career. It's also likely that she's included here based on her recent appearance in the Frankie Howerd vehicle *Up the Chastity Belt* (1971). Ned Sherrin (Ep. 5) produced the film.

– L –

large Chinese crowds—(PSC; "Bingo-Crazed Chinese") This film stock is "Red Guards 1376/67" and "961/67" (WAC T12/1,440). These newsreels would have been

recorded during the mass demonstrations in places like Wuhan, China in July 1967.

"Lenin"—("Clodagh Rogers") V.I. Lenin (1870-1924) led the Soviet state 1917-1924. The footage used when Lenin "sings" is Pathe film stock (WAC T12/1,440). Lenin earlier appeared as a befuddled contestant on *Communist Quiz*, and wasn't able to utter a word (Ep. 25).

The depiction of Trotsky's relationship with Lenin is significant here. Stalin and comrades moved against Trotsky as Lenin tried to recuperate from several strokes, and Lenin over and over again wrote from his bed that Trotsky was essential to the future of the Soviet Union he'd (Lenin) envisioned, characterizing such dismissive moves as the "height of stupidity" (Document 106, *The Unknown Lenin*). So Gulliver as Trotsky having some kind of an emotional connection to Lenin is in character for both men and historically justifiable.

"line of gentlemen with rifles"—("Jack in a Box") During Stalin's purges in the 1930s, thousands of "disloyal" and "counterrevolutionary" types were executed by firing squad, most innocent of the charges brought against them, but caught up in Stalin's consolidation of power machinations. Estimates of those killed during Stalin's purges and recriminations mount into the tens of millions (*EBO*).

"Little White Bull"—("Clodagh Rogers") A song from the film *Tommy the Toreador* (1959), and written by Lionel Bart, Michael Pratt, and Jimmy Bennett. The film starred Tommy Steele.

"Lyons, Joe"—("Bingo-Crazed Chinese") Joe Lyons Corner Houses were ubiquitous food establishments, catering royal gatherings and becoming Europe's largest food company before falling prey to the recession of the 1970s. Lyons' Kup Kakes are mentioned prominently in Ep. 33, when Mrs. Neves (Jones) has gone to sea for cakes and macaroons.

– M –

Mao-suited Chinese people—("Bingo-Crazed Chinese") These actors include Arnold Lee (*Dr. Who*), George Laughing-Sam, Kelwin Sue-a-Quan, C.H. Yang, Jack Tong, and Ken Nazarin (*A Casual Affair*). These actors were cast simply because they were Asian, and were even from a different talent agency than most of the other extras the show acquired (WAC T12/1,440).

"me Blitish consul"—("Bingo-Crazed Chinese") Continuing the Python (and music hall) tradition of outrageous racial stereotyping, substituting "r" for "l" and squinting for an Asian character (last seen and heard in Ep. 29), though the presence of Chinese infiltrators becomes the more interesting specter here. Again, relations between the Russians and the Chinese were deteriorating at this point, with differing socialist interpretations (Soviet Marxism vs. Chinese Maoism) leading to border concerns as the Chinese military flexed its muscles, and the USSR flexed right back. In this case the Chinese have killed the British ambassador, replaced him, and Chinese minions are actually hiding in the woodwork, emerging at the call of "Housey!"

"Monte Carlo"—("Smolensk") The helpful Military Man (Idle) has trouble distinguishing direction, especially the difference between west and east. Monte Carlo, Monaco is about 100 miles south of Turin, Italy, about 177 miles (along the coast) *west* of Pisa, Italy (not east), and about 520 miles *east* of Bilbao, Portugal (not west).

Shakespeare, of course, provides similarly bad (and probably memorial) directions in *Richard III*:

[He confuses] travel directions from Northampton to London: "Last night, I [hear], they lay at Stony-Stratford/ And at Northampton they do rest to-night./ Tomorrow, or next day, they will be here" (2.4.1-3). Following these directions it certainly would not be tomorrow or the next day; one would find the Irish Sea quicker than the city of London. Phyllis Rackin offers that Shakespeare's dubious geography was certainly "careless only because he had better things to do with his settings than plot their locations on a map. . . ." (Larsen, *MPSERD*)

As has been seen, Python has relied less on hyper-accurate research and more on the group memory of names, places, and events. In Ep. 33, for instance, Mousebender says he's been reading *Horace* Walpoling, when he clearly meant he'd been reading *Hugh* Walpole. See notes to the "Cheese Shop" sketch.

– N –

"North Cornwall"—("Mr. Pither") Though he says he's enjoying North Cornwall, most of the locations Mr. Pither mentions are in Devon, where the Pythons spent a great deal of time shooting locations in May 1970. In additon, every bit of the country he's currently riding through is found on the island of Jersey, where the Pythons spent much of the March-May 1972 period.

– O –

"Okehampton by-pass"—("Jack in a Box") Okehampton is in Devon just north of Dartmoor.

"old fashioned girl"—("Jack in a Box") Lyrics from the 1957 song "Just an Old-Fashioned Girl" by Marve Fisher.

"Ottery St. Mary"—("Mr. Pither") Also in Devon, Ottery St. Mary lies about ten miles east of Exeter.

– P –

"Permanent Revolution"—("Jack in a Box") A concept adapted by Trotsky from Marx's writings, Trotsky defines "permanent revolution" this way:

The complete victory of the democratic revolution in Russia is conceivable only in the form of the dictatorship of the proletariat, leaning on the peasantry. The dictatorship of the proletariat, which would inevitably place on the order of the day not only democratic but socialistic tasks as well, would at the same time give a powerful impetus to the international socialist revolution. (*Permanent Revolution*)

Part of the purpose of Trotsky's definition—placing all power in the hands of the working proletariat and shared with the peasantry, and pressing for social revolution worldwide—was to illumine the dangers of Stalin and Bukharin's centralized grab for power in the late 1920s. Stalin would, of course, eventually win that battle, too, and then have Bukharin executed in 1938, and Trotsky in 1940.

Trotsky probably didn't intend the concept to be as sensual as delivered by the Eartha Kitt character here, however. Kitt—American television's "Catwoman"—was known to "purr" a sultry introductory "I'm here" when she took the stage in concert.

Petrograd . . . Moscva—("Jack in a Box") St. Petersburg was only known as Petrograd between 1914 and 1924, when its name was changed officially to Leningrad.

"Lewgrad" is a reference to Sir Lew Grade (1906-1998), producer of myriad entertainments—movies, television, theater productions, etc.—in the UK, and founder of ATV. The Goons mention Lord Grade ("Lew Grade in rags?"), as well.

"Lesliegrad" is a reference to Lew Grade's brother, Leslie (1916-1979), a partner in Grade's production company.

Pither is writing up his diary—(PSC; link into "Trotsky") Portions of this Pither character may be a parody of Palin himself, as he was and is a devoted diarist. The first volume (1969-1979) was published in 2006.

"Pogrom"—("Smolensk") A pogrom is an official or at least officially *tolerated* riot action against the Jewish population in Russia.

– R –

Red Book—("Bingo-Crazed Chinese") The collection of Mao's writings made official and required reading, and called *The Quotations of Mao Tse-Tung*, first printed in 1964.

"reputedly self-sealing"—("Mr. Pither") A terrific example of Pither's empiricist philosophy (see "Cycling Tour" entry above). His a priori knowledge turns out to be secondhand, of course, and therefore unreliable when the real-world experience—where the Tupperware hits the road—presents itself to him after a cycling crash. The lesson learned is that firsthand experience counts in the world, and he even attempts to prepare himself for the next (and inevitable) crash by asking the Woman (Cleese) where she keeps her eggs. English philosopher John Locke (1632-1704) notes that it is only through "sensation" and "reflection" that we acquire ideas; and Pither is certainly the wide-eyed "white paper" Locke describes where experience is written.

Locke has already been mentioned by the Pythons in Ep. 22, where he is one of the subjects to be taught by the new Bruce, Michael (Jones). Locke is also mentioned as a member of the defeated English football team in the second *Fliegender Zirkus* episode.

"Rich, Buddy"—("Clodagh Rogers") American jazz and Big Band drummer, 1917-1987.

Rogers, Clodagh—("Clodagh Rogers") Irish-born singer whose "Jack in the Box," Britain's entry in the 1971 Eurovision Song Contest (3 April 1971) held in Dublin, came fourth. This is the song Pither is talking about when he tries to comfort her as she becomes Trotsky: "I did enjoy your song for Europe, Clodagh."

Russian 42nd International Clambake—("Jack in a Box") The First International (International Workingmen's Association) was convened in Geneva in 1866, and at later Internationals Trotsky would argue his anti-Stalinist policies, essentially sealing his own demise.

– S –

"SCENE MISSING"—("Jack in a Box") In the early days of film censorship, offending reels of film or just shots were often removed (by local or national review boards, or even projectionists) with little thought to continuity. This removal creates a deus ex machina for Pither and Gulliver, allowing them a fantastical escape. In this case, the narrative metalepsis or disruption means that the characters necessarily miss the execution scene, which is cut from the film, and end up safe and happy in the Devon (Jersey) countryside, no worse for the wear.

"Smolensk"—("Smolensk") A Russian city approximately 190 miles *east* of Minsk (not west), about 289 miles north of Kursk, and 1,644 miles west of Omsk. Smolensk is also about 1,544 miles from Tavistock, give or take a few miles.

"Solzhenitzhin"—("Jack in a Box") Most of this Russian is gibberish, but there are a few recognizable words, including a variation of the name of the noted author and former prison camp inmate Aleksandr Solzhenitsyn (b. 1918), author of *One Day in the Life of Ivan Denisovich* (1962). Solzhenitsyn was awarded the Nobel Prize in 1970.

"oblomov"—The central and titular character in *Oblomov* by Ivan Goncharov (1858).

"Stalin has always hated me"—("Trotsky") Cricket journalist and adept world historian C.L.R. James, writing in *World Revolution 1917-1936* (1937), defined this particularly venal enmity:

> Yet, as Lenin, quite obviously saw, the immediate origin of the danger was personal. Lenin did not say so in so many words. *The Testament* is very carefully phrased, but all through the civil war there had been clashes between Trotsky and Stalin. Stalin, with Zinoviev and Kamenev, who supported him at first, hated Trotsky, but Stalin hated him with a hatred which saw in him the chief obstacle to his power; Zinoviev and Kamenev Stalin knew he could manage. (chapter 6)

Stock film of Kremlin—("Jack in a Box") The stock film is a Pathe reel called "Kremlin." The music in this transition is "Variety Playoff" by M. Hunter (WAC T12/1,440).

– T –

"Taisez-vous"—("Clodagh Rogers") "Who's there?" Translations of the balance of the sometimes fractured Python French:

> M. Brun (Cleese): "Taisez-vous. Qu'est-ce que le bruit? C'est impossible! ("Who is it? What's that noise? It's impossible!")
>
> Mme. Brun (Idle): "Mais oui - c'est Clodagh Rogers!" ("Yes, it's Clodagh Rogers!") . . . "C'est Clodagh Rogers la fameuse chanteuse Anglaise." ("It's Clodagh Rogers the famous English singer!")
>
> Genevieve (Chapman): "Excusez-moi Madame Clodagh. Ecrivez-vous votre nom dans mon livre des hommes célèbres, s'il vous plait. Là, au-dessous de Denis Compton. Maman! Ce n'est pas la belle Clodagh. ("Excuse me, Madame Clodagh. Could you write your name in my book of male celebrities. There, below Denis Compton. Mama! This isn't the beautiful Clodagh!")

Mme Brun: "Quoi?" ("What?")

Genevieve: "C'est Trotsky le révolutionaire." ("It's Trotsky, the revolutionary!")

Mme. Brun: "Mais Trotsky ne chante pas." ("But Trotsky doesn't sing.")

M. Brun: "Il chante un peu." ("He sings a little.")

Mme. Brun: "Mais pas professionalement. Qu'il pense de Lenin." ("But not professionally. Then you'd think of Lenin.")

M. Brun: "Ah! Lenin!! Quel chanteur." ("Ah, Lenin! What a singer.")

M. Brun: "Et aussi Monsieur Kerensky avec le 'Little White Bull', eh?" ("And Mr. Kerensky with 'The Little White Bull,' eh?")

And moments later when the lovers are in the car:

Frenchman: "Je t'aime." ("I love you.")

French Girl: "Maurice! Regardez! C'est la chanteuse anglaise Clodagh Rogers." ("Maurice! Look! It's that English singer Clodagh Rogers.")

Frenchman: "Ah mais oui! Jacques dans la boîte. . . ." ("It is! 'Jack in the Box'. . . .")

"tarmacadam surface"—("Mr. Pither") "Tar penetration macadam" is a highway surface type, though these roads are most likely asphalt.

"Taunton"—("Clodagh Rogers") Taunton is in Somerset, while the A237 runs through Greater London and runs south from Wandsworth, and past Croydon.

"Tavistock"—("Mr. Pither") Pither falls off in front of the Pierson Hotel on Pierson Road in St. Helier, Jersey, and not in Tavistock, Devon.

"ten woods"—("Mr. Pither") Colloquialism for half a pack of cigarettes.

Theme music—("Mr. Pither") Pither's cycling theme music is a snippet of the Vienna Philharmonic playing "Waltz from Faust" by Gounod (WAC T12/1,440).

through the streets—("Jack in a Box") The music behind this chase scene is the London Symphony Orchestra playing "Gayaneh Ballet Suite: Dance of the Young Kurds" and "Fire" by Khachaturian (WAC T12/1,440).

The frantic ending to this film plays very much like a Peter Sellers or even Terry-Thomas film of the 1950s and 1960s.

tiny village high street—("Mr. Pither") These scenes were actually shot on Jersey, in and around St. Helier and St. Ouen.

"Tiverton"—("Mr. Pither") Tiverton is also in Devon, on the Exe and Lowman rivers.

"Tizer"—("Mr. Pither") A soft drink, in 1972 A.G. Barr had purchased the Tizer brand, probably accounting for the red drink's mention here.

"Tonblidge Wells"—("Bingo-Crazed Chinese") Tunbridge Wells is in Kent, south of London. Baden-Powell (mentioned above) went to school in Tunbridge Wells.

train wheels in the night—("Jack in the Box") The incidental music under this unnamed film stock is played by the International Studio Orchestra, from the album *Modern Transport*, and is called "Long Haul" by Keith Papworth (WAC T12/1,440).

transport café—("Mr. Pither") Essentially, a truck stop (or lorry stop).

"Trotsky"—("Clodagh Rogers") Leon Davidovich Trotsky (1879-1940) had, with Lenin, spent time in London planning their revolutionary activities, and then became the military mind of the Revolution. It was in the period 1922-1923, when Lenin's health was failing, that Stalin and friends consolidated their power against Trotsky. Stalin would later have most of those same "friends" eliminated, as well. It's somewhat ironic that one of the charges leveled against Trotsky in 1924 (by Stalin's associates) was that he had "distorted" his role in the October Revolution—raising his level of action and reducing the influence of others. In other words, he changed as the current situation demanded, not unlike Gulliver-Clodagh-Trotsky-Eartha Kitt in this episode.

– W –

Watney's pub—("Mr. Pither") Pubs that sold the line of Watney beers, including the Red Barrel so loathed by the Tourist (Idle) in Ep. 31.

– Y –

"Young Generation"—("Clodagh Rogers") The Young Generation were actually performing with Engelbert Humperdink in 1972 for a West German television variety show, not with Buddy Rich. The Young Generation had also appeared fairly recently on the BBC in *Christmas With the Stars* (December 1971), appearing with Englebert Humperdink (Eps. 18 and 19) and Lulu (Eps. 21 and 28).

"Young Men's Anti-Christian Association"—("Jack in the Box") The YMCA had been in Russia since 1900, but as an admitted evangelical Christian society, was officially shut down by Soviet authorities in 1919.

The Desk Clerk's (Gilliam) later "Lack of God!" oath is another reminder of the so-called godless society of Soviet Communism.

Episode 35

– A –

"accidentally hanged"—("Mortuary Hour") There may have been an "accidental" hanging in UK, and fairly recently. In April 1962, James Hanratty was hanged for murder and attempted murder, in the so-called A6 Murders, a crime for which another man, Peter Alphon, later allegedly confessed. Hanratty's family and many others campaigned actively for years to exonerate him. This followed the conviction and execution of Timothy Evans, well-known for his alleged role in the 10 Rillington Place murders referenced in Ep. 27. Evans was characterized by many as mentally deficient, offering several different accounts of the deaths, eventually accusing a neighbor, John Reginald Christie. Evans was hanged in March 1950. Christie would be found to have killed a number of women and hidden them around his house just a few years later. Writer Ludovic Kennedy (see notes to Ep. 37) championed Evans' innocence for many years.

Adam and Eve—("M1 Interchange Built By Characters From *Paradise Lost*") These two actors—Paul Barton and Laurel Brown—signed "nudity" contracts with the BBC to appear partly clothed here. This scene seems to have been filmed on 16 March 1972 (WAC T12/1,460).

"Aldebaran"—("Prices on the Planet Algon") This bright star is actually in the constellation Taurus and, connecting it back to the Brigadier's (Cleese) rant, is called "The Bull's Eye."

Algon 1—("Prices on the Planet Algon") Launched in March 1972, on 15 July 1972 the Pioneer 10 spacecraft passed through the asteroid belt on its journey toward Jupiter, and was the subject of much media coverage and intense scientific speculation. Pioneer 10 is currently on the way toward Aldebaran (see above),

which is more than sixty-five light years distant—scientists estimate the trip can be made in about two million years (*EBO*).

The Apollo program (1969-1972) had completed six manned missions to the Moon by this time. This frenetic, over-the-top coverage is yet another jab at the BBC's exhaustive coverage of the recent Apollo lunar landings, which James Burke (see "M'Burke" below) also covered.

"an 1100"—("Prices on the Planet Algon") This could be either a Morris or Simca 1100, both small cars available in the UK at this time. The Morris was a British car, which makes it the more likely reference, and the Simca was built by Chrysler for the Continental market.

"Antony has his Cleopatra"—("Mystico and Janet—Flats Built by Hypnosis") This photographic still is from the Mansell Collection, "Anthony & Cleopatra" B127 (WAC T12/1,443).

"Archangel Gabriel"—("M1 Being Built by Characters From *Paradise Lost*") An angel of mercy, Gabriel actually captures Satan attempting to seduce Adam and Eve to evil, and forces him to leave their presence (*Paradise Lost*, chapter 8).

"asbestos-lined ceilings"—("Housing Project Built by Characters From Nineteenth-Century English Literature") It was just recently, in 1971, that the installation of asbestos materials in construction was banned in the United States. These nineteenth-century characters, however, would have carried on the asbestos installation without pause—it was ubiquitous as an insulation material after the advent of the Industrial Revolution.

Asbestos was much in the news during this period, especially as ships like the celebrated QE2, being built in the financially struggling Clyde shipyards, experienced lengthy delays as installed asbestos linings (approved in 1968, declared hazardous not long after) had to be completely removed by special covered saws (*Private Eye* 2 July 1971, 20). Stopgap funding from the sitting Labour government helped pay for these snafus.

Austin 30—(PSC; "Mystic and Janet—Flats Built by Hypnosis") A small car introduced in 1951 from the Austin Motor Company.

– B –

Badger, Mr.—(PSC; "Bomb on Plane") With this appearance and his previous appearance in Ep. 32, Mr. Badger (Idle) has begun living up to the metaphoric meaning of his name, as he tends to good-naturedly badger anyone he contacts.

"Bassey, Shirley"—("*Mortuary Hour*") Welsh-born singer Bassey (b. 1937) had recently performed the hit song "Diamonds Are Forever" from the James Bond film of the same name (1971). The song was composed by John Barry.

"Battersby"—("*Mortuary Hour*") Roy Battersby (b. 1936) had produced and directed a landmark film, *The Body* (1970), which took viewers on an unprecedented, endoscopic guided tour of the human body. Battersby had worked for the BBC in the Science and Features area since at least 1963, and is also credited with co-founding *Tomorrow's World*, a show mentioned in Ep. 20.

"Bergsonian"—("Naked Man") Theorist Henri Bergson (1859-1941) has been mentioned a number of times in *FC*, especially by and in relation to Cleese. Specifically, Bergson wrote:

> Laughter is, above all, a corrective. Being intended to humiliate, it must make a painful impression on the person against whom it is directed. By laughter, society avenges itself for the liberties taken with it. It would fail in its object if it bore the stamp of sympathy or kindness. . . . In this sense, laughter cannot be absolutely just. Nor should it be kind-hearted either. Its function is to intimidate by humiliating. Now, it would not succeed in doing this, had not nature implanted for that very purpose, even in the best of men, a spark of spitefulness or, at all events, of mischief. Perhaps we had better not investigate this point too closely, for we should not find anything very flattering to ourselves. (chapter V)

So if in Bergson's terms rigidity is the comical, and laughter is its corrective, then the Pythons clearly share that definition. With a certain glee of "spitefulness" they puncture straight-laced types in every level of society—from middle-class Tory Housewives to the Upper Class to the Monied Elite (City Gents and Merchant Bankers), and any inflexible organization—the Church,

the Military, the Monarchy, the Constabulary—in British society or history.

"Bob Cratchett on his father's back"—("Housing Project Built by Characters From Nineteenth-Century English Literature") A mistake here, probably intended to be "Tim Cratchett on his father's [Bob's] back." Tim is played by the child actor Balfour Sharp, who was attending the Corona Stage School (26 Wellesley Road W4), and his mother may have picked up his check, according to BBC payroll records (WAC T12/1,460). The Pythons also switched the Walpoles, Horace and Henry, earlier in Ep. 33. Shakespeare did this fairly regularly, as well, especially in his history plays. In *1 Henry IV*, for example, he mixes his Mortimers, moves battles around to suit his chronological and dramatic needs, and changes ages of his characters when necessary.

See notes to *1 Henry IV* in Evans' *The Riverside Shakespeare*, as well as Larsen's *MPSERD* for more.

brief funny noises—("*Mortuary Hour*") Shows from BBC1 deejays like Bob Callan, whose theme song—"Can You Dig Bob Callan?"—is of the ilk the Pythons seem to be lampooning here, complete with inane radio babble and sound effects. Early BBC1 deejays Tony Blackburn and David Gregory could also qualify for this dubious honor. *The Guardian* stood with the Pythons, reporting in October 1971: "Radio 1 and 2 were the deeper part in the warm sea of mediocrity" (quoted at radiorewind.co.uk, where clips of these shows can be heard). Blackburn and Gregory are featured on a 1970 "Top of the Pops" cover of the *Radio Times*.

"Brontë, Anne"—("Housing Project Built by Characters From Nineteenth-Century English Literature") A Northern-born author (Yorkshire), Anne (1820-1849) was the younger sister of authors Emily (*Wuthering Heights*) and Charlotte (*Jane Eyre*). Anne's *The Tenant of Wildfell Hall* appeared in 1848, not long before she died at Scarborough. See the "*Tenant . . .*" entry below for more on the novel.

"building site"—("Housing Project Built by Characters From Nineteenth-Century English Literature") This construction site was found at Sussex Gardens, where Wates Ltd. were building the towers. The shots were recorded on 16 March 1972.

– C –

castle—(PSC; "The Olympic Hide-and-Seek Final") Don (Chapman) is hiding in Mont Orgueil Castle in Jersey, and specifically in the Long Cellar, also called the Crypt Chapel of St. George.

"Clochmerle"—(link into "The Cheap-Laughs") *Clochemerle* was a short-lived (nine episodes, all in 1972) BBC2 comedy about a French town that builds a urinal as a war memorial. The show was co-produced by Bavarian television (Bavaria Atelier GmbH, which produced the *Fliegender Zirkus* episodes in 1971), and was shot on location in France, which would have greatly increased production costs in relation to other contemporary BBC shows.

"Coward, Noël"—(PSC; "Naked Man") Noël Coward (1899-1973) was the quintessentially English playwright, novelist, screenwriter, singer, and songwriter, who breathed life back into British live theatre in the 1920s and then carried the stage through the Depression and war years. By the 1950s, though, the bloom was off his rose, leading social critics like Richard Hoggart to dismiss him as hopelessly passé. (See the entry for "pantomime Princess Margaret" in Ep. 30 for more on Hoggart's dim view of the decade.) By 1972 he was the venerable old man of London stage and screen letters, and is seen by the Pythons, at least, holding court like Dr. Johnson or John Dryden might have. The Goons mention Coward's work often—kiddingly, "Noël Coward–type dialogue"—whenever their subject matter is less than urbane.

current-affairs-type programme—(PSC; "Bull-Fighting") The music used here is from "Music for Technology," "Industrial Sounds" by Walter Scott (WAC T12/1,443).

cut to Trafalgar Square—(PSC; "The Olympic Hide-and-Seek Final") The stirring music used here is Jack Trombey's "March Trident" as played by the International Studio Orchestra (WAC T12/1,443). This track can be heard at the DeWolfe website. (The DeWolfe catalogue of program music would provide much of the incidental music for *Holy Grail*, incidentally.)

– D –

donkey jacket—(PSC; "Housing Project Built by Characters From Nineteenth-Century Literature") The character is wearing a "donkey jacket," a workman's jacket designed for warmth and rain protection.

Don Roberts hails a cab—("The Olympic Hide-and-Seek Final") The music here is from the Pul Piotet et son Grand Orchestre, "Dance Mood Music, Les fous de soleil" by St. George (WAC T12/1,443).

– E –

"East Scottish Airways"—("Bomb on Plane") A fictional airline. BEA had taken over regional airlines like

Scottish Airways in 1947. Scottish-based Caledonian Airways had been founded in 1961.

"eighteen-level motorway interchange"—("M1 Interchange Built By Characters From *Paradise Lost*") A reference to the then new and novel (and celebrated) "four-level stack" interchanges that began appearing in the UK in 1966, when the Almondsbury, Bristol stack opened at the M4-M5 exchange. As with many other hobbies in the UK, there is at least one website dedicated to spotting and cataloguing these interchanges (see, for example, cbrd.co.uk/reference/interchanges).

Episode 35—This episode was recorded ninth in the third series, on 11 May 1972, and was broadcast on 14 December 1972.

Also appearing in this episode as extras or in photos: Paul Lindley (Eps. 3, 14, 29; *Dixon of Dock Green*), Henry Raynor (*Dixon of Dock Green*), Emmett Hennessy (*Dr. Who*; *Softly Softly*), Laurel Brown (Ep. 39), Frank Lester (Eps. 31, 36, 37, 40; *Jackanory*), Alf Coster (*Law & Order*); on film: Marie Anderson (photo work, too), Laurel Brown, Balfour Sharp (child; *Till Death Do Us Part*), Cyma Feldwick (*Doctor in the House*), Paul Barton (*Z Cars*; *Dr. Who*), David Pike (*Survivors: Lights of London*), Katie Evans (*Softly Softly*) (WAC T12/1,443).

– F –

Frank Bough man—(PSC; "The Olympic Hide-and-Seek Final") Bough (b. 1933) presented *Grandstand*, *Sportsnight*, and *Nationwide*, and was already a ubiquitous television personality, and very much connected to sport.

– H –

"hanged at Leeds"—("Mystico and Janet—Flats Built By Hypnosis") The death penalty had been abolished in the UK in 1965, so this execution would truly have been a miscarriage of justice. Leeds had been a site for state executions since the nineteenth century.

Heathcliff and Catherine—(PSC; "Housing Project Built by Characters From Nineteenth-Century Literature") The love-tossed characters from the novel *Wuthering Heights*, who were earlier satirized in the "Semaphore Version of *Wuthering Heights*" sketch, in Ep. 15.

"Here's your pound"—("Bomb on Plane") This is borrowing from Bugs Bunny's classic turnabouts performed, most memorably, with Daffy Duck (*Rabbit Fire* [1951]; *Rabbit Seasoning* [1952]; *Duck! Rabbit, Duck!*

[1953]), where the argument is completely reversed by Bugs' taking the opponent's position in the middle of the debate. Bugs also uses this topos with the umpire in *Baseball Bugs* (1946), and the stranded men on the desert island in *Wackiki Rabbit* (1943). Cartoons admittedly played a profound influence on both the Pythons and their comedy mentors, The Goons. See the "squawk" entry in the notes for Ep. 1 for more on the cartoon connection to both the Goons and *Flying Circus*.

High-rise development area—("Mystico and Janet—Flats Built By Hypnosis") This building site is most likely in Sussex Gardens, and was being constructed by Wates Ltd. when shooting took place on 16 March 1972 (WAC T12/1,428).

"Hinckley in Leicestershire"—("The Olympic Hide-and-Seek Final") Hinckley lies between Birmingham and Leicester, near where Chapman grew up.

"his brain is so tiny"—("*Mortuary Hour*") Another in a long line of jabs at the upper class, this one very much in line with the scathing depictions in "The Upperclass Twit of the Year" discussed earlier in Ep. 12. A similar brain difficulty is troubling British "Great White Hope" boxer Ken Clean-Air Systems (Cleese) in Ep. 18, with removal of the brain being the only sure remedy.

huge hammer strikes him on the head—("The British Well-Basically Club") This sort of violent, cartoony, retributive action—to beat the campiness out of a character—goes right along with the often violent, retributive actions taken against homosexuals (the Mason in Ep. 17, the "Rabelaisian" clam squashed flat in Ep. 32, the admittedly "gay" Algy shot in Ep. 33) and women ("She" in the "Science Fiction Sketch") in *FC*. The character Alex (Malcolm McDowell) was subjected to violent therapies in *A Clockwork Orange* (1971), ostensibly to rid him of his violent, sexualized, anti-social behaviors.

"Huntingdon, Arthur"—("Housing Project Built by Characters From Nineteenth-Century Literature") Arthur Huntingdon is a character from Anne Brontë's *The Tenant of Wildfell Hall* (1848); the visitor Huntingdon does pore over a series of Miss Hargrave's drawings in chapter 17, all the while making "clever" and "droll" remarks. Anne's older sister Emily's 1847 novel, *Wuthering Heights*, is featured in Ep. 15 in semaphore version.

– I –

"Is this character giving you trouble?"—("Bomb on Plane") Identifying the artificial nature of the narrative,

the poorly received performance of a Scottish character is blamed for the demise of the sketch, not the writing or production value. In Ep. 1 a guest being interviewed is similarly labeled and summarily tossed off the interview set ("Arthur 'Two-Sheds' Jackson"). So rather than work out a difficult character situation within the narrative, the Pythons increasingly bring in deus ex machina–type characters and situations (the intruding Scotland Yard detectives in Ep. 29, the "Missing Scene" in Ep. 34, e.g.) to bring scenes and episodes to a close.

– J –

"Janet"—("Mystico and Janet—Flats Built By Hypnosis") Marie Anderson plays the character of Janet, appearing on film and in still photos (WAC T12/1,460).

– K –

"Khan, Professor Herman"—("Prices on the Planet Algon") Khan (1922-1983) was a RAND Corporation military thinker, and can be credited with popularizing the MAD theory—the "Mutual Assured Destruction" scenario should the Soviets attempt an all-out preemptive nuclear strike against the United States. Khan may have been especially frightening to many because he talked openly about "winnable" nuclear wars, and has been seen by many as the influence for the military mindset exhibited in *Dr. Strangelove* (1964). See Bruce-Briggs' *Supergenius: The Mega-Worlds of Herman Khan* for more.

This frightening man is rendered silly and perhaps less threatening here as he discusses sexy women's underwear—a typical Python method of Bergsonian diminution for the inflexible authority figure.

"Kilmarnock"—("The Olympic Hide-and-Seek Final") Town in East Ayrshire, Scotland.

– L –

"Little Nell from Dickens' *Old Curiosity Shop*"—("Housing Project Built by Characters From Nineteenth-Century Literature") Peter Ackroyd points out that girls of Nell's age would most definitely have been working in 1841 London, but that child prostitution would have been their trade, primarily. She would have been the "young woman . . . betrayed by the great metropolis," and mourned by the Victorian reader (*London* 621). In Dickens' work she is found wandering at night by the narrator, and taken to her "grandfather." The actress here may have been adolescent

Cyma Feldwick, who, along with Balfour Sharp (playing Tiny Tim), was attending the Corona Stage School in London when they were cast for this brief appearance (WAC T12/1,460).

"Tess of the D'Urbervilles"—Thomas Hardy's 1891 novel. In Ep. 17, Hardy (1840-1928) was a novelist installed in the Housewife's (Jones) bedroom ("Poets"), and he is also featured on a Monty Python LP, where he is attempting to begin a new novel in front of a large football-type crowd ("Novel-Writing" from *The Monty Python Instant Record Collection* album). The "farmhands" depicted would be the Dorset-area people he grew up with and spent his life writing about as inhabitants of his fictional "Wessex." The novel calls into question Victorian morality and judgment, which is perhaps why it is included here.

"Mrs Jupp, from Samuel Butler's Way of All Flesh"—Another Northerner (like the Brontës), Butler (1825-1902) was born in Nottinghamshire and finished this almost anti-Victorian novel in 1885, though it would not be published until after his death in 1902.

"Milton's Paradise Lost"—John Milton's magnum opus, *Paradise Lost* is a seventeenth-century English poem of epic proportions, and also upset traditionalists as he looked creatively at the pre- and postlapsarian existences.

– M –

making rather a noise—(PSC; "Mystico and Janet—Flats Built By Hypnosis") The radio is playing a version of "Jack in a Box," as sung by the Pythons. The Clodagh Rogers song was featured prominently in Ep. 34.

M'Burke, James—(PSC; "Prices on the Planet Algon") BBC Science correspondent James Burke (b. 1936) covered the Apollo missions for the network in 1969 and beyond, and has already been spoofed in Ep. 28. It's not clear why the printed script terms him "M'Burke," except as a simple joke. Burke was also the cohost for *Tomorrow's World*, mentioned in Ep. 20. It's possible that the Pythons are Africanizing Burke's name—an Edgar Rice Burroughs character in the Tarzan series is named "M'buku," for example—just as they created Scots names in Ep. 2 ("McWoolworths"), and Jewish-sounding names in Ep. 6 ("Chapmanberg").

"Mrs. Equator sort of lady"—("The Cheap Laughs") One of the standardized "type" requests possible as the show goes on—the production design team merely has to seek out wardrobe and hair and makeup requests for Ep. 9, "The Visitors" sketch. Many of these requests and the weekly costuming needs forms are part of the archival WAC collection.

– N –

Nelson, Mr. Beadle—(PSC; "Housing Project Built by Characters From Nineteenth-Century Literature") Admiral Nelson has already made appearance in *FC*, while Mr. Bumble the Beadle—from Dickens' *Oliver Twist*—makes a first appearance. These characters aren't seen long enough or clearly enough amid the scaffolding and smoke to really be identifiable. Most of the actors are just dressed in period clothing.

"new town site"—("M1 Being Built By Characters From *Paradise Lost*") A New Town is a purpose-built, planned town, generally away from existing cities, and became vogue especially in Europe and the UK after the destruction and social upheaval of WWII. These types of "new towns" were just the answer, for Modernists, to the Victorian dilapidation of England's larger cities, providing the opportunity to tear down miles of maze-like structures and design clean, orderly, and efficient spaces for the working poor. The Gustave Doré etching "Over London by Rail" (1870) illustrates the cramped, sooty, oppressive neighborhoods London's working classes called home. New towns like Milton Keynes, Stevenage, and Peterborough were just such planned cities, the last emerging just before *FC* went on the air, in 1968.

"new world record time"—("The Olympic Hide-and-Seek Final") This may be a comment on the interminable cricket test matches, the record for which was set in 1939 at more than forty-three total playing hours over eleven days. Test cricket is played to a limit of five days, generally. It wouldn't be until 1963 that one-day cricket was introduced, mostly to try and bolster sagging attendance figures across the UK.

"no need to panic"—("Bomb on Plane") Yet another swipe at one of the Pythons' favorite targets, the Scots, treating the plane's Glaswegian destination as if it is Havana or the Middle East in a hijacking situation.

"note from the Council"—("M1 Being Built By Characters From *Paradise Lost*") After the Ronan Point disaster in 1968, the local Council made sure gas supply was cut off to the entire development (nine buildings), and the residents had to wait for electric appliances to be installed. See the British Cartoon Archive for editorial page mentions of the problem.

Local or borough councils were (and often still are) charged with providing adequate housing for their citizens, whether the structures are high-rises or apartment blocks (both Ep. 17), semi-detached houses (duplexes; see Ep. 28), bungalows (Ep. 31), or rowhouses (Mrs. Pinnet's house, Ep. 14).

nude organist—(PSC; "A Naked Man") This and the following introduction scenes (including the "It's Man") were shot in Jersey, in the same area as the Reg Pither's "Cycling Tour" scenes.

– O –

"Olympic Hide-and-Seek"—("The Olympic Hide-and-Seek Final") The silliness of this event may be in response to the upcoming appearance in the 1972 Summer Olympics of events like handball, slalom canoeing, and water skiing. The episode was recorded in May 1972, months before the 26 August 1972 opening ceremonies in Munich. In these summer Olympics Britain managed four gold medals—sailing, equestrian (two), and women's pentathlon.

"Onan, Clement"—("Mystico and Janet—Flats Built by Hypnosis") Hardly a surprise that this "well-dressed authoritative person" is tagged by the Pythons as a sexual deviant. Onan is a character in the Old Testament who was destroyed by God when he "spilled his seed" rather than impregnate his brother's widow. See Genesis 38. A Chapman character admitted his onanism back in Ep. 31, when Harry Bagot listed his hobbies at the "All-England *Summarize Proust Competition*."

"Oppenheimer spy ring"—("Mystico and Janet—Flats Built By Hypnosis") Klaus Fuchs (1911-1988) and others who worked with Robert Oppenheimer (1904-1967) at the Los Alamos site in the war years were eventually arrested and tried for spying for the Soviet Union, but not until 1950.

– P –

palm court set—(PSC; link out of "Ten Seconds of Sex") This "palm court set" description in the printed script is a shorthand for the show's production designers to build a very simple chair, table, and curtained backdrop set, designed for a presenter (or linkman) only. The Pythons will use it often, and it will comprise the final set for their final feature film, *The Meaning of Life* (1983).

"Paraguay"—("The Olympic Hide-and-Seek Final") Paraguay wouldn't send an athlete to the Olympics, summer or winter, until 1988. The Pythons may also be referencing Great Britain's medal paucity in the 1968 and 1972 Olympics, the proud nation accounting for only 31 medals in both games. By comparison, the United States took home 107 medals in 1968 and

94 medals in 1972, and Australia even accounted for 34 medals over the same two games. This same kind of British athletic performance lamentation is also seen in Ep. 7, when the UK must rely on a Scotsman (Palin) to defeat extraterrestrial blancmanges and win Wimbledon.

peer of the realm—(PSC; "Mortuary Hour") One who is a member of the peerage, who can sit in the House of Lords. This Peer (Palin) is probably a duke, since he is called "Your Grace." This treatment is similar to what the Upperclass Twits receive in Ep. 12—as a class, the aristocracy (to the Pythons) seems just too collectively dim to even survive.

"perspicacious Paraguayan"—("The Olympic Hide-and-Seek Final") Probably just a bad word choice, when the character probably meant to use "peripatetic," which both continues the alliteration and the hide-and-seek theme.

"Peterborough"—("Housing Project Built by Characters From Nineteenth-Century Literature") North of London, Peterborough was designated a New Town in 1968, with the new townships to be Bretton, Orton, and Paston/Werrington. See the entry for "new town site" above for more.

"plane"—("Bomb on Plane") Skyjackings began in earnest in about 1961, with a number of domestic American flights being rerouted to Cuba. Skyjacking was seen as a significant political tool for smaller, leftist terrorist cells such as the Popular Front for the Liberation of Palestine (PFLP), which began skyjacking planes in 1968, the first an international El Al flight from Rome to Tel Aviv. The phenomena had become so prevalent during the late 1960s that *Time* magazine devoted its 21 September 1970 cover to these "Pirates in the Sky."

This particular sketch may well have been spurred by the infamous skyjacking in the northwestern United States of 24 November 1971, where a man initially identified as "D.B. Cooper" indicated to a flight attendant that a bomb on the plane would explode unless he was given money and parachutes at the next stop. Mr. Badger, naturally, isn't given the foresight to consider bringing a parachute or foment any kind of escape strategy. Cooper had demanded (and received) $200,000, and is assumed to have jumped from the plane. In Ep. 16, a Gunman (Palin) hijacks a plane to Luton, but then decides it's less bothersome to be thrown out over Basingstoke.

"prefabricated concrete slabs"—("Housing Project Built by Characters From Nineteenth-Century Literature") This was the very type of construction—prefab concrete—that would be at least partly to blame for the collapse at Ronan Point. The joining and bolting procedures weren't properly followed in that high-rise project, and the vulnerable seams came right apart in the moderate gas explosion in May 1968 that killed four. See notes to Ep. 17.

Pre-fabricated concrete slabs were also key to the Bauhaus-inspired (thus continental in origin, thus suspect) design and construction dreams of the Modernist architects of the 1930s and beyond in England. These architects embraced the pre-fab simplicity of concrete slabs, piecing together new buildings onsite, and fairly quickly. Government embraced the new technology as well, since Labour had promised to build myriad new homes after the 1964 General Election:

> In the next five years we shall go further. We have announced—and we intend to achieve—a target of 500,000 houses by 1969/70. After that we shall go on to higher levels still. It can be done—as other nations have shown. It must be done—for bad and inadequate housing is the greatest social evil in Britain today. (*Labour Manifesto*, 1964)

The shadow government Conservatives were also making big promises for thousands of new homes, and the Pythons had already lampooned this hyperbole in Ep. 14, when an interviewer asks pointedly about the government's promise to build "88 million, billion" homes in a single year. The crossdressed minister answers in a high-pitched squeal.

For more, see the series of articles on Modernism and Modernist architecture—"From Here to Modernity"—at the Open University website.

"Premier Chou En Lai"—(*"Mortuary Hour"*) Probably referring to the "major breakthrough" that was the February 1972 "Shanghai Communiqué," signed by the United States and China, pledging mutual work toward normalized relations. This was Nixon's backdoor way to improved security not only in Southeast Asia, but farther north and west, as a U.S. friend in China meant the Soviet's sabers had to rattle more quietly.

"provided of course people *believe* in them"—("Mystico and Janet—Flats Built By Hypnosis") Certainly another comment on the still-fresh events at Ronan Point, when a high-rise block partially collapsed after a faulty cooker blew up. See notes to Ep. 17, the "Architect Sketch" for more on that disaster. Local councils continued to "believe in" these high-rises (tower blocks) because they housed so many people so efficiently, and they also believed a greatly reduced cost-per-tenant ratio (whether in the end that was true or not) for towers as opposed to rowhouses was a main consideration. The 1956 Housing Act had even put subsidies on the table for local councils willing to build

higher than five stories, so there was great incentive to go skyward during this period.

Also, in 1967, the Wilson government had devalued the pound after many months of denying that any such move was imminent, with Wilson asking, essentially, that the British people still believe in the value of the pound in their "pocket or purse," and that better financial times were just ahead. The pound would be floated again in June 1972, during the Heath administration, just days after Chancellor Anthony Barber had reaffirmed the government's position against such a move on the BBC's *Panorama*.

– R –

"Radio Four"—(*"Mortuary Hour"*) BBC Radio 1, 2, 3, and 4 went on the air on 30 September 1967. Tony Blackburn was the morning DJ on Radio One, having worked for a pirate radio station previously.

Redcoat—(PSC; link into "Cheap-Laughs") Described in the printed script as a "Redcoat," which is the nickname for hosts at Butlin's Holiday Camps. Palin has already appeared as a Redcoat in Ep. 7, introducing the "Science Fiction Sketch," and the crew shot the Lake Pahoe scene at the Butlin's Holiday Camp pool in Bognor Regis on 18 October 1971 (WAC T12/1,428). These camps would have entertained millions of families on school and bank holidays, and were generally within driving (or train) distance for most in at least the south.

"Robinson, Roger"—("The Cheap-Laughs") This could be a reference to the Roger Robinson who attended Cambridge at the same time as the Pythons. Coincidentally, Robinson edited the Pan Classics 1976 edition of Samuel Butler's *The Way of All Flesh*. (See entry for "Mrs Jupp . . . " above.)

"rota"—("Housing Project Built by Characters From Nineteenth-Century Literature") A rotation of persons, simply.

– S –

Sardinia—("The Olympic Hide-and-Seek Final") Castelsardo is a prominent castle in Sardinia, and was probably the inspiration for the location in Jersey where Don Roberts (Chapman) actually hides.

"Scottish money"—("Bomb on Plane") The Scottish pound is, indeed, numbered, meaning it can be traced.

"self-generating"—("Housing Project Built by Characters From Nineteenth-Century Literature") The obsession for self-perpetuating machines in the nineteenth century was quite unequaled in history, and wouldn't cool until the law of conservation of energy was discovered/published in the early 1840s, and then slowly disseminated to the world. *Wildfell Hall* appeared in 1848, though the setting is 1827, so Mr. Huntingdon could very well have still been quite enamored of this supernal energy potential.

"shtoom"—("*Mortuary Hour*") Already heard in Ep. 14, when Vercotti (Palin) is on the phone, the word is used here in its Cockney vein, generally meaning "shut it." Mr. Wang (Cleese) just wants Battersby (Jones) to shut up and prepare for the peer's visitation.

"sorry about Mon-trerx"—(link into "The Cheap-Laughs") In 1971 the Pythons were invited by the BBC to submit a compilation episode to the Golden Rose of Montreux competition. They then compiled a sort of "best of" the available episodes and set about reshooting (to put everything on film stock). They did not win, finishing behind an Austrian-produced show, and brought home a silver rose. *The Marty Feldman Comedy Machine* show would win the prize the following year.

The compilation episode included the following sketches, most reshot specifically for the competition, in this order: "*Scott of the Sahara*," a drag minister, "The New Cooker Sketch," "Conrad Poohs and his Dancing Teeth," "It's the Arts," "Wuthering Heights/Julius Caesar," the fig leaf animation, the "Exploding Version of the Blue Danube," "Newsagent Shop," "Silly Walks," "Birdman," "Butterfly Man" animation, "Blackmail," "Newsreader," "Erotic Film," the Women's Institute footage, "Upperclass Twits," and the end credits run over "Battle for Pearl Harbor" footage, and ending with "Ramsay MacDonald" (WAC T12/1,413). Most of the scenes were shot in late March 1971, and the show was aired 16 April 1971.

Others appearing in this reshoot included: Derek Chafer (*Dr. Who*), John Hughman, David Ballantyne, and Stanley Mason (all Gasmen), Helena Clayton (*The Sex Killer*) as the "Blackmail" dominatrix and twenty extras (to play Gasmen on 24 March 1971). The Gasmen were: Richard Lawrence (*Dr. Who*), Ivor Owen, Donald Campbell (Eps. 27, 28), William Curran (Ep. 3), David Pike (Ep. 35; *Survivor: Lights of London*), John Baker (*Dr. Who*), Richard Kirk (Ep. 39), Bob Raymond (Eps. 40, 42-45; *Secrets of Sex*), Mike Urry (*Public Eye*), Roger Minnis, Michael Earl (*Doctor in the House*), Terry Leigh (Ep. 32; *Dr. Who*), Leslie Bryant (Eps. 25, 40; *The Wednesday Play*), Alan Wells (*Dr. Who*), Bill Richards (*Dixon of Dock Green*), David Melbourne (*Z Cars*), Harry Tierney (*Dr. Who*), Emmett Hennessey (*Dr. Who*), Eric Kent (*Dr. Who*), and Reg Lloyd (*Softly Softly*). Daphne Davey (*Troubleshooters*) also appears in an insert (WAC T12/1,413).

"Swalk, Harry 'Boot-in'"—("Mystico and Janet—Flats Built by Hypnosis") Another indictment of the police as simple thugs ("Boot-in"), "Swalk" isn't even a name, but an ironic acronym for "Sealed With a Loving Kiss."

– T –

"*Tenant of Wildfell Hall, The*"—("Housing Project Built by Characters From Nineteenth-Century Literature") An epistolary novel, Anne Brontë's second work appeared in 1848, and *The Spectator* reviewed the book as "brutal" and filled with "a morbid love for the coarse" (21: 662-63). In the novel, the estranged wife does come "running back," as Huntingdon asserts, but only to nurse him in his infirmities and convince him to come to God. See the *ODNB* for more on the Brontës, their lives and published works.

Trafalgar Square—("The Olympic Hide-and-Seek Final") To capture this long shot from across the street and above, a request for filming and location permissions at the fourth floor front office of Trafalgar Buildings, on 14 Mar 1972 was submitted. Permission was granted from The Electricity Council, 30 Millbank SW1, and they shot between 10 a.m. and noon (WAC T12/1,428).

Tottenham Court Road—("The Olympic Hide-and-Seek Final") A central London road that runs north-south. This area was known for electronics (hobby) shops for many years. This sketch was shot in both London and Jersey.

Tretchikoff picture of the Chinese girl—("The Cheap-Laughs") This odd, green-and-blue-faced portrait has been used in previous episodes, most recently behind the documentary presenter (Cleese) in the "Molluscs" sketch for Ep. 32. It is also on the cover of an LP of light music from this period, and was a very popular framed print after its original painting in 1950.

In this scene she's been given a penciled-in mustache, probably low art's (and Monty Python's) version of the famous Duchamps treatment of the *Mona Lisa* in the portrait *L.H.O.O.Q.* (1919).

"train"—("Bomb on Plane") This is a mnemonic device designed to allow Mr. Badger to correctly remember just where he's put the bomb.

"two separate strands of existence"—("Naked Man") Probably a reference to the fairly recent and (for some) revolutionary book, William Carlo's *The Ultimate*

Reducibility of Essence to Existence in Existential Metaphysics (1966), where Carlo (1921-1971) examines the metaphysics of St. Thomas Aquinas. Carlo's writing and reputation may have been more prominent during this period due to his untimely death at age fifty in 1971. Carlo was a visiting professor at Oxford 1959-1961. (Jones was at Oxford 1961-1964.)

– U –

"Unless you give me the bomb"—("Bomb on Plane") This befuddled-would-be-criminal-meets-helpful-victims scenario is seen a few years earlier in the Woody Allen film *Take the Money and Run* (1967), where earnest but nervous bank robber Allen has to help the bank staff decipher his scrawled stick-up note.

– W –

"Whitby"—(*"Mortuary Hour"*) Whitby is in Yorkshire, but has no record of a significant assize history, unlike York, for example. There is a traditional song called "The Whitby Lad" about a ne'er-do-well who, after punching up a woman, is condemned at the assizes to Botany Bay, the Australian penal colony.

– Y –

"Yeovil, Somerset"—(link out of "Mystico and Janet—Flats Built by Hypnosis") North and east of Paignton and Torquay, where the Pythons shot significant second series footage. Not far off the A303, the Pythons could have traveled through the town on their way to and from these locations and London.

"Younger Generation"—("British Well-Basically Club") The Brigadier (Cleese) offers a list of active and semi-active dance troupes in the London area, circa 1972:

"Lionel Blair Troupe"—Some of the Pythons would have met dancer/choreographer Blair (b. 1931) when he choreographed *The Magic Christian* (1969), for which Chapman and Cleese contributed material. Blair and his dancers appeared in The Beatles' 1964 film *Hard Day's Night*, as well.

"Irving Davies Dancers"—Welsh-born Davies (1926-2002) was also a dancer and choreographer who ap-

peared on Ed Sullivan's *Toast of the Town* (1955) and choreographed for Cicely Courtneidge (Ep. 6) and even Twiggy.

"Pan's People"—Dance troupe attached to the very popular *Tops of the Pops* (1964-2006), the BBC's long-running pop music show. Their choreographer was Flick Colby. Both Colby and Pan's People have already been mentioned in the printed scripts, in Ep. 21.

"SAM missiles"—These are Surface-to-Air Missiles, and they can be launched from silos. These missiles became newsworthy during the early years of the Vietnam War (beginning in 1965), when Soviet-made missiles manned by North Vietnamese forces began shooting at (and shooting down) American jets. Also during this period, the Soviets deployed myriad SAMs in underground silos around Moscow, Leningrad, Kiev, for example.

"send in Scottish boys with air cover"—One such regiment has already been mentioned prominently, the Argyll and Southern Highlanders, deployed to Aden in 1967 during mass uprisings. See notes to Ep. 26 for more.

"George Balanchine and Martha Graham"—Balanchine (1904-1983) was a Russian émigré who led American ballet from the 1930s through the 1960s, while Graham (1894-1991) was an American-born ballet dancer and choreographer during that same period.

"Sadler's Wells"—A dance and performance theater in Clerkenwell—there has been a theater space on the property since the late seventeenth century.

"auxiliary role in international chess"—The chess world began to "hot up" in the 1970-1972 period, when a Python-aged grand master would emerge and tweak the nose of international chess. American sensation Bobby Fischer (b. 1943) would beat Soviet champion Boris Spassky (b. 1937) in Reykjavik, Iceland in September 1972, a few months after this episode was recorded. Leading up to this world championship match, however, the international interest in this mercurial and erratic but entirely watchable young challenger boomed as Fischer beat virtually all comers by staggering margins. He would string together twenty consecutive wins during this period (*EBO*).

Fischer is also significant in his connection to the Worldwide Church of God and the Armstrongs (Ep. 24), all in the news in May 1972. He would donate a large portion of his winnings in September 1972 to the church, but later renounce both the church and its infighting leadership.

Episode 36

– A –

"Acton"—("Pornographic Bookshop") Acton is a part of Greater London, and is just west of Shepherd's Bush, where BBC Television Centre is located. The Uxbridge Road (Ep. 33) runs through Acton.

Aldwych Theatre—(PSC; "Elizabethan Pornography Smugglers") The Aldwych Theatre was the home of the Royal Shakespeare Company of Stratford-upon-Avon between 1960 and 1982, and the "Theatre of Cruelty" in the mid-1960s (see below).

The 1950s and 1960s saw a significant increase in the sexual frankness of London stage plays, including Joe Orton's *Entertaining Mr. Sloane* (1964), which raised the hackles of many in the London theater industry, while encouraging as many others. The so-called Theatre of Cruelty season at the Aldwych Theatre in 1964 also upset and disturbed many, with *Marat/Sade* (Peter Weiss) drawing condemnation from the establishment types, though audience members leaving the theatre voiced support for the production, as well as optimism for the future of the English stage (*Eyewitness: 1960-69*, "'New Writing' and the 'Theatre of Cruelty' Season").

An nimated excerpt . . . —(PSC; link out of "Elizabethan Pornography Smugglers") Gilliam borrows (and animates) images of nude men from some of Eadweard Muybridge's 1880s photographic experiments.

– B –

"Bridget—Queen of the Whip"—("Pornographic Bookshop") Some actual erotic titles from the period include *Love Lottery* (1961), *Sleep-In Maid* (1968), and the almost-too-good-to-be-true *Hillbilly Nympho* (1961). Olympia Press' (see below) Frankfurt, Germany office published titles that included *Königin der Lust* (*Great Balls of Fire*) in 1970 and *Die Sexfarm* (*Meanwhile, Back at the Sex Farm*, 1971).

– C –

"Call My Bluff"—("Thripshaw's Disease") A BBC2 quiz show debuting in 1965, the show ran to 1988, and featured celebrity guests presenting real and fake definitions for *Oxford English Dictionary* words.

"cleaned up a packet"—("Elizabethan Pornography Smugglers") A colloquialism meaning to obtain (illicitly) a large amount of money.

– D –

"de Vega, Lope"—("Elizabethan Pornography Smugglers") Spain's most accomplished and prolific playwright, de Vega (1562-1635) was also a well-known womanizer throughout his life, even after taking vows. He wrote what many call "cloak and sword" plays and poems steeped in intrigue and Spanish history.

"Devon and Cornwall"—("Pornographic Bookshop") The area in the southwestern portion of England where Pither had supposedly been riding in "The Cycling Tour" (Ep. 34), and where the Pythons had spent weeks shooting location footage for the first series.

"Devonshire Country Churches"—("Pornographic Bookshop") John Stabb published the trilogy *Some Old Devon Churches* in 1908-1916 (London: Simpkin), a fairly exhaustive examination of area churches as they existed in the Edwardian era.

"Dirty books, please"—("Pornographic Bookshop") The Obscene Publications Acts of 1959 and 1964 were created to control "the publication of obscene matter; to provide for the protection of literature; and to strengthen the law concerning pornography." The acts test the obscenity of an "article" (picture, magazine, book, film, etc.) as well as provide punishment guidelines for those convicted of publishing and/or distributing such matter. These rather strict laws forced many publishers of pornography in the UK to either close shop or move to more favorable climes, including the Netherlands and Germany.

"doing five years bird"—("Elizabethan Pornography Smugglers") "Bird-lime" is rhyming slang for "doing time," and often shortened to just "bird."

"Drake"—("Tudor Jobs Agency") Sir Francis Drake (1540-1596) led Elizabeth's navy against the Spanish Armada in 1588, and was also a bit of a privateer and explorer. Drake was last mentioned in Ep. 29 by Elizabeth (Chapman) in the sketch "*Erizabeth L.*"

– E –

Elizabethan music—(PSC; "Elizabethan Pornography Smugglers") These two musical pieces (here and under the credit) seem to be "Lady Margaret's Pavan" and "Sir William Galiard" by composer Gareth Walters (WAC T12/1,447).

"Elizabeth, we supplied the archbishops for her coronation"—("Tudor Jobs Agency") Elizabeth I (1533-1603) was crowned in January 1559 after the death of her half-sister Mary. According to histories of the period, the church officials needed for the coronation were very nearly "temped" out, since the requisite bishops were severally unavailable. The Archbishop of Canterbury had died just months before, and the remaining high-ranking clergy were, according to Collinson, "either dead, too old and infirm, unacceptable to the queen, or unwilling to serve" (*ODNB*). The bishop of Carlisle eventually carried out the ceremony, clearly temping for Canterbury.

Episode 36—Recorded 25 May 1972, and broadcast 21 December 1972. This episode was recorded thirteenth, and transmitted tenth.

Others appearing in this episode (or billed to this episode by BBC accountants) but not officially credited include: The Fred Tomlinson Singers, The Cittie Waites (a Tudor Minstrel group), Frank Lester (Eps. 31, 35-37, 40; *Jackanory*), Caron Gardner (Ep. 39; *The Saint*), Peter Kodak (Eps. 27, 29; *Dr. Who*), Graham Skidmore (Eps. 27-29; *Dixon of Dock Green*), John Beardmore (Ep. 34; *Softly Softly*), Bob Midgley (drums), Ralph Dollimore (piano), and Rosalind Bailey (WAC T12/1447). Some of these have been "charged to another episode," but

Bailey appears here as the crying Elizabethan Girl, according to IMDb.com. Midgley had played drums on the Frank Sinatra track "Roses of Picardy" in 1962, from *Sinatra Sings Great Songs From Great Britain*. Dollimore had played piano on many albums for the Studio To Stereo label, and in Eric Winstone's band.

– F –

"Frances"—("Elizabethan Pornography Smugglers") Frances Walsingham (1569-1631) married Sir Philip Sidney in 1583. Her father, Sir Francis Walsingham, was Elizabeth's head of secret police activities. See "Walsingham" entry below.

– G –

"Gargoyle Club"—("Pornographic Bookshop") Located on Meard's Street in Soho, the club was by this period a low-rent bar. The Club had been the hangout for artists and writers in the 1950s, including Dylan Thomas, Francis Bacon, and journalist/presenter Daniel Farson, and was frequented by men seeking the company of other men (or boys).

"Gilbert, Sir Humphrey"—("Tudor Job Agency") Explorer and politician Gilbert (1537-1583) served under Philip Sidney and was Walter Raleigh's half brother, both mentioned elsewhere in this scene. Gilbert shares the Northwest Passage exploration honors with a number of other explorers.

"Cabot"—Sebastian Cabot (1484-1557) had also looked for the fabled Northwest Passage, but much earlier, in 1522, landing in Nova Scotia or Newfoundland.

"Cathay"—The period name for China.

"Gloucester"—("Pornographic Bookshop") Probably a reference to Shakespeare's Gloucester in *1 Henry VI*, who appears together with Warwick in the play's opening scene.

group of Spanish singers—("Sherry-Drinking Vicar") These are the Fred Tomlinson Singers, and the song, "Amontillado," was penned by Tomlinson. The taping was scheduled for 25 May 1972 (WAC T12/1,428).

– H –

"Hamlet"—("Elizabethan Pornography Smugglers") Written and performed about 1601.

"Harley Street"—("Thripshaw's Disease") The area in London where myriad medical offices are found.

"Fleet Street"—The center of Britain's publishing industry until the late twentieth century, it was named for the River Fleet.

– I –

"Imperial War Museum"—(*"Is There? . . . Life After Death?"*) A London museum featuring exhibits from various British military campaigns, and located in Lambeth in the former Bedlam Hospital.

The museum was at this time assisting in the production of the epic *World at War* documentary series that would debut on Thames TV in 1973.

"Introduced by Roger Last"—(*"Is There? . . . Life After Death?"*) Roger Last is one of the Floor Managers for the show during this period, often responsible for props, and he appeared in the lingerie shop in Ep. 10.

"J. Losey"—Joseph Losey (1909-1984) was an American-born expatriate who led Britain's New Wave filmmakers into the 1960s and beyond, directing class-conscious social satire films like *The Servant* (1963) and *Accident* (1967), both written by Harold Pinter (Ep. 10).

"L. Anderson"—British filmmaker Lindsay Anderson (1923-1994) has already been mentioned in Ep. 19, where his controversial 1968 film *If. . . .* is satirized.

"S. Kubrick"—Another American expatriate director working in the UK, Kubrick (1928-1999) had recently directed the infamous *A Clockwork Orange* (1971). A *FC* extra from the first series, Katya Wyeth, also appeared in a small part in this film.

"P.P. Pasolini"—Pier Paolo Pasolini (1922-1975) was an Italian New Wave director who had directed some of the most important (and Marxist) films of the recent past, including *Accatone* (1964) and *The Decameron* (1971).

"O. Welles"—Iconic American film director and actor Orson Welles (1915-1985).

"B. Forbes"—Bryan Forbes (b. 1926) is a British actor/writer/director already mention in Eps. 20 and 23.

"Is There?"—(*"Is There? . . . Life After Death?"*) The music under the closing credits for *Is There?* is from Prokofiev's "Symphony No. 3," as performed by the London Symphony Orchestra (WAC T12/1,447).

This panel of experts set-up is probably modeled after the popular radio and then TV program *The Brains Trust* (1955). Topics included questions like "What is Civilisation?" for example, and various eminent church men, philosophers, scholars, novelists, and even Dr. Bronowski (Ep. 22) appeared on the show (Vahimagi 47).

"I think I will"—("Elizabethan Pornography Smugglers") Here, Gaskell (Palin) crosses over not only into the appearance of the Elizabethan world, but allows himself to become part of that world by admitting its possible existence, and eventually partaking of its niceties. And whether Gaskell is actually Sidney isn't important—for the remainder of the episode he *is* Sir Philip Sidney. He is either acting the part, which is quite possible, or we have crossed the fringes of time (as is apt to happen in the world of Python) and are back in Tudor times.

– J –

"job on the buses, digging the underground" ("Pornographic Bookshop") As recently as the 1950s, the UK government had resorted to inviting/imploring Caribbean workers to staff the buses, trains, and underground service positions in London, due to a severe shortage of interested native workers (Judt 335-36). This welcome mat would be yanked in the early 1960s, when the flood of former-colonial-now-Commonwealth-workers inundated the UK work force, making even menial labor very hard to come by for native Englishmen. The immigration problem became so vexing that even the sitting Labour government took up the cause, sponsoring laws to curb Commonwealth immigration—a damaging public relations move for the party of the underrepresented.

– L –

"London 1583"—("Elizabethan Pornography Smugglers") It was during this period that Sidney was doing more writing than courtly duties, and he wouldn't be married until September 1583 ("Philip Sidney" at *ODNB*).

loud silly noises—("Silly Disturbances [The Rev. Arthur Belling]") The hooting Belling (Palin) voices are borrowed from the "Language Laboratory" (Ep. 31). The episodes were recorded approximately one month apart.

– M –

Maddox pauses only to pick a book from the bookcase near the door—(PSC; "Pornographic Bookshop") The scope of the corruption discovered in the Flying Squad and Metropolitan Police rank and file during the "Soho porn merchants" investigations in the early 1970s led to approximately 400 actions against officers—ranging from reprimands to reassignments to criminal prosecution. Maddox (Chapman) is offering an accurate example of the contradictory nature of the times—the policemen in charge of ferreting out pornography and pornographers were themselves enjoying and profiting from that same industry. Many in the police force seemed to believe that as long as the pornography wasn't targeting or exploiting children, for instance, then it should be monitored but essentially left alone (*Eyewitness 1970-79*, "The Oz Trial"). See the entry for "sad I am" below for specifics on the Soho investigations.

magazines in racks—("Pornographic Bookshop") Most of these are images from actual "dirty books," but the magazine prominently displayed behind the Second Assistant (Idle) is *Woman & Home*, a popular (and non-pornographic) UK ladies' magazine still published today.

man emerges from a barrel—(link out of "Thripshaw's Disease") This transitional gag had already been seen on *The Benny Hill Show* (BBC, 1955-1989), Cook and Moore's *Not Only . . . But Also* (1965), as well as the American comedy show *Laugh-In* (1968). In recycling the recognizable gag, the Pythons could be reminiscing with the audience, relying on the gag's commonality.

"master joiners and craftsmen"—("Tudor Job Agency") A joiner is a woodworker, not unlike a finish carpenter. The Globe Theatre was built in 1599, then destroyed by fire and rebuilt in 1614. Joiners and craftsmen would have been much needed as the Globe was originally built from the timbers and material of The Theatre (owned by the Burbages), having been completely dismantled and moved from Shoreditch to Southwark.

messenger on a horse—("Elizabethan Pornography Smugglers") The horse for this sequence was acquired from Henry Woodley at Elm Farm, Boveney (still a riding/stable business today), and was shot on 6 April 1972 (WAC T12/1,428).

minstrels in attendance—("PSC; "Elizabethan Pornography Smugglers") These minstrels are The Cittie Waites (WAC T12/1,447).

"morass of filth"—("Elizabethan Pornography Smugglers") Historically, of course, Sir Philip Sidney did fight the Spanish, and he was also a Tudor gentleman, scholar, poet, and courtier. The Pythons are shaping a new history for and with the admittedly Petrarchan Sidney, drawing here, instead, on coarser, *Ovidian* elements in Sidney's work. It is known that Sidney was more than a little taken with the physical attributes of his fancy, Penelope Rich, so much so that some recent analysis of his "Astrophil and Stella" sonnet sequence purports to reveal a man corporeally obsessed. In 1991 Paul Allen Miller may have unconsciously supported Python's reading of Sidney when he argued that rather than the announced Petrarchan tradition of chaste love from afar, Sidney just as often embraced the Ovidian fascination with body parts and sexuality (see Miller's

"Sidney, Petrarch and Ovid, or Imitation as Subversion"). This attraction to the body is a noteworthy element when the specter of Python's Sidney as a fighter *against* pornography ("where the female body is objectified for its sexual parts") is presented in the Python sketch. Miller sees Sidney's approach as descriptive of Bakhtin's later phenomenon of "grotesque degradation," or the "bringing down" of both the object of affection/obsession and the objectifier.

So is Python appropriating Sidney the respected public figure, the gentleman who lives up to his station and waxes Petrarchan in writing? This Sidney would naturally, rightfully, be against the practice of pornography and "porn-merchanting." Or is this the more licentious, Ovidian Sidney who lusts where he cannot love and describes in what must have been considered at least mildly pornographic detail ("her belly," her "Cupid's hill," "spotless mine," and "her thighs") the object of his unfulfilled carnal desire for a married woman? For the Oxbridge-educated Pythons, the more "earthy" Sidney must have been at least unconsciously appreciated, and the irony of Sidney the porn fighter then becomes possible.

"My particular prob or buglem bear"—("Thripshaw's Disease") Once again, the source of the conflict here is miscommunication, as was seen just moments before in the stilted "vignette" scene. This Python trope often involves at least two people and their inability to effectively communicate, leading to confusion and, sometimes, dire consequences. Python characters create offensive sales campaigns (Ep. 24), use mistranslated Hungarian phrasebooks (Ep. 25), ask pop culture questions of Marxist leaders (Ep. 25), speak only certain parts of words (Ep. 26) or in hopelessly fractured English (Ep. 29), or even in anagrams and jumbles (Ep. 30). The comedy of "misunderstanding" (as discussed in the author's *MPSERD*) is ubiquitous.

– P –

"Panther, Maudling"—("Pornographic Bookshop") Police dog names here ticked off by the flustered Gaskell, but earlier "Panther" was Inspector Leopard's (Cleese) original name (Ep. 29), and "Maudling" is yet another reference to the unpopular Conservative Home Secretary. Maudling would be forced to resign less than three months after this episode was recorded, when the Metropolitan police opened an investigation into one of his former business partners, John Poulson (*ODNB*).

"Parkhurst"—("Elizabethan Pornography Smugglers") A prison on the Isle of Wight. The Kray brothers (Ep. 14) spent time in Parkhurst.

"Penshurst"—("Elizabethan Pornography Smugglers") Penshurst Place was the Sidney's ancestral home in Kent.

"Philip of Spain"—("Tudor Job Agency") Born in 1527, Philip ruled Spain from 1556 to his death in 1598, and was in power during Spain's most expansive colonial, military, and mercantile endeavors.

"porn merchant"—("Elizabethan Pornography Smugglers") The definition of pornography would have been quite different in Elizabethan times. According to Lynda Boose, pornography in the time of Shakespeare and Elizabeth was "a language not of lascivious delight but of sexual scatology—of slime, poison, garbage, vomit, clyster pipes, dung, and animality—that emerges connected to images of sexuality in the vocabulary" (193). The Pythons, then, have transposed the pornography of the twentieth century into Elizabethan times, an anachronistic incongruity common for the troupe. The fear of sexual license was very real, of course, but only as it threatened to contaminate and confuse lineage lines with bastard children making inheritance claims. The homosexual (or "sodomitical," in the period terminology) exploits of men, especially, were less threatening—no procreation, simply recreation—so dallying with a catamite or ingle was frowned upon, but not often punished. See the author's chapter six in *MPSERD* for more.

"Professor Thynne"—(*"Is There? . . . Life After Death?"*) Probably a reference to the well-loved *Goon Show* character Hercules Grytpype-Thynne, played by Peter Sellers.

– R –

"Raleigh, Sir Walter"—("Tudor Job Agency") Adventurer and courtier to Elizabeth I, Raleigh (1552-1618) commissioned the first Ark Royal, and established settlements in the New World in the years before the Armada. Raleigh was last mentioned in Ep. 29, in the "Erizabeth L" sketch.

"Royal College of Surgeons"—("Thripshaw's Disease") The RCS received its Royal Charter in 1800.

running into a church—("Silly Disturbances [The Rev. Arthur Belling]") This setting is The Old Place, Boveney, Windsor, and was used before as a location for Ep. 2.

– S –

"sad I am to see you caught up in this morass of filth"—("Pornographic Bookshop") The image of a "fighter against filth" being caught up in the trafficking of that same material is likely a very contemporary reference to Detective Chief Inspector George Fenwick and his relation with the Soho pornographic industry. Fenwick had led the investigation and arrest of the *Oz* publishers in 1971 for obscenity, but was himself soon thereafter revealed as the controller of a "Soho porn merchant" ring that the Metropolitan Police had been ignoring altogether or assisting outright. Another police official, Flying Squad Chief Kenneth Drury, had been on holiday to the Continent with a Soho porn merchant in 1972, it was discovered. Both Drury and Fenwick would eventually be arrested, tried, and imprisoned by the mid-1970s, along with a dozen other policemen (*Eyewitness: 1970-79*, "The Oz Trial").

second Spaniard leaps out—("Elizabethan Pornography Smugglers") This second costumed actor is Cleese, who has already appeared in this very costume and in this very location in Ep. 33, when he admits that the show's run long and the audience needs to trundle on home. They would have shot as much seashore footage as they might have needed for the entire third series in this location.

"Seltzer, David O."—("Thripshaw's Disease") The stock Hollywood producer name used before by the Pythons, and modeled after David O. Selznick, producer of *Gone With the Wind* (1939), and earlier adventure films like *Prisoner of Zenda* (1936) and *Viva Villa!* (1934).

"Shakespeare's latest works"—("Elizabethan Pornography Smugglers") In 1583, Shakespeare was just meeting/forming up with the Queen's Company, and was several years away from professional playing and writing in London (commencing about 1587). Sidney was getting married this year, and would be dead in three years from a wound received in the battle he'd so hoped for in the Netherlands.

sherry—("Sherry-Drinking Vicar") A Spanish fortified wine. The Pythons may have been thinking of the popular (low-priced and available) QC brand of sherry.

"Amontillado"—A wine produced originally in Montilla, it is a more mature sherry than the "dry" sherry mentioned by the Vicar (*OED*).

"Sidney, Sir Philip"—("Pornographic Bookshop") Sidney (1554-1586) was a poet, a man of the court, and an accomplished soldier. The title misspells his name as "Phillip."

"since 1625"—("Tudor Job Agency") It's not clear why the Tudor job market would last this long, since the Tudor era officially ended with Elizabeth's death in 1603, and the Stuart era (under James) began that same year. James would die in 1625, which may be the reason this date is mentioned, but then Charles ascended the throne, and the (Carolean-) Stuart period continued until 1714.

This may also be alluding to the Tudor Job Agency actually putting Charles I on the throne in 1625. A temp job, certainly—Charles would lose both the job and his head in 1649, signaling the beginning of the Interregnum.

"Sir Philip! Not alone!"—("Elizabethan Pornography Smugglers") Historically, Sidney had been frustrated many times in his attempts to gain Elizabeth's favor and secure both a knighthood and important foreign service, so this moment of bravado isn't out of character.

Soho dirty bookshop—(PSC; "Pornographic Bookshop") Located in the West End of London, Soho has been the home to illicit (meaning sexual) activities since the area was left out of upscale development in the sixteenth and seventeenth centuries, and a mixed immigrant and English working-class population flourished. Popular entertainment venues dotted the streets, including music halls and pubs and houses of ill repute, and soon these included "dirty bookshop"–type stores, as well. The sex trade (prostitutes, clip joints, sex shops) called Soho home for much of the latter half of the twentieth century. See Ackroyd.

"Spaniards have landed in the Netherlands"—("Elizabethan Pornography Smugglers") Probably a reference to the then-notorious Maurice Girodias (1919-1990), owner/publisher of Olympia Press in Paris. Girodias was watched carefully by British authorities, and was hounded from Paris to Denmark to the United States. His "dirty books" were intercepted and destroyed on a regular basis as pornography. Among the naughty titles were also included other innovative, more avant-garde works, as well. Python mate Terry Southern (*The Magic Christian*; *Dr. Strangelove*) was published through Girodias' Traveller's Companion press (within Olympia), as were luminaries including Genet and Beckett.

stock film of Elizabethan London—(PSC; "Elizabethan Pornography Smugglers") The WAC records for this episode offer no source for this film stock, nor for the later shot of a seventeenth-century sailing ship. It appears that sometimes, when the film stock or photograph is from the BBC Library, the official request/copyright notation does not appear on the paperwork that normally includes all cast members, extras, musicians, film and photographic stock, and music clips charged to that particular episode. This may be the case when there is no need to request copyright permission for an item already owned by the BBC.

stock film of marauding knights—(PSC; "Thripshaw's Disease") This is the same film stock used in Ep. 20 for the *Attila the Hun Show* sequence, and is simply titled "*Attila the Hun*" in the BBC records. It may have been borrowed from film critic Philip Jenkinson's film stock collection, who is lampooned in Ep. 33.

string quartet—("The Free Repetition of Doubtful Words Sketch, by an Underrated Author") These men are most likely some of Fred Tomlinson's singers, pretending to play Mozart's "String Quartet in G" (K.516), originally played by the Weller Quartet (WAC T12/1,447).

"Stuart period nothing. Hanoverians nothing . . . "—("Tudor Jobs Agency") The Stuart line began with James I and continued to 1714, followed by the German-bred Hanoverians from 1714-1901 (including Victoria), and the Saxe-Coburgs (also German, through Prince Albert), before Windsor was chosen as the English royal family name in 1917, during the height of WWI.

– T –

"That's all you say?"—("Tudor Job Agency") It's unclear whether this is a reference to the printed script for the sketch itself, which has been referred to in past shows (Eps. 17 and 29, e.g.), or if this is the first cracking of the "Tudor" façade with the customer. The back-and-forth trading of code phrases was last seen in Ep. 4, and was already a staple of the pulp spy film/novel genre.

Thripshaw at a desk evidently in a castle—("Thripshaw's Disease") The Hollywood-ization of historical subjects has been going on since the movies began, and "biopics" had been a staple of various studios' output since *Napoleon* (1927), *I Am A Fugitive From a Chain Gang* (1932), and *The Life of Emile Zola* (1937).

"thy sharp-tongued wit"—("Elizabethan Pornography Smugglers") His sharp-tongued (and sharp-penned) reputation did get Sidney into trouble on a few occasions, as, for example, he quarreled with the earl of Oxford over a tennis court at Greenwich Palace, essentially since the higher-born Oxford hadn't said "please." The Queen would later "remind" Sidney of his place, and the row subsided (Woudhuysen, *ODNB*).

"'tis a story of man's great love for his . . . fellow man"—("Elizabethan Pornography Smugglers") The homoerotic was not nearly as stigmatized during the Elizabethan period as it has become, mostly due to the fact that same-gender sexual activity (man-to-man, even man-to-boy) couldn't upset bloodlines and introduce bastards or multiple claimants to the gentry's fortunes. See the entry for "porn merchant" above for more.

"Tudor"—("Tudor Job Agency") The Tudors were the ruling family named for Owen Tudor (1400-1461), who married Henry V's widow.

– U –

"underground"—("Tudor Job Agency") The colloquial name for London's subway system, which opened in 1863.

– V –

"vittler"—("Tudor Job Agency") One who provides food and drink.

– W –

"Walsingham"—("Elizabethan Pornography Smugglers") Frances Walsingham (1530-1590) was Elizabeth's spymaster, rooting out Popish types and any family (especially the old Catholic-leaning nobility in the north) who might be inviting Catholic priests and/or spies into England. Sidney—Walsingham's son-in-law—is said to have found safe haven in Walsingham's Paris home as a Protestant refugee in the early 1570s.

"Warwick"—("Pornographic Bookshop") Ambrose Dudley, third Earl of Warwick (abt. 1528-1589) was Master-General of the Ordnance with Philip Sidney in 1585-1586, and another favorite of Elizabeth I.

"We live in Esher"—("Thripshaw's Disease") As in previous episodes, Esher seems to be the center of the swinging London borough lifestyle.

– Y –

"You'll do time for this"—("Elizabethan Pornography Smugglers") The Obscene Publications Acts of 1959 and 1964 did outline sentencing guidelines, including prison sentences lasting up to three years, as well as fines, probations, etc. Technically, however, since the Acts also determine that "[a] prosecution . . . for an offence against this section shall not be commenced more than two years after the commission of the offence," Maddox may have a hard time making the charges stick almost 400 years after Sidney/Gaskell allegedly committed them.

Episode 37

– A –

"all so meaningless"—("Dennis Moore") Here Moore slips the twentieth-century philosophy of Jean-Paul Sartre into the eighteenth century, spouting the Paris coffee-house nihilism of Sartre's *Being and Nothingness*, the hopeless anxiety of the academic and the intellectual in a godless and technological world that festered into student riots in the late 1960s.

"Amalgamated Money TV"—("*TV4 or Not TV4* Discussion") Since at least the early 1950s there had been ongoing discussions in the UK regarding commercial television. The BBC and various sitting governments (Wilson, Heath) had been very concerned about the effect commercial TV would have on the electorate, and whether the subsidized BBC could survive in the new commercial world. Labour spent a good deal of time pointing at the big money owners of various independent television networks, seeing a Conservative mouthpiece at each commercial-driven channel. See Buscombe, Crisell (2002), and Freedman for more.

"Amontillado"—("Off-Licence") See the entry in Ep. 36 for more on sherry, the "Sherry-Drinking Vicar" sketch.

– B –

"Basil"—("What the Stars Foretell") Basil was the name of the clever sheep in Ep. 2, "Flying Sheep." The star sign for June 21-22 is actually Cancer.

"Bodell, Jack"—("*Boxing Tonight*") Played by Nosher Powell (b. 1928), who went on to perform stunts and act as stunt coordinator for James Bond films and *Star Wars* (1977). Powell also did stuntwork for Leone's spaghetti Westerns and *The Magic Christian* (1969), where he probably met at least Chapman and Cleese.

"British and Empire Heavyweight Champion"—Indicating that the fighter holds the titles for both Britain and the Commonwealth. In 1959, for example, the British and Empire Heavyweight Champion was Henry Cooper, who had defeated Brian London (already mentioned in Ep. 13) in January.

Braddon, Russell—(PSC; "*Prejudice*") The printed script notes that this character is Russell Braddon (1921-1995, Australia), who wrote the novel upon which the camp film classic *Night of the Lepus* (1972) was based. Braddon also wrote the celebrated *The Naked Island* (1952), detailing the horrors of his four years in a Japanese concentration camp. Braddon was living and working in the UK during this period.

"Bremen and Verdun"—("Lupins") Sweden had ceded both Bremen and Verdun to George in his capacity as Elector of Hanover, and these were significant northern ports for the landlocked Hanover.

Incidentally, Jones had read English and Palin modern history at Oxford, and they had worked together writing the London Weekend Television show *The Complete and Utter History of Britain* (1969).

"Buckingham"—("Lupins") There were multiple Buckinghams, though only two from the eighteenth-century period depicted in "Dennis Moore"—George Nugent-Temple-Grenville (1753-1813) and his son, Richard Temple-Nugent-Brydges-Chandos-Grenville (1776-1839).

– C –

"cell'd"—("Off-Licence") A poetic contraction meaning enclosed within a cell or cellar, the wine would have been aged in caves in the region.

"vinous soil"—Meaning the soil has the "nature" of wine.

"Pluto's hills"—There is an area in Fuentes de Andalucia Sevilla known as "Pluto."

"Charles XII"—("Lupins") Charles (1682-1718) was indeed the central figure in the Great Northern War, campaigning as king of Sweden against Denmark, Poland, Russia, and collections of northern forces banding together to answer Charles' overreaching foreign policy.

"Clark, Petula"—("What the Stars Foretell") Born in 1932, Clark is a British singer and actress already mentioned in Ep. 3.

"Clark, Sir Kenneth"—(*Boxing Tonight*) Lord Clark (1903-1983) was an author, presenter, museum director and academic, and for many years was Britain's most visible and respected critical art figure. His 1969 television series *Civilisation* (BBC2) was a hit in both the UK and United States, and Clark's reputation and stature would have been enormous in 1972, when this episode was broadcast.

Clark does indeed wander around as he lectures in *Civilisation*, hands in pockets under a casual tweed jacket—Chapman mimics this quite well.

" . . . cock may chance an arm"—("Off-Licence") This trumped-up Elizabethan stage dialogue is a cobbling of Shakespeare and Marlowe mixed in with Lewis Carroll–type frippery. Idle did this once before, in Ep. 3, as the Olivier-like prisoner trying to beat a parking ticket. The *Beyond the Fringe* group also created a full mock-Shakespeare sketch called "So That's the Way You Like It." See the entry for "Olivier impression" in Ep. 3 for more.

"Colwyn Bay"—("Ideal Loon Exhibition") Jones was born in Colwyn Bay, Wales.

"Concorde"—("Dennis Moore") This name elicits a generous laugh from the studio audience, perhaps because the horse's namesake—the still new Concorde SST aircraft—was very much in the public's view and imagination. There are, for example, more than 300 political cartoons treating the subject (Concorde's noise levels, cost overruns, the challenges of cooperating with the French, the expense of operating even one plane, etc.) that appeared in English newspapers during the 1964-1972 period. Also, the significant experienced and projected costs (and cost overruns) for the cooperative program had many asking how such a boondoggle could be justified in times of inflation, and preservationists worried about the sonic booms' deleterious effect on fragile stone cathedrals and churches throughout the country (*Private Eye* 9 October 1970, 21-22).

The horse ridden by Cleese appears to have been obtained from Chris Le Boutillier of Le Chassine, St. Ouen, Jersey, and was used 21, 26, and 29 May 1972 (WAC T12/1,460).

"crofter's daughter"—(link out of "*TV4 or Not TV4*") Victoria (1819-1901) was, of course, the daughter of a duke and a princess, and thus not a commoner. The show *Victoria Regina* had been produced in 1961 for American television on George Schaefer's Showcase Theatre, with Julie Harris in the title role.

Probably a well-worn comedy phrase (it's heard in *The Goon Show*, for example), the *Private Eye* staff earlier describe PM Macmillan as a "humble crofter's grandson" (Ingrams 82). Macmillan (1894-1986) was actually born well and married even better, leading a patrician life that provided ample ammunition to his opponents.

"Curtis, Tony"—("What the Stars Foretell") In 1972 the American Hollywood star Curtis (b. 1925) was appearing with Englishman Roger Moore (b. 1927) in the British television show *The Persuaders* (Tribune Productions/ITC, 1971-72), and would have been featured in the very newspapers being read by Mrs. Trepidatious and Mrs. O.

– D –

Daily Express—("Ideal Loon Exhibition") Long-standing Conservative-leaning newspaper, the *Express* would have been both run by and favorable to the Heath-led "loons" the Pythons lampoon in this sketch.

"Derry and Toms"—("What the Stars Foretell") A popular Kensington High Street department store that had just closed in January 1972, and was earlier mentioned in Ep. 35.

"digger duffer"—("Ideal Loon Exhibition") Probably a colloquialism meaning a luckless, fortune-less miner. The editors of *Private Eye* had nicknamed Australian media mogul Rupert Murdoch "Digger" and "Dirty Digger" (*PE* 1 January 1971, 3).

DJ—("*Boxing Tonight*") Dinner Jacket. This is the uniform, as well, of BBC announcers as portrayed by the Pythons.

doctor is lowered on a wire—("What the Stars Foretell") In Groucho Marx's (1890-1977) popular television show *You Bet Your Life* (1950-1961), the "Secret Word Duck" would drop from above if the secret word was uttered, though brother Harpo (1888-1964) also made an entrance this way at least once. Mr. and Mrs. Bun (Idle and Chapman) arrived into and then departed the "Spam" sketch in this same manner in Ep. 25.

Down Your Way—("*Prejudice*") The printed script describes this set-up as the visual equivalent ("a TV version") of *Down Your Way*, a popular and long-running BBC radio show (1946-1992). The show had been hosted by Richard Dimbleby (Ep. 23) and later Brian Johnston (Ep. 21), and focused on life and people in smaller English villages and towns, not the big cities or New Cities being built after the war. (Hence, the sketch begins "from the *tiny village* of Rabid in Buckinghamshire.") The Pythons' joke, then, could be either (a) the backward provinciality of these simpler folk allowed for time-honored ignorant bigotry or (b) the squeaky-clean "hominess" of the characters and settings (the show was broadcast Sundays at teatime) were a perfectly incongruous backdrop for such bald-faced prejudices.

– E –

"Eddy, Duane"—("What the Stars Foretell") Eddy is an American born in 1938, and had become known in this period for myriad instrumental hits, and for his rock-and-roll "twangy" guitar-playing.

Edward Heath opening something—("Ideal Loon Exhibition") This film footage is BBC stock, titled "Heath & Queen at Ideal Home" (WAC T12/1,460). Heath was Prime Minister from 1970 to 1974, and, as a Conservative, a constant target of the Pythons.

"Empire Pool, Wembley"—("*Boxing Tonight*") Empire Pool is the nickname of Wembley Arena, and is across the street from Wembley Stadium in Greater London.

empties his wallet—("Doctor") In Britain the National Health Service (NHS) had been providing socialized medicine since 1948, with every citizen able to receive "free" medical treatment from cradle to grave. This universal coverage led to long waiting times for treatment (and especially surgery) as well as dips in levels of service quality and the quality of people willing to embark on medical careers. (See Klein for more.) However, forcing the patients to pay for expensive procedures has not been one of the NHS's real problems, though "co-pay" type charges (minimal fees for dental visits and prescriptions, for example) have been utilized for many years to offset the enormous expense of truly "universal" NHS coverage.

Also, so-called amenity beds have become available for those with sufficient funds to pay for more services and comfort, especially in hospitals. The state of London-area and provincial hospitals is broached in Eps. 26 and 34, as well.

Episode 37—Recorded 17 April 1972, and broadcast 4 January 1973. The episode was recorded eighth and broadcast eleventh in the series.

Others included on the BBC's repeat list (for royalty payment purposes) include: Frank Lester (Eps. 31, 35-37, 40; *Jackanory*), Henry Rayner (Ep. 35; *Dixon of Dock Green*), Paul Lindley (Eps. 3, 14, 28, 35), Francis Mortimer (*The Brontes of Haworth*), Michael Fitzpatrick, Derek Allen, Richard Burke, Adrien Wells, Reid Anderson (*Secrets of Sex*), Adam Day, Micki Shorn, Nosher Powell, Peter Roy (*Engelbert with The Young Generation*), Fred Tomlinson, Helena Clayton (*FC* Montreux episode; *The Agony of Love*), Jean Clarke (Eps. 29, 33, 39; *The Borderers*), Frances Pidgeon (Eps. 29, 33; *Value For Money*), and Peter Kodak (Eps. 27, 29, 36; *Dr. Who*) (WAC T12/1,460).

"*Erratum*"—(link out of "*Prejudice*") This bit of errata is correct—Bodell was born in Swadlincote, Derbyshire in 1940, and not Lincolnshire. Derbyshire is west of Lincolnshire, in the East Midlands.

– F –

"Flan-and-pickle"—("What the Stars Foretell") An unusual dessert combination, at the least, and here pronounced more like "flannem pickle."

fop—(PSC; "Lupins") An eighteenth-century foolish-dandy character of the stage and page, the fop is based originally on Sir Fopling Flutter from Etherege's *Man of Mode* (1676).

"Frederick William busily engaged"—("Lupins") Again, the Pythons have plundered eminent historian Trevelyan and given a fair accounting of Frederick William's travails regarding Silesia, an Austrian province, which would include the Seven Years' War. Note the linguistic similarity of Buckingham (Jones) and Grantley's (Palin) description of the period to Trevelyan's, from *The History of England*:

> During the Seven Years' War, Frederic was engaged in defending against the three great military powers of Europe the Silesian province, which he had seized in the War of Austrian Succession in spite of his pledged word. The heroism of the defence covered the baseness of the original robbery. Yet even Frederic must have succumbed but for Pitt's subsidies. (544)

The Pythons are quoting Trevelyan (the 1952 edition), essentially, as they've done before—though previously with acknowledgment (see Ep. 26).

"Pitt's subsidies"—Britain was one of Frederick's few allies during this period, with William Pitt arranging ample subsidies to support Frederick's efforts and underscore Britain's burgeoning Continental and even global influence.

"Free French"—("Ideal Loon Exhibition") The Free French forces fought against the Axis forces during WWII, generally outside of established war zones. Exiled General de Gaulle claimed at least nominal leadership of these forces.

"Frost, David"—("What the Stars Foretell") The one-time Python associate and boss, Frost (b. 1939) by this time was appearing in another of his own shows, *The Frost Programme*, and was well-known enough to already be featured on *This Is Your Life* in 1972, and regularly travel on the Concorde between London and New York. See the earlier entries (Eps. 10 and 19) for the ubiquitous and successful Frost—the Pythons' simpering, glad-handing, and irritatingly successful bête noire.

– G –

Gathering Storm, The—(*George I* link out of "Doctor") This is the title of the first volume of Sir Winston Churchill's (1874-1965) six-volume work covering WWII and the immediate pre- and postwar years, the entire series published between 1948 and 1953. The title will be soberly used again in the "Penguins" section of Ep. 38.

"George"—("Lupins") A reference to George III (1738-1820) and his involvement in the post–French Revolution struggles in Europe against the seemingly unstoppable Napoleon Bonaparte (1769-1821; Eps. 2, 5, 12, 13, 23, 35, and 44).

"Grantley"—("Lupins") The Baron Grantley during this period was William Norton (1742-1822).

"green, scaly skin . . . arid subtropical zones"—("What the Stars Foretell") This fanciful description is somewhat close to the Komodo Dragon of Indonesia, though thirty feet is a bit long even for these top-of-the-food-chain predators.

– H –

"Hanover"—("Lupins") English kings George I, II, and III were all Electors of Hanover, a German city in Lower Saxony. The Hanoverian line has been mentioned in Ep. 36, in the "Tudor Jobs Agency" sketch. The German "Saxe-Coburg" heritage of the English royal house was officially made unofficial during WWI, when the more politically correct "Windsor" became the family name.

"height of the English Renaissance"—(*Boxing Tonight*) Inigo Jones (Ep. 7) is given credit for insti-

gating this renaissance movement in English architecture, with the designs for Covent Garden and the Banqueting House at Whitehall (Ep. 40).

"He seeks them here"—("Lupins") Adapted from Baroness Orczy's very popular *The Scarlet Pimpernel* (1905):

> They seek him here, they seek him there
> Those Frenchies seek him everywhere
> Is he in heaven or is he in hell?
> That demned elusive Pimpernel.

The hero of that work, Sir Percy Blakeney (aka "The Scarlet Pimpernel"), played a dandified fop character to hide his true identity from evil Revolutionaries.

highwayman—("Dennis Moore") Moore may be patterned after the Robin Hood–like English highwayman Humphrey Kynaston (1474-1534), who is said to have robbed the rich to help the poor. Kynaston's mount was allegedly called "Beelzebub."

"hip injuries"—("Ideal Loon Exhibition") Though not made clear in the sketch, this comment must refer to the dangers of counter-marching near another player wearing a very large bathtub.

– I –

"Ideal Loon Exhibition"—("Ideal Loon Exhibition") *The Daily Mail* (not *Daily Express*) has sponsored the Ideal Home Exhibition (now Ideal Home Show) since 1908. New furniture, appliance, and decorating ideas galore greeted Ideal Home attendees. *The Daily Mail*, along with the *Daily Express*, have been termed "conservative" (and even "nationalist") British newspapers.

"I know one of them isn't"—("Dennis Moore") At this point Moore digresses from the narrative trajectory, and even after all the verisimilitude of eighteenth-century costumes, props, and overall production design, we're quickly thrust sideways into the world of Laurence Sterne's Uncle Toby and Tristram (from *Tristram Shandy*) where diversions, backtracks, and self-conscious narrative hiccoughs keep the story from ever actually progressing. (Palin did this earlier, in Ep. 30, "Gestures to Indicate Pauses in a Televised Talk," where he qualifies and hedges and qualifies some more, creating brackets of reference and speech within other brackets.)

In this the Pythons are anticipating their feature film *Holy Grail*, where the grimy reality of the sets and Middle Ages design are consistently undercut by the temporal and spatial narrative transgressions—

the appearance of coconuts, argumentative peasants, a film production member's death (the Animator), and the "out of bracket" Historian who attempts to narrate the story, only to be killed by someone "inside the bracket."

The digressions in "Dennis Moore" also suffer digressions (as seen earlier in "Njorl's Saga"), with the discussion moving from the remaining loaded pistol to Moore's accuracy to his practice schedule to the target to size of the target hillock to the particular tree that can be hit to how often he can hit that target tree. They then disagree which tree Moore might be aiming at and discuss trees in general. The narrative doesn't get retracked until Moore takes control of the situation again, narratively, sidetracks the sidetracking digressions, and reminds the coach travelers that they are his victims.

"Ikon, Mrs."—("What the Stars Foretell") This spelling of "icon" is generally not used, but this also could be a reference to the Ikon Gallery, a modern art gallery in Birmingham, opened in the city's Bull Ring section in the 1960s. Also, the figure of a "Mrs. Trepidatious" may actually have become iconic by this time, in the Python world at least, meaning a fussy, ratbag of a mannish-woman.

"it's all so meaningless"—("Lupins") This existentialist moment is certainly an intrusion of the twentieth-century on the eighteenth, with Moore (Cleese) voicing the Sartrean discipline already covered in Ep. 27 by the Pepperpots, where possessions and the "wants" of life can only preclude or put off the search for a meaningful existence. With further prodding, however, Moore switches to a more practical mode of existence, outlining "the usual things" he and everyone wants—home and marriage—the sort of cheerful "hearth, children and home" trope seen so often in the eighteenth-century English pastoral tradition (see Thomson's "The Seasons," and Grey's "Elegy Written in a Country Church-Yard").

– L –

"Ludovic Ludovic"—("*TV4 or Not TV4* Discussion") This is more than likely a reference to the working journalist/author Ludovic Kennedy (b. 1919), an Oxford grad who would become a newsreader for ITV and a presenter/interviewer for the public affairs program *This Week*.

"Ludo" Kennedy was also the screenwriter for *10 Rillington Place* (1971), starring "Dickie" Attenborough, the film detailing the John Christie murders alluded to in Ep. 27, the "Court Scene—Multiple Murderer" sketch.

– M –

"Massed Pipes and Toilet Requisities"—("Ideal Loon Exhibition") There are many Massed Pipes and Drum groups in the UK, often appearing at Military Tatoos and Highland games.

McGough—(PSC; "Off-Licence") The poet named in the scripts as "McGough" (Idle) is certainly based on Roger McGough (b. 1937), the Liverpudlian poet/playwright who was also a member of the 1960s music/poetry group The Scaffold. McGough would later appear in *All You Need Is Cash* (1978), written by Idle. McGough and friends may have been at least partly the inspiration for the Scottish poet McTeagle seen earlier in Ep. 16.

The short rhyme beginning with "Just one bottle . . ." is much like McGough's playful poetry, for example, his 1967 poem "Cake":

> i wanted one life
> you wanted another
> we couldn't have our cake
> so we ate each other. (*The Mersey Sound*)

"Mike Sammes Singers"—("What the Stars Foretell") Originally a working solo backup singer, Sammes founded his backup group and performed almost non-stop on commercials, jingles, pop records, and on until the mid-1970s.

Sammes and his singers were performing with Petula Clark in 1970 on *Petula*, a 1970 American television special.

"Millichope"—("Doctor") Ray Millichope was the editor for much of the run of *Flying Circus*.

Miss World—(PSC; "Ideal Loon Exhibition") The printed script mentions that this judging scene is to mimic the "Miss World" pageant look, which debuted in the UK in 1951.

"Moore, Roger"—("What the Stars Foretell") Soon-to-be popular British TV and film actor who in the following year would take on the James Bond role in *Live and Let Die* (1973). In 1972, however, Moore was merely a mid-level television actor appearing with former Hollywood star Tony Curtis in *The Persuaders*.

"Mrs Ikon"—("What the Stars Foretell") It's not clear why Mrs. Trepidatious (Chapman) has become Mrs. Ikon, nor why she doesn't correct the doctor, except perhaps that this is a comment on the strained doctor-patient relationship in the inefficient and overburdened National Health Service. Since the creation of the NHS in 1948 there have been lingering complaints about waiting lists for certain treatments and extended waiting times for appointments and in doctors' offices.

The robbery going on in the following scene may just be this particular doctor or hospital trying to make ends meet, since budgets for state-owned and funded medical services were/are always at least meager, and certainly cost-conscious.

"Mrs. Trepidatious"—("Doctor") Mrs. Trepidatious (identified in both the script and by Mrs. O) will later be called "Mrs. Ikon" by the Doctor (Jones). And though "trepidatious" is an overstated way of saying "timid," the character as played by Chapman seems anything but timid or timorous, complaining loudly about her health and arguing with her friend regularly. She doesn't even seem overly frightened when the doctor robs them at gunpoint.

Music starts—(link out of "Doctor") The musical piece used under the *George I* promo is an overture from the Paul Bonneau Orchestra Terpsichoreau Festival by F. de Boisvalle. The music that follows as the nobles chat in "Dennis Moore" is "Musiques pour les fetes d'eau Face" (WAC T12/1,460).

– N –

"Nae Trews"—("Ideal Loon Exhibition") Literally, "without trousers."

"Nesbitt"—("What the Stars Foretell") The name Nesbitt has been used at least twice to indicate a Pepperpot type, in Eps. 24 and 26, and Mrs. Trepidatious (Chapman) appears to fit that profile well.

– O –

"On ITV now the" (*sound of a punch*)—("*George I*" link into "Dennis Moore") The possibility of a BBC announcer giving programming information for the rival networks is remote, and punished here rather finally.

"Oxford Professor of Fine Art"—("*Boxing Tonight*") In the immediate postwar years, Sir Kenneth Clark was the Slade Professor of Fine Art at Oxford. In Ep. 25, Clark is mentioned as a volunteer negotiator between museums and the striking artworks.

– P –

"Palladio's villas"—("*Boxing Tonight*") Ornate, groundbreaking, and, yes, "ordered" villas designed by the Italian architect professionally known as Palladio (1508-1580), whose influence would be carried into England by Inigo Jones (see above) and Christopher Wren (1632-1723).

pan across idyllic countryside—("Dennis Moore") The music underneath this opening is "Early Dusk" from the album *Pastoral Music* by Ivor Slaney (WAC T12/1,460).

"party feeling"—("Lupins") A specialized phrase meaning action in favor or support of partisanship. According to the *OED*, the phrase dates just to the early nineteenth century, though Trevelyan—whom the Pythons are very nearly quoting in this scene—does employ the phrase. This indicates that the eighteenth-century characters portrayed by the Pythons are speaking in the later vernacular of their chroniclers, like Trevelyan.

phony mouthing way—(PSC; "Dennis Moore") This refers to the time-honored stage and television tradition of secondary actors speaking sotto voce when the microphones are hot and only the principals are meant to be heard. Rather than mic up everyone in the scene (time-consuming and costly), the overhead boom mic is placed as near the action as possible, so all "crowd" actors have to pretend to talk normally—which often does look quite phony, since these actors tend to overplay their dumb-show to compensate.

postilion—(PSC; "Dennis Moore") This man essentially "rides shotgun" on the coach, though this doesn't seem to fit the historical demands for the job—which was to ride along with multiple-horse carriages as an assistant.

"Pretty Girl is Like a Melody, A"—("Ideal Loon Exhibition") This performance is by Stanley Black, and the song is composed by Irving Berlin (WAC T12/1,460).

pulls out a stethoscope—("Doctor") This is a very clever sight gag—a doctor being frightened of a stethoscope—the likes of which are disappearing as the series progresses, in favor of either non-sequitur moments/transitions or just more homogenous narrative structures.

– R –

"redistribution of wealth"—("Lupins") This may be a comment on the UK's non-proportional income tax, where incomes above certain levels take on more and more of the tax burden, with that money being "redistributed" via social programs, creating a kind of "Robin Hood" (or here, "Dennis Moore") effect. Trade unionists (and syndicalists, even) made similar demands of owners of industrial concerns in this period, that profits should be more evenly distributed among workers and owners. Economist and former Harvard professor Simon Kuznets (1901-1985) had won the

Nobel Prize in October 1971 for his work along these lines (income inequality and economic growth correlations), the notoriety of which may accounts for the Pythons' treatment of the subject.

Rhodesian police—("*Prejudice*") The Rhodesian situation has been treated before (Eps. 28 and 31), and will be again (in Ep. 45). The Rhodesian police force had gained quite a reputation for firm crowd control tactics and enforcing the white minority government's segregation laws. The Judge (Chapman) in Ep. 15 wishes aloud that he could emigrate to Africa and "get some real sentencing done."

– S –

"**skivers**"—("*Prejudice*") Those who shun their duties; the lazy and shiftless.

song is heard—("Dennis Moore") There are numerous songs about highwaymen (most dating from the nineteenth century), including "Whiskey in the Jar," and "Brennan on the Moor." The song used by the Pythons was originally titled "Robin Hood" and penned by Fred Tomlinson, and is sung by the Fred Tomlinson Singers (WAC T12/1,460).

Sports programme music—(PSC; "*Boxing Tonight*") This recording on film is the Scots Guard playing "Drum Majorette" by Steck (WAC T12/1,460).

"**Stand and Deliver!**"—("Dennis Moore") According to Alexander Smith in his 1714 book on English highwaymen, this was the well-known and much-feared cry of the rogue beginning his work.

"**Stars Spangled Banner**"—(PSC; "Ideal Loon Exhibition") This music used here is listed in the printed scripts as "Souza's Star Spangled Banner," but is actually Sousa's "Stars and Stripes Forever." This particular performance is by the Band of Royal Military Academy, Sandhurst (WAC T12/1,460).

Stern music—("*TV4 or Not TV4* Discussion") This and the closing titles music are short clips from Shostakovich's "Symphony No. 12, First Movement" performed by the Leningrad Philharmonic Orchestra (WAC T12/1,460).

swag—(PSC; "Lupins') Slang for ill-gotten booty.

"**sward**"—("Dennis Moore") A green, grassy slope (*OED*), and probably only used because it nearly rhymes with "Concorde."

– T –

"**through that stage**"—("Lupins") Though this obviously sounds like a very modern, psychoanalytic phrase, the *OED* makes it clear that as early as the fourteenth-century this more abstract usage of the term was extant, though not common.

"**Treaty of Westphalia**"—("Lupins") Already argued about in Ep. 13, the Treaty ended the Thirty Years' War, and did cede significant northern lands to Sweden.

"**trencherman**"—("Off-Licence") A preparer or purveyor of food. Sir Philip Sidney (Ep. 36) uses the term in *Arcadia* (1586).

TV4—("*TV4 or Not TV4* Discussion") There never has been, technically, a TV4 in Britain. The third and fourth BBC television channels (by number) wouldn't appear until 2002-2003. The proliferation of commercial channels via the Independent Television Authority was active during this period, which did lead to debate concerning the need for myriad broadcast channels and those channels' sometimes spurious, commercially driven content.

"**Two say will**"—("*TV4 or Not TV4* Discussion") Again, as in the previous episode where life after death is briefly discussed, the terseness of the scene might indicate the Pythons' waning interest in writing more complex sketches, though the cleverness of the announced *Great Debate* episode being "cancelled mysteriously" is admitted, and saves the scene from the cynicism it seems to embrace.

– V –

"**Velasquez**"—("Lupins") Spanish painter Diego Velasquez (1599-1660) was a baroque artist; he highly influenced the later Impressionists. According to biographers, Velasquez was a fairly well-kept secret outside of his home country until the nineteenth century, meaning well after Dennis Moore's peasants could have demanded his work for the loo (*Gardner's*).

For the Pythons' reference, however, Velasquez work has been displayed in the National Gallery since at least 1846. The Female Peasant (Jones) may be referring to Velasquez's earlier work, as well, where depictions of "tavern scenes" and the common life abounded—just right for her "outside loo," perhaps.

"**very good about the spectacles**"—("What the Stars Foretell") A comment on the generalized nature of many newspaper-based horoscopes, which could with finessing fit any reader, as well as the willingness of horoscope readers to overlook these vagaries and embrace any accidental specificity.

– W –

What's My Line?—("*Prejudice*") BBC television game show appearing in 1951 in the UK, and which would run through 1962.

"Wiltshire"—("Off-Licence") County just east of Somerset, where Cleese was born and raised. There were a number of noted Wiltshire highwaymen, including a man known as "Biss," one William Davies, and another Thomas Boulter, who allegedly cut quite a nice figure (expensive clothes, impeccable manners, etc., not unlike Dennis). See Spraggs' *Outlaws and Highwaymen* for more.

"Wops, Krauts, Nigs . . . "—("*Prejudice*") A laundry list of insulting appellations: "Wops": Italians; "Krauts": Germans; "Nigs": blacks; "Eyeties": Italians; "Gippos": Egyptians; "Bubbles": Greeks; "Froggies": French; "Chinks": Chinese; "Yidds": Jews; "Jocks": Scots; "Polacks": Poles; "Paddies": Irish; and "Dagoes": Spanish/Portuguese. Use of such terms was still fairly common on British radio and television (especially comedies)—listen to or watch *The Goon Show*, *Benny Hill*, *Beyond the Fringe*, and *Not Only . . . But Also*, etc., for more.

"Wyngarde, Peter"—("What the Stars Foretell") Wyngarde (b. 1933; France) was appearing in the spin-off series *Jason King* in 1972, after having created the role in *Department S* (1969). His role is that of a pleasure-seeking womanizer, which may account for the Pepperpots' negative reaction to the mention of his amorous attentions.

– Y –

"Your money, your jewellery . . . "—("Lupins") Spraggs and others note that with the advent of bank checks in the later eighteenth century, the instances of wealthy travelers carrying chests of cash and goods dropped significantly, one of the reasons that highway robberies began to trail off in the same period. Moore here is covering his bases, then, asking for all manner of valuables that still might be carried on their persons.

"snuff"—Generally, powdered tobacco.

– Z –

"zodiacal signs"—("What the Stars Foretell") The mention of the "horoscopic fates" here (Aries, Taurus, Gemini, etc.) initiates one of the show's few "on the nose" thesaurus moments, even to the point of a placard descending from above to continue the list and allow audience participation. In previous sketches, including "Cheese Shop" (Ep. 33), the thesaurus structure is at least woven into the fabric of the diegetic world, but here that list element is forwarded in all its artificiality. Other listings include:

"genethliac prognostications"—The castings of nativities (fortune-telling, to some).

"mantalogical [*sic*] harbingers"—Misspelled here, a "mantologist" is one who practices divination.

"vaticinal utterances"—Utterances that are prophetic, "vatic."

"fratidical [*sic*] premonitory uttering of the mantalogical omens"—Another misspelling here, "fatidical" utterings are those that are prophetic.

Episode 38

– A –

"abandoned in 1956"—("Penguins") Australians Lew Hoad and Ken Rosewall were dominating men's international tennis in 1956. See their biographical entries below.

***"All Answers Verified By* Encyclopaedia Britannica"**—("Spot the Loony") This may be a slight, actually, since this was the era when *EB* was owned and operated by American business interests, and when the scholarly thicket of entries was consistently winnowed for the more modern reader's understanding and accessibility. In other words, these "silly" facts and identifications of loonies may be just what the American editors thought the publication needed to command a larger *paying* audience.

***animated line showing the route*—**(PSC; *2001* animation) The music Gilliam uses in this *2001: A Space Odyssey* send-up is the Scholar Canforiuno of Stuttgart singing "Lux Aeterna, New Music for Chorus" by Ligeti, followed by "The Blue Danube" by Strauss (WAC T12/1,462).

This incongruous juxtaposition isn't as unusual as it might appear, even three years after the movie's debut. After the release of Kubrick's 1968 film, fashionable handbag maker John Romain released a movie tie-in poster that featured a star-dotted backdrop; a beautiful, leather-clad, floating model clutching a modish handbag; and a small insert of a *2001* lobby title card. This particular card, however, depicts the pod (piloted by Dave Bowman) retrieving the dead body of Bowman's shipmate Frank Poole. The leaping model and the floating, spacesuited body do look similar, even ethereally beautiful, but it probably indicates the ad agency had not screened the film before choosing the image.

"Ann Sewell's *Black Beauty*"—("*Book at Bedtime*" link into "*Dad's Doctors*") Anna Sewell (1820-1878) published *Black Beauty* in 1877-1878, just before her death.

– B –

"Ben Medhui"—("*Spot the Loony*") Actually spelled Ben *Machdui*, it is the highest peak in the Cairngorms (and the second-highest in Scotland), connecting this reference right back to the *Redgauntlet* reading earlier in the episode. This is also a reference to the Himalayan theme in Ep. 31 ("Everest Climbed By Hairdressers"), though here it's a bit of a mock heroic, since Machdui is just under 4,300 feet high.

This scene was shot on the troupe's location visit to the Oban area in Scotland, where much of the exterior work for the "Walter Scott" bits, "Rival Documentaries," and "Expedition to Lake Pahoe," etc., was recorded for the third series.

***Book at Bedtime, A*—**("*A Book at Bedtime*") Title of a long-running BBC4 radio show, selected books have generally been read by well-known actors.

"Britain's timber resources"—("Rival Documentaries") According to the Royal Scottish Forest Society, forests covered only about 4 percent of Scotland during Sir Walter Scott's lifetime, which seems to be the time period being struggled over here. By 1972, when the faux documentaries are being produced, that number had risen to somewhere around 14 percent.

– C –

"common parlance"—("Kamikaze Scotsmen") Again, communication between seemingly compatible people (military men) is always a struggle in the Python world. There is the possibility that the rank and class of these individuals—one a captain, the other a sergeant major—figures in, preventing them from speaking the same language, while the lowly, suicidal Scotsman recruit can't be reached at all.

"coniferous cornicopia"—("Rival Documentaries") This verbiage harks back to Ep. 27 and "Whicker Island," where jetsetting interviewer Alan Whicker is satirized for his recognizable euphuistic language.

"Conservative and Unionist"—(PSC; "Party Political Broadcast [Choreographed]") The official name of the Conservative Party, and which stresses the significance of Ireland, Wales, and Scotland as part of the kingdom. This entire opening sketch is missing from the more recent (1999 and beyond) editions of *Flying Circus* on VHS and DVD.

Crescendo of music—("*Spot the Loony*") The intro music for *Spot the Loony* is "Opening Number" by Len Stevens (WAC T12/1,462).

"Curb inflation, save the nation"—(PSC; "Party Political Broadcast [Choreographed]") The years 1971-1972 were fairly unforgiving to British workers, with some wages rising artificially to stay ahead of "rising prices," and unemployment reaching record post-Depression numbers in January 1972. Heath's government attempted intervention by spending—that is, increasing capital expenditures in national industries to stimulate the economy via new cash and employment—but inflation figures forced businesses to hive off workers and downsize to stay competitive. This cycle kept prices high and jobs scarce.

The "wages spiral" had been lamented since at least the late 1950s, when Macmillan's Conservative government struggled with the specter of rising wages and wage demands in a time of poor economic performance, with Lord Cohen's (1900-1977) Council on Prices, Productivity and Incomes reports offering sometimes painful solutions. (See the entry for Lord Cohen in *ODNB* for more.) And according to financial statistics provided by HM's government, the inflation rate in 1972 (a little over 7 percent) was a bargain compared to the rates of 16 percent and more than 24 percent by 1974 and 1975, respectively. Again, the sagging economy played into the Opposition's hand (as it had in 1970 for the Conservatives), this time bringing Labour back into power in 1974.

Cut to film (no sound) of Edward Heath—("*Spot the Loony*") This footage is not accounted for in the WAC records.

– D –

"Dad's Pooves"—(PSC; "*Dad's Pooves*") Like the opening "Party Political Broadcast" sketch, this trailer sketch is missing completely from the latest (1999) DVD and earlier VHS versions of this episode. As it doesn't seem particularly more naughty or libelous than anything else in the third series, it may be that the scenes are missing due to a film transfer oversight. (This scene *is* included on the laser disc versions of the episodes.) One particular show—*Dad's Army*—may be the target here due to *Flying Circus* losing out to *Dad's Army* for the Light Entertainment Production award at BAFTA in 1971. The Pythons had won two special awards from BAFTA in 1970, but not in any of the usual (read: prestigious) categories.

"Dame Elsie Occluded"—(PSC; "*Spot the Loony*") The printed script lists this character as being played by Palin, but it isn't, and instead looks very much like John Hughman.

diving rugger tackle—(PSC; "Rival Documentaries") This competition between documentarists has appeared before, in Ep. 30, when documentarists Heinz Sielmann, Peter Scott, and Jacques Cousteau get into a punch-up with the Duke of York, Terence Rattigan, and the Dummy Princess Margaret over repeat fees.

The competition the Pythons could have been referring to was the struggle for primetime viewing slots not only between documentary shows, but between Light Entertainment fare and drama or documentary productions—all equally interested in the largest British viewing audience. The Pythons complained over and over again with the BBC programmers (whom they take to task in this episode) for the erratic scheduling and repeat broadcast difficulties. There are memos and letters throughout the WAC archives from the Pythons and their representation as well as responses from BBC departments in regard to programming.

– E –

"Edinburgh Castle"—("Kamikaze Scotsmen") This castle is actually Norwich Castle, in Norfolk, and the scene was shot on 9 November 1971. WAC records indicate that the keepers of Edinburgh Castle (likely the Ministry of Defence) had politely declined to allow the Pythons access for filming purposes in October 1971 (WAC T12/1,428). The exterior scenes (where the RSM [Jones] drives MacDonald [Chapman] in the lorry) were also shot around the Norfolk-area castle.

Episode 38—Recorded 18 December 1971, and broadcast 11 January 1973. The episode was recorded third in the series and broadcast twelfth, meaning there passed a very long period (about thirteen months) between its initial recording date in mid-December 1971 to its transmission in mid-January 1973.

The entire first sketch for this episode—"Party Political Broadcast for the Conservative and Union Party"—is missing from most surviving video copies of Ep. 38, as is the Wilson and Heath dancing animation that follows. Variously, compilers of the recent A&E versions of the shows (on VHS/DVD) have stated that the original prints they were provided for copying purposes were missing bits and pieces, but also that due to "rights issues" some changes had to be made.

Also appearing in this episode: (in-studio) John Hughman, Karen Burch, and Peter Kodak (Eps. 27, 29, 36, 37; *Dr. Who*) (all scheduled to appear at TC 6 for taping on 18 December 1971); Robyn Williams (Ep. 29, 32; *Jackanory*), Jeff Witherick (*Dr. Who*; *Z Cars*), Roy Pearce (Ep. 29, 33; *Dr. Who*; *Z Cars*), Kevan Morgan, David Waterman (Ep. 33; *Dr. Who*), Ron Tingley (Eps. 29, 33; *Z Cars*); (on film) Bernard Mistovski (*Colditz*), Colin Richmond (Ep. 29), Sabu Kimura (*Tenko*), Omo Aide (Ep. 29), Kock Chuan, Peter Moore, Graham Skidmore (Eps. 27-30, 36; *Dixon of Dock Green*), Peter Kodak; (in Norwich) Anne Hall; (and dancers) Arthur Sweet (*Slipper and the Rose*), Peter Walker (*Dr. Who*), David Ellen, and Christopher Robinson (WAC T12/1,462).

The complete list of music requests for this episode (many of which are identified elsewhere in these notes by their final place in the recorded show) includes the following:

Music dubbed onto film: M. Burgess "Lament for Viscount Dundee"; Orchestra de Suisse Romande, French Overtures: Orpheus, "Scenic and Romance: Desert Morning" by Cliff Johns, and "Industrial and War: Action Line" by David De Lara, and "Scenic and Romance: After Midnight" by James Harpham; Moscow PO "The Execution of Stepan Razin" by Shostakovich, and "Dramatic Background: Approaching Menace" by Neil Richardson; "I Belong to Glasgow"; ISO Pastoral Music "The Big Country" by Keith Papworth; "Locations and Comedy: Comic Giggles" by John Pearson, and "Viennese Party" by Harry Wild; Ensemble de Guivres de Paris "Fanfares de Tour les Temps Face" by Paul Dukas; "Towers and Spires: Brandle de Bourgogne" by Spencer Nakin; Scholar Canforiuno of Stuttgart "Lux Aeterna New Music for Chorus" by Ligeti, and "Blue Danube" by Strauss; (music on disc) English Chamber Orchestra "Welsh Music for Strings Fifth Movement" by Gareth Walters; Ronnie Aldrich "Silent Movie Piano Suite No. 6: Hearts and

Flowers" by Czibulka/Warren, and "Opening Number" by Len Stevens; Queens Hall Light Orchestra "Devil's Gallop"; and London Big Sound "Big City Story: Beyond the Night" by Peter Reno.

Music on records (additional): European Stage Orchestra "Pleasure Spectacle: Picnic in the Park" by Syd Dale; Das Orchester Heinz Kiessling "A La Bonheur"; London Studio Group "Looney Tunes: Pit Overture" by R. Wale, and "Luva Duck" by Peter Reno; LSO "P&C" by Elgar; "Selling Sounds: Skip Along" Barry Stoller (WAC T12/1,462).

– F –

fanfare as for historical pageant—(PSC; "*Spot the Loony*") The fanfare used is Spencer Nakin's "Brandle de Bourgogne" from "Towers and Spires" (WAC T12/1,462). Nakin's fanfares have been used before, in Ep. 29.

few bars of bagpipe music—("Kamikaze Scotsmen") The music here is M. Burgess' (most likely Pipe Major John Burgess) performance of "Lament for Viscount Dundee" (WAC T12/1,462).

"fifth state"—("Kamikaze Scotsmen") There was an approximately thirty-day training course for kamikaze pilots, and it's reported that their practiced positive attitude (including smiling) and stoicness in the face of sure death kept most pilots focused on their goal—not suicide, but the destruction of enemy materiel and personnel, and furthering of the war effort.

"Fleming, Sir Alexander"—("Penguins") Fleming's discovery of penicillin was, indeed, something of an accident, when his culture dishes became contaminated after being left out. Fleming (1881-1955) and others had been working to find anti-bacterial agents since at least the end of WWI.

"James Watt"—Scottish inventor Watt (1736-1819) didn't invent the steam engine, but did modify and improve steam power to make it more industry-friendly.

"Albert Einstein"—Einstein's (1879-1955) cleverness improved upon existing theories of Galileo and Lorentz, among others, in producing the special and general theories of relativity in the first years of the twentieth century.

"Rutherford"—Ernest Rutherford (1871-1937) first split the atom in 1919.

"Marconi"—Marconi (1874-1937) developed a practical radiotelegraph system, and would win the Nobel Prize in 1909.

A commonality exists for most of these mentioned: Einstein, Rutherford, Fleming, and Marconi were awarded Nobel Prizes for their work. (James Watt lived and worked before the institution of the Nobel Prize, but he was a Scotsman.) See Watson's *The Modern Mind* for more on most of these inventors and innovators and the ideas that shaped the world of the twentieth century. The Pythons continue to betray a fascination with and deep knowledge of the great ideas of their century, flavoring their "silly" narratives with astute cultural references and recognizable philosophic undertones.

There is also a structural unity here, the "rule of three," or a staple of the comedic monologue (and, incidentally, speech and oratory in general). The Presenter (Cleese) mentions Fleming and his accomplishments, Watt and his accomplishments, and Einstein and his accomplishments—all fairly straight ahead and even accurate—immediately followed by a comedic twist ("if he hadn't been clever"). The comic cadence is "set-up, set-up, set-up, pay-off." There is then an interstitial bridge, a pause ("All these tremendous leaps forward have been taken in the dark"), followed by the next threesome: Rutherford, Marconi, and the generalized "amazing breakthroughs"—followed by the comedic "Of course not." The same cadence is heard in Ep. 7, when the Camel Spotter (Idle) admits that he's (1) seen one yeti, (2) seen a little yeti, (3) seen a picture of a yeti, and, finally, he's (4) only heard of a yeti, and after only three, four, five, and actually seven years of spotting. This is the classic set-up and pay-off structure of the stand-up comedian, monologist, mythology, and fairy/folk tales (see Propp), memorable addresses ("Life, liberty, and the pursuit of happiness"), and, very often, Python's humor in *Flying Circus*. Even as the Pythons admittedly attempt to fly in the face of conventional comedic structures, they very often obey those time-honored tenets.

"Frontiers of Medicine"—("Penguins") This mock documentary is inspired by earlier and memorable BBC programming, including Laurens van der Post's *The Lost World of the Kalahari* (1957), which includes the author's Afrikaans-tinged voiceover narration, as well as the series *Frontiers of Science*, which appeared on the BBC in the late 1950s, and then BBC2 in the late 1960s. *Frontiers of Science* themes were primarily space- and environmentally oriented.

– G –

Gathering Storm, The—("Penguins") Once again, this is the title of the first volume of Churchill's massive WWII book project. The music under this title is "Industrial and War: Action Line" by David De Lara (WAC T12/1,462).

Gentle classical music—(PSC; "Rival Documentaries") The printed script mentions accompanying music to this section, but there is none provided in the final broadcast version of the episode.

"going from 'unemployment' through 'pensions'"—(PSC; "Party Political Broadcast [Choreographed]") This entire scene has been elided from recent broadcast and recorded versions of the episode. It wasn't until 1972 that the British Pensioners and Trade Union Action Association was formed, to organize and mobilize millions of retired trade union members into continuing political action. These voters tended to lean toward Labour and promises of full employment, higher wages, and increased pensions.

"group of mad medicos"—(PSC; "*Dad's Doctors* [Trail]") "*Dad's Doctors*" is a variation on the very popular BBC sitcom *Dad's Army* (1968-1977), which featured the exploits of the old and creaky Home Guard in London during WWII. The *Dad's* humor was often warm and broad, just the type of show for the Pythons' incongruous sexually deviant remakes.

"RAMC"—The Royal Army Medical Corps. These references may also point to the currently popular *Doctor at Large* series, contributed to by Chapman and Cleese in 1971, or even the award-winning Robert Altman film *M*A*S*H* (1970).

"Guy Mannering"—("Rival Documentaries") One of Scott's "Waverley" novels, and published anonymously in 1815.

– H –

"Heart of Midlothian"—("Rival Documentaries") *Heart of Midlothian* was not one of Scott's "Waverley" novels, but was gathered in a series called "Tales of My Landlord," and originally appeared in 1818. *Old Mortality* (1816) was part of the first series of "Tales" novels, and was set in West Scotland in the late seventeenth century. What both are "preserving," probably, is the Scottish language and way of life of the recent past.

– I –

"I can't go on with this drivel"—("Kamikaze Scotsmen") Another moment of self-consciousness, with the usually controlled and unflappable BBC announcer (Palin) actually critiquing the words he's hired to read. Earlier, in Ep. 30, BBC Announcers are reminded that they aren't to think about what they're reading ("Neurotic Announcers"). The silliness of

MacDonald's suicide attempts just following supports the announcer's assessment of the drama.

"it's so much harder with the words"—("Party Political Broadcast") In the "Colour Section" of *Private Eye*, where actual news tidbits are offered for their innate silliness, the goings-on in preparation for the Conservative Party political broadcast (probably for a 1965 by-election) were described:

> Something that seemed to sum up the election campaign was seen in a BBC studio last week.
> Mr. Heath was rehearsing for his party political broadcast. On the tele-prompter could be seen the words:
>
> I CARE DEEPLY ABOUT . . . ..
>
> The word "deeply" was underlined no less than three times. (Ingrams 132)

Again, this sketch has been left out of most recent versions of Ep. 38 on DVD or VHS, and can only be found in the printed scripts.

Ivanoe—(PSC; "*Spot The Loony*") Spelled correctly on the screen, in the printed scripts, the subtitle reads "Ivanoe," which is a misspelling of Scott's very popular historical adventure novel *Ivanhoe* (1819).

– J –

"Jacklin, Tony"—("*Spot the Loony*") Well-known British golfer (b. 1944) who's already been mentioned by two ranters—the abbatoir architect (Cleese) in Ep. 17, and the Tourist (Idle) in Ep. 31, both of whom see owning "Tony Jacklin golf clubs" as a significant and execrable British status symbol.

"Anthony Barber"—Barber (1920-2005) was the Chancellor of the Exchequer during the Heath administration, thus a Conservative and certainly a potential "loony" to the Pythons. Throughout 1972 inflation was rising dramatically in the UK, and Barber was persona non grata to many who felt the pinch of their weakening purchase power. Barber has already been mentioned (in Ep. 28) as appearing in a Ken Russell film where he, "sadly, was unable to cope," a comment on his perceived ineffectiveness at the helm of Britain's listing economic ship. Barber was much in the news in 1972, having recently reaffirmed the government's position against floating the pound. (It would be floated just four days later, 23 June 1972.)

"Edgar Allan Poe"—A noted American poet, Poe (1809-1849) is probably the only celebrity in this list of possible "loonies" who might have actually fit the appellation, given his alleged penchant for alcohol and drug abuse, his morose published work (and life), and untimely death.

"Katie Boyle"—Boyle (b. 1926) was indeed a television presenter, hosting *It's a Knockout* in 1966. Boyle would also host the *Eurovision Song Contest* in 1968, and was likely the inspiration for Idle's "Girl" character in Ep. 22 who hosts a similar international singing contest. It may well be that the Pythons pulled back on this "loony" reference to Boyle to avoid complaints from the BBC and/or attorneys representing Boyle or the various popular shows she hosted.

"Reginald Maudling"—Yet another Conservative figure. Due to a financial scandal that indirectly implicated him, Maudling (1917-1979) had resigned as Home Secretary in July 1972, before this episode was broadcast (but long after studio recording had been accomplished, in December 1971). Barber (mentioned above) had served as Financial Secretary to the Treasury under Maudling in the early 1960s.

– L –

"late Pleistocene era"—(PSC; closing link out of "*Dad's Pooves* [Trail]") Probably pulling a geological era out of the blue, the Pythons have identified this fairly recent epoch as the time when Britain's rock strata was forming. However, the earliest formations in the islands date back at least 2.7 million years (especially in Scotland). The Pleistocene epoch in Great Britain, more precisely, was a time of ice ages and glaciation.

"Limestone, Dear Limestone"—The sappy title is a play on the popular *Father, Dear Father* (1968), a Thames TV farcical comedy about a single father and his rambunctious household. The show was a star vehicle for Patrick Cargill (1918-1996), who also appeared in *The Magic Christian* and *The Frankie Howerd Show*.

Most of the UK's limestone was formed during the Jurassic period, much earlier than the Pleistocene. There are small limestone deposits in the northern area (Oban, Scotland) where the Pythons were shooting this location footage, but much larger ones to the south, especially in southern Scotland and northern England.

"Leicester . . . Gatwick"—("*Spot the Loony*") Leicester is Chapman's birthplace and is found in Leicestershire, Buxton is located in Derbyshire, and Gatwick is in Crawley, West Sussex, and is really just the name of the airport located there (and the medieval manor house in the area).

lorry emerges—(PSC; "Kamikaze Scotsmen") This lorry travels down the main road from Norwich Castle.

The swelling music underneath is "Scenic and Romance: Desert Morning" by Cliff Johns (WAC T12/1,462).

– M –

Map with an animated line—(PSC; "Kamikaze Scotsmen") Wartime documentaries and animated training films featured this type of animated map work. See the "Why We Fight" series (1943-1944), *Memphis Belle*, and Disney's *Victory Through Air Power* (both 1943) for myriad examples.

Morris Minor speeds up—(PSC; "Rival Documentaries") The music used in this chase sequence is "Devil's Gallop" played by the Queens Hall Light Orchestra (WAC T12/1,462). This chase music was also used in the wrap-up for "The Spanish Inquisition" sketch in Ep. 15, as well as a similar chase scene in Ep. 30, *"The Pantomime Horse is a Secret Agent* Film" sketch. Also, Janet (Marie Anderson) and Mystico (Jones) drive a Morris in Ep. 35.

– N –

"no time to lose"—("Kamikaze Scotsmen") The Pythons often take something very familiar—a bedtime story, a stock market report, a newscast, a colloquialism—and defamiliarize it for comedic purposes. The horror film genre, of course, performs the same type of defamiliarization, but for uncanny results (a harmless stuffed doll becomes a threat, e.g.). Additionally, just spending time examining a word or phrase serves the same purpose, detaching that phrase from its context and rendering it abstract, thus difficult to comprehend. Later, Man (Palin) will struggle greatly with this seemingly simple phrase, putting the emphasis on the wrong word, etc., and demonstrate no ability to understand how to "turn a phrase."

This entire stilted conversation will be revisited in the feature film *Life of Brian*, when Pontius Pilate (Palin) and Centurion (Cleese) attempt to discuss Brian's fate, with Centurion mishearing, but responding anyway.

The music under the animation following this sketch is from the Orchestra de Suisse Romande's album *French Overtures*, "Orpheus in the Underworld" (WAC T12/1,462).

– O –

"On the Dad's Liver Bachelors at Large"—(PSC; *"Dad's Pooves* [Trail]") Certainly a reference to another Chapman and Cleese show (where they contributed as writers), *Doctor at Large*, starring Barry Evans, and appear-

ing on London Weekend Television (LWT), followed by *Doctor in Charge* (premiering in April 1972). Only Chapman contributed material to this latter series.

– P –

"Party Political Broadcast"—(PSC; "Party Political Broadcast [Choreographed]") Broadcast time given to the major political parties prior to elections. The staginess and stiffness of the (especially) earlier broadcasts from both parties is well documented, with surviving party broadcast scripts available through the "UK Elections" site at Keele University. Some of these broadcasts featured carefully written and rehearsed scripts with trained actors, vox pops, and the party leaders themselves trying to smile through the clumsy staged events. In the lead-up to the 1970 General Election, the Conservatives created a *News at Ten*–lookalike set on which their presenters were to act, with presenters delivering the anti-Labour message like coverage of a rail disaster:

> Voice Over: Last night Mr. Heath spoke in Birmingham, one of his themes was care and compassion. And that's the theme of tonight's edition of "A Better Tomorrow."
>
> Geoffrey Johnson Smith: We're hearing a lot about care in this election. Mr. Wilson calls it compassion, and you'd think he'd invented the word. But just how much does Mr Wilson's caring count?
>
> Christopher Chataway: The fact is that today after five years of Labour government the poor are getting poorer, things are actually getting worse. Two million families are living in sub-standard conditions, yet this year fewer homes are being built than when Labour took over.
>
> G.J. Smith: As for people on pension, well Labour meant well. When they came to office, they put pensions up by four shillings in the pound.
>
> C. Chataway: The only trouble was that in the next five years prices rose faster than pensions . . . ("UK Party Election Broadcasts 1970: Conservative Party")

These in-studio portions were matched by man-on-the-street Vox Pops moments with disaffected folk on the street, and usually ended with a short address by Heath himself. The Conservatives would surprise Labour and win the 1970 General Election, largely on the basis of the electorate's hope that the ailing economy could be "fixed."

penguin pool—(PSC; "Penguins") This scene was shot at Penguin Pool, Children's Zoo, Hotham Park, on 18 October 1971, with permission received from the Bognor Regis Urban District Council (WAC T12/1,428).

"Penguins, yes penguins"—("Penguins") The affordable and attractive line of pocket-sized Penguin books (est. 1935) featuring readable titles from myriad authors and genres—titles from *Lady Chatterley's Lover* to *Gidget*—made Penguin books a national phenomenon. These color-coded (orange, green, maroon, blue) and simple books were, literally, everywhere as the Pythons grew up. In *FC*, penguins appear in as many settings—in stage shows, on TV sets, in boardrooms, and as killer creatures in bad Hollywood films. See notes to Eps. 4, 5, 22, and 23 for more.

Lastly, the celebrated case in the UK when Penguin Books was taken to court for violating the Obscene Publications Act of 1959 with the belated publication of *Lady Chatterley's Lover* brought penguins into court, literally, and forcing the name in the public consciousness.

"Phillips-Bong"—("*Dad's Pooves* [Trail]") The character Kevin Phillips-Bong (Palin) appeared in Ep. 19 as a candidate from the Slightly Silly Party, and received no votes.

"post-Impressionists"—("No Time To Lose") Toulouse-Lautrec is considered to be a member of the post-Impressionists, with notable others including Gauguin, Cezanne, Van Gogh, and Seurat. If they can be described as "lawless," it must be due to the post-Impressionists' purposeful move away from the rules of classical composition, use of color, and perspective.

– Q –

"Queen's Own"—("Kamikaze Scotsmen") Indicating that the unit or materiel belongs to the government (*OED*).

– R –

"Ratings Game, The"—(PSC; "*Dad's Pooves* [Trail]") *The Dating Game* was a very popular American game show that made its debut in 1965.

Redgauntlet—("*A Book at Bedtime*") Sir Walter Scott's 1824 novel looks at a further return to Scotland by Bonnie Prince Charlie.

Red Square—("Unexploded Scotsman") The transition music under this title and footage is Shostakovich's "The Execution of Stepan Razin" as played by the Moscow Philharmonic Orchestra (WAC T12/1,462).

"remember you're cabinet ministers"—(PSC; "Party Political Broadcast [Choreographed]") Prime Minister Heath's Cabinet included Robert Carr, Quintin Hogg, Anthony Barber (Ep. 28), Alec Douglas-Home (Ep. 30), Reginald Maudling (Eps. 12, 22, 36, etc.), Jim Prior,

Lord Carrington (Ep. 42), Margaret Thatcher (Ep. 30), and others.

"Rosewall"—("Penguins") Australian tennis player Rosewall (b. 1934) competed at the international level from the 1950s through the 1970s. What follows is another laundry list of professional tennis players first visited in the initial series, in Ep. 7, when alien blancmanges winning Wimbledon was the subject.

"Laver"—Rod Laver (b. 1938) was of the tennis generation just following Rosewall; he was also Australian, and held the number one ranking for five consecutive years.

"Charles Pasarell"—American Pasarell (b. 1944) and partner lost to Rosewall and partner in the 1969 U.S. Open.

"Dr. Peaches Bartkowicz"—American Jane Bartkowicz (b. 1949) had retired from tennis very recently, in 1971.

"Dr. Kramer"—Born in 1921 and still very much alive at the time this episode was produced, Jack Kramer was a star player and then promoter for/of international tennis.

"Dr. Lewis Hoad"—Yet another Australian tennis player, Hoad (1934-1994) and Rosewall were a very successful doubles team, and Hoad won the singles title at Wimbledon in both 1956 and 1957.

– S –

"Sapper"—("Kamikaze Scotsmen") A "sapper" is the colloquial or unofficial term for a private in the Royal Engineers (*OED*).

"Scott, Sir Walter"—("*Spot the Loony*") Noted Scot novelist (1771-1832) whose Waverley novels popularized historical fiction and especially "folk" romance fiction involving "real" Scottish families and settings. As for being "disllusioned and embittered," Scott seems to have escaped that fate, with the exception of some financial concerns that kept him writing for a living well into his retirement years.

"Charles Dickens"—Victorian novelist Dickens (1812-1870) produced all of his major works much later than Scott (his first, *The Pickwick Papers*, appeared in 1836), and his settings and characters were inseparably connected to the south and especially the city of London.

six male dancers—(PSC; "Party Political Broadcast [Choreographed]") These dancers (none pictured in the latest episode versions, however) include Arthur Sweet (*The Slipper and the Rose*), David Allen (*40 Pounds of Trouble*), Chris Robinson, and Peter Walker (*Amahl and the Night Visitors*), who also dances in Ep. 39.

sixty-six feet high penguin—("Penguins") This model as built by the BBC prop crew measured about 10 feet tall and 16 feet wide (WAC T12/1,445). The giant penguin motif was last seen in Ep. 23, "*Scott of the Antarctic.*"

"Spot the Looney"—(PSC; "*Spot the Loony*") In the printed scripts, "loony" is more often spelled "looney." On the set created for the sketch, for example, it is spelled "Looney" in flashing lights.

stock film of penguins—(PSC; "Penguins") This footage is listed as "GR 2091A Reduction Print from T/R" in the WAC records (WAC T12/1,462). Much of the stock footage used in this episode—for example, the Kremlin and the "investiture of the Prince of Wales"—is not source-identified in the WAC records.

"stop the rising unemployment at a stroke"—(PSC; "Party Political Broadcast [Choregraphed]") Part of Heath's proposed political platform for his eventual (and surprising) Conservative government win in the 1970 General Elections was a drastic upswing in the economy: "This would, at a stroke, reduce the rise in prices, increase production and reduce unemployment." This sweeping comment on the effects of reduced taxation was actually deleted from Heath's speech when delivered as part of a political party broadcast, but the line remained in the material given to the press. The line became fodder for op-ed pages and cartoonists, especially as the Heath government struggled through the economic crises of 1971 and 1972. The oft-heard joke became "At a stroke, lose your jobs," etc. See the British Cartoon Archive for these UK political cartoons.

sunlit university quad with classical pillars—(PSC; "Rival Documentaries") This shot was actually recorded way back on 12 November 1971 at Felbrigg Hall, where the exterior shot for "*Erizabeth L*" (Ep. 29) was also shot (WAC T12/1,428). The specific location is the stables and courtyard area at the extreme east of the structure.

"sunset was dying over the hills . . . "—("*A Book at Bedtime*") This is an imagined passage from an imagined Scott novel, no doubt, as it appears nowhere in *Redgauntlet* or in any of Scott's existing works. There is a similarly themed passage which the Pythons may have remembered as they wrote the sketch, from the opening paragraph of "Letter IV":

> The whole was illuminated by the beams of the low and setting sun, who showed his ruddy front, like a warrior prepared for defence, over a huge battlemented and turreted wall of crimson and black clouds, which appeared like an immense Gothic fortress, into which the lord of day was descending. His setting rays glimmered bright upon the wet surface of the sands, and the numberless pools of water by which it was covered, where

the inequality of the ground had occasioned their being left by the tide (35).

As can be seen, the imagery is very similar, but without the specifics of "Edinburgh Castle," for example. Coincidentally, the origination for this letter in the Scott novel is "Shepherd's Bush," where BBC Television Centre would be built some 136 years later.

– T –

tennis courts in the background—(PSC; "BBC Programme Planners") These tennis court scenes were shot in Salt Hill Park, Slough (WAC T12/1,428).

"That's where you'll get the balloons and the ticker tape, Chris"—(PSC; "Party Political Broadcast [Choreographed]") The "Chris" mentioned by the Choreographer (Idle) is likely to refer to Chris Chataway (b. 1931), a presenter on *Panorama* and *ITV News* and who appeared in Conservative Party Political Broadcasts leading up to the 1970 General Election.

"Toulouse"—("No Time To Lose") Larger city (population of about 475,000 in 1968) located in southwest France.

"Toulouse-Lautrec"—Noted French painter, the diminutive Toulouse-Lautrec (1864-1901) has already been mentioned (and spoofed, riding a tricycle while painting) in Ep. 1. His favorite subjects were the "real" people in the lower-class Montmartre section of Paris, and especially the theatres and brothels.

tragic, heart-rending music—(PSC; "No Time to Lose") This is Ronnie Aldrich's (1916-1993) "Silent Movie Piano Suite No. 6: Hearts and Flowers" by Czibulka/Warren (WAC T12/1,462).

"trans at eight, so nobody be late"—(PSC; "Party Political Broadcast [Choreographed]") Once again, the sing-song delivery of a gay male is the "type" identifier, along with the dance and "luv" references. "Trans" is the diminution of "transmission," though it may not be accidental that it also bears sexual connotations.

– U –

Unexploded Scotsman—("Unexploded Scotsman") There were thousands of unexploded bombs—known as "UXB"—left in and under England after WWII, and hundreds remain under London homes and buildings today, untouched and undetonated.

The music under the defusing of the Scotsman is Neil Richardson's "Dramatic Background: Approaching

Menace," which was also used by the popular BBC quiz show *Mastermind* (1972-).

"Up the Palace"—(PSC; *"Dad's Pooves* [Trail]") *Carry On . . . Up the Khyber* (1968) and *Carry On . . . Up the Jungle* (1970) were part of a series of slapstick, Empire-bashing film comedies starring Frankie Howerd, who also later starred in the popular *Up Pompei!!* television series for the BBC. The Pythons, of course, quite easily connect these ribald, pratfall-rich sources with the investiture of Charles as the Prince of Wales (by his mother, the Queen), accomplished in July 1969, just as the first series of *FC* was being cobbled together.

– V –

"Very good sergeant major"—("No Time To Lose") This structure is a revisitation of the "Being Hit on the Head Lessons" section from Ep. 29, "Argument Clinic." The repetitiveness of the writing and structure of the show is what put Cleese off as early as midway through the second series (see Morgan [1999].)

Very impressive stirring music—(*"Spot the Loony"*) The music used in the first part of the sequence is Keith Papworth's "The Big Country," from De Wolfe Music (WAC T12/1,462). This same music will also be used later in the feature film *Holy Grail*. Budgetary constraints precluded hiring a composer, and the fallback—paying very reasonable one-use licensing fees for program music—had worked very well for *FC* (and myriad BBC shows).

The music changes to "Locations and Comedy: Comic Giggles" by John Pearson (WAC T12/1,462).

Voice Over—(PSC; "Kamikaze Scotsmen") The printed script lists this as being voiced by Palin, but it clearly is not Palin in each speech. The WAC records don't indicate directly who took the role in the "conditions of extreme secrecy" speech, but it may have been (actual Scotsmen) director Ian MacNaughton or even cameraman James Balfour.

– W –

"What makes these young Scotsmen so keen to kill themselves?"—("Kamikaze Scotsmen") Yet another swipe at the easy targets to the north (and once again avoiding similar attacks on the Irish, for example), the typical young Scot, it seems, will fall prey to the British military's recruiting drives that actually do mention sports and fun as part of service. The good money quote, of course, is silly in that the dead Scotsmen won't be spending his paycheck anyway.

But lack of jobs could have also played a significant part in this willingness to join the military. In January 1972 *International Socialism* announced that unemployment in Great Britain and Ireland had exceeded one million, and in Scotland, unemployment among men stood at more than 9 percent in that same year, second only to Northern Ireland (*International Socialism* 51 [April-June 1972]: 31). Suicide rates in Scotland were also increasing rapidly during this period, and would continue to rise into the 1980s, according to NHS figures.

– Y –

"Yes excellent"—("No Time To Lose") The Consultant (Idle) is kneeling away from Man (Palin) and everything else, indicating he's about to have the sixteen-ton weight dropped on him, but there is a cutaway before the weight drops. This was either cut out during the editing for the show or, more likely, did not make the transfer cut when the latest DVDs were being produced. The opening scene and following animated link also suffered the same fate, disappearing before transfer to DVD.

Episode 39: "Grandstand"

– A –

"Are you the man from Curry's?"—("New Brain From Curry's") The Cleese character is wearing a hat with a very prominent tag that reads "L.H. Nathan." L.H. Nathan was actually a costumier who had recently costumed for the film *Carry On Henry* (1971) and *The Lion in Winter* (1968).

Around the World in 80 Days' *music*—(PSC; "David Niven's Fridge") Niven's 1956 film based on Jules Verne's novel, and scored by Victor Young (1899-1956). The Pythons do use a snippet of the popular theme from the film, but that use isn't accounted for in the WAC records for some reason.

Composer Victor Young would score this film using all sorts of recognizable musical cues—including *Rule Britannia*, *Yankee Doodle*, and *La Cucaracha*—a technique the Pythons obviously picked up on as they approached "scoring" the *Flying Circus* series.

Attenborough, Dickie—("Light Entertainment Awards") Richard Attenborough (b. 1923) is an actor, director, and producer who was busy directing *Young Winston* in 1972 (which was nominated for but lost the Academy Award). His 1969 film *Oh! What a Lovely War* had been nominated for a BAFTA award in 1970. In 1972, Attenborough's co-star in *10 Rillington Place*, John Hurt, had been nominated for a best supporting actor BAFTA, while Attenborough wasn't, even though he was the "star" of the film. Dustin Hoffman (*Little Big Man*), Dirk Bogarde (*Death in Venice*), Albert Finney (*Gumshoe*), and Peter Finch (eventual winner, for *Sunday, Bloody Sunday*) had been the best actor nominees that year.

Attenborough is earlier lampooned, also by Idle, in his portrayal of the multiple murderer in Ep. 27.

audience standing in a rapturous applause—(PSC; "Dickie Attenborough") The film stock of the applauding audience is EMI's "Theatre Audience" (WAC T12/1,461).

awful continuity music—(PSC; "*Light Entertainment Awards*") This canned music is "Aces to Open" by Syd Dale (WAC T12/1,461).

– B –

"Best Foreign Film Director"—("David Niven's Fridge") As the BAFTA awards were earmarked for British performers and performances, there were no foreign film categories.

The winner of the "Best Foreign Language" film award in the 1972 Academy Awards was Vittorio de Sica's *The Garden of the Finzi-Continis* (1970). The same award in 1971 was also collected by an Italian film, though not directed by Pier Pasolini, while Costa Gavras' *Z* (1969) took the award the year before.

Bough, Frank—(link out of "International Wife-Swapping") Frank Bough (b. 1933) presented *Grandstand* (1958), *Sportsnight* (1968), and *Nationwide* (1969), among others. Bough was depicted earlier, also by Palin, in Ep. 35, presenting "The Olympic Hide and Seek Final."

"Boycott, Geoff"—("Pasolini's Film *The Third Test Match*") Boycott (b. 1940) was a Yorkshire and English cricket player who went on to become a cricket broadcaster. According to cricinfoengland.com, Boycott's Test batting average (for his career) stands at 47.72.

"Fred Titmus"—Another cricketer, Titmus (b. 1932) was a cricketer and footballer. Titmus played for England, and in 1964 batted with Boycott against Australia in Nottinghamshire, which is probably the match the Pythons are referencing.

"Ray Illingworth"—Born in 1932, Illingworth played for Yorkshire, Leicestershire, and England, and was the English national cricket team captain during this period. (See cricinfo.com and *Wisden* for much more.)

British Showbiz Awards—("*Light Entertainment Awards*") On 4 March 1971 the "British Screen Awards: A Gala Night for Television and Film" were held in the Royal Albert Hall, and hosted by Richard Attenborough. This show was broadcast on BBC1. On 23 April 1972 Attenborough hosted the "British Screen Awards," also know as the "Society of Film and Television Arts Awards," also at the Royal Albert Hall. These awards actually were aired on Thames Television, for ITV.

– C –

"Come Wife-Swapping—North West v the South East"—(link out of "International Wife-Swapping") Spoofing the *Come Dancing* ballroom dance show that made its debut on the BBC in 1949. Regions of England competed against each other. *Come Dancing* was presented by Peter West and Brian Johnston, among others. This long-running and popular interregional competition show has already been mentioned in the "Test Match" sketch in Ep. 20.

Incidentally, the title "Come Wife-Swapping" is misspelled on screen, being printed as "Wife-Swopping."

Cotton, Bill—("Light Entertainment Awards") Born in 1928, Cotton was the head of BBC Light Entertainment and is credited with giving Cleese and the Pythons a shot at a new BBC show in 1969.

Cotton appears in the WAC archives for *Flying Circus*, but only for his responses to some of the show's lapses in "good taste," as well as fielding memos from agents asking/demanding more money and better time slots for their clients (the Pythons, severally).

"Curry's"—("New Brain From Curry's") Currys was an electrical appliance store chain in the UK, with stores conveniently close to the Pythons in Uxbridge, Staines, Harrow, Pinner, Ruislip, and the nearest located in Southall.

– D –

"Dirty Vicar Sketch"—("The Dirty Vicar Sketch") This set-up may be a poke at BAFTA awarding *The Benny Hill Show*—flatulence, jiggling breasts, and "wink-wink" jokes—with the Light Entertainment Award in 1972 for the best comedy program *and* best comedy script.

Also, *Jude the Obscure* (based on the Hardy novel) appeared on the BBC in 1971, with the requisite setting (Victorian) and characters (including a "Chivers" and a vicar) for the Pythons to have borrowed. The serialized book was greeted with much public denunciation due to its "libertine" and sexualized characters, something not lost on the Pythons as they created their Vicar character.

"Doncaster"—("Wife-Swapping") Doncaster was one of the sites for ITV's race coverage of the *ITV Seven*, while Cheltenham was actually a BBC-covered event for the more affluent horse racers (see Aylett).

"dose of clap"—("The Oscar Wilde Sketch") The term "clap" has been in common (albeit vulgar) parlance since the late sixteenth century, at least. The widespread presence and virulence of venereal diseases in the UK, and especially larger cities, had been reported and fretted over for generations. The numerous Contagious Disease Acts enacted, re-enacted, reinforced, and reinvigorated in the nineteenth century alone attests to an almost epidemic infection rate in the crowded metropolis. Hundreds of professional books and articles were published in the UK and on the Continent on the subject, and the ravages of syphilis became the stock-in-trade of many dramatists and literary types, including Voltaire, Shakespeare, Swift, Hogarth, and Charlotte Brontë, and hundreds of lesser scribes and broadside balladeers. The royal hospital St. Bartholomew's (where Chapman had worked) was a well-known venereal disease treatment facility through much of preceding two hundred years.

– E –

Episode 39—This episode was recorded on 18 May 1972, and first broadcast 18 January 1973. It was the twelfth episode recorded and was broadcast thirteenth, and was Cleese's last official (broadcast) episode as a full member of the troupe. His written contributions would continue into the abbreviated fourth series. He is even scheduled to appear in Ep. 42, but does not, with Douglas Adams appearing in his place.

The assorted extras and walk-ons appearing in this episode include: Giovanna de Domenici, Gillian Phelps (Eps. 12, 17, 32), Annetta Bell (*Microbes and Men*), Jill Shirley, Cathy Holland, Alison McGuire (*Dial M For Murder*), Antonia McCarthy, Jack Fulton, Barry Ashton (*Dr. Who*), Roy De Wynters, Richard Kirk, Colin Thomas (*Dr. Who*), Jenifer Nicholas, Laurel Brown (Ep. 35), Emmett Hennessey (Ep. 35; *Z Cars*; *Softly Softly*), Clive Rogers (Ep. 30; *Z Cars*) (WAC T12/1,461).

– F –

"five-and-a-half"—("New Brain From Curry's") This reflexive moment connects the audience back to the obviously remembered and popular (they applaud and laugh) moments in Ep. 31, the "Our Eamonn" sketch, when characters answering the phone have to give their shoe sizes in a string of "yes" answers. Other reflexivities—Spiny Norman, Cardinal Ximinez, the Nudge Nudge Man, Richard Baker—continue to erase boundaries between episodes and create a sort of everpresent in the *Flying Circus* world.

four screens of naughty activity—(PSC; link out of "International Wife-Swapping") The *Grandstand* titles did feature a similar four corners effect, but with different sports depicted in each section.

"friends of the society"—("*Light Entertainment Awards*") Meaning the "Society of Film and Television Arts" established in 1958.

– G –

"Graham Chapman and Mr. Sherlock"—("Credits of the Year") David Sherlock is acknowledged here as Chapman's partner, or spouse. Sherlock was a writer for *Doctor in the House* (1973) and *Doctor in Charge* (1969), and has spoken for Chapman in Python-related interviews since Chapman's death in 1989.

Grandstand—(introductory titles) *Grandstand* was a popular BBC sports show that made its debut in 1958, and was hosted by Frank Bough and David Coleman, among many others.

– H –

Hamilton, David—(PSC; "Thames TV Introduction") Hamilton (b. 1939) was a Thames TV announcer, specifically for ABC Weekend Television (ATV), the broadcast organization awarded a license by the government to conduct weekend programming in London beginning in 1956. This same license was given over to London Weekend Television (fronted by David Frost) in 1968. Hamilton also announced for the popular *Top of the Pops*, and would have been a very familiar face to Pythons' studio and home audience.

hansom cabs—(PSC; "*Light Entertainment Awards*") This film stock is from the British Movietone News Library (WAC T12/1,461).

"he has sent his fridge"—("David Niven's Fridge") Just two months later, in March 1973, Hollywood icon

Marlon Brando would send an actress dressed as an American Indian to reject his Academy Award for Best Actor.

HRH The Dummy Princess Margaret—("*Light Entertainment Awards*") At the 1971 "British Screen Awards: A Gala Night for Television and Film" show, Princess Anne (b. 1950) actually served as the royal guest, not Margaret. This is the third episode where Margaret has appeared in this "pantomimetic" form.

There is no indication in the WAC records that either the princess or the royal family officially or unofficially complained about these continuing, unflattering references to the Queen's younger sister. Perhaps Margaret's more public (and sometimes profligate) lifestyle made such barbs inevitable, and the royal family and equerry took them as unavoidable.

– I –

"I never said that"—("The Oscar Wilde Sketch") The friendship and competition between Wilde and Whistler is attested to in each man's own words from the period, as well as in many incidents recorded by friends and associates. Desmond McCarthy (a member of the Bloomsbury Group) notes that Wilde did indeed host and attend the type of socially and artistically elevated parties as depicted by the Pythons, and that Wilde's goal wasn't ridicule or scorn, necessarily, but to "play others off the stage" in good fun (see Nelson's *English Wits*, 50). Wilde would come to such events prepared with witticisms and bon mots; his stories and amusements were carefully crafted to lead to a witty finish, to the delight of all in attendance. In *The Whistler Journal* by E. R. and J. Pennell (1921), one such party conversation moment is recorded, with the theatricalized and rehearsed Wilde being suddenly upstaged, to Whistler's great satisfaction. From the Pennells:

> A characteristic of a still different mood and manner was a story John Alexander [an American painter, 1856-1915] used to tell. He was dining at the Walter Gays [Gay was also an American painter, 1856-1937] and Whistler was there, though at the other end of the table. Alexander was recalling another dinner some years before where he met Oscar Wilde. As usual Wilde's talk was designed to lead up to carefully prepared witticisms. In the midst of it the lady he had taken in to dinner asked, "And how did you leave the weather in London, Mr. Wilde?" and that was the end of the talk and the witticisms. Alexander had no idea that Whistler was listening or even could hear, but, at this point he heard the familiar "Ha! Ha!" and Whistler leaning over said to him, "Truly a most valuable lady!" (228; bracketed descriptions added)

It is just this type of elevated one-upsmanship that the Pythons employ in the sketch, with the target being the good-natured Prince of Wales (Jones), and Shaw (Palin) getting played off the stage.

ink all over Mr. Heath—(PSC; "*Light Entertainment Awards*") On 22 January 1972 a young woman (a native German living in London) approached PM Heath in Brussels and splattered him with ink. Heath was in Belgium to sign the accession pact (along with Ireland, Norway, and Denmark) for entry into the European Union. Political cartoonists of the day had fun with this incident for weeks afterward (see the British Cartoon Archive).

The film stock is BBC Film DO23/72/41 "Heath" ("WAC T12/1,461). The photo of the attack graced the front page of hundreds of newspapers and magazines, as well.

– J –

John Rickman type person—("International Wife-Swapping") Rickman (who died in 1997) was ITV's host for its popular racing program, *ITV Seven*, which featured seven horse races, and went on the air in 1969. The audience obviously recognizes the caricature, laughing as soon as Palin appears.

– K –

"Keighley"—(Rugby link into "Credits of the Year") Keighley and Hull Kingston Rovers played for the Yorkshire Cup, a county cup, though Keighley never won the cup. Hull K.R. won the cup in 1971-1972, defeating Castleford 11-7, after having won the Yorkshire in 1966-1967 and 1967-1968.

– L –

lady rushes across the street—("International Wife-Swapping") An accident report was filed with the BBC for this episode, according to WAC archives. Actress Antonia McCarthy fell and skinned her knee (on 13 Mar 1972) as she ran from one house to another on Aldbourne Road, Hammersmith, Greater London, where this scene was shot. After a visit to the "surgery," she returned to the set to work (WAC T12/1,428).

"latest play"—("Oscar Wilde Sketch") Wilde's *The Importance of Being Earnest* made its premiere in February 1895, to strong reviews (excepting Shaw's, coincidentally) and full houses. Unfortunately, Wilde's homosexuality was soon to be revealed, and his career took

a fairly precipitous downward spin thereafter (including a trial for sodomy and then prison).

"Light Entertainment Award"—("*Light Entertainment Awards*") In 1972, BAFTA gave its "Best Light Entertainment Performance Award" to Ronnie Corbett and Ronnie Barker of *The Two Ronnies*, with the runner-up nod going to *Benny Hill*. The "Best Light Entertainment Production Award" went to *The Benny Hill Show*. *Monty Python's Flying Circus* did not make the final nominations.

FC had been nominated twice the previous year at the same awards show. Cleese was nominated for the "Performance" award but lost out to Eric Morecambe and Ernie Wise (*The Morecambe and Wise Show*), while *FC* was nominated for the "Production" award, losing to the atavistic *Dad's Army*. This latter loss may be the reason the Pythons gleefully, deviantly skewer *Dad's Army* in the final scene of Ep. 38, "*Dad's Pooves*."

FC would finally win the award for "Best Light Entertainment Programme" in 1973. See the Internet Movie Database for a complete list of BAFTA winners and nominees.

"like a big jam doughnut"—("Oscar Wilde Sketch") Both Wilde and Shaw were well-known for aphorisms and memorable one-liners. From Wilde: "Those whom the gods love grow young" (from "A Few Maxims for the Instruction of the Over-Educated," *Saturday Review* [London, 17 November 1894]); and from Shaw: "There are no secrets better kept than the secrets everybody guesses" (from *Mrs. Warren's Profession*).

– M –

Mambo music starts its intro—(PSC; "International Wife-Swapping") The music here is from the Edmundo Ros Orchestra album *The Wedding Samba*, "Dance Again" by Ellestein (WAC T12/1,461).

"Manchester United"—(link into "Credits of the Year") Manchester United, Southampton, and Coventry are all English football teams.

man in a brown coat—(PSC; "*Light Entertainment Awards*") This is Frank Lester, who appeared as a loony in Ep. 31 (WAC T12/1,461).

"Marsh, Alec"—("International Wife-Swapping") Alec Marsh (1908-1996) was first a jockey then a horse racing official (*ODNB*). "Mrs. Alec Marsh" at this time was Marjorie Minnie Cole, Marsh's second wife. They had married in June 1972, meaning the starter here had very recently swapped his own wife for a newer model.

"Match of the Day"—(Rugby link into "Credits of the Year") A BBC2 sports show that appeared in 1964 and

broadcast football highlights. David Coleman (b. 1926), mentioned later, assumed the role of presenter in 1970.

"Mountbatten"—("Credits of the Year") Lord Mountbatten (1900-1979), also known as "Dickie," was a great-grandson of Queen Victoria and the last viceroy of India. The naming of the award here after him might be in reference to the unreleased home movie Charlie Chaplin made with the newly married Mountbattens on their honeymooon in America, titled *Nice and Friendly* (1922), or the later marital infidelities and fireworks the Mountbattens would endure. As early as 1953 many would hint at Mountbatten's allegedly homosexual flings with naval cadets (calling him "Mountbottom"), these sexual indiscretions fitting into the "Wife-Swapping" theme rather well (see Wilson's *After the Victorians*).

Music comes in—("Pasolini's Film *The Third Test Match*") This dramatic music is from Prokofiev's score for *Alexander Nevsky*, the "Battle on the Ice" (specifically the "Ice Breaks" section) as played by the Czech Symphony Orchestra (WAC T12/1,461).

"Muskie, Senator"—("New Brain From Curry's") Edmund Muskie (1914-1996) was a U.S. senator from Maine, and had run for vice president in 1968 on the Humphrey Democratic ticket, losing to Nixon and Agnew. During the contentious primaries for the 1972 Democratic Party presidential nominations, Muskie was perceived as crying in an address to the media, and this may have prompted the Pythons to ratchet up the Attenborough "waterworks" as seen in this episode.

– N –

"Niven, David"—("*Light Entertainment Awards*") Actor Niven (1910-1983) had appeared most recently in *The Statue* (1971), in which Cleese also makes a brief appearance.

"np"—("New Brain From Curry's") "Old pence" and "new pence" ("op" and "np") indicate the pre- and post-decimalization valuation of the penny in the UK.

– O –

"Old Sketch Written Before Decimalisation"—("New Brain From Curry's") In 1971 the UK adopted the system where the pound was divided into one hundred equal parts, as opposed to the pound being earlier divided into twenty shillings, and each shilling then divided into twelve pence. This Labour-spawned

but Tory-managed changeover was such a momentous event that a mass advertising campaign was created by the government, including memorable radio and TV spots. One such announcement offers a shouting Cockney hawker-type followed by a musical jingle:

> *Jingling sound of a new penny dropped on a counter.*
> Hawker (*shouting*): The new penny! It's lighter than the old penny, it's smaller, and it's worth over twice as much!
> *Then a jaunty piano and male choir chime in*:
> Singers: One pound is a hundred new pennies,
> A hundred new pence to the pound.
> One pound is a hundred new pennies,
> A hundred new pence to the pound. (*Eyewitness: 1970-79*, "General Election, 18 June 1970")

Significantly, this mention also points up the increasing delay between the team's writing of the show and the eventual production. For the third series, writing would have been under way in the fall of 1971, with studio recording beginning in December 1971. Broadcasting these episodes for the first time wouldn't be complete until January 1973, eighteen months after decimalization.

"only thing worse than being talked about"—("Oscar Wilde Sketch") A quote actually attributed to Wilde.

– P –

"Pasolini, Peir Paolo"—("*Light Entertainment Awards*") Italian New Wave film director Pasolini (1922-1975) had recently directed *Teorem* (1968), *Porcile* (1969), and *The Decameron* (1971), all "experimental" in their approaches to classical filmmaking. Pasolini may have faced this kind of interpretive scrutiny as he created his version of an English treasure, Chaucer's *The Canterbury Tales* in 1972, where he would drift away from Chaucer with his own written material and characterizations.

The Third Test Match sketch is probably satirizing Pasolini's raucous *Il Decameron* (1971), but there are also images (tight close-ups, crash zooms, face offs) borrowed from at least two other Pasolini films, *Oedipus Rex* (1967) and his most rcent, *Canterbury Tales* (1972). It's abundantly clear, for example, that at least some of the Pythons had watched Pasolini's Oedipus adaptation before embarking on the Holy Grail film project.

paying him with invisible money—("New Brain From Curry's") This "pretending" is a fairly new development in the show, where a bit of "business" in a sketch is feigned as opposed to enacted. It could be said that the Pythons are less reliant on fastidiousness when it comes to use of props and common exchanges because they're tiring of the show itself, but it's also arguable that the show is becoming less reliant on normal, accepted theatrical conventions, and edging further into television's avant garde. But the dumb show is hodge podge—just moments before when Mrs. Zambesi is asked to sign the severed leg, she takes a pencil and attempts to do so. She (Chapman) accidentally drops the pencil, then bothers to pick it up and complete the signature, so the skirting of theatrical convention hasn't been completely embraced by (all of) the Pythons.

photo of Picadilly Circus—(PSC; "*Light Entertainment Awards*") The swelling music beneath this photo and the titles of the show is from "Academy Awards: The Music of Stanley Black" by Stanley Black (WAC T12/1,461).

"Prince of Wales"—("Oscar Wilde Sketch") HRH Albert Edward was the Prince of Wales between 1841 and the death of his mother, Victoria, at the turn of the century, when he became George V. The prince was an avid patron of the arts, and he did have a social relationship with Wilde and even Whistler. The Prince and Princess of Wales, for example, took in a private tour of Whistler's etching exhibition at the Fine Art Society in 1883.

The Prince also answered to a nickname not unlike "Shaw-y"—for G.B. Shaw heard here—the Prince was called "Bertie."

– R –

"Redcar"—("International Wife-Swapping") There remains a racecourse in Redcar (in Redcar & Cleveland), off of Redcar Road.

"Richard Baker for Lemon Curry"—("*Light Entertainment Awards*") This insert appeared originally in Ep. 33, and was most likely recorded during the taping of Ep. 30 (on 11 December 1971), when Baker appears as himself and "gestures" the day's news.

"rotten old BBC"—("Thames TV Introduction") The government-funded "Auntie Beeb" was often characterized as producing dated, tired, and very "safe" programming, especially during the tenures of John Reith (1932-1939) and Ian Jacob (1952-1959), whose programming choices and management styles tended to mirror their own conservative, even didactic beliefs.

Ironically, the Pythons had only come into existence thanks to a general thaw in this corporate conservatism, when Hugh Green headed the BBC (1960-1969) and expanded the new show directions into the youth and even counterculture markets. What they are likely complaining about here is the current administration, under Charles Curran (1969-1977), which had

regressed back into more conservative and family-friendly programming in the wake of threats and bluster from Mary Whitehouse and her followers.

Lastly, this "rotten old" show so spurned by Hamilton and Thames TV, the "British Screen Awards," would the following year appear on Thames TV, and not on the BBC.

"Russell, Bertrand"—("New Brain From Curry's") Noted British philosopher and mathmetician Russell (1872-1970) was a Nobel laureate, anti-war activist, and anti-nuclear demonstrator. He is mentioned in the notes to Ep. 31, and his writings are being burned by crusading Pepperpots ("Tory Housewives") in Ep. 32.

– S –

"Shaw"—("Oscar Wilde Sketch") George Bernard Shaw (1856-1950) was an Irish playwright and wit, and younger than either Wilde or Whistler. Shaw had been one of the few critics to react negatively to Wilde's very popular 1895 play *The Importance of Being Earnest*, admitting its engaging qualities but bemoaning its lack of "humanity," but was for the most part a supporter of his fellow Irishman, even campaigning for Wilde's early release from prison and against censorship of Wilde's controversial *Salome*. Both Shaw and Wilde had written for the *Pall Mall Gazette*, developing at least a mutual respect for each others' work there (see Gordon). There seems to be no evidence for the convivial triumvirate of Whistler, Wilde, and Shaw, especially as late as 1895, when Whistler was caring for his terminally ill wife and Wilde was in the early stages of his fall from grace.

"south of Sidcup"—("New Brain From Curry's") Part of Greater London, Sidcup is in Bexley, about twelve miles from the City of London.

"split the urban Republican vote"—("New Brain From Curry's") Probably a campaign plan of both Senators Ed Muskie (mentioned moments earlier) and George McGovern, front-runners for the Democratic nomination for U.S. president in 1972. Eventually, Muskie dropped out of the race, and incumbent Richard Nixon was re-elected.

Suitable classy music—("Oscar Wilde Sketch") The music clip is from "Strauss at the Waltz" by Harry Wild (WAC T12/1,461).

– T –

Talk-back—(PSC; "Pasolini's Film *The Third Test Match*") *Talkback* was a BBC show designed to let viewers give comments on sports and BBC coverage of sport. The show was presented by Michaerl Barratt.

Thames Television logo —(PSC; "Thames TV Introduction") Thames was the weekday company serving London for ITV (commercial broadcasting) after 1968. The re-recording (for use here in the show) of the "Thames Opening Symbol" theme sparked plenty of controversy, it seems, with memos flying back and forth between various departments and the BBC legal personnel. The BBC eventually agreeed to pay the Musician's Union about £157 (WAC T12/1,462).

"the other side"—("New Brain From Curry's") Indicating that these Pepperpots still see the available television stations as they would an LP—there are only two sides, BBC1 and BBC2.

"Third Parachute Brigade Amateur Dramatic Society"—("The Oscar Wilde Sketch") The Third Parachute Brigade was a WWII-era unit that participated in the Normandy D-Day invasion on 6 June 1944.

There are literally hundreds of amateur dramatic and operatic societies in the UK, most, however, associated with municipalities. These societies did (and do) perform Wilde's repertoire. For example, the Macclesfield Amateur Dramatic Society staged a version of *The Importance of Being Earnest* in 1951-1952. The incongruous combination of a military unit and dramatic society may be a result of the well-known dramatic efforts of WWII Allied prisoners of war staging sometimes lavish performances (very often featuring cross-dressed characters). Some of these performances are recounted by participants in *Eyewitness 1940-49*, "Getting Through," with those who took woman's parts being described as often assuming feminine qualities and allurements that went with them after the camps were liberated.

– V –

vast applause—(PSC; "David Niven's Fridge") At the 1971 Academy Awards (broadcast in April 1972), Charles Chaplin (1889-1977) received a lifetime achievement award and a lengthy standing ovation. Chaplin did attend the ceremony in Los Angeles. In the previous year's Oscar ceremony, Orson Welles (1915-1985) was also given a lifetime award, but sent actor/director John Huston (1906-1987) to collect the statuette.

very patriotic music—("Dirty Vicar Sketch") This is Edward Elgar's "Enigma Variations" as played by the London Symphony Orchestra (WAC T12/1,461).

– W –

Waring, Eddie—(PSC; Rugby link into "Credits of the Year") Idle is listed in the printed script as playing Eddie Waring (1910-1986), who was earlier mentioned in the script for Eps. 1 and 13. Waring was a Rugby League commentator for many years.

West, Peter—(PSC; "International Wife-Swapping") Peter West (1920-2003) was a journalist who covered cricket, rugby, tennis, and even dancing for the BBC. West has already been mentioned along with fellow broadcaster Brian Johnston in Ep. 21.

"Whistler, James McNeill"—("The Oscar Wilde Sketch") American-born painter who spent most of his adult life in the artist colonies of London and Paris, Whistler (1834-1903) did have a much-publicized epistolary and in-person relationship with Wilde, whom many considered Whistler's disciple (including Whistler). The two allowed for the publication of their satiric and witty (and sometimes vitriolic) correspondences in *The World* in 1883 (and Wilde published art criticism in the *Pall Mall Gazette*), and it seems that by this point Whistler was already beginning to worry that his protégé was surpassing him at the forefront of modern British society and as leader of the avant garde (Anderson and Koval). The competition for the crowd's affections as shown in the *FC* sketch is a reflection of the two artist's real-life competition to be the most respected artist in Britain.

In 1895 (when this sketch is said to be staged) Whistler was spending much time in London, where his wife was terminally ill, and Wilde was on the verge of a two-year prison sentence. See entries in the *ODNB* for more on both men.

"Wife-Swapping"—("International Wife-Swapping") There is a healthy car swapping market in the UK, where interested parties swap cars rather than buying and selling them. The swapping theme was earlier broached in Ep. 28, as was the "Ford Popular" reference.

"Wife Swapping with Coleman"—(link into "Credits of the Year") Frank Bough did replace David Coleman as the host of *Grandstand* in 1968. See the "*Match of the Day*" entry for more.

Wilde, Oscar—(PSC; "The Oscar Wilde Sketch") During this fin-de-siècle period Wilde (1854-1900)—a very prominent and flamboyant British writer, aesthete, and bon viveur—lived in Paris, where he and Whistler would, indeed, hobnob and exchange witty ripostes with astonishing alacrity. By 1895, however, their mutual acrimony and personal life struggles prevented any real social or personal encounters

(Whistler's wife reportedly "loathed" Wilde)—this scene could have better been set in 1880-1883, when they were still at least mostly on speaking terms (see Anderson and Koval).

– Y –

"Yorkshire"—("Pasolini's Film *The Third Test Match*") The Yorkshire County Cricket Club featured Brian Close, Geoff Boycott, and Ray Illington during the 1960s. These are meant to be Yorkshire cricketers, hence the accents, and the references to popular professional Yorkshire cricketers.

"You will, Oscar, you will"—("The Oscar Wilde Sketch") Yet another famous riposte by Whistler (allegedly spoken c. 1888), acknowledging his friend/ foe Wilde's penchant for incorporating bits and pieces from other wits into his own repertoire. In 1886 Whistler would write to *The World*, illustrating the growing rift between him and former disciple Wilde:

What has Oscar in common with Art? except that he dines at our tables and plucks from our platters the plums for the puddings he peddles in the provinces. Oscar—the amiable, irresponsible, esurient Oscar— with no more sense of a picture than of the fit of a coat, has the courage of the opinions—of others! (qtd. in Anderson and Koval 314).

"You might even need a new brain"—("New Brain From Curry's") This was the miraculous era when heart transplants and artificial hearts, for example, had stormed the news internationally, originating in South Africa and Texas and moving into developed countries around the world. These pioneering surgeons (Barnard and Du Bakey) are mentioned in Ep. 29, "Argument Clinic."

– Z –

Zambesi—("New Brain From Curry's") The Zambezi is a river in Africa, and yet another silly name for a Python character.

Episode 40:
"The Golden Age of Ballooning"

– A –

Animation of balloons ascending—(PSC; "Montgolfier Brothers") Though not even mentioned in the printed scripts, the music for the titles here sounds to be Salieri's "La Fiera di Venezia" as performed by the Richard Bonynge English Chamber Orchestra (WAC T12/1,469).

"Annencay"—("Montgolfier Brothers") Actually "Annonay," the first Montgolfier balloon flight in 1783 was conducted just south of St. Étienne at Annonay in southwestern France. This first balloon was made of paper (the brothers were papermakers by trade), and the next flight in September 1783 carried a duck, a chicken, and a rooster as passengers. The first manned flight occurred on 21 November of that same year.

– B –

"ballcock . . . bang"—("Montgolfier Brothers") The first is an apropos plumbing reference, as it is a toilet requisite reportedly invented by Englishman Thomas Crapper much later than the Montgolfiers' flight. The latter might refer to the sound of an exploding balloon, or have a sexual context based on the later comments made by Jacques (Jones) as his fiancée hangs from the gas bag. Joseph (Idle) also follows the dictionary entry by saying, "What a position!"

"Bartlett"—("Louis XIV") It's not clear why Mr. Bartlett (played here by Peter Brett) wants to see the brothers, nor whether he is connected at all to the Glaswegian Louis, nor why the Irishman O'Toole (Chapman) has such a difficult time pronouncing what should be a fairly recognizable name. The continuity breaks in this period piece are myriad, however, and include a modern plumber who narrates (Palin), the

introduction of stage hands and projection equipment for voiceover assistance, a Scotsman (Palin again) impersonating a dead French king, etc. The last six shows of the series vary greatly in their cohesiveness and even watchability, as Cleese had long since left for greener pastures, prepping elsewhere for *Fawlty Towers* (1975-1979).

"Bartlett" is also the name of Counsel in Ep. 3, there played by Cleese.

"better things to do"—("Louis XIV") One of the concerns about a monarch such as Louis XIV was that he did attempt to rule every aspect of his kingdom, making decisions and commands without utilizing a strong network of more regional or local controlling bodies. In short, he took on too much, and the slippages (angry dukes, unhappy commoners, unsuccessful military endeavors, unfinished roads) became inevitable (*EBO*).

"Bismarck"—("Zeppelin") First chancellor of the German Empire, Bismarck (1815-1898) was a driving force behind German unification.

"bits and pieces of balloons"—("Louis XIV") After the Montgolfier brothers' successful flight, there was an explosion in balloon paraphernalia throughout France, with balloon-emblazoned crockery and figurines available in many French stores.

black and white film of Barry—("Zeppelin") The tearful piano music used behind this footage is Peter Reno's "The Poor Soul" as performed by Rose Treacher. The scene was shot near Motspur Park, with the South East Gas Holders looming in the background, on 3 October 1974 (WAC T12/1,469).

"Bo-sankway, Reginald"—(link out of "Zeppelin") Another reference to newsreader Reginald Bosanquet, who has been mentioned earlier in Eps. 20 and 26.

– C –

"canal"—("Louis XIV") In the seventeenth and eighteenth centuries the French did speculate about a canal through the isthmus in Egypt, attempting to counter the dominance of East Indian trade by the Portuguese, Dutch, and then English. The French didn't survey the area until around 1800, however. The Suez Canal—financed by France and Egypt—was finally completed in 1869. Britain, however, would come late and pick up a significant interest in the canal by 1875, culminating in an embarrassing military exercise in 1956 that essentially put the lid on Britain's world power dreams.

"Constance"—("Zeppelin") Or Konstanz, in Baden, Germany.

Cut to a throne room—("George III") The music here is from Handel's "Concerto Grosso in C Major, Alexander's Feast, First Movement (Allegro)" as performed by Granville Jones' Philomusica of London (WAC T12/1,469).

– D –

"drawing room . . . sitting room"—("Zeppelin") This type of corrective badinage (*"Drawing* room") will be revisited in *Holy Grail,* when King Arthur (Chapman) constantly says "five" and is corrected to "three."

"dukes"—("Louis XIV") The "dukes" Louis is trailing behind him are played by Frank Lester (Eps. 31, 35-37; *Jackanory*) and Bob Raymond (*FC* fourth series; *Secrets of Sex*) (WAC T12/1,469).

– E –

Edwardian photo—(PSC; "Zeppelin") These black-and-white photos were and are available in London shops and stalls. The advent of photography in the nineteenth century caught the general public's imagination quickly and many—not just the upper class—began sitting for photos. Most of the images Gilliam employs appear to be common folk sitting for dignified "picture portraits." Gilliam mentions that comedian Ronnie Barker (1929-2005) gave him a boxful of the mildly erotic photos—Gilliam called the Edwardian-era models "round and squidgy"—and the photos then begin to appear in his animations (*Gilliam on Gilliam* 41).

Episode 40—This is the first of the last six episodes recorded for the entire *Flying Circus* series, and the episodes are broadcast in the precise order of recording. The Pythons had been officially "separated" since the completion of recording for Ep. 36, which was finished 25 May 1972. The fourth series wouldn't start taping until 12 October 1974, and they were finished just five weeks later, when Ep. 45 would be recorded on 16 November 1974.

Ep. 40 "The Golden Age of Ballooning" was recorded on 12 October 1974, and broadcast on 31 October 1974. This episode is also featured on the cover of the *Radio Times* for 26 October 1974, complete with a Gilliam animation and a synopsis of the major sketches. The BBC was also making it clear both in internal memos and advertising blurbs for the final series that the shows were "similar but different" to the previous three series, especially in that there was a theme for each episode (WAC T12/1,469).

The BBC had convinced the remaining Pythons (Chapman, Gilliam, Idle, Jones, and Palin) to create a half-season schedule for 1974, but the writing was clearly on the wall. By December 1974, according to the BBC's regularly gathered ratings figures, the percentage of available audience watching *FC* on BBC2 had dropped to 8.4 percent (while competing shows on BBC1 and ITV experienced viewership increases during this same period). Many canvassed viewers commented that without Cleese the show wasn't as funny or appealing, that it had grown completely tasteless and offensive, and seemed to be reaching for shocks, not laughs (WAC T12/1,469).

Various actors brought in and dressed in period costumes for "The Golden Age of Ballooning" include the following: Reg Turner (*Z Cars*), Rory O'Connor (*Blakes 7*), Hattie Riemer (*Z Cars; The Wednesday Play*), Leslie Bryant (Ep. 25; *The Wednesday Play*), Leslie Glenroy (*Dr. Who*), Bill Lodge (*Upstairs, Downstairs*), Nicholas Kane (*The Ribald Tales of Robin Hood*), Simon Joseph (*Softly Softly*), Harry Davis (*Dixon of Dock Green*), Cecil Lloyd (*Microbes and Men*), George Lowdell (*The Saint*), John Kimberlake, Bill Earle, Jim O'Neill, Charles Rayford (*Dr. Who*), Raymond St. Clair (*Track of the Moon Beast*), Ronald Musgrove (*Z Cars*), Richard Cash, D. Southern, Les Conrad (*Softly Softly*), Annet Peters (*The Fall and Rise of Reginald Perrin*), Judy Roger, Sylvia Lane, Audrey Searle (*The Debussy Film*), Stella Conway, Mike Barrymore, and Noel Pointing (WAC T12/1,469).

– F –

"failure to buy it"—("Louis XIV") The Goons dedicated an entire show to the Big Brother–type corporation BBC forcing listeners and viewers (and actors and announcers) to watch and listen. Listen to the "1985" episode from *The Goon Show* (BBC Radio Collection).

Fanfare. Enter Louis XIV—("Louis XIV") The fanfare is from "The Fanfares" by Charles Williams (WAC T12/1,469).

"fire balloon"—("Montgolfier Brothers") The Montgolfiers' creation utilized a fire at the mouth of the balloon to inflate and lift the balloon.

"flannel"—("Montgolfier Brothers") A colloquialism for "wash cloth," the *OED* points out that it won't be until 1819 that the term appears (in English) in print.

– G –

"George-Brown, Lord"—("Party Political Broadcast") Higher-up in the Labour Party during the 1960s, George-Brown (1914-1985) had won a Labour seat in 1945 and was in the running for the party leadership before Harold Wilson came to the fore. In 1966, George-Brown became Foreign Secretary, only to lose that position in 1968, and then lose his seat completely in the Conservative-friendly 1970 General Election. It was Brown's alleged increasing dependence on alcohol that prompted *Private Eye* to coin the euphemism "tired and emotional," mostly to avoid libel or slander charges while still taking their shots at the Labour leader.

George III—("George III") This song is written by oft-contributor Neil Innes (b. 1944), who will go on to get squashed by a catapulted rabbit in *Holy Grail* and write all the songs for Idle's *Meet the Rutles* (1978) parody film. Innes was part of the Bonzo Dog Doo-Dah Band who appeared regularly on the Palin/Jones/Idle pre-Python show, *Do Not Adjust Your Set* (1967).

The historical person George III (1738-1820) was the English monarch from a German background (a Hanoverian king) who at this time (1781-1782) was losing the American colonies to independence. France had signed agreements with the upstart colonies to supply material support in the revolutionary effort, which probably accounts for the international intrigue at the heart of this episode (*ODNB*). George (Chapman) will ask the faux-Frenchman Louis (Palin) to stop this assistance as part of the balloon plan deal.

"George IV"—("George III") George IV (1762-1830) would act as regent for his father in later years, coinciding with the king's here-and-there mental stability. George III is reported to have disliked his son for his epicurean proclivities, so this mistaken identity might have bothered him even more (*ODNB*).

"Glaisher and Coxwell"—("Louis XIV") Henry Coxwell (1819-1900) and James Glaisher (1809-1903) did, in fact, reach record heights in 1862 in their balloon. See the entry for Coxwell in the *ODNB* for more.

"Glaswegian"—("Louis XIV") Louis (Palin) speaks with the accent peculiar to Glasgow, Scotland's largest city, which sits on the Clyde River. Even among the Scots, it seems that a Glaswegian accent is more "coarse" and even "shorthand" than other dialects.

"Golden Age"—("Montgolfier Brothers") Other similar titles available to the Pythons as they wrote included *The Golden Age of Comedy* (1957), and *Greece: The Golden Age* (1963), the latter narrated by Trevor Howard.

"Golden Years of Colonic Irrigation"—(link out of "Zeppelin") The music under this title card is John Reid's "Market Research" (WAC T12/1,469).

"Government has collapsed"—("Decision") This is a reference to the recent 1974 General Election that saw the Tories lose many seats (in the House of Commons) while retaining a slim lead over Labour, but not enough to form a government without coalition. When the Liberals didn't cooperate, rendering a coalition impossible, Heath and his group had to resign, bringing Wilson and Labour's return to power. Labour, however, did not enjoy anything like a mandate. (Exact figures on the change of power can be found at Keele's "UK Elections" website.) In the 1974 election, both Northern Irish and Welsh seats were won by local parties/candidates, a startling change that certainly illustrated the government's incapability "of providing any sort of unifying force," as Dividends (Chapman) asserts. The Pythons' Tory bashing continues unabated.

– H –

Hamer, Dr.—(PSC; "George III") In the printed scripts, Gilliam's butler character is named "Dr. Hamer," and there's even a textual comment on the fact that he is to look like a "period butler," and not a doctor. There was a Dr. Neil Hamer at Trinity College, Cambridge (from 1964) who may have been the inspiration for Gilliam's affected performance here, probably as coaxed by the remaining Cantab Pythons, Idle and Chapman.

health and efficiency nudist camp—("Zeppelin") *Health & Efficiency* is an international nudist magazine.

"heavier than air dirigible"—("Louis XIV") These types of balloons are typically heavier than the air around them, meaning buoyancy must be created by filling the balloon with heated air, allowing for lift. From a man so obsessed with balloons, of course, Antoinette (Cleveland) should have interpreted this remark as the ultimate compliment.

"hen"—("George III") A very familiar term, and one which wouldn't usually be used with royalty, which is probably why it's here—the impostor Louis, like the

484 Monty Python's Flying Circus

Peasant Dennis in *HG* (both played by Palin), doesn't recognize such things.

He reappears, takes a bow—(PSC; "Louis XIV") The adulation for this seemingly minor character is probably a reference to Angus Hodson, a butler character played by Gordon Jackson in *Upstairs, Downstairs* (1971-1975, LWT), one of British television's "classic" serials.

"Hollweg"—("Zeppelin") Theobald Bethmann-Hollweg (1856-1921) was German imperial chancellor before and during WWI.

– I –

"I could hardly wash"—("Montgolfier Brothers") If a washing was sought at all during the late eighteenth century, it usually included face and hands—or just those body parts not covered by thick clothing. Most people washed only when they had to, and the resulting odors would have been quite the standard. It will become clear that this entire episode does have a lavatorial bent—a plumber-narrator, bathing animation, Joseph in his towel and shower cap, etc.

This is also a traditional (by now) structure for the Pythons—introducing a serious or important historical topic or personage (the first manned balloon flight), then undercutting that seriousness by silliness or diminution (inadequate personal hygiene).

"Ik tvika nasai"—("Party Political Broadcast") This is jabberwock Norwegian, and actually structured more like a Slavic language than anything Nordic. "Good evening," for example, in Norwegian would be "God aften." The next two lines would translate something like: "De tror det merkelig at vi spør De stemme Norsk på den neste valg" and "Men betrakter fordelene." The Pythons have demonstrated abilities in French, German, and even Spanish and semaphore code in *FC*, but when it has come to Russian and now Norwegian, they have clearly attempted just the "sound" of those languages and avoided trying for any linguistic accuracy.

– K –

"kiddy-winkies"—("Zeppelin") A little-used colloquialism meaning "children," the term earlier appears in *Private Eye* in Christopher Logue's "True Stories" section, the 6 August 1965 edition (Ingrams 125).

– L –

"least talented"—("George III") Not unlike the lesser-known Marx brothers, including Zeppo (1901-1979),

who played the straight man and/or romantic lead in several of their films, and Gummo (1893-1977), who appeared in no films at all. The actual Ferdinand Zeppelin had one brother and one sister.

Lord North—(PSC; "George III") Not mentioned by name in the episode, Jones is playing Lord North (1732-1792), who was prime minister 1770-1782, and who suffered greatly (politically, personally) when the American colonies were lost.

"Louis XIV died in 1717"—("Louis XIV") French monarch (1638-1715) actually died 1 September 1715, at Versailles, thirty-five years before Joseph Montgolfier was born.

In Ep. 3, Inspector Dim (Chapman) points out that Cardinal Richelieu (Palin) has been dead since 1642—"I put it to you that you died"—making it impossible for him to be testifying as a character witness for the also-dead Harold Larch in 1969 London.

"Louis XV"—("Louis XIV") Louis XV was the great-grandson of Louis XIV, and was just five years old when he assumed the crown (under a protectorate). He would die in 1774, and his grandson would become Louis XVI, and would be the last French monarch. Louis XVI was beheaded in 1793 during the French Revolution.

– M –

"make a list"—("Zeppelin") The Pythons are by now clearly poking fun at the perceived German penchant for order and rigor—reading alphabetical listings of food items, correcting room designations, sorting out dead government men by job description, and making lists. German critic and essayist Jürgen Syberberg characterizes the perceived mania this disturbing way:

The problem is that Germans are too well organized for the messiness of liberal democracy. We attempt to organize democratic opinion, to keep the system running smoothly and efficiently. When something disrupts the system, or doesn't fit where it's supposed to, there are problems. The concentration camps also belong to this chapter of German thoroughness, of starting from basics, thinking radically, totally, absolutely, getting to the very root of things. Expressed in vulgar terms, this means German orderliness. (*NPQ* 10.1 [Winter 1993])

Men racing through the gardens—(PSC; "Louis XIV") Very faintly the Wick Scottish Dance Band can be heard (as chase/transition music) playing "Mrs. McLeod of Raasay (Reel)" (WAC T12/1,469).

"Mill on the Floss"—(link out of "Zeppelin") The music underneath this "balloonic" version of George

Eliot's novel *Mill on the Floss* (1859) is Sir Adrian Boult and the London Philharmonic Orchestra playing "Symphony No. 2 in E Flat Major" by Elgar (WAC T12/1,469).

The realism that Eliot so often employed in the depicting of characters' lives and worlds is sent up, literally, as the lovers float away gently like balloons.

"Minister for Colonies"—("Zeppelin") The "State Secretary for the Colonies" for Germany in 1908 was Bernhard Dernburg.

"Mirabeau's . . . 'assignats'"—("George III") The "assignats" (or a form of paper currency) weren't issued in France until 1789, during the period of the Revolution, or fully eight years after this sketch is said to be set. Honoré Gabriel Riqueti, Comte de Mirabeau (1749-1791) very much believed in the program, which would spiral the country into hopeless inflation by 1795 (*Mirabeau and the French Revolution* 368-70).

"Montesquieu"—("Montgolfier Brothers") A leading figure of the French Enlightenment, Montesquieu (1689-1755) forwarded the "separation of powers" theory of government, and his work was very popular in Great Britain (and America). His *Persian Letters* (1722) poked fun at Louis XIV's court, which may be why the Pythons reference both in this episode. (See the entry for Montesquieu in the *Catholic Encyclopedia* for more.) Mozart has already been mentioned in the initial *Flying Circus* episode, hosting a "famous deaths" television show, and in Ep. 21, as the father of Colin Mozart, Ratcatcher.

"Montgolfier"—("Montgolfier Brothers") Actual historical personages, the Montgolfier brothers—Joseph-Michel (1740-1810) and Jacques-Étienne (1745-1799)—are credited with developing the hot air balloon and conducting the first untethered flights.

Muybridge—(PSC; "Zeppelin") This particular photo does not appear to be a Muybridge photo. Eadweard Muybridge (1830-1904) was an early experimental photographer. Gilliam has used Muybridge's series photography before, however, earlier in this episode (as the Montgolfier brothers wash, supposedly), and even earlier in Ep. 36.

– N –

"Necker"—("George III") Necker (1732-1804) was a Swiss banker and a director general of finance (1771–1781, 1788–1789, 1789–1790) under Louis XVI. The "wee bit of trouble" Louis mentions probably refers to Necker's 1781 financial state-of-the-kingdom report that painted a very positive picture of France's fiscal health, and which would eventually cost him his job (*Catholic Encyclopedia*). He would resign finally in 1790, leaving the country to the devices of Mirabeau and the "assignats" (see above).

"Norwegian Party"—(PSC; "Party Political Broadcast") The printed script notes that Idle is essentially ad-libbing here, and that his "Norwegian" should be "earnestly" delivered as the subtitles pass. This jabberwock approach is used by Idle earlier, in "The Cycling Tour" episode (Ep. 34), when he plays a Soviet compère telling a joke in faux-Russian.

"not a balloon"—("Zeppelin") Zeppelin was, from the beginning when he observed American balloon reconnaissance activities during the Civil War, determined to create balloons that could be guided, or "airships."

"not supposed to go mad until 1800"—("George III") Actually, George III was completely overtaken by mental disease in 1810, after severe breakdowns in 1788 (when he tried to kill his son, the Prince of Wales), 1801, and 1804 (*ODNB*).

– O –

"orangery"—("Louis XIV") A room in many of the more impressive manors in both France and England where orange (or citrus) trees were grown—the glassed-in rooms are kept warmer and very well-lit. Orangeries can be found at both Kew and Kensington.

– P –

palm court orchestra playing—(PSC; "Zeppelin") This small group is pretending to play the Palm Court Trio's version of "On Wings of Song" by Mendelssohn (WAC T12/1,469).

"Party Political Broadcast"—("Party Political Broadcast") Air time given over to the leading political parties prior to elections. Python lampoons these regular broadcasts in Eps. 12, 32, 38, and 45 (latterly, the Labour candidate performing martial arts in a hallway). See entries in those episodes for more.

Pleasant elegant eighteenth-century music—(PSC; "Montgolfier Brothers") This is a snippet of organ music, specifically Corette's "Concerto in D Minor" performed by the Helmuth Rilling Wurttemberg Chamber Orchestra (WAC T12/1,469).

plumber—("Montgolfier Brothers") A Plumber (Palin) relates the story of the Montgolfiers, and a plumber is included in every scene at the Montgolfiers' residence, working away in the near background. This privileged view is much like the evidence of memorialized versions of some of Shakespeare's works, wherein all the lines of a minor character like Marcellus (*Hamlet*) are included and even added upon, while other areas/characters are given significantly less attention. Scholars can conclude, then, that a particular version could have been provided by an actor who had played Marcellus at one point (or been recreated from a particular prompt book), thus the favoritism toward his own lines and his elevated significance in the memorialized version. (See *The Oxford Shakespeare: Histories with the Poems and Sonnets* xxvi.) The Plumber's version of the Montgolfier story, then, might understandably include otherwise insignificant details about washing and hygiene.

The plumber working in the background in most of the scenes (excepting the initial scene where Palin narrates) is played by Stenson Falke (*Dr. Who*) (WAC T12/1,469).

"Portland, Duke of"—("George III") The Duke of Portland (1738-1809) was the British prime minister from 2 April to 19 December 1783, and again 1807-1809.

"published by the BBC"—("Louis XIV") The BBC did produce (or provide) accompanying texts to many of its documentary-type programs, with representative titles including *Colour in Britain* (1965), from a radio feature of the same name, and *Europe and the Indies: The Era of the Companies, 1600-1824* (1970), from a multipart television serial.

– R –

racing through the gardens—("Montgolfier Brothers") These chase scenes are shot at Bicton Gardens, East Budleigh, Devon on 11 September 1974 (WAC T12/1,469). Much of the location work for the abbreviated fourth series was accomplished in Devon.

"railway between the towns"—("Louis XIV") Serious talk about railway-building in India didn't begin until the 1840s, and the Lahore sections of railway were constructed in the 1860s, well after this sketch is allegedly set.

"Reginald Bo-sankway"—("Zeppelin") Reginald Bosanquet (1932-1984) was an ITV newsreader and the BBC's *News at Ten* anchor. Bosanquet has already been mentioned in Ep. 20, and he appears in Ep. 26, standing to attention for the Queen.

– S –

"salle à manger"—("Louis XIV") A dining hall. Perhaps because the Montgolfiers' butler is Irish

("O'Toole"), they feel they must translate from French to English for him.

"seventeen square feet of body area"—("Montgolfier Brothers") Since most adults can claim about twenty square feet of skin area, Joseph and Jacques are *still* missing some vital areas in their washing.

"shit"—("Louis XIV") The Pythons generally used veiled vulgarisms, rather than straightforward swearing, but the swearing and violence does increase during the third and especially fourth seasons of *FC*. They have used "merde" in previous episodes, which might have been expected from the Frenchman Joseph, though their butler is obviously an Irishman ("O'Toole") who for some reason struggles with the pronunciation of British-type names like "Bartlett." They have also used "excrement" in Eps. 17 and 19.

"six months later"—("George III") It's 1781 now, so "six months later" is actually two years earlier than the historical Montgolfier setting. George (1738-1820) was a Hanoverian king who did suffer periods of dementia or "madness" that forced him from the throne for months at a time. In 1781, George's forces in America were losing, and suing for peace would begin the following year.

"sixteen years of work"—("Louis XIV") The Montgolfiers had been working on balloons since 1782, or about one year.

The question of France being "in the grip of a Glaswegian monarch" is relevant when Louis XIV's Catholicism (or anti-Protestantism, more precisely) allied him with the Scottish Stuarts and their claim to the English throne against William of Orange, who would become William III. So Louis could have been known as a "Glaswegian (French) monarch" more readily than a "Londoner (French) monarch," certainly.

"smartarse"—("Louis XIV") A would-be clever person, a know-it-all, and one who talks back (*OED*).

some men—("Montgolfier Brothers") These men who enter carrying film projection equipment are meant to look like black-draped stagehands from the modern theatre, but they certainly clash with the otherwise period settings and dress. These two actors are Mike Britton (variously spelled "Bridon," "Briton," or "Brydon" in WAC records; *Secrets of Sex*) and David Wilde (WAC T12/1,469).

"spotty sassenach pillock"—("George III") Literally, the insult means a pimpled/blemished Saxon fool (or even "dick"), according to the *OED*. Not unlike Shakespeare's often-used three-part insults: "damned tripe-visaged rascal" (*Henry IV*, part 2, 5.4); "scurvy jack-dog priest" (*Merry Wives of Windsor* 2.3); or "foul indigested lump" (*Henry VI*, part 2, 5.1).

"St. James Palace"—("George III") The official residence of the English monarch, and was built by Henry VIII, but hasn't been lived in as such since the nineteenth century.

"suppositories"—(link out of "Zeppelin") This simply continues the lavatorial (and now excretory) emphasis of the episode, which will be once again reinforced when the "Golden Years of Colonic Irrigation" title card is presented later.

"Surely he gave you some money for it"—("Zeppelin") Graf Zeppelin seems to have raised money for his designs and experiments by both private donation and government contracts, mostly for possible military applications of the new airships. (See De Syon.)

– T –

tam o'shanters—("George III") The Scotsmen posing as the French court are wearing the colorful Scottish caps more often worn by young Scots *women* in the nineteenth century, according to the *OED*. Like the Interviewer (Cleese) slowly becoming a pirate in Ep. 32, the Glaswegian Louis is looking more and more like a Scotsman as the episode moves along.

"thousand francs"—("Louis XIV") The Montgolfier brothers were essentially self-funded, their family owning a very prosperous paper factory. They did benefit from their close relationship with the French government as an industry of rather advanced technology.

Three black ladies—(PSC; "George III") These performers are Sue Glover, Rosetta Hightower, and Joanna Williams (WAC T12/1,469). Glover would release a handful of solo albums in the mid-1970s in the UK, including *Solo* in 1976; Hightower had been a member of the Ronettes-like The Orlons until 1968, according to the *All Music Guide*; and Joanna (perhaps "Joanne") Williams was a studio background singer who participated in Roger Glover projects, including "Butterfly Ball" in 1974. Dr. Hamer (Gilliam) actually introduces them as "The Ronettes," a 1960s girl group singing rock and roll and the blues, specifically the Motown sound. The real Ronettes were Veronica Bennett, Estelle Bennett, and Nedra Talley.

time-honoured Glaswegian way—("Louis XIV") This headbutt has become known as a "Glasgow kiss."

"Tirpitz"—("Zeppelin") Alfred von Tirpitz (1849-1930) was a German admiral and chief builder of the German Navy prior to WWI. Tirpitz and Hollweg (thrown out next) are given significant historical culpability for World War I and its horrors, which may account for their early (and fatal) exit from the airship.

"Titty"—("George III") There is a character named Titty in Englishman Arthur Ransome's book series "Swallows and Amazons," about siblings' adventures on school breaks in the wilds of Britain. The book the Reader (Idle) is reading from appears to be a "Little Golden" title (est. 1942).

"Trondheim"—("Party Political Broadcast" link out of "Zeppelin") Third-largest city in Norway, seat of Sør-Trøndelag fylke (county) and situated in central Norway. Trondheim has already been mentioned in Ep. 25 as the "Spam" Vikings' launch point for coastal invasions.

two naked men boxing—("Montgolfier Brothers") These images seem to be either Eadweard Muybridge photos, perhaps the "Athletes Boxing" series from 1879, or modified images from one of Edison's films, à la "Glenroy Brothers: Comic Boxing," c. 1894.

– V –

"verified by *Encyclopaedia Britannica*"—("George III") The Pythons have, in fact, leaned on reference texts in the past, nearly quoting historian Trevelyan in the "Dennis Moore" episode (Ep. 37), after mentioning him by name in Ep. 26. The "facts" found in the game show *Spot the Loony* (Ep. 38) were also allegedly verified by the *American*-owned and controlled EB.

Victorian couple in the countryside—(PSC; "Zeppelin") The music beneath this ballooning couple is from Sir Adrian Boult and the London Philharmonic Orchestra playing "Symphony No. 2 in E Flat Major" by Edward Elgar.

"Von Bülow"—("Zeppelin") Bernhard von Bülow (1849-1929) was the German Imperial Chancellor and Prussian Prime Minister under William II, and was probably elsewhere dealing with the international reputation of his Emperor and country, and not with Zeppelin. His is a recognizable old German name, certainly, hence its inclusion.

"Von Moltke"—("Zeppelin") Probably referring to the younger von Moltke (1848-1916), who led the German army into WWI. *Karl* von Müller may be the naval officer who was captured by the British and interned in a Nottinghamshire prison camp for the duration of the war. Most of the other names listed (Reichner, Von Graunberg, Zimmerman, Kimpte) don't appear to be anything other than part of the usual Python laundry listing of historical and made-up names.

– W –

"waggle"—("Louis XIV") One of the initial problems with the Montgolfier balloons was their instability—test flights indicated that human occupants ("aeronauts") might incur serious injury on even low-altitude ascents, so animals were sent up first. By the time the United States and USSR had achieved extraterrestrial capability in the 1950s and 1960s, it was a dog and then a monkey making the initial space flights, and not humans.

"Will Louis XIV get away with . . . "—("Louis XIV") This is structured much like a Saturday matinee serial (*Buck Rogers, The Perils of Pauline*, both 1934) where a cliffhanger ending keeps the audience waiting for the next exciting episode. This cliffhanger structure and the "burning questions" trope ("Is France really in the grip . . . ") were also played up on the long-running *Rocky & Bullwinkle* cartoon series (1959-1973) produced by Bill Scott and Jay Ward for ABC and NBC.

Here also the artifice of using both videotape and film in a continuing narrative is broached. In most cases, the Pythons just have done what other shows also did—cut between tape and film when the characters/story head out of doors, without comment. Most UK audience members would have by this time become quite accustomed to the transition, which may seem quite jarring to modern audiences. Here the film projection equipment is made manifest (the man-behind-the-curtain-is-the-wizard scenario), drawing attention to the filmed images as separate and distinct from the videotaped images. Earlier, characters have discussed filmed images—Ep. 8, stopping a filmed sketch; Ep. 15, as a "link"; Ep. 18 when characters are "trapped" on film; and Ep. 29, when film is capturing the explorer's last words. The introduction of the projector and screen as such an artificial and theatricalized linking device was earlier seen in the "Silly Walks" sketch, though in that instance the character is merely illustrating a referenced point—that other silly walks exist—and the original narrative is rejoined when the film stops.

– Y –

"year 1908 was a year of triumph"—("Zeppelin") The first successful flight was in 1900, though in 1908 a crash of one of the airships created a rush to donate funds to continue Graf Zeppelin's work, rendering an ironic triumph.

At the end of the episode, the narrator (Palin) mentions that the momentous flight occurred in 1900, not 1908.

"Yours has been the work"—("Montgolfier Brothers") Spoken in the episode by Jacques (Jones) to Joseph (Idle), the historical accounts seem to support this, as well. Joseph initiated the experiments in 1782 and performed much of the early balloon research (*EBO*).

– Z –

"zabaglione . . . Zakuskie"—("Zeppelin") Helmut seems to be at the end of a kind of food encyclopedia, yet another "list" moment for these German characters.

Zeppelin—("Zeppelin") Ferdinand von Zeppelin (1838-1917) was the first major designer and builder of rigid airships for commercial purposes. The initial flight of his airship was on 2 July 1900 near Lake Constance.

Episode 41: "Michael Ellis"

– A –

"Abanazar"—("Buying an Ant") The evil character in the popular pantomime *Aladdin*, as well as Kipling's *Slaves of the Lamp* (from *Stalky and Co.*, 1899). Jones and Palin had written a version of the *Aladdin* panto, and were able to watch a performance of that pantomime in Glasgow in January 1971 (Palin 51-52).

Albert's coffin—(PSC; "Poetry Reading [Ants]") Victoria's husband HRH Prince Albert died in 1861, leaving the Queen devastated and in seclusion and mourning for years. The first cover photo for the satirical magazine *Private Eye* featured the Albert Memorial, characterizing it as a spaceship ready to take Albert into orbit (7 February 1962).

"Allison, Malcolm, Brian Clough . . . Jimmy Hill"—("Different Endings") Footballer Malcolm Allison (b. 1927) retired from play in 1958. Allison was managing Crystal Palace in 1974. Brian Clough (1935-2004) was a former footballer who was managing Brighton & Hove Albion in 1974.

Former player and coach Jimmy Hill (b. 1928) was presenting the BBC's *Match of the Day* in 1974. Hill had pioneered the panel set program for football discussion when working for London Weekend Television in the late 1960s. He will appear in Ep. 43 dressed as Queen Victoria.

"Ayrshire"—("Buying an Ant") A breed of cattle from Ayr, Scotland. A "King George bitch" is probably a play on the dog breed "King Charles spaniel." King George III (played by Chapman) is featured in Ep. 40,

"The Golden Age of Ballooning." An "Afghan" is a furry greyhound.

– B –

"Blancmange"—("Buying an Ant") He says "blancmange" because a race of these giant pastries from outer space menaced Earth in Ep. 7, in the "Science Fiction Sketch." This intertextuality pops up occasionally in *FC*, with reappearances of recognized characters from previous episodes, including the "Nudge, Nudge" character (Idle), Cardinal Ximinez (Palin), characters answering the phone and immediately looking at their shoe size, etc.

The Pythons do "quote themselves," as well (as did Shakespeare), in revisiting character situations and incidents of miscommunication episode after episode, accessing the show's history as it becomes institutionalized (see *MPSERD*). See notes to Ep. 45, where a character sings a bit of an original song first heard in Ep. 42. This familiarity is part of the reason that the show could build an audience—the flip side is, of course, that troupe members (like Cleese) could quickly tire of the repetitiveness and revisitation.

"book on ants"—("Buying an Ant") Episode 12 is subtitled "The Naked Ant," which is a play on the Desmond Morris book *The Naked Ape: A Zoologist's Study of the Human Animal*, published in 1967. A poster for *The Naked Ape* is featured prominently in Ep. 4, the "Secret Service Dentists" sketch.

"Bradlaugh"—("Poetry Reading [Ants]") Charles Bradlaugh (1833-1891) was a well-known atheist and "freethinker" during Victoria's reign.

– C –

customer whose back is on fire—("Department Store") This actor is Tim Condren—listed as "Smoldering Man"—a stuntman who did stunt work for the early Bond films, *Star Wars*, and Gilliam's *Brazil* (WAC T12/1,467). He died in 2006.

The young woman talking to him in this shot is Annett Peters ("Lady in Twin-Set") (WAC T12/1,467).

– D –

developing a German accent—(PSC; "Poetry Reading [Ants]") Victoria was of German descent, being from the House of Hanover, and she was perhaps raised speaking German first, then English, and later became fluent in other languages. Victoria was never the ruler of Hanover, since German law forbade a female ruler, and that title transferred away from her and to her uncle ("Victoria" in *ODNB*).

The essentially German pedigree of portions of the English royal family is alluded to earlier in Ep. 33, when Biggles dictates a letter to the "*real* Princess Margaret," coyly reminding her of the "Saxe-Coburg canasta evening."

"dinner-wagon"—("Buying an Ant") A dinner wagon is a wheeled serving table.

– E –

"Eighth Floor: Roof Garden"—(PSC; "Department Store") Certainly another reference to the celebrated roof garden at the Derry & Toms department store, which closed in 1972. Derry & Toms has been referenced before in *FC*, in Eps. 23 and 37, and will be mentioned later in Ep. 42. See notes to those episodes for more.

"Ellis, Michael"—("Buying an Ant") The mysterious Michael Ellis was an assistant editor on Lindsay Anderson's controversial 1968 film *If. . . .*, referenced earlier in Ep. 19. Throughout this *Flying Circus* episode Ellis is a Harry Lime–like apparition—the childhood friend/black marketeer (Orson Welles) to Holly Martins (Joseph Cotten) from *The Third Man* (1949)—who is much talked about and sought-after through the noir-ish streets (and sewers) of postwar Vienna.

ending up in an aerial view of London—(PSC; "Different Endings") This film stock is "Aerial Views of London" from World Background, Elstree Studios (WAC T12/1,467).

Episode 41—This episode was recorded 19 October 1974, and broadcast 7 November 1974, and was officially titled "Michael Ellis." All six episodes in the fourth series are given titles, long after Light Entertainment higher-ups worried that such subsidiary titles might be confusing to the typical BBC viewer. See notes to Ep. 2 for more on this request, and WAC T12/1,242.

The actors/extras used in the episode include the following: Tim Condren (*Dr. Who*; *Star Wars*); J. Hughman; Annet Peters and Pam Wardell (*The Avengers*); (extras) Steve Kelly (*Barlow at Large*), Eric French (*Z Cars*), Derrick (or "Derek") Hunt (*Z Cars*), Dennis Hayward (*Play For Today*), James Muir (*Z Cars*), Reg Turner (*Dr. Who*), Keith Norrish (*Dr. Who*), James Haswell (*Wednesday Play*), Alec Pleon (*Up the Chastity Belt*), Lyn Howard, Vi Delmer (*Z Cars*), Peggy Sirr (*Dr. Who*), Vi Kane (an Equity Council rep; *Wednesday Play*), Barbara Faye, Mary Maxted (aka Mary Millington [1945-1979]; *Dr. Who*), Suzy Mandel (*The Benny Hill Show*), Jackie Street (*A Little of What You Fancy*), Kathleen Heath (*Emma*), Susanne Fleuret (*Z Cars*), Rita Tobin (*Anne of the Thousand Days*), Beatrice Greek (*Frankenstein and the Monster From Hell*), Vi Ward (*Engelbert with the Young Generation*), Eileen Matthews (*Agatha Christie's Miss Marple: Nemesis*), Pat Prior (*Dr. Who*), Bob Raymond (*Softly Softly*), Eve Aubrey (*Mini Weekend*), Elsa Smith (*Arthur of the Britons*), Peter Holmes (*Play For Today*), Simon Joseph (*Softly Softly*), Lionel Sansby (*Dr. Who*), Constance Reason (*Z Cars*), Willie Shearer (*Private Life of Sherlock Holmes*).

– F –

Fourth Floor—(PSC; "Department Store") In the "Granite Hall" are non-granitic rocks including "shale" (a sedimentary rock), "alluvial deposits" (which can contain some granite), and "felspar" ("*feldspar*," a mineral-forming rock). Also, there seem to be mountain ranges in this hall, including the "Carpathians" (Central Europe), the "Andes" (South America), and "Urals" (Russia). Though shot in Croydon, this store is modeled on Harrods, the fashionable Knightsbridge department store offering virtually everything—clothing, electronics, food, jewelry, pet supplies, appliances, and legendary service—since the beginning of the twentieth century.

– G –

gaggle of customers—(PSC; "Department Store") These Pepperpots and Customers include Peter Holmes (Man in Bad Suit), Reg Turner, and Alec Pleon (both Pepperpots) (WAC T12/1,467). The extras in the fourth series often appear in multiple episodes, with calls at Television Centre arranged for maximum efficiency. See the WAC records for these episodes for more.

Greek national costume—(PSC; "Ant Communication") The actor is listed as Dennis Hayward, though it looks very much like Terry Jones has taken the role (WAC T12/1,467). WAC records have previously indicated in error a particular actor brought in to play a particular role, so this type of personnel change (sometimes due to an actor missing call for various reasons) isn't unusual.

– H –

"Half an inch"—("Poetry Reading (Ants)") A play on the initial lines of Tennyson's *Charge of the Light Brigade*, a very early wax recording of which (voiced by Tennyson himself) was extant at the time the Pythons wrote and performed this episode. The first stanza, as written by Tennyson:

Half a league, half a league,
Half a league onward,
All in the valley of Death
Rode the six hundred.
"Forward, the Light Brigade!
Charge for the guns!" he said:
Into the valley of Death
Rode the six hundred.

Harrods-type store—("Department Store") The show received permission to shoot much of the episode at Grants Department Store, High Street, Croydon (WAC T12/1,469).

The music used underneath this scene is from Eric Coates, "London Suite (London Everyday): No. 3 Knightsbridge," here played by the Royal Liverpool Philharmonic Orchestra (WAC T12/1,467). This familiar music is also used earlier, in Eps. 7 and 16.

"Hillman"—("At Home with the Ant and Other Pets") A Hillman was a small car designed to be a competitor to the very popular Mini.

"how about a chase"—("Different Endings") The music used here is "Devil's Gallop," from the *Dick Barton* series, which was used in Eps. 15 and 30, both in chase sequences.

– I –

"I can assure you they do"—("Ant Communication") Open University (or University of the Air) broadcasts tended to be prerecorded and then just transmitted at a slotted time, but here the Pythons are positing a more traditional, in-class kind of experience where the teacher can answer questions directly to the students. In this the effectiveness of the Open University model—a single message transmitted simultaneously to thousands of potential recipients—is made far less efficient, becoming a one-on-one teacher-student experience where the teacher also must sit and wait for the student to be available for instruction.

Early on, there was much ridicule of the new educational endeavor, including hundreds of op-ed page cartoons depicting Open University–trained surgeons, non-traditional (as in OAP) student demonstrations, and airtime competition with the likes of Basil Brush, etc. See the many cartoons lampooning the new educational endeavor at the British Cartoon Archive.

"I met a traveller . . . "—("Poetry Reading [Ants]") Shelley's "Ozymandias," published in 1818, is a sonnet that reads more precisely:

I met a traveller from an antique land
Who said:—Two vast and trunkless legs of stone
Stand in the desert. Near them on the sand,
Half sunk, a shatter'd visage lies, whose frown
And wrinkled lip and sneer of cold command
Tell that its sculptor well those passions read
Which yet survive, stamp'd on these lifeless things,
The hand that mock'd them and the heart that fed.
And on the pedestal these words appear:
"My name is Ozymandias, king of kings:
Look on my works, ye mighty, and despair!"
Nothing beside remains: round the decay
Of that colossal wreck, boundless and bare,
The lone and level sands stretch far away.

"inflation I'm afraid"—("Buying an Ant") In 1974, the inflation rate in the UK reached 16 percent by mid-year and was still climbing, peaking at 24 percent in 1975 (UK Composite Price Index). The Heath administration would lose its hold on the government in 1974 due in large part to the very weak economy. The Wilson Labour government wouldn't be able to work wonders with the moribund economy, either, ushering in Margaret Thatcher (Eps. 21-22, 30) and the Tories in 1979.

"intraspecific signalling codes"—("At Home With the Ant and Other Pets") These would be signals used *within* a certain species, not between species, so from one ant to another ant.

"I wandered . . . "—("Poetry Reading [Ants]") Wordsworth's Romantic-era poem, written in 1804, and preceding the Victorian age. Instead of "worker ants," Wordsworth (and his sister, autobiographically) saw "daffodils."

This same poem has already been read aloud in Ep. 17, in the "Poets" sketch, from a Wordsworth (Idle) kept under the stairs.

– J –

"Jehovah's witnesses"—("At Home with the Ant and Other Pets") A well-known proselytizing religious group, the "Watchtower Bible and Tract Society" would have been in the news significantly during this period. In 1969 a mass meeting of Jehovah's Witness faithful at Yankee Stadium was hailed by many as the final gathering of the international church before the end of the world, which was calculated to take place in late 1975, just months after these *FC* episodes were being written and recorded.

The mention of this eschatological sect in the midst of an episode so obviously satirizing a corrupt, debased consumer society is no surprise, nor is the mention that the tiger has consumed the witnessing faithful, further evidence that a cleansing is imminent. In the early 1970s, Witnesses were patiently waiting for "Jehovah God to bring an end to a corrupt world drifting toward ultimate disintegration," according to one of their inedible tracts, *Awake!* (8 October 1968). In fact, this particular issue of *Awake!* (probably meant to spur the faithful to attend the New York gathering) provides a laundry list of the woes of the world—mammon before God, violence, drug use, material worship, pestilences, lawlessness, disobedience to parents—*all* coincidentally encountered by Chris (Idle) as he wanders through the department store and even his home in this episode.

Lastly, the *Private Eye* had announced in late 1969 that then-Prime Minister Harold Wilson was converting to the Jehovah's Witness faith (26 September 1969).

– L –

ladies in German national costume—(PSC; "Ant Communication") Suzy Mandel (*Benny Hill*) plays one of these German girls (WAC T12/1,467).

line of ten people—(PSC; "Complaints" link into) These actors, according to WAC records, include: "Tyrolean Man"—Keith Norrish (*Dr. Who*); "Icelandic Man"—Steve Kelley; "Greek Man"—Dennis Hayward (*Play For*

Today); "Man With Lawn Mower"—Lionel Sansby (*Dr. Who*); "Man with Dog"—James Muir (*Z Cars*); "Bandaged Nose Lady"—Constance Reason (*Z Cars*); "Lady with Pram"—Barbara Fay; "Lady with Tennis Racquet"—Pat Prior (*Dr. Who*); "Man with Cigar"—Simon Joseph (*Sunday Bloody Sunday*); "Man in Bad Suit"—Peter Holmes (*Dr. Who*) (WAC T12/1,467).

– M –

"Mac Fisheries"—("Toupee") A chain of UK fish shops set up in 1919 by William Lever. The intended insult is likely that the toupee looks woven, like a fishnet.

"mandies"—("At Home with the Ant and Other Pets") A "mandy" is a dose of the sedative methaqualone, used as a sleep inducer in this period.

"My heart aches . . . "—("Poetry Reading [Ants]") Inspired by Keats' "Ode to a Nightingale," the first stanza of which is actually as follows:

My heart aches, and a drowsy numbness pains
My sense, as though of hemlock I had drunk,
Or emptied some dull opiate to the drains
One minute past, and Lethe-wards had sunk:
'Tis not through envy of thy happy lot,
But being too happy in thine happiness,—
That thou, light winged Dryad of the trees,
In some melodious plot
Of beechen green, and shadows numberless,
Singest of summer in full-throated ease.

– N –

"No, I want a *different* assistant"—("Buying an Ant") This is the beginning of yet another difficult transaction (a communication, of sort) in the Python world, where it's never as simple as choosing an item, paying for that item, and completing the transaction (that wouldn't be funny, on its own). In many cases, the item isn't available or as advertised ("Cheese Shop," "Tobacconists," "Dead Parrot," "Argument Clinic"), or the exchange is abrogated as the narrative moves off tangentially ("Off-Licence," "Police Station," "Fish Licence"). In this case, Mr. Quinn (Idle) has to go through two assistants (Chapman and Palin) and a manager (Jones) before successfully completing his purchase, one of the few such successful transactions in all of *Flying Circus*. The success is short-lived, of course, as Chris realizes later that the ant is damaged, and he has to return to the store for an attempt (à la the "Dead Parrot" sketch) at a refund.

– O –

"Only useful animal you ever bought, that"—("At Home with the Ant and Other Pets") Since the "orange-rumped agouti" (a rodent) is about the size of a hare, it's unlikely that this pet would be the one opening the door.

– P –

Paisley—("Buying an Ant") A department store "Paisley Counter" would have offered items featuring the distinctive Paisley print (ties, scarves, shawls, etc.), created by weavers in the lowland Scotland town of the same name.

Ian Paisley (b. 1926) represented the North Antrim, Ireland constituency in this period, and was a leading voice in the Irish "situation" for many years. The Reverend Paisley was instrumental in opposing the sharing of power in Ireland with all entities, including England, Ireland, and Northern Ireland. Paisley was featured on the cover of *Private Eye* on 31 January 1969.

The lady passing with a bandaged nose in this shot is Constance Reason (WAC T12/1,467).

"pangolin"—("At Home with the Ant and Other Pets") A pangolin is a scaly (armored) anteater, essentially.

"parky"—("Buying an Ant") Chilly, cold.

– Q –

Queen Victoria with a fanfare—("Poetry Reading [Ants]") The fanfare used here is "Investiture Fanfare" by Charles Williams. Victoria's attendants (carrying Albert's coffin) are Bob Raymond and William Shearer (WAC T12/1,467).

– R –

"rag week"—("Buying an Ant") A university tradition where students help raise money (via sideshow-type performances) for charities. Both Cambridge and Oxford participate in the long-standing "raising and giving" tradition. The student fun and games during rag week could be rather over the top. In 1967 Surrey University rag week participants kidnapped a popular Radio 1 deejay, Tony Blackburn, demanding he play a sort of commercial tape for their rag week activities (see "Radio Rewind," 1967).

"recent discoveries in the field"—("At Home with the Ant and Other Pets") Both the focus on ants and this specific scientific section are perhaps attributable to the front-page presence of the ant work of Harvard professor E. O. Wilson, who had released *The Insect Societies* in 1971.

Also, poet Sir Osbert Sitwell (1892-1969) had depicted the ant as one of the paragons of humanity's interwar pugnacity.

"Ribena"—("Buying an Ant") A popular blackcurrant soft drink in the UK.

"rotten ending"—("Different Endings") The traditional structure of the traditional BBC show is just what the Pythons were intending to upend when *Flying Circus* was being talked about back in early 1969. They have flirted with all sorts of endings in the preceding three series, but here is the first time they actually lay bare the various possibilities and weed through them, one by one.

– S –

shopping trolley is smoldering—(PSC; link out of "Ant Communication") This burning lady is Pam Wardell (WAC T12/1,467).

"Snetterton"—("Buying an Ant") Snetterton is a village in Norfolk, where the Pythons shot location scenes for much of the second series. The "nailed-my-head-to-the-floor" character from "The Piranha Brothers" (Ep. 14) is named Vince Snetterton Lewis.

switches it on and settles down to watch it with Marcus—("At Home with the Ant and Other Pets") The snippet of introductory music used for the University of the Air is from Benjamin Britten's "Lisbon Bay," and is played by the Members of the English Chamber Orchestra (WAC T12/1,467).

– T –

twenty old televisions—(PSC; "At Home with the Ant and Other Pets") The overarching theme of this episode seems to be rampant consumerism in an existential world, or the materialist, "acquisitive" quagmire bemoaned by many in twentieth-century Western culture. The myriad televisions, the profligate menagerie, and the "anything-you-could-want" department store setting point toward Thorstein Veblen's "conspicuous consumption," or the middle-class accumulation of consumer goods in place of active political or social commitment. See Veblen's *Theory of the Leisure Class*. In Ep. 27 Mrs. Premise (Cleese) and Conclusion (Chapman) agree that man can only be free when he's rid himself of his worldly possessions, which Mrs. Premise sees as the central argument of Sartre's *Roads to Freedom*. See notes to Ep. 27 for more on the Pythons' existentialism.

– U –

"University of the Air"—("At Home with the Ant and Other Pets") Open University was established in 1969, broadcasting on the BBC, and was designed to offer the university experience to non-traditional students (disabled, non-traditional students, post-grads, distance learners, etc.). Palin is depicted wearing the typically drab "coat-and-kipper-tie" uniform of the early on-air lecturers.

– V –

"Victorian poetry reading hall"—("Poetry Reading [Ants]") The ladies in the audience in this scene include Lyn Howard, Elsa Smith, Eve Aubrey, Pamela Wardell, Mary Maxted, and Vi Delmar (WAC T12/1,467).

For most of the poets in this line-up, Victoria (1819-1901) would have been an infant when they died, though, perhaps, she was no more German than when she was very young.

– W –

"Walking into the sunset?"—("Different Endings") The music used in this romantic moment is "Elm Street" by Johnny Burt (WAC T12/1,467).

"was ist das schreckliche Gepong . . . es schmecke wie ein Scheisshaus . . . "—("Poetry Reading [Ants]") Essentially, in very fractured German, she's asking: "What is that awful smell? . . . It smells/tastes like a shithouse . . . and so on."

"We are not . . . amusiert?"—("Poetry Reading [Ants]") The "We are not amused" catchphrase is credited to Queen Victoria by one Caroline Holland in *Notebooks of a Spinster Lady* (London: Cassell, 1919), though its authenticity can certainly be challenged, as the book was originally published anonymously. What cannot be challenged is the phrase's significance to the Pythons in their depictions of the somewhat dour Queen—she is not amused when she's earlier given a

hole in her head in a Gilliam animation (Ep. 15), and she's not "amusiert" by the ant references here.

Wordsworth, Shelley, Keats, Tennyson—(PSC; "Poetry Reading [Ants]") All writers included, for example, in Harrison and Bates' 1959 collection *Major British Writers II*, from Harcourt, and yet three of the four are actually from the English Romantic period, which preceded the Victorian Age.

Wordsworth—An English Romantic poet, William Wordsworth (1770-1850) was Poet Laureate the last seven years of his life.

Shelley—Another English Romantic poet, Percy Bysshe Shelley (1792-1822).

Keats—Active in the English Romantic period, John Keats (1785-1821) is also a bit out of place in this Victorian setting.

Tennyson—(1809-1892) He assumed the laureateship after Wordsworth, and was the poet installed in the bathroom in Ep. 17. See entries in the *ODNB* for more on all these writers.

– Y –

"Yes, the book on ants"—("Buying an Ant") Probably an unintended pun, as the "book on ants" is slammed down *on the ants*. The joke becomes the ants being thoughtlessly crushed, not thoughtlessly crushed by a book on ants. The audience doesn't seem to get the joke, anyway, intended or not.

"You can see the join"—("Poetry Reading [Ants]") The "join" would be the place where the toupee is supposed to mesh invisibly with the remaining natural hair. In the *Beyond the Fringe* sketch "Bollard," one of the models, is fretting about his hair, and another assures him that he can "scarcely see the join." When Chris finally makes it to the Toupee Hall, the assistants' bad hair joins are all quite visible.

"You let them die, then you buy another one"—("Buying an Ant") This is a moment where the normally unspoken part of the commodity transaction in a consumer culture is voiced—buying for the long-term isn't as good for business as buying, then buying again, and again and again. Watson notes in *The Modern Mind* both the increasing importance of "things" in the twentieth century and the literary/artistic reaction to that acquisitiveness:

> What Joyce, Eliot, Lewis, and the others were criticising, among other things, was the society—and not only the [WWI-era] war society—which capitalism had brought about, a society where value was placed on possessions, where life had become a race to acquire

things, as opposed to knowledge, understanding, or virtue. In short, they were attacking the acquisitive society. (186)

The Pythons' firm reliance on the masterpieces and ethoi of the Modernist movement(s) has been mentioned throughout these notes; coupled with the more hopeful existentialism of the postwar Sartre, the Pythons' attacks on consumer society (they grew up in a culture forever changed by capitalism) reach a significant level of maturity in this self-contained episode.

Episode 42:
"Light Entertainment War"

"198 feet high . . . "—("Show Jumping [Musical]") The Coliseum is actually about 157 feet high. Why the biblical epic *Ben Hur* (novel 1880; Charlton Heston film 1959) is included as a jump in this event featuring musicals isn't clear. By 1974, the Lew Wallace story had been filmed at least three times.

"4th Armoured Brigade"—("Trivializing the War") This brigade saw significant action in North Africa, Italy, and Germany during WWII, and was disbanded after the war.

– A –

"Agnelli, Gino"—("*Up Your Pavement*") Italian billionaire Gianni Agnelli (1921-2003) had been the principal owner of Fiat since 1966.

"Alan Jones knocked down poor Judd"—("Show Jumping [Musical]") Jones (b. 1946) was an Australian Formula 1 driver racing in the UK during this period, and not affiliated with horse jumping. Judd is a character in *Oklahoma!*, and he is mock-lamented in the song "Poor Judd is Dead."

ANIMATION: **"What a lovely day"**—(animated link into "Woody and Tinny Words") This Gilliam animation, where the "bloody weather" becomes noisily exasperating, will be revisited in *Holy Grail*.

Arsenal—(closing credits) After winning the FA Cup in 1970-1971, Arsenal FC had slipped steadily, and by 1974 were on their way to a sixteenth-place finish.

– B –

"Basing House, burned down . . . "—("Basingstoke in Westphalia") Basing House (est. 1535) would burn down as a result of the English Civil War in 1645. Cromwell would empty the buildings of valuables, and the local villagers came in and took the bricks to rebuild their homes. Earthworks and some gating still stand today. See entries for "John Paulet" and "Cromwell" in the *ODNB* for more.

"bored"—("Woody and Tinny Words") Father (Chapman) here is expressing a Kierkegaardian complaint voiced in *Either/Or*, namely that for the aesthete—whose life is devoted to the pursuit of pleasure and amusement—boredom is the single greatest evil. When discussing pleasingly "woody" and unpleasant "tinny" words, as well as admiring the fecundity of the "woody" croquet hoops or the sensuality of "woody" words grows tiresome, boredom sets in for Father, and he's off to his tenth bath of the day, or to build another useless Babel, in Kierkegaard's terms:

> The gods were bored, and so they created man. Adam was bored because he was alone, and so Eve was created. Thus boredom entered the world, and increased in proportion to the increase of population. Adam was bored alone; then Adam and Eve were bored together; then Adam and Eve and Cain and Abel were bored *en famille*; then the population of the world increased, and the peoples were bored *en masse*. To divert themselves they conceived the idea of constructing a tower high enough to reach the heavens. This idea is itself as boring as the tower was high, and constitutes a terrible proof of how boredom gained the upper hand. (228)

And when his wife (Cleveland) dissuades him from his next bath, he opts instead to sack a "tinny" (and thus unpleasant) servant, enacting just the type of change (what Kierkegaard called a "crop rotation") that focuses him away from one moment and onto another, an act that can, for a time, stave off boredom.

Bovril—(PSC; "RAF Banter") The character played by Jones is in the printed scripts identified as "Bovril," a proprietary name for a beef extract spread.

"B roads"—("The Last Five Miles of the M2") A "B" road is a more local road separate from the larger, longer A and AA roads in the UK. The "B roads" series idea might have played better, then, in the regional markets (Midlands, for example), where, ironically, *Flying Circus* tended to struggle, thanks to on-again-off-again programming decisions by individual regions.

– C –

"can't say 'sodding' on the television"—("The Last Five Miles of the M2") This should be *couldn't* say sodding on television, since the word was elided in Ep. 17, the "Architect Sketch," when Cleese's line reads "Oh (*blows raspberry*) the abbatoir," instead of "Oh sod the abbatoir," which it had read originally. By the fourth series (several years later) words like "sod" and "bugger" and "shit" were being heard more regularly on *FC*, which led some viewers (general audience and BBC types alike) to lament the too-easy shock value of the formerly creative, edgy show.

"Captain Phillips"—("Show-Jumping [Musical]") Captain Mark Phillips (b. 1948) was the husband of Princess Anne (Elizabeth's daughter), and won an equestrian team gold medal in the 1972 Munich Olympics. (Princess Anne had officiated at the British Screen Awards in 1971, and was lampooned in Ep. 39, "Grandstand.") According to the United States Event Association, Phillips successfully rode mounts Rock On, Great Ovation, Maid Marion, and Columbus between 1967 and 1974.

"Streuth" is an invective (a contraction of "God's truth") that's been used (mostly by Chapman) several times in the series, including Eps. 1 and 2.

"CAPTION: '1942 . . . "—("Woody and Tinny Words") The British Empire did at one time extend to Africa, the Middle East, and South America, where landed men like Father (Chapman) would have performed foreign civil or military service before retiring to woody pursuits back home.

car park below—("Programme Titles Conference") This scene was shot from the roof of Clarendon House, Western Way, Exeter on 13 September 1974 (WAC T12/1,469).

"Carrington, Lord"—(*Up Your Pavement*) Lord Carrington (b. 1919) was leading the Conservative opposition in the House of Lords after the Labour victory in 1974, and had been Chairman of the Conservative Party between 1972 and 1974, as well as Defence Secretary. His education qualifies him for special vituperation, at least in the Python world: Eton, Sandhurst, and the Guards (see Ep. 20). For the Pythons, Carrington would have been just the stuffy, establishment type—along with a reverend and spouse—to have concocted such a traditional, corny kind of show as the one lampooned.

"Chiropodist"—("Up Your Pavement") This corn and bunion specialization was earlier featured in Ep. 31, when Everest was being climbed by hairdressers and chiropodists.

"Conceived and Written By"—(closing credits) Cleese is given a writing credit here, though not a performing credit. (He is listed as performing in the script, but does not appear in the finished segment.) Neil Innes also receives a writing/conception credit here.

Other tidbits from the "Social Class" credits section include: Another mention of the now-defunct department store ("Derry and Toms"); body measurements for the costumer ("35 28 34"); an f-stop reading for the cameraman ("f8 at 25th sec."); a school mention ("Lower Sixth"); director Ian MacNaughton's drink of choice ("a bottle of Bell's"); and a reference to Eps. 9 and 41 ("Ant").

Crossroads *type theme music*—(PSC; link out of "Woody and Tinny Words") *Crossroads* (ATV, 1964-1988) was a very popular family drama set in a Midlands motel.

– D –

"Dad's Navy"—("The Last Five Miles of the M2") Playing on well-known extant BBC shows, including *Dad's Army* (1968-1977), already satirized in Ep. 38, and the feature film/BBC play *Up the Junction* (1968), a gritty kitchen sink drama (and *Up Pompeii!*, etc.). Chapman makes fun of himself in mentioning "*Doctor at Bee*," "*Doctor at Three*," and "*Doctor at Cake*," seeing that he contributed significantly (as a writer) to *Doctor in Charge* (1972-1973), *Doctor at Large* (1971), and *Doctor in the House* (1969). *And Mother Makes Three* was a 1971 British comedy written by Peter Robinson, who also wrote for *The Two Ronnies*.

There are bunches of *I Married . . .* titles extant, including *I Married a Communist* (1958), *I Married a Witch* (1942), and *I Married a Heathen* (1974).

"Diamond, Alex"—("*Up Your Pavement*") Alexandros Diamantis is a Greek filmmaker whose screen name in the mid-1970s was Alex Diamond.

"Drummond-Hay, Anneli"—("Show Jumping [Musical]") She's already been mentioned in Ep. 28, when she was jumping with her horse in a family's flat (when the BBC were short of money). See notes to Ep. 28, "Puss in Boots."

– E –

Episode 42—Recorded 26 October 1974 and transmitted 14 November 1974.

Additional actors for this episode include the following: Neil Innes, Bill Olaf, Marion Mould (rider), Peter Woods (*Morecambe & Wise*), Judy Roger, Angela Taylor, Ann Payot (*Health & Efficiency*), Elsa Smith (*Adventures of Barry Mackenzie*), Annet Peters (Eps. 40-43; *Fall and Rise of Reginald Perrin*), Sylvia Laine (*Thief of Baghdad*), Lyn Howard, Jean Channon (*Z Cars*), Stella Conway, Sylvia Brent, Stuart Myers (*Microbes and Men*), Rory O'Connor (*Blakes 7*), Michael Finbar (*Blakes 7*), Fred Davies (*Blackpool Show*), Ron Musgrove (*Z Cars*), Eden Fox (*Doctor in the House*), Paul Phillips (*Doctor Who*), Les Shannon (*Blakes 7*), Bill Hughes (*Barlow at Large*), Colin Thomas (*Love Among the Ruins*), Sue Bishop (*Dad's Army*), Sally Foulger, Belinda Lee (*Are You Being Served?*), Diane Holt, Sally Sinclair (*Doctor Who*), Jackie Street (*A Little of What You Fancy*), Dominic Plant, Tania Simmons, Laura Hannington, Sharon Parmee, Deborah Jones, Matthew Jones, Bob Raymond (*FC* fourth series), John Hughman, Donald Stratford (*Barlow at Large*), Garth Watkins (*The Liver Birds*), Reg Turner (*Dr. Who*), James Haswell (*Z Cars*), Harry Davis (*Dixon of Dock Green*), Kathleen Heath (*Doctor in the House*), Mike Barrymore, Peter Leeway, John Casley, and Cliff Anning.

– F –

"fairy wands with big stars on the end"—("Trivializing the War") This lighthearted or even disinterested approach to The Great War may be a reference to the fact that in Britain, during 1938-1940, the continental affairs were known as the "Phoney War," since no direct hostilities against or by British troops and installations had been undertaken, nor had the Axis powers directly engaged British interests. Many in the UK felt that as Czechoslovakia, The Netherlands, and even France fell into German hands, it still had nothing to do with Great Britain. Part of the problem was, of course, that British authorities called for wartime measures—austerity, vigilance, gas masks, internment, billeting—a full year before any bomb fell on London.

– G –

"gaiters"—("Courtmartial") Military-issue legwear, specifically to be worn between the heel and knee.

Ceremonial attire is usually reserved to swords, adornments, etc.

"Get me the Prime Minister"—("Trivializing the War") A phrase heard in many of the British WWII films, especially when a discovery's been made (like a decoded communiqué or the identification of incoming "cabbage crates"), and it's always meant "get the PM on the phone." Here, again, Python's penchant for literality is expressed. In Ep. 20, it is the Chief of Police (Ian Davidson) who appears from a morgue drawer just when he's summoned.

"Gorn"—(PSC; "Woody and Tinny Words") Probably a nonce word, but the pronunciation is very much like the Yorkshire version of "go on" or even "gone," and when hearing it (as the audience does), it's probably too homonymic to accurately identify.

In fact, when Mother (Idle) asks, "What's gorn, dear?" and Father (Chapman) answers, "Nothing," she is asking, essentially, "What's gone, dear?" Later in the scene this reading is underscored when Father shoots the caribou, then quips "Caribou gorn."

– H –

high street—(PSC; "Up Your Pavement") The printed script describes the setting as a "high street," which would be the main shopping district in most smaller towns during this period. This high street may have been in Crediton, Exeter.

"Hills Are Alive, The"—(PSC; "Show Jumping [Musical]") The Rodgers and Hammerstein song performance here is by Ann Rogers with Ainsworth and his Orchestra. The following number from *Oklahoma!* (also Rodgers and Hammerstein) is performed by Tony Adams and Singers, and then the Black and White Minstrels sing "Let's Face the Music" by Irving Berlin (WAC T12/1,469).

Incidentally, the use of the song from *Oklahoma!* generated an angry letter from copyright holders, though BBC lawyers argued that since the song wasn't parodied there was no recourse either possible or justified (WAC T12/1,469).

Leslie Crowther (1933-1996)—flicked by Drummond-Hay on a jump—hosted *The Black & White Minstrel Show* in 1958.

– I –

"I Married Lucy"—("The Last Five Miles of the M2") *I Love Lucy* (1951-1957) was the top-rated U.S. television show throughout most of the 1950s, and first appeared in syndication on ITV in 1955 (Vahimagi). During the run of *Flying Circus*, Lucille Ball (1911-1989) was starring in another version of the show, *Here's Lucy* (1968-1974).

impressive college grounds—(PSC; "Up Your Pavement") These are the grounds not of Bicton College, but of the Bicton Park Botanical Gardens, in East Budleigh, Devon, and this footage was shot on 11 September 1974 (WAC T12/1,469).

interior of a bomber—(PSC; "Film Trailer") These were recorded at the RAF Museum, Hendon, where they shot in a Lancaster bomber on 4 October 1974 (WAC T12/1,469). The Lancaster is still on display there.

The footage here is shot as a straight-ahead dramatic combat scene, with no indication that the sexualized voiceover ("hot bloodedly bi-sexual navigator") has any connection to the characters or images displayed. In this the scene plays much like the 1966 Woody Allen project *What's Up Tiger Lilly?*, where Allen and friends remove the soundtrack from a Japanese gangster B-movie and replace it with their own silly, self-conscious, and sexualized dialogue and sound effects.

"It's the World War series . . . "—(link out of "Programme Titles Conference") In addition to the admittedly, unashamedly sentimentalized *Dad's Army*, this may be a reference to the very new *The World at War* series (from Jeremy Isaacs) produced by BBC competitor Thames and sponsored by the Imperial War Museum. The twenty-six-part series made its debut in October 1973 and ran through May 1974—in time for the Pythons to make fun of the series' very sober approach to the war.

– J –

Joseph, Sir K.—(PSC; closing credits) Sir Keith Joseph (1918-1994) was a powerful Conservative politician who helped push Thatcherism into the public eye in the 1970s and beyond. In 1974, Mary Whitehouse lauded Joseph for toting the banner of anti-permissiveness, which is probably why the Pythons mention him here, as well as later in the "Dramatis Personae" for Ep. 43.

– K –

Kildare theme—(PSC; "Up Your Pavement") This performance of the well-known "Dr. Kildare Theme" (Jerry Goldsmith) is by Johnnie Spence (WAC T12/1,469), and has been used whenever a pseudo-serious medical setting is demanded (Eps. 13, 26, and 32).

The actor playing the doctor here is supposed to have been Cleese, according to the printed script, but since he was no longer attached to the show by this time, the part seems to have been given to Douglas Adams (*Hitchhiker's Guide*). Adams will appear briefly in two more episodes, and get screen credit for Ep. 45.

Interestingly, Adams' name does not appear in the BBC records for the series, which is unusual. If nowhere else, the participants' names for repeat fees assignation purposes should be extant—his is not.

"Kissinger, Henry"—(*"Up Your Pavement"*) U.S. Secretary of State during this period, Kissinger (b. 1923) was in the headlines often, making agreements with Communist China in 1972 and winning the Nobel Prize in 1973. A German-born American, Kissinger may be implicitly connected to the Hanoverian Victoria's appearance in the previous episode, but he also represents the increasing international presence of the United States, its policies and culture, and the concomitant decline of Great Britain's international significance during this period.

– L –

large, tasteful, Georgian rich person's house—(PSC; "Woody and Tinny Words") The printed set-up for this shot belies the actual finished shot, with a significant amount of detail included for the reader only:

> *Sound of lawnmowers and cricket in the distance. Laughter from the tennis court. Sound of gardener sharpening spades in the potting shed. Out of vision, a Red Indian struggles to free himself from the rope bonds that bind him.*

There are no lawnmower or cricket or gardener or tennis sounds, and no Indian anywhere. There is the sound of a single-engine propeller-driven plane, however, which may have been "wild" sound (meaning accidentally recorded on location). At some points the Pythons have included such script details for either the production design team (to assist in gathering props and finding locations) or just to amuse themselves—inside jokes for the other Pythons only.

"Len Hanky!"—(*"Up Your Pavement"*) The music beneath this section (as the character emerges from behind the shrubbery) is George Malcolm's "Bach Before Breakfast" (WAC T12/1,469).

"lower middle"—("Woody and Tinny Words") The indication by Mother (Idle) here is that "tinny" words are those spoken by the lower classes, those who would also occupy mock-Tudor homes, and dress in the twin-set-and-pearls outfits seen earlier with Mrs. Elizabeth III (Jones) and Mrs. Mock Tudor (Chapman).

Luke 17, verse 3—(PSC; "RAF Banter") "Take heed to yourselves: If thy brother trespass against thee, rebuke him; and if he repent, forgive him." Rather than the usual pinup girl nose art and accompanying clever or naughty slogan, the chaplains have chosen scriptural passages. There are actually a few records showing that chaplains did indeed pilot aircraft, including C.S. "Bam" Bamberger, a Jewish Chaplain who was awarded the Distinguished Flying Cross in 1943, and who was Sergeant Pilot, then Squadron Leader. Bamberger took part in the Battle of Britain, significantly. (See battleofbritain.net.)

– M –

"Marquetry"—("Film Trailer") Intricate carvings, often found in handmade furniture. This type of film trailer was common through the 1960s.

"micturate"—("The Public Are Idiots") To urinate.

Mock Tudor—(PSC; "The Public Are Idiots") The characters' names here, not voiced, are Mrs. Mock Tudor (Chapman) and Mrs. Elizabeth III (Jones). A "Mock Tudor" is a contemporary version of the well-known Tudor-style home/building—there are countless such homes in the UK and United States. There has been no Elizabeth III, and with the succession clearly leaning toward the male side of the Windsors, at least for the present, there's little chance of a third ruling Elizabeth in the near future.

modern casa-type Italian office—(PSC; "Up Your Pavement") The music beneath this Italian interlude is lifted from the Nino Rota soundtrack for *La Dolce Vita* (1960), and is performed by Gordon Franks and Orchestra (WAC T12/1,469).

momentary flash of a still of each—(PSC; "Up Your Pavement") This stream-of-consciousness structure (photos and narration) was earlier used in Ep. 40 to wrap up the episode.

mounted female rider—(PSC; "Show Jumping [Musical]") The rider/actress is Marion Coakes Mould (b. 1947), the horse is most likely Stroller, and the jumping scenes are being shot at the All English Jumping Course, Hickstead on 23 September 1974 (WAC T12/1,469). Mould had jumped in the 1968 Mexico City Olympics for Great Britain.

"Mr. Heath"—("The Last Five Miles of the M2") Ted Heath had resigned the PM position in March 1974 after failing to create a viable coalition government in the wake of a Conservative backslide (in seats, not votes) in the 1974 General Election. Harold Wilson and Labour (with more Commons seats) returned to power in the transition, but without a mandate, and Wilson would resign in 1976, leaving the party leadership (and the country's fiscal mess) to James Callaghan (1912-2005). By 1979, the Tories would be back in 10 Downing Street thanks in great part to a doleful economy. See the University of Keele's "UK Elections" website for more on the pivotal election.

"M2"—("The Last Five Miles of the M2") The M2 motorway was finished in 1965, reaching into Faversham, Kent, which is what/where these "idiot" viewers would have been watching.

"municipal borough . . . cavalry in 1645"—("Court-martial") The information here is accurate, meaning the Pythons probably checked their facts as they wrote, rather than relying on memory. Even the distance between Southampton and Basingstoke is accurate (about twenty-seven miles). In Ep. 37, the historical recitation given by Grantley (Palin) and Buckingham (Jones) is also quite accurate, there drawn from G.M. Trevelyan's work on the period.

music instantly changes to the heroic—(PSC; "Up Your Pavement") This is Elgar's "Pomp & Circumstance March" as played by the London Symphony Orchestra (WAC T12/1,469).

music turns more urgent and transatlantic—(PSC; "Up Your Pavement") The new bit of music is Neil Richardson's "Full Speed Ahead" (WAC T12/1,469).

– N –

Nissen hut—(PSC; "RAF Banter") Quonset-type huts installed at airbases across the UK, used for mess halls, officer's clubs, barracks, etc.

"not only fighting this war on the cheap . . . they're also not taking it seriously"—("Trivializing the War") American broadcaster Edward R. Murrow (1908-1965) visited London in April 1940 just as the possibilities of Britain's participation in war in Europe were being heatedly discussed, and the baggage-heavy, "peace in our time" Chamberlain government was essentially being shown the door in a Commons no-confidence vote. Murrow reported the following:

> This is London. I spent today in the House of Commons. The debate was opened by Mr. Herbert Morrison, one of the ablest members of the Labour Party. He doubted that the government was *"taking the war seriously."* Mr. Morrison said that the Labour Party had decided to divide the House—in other words, call for a vote. Mr. Chamberlain, white with anger, intervened in the debate and accepted the challenge. In fact, he welcomed it. . . . When he had finished, Mr. David Lloyd George rose and placed his notes upon the dispatch box, and members surged into the room through both doors, as though the little, grey, square-shouldered, white-haired Welshman were a magnet to draw them back to their seats. He swept the house with his arm and said: *"If there is a man here who is satisfied with our production of planes, of guns, of tanks, or the training of troops, let him stand on his feet."* No one stood. (Audio

transcription, *Eyewitness 1940-49*, "'No Confidence' Debate")

In this one dispatch from London to America before the war even begins Murrow voices the concern that the Pythons will comedically lament in this episode—the war is being trivialized and fought on the cheap. In the aftermath of the Commons vote, Chamberlain's grip on power was greatly eroded, he resigned, and the king asked Winston Churchill to form a coalition government.

This sketch is also likely an indirect result of significant BBC tongue-clucking over the *"Ypres 1914"* sketch(es) that appeared in Ep. 25. The weekly assessment meetings of the various Light Entertainment shows (attended by higher-ups representing most major departments at the BBC) revealed the dismay with which this episode—and especially the ridicule of the amputee Padre (Cleese)—was met by BBC officials and viewers alike. (Also, the silliness of war-themed comedy shows like *Dad's Army* [1968] may have contributed to the WWII veterans' dismay over their fading public and historic valorization.)

In *Hard Day's Night* (1964), the stuffy gentleman on the train reminds The Beatles that he had "fought the war" for them, a rhetorical flag that had been flown and saluted by WWII vets (and their political reps) for almost two decades by that time, and almost three decades by 1974. In the "Programme Titles" sketch from Ep. 42, the security guard (Gilliam) with the "oriental sword" (read: Japanese) through his head is obviously a WWII-era vet, and wears his battle wounds from the Great War with on-the-sleeve pride—in fact, the wound can't help but be noticed. The "not taking it seriously" malaise may be an indication that the unpopularity and evening news ugliness of the Vietnam War was by this time supplanting the patriotic memories of the WWII generation in the (especially younger) public's eye, and the WWII generation may have begun to miss the limelight.

"not understanding"—("RAF Banter") The Pythonesque miscommunication trope, again. This can be referred back to the sketch in the police station (Ep. 12) where each officer hears in his own way (low pitch, high pitch, faster, slower), meaning they each must learn each others' idiom/delivery in order to communicate, and strangers (like the man trying to report a crime) are left in a sea of babel.

– O –

"oblige them sir"—("Courtmartial") From the earliest *FC* episodes the specter of "sodomitical" behavior

(read: buggery), or man-on/in-man sexuality has been a source of humor for the troupe, even though one of their members (Chapman) was by this time an "outed" gay man active in the gay community. The stigma of gay relationships had lessened recently, with the decriminalization of homosexuality in the UK in 1967, and following the publication of the polarizing Wolfenden Report in 1957, which had recommended the sweeping public policy move. Still, "gay" jokes appear often in *FC* (and *Benny Hill* and many other contemporaneous comedy shows), and seem to go over fairly well with the studio audience, including the later "one man's love for another man in drag" and "night emission" quips.

– P –

"Porter, Cole"—("Courtmartial") American songwriter Porter (1891-1964) did write "Kiss Me Kate" in 1948, as well as "Anything Goes" in 1934.

"public are idiots"—("Programme Titles Conference") The premise that British viewers would sit and watch just about anything might not have been far wrong, especially when it's considered what hobbies were/are popular in the UK, including trainspotting and bridge identification.

If anything, however, the BBC as discovered in the WAC records seems overly considerate of the viewing audience, with most of the recorded comments illustrating concern over how portions of the episodes would be received. The admitted competition with newer, flashier commercial television networks like ITV kept attractive programming very high in the minds of Light Entertainment officials, while at the same time disturbing parliamentary, purse-string powers who wished the BBC to retain her brilliance as a moral beacon.

"PVC"—("Woody and Tinny Words") An acronym for polyvinyl chloride, a plastic used in construction materials around the world, including mock Tudor homes in the UK. The initials are pronounced "pee-vee-cee," a definite "tinny" sound.

– R –

"repeats"—("The Public Are Idiots") The Pythons as a group probably liked repeats, actually. As early as 1971 the Pythons were reaping tidy sums from repeats of the first *FC* season (£80 per troupe member), and the WAC files are thick with repeat information in the following months and then years. Paul Fox (Controller

BBC1) and David Attenborough (BBC Television's Director of Programmes) were even working overtime, it seems, to make sure that the repeat slots for *FC* were as favorable as possible for a burgeoning audience (WAC T47/216).

– S –

sailor on a ship—("Film Trailer") These scenes were shot aboard the HMS *Belfast* at Symons Wharf on 27 September 1974.

"sausage squad . . . briny"—("RAF Banter") These may not have been true RAF banter phrases, but they at least make some sense, and are much more on-the-nose. The first—"Sausage squad up the blue end"—is clearly to be translated as the presence of Germans (eaters of sausage) "up the butt" (meaning many of them). The second is even easier. Since Germans were also known as Krauts (from sauerkraut, which is made from fermented cabbage), the German planes are the "cabbage crates" on their way over the "briny" sea. (The latter may date from WWI, actually.)

So the Pythons are mixing traditional banter with colorful period slurs and just nonsense. The point seems to have been that it didn't used to matter what was said, but it had to be said quickly—it can't be banter if it's slow, or if it's explained. Here, the Pythons have taken the RAF-speak—a privileged vernacular reserved for "members only" as a means of communication and quick identification of other members—and Babel-ized it, meaning even those on the inside, those who allegedly speak the lingo, can no longer understand. Earlier, in the "Architect Sketch" (Ep. 17), the Masonic "language" is used to exclude non-members.

"Second World War has entered a sentimental phase"—("Newsflash [German]") The sentimentalizing of both the war and its servicemen and women began not long after the war, and continues to a significant degree to this day. The Home Guard portion of the war effort, depicted warmly in *Dad's Army*, which was busy winning entertainment awards (and perhaps inciting a bit of jealousy), may have inspired this reference.

seedy fellow in a terrible lightweight suit—(PSC; "Up Your Pavement") The script describes this character differently from the finished version, and even has Palin playing the part as a sort of Ken Shabby. In the filmed version, Jones takes the part, looking more like one of the "rapists" from *Fliegender Zirkus 1*.

"She's going to marry Yum Yum"—("Woody and Tinny Words") A song from the comic opera *The Mikado*, which is actually titled "For He's Going to Marry Yum Yum," and penned by Gilbert and Sullivan (Ep. 16).

Shots of big coastal guns—("Film Trailer") This is Pathé film footage (WAC T12/1,469). All of the stock film in this episode is borrowed from the Pathé film stock archives, though the WAC records do not indicate which particular bits of stock are being used. In past episodes, most film stock is both requested and accounted for, by name and/or file number.

"Show-Jumping from White City"—("Show-Jumping [Musical])") Show-jumping has already been lampooned in Ep. 28, and the White City Stadium setting was a typical event location. (This location is the All English Jumping Course in Hickstead.) Rider David Broome was actually astride Mr. Softee in the 1968 Summer Olympics in Mexico City, and not Drummond-Hay, who rode Xanthos II to the British Jumping Derby crown in 1969.

White City was a stadium built originally for the 1908 Olympic Games. The stadium is used as a location in *The Blue Lamp* (1950), the film that presented PC Dixon—later of *Dixon of Dock Green*—to the grateful British viewing public.

silver halos . . . stars—("Film Trailer") This type of fairy has appeared before, in Ep. 13, when policemen became fairies to more successfully fight crime.

Skating Vicar—(PSC; "Courtmartial") The Skating Vicar is played here by Bill Olaf (WAC T12/1,469).

"Somewhere in England"—("RAF Banter") The exact location of RAF and U.S. military airfields and hangars in the UK were kept as secret as possible during the war, and also far away from London and strategic targets. Many were hidden in plain sight in and near country villages—including Winkleigh and Okehampton in Devonshire—and the Local Defence Volunteer (Home Guard) units would even remove or rearrange road signs to further confuse any invading German force.

Spitfire—(PSC; link into "RAF Banter") This plane was located at the Torbay Airport Museum, and the shot was recorded on 9 September 1974 (WAC T12/1,469). The Spitfire was the star of the Battle for Britain during the early days of WWII.

"Squiffy"—("RAF Banter") Squiffy has been a nickname for the surname "Asquith."

Steptoe and Son—(PSC; "Up Your Pavement") The printed script mentions that the theme music here is supposed to sound like that of *Steptoe and Son* (1962-1974), a popular BBC comedy starring Wilford Brambell (Paul's grandfather in *Hard Day's Night*), and which later would be adapted into *Sanford and Son* on American television.

The specific title/artist procured is not accounted for, however, in the WAC records for the episode.

stock film of a big car-producing plant—("*Up Your Pavement*") This stock (photo, not film) is listed as a photo of a Fiat car factory (WAC T12/1,469).

"studio five"—("The Last Five Miles of the M2") Actually one of Television Centre's smallest studio spaces, it's unlikely that a WWII drama would have been relegated to the Studio 5 space, which was used for game shows and the like. *Flying Circus* shot most of its in-studio scenes in Studio 6, but also used Studios 1 and 8 and the nearby Ealing Television Film Studio when more space was needed (see WAC records for call locations).

– T –

Tense music—(PSC; "Film Trailer") The mood music here is also from Eric Coates, and called "633 Squadron" (from the 1964 movie of the same name), and is performed by Geoff Love and Orchestra (WAC T12/1,469).

"tinny sort"—("Woody and Tinny Words") In an episode of *The Goon Show*, a Peter Sellers character mentions the "certain thin" sounds of the studio orchestra, giving a mass or shape to the anticipated music.

"Top-hole . . . Bertie"—("RAF Banter") Most of this is actually identifiable RAF-speak, though some, as usual, has been manufactured by the Pythons.

"Top-hole" means first rate, "bally" is a euphemism for bloody, while "Jerry" is one of the nicknames given to German troops during the war. To prang something is to smash it, a "kite" is an airplane, and "how's your father" is a euphemism for sex or sexual organs (probably from a music hall derivation). A "hairy blighter" is merely a rude, hirsute fellow, and a "dicky birdie" is a small, inconsequential bird, like a sparrow, which could die and none would notice. See the *OED*.

"trivializing this war"—("Trivializing the War") Elgar's "Pomp & Circumstance March" is used here again, the same recording as used before in the "*Up Your Pavement*" sketch.

twin-set-and-pearls ladies—(PSC; "The Public Are Idiots") These ladies (Chapman and Jones) are decidedly less frumpy than the normal Python Pepperpot, though certainly no more attractive. Their elevated social position (and membership in the colonial club, as it were) might be indicated by the "Arab Boy remote control" (Gilliam) they've had installed.

– U –

"Up Your Pavement"—("*Up Your Pavement*") Yoko Ono had produced an experimental film in 1970 called *Up Your Legs Forever*. This type of title has been spoofed before, and is probably based on the popular *Up Pompeii!* and *Carry On*-type films noted in Ep. 38.

– V –

"Vauxhall Vivas"—(link out of "Woody and Tinny Words") Vauxhall is a British car company owned by General Motors since the 1920s. Vivas were small cars built by the thousands during the gas crunch times of the late 1960s and into the 1970s, designed to compete with Datsun, Toyota, and Opel imports.

veers off away—(PSC; "*Up Your Pavement*") This active, restive camera in relation to the supposed narrational object/subject was first glimpsed in Ep. 7, when the first protagonists introduced, Mr. and Mrs. Brain Sample (Chapman and Idle), are found to be too dull, and the camera and narrator veer away to Mr. Harold Potter (Palin), so that the exciting sci-fi story can begin. A similar wandering camera finds a helpful, "moustachioed Italian waiter" in Ep. 26, on its way to Herbert Mental (Jones), who collects birdwatchers' eggs. Nouvelle Vague filmmaker Godard (Ep. 23) employs this type of camera work in *Week End* (1967), as well.

victory-at-sea music—(PSC; "Film Trailer") The printed scripts call for "victory-at-sea" type music, referring to the 1952-1953 WWII documentary series, *Victory at Sea*. Music for the actual series was created by Richard Rodgers. The stirring music used here is Eric Coates' "Dambusters" played by Geoffrey Love and Orchestra (WAC T12/1,469). Coates' "633 Squadron" will be used later in the episode.

– W –

WAAF—(PSC; "Trivializing the War") A member of the Women's Auxiliary Air Force.

"we never actually see the horses jump"—("Show Jumping [Musical]") A comment on the budgetary constraints for most BBC shows, constraints that reduced the levels of acceptable verisimilitude for most shows and most genres. (It would also have been quite dangerous to have a shod horse leaping over extras, admittedly.) The "cutaway" shot is the standard obfuscation method for the medium—the Pythons have used it since the first episode, when the Rustic (Chapman) and the City Gent (Jones) watch and comment upon action taking place well offscreen. This comment also points up the artificiality of the medium, of the episode being taped, filmed, and broadcast.

"Western Front"—("Trivializing the War") A term not used as readily after WWI, especially in the West.

When the Germans during WWII referred to a front, it was the Eastern Front, as they were fighting Russia there. The Pythons may have mixed up their Mortimers here, so to speak (see the discussion on anachronisms in *MPSERD*).

"When Does a Dream Begin?"—("Trivializing the War") This original song is orchestrated and accompanied by Bill McGuffie and written/sung by Neil Innes (WAC T12/1,469). The orchestra is being led by Bobby Midgley. Later as the "Woody and Tinny Words" sketch begins the printed script mistakenly calls this song "*Where* Does a Dream Begin."

Whitehall war office room—("Trivializing the War") There were and are subterranean "war rooms" beneath Whitehall and HM Treasury in London, secure locations where the Cabinet, military, and PM could meet and conduct the war.

Williams, Dorian—(PSC; "Show Jumping [Musical]") Author, host, and presenter Williams (b. 1914) was the voice of the BBC's show jumping broadcasts since 1962, as well as the *Horse of the Year* show since 1949.

Wingco—("RAF Banter") Short for "Wing Commander."

Woods, Peter—(PSC; "Newsflash [German]") Woods (1930-1995) was a BBC reporter and then newsreader.

"woody"—("Woody and Tinny Words") There is a precedent for this type of seemingly nutty nomenclature. A sound (of a musical instrument, for an example) that is more "dull of tone" can be called "woody," meaning it's not as bright or piercing as a "tinny" sound, which is most often used pejoratively, and refers to a "cheaply contrived" high frequency sound (*OED*).

The "woody" words chosen by the Pythons tend to contain vowels—as found on the International Pho-

netic Association chart—that are generally voiced toward the "back" and "open" (like "gorn" and "vole"), while the more "tinny" words like "tit" and "leap" voiced nearer the "front" and more "closed." The "woody" words then sound more rich and full, while the "tinny" words are clipped and even shrill—just the sort of distinction one might make while sitting about with nothing to do (suffering Kierkegaardian boredom, see above) in a stuffy and expensive Georgian drawing room.

– X –

"Xerxes"—("Programme Titles Conference") A king of Persia (c. 485 BC), and obviously a random thought from the dementia-tinged mind of the planner (Palin). The planner goes from "Joey" to "Xerxes" and finally to "Mr. Heath" as the name of his long-lost pet budgie.

– Y –

"You don't re-heat cakes"—("The Last Five Miles of the M2") Based on the hand-wringing and general tsk-tsk-ing apparent in the department heads' meetings in regards to broadcast *FC* episodes, the dotty, fuddy-duddy depictions here might be somewhat justified. Comments from these post-morta include words like "disgusting," "over the edge," "awful," "appalling," and "not . . . amusing" (WAC T47/216).

young, inspired and devoted nurse—(PSC; "*Up Your Pavement*") The music changes to a version of Siebert's "Rule Britannia" as performed by the All Star Brass Band (WAC T12/1,469).

Episode 43: "Hamlet"

– A –

"And then . . . "—(link out of "Queen Victoria Handicap") This is Palin, but clearly not the "It's Man" character—perhaps this is an attempt to make this linking role more Shakespearean. The phrase does appear in *Hamlet* on six occasions.

Archers *theme tune*—(PSC; "Piston Engine [A Bargain]") The theme song to the popular radio show *The Archers* is called "Barwick Green" and was composed by Arthur Wood. This BBC Radio drama has been running since January 1951, and was originally created to offer postwar farming and husbandry support to a nation recovering from years of privation, and was even a not-so-subtle reminder of the importance of UK price supports and subsidies in the face of the flood of incoming European goods (see Smethurst). During WWII, as well, when material and personnel were at a premium in the UK, feature filmmaking could only be truly justified as part of the war effort, and it was with tacit Ministry of Information approval and assistance that such films of Englishness like *Henry V* could be produced, and on such a massive scale.

This crossing of purposes in entertainment shows was not lost on the Pythons, as various sketches have wandered into similarly divergent storylines, including a wrestling match to prove the existence of God (Ep. 2), the Careers Advisory Board hosting of a "Silly Job Interview" (Ep. 5), and all of Ep. 45 as a Party Political Broadcast for the dark horse Liberal Party.

"arrived here by train"—("Police Helmets") The nearest train station to the Westminster Bridge site is Waterloo, to the south.

Assistant—(PSC; "Boxing Match Aftermath") The Assistant is played by Bob Raymond, who appears in most of the fourth series episodes.

– B –

"bachelor friend"—("Dramatis Personae") A Victorian-era euphemism for a homosexual man, which fits, considering Chapman's admitted sexuality. Gilliam is credited as being a "butch" bachelor friend to Hamlet—he had been married since the previous year. In the "Dramatis Personae" provided for the actual Shakespeare play, Horatio is listed as "friend to Hamlet" (*Riverside Shakespeare* 1141).

"bogus psychiatrists"—("Bogus Psychiatrists") This may be a comment on the significant anti-psychiatry bias that appeared after WWII, especially, and which came to a head in the 1960s and 1970s. The practices of the Nazi, Japanese, and then Soviet mental health communities in regard to political and criminal prisoners as well as mentally ill citizens before, during, and then after the war called into question all invasive and so-called traditional treatments of mental disease.

This section is probably a reference to then-infamous American con artist Frank Abagnale, Jr., who had impersonated a teacher, a pilot, an attorney, and even a physician before being apprehended in 1969. Abagnale was in the news in 1974, when he was released from prison to assist the U.S. government in fraud investigations.

boxer on a stretcher—(PSC; "Boxing Match Aftermath") The decapitated boxer is played by Reg Turner (WAC T12/1,468).

The setting, according to the printed script, is New York's Madison Square Gardens (*sic*), and the actors all attempt (with varying success) tough, East Coast American accents.

In a connection with the later mention of Nazis Martin Boorman and Heinrich "Gus" Himmler, author Ladislas Farago (see "Sinatra" note below) is quoted by *Time* magazine as saying: "Even if I bring Martin Bormann back with me personally and exhibit him in the Felt Forum of Madison Square Garden, people will still say it's just another hoax" (11 December 1972).

"Brian"—(link out of "Queen Victoria Handicap") Another reference to Brian Clough, football player, coach, and analyst, who was mentioned and lampooned in Ep. 41, where he slouches through another football analysis.

Burlington Wall-banger—(PSC; link out of "Father-in-Law") This reference is most likely an amalgam. First, Burlington-Ware launched the upscale Burlington Arcade (in Piccadilly) in 1819, a fashionable mall before there were shopping malls. Stores within tended to be very high-end, and would have sold gold-leafed wall-bangers, if such things were available for sale. Secondly, the drink Harvey Wallbanger had been introduced (in the United States) just a few years prior to this episode's creation. The script also mentions that the weapon looks like an "Indian club," which was a piece of athletic equipment (not unlike a thin bowling pin) popular in Victorian times modified from an ancient Indian weapon.

– C –

"Chaldeans"—("Police Helmets") From the Babylonian empire of about the seventh century.

The episode seems to hinge thematically on "authenticity," with credentials proving the qualified psychiatrist, a number and helmet proving the true Metro policeman, Edgeworth's name on the bottom of her chair, and Hamlet's inability to do anything other than what has historically made him "authentic." Previously an authentic BALPA spokesman wore the appropriate cufflinks, etc. (Ep. 16), and a "bona fide" animal lover would not have tried to feed goldfish sausages (Ep. 13). This struggle with authenticity continues the Pythons' fascination (conscious or otherwise) with the Sartrean notion of *choosing* freedom and living life as it can/should be lived.

Charlton, Michael—(PSC; "*Nationwide*") Charlton (b. 1927) was a presenter on *Panorama* (1953-) and reported on both the 1964 General Election and the Apollo 11 landing for the BBC.

"completely bona fide psychiatrist"—("Bogus Psychiatrists") This fixation on authenticity is also a Sartrean conceit, with the Pythons playing on Sartre's examinations of his own characters as they do or do not live "authentically." Essentially, are they so afraid of the freedoms of this life that they choose (in bad faith) to live by the strictures of class and race and religions and gender, eschewing complete (and frightening) freedom

for the comforts of restraint and submission? See Sartre's *Being and Nothingness* for much, much more.

"Cutty Sark"—("Father-in-Law") A clipper ship commissioned in 1869.

– D –

deafening sound track—("Bogus Psychiatrists") This chase music is "The Good Word" from Johnny Scott and his Orchestra (WAC T12/1,468).

"Dull, John"—("Police Helmets") The name here is certainly a comment on the perceived interest level in a show like *Nationwide*, its subject matter, and on-air staff. Besides Frank Bough, others presenting on *Nationwide* in these early years included Michael Barratt, Bob Wellings, and Sue Lawley.

This "John Dull" reference, however, would have meant one of the myriad reporters sent out on assignment across the UK for the show's regional human interest stories. Contributor Philip Tibbenham, for example, reported on the effects of the new three-day work week (thanks to power and goods shortages) on the town of Hartlepool, Durham. Due to a prolonged coal miners' work-to-rule action in 1973, most areas of the country were rationed to three days per week of electricity transmissions by January and February of 1974. This episode of *Nationwide* was broadcast on 18 January 1974 (BFI).

– E –

Episode 43—Recorded 2 November 1974, and transmitted 21 November 1974, this episode was given the subtitle "Python's Playhouse," indicating the troupe's movement away from the previous three series. A quote probably submitted by the show to the *Radio Times*: "Programme Four: Monty Python has decided to change its image. Towards Shakespeare seemed to be the logical departure and the MP Repertory Company present their production of *Hamlet*" (WAC T12/1,468).

Also appearing: Jimmy Hill (*Match of the Day*), Connie Booth; (stuntmen playing Queen Victorias) Marc Boyle (*You Only Live Twice*), Tim Condren (Ep. 41; *Star Wars*), Billy Horrigan (*Dr. Who; Raiders of the Lost Ark*), Tony Smart (*Casino Royale*), and Bob Raymond (Eps. 40-45; *Softly Softly*); (extras) Richard Sheekey (*Some Mothers Do 'Ave 'Em*), Bill Barnsley (*Z Cars*), Victor Charrington (*Dixon of Dock Green*), Martine Holland, Jackie Bristow, Katie Evans (*Softly Softly*), Freda Curtis, Mrs. Kitty, Eileen Rice, Rosemary Parrot, Babs Westcott, Edna Wood (*Wanted For Murder*), Edith Crump, Hilary Abbot, Reg Turner (*Z Cars*), James Haswell (*Dr. Who*),

Tony Snell, Michael Dalton, Stuart Myers (*Microbes and Men*); (Asian actors) Vincent Wong (Ep. 22; *Birds on the Wing*), Edgar Hing, Ken Nazarin (Ep. 34; *A Casual Affair*), and Robert Ng; Annet Peters (Eps. 40-42; *The Fall and Rise of Reginald Perrin*), Pamela Wardell (Ep. 41; *Microbes and Men*), Donald Groves (*Jackanory*), Reg Thomason (*Some Mothers Do 'Ave 'Em*), Lionel Sansby (Ep. 41; *Blakes 7*), Michael Finbar (Ep. 42; *Blakes 7*), Michael Brydon (*Dr. Who*), Harry Davis (Ep. 40; *Dixon of Dock Green*) (WAC T12/1,468).

A number of these extras are "locals," meaning they were cast in the areas where the Pythons shot location footage for this final series.

"Epsom"—(link into "Dentists") Epsom Downs is a racecourse that hosts the Epsom Derby, and is the second race of the English Triple Crown.

The racecourse used here is not Epsom, but actually Lingfield Racecourse, Lingfield, Surrey, south of London. The footage was shot on 24 September 1974 (WAC T12/1,469).

"European Cup"—(link into "Dentists") FC Bayern-Munich did win the Cup for the first time in 1973-1974, and would win again the following two championships, beating Leeds United FC 2-0 in the 1974-1975 final match. There were some significant blow-outs during the 1973-1974 European Cup, with established football powers like Club Brugge KV beating Floriana FC 10-0, and the Irish team Crusaders FC losing badly to the Romanian team Dinamo Bucuresti 12-0 (see Motson and Rowlinson).

– F –

Frank Bough type presenter—(PSC; link into "Dentists") Frank Bough (b. 1933) presented for *Nationwide*, *Grandstand*, and myriad sports programs. He has already "appeared" in Ep. 35, covering the Olympic Hide-and-Seek finals, and then in Ep. 39, where he presents rugby league highlights (where Mrs. Colyer is tossed into the scrum).

– H –

Hamlet—("Bogus Psychiatrists") Shakespearean tragedy written about 1599, the play has become the *locus classicus* for both the Elizabethan revenge tragedy corpus and the "troubled" dramatic character.

Many critics have put Hamlet "on the couch," including J. Dover Wilson in *What Happens in Hamlet* (1935):

> From the *point of view of analytic psychology* such a character may even seem a monster of inconsistency. This

does not matter, if as here it also seems to spectators in the theatre to be more convincingly life-like than any other character in literature. (219; italics added)

This very "life-like" character of Hamlet can be assumed, in the Pythons' world, to be so real that he must be obsessed with sex and the body, as indicated by years of Shakespeare scholarship and the Pythons' own penchant for such corporeality. The popularization of Freud's theories of the unconscious—emerging and being engaged by scientists, critics, and laymen alike between the wars—accounts here for the frustrated, sexualized, psychoanalyzed Hamlet.

Harley Street type—(PSC; "Bogus Psychiatrists") Harley Street has been the upscale home of the London medical establishment for many years, and has already been mentioned in the scripts for Eps. 13 and 22. See notes to those episodes for more.

"head came off"—("Boxing Match Aftermath") This oft-injured fighter could be a very topical reference to the then-heavyweight contender Gerry Quarry (1945-1999), an American fighter who suffered many stopped fights due to facial/head cuts that could not be adequately treated.

"Hill, Jimmy"—("Queen Victoria Handicap") A football player, coach, and broadcaster, Hill (b. 1928) was hosting *Match of the Day* during this period.

hospital ward—(PSC; "Boxing Commentary") In this scene are bandaged patients (Reg Turner, James Haswell, Donald Grove, and Lionel Sansby), as well as patients Wong, Hing, Nazarin, and Ng (WAC T12/1,468).

– I –

"I am myself indifferent honest . . . "—("Hamlet and Ophelia") Slightly misquoted from *Hamlet* 3.1: "I am myself indifferent honest, but yet I could accuse me of such things that it were better my mother had not borne me" (3.1.121-23).

The following "O fair Ophelia" lines come from earlier in this same act, so are played here out of order: "The fair Ophelia. Nymph in thy orisons / Be all my sins remb'red" (3.1.87-88).

identically dressed Queen Victorias—(PSC; "Queen Victoria Handicap") This costume is based on the well-known depiction of the mourning Victoria painted by Heinrich von Angeli (1840-1925) in 1899. Albert had died in 1861. There were also several paintings created in the Angeli style (and featuring Victoria in the same black dress) in later years, as well as a few photographs featuring the same attire.

"It's the sex, is it"—("Bogus Psychiatrists") The long-held bias against Freud's psychoanalytical approach through the subconscious, at least in popular culture, is the seemingly unwavering focus on sex or the libido as the foundation of many/all psychological problems.

– J –

Japanese businessmen . . . Tour de France—(PSC; link out of "Father-in-Law") The "Japanese businessmen" are played by Wong, Hing, Nazarin, and Ng (see Episode 43 notes above for their credits); the "lady American tourists" are Annet Peters and Pam Wardell; the "English gentlemen in pyjamas" are Tony Snell, Donald Grove, and Reg Thomason; the "Tour de France riders" are Michael Dalton and Stuart Meyers; the "Swedish businessmen" are Lionel Sansby, Michael Finbar, and Michael Bridon; and Harry Davies plays the "Winston Churchill" character (WAC T12/1,468).

Joseph, Sir K.—("Dramatis Personae") Conservative politician already mentioned in the credits to Ep. 42, it's no surprise he's characterized by the Pythons as a "loony."

– L –

"Let four captains . . . "—(link out of "Queen Victoria Handicap") From Hamlet 5.2, the actual lines, as spoken by Fortinbras, not Victoria:

> *Fort.*   Let four captains
> Bear Hamlet like a soldier to the stage,
> For he was likely, had he been put on,
> To have prov'd most royal. . . . (395-98)

lyrical music—(PSC; "Father-in-Law") Even though the printed script calls for transition music here, none is included, and there is no indication in the WAC records that any such music was requested for copyright clearance.

– M –

"Mau Mau, Ronnie"—("Live From Epsom") A tidbit from recent British colonial history, the Mau Mau Uprising involved Kenyan rebels sniping at the British troops and administrative authority in Kenya between 1952 and 1960, with a number of white settlers gruesomely hacked to death by local insurgents. Earlier references to the Mau Mau incidents occurred in Eps. 9 and 31.

– N –

Natal—(PSC; "Bogus Psychiatrists") Dr. Natal (Idle) isn't named outside of the printed scripts. The Colony of Natal in eastern South Africa was a British Colony throughout the second half of the nineteenth century.

"Nationwide"—("*Nationwide*") A very popular current affairs program that adroitly gave attention to most of the regions covered by the BBC, *Nationwide* (BBC1, 1969-1984) was ensured a wide and loyal viewership. Herbert Mental (Jones), the man who collects birdwatchers' eggs in Ep. 26, mentions an appearance as an "eccentric" on the regional section of *Nationwide*.

The *Nationwide* theme music is from Johnny Scott, "The Good Word" (WAC T12/1,468).

Nationwide had made its debut on the BBC less than one month before *Monty Python's Flying Circus* came on the air on 5 October 1969.

New York Times *headline*—(PSC; "Boxing Match Aftermath") The copy of the *Times* is from 29 October 1974.

– O –

"O/C lights"—("Father-in-Law") Probably from the military, and here means "Officer in Charge" of the lights.

"on aggregate"—(link into "Dentists") In English football an aggregate score is achieved when the scores for two matches are combined, the winner having the higher aggregate score. This can only mean that Wrexham, in the first leg of this match, must have scored more than 4,397 points against Bayern-München.

– P –

"Peter"—("Queen Victoria Handicap") This is likely a reference to Peter Bromley (1929-2003), the voice of English horse racing, especially on BBC radio, for more than forty years. The "Brian" mentioned may be Brian Moore (1932-2001), another well-known sports broadcaster, but associated with ITV.

"Pinner"—("Police Helmets") Pinner is a small town in northwest London, near Harrow. Pinner is just west of other *FC* locations, including Golders Green (Ep. 8), Edgware Road, and Willesden (WAC T12/1,416).

policeman runs up to him, grabs his arm, twists it . . .—("Police Helmets") The insensitive and downright brutal police officer of the *Flying Circus* world appears throughout the series. In Ep. 42 the wheelchair-bound Security Guard (Gilliam) at the BBC is described as looking "neo-fascist." Earlier, in Ep. 29, Inspector Leopard (Cleese) knees his PC (Gilliam) and arrests Queen Elizabeth I because she's handy and "there's violence to be done." Earlier still the testifying policeman (Palin) truncheons everyone within reach (Ep. 27), and in Ep. 17 PC Pan Am (Chapman) arrests a man (Idle) for simply reporting a crime.

The oft-captured images of policemen in the United States, UK, and across Europe (especially in the mid- to late-1960s) dealing with angry "rights" protesters contributed to this easy depiction. More recently and closer to home, a demonstrator (a Warwick University student) had died in June 1974 at an anti-fascist counterdemonstration in Red Lion Square. In this raucous demonstration there were at least three combatant parties—fascists, anti-fascists, and police. The popular claim was that a policeman's club had killed the young man, but no evidence supports any final conclusion. The story was well-covered in period newspapers; also, see "On This Day" at bbc.co.uk, 15 June 1974.

Press Photographer—(PSC; "Boxing Match Aftermath") The two press photogs in this scene are played by Michael Bridon and Michael Finbar, while Bob Raymond carries one end of the litter, and extra Ken Cranham may be on the other end (WAC T12/1,468).

– R –

"Real Madrid"—("Queen Victoria Handicap") Considered to be one of the best football teams in the world in this period (and the twentieth century), Real Madrid had won the UEFA championship 1956-1960 and 1966, and had played for second place in 1962 and 1964.

"Robinsons"—("Piston Engine [A Bargain]") Based on the Archers family from *The Archers* radio series (1951-), which follows the lives and travails of a farm family in rural (and mythical) Ambridge, England.

The visual cutting from radio set to radio set is probably a comment on the huge radio broadcast presence *The Archers* enjoyed since it first took to the airwaves in 1951—reaching an unprecedented 60 percent market share at one point.

"room in Polonius's house"—("A Room in Polonius's House") This particular setting occurs in act one, scene three (1.3) and act two, scene one (2.1) in *Hamlet*. Ophelia and Hamlet have no exchanges in these scenes from the original play, and aren't even in the room together.

– S –

"sent off"—(link out of "Queen Victoria Handicap") There is a reason these rather silly send-offs are mentioned here, in the 1974 *FC* series. The "red card" in international football—issued to a player for an ejectionable incident of misconduct—had been instituted in 1970 in FIFA play (along with the "yellow card"). In the 1974 tournament (13 June through 7 July) the first red card was issued to Carlos Caszely of Chile, and he was sent off in the match against West Germany.

"she's all ready for it"—("Bogus Psychiatrist") The debate rages on today as to the level of sexual intimacy Hamlet and Ophelia may have reached—equally strident voices (on scholarly Shakespeare listserv sites, for example) argue for everything from unblemished chastity to heavy petting to either a hysterical or real pregnancy contributing to the characters' states of mind. It's interesting to note that the surviving quarto and folio versions of the play—Q1, Q2, and F1—also disagree in their characterizations of Ophelia, Hamlet, and their physical relationship.

"Sinatra, Frank"—("Boxing Match Aftermath") The legendary singer Sinatra (1915-1998) was also a lifelong boxing fan, and even co-promoted several fighters over the years. He was ringside in Madison Square Garden in 1971 when Frazier beat Ali (see *Boxing Monthly* July 1998). Sinatra and actor George Raft (1895-1980), a former boxer himself, attended fights at Hollywood Legion Stadium in the 1940s and 1950s (Springer).

"Martin Bormann"—Bormann (c. 1900-1945) was one of Hitler's most trusted henchmen, and allegedly died in 1945 as Berlin fell. The mention of Nazis Bormann and Himmler (1900-1945) here—as well as the subtitle of this scene—is probably due to the recent and controversial release (in 1974) of the book *Aftermath: Martin Bormann and the Fourth Reich* by Ladislas Farago. The author purported to have found that Bormann not only survived the war but escaped Berlin and Europe, and as late as 1972 was alive and well in Argentina. A lively denunciation of the book and these "facts" was waged in the newspapers of the time, with an especially interesting exchange found in the *New York Review of Books* between reviewer Hugh Trevor-Roper and Farago attorney Joel Weinberg (14 November 1974 and 20 February 1975). Farago's assertions about Bormann appeared first in a series of articles in *The Daily Express*, which is where the Pythons probably encountered them.

six pairs of legs—(PSC; "Bogus Psychiatrists') These actors under the prop computer are Tony Snell, Michael Dalton, and Stuart Myers, and there are six legs in toto (WAC T12/1,468).

sports pictures—(PSC; link into "Dentists") The pictures behind the Bough-like character include images of show jumping, cricket, track and field sprinting, Formula 1 racing, and football, as well as an image of Mark Spitz swimming in a butterfly (or the 4 x 100 medley relay) event in the 1972 Olympics.

– T –

Third Jockey—(PSC; "Live From Epsom") The Third Jockey (wearing the green silks) appears to be Neil Innes, who is listed as appearing, per WAC records (WAC T12/1,468).

"To be or not to be"—("Bogus Psychiatrists") Probably the most famous speech in all dramatic history, this is found in *Hamlet* 3.1. The "too too solid flesh should melt" lines are found earlier, in *Hamlet* 1.2, after Hamlet's been left alone by Claudius and Gertrude:

> *Ham.* O that this too too sallied flesh would melt,
> Thaw, and resolve itself into a dew!
> Or that the Everlasting had not fix'd
> His canon 'gainst [self-]slaughter! O God, God. . . .
> (129-32)

Lastly, the abbreviated mention of the "Alas poor Yorick" is drawn from the fifth act, first scene.

tragic music—(PSC; "Bogus Psychiatrists") The "tragic music" is actually somewhat martial, and is from Walton's "*Henry V* Suite: Globe Playhouse," as played by Walton's Philharmonic Orchestra (WAC T12/1,468).

The chase music that follows is not listed in the records for the episode.

"Tsar's private army"—("Police Helmets") The Alexander tsars installed "Internal Guard" cadres in the nineteenth century, while earlier and more bloodthirsty black-clad operatives served Ivan in the sixteenth century. The groups were essentially secret police units.

two men in white coats—(PSC; "Bogus Psychiatrists") These actors hustling the Bogus Psychiatrist off are Reg Turner and James Haswell. Their credits are listed above in the "Episode 43" note.

– U –

"University of Oxford"—("Bogus Psychiatrists") Palin is one of the two Pythons who graduated from Oxford.

"British Psychiatric Association"—The British Psychological Society was founded in 1901, was located at

Tavistock House, South Tavistock Square, WC1, and was earlier referenced in Ep. 16 by the BALPA spokesman (Idle).

"Psychiatry Today"—Probably meaning *The British Journal of Psychiatry*, established in 1965 in the UK.

– W –

West End surgery—(PSC; "Bogus Psychiatrists") London's West End has been the home to most of the city's live theatres for many years, and has been a trendy spot for business and living since at least the eighteenth century. The BBC's Portland Place flagship building is not far northwest of the West End.

"Westminster Bridge"—("Police Helmets") The bridge spans the Thames from Westminster (at the Houses of Parliament) to Lambeth, and is still a very busy bridge.

"wet things"—("Nationwide") There were some viewers who complained that the regionalized eccentricity of *Nationwide* made for dull, provincial viewing—including roller-skating ducks, beer-drinking snails—and that serious news was to be had elsewhere. The complex *Nationwide* broadcast structure—where broadcast from Lime Grove Studios (BBC) would be the "home base" and hand-offs to regional broadcast centers would happen periodically—is also touched on in the sketch, as Charlton (Idle) waits nervously for the first such switch.

"What d'you buy that for?"—("Piston Engine [A Bargain]") The answer: "It was a bargain!" This is a return to a previous episode's fixation of the acquisitive culture (Ep. 41) which had settled in on the UK with the prosperities of the 1950s and beyond. Not only is the engine being casually purchased for no discernible reason, but it's then resold just as casually. In addition, Mrs. Non-Smoker (Jones) isn't consuming her goods; she's using her purchases as weapons, smashing birds left and right.

It's probably no accident that these ladies have been listening to a version of *The Archers*, a radio program originally designed to encourage consumer spending, build consumer confidence, and reaffirm the government's pivotal role in recovering the agricultural economy (and fending off the alliance-happy Europeans and culturally barbaric Americans) during the lean postwar years.

"wondrous strange"—("Piston Engine [A Bargain]") From Horatio and Hamlet's conversation in act one, scene five, when the Ghost has appeared beneath the stage, demanding they both take an oath (*Hamlet* 1.5.163-90). The Pythons abridge Hamlet's speech quite a bit, eliding most of his lines between 169 (in the *Riverside Shakespeare*) and 187, picking up again at line 188:

> Hamlet: The time is out of joint—O cursed sprite,
> That ever I was born to set it right!
> Nay, come, let's go together.　　　　*Exeunt.* (1.5.188-90)

"wouldn't put up much of a fight"—("Live From Epsom") This specter of forceful redevelopment isn't terribly unrealistic. The influx of Commonwealth foreigners coupled with the postwar baby boom meant housing was at a premium in the UK in the 1960s, while retail expansion tended to trump older apartments and neighborhoods, and there were plenty of unscrupulous types (including the notorious Notting Hill slumlord Peter Rachman) taking advantage of the situation. According to Donald Chesworth (1923-1991), a London Councillor:

> There were, however, enormous profits to be made . . . there were people who specialized in getting rid of existing tenants—old people, all kinds of people—and replacing them substantially by newcomers to Britain, who were in desperate need for themselves and their families. . . . They were willing to pay very substantial rents. (Audio transcription, *Eyewitness: 1960-69*, "Rachmanism 1")

Rachman has already been lampooned in Ep. 14, as the low-end gangster Dino Vercotti (Palin) being menaced by the Piranha brothers. See notes to Ep. 14 for more on that real-life intimidation scheme.

Secondly, in the early 1970s there were significant razings of housing in London to take advantage of a new hotel tax break that paid off by the rentable room, and dozens of new hotels began to spring up. Thousands of residents found themselves out of their apartments and, thanks to the rather cozy arrangement between local councils and developers, those displaced

had little opportunity to "put up much of a fight," either (*Private Eye* 20 Feb 1970, 20-21).

"Wrexham"—(link into "Dentists") A football club located in Wrexham, Wales, Wrexham FC first appeared in European Cup competition in 1970. Wrexham is about forty-four miles southeast of Colwyn Bay, where Jones was born.

– Y –

"Yes, a private dick!"—("Bogus Psychiatrists") So, is Hamlet also participating in acts of Sartrean bad faith as he laments his lot in life yet chooses to continue in that lot? The chartered accountant who wants to be a lion tamer (played by Palin) also clings to his dull but safe profession in Ep. 10. (See notes to Eps. 9 and 13 for more of this "bad faith" phenomenon as it appears throughout *FC*.) In the world of the play, of course, Hamlet does act the investigator, the discoverer (meaning he reveals and discloses), as he entertains the Ghost's charges and demands, and seeks out the truth of not only his father's death but his uncle's duplicity and his mother's unwitting betrayal. He also "discovers" the depths of his sadness to Rosencrantz and Guildenstern, as well as Polonius behind the arras (with the point of a sword). But in true "bad faith" form, Hamlet won't free himself of everything and become that private dick, he won't escape his role in this 400-year-old tragedy—instead, he goes to a modern-day anguish manager (a psychiatrist), to deal with the bad faith issues.

"you sure it doesn't put you off?"—(link into "Father-in-Law") The incongruity here, of course, is that this publicly affectionate couple isn't put off by the cold, wet pavement or a busy sidewalk in the heart of workaday London, but will struggle with intimacy when her dad's in bed with them in the following scene.

Episode 44: "Mr. Neutron"

– A –

"a bit flash"—("Mr. Neutron") Meaning Shirley is a bit showy or ostentatious.

American government building—(PSC; link into "Teddy Salad") The still image used as the headquarters for FEAR is an image of the Federal Reserve Board Building in Washington, D.C. There is no record in the WAC records to indicate a copyright clearance search for this photo.

American military music—(PSC; link into "Teddy Salad") The music here is Sousa's "Stars and Stripes Forever" as performed by the British Grenadier Guards (who also perform every iteration of "Liberty Bell" in the series) (WAC T12/1,469).

"Anouk"—("Teddy Salad [CIA Agent]") Not an Eskimo but a Dutch name, "Anouk" was probably chosen because (1) it sounds like "Nanook," the star of the Robert Flaherty Eskimo pseudo-ethnography *Nanook of the North* (1922), and (2) Anouk Aimee (b. 1932) is a French actress who would have been known to the Pythons, having appeared in *La Dolce Vita* (1960, musical theme used in Ep. 42) and *8½* (1963).

– B –

"Ballet Rambert"—("Teddy Salad [CIA Agent]") This company (established in 1935) had by this time switched from ballet to modern dance.

"Petrouchka"—Also *"Petrushka,"* this was a controversial (thanks to the avant garde music) Igor Stravinsky ballet first performed in 1911. The Pythons use an audio snippet from another controversial Stravinsky ballet, *The Rite of Spring* (1913)—which, along with its dance, caused a riot—in Ep. 30.

"Fille Mal Gardée"—A late eighteenth-century pastiche French ballet.

"Benidorm"—("Teddy Salad [CIA Agent]") Another seaside resort town, this one in Alicante, Spain. The other mentioned in this episode is Shanklin, Isle of Wight (see below). The Mediterranean vacation spots have been mentioned several times by the Pythons, most notably by Idle's rambling Tourist (Idle) in the "Travel Agent" sketch in Ep. 31, but also as a past vacation spot for Captain Biggles (Chapman) in Ep. 33.

"bream"—("Teddy Salad [CIA Agent]") Certain types of bream (bluegill, e.g.) are found in Canada, so this request wouldn't have been so out of line. Bream was also one of the possible "toilet requisites" proffered by the Chemist (Palin) in Ep. 17.

– C –

C & A twin set—(PSC; "Teddy Salad [CIA Agent]") The uniform of the smart, mid-1970s Pepperpot, this outfit is also employed in the Batley Townswomen's Guild re-enactments, as well as Ep. 41 (in the department store), and the Wife in "The Restaurant Sketch" in the second *FZ*.

"C & A" was a clothing store chain founded in the Netherlands in the nineteenth century, and was considered a high street–type (downtown) store when it reached the UK in 1922. The stores sold moderately priced (and modestly fashioned) clothing ideal for the Pepperpot wanting to step out.

"canelloni"—("Teddy Salad [CIA Agent]") Misspelled in the printed scripts, "cannelloni" is a meat-stuffed pastry, and has already been mistaken for fish by Mrs. Scum (Jones) in Ep. 20. Mrs. S.C.U.M. will appear later in Ep. 44, also played by Jones, though in her C&A twin set she looks decidedly more modish.

Carpenter is trekking along—("Teddy Salad [CIA Agent]") The background music here is Sibelius' "Finlandia Op. 26 No. 7," as performed by the London Proms Symphony Orchestra (WAC T12/1,469).

"CIA"—("Teddy Salad [CIA Agent]") The Central Intelligence Agency was very active internationally during the Cold War. Intelligence gathering and anti-Communist activities dominated the work, with CIA agents and mercenaries active—especially in the Third World—wherever a democratic-styled (or just anti-Communist) government might be losing support, or a Marxist government showing signs of weakness.

The silliness of Teddy Salad and this sketch in general might be a result of incidents like the Bay of Pigs debacle, where the CIA's reputation had been badly tarnished.

contributions of arms from householders—(PSC; link into "Post Box Ceremony") The Firearms Act of 1968 in the UK had banned all sorts of automatic weapons, as well as weapons not deemed ordinary for target shooting or self-defense. This newest Act had consolidated a jumbled handful of earlier ordinances into one, which may account for the array of weapons the housewives are producing. Also, the Firearms Act of 1968 defined a firearm as "a lethal barreled weapon of any description from which *any shot, bullet or other missile can be discharged*" (italics added). This looks like it would include bazookas, grenade launchers, rocket-propelled grenades, etc.

"Corsair"—("Teddy Salad [CIA Agent]") Originally an African coast pirate, the Ford Corsair was built by American automaker Ford in the UK. This family-style car wasn't made after 1970. (There are, of course, Ford Corsair car clubs in the UK.)

"Cotton, Mr."—("Teddy Salad [CIA Agent]") Bill Cotton (b. 1928) was the head of BBC Light Entertainment Group, and is the man who had to respond to most of the Pythons' (personally and via their agents) complaints about salaries, repeat fees, time slots, repeat time slots, and on and on. Cotton would also have been fielding many of the complaints lodged against the show, not only from viewers, but weekly from other heads of BBC departments.

– **D** –

décor of a rather exclusive restaurant—(PSC; "Teddy Salad [CIA Agent]") Characteristic of this fourth and final series is the escalating budget for each episode. In the first series, for example, blank backdrops or extant sets (at Television Centre, Golders Green, and Ealing TFS) were used for all sorts of set-ups, and even as late as Ep. 29 (third series) the very clever "Argument Clinic" sketch was staged in a bare bones office set. By the latter third of the third series (i.e., Ep. 37 and beyond), costumes and set dressing had become increasingly intricate and baroque, while at the same time audiences were complaining that the show wasn't as funny as it had been (especially without Cleese) (WAC T12/1,469).

In this episode there are also at least two (expensive) process shots (masked screen or green screen special effects shots) that had no place in the earlier series, when the show's shoestring budget seemed to ratchet up the creativity level.

disembodied voice—(PSC; "Mr. Neutron") Not unlike a Bond-type villain or henchman, or even a cartoon supervillain of the period, which Mr. Neutron (Chapman) clearly resembles. The recent Bond-spoof films *Our Man Flint* (1966) and *In Like Flint* (1967) may also be precursors to this parody, as was the silly "Captain Fantastic" serial that appeared as a recurring segment in Palin/Jones/Idle's children's show *Do Not Adjust Your Set* (1967).

– **E** –

Episode 44—Entitled "Mr. Neutron," this themed episode was recorded on 9 November 1974 and broadcast 28 November 1974.

The additional cast for this episode include: Len and Dot Webb (husband and wife mayor and mayoress), Muriel Evans, Betty Budd, Barry Casley, Mrs. Please, Mrs. Richards, Freda Curtis, Mrs. Bradwell, Rosemary Parrot, Edna Wood (*Wanted For Murder*), Johnathon, Andrew and David Chandler, Noel Pointing, Araby Rio, Tony Marshall, Jasmine Rio, Helen Fishlock, Reg Turner, Bob Raymond, Eden Fox, Rory O'Connor, Ronald Musgrove (*Colditz*), Bill Hughes (*Z Cars*), Belinda Lee (*Are You Being Served?*), Annet Peters (*The Fall and Rise of Reginald Perrin*), Pam Wardell (*Microbes and Men*), Diana Holt, Alison Kemp, Jane von Arrensdorff, Leslie Conroy, and Bill Earle (WAC T12/1,469). Many of these extras are locals (living outside of Greater London) brought in for location shooting.

"Everyone's really scared of us"—("Mr. Neutron") This "show of force" or Monroe Doctrine–type mentality had been apparent in the U.S. foreign policy since the Spanish-American War, at least, and had reached something of a zenith during the Vietnam and Cold War era, when U.S. military strength (what the

Brit press would call "gunboat diplomacy") was constantly on display, even in Britain. (From 1962 the United States had, for example, been supplying the UK with all of its nuclear-tipped ballistic missiles, including the Polaris ICBM, and in return occupied nuclear submarine berths in Scotland.)

According to the "Department of the Army Historical Summary," however, in 1974 (fiscal year) there were no U.S. combat units "engaged in military action" anywhere in Southeast Asia, for instance, and the armed forces were able to make enlistment quotas without conscription for the first time since 1948 (1). There had been significant military exercises with NATO allies in the recent past which would have made the news, including "Operation Reforger" in fall 1973 in Germany (2.4).

"expensive and lavish scenes"—("Teddy Salad [CIA Agent]") These episodes were, in fact, much more expensive than previous episodes, and this sketch is most likely a comment on the BBC's continuing prate (via memo) about salaries and costs.

– F –

"FEAR"—("Mr. Neutron") There are and were innumerable American military acronyms available for spoofing, including DARPA (Defense Advanced Research Projects Agency), NORAD (North American Aerospace Defense Command), and FOB (Forward Operating Base), the last of which would have been mentioned often in newscasts and reports during the recently concluded Vietnam conflict.

"fifty-six stone"—("Teddy Salad [CIA Agent]") Approximately 784 pounds.

flash, a jump cut—(PSC; "Teddy Salad [CIA Agent]") The special effect sound used here as Mrs. S.C.U.M. is made more beautiful is borrowed from Ilhan Mimaroglu's "Agony," an electronic music piece composed in 1965 (WAC T12/1,469). The prompt for this sound effect is not included in the printed script.

"Fonteyn, Margot"—("Teddy Salad [CIA Agent]") The prima ballerina of her time, Fonteyn (1919-1991) danced initially at Sadler's Wells Theatre, already mentioned by Cleese in his military/dance rant in Ep. 35. *Les Sylphides* is a non-narrative ballet first performed in 1893, and performed by Fonteyn in 1938 at Sadler's Wells, according to Helpmann's "Prompt Collection."

"Lionel Blair"—Born in 1931, Blair headed his own dance troupe in the 1960s, appearing in *Hard Day's Night* (1964) and myriad variety programs. Blair has also been mentioned in Ep. 35.

"fruit machine"—("Teddy Salad [CIA Agent]") A fruit machine is a slot machine, in tabloid and underworld lingo. The Piranha brothers strongarm their targets by forcing them to buy overpriced "fruit machines" in Ep. 14; the Kray brothers had practiced a similar shakedown.

– G –

"Gobi Desert"—("Teddy Salad [CIA Agent]") The Chinese/Mongolian desert is the setting for one of this episode's special effects shots, where a portion of the image is matted out, and a dunescape is inserted.

GPO van—(PSC; "Post Box Ceremony") From the General Post Office, these are still very recognizable red vans. The GPO had actually been dissolved in 1969, with postal service duties being assumed by the Post Office Corporation, formed by an Act of Parliament.

"gunga"—("Teddy Salad [CIA Agent]") A reference to the water-bearer in Kipling's 1892 poem "Gunga Din," here used as a catch-all for calling the ethnic help.

– H –

"Harrow, Hammersmith, Stepney, Wandsworth and Enfield"—("Teddy Salad [CIA Agent]") Following this route executes a large "U" around London, and would be an effective bombing path if killing civilians were the goal. The collateral damage of the Cold War was significant—including the support of brutal anti-Communist dictators, death by terrorist and anti-terrorist activity, civilians dying in B-52 carpet bombing runs in Southeast Asia, etc.

"hen-teaser"—("Teddy Salad [CIA Agent]") The Fiat chairman (played by Idle) has already asked this question back in Ep. 42.

his little tadger tiny as a tapir's tits—(PSC; "Teddy Salad ["CIA Agent]") Another example where portions of the printed script are included by the Pythons just for the Pythons, meaning the described action or item never actually appears on the screen (in this case, because it's an alliterative metaphor), and is never spoken by a character. These kinds of "in jokes" are obviously just designed for the mutual amusement of the Pythons, and don't exist for the viewer at all.

"Tadger" is Yorkshire slang for "penis," while a tapir is a tropical climate ungulate.

"Horse of the Year Show"—("*Conjuring Today*") Already mentioned in *FC* in Ep. 28, where the show was being broadcast from the Kellys' flat due to BBC budget cuts. A very popular show in its own right, but with an older demographic, *Horse of the Year* would have been one of those "rubbish" shows to the younger generation.

housewife brings out a rather sophisticated-looking ground-to-air missile—(PSC; link into "Post Box Ceremony") In the immediate months after WWII, only four countries—the United States, Britain, France, and the UK—competed for and with missile technology, much of it brought home from the Nazi works at Peenemünde (Ep. 1). By 1973, however, missiles had proliferated throughout Central and Eastern Europe, across the Middle East and the Asian diaspora, and Khrushchev had even tried to install them in Cuba, instigating the Cuban Missile Crisis in 1962.

The (a) success the North Vietnamese forces enjoyed in deploying and then effectively using ground-to-air missiles against American aircraft in the Vietnam conflict and (b) the significance of Syrian missiles (all Soviet-made) launched against Israel in the Arab-Israeli conflict of 1973 certainly led to this depiction—that anyone, even housewives, could acquire (and successfully use) advanced missile systems.

– I –

"introduce conscription"—(link into "Teddy Salad") The U.S. military had abandoned "the draft" in 1973, after the long and unpopular Vietnam War. In 1974 President Gerald Ford was making headlines by declaring amnesty for many draft evaders.

– K –

"Kellogg's Corn Flake Competition"—("Mr. Neutron") Kellogg's is a well-known American breakfast cereal company. The Kellogg's Corn Flakes brand cereal has been around since 1906, and Kellogg's began running mail-in and cereal box promotional events during the 1920s.

"King Edwards"—("Teddy Salad [CIA Agent]") A popular British baking potato.

– L –

"Laine, Frankie"—("Teddy Salad [CIA Agent]") Laine (b. 1913), an American pop singer, was married to Nan Grey. Laine may have been best known during this period for having sung the theme for the popular television show *Rawhide*.

Lord Mayor is ushered out . . .—(PSC; "Post Box Ceremony") The Lord Mayor and wife are here played by locals Len and Dot Webb, then of 13 Haddington Road, Stoke, Plymouth.

– M –

"Man From the *Radio Times*"—("Teddy Salad [CIA Agent]") Idle is reading the *Radio Times* edition that featured a *Flying Circus* cover story, dated 24 October 1974 (*RT* 2659). This cover story was an attempt by the BBC to usher in the fourth and final series with as large a viewing audience as possible, and promised a new and improved show.

"Moscow! Peking! and Shanklin"—("Teddy Salad [CIA Agent]") The seats of power and struggle during the Cold War period, excluding Shanklin, which is a quiet resort town on the Isle of Wight. Moscow (USSR) and Peking (PRC) were alternately at each other's throats and rattling their sabers at their common ideological enemy, the United States.

"Mr. Neutron"—("Mr. Neutron") This character's name may come from the then-current "neutron bomb" technology and testing, which had been under way since 1962, when the bomb was created by American scientists. The neutron bomb was a *tactical* nuclear weapon, meaning it was designed to be a more focused attack weapon, and not just an umbrella-blast against military installations or even cities, for which larger nuclear devices were designed.

This actually fits the Pythons' positioning of Mr. Neutron (Chapman) in Sutton, a London borough, where "the most dangerous man in the world" can be more concerned about proximity to shops and the West End than global domination, and where his "strike" amounts to attempting to woo away Mrs. S.C.U.M. (Jones) from her husband Ken.

Music: "Rule Britannia" type theme—(PSC; "Teddy Salad [CIA Agent]") This version of "Rule Britannia" is from the All Stars Brass Band, as led by Siebert (WAC T12/1,469).

– N –

"Nous sommes ici . . . "—("Post Box Ceremony") This translation is fairly accurate, as is the German version that is to follow.

– O –

"Oldham"—("Teddy Salad [CIA Agent]") In northwest England, and part of Greater Manchester.

"Ottershaw"—("Mr. Neutron") A village in Surrey, and mentioned in H.G. Wells' *War of the Worlds* as the place where the narrator first hears of the Martian eruptions.

– P –

"perfectly ordinary morning"—("Mr. Neutron") This utopian, bucolic serenity, borrowed from scores of lesser science fiction sources, but also reminiscent of the infamous 1938 radio broadcast of H.G. Wells' *War of the Worlds*, as introduced by a very young Orson Welles:

> With infinite complacence people went to and fro over the earth about their little affairs, serene in the assurance of their dominion over this small, spinning fragment of solar driftwood which, by chance or design, man has inherited out of the dark mystery of Time and Space.

In the case of Wells' original work, the English suburbs were Woking, Ottershaw, Winchester, and Weybridge, etc., and every smaller town "in Berkshire, Surrey, and Middlesex," where the invasion begins (chapter 2).

The "Science Fiction Sketch" in Ep. 7 also begins very much in this form.

photo of Eisenhower—(PSC; "Mr. Neutron") The sitting PM during this period was the newly re-elected Harold Wilson, though Idle is clearly not lampooning him (Wilson was round-faced and sucked on an ever-present pipe), nor the recent Conservative PM Heath. Instead, Idle seems to be reaching back to the height of the Cold War and former Conservative PM Harold Macmillan, who had been such a consistent target of contemporary satirists, including the *Beyond the Fringe* troupe, *Private Eye*, and Frost's *That Was the Week That Was*. Macmillan (distinguished, mustachioed, and eminently deflatable) enjoyed a special relationship with Dwight Eisenhower, both in the war years in Africa and when Eisenhower was U.S. president and Macmillan was PM. Many (including the Pythons, clearly) saw Macmillan as too much of an American lapdog during this period, especially in military and foreign policy terms. (Macmillan was, coincidentally, half-American by birth.) Many political cartoons of the period echo this concern about Macmillan's "special" U.S. relationship. See the British Cartoon Archive.

The worshipful shrine seen in the sketch isn't so out of left field, either. In his review of Geelhoed and Ed-

monds' *Eisenhower, Macmillan and Allied Unity, 1957-1961* (2003), Christopher A. Preble of The Cato Institute, notes that "Macmillan deliberately played on British affection for Eisenhower for his own political gain, shamelessly flaunting Eisenhower during a visit to England in August 1959" (see Preble).

"pillar box"—(PSC; "Post Box Ceremony") A postal receptacle shaped like a pillar.

"Post Office . . . complete world domination"—("Teddy Salad [CIA Agent]") A queer claim seeing that as of 1969 the GPO had ceased to exist as a government department, though maybe the "domination" could only begin when the Post Office became a state-owned company, with the Royal Mail as part of its mandate. This is probably a very tongue-in-cheek reference, also, to the fifteen-year GPO project of assigning postal codes to every corner of the UK, just completed in 1974. The acronym fixation seen earlier can also be credited to this postal code changeover, with acronyms assigned to cities across the country—"CRO" for Croydon, "NPT" for Newport, and "NOR" for Norwich, for example. Between 1959 and 1974 the new system was implemented for the entire country.

"Prime Minister"—("Teddy Salad [CIA Agent]") Harold Wilson was back in Number 10 Downing Street during this period, Labour having wrested at least a coalition-driven control of the Commons from the Tories in the 1974 General Election.

– R –

"roses bloom anew"—("Teddy Salad [CIA Agent]") Perhaps a reference to popular WWII-era big band song "When the Roses Bloom Again" ("When the roses bloom again / And the fields feel the plough / We will meet again sweetheart / Somehow") by Nat Burton and Walter Kent, and sung (in 1942) by Deanna Durbin, among others.

Ruislip—(PSC; "Post Box Ceremony") According to WAC records, the troupe and crew shot in Harefield, which is about 2.5 miles from Ruislip, Hillingdon, Greater London. The street where the scrap cart is gathering missiles may have been in Ruislip, though WAC records give no specific location request for the area (WAC T12/1,469).

– S –

Sainsbury's—(PSC; "Mr. Neutron") A grocery store chain in the UK.

scrap cart—("Post Box Ceremony") This cart notion will reappear in the feature film *Holy Grail*, there collecting plague victims.

The music beneath this section sounds like "Serenade for Summer" by King Palmer (WAC T12/1,469).

Secretary of State—(PSC; "Teddy Salad [CIA Agent]") This is most likely either the Secretary of State for Foreign Affairs or Defence, Sir Alec Douglas-Home (1903-1995) or Roy Mason (b. 1924), respectively, in the second half of 1974.

"She's 206!"—("Teddy Salad [CIA Agent]") Margot Fonteyn's age was a news item during this period—at fifty-three, she was still dancing at peak performance, and wouldn't retire until she was sixty.

Smailes, Frank—("Teddy Salad [CIA Agent]") An English cricketer, Thomas "Frank" Smailes (1910-1970) played for England in 1946, and for Yorkshire in his early years.

sniffs his left armpit—("Mr. Neutron") Once again the Pythons are harnessing a powerful leadership presence (in this case military, but just as often political or social) to a diminishing fetish or embarrassing peccadillo. This particular characterization may be related to the preoccupation of General Ripper (Sterling Hayden) with "precious bodily fluids" in Kubrick's 1964 black comedy *Dr. Strangelove*, co-written by Python intimate Terry Southern (1924-1995). In that film, Ripper's paranoia about the sanctity of his (and all Americans') bodily fluids leads him to launch a nuclear strike against those he sees as perpetrating this public health attack, the Soviet Union.

"Staines"—("Mr. Neutron") In Middlesex, where the initial events of the Martian invasion occurred, the rest of Mrs. S.C.U.M.'s list includes Stanmore, in Greater London, Leytonstone, in Walthamstow, and Deauville, which is quite a bit further away. The action of this apocalyptic adventure continues to focus on the same areas Wells (and the Martians) targeted in *War of the Worlds*.

The Pythons had shot some location footage at the Staines Recreation Grounds, including at a pool and a ballroom setting, early in the first series (WAC T12/1,086).

stock film—("Teddy Salad [CIA Agent]") The stock film used in this episode is not accounted for in the surviving WAC records.

sudden explosion—("Teddy Salad [CIA Agent]") This begins to look and be structured more and more like Kubrick's above-mentioned *Dr. Strangelove* (1964), where hypersexualized, paranoid, and somewhat dim

military and political figures (mostly American) end up destroying the world in a nuclear conflagration.

"Supreme Commander"—("Mr. Neutron") The Chairmanship of the Joint Chiefs of Staff of the United States' military in 1974 was held by two men, Thomas H. Moorer (1912-2004), then George S. Brown (1918-1978). The Supreme Commander of Allied forces during WWII was General Dwight Eisenhower, who will be referenced later in the episode.

"Sutton"—("Mr. Neutron") A London borough southwest of the City.

– T –

"Time-Life"—("Teddy Salad [CIA Agent]") The BBC and Time-Life co-produced or shared distribution credits for many expensive/expansive film projects, including the recent and very popular *Ascent of Man* series (from Dr. Jacob Bronowski [Ep. 22]) released in 1973, and *David Copperfield* (1974).

Time-Life has been referenced earlier, in notes to Ep. 30, with *To the South Pole with Peter Scott*, a BBC and Time-Life Film from 1967, as well as Ep. 31, in the "Summarize Proust" sketch.

train stops at the station—(PSC; "Mr. Neutron") The station is in Lingfield, Surrey, where the Lingfield Racecourse is also located. The "Queen Victoria Handicap" (Ep. 43) was shot at this course on 24 September 1974.

"Turner's Parade"—("Post Box Ceremony") An urban shopping area, similar to a strip mall, usually in a smaller town. There are several in Ealing, for example, where the Pythons shot much of the first series' exteriors (including Lammas Park Road, Elers Road, and Walpole and Lammas Park, all within a stone's throw of Ealing TFS).

– U –

"Ulverston Road and Sandwood Crescent"—("Post Box Ceremony") A concatenation of locations, since these street names—including Esher Road and Wyatt Road—can be found in multiple towns and counties up and down the UK, from Glasgow south to Devon.

– Y –

"Yellow River"—("Teddy Salad [CIA Agent]") There is no Yellow River in the Yukon (it's actually in China), but there is a White River. The Yukon Territory is about 2,700 miles from Montreal, meaning this ballet road trip would have been substantial.

"You're not Jewish, are you?"—("Mr. Neutron") Anti-Semitism hasn't been any more of a fixation in *FC* than any other type of fairly good-natured racial ribbing. And with the more relaxed attention to racial and ethnic slurring on television in general during this period, these barbs would be expected. (See the entries of the cartoony-ness of *FC* in Eps. 1 and 6 for more.) Specifi-cally, a "Jewish Figure" (Palin) is depicted in Ep. 7, though he's no Fagin-ish stereotype—in fact, viewers seem to have not recognized the type at all.

Yukon—("Teddy Salad [CIA Agent]") These scenes (the ones not in an indoor set) were shot on and around Hookney Tor, Dartmoor on 18-19 September 1974 (WAC T12/1,469). The Pythons had been here before, shooting, for example, the exterior scenes for "The Semaphore Version of *Wuthering Heights*" for Ep. 15.

Episode 45: "Party Political Broadcast"

– A –

"AA"—("BBC News [Handovers]") Britain's Automobile Association, earlier mentioned by Mrs. S.C.U.M. (Jones) in the "Mr. Neutron" sketch in Ep. 44.

"Adams, Douglas"—(closing credits) Douglas Adams (1952-2001) was a science fiction writer and avowed technologist, who, in 1974, was a protégé of Chapman's in Cleese's absence, contributing some material to *FC*. Adams would go on to create the popular *The Hitchhiker's Guide to the Galaxy* (1981), originally as a BBC Radio Series program.

Ano-Weet—(PSC; "*Most Awful Family in Britain*") Probably a play on high-fiber cereals from the Weetabix company (est. 1932), a cereal company founded, coincidentally, by South Africans (see "Rhodesia" below). Also, as early as the war years American cereal company Nabisco was marketing its "Nabisco 100% Bran" for its encouragement of bowel regularity: "And that's the reason Nabisco 100% Bran offers such mild, gentle relief from constipation due to insufficient bulk" (Nabisco newspaper print ad, 1944).

"*Anything Goes*"—(link out of "The Man Who Finishes Other People's Sentences") Another intertextual moment, where the Pythons "quote themselves," Jones' character humming a bit of the "other Cole Porter" song that was first heard in Ep. 42. The audience doesn't seem to respond to the quoting —at least, not nearly as much as when Cardinal Ximinez (Palin) and the Nudge, Nudge Man (Idle) reappeared well after their debut episodes.

"Amazellus Robin Ray"—("The Walking Tree of Dahomey") Robin Ray (1934-1998) was an actor (*Doctor in Love*; *Hard Day's Night*) and quiz show panelist (*Face the Music*), which connects him to Gascoigne men-

tioned just above. Nicholas Parsons (see below) was also a cast member of *Doctor in Love*.

"Arborus Bamber Gascoignus"—("The Walking Tree of Dahomey") Born in 1935, Bamber Gascoigne was quizmaster for the very popular *University Challenge* (Granada, then BBC1, 1962).

Attenborough, David—(PSC; The Walking Tree of Dahomey") Brother to previously lampooned Sir Richard Attenborough (who blubbered through Ep. 39's "*Light Entertainment Awards*"), David had produced the popular nature documentary series *The World About Us* (1967-1986). The music used here is actually the theme from *The World About Us*, and is played by Stuart Crombie and Orchestra (WAC T12/1,469).

– B –

"Batsmen of the Kalahari"—("Batsmen of the Kalahari") A play on "Bushmen" of the Kalahari. The BBC had commissioned a very popular six-part series in 1956 from Laurens van der Post (1906-1996), called *The Lost World of the Kalahari*, based on his book of the same name. The two batsmen pictured here are Derrick Southern and Ken Tracey (WAC T12/1,469).

"Berkshire"—("*Most Awful Family in Britain*") The "home" to Queen Elizabeth and Windsor Castle, as well as the Second-Most Awful Family, the Fanshaw-Chumleighs, the Royal County of Berkshire is also home to Reading, where the family depicted in the BBC's reality series *The Family* (1974) lived.

Big Country *theme*—(PSC; link out of "Icelandic Honey Week") Performed by Geoff Love and His Orchestra, the movie theme (from *Big Country*, 1958) was composed by Jerome Moross (WAC T12/1,469).

big county grand pavilion—(PSC; "The Batsmen of the Kalahari") This is the Exeter Cricket Club on Prince of Wales Road, Exeter, and the scenes were shot in September 1974 (WAC T12/1,469).

"Bogarde, Dirk"—("Brigadier and Bishop") Actor already mentioned in Ep. 29, Bogarde (1921-1999) appeared in *Death in Venice* (1971) and *The Damned* (1969). The first volume of Bogarde's autobiography, *A Postillion Struck by Lightning*, would not appear until 1977.

"Book of Maccabee"—("Brigadier and Bishop") Actually Books of Machabees, these are four scriptural/historical texts—two accepted by the Catholic Church as doctrinal, and all treated as apocrypha by most Protestant faiths. This pseudo-scriptural recitation delivered by Palin will be revisited in *HG*, in the "Holy Hand Grenade" scene, and in *ML* in the "Growth and Learning" chapel scene.

– C –

"Cedron"—("Brigadier and Bishop") Cedron is actually a brook or streambed on the east side of Jerusalem, and is mentioned in the scriptures in relation to King David, King Asa, and in 2 Chronicles and Jeremiah.

Centre Point—(PSC; "Appeal on Behalf of Extremely Rich People") A controversial and empty office building at the writing of this episode, Centre Point had been designed for a single, upscale company tenant, and was sitting empty (as it had been since 1964) when that tenant failed to materialize. Homeless activists (squatters, Ep. 13) had even managed to briefly occupy a portion of the building in January 1974, which may account for its mention in the episode. There are also a handful of political cartoons equating the empty Centre Point with the emptiness of Parliament in 1972. See the British Cartoon Archive. The Centre Point debacle is also addressed a number of times in the pages of *Private Eye*.

"Chandler, Raymond"—("Brigadier and Bishop") Hard-boiled crime writer Chandler (1888-1959) set many of his stories in the hot, dry streets of Los Angeles, and used similes with great success. Chandler created the Philip Marlowe character, who would, in *Farewell My Lovely*, think: "Her voice came from her mouth sounding like a worn out phonograph record" (101). The Pythons even picked up on the fact that many of Chandler's similes utilized "aspects of the natural world" (Newman).

"China Declares War"—("*Most Awful Family in Britain*") Another mention of the Chinese, a regime that's appeared in some way in at least five other episodes, most of the references hinting at a kind of "sleeping giant" threat.

commentator—("Batsmen of the Kalahari") This may be a parody of probably the most well-known and beloved cricket commentator of the period, Brian Johnston (1912-1994), who has been mentioned in earlier episodes (Eps. 20 and 21) . The hirsuteness of the mask isn't characteristic of "Johnners," but the nose and facial features are nearly identical.

"corn-plasters"—(link into "Icelandic Honey Week") A topical application for the treatment of corns, and earlier mentioned as being worn by French chiropodists trying for the summit of Everest (Ep. 31).

"Council re-housing"—("*Most Awful Family in Britain*") Local city and village councils were faced with re-housing their citizens after myriad slum razings in the post-Victorian era, and which continued into at least the 1970s in the UK. Both the New Towns Act of 1946 and the Town and Country Planning Act of 1947 were instrumental in jumpstarting the postwar re-housing boom, with semi-detached homes and then tower blocks springing up around the country. Entire towns were also laid out, along the newer motorways. See notes for Ep. 14 for more on Britain's postwar housing crunch, as well as notes to Ep. 17 for the tower block phenomenon.

The scarcity of housing even years after the war is demonstrated in Caledon, Ireland, where in 1968 an Irish MP Austin Currie squatted in protest in a council house that had been allocated to a young woman. The nineteen-year-old had been bumped ahead of hundreds of families on the council housing waiting list largely due to her religious affiliation, and protests followed (*Eyewitness: 1960-69*, "Dungannon Housing Protest").

Cowdrey, Colin—(PSC; "The Batsmen of the Kalahari") The printed script compares this performance (the cricketer being impaled) to celebrated cricketer Cowdrey (1932-2000) "caught clean bowled." Cowdrey, still active in 1974, would retire from play in 1976. A "clean bowl" occurs when the batsmen makes no contact with the ball and the wickets are put down.

Cowdrey would have been one of the most recognized cricketers for most of the Pythons' lives, being active in First-Class play 1950-1976; he played for both the Kent and Oxford University teams, as well as England.

– D –

"Dad"—("Icelandic Honey Week") Dad here is cross-dressed a bit, wearing a sweater vest over a dress, a wig, and obviously a stuffed bra. The characters are

Pepperpots underneath, and father, mother, and son on the surface.

"Dahomey"—("The Walking Tree of Dahomey") The African nation of Dahomey would be renamed Benin in 1975.

"Delaney, Hugh"—("BBC News [Handovers]") A radio and television presenter.

drinking and celebrating—(PSC; "BBC News [Handovers]") The Liberals did have much to celebrate after the February 1974 General Election, where they picked up an additional eight seats in the Commons, bringing their total to fourteen. The Liberals garnered almost 20 percent of the total vote, indicating how frustrated the average voter had become with the two seemingly inept governments, Tory and Labour, especially in the throes of runaway inflation.

"Droitwich"—(*Most Awful Family in Britain*) In Worcestershire, Droitwich is a suburb of the greater Birmingham area, and south from Idle's stomping grounds in Wolverhampton.

"Dunaway, Faye"—(*Most Awful Family in Britain*) Mrs. Garibaldi (Idle) is fielding an offer from a Hollywood studio, obviously, though it's not clear yet that this is a *television* family we're watching. In 1974, American actress Faye Dunaway (b. 1941) had appeared in *Chinatown* and *Towering Inferno*, and had been the most sought-after Hollywood actress since her appearance in *Bonnie and Clyde* in 1967.

"Durham"—(*Most Awful Family in Britain*) Located in northeast England, Durham has been mentioned in passing in Eps. 24 and 30.

– E –

"East Midlands"—(*Most Awful Family in Britain*) Essentially Idle's old stomping grounds, growing up in the Wolverhampton area. Idle's "Tourist" rant from Ep. 31 is focused on the Midlands, its people, and places. The "East Midlands Poet Board" also figured into Ep. 17.

"Elsan"—(*Most Awful Family in Britain*) A portable chemical toilet, which may mean that this public housing building has no working toilet facilities of its own, which is yet another comment on the situation of both the family and housing in Britain in 1974.

Episode 45—Recorded 16 November 1974, and broadcast 5 December 1974.

Additional actors and extras appearing in this episode include: Peter Brett (Ep. 40; *Dixon of Dock Green*), Ernest Blythe (*Play For Today*); Bikini Girls: Teresa Wood (*The Office Party*), Diane Holt, Pip (*On the Bright Side*),

Alison Kemp; Everett Mitchell, Harold Coward, Bill Shani, Ade Jumal, Fernando Benito, Cecil Calston, Louis St. Just, Tony Regar, Louie McKenzie, Horace McKenzie, Bowle Williams, Derrick Southern and Ken Tracey (both Batsmen), Bola Omoniyi, John Hughman (Eps. 14-15, 17-18, 26, 29-30, 32, 36, 38, 41-42, 45, Montreux compilation), Bob Raymond (Eps. 40-44, Montreux compilation), Douglas Barlow (*Malice Aforethought*).

"Eton"—(*Most Awful Family in Britain*) Exclusive school for training Britain's young elite, Eton was established in 1440 by Henry VI, and is mentioned in Eps. 16 and 20.

– F –

"forced to live in conditions of extreme luxury"—("Appeal on Behalf of Extremely Rich People") In the 13 May 1966 edition of *Private Eye*, the "Personal" section features a similar appeal: "Don't miss the Rt. Hon. Selwyn Lloyd's appeal on behalf of distressed Toryfolk. BBC Home Service. Sunday May 16. 6:30 p.m." (Ingrams 133). The Tories had been out of power since the 1964 General Election.

"Free Inside—The Pope + Demonstration Record"—(*Most Awful Family in Britain*) During the 1960s and beyond a number of breakfast cereal companies included short-play "45s" in cereal boxes as promotional giveaways. The records were also included in the packaging, having to be cut out of the back material by the eager listener. Post, General Mills, and Kellogg's provided such prizes (the records often made of plastic or even cardboard), with songs from groups like The Monkees, The Jackson 5, and teen heartthrob Bobby Sherman.

The fact that the family is at least nominally Italian may account for the inclusion of the Pope in the cereal box, along with a record demonstrating how he works.

– G –

Garibaldi—(PSC; "*Most Awful Family in Britain*") This spoof is based at least partly on the recent and very popular BBC reality show *The Family*, wherein a real Reading family was the subject of the twelve-part documentary series. The series was initially broadcast between April and June 1974, and was adapted from an American show, *An American Family* (1973). The artificial nature of the setting (when the "show"-ness is made clear) supports this parody of a recent television reality.

"George, Lloyd"—(closing credits) Former Prime Minister David Lloyd George (1863-1945) was often privately (and even publicly) attacked for his "absolutist" demeanor and policies, which is probably why the Pythons surrender producer credit to him. One of the Pythons' favorite historians, A.J.P. Taylor (satirized as "Prof. R.J. Gumby" in Ep. 9, and later in *HG*), describes the former Liberal PM as "the nearest thing England has known to a Napoleon, a supreme ruler maintaining himself by individual achievement" (qtd. in A.N. Wilson 242). George, then, is just the kind of larger-than-life, politically hungry character the Pythons would have allowed to purloin a producer credit for the episode. Plus, he was a Liberal, the obvious party of choice for this episode.

girls in bikinis—(PSC; "Appeal on Behalf of Extremely Rich People") These actresses/models are Teresa Wood, Diane Holt, Pip, and Alison Kemp. See notes for "Episode 45" for more on these actresses.

"Grimond, Jo"—(closing credits) Grimond (1913-1993) was essentially the public face of the Liberal Party in the 1950s and 1960s, when the party enjoyed a resurgence in popularity and votes. Grimond represented Orkney and Shetland in Parliament.

– H –

He has no iguana on his shoulder—(PSC; "The Man Who Finishes Other People's Sentences") This statement is apropos of nothing that can be seen in the scene, and is merely included for the other Python readers. It follows the absurd textual naming (never uttered) of "Mrs.-What-a-long-name-this-is-hardly-worth-typing-but-never-mind-it-doesn't-come-up-again's-living-room" in the same section of stage direction.

"Hippocratic"—("A Doctor Whose Patients Have Been Stabbed By His Nurse") A reference to the oath taken by doctors to provide relief and cause no injury, this scene is structured almost exactly like the "Merchant Banker" scene in Ep. 30, except that the phrase being looked up is "inner life" there. This rehearsal of earlier themes and narrative structures is the very reason Cleese (who played the Merchant Banker) left the show after the third series was completed.

"howzat"—("The Batsmen of the Kalahari") The native fielders respond to Pratt's (Jones) death at the crease with an appeal to the umpire for a ruling on the impaled batsman, called a "howzat."

– K –

"Kentucky Fried Chicken"—("BBC News [Handovers]") KFC opened its first outlet in the UK in 1965, after debuting in the United States (in South Salt Lake, UT) in 1952. In Ep. 42 the loveable rogues from *Up Your Pavement* (Palin and Jones) saunter past a Kentucky Fried Chicken store before being run down by Alex Diamond (Chapman).

– L –

lavender tutu . . . high heels—("Brigadier and Bishop") A nexus moment for the Pythons and their playful-derision-of-authority-figures hobbyhorse, here they've posited a representative of both the church and the military in ridiculous attire and a compromising sexual situation. Throughout the series the Pythons have diminished such respectable, stentorian figures of "The Establishment" by means of effeminate dress, effeminate behaviors, and "aberrant" sexualities (including homosexuality, bestiality, self-abuse, etc.). The humor often works so well, as it does in this scene, because the respected figures retain their gravitas even as they ponce about.

"lbw"—("The Batsmen of the Kalahari") Meaning "leg before wicket," which an umpire can call if the batsmen places any part of his body in front of the wicket to protect it, and the ball hits him. If the wicket is hit, the batsman is bowled out. The fielding team can "howzat" for an appeal (see "howzat" above) if they feel an lbw has occurred.

"Leicester North"—(closing credits) These constituencies listed in the closing credits represent the home towns, essentially, of each of the Pythons.

Leicester North (representing Chapman) was not an official constituency in the October 1974 General Election, but Labour did hold or gain the three Leicester seats—East, West, and South—with the Liberal candidates polling less than 13 percent in each area. For South Shields (Idle), Labour also held easily, though the Liberal candidate polled more than 17 percent. Of the six Sheffield constituencies (Palin), Labour held five and the Conservatives held one in 1974. In Sheffield Park the Liberals came second, an unusually strong showing. Most northern Wales (Jones' Colwyn Bay is situated between Conwy and Denbigh) parliamentary seats were held by the Conservatives during this period.

"Liberal Party"—("Party Political Broadcast") The Liberal Party has been the atrophied "third leg" party since 1922, when Labour became the official opposition party to the Conservatives—the Labour-Conservative ruling tandem becoming de rigeur, and remaining so. In the 1950s and 1960s the Liberals made a bit of a comeback under Joe Grimond and then Jeremy Thorpe, the latter lampooned by the Pythons later in this episode. In 1970, the Liberals were reduced to six MPs, though under Thorpe's leadership the Liberal Party claimed a total of fourteen seats in the February 1974 election (which then fell to thirteen seats in the October 1974 General Election).

"Liberals a very close third"—("BBC News [Handovers]") In the October 1974 General Election the Liberal Party managed to garner just over 18 percent of the total votes cast, a *distant* third behind Labour (39.2 percent) and the Conservatives (35.8 percent). The Liberals gained one seat and lost two, for a total of thirteen seats in the Commons. Just five years later the country would witness a significant swing to the Conservative camp (behind the leadership of Margaret Thatcher), when Labour would lose fifty seats, and the Liberals would surrender two seats.

"Lost Deposit"—(closing credits) If the candidate does not receive a minimum number of votes in a particular election, that candidate must forfeit his/her filing deposit. The "back marker" in many of these elections for many years has been Liberal Party candidates, though fringe candidates (e.g., National Front, Marxist-Leninist) also regularly suffer the same fate.

In the February 1974 General Election, eight Conservatives, twenty-five Labour, and twenty-three Liberal candidates lost their deposits.

– M –

man in a dark suit—("*Most Awful Family in Britain*") This actor is Peter Brett, who also appeared in Ep. 40.

"Merchant of Venice . . . Virginia Wade"—("A Doctor Whose Patients Are Stabbed By His Nurse") *Merchant of Venice* (c. 1597) is one of Shakespeare's so-called problem plays, and was performed by the cows of the Bad Ischl Dairy in Python's *FZ* 1 (1971); the Treaty of Versailles (signed 1919) put into writing the surrender and then reparations promised by Germany to France and the allies after WWI; Emerson Fittipaldi (b. 1946) was racing Formula One in 1974; and British-born Virginia Wade (b. 1945) was ranked in the women's top five, winning the U.S. Open and Australian Open, etc.

"Most Awful Family in Britain"—("*Most Awful Family in Britain*") The depictions of the institution of the family in *FC* have ranged from benign to appalling across the span of the four series, but such depictions are primarily conspicuous by their absence. With the exception of myriad dowdy married couples (e.g., Mr. and Mrs. Brain Sample), the nuclear family doesn't figure prominently in *FC*, partly due to the relatively few ju-

venile roles the Pythons wrote for themselves to perform. There are just a few examples to draw on.

In Ep. 2, the Pythons borrow a scene from Lawrence's *Sons and Lovers* to depict the harsh life of a working-class playwright, with the coal miner son coming home to his father's scorn. This scene is an inversion, of course, of the typical Lawrence drawing room, where the blue-collar father might confront the angry, disaffected son who wants a life outside the mines. In Ep. 9 the extended nuclear family has run into trouble as the grannies take to the streets in "Hell's Grannies"; there's a benign family in Ep. 10, with a "Man" and "Wife" and offscreen "Dad" figure in a walk-on part for the BBC, and Chapman plays a school boy (he wears the typical grammar school uniform) in Ep. 29, "Salvation Fuzz," part of a "Man" (Idle), "Woman" (Jones), and "Son" family grouping. Episode 21 offers Michelangelo (Palin) lost in a sea of newborns, and his wife is having more, while Mozart wishes his son a better life than that of a composer. In "Salvation Fuzz" the family operates simply as a narrative tool, with each member playing a part in the eventual discovery and arrest of the murderer, the Man (Idle). Most of the familial depictions, then, are narratively useful rather than revealing, and can be traced back to the *Beyond the Fringe*–type scenes typical of the university revues, where the Pythons honed their writing and performing skills.

Finally, it may well be that the other "broadcast families" of the period (including the Archers [BBC Radio], the Richardsons of *Crossroads* fame, and even the denizens of *Hancock's Half Hour*) were so banal and "cosy," as Vahimagi notes, that they just didn't merit parody through most of *FC*, so the depiction in Episode 45 becomes a full-choke shotgun blast at the family (*British Television* 123).

Mrs. Long Name leaves—(link out of "Icelandic Honey Week") In Ep. 14, Mrs. G. Pinnet (also Jones) answers the door only to discover she's been watching TV in the wrong house. She clambers outside, across the brick fence, and into the house next door, and the "New Cooker Sketch" can begin. (In the printed script she's called "Mrs. What-a-long-name-this-is-hardly-worth-typing-but-never-mind-it-doesn't-come-up-again's-living-room," another in-joke for the other Pythons, and not the viewer.)

It seems that here, in addition, Mrs. Long Name (Jones) has been empowered by her ability to finish her own sentences, and she can leave her workaday drudgery and head out into the exciting world, perhaps for the first time. She encounters other Pepperpot-types doing road construction work as she goes, and eventually ends up staring in rapture at Stonehenge.

– N –

National Health glasses—(PSC; "*Most Awful Family in Britain*") Eyeglasses provided by Britain's National Health Service (NHS), in styles that tended to be quite uniform, sturdy, and unflattering.

Fair-Isle jersey—Traditional knitted wear from Fair Isle, north of Scotland, near the Orkneys.

– O –

"Odinga"—("Batsmen of the Kalahari") Jaramogi Oginga Odinga was a popular Kenyan political leader in the 1960s, and was often in the news, including the pages of *Private Eye*.

"P.B.T.R."—An acronym for "Play By the Rules, " which the Assegai clearly are flaunting.

"jacksey"—Meaning "arse" or "backside," the term is usually spelled "jacksy."

– P –

"Party Political Broadcast"—(link into "BBC News [Handovers]") A staple on radio and TV for many years in Great Britain, PPBs were designed to give the more prominent political parties free access to the mass listening/viewing voting audience, both just before and in between elections.

Formats were initially rather dull, with a somewhat stentorian delivery by a single, precise voice offering the Conservative, Labour, and Liberal party platforms to anyone who would listen. Martin Rosenbaum notes that after 1955 (probably due to television's influence) skits, celebrity readers, vox pops, and signature music became part of many of these broadcasts, which is probably where the Pythons found inspiration for the lunacy depicted in their PPB sketches. See Martin Rosenbaum's *From Soapbox to Soundbite*.

played very hesitantly on guitar—(PSC; closing titles) For the first time in the series, the closing "Liberty Bell" theme is not the Band of the Grenadier Guards version.

"Pratt, M.J.K."—("The Batsmen of the Kalahari") Meant to remind viewers of eminent English cricketer M.J.K. Smith (b. 1933), who had played for Oxford University, Warwickshire (see below) and Leicestershire, as well as England. Cowdrey (see above) followed him as English National Cricket Captain.

"W.G. Pratt"—Styled after the pre-eminent batsman W.G. Grace (1848-1915), who popularized cricket as a mass spectator sport. Noted cricket histo-

rian Peter Wynne-Thomas calls Grace "the greatest of cricketers" (1983). Grace's bearded image appears in *Holy Grail* as God calling Arthur to his quest. For more on Grace and his stature in the cricket world, see "Muscular Christianity and Cricket" (*Eyewitness: 1900-09*).

"Z. Pratt"—Perhaps a reference to noted batsman Z. Harris (1927-1991), who played internationally for New Zealand in the 1950s and 1960s.

– Q –

"Quercus Nicholas Parsonus"—("The Walking Tree of Dahomey") "Quercus" is the Latin term for "oak," while Nicholas Parsons (b. 1923) is a Brit TV and radio personality who has participated in the BBC radio panel game *Just a Minute* since 1967. Derek Nimmo (mentioned in Ep. 25) was one of the early panelists.

quite appalling accents—(PSC; "*Most Awful Family in Britain*") The upper-crust dinner party participants sound very much like the Upperclass Twits from Ep. 12.

– R –

"recommend you for hospital"—("A Doctor Whose Patients Are Stabbed by His Nurse") The doctor is running his office here as if it were an English prep school, where test performance can recommend a student to Cambridge or Oxford, or keep a student at one of the newer universities, or out of higher education entirely.

"Rhodesia"—("*Most Awful Family in Britain*") See entry for "Ian Smith" below. Named in 1965 after Cecil Rhodes, Southern Rhodesia (now Zimbabwe) was hit with United Nations sanctions after Smith's UDI (Unilateral Declaration of Independence), and quickly became an international pariah. See notes for "Rhodesia" in Eps. 3, 10, and 28, as well.

"Rostrum Camera"—(closing credits) A special effects camera platform, allowing precise camera movement across, "into" and "out of" still images, for example, to create animated special effects. This camera was used only in this fourth and more expensive/expansive series. There are two special effects shots in Ep. 44 (composite shots) that may have demanded such a camera.

– S –

saxophone-wearing natives—("The Walking Tree of Dahomey") A barefaced but still fairly clever comment on the lingering perception of blacks being capable of only performing as either African natives or jazz musicians on British television. Black characters in *FC* are few and far between, however, with Idle putting on a broadly stereotyped "Rochester"-type performance, in black-face, for "*The Attila the Hun Show*," and Cleese and extras donning black-face to portray the West Indies' cricket team, both in Ep. 20. Black actors are even scarcer still. This racial mix paucity probably reflects both the "whiteness" of Cambridge and Oxford (and especially their respective dramatic clubs) as well as the BBC in general, which tended to produce shows aimed at its predominately Caucasian audience. (Just leaf through Vahimagi's *British Television* to view the predictable sea of white faces, spanning broadcast years 1930-1995—and where the few black performers are almost exclusively pictured in relation to jazz music variety shows.)

During this period (1958-1978), the very popular *Black and White Minstrel Show* was also airing on BBC, offering black-face performers singing primarily American music. As early as 1967 there were public outcries for the program's change or elimination, but it stayed on the air for another ten years.

Scun—(PSC; "*Most Awful Family in Britain*") A play on the sensationalistic *Sun* tabloid newspaper, which continues to feature scantily clad women along with some news to this day. The paper had been a fairly Labour-friendly mouthpiece during its early years (1964-1974).

sets off purposefully up the road—(PSC; link out of "Icelandic Honey Week") Mrs. Long Name (Jones) walks "purposefully" to the sounds of the Vienna Philharmonic Orchestra's performance of "Ride of the Valkyrie" by Richard Wagner (WAC T12/1,469).

This same music was used quite effectively a decade earlier in Federico Fellini's *8½* (1963), when Guido is trying to rein in his harem.

This is also quite reminiscent of the penultimate scene in Pier Pasolini's *Teorema* (1968), when the sanctified Emilia sets out suddenly from the village to go to her "burial" site—she strides purposely, knows just where she's going, and is accompanied by a musical score (from Ennio Morricone), as well.

"Smith, C."—(closing credits) Continuing the Liberal Party slant of the entire episode, Cyril Smith (b. 1928) was the portly Liberal MP for Rochdale 1972-1992.

"L Byers"—Lord (Charles) Byers led the handful of Liberal MPs in the House of Lords from 1967 until his death in 1984.

Smith, Ian—(PSC; "*Most Awful Family in Britain*") Leader of the white minority and ruling government in Rhodesia, Smith declared a unilateral independence

from Great Britain in November 1965. Smith was vilified by the international community and press for his party's minority rule policies, and would eventually have to surrender power (in 1979). Smith and the Rhodesia situation have already been mentioned in Ep. 10.

"Spring of 1863"—(link out of "Icelandic Honey Week") A bevy of cobbled-together names and facts, in 1863 the Comanche were fighting battles with other tribes on the Great Plains, with Texas having become inhospitable to the tribe several years earlier.

Stonehenge—(link into "David Attenborough") One of many distinct locations employed by the show during the production of this final series (this one used only as a fleeting link), the Pythons seemed to be less concerned with keeping costs at a minimum by shooting all exteriors in a single geographical area, as had been the case in at least the first and second series. For this series they filmed in: Torbay, Exeter and Hookney Tor, Devon; Bicton, East Devon; Lingfield, Surrey; Turners Hill and Hickstead, West Sussex; Croydon, Greater London; Motspur Park, West London; Hendon, Barnet, Greater London; and Harefield, Hillingdon, Greater London (WAC T12/1,469).

"strewth"—("Icelandic Honey Week") Again, it's Chapman uttering this mild invective, as he's done in Eps. 1 and 2.

- T -

Thorpe, Jeremy—(PSC; "Icelandic Honey Week") Without the script notation it's probably not clear who this masked figure is supposed to be (and the studio audience's lack of response supports this). Liberal Party leader during this period, Thorpe (b. 1929) was an Eton grad (see above), and had been in the news as he responded to allegations about his alleged homosexuality. To be more recognizable, the masked Thorpe is also wearing the yellow badge of the Liberal Party candidates. Thorpe represented the North Devon constituency 1955-1975.

The satirical magazine *Private Eye* published a cover featuring Thorpe in this very outfit on 15 December 1972.

"Tits and Inflation"—(PSC; "*Most Awful Family in Britain*") Beginning in 1969, bikini-clad (and then topless) models began to appear in Rupert Murdoch's tabloid newspaper *The Sun*, called "Page Three Girls"—they helped the paper's circulation jump significantly in the early 1970s. See note for "*Scun*" above.

– U –

"Umbonga's hostile opening"—("Batsmen of the Kalahari") A reference to the practice of "fast bowling" in modern cricket. In 1932-1933, the English bowler (and Captain) Douglas Jardine (1900-1958) upset much of the cricket world with his purposefully intimidating bowling style—designed to brush the batsman back and force a bad swing. In the so-called Bodyline series, English bowlers attempted to mitigate Australia's highly effective batsman Don Bradman (1908-2001) by throwing the ball directly at him (and other Australian hitters), causing various injuries (including a fractured skull) and leading to a diplomatic row between England and Australia. For Jardine's version of the events (he called it "Fast Leg Theory") see his *In Quest of The Ashes* (1933).

See notes for "Gubby Allen" in Ep. 20 for another reference to the Bodyline Tour.

– W –

"Walking Tree"—("The Walking Tree of Dahomey") There are species of trees (including mangroves) that reportedly re-root themselves—very, very slowly—in whatever direction provides the best/better soil. They would have been a suitable subject for a *World About Us*–type show, however.

"Warwickshire"—("The Batsmen of the Kalahari") The Warwickshire County Cricket Club had won a County Championship in 1972.

Bibliography

Abrams, Mark. "The Opinion Polls and the 1970 British General Election." *Public Opinion Quarterly* 34, no. 3 (1970): 317-24.

Abrams, M.H. *A Glossary of Literary Terms*. 4th ed. New York: Holt, Rhinehart and Winston, 1981.

Ackroyd, Peter. *Albion*. London: Doubleday, 2003.

———. *J.M.W. Turner*. New York: Nan A. Talese, 2006.

———. *London: The Biography*. London: Doubleday, 2000.

Aldgate, Anthony. *Censorship and the Permissive Society: British Cinema and Theatre, 1955-1965*. London: Oxford University Press, 1995.

Aldous, Richard. *Macmillan, Eisenhower and the Cold War*. Dublin, Ireland: Four Courts Press, 2005.

Allen, Grant. *What's Bred in the Bone*. New York: Knight & Brown, 1898.

Altman, Rick. *The American Film Musical*. Bloomington: Indiana University Press, 1989.

Anderson, Ronald, and Anne Koval. *James McNeill Whistler: Beyond the Myth*. London: John Murray, 1994.

Andors, Stephen. "Mao and Marx: A Comment." *Modern China* 3, no. 4 (1977): 427-33.

Araloff, Simon. "The Internal Corps—The Kremlin's Private Army." Global Challenges Research website: http://www.axisglobe.com/article.asp?article=178. Accessed 18 November 2006.

Argyle, John Michael. *Psychology and Social Problems*. London: Methuen, 1964.

Attfield, Judy. *Utility Reassessed: The Role of Ethics in the Practice of Design*. Manchester, NY: Manchester University Press, 1999.

"Attila" *World Encyclopedia*. Philip's, 2005. *Oxford Reference Online*. Oxford University Press. Brigham Young University (BYU). http://www.oxfordreference.com/views/ENTRY.html?subview=Main&entry=t142.e793. Accessed 1 May 2006.

Aylett, Glenn. "The Sporting Class." Transdiffusion Broadcasting System website: http://www.transdiffusion.org/emc/worldofsport/the_sporting_cl.php. Accessed 17 October 2006.

Bakhtin, Mikhail. *Rabelais and His World*. Trans. Helene Iswolsky. Bloomington: Indiana University Press, 1984.

Baldick, Chris. *Oxford Concise Dictionary of Literary Terms*. Oxford: Oxford University Press, 2001.

Baldwin, T.W. *Organisation and Personnel of the Shakespearean Company*. Princeton: Princeton University Press, 1927.

Beck, Jerry. *Looney Tunes and Merrie Melodies: A Complete Illustrated Guide to the Warner Bros. Cartoons*. New York: Henry Holt, 1989.

Bennett, Alan, Peter Cook, Jonathan Miller, and Dudley Moore. *Beyond the Fringe*. New York: Random House, 1963.

Bergeron, David M. "Shakespeare Makes History: 2 *Henry IV*." *Studies in English Literature* 31, no. 2 (1991): 231-45.

Bergson, Henri. *The Creative Mind: An Introduction to Metaphysics*. 1946. New York: Dover, 2007.

———. "Laughter: An Essay on the Meaning of the Comic." Trans. Brereton and Rothwell. London: Macmillan, 1911.

Biao, Lin. "Advance Along the Road Opened up by the October Socialist Revolution." Foreign Languages Press, 1967.

Bird, Peter A. *First Food Empire: A History of J. Lyons & Co.* Chichester: Phillimore, 2000.

Bishop, Ellen. "Bakhtin, Carnival and Comedy: The New Grotesque in Monty Python and the Holy Grail." *Film Criticism* 15, no. 1 (1990): 49-64.

Bogle, Donald. *Toms, Coons, Mulattoes, Mammies, & Bucks*. New York: Continuum International, 2003.

Bond, Maurice Francis. *The Gentleman Usher of the Black Rod*. London: HMSO, 1976.

Boose, Lynda. "Let it be Hid: The Pornographic Aesthetic of Shakespeare's *Othello*." *Women, Violence, and English Renaissance Literature*. Ed. Linda Woodbridge and Sharon Beehler, *Medieval and Renaissance Texts and Studies*. Phoenix: Arizona State University Press, 2003, 34-58.

Bordwell, David, Janet Staiger and Kristin Thompson. *The Classical Hollywood Cinema*. London, Melbourne and Henley: Routledge and Kegan Paul, 1985.

Bordwell, David and Kristin Thompson. *Narration in the Fiction Film*. University of Wisconsin Press, 1985.

"Boxing's Loss, Too." *Boxing Monthly* 10, no. 3 (July 1998).

Bradman, Sir Don. *The Art of Cricket*. London: Hodder & Stoughton, 1990.

Brettell, Richard R. *Modern Art 1851-1929*. London: Oxford University Press, 1999.

Brontë, Anne. *The Tenant of Wildfell Hall*. Kessinger, 2004.

Brontë, Elizabeth. *Wuthering Heights*. 1847. New York: Bantam, 1983.

Browning, Robert. *Home Thoughts, from Abroad*. 1845. http://www.emule.com/poetry/?page=poem&poem=297. Accessed 28 November 2007.

Bruce-Briggs, B. *Supergenius: The Mega-Worlds of Herman Khan*. North American Policy Press, 2000.

Bryk, William. "Defender of the Faith." *The New York Press*. 16 March 2000.

Buscombe, Edward. *British Television: A Reader*. Oxford: Oxford University Press, 2000.

Butler, David, and Michael Pinto-Duschinsky. *The British General Election of 1970*. London: Macmillan, 1971.

Caesar, Julius. *Commentarii De Bello Gallico*. http://www.gutenberg.org/etext/10657. Accessed 26 November 2007.

Cambridge History of English and American Literature, The. New York: Putnam, 1907-1921.

Campbell, John. *Edward Heath: A Biography*. London: Jonathan Cape, 1993.

Canetti, Elias, and Michael Hofmann. *Party in the Blitz: The English Years*. New York: New Directions, 2005.

Carpenter, Humphrey. *The Angry Young Men: A Literary Comedy of the 1950s*. London: Penguin, 2004.

———. *A Great Silly Grin: The British Satire Boom of the 1960s*. London: Da Capo Press, 2003.

———. *That Was Satire, That Was*. London: Victor Gollancz, 2000.

Catholic Encyclopedia, The. http://www.catholic.org/encyclopedia/. Accessed 19 November 2007.

Chamberlain, Gethin. "Threatened Regiments Take Courage From Past." *The Scotsman*. 10 July 2004. http://thescotsman.scotsman.com/index.cfm?id=789542004. Accessed 25 January 2006.

Chapman, George, Ben Jonson, and John Marston. *Eastward Ho*. Schelling, ed., 1903. Complete digital reproduction at http://books.google.com/books?as_brr=1&id=qlL1LVR0xj8C&vid=OCLC05138166&jtp=1. Accessed 27 November 2007.

Chapman, Graham, John Cleese, Terry Gilliam, Eric Idle, Terry Jones, and Michael Palin. *The Complete Monty Python's Flying Circus: All the Words*, 2 vols. New York: Pantheon, 1989.

Chapman, Graham, et al. *The Monty Python Song Book*. New York: Harper Trade, 1995.

———. *Monty Python's Big Red Book*. New York: Contemporary Books, 1980.

Chesneau, Roger. *Aircraft Carriers of the World, 1914 to the Present: An Illustrated Encyclopedia*. Annapolis: Naval Institute Press, 1984.

Christie, Ian. *Gilliam on Gilliam*. London: Faber and Faber, 1999.

Clark, Kenneth. *Civilisation: A Personal View*. New York: Harper & Row, 1970.

Clarke, Peter. *Hope and Glory: Britain 1900-1990*. London: Penguin, 1996.

Cockerell, Michael. *Live From Number 10: The Inside Story of Prime Ministers and Television*. London: Faber, 1989.

Coleman, Alice. *Utopia on Trial: Vision and Reality in Planned Housing*. London: Hilary Shipman, 1985.

Cook, Chris, and John Stevenson, eds. *Modern British History: 1714-2001*. London: Longman, 2001.

Corner, John. *Popular Television in Britain: Studies in Cultural History*. London: BFI, 1991.

Cox, John D., and David Scott Kastan, eds. *A New History of Early English Drama*. New York: Columbia University Press, 1997.

Crab, Roger. *The English Hermite, or, Wonder of this Age*. London, 1655. http://wwwlib.umi.com/eebo/image/42017 (Huntington Library reproduction).

Crawford, Robert. *The Savage and the City in the Work of T.S. Eliot*. Oxford: Oxford University Press, 1991.

Creaton, Heather. *Sources for the History of London 1939-45*. London: British Records Association, 1998.

Crisell, Andrew. *An Introductory History of British Broadcasting*. New York: Routledge, 2002.

———. "Filth, Sedition and Blasphemy: The Rise and Fall of Television Satire." *Popular Television in Britain: Studies in Cultural History*. Ed. John Corner. London: BFI, 1991.

Crisp, Quentin. *The Naked Civil Servant*. London: Penguin, 1997.

Crowe, Brian L. "British Entry into the Common Market: A British View." *Law and Contemporary Problems* 37, no. 2 (Spring 1972): 228-34.

Davis, John. "The London Drug Scene and the Making of Drug Policy, 1965–73." *Twentieth-Century British History* 17, no. 1 (2006): 26-49.

DeAndrea, William L. *Encyclopedia Mysteriosa: A Comprehensive Guide to the Art of Detection in Print, Film, Radio, and Television*. New York: Prentice Hall, 1994.

Dekker, Thomas. *The Shoemaker's Holiday. Drama of the English Renaissance: The Tudor Period*. Ed. Russell A. Fraser and Norman Rabkin. New York: Macmillan, 1976.

D'Emilio, John. *Sexual Politics, Sexual Communities*. Chicago: University of Chicago Press, 1983.

Denning, Lord Alfred Thompson. *Lord Denning's Report, Presented to Parliament by the Prime Minister by Command of Her Majesty*. London: HMSO, 1963.

De Syon, Guillaume. *Zeppelin!: Germany and the Airship, 1900-1939*. Baltimore: Johns Hopkins University Press, 2002.

Deutscher, Isaac. *The Prophet Outcast: Trotsky 1929-1940*. New York: Verso, 2003.

Diamond, John. "Once I Was British." *The Times*. 14 January 1995, 1.

Dictionary of National Biography. Oxford: Oxford University Press, 2004.

Dixon, T.J. "The Civil Service Syndrome." *Management Today* (May 1980): 74-79, 154, 158, 162.

Dodge, Mabel. "Speculations, or Post-Impressionism in Prose." *Arts and Decoration* (March 1913).

Dollimore, Jonathan and Alan Sinfield, eds. *Political Shakespeare: Essays in Cultural Materialism*. Manchester: Manchester University Press, 1999.

Dover, Harriet. *Home Front Furniture*. England: Scolar Press, 1991.

Doyle, Arthur Conan. *The Lost World*. New York: Tor Classics, 1997.

Drabble, Margaret. *For Queen and Country: Britain in the Victorian Age*. New York: Seabury Press, 1978.

———. *The Oxford Companion to English Literature*, 5th ed. Oxford: Oxford University Press, 1985.

Duberman, Martin. *Stonewall*. New York: Dutton, 1993.

Dynes, Wayne. *Homosexuality: A Research Guide*. New York: Taylor and Francis, 1987.

Ebert, Roger. *Julius Caesar.* 17 March 1971. http://rogerebert
.suntimes.com/apps/pbcs.dll/article?AID=/19710317/
REVIEWS/103170301/1023. Accessed 28 November 2007.

Eirik The Red and Other Icelandic Sagas. London: Oxford University Press, 1999.

Eliot, T.S. *Murder in the Cathedral.* 1935. San Diego: HBJ, 1988.

———. "The Waste Land." 1922. *The Norton Anthology of World Masterpieces,* Vol. 2, 5th ed. Ed. Maynard Mack, et al. New York and London: Norton, 1985.

Ellsworth, Scott. "Interview with Amil Gargano." *Advertising and Society Review* 2, no. 4 (2001). Website: http://muse.jhu.edu/journals/asr/archives/archives.html. Accessed 18 January 2006.

Esher, Lionel. *A Broken Wave: The Rebuilding of England, 1940–1980.* London: Allen Lane, 1981.

Evans, G. Blakemore, ed. *The Riverside Shakespeare.* New York: Houghton Mifflin, 1974.

Evelyn, John. *The Diary of John Evelyn.* Trans. E.S. de Beer. Oxford: Oxford, 1955.

Eyewitness: 1940–1979. Wr. Joanna Bourke, narr. Tim Pigott-Smith. CD. BBC Books, 2005.

Fielding, Henry. *Tom Thumb (The Tragedy of Tragedies).* http://www.gutenberg.org/etext/6828. Accessed 28 November 2007.

Fraser, Rebecca. *The Story of Britain.* New York: W.W. Norton, 2003.

Fraser, Russell, and Norman Rabkin, eds. *Drama of the English Renaissance, I and II.* New York: Macmillan, 1976.

Freedman, Des. "Modernising the BBC: Wilson's Government and Television, 1964–66." *Contemporary British History* 15, no. 1 (Spring 2001): 21–40.

Gable, Jo. *The Tuppenny Punch and Judy Show—25 Years of TV Commercials.* London: Michael Joseph, 1980.

Gabler, Neal. *An Empire of Their Own: How The Jews Invented Hollywood.* New York: Random House, 1989.

Gage, John. "The Distinctness of Turner." *Journal of the Royal Society of Arts* 123 (1975): 448–57.

Gardner's Art Through the Ages, 7th ed. Horst de la Croix and Richard Tansey, eds. New York: Harcourt Brace Jovanovich, 1980.

Genette, Gérard. *Narrative Discourse: An Essay in Method.* Ithaca, NY: Cornell University Press, 1980.

"Germany's Heart: The Modern Taboo." Interview with Jurgen Syberberg in *NPQ* 10, no. 1 (Winter 1993).

Giddings, Robert, and Keith Selby. *The Classic Serial on Television and Radio.* New York: Palgrave-Macmillan, 2001.

Gilbert, Martin. *The First World War.* New York: Owl Books, 2004.

Gilbert, W.S., and Arthur Sullivan. *The Pirates of Penzance.* 1879.

Giles, Colum. *Yorkshire Textile Mills, 1770–1930.* London: HMSO, 1992.

Gilliam, Terry. *Gilliam on Gilliam.* Ed. Ian Christie. London: Faber and Faber, 1999.

Gillispie, Charles. *The Montgolfier Brothers and the Invention of Aviation, 1783–1784.* Princeton, NJ: Princeton University Press, 1983.

Glendinning, Miles, and Stefan Muthesius. *Tower Block: Modern Public Housing in England, Scotland, Wales and Northern Ireland.* New Haven: Yale University Press, 1994.

Goon Show, The. Starring Spike Milligan, Peter Sellers, and Harry Secombe, 1951–1960. "*The Goon Show* Old Time Radio MP3 Collection," 2007.

Gordon, David. "Shavian Comedy and the Shadow of Wilde." *The Cambridge Companion to George Bernard Shaw.* Ed. Christopher Innes. Cambridge: Cambridge University Press, 1998.

Grafton, Roger, and Roger Wilmut. *The Goon Show Companion: A History and Goonography.* London: Robson, 1976.

Gray, Andy, with Jim Drewett. *Flat Back Four: The Tactical Game.* London: Macmillan, 1998.

Grimm's Teutonic Mythology. Trans. James Steven Stallybrass. London: Routledge, 1999.

Gurr, Andrew. *The Shakespearean Stage, 1574–1642.* Cambridge: Cambridge University Press, 1992.

Hamilton, A.C., ed. *The Faerie Queene.* London and New York: Longman, 1977.

———. *The Spenser Encyclopedia.* Toronto: Toronto University Press, 1997.

Hazewell, Charles Creighton. "The Indian Revolt." *The Atlantic Monthly* 1, no. 2 (Dec. 1857): 217–22.

Henke, James. *Courtesans and Cuckolds.* New York: Garland, 1979.

Henri, Adrian, Roger McGough, and Brian Patten. *The Mersey Sound.* London: Penguin, 1967.

Hewison, Robert. *In Anger: British Culture in the Cold War 1945–60.* New York: Oxford University Press, 1981.

———. *Monty Python: The Case Against.* London: Eyre Methuen, 1981.

Heyerdahl, Thor. *Kon Tiki: Across the Pacific By Raft.* Chicago: Rand McNally, 1950.

———. *The Ra Expeditions.* New York: Doubleday, 1971.

Holland, Steve. *The Mushroom Jungle: A History of Postwar Paperback Publishing.* Wiltshire, England: Zeon, 1993.

———. *The Trials of Hank Janson.* Richmond, KY: Books Are Everything, 1991.

Hopkins, Gerald M. "Felix Randal." http://www.bartleby.com/122/29.html. Accessed 28 November 2007.

Hopkins, James K. *A Woman to Deliver Her People: Joanna Southcott and English Millenarianism in an Era of Revolution.* Austin, TX: University of Texas Press, 1981.

Hoppenstand, Gary, Garyn G. Roberts, and Ray B. Browne, eds. *More Tales of the Defective Detective in the Pulps.* Bowling Green: Bowling Green University Press, 1985.

Hughes, Merritt Y. *John Milton's Complete Poems and Major Prose.* Indianapolis: Odyssey, 1957.

Hughes, Robert. *The Shock of the New.* New York: Knopf, 1991.

Hughes, Ted. *Crow: From the Life and Songs of a Crow.* London: Faber, 1970.

Index to the Times. London: Times Publishing Co., 1969–1974.

Ingrams, Richard, ed. *The Life and Times of Private Eye: 1961–1971.* New York: McGraw-Hill, 1971.

Jardine, Doug. *In Quest of the Ashes.* London: Methuen, 2005.

Jenkins, Steven. *Cheese Primer.* New York: Workman, 1996.

Johnson, Kim. *The First 20 Years of Monty Python.* New York: St. Martin's Press, 1989.

———. *The First 28 Years of Monty Python.* New York: St. Martin's Press, 1998.

Jones, Robert K. *The Shudder Pulps*. New York: Dutton/Plume, 1978.

Jonson, Ben. *The Alchemist. Drama of the English Renaissance II: The Stuart Period*. Ed. Russell Fraser and Norman Rabkin. New York: Macmillan, 1976.

———. *Bartholomew Fair. Drama of the English Renaissance II: The Stuart Period*. Ed. Russell Fraser and Norman Rabkin. New York: Macmillan, 1976.

———. *Volpone. Drama of the English Renaissance II: The Stuart Period*. Ed. Russell Fraser and Norman Rabkin. New York: Macmillan, 1976.

Judt, Tony. *Postwar: A History of Europe Since 1945*. New York: Penguin, 2005.

Keynes. John Maynard. *The Economic Consequences of the Peace*. New York: Prometheus, 2004.

"KGB's 1967 Annual Report, The." Woodrow Wilson International Center for Scholars, Cold War International History Project (TsKhSD f. 89, op. 5, d. 3, ll. 1–14). Trans. Vladislav Zubok (6 May 1968).

Kierkegaard, Søren. *Either/Or: A Fragment of Life*. London: Penguin, 1992.

Klein, Rudolf, M.A. "The Troubled Transformation of Britain's National Health Service." *NEJM* 355, no. 4 (July 2006): 409–15.

Koszarski, Richard. *An Evening's Entertainment: The Age of the Silent Feature Picture, 1915–1928*. New York: Scribner, 1990.

Larsen, Darl. "'Is Not the Truth the Truth?' or Rude Frenchman in English Castles: Shakespeare's and Monty Python's (Ab)Uses of History." *Journal of the Utah Academy of Sciences, Arts, and Letters* 76 (1999): 201–12.

———. *Monty Python, Shakespeare, and English Renaissance Drama*. Jefferson, NC: McFarland, 2003.

Lawrence, D.H. *Lady Chatterley's Lover*. London: Penguin, 1960.

———. *The Rainbow*. London: Penguin, 1915.

———. *Sons and Lovers*. New York: Signet, 1953.

———. *Women in Love*. London: Penguin, 1921.

Laws of Cricket, 2003. 2nd edition. London: Lord's, 2003.

Laxdaela Saga. Trans. Magnus Magnusson. London: Penguin, 1969.

Lenin, V.I. *Lenin Collected Works, Volume 8*. Moscow: Foreign Languages Publishing House, 1962.

Loemker, Leroy E., ed. *G.W. Leibniz: Philosophical Papers and Letters*, 2nd ed. Dordrecht, 1969.

Machen, Arthur. *The Great God Pan*. http://www.gutenberg.org/etext/389. Accessed 28 November 2007.

Mack, Maynard, et al., ed. *The Norton Anthology of World Masterpieces*, vols. 1 and 2. 5th ed. New York: W.W. Norton, 1985.

Mailik, Zaiba. "Watery Grave." *The Guardian*. 15 Dec. 2004.

Malik, Sarita. "The Black and White Minstrel Show." Museum of Broadcast Communication. http://www.museum.tv/archives/etv/B/htmlB/blackandwhim/blackandwhim.htm. Accessed 29 April 2006.

Marwick, Arthur. *British Society Since 1945*. London: Penguin, 2003.

Marx, Karl, and Frederick Engels. *The Manifesto of the Communist Party*. Chicago: Kerr and Co., 1906.

Matyszak, Philip. *The Enemies of Rome*. London: Thames and Hudson, 2004.

McCabe, Bob. *The Pythons*. New York: St. Martin's Press, 2003.

Miller, Fredric. "The British Unemployment Crisis of 1935." *Journal of Contemporary History* 14, no. 2 (April 1979): 329–52.

Miller, Paul Allen. "Sidney, Petrarch, and Ovid, or Imitation as Subversion." *ELH* 58, no. 3 (Autumn 1991): 499–522.

Milligan, Spike. *The Goon Show Scripts*. New York: St. Martin's, 1972.

Mills, A.D. *A Dictionary of British Place Names*. Oxford: Oxford University Press, 2003.

Monty Python and the Holy Grail. Dir. Terry Gilliam and Terry Jones. EMI Films, 1975.

Monty Python's Flying Circus. Dir. John Howard Davies and Ian MacNaughton. BBC, 1969–1974.

Monty Python's Life of Brian. Dir. Terry Jones. HandMade Films, 1979.

Monty Python's The Meaning of Life. Dir. Terry Gilliam and Terry Jones. Universal Pictures, 1983.

Morgan, David. *Monty Python Speaks!* New York: Avon Books, 1999.

Morgan, Kenneth O. *Britain Since 1945: The People's Peace*. Oxford: Oxford University Press, 2001.

———. *The Oxford History of Britain*. Oxford: Oxford University Press, 2001.

Motson, John, and John Rowlinson. *The European Cup 1955–1980*. London: Queen Anne Press, 1980.

Musser, Charles. *The Emergence of Cinema: The American Screen to 1907*. New York: Scribner, 1990.

Nelson, Russell. *English Wits*. London: Hutchinson, 1953.

Nettleton, George, and Arthur Case, eds. *British Dramatists from Dryden to Sheridan*. Boston: Houghton Mifflin, 1939.

Newman, Ray. "The Dialectic Aspect of Raymond Chandler's Novels." http://home.comcast.net/~mossrobert/html/criticism/newman.htm. Accessed 24 December 2006.

Nietzsche, Frederich. *The Will to Power*. New York: Vintage, 1968.

Nixon, Richard. "Building for Peace: A Report by President Richard Nixon to the Congress, 25 February 1971." http://www.state.gov/r/pa/ho/frus/nixon/e5/54812.htm. Accessed 28 November 2007.

Njal's Saga. Trans. Robert Cook. London: Penguin, 2002.

Nowell-Smith, Geoffrey. *The Oxford History of World Cinema*. Oxford: Oxford University Press, 1996.

Nuttgens, Patrick. "From Utopia to Slum." *The Tablet* (26 September 1998). www.thetablet.co.uk. Accessed 6 April 2006.

Orczy, Baroness. *The Scarlet Pimpernel*. 1905. First World Library, 2005.

Orlova, Alexandra. "Tchaikovsky: The Last Chapter." *Music & Letters* 62, no. 2 (1981): 125–45.

Ostrom, John. "*Archaeopteryx*: Notice of a 'New' Specimen." *Science* 170, no. 3957 (30 October 1970): 537–38.

Oxenham, John. *Bees in Amber: A Little Book of Thoughtful Verse*. New York: American Tract Society, 1913.

Oxford Dictionary of Modern Quotations. Ed. Elizabeth Knowles. Oxford: Oxford University Press, 2003.

Oxford Dictionary of National Biography. Oxford: Oxford University Press, 2004. Online version at: http://www.oxforddnb.com/.

Palin, Michael. *Michael Palin Diaries 1969–1979: The Python Years*. London: Weidenfeld & Nicholson, 2006.

Partridge, Eric. *Shakespeare's Bawdy*. London: Routledge, 1991.

Paxman, Jeremy. "The English." *The Sunday Times*. 27 September 1998, 1–8.

Pearson, Cynthia, and Norbert Delatte, M.ASCE. "Ronan Point Apartment Tower Collapse and its Effect on Building Codes." *Journal of Performance of Constructed Facilities* 19, no. 2 (May 2005): 172–77.

Pennell, E. R. and J., eds. *The Whistler Journal*. Philadelphia: Lippincott, 1921.

Pepys, Samuel. *Passages From the Diary of Samuel Pepys*. Ed. Richard Le Gallienne. New York: The Modern Library, 1964.

Perez, Joseph. *The Spanish Inquisition: A History*. New Haven, CT: Yale University Press, 2005.

Perry, Elizabeth J. *Patrolling the Revolution: Worker Militias, Citizenship, and the Modern Chinese State*. New York: Rowman & Littlefield, 2005.

Pickering, J.F. "The Abandonment of Major Mergers in the UK." *Journal of Industrial Economics* 27, no. 2: 123–131.

Pincus, Edward. *The Filmmaker's Handbook*. New York: New American Library, 1984.

Preble, Christopher A. "Review of E. Bruce Geelhoed and Anthony O. Edmonds, *Eisenhower, Macmillan and Allied Unity, 1957–1961*," H-Diplo, H-Net Reviews, February, 2005. http://www.h-net.org/reviews/showrev.cgi?path=125481117220884. Accessed 29 November 2006.

Propp, Vladimir. *Morphology of the Folk Tale*. Austin, TX: University of Texas Press, 1968.

Proust, Marcel. *In Search of Lost Time*. Trans. Lydia Davis. London: Penguin, 2004.

Quicherat, Jules. *Histoire du costume en France*. Paris, 1875.

Rainey, Laurence. "The Cultural Economy of Modernism." *The Cambridge Companion to Modernism*. Ed. Michael Levenson. Cambridge: Cambridge University Press, 1999.

Rampa, T. Lobsang. *The Third Eye*. 1956. New York: Ballantine, 1986.

Ratcliffe, Stephen. "MEMO/RE: Reading Stein." *Corner* 2 (Spring 1999). http://www.cornermag.org/corner02/page07.htm#anchor76741. Accessed 2 February 2007.

Rattigan, Terence. *The Collected Plays of Terence Rattigan*. Ed. Elizabeth Knowles. Oxford University Press, 2002. Oxford Reference Online. Oxford University Press. Accessed 6 October 2003.

The Renaissance in Italy. New York: Modern Library, 1935.

Rigby, T.H. "The Soviet Leadership: Towards a Self-Stabilizing Oligarchy?" *Soviet Studies* 22, no. 2 (1970): 167–91.

Robertson, Jean. "Philip Sidney." *The Spenser Encyclopedia*. Ed. A.C. Hamilton, et al. Toronto: University of Toronto Press, 1990.

Rosenbaum, Martin. *From Soapbox to Soundbite: Party Political Campaigning in Britain Since 1945*. London: Macmillan, 1997.

Ross, Charles. *The Wars of the Roses: A Concise History*. London: Thames and Hudson, 1986.

Rundell, Michael. *The Dictionary of Cricket*. 2nd ed. Oxford: Oxford University Press, 1995.

Russell, Bertrand. *The Autobiography of Bertrand Russell*. London: Routledge, 2000.

———. *The Problems of Philosophy*. Oxford: Oxford University Press, 1997.

Rutherford, Jonathan. *Forever England: Reflections on Race, Masculinity and Empire*. London: Lawrence & Wishart, 1997.

Sachs, Albie. *Justice in South Africa*. London: Chatto & Heinemann, 1973.

Salmond, Dame Anne. *Two Worlds*. New Zealand: Penguin, 1991.

Santayana, George. *Soliloquies in England*. New York: Charles Scribner's Sons, 1922.

Sartre, Jean Paul. *Being and Nothingness*. Trans. Hazel Barnes. New York: Washington Square Press, 1966.

Schmidt, Steven C. "United Kingdom Entry into the European Economic Community: Issues and Implications." *Illinois Agricultural Economics* 12, no. 2 (July 1972): 1–11.

Schroth, Raymond A. "The One and Only." *National Catholic Reporter* 38, no. 14 (8 February 2002): 11.

Schur, Norman. *British English, A to Zed*. New York: Facts on File, 2007.

Scott, Walter, Sir. *Redgauntlet*. Boston: Estes and Lauriat, c1894.

Shakespeare, William. *A Midsummer Night's Dream. The Riverside Shakespeare*. Ed. G. Blakemore Evans. Boston: Houghton Mifflin, 1974.

———. *Cymbeline. The Riverside Shakespeare*. Ed. G. Blakemore Evans. Boston: Houghton Mifflin, 1974.

———. *Hamlet. The Riverside Shakespeare*. Ed. G. Blakemore Evans. Boston: Houghton Mifflin, 1974.

———. *1 Henry IV. The Riverside Shakespeare*. Ed. G. Blakemore Evans. Boston: Houghton Mifflin, 1974.

———. *2 Henry IV. The Riverside Shakespeare*. Ed. G. Blakemore Evans. Boston: Houghton Mifflin, 1974.

———. *Henry V. The Riverside Shakespeare*. Ed. G. Blakemore Evans. Boston: Houghton Mifflin, 1974.

———. *Henry VIII. The Riverside Shakespeare*. Ed. G. Blakemore Evans. Boston: Houghton Mifflin, 1974.

———. *Julius Caesar. The Riverside Shakespeare*. Ed. G. Blakemore Evans. Boston: Houghton Mifflin, 1974.

———. *King John. The Riverside Shakespeare*. Ed. G. Blakemore Evans. Boston: Houghton Mifflin, 1974.

———. *The Merchant of Venice. The Riverside Shakespeare*. Ed. G. Blakemore Evans. Boston: Houghton Mifflin, 1974.

———. *Much Ado About Nothing. The Riverside Shakespeare*. Ed. G. Blakemore Evans. Boston: Houghton Mifflin, 1974.

———. *The Rape of Lucrece. The Riverside Shakespeare*. Ed. G. Blakemore Evans. Boston: Houghton Mifflin, 1974.

———. *Richard II. The Riverside Shakespeare*. Ed. G. Blakemore Evans. Boston: Houghton Mifflin, 1974.

———. *Richard III. The Riverside Shakespeare*. Ed. G. Blakemore Evans. Boston: Houghton Mifflin, 1974.

———. *Romeo and Juliet. The Riverside Shakespeare*. Ed. G. Blakemore Evans. Boston: Houghton Mifflin, 1974.

———. *The Tempest. The Riverside Shakespeare*. Ed. G. Blakemore Evans. Boston: Houghton Mifflin, 1974.

Shaw, George Bernard. *Pygmalion*. 1916. http://www.bartleby.com/138/2.html. Accessed 28 November 2007.

Shaw, Harry E. *Critical Essays on Sir Walter Scott: The Waverley Novels*. London: Prentice Hall, 1996.

Shelley, Percy Bysshe. "Ozymandias." *Shelley's Poetry and Prose: Authoritative Texts, Criticism*. New York: Norton, 1977.

Sherrin, Ned. *I Wish I'd Said That*. Oxford: Oxford University Press, 2004.

Sickert, Walter P. "The Idealism News." In *A Free House! Or The Artist as Craftsman; Being the Writings of Walter Richard Sickert*, ed. Oscar Sitwell. London: Macmillan, 1947.

Smethurst, William. *The Archers—The True Story: The History of Radio's Most Famous Programme*. London: Michael O'Mara Books, 1996.

Smith, Alexander. *A Complete History of the Lives and Robberies of the Most Notorious Highwaymen* (1714). London: Routledge, 1926.

Smollett, Tobias. *Humphry Clinker*. Ed. James L. Thorson, Norton Critical Editions. London: W.W. Norton, 1983.

———. *The Letters of Tobias Smollett*, ed. L. M. Knapp. Oxford: Clarendon Press, 1970.

Somerville, Christopher. "Woodstock Oxfordshire Walk." *Weekend Telegraph*. http://www.woodstock-oxfordshire.co.uk/pages/sport_and_entertainment/walk/walk.htm. Accessed 31 January 2007.

Spraggs, Gillian. *Outlaws and Highwaymen: The Cult of the Robber in England from the Middle Ages to the Nineteenth Century*. London: Pimlico, 2002.

Springer, Steve. "The City Was Full of Fight." *Los Angeles Times*. 30 March 2006. Website accessed 24 November 2006.

Stam, Robert. *Reflexivity in Film and Literature: From Don Quixote to Jean-Luc Godard*. New York: Columbia University Press, 1992.

Stein, Gertrude. "Melanctha." *Three Lives*. New York: Vintage, 1909.

Stevenson, Robert Louis. *Treasure Island*. 1883. http://www.online-literature.com/stevenson/treasureisland/. Accessed 29 November 2007.

Stewart, Gordon. "Tenzing's Two Wrist-Watches: The Conquest of Everest and Late Imperial Culture in Britain, 1921–1953." *Past & Present* 149 (Nov. 1995): 170–97.

Swift, Jonathan. *Gulliver's Travels*. The Writings of Jonathan Swift. Robert A. Greenberg and William B. Piper, eds. London: Norton, 1973.

———. *The Lady's Dressing Room*. The Writings of Jonathan Swift. Robert A. Greenberg and William B. Piper, eds. London: Norton, 1973.

Tansey, Richard, et al. *Gardner's Art Through the Ages*, 7th ed. New York: HBJ, 1980.

Taylor, Basil. *Constable: Paintings, Drawings, and Watercolours*. London: Phaidon, 1973.

"Ten Years of TV Coverage." *Belfast Bulletin* 6 (Spring 1979): 20–25, published by the Belfast Workers Research Unit.

Tennyson, Alfred Lord. *A Dream of Fair Women*. 1832. http://whitewolf.newcastle.edu.au/words/authors/T/TennysonAlfred/verse/ladyshalott/dreamfairwomen.html.

———. *Mariana*. http://www.web-books.com/Classics/Poetry/anthology/Tennyson/Mariana.htm.

———. *The Princess: A Medley*. 1847, 1850. http://classiclit.about.com/library/bl-etexts/atennyson/bl-aten-princess.htm.

Thompson, John O. *Monty Python: Complete and Utter Theory of the Grotesque*. BFI: London, 1982.

Tillyard, E.M.W. *Shakespeare's History Plays*. London: Chatto and Windus, 1944.

Took, Barry. *Laughter in the Air*. London: BBC, 1981.

Trevelyan, G.M. *History of England*, 2nd ed. New York: Longmans, Green and Co., 1926.

———. *History of England*, 3rd ed. New York: Longmans, Green and Co., 1952.

This Sceptred Isle: The Twentieth Century. Wr. Christopher Lee. CD. *BBC Radio 4 Series*, BBC Audiobooks, 1999.

Unger, Roberto. *Passion: An Essay on Personality*. New York: Free Press, 1986.

Vahimagi, Tise. *British Television*. Oxford: Oxford University Press, 1996.

Veblen, Thorstein. *The Theory of the Leisure Class*. 1899. New York: Dover, 1999.

Voltaire. *Candide*. London: Penguin, 1950.

Warburton, Nigel. *Philosophy: The Classics*, 3rd ed. London: Routledge, 2006.

Warwick, Charles and John R. Neill. *Mirabeau and the French Revolution*. Whitefish, MT: Kessinger, 2005.

Watson, Peter. *The Modern Mind: An Intellectual History of the 20th Century*. New York: Harper Collins, 2002.

Waugh, Thomas. *Hard to Imagine: Gay Male Eroticism in Photography and Film from Their Beginnings to Stonewall*. New York: Columbia University Press, 1996.

Webster, Charles. *The National Health Service: A Political History*. Oxford: Oxford University Press, 2002.

Weintraub, Stanley, ed. *Bernard Shaw on the London Art Scene, 1885–1950*. Penn State: University Park University Press, 1989.

Wells, Stanley, and Gary Taylor, eds. *The Oxford Shakespeare: Histories with the Poems and Sonnets*. Oxford: Oxford University Press, 1994.

Weston, Richard. *Modernism*. London: Phaidon, 1996.

Westman, Andrew and Tony Dyson. *Archaeology in Greater London, 1965–1990*. London: Museum of London, 1998.

Westwood, J.N. *Railways of India*. Newton Abbot, UK: David & Charles, 1975.

"What Will the 1970's Bring?" *Awake!* 8 October 1969, 14–16.

Williams, Eric. *The Wooden Horse*. New York: Harper, 1949.

Wilmut, Roger. *From Fringe to Flying Circus*. London: Methuen, 1987.

Wilson, A.N. *After the Victorians: The Decline of Britain in the World*. London: Picador, 2005.

Wilson, J. Dover. *What Happens in Hamlet*. Cambridge: Cambridge University Press, 1935.

"Witnessing the End." *TIME*. 18 July 1969. http://www.time.com/time/magazine/article/0,9171,901074-1,00.html. Accessed 28 October 2006.

Wolfe, Tom. *From Bauhaus to Our House*. New York: Farrar Straus Giroux, 1981.

Wooden Horse, The. Dir. Jack Lee, 1950.

Woodward, Rachel. "'It's a Man's Life!': Soldiers, Masculinity and the Countryside." *Gender, Place and Culture: A Journal of Feminist Geography* 5, no. 3 (1 Nov. 1998): 277–300.

Wynne-Thomas, Peter. *Hamlyn A–Z of Cricket Records*. London: Hamlyn, 1983.

SELECTED INTERNET RESOURCES

1970 General Election, review of the rebroadcast: http://www.offthetelly.co.uk/reviews/2003/election70.htm

Affected "gay" speech (by Caroline Bowen): http://www.speech-language-therapy.com/caroline.html. Accessed 16 Aug. 2006

All Blacks Rugby: http://www.allblacks.com/

"Anarcho-Syndicalism, History of." *Self-Ed Education Collective*, http://www.selfed.org.uk/units/2001/index.htm

Argyll Regiment: http://argylls.co.uk/today.html

At Last the 1948 Show information: http://orangecow.org/pythonet/1948show/

Avengers, The, TV show: http://theavengers.tv/forever/

Barr Soft Drinks: http://www.agbarr.co.uk

Baths, UK: http://www.localhistory.scit.wlv.ac.uk/interesting/htbaths/htbaths04.htm

BBC History: http://www.tvradiobits.co.uk/

BBC Programme Catalogue: http://open.bbc.co.uk/catalogue/infax/

BBC Radio (1967): http://www.radiorewind.co.uk/1967_page.htm. Accessed 1 January 2007

BBC Radio (1971-1972): http://www.radiorewind.co.uk/1971_page.htm

BBC Television Centre history: http://www.martinkempton.com/TV%20Centre%20history.htm#stage%206

Best, George obituary: http://www.timesonline.co.uk/article/0,,2-1890892,00.html, and http://www.manutdzone.com/legends/GeorgeBest.htm

BFI Film and TV Database: http://www.bfi.org.uk/filmtvinfo/ftvdb/

Board of Trade: http://dti.gov.uk/history/board.htm

British Broadcasting Corporation: http://www.bbc.co.uk

British Cartoon Archive: http://opal.kent.ac.uk/cartoonx-cgi/ccc.py

British Telephone Historical Archives (accessed through ancestry.com): http://content.ancestry.co.uk/iexec/?htx=List&dbid=1025&offerid=0%3a7858%3a0

British TV, anecdotal history: http://www.whirligig-tv.co.uk/

British TV, history: http://www.teletronic.co.uk/

Brown, Arthur obituary: http://www.guardian.co.uk/obituaries/story/0,3604,969745,00.html (penned by Andrew Phillips)

Cambridge University prizes in Classics: http://www.admin.cam.ac.uk/reporter/2003-04/special/05/b5.html

"Catenaccio defense": http://naccio.cs.virginia.edu/catenaccio.html

Celtic FC: http://www.lonestarceltic.com/25_may_1967.php

Chichester Festival history: http://www.cft.org.uk/content.asp?CategoryID=1107.

Churchill Centre "darker days" speech: http://www.winstonchurchill.org/i4a/pages/index.cfm?pageid=423

Clergy Lists, UK: *Kelly's Clergy List, 1909*: http://midlandshistoricaldata.org

Commonwealth Immigration Act of 1968: http://britishcitizen.info/CIA1968.pdf

Corporal punishment in South Africa: http://www.corpun.com/jcpza9.htm

Courtauld Gallery collection search: http://www.courtauld.ac.uk/index.html

Cowdrey, Colin obituary (by John Thicknesse): http://content-www.cricinfo.com/ci/content/player/10846.html

Cricket info.: http://content-usa.cricinfo.com/england/content/player/20159.html

Crystal Palace FC: http://www.cpfc.co.uk

DeWolfe music: http://www.dewolfe.co.uk/

Dorking Dramatic Society Archives: http://www.ddos.org.uk/archives.asp

Encyclopedia Britannica: http://www.ebo.com

Encyclopedia of Fantastic Film & Television: http://www.eofftv.com/

Everest Climbing History: http://www.everestnews.com/everest1.htm

FBI files on Burgess, Maclean: http://foia.fbi.gov/filelink.html?file=/philby/philby1a.pdf

Forestry Commission UK: http://www.forestry.gov.uk

Freemasonry watchdog: http://freemasonrywatch.org/

Gas Boards history: http://www.gasarchive.org/Nationalisation.htm and http://www.centrica.co.uk/index.asp?pageid=397

Gay characters on British TV: http://www.queertv.btinternet.co.uk/

Gay men's magazines: http://www.planetout.com/news/history/archive/09271999.html

Guardian Century: http://century.guardian.co.uk/

Highwayman Humphrey Kynaston: http://www.bbc.co.uk/shropshire/features/halloween/kynaston.shtml

Hitler's speeches: http://hitler.org/speeches/

Homelessness in the UK in 1969: http://news.bbc.co.uk/onthisday/hi/dates/stories/september/11/newsid_3037000/3037650.stm

An Incomplete History of London's Television Studios: http://www.tvstudiohistory.co.uk/tv%20centre%20history.htm

Julian Slade obituary (by Dennis Barker): http://arts.guardian.co.uk/news/obituary/0,,1801400,00.html

"Kray Brothers" (by Thomas Jones): http://www.crimelibrary.com/gangsters_outlaws/mob_bosses/kray/index_1.html

Labour Manifesto, 1966: http://www.psr.keele.ac.uk/area/uk/man/lab66.htm

Labour Market Trends, Office for National Statistics, June 1999: http://www.statistics.gov.uk/

London School of Economics riots (January 1969): http://news.bbc.co.uk/onthisday/hi/dates/stories/january/24/newsid_2506000/2506485.stm

Lord's (MCC) Laws of Cricket: http://www.lords.org/laws-and-spirit/laws-of-cricket/

"Men of Harlech": http://www.data-wales.co.uk/harlech.htm

MPFC Scripts: http://www.ibras.dk/montypython/justthewords.htm

National Film Theatre: http://bfi.uk.org

National Gallery collection archive: http://www.national-gallery.org.uk/

National Portrait Gallery collection search: http://www.npg.org.uk/live/collect.asp

North Yorkshire photos (Unnetie Digitisation Project) http://www2.northyorks.gov.uk/unnetie/

Man Alive: http://www.offthetelly.co.uk/features/bbc2/forty1.htm

McGuffie, Mary (McCheane) information, Farnon Society: http://www.rfsoc.org.uk/jim3.shtml

Mont Orgueil Castle: http://www.bbc.co.uk/jersey/content/image_galleries/mont_orgueil_one_gallery.shtml?5

"Northern Ireland Conflict and Politics (1968 to the Present)": http://cain.ulst.ac.uk/othelem/media/tv10yrs.htm

Notting Hill "pop" history (by Tom Vague): http://www.historytalk.org/Tom%20Vague%20Pop%20History/Tom%20Vague%20Pop%20History.htm

Nova (magazine) listserv: http://listserv.uel.ac.uk/pipermail/centrefornarrativeresearch/Week-of-Mon-20050411/000319.html

Online Medieval & Classical Library: http://omacl.org/

Open University ("From Here to Modernity"): http://www.open2.net/modernity/

"Overcrowding in London" (March 2004): http://www.lhu.org.uk

Oxford English Dictionary: http://dictionary.oed.com/

Party Political (or Election) Broadcasts: http://www.psr.keele.ac.uk/area/uk/peb.htm

Peerage listings: http://www.thepeerage.com/

Pinball machines, vintage: http://dguhlow.tripod.com/pinballs/htmls/bankaball.html

Pontiac Firebirds in movies: http://www.imcdb.org/vehicles_make-Pontiac_model-Firebird.html

Positivism: http://radicalacademy.com/philpositivists.htm

Postwar fireplaces (and fireplace inserts): http://www.c20fires.co.uk/fireplaces/original/postfires.htm

Pound devaluation, 1972: http://news.bbc.co.uk/onthisday/low/dates/stories/june/23/newsid_2518000/2518927.stm

"Poverty in England" (by Charles Booth): http://booth.lse.ac.uk/

Proust, Marcel and *À la recherche du temps perdu*: http://tempsperdu.com/

Queen's itinerary and speeches, 1970: http://www.nla.gov.au/ms/findaids/9174.html#1970

Queen's Park Rangers FC: http://www.qpc.co.uk

Radio Times official website: http://radiotimes.beeb.com

Radio Times (unofficial) cover art site: http://www.vintage-times.org.uk/

Railroad music: http://www.musicweb.uk.net/railways_in_music.htm

Railway signal boxes: http://www.signalbox.org/gallery/be.htm

Railway violence: http://btp.police.uk/History

Reith Lectures: http://www.bbc.co.uk/radio4/reith/reith_history.shtml

Richter, Sviatoslav (chronology): http://www.trovar.com/str/dates/index.html

Rijksmuseum Rembrandt collection: http://rijksmuseum.nl/index.jsp

Rock climbing jargon: http://www.myoan.net/climbing/jargon.html

Roirama Expedition: http://www.lastrefuge.co.uk/data/adrian2.html

Royal Scottish Forestry Society: http://www.rsfs.org/

Scott, Peter entry at WordIQ: http://www.wordiq.com/definition/Peter_Scott

Scottish politics: http://www.alba.org.uk/nextwe/snp.html

Semaphore signals: www.cs.dartmouth.edu/~rockmore/semaphore.jpg

Shakespeare listserv: http://www.shaksper.net/www.shaksper.net

Society of Film and TV Arts (UK): http://www.bafta.org

"Squatting in London" (Andrew Friend): http://squat.freeserve.co.uk/story

St. Albans Operatic Society: http://www.saos.org.uk

Strike activity in the UK: http://www.eiro.eurofound.eu.int/1999/07/feature/uk9907215f.html

Tate Gallery Collection: http://www.tate.org.uk/britain/

Tax Freedom Day in the UK: http://www.adamsmith.org/tax/short-history.php

Tennis information: http://www.tennisfame.org/enshrinees/

Time Magazine online archives: http://www.time.com/time/magazine/archives

UK Announcers archive: http://tvannouncers.thetvroomplus.com/channel-19.html

UK General Elections (including results since 1832): http://www.psr.keele.ac.uk/area/uk/edates.htm

UK motorway exchanges: http://www.cbrd.co.uk/reference/interchanges/fourlevelstack.shtml

UK Parliament: http://www.parliament.uk/

UK postwar politics: http://politics.guardian.co.uk/politicspast/story/0,9061,471383,00.html

UK postwar spending: "Long-Term Trends in British Taxation and Spending" (Tom Clark and Andrew Dilnot) from the Institute for Fiscal Studies: http://www.ifs.org.uk/bns/bn25.pdf

UK street maps: http://www.streetmap.co.uk

Victoria & Albert Museum collection: http://www.vam.ac.uk/collections/

Vladimir Horowitz concert information: http://web.telia.com/~u85420275/index.htm

Wimbledon archives: http://www.wimbledon.org

Wisden Cricketer, The: http://www.cricinfo.com/wisdencricketer/

YMCA in Russia: http://www.ymca.ru/english/history/

Index

Index of *Monty Python's Flying Circus* Extras and Walk-Ons (As Scheduled)

About the Author

Darl Larsen was born in California in 1963 and has been part of the film faculty at Brigham Young University since 1998. He took degrees at UC Santa Barbara (1990), Brigham Young University (1994), and Northern Illinois University (2000). At BYU he teaches film history, screenwriting, animation, and genres, and he researches popular culture. He published *Monty Python, Shakespeare and English Renaissance Drama* in 2003, and lives in beautiful Provo, Utah, with his family.